College Scholarships and Financial Aid

With

ARCO's Scholarship Search Software

Wintergreen/Orchard House, Inc.

New Orleans, Louisiana • Brunswick, Maine

John Schwartz, Staff Reporter, *Washington Post*

MACMILLAN • USA

Sixth Edition

Macmillan General Reference
A Simon & Schuster Macmillan Company
1633 Broadway
New York, NY 10019

An Arco Book

MACMILLAN is a registered trademark of Macmillan, Inc.
ARCO is a registered trademark of Prentice-Hall, Inc.

ISBN: 0-02-860585-3

Manufactured in the United States of America

10 9 8 7 6 5 4 3 2 1

GETTING STARTED

INTRODUCTION

What is *Scholarship Search*?

Scholarship Search is a hypertext computer program designed to supplement Arco's *College Scholarships and Financial Aid* book. While the scholarship data contained in the book and on the disk is the same, the disk is intended to give you some alternative ways to find information quickly. For instance, say you are interested in which scholarships are given for a particular ethnicity or race. Instead of reading through the entire Race/Ethnicity section of the book, you can use the software's Index function to find the available scholarships for your designation. *Scholarship Search* will tell you exactly which scholarships meet your criteria.

What are the System Requirements for *Scholarship Search*?

In order to run *Scholarship Search*, you will need the following minimum system requirements:

80386SX processor (running at 16 MHz)
2 MB RAM (4MB recommended)
5 MB hard–disk storage available
4–bit VGA graphics adapter with color VGA monitor
Two–button, Microsoft–compatible mouse
101–key keyboard
MS–DOS version 3.3 or later
Microsoft Windows operating system version 3.1 or later (enhanced mode)

INSTALLING *SCHOLARSHIP SEARCH*

How do I install *Scholarship Search*?

1. Insert the 3.5" floppy disk into your computer's drive.
2. On the File menu in your Program Manager, choose **Run**.
3. In the dialog box that comes up, you can do either of the two following options:
   type "a:\setup" at the blinking cursor in the Command Line box and click **OK**; or click **Browse** and select the drive in which you have inserted your disk. Choose "setup" as the file name and click **OK**.
4. You will see a dialog box that welcomes you to *Scholarship Search*. Click **OK** to begin the installation.
5. You must next choose the destination directory for the *Scholarship Search* program on your computer. The default option is c:\arcoscho. If you would like to place it somewhere else, you can use the scroll bar to move up and down the list of available locations. You can also select the destination drive if c: is not where you would like to place *Scholarship Search*.
6. At the prompt for the Program Manager Group, you can choose exactly where you would like to put *Scholarship Search* on your computer. The default location is a new folder on your hard drive entitled "Arco's Scholarship Search." You can put the program in a different place by using the scroll bar to move down the list and clicking on a title. Click **OK** when you are ready. Your program manager will appear on your screen; the folder where *Scholarship Search* was installed will be highlighted.

How do I uninstall *Scholarship Search*?

If you would like to remove *Scholarship Search* from your hard drive, double–click the "Uninstall" icon in the "Arco's Scholarship Search" folder. A dialog box will appear asking you to choose the method of uninstallation: automatic or custom. Automatic quickly removes the software and data files from your computer. This option is not only faster and easier than the custom option, but it is much safer for your computer. With automatic, you can be assured only the data and files related to *Scholarship Search* will be removed from your computer. Custom allows you to control every step of the uninstallation process. Press **Cancel** if you do not want to uninstall.

NAVIGATING THROUGH *SCHOLARSHIP SEARCH*

How do I begin?

To begin exploring *Scholarship Search*, double–click the "Arco's Scholarship Search" icon. You will now see the program's main screen which resembles the cover of the book. When held over this graphic, the cursor becomes a pointing hand. This pointing–hand icon signifies a "hot spot": a word, phrase or picture that allows you to jump from one topic to another within *Scholarship Search*. Clicking your mouse once anywhere the cursor appears as a hand will bring you to the Table of Contents. From here you can get to the information you need by clicking on a general topic highlighted in yellow and then on any of the sub–topics with green lettering.

What is hypertext?

Scholarship Search is a program created in *hypertext*: literally, enhanced text. The scholarship data is arranged so that instead of flipping through pages to find information, all you have to do is click on certain portions of the text and the program will bring you to the information you need. There are several distinguishing features of the hypertext program that make it fast and easy for you to access scholarship information:

● SEARCHING Using either the full–text or the keyword search engines, you can jump to topics in which you are interested. *Keyword* searching lets you choose pre–programmed topics as if you were looking in an index in the back of a book. *Full–text* searching enables you to customize your search for specific words or phrases. See "Index" and "Search" for more detailed descriptions of keyword and full–text searching.

● MENUS Four pull–down menus allow you to print, copy, and annotate scholarship data.

File Menu:

    ● **Print Topic** prints the topic that is currently displayed on the screen.
    ● **Print Setup** displays a dialog box where you can select a printer and change printer–setup information.
    ● **Exit** quits *Scholarship Search*.

Edit Menu:

    ● **Copy** displays a dialog box where you can copy topic text you've selected onto the clipboard.
    ● **Annotate** attaches a note to the currently displayed topic.

Bookmark Menu:

    ● **Define** displays a dialog box for placing a bookmark at the current topic.

Help Menu:

    ● Offers general information about your *Scholarship Search* software.

● BUTTONS Seven keys on the button bar enable you to move around within a given topic and also to move outside it to search for other topics.

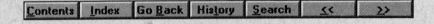

1. **Contents** returns you to the table of contents. From there you can select and view any topic.

2. **Index** allows you to find a specific topic. A dialog box, as shown below, will appear on your screen.

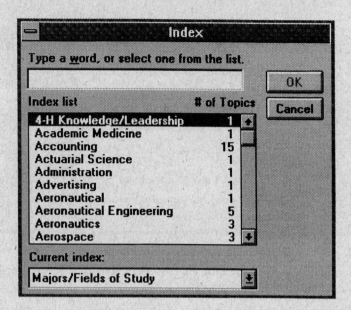

You can either type in the topic you are looking for or scroll down the list and click on your area of interest. You can also specify in which of the following indexes you would like to search in the *Current Index* box:

- Majors/Fields of Study
- Academic Record
- Business/Corporation Affiliation
- City/County of Residence
- Club Affiliation
- Gender/Marital Status
- Handicapped Students
- National Merit Status
- Race/Ethnicity
- Religious Affiliation
- Sports
- State/County of Residence
- Union Affiliation

Click **OK** once you have found the desired listing. If there is only one scholarship that contains your topic, *Scholarship Search* will go directly to it. If there is more than one scholarship, a dialog box labeled "Topics Indexed" will appear on your screen with a list of all the scholarships that contain your chosen topic. Select a topic and click **Go To**. If you wish to choose a different topic, change your search, or narrow it down, click **To Index** to return to the original Index box:

3. **Go Back** displays the topic you viewed prior to the topic on the screen..

4. **History** lists up to 40 topics from your current session. The topics appear in the order in which you viewed them. To return to a topic simply click **Go To**.

5. **Search** enables you to find a topic through different search methods. A dialog box, as shown below, will appear on your screen.

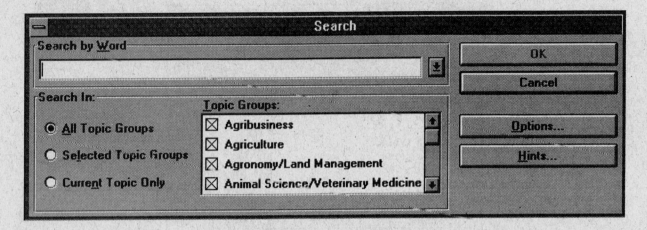

Enter the word or phrase you would like to search for at the cursor, and then choose in which of the following categories you would like *Scholarship Search* to look for it:

- **All Topic Groups** searches every instance your word/phrase appears in the entire program.
- **Selected Topic Groups** lets you search for your word/phrase in your choice of a pre–programmed grouping of topics.
- **Current Topic Only** looks for your word/phrase in the listing that currently appears on the screen behind the Search dialog box.

The **Options** button lets you choose whether you want to search for your word/phrase in topic titles only or in a list of the previous topics you've viewed. If you are doing a search for two or more words that appear near each other in context, you can define their proximity by entering a different number in the "NEAR means within 8 words" line.

The **Hints** button provides you with tips on quickening and narrowing your search by using four key words: AND, OR, NOT, and NEAR. Make sure that if you are searching for a connected phrase, such as "college–preparatory," you enter it in the *Search by Word* line with quotes around it. If you enter two or more words without quotes to tie them together, *Scholarship Search* will find all instances of *each* word.

NOTE: *Scholarship Search* will not search the following words/phrases:

- Minimum/Maximum/Average Award
- Minimum/Maximum/Number of Awards
- College Level
- Deadline
- Majors/Fields of Study
- Criteria

If you would like to do a search using one of these words/phrases, such as college level, you can do so by searching on a more specific criterion such as "Doctoral" or "Undergraduate."

When you are ready for the program to begin the search, click **OK**. A dialog box will appear with a list of the search results. Select the listing you want to view and click **Go To**. The scholarship will appear on your screen with your word/phrase highlighted in every instance it appears in the text. If the "Search Results" box blocks the listing, you can drag it to another location on the screen. Click **To Search** if you would like to begin a new search or narrow down your search criteria even more. To return to your search results, click **Cancel**.

In addition, *Scholarship Search* keeps a record of the words/phrases for which you search. To recall a previous search, click the down–arrow on the right–hand side of the *Search by Word* line and a list of your words/phrases will appear. Highlight one of the items on the list and click **OK**.

6., 7. Click either the [<<] or the [>>] key to browse through topics near the topic you are currently viewing on the screen. If the >> key is dimmed you have reached the last topic in the sequence; if the << key is dimmed you are at the first topic in the sequence. Topics are arranged alphabetically. If you are at the Table of Contents, both buttons appear dimmed because you are not in any particular topic. If you would like to "browse" through the Contents, click on any of the topics highlighted in yellow at the top of the Contents screen or use the scroll bar on the right–hand side of the screen.

How do I quit?

To end your *Scholarship Search* session, simply click **Exit** from the File menu.

We hope you enjoy using *Scholarship Search* and that it is beneficial in your college and scholarship search.

College Scholarships and Financial Aid

Wintergreen/Orchard House, Inc.

New Orleans, Louisiana • Brunswick, Maine

John Schwartz, Staff Reporter, *Washington Post*

MACMILLAN • USA

Sixth Edition

Macmillan General Reference
A Simon & Schuster Macmillan Company
1633 Broadway
New York, NY 10019

An Arco Book

MACMILLAN is a registered trademark of Macmillan, Inc.
ARCO is a registered trademark of Prentice-Hall, Inc.

ISBN: 0-02-860329-X

Manufactured in the United States of America

10 9 8 7 6 5 4 3 2 1

Contents

Introduction   page 3

Anyone Can Pay for College   5

Financial Aid News Update   10

You and the Tax Laws: What the IRS Has Done
   to Higher Education   14

Intermission—The Loan Route   16

The World of Available Aid—Public Channels   18

Intermission—Righting the Balance   54

The World of Available Aid—Private Channels   57

Cooperative Education   65

Getting the Most College for the Money   108

Putting Your Financial Aid Package Together   114

Glossary of Financial Aid Terms   119

At-A-Glance Financial Aid Calendar   122

Financial Aid Forms Update   123

Bibliography   124

Directory of Scholarships and Grants   127

Index of Majors   410

Index of Criteria   415

Alphabetical Index to Scholarships   424

A Word of Thanks

This is the sixth edition of *College Scholarships and Financial Aid*. When I first approached the project, I was a newly-minted reporter for *Newsweek On Campus*, the famous newsweekly's five-year experiment in producing a magazine for the college market. College financial aid was an interesting, if abstract, subject. A lot has changed in the ensuing years—I now write about science and other topics for *The Washington Post*, have two kids, and have begun to worry in earnest about paying for their college educations. That's justice, I suppose.

A book like this would not be possible without the selfless work of professionals in the financial aid field whose job it is to get the word out and who don't seem to mind when guys like me recycle their labors for money. Madeleine McLean Longano, Associate Director of Communications for the National Association of Student Financial Aid Administrators, has been a consistent source of good stuff. So has Jerry S. Davis, Research Director for SALLIE MAE, the Student Loan Marketing Association, who in his previous incarnation at the Pennsylvania High-er Education Authority compiled an annual goldmine of state financial aid information. Mr. Davis has shown a geniality and grace under pressure that all of us could learn from. Barbara Gilson, the editor who has ridden this project from the beginning, has been patient, alert, insistent–and a good counselor on child-raising besides. Thanks also to the good folks at Wintergreen/Orchard House, who compile the databases and make this book work. This year, Judith Lewenthal again came to the rescue as researcher. Overqualified for all that she tackles, Judy nonetheless consented to lend her considerable skills to the effort.

As I write this, my family is asleep nearby, so rather than wake them I'll just thank them here. Jeanne, my wife, has suffered through my awful work hours and worse work habits. The kids, too, are a powerful incentive for me to learn as much as possible about paying for college: daughter Elizabeth, now almost eight, is a constant source of wonder; Sam Austin has charged toward the five-year mark pretty much intact. Without them, none of this would be necessary.

Introduction

The times, they are a-changing. The last time we published this book we were just beginning a new Democratic administration in Washington. The previous administration didn't spend a lot of time worrying about making college more affordable, but Bill Clinton made improving financial aid one of his top priorities. His campaign was focused on a single issue—"It's the economy, stupid" was the sign in the War Room in Little Rock—and paying for college was a perfect middle-class hot button. More important, it was one of the issues Clinton seemed actually to care deeply about. As he spoke of a program of national service that would encourage volunteerism and defray college costs, you could tell that it came from the heart. Arkansas, after all, is not a rich state. Clinton could see daily what needed to be done. And while promises of financial aid reform alone did not elect Bill Clinton, it's clear that it was part of the package of planned reforms that helped to put him over the top.

At this writing, some two and a half years into the new administration, Clinton and his policies are under serious attack by the new Republican majority in Congress. Though Clinton passed a national service program and created a new "direct lending" system that bypasses commercial institutions, the Republican political leadership has targeted each of those programs for caps, cuts, or dismantling.

More on that later. For the purposes of this introduction, let me simply say that times really are changing. Read your newspaper: The news, now more than any time in the last two decades, could create new opportunities—or take them away—overnight.

The positive early response to Clinton's proposals underscores the basic point of this book: Financial aid is not just for the needy any more. Considering the high cost of college today, *everyone* is needy. Everybody could use a little help paying for the kids' college education—well, maybe not Ross Perot, but certainly the rest of us. Tuition has long had a habit of rising faster than the rate of inflation. The costliest schools demand some $26,000 in tuition and residential fees each year, and the College Board estimates that the average four-year private college costs nearly $16,500 annually when tuition, fees, and room and board are added together. Public schools, while cheaper, top $6,500 annually, on average.

The good news is that a college education is still not out of reach for just about anybody who really wants it. Things are not getting any easier, but it can be done. "Although tuition increases continue to run ahead of inflation, the fact remains that college is still affordable for most students," College Board president Donald M. Stewart said in September 1994. "Students and their families must keep the issue of college costs in perspec-

tive and not focus on the cost of a relatively small number of high-priced colleges."

Schools know that they cost too darned much, and many of them are now struggling to find ways to provide value—or, at least, the *image* of value—to students. In a recent story on offbeat tuition plans, *Washington Post* staff writer Rene Sanchez wrote that "Colleges across the country have begun trying to recruit and keep students worried about soaring tuition costs with a brand-new sales pitch: Let's make a deal." While warning that some bargains could be exaggerated, Sanchez cited several innovative schemes:

• Michigan State has pledged to incoming freshmen that tuition won't rise any faster than inflation for the next four years.

• Indiana University promises that some students who can't take all of their required course work within a four-year program (since some required courses aren't available every semester) will get the fifth year for free.

• Middlebury College in Vermont, like several other small, expensive liberal arts colleges, has created a three-year degree program to help cut costs by as much as $18,000 overall.

Cost consciousness has put more pressure than ever on schools, David Warren, president of the National Association of Independent Colleges and Universities, told Sanchez, "creating a lot of experiments with tuition prices. I don't know a university president who is not engaged in strategic planning along these lines."

We put together this book to help you do a little strategic planning of your own, to help you get the money you need to pay for college. The aid maze is so complex that most of us could use a friendly guide. Yet so many of the guides to getting financial aid are not what computer types call "user-friendly." In fact, some seem almost user-hostile. Most could put Sominex out of business. They are dull, wordy, and overly complex. This book is intended to be different—lively, easy to read, and to the point. The book describes the many avenues to financial aid. It shows how you can plan to pay for your college education. And it even takes you by the hand in filling out cumbersome financial aid applications. We have tried to make this the most useful, readable guide to financial aid on the market today. But it is not a guide for everyone: In the first place, we have chosen principally to provide information pertaining to undergraduates looking for financial aid.

We've done some selecting for you already. Several scholarship guides we have come across fatten their pages with thousands of scholarships that are next to useless. They may apply to too few people, offering money to, say, blue-eyed virgins from Lourdes, Tennessee. If you qualify, you probably already know about that scholarship. And if you aren't a blue-eyed virgin from Lourdes, Tennessee, you can't get the money. So why include it? Other scholarships are a little, well, chintzy—some don't even cover the cost of textbooks. We decided to provide you with a realistic list. Most scholarship sources in this book provide an award of at least $1,000 annually.

At the same time, you need to keep in mind that more than 80 percent of all aid comes from federal and state programs, not the private scholarships listed here. So while we give you a healthy list of private scholarships, we encourage you to focus your attention on the sources of aid that matter—the government programs discussed here in the front of the book—before you spin your wheels applying to every program under the sun.

This guide is regularly updated. Financial aid programs aren't etched in stone; they change from year to year depending on factors ranging from the whims of Congress to losses incurred by the stock portfolios of the foundations behind their grants. Often factors affect higher education funding from directions no one could ever predict. Take for example the effects of fuel prices on the University of Texas. During the mid-1980s, the Organization of Oil Producing and Exporting Countries lost its self-discipline and flooded world markets with oil, dropping fuel prices and setting off a disastrous recession in oil-producing American states like Texas. The Texas recession spun out of control, dragging down with it the banking, real estate, and agriculture sectors of the economy. The Texas legislature, scrambling to make up for the lost tax revenues, raised college tuition across the board—without commensurately raising financial aid. Thus what was widely considered one of the best bargains in American higher education became a mere good deal. Using an up-to-date guide gives you the edge in calculating tuition dollars, shopping for aid money, and anticipating unpleasant surprises.

Before you go any further—Do you really want to go to college? Ask yourself that question. If you have bought this book, you probably have already decided that college is the way to go. But what if you're not planning to follow the standard business route? Maybe deep in your heart of hearts you know you're a plumber. You have loved pipes and joints since infancy. You have a plumber's soul. Though a degree in mechanical engineering might enhance your appreciation of the plumbing aesthetic, you don't need it to get started. Considering that a Manhattan plumber makes more than $50 an hour, college begins to look like a lot of time and money down the drain.

If you do decide to skip college, you'll be in good company. Among the noncollegiate, you will find such well-known authors as Ernest Hemingway and Rudyard Kipling, as well as Abraham Lincoln and Wee Kim Wee, president of Singapore. Other famous people, like Walter Cronkite and Apple Computer cofounder Steven Jobs, left college before graduating.

In all fairness to the colleges, it should be noted that many of the noncollege success stories decided not to go onto higher education at a time (or in a culture) in which a degree was less than essential. Uncle Sam democratized college after World War II by paying for the educations of millions of returning servicemen. That college-educated generation expected its kids to go to college, too. More and more Americans are going to college: According to the Bureau of Labor Statistics, nearly half of workers aged 25 to 64 in the U.S. have had some college experience, and 26 percent of workers in that group have had at least four years of college. So it's harder than before to buck the trend.

Besides—while there are a lot of college-educated taxicab drivers, there's also plenty of evidence that going to college pays. Studies regularly show that college graduates earn more than those who do not attend. Higher education simply gives you a leg up in the job market. The Bureau of Labor Statistics reports that nearly 90 percent of people with four or more years of college are in the labor force: that means that they are either working or looking for work. People with a high school degree alone don't fare so well: only 77 percent of that group is in the labor force. A January 1988 report entitled *The Forgotten Half: Non-College Youth in America* says, "The plight of the young person without advanced education, never easy, has become alarming in recent years." The report went on to say, "In a fast-changing economy that demands increasingly specialized skills, these young people are in danger of being left at the starting gate." The business world pays attention to credentials (maybe too much attention, but that's a subject for a different book), and a college degree is one of the basics. And the professions are getting more specialized, not less.

Ultimately, the value of a college education has to be measured in terms that go beyond the balance sheet. Something about dollar signs and decimal points flattens the wonder inherent in the college experience. It's about forming lifelong friendships, and more. I met my wife the week before classes started my freshman year; we first kissed in a dorm lounge while studying for a history exam. Friends from college days now work all over the world—as lawyers, political consultants, journalists, cartoonists and more. I'd be much poorer for not having known them.

Treated right, higher education is a four-year excursion into the life of the mind, with opportunities for gaining knowledge and personal growth. At its best, college teaches you how to learn, so that you can tackle any task set before you. With the right courses, you can heighten your appreciation of literature and the arts, making the acquisition of knowledge a lifelong pleasure. Yes, it's important to find the money to pay for school. But once the financial side is taken care of, enjoy! Take advantage of this unique opportunity to broaden your horizons and expand your powers of thought.

Anyone Can Pay for College

1. The Short Course: What This Section Will Tell You

In effect, this chapter serves as a short version of the book, with fundamental information about financial aid for people in a hurry. You'll find capsule descriptions of the basic kinds of financial aid, some tips here and there, and a few warnings to make sure you don't lose out. The chapter also includes a long-term and short-term view of trends in paying for college that could help you plan for the near and distant future.

2. There Are Right and Wrong Ways to Pay for College

In *Citizen Kane*, Charles Foster Kane tells an associate, "It ought to be easy to make money—if that's all you want to do." When he made that statement, Kane—like the man he was modeled on, publishing magnate William Randolph Hearst—was a millionaire many times over. You, the reader, are probably not a millionaire many times over. Even if Kane was right, college is not the time to make moneymaking your sole goal. When you're going to college, the last thing you want to do is to spend so much time trying to pay the bills that you can't enjoy the experience—or worse, can't keep up with your studies.

There are plenty of bad ways to pay your way through college. The most common is simple overwork: taking on two or more jobs to make ends meet. One friend of mine worked his way through law school with no less than three part-time jobs. He ended up spending a semester recuperating from hepatitis, and almost had to put off graduating. (Today he's a successful attorney—still overworked, but getting paid handsomely for it.) Other diseases, such as mononucleosis, commonly spring from exhaustion. Why ruin four great years of your life by keeping your nose so close to the grindstone that you can't even enjoy your studies, much less develop a social life? If you decide to work through your college days, choose your employment wisely. Later in this book, we give you some tips on creating your own small business in order to earn money, and direct you to guides that show schemes that have worked for students in the past.

Another way to pay college expenses that gets students into trouble is taking on an oversized debt burden.

Education funding experts have warned that taking on too heavy a burden of debts may cause students to look toward safer, higher-paying careers than they might otherwise be attracted to. The same experts also fear that the prospect of being in debt could be enough to scare many lower-income students away from college, or from majors they might find personally fulfilling (say, teaching or fine arts) but which they feel will never allow them to repay the loans. We lose a lot of good teachers to the ranks of lawyers and engineers that way. While student loans are an increasingly important part of financial aid packages, most schools still have some discretion as to how much of your aid package should be made up of loans and how much should be made up of outside grants. (It is sometimes possible to get a college financial aid officer to alter the makeup of a financial aid package.) Parents have to decide, when looking at financial aid packages, how much pain they can stand—and how much of the debt burden they can, in good conscience, shift to their kids. We'll return to these topics a little later.

Some ideas aren't just bad: they're illegal. Shady moneymaking schemes attract a number of students for the same reason that they attract criminals: quick money, and lots of it. However, the risk often outweighs the reward, and few students show the street smarts to escape the long arm of the law. In my college days, a few acquaintances tried to hustle up extra money by dealing drugs. None of them were arrested, but most found they lost money more often than made it. Their college education had not yet honed their business skills, and besides, they generally had trouble keeping out of the inventory. One friend was clubbed to death, apparently because of a deal gone sour. There have got to be better ways to raise a buck than that. (In case you were wondering, most of my college friends, like the overworked law student, were fine, upstanding young people who have terrific jobs today.)

The purpose of this book is to help you spend your time wisely and to get the maximum amount of financial aid funds from the most lucrative sources. That way, you'll be less likely to run yourself into the ground trying to make up for aid money you might otherwise have gotten.

3. Figuring Out What College Will Really Cost

The student is more than just a seeker of knowledge—he or she is also a consumer in the academic marketplace. And all good shoppers know the value of comparison shopping. Comparing colleges, while a complex task, pays off. The main areas of comparison are these: tuition and fees, books and supplies, room and board, transportation, and personal expenses. Most colleges publish a "consumer brochure"—a handy resource that sets out expenses. That brochure is a helpful starting point for any student or family.

Tuition and fees vary widely, but the most basic dividing line between institutions is public versus private. Private schools simply tend to be pricier. But before you strike all private schools from your list, consider this: Public schools are far from cheap—and out-of-state tuition at many of the most respected public universities rivals that of the average private school.

Books and supplies don't vary as much from school to school as do tuition and fees, but they can add hundreds of dollars each semester to the bill and must be counted in. These costs vary depending on the field of study, so it is important to find out typical figures from the academic department or from students within the major.

Room and board can make up a huge chunk of college costs. Room and board can be measured simply if the student is living in a dormitory: it's part of the total bill. According to the College Board, during the 1993–94 school year the average cost of room and board at four-year private colleges was $4,976; at public schools, $3,826. Both had risen about four percent over the previous year's figure. But don't think living at home will simply clear that cost from the college budget. For one thing, you won't save as much money as you think on wholesome, home-cooked meals. Irregular class hours will force the student to buy at least one meal a day on or near campus. And if the student is going to live off campus, living expenses could run even higher, with variations from school to school. The differences between paying for an apartment in Athens, Georgia, and Cambridge, Massachusetts, are enough to skew comparisons of schools that might otherwise appear to be similarly priced.

Personal expenses may add up to more than parents expect. Although students have historically lived on the cheap, the Benetton generation is more prone to fancy accessories than its grubbier parents, for whom a year-old pair of (non-designer) blue jeans could be considered formal wear. Even the Seattle/Grunge look could be expensive if you went to fancy department stores for those fashionably worn-out lumberjack shirts. Again, geographic variation wreaks havoc on expense estimates. Travel expenses might include air fare for out-of-state students or simply gas and car repair for commuters. In any case, this easily overlooked category can add thousands to the college bundle of costs. Finally, don't forget to add in known medical costs, such as treatment and pharmaceuticals for an existing medical condition.

When you start to see the real cost of college, you might give serious consideration to getting a degree from one of those institutions that advertises on matchbook covers, or to exploring a career in auto repair. DON'T PANIC! Expensive institutions know that they cost more than most people can pay, and they often have the resources to help you. After all, if the students don't come, they have to shut their doors.

Once you know what different schools might cost, it's time to work out what you and your family can afford to pay. Taking the difference between what the college costs and what you can afford to pay gives you the amount of your need. This deceptively simple term, "need," doesn't necessarily mean what you think it ought to mean, or what you would like for it to mean. It's a specific, technical term for the amount you cannot pay on your own, and is the amount left after your Expected Family Contribution (EFC) is subtracted from your cost of education. Schools determine how much families should pay based on sets of formulas that each institution chooses. Some choose the federal formulas established by Congress, while others go by what's known as the Institutional Methodology. So it's important to make sure you know what each school you'll be applying to expects to know; one size does not fit all.

Financial assistance comes in three basic flavors: grants, loans, and work-study. Grants do not need to be repaid, while loans must be repaid some day. Work-study lets students work in order to gain the money to pay for school. You and the financial aid administrator at the college of your choice will negotiate a financial assistance package that will probably contain some combination of these three varieties of aid. During the 1993–94 school year, 54 percent of all aid was in the form of loans.

Your aid will come from a number of sources, from the most massive federal programs down to institutional funds unique to your school. Aid might come from the state, private foundations, the school, or even an employer. If the aid comes from a federal government program or a state agency, it is known as public aid; sources such as employers, donors, or foundations are known as private aid.

4. Financial Aid: What It Is

Federal Aid

Since the federal government is the largest source of student aid, it pays to know something about the major federal programs. The federal government, through the Department of Education, offers the best-known college financial aid programs. These are:

Pell Grants

In 1994, some 14 percent of American college students received Pell Grants. This program was once known as the

Basic Educational Opportunity Grant program, and you might see it referred to as such in older materials. These grants are distributed based on family need and education costs at your school. The maximum available in the 1995–96 school year is $2,300 per year, though the maximum amount changes from year to year depending on how Congress funds the program. The average grant reported in a 1994 study by the census bureau was $1,375. Eligibility is determined by a standard formula which was passed into law by Congress; that calculates your Expected Family Contribution. If that EFC figure falls below a certain threshold, you'll be eligible for a Pell. Once you've applied for aid, you'll receive a Student Aid Report that gives your Expected Family Contribuion number and tells you if you qualify. The amount of the grant you may receive is not standardized. Different schools, with their varying tuitions, disburse different amounts. Pell Grants are available until you get your undergraduate degree. While Pell Grants once went only to students who attend school at least half-time (another term with a strict definition—see the glossary for more details), part-time students are now eligible so long as their expected family contribution is in line with federal requirements. By the way—even if you think you will not qualify for a Pell Grant, you need to apply. Many schools won't consider you for aid until they see your Pell results.

Other Aid

■ There are two main kinds of low-interest loans for students and parents these days: the Federal Direct Student Loans (Direct Loan) Program and the Federal Family Education Loan (FFEL) Program. Direct Loans come directly from the federal government. The FFEL loans involve private lenders such as banks, credit unions, and savings and loans. Aside from that difference, the loans are pretty much the same; which program you get your money from depends on which program your school participates in. We'll get deeper into the details of these programs in the chapter entitled "The World of Available Aid—Public Channels."

■ Payment on some of these loans can be deferred, postponed, or even reduced, depending on your circumstances. Loans can be deferred while you continue your studies, or if you encounter economic hardship or are unable to find full-time employment for up to three years.

■ Parents who are applying for the financial aid go for what are called PLUS Loans. Like the Staffords, PLUS Loans are available from both the Direct Loan and the FFEL program. The interest rate varies from year to year, running as high as 9 percent.

■ The Direct and FFEL programs also allow what are called "Consolidation Loans" to help borrowers combine different kinds of student loans into a simpler payment scheme.

■ Three of the federal programs are "campus-based": Federal Supplemental Educational Opportunity Grants (FSEOG), Federal Work-Study (FWS), and Federal Perkins Loans. "Campus-based" simply means that the programs are administered by financial aid officers at each school. As we mentioned above, these are not entitlement programs like the Pell Grant or the Stafford Loans. The government gives each school a set amount of cash; when it's gone, it is really gone—no more campus-based aid can be had until the next year's allotment comes through. The schools set their own deadlines for these programs, so ask at your school's financial aid office and apply as early as possible to catch some of the money before it runs out.

■ Federal Supplemental Educational Opportunity Grants (FSEOG) are administered by the schools. Not all schools participate in the program, and the grants are awarded based on financial need—"exceptional financial need" is the way the government brochures put it. Unlike the Pell Grants program, which provides some money to every eligible student, the FSEOG programs only get a certain amount of funds each year. That means that once the fund dries up, there's no more until next year.

■ Federal Work-Study (FWS): This is basically a part-time job, funded by the federal government and administered by your school. Most undergraduates are paid by the hour, and often at the minimum wage. Graduate students may be paid by the hour or may receive a salary. The jobs are awarded on the basis of need, the size of FWS funds at your school, and the size of your aid package.

■ Federal Perkins loans are low-interest loans for students with "exceptional" financial need. They're also an exceptionally good deal at just 5 percent interest. The program is administered by the school; undergraduates can borrow $3,000 a year up to a total of $15,000. Perkins loan payment can be deferred in case of unemployment, and reduced or even cancelled if you pursue certain much-needed professions, including teaching in designated low-income schools, or in certain child family service agencies, or in Head Start, VISTA, the Peace Corps, and other options.

The federal government has several other ways of helping students get through school. The government provides a tuition-free education for thousands of students. The only catch is that the schools are owned by Uncle Sam: They are the military academies. If you don't mind the haircut and want to serve your country through the military, the service academies are an excellent way to do so while getting your degree. If you don't get into these highly competitive academies, the service branches maintain ROTC units on many campuses. The ROTC is another rich lode of scholarships. The ROTC also has a number of scholarships geared toward helping minority students, and to boost the number of students entering important-but-strained career fields such as the health professions. There's more on those programs in the chapter, "The World of Available Aid—Public Channels."

State Aid

In 1993–94, states expected to award just under $3 billion in total grant aid to more than 1,900,000 postsecondary students. About 75 percent is in need-based aid to undergraduates—states collectively award nearly $2 billion in need-based grants to undergraduates, according to the most recent survey by the authoritative National Association of State Scholarship and Grant Programs. That group expected to see a 12 percent increase in the 1993–94 school year. It's part of a continuing trend among the states to increase their support for higher education. However, each state is different, and some states spend far more than others. The top quarter of the states spend three-quarters of the grant dollars; the seven states that estimated they would pay more than $100 million in the 1993–94 school year—New York, California, Illinois, Pennsylvania, New Jersey, Ohio, and Minnesota— accounted for more than 61 percent of the total aid pie. New York alone estimated it would spend $667 million—23 percent of the national total.

Also, states go through cycles of generosity and stinginess that are virtually impossible to predict. But look for programs that state legislatures have instituted in order to attract more students to certain career fields, such as teaching, and so-called "non-need-based" programs (usually academic scholarships), which are booming.

College Funds

This money includes everything from athletic to academic, or merit, scholarships. The last few years have also been building years for college and university endowments, with hundreds of millions of dollars flowing into schools as diverse as Harvard University and the University of Washington (thanks, Bill Gates!). Some, but certainly not all, of this endowment money has gone into scholarship funds. Other college funds might find their way to students in the form of tuition discounts for prepayment, aid in receiving loans, and other innovative programs. Most schools also keep funds on hand for short-term emergency loans for students.

Employers

Many employers help put students through college through the burgeoning field of cooperative education, in which students alternate semesters of school with semesters of work. Not only does this provide professional skills and a leg up in the employment game, it also puts money in the student's pocket. It is best developed at technical and engineering schools like Georgia Tech, which places hundreds of students into positions in a five-year degree program, but all kinds of institutions offer cooperative education programs—almost 1,000 schools boast such programs. (See page 66 for a table of cooperative programs.)

Many employers also pay their employees to go to school. Millions of employees have the right to go back to school on their company tab, though relatively few choose to take the time. Other programs pay for the dependents of employees to attend school.

Private Scholarships

This is a relatively small part of the financial aid picture, and many carry daunting eligibility requirements—the old "red-haired Methodist from Georgia" problem. There's a lot more money to be drawn from federal and state programs, but hundreds of millions of dollars are nonetheless available in private scholarships—not an amount to turn your nose up at. There really are scholarships for left-handed students; Juniata College in Huntington, Pennsylvania, has had one since 1978. Just remember to go after the big money first and early, and then look around for whatever private scholarships you might be able to pick up.

5. The Long-Term Trends in Paying for College

The long-term trends in paying for college have repercussions for every student and every family. Three main trends have shown up lately: Families are paying a larger share of college costs these days and will continue to do so; financial aid funding is shifting away from grants and toward loans; and the number of college-age students is decreasing. Let's look at each individually.

Students and parents are indeed paying an increasing share of college costs, because federal aid to education hasn't kept up with student need. During the Reagan years, the emphasis in federal aid shifted to the needs of the poorer students as funds dwindled. Between 1980 and 1988, the number of students overall who received federal aid plummeted, and Pell Grants went from being a program for middle- and low-income students to being almost exclusively a low-income program. In 1980, 31.5 percent of all freshmen received Pell Grants; in 1988 the percentage had dropped to just 15.6 percent—the lowest level in the history of the program, according to the Cooperative Institutional Research Program. Other federal aid programs showed similar declines. The percentage of freshmen receiving Supplemental Educational Opportunity Grants dropped from eight percent in 1980 to less than four percent in 1988. And fewer students than ever are entering the federally funded Federal Work-Study program, which, during the same time dropped to less than seven percent from 14.5 percent.

The dropoff in federal assistance has sent students to other sources to make up their college funds. "These trends suggest that the burden of paying for college is increasingly falling on students, their families, and the nation's colleges," said Alexander W. Astin, professor of higher education at UCLA's Graduate School, who directs the annual survey of freshmen that provides the information cited above for the American Council on Education. Family contribution, savings, loans, and institutional grants are on the rise. A 1985 study by the National Institute of Independent Colleges and Universities points out that between 1979–80 and 1983–84, the average family contribution toward paying the price of attending an independent college or university grew from $3,313 to $5,705 for recipients of federal aid—a jump from 53 to 62 percent. The rate of increase was largest for low-income families, soaring 97 percent from $329 to $648 for families with annual incomes of less than $20,000. Nearly 80 percent of freshmen depended on their families for meeting college costs in 1988—a record high, up from about 70 percent in 1980. The percentage of freshmen relying on college grants and scholarships jumped from about 13 percent in 1980 to 20 percent in 1988.

At the same time that families have been required to shoulder more of the burden of college costs, the nature of the remaining aid has changed radically. The past few years have seen a marked shift in aid away from grants, which do not need to be repaid, and toward loans, which must eventually be repaid. Today loans make up about half of the aid that goes to college students, which means that recent graduates go into the world with a debt burden that is nothing short of massive—especially for graduates of professional and medical schools.

One trend that shows an eventual silver lining is the sweep of demographics. The post-World War II baby boom is coming to an end. Demographic predictions indicated higher education enrollments would have already started to drop off in the 1980s as the baby boomers waned. The dropoff has not happened yet—largely because of a 15 percent growth in the enrollment of 22- to 34-year-olds between 1980 and 1988. Still, the 18-year-old population will continue to ebb into the 1990s, until a baby "boomlet" that is expected to push enrollments back to mid-70s levels by the year 2000. All this means a coming drop in the pool of college-age students. While the best-known and most prestigious public and private schools will continue to attract a steady stream of applicants, the nation's smaller private schools will suffer. In the last decade nearly 150 small liberal arts colleges shut down, as more students in a shrinking overall pool of college-age students opted for less expensive public education.

The reason that this news is good news for students is that it means many colleges are working harder to attract students. As a corollary to that trend of a diminishing pool of college-aged students, we can expect to see continued strong demand for students with high scholastic achievement. Such scholarships are not based on need, and will remain popular since bringing these students into a school helps the reputation and academic climate of a campus—and because such programs are the easiest student aid to sell to alumni and other sources of contributions.

Of course, the shrinking population of college-age students could also be bad news. The danger is that fewer students will mean less tuition for the schools. That could start a vicious cycle in which schools, pressed for money, will have to raise their tuition to bring in more bucks; that will in turn drive away more students, so the remaining students will have to pay even more, and so on. It makes sense, then, to think about the nature of a school's endowment in making your choice of a college. Schools that are largely dependent on tuition for their income will be more likely to raise tuition in this environment than those that have cushy endowments. Most schools publish a breakdown of the sources of their money; read it and choose wisely.

One final note on demographics: While minority enrollment has been growing over the past few years, it has not kept pace with the minority groups' greater representation within the larger population. At the same time, the portion of the school-age population that is made up of minority students is growing; minority students could make up almost a third of Americans between the ages of 18 and 24. The effects of such changes can only be guessed at so far, but there is a distinct possibility of a greater percentage of aid money being committed to providing educational opportunities for black and Hispanic students in coming years.

Financial Aid News Update

■ **Hold the presses!** As this edition of *College Scholarships and Financial Aid* went to press, the future of aid is harder to predict than at any time in recent memory. The Republican majority in both houses of Congress had announced sweeping cuts in federal programs across the board, and many deficit-cutting measures included massive cuts in financial aid programs—or complete elimination of some of them. This comes on the heels of President Clinton's attempts to get the federal government MORE directly involved in financial aid by setting up a pilot program for direct lending to students and their families by the government. It's impossible at this time to say where this whipsawing will end, or what the ultimate effect on financial aid and the tax code will be. But it's vitally important that people who receive or want to receive financial aid to be ready to act quickly if the environment changes. These are times of rapid change and uncertainty; the best advice is to read your newspaper and try to follow what's going on.

■ **Monies for financial aid: What was up, what was down:** The grant picture has been mixed. Between 1987 and 1994 Pell Grants rose from $3.9 billion to over $5.5 billion. The current maximum: $2,300 per year. But since Congress often appropriates less than the administration requests for the grants, more students will be worried about getting money at all than getting the maximum. Other programs are each feeling the squeeze, too, as President Clinton and Congress look for ways to trim the monumental budget deficit. Today's programs are going to feel a lot of pain, whichever side ends up winning.

Since the amount of federal money allocated to higher education has not kept up with the overall rate of inflation, and since college tuition has risen at about twice the rate of overall inflation, it means that college will be harder than ever to pay for. No surprise there.

State aid has been trying to catch up with college costs and to make up for losses from federal shortfalls. In 1990–91 states awarded more than $2.15 billion in grant aid to more than 1.7 million students, according to the National Association of State Scholarship and Grant Programs; in 1993–94, the number was more like $3 billion for 1.9 million students. About 75 percent of that amount goes to need-based programs. There has been a strong rise in the money allotted to non-need-based programs, such as merit scholarships. However, the money spent on that kind of scholarship still pales in comparison to the sums that go to need-based aid.

At the same time, it's worth outlining the broad areas that are obviously important to Bill Clinton, because those are programs he will be working the hardest to enact. Those fall into two main areas: a program of national service and an attempt to take over a large portion of the student loan business.

■ **Putting kids to work:** Candidate Clinton spoke in glowing terms of programs like Vista and the Peace Corps, in which young people got a chance to do good for others for a couple of years before doing well for themselves in their careers. During the campaign, Clinton said that by 1996, he would double the amount of financial aid for higher education, spending billions on national service alone. He pledged to create a program of national service that would allow college students to pay off their loans by helping to rebuild America—to put "a new generation of Americans" to work, serving in hospitals, schools, and shelters. Its core would be college-age students, paid the minimum wage while in service, of which the feds would pick up 85 percent. For each year's service (up to two years) the student would also earn up to an additional $5,000 to be applied by the government toward a year of college or other advanced study.

It sounded great to many Americans. The media loved it. But conservatives looked at the plan and had a pronounced case of sticker shock: The maximum price tag per student, spread over four years, would be $22,580, plus health benefits, all paid by taxpayers. By 1997, some $3.4 billion would be needed to run the program and support 150,000 participants.

It wasn't just the Bob Dole crowd criticizing this one. Some critics noted that the $3.4 billion was more than a quarter of the $12.7 billion we were spending in 1993 on student financial aid—and reaching far fewer kids. Those lucky few would get nearly twice the money the average student on financial aid received in guaranteed student loans, and wouldn't have to pay anything back. The numbers looked scary—especially if it meant money for the new program might come at the expense of the old. Clinton's proposed 1994 budget cut $1.2 billion from student aid.

So Congress took a cleaver to the national service plan. What emerged was a smaller, $10 million pilot program begun with great fanfare in the summer of 1993. It allows 1,000 to 1,500 students to tutor and counsel youths and clean up neighborhoods in exchange for money for college or job training.

Sounds like small potatoes, right? But if it gets good reviews, the program could expand. If it gets anywhere near the dreams that Clinton proposed at first, National Service could end up as a revolutionary way to pay for college. Watch it closely. Whatever such a program might mean for the fiscal health of the country, it could be a fabulous deal for the individual students lucky enough to get in.

As of this writing, the Republican majority in Congress had targeted Clinton's pet project for even deeper cuts or elimination.

Uncle Sam takes on SALLIE MAE: The second broad initiative in the Clinton administration could turn out to be the biggest change to financial aid in decades. Known as the Direct Student Loan program, it is intended to take the business of taking student loans away from the businesses that have handled it in the past and giving the job to the federal government. The goal: to save more than $2 billion a year.

How? The flaws in the system are expensive, Clinton said. The amount of money that the U.S. loses because of students who don't pay their college loans is nothing short of astonishing—about $3 billion each year. At a 1993 speech to Illinois high schoolers, Clinton pointed out that part of the reason the default rate is so high is that "a lot of people. . . are making money out of the present system." Clinton went on to explain that the system was set up to make money for lenders whether students paid their loans or not. That's the "guaranteed" part of guaranteed student loans; many financial institutions are just as happy to get their payments from Uncle Sam as from students, who might have more trouble paying. The system, Clinton said, "is confusing and it's costly, and the more money that goes to other things, the less money that's available to provide low cost loans to the students of America."

Clinton took special aim at SALLIE MAE, the Student Loan Marketing Association, which made $394 million of the total $1 billion profit that all lenders made on student loans in 1992. Clinton's blunt proposal: Get rid of the middlemen and take over the loan business. Students could then pay off the loans after graduation through a payroll deduction of a percentage of salary or through, yes, performing national service.

It's another interesting idea, but it's even more controversial than the national service plan. A trial run of the system is now in effect, right alongside the old student loan system of applying for loans through private lenders. Will it expand? Will it last? Stay tuned—and read those newspapers.

■ **Colleges feel the heat:** Schools hardly need to be reminded that they need to cut costs. While tuition continues to rise at an annual rate of seven percent—far higher than the inflation rate for the rest of the economy—schools are feeling the financial squeeze more than ever. Expensive research programs and physical costs are making schools reconsider their funding priorities. The Johns Hopkins University is in the middle of a five-year plan to cut costs—a plan that includes eliminating programs in its prestigious arts and sciences school. Washington University has shut down its dentistry school, and has announced plans gradually to close its department of sociology. And Columbia University has been phasing out such prestigious programs as its archival management program, geography, and linguistics departments, transferring some courses to other departments and dropping others entirely. These aren't podunk schools —these are high-powered, wealthy institutions. So you can imagine what this means for smaller schools without the prestige and fancy endowments. And you can bet that the impact on financial aid, already severe, will only get worse. With school costs increasing and with government funds decreasing—especially state budgets, which look sickly across the nation and which are causing legislators to eye state school tuition increases more hungrily than ever—colleges are looking for every way to make students pay more of their share of education.

Students, too, appear to be making college choices with more emphasis on affordability and financial aid. In a recent survey by the College Bound, a publication for admissions advisers, nearly 92 percent of colleges said economic factors are "casting an ominous shadow on college admissions and creating personal and institutional tensions." The newsletter quoted a Purdue University administrator who said "Most students who cancelled admissions at Purdue did so because of little or no financial aid or scholarships."

Some analysts say that the whole question of college costs has been miscast—that the skyrocketing price of college is at least partly an illusion, albeit one that drives away prospective students. The *New York Times* reported in 1991 that applications to many private institutions had declined between 5 and 15 percent in the past year, a combination of smaller student population and recessionary pressures on the families footing the bills. Applications were up at the better public institutions. Consultant Peter Drucker writes in the *Wall Street Journal*: "The market share of the prestige colleges has been falling steadily these past five years, perhaps by as much as one-fifth. . . There is only one reason for this decline in market share: 'sticker shock'." Drucker's point is that even though private college costs hit the $20,000 range, the average student in private schools pays closer to $11,000 after financial aid—not pocket change, but a lot closer to what the prestigious public schools charge for out-of-state tuition. Financial aid administrators recognize the coming crisis, too: in a recent edition of the administrator magazine, *Student Aid Transcript*, Robin Jenkins, Director of Financial Management Center of the National Association of College and University Business Officers, wrote that institutions need marketing strategies "based on cost containment and educational value (price/cost) rather than manipulating price (and calling it financial aid) if they are to successfully meet consumer demand and public policy expectations."

Will a price war ensue? Don't hold your breath: The colleges aren't really set up for deep discounts, especially at tuition-dependent private schools. But schools with less arrogant and self-destructive administrations will find that they can limit their budget increases; in late 1994, Michigan State President Peter McPherson guaranteed that new students arriving in 1995 would see their tuition rise no more than the rate of inflation for the next four years. It's not a cut, and it's not even a guarantee: McPherson said the promise was "contingent upon state appropriation increases for MSU's general fund of at least the rate of inflation. But it's the kind of promise students and parents are going to want to hear, more and more—and the kind of promise that they will examine carefully before signing on the dotted line.

Other Trends to Watch

If you've been accepted to a top school, you might find good news in a 1992 trial that declared the practices of an organization called the Overlap Group illegal. Since 1958, MIT and the eight Ivy League universities have met several times a year to set joint principles for awarding financial aid and to negotiate individual aid awards for students who applied to at least two of the institutions. The result of the overlap process was that a student's cost of attending any of the schools was approximately the same. In the world of business, such practices are called price fixing, and invoke the wrath of antitrust laws. The universities seemed to feel that they were above all that, since by conserving their precious endowments they were furthering the cause of education. Soon after the suit was filed in May 1991, the Ivies originally named as defendants—Harvard, Yale, Brown, Dartmouth, Columbia, Princeton, Cornell, and the University of Pennsylvania—signed a consent decree, admitting to no wrongdoing but agreeing to stop the overlap activities. MIT decided to fight—and lost.

What does all of this legal stuff mean for the average applicant? For one thing, it means that the schools can't collude to set the same amount of financial aid for all applicants; a strong negotiator can play one school against another and shop for the best deal. The schools also agreed to base financial aid solely on need, and not merit. Ultimately, of course, this high-minded legal action might mean that the schools have less money for financial aid altogether, and so fewer students will receive financial aid.

But for now, it means it's time to play "Let's make a deal!" The Justice Department also is investigating a group of 14 smaller colleges that engaged in similar activities of meeting to discuss financial aid practices. These colleges include Williams, Amherst, Bowdoin, Wellesley, Vassar, Middlebury, and Tufts.

Colleges have been trying to fight their big-spender images with a variety of programs. Many of them can help students shave thousands of dollars from their higher education costs, while others have an almost hucksterish quality that seems more calculated to generate headlines and attract students than to help a large number of students pay for college. So when you hear about a program, ask yourself who will benefit from the program and how much it will do for them. Is it a continuing program, or a one-shot promotion? You'll find a full discussion of alternative financing methods for the chapter, "Getting the Most College for the Money."

Endnotes: Tips on Filling Out the Application

Here are a few tips on filling out your financial aid application for the filer who is in a hurry. The most important point for applicants to specific scholarships is: Don't apply if you're not eligible. Some students try a scattershot approach, submitting hundreds of letters for awards they couldn't possibly receive because of everything from academic standards to geographic requirements. The glut of these semifraudulent applications has caused many foundations actually to ask that their names be removed from the scholarship rolls—thus injuring deserving students who might not otherwise find out about the programs.

The second tip—and this is a deceptively obvious point—is to fill out the entire application properly. The late, great, legal educator Bernard Ward used to talk about judging essays for civic competitions. To weed out the flood of entries, the first thing he recalled doing was to measure the margins on each page. If the applicant's typing slopped over the prescribed margins, Ward would blithely chuck the essay without a thought as to its content. Heed Ward's example: fill out the forms letter-perfectly. Leave no blanks: where a question doesn't apply, simply write in "n/a" and move on. Some agencies return forms that have blanks, and the paper runaround can make you miss important deadlines. If you're having trouble making sense of the federal Financial Aid Application, you can call a new toll-free hotline at the Department of Education. The number is 1-800-4-FED-AID. In numbers, that's 1-800-433-3243. The TTD number for the hearing-impaired is 301-369-0518.

A third tip, or warning: Use common sense if you pay an outsider to help you with your financial aid search. Most students still hear about financial aid opportunities through high school guidance counselors or college financial aid officers. While this is often a good route to take, sometimes such officials are overworked, or can't keep up with changes in the financial aid scene on top of their other duties. Thus families often can't get the high-quality, individual attention they desire from the usual free channels. At the same time, many families look for help simply in filling out financial aid forms and in managing the complex applications process—the same way families hire experts to help file their tax forms. That is why many families have turned to independent financial counselors, many of whom are former guidance counselors and financial planners. They also pay $40 or more for computerized scholarship searches. But some of these firms walk a fine line between what is acceptable, what is unethical—and what is illegal.

Independent financial aid finding services might help find more money, but it might come at the expense of your conscience. While a college financial aid officer is likely to describe the world as it is, a paid financial planner is likelier to describe that world as it could be, going so far as to offer suggestions of ways for parents to hide income from disclosure requirements on financial aid forms. Advisers might recommend shifting assets into retirement accounts, annuities, or universal life insurance policies—none of which need to be listed on financial aid applications. Though not illegal, some college financial aid officers claim the practices are unethical at least, and that they take aid money away from truly needy students. Financial aid professionals don't look kindly on the "bend the rules" financial guys. SALLIE MAE executive Jerry Davis recalls sitting down with a financial adviser to talk about his investments when the young whiz kid started telling Davis about how he advises parents on how to hide their assets to escape their being accounted for in a needs analysis. Some of the advice was a little, shall we say, dishonest. Davis said nothing at the time, but did sit down and write a letter the next evening to the young man telling him that if he had indeed found a loophole, he could be sure that Davis would work to close it. Davis takes such things seriously—but so should you. The penalty for lying on federal aid forms is as much as ten years in jail; you can read that part right by where you sign your name.

Some for-profit financial aid services go over the line. A while back, officials at Canisius College, a small Buffalo, New York, school, noticed that 350 of the school's 3,000 financial aid requests had been put together by a local aid-search firm. (The official realized that many of the forms were filled out in the same handwriting.) Nothing wrong with that, but the school did more checking and discovered that the forms contained many interesting errors, from undervalued homes to claims of more children in college than were actually attending. According to the *Wall Street Journal*, if the misinformation had not been detected Canisius could have paid $400,000 more for aid than it should have—about five percent of its annual financial aid budget.

Beyond the familiarity with fancy footwork, many experts question whether these financial aid entrepreneurs provide much of a service. Orlow Austin, financial aid director for the University of Illinois–Urbana-Champaign, performed an informal check on such services. Austin asked students who were already receiving financial aid from his office to file with financial aid finding services. He found that once the services had gotten their $40 or more from the students, they rarely uncovered more sources of financial aid than the students had already procured through the school's own financial aid office. Austin also points out that while many of these services offer a money-back guarantee, it is a rare student who actually takes the trouble to ask for a refund—largely because the aid process is so complex that students are unlikely to know when they have not been well served, and are also likely to blame themselves for not working hard enough to pursue financial aid avenues.

Finally, many of these self-proclaimed financial "experts" know a lot less than you will after having read this book. They could be stockbrokers or financial wizards who have sniffed an opportunity in education costs, but many of them haven't done the necessary homework needed to serve the individual student. And like stockbrokers, many of them are just pushing the hot instrument of the moment—a tuition aid plan that has recently burst on the scene that will earn them a healthy commission if they can force it on you. The one-size-fits-all approach wasn't appreciated in Procrustes' day, and works no better today. If you do decide that you need to speak with a financial adviser, protect yourself. Anyone can call himself an investment adviser, so it's important to find someone with special expertise. Certified Financial Planners have at least three years of experience and have taken at least a two-year course in financial planning and a six-part certification exam. College finances make up a part of that training and testing. "That's one of the most-requested strategies—to set up a game plan for sending a kid through college," says Mark Tuttle of the Institute of Certified Financial Planners, the nonprofit organization that polices the profession. To track down a CFP in your area, call the Institute at 1-800-282-PLAN (7526). They can even refer you to CFP's who specialize in college planning.

The lesson: it pays to establish a strong relationship with the financial aid officers at your school. They are most likely to know the field well and to have special knowledge about what is available at your school. And if you must go outside for help, remember Jiminy Cricket's credo: Let your conscience be your guide.

You and the Tax Laws: What the IRS Has Done to Higher Education

During the 1980s, tax law changes were not kind to parents, or students, trying to meet the costs of higher eduation. Congress made it more difficult for parents to shift income to children in lower tax brackets and for students to obtain tax-free treatment for scholarships and grants. Interest deductions for education loans were also cut.

However, tax-saving opportunities remain and there is talk in Washington of providing new tax breaks to help shoulder the cost burdens of college.

This chapter will give you the outlines, but of course you should sit down with your family's investment adviser to see how the tax laws apply directly to you. Let's look at each broad category individually.

Income Splitting Has All But Split, But Some Help Is on the Way

Once upon a time parents could spin off their income to their kids and their lower tax bracket, which would mean less taxes paid while keeping money all in the family. Tax shelters like the Clifford Trust proliferated. Nowadays the tax laws have gotten tough on kiddie tax shelters—though income splitting is still a good idea, if you do it right. If you give your child investments that produce income of $1,300 or less a year—and this amount changes annually with inflation—the first $650 (also changes annually) is tax free and the next $650 is taxed to the child at the child's tax rate. However, if a child under age 14 has investment income exceeding $1,300 (as adjusted for inflation), the so-called "Kiddie-Tax" subjects the excess to tax at the parent's higher tax rate. Children who are at least age 14 at the end of the year are taxed on all of their investment income at their own tax bracket rate.

In order to shift any income to a child, you must acutally transfer ownership of the income-producing asset to the child. You cannot instruct the bank to credit the interest from your account to the child. You have to transfer ownership of the account itself.

When you transfer substantial assets to your child, there is a potential gift tax liability, but under the annual exclusion, you can give up to $10,000 per child, per year, without triggering the gift tax, and this amount is increased to $20,000 if you are married and your spouse agrees to split the gift.

Parents can accomplish a degree of income splitting by creating custodial accounts for their children through a bank, mutual fund, or brokerage firm.

In the case of a custodial account handled through a brokerage, for example, an adult—parent, grandparent, guardian, or any adult—opens a stock account at a broker's office in the child's name. The custodian then can buy and sell the securities, collect the income from sales and investment, and spend it on the child or plow it back into the account. The custodian need not be that adult—in fact, a bank or trust company can serve as custodian. When the child comes of age, he or she can take over the account and sell off the securities, or keep the ball rolling. But remember the caveat above: If the child is under 14 years of age and the income rises above $1,300 a year, the excess will be taxed at the parent's rate. Also, income from the account that is used to discharge a parent's support obligation is taxable to the parent. The rules governing custodial accounts vary from state to state, but those differences don't generally affect tax consequences of having the accounts.

What sort of properties make good gifts to minors? Gifts that require little attention; if you exercise too much control over the child's property, the IRS might not let you call it a gift for the purposes of shifting income. Some of these set-it-and-forget-it investments include bonds, which you can buy in the minor's name and which sit quietly until the date of maturity—the bond's that is, not the child's. Many savvy investors are buying zero-coupon municipal bonds, which are tax-free and can be timed to reach maturity when your child is ready for college. Also, mutual fund shares provide steady supervision for an investment. Even good old U.S. Savings Bonds can make an attractive gift investment when you consider that you don't have to report the interest income until the year the bond is cashed in or matures. That means you can buy bonds for an under-14-year-old and defer interest reporting until the child has reached 14 years of age, when the income will be taxed at the child's lower rate.

The tax law provides some families with a break that makes Series EE Savings Bonds even more attractive. If you use those bonds to pay tuition or other educational fees for yourself or your family, the accrued interest on the redeemed bonds may be excluded from your reported income. There are a few requirements, of course. The new law only applies to EE bonds issued after 1989, and the purchaser has to be older than 24. So if you bought them in your child's name, or if you jointly own them with your child, you don't qualify. You must elect to defer the reporting of interest accrued on the bonds to the time when you redeem them, instead of reporting the interest annually. The full tax exclusion on that interest income only applies to taxpayers with modified adjusted gross incomes below an annual threshold. For example, the exclusion for 1995 was available to unmarried persons with modified adjusted gross income of up to $42,300, and to married couples filing jointly with up to $63,450. If your income exceeds the threshold, the exclusion is phased out over the next $15,000 of income for unmarried persons, or $30,000 on a joint return. (The exclusion doesn't apply to a married person filing separately.) If by happy chance your interest income exceeds your educational expenses, then you will have to pay taxes on the portion of the interest income that spills over the top.

Several states now offer a local version of this deal, commonly known as "Baccalaureate Bonds." They act like zero-coupon bonds, which is to say your kid gets no income until they mature.

A word to the investment-wise: Many investment advisers have taken a long look at the Savings Bond plan and have decided that they don't offer as sweet a deal as you might like. The income restrictions make them a difficult game to play—if your earnings power increases, you lose the tax benefit of all your scrimping. Besides—there are a lot of relatively safe investments out there, such as stock-based mutual funds, that tend to generate far more income than bonds do. The stock market may go up and down, but its general trend over the years has been a steady rise that beats almost any other investment you could name.

What about those headline-grabbing programs that let you prepay tuition—even years ahead of time—at a steep discount? (More on such plans in the chapter, The World Of Available Aid—Private Channels.) The IRS has set its sights on the plans that are being administered by the states to make sure that they will not be Clifford Trusts in sheep's clothing. Parents must file a gift tax return, though in most cases they will not have to pay any taxes until the child enters college. Until then, the state trust takes the tax hit. When the trust does start to pay off for the college student, the IRS will be waiting. The student will have to pay tax on the "gain element" provided by the parent's gift—a far larger sum than the amount the parents first put into the fund. Each year, the student will pay taxes on the excess over the current tuition costs over 25 percent of the par-

ent's prepayment. If the child does not enter college, then the refund from the state will also be taxed to an extent.

Scholarships and Grants

Students receive a tax break for scholarships and fellowship grants, but it is limited. Tax-free treatment is allowed only to degree candidates, and only to the part of the grant used to pay for tuition and course-related supplies. If you use the grant for room and board, it is taxable. Also taxable is a grant that pays for teaching or research services that are required as a condition of receiving the grant.

The Loan Ranger: Hi-Yo Silver, Away!

Under the tax law, not all mortgages are alike. Those mortgages taken out on or before October 14, 1987, are simple: all interest payments are deductible, whether the mortgage was for your principal residence or for a second home. The same goes for home equity loans taken out before that date. On the other hand, mortgages incurred after October 13, 1987, are only fully deductible if:
(1) the debt that you have taken on to buy, build, or improve your principal residence does not exceed $1,000,000 (or $500,000 if married filing separately); or
(2) you have taken out a home equity loan of up to $100,000 (or $50,000 if married filing separately). This applies to either your primary residence or second home. Interest payments on any amount above that are not deductible.

Letting the Boss Pay Gets a Little Less Cushy

Until the beginning of 1995, employees enjoyed a great gift from the government: If their employer was willing to foot the bill for college, Uncle Sam wouldn't tax the first $5,250 of benefits. Unless Congress restores this tax break, the money spent on courses will be considered taxable pay by the IRS—though in some cases, employees still might be able to deduct the expenses if they can prove the courses they took were job-related.

Keep an Eye on Congress

Congress has been feeling the heat from angry parents who fear they will not be able to pay for their child's education; you can expect more plans will emerge to allow parents to save for their kids' education. For example, Congress may decide to allow a tax deduction for tuition or allow tax-free withdrawals from IRAs to pay college costs. However you decide to proceed, do so with care. When someone tells you about a great tax shelter, make sure that it is still in effect before you spend any money on it. Keep up with the tax news (or hire a good accountant) so you'll know if Congress takes your shelter away.

Intermission—The Loan Route

No other aspect of paying for college is as bewildering—or as frightening—as loans. Other forms of assistance make more sense. The concepts behind work-study and other forms of work are pretty familiar: you work, you get paid. As the lawyers say, quid pro quo—something for something. The concept of grants is pretty easy, too: Someone gives you money, you spend it. You don't give it back. In effect, you are getting something for nothing. (No wonder grants are so hard to get.)

Owing money is just plain unpleasant. Polonius told Hamlet, "Neither a borrower nor lender be," and most of us wish we could take his advice. We don't like being in someone's debt. But for a lot of middle-class families, borrowing is a fact of life. It is the leverage that got the folks their house, their car, and probably helped them along toward other major purchases on the way.

But there are differences between their time and yours. For many of our parents, loans have been a way of life—and a pathway to riches. Parents getting started in the 1950s and the 1960s took out loans with relatively low interest rates and bought homes, which appreciated greatly in value. The value of the homes ballooned through the 1970s and 1980s, exceeding the cost of the mortgage and making it possible to generate even more money through second mortgages and home equity loans. This isn't the way it worked out for everyone, of course, but it served as a pattern of success for a generation.

The succeeding generations haven't had it so lucky. Runaway inflation in the 1970s raised both the value of property and the cost of credit. Not only are homes out of the reach of many young people today, but also loans for college are beginning to look quite forbidding. When deciding how much they can afford to pay up front, parents who have benefitted from the real estate and interest rate ride might have to dig deeper than they'd like to, since the alternative means shifting the financial burden to a generation that looks like it will end up having less ability to pay those debts back, on the whole.

Perhaps the scariest result of the growth in borrowing to pay for higher education is that borrowing could be squeezing many people out of the world of financial aid—and thus college. A recent report sponsored by Congress and the College Board warned that the growing debt burden might represent a threat for society at large, perhaps burdening the current generation beyond its ability to pay. The report further speculated that borrowing was a tougher concept for the poor than for the middle class, and that these groups would have more trouble repaying their loans than better-off students. So the trend toward borrowing was most threatening to the poor, and especially to minorities. Some prospective students, uncertain of their ability to find a job lucrative enough to allow repaying a loan, might simply avoid loans, and college, altogether. Thus borrowing could be part of what's behind the fact that black and Hispanic students do not attend college in numbers commensurate with their percentage in the population as a whole.

The sad fact is that borrowing is here to stay; you will almost certainly have to borrow to complete your education. Even if Bill Clinton saves his Direct Loan program from the Republican budget knife, you'll still end up owing money—but the creditor will be Uncle Sam, the guy who brought you the Internal Revenue Service. But getting a loan is not a death knell. Many programs, especially the federal loan programs, have provisions to make your debt burden more manageable. For one thing, several of them (such as the Perkins Loan) give you a grace period of six months. And some of the programs even let you delay payment for other reasons, like joining the Peace Corps. More and more programs are allowing students to defer or reduce loan payments in return for working in much-needed professions such as nursing; the current administration in Washington wants to expand such options.

It's also important to keep in mind that those earlier generations had the right idea—that borrowing is still a smart way to make big-ticket expenses like an education more manageable. Karl E. Case, Professor of Economics at Wellesley College, has published a paper in the Journal of Student Financial Aid that looks at how different ways of meeting college costs affect the percentage of family income that the colleges get. While his basic point is that long-term saving and financial planning is the best way to reduce the burden of college costs, his comparisons of loans and burdens are nonetheless eye-opening. He writes:

"A household with a $40,000 income takes home about $2,150 a month after taxes. A yearly parental contribution of $5,430, if paid out of a year's income would be $453 a month or 21% of take home pay. Since the child is in school for four years, that would be $453 per month for four years. But...

"Using a parent loan with a 9% interest rate for 10 years the monthly payment would be cut to $174 per month or 8.1% of take home pay.

"If parents had started saving six years prior to college earning 6% on their savings, the whole bill could have been paid for $150 per month over 10 years (6 years before and 4 years during college)—7.1% of income with no borrowing.

"If parents had started when the child was 8 years old and took out an 8-year parent loan, the whole thing could have been financed for $75 per month or 3.5% of income."

Case goes on in the paper to show that the same logic applies to families with higher or lower income.

Complex numbers aside, Case's basic principles apply to all debt burdens: paying over a longer period of time reduces the amount that you have to pay each year or each month. And since savings generate income for you in the form of interest, it is an even better way to prepare for any debt burden. Unfortunately, it is probably too late for you to do this kind of long-range planning for your education; most buyers of this book are headed for college within a year or so, but Case's advice can well apply to a younger family member. Look again at the difference between the effect on income of long-term borrowing as opposed to paying out tuition semester by semester, and you'll see that borrowing is a necessary evil—more necessary now than ever. That's why so many colleges, states, and private institutions are presenting innovative loan programs and programs to allow installment payment of tuition.

Of course, government programs are political footballs—you can expect everything from funding levels to entitlement rules to be tinkered and tampered with from year to year. So it's important to keep up with financial aid news to know what's coming your way.

The World of Available Aid—Public Channels

What This Chapter Will Do

O.K.—let's get back to work. In this chapter we will go into greater detail about the publicly funded sources of financial aid. We will cover federal programs and state programs. The federal programs make up the bulk of all funding for financial aid. On the state side, we will compare state appropriations to show which states are the big spenders and which are the skinflints. We will describe the range of programs available from the states. We also include the state offices that oversee financial aid so that you can continue the hunt for specific state programs on your own.

Federal Government Programs

Pell Grants

Before we even describe Pell Grants and how tough it is to get money out of this need-based federal program, here's a point about them that we can't stress enough: EVEN IF YOU THINK YOU COULDN'T POSSIBLY BE ELIGIBLE FOR A PELL GRANT, YOU SHOULD APPLY. Many other aid programs require that you first apply for a Pell. If you bypass the Pell, you pass up a great deal of possible aid, including the Stafford Loan program. So if you're serious about applying for financial aid, APPLY FOR A PELL GRANT EVERY YEAR THAT YOU ARE IN COLLEGE.

What it is: Pell Grants are, as the name implies, grants—they need not be repaid. Though the funding for Pell Grants comes from the federal government, your school gives you the money—or, in some cases, merely credits your tuition account. Your school will tell you which forms you must fill out to apply for a Pell Grant; different schools require different forms. (We will go into more detail on the different financial aid forms in the chapter, "Putting Your Financial Aid Package Together.")

Prior to 1980, Pell Grants were called Basic Educational Opportunity Grants; older materials might refer to them as such. If you see terms like BEOG or Guaranteed Student Loan (until recently, the name for the FFEL Stafford Loan Program), you shouldn't use those outdated materials. Times change, and the old stuff can steer you wrong.

The budget for Pell Grants is not limited: there is no cap on the number of Pell Grants that will be handed out in a given year. Washington budgets according to its expectations and hopes for the best. However, if program budgets get tight, the maximum award can be shaved somewhat by the Secretary of Education. The important thing to remember with Pell Grants is that if you qualify and apply on time—no later than May 1—you will get your money. The early bird doesn't get a better worm when it comes to Pells, but missing your deadline means getting no money at all.

Pell Grants can be used for five years of undergraduate study, or six if the student is pursuing a course of study that requires more than four years. Factors that exempt students from the five- and six-year limits include death of a relative, personal illness or injury to the student, or the need to take remedial courses. Your school might have other rules for extending Pell support.

How to qualify: Students must be U.S. citizens and must be attending school at least half-time. These undergraduate grants go to students who are enrolled at least half-time. (As you can imagine, "half-time" is a term with a very specific definition. The Department of Education defines that this way: "At schools measuring progress by credit hours and academic terms (semesters, trimesters, or quarters), 'half-time' means at least six semester hours or quarter hours per term. At schools measuring progress by credit hours but not using academic terms, 'half-time' means at least twelve semester hours or eighteen quarter hours per year. At schools measuring progress by clock hours, 'half-time' means at least twelve hours per week." If that isn't confusing enough, individual schools can set higher minimum requirements—which means you should check with your school to find out its definition.)

Whether or not you will get a Pell Grant depends on a formula, passed into law by Congress, that is applied to the information you provide in your financial aid application. The formula produces a Student Aid Index number. The lower the Student Aid Index number, the more money you can get in your grant. The maximum available for the 1995–96 school year is $2,300. These grants are distributed based on family need and education costs at your school. The formula that the Education Department uses to determine your Expected Family Contribution

(EFC) is established by Congress; it shows up on the Student Aid Report that comes back after you've applied. If you want to know everything there is to know about how that magic number comes about, the Department of Education publishes a booklet, "Expected Family Contribution (EFC) Formulas," which you can order from the Federal Student Aid Information Center, P.O. Box 84, Washington D.C. 20044.

Federal Supplemental Equal Educational Opportunity Grants

What it is: FSEOG is another grant for undergraduates. As grants, FSEOG's do not need to be repaid. This is a campus-based program, which means it is administered by the schools—but not all schools participate, so check with your financial aid office. It provides up to $4,000 a year, depending on your need. Unlike Pell Grants, SEOG funds are "campus-based," which means they come to schools in a set amount. Once that fund is depleted, there's no more until next year. The lesson: Apply early (your school sets its own deadline for these grants).

How to qualify: They are earmarked by Congress for students with exceptional financial need, and first priority goes to Pell Grant recipients. Schools decide whether to give FSEOG's to students who do not attend more than half-time.

Federal Work-Study

What it is: FWS lets you earn while you learn in jobs either on- or off-campus, administered through the financial aid office. The amount you earn will be at least the federal minimum wage, but you can earn more depending on the kind of work that the school finds for you. The total amount you earn will be determined by the school; working more hours than those assigned will not get you more money.

The range of work-study jobs is limited only by the imagination of your school aid office, and many aid officers have surprisingly broad imaginations. Thus your school might have arranged myriad jobs on campus in each academic department, from cleaning out the baboon cages to helping run the projectors for college movies. Off-campus jobs abound, too, and often involve working for a private or public nonprofit organization or a local, state, or federal agency. And many schools have linked up with private employers near the campus to give you valuable real-world job experience. Some colleges even have large employment offices to help students sort out all their options. (College Work-Study is not the same as cooperative education, in which the school helps students divide their time between school and a career-oriented job. A description of cooperative education begins on page 65.)

How to qualify: Both undergraduates and graduate students are eligible for this campus-based program. Financial aid administrators dole out work study jobs based on your need. Part-time students may be eligible, depending on the school. Again, since work-study is campus based, the money is allocated to the school in a lump. Once it's gone, it's gone. Pay attention to the school's application deadlines.

Federal Perkins Loans (formerly National Direct Student Loans)

What it is: This is a broad program of federal loans—and loans have to be paid back, with interest. However, Perkins Loans offer extremely low interest—five percent—which is far better than you can get at a commercial lending institution. The school will either pay you directly or credit your tuition account.

Depending on how much money you need and how much money the school can give out, Perkins Loans can give you quite a bit of money. You can borrow up to $15,000 as an undergraduate—$3,000 for each year. Some schools that have extremely low default rates on their loans are allowed to give out even more Perkins Loan money; check to see if your school is one of the lucky few.

How to qualify: Of course, with money this cheap there's a catch. Perkins Loans are only available to students who demonstrate exceptional financial need. Though the loans go primarily to full-time students, some schools also give them to part-time and half-time students. These loans are made through your school's financial aid office. This is another campus-based program, which means that the amount of funds are limited by how much money your school got from Washington. So find out the application deadlines at your school and get the applications in early.

When to pay it back: If you are a "new borrower"— that is, if you enroll after July 1, 1987, and you have no other outstanding Perkins Loans or Federal Direct Student Loans or have paid off your own loans—then you have a grace period of nine months after you graduate, leave school, or drop below half-time attendance. Your school might have different rules concerning payback for students who drop below half-time, so check with your school's financial aid office before dropping too many classes. If you are not a new borrower, your grace period is six months. In either case, you will have as much as ten years to repay your loan.

You can stop the clock on your Perkins Loan so long as you continue your studies at least half-time. You can also hold off repayment for up to three years by working in the Peace Corps or VISTA Programs, or comparable full-time volunteer work for a qualified tax-exempt organization; active duty in the Armed Forces or in the commissioned corps of the U.S. Public Health Service; or serving in the National Oceanic and Atmospheric

Administration Corps. Uncle Sam also now allows deferments if you work as a teacher in a federally-defined "teacher shortage area"; your school's education department should have information on which programs qualify you for that deferment. You can also hold off payments for as much as three years if you become temporarily totally disabled, or can't work because you're caring for a spouse or other dependent who becomes temporarily totally disabled. Certain internships can get you a two-year deferment, and mothers of preschool-aged children who are working at a salary that pays no more than a dollar above minimum wage get a one-year deferment. There's even a parental leave deferment of up to six months for pregnant borrowers, or borrowers who are caring for newborn or newly adopted children. If you become unemployed, your school may have programs to defer the principal of your loan during your period of unemployment. Being on your way to employment can also get you a deferment: under certain conditions, an internship or residency program that is required to begin professional practice or service. But none of these deferments is automatic; you have to apply for a deferment through your school, and you have to continue paying off your loans until the deferment goes through. Otherwise, you could be found in default. You can even get all or part of your loan forgiven altogether. Part of your loan will be wiped off the books if you become a teacher of handicapped children, or teach in a designated elementary or secondary school that serves low-income kids. In either case, your entire loan will be cancelled in the fifth straight year of full-time teaching. Your college can provide you with a list of designated schools that will help you do well for yourself by doing good. Working in certain Head Start programs will also cancel up to 100 percent of your loan; by your seventh Head Start year, the slate will be wiped clean for your entire loan. And as much as 70 percent of your loan can be cancelled if you volunteer for the Peace Corps or VISTA. Finally, the military often repays a portion of your loan as an incentive to sign up.

Direct and FFEL Program Loans

What it is: Life used to be much simpler when this program was just known as the Stafford Loan. In recent years, a number of new Federal loan programs have proliferated, thanks in part to the government's entry into the direct loan field. But before you wander into the maze of program titles, you need to know one thing: there are differences in benefits between Federal direct loans and the old-fashioned federally subsidized loans.

The two broad programs are now known as the Federal Direct Student Loan Program and the Federal Family Education Loan (FFEL) Program. Under the Direct Loan Program, Uncle Sam makes the loans directly to students and parents through the school. With FFELs, you get the money from banks, credit unions, or savings and loans.

Direct Loans and FFEL Program Loans come in two flavors: subsidized or unsubsidized. If your financial need is great enough that you qualify for a subsidized loan, the federal government will pay the interest on the loan until you begin paying the loan back—usually, after college. An unsubsidized loan is not awarded on the basis of need, but it's more expensive than the subsidized kind. If you qualify for an unsubsidized loan, your interest charges will begin from the time you first get the loan until you pay it in full.

If you're entering the FFEL program (getting the money from a financial institution like a bank), then the programs are either known subsidized or unsubsidized Stafford Loans. If you sign up for a Direct Loan program (that is, the government is handing out the money through the school), the programs are known as the Direct Stafford Loans (the subsidized kind) or the Direct Unsubsidized Stafford Loan. You can mix and match subsidized and unsubsidized money, so long as both loans are from the same program—either FFEL or the Direct Loan Program.

Stafford Loans, like Federal Perkins Loans or any loans, have to be repaid with interest. If you get a Direct Loan, your lender is the U.S. Department of Education; the loan is processed by the school and you don't have to seek out a lender. If you get an FFEL loan, you'll be dealing with a private lender such as a bank, a credit union, or a savings and loan. Your school's financial aid officer or state guaranty agency can help you connect with a lender. Sometimes the school itself is the lender. (A list of state guaranty agencies begins on page 25 along with the list of state financial aid offices.) The federal government reinsures the loans that the lender has made, making them more amenable to the idea of lending to students. While the rate of interest isn't as low as with Perkins Loans, Stafford Loans are easier to obtain—and the rate is awfully good.

How good are they? The interest rate charged on all flavors of Stafford Loans has fluctuated over time, but has consistently remained below market value for loans—and, in fact, is a better deal than can be found anywhere this side of the five percent Perkins Loan. The rate fluctuates from year to year, but cannot exceed 8.25 percent; in 1995, the rate was 7.43 percent for the first four years of repayment. Depending on your need, Stafford Loans can add up to a total of $23,000 for a dependent undergraduate student or $46,000 as an independent undergraduate student, with no more than $23,000 of that amount in subsidized loans.

These loans cost some money up front: an "origination fee" of four percent, which is deducted from the loan in installments. The state guaranty agency might also take its cut—up to three percent—also to be taken out proportionately from each loan disbursement as an insurance premium. You could also be charged late fees and collection costs if you don't keep up with your payments.

How to qualify: Students must be attending school at least half-time. (For a definition of "half-time," see the entry under "Pell Grants" or turn to the glossary.) Both undergraduate and graduate students are eligible. Students must demonstrate need. But like the Pell Grant program, there is no cap on the number of students who can receive these loans.

When to pay it back: You have to dig into your pocket six months after you graduate, leave school, or drop below half-time status. You usually have five years to repay the debt, though some allow as much as 10 years. As with Perkins Loans, Uncle Sam has made provision for deferments: up to three years for students unable to find full-time employment, or who can show economic hardship.

As with Perkins Loans, you can even get all or part of your loan forgiven altogether. If you become totally and permanently disabled or file for bankrupcy (in some cases), or if you die, the loan will be forgiven. That's cold comfort.

PLUS Loans for Parents

What they are: Like Stafford Loans, PLUS Loans provide additional funds for educational expenses—but these are not need-based. PLUS loans go to parents. As with Stafford Loans, these low-interest loans can either come directly from the Federal government, or from a lender such as a bank, a credit union, or a savings and loan. The Direct Loan Program offers the Federal Direct PLUS Loan; the FFEL Program offers the Federal PLUS Loan. If you enter the FFEL program, your financial aid officer or state guaranty agency can help you connect with a lender. Sometimes the school itself is the lender. (See the list of state guaranty agencies on page 25.) PLUS loan interest rates are variable, though they cannot rise higher than 9 percent. During the 1994–95 award year the rate was set at 8.38 percent. Parents can borrow as much as is needed to meet the cost of attendance minus the student's other financial aid.

How to qualify: PLUS loans are open to parents who have a child who is enrolled at least half-time and is a dependent student. (See discussion of dependency in the glossary, page 115.)

When to pay it back: Debtors usually must begin repaying interest on these loans within sixty days after first getting the money, with no grace period. Deferments are possible in times of economic hardship or unemployment, but only on the loan principal; interest continues to pile up during the deferment period. There are very few avenues for cancellation or reduction of these loans: They include death (but not disability) of the student, or if the school closes its doors before the student can complete the program of study.

A Note on Repayment

Loan consolidation: Until 1983, students could lump together all of their education loans into one loan with a low, federally subsidized interest rate under a program known as OPTIONS. Consolidation disappeared for a while while Congress tried to figure out how to make the program, which was convenient for students and their families, less costly for the government.

The government brought back consolidation with the Higher Education Amendments of 1986. Today's consolidation is more tightly controlled and costs the borrower more. Here are the details:

Consolidation loans can replace combinations of loans that you would normally pay individually into one payment each month. Like all of the other loan programs, consolidation loans can now come from lenders or directly from the Federal government.

There are three kinds of Direct Consolidation Loans: Direct Subsidized Consolidation Loans, Direct Unsubsidized Consolidation Loans and Direct PLUS Consolidation Loans. In the case of Direct Subsidized and Unsubsidized Consolidation Loans, you'll pay an interest rate that can't go higher than 8.25 percent; for the 1994–95 school year that rate was 7.43 percent. With Direct PLUS Consolidation Loans, the rate can't go higher than 9 percent, and sat at 8.38 percent during the 1994–95 school year. The Direct Consolidation Loan programs offer a range of repayment options. The FFEL Consolidation Loans are similar to the Direct Program's loans, but come from financial institutions. The financial institution will charge an interest rate based on the weighted average of the original interest rate on the loans being pooled together. If you need more information on the Consolidation process, call 1-800-848-0982.

Other Avenues to Federal Funds

The Military

How you feel about the military in general will determine whether you skip the next few paragraphs or not. The simple point is this: unless you have conscientious objections to serving in the Armed Forces, the military could be a way to help finance your college education. The military offers a number of ways to help students pay for college, though none of today's programs match the largesse of the GI Bill that educated the post-World War II generation. In return for the years of military service, you receive everything from a cheaper education to one that costs you no money at all. Service academies such as West Point offer a tuition-free college education. Each branch of the service has its own academy with its own character and traditions. These academically rigorous institutions are excellent, especially for the technical fields, and you can't beat the price.

If you'd rather not attend a service academy—or can't get in—chances are that your school will have a Reserve Officer Training Corps—and that organization, too, can help you pay for college. Standing scholarships are available that put $100 each month into your pocket for as much as five years, and ad hoc scholarships are announced all the time to attract students into areas the military feels a need to beef up—usually in the technical fields. Even without ROTC scholarships, students in the ROTC earn $100 each month in their junior and senior years (though they receive nothing as freshmen and sophomores). Once on active duty, students stand a good chance of being sent back to school and having all or part of their tuition picked up by Uncle Sam. The New GI Bill matches the soldier's contribution to a college fund; after emerging from the Armed Services, a student-to-be can amass a war chest of more than $10,000. There are also state programs to help members of the military, as well as funds from public and private sources for families of former military. Healthy benefits are also available to those who enlist in the National Guard.

Whether or not you care for the military, be sure that you have registered for the draft if you are male. Uncle Sam is now tying aid to draft registration: if you don't sign up, you can't sign up for aid.

Federal Programs Offered Through the Department of Health and Human Services

Other federal programs that do not come from the Education Department have millions of dollars to spread around. Many of them are directed toward influencing career choices—say, producing more medical professionals. Here are a few of the most prominent ones:

Several campus-based programs get their funding from the Department of Health and Human Services. As campus-based programs, they are administered by the school and funded in a lump sum from the federal government. Campus-based programs can run out of money, and so it is important to check your school's deadline and apply early in order to be sure to get all the money you can get.

■ Nursing Student Loan Program applies to nursing students attending certain nursing schools. Both full-time and half-time students are eligible, depending on the school. Students must demonstrate financial need. The student can then receive up to $2,500 each year (and $4,000 annually in the last two years of your program) for a maximum of $13,000. Repayment of the five percent

loans begins nine months after the borrower leaves school and can stretch over ten years, with deferments for active duty in the armed forces, Coast Guard, National Oceanic and Atmospheric Administration, or the U.S. Public Health Service or as a Peace Corps volunteer.

■ Financial Assistance for Disadvantaged Health Professions Students provides up to $10,000 per year to full-time students in medicine, osteopathic medicine, and dentistry. Not only must students prove exceptional financial need, but they must also come from a disadvantaged background.

■ Undergraduates pursuing degrees in Pharmacy can also qualify for two programs that are otherwise restricted to graduate students. These are the Health Profession Student Loan (HPSL) and the Health Education Student Loan (HEAL). Your departmental financial aid advisor should be able to help you with information on these programs.

For More Information on Federal Financial Aid Programs

Write or call one of the regional offices of the U.S. Department of Education:

REGION I

Connecticut, Maine, Massachusetts, New Hampshire, Rhode Island, Vermont

U.S. Department of Education
Office of Student Financial Assistance
J.W. McCormack Post Office and Courthouse Building
Room 502
Boston, MA 02109
(617) 223-9338

REGION II

New Jersey, New York, Puerto Rico, Virgin Islands, Panama Canal Zone

U.S. Department of Education
Office of Student Financial Assistance Programs
26 Federal Plaza, Room 3954
New York, NY 10278
(212) 264-4046

REGION III

Delaware, District of Columbia, Maryland, Pennsylvania, Virginia, West Virginia

U.S. Department of Education
Office of Student Financial Assistance
3535 Market Street, Room 16200
Philadelphia, PA 19104
(215) 596-0247

REGION IV

Alabama, Florida, Georgia, Kentucky, Mississippi, North Carolina, South Carolina, Tennessee

U.S. Department of Education
Office of Student Financial Assistance
101 Marietta Tower, Suite 2203
Atlanta, GA 30323
(404) 331-0556

REGION V

Illinois, Indiana, Michigan, Minnesota, Ohio, Wisconsin

U.S. Department of Education
Office of Student Financial Assistance
401 South State Street, Room 700D
Chicago, IL 60605
(312) 353-8103

REGION VI

Arkansas, Louisiana, New Mexico, Oklahoma, Texas

U.S. Department of Education
Office of Student Financial Assistance
1200 Main Tower, Room 2150
Dallas, TX 75202
(214) 767-3811

REGION VII

Iowa, Kansas, Missouri, Nebraska

U.S. Department of Education
Office of Student Financial Assistance
10220 North Executive Hills Boulevard, 9th Floor
Kansas City, MO 64153-1376
(816) 891-8055

REGION VIII

Colorado, Montana, North Dakota, South Dakota, Utah, Wyoming

U.S. Department of Education
Office of Student Financial Assistance
1244 Speer Boulevard, Suite 310
Denver, CO 80204-3582
(303) 844-3676

REGION IX

Arizona, California, Hawaii, Nevada, American Samoa, Guam, Federated States of Micronesia, Marshall Islands, Republic of Palau, Wake Island

U.S. Department of Education
Office of Student Financial Assistance
50 United Nations Plaza
San Francisco, CA 94102
(415) 556-5689

REGION X

Alaska, Idaho, Oregon, Washington

U.S. Department of Education
Office of Student Financial Assistance Programs
915 Second Avenue, Room 3388
Seattle, WA 98174-1099
(206) 220-7820

Endnotes on Federal Aid

If reading about federal sources of aid makes your brain hurt and you still need answers, there is a Federal Student Aid Information Center. Its toll-free number is 1-800-433-3243. The people on the other end of the line can tell you if the school you're applying to participates in federal aid programs, help you file an application, explain student eligibility requirements, and more. They accept calls between the hours of 9:00 a.m. and 5:30 p.m. Eastern Standard Time, Monday through Friday. Usually, they are even pleasant—no small trick these days.

Getting Financial Aid from the States

The fifty states vary widely in the amount of aid that each gives to education, according to the authoritative National Association of State Scholarship and Grant Programs. In 1993–94, states expected to award more than $3 billion in total grant aid to more than 1.9 million college-aid students—about 12 percent more than the previous year's spending. $2 billion of that money went to undergraduates for need-based aid. The National Association of State Scholarship and Grant Programs predicts the numbers will continue to rise.

Some states are haves, others are have-nots. Whether the states like it or not, some do spend more than others. A lot more. In the 1993–94 school year—the last year for which detailed figures are available—New York state alone spent $619 million on need-based undergraduate aid. The top six states—New York, California, Illinois, Minnesota, New Jersey, and Pennsylvania, spent

$1,468,549,000 in that year. The bottom dwellers—Alaska, Hawaii, Idaho, Montana, Nevada, New Hampshire, South Dakota and Wyoming, spent a total of $4,258,000 during the same period.

Don't pack the car and head for New York yet. While there are plenty of ways to look at how much money states spend on their college students, it's hard to come by numbers that make sense. Less populous states argue that just citing raw dollar amounts spent overall is misleading, because they end up spending more per capita on their small number of students. Some also complain that the full extent of their aid doesn't show up in standard measures: for instance, several states argue that their schools are so inexpensive that students don't need much financial aid—so that the states are penalized in the rankings for having a strong economic climate and helping students out with low tuition.

Not all of the arguments can be addressed, but the NAASP has tried to address some of them. Rather than be accused of unfairness, the NAASP tries to look at other measures of spending, such as how much the states spend per student. One listing the organization provides ranks states by how much each spends on its undergraduates, both full- and half-time—an imperfect measure, but within the ballpark. The estimated top ten spenders of need–based grant aid per full-time undergraduate for 1993–94 were:

New York	$1,148
New Jersey	$941
Minnesota	$782
Illinois	$675
Pennsylvania	$543
Vermont	$504
Indiana	$335
Iowa	$335
Washington	$330
Michigan	$316

Source: *National Association of State Scholarship & Grant Programs 25th Annual Survey Report.*

Types of Programs Administered by the States

The range of state aid is dizzyingly broad, and shows the political process at work. Along with the standard varieties of need-based aid, states are now moving heavily into non-need-based aid programs that reward, say, outstanding academic achievement. The state legislatures also try to influence future careers by offering money to students who pursue certain areas of study or professions, just as the federal government rewards students entering the health professions. Many states push math and science studies for

students who intend to go into teaching, while others boost a kaleidescopic array of professions ranging from bilingual education to teaching.

Other state programs try to reward people less for what they do than who they are. Minority group programs and programs to aid the dependents of prisoners of war or police officers killed in active duty all fall under this broad heading. Many also offer low-interest loan programs that are similar to federal loan aid. And to make the state's private colleges more attractive, several states now offer "equalization" money to help the private colleges' tuition match that of the public institutions.

The best benefit a state offers is the protection it gives its own citizens in the form of in-state tuition at its public institutions. Resident status is also a requirement for eligibility for certain aid programs. If you plan to attend a public school out of state, some students find it worthwhile to take the time beforehand to establish residency in the state of choice—often by moving there early and getting a job. But since establishing residency takes two years in some states, many students feel they just don't have the time.

Attracted to an academic program offered in another state but don't want to give up possible aid from your own state? Many states have established agreements to allow you to take advantage of your home state's aid while studying elsewhere.

The No-Need Aid Trend: Some Information and a Little Advice

Remember that trend toward non-need-based aid? In all during the 1992–93 school year, 31 states had such programs, and they doled out some $244.5 million. Those programs have been growing, though over 90 percent of grant dollars that states award to undergraduates are need based, according to the National Association of State Scholarship and Grant Programs. Of the non-need pool, the biggest chunk of cash went into academic scholarships. So study up! It pays.

Non-need-based aid is usually broken down into three categories:

(1) Tuition equalization programs, which help reduce the difference in tuition costs between public and private schools;

(2) Scholarship programs or merit awards, which reward academic achievement and are largely aimed at charming academic talent into staying in state;

(3) Categorical aid programs, which encourage students to go into particular fields of study such as math and science, or which help special constituencies like veterans and policemen.

As with all state programs, some give a lot more money than others. In the 1993–94 school year, for example, most of the growth in non-need-based programs could be attributed to Florida and Georgia, which bumped up spending by more than $26 million.

As you've probably figured out from the list of states above, having a new program doesn't automatically mean that money will shower upon you. The spurt in no-need monies is still puny compared to the massive $2 billion that go to undergraduates based on need annually. Starting new programs makes legislators feel good; actually giving those programs enough money to make a difference makes state legislators feel decidedly less good. Thus when you exclude behemoth programs like, New York's Part-Time Student Grant Program and Ohio's Student Choice Program, the average allotment for these programs drops off dramatically. That's why the 19th annual report from the National Association of State Scholarship and Grant Programs said that "adding new programs has contributed little to the growth of state grant aid." Of course, a million dollars is not pocket change; most of us would be very happy with just a fraction of that. Simply keep this advice in mind: Don't get so hung up on cashing in on the new that you ignore the larger sums that are available from more traditional programs.

State-Administered Aid Programs That Get Their Funding from the Federal Government

Several federally funded aid programs are administered by individual states. This gives a little more consistency to the crazy quilt of state aid programs, giving you some program names to look out for when going over state aid information.

■ State Student Incentive Grants: While the states administer the program and decide individually whether the grants apply to full- or half-time students, the program is partially funded by the federal government. Annual maximum: $2,500.

■ Robert C. Byrd Honors Scholarship Program: This program recognizes ten students from each congressional district for outstanding academic achievement, providing $1,500 for the first year of higher education study.

■ Paul Douglas Teacher Scholarship Program: a merit-based, state-administered program intended to encourage students who graduate in the top 10 percent of their classes to enter the field of teaching. The states may give each student up to $5,000 a year for up to four years; the student is then obligated to teach for two years.

The State of the States

The entry for each state in the list below consists of addresses and phone numbers. These refer to the agencies that oversee most of the student aid. You should be able to get current information from counselors at your high school or at the college financial aid office, but sometimes the world does not work as well as we would like. If you can't get the facts from those sources and need more than what the list below provides, the state agencies have the most up-to-date and comprehensive information.

State Guarantee Agency

This heading refers to the state guaranteeing agency or nonprofit organization that administers the FFEL Stafford and PLUS loans. While the federal government sets the loan limits and interest rates for these programs, the states set their own limitations and conditions. You will want to contact them for the latest information on loan availability and repayment and deferment conditions; the guaranty agency can also put you in touch with willing lenders.

State Aid

This office is a central clearinghouse for the aid programs provided within the state. Since even programs that sound similar vary in their particulars from state to state, this office can help you sort out the differences.

Under the category of state aid, we list the different state programs administered by that state aid agency, and also list programs administered by other agencies.

Alabama

One agency for information on Stafford Loan/PLUS and state aid:
Alabama Commission on Higher Education
3465 Norman Bridge Road
Montgomery, AL 36105
(205) 281-1921

Alaska

State Guaranty Agency for Stafford Loan/PLUS:
U.S. Department of Education
Office of Student Financial Assistance Programs
915 Second Avenue, Room 3388
Seattle, WA 98174-1099
(206) 220-7820

For information on state aid:
Alaska Commission on Postsecondary Education
3030 Vintage Boulevard
Juneau, AK 99801-7109
(907) 465-2854

Arizona

USA Group, Incorporated
Arizona Education Loan Program
25 South Arizona Place, Suite 400
Chandler, AZ 85228
(602) 814-9988
(800) 824-7044

For information on state aid:
Contact the individual college/institutions.

Arkansas

State Guaranty Agency for Stafford Loan/PLUS:
Student Loan Guarantee Foundation of Arkansas
219 South Victory
Little Rock, AR 72201
(501) 372-1491

For information on state aid:
Department of Higher Education
114 East Capitol
Little Rock, AR 72201
(501) 324-9300

California

State Guaranty Agency:
California Student Aid Commission
P.O. Box 510845
Sacramento, CA 94245–0845
(916) 323-0435

Colorado

State Guaranty Agency for Stafford Loan/PLUS:
Colorado Student Loan Program
999 Eighteenth Street, Suite 425
Denver, CO 80202
(303) 294-5050

For information on state aid:
Colorado Commission on Higher Education
1300 Broadway, Second Floor
Denver, CO 80203
(303) 866-2723

Connecticut

State Guaranty Agency for Stafford Loan/PLUS:
Connecticut Student Loan Foundation
525 Brook Street
Rocky Hill, CT 06067
(203) 257-4001

For information on state aid:
Connecticut Department of Higher Education
61 Woodland Street
Hartford, CT 06105
(203) 566-2618

Delaware

State Guaranty Agency for Stafford Loan/PLUS:
Delaware Higher Education Loan Program
Carvel State Office Building
820 North French Street, 4th Floor
Wilmington, DE 19801
(302) 577-6055

For information on state aid:
Delaware Higher Education Commission
Carvel State Office Building
820 North French Street, 4th Floor
Wilmington, DE 19801
(302) 577-3240

District of Columbia

State Guaranty Agency for Stafford Loan/PLUS
Higher Education Loan Program of Washington, D.C.
1413 K Street NW, Suite 900
Washington, D.C. 20005
(202) 682-1996

For information on state aid:
Office of Postsecondary Education
Research and Assistance
D.C. Department of Human Services
2100 Martin Luther King, Jr. Avenue SE, Suite 401
Washington, D.C. 20020
(202) 727-3688

Florida

State Guaranty Agency for Stafford Loan/PLUS:
Office of Student Financial Assistance
Department of Education
1344 Florida Education Center
Tallahassee, FL 32399-0400
(904) 488-8093
(800) 366-3475

For information on state aid:
Office of Student Financial Assistance
Department of Education
325 West Gaines Street, Suite 1344
Tallahassee, FL 32399-0040
(904) 487-0049

Georgia

One agency for information on Stafford Loan/PLUS and state aid:

Georgia Student Finance Commission
2082 East Exchange Place, Suite 200
Tucker, GA 30084
(404) 414-3200

Hawaii

State Guaranty Agency for Stafford Loan/PLUS:

Hawaii Education Loan Program
P.O. Box 22187
Honolulu, HI 96823
(808) 536-3731

For information on state aid:

State Postsecondary Education Commission
209 Bachman Hall
University of Hawaii
2444 Dole Street, Room 209
Honolulu, HI 96822
(808) 956-8213

Idaho

State Guaranty Agency for Stafford Loan/PLUS:

Student Loan Fund of Idaho, Inc.
P.O. Box 730
Fruitland, ID 83619–0730
(208) 452-4058

For information on state aid:

Office of State
Board of Education
P.O. Box 83720
Boise, ID 83720–0037
(208) 334-2270

Illinois

One agency for information on Stafford Loan/PLUS and state aid:

Illinois Student Assistance Commission
1755 Lake Cooke Road
Deerfield, IL 60015
(708) 948-8550

Indiana

One agency for information on Stafford Loan/PLUS and state aid:

State Student Assistance Commission of Indiana
150 West Market Street, Suite 500
Indianapolis, IN 46204
(317) 232-2366

Iowa

State Guaranty Agency for Stafford Loan/PLUS:

Iowa College Student Aid Commission
201 Jewett Building
914 Grand Avenue
Des Moines, IA 50309
(515) 281-4890

For information on state aid:

Iowa College Student Aid Commission
201 Jewett Building
914 Grand Avenue
Des Moines, IA 50309
(515) 281-3501

Kansas

State Guaranty Agency for Stafford Loan/PLUS:

USA Services, Incorporated
3 Townsite Plaza
Suite 220
120 SE Sixth Street
Topeka, KS 66603
(913) 234-0072

For information on state aid:

Kansas Board of Regents
Student Financial Aid Section
700 SW Harrison Street, Suite 1410
Topeka, KS 66603
(913) 296-3517

Kentucky

One agency for information on Stafford Loan/PLUS and state aid:

Kentucky Higher Education Assistance Authority
1050 U.S. 127 South
Suite 102
Frankfort, KY 40601
(502) 564-7990

Louisiana

One agency for information on Stafford Loan/PLUS and state aid:
Louisiana Office of Student Financial Assistance
P.O. Box 91202
Baton Rouge, LA 70821-9202
(504) 922-1011

Maine

One agency for information on Stafford Loan/PLUS and state aid:
Finance Authority of Maine
State House Station 119
1 Weston Court
Augusta, ME 04333
(207) 287-2183

Maryland

State Guaranty Agency for Stafford Loan/PLUS:
Maryland Higher Education Loan Corporation
2100 Guilford Avenue, Room 305
Baltimore, MD 21218
(410) 333-6555

For information on state aid:
Maryland State Scholarship Administration
16 Francis Street
Annapolis, MD 21401
(410) 974-5370

Massachusetts

State Guaranty Agency for Stafford Loan/PLUS:
American Student Assistance
Berkeley Place
330 Stuart Street
Boston, MA 02116
(617) 426-9434

For information on state aid:
Office of Student Financial Assistance
330 Stuart Street
Boston, MA 02116
(617) 727-9420

Michigan

State Guaranty Agency for Stafford Loan/PLUS:
Michigan Guarantee Agency
P.O. Box 30047
Lansing, MI 48909
(517) 373-0760 or (800) MGA-LOAN

For information on state aid:
Michigan Department of Education
Student Financial Aid
P.O. Box 30008
Lansing, MI 48909
(517) 373-3394

Minnesota

State Guaranty Agency for Stafford Loan/PLUS:
Northstar Guarantee Incorporated
P.O. Box 64102
St. Paul, MN 55164-0102
(612) 290-8795
(800) 366-0032 (in state)

For information on state aid:
Minnesota Higher Education Coordinating Board
Capitol Square, Suite 400
550 Cedar Street
St. Paul, MN 55101-2292
(612) 290-8795
(800) 366-0032 (in state)

Mississippi

State Guaranty Agency for Stafford Loan/PLUS:
Board of Trustees of State Institutions of Higher Learning
3825 Ridgewood Road
Jackson, MS 39211-6453
(601) 982-6570

For information on state aid:
Mississippi Postsecondary Education Financial Assistance Board
Student Financial Aid
3825 Ridgewood Road
Jackson, MS 39211-6453
(601) 982-6570

Missouri

One agency for information on Stafford Loan/PLUS and state aid:
Coordinating Board for Higher Education
CBHE/MSLP
P.O. Box 6730
Jefferson City, MO 65102
(314) 751-3940
(800) 473-6757 (in-state)

Montana

One agency for information on Stafford Loan/PLUS, and state aid:
Montana Guaranteed Student Loan Program
2500 Broadway
Helena, MT 59620-3103
(406) 444-6594

Nebraska

Stafford Loan/PLUS:
Nebraska Higher Education Loan Program
P.O. Box 82505
Lincoln, NE 68501
(402) 475-7272

For information on state aid:
Coordinating Commission for Postsecondary Education
P.O. Box 95005
Lincoln, NE 68509-5005
(402) 471-2847

Nevada

State Guaranty Agency for Stafford Loan/PLUS:
United Student Aid Group
P.O. Box 3028
Reno, NV 89557

For information on state aid:
University of Nevada–Reno
Student Financial Services
Mailstop 076
Reno, NV 89557
(702) 784-4666

New Hampshire

State Guaranty Agency for Stafford Loan/PLUS:
New Hampshire Higher Education Assistance Foundation
P.O. Box 877
Concord, NH 03302
(603) 225-6612

For information on state aid:
New Hampshire Postsecondary Education Commission
2 Industrial Park Drive
Concord, NH 03301-8512
(603) 271-2555

New Jersey

State Guaranty Agency for Stafford Loan/PLUS:
New Jersey Department of Higher Education Assistance Authority
4 Quaker Bridge Plaza
C.N. 543
Trenton, NJ 08625
(609) 588-3200 or (800) 356-5562

For information on state aid:
New Jersey Department of Higher Education
Office of Student Assistance, Grants and Scholarships
C.N. 540
Trenton, NJ 08625
(609) 588-3230/31
(800) 792-8670 (in-state)

New Mexico

State Guaranty Agency for Stafford Loan/PLUS:
New Mexico Educational Assistance Foundation
P.O. Box 27020
Albuquerque, NM 87125
(505) 345-3371

For information on state aid:
Commission on Higher Education
1068 Cerrillos Road
Santa Fe, NM 87501
(505) 827-7383

New York

State Guaranty Agency for Stafford Loan/PLUS:
New York State Higher Education Services Corporation
Loans Division
99 Washington Avenue
Albany, NY 12255
(518) 473-1574
(800) 642-6234

For information on state aid:
New York State Higher Education Services Corporation
99 Washington Avenue
Albany, NY 12255
(518) 474-5642

North Carolina

State Guaranty Agency for Stafford Loan/PLUS:
College Foundation
P.O. Box 12100
Raleigh, NC 27605-2100
(919) 821-4771

For information on state aid:
North Carolina State Education Assistance Authority
P.O. Box 2688
Chapel Hill, NC 27515
(919) 549-8614

North Dakota

State Guaranty Agency for Stafford Loan/PLUS:

Bank of North Dakota
Student Loan Program
P.O. Box 5509
Bismarck, ND 58506-5509
(701) 224-5600 or (800) 472-2166

For information on state aid:

North Dakota Student Financial Assistance Program
10th Floor, State Capitol
600 East Boulevard
Bismarck, ND 58505-0230
(701) 224-4114

Ohio

State Guaranty Agency for Stafford Loan/PLUS:
Ohio Student Aid Commission
P.O. Box 16610
Columbus, OH 43266-6610
(614) 466-3091

For information on state aid:
Ohio Student Aid Commission
309 South Fourth Street
Columbus, OH 43218-2452
(614) 466-7420

Oklahoma

State Guaranty Agency for Stafford Loan/PLUS:
Oklahoma Guaranteed Student Loan Program
P.O. Box 3000
Oklahoma City, OK 73101-3000
(405) 552-4300

For information on state aid:
Oklahoma State Guaranteed Student Loan Program
621 North Robinson, Suite 201
Oklahoma City, OK 73102
(405) 552-4300
Scholarship hotline: (800) 858-8642 (in-state)

Oregon

One agency for information on Stafford Loan/PLUS and state aid:
Oregon State Scholarship Commission
1500 Valley River Drive, Suite 100
Eugene, OR 97401
(503) 687-7400 or (800) 452-8807 (in-state)

Pennsylvania

State Guaranty Agency for Stafford Loan/PLUS:
Pennsylvania Higher Education Assistance Agency
1200 North Seventh Streeet
Harrisburg, PA 17102
(717) 257-2860 or (800) 692-7392

For information on state aid:
Pennsylvania Higher Education Assistance Agency
1200 North Seventh street
Harrisburg, PA 17102
(717) 257-2800 or (800) 692-7435

Rhode Island

One agency for information on Stafford Loan/PLUS and state aid:
Rhode Island Higher Education Assistance Authority
560 Jefferson Boulevard
Warwick, RI 02886
(401) 736-1100 (in-state)
(800) 922-9855 (out-of-state)

South Carolina

State Guaranty Agency for Stafford Loan/PLUS:
South Carolina Student Loan Corporation
Interstate Center, Suite 210
P.O. Box 21487
Columbia, SC 29221
(803) 798-0916

For information on state aid:
Higher Education Tuition Grants Commission
Room 811 Keenan Building
P.O. Box 12159
Columbia, SC 29211
(803) 734-1200

South Dakota

State Guaranty Agency for Stafford Loan/PLUS:
Education Assistance Corporation
115 First Avenue, SW
Aberdeen, SD 57401
(605) 225-6423 or (800) 592-1802

For information on state aid:

Department of Education and Cultural Affairs
Office of the Secretary
700 Governor's Drive
Pierre, SD 57501
(605) 773-3134

Tennessee

One agency for information of Stafford Loan/PLUS, and state aid:

Tennessee Student Assistance Corporation
404 James Robertson Parkway
Suite 1950, Parkway Towers
Nashville, TN 37219
(800) 342-1663 (in-state)
(615) 741-1346 (out-of-state)

Texas

State Guaranty Agency for Stafford Loan/PLUS:
Texas Guaranteed Student Loan Corporation
P.O. Box 201635
Austin, TX 78720-1625
(512) 219-5700

For information on state aid:
Texas Higher Education Coordinating Board
Student Services
P.O. Box 12788
Austin, TX 78711
(512) 483-6340

Utah

State Guaranty Agency for Stafford Loan/PLUS:
Utah Higher Education Assistance Authority
355 West North Temple, Suite 550
Salt Lake City, UT 84180
(801) 321-7100

For information on state aid:
Utah State Board of Regents
Three Triad Center, Suite 550
355 West North Temple
Salt Lake City, UT 84180-1205
(801) 321-7100

Vermont

One agency for information on Stafford Loan/PLUS, and state aid:
Vermont Student Assistance Corporation
Champlain Mill
P.O. Box 2000
Winooski, VT 05404
(802) 655-9602 (out-of-state)
(800) 642-3177 (in-state)

Virginia

State Guaranty Agency for Stafford Loan/PLUS:
Virginia Student Assistance Authority
411 East Franklin, Suite 300
Richmond, VA 23219
(804) 775-4000

For information on state aid:
State Council of Higher Education for Virginia
James Monroe Building
101 North 14th Street
Richmond, VA 23219
(804) 225-2141

Washington

State Guaranty Agency for Stafford Loan/PLUS:
Northwest Education Loan
500 Colman Building
811 First Avenue
Seattle, WA 98104
(206) 461-5470

For information on state aid:
Higher Education Coordinating Board
917 Lakeridge Way
Olympia, WA 98504-3430
Attention: Financial Aid Office
(206) 753-3571

West Virginia

State Guaranty Agency for Stafford Loan/PLUS:
West Virginia Education Loan Services
P.O. Box 591
Charleston, WV 25301
(304) 345-7211

For information on state aid:
State College & University Systems of West Virginia
Central Office
West Virginia Higher Education Grant Program
3110 MacCorkle Avenue SE
P.O. Box 4007
Charleston, WV 25364-4007
(304) 347-1211

Wisconsin

State Guaranty Agency for Stafford Loan/PLUS:
Great Lakes Higher Education Corporation
Borrower Contract Department
P.O. Box 7860
Madison, WI 53704
(608) 246-1800

For information on state aid:
Wisconsin Higher Educational Aids Board
P.O. Box 7885
Madison, WI 53707
(608) 267-2206

Wyoming

State Guaranty Agency for Stafford Loan/PLUS:
USA Group
1912 Capitol Avenue, Suite 320
Cheyenne, WY 82001
(307) 635-3259

For information on state aid:
Student Financial Aid Office
University of Wyoming
P. O. Box 3335
Attn: Terry Smith
Laramie, WY 82710-3335
(307) 766-3886

Puerto Rico

State Guaranty Agency for Stafford Loan/PLUS:

University of Puerto Rico
Financial Aid Office
P.O. Box 364894
San Juan, PR 00936
(809) 764-3710

For information on state aid:
Council on Higher Education
P.O. Box 23305–UPR Station
Rio Piedras, PR 00931
(809) 764-3256

State Aid Programs for Undergraduates— Estimates for 1993-94

STATE/PROGRAM	MAX. AWARD	NUMBER OF AWARDS	NEED-BASED?
Alabama			
Student Assistance Program	$2,500	4,680	Y
Student Grants Program	$1,200	7,245	N
National Guard Education Assistance Program	$1,000	580	N
Police Officer's and Firefighter's Survivor's Education Assistance Program	$3,000	26	N
Alaska			
Student Incentive Grant	$1,500	315	Y
Arizona			
Incentive Grant Program	$2,500	3,194	Y
Arkansas			
Student Assistance Grant	$624	8,300	Y
Academic Challenge Scholarship	$1,000	4,000	Y
MIA/KIA Dependents Scholarship	$5,000	9	N
Law Enforcement Officers' Dependents Scholarship	$4,000	19	N
Governor's Scholars Program	$2,000	380	N
Second Effort Scholarship	$1,000	17	N
California			
Cal Grant A	$5,250	40,623	Y
Cal Grant B	$6,600	32,268	Y
Cal Grant C	$2,890	2,506	Y
Law Enforcement Personnel	$1,500	10	Y
Colorado			
Student Incentive Grants	$5,000	2,943	Y
Student Grants	$5,000	18,681	Y
Part-Time Student Grant	tuition, fees,books, supplies	1,342	Y
Extended Studies Grant	tuition	N/A	Y
Undergraduate Merit Awards	tuition, fees	10,627	N
Diversity Grants	N/A	3,188	N
Connecticut			
Aid for Public College Students Grant Program	$8,000	10,200	Y
Independent College Student Grant Program	$6,700	4,000	Y
Scholastic Achievement Grants	$2,000	4,200	Y

STATE/PROGRAM	MAX. AWARD	NUMBER OF AWARDS	NEED-BASED?
Delaware			
Diamond State Scholarships	$1,000	163	N
Postsecondary Scholarship Fund	$1,000	1,478	Y
Educational Benefits for Children of Deceased Military and Police	full tuition	2	N
Governor's Workforce Development Grant	$1,000	97	Y
Bradford Barnes Scholarship	tuition, fees, room & board	4	N
District of Columbia			
Incentive Grants	$1,500	1,107	Y
Florida			
Student Assistance Grants	$1,030	42,918	Y
Seminole/Miccosukee Indian Scholarships	cost of education	13	Y
Tuition Voucher Fund	$1,090	17,119	N
Undergraduate Scholars' Fund	$2,500	13,426	N
Scholarships for Children of Deceased/Disabled Veterans/POW/MIA	tuition, fees	69	N
Jose Marti Scholarship Challenge Grant	$2,000	64	Y
Exceptional Student Education State Training Grant	$1,800	255	N
Critical Teacher's Shortage Tuition Reimbursement Program	$702	2,400	N
Challenger Astronauts Memorial Scholarships	$4,000	62	N
M.M. Bethune Scholarship Challenge Grant	$3,000	105	Y
Vocational Gold Seal Endorsement Scholarships	$1,860	2,925	N
Most Promising Teacher Scholarship	$950	246	Y
Postsecondary Education Planning Commission Student member Scholarship	$4,859	n/a	N
State Board of Community Colleges Student Member Scholarship	$4,859	n/a	N
Georgia			
Student Incentive Grant Program	$2,500	11,103	Y
Tuition Equalization Grants	$1,000	17,511	N
Law Enforcement Personnel Dependents Grants	$2,000	19	N
Governor's Scholarship Program	$1,540	1,754	N
North Georgia College/ROTC Grants	$300	265	N
HOPE Grant	$1,800	10,620	Y

STATE/PROGRAM	MAX. AWARD	NUMBER OF AWARDS	NEED-BASED?
Hawaii			
Student Incentive Grants	$2,000	700	Y
Idaho			
Student Incentive Grants	$5,000	1,608	Y
State of Idaho Scholarship	$2,650	100	N
Illinois			
Monetary Award Program	$3,500	119,000	Y
Student-to-Student Matching Grants	$1,000	2,000	Y
National Guard Scholarships	$3,500	5,000	N
Descendants Grants	$3,500	40	N
Veteran Grants—Undergraduates	$3,500	18,000	N
Merit Recognition Scholarships	$1,000	2,100	N
College Bond Incentive Grant	$80	200	N
Indiana			
Higher Education/Freedom of Choice Grants	N/A	55,846	Y
Hoosier Scholarships	$500	794	N
Iowa			
Scholarship Program	$400	1,815	both
Tuition Grant Program	$2,650	14,200	Y
Vo-Tech Tuition Grants	$600	4,000	Y
Iowa Grant	$1,000	1,150	Y
Kansas			
State Scholarships	$1,000	1,159	Y
Independent College Tuition Grants	$1,700	3,200	Y
Vocational Scholarship Program	$500	120	N
Regents Institution Grants	N/A	2,548	Y
Minority Scholarships	$1,500	205	Y
Kentucky			
College Access Grant Program	$840	17,600	Y
Tuition Grant Program	$1,200	7,370	Y

STATE/PROGRAM	MAX. AWARD	NUMBER OF AWARDS	NEED-BASED?
Louisiana			
Incentive Grants	$2,000	3,600	Y
Tuition Assistance Plan	$2,631	2,040	Y
T. H. Harris Scholarships	$400	1,770	N
Honors Scholarship	$2,631	2,090	N
Maine			
Incentive Grants	$1,000	9,500	Y
Maryland			
General State Scholarships	$2,500	13,000	Y
Senatorial Grants	$2,000	8,598	Y
Jack T. Tolbert Scholarships	$1,500	700	Y
Delegate Scholarships—Undergraduates	$6,000	2,145	N
Edward T. Conroy Memorial Program	$3,056	63	N
Distinguished Scholar Program	$3,000	1,400	N
Professional Scholarships	$1,000	13	
Part-Time Grant program	N/A	2,500	Y
Massachusetts			
General Scholarships	$2,500	32,600	Y
Christian Herter Memorial Scholarship	1/2 financial need	100	Y
Cash Grants	tuition	13,000	Y
Public Service Grant	$2,200	64	N
Michigan			
Competitive Scholarships	$1,200	25,900	Y
Tuition Grants	$1,900	28,954	Y
Educational Opportunity Grants	$1,000	5,000	Y
Adult Part-Time Grants	$600	6,100	Y
Minnesota			
State Grant Program	$5,889	67,000	Y
Rural Nursing Grant	$1,169	255	Y
Non-AFDC Child Care Grant	N/A	1,260	Y
Safety Officers Survivor Grant	N/A	9	N
Mississippi			
Student Incentive Grants	$1,500	2,051	Y
POW/MIA/Law/Fireman Scholarship	based on tuition and room charges	23	N

STATE/PROGRAM	MAX. AWARD	NUMBER OF AWARDS	NEED-BASED?
Missouri			
Student Grants	$1,500	9,000	Y
Higher Education Academic Scholarships	$2,000	5,125	N
Public Service Survivor Grants	full tuition at U. of Missouri	12	N
Vietnam Veterans Survivor Grants	avg. tuition at 4-yr. public regional instition	12	N
Montana			
Student Incentive Grants	$900	1,325	Y
Nebraska			
State Scholarship Award Program	$5,000	3,720	Y
Scholarship Assistance Program	Det. by school	2,600	Y
Postsecondary Education Award Program	Det. by school	650	Y
Nevada			
Student Incentive Grants—Undergraduates	$5,000	656	Y
New Hampshire			
Incentive Grants	$1,000	1,100	Y
Nursing Education Grants	$1,000	86	Y
War Orphans Scholarships	$1,000	10	N
New Jersey			
Tuition Aid Grants	$5,030	55,000	Y
Garden State Scholarships	$500	4,200	N
Educational Opportunity Fund—Undergraduates	$1,950	12,000	Y
Public Tuition Benefits	$3,998	17	N
Edward J. Bloustein Distinguished Scholars Program	$1,000	3,910	N
Part-Time Tuition Aid Grants	$3,772	350	Y
Garden State Urban Scholars Program	$1,000	2,013	N
New Mexico			
Incentive Grants	$2,500	8,000	Y
Student Choice	$2,273	360	Y
Scholars Program	$2,490	445	Y
Vietnam Veterans Scholarships—Undergraduates	$2,000	N/A	N

STATE/PROGRAM	MAX. AWARD	NUMBER OF AWARDS	NEED-BASED?
New York			
Tuition Assistance Program	$4,050	299,576	Y
Aid for Part-Time Study	$2,000	22,337	Y
Children of Veterans Awards	$450	650	N
Memorial Scholarships for Children of State Deceased Police Officers & Firefighters	state tuition, other costs	80	N
Regents Professional Opportunity Scholarships—Undergraduates	$5,000	323	N
Vietnam Veterans Tuition Awards	$2,000 (full-time) $1,000 (part-time)	680	N
Empire State Scholarships of Excellence	$2,000	250	N
Police Officer/Firefighter/Corrections Officer Awards	$450	3	N
Health Services Corps—Undergraduates	$15,000	236	N
Empire State Public Employees Scholarships	$8,785	12	N
North Carolina			
Student Incentive Grant	$1,500	3,891	Y
Legislative Tuition Grants	$1,150	21,550	N
State Contractual Scholarships	cost of education	7,775	Y
North Dakota			
Student Incentive Grants	$600	3,400	Y
Scholars Program	$1,986	153	N
Ohio			
Instructional Grants	$3,606	80,000	Y
Academic Scholarship	$1,000	4,000	N
War Orphans Scholarship Program	full tuition	1,111	N
Student Choice Grants	$588	41,462	N
Part-Time Student Instructional Grants	$3,600	N/A	Y
Oklahoma			
Tuition Aid Grants	$1,000	16,849	Y
Future Teachers Scholarship Program Undergraduates	$1,500	198	N
William P. Willis Scholarship Program	$3,050	26	Y
Academic Scholars Program—Undergraduates	$4,500	1,346	N

STATE/PROGRAM	MAX. AWARD	NUMBER OF AWARDS	NEED-BASED?
Oregon			
Need Grants	$3,150	16,849	Y
Pennsylvania			
State Grants	$2,500	132,441	Y
POW/MIA Program	$1,200	1	Y
Scholars in Education Awards	N/A	76	N
Rhode Island			
Scholarship and Grant Program	$1,000	13,700	Y
South Carolina			
Tuition Grants	$2,890	9,100	Y
South Dakota			
Student Incentive Grants	$600	1,200	Y
Tuition Equalization Grants	$300	900	Y
Superior Scholar Scholarship	$1,500	45	N
Tennesee			
Student Assistance Awards	$1,482	19,388	Y
Academic Scholars Program	$5,000	191	N
Dependent Children Scholarship	$5,951	3	N
Community Colleges Program	$2,000	9	N
Student Assistance Award Restoration Act	$408	3,063	Y
Texas			
Tuition Equalization Grants	$3,684	15,831	Y
Public Educational SSIG Grants	$2,500	4,286	Y
State Scholarship Program for Ethnic Recruitment	$1,000	464	Y
Tax Reimbursement Grants (undergrad)	$2,500	42	Y
Nursing Scholarships (undergrad)	$3,000	268	Y
Utah			
Incentive Grants	$2,500	2,600	Y

STATE/PROGRAM	MAX. AWARD	NUMBER OF AWARDS	NEED-BASED?
Vermont			
Incentive Grants	$5,050	9,053	Y
Part-Time Student Grants	$3,785	2,943	Y
Non-Degree Student Grant Program	$325	1,526	Y
Virginia			
College Scholarship Assistance Program	$2,000	7,200	Y
Tuition Assistance Grant Program—Undergraduates	$1,500	11,776	N
Virginia Scholars Program	$3,000	190	N
Virginia Transfer Grant	$4,500	740	N
Undergraduate Student Financial Assistance Program	$4,500	600	Y
Eastern Shore Tuition Assistance Program	$2,400	50	N
Virginia Assistance Program	N/A	160	Y
Washington			
Need Grant Program	$2,625	38,000	Y
Assistance to Blind Students	$300/semester	3	N/A
Educational Opportunity Grant	$2,500	275	Y
American Indian Endowed Scholarship	$1,000	N/A	Y
West Virginia			
Higher Education Grant Program	$1,968 (in-state, private) $1,428 (in-state, public) $600 (out-of-state)	4,421	Y
Wisconsin			
Tuition Grant Program	$2,172	9,100	Y
Higher Education Grants	$1,800	42,500	Y
Indian Student Grants	$2,200	1,010	Y
Handicapped Student Grants	$1,800	75	Y
Talent Incentive Grants	$1,800	5,200	Y
Vo-Tech Student Minority Grants	$2,500	240	Y
Private School Student Minority Grant	$2,500	375	Y
Independent Student Grants	$6,000	152	Y
Academic Excellence Scholarship	$2,545	2,010	N

STATE/PROGRAM	MAX. AWARD	NUMBER OF AWARDS	NEED-BASED?
Wyoming			
Incentive Grants	$2,500	592	Y
Puerto Rico			
Supplementary Assistance Program	N/A	26,644	Y
Educational Fund	N/A	23,555	Y
Legislative Awards	N/A	14,864	Y
Student Incentive Grants	$1,000	3,421	Y

Federal Programs Administered by State Agencies– Estimates for 1993-94

STATE/PROGRAM	APPROX. VALUE OF AWARDS	APPROX. NUMBER OF AWARDS	MERIT BASED?	NEED-BASED?
Alabama				
Guaranteed Student Loan Program	$90,000,000	35,000	N	Y
Paul Douglas Teacher Scholarship	$243,012	61	Y	Y
Appalachian Youth Scholarship	$25,000	15	Y	Y
Alaska				
Student Loan Program	$55,000,000	14,500	N	N
Paul Douglas Teacher Scholarship	$44,500	9	Y	N
Arizona				
Paul Douglas Teacher Scholarship	$227,325	86	Y	N
Arkansas				
Emergency Secondary Education Loan	$81,717	37	Y	N
Teacher and Administrator Grant Program	$170,000	775	N	N
Paul Douglas Teacher Scholarship	$144,916	31	Y	N
Faculty/Administrator Development Fellows	$21,350	1	N/A	N
California				
California Loan Programs				
Stafford Loan Programs	$987,500,000	304,408	N	Y
PLUS/SLS	$323,183,000	101,534	N	N
Assumption Program of Loans for Education	$1,600,000	660	Y	N
Robert C. Byrd Honors Scholarship	$1,014,000	676	Y	N
Work-Study	$607,000	N/A	N	Y
Paul Douglas Teacher Scholarship	$1,954,532	397	Y	N
Colorado				
Work-Study	$9,872,408	7,384	N	Y
Nursing Scholarship	$221,192	172	Y	N
Paul Douglas Teacher Scholarship	$200,000	40	Y	N
NDSL Loan Match	$283,416	241	N	Y
Connecticut				
Paul Douglas Teacher Scholarship	$228,000	46	Y	N
Robert C. Byrd Honors Scholarship	$96,000	64	Y	N

STATE/PROGRAM	APPROX. VALUE OF AWARDS	APPROX. NUMBER OF AWARDS	MERIT BASED?	NEED-BASED?
Delaware				
Christa McAuliffe Teacher Loan	$157,000	71	Y	N
Paul Douglas Teacher Scholarship	$40,000	8	Y	N
Optometric Institutional Aid	$16,000	4	N	N
Robert C. Byrd Scholarship	$22,500	15	Y	N
Nursing Incentive Loan	$97,400	39	Y	N
District of Columbia				
Paul Douglas Teacher Scholarship	$35,000	7	Y	Y
Nurses Training Corps Program	$250,000	17	Y	Y
Florida				
Most Promising Teacher Scholarship/Loan	$3,204,000	856	Y	N
Student Loan Forgiveness	$1,440,000	647	N	N
Public School Work Experience Program	$64,285	50	Y	N
College Career Work Experience Program	$534,958	280	N	Y
Robert C. Byrd Honors Scholarship	$387,000	258	Y	N
Teacher Scholarship Loan Program	$1,170,000	325	N	N
Masters' Fellowship Loan for Teachers	$232,800	23	N	N
Paul Douglas Teacher Scholarship	$778,124	156	Y	N
Georgia				
Osteopathic Cancellable Medical Loan	$160,000	16	Y	Y
N. Georgia College Cancellable Military Loan	$501,720	120	Y	N
Critical Fields Cancellable Loan (GSL)	$2,660,000	1,330	Y	N
Paul Douglas Teacher Scholarship	$400,000	80	Y	N
Idaho				
Work-Study	$810,000	934	N	Y
Education Incentive Loan Forgiveness	$54,400	28	Y	N
Paul Douglas Teacher Scholarship	$70,000	14	Y	N
Fowler Memorial Scholarship	$7,085	5	Y	N
Illinois				
Stafford Loan Program	Revolving fund for defaulted loans		N	Y
SLS	Revolving fund for defaulted loans		N	N
PLUS	Revolving fund for defaulted loans		N	N
Uniloan	Revolving fund for defaulted loans		N	N
Paul Douglas Teacher Scholarship	$700,000	150	Y	N
Minority Teachers Scholarship	$500,000	125	Y	N

STATE/PROGRAM	APPROX. VALUE OF AWARDS	APPROX. NUMBER OF AWARDS	MERIT BASED?	NEED-BASED?
Indiana				
State Summer Work Study	N/A	N/A	N	Y
Minority Teacher Scholarship	N/A	N/A	N	N/A
Paul Douglas Teacher Scholarship	N/A	N/A	Y	N/A
Lilly Endowment Educational Awards	N/A	N/A	Y	N/A
Iowa				
Stafford Loan	$202,201,338	84,000	N	Y
PLUS/SLS	$55,806,848	29,680	N	N
College Work Study	$2,898,840	5,000	N	Y
Osteopathic Forgivable Loan	$291,500	110	N	N
Kansas				
Osteopathic Loan	$500,000	50	N	Y
Teacher Scholarship	$508,764	104	Y	N
Nursing Student Scholarship	$897,000	299	N	N
Optometry Loan Program	$116,200	35	Y	N
Paul Douglas Teacher Scholarship	$150,000	31	Y	N
College Work-Study	$463,729	300	N	N
Youth Education Services	$39,303	30	N	N
Kentucky				
Stafford Loan Program	$101,310,700	43,600	N	Y
PLUS/SLS	$15,081,900	5,300	N	N
Teacher Scholarship	$1,575,000	375	Y	N
Work-Study	$880,000	1,000	N	N
Paul Douglas Teacher Scholarship	$228,281	47	Y	N
Consolidated Loans	$3,000,000	90	N	N
Louisiana				
Paul Douglas Teacher Scholarship	$255,531	51	Y	N
Stafford Loan/LA–OP	$100,100,742	38,500	N	Y
PLUS/SLS	$11,001,200	4,200	N	(SLS)Y (PLUS)N
Maine				
Osteopathic Loan Fund	N/A	N/A	Y	N
Postgraduate Health Professions Program	N/A	N/A	Y	N
Blaine House Scholars	$1,800,000	1,200	Y	N
Paul Douglas Teacher Scholarship	$22,500	15	Y	N
Robert C. Byrd Honors Scholarship	$50,000	29	Y	N

STATE/PROGRAM	APPROX. VALUE OF AWARDS	APPROX. NUMBER OF AWARDS	MERIT BASED?	NEED-BASED?
Maryland				
Paul Douglas Teacher Scholarship	$287,571	52	Y	N
Christa McAuliffe Teacher Education Tuition Assistance	$205,546	46	Y	N
Loan Assistance Repayment Program	$170,000	64	N	Y
Tuition Reimbursement for Firemen, Ambulance, and Rescue Squad Members	$135,135	160	N	N
Nursing Scholarships	$544,100	227	Y	N
Nursing Living Expenses Grant	$47,200	80	N	Y
Physical and Occupational Therapy	$15,000	8	N	N
Child Care Provider	$53,250	47	Y	N
Distinguished Scholarship Teacher Education	$145,500	49	Y	N
Family Practice Medical Scholarship	$60,000	8	Y	N
Massachusetts				
Gilbert Matching Grant Program	$3,000,000	3,000	N	Y
Tuition Waiver for Public Institutions	$9,876,186	11,100	N	Y
No Interest Loan Program	$9,000,000	3,000	N	Y
Michigan				
Federal Family Educational Loans	$330,000,000	140,000	N	Y
Work-Study	$6,000,000	6,100	N	Y
Degree Reimbursement	$9,100,000	9,800	N	Y
Michigan Loan Program	$5,000,000	1,000	N	N
Robert C. Byrd Honors Scholarship	$349,500	233	Y	N
Paul Douglas Teacher Scholarship	$605,000	121	Y	N
Indian Tuition Waiver	$1,900,000	2,000	N	N
Minnesota				
Work Study	$5,800,000	6,800	N	Y
Student Education Loan Fund (SELF)	$37,000,000	14,000	N	N
Mississippi				
Medical Education Loan/Scholarship Program	$126,000	21	Y	N
Academic Common Market	N/A	200	Y	N
Paul Douglas Teacher Scholarship	$154,761	35	Y	Y
Special Nursing Education Loan/Scholarship	$72,000	36	Y	Y
William Winter Teacher Scholar Program	$245,500	93	Y	N
Stafford/SLS	$340,000	50	N	Y

STATE/PROGRAM	APPROX. VALUE OF AWARDS	APPROX. NUMBER OF AWARDS	MERIT BASED?	NEED-BASED?
Mississippi (cont'd)				
Graduate and Professional Degree Loan/ Scholarship Program	$110,542	18	Y	N
Southern Regional Education Board Loan/ Scholarship Program	$205,800	33	Y	N
Dental Education Loan/Scholarship Program	$52,000	13	Y	N
African-American Doctoral Teacher Scholarship	$50,000	5	Y	N
Career Ladder Nursing Loan/Scholarship Program	$28,500	19	Y	N
Health Care Professions Scholarship/Loan	$6,000	4	Y	N
Nursing Education Loan/Scholarship Program	$176,000	55	Y	N
Missouri				
Stafford Student Loan	$15,000,000	48,550	N	Y
PLUS	$8,000,000	2,450	N	Y
SLS	$12,500,000	4,500	N	Y
Montana				
Work Study	$496,790	552	Y(70%)	N(30%)
New Hampshire				
Medical Education Capitation and Loan	$200,000	10	N	N
Veterinary Education Capitation and Loan	$163,000	13	N	N
Optometry Education Capitation and Loan	$18,000	7	N	N
Paul Douglas Teacher Scholarship	$64,303	13	N/A	N
New Jersey				
Stafford Loan	$210,000,000	70,000	N	Y
PLUS	$20,000,000	6,000	N	N
Paul Douglas Teacher Scholarship	$504,750	104	Y	N
SLS	$30,000,000	8,000	N	N
NJCLASS Loan	$25,000,000	5,000	N	N
New Mexico				
Work Study	$3,670,920	3,240	N	Y(33%)
Osteopathic Student Loan	$132,000	11	N	Y
Nursing Student Loan	$410,000	164	N	Y
Physician Student Loan	$360,000	30	N	Y
Minority Doctoral Assistant Student Loan	$100,000	4	Y	N
Minority Teachers Program	N/A	N/A	Y	N/A

STATE/PROGRAM	APPROX. VALUE OF AWARDS	APPROX. NUMBER OF AWARDS	MERIT BASED?	NEED- BASED?
New York				
Stafford Loan Program	$785,497,564	269,789	N	Y
SLS	$150,135,826	54,496	N	Y
PLUS	$74,290,400	22,515	N	Y
Loan Forgiveness Program	$1,600,000	80	N	N
Paul Douglas Teacher Scholarship	$1,081,997	225	Y	N
Robert C. Byrd Honors Scholarship	$605,350	370	Y	N
Loan Repayment Program	$300,000	20	N	N
Transit Corps of Engineers	N/A	N/A	Y	N
North Carolina				
Health, Science and Math Scholarship/Loan	$2,600,000	450	N	Y
Nurse Education Scholarship/Loan	$1,050,000	950	N	Y
Nurse Scholars	$3,276,000	909	Y	N
Oklahoma				
Stafford Guaranteed Student Loan	$116,423,363	32,749	N	Y
State Regents' Fee Waiver	$21,289,157	N/A	Y	Y
Paul Douglas Teacher Scholarship	$201,589	43	Y	N
PLUS/SLS	$36,896,379	9,737	N	Y
Oregon				
Medical/Dental Student Loan	$850,000	240	N	Y
Teacher Corps Loan	$7,998	5	Y	N
Nursing Loan	$48,000	32	Y	Y
Pennsylvania				
Federal Stafford Loan	$1,028,000,000	369,000	N	Y(Sub) N(Non-Sub)
Institutional Assistance Grants	$32,997,728	35,300	N	N
Matching Funds/Work-Study Program	$6,341,000	49,905	N	Y
Health Education Assistance Loan	$65,000,000	6,000	N	Y
ITEC (tuition) and ITEC (grants)	N/A	N/A	N	N
Higher Education Loan Plan (Federal Stafford only)	$6,000,000	1,500	N	Y
Loan Forgiveness Program	$524,400	276	N	N
Science Teachers Education Program	$530,000	800	N	N
Robert C. Byrd Honors Scholarship	$411,000	274	Y	N
Urban/Rural Loan Forgiveness	$3,883,000	1,900	N	N

STATE/PROGRAM	APPROX. VALUE OF AWARDS	APPROX. NUMBER OF AWARDS	MERIT BASED?	NEED-BASED?
Pennsylvania (cont'd)				
Federal PLUS/SLS	$206,000,000	57,800	N	N
Paul Douglas Teacher Scholarship	$635,000	131	Y	N
Rhode Island				
Intern Program	N/A	300	N	N
Consolidation Loan	$1,139,022	86	N	N
Stafford Loan Program	$50,492,586	17,978	N	Y
PLUS/SLS	$10,907,312	3,455	N	N
Paul Douglas Teacher Scholarship	$90,000	18	Y	N
Best and Brightest Teacher Scholarship	$180,000	36	Y	N
Community Service	$137,000	65	Y	N
South Dakota				
Paul Douglas Teacher Scholarship	$41,860	13	Y	N
Robert C. Byrd Honors Scholarship	$36,000	24	Y	N
Tennessee				
Stafford Loan	N/A	N/A	N	Y
PLUS	N/A	N/A	N	Y
Teacher Loan Scholarship Program	$300,000	225	Y	N
SLS	N/A	N/A	N	Y
Paul Douglas Teacher Scholarship	$330,000	69	N	N
Disadvantaged Areas	$27,000	20	Y	N
Minority Fellows	$285,000	57	N	N
Robert C. Byrd Honors Scholarship	$171,000	114	Y	N
Texas				
Hinson-Hazlewood Loan Program	$87,900,000	23,700	N	Y
College Work-Study	$2,800,000	4,357	N	Y
Public Educational Grant (on campus)	$32,000,000	48,000	N	Y
Good Neighbor Scholarship Program	N/A	N/A	N	N/A
Baylor Medical Scholarship	$31,800,000	N/A	N	N
Baylor Dental Scholarship	$13,400,000	N/A	N	N
Paul Douglas Teacher Scholarship	$1,000,000	318	Y	N
Robert C. Byrd Honors Scholarship	N/A	N/A	N	N/A
Utah				
Career Teaching Scholarship	$674,000	360	Y	N
SLS/PLUS	$16,300,000	5,800	N	N
Stafford Student Loans	$111,400,000	38,000	N	Y

STATE/PROGRAM	APPROX. VALUE OF AWARDS	APPROX. NUMBER OF AWARDS	MERIT BASED?	NEED-BASED?
Vermont				
Honors Scholarship	N/A	N/A	N	N/A
Student Employment Program	$250,000	200	N	Y
Robert C. Byrd Honors Scholarship	N/A	N/A	N	N/A
Paul Douglas Teacher Scholarship	N/A	N/A	Y	N/A
Virginia				
Work-Study Program	$1,795,000	1,400	N	Y
Washington				
State Work Study	$12,211,650	6,023	N	Y
Health Professions Loan Repayment Program	$214,000	5	N	N
WICHE	$113,600	16	N	Y
Future Teacher Conditional Scholarship	$279,155	93	Y	N
Paul Douglas Teacher Scholarship	$323,982	70	Y	N
Paul Fowler Academic Excellence Scholarships	$30,570	15	Y	N
Rural Physician, Pharmacist, and Midwife Scholarship	$36,000	9	Y	N
Scholars Program	$855,827	355	Y	N
Nurses Conditional Scholarship Program	$156,847	52	Y	N
West Virginia				
Institutional Undergraduate Tuition and Fee Waiver Program	$5,000,000	N/A	N	N/A
Institutional Graduate and Professional Tuition and Fee Waiver Program	$2,000,000	N/A	N	N/A
Paul Douglas Teacher Scholarship	N/A	24	N	N/A
Robert C. Byrd Honors Scholarship	N/A	42	N	N/A
Underwood-Smith Teacher Scholarship	N/A	163	N	N/A
Medical Student Loan Program	$775,490	155	N	N
Wisconsin				
Nursing Loan	$333,000	225	N	Y
Minority Teacher Loan Program	$50,000	15	N	Y
Paul Douglas Teacher Scholarship	$294,205	70	N	N

Other State Aid Programs

STATE/PROGRAM/AGENCY	APPROX. VALUE OF AWARDS	APPROX. NUMBER OF AWARDS	MERIT-BASED?	NEED-BASED?
Alabama				
Alabama G.I./Veterans Affairs	$99,789	46	N	N
Vocational Rehabilitation/Dept. of Education	$4,028,209	1,919	N	Y
American Legion Scholarships	$100,000	200	Y	N
Department of Blind Parents	$15,000	10	Y	Y
California				
Educational Opportunity Grant Program	$13,962,484	17,900	N	Y
Extended Opportunity Programs and Services	$6,293,000	25,500	N	Y
State University Grants	$79,115,869	72,631	N	Y
Board of Governors Grants	N/A	349,715	N	Y
Cooperative Agencies Resources for Ed.	$1,000,000	n/a	N	Y
Colorado				
National Guard Tuition Assistance	$233,930	724	N	N
Connecticut				
Tuition Set Aside Program	$21,306,036	N/A	N	Y
Delaware				
Ivy Davis Scholarships	$28,050	11	Y	Y
Georgia				
Regents Scholarship	$191,250	306	Y	Y
Regents Opportunity Grant	$693,750	185	Y	Y
Regents Scholarship	$200,000	300	Y	Y
Illinois				
Math/Science Scholarships	N/A	42	N	N
Teacher Shortage Area Scholarships	N/A	51	N	N
Gifted Program Fellowships	N/A	25	N	N
General Assembly Scholarships	N/A	8	Y	N
Teacher of Secondary Science/Math	N/A	14	N	N
Equal Opportunity Scholarship	N/A	150	N	Y
Bilingual Special Education Program	N/A	46	N	N
Christa McAuliffe Fellowship	N/A	1	N	N
Robert C. Byrd Honors Scholarship	N/A	266	Y	N
Iowa				
Vocational Rehabilitation	$3,998,500	5,500	N	Y
Commission for the Blind	$100,000	400	N	N

STATE/PROGRAM	APPROX. VALUE OF AWARDS	APPROX. NUMBER OF AWARDS	MERIT-BASED?	NEED-BASED?
Kentucky				
Vocational Rehabilitation	N/A	N/A	N/A	N/A
Federal Work-Study	$1,734,400	N/A	N	Y
Perkins Loans	$177,800	N/A	N	Y
SEOG	$983,000	N/A	N	Y
Statutory Programs	$1,600,300	N/A	N	N
Commonwealth Scholars	$1,714,500	N/A	Y	N
Tuition Reciprocity	$5,670,000	N/A	N	N
Louisiana				
Education Majors Scholarship	$1,777,000	1,177	Y	N
Massachusetts				
Massachusetts Plan Program	N/A	4,000	N	N
Michigan				
Tuition Incentive Program	N/A	N/A	N	Y
Education Trust Program	N/A	N/A	N	N
Mississippi				
Vocational Rehabilitation	$1,150,000	300	N	N
Missouri				
Teacher Education Scholarship	$250,000	250	Y	N
Nebraska				
Rural Health Opportunity Program	N/A	27	N	N
Vocational Rehabilitation	N/A	1,281	N	Y
New Hampshire				
Leveraged Incentive Program	N/A	N/A	Y	Y
Nursing Leveraged Grant	N/A	N/A	N/A	N/A
Robert C. Byrd Honors Scholarship	N/A	N/A	N/A	N/A
New Jersey				
Veterans Tuition Credit	N/A	240	N	N
Vietnam Veterans Tuition Aid	N/A	20	N	N
POW/MIA Program	N/A	1	N	N
War Orphans	N/A	6	N	N
New Mexico				
Three Percent Scholarships	N/A	N/A	N/A	Y
National Guard	N/A	N/A	N	N
Athletic Scholarships	N/A	N/A	N/A	N
Competitive Scholarships	N/A	N/A	N/A	N

STATE/PROGRAM	APPROX. VALUE OF AWARDS	APPROX. NUMBER OF AWARDS	MERIT-BASED?	NEED-BASED?
New York				
Native American Postsecondary Aid	$458,269	715	N	N
North Carolina				
Community College Scholarships	$280,000	N/A	N	Y
Teaching Fellows	$7,706,000	N/A	Y	N
Prospective Teacher Scholarship/Loan	$1,876,033	N/A	N	N
Freshman Scholars Program	$1,000,000	N/A	N	Y
American Indian Scholarship	$155,200	477	N	Y
Minority Presence Grants	$1,500,000	2,890	N	Y
Tuition Remission	$14,389,457	N/A	N	Y
Appropriated Grants	$8,136,426	N/A	N	Y
Veterans Scholarships	$3,509,160	N/A	N	N
Vocational Rehabilitation	$2,800,000	N/A	N	Y
Incentive Grants	$2,700,000	N/A	Y	N
Federal College Work-Study	$1,436,400	N/A	N	Y
Ohio				
National Guard Scholarships	$3,600,000	2,000	N	N
Rhode Island				
Vocational Rehabilitation	$340,000	280	N	Y
South Carolina				
Teacher Loan Program	$4,968,000	1,242	Y	N
State Grant Program	$24,750	33	Y	N
Graduate Incentive Fellowship	N/A	N/A	Y	Y
Other Race Grant Program	$44,000	44	Y	Y
SREB Contract Program (Veterinary and Optometry)	$726,184	86	Y	Y
Contract with North Carolina School of Arts	$16,106	12	Y	N
Palmetto Fellows Scholarships	$100,000	40	Y	N
Tennessee				
Vocational Rehabilitation	$58,000,000	30,000	N/A	N/A
Texas				
Resident Tuition Exemptions	$7,600,000	213,819	N	N
Non-Resident Tuition Waivers	$65,400,000	41,500	N	N
Line Item Scholarships	$3,300,000	5,000	N	Y

STATE/PROGRAM	APPROX. VALUE OF AWARDS	APPROX. NUMBER OF AWARDS	MERIT-BASED?	NEED-BASED?
Utah				
Tuition Waivers	$9,750,000	N/A	Y	Y
Educationally Disadvantaged	$491,300	2,300	N	Y
SEOG	$3,629,677	9,400	N	Y
Federal Work-Study	$3,508,370	3,600	N	Y
Perkins Loans	$9,352,058	6,500	N	Y
College Work-Study	$3,482,800	3,000	N	Y
Perkins Loan	$9,124,300	6,000	N	Y
Virginia				
Nursing Scholarships	$100,000	250	Y	N
National Guard	$195,000	600	N	Y
Discretionary Aid Program	$47,660,169	33,000	N	N
West Virginia				
State War Orphan Act	$1,800	4	N	N
Vocational Rehabilitation	$1,300,000	1,200	N	Y
Public Health Trust Scholarship	$3,750	5	N	Y
Veterans Benefits	$720,000	1,200	N	N
West Virginia				
State War Orphan Act	$1,500	3	N	N
Vocational Rehabilitation	$1,300,000	1,200	N	Y
Veterans Benefits	$698,400	1,000	N	N
Wisconsin				
Lawton Minority Grant	$1,875,600	1,250	N	Y
Minority Tuition	$132,000	60	N	Y
Minority Teacher Loan Forgiveness	$100,000	50	N	N

Intermission — Righting the Balance

Before we move from the governmental sources of aid into the private realm, we should discuss two broad categories of assistance that span both public and private assistance. The first is aid to certain minorities: If you are a member of a group that has suffered from discrimination past or present, there's a category of student aid that you should know about that doesn't fit into neat pigeonholes. These are broad areas that have contributions kicked in from all sources of aid—federal, state, the schools themselves, and private groups—and which attempt to correct past wrongs by providing new opportunities.

A second type of program attempts to correct a very different type of imbalance: the lack of students entering certain professions, such as teaching or the health professions. To get more students into these areas, government and private organizations are holding out the promise of cash. You can even find programs intended to promote these fields for minority students—an interesting twofer that students with the right qualifications can't afford to pass up.

We don't list every program offered at the federal, state, college, and local level here. We will concentrate on the federal level, where much of the money is. You can then run through the state aid programs that begin on page 33, and write to the state aid agency (pages 26–32) for more detailed information. By using the index to the roster of other scholarships that begins on page 424 you should be able to locate a lengthy list of organizations that provide other monies. And of course, check in with your high school counselor or your college financial aid office for more information.

Minorities

Minorities students looking for financial aid will not find much of interest at the federal level; federal monies are concentrated in counseling for minority students. Still, many colleges have implemented minority recruitment and retention programs and can direct you to funds available at the schools you're most interested in. For a list of reference guides to the more prominent scholarships for minority students, see the bibliography on page 124.

To find money, students should look to the states, colleges, and private organizations. Several states have funded programs to enhance the opportunities of minority students, from the Cal Grant B program to the Florida Seminole-Miccosukee Indian Scholarship Program. Consult the list of state aid programs (page 33), or contact your state agency for information. (List, page 26.)

Colleges are trying to fulfill their federal commitment to affirmative action programs by working harder to recruit and retain qualified minority students. Even in these times of political attacks and reassessment of affirmative action guidelines, many schools still recruit vigorously and many have minority affairs officers on campus who, in conjunction with the financial aid office, can help you find your way to academic funding.

Think the days of minority scholarships are over? Try telling it to Anne Connolly, a college student from the Washington, D.C. area, who was flooded with scholarship offers as she neared high school graduation in 1994. In all, she had offers from 47 schools that totalled $1.2 million. Of course, she had a 4.0 grade point average and perfect attendance since kindergarten. According to a story in the Washington Post, another student, Patrice Arrington, got a similar bounty of offers based on her 3.4 grade point average; she was also an all-American volleyball player. They are unusual cases, sure—but they're for real. It happens.

Private organizations also do what they can to add to the numbers of minority students in higher education. One such program is the Wilkins Educational Scholarship Program, which is offered by the National Association for the Advancement of Colored People and funded by major corporations.

About a dozen of these $1,000 scholarships are awarded annually; contact:

Youth and College Division
NAACP
4805 Mount Hope
Baltimore, MD 21215
(410) 358-8900

For more programs, look up minority scholarships in the index to our own roster of scholarships, which begins on page 420. While some come from religious organizations and civic groups, many of these scholarships are supplied by professional associations. The best-known program aids minority students interested in engineering careers; the program is funded through the schools. For a list of schools that participate in the program, write:

National Action Council for Minorities in Engineering
3 West 35th Street, 3rd floor
New York, NY 10001
(212) 279-2626

The federal government has also developed a number of programs to aid American Indians. The Bureau of Indian Affairs Higher Education Program provides need-based scholarships and loans to Indian tribal members who have at least one-fourth degree Indian blood. The school's financial aid office should have information on the different programs, or you can get applications from your home agency, tribe, or regional office. Or write:

Bureau of Indian Affairs Higher Education Program
Office on Indian Education
1849 C Street, NW
Washington, DC 20240
(202) 208-4871

To find out if your chosen profession has a minority scholarship program, first look up the group in a reference work such as Gale's *Encyclopedia of Associations*. Contact the group and ask whether minority scholarships exist.

Women

The money for women in higher education comes almost exclusively from the colleges and private sources. College money most often takes the form of athletic scholarships; for the most exhaustive and up-to-date listing of such awards, buy the January issue of *Women's Sports and Fitness*, which runs a lengthy annual roster. Or send for reprints by mailing $5.00 to:

Women's Sports Foundation
P.O. Box 472
Mount Morris, IL 61054
(516) 542-4700

Another lode of scholarship and loan money for women is through professional organizations such as the Society of Women Engineers (United Engineering Center, 120 Wall Street New York, NY 10005), and the Business and Professional Women's Foundation (2012 Massachusetts Avenue, NW, Washington DC 20036; (202) 293-1200).

If you are a female student with small children, you should find out whether your school offers day care for free or at low cost. Some schools do this now—often through their school of social work, which means enthusiastic, careful attention. In any case, the expenses associated with raising kids should be reflected in your financial need, which could get you more aid.

Handicapped Students

Along with the assorted state programs for blind students, the Qualls Memorial Scholarships provide ten to twenty scholarships for blind students each year that range in value from $1,000 to $2,500. Contact the Floyd Qualls Memorial Scholarship Committee, American Council of the Blind, 1155 15th Street, NW, Suite 720, Washington, DC 20005; (202) 467-5081.

Gallaudet University, the nation's leading institution of higher education for the deaf, has developed a vigorous financial aid program that combines government aid with its own funds. For more information write the Director of

Financial Aids, Gallaudet University, 800 Florida Avenue, NE, Washington, DC 20002; (202) 337-5220/TTD: same.

The Alexander Graham Bell Association for the Deaf, Inc. (3417 Volta Place, NW, Washington, DC 20007) also provides many scholarships for deaf students attending higher education institutions for hearing students.

Attracting Students into Necessary Professions

Teaching

The federal government's most lucrative program to attract bright students into the field of teaching is now known as the Paul Douglas Teacher Scholarship Program. It was formerly known as the Carl D. Perkins Teacher Scholarship and the Congressional Teacher Scholarship. The program is administered by the states, and goes to students who rank in the top 10 percent of their graduating class (or who have GED scores recognized by the state to match that ranking). Washington allows the states to award each recipient up to $5,000 each year. Sound great? It is. But look out for the catch—each year that the student receives the scholarship has to be paid back with two years of teaching. If the student doesn't fulfill this requirement, the money has to be repaid, with interest. For more information, check with your state aid agency for specific eligibility criteria, which varies from state to state.

When contacting the state agency about the Douglas scholarships, be sure to ask about other teaching programs the state may offer—many promote teaching heavily. Private foundations also offer teaching scholarships; see the index of scholarships by major beginning on page 412.

Health Professions

On the federal level, there exist several well-funded programs intended to draw students into what the Department of Health and Human Services calls "shortage areas" in the health professions. Most of these are directed toward graduate study—fields such as medicine, osteopathy, dentistry, veterinary medicine, optometry, podiatry, pharmacy, chiropractic, and public health. Rest assured that when you finish your premed program, there are several federal programs to help students who can demonstrate need. Remember, too, that the military provides many scholarship opportunities within the health professions for students who join ROTC or who enlist in the Armed Forces. Programs that benefit undergraduates and which are sponsored by the Department of Health and Human Services include:

Health Professions Student Loan Program: Helps full-time students who can demonstrate need and who are pursuing Bachelor of Science degrees in pharmacy; it also applies to certain graduate studies. Students may receive a maximum of $2,500 on top of tuition each academic year; selection is made by the school. The nine percent loans have a ten-year payback time that begins a year after the student finishes full-time studies. Students can get deferments of three years while serving in the uniformed service or as a Peace Corps volunteer, or while pursuing advanced professional training.

Nursing Student Loan Program: Applies to nursing students attending certain nursing schools. Both full-time and half-time students are eligible, depending on the school. Students must demonstrate financial need. The student can then receive up to $2,500 each year for a maximum of $10,000. Selection is made by the individual school. Repayment of the six percent loans begins nine months after the borrower leaves school and can stretch over ten years, with deferments for active duty in the armed forces, Coast Guard, National Oceanic and Atmospheric Administration, U.S. Public Health Service, or as a Peace Corps volunteer.

For additional information on nursing aid, get the booklet, *Scholarships and Loans for Nursing Education*, by sending $15.95 plus $3.75 shipping and handling to:

National League for Nursing
350 Hudson Street
New York, NY 10014
(212) 989-9393

For information on state and private programs in the health professions, check with your college financial aid office, as well as the advising office within your academic department. Several private programs can be found through the index of scholarship sources by major that begins on page 412. Looking through a directory of associations, such as *Gale*'s *Encyclopedia of Associations*, can give you the addresses of the professional associations that represent your specialty within the health professions. These associations can be a good source of information on additional sources of financial aid.

Public Service

The Harry S Truman Scholarship is offered to more than 100 students each year who wish to pursue careers in public service. The foundation pays tuition, fees, books, and room and board up to a maximum of $6,500 each year for four years. Your school must nominate you for this award. For more information, contact:

Harry S Truman Scholarship Foundation
712 Jackson Place, NW
Washington, DC 20006
(202) 395-4831

The World of Available Aid— Private Channels

In this chapter we discuss the many sources of financial aid outside of the government. The world of private aid is more complex than that of public aid—and the public aid, as we have already seen, is pretty complex. But the sources of public aid are limited to the federal government and the fifty states. Private sources of aid are not only more numerous, but are also tougher to track down—they range from the colleges themselves to private foundations, companies, and other programs such as the National Merit Scholarship Corporation. Trying to keep track of all of these sources on your own borders on the impossible. We list many of them here, and have provided an extensive scholarship directory later in this book.

Since the field of private financial aid is so dauntingly broad, we recommend that you not try to master it on your own. Find out who knows about sources of aid and pick their brains. Your search should take you to those people who know about the financial aid sources for your school and for your career area. High school counselors can provide the information you need on locally available scholarships. For special programs available through your college, consult the school's financial aid office— America's colleges have about $5 billion in their own funds to help students. For corporate programs, ask your boss (or your parents' bosses) or the company officer in charge of employee benefit programs. This may mean a lot of telephone calls, personal visits, and letters. But this will be time well spent.

About the organization of this chapter: We have placed aid from the colleges' own funds in this chapter on "private sources." Of course, this broad heading none-theless includes state-run, "public" institutions. But since many of these public schools have endowments that go to helping their students, we have put them in the same category as the private schools for the purposes of this section, if for no other reason than to simplify things.

A Warning about the True Value of Scholarships

There's a caveat that we should deal with before getting to the goods: Getting a scholarship may not help you pay for college. That's because the school will probably either count the award into what it was already going to give you, or add it to your ability to pay. Either way, you are left digging into your pocket for the same amount of money as before. The school is then able to divert the money that would have gone to you to another student who has not been as enterprising as yourself. Sound like a ripoff? Maybe. But it's one way schools have found to stretch their

much-needed aid dollars. And remember: Getting the scholarship gives you plenty of what you might call "prestige points." These honors look good on your resume, which could help you in your later application to graduate school or job hunt. That warning behind us, let's look at the sources of funds.

The Schools Do Their Part: The $5 Billion Question

In days gone by, many schools held out a "need-blind" admissions policy. The phrase means that if a student is accepted at a college, that student will be able to attend; money will be found somewhere. A lofty concept, few schools have been able to preserve "need-blind" as anything more than a concept in these cash-tight days.

In fact, "need-blind" puts schools in an uncomfortable cycle: by guaranteeing to subsidize the costs for so many of their students, they often find themselves needing to raise tuition—creating even more need for the school to have to fill somehow. The result can be chilling: Smith College, facing 20 percent annual increases in its financial aid budget over the last five years, decided that enough is enough. Starting in 1991, the school decided it would rank students who have been accepted for admission and hand out the money from the top down. Students highest on the list will see all of their financial aid needs met; below the fateful line, students will be on their own unless Smith can find the money elsewhere.

So again, a little investigative work is in order on your part. You should check in with the college financial aid office to see if the school maintains a "need-blind" policy. You might be surprised—it's not just the Ivies. Smaller schools like Franklin and Marshall College in Pennsylvania have managed to hold on to need-blind values. Still, if a school tells you it has need-blind admissions, try to find out what that actually means in practice. Don't be afraid to ask tough questions; for the kind of money you'll be spending, you deserve answers.

Today we look to the colleges for supplements to our education funding that include endowed scholarships, scholarships for athletic or academic prowess, work-study, and even loans from the school's own funds. Some private schools even offer "tuition remission"—that is, a discount on the official cost of tuition. (For a look at other innovative ways that schools have used to make paying for college less burdensome, see the next chapter, "Getting the Most College for the Money.")

All of these college gambits cost money. As a practical matter, this means that it behooves you as an academic consumer to keep in mind the school's bottom line while you are trying to make your college choice. It may seem an obvious point, but a school with a bountiful endowment like billionaire Harvard is going to be in a better position to offer you financial aid than a less wealthy institution. And a school that is truly strapped financially could burden you with tuition increases once you enter—or even fold. It happens.

With that chilling thought behind us, let's look at each broad category of student aid from the colleges.

Grants and Scholarships

Academic scholarships: Just as the states have been providing increasing amounts of money for programs to attract academic stars, the individual schools have been hustling to gain the prestige of enrolling academically talented students. If you earn a certain grade point average, or score higher than a certain level on the SAT or ACT, most schools will offer enticements to attend. Some schools also provide special lures for valedictorians or students who have achieved other academic honors. Not every school promotes academic scholarships; the nation's most prestigious institutions attract a consistently high level of scholar, so many don't refer to academic scholarships as such. Academic scholarships are most important to schools on the make: those institutions that are trying to build an academically strong student body but don't have the academic traditions of the Ivy League schools as a draw.

Money comes to scholars in a number of ways. The school may offer the awards according to a formula or set of conditions, such as a set SAT score. In addition to the funds available under the standard formula, the school might hold money in reserve to offer to especially promising students in order to sweeten the pot. Instead of actually spending money on bright students, many private schools simply offer tuition remission.

Need is a factor in most academic scholarships. Most of them offer a no-need minimum of a small amount —often less than $300. Beyond that, demonstrated need can up the annual award into the thousands. It's worth asking your school whether there are special no-need scholarships above the need-based variety, and whether you can qualify.

Athletic scholarships: Don't laugh. Even if you're not going to win the Heisman Trophy, there could be athletic scholarships for you out there. (If you are going to win the

Heisman Trophy, you're not going to be reading this book, anyway.) Sure, the super-jocks have got football, basketball, baseball, and the like sewn up. But most colleges also have money to help students who show promise. The best jocks will be wooed by the biggest schools. But one of the smaller schools you are considering may have an ambitious sports program in a sport you might be pretty good at. Though your skills might not have gotten you far at Big State U, the other school might be happy to have you—and willing to supply a little money to entice you. And not just in football, basketball, or baseball. Many schools offer scholarships in sports you might never have thought of, including: archery, badminton, bowling, crew, fencing, gymnastics, lacrosse, sailing, skiing, synchronized swimming, and volleyball. Come on—if they're going to make curling an Olympic sport, can varsity tiddly-winks be far behind?

At the beginning of this chapter, we talked about contacting the people who know where the money is. In this case you need to talk not just with your high school guidance counselor but also with your coach. Together you can figure out which schools' athletic programs might want you. Numerous college guides break down athletic scholarships by sport to make your search easier. Contact the college coaches at the most likely schools with a letter detailing your athletic achievement and pointing out that you would need financial aid. Be ready to provide the coaches who respond to your letter with more information and letters of recommendation.

The college as bank: Many colleges now offer long-term or short-term emergency loans out of their own funds. Ask at your financial aid office to see if your school has such a program. Many of them help students who do not otherwise qualify for need-based aid, and offer lower interest than commercial banks. Fairleigh Dickinson University of New Jersey uses its foundation money to subsidize interest on parent loans to keep the interest rates low. Other schools such as Lafayette College in Pennsylvania pay the interest on student loans while the student is in college, taking the pressure off students and their families during the college years. The school must be paid back within twelve years of graduation.

Looking for more funding power, thirty of the most prestigious colleges in New England banded together to form a group known as The Consortium on Financing a Higher Education; together with private enterprises such as the New England Loan Marketing Corporation (NELLIE MAE) and the Educational Resources Institute, they have created a loan program that they dubbed SHARE. Parents can borrow up to $20,000 annually at a reasonable interest rate. (See a fuller description of NELLIE MAE's offerings in the chapter, "Getting the Most College for the Money.")

Other Private Sources of Funds

Student organizations: You can make your social life pay off. Many student organizations sponsor scholarships for deserving students. Many fraternities, sororities, honor societies, and campus professional groups, among others, have programs, which are almost always limited to their members. If you're a joiner, you might open up some financial aid opportunities. Your school's financial aid office should have the breakdown of programs by organization, as will the organizations themselves.

National Merit Scholarships

Just about everybody who intends to go on to college ends up taking the PSAT/NMSQT test in their junior year of high school. It's preparation for the SAT—and more important, it puts you into competition for financial awards that can put a good deal of money in your pocket. But the competition is stiff: a mere 13,500 of the million students who take the PSAT/NMSQT each year are eligible to compete for these awards. Some schools, like Texas A&M University, work extra hard to recruit National Merit finalists and scholars because of the prestige that winning the award brings to the institution. So even though the actual amount of money received by finalists is usually not that great, it can get you offers of more attractive financial aid packages as schools vie for you. The three types of awards are:

■ $2,000 National Merit Scholarship. There are about 1,800 of these awarded each year; they are one-time-only awards. Need is not considered in these awards.

■ College-sponsored scholarships. Schools offer finalists scholarships out of their own pockets. Fewer than 250 colleges offer about 2,100 scholarships to National Merit finalists each year, including institutions ranging from the University of Chicago to Texas A&M University. The scholarships range from an annual $250 non-need grant to a maximum of $2,000 annually. Beyond that $250 minimum, the award must make up half of the student's calculated need.

■ Corporate-sponsored scholarships. Like the school-sponsored awards, the roughly 1,700 corporate-sponsored awards are renewable and can be received for all four years of college. And like the school-sponsored awards, they range from a minimum of $250 to $2,000 per year, though some go higher. While some of these programs apply to students with no direct tie to the corporation—say, those who live in the vicinity of one of the sponsoring company's plants—very, very few of these awards go to students whose parents do not work for the sponsoring corporation. For the most up-to-date information available on the National Merit Scholarships program, call the organization directly at (708) 866-5100.

Some of the Schools that Sponsor National Merit Scholarships

American University
Arizona State University
Auburn University
Baylor University
Boston University
Bowling Green State University
Carleton College
Case Western Reserve University
College of the Holy Cross
College of William and Mary
DePauw University
Emory University
Florida State University
Furman University
George Washington University
Georgia Institute of Technology
Grinnell College
Harvey Mudd College
Iowa State University
Johns Hopkins University
Louisiana State University
Macalester College
Miami University
Michigan State University
Mississippi State University
New York University
Northwestern University
Oberlin College
Ohio State University (all campuses)
Rensselaer Polytechnic Institute
Rice University
Rose-Hulman Institute of Technology
Rutgers, The State University of New Jersey
  (all campuses)
Southern Methodist University
Texas A&M University (all campuses)
Trinity University
Tulane University
University of Alabama
University of Arizona
University of California at Davis
University of California at Los Angeles
University of California at San Diego
University of Chicago
University of Delaware

University of Florida
University of Georgia Foundation
University of Houston
University of Maryland (all campuses)
University of Miami
University of New Orleans
University of Missouri–Columbia
University of Nebraska–Lincoln
University of Oklahoma
University of Rochester
University of South Carolina (all campuses)
University of Southern California
University of Texas at Austin
University of Washington
Vanderbilt University
Virginia Polytechnic Institute and State University
Washington University
Wheaton College (Illinois)

Some of the Corporations that Provide National Merit Scholarships

These are some of the corporations listed in the fall 1992 Student Bulletin of the National Merit Scholarship Corporation. Since the American corporate landscape is changing rapidly due to mergers, acquisitions, and general belt-tightening, this list tends to shift a great deal from year to year. Check with your employer even if it is not mentioned on this list, and make sure your company still supports the program if it is on the list.

Abbott Laboratories
ADT Security Systems
Allied-Signal
American Cyanamid
American Home Products Corporation
Amoco
ARCO
Armstrong World Industries
Arthur Andersen
Avon Products
B & W Nuclear Technologies
BASF Corporation
Bechtel
Bell & Howell
BellSouth
BFGoodrich
BFI Corporation
Black & Decker
Blount

Boeing
Boston Edison
BP America
Bridgestone/Firestone
Bristol-Myers
Brown & Williamson Tobacco
Burroughs Wellcome
California Medical Education and Research
Capital Cities/ABC
CIBA-GEIGY
CIGNA Corporation
Collins & Aikman Corporation
ConAgra
CONSOL
Consolidated Papers
Continental Corporation
Cooper Industries
Crum and Forster
CSX Corporation
Data General
Deluxe Corporation
Digital Equipment Corporation
Dow Chemical Company
Dow Corning
Dow Jones
Dresser Industries
Dun & Bradstreet
Duracell
Eastman Kodak
Eaton Corporation
Equitable Life Assurance Society of the U. S.
Ethyl Corporation
Fisher-Price
Fleming Companies
FMC Corporation
GATX Corporation
General Mills
Georgia-Pacific Corporation
Gillette
Goodyear Tire & Rubber
Greyhound Lines
GTE Corporation
Harsco Corporation
Hoechst Celanese Corporation
Honeywell
ICI Americas
Ingersoll-Rand
Inland Steel-Ryerson
Interlake
International Paper

ITT Hartford Fire Insurance
K mart
Thomas J. Lipton
Litton Industries
Lockheed
Loews
LTV Corporation
Lucky Stores
MAXUS Energy Corporation
May Department Stores
Maytag
McDermott
McDonald's Corporation
McGraw-Hill
McKesson Corporation
Meredith Corporation
Metropolitan Life
Miles
Minnesota Mining and Manufacturing (3M)
Mobil
Monsanto
Motorola
National Distillers Distributors
National Medical Enterprises
Navistar
New Jersey Bell Telephone
New York Times Company
Norfolk Southern
Occidental Petroleum
Olin Corporation
Owens-Corning Fiberglas
Paramount Communications
Parker Hannifin Corporation
Penn Mutual
Pennsylvania Power & Light
PepsiCo
Pet
Pfizer
Phelps Dodge
Philadelphia Electric
Polaroid
PPG Industries
Prudential
Public Service Enterprise
Quaker Oats
Quantum Chemical
Raytheon
Rexham Corporation
RJR Nabisco

Rockwell International
Rohm and Haas
Santa Fe Pacific Corporation
Sara Lee
Schering-Plough Corporation
Shell Oil
Siemens
Sony Corporation of America
State Farm Companies
Sterling Winthrop
Stone & Webster
Sun Company
Tenneco
Textron
Times Mirror Company
Transamerica Corporation
Transco Energy Company
TRINOVA Corporation
Unilever United States
Union Electric
Union Pacific Corporation
United Airlines
United Services Automobile Association
United States Fidelity & Guaranty
United States Shoe Corporation
Upjohn
UPS
USG Corporation
Warner-Lambert
Weyerhaeuser Company
Robert W. Woodruff Foundation
Xerox

A number of other programs are looking for ways to give a hand to academically gifted students. By looking though the scholarship index, you will be able to find programs that provide such aid, like the National Honor Society, which provides about 250 scholarships worth $1,000 each year. (You apply through the chapter at your high school, but the main number is (202) 785-2255.) The famous Westinghouse Science Scholarships program distributes about $140,000 among forty winners. (Write Science Service, 1719 N Street, NW, Washington, DC 20036.) The federal government has weighed in with programs like the Robert C. Byrd Honors Scholarship Program, a state-administered gold mine that recognizes outstanding academic achievement by giving ten students from each congressional district a one-time, $1,500 scholarship for their first year of college study. Another program, the Presidential Scholars, rewards about 120 high scorers on standardized entrance exams with a free trip to Washington; the Dodge Foundation then gives each recipient $1,000. You don't apply for this one, though—

the program chooses you. And, of course, more and more states are trying to help bright students. Some of these programs are based on financial need, but a growing number are not. See the section on state aid for the non-need-based programs, or write the state aid agency for more detailed information. The list of agencies begins on page 25.

Letting the Boss Pay

Employer tuition plans: This is the great unclaimed area of financial aid, with billions of dollars available to millions of employees. Unfortunately, there's a Catch-22 involved: many companies won't hire you for a good position until you have your college degree. But if you are willing to attend college part-time, and to start in a lowly position, you will find many companies that will pay for your higher education. Though guides to employers with such programs are commercially available, they also tend to be expensive; you can also find them in the public library or through your school library or guidance counselor.

The company wants to make sure it will get its money's worth, so plans generally come with a hitch or two. The most important hitch: you have to make the grade. In "reimbursement" plans, in which you have to put up the tuition money at first, you get the money back only when you have successfully completed the course—in some programs, that means with a grade of "B" or better. In other programs the company pays up front—but you will still have to repay the company if you drop out or flunk. Also, you might have to prove that the courses you are taking are somehow related to your work. Still, an understanding boss can help you to frame your educational needs in such a way that they fit in nicely with the company objectives.

The cooperative way: In co-op education, you combine your time in the classroom with practical experience on the job. It's something for everyone: You the student get a job and the employer gets a highly motivated work force. Co-op programs not only put money in your pocket—roughly $1 billion a year in co-op wages nationwide—they also provide you with job contacts for the future. You get to try out your chosen profession—kick the tires, drive it around the block—to see if it's really what you would like to do. If it is, you have another advantage: Often the firm you worked for is the one that hires you after graduation. Fully 40 percent continue working for their co-op employer after graduation. Another 40 percent find work in fields directly related to their co-op assignments, while about 15 percent enroll in law or other professional schools. Add up those percentages, and its pretty easy to see that co-oping it leads to jobs.

Roughly 1,000 colleges have cooperative programs of some kind or another—including some schools where virtually all of the students are in cooperative education programs, such as Antioch College in Yellow Springs, Ohio, Drexel University in Philadelphia, and Northeastern University in Boston. Some 50,000 employers hire on the co-op plan—including the largest provider of co-op jobs, the federal government, which hires nearly 12,000 students each year.

Co-oping takes time. Whether you alternate semesters of work and study or work part-time while attending school, the programs usually require five years. Still, 200,000 students each year seem to feel the time is worth spending. See pages 66 to 107 for information on co-op programs. You can get more data on all schools with co-op programs by writing:

National Commission for Cooperative Education
360 Huntington Avenue
Boston, MA 02115
(617) 373–3770 or 3778

Getting help from your future colleagues: If you have made your career choice, you might be eligible for aid from the professional association, or associations, that serve the field. Of course, if you really want to get financial aid in your chosen career field and want to get a head start besides, you should consider attending a college that has a cooperative education program. (See co-op programs, page 66.) But if your school doesn't provide such programs, then you might be able to get help from the professional association. There is an industry group for every trade and profession, from dental hygienists to hotel management to wine experts. Of course, most of this money gravitates toward schools that have well-regarded programs in the field, such as journalism at Northwestern University or meat science at Sul Ross State University. For suggestions on the strongest schools in your career area, you should consult guides such as *Rugg's Recommendations on the Colleges*. Still, many professional groups offer "portable" scholarships that are not tied to a particular school.

We have listed many career-connected scholarships in the index of majors that begins on page 412; there you can find scholarships for diverse fields such as acting, aviation, entomology, and criminal justice. However, there are thousands of such associations, and we could not include all of them or their programs in our list. So it is worth your while to find out about any other opportunities offered by your professional group. Trade groups are easy enough to find: reference works like *Gale's Encyclopedia of Associations*, available at the library, can give you the addresses and telephone numbers. Once you have the addresses, write to request their scholarship information, including a stamped, self-addressed envelope.

Working for Uncle Sam through the Junior Fellowship Program

The Junior Fellowship program resembles cooperative education, but with some important differences: for one thing, your boss is the federal government. Also, you join the Junior Fellowship program in high school—though you don't begin working until college—and apply through your high school guidance counselor. Unlike cooperative education, which is only offered through certain schools, Junior Fellows can attend any school—you work during breaks in the college term. You also have to have very good grades and prove financial need. And here's the good part: though the program is limited to 5,000 participants at a time, it has historically had thousands of vacancies. If your high school guidance counselor doesn't have information on this program, you can write for it yourself:

Director, Office of Personnel Management
1900 E Street, NW
Washington, DC 20415

Other Private Sources of Aid

Many organizations provide scholarships, though the amount is usually small. If you have already gotten all you are going to get from the big-ticket sources of financial aid, like federal and state programs and your college resources, you may be able to get a little extra from sources you might not have considered. Here's a list to start you on your way:

Your local government: Your city, county, or even your school district might have scholarship money or other special programs. Though many of these only amount to a few hundred dollars, some offer funds in the thousands. Finding them involves investigative work on your part, since relatively few of these make their way into the big scholarship databases. But you can find them: your high school or college financial aid officer should have some information about these programs. The Chamber of Commerce and public library might have leads, too. Keep an eye out for scholarships in the local news section of your newspaper.

Unions: Despite the tough times that America's unions are going through, many still offer funds for the education of their members' children. Information about some of these programs can be found in the scholarship roster; for more specific information you should contact the secretary of your union local. Union programs are offered both by the national organization and by the local chapters. You can get some information from your local; to get the fullest amount of information, write for the comprehensive AFL-CIO guide, which is free to members: *AFL-CIO Guide to Union Sponsored Scholarships, Awards and Student Financial Aid.*

Department of Publication, AFL-CIO
815 16th Street, NW
Washington, DC 20006
(202) 637-5000

Foundations: Many private foundations and educational trusts provide funds for students. Organizations like the Hattie M. Strong Foundation provide Strong Foundation Loans from $1,000 to $2,500 per year, on average, to students who are a year away from college graduation. Some have rather odd restrictions: the Ernestine Matthews Trust Scholarships, for example, offers around $750 per year—but recipients must sign a statement that they will neither smoke nor use alcoholic beverages while receiving the scholarship. You can find others in the scholarship directory.

Community organizations in general: Don't forget to check into scholarship programs available as a multitude of awards, including a $2,000 scholarship at the national level for children of veterans called The American Legion Auxiliary National President's Scholarship. There's also a National High School Oratorical Contest with a grand prize of $16,000 and many $1,000 scholarships. More important, each state organization and its auxiliary offer scholarships. The Legion is most valuable to students who are the children of veterans, but not exclusively to them. For the most up-to-date listing of the Legion's programs and contests, you should send three dollars to get a copy of *Need a Lift?* Write to:

The American Legion
National Emblem Sales
P.O. Box 1050
Indianapolis, IN 46206
(317) 630-1200

Religious organizations: Churches and religious organizations also have money to give. Groups like the Aid Association for Lutherans host contests and offer scholarships and loans. Find these groups through your church, your campus Bible Chair, or in *Gale's Encyclopedia of Associations.* You might run into a number of restrictions, including a requirement of religious study or of attending a church-sponsored school.

Ethnic societies: Sure, you're proud to be an Armenian. But did you know that your Armenian ancestry could qualify you for scholarships? The Armenian Relief Society (80 Bigelow Ave, Watertown, MA 02172) has many available. So does the Armenian General Benevolent Union, which offers both scholarships and loans (31 West 52nd Street, New York, NY 10019 (212) 765-8260). Are you a woman of Greek descent? Perhaps you have a relative in the Daughters of Penelope. If so, you might qualify for one of that organization's awards, such as the Helen Karagianis Memorial Award or the Pota Sarastis Memorial Award. (Scholarship Committee,

Daughters of Penelope, Supreme Headquarters, 1422 K Street, NW, Washington, DC 20005.)

We've only scratched the surface of ethnic funds available. Many national groups in the U.S. sponsor programs to help each new generation better itself through higher education. If you or your parents aren't members of such organizations, you can find their names and addresses in *Gale's Encyclopedia of Associations*, available in your library. Send them a request for information on college aid along with a stamped, self-addressed envelope.

Youth clubs and jobs: Think back to your childhood—or to more recent high school experience. You can find scholarships for former Boy Scouts, newspaper carriers, and even golf caddies. Really. The Western Golf Association maintains an Evans Scholars House, where lucky former caddies live for free, at fourteen universities—Colorado, Illinois, Indiana, Marquette, Miami (Ohio), Michigan State, U of Michigan, Minnesota, Missouri, Northern Illinois State U at DeKalb, Northwestern, Ohio State, Purdue, and Wisconsin. The sponsoring organization also covers tuition. Students at state universities that do not have an Evans House can get their tuition and a housing allowance paid by the sponsoring organization. Caddies who served for more than two years and show financial need may apply to:

Western Golf Association, Evans Scholarship
One Briar Road
Golf, IL 60029
(708) 724-4600

As for your participation in high school activities, you might have made yourself eligible for scholarships if you were a member of 4-H, Future Homemakers of America, or distributive education programs. You might also want to check with your high school counselor for other awards that get overlooked.

The contest route: Many of the organizations alluded to above sponsor contests in essay writing and oratory. That's just the tip of the iceberg for competitions ranging from science competitions to beauty pageants. Many of them sponsor scholarships for prizes. Each summer, the National Association of Secondary School Principals puts its stamp of approval on a long roster of these programs in its Advisory List of National Contests and Activities. For a copy of this list, send a request for publication #210-9295, $8.00 plus $3.00 for shipping and handling to:

National Association of Secondary School Principals
Attention: Sales Office
1904 Association Drive
Reston, VA 22090
(703) 860-0220

Warning: Entering a lot of contests can be time-consuming—and you're going to need a lot of time to apply for the traditional channels of financial aid. Don't get lost on a rabbit trail—go after the big game first by applying for financial aid through your school's financial aid office. Once you've done that, and if you have a little extra time, you might give some of the contests listed by the principals a try—your odds of winning are no worse than those on getting many of the private foundation scholarships mentioned in this book.

If there's any lesson to take away from this chapter, it is simply this: Get to know your college financial aid officer. This is the person who can help you ferret out money, and who has some power, however limited, to ease your financial aid burden. The position of student aid administration is fast becoming a hardship post. Aid officers report that angry students have hit them and threatened their lives. And one tragic case a few years back ended in death. A student threw coffee on Willie Pappas, director of financial aid at Delgado Community College in Louisiana. When Pappas followed the student out into a parking lot, the student shot him.

Obviously, this is no way to get your financial aid package improved. Financial aid officers don't take the job to abuse students and pinch pennies; they are in the business of helping students. Unfortunately, they are also working within the school's budgetary limits—and the school is juggling the financial needs of students with its own priorities for research, faculty pay, physical improvements, and shiny new leather chairs for the trustees to sit on at their meetings. And so they are tough.

But not necessarily heartless. They will listen to reason and respond to real problems. With solid negotiation, you might be able to get your financial aid officer to adjust the formula for computing your need: The officer can adjust your family contribution down or the cost of education up to reduce your aid burden. The key is to deal with financial aid officers politely and responsibly. Don't try to con them—students sharper than you have tried, and failed. Have all your ducks in a row: Keep track of your financial records and be ready to back up your case with documentation.

Cooperative Education

Cooperative education lets you mix career-oriented jobs with your college education over the course of your degree program. Unlike internships, which tend to be nonpaying jobs that students work into their schedules as best they can, cooperative programs can pay the bills and are an integral part of the school's degree program and your career plans. About 40 percent of co-op students end up working for their co-op employer after graduation, and another 40 percent find employment in their co-op job field. Depending on the money you earn, a co-op job can cover a great deal of your college costs. And since co-op graduates tend to have higher starting salaries than non-co-op grads, you can pay off college debts earlier. That's why we have included this list of institutions that participate in cooperative education programs: to let you know where to apply if you decide that cooperative education is the route you want to take. Once you have used this chart to identify colleges with programs in your field of interest, contact the school's Cooperative Education department and ask for more information on the program.

For more information about cooperative education, see page 62, "Letting the Boss Pay."

The categories covered by this list are as follows:

1. **Agriculture (AG):** includes natural resources, animal and poultry sciences, livestock, plant and soil science
2. **Art (AR):** arts, including architecture, commercial art, communications, crafts, fine arts, and performing arts
3. **Business (BU)**
4. **Computer Science (CS)**
5. **Education (ED)**
6. **Engineering (EN)**
7. **Health Professions (HP)**
8. **Home Economics (HE)**
9. **Humanities (HU)**
10. **Natural Sciences (NS):** includes biology, mathematics, and physical sciences
11. **Social and Behavioral Science (SB)**
12. **Technologies (TE)**
13. **Vocational Arts (VA):** includes trade and industrial courses

Many schools offer more than one category.

Undergraduate Programs in Cooperative Education

State/Institution	AG	AR	BU	CS	ED	EN	HP	HE	HU	NS	SB	TE	VA
Alabama													
Alabama A&M U Normal, AL 35762	✔	✔	✔	✔			✔	✔	✔	✔	✔	✔	✔
Alabama St U Montgomery, AL 36101-0271		✔	✔	✔	✔	✔		✔	✔	✔			
Alabama, U of, Birmingham Birmingham, AL 35294-0104				✔		✔							
Alabama, U of, Huntsville Huntsville, AL 35899			✔	✔		✔				✔			
Alabama, U of, Tuscaloosa Tuscaloosa, AL 35487-0132			✔	✔	✔	✔				✔	✔	✔	
Auburn U Auburn University, AL 36849	✔	✔	✔	✔		✔			✔	✔			
Auburn U, Montgomery Montgomery, AL 36117-3596		✔	✔	✔	✔	✔	✔		✔	✔	✔		
Huntingdon Coll Montgomery, AL 36106-2148			✔										
Jacksonville St U Jacksonville, AL 36265-9982			✔	✔								✔	✔
Miles Coll Fairfield, AL 35064						✔							
Mobile, U of Mobile, AL 36663-0220						✔	✔						
Montevallo, U of Montevallo, AL 35115-6000						✔							
Samford U Birmingham, AL 35229			✔	✔					✔				
South Alabama, U of Mobile, AL 36688-0002		✔	✔	✔	✔	✔	✔			✔	✔	✔	
Tuskegee U Tuskegee, AL 36088	✔		✔	✔	✔	✔	✔	✔		✔	✔		

State/Institution	AG	AR	BU	CS	ED	EN	HP	HE	HU	NS	SB	TE	VA
Alaska													
Alaska Southeast, U of, Juneau Campus Juneau, AK 99801				✔	✔					✔			
Alaska, U of, Anchorage Anchorage, AK 99508		✔	✔			✔						✔	✔
Sheldon Jackson Coll Sitka, AK 99835-7699		✔			✔					✔			
Arizona													
Arizona, U of Tucson, AZ 85721-0007	✔	✔	✔	✔	✔	✔	✔	✔	✔	✔	✔	✔	
Embry-Riddle Aeronautical U Prescott, AZ 86301		✔	✔			✔						✔	
Northern Arizona U Flagstaff, AZ 86011			✔			✔	✔						
Arkansas													
Arkansas, U of, Fayetteville Fayetteville, AR 72701	✔	✔	✔	✔		✔		✔	✔	✔	✔		
Arkansas, U of, Little Rock Little Rock, AR 72204		✔	✔			✔			✔	✔		✔	
Harding U Searcy, AR 72149		✔	✔	✔	✔		✔	✔	✔	✔	✔		
Ouachita Baptist U Arkadelphia, AR 71998-0001			✔							✔	✔		
California													
Acad of Art Coll San Francisco, CA 94105		✔											
Biola U La Mirada, CA 90639	✔	✔	✔	✔	✔	✔	✔			✔	✔	✔	✔
California Lutheran U Thousand Oaks, CA 91360-2787		✔	✔	✔			✔		✔	✔	✔		

State/Institution	AG	AR	BU	CS	ED	EN	HP	HE	HU	NS	SB	TE	VA
California Maritime Acad Vallejo, CA 94590						✓							
California Polytechnic St U, San Luis Obispo San Luis Obispo, CA 93407-0005	✓		✓	✓		✓							
California St Polytechnic U, Pomona Pomona, CA 91768-4019	✓		✓	✓		✓					✓		
California St U, Bakersfield Bakersfield, CA 93311-1099		✓	✓	✓	✓				✓	✓	✓		
California St U, Chico Chico, CA 95929-0720	✓	✓	✓	✓	✓	✓	✓	✓		✓	✓	✓	✓
California St U, Fresno Fresno, CA 93740-0047	✓	✓	✓	✓	✓	✓	✓	✓	✓	✓	✓	✓	✓
California St U, Fullerton Fullerton, CA 92634		✓	✓	✓	✓	✓	✓		✓	✓	✓		
California St U, Hayward Hayward, CA 94542		✓	✓	✓	✓		✓		✓	✓	✓		
California St U, Long Beach Long Beach, CA 90840		✓	✓	✓	✓	✓	✓	✓	✓	✓	✓	✓	✓
California St U, Sacramento Sacramento, CA 95819			✓	✓	✓	✓			✓	✓	✓		
California St U, San Bernardino San Bernardino, CA 92407-2397	✓	✓	✓			✓					✓		
California St U, Stanislaus Turlock, CA 95382		✓	✓	✓	✓		✓		✓	✓	✓		✓
California, U of, Berkeley Berkeley, CA 94720	✓	✓	✓	✓	✓	✓	✓	✓	✓	✓	✓	✓	✓
California, U of, Davis Davis, CA 95616-8678												✓	
California, U of, Riverside Riverside, CA 92521			✓		✓	✓				✓	✓		
Chapman U Orange, CA 92666			✓	✓	✓					✓			

State/Institution	AG	AR	BU	CS	ED	EN	HP	HE	HU	NS	SB	TE	VA
Concordia U Irvine, CA 92715			✔		✔						✔		
Design Inst of San Diego San Diego, CA 92121	✔												
Golden Gate U San Francisco, CA 94105		✔	✔									✔	
Humboldt St U Arcata, CA 95521					✔				✔				
Humphreys Coll Stockton, CA 95207-3896		✔	✔								✔		✔
John F. Kennedy U Orinda, CA 94563				✔									
New Coll of California San Francisco, CA 94131				✔									
Pacific Christian Coll Fullerton, CA 92631	✔		✔	✔	✔				✔	✔			
Pacific Union Coll Angwin, CA 94508		✔	✔									✔	
Patten Coll Oakland, CA 94601		✔											
Pepperdine U Malibu, CA 90263-4392					✔								
St. Mary's Coll Moraga, CA 94575					✔								
San Diego, U of San Diego, CA 92110-2492					✔								
San Jose St U San Jose, CA 95192-0009	✔	✔		✔	✔	✔		✔	✔	✔			
Santa Clara U Santa Clara, CA 95053					✔								
Sonoma St U Rohnert Park, CA 94928									✔	✔			

State/Institution	AG	AR	BU	CS	ED	EN	HP	HE	HU	NS	SB	TE	VA
Southern California, U of Los Angeles, CA 90089						✔							
Whittier Coll Whittier, CA 90608						✔							

Colorado

State/Institution	AG	AR	BU	CS	ED	EN	HP	HE	HU	NS	SB	TE	VA
Colorado Christian U Lakewood, CO 80226		✔											
Colorado Coll Colorado Springs, CO 80903				✔		✔						✔	
Colorado Sch of Mines Golden, CO 80401-9952				✔		✔							
Colorado St U Fort Collins, CO 80523	✔												
Colorado Tech Colorado Springs, CO 80907				✔		✔						✔	
Colorado, U of, Boulder Boulder, CO 80309						✔							
Colorado, U of, Denver Denver, CO 80217-3364			✔	✔		✔							
Metropolitan St Coll of Denver Denver, CO 80217-3362	✔	✔	✔	✔	✔	✔	✔		✔	✔	✔	✔	✔
Southern Colorado, U of Pueblo, CO 81001						✔						✔	
Western St Coll of Colorado Gunnison, CO 81231			✔			✔							

Connecticut

State/Institution	AG	AR	BU	CS	ED	EN	HP	HE	HU	NS	SB	TE	VA
Bridgeport, U of Bridgeport, CT 06601		✔	✔	✔		✔			✔	✔	✔		
Central Connecticut St U New Britain, CT 06050		✔	✔	✔	✔				✔	✔	✔	✔	✔
Connecticut, U of Storrs, CT 06269	✔	✔	✔	✔	✔	✔			✔	✔	✔		

State/Institution	AG	AR	BU	CS	ED	EN	HP	HE	HU	NS	SB	TE	VA
Eastern Connecticut St U Willimantic, CT 06226			✔	✔					✔	✔	✔		
Fairfield U Fairfield, CT 06430-7524						✔							
Hartford, U of West Hartford, CT 06117		✔	✔	✔		✔				✔			✔
New Haven, U of West Haven, CT 06516		✔	✔	✔		✔			✔	✔	✔		
Sacred Heart U Fairfield, CT 06432-1000		✔	✔	✔			✔		✔	✔	✔		
Southern Connecticut St U New Haven, CT 06515	✔	✔	✔	✔			✔		✔	✔	✔	✔	✔
Teikyo Post U Waterbury, CT 06723-2540			✔		✔				✔		✔		
Western Connecticut St U Danbury, CT 06810	✔	✔	✔						✔	✔	✔	✔	✔

Delaware

State/Institution	AG	AR	BU	CS	ED	EN	HP	HE	HU	NS	SB	TE	VA
Delaware St U Dover, DE 19901-2275			✔		✔		✔	✔			✔		
Delaware, U of Newark, DE 19716			✔			✔							
Goldey-Beacom Coll Wilmington, DE 19808			✔	✔									

District of Columbia

State/Institution	AG	AR	BU	CS	ED	EN	HP	HE	HU	NS	SB	TE	VA
American U Washington, DC 20016-8001	✔	✔	✔	✔			✔		✔	✔	✔		
District of Columbia, U of the Washington, DC 20008			✔	✔					✔			✔	
George Washington U Washington, DC 20052			✔		✔	✔							
Strayer Coll Washington, DC 20005			✔	✔									

State/Institution	AG	AR	BU	CS	ED	EN	HP	HE	HU	NS	SB	TE	VA
Florida													
Bethune-Cookman Coll Daytona Beach, FL 32114-3099			✔	✔	✔				✔	✔	✔		
Central Florida, U of Orlando, FL 32816		✔	✔	✔	✔	✔	✔		✔	✔	✔	✔	
Embry-Riddle Aeronautical U Daytona Beach, FL 32114-3900			✔	✔		✔			✔	✔	✔	✔	✔
Florida Atlantic U Boca Raton, FL 33431-0991			✔	✔		✔	✔		✔	✔	✔		
Florida Inst of Tech Melbourne, FL 32901-6988			✔	✔	✔	✔			✔	✔	✔		
Florida International U Miami, FL 33199		✔	✔	✔	✔	✔	✔		✔	✔	✔	✔	✔
Florida, U of Gainesville, FL 32611	✔		✔	✔		✔				✔			
Jacksonville U Jacksonville, FL 32211						✔							
North Florida, U of Jacksonville, FL 32224-2645			✔	✔		✔	✔					✔	✔
Nova Southeastern U Fort Lauderdale, FL 33314			✔	✔									✔
Orlando Coll Orlando, FL 32810		✔		✔			✔						
South Florida, U of Tampa, FL 33620		✔	✔	✔		✔	✔				✔	✔	
West Florida, U of Pensacola, FL 32514-5750			✔	✔									
Georgia													
Albany St Coll Albany, GA 31705			✔	✔			✔				✔	✔	
Armstrong St Coll Savannah, GA 31419				✔		✔							

State/Institution	AG	AR	BU	CS	ED	EN	HP	HE	HU	NS	SB	TE	VA
Atlanta Coll of Art Atlanta, GA 30309		✓											
Augusta Coll Augusta, GA 30910			✓	✓					✓	✓	✓		
Berry Coll Mt Berry, GA 30149			✓	✓				✓	✓	✓	✓		
Clark Atlanta U Atlanta, GA 30314						✓							
Clayton St Coll Morrow, GA 30260			✓	✓			✓					✓	
Georgia Coll Milledgeville, GA 31061	✓	✓	✓						✓	✓	✓		
Georgia Inst of Tech Atlanta, GA 30332				✓		✓						✓	
Georgia Southern U Statesboro, GA 30460-8024			✓			✓						✓	
Georgia Southwestern Coll Americus, GA 31709-4693			✓	✓								✓	
Georgia St U Atlanta, GA 30303	✓	✓	✓	✓		✓			✓	✓	✓		
Georgia, U of Athens, GA 30602	✓	✓	✓	✓	✓			✓	✓	✓	✓	✓	✓
Kennesaw St Coll Marietta, GA 30061		✓	✓	✓					✓	✓	✓		
Mercer U Macon, GA 31207			✓			✓							
Morehouse Coll Atlanta, GA 30314			✓	✓		✓	✓				✓		
Oglethorpe U Atlanta, GA 30319-2797	✓	✓	✓	✓	✓	✓			✓	✓	✓		
Paine Coll Augusta, GA 30910			✓	✓									

State/Institution	AG	AR	BU	CS	ED	EN	HP	HE	HU	NS	SB	TE	VA
Southern Coll of Tech Marietta, GA 30060-2896				✔								✔	
Valdosta St U Valdosta, GA 31698	✔	✔	✔	✔	✔			✔	✔	✔			✔

Guam

State/Institution	AG	AR	BU	CS	ED	EN	HP	HE	HU	NS	SB	TE	VA
Guam, U of Mangilao, GU 96923	✔	✔	✔	✔	✔			✔	✔	✔	✔		

Hawaii

State/Institution	AG	AR	BU	CS	ED	EN	HP	HE	HU	NS	SB	TE	VA
Brigham Young U, Hawaii Campus Laie, HI 96762-1294			✔							✔			
Hawaii Pacific U Honolulu, HI 96813			✔	✔				✔					
Hawaii, U of, Hilo Hilo, HI 96720-4091				✔									
Hawaii, U of, Manoa Honolulu, HI 96822	✔	✔	✔	✔	✔	✔		✔			✔	✔	

Idaho

State/Institution	AG	AR	BU	CS	ED	EN	HP	HE	HU	NS	SB	TE	VA
Albertson Coll Caldwell, ID 83605						✔	✔						
Boise St U Boise, ID 83725						✔	✔						
Idaho, U of Moscow, ID 83844-3133	✔	✔	✔	✔	✔	✔		✔	✔	✔	✔		✔
Lewis-Clark St Coll Lewiston, ID 83501-2698			✔		✔			✔			✔	✔	✔
Northwest Nazarene Coll Nampa, ID 83686						✔	✔						

Illinois

State/Institution	AG	AR	BU	CS	ED	EN	HP	HE	HU	NS	SB	TE	VA
Art Inst of Chicago, Sch of the Chicago, IL 60603		✔											

State/Institution	AG	AR	BU	CS	ED	EN	HP	HE	HU	NS	SB	TE	VA
Bradley U Peoria, IL 61625		✔	✔	✔	✔	✔	✔	✔			✔		
Chicago St U Chicago, IL 60628					✔								
East-West U Chicago, IL 60605			✔	✔		✔					✔		
Elmhurst Coll Elmhurst, IL 60126-3296						✔							
Greenville Coll Greenville, IL 62246	✔	✔	✔						✔	✔	✔		
Illinois Inst of Tech Chicago, IL 60616		✔				✔							
Illinois St U Normal, IL 61761-6901			✔	✔						✔	✔		
Illinois, U of, Chicago Chicago, IL 60680	✔	✔				✔	✔		✔	✔	✔		
Illinois, U of, Urbana-Champaign Urbana, IL 61801						✔							
Lincoln Christian Coll and Sem Lincoln, IL 62656-2111					✔								
Northern Illinois U DeKalb, IL 60115	✔	✔	✔	✔	✔	✔	✔		✔	✔	✔	✔	
Northwestern U Evanston, IL 60204-3060				✔		✔							
Principia Coll Elsah, IL 62028						✔							
Southern Illinois U, Carbondale Carbondale, IL 62901	✔		✔			✔	✔					✔	
Trinity Christian Coll Palos Heights, IL 60463													✔
Western Illinois U Macomb, IL 61455	✔		✔	✔				✔	✔	✔	✔	✔	

State/Institution	AG	AR	BU	CS	ED	EN	HP	HE	HU	NS	SB	TE	VA
Indiana													
Ball St U Muncie, IN 47306		✔	✔	✔	✔		✔	✔		✔	✔	✔	
Calumet Coll of St. Joseph Whiting, IN 46394			✔										
Earlham Coll Richmond, IN 47374			✔			✔							
Evansville, U of Evansville, IN 47722				✔		✔							
Franklin Coll Franklin, IN 46131						✔	✔						
Huntington Coll Huntington, IN 46750					✔								
Indiana Inst of Tech Fort Wayne, IN 46803		✔	✔										
Indiana St U Terre Haute, IN 47809		✔	✔	✔			✔	✔		✔	✔	✔	
Indiana U Bloomington Bloomington, IN 47405		✔	✔	✔		✔		✔	✔	✔			
Indiana U Northwest Gary, IN 46408		✔	✔										
Indiana U-Purdue U, Fort Wayne Fort Wayne, IN 46805-1499				✔		✔						✔	
Indiana U-Purdue U, Indianapolis Indianapolis, IN 46202-5143	✔	✔	✔	✔	✔	✔			✔	✔	✔	✔	
Indianapolis, U of Indianapolis, IN 46227-3697		✔	✔	✔		✔			✔	✔	✔		
Oakland City U Oakland City, IN 47660													✔
Purdue U West Lafayette, IN 47907	✔		✔	✔		✔				✔		✔	
Purdue U, Calumet Hammond, IN 46323				✔		✔						✔	

State/Institution	AG	AR	BU	CS	ED	EN	HP	HE	HU	NS	SB	TE	VA
Southern Indiana, U of Evansville, IN 47712			✔			✔							
Taylor U, Fort Wayne Campus Fort Wayne, IN 46807			✔										
Tri-State U Angola, IN 46703-0307			✔	✔		✔						✔	
Valparaiso U Valparaiso, IN 46383-6493			✔	✔		✔	✔		✔	✔	✔		

Iowa

State/Institution	AG	AR	BU	CS	ED	EN	HP	HE	HU	NS	SB	TE	VA
Coe Coll Cedar Rapids, IA 52402						✔							
Cornell Coll Mount Vernon, IA 52314						✔	✔						
Iowa St U Ames, IA 50011-2010	✔		✔	✔		✔		✔		✔	✔		
Iowa Wesleyan Coll Mount Pleasant, IA 52641						✔						✔	
Iowa, U of Iowa City, IA 52242-1396		✔	✔	✔	✔	✔	✔	✔	✔	✔	✔		✔
Morningside Coll Sioux City, IA 51106						✔	✔						
Northern Iowa, U of Cedar Falls, IA 50614-0033		✔	✔	✔	✔		✔	✔	✔	✔	✔		✔
Northwestern Coll Orange City, IA 51041						✔							
St. Ambrose U Davenport, IA 52803		✔	✔	✔	✔	✔	✔				✔	✔	
Simpson Coll Indianola, IA 50125		✔	✔	✔	✔	✔	✔			✔	✔		✔
Teikyo Marycrest U Davenport, IA 52804-4096		✔	✔	✔			✔			✔	✔		✔
Vennard Coll University Park, IA 52595			✔		✔								

State/Institution	AG	AR	BU	CS	ED	EN	HP	HE	HU	NS	SB	TE	VA

Kansas

State/Institution	AG	AR	BU	CS	ED	EN	HP	HE	HU	NS	SB	TE	VA
Bethany Coll Lindsborg, KS 67456-1897						✓							
Bethel Coll North Newton, KS 67117						✓							
Emporia St U Emporia, KS 66801			✓	✓	✓	✓	✓		✓	✓	✓		
Kansas Newman Coll Wichita, KS 67213	✓	✓	✓	✓	✓		✓		✓	✓	✓	✓	
Kansas St U Manhattan, KS 66506	✓	✓	✓	✓	✓	✓		✓		✓	✓		
Kansas, U of Lawrence, KS 66045						✓							
Manhattan Christian Coll Manhattan, KS 66502	✓		✓	✓	✓			✓	✓		✓		
McPherson Coll McPherson, KS 67460			✓										
Pittsburg St U Pittsburg, KS 66762		✓	✓	✓	✓	✓	✓	✓		✓	✓	✓	✓
Wichita St U Wichita, KS 67260-0113			✓	✓	✓	✓	✓	✓	✓	✓	✓	✓	

Kentucky

State/Institution	AG	AR	BU	CS	ED	EN	HP	HE	HU	NS	SB	TE	VA
Eastern Kentucky U Richmond, KY 40475-3101	✓	✓	✓	✓	✓	✓	✓	✓	✓	✓	✓	✓	✓
Kentucky, U of Lexington, KY 40506	✓		✓	✓		✓							
Lindsey Wilson Coll Columbia, KY 42728			✓									✓	
Louisville, U of Louisville, KY 40292			✓	✓	✓	✓							
Murray St U Murray, KY 42071	✓	✓	✓	✓	✓	✓	✓	✓	✓	✓	✓	✓	✓

State/Institution	AG	AR	BU	CS	ED	EN	HP	HE	HU	NS	SB	TE	VA
Northern Kentucky U Highland Heights, KY 41099-7010		✓	✓							✓	✓	✓	
Thomas More Coll Crestview Hills, KY 41017		✓	✓	✓			✓		✓	✓	✓		
Union Coll Barbourville, KY 40906			✓								✓		
Western Kentucky U Bowling Green, KY 42101	✓	✓	✓	✓	✓	✓	✓	✓	✓	✓	✓	✓	✓

Louisiana

State/Institution	AG	AR	BU	CS	ED	EN	HP	HE	HU	NS	SB	TE	VA
Grambling St U Grambling, LA 71245			✓	✓			✓	✓	✓	✓	✓	✓	
Louisiana St U & A&M Coll Baton Rouge, LA 70803-2750	✓	✓	✓	✓		✓				✓	✓		
Louisiana St U, Shreveport Shreveport, LA 71115			✓										
Louisiana Tech U Ruston, LA 71272	✓					✓	✓						
McNeese St U Lake Charles, LA 70609-2495						✓							
New Orleans, U of New Orleans, LA 70148		✓	✓	✓	✓	✓	✓		✓	✓	✓		
Nicholls St U Thibodaux, LA 70310			✓										
Southeastern Louisiana U Hammond, LA 70402			✓									✓	
Southern U & A&M Coll Baton Rouge, LA 70813				✓									
Xavier U of Louisiana New Orleans, LA 70125		✓	✓	✓			✓	✓		✓	✓	✓	

Maine

State/Institution	AG	AR	BU	CS	ED	EN	HP	HE	HU	NS	SB	TE	VA
Husson Coll Bangor, ME 04401		✓	✓	✓			✓						

State/Institution	AG	AR	BU	CS	ED	EN	HP	HE	HU	NS	SB	TE	VA
Maine Coll of Art Portland, ME 04101		✓											
Maine Maritime Acad Castine, ME 04420						✓							
Maine, U of Orono, ME 04469	✓		✓	✓	✓	✓	✓	✓	✓	✓	✓		
Maine, U of, Augusta Augusta, ME 04330-9410			✓										
Maine, U of, Machias Machias, ME 04654			✓		✓				✓		✓		
Southern Maine, U of Gorham, ME 04038		✓	✓	✓	✓	✓	✓		✓	✓	✓	✓	✓
Thomas Coll Waterville, ME 04901-9986			✓										
Unity Coll Unity, ME 04988-0532	✓								✓				

Maryland

State/Institution	AG	AR	BU	CS	ED	EN	HP	HE	HU	NS	SB	TE	VA
Baltimore, U of Baltimore, MD 21201			✓	✓					✓		✓		
Bowie St U Bowie, MD 20715	✓	✓	✓	✓		✓			✓	✓			
Capitol Coll Laurel, MD 20708				✓		✓							✓
Columbia Union Coll Takoma Park, MD 20912			✓	✓	✓	✓	✓						
Coppin St Coll Baltimore, MD 21216				✓	✓	✓							
Frostburg St U Frostburg, MD 21532			✓										
Johns Hopkins U Baltimore, MD 21218				✓	✓	✓							
Maryland, U of, Baltimore County Baltimore, MD 21228	✓	✓	✓			✓	✓		✓	✓	✓	✓	✓

State/Institution	AG	AR	BU	CS	ED	EN	HP	HE	HU	NS	SB	TE	VA
Maryland, U of, College Park College Park, MD 20742			✔	✔		✔							
Maryland, U of, Eastern Shore Princess Anne, MD 21853	✔		✔		✔	✔				✔		✔	
Maryland, U of, University College College Park, MD 20742-1600		✔	✔	✔					✔	✔	✔		
Mt St. Mary's Coll Emmitsburg, MD 21727			✔		✔		✔		✔	✔	✔		
Salisbury St U Salisbury, MD 21801			✔										
Towson St U Towson, MD 21204-7097		✔	✔	✔			✔		✔	✔	✔		
Villa Julie Coll Stevenson, MD 21153			✔	✔					✔	✔	✔	✔	
Western Maryland Coll Westminster, MD 21157					✔	✔					✔		

Massachusetts

State/Institution	AG	AR	BU	CS	ED	EN	HP	HE	HU	NS	SB	TE	VA
Atlantic Union Coll South Lancaster, MA 01561		✔	✔	✔	✔		✔		✔		✔		
Bay Path Coll Longmeadow, MA 01106			✔		✔		✔						
Boston U Boston, MA 02215						✔							
Eastern Nazarene Coll Quincy, MA 02170						✔							
Gordon Coll Wenham, MA 01984	✔	✔	✔	✔	✔	✔			✔	✔	✔		
Massachusetts Coll of Art Boston, MA 02115-5882		✔											
Massachusetts Inst of Tech Cambridge, MA 02139						✔							
Massachusetts Maritime Acad Buzzards Bay, MA 02532-1803						✔						✔	

State/Institution	AG	AR	BU	CS	ED	EN	HP	HE	HU	NS	SB	TE	VA
Massachusetts, U of, Amherst Amherst, MA 01003	✔	✔	✔	✔	✔	✔	✔	✔	✔	✔	✔	✔	
Massachusetts, U of, Boston Boston, MA 02125-3393		✔	✔	✔	✔		✔		✔	✔	✔		
Merrimack Coll North Andover, MA 01845			✔	✔		✔	✔		✔	✔			
Montserrat Coll of Art Beverly, MA 01915		✔			✔								
Museum of Fine Arts, Sch of the Boston, MA 02115		✔											
Northeastern U Boston, MA 02115		✔	✔	✔	✔	✔	✔		✔	✔	✔		
Springfield Coll Springfield, MA 01109-3797		✔	✔	✔	✔		✔		✔	✔	✔		
Suffolk U Boston, MA 02108			✔	✔	✔	✔	✔		✔	✔	✔		
Wentworth Inst of Tech Boston, MA 02115				✔		✔						✔	
Westfield St Coll Westfield, MA 01086	✔	✔	✔	✔					✔		✔		
Worcester Polytechnic Inst Worcester, MA 01609				✔		✔				✔			

Michigan

State/Institution	AG	AR	BU	CS	ED	EN	HP	HE	HU	NS	SB	TE	VA
Aquinas Coll Grand Rapids, MI 49506-1799	✔	✔	✔	✔			✔		✔	✔	✔		
Baker Coll of Auburn Hills Auburn Hills, MI 48326-2642			✔				✔						
Baker Coll of Cadillac Cadillac, MI 49601-9169			✔										
Baker Coll of Flint Flint, MI 48507							✔						
Baker Coll of Jackson Jackson, MI 49201-2328			✔				✔						

State/Institution	AG	AR	BU	CS	ED	EN	HP	HE	HU	NS	SB	TE	VA
Baker Coll of Mt Clemens Clinton Township, MI 48035-4701			✓				✓						
Baker Coll, Muskegon Muskegon, MI 49442			✓	✓			✓					✓	
Baker Coll, Owosso Owosso, MI 48867-4400			✓				✓						
Baker Coll of Port Huron Port Huron, MI 48060-2597			✓				✓						
Calvin Coll Grand Rapids, MI 49546			✓			✓							
Central Michigan U Mount Pleasant, MI 48859												✓	✓
Cleary Coll Ypsilanti, MI 48197			✓										
Concordia Coll Ann Arbor, MI 48105			✓										
Cornerstone Coll Grand Rapids, MI 49505				✓									
Detroit Coll of Business Dearborn, MI 48126			✓				✓						
Detroit Mercy, U of Detroit, MI 48221			✓	✓	✓	✓	✓		✓	✓	✓	✓	
Eastern Michigan U Ypsilanti, MI 48197	✓	✓	✓			✓	✓	✓	✓	✓	✓	✓	✓
Ferris St U Big Rapids, MI 49307-2251			✓	✓	✓		✓				✓	✓	✓
GMI Engineering & Management Inst Flint, MI 48504-4898			✓	✓		✓							
Grand Valley St U Allendale, MI 49401				✓	✓	✓							
Kendall Coll of Art & Design Grand Rapids, MI 49503-3194	✓												

State/Institution	AG	AR	BU	CS	ED	EN	HP	HE	HU	NS	SB	TE	VA
Lawrence Tech U Southfield, MI 48075						✓							
Marygrove Coll Detroit, MI 48221-2599	✓	✓	✓	✓									✓
Michigan St U East Lansing, MI 48824-0590						✓							
Michigan Tech U Houghton, MI 49931			✓	✓		✓						✓	✓
Michigan, U of, Ann Arbor Ann Arbor, MI 48104-2210						✓							
Michigan, U of, Dearborn Dearborn, MI 48128-1491	✓	✓	✓	✓	✓	✓	✓		✓	✓	✓		
Michigan, U of, Flint Flint, MI 48502			✓	✓	✓	✓	✓		✓	✓	✓	✓	
Oakland U Rochester, MI 48309			✓	✓	✓	✓	✓		✓	✓	✓		
Olivet Coll Olivet, MI 49076	✓	✓	✓						✓	✓	✓		
St. Mary's Coll Orchard Lake, MI 48324			✓	✓						✓	✓		
Siena Heights Coll Adrian, MI 49221	✓	✓	✓	✓		✓			✓	✓	✓		
Wayne St U Detroit, MI 48202					✓		✓				✓		
Western Michigan U Kalamazoo, MI 49008			✓	✓		✓							✓

Minnesota

State/Institution	AG	AR	BU	CS	ED	EN	HP	HE	HU	NS	SB	TE	VA
Augsburg Coll Minneapolis, MN 55454	✓	✓	✓	✓	✓	✓			✓	✓	✓	✓	
Concordia Coll, Moorhead Moorhead, MN 56562	✓	✓	✓			✓	✓		✓	✓	✓		
Hamline U St. Paul, MN 55101					✓	✓							

State/Institution	AG	AR	BU	CS	ED	EN	HP	HE	HU	NS	SB	TE	VA
Minneapolis Coll of Art & Design Minneapolis, MN 55404		✓											
Minnesota, U of, Morris Morris, MN 56267		✓	✓	✓					✓	✓	✓		
Moorhead St U Moorhead, MN 56563	✓					✓	✓	✓					
North Central Bible Coll Minneapolis, MN 55404				✓			✓						
Northwestern Coll St. Paul, MN 55113	✓						✓						
St. Catherine, The Coll of St. Paul, MN 55105						✓	✓			✓			
St. Mary's Coll of Minnesota Winona, MN 55987-1399						✓	✓						

Mississippi

State/Institution	AG	AR	BU	CS	ED	EN	HP	HE	HU	NS	SB	TE	VA
Alcorn St U Lorman, MS 39096	✓		✓	✓	✓	✓	✓	✓		✓	✓		
Belhaven Coll Jackson, MS 39202					✓								
Jackson St U Jackson, MS 39217			✓	✓						✓			
Mississippi St U Mississippi State, MS 39762	✓	✓	✓	✓	✓	✓		✓			✓		
Mississippi U for Women Columbus, MS 39701		✓	✓										
Mississippi Valley St U Itta Bena, MS 38941--400			✓	✓								✓	
Rust Coll Holly Springs, MS 38635			✓	✓					✓	✓	✓		
Southern Mississippi, U of Hattiesburg, MS 39406		✓	✓	✓	✓			✓	✓	✓	✓		
Tougaloo Coll Tougaloo, MS 39174			✓							✓	✓		

State/Institution	AG	AR	BU	CS	ED	EN	HP	HE	HU	NS	SB	TE	VA
Missouri													
Central Missouri St U Warrensburg, MO 64093						✔							
Culver-Stockton Coll Canton, MO 63435-1299			✔			✔	✔						✔
Drury Coll Springfield, MO 65802			✔			✔	✔						
Fontbonne Coll St. Louis, MO 63105		✔	✔	✔	✔		✔	✔		✔	✔	✔	
Lincoln U Jefferson City, MO 65102-0029	✔												
Lindenwood Coll St. Charles, MO 63301			✔	✔									
Maryville U of St. Louis St. Louis, MO 63141-7299		✔	✔	✔	✔		✔		✔	✔	✔		
Missouri, U of, Columbia Columbia, MO 65211		✔	✔				✔		✔	✔	✔		
Missouri, U of, Kansas City Kansas City, MO 64110			✔	✔			✔				✔	✔	
Missouri, U of, Rolla Rolla, MO 65401			✔	✔			✔		✔	✔	✔		
Missouri, U of, St. Louis St. Louis, MO 63121			✔				✔				✔		
Northwest Missouri St U Maryville, MO 64468	✔												
Ozarks, Coll of the Point Lookout, MO 65726	✔	✔	✔	✔	✔	✔	✔	✔	✔	✔	✔	✔	✔
Rockhurst Coll Kansas City, MO 64110-2508			✔	✔					✔	✔	✔		
Southeast Missouri St U Cape Girardeau, MO 63701			✔										
Southwest Baptist U Bolivar, MO 65613-2496							✔	✔					

State/Institution	AG	AR	BU	CS	ED	EN	HP	HE	HU	NS	SB	TE	VA
Southwest Missouri St U Springfield, MO 65804	✓	✓	✓	✓	✓		✓	✓	✓	✓	✓	✓	✓
Washington U St. Louis, MO 63130			✓			✓							
Webster U St. Louis, MO 63119-3194		✓	✓	✓	✓		✓		✓	✓	✓		

Montana

State/Institution	AG	AR	BU	CS	ED	EN	HP	HE	HU	NS	SB	TE	VA
Carroll Coll Helena, MT 59625			✓										
Great Falls, Coll of Great Falls, MT 59405			✓	✓					✓		✓		
Montana Tech of the U of Montana Butte, MT 59701-8997			✓	✓		✓		✓					
Montana, U of Missoula, MT 59812			✓	✓	✓		✓		✓		✓		
Northern Montana Coll Havre, MT 59501	✓		✓	✓					✓	✓	✓	✓	✓
Rocky Mountain Coll Billings, MT 59102-1796		✓	✓	✓	✓	✓	✓		✓	✓	✓	✓	

Nebraska

State/Institution	AG	AR	BU	CS	ED	EN	HP	HE	HU	NS	SB	TE	VA
Grace U Omaha, NE 68108	✓	✓	✓	✓	✓		✓					✓	✓
Nebraska, U of, Lincoln Lincoln, NE 68588	✓	✓	✓	✓	✓	✓	✓	✓	✓	✓	✓	✓	✓
Nebraska, U of, Omaha Omaha, NE 68182-0005			✓			✓							
Peru St Coll Peru, NE 68421-0010		✓	✓	✓	✓				✓	✓	✓	✓	
Wayne St Coll Wayne, NE 68787	✓	✓	✓	✓	✓		✓	✓	✓	✓	✓	✓	✓

State/Institution	AG	AR	BU	CS	ED	EN	HP	HE	HU	NS	SB	TE	VA
Nevada													
Nevada, U of, Reno Reno, NV 89557-0002	✓	✓		✓		✓							
New Hampshire													
Keene St Coll Keene, NH 03431		✓	✓	✓	✓	✓	✓	✓		✓	✓	✓	✓
New Hampshire Coll Manchester, NH 03106-1045			✓	✓	✓				✓		✓		
New Jersey													
Caldwell Coll Caldwell, NJ 07006		✓	✓	✓			✓	✓	✓	✓			
Drew U Madison, NJ 07940						✓							
Fairleigh Dickinson U Teaneck, NJ 07666		✓	✓	✓	✓	✓			✓			✓	✓
Georgian Court Coll Lakewood, NJ 08701-2697		✓	✓			✓				✓	✓		
Jersey City St Coll Jersey City, NJ 07305		✓	✓	✓			✓	✓	✓	✓			
Medicine & Dentistry of New Jersey, U of Newark, NJ 07107				✓	✓			✓			✓		
Monmouth Coll West Long Branch, NJ 07764-1898		✓	✓	✓	✓	✓	✓		✓	✓	✓	✓	
Montclair St U Upper Montclair, NJ 07043-1624		✓	✓	✓			✓	✓	✓	✓	✓	✓	
New Jersey Inst of Tech Newark, NJ 07102-1982			✓	✓		✓				✓	✓	✓	
Ramapo Coll of New Jersey Mahwah, NJ 07430		✓	✓	✓						✓	✓	✓	
Rider U Lawrenceville, NJ 08648-3099			✓										

State/Institution	AG	AR	BU	CS	ED	EN	HP	HE	HU	NS	SB	TE	VA
Rowan Coll of New Jersey Glassboro, NJ 08028			✔		✔								
St. Peter's Coll Jersey City, NJ 07306		✔	✔	✔	✔				✔	✔	✔		
Seton Hall U South Orange, NJ 07079-2689			✔	✔		✔	✔			✔	✔		
Stevens Inst of Tech Hoboken, NJ 07030			✔	✔		✔	✔		✔	✔	✔		
Stockton Coll of New Jersey Pomona, NJ 08240	✔	✔	✔	✔			✔			✔	✔	✔	

New Mexico

State/Institution	AG	AR	BU	CS	ED	EN	HP	HE	HU	NS	SB	TE	VA
Eastern New Mexico U Portales, NM 88130		✔	✔	✔	✔			✔		✔			
New Mexico Highlands U Las Vegas, NM 87701			✔	✔		✔				✔			
New Mexico Inst of Mining & Tech Socorro, NM 87801			✔	✔	✔	✔				✔	✔		
New Mexico St U Las Cruces, NM 88003-8001	✔		✔	✔	✔	✔		✔	✔	✔	✔	✔	✔
New Mexico, U of Albuquerque, NM 87131			✔			✔							
Western New Mexico U Silver City, NM 88062			✔		✔								✔

New York

State/Institution	AG	AR	BU	CS	ED	EN	HP	HE	HU	NS	SB	TE	VA
Alfred U Alfred, NY 14802			✔			✔							
Audrey Cohen Coll New York, NY 10014			✔		✔		✔		✔		✔		
Cornell U Ithaca, NY 14853	✔					✔							
CUNY, City Coll New York, NY 10031						✔			✔		✔		

State/Institution	AG	AR	BU	CS	ED	EN	HP	HE	HU	NS	SB	TE	VA
CUNY, York Coll Jamaica, NY 11451			✔	✔			✔						
Dominican Coll of Blauvelt Orangeburg, NY 10962			✔	✔	✔		✔		✔			✔	
Dowling Coll Oakdale, NY 11769			✔	✔	✔		✔		✔	✔	✔	✔	
Fashion Inst of Tech New York, NY 10001-5992		✔	✔										
Five Towns Coll Dix Hills, NY 11746-6055			✔		✔							✔	✔
Insurance, Coll of New York, NY 10007			✔										
Iona Coll New Rochelle, NY 10801			✔	✔	✔				✔	✔	✔		
Keuka Coll Keuka Park, NY 14478						✔							
Long Island U, Brooklyn Campus Brooklyn, NY 11201	✔	✔	✔									✔	
Long Island U, C.W. Post Campus Brookville, NY 11548	✔	✔	✔	✔	✔		✔		✔	✔	✔		
Manhattan Coll Riverdale, NY 10471	✔	✔	✔	✔	✔	✔			✔	✔	✔	✔	
Marist Coll Poughkeepsie, NY 12601	✔	✔	✔	✔					✔	✔	✔	✔	
Marymount Manhattan Coll New York, NY 10021			✔										
Mercy Coll Dobbs Ferry, NY 10522					✔						✔		
Mt St. Mary Coll Newburgh, NY 12550-3598			✔	✔	✔		✔		✔	✔	✔	✔	
Nazareth Coll of Rochester Rochester, NY 14618										✔			

State/Institution	AG	AR	BU	CS	ED	EN	HP	HE	HU	NS	SB	TE	VA
New Rochelle, Coll of New Rochelle, NY 10805		✔	✔		✔		✔		✔	✔	✔		
New York St Coll of Ceramics at Alfred U Alfred, NY 14802		✔					✔						
Polytechnic U Brooklyn, NY 11201			✔			✔			✔	✔	✔		
Rensselaer Polytechnic Inst Troy, NY 12180		✔	✔			✔			✔	✔	✔		
Roberts Wesleyan Coll Rochester, NY 14624-1997						✔							
Rochester Inst of Tech Rochester, NY 14623	✔	✔	✔			✔	✔			✔	✔	✔	
Russell Sage Coll Troy, NY 12180	✔	✔	✔	✔			✔		✔	✔	✔		
St. Thomas Aquinas Coll Sparkill, NY 10976-1050						✔							
SUNY at New Paltz New Paltz, NY 12561-2499		✔	✔			✔						✔	
SUNY Coll at Buffalo Buffalo, NY 14222	✔	✔	✔	✔						✔	✔	✔	✔
SUNY Coll at Cortland Cortland, NY 13045	✔	✔	✔	✔			✔		✔	✔	✔		
SUNY Coll at Oneonta Oneonta, NY 13820	✔				✔	✔	✔						
SUNY Coll at Plattsburgh Plattsburgh, NY 12901	✔	✔	✔	✔			✔		✔	✔	✔		
SUNY Coll at Potsdam Potsdam, NY 13676-2294	✔	✔	✔			✔	✔		✔				
SUNY Inst of Tech at Utica/Rome Utica, NY 13504-3050			✔				✔					✔	
SUNY, Purchase Coll Purchase, NY 10577				✔									

State/Institution	AG	AR	BU	CS	ED	EN	HP	HE	HU	NS	SB	TE	VA
Syracuse U Syracuse, NY 13244						✓							
U.S. Merchant Marine Acad Kings Point, NY 11024-1699						✓							
Utica Coll of Syracuse U Utica, NY 13502-4892			✓	✓		✓							
Webb Inst Glen Cove, NY 11542						✓							

North Carolina

State/Institution	AG	AR	BU	CS	ED	EN	HP	HE	HU	NS	SB	TE	VA
Barber-Scotia Coll Concord, NC 28025			✓										
Campbell U Buies Creek, NC 27506					✓							✓	
East Carolina U Greenville, NC 27858-4353		✓	✓	✓	✓	✓	✓	✓	✓	✓	✓	✓	✓
Elizabeth City St U Elizabeth City, NC 27909		✓	✓	✓		✓				✓	✓	✓	
Elon Coll Elon College, NC 27244			✓	✓			✓		✓				
Fayetteville St U Fayetteville, NC 28301		✓											
Johnson C. Smith U Charlotte, NC 28216		✓	✓	✓	✓		✓		✓				
Livingstone Coll Salisbury, NC 28144			✓	✓	✓				✓	✓	✓		
Mars Hill Coll Mars Hill, NC 28754						✓							
Methodist Coll Fayetteville, NC 28311			✓		✓								
Mt Olive Coll Mount Olive, NC 28365		✓	✓	✓					✓	✓	✓		
North Carolina A&T St U Greensboro, NC 27411			✓		✓								

State/Institution	AG	AR	BU	CS	ED	EN	HP	HE	HU	NS	SB	TE	VA
North Carolina St U Raleigh, NC 27695-7103	✔	✔	✔	✔	✔	✔			✔	✔	✔	✔	
North Carolina Wesleyan Coll Rocky Mount, NC 27804			✔	✔					✔	✔	✔		
North Carolina, U of, Charlotte Charlotte, NC 28223		✔	✔	✔		✔			✔	✔	✔		
Pfeiffer Coll Misenheimer, NC 28109		✔	✔	✔					✔	✔	✔		
St. Augustine's Coll Raleigh, NC 27610			✔		✔				✔				
Wake Forest U Winston-Salem, NC 27109					✔	✔							
Warren Wilson Coll Asheville, NC 28815	✔	✔	✔			✔			✔	✔	✔		
Western Carolina U Cullowhee, NC 28723		✔	✔	✔	✔	✔	✔	✔	✔	✔	✔		
Wingate Coll Wingate, NC 28174-0157						✔							
Winston-Salem St U Winston-Salem, NC 27110			✔	✔					✔	✔			

North Dakota

State/Institution	AG	AR	BU	CS	ED	EN	HP	HE	HU	NS	SB	TE	VA
Jamestown Coll Jamestown, ND 58405		✔											
Mary, U of Bismarck, ND 58501-9652			✔	✔	✔		✔						
North Dakota St U Fargo, ND 58105	✔	✔	✔	✔	✔	✔	✔	✔	✔	✔	✔	✔	
North Dakota, U of Grand Forks, ND 58202-8172		✔	✔	✔		✔	✔	✔	✔			✔	✔	✔
Valley City St U Valley City, ND 58072-4098		✔	✔		✔				✔	✔	✔		

State/Institution	AG	AR	BU	CS	ED	EN	HP	HE	HU	NS	SB	TE	VA

Ohio

State/Institution	AG	AR	BU	CS	ED	EN	HP	HE	HU	NS	SB	TE	VA
Akron, U of Akron, OH 44325	✔	✔	✔			✔		✔	✔	✔		✔	
Art Acad of Cincinnati Cincinnati, OH 45202	✔												
Bowling Green St U Bowling Green, OH 43403	✔	✔	✔	✔		✔	✔	✔	✔	✔	✔		
Case Western Reserve U Cleveland, OH 44106			✔			✔			✔				
Central St U Wilberforce, OH 45384			✔	✔									
Cincinnati Bible Coll Cincinnati, OH 45204-3200					✔								
Cincinnati, U of Cincinnati, OH 45221-0127			✔	✔		✔			✔				
Cleveland St U Cleveland, OH 44115	✔	✔	✔	✔	✔				✔	✔	✔	✔	
Dayton, U of Dayton, OH 45469-1660			✔	✔		✔				✔		✔	
Defiance Coll Defiance, OH 43512			✔		✔				✔	✔	✔		
Dyke Coll Cleveland, OH 44115-1096			✔			✔					✔		
Franciscan U of Steubenville Steubenville, OH 43952-6701						✔							
Heidelberg Coll Tiffin, OH 44883						✔							
Kent St U Kent, OH 44242-0001												✔	
Kenyon Coll Gambier, OH 43022-9623				✔	✔								
Malone Coll Canton, OH 44709			✔	✔	✔		✔		✔	✔	✔		

State/Institution	AG	AR	BU	CS	ED	EN	HP	HE	HU	NS	SB	TE	VA

State/Institution	AG	AR	BU	CS	ED	EN	HP	HE	HU	NS	SB	TE	VA
Miami U Oxford, OH 45056				✔		✔						✔	
Mt St. Joseph, Coll of Cincinnati, OH 45233-1672		✔	✔	✔	✔		✔		✔	✔	✔		
Mt Union Coll Alliance, OH 44601			✔	✔	✔		✔		✔	✔	✔		
Notre Dame Coll of Ohio South Euclid, OH 44121		✔	✔				✔		✔	✔	✔		
Ohio Northern U Ada, OH 45810						✔						✔	
Ohio St U, Columbus Columbus, OH 43210-1200	✔		✔	✔		✔			✔	✔	✔		
Ohio St U, Newark Newark, OH 43055			✔			✔							
Ohio U Athens, OH 45701-2979				✔		✔							
Rio Grande, U of Rio Grande, OH 45674		✔	✔		✔		✔		✔	✔	✔	✔	
Toledo, U of Toledo, OH 43606			✔	✔	✔	✔	✔		✔	✔	✔	✔	✔
Ursuline Coll Pepper Pike, OH 44124		✔	✔	✔	✔		✔		✔	✔	✔		
Walsh U North Canton, OH 44720			✔	✔			✔						
Wilberforce U Wilberforce, OH 45384		✔	✔	✔			✔		✔	✔	✔		
Wooster, Coll of Wooster, OH 44691					✔	✔				✔			
Wright St U Dayton, OH 45435			✔	✔		✔				✔	✔		

Oklahoma

State/Institution	AG	AR	BU	CS	ED	EN	HP	HE	HU	NS	SB	TE	VA
Northeastern St U Tahlequah, OK 74464			✔		✔							✔	

State/Institution	AG	AR	BU	CS	ED	EN	HP	HE	HU	NS	SB	TE	VA
Oklahoma Baptist U Shawnee, OK 74801		✔	✔	✔						✔	✔		
Oklahoma St U Stillwater, OK 74078						✔							
Oklahoma, U of Norman, OK 73019						✔							
Oral Roberts U Tulsa, OK 74171							✔				✔		
Panhandle St U Goodwell, OK 73939	✔												

Oregon

State/Institution	AG	AR	BU	CS	ED	EN	HP	HE	HU	NS	SB	TE	VA
Bassist Coll Portland, OR 97201													✔
Eastern Oregon St Coll LaGrande, OR 97850	✔	✔	✔		✔								
George Fox Coll Newberg, OR 97132						✔							
Oregon Inst of Tech Klamath Falls, OR 97601-8801			✔	✔		✔						✔	
Oregon St U Corvallis, OR 97331	✔	✔	✔	✔	✔	✔	✔	✔	✔	✔	✔		✔
Portland St U Portland, OR 97207-0751		✔	✔	✔	✔	✔			✔	✔	✔		
Reed Coll Portland, OR 97202		✔	✔	✔		✔							

Pennsylvania

State/Institution	AG	AR	BU	CS	ED	EN	HP	HE	HU	NS	SB	TE	VA
Acad of the New Church Coll Bryn Athyn, PA 19009		✔	✔	✔	✔	✔				✔	✔		
Albright Coll Reading, PA 19612-5234						✔					✔		
Beaver Coll Glenside, PA 19038-3295		✔	✔	✔					✔	✔	✔		

State/Institution	AG	AR	BU	CS	ED	EN	HP	HE	HU	NS	SB	TE	VA
Cabrini Coll Radnor, PA 19087-3699		✔	✔	✔	✔		✔		✔	✔	✔		
California U of Pennsylvania California, PA 15419	✔	✔	✔	✔	✔	✔	✔		✔	✔	✔	✔	✔
Chatham Coll Pittsburgh, PA 15232					✔	✔	✔						
Chestnut Hill Coll Philadelphia, PA 19118-2695		✔	✔	✔	✔		✔		✔	✔	✔		
Cheyney U of Pennsylvania Cheyney, PA 19319		✔	✔	✔	✔		✔	✔	✔	✔	✔	✔	✔
Clarion U of Pennsylvania Clarion, PA 16214						✔							
Delaware Valley Coll Doylestown, PA 18901	✔		✔	✔	✔								
Drexel U Philadelphia, PA 19104		✔	✔	✔		✔			✔	✔	✔	✔	✔
Duquesne U Pittsburgh, PA 15282							✔						
Gannon U Erie, PA 16541			✔			✔							
Geneva Coll Beaver Falls, PA 15010							✔						
Holy Family Coll Philadelphia, PA 19114			✔	✔	✔		✔			✔	✔	✔	
Juniata Coll Huntingdon, PA 16652-2119					✔	✔				✔			
King's Coll Wilkes-Barre, PA 18711			✔	✔	✔					✔	✔	✔	
LaSalle U Philadelphia, PA 19141-1199			✔	✔	✔					✔	✔	✔	
Lebanon Valley Coll Annville, PA 17003					✔	✔							

State/Institution	AG	AR	BU	CS	ED	EN	HP	HE	HU	NS	SB	TE	VA
Lehigh U Bethlehem, PA 18015-3035						✔							
Lincoln U Lincoln University, PA 19352		✔	✔	✔		✔			✔	✔	✔		
Lock Haven U of Pennsylvania Lock Haven, PA 17745						✔							
Lycoming Coll Williamsport, PA 17701-5192						✔			✔				
Mercyhurst Coll Erie, PA 16546	✔	✔	✔	✔			✔	✔	✔	✔	✔		
Millersville U of Pennsylvania Millersville, PA 17551-0302	✔	✔	✔	✔	✔	✔			✔	✔	✔	✔	✔
Moore Coll of Art & Design Philadelphia, PA 19103	✔			✔									
Moravian Coll Bethlehem, PA 18018						✔							
Muhlenberg Coll Allentown, PA 18104-5586						✔	✔						
Neumann Coll Aston, PA 19014-1297		✔	✔	✔	✔				✔	✔	✔		
Pennsylvania St U University Park, PA 16802						✔							
Pennsylvania St U, Harrisburg Middletown, PA 17057												✔	
Philadelphia Coll of Bible Langhorne, PA 19047-2992		✔	✔										
Philadelphia Coll of Pharmacy & Science Philadelphia, PA 19104-4495											✔		
Philadelphia Coll of Textiles & Science Philadelphia, PA 19144	✔	✔	✔			✔			✔	✔	✔		✔
Pittsburgh, U of, Bradford Bradford, PA 16701-2898						✔							

State/Institution	AG	AR	BU	CS	ED	EN	HP	HE	HU	NS	SB	TE	VA
Pittsburgh, U of, Pittsburgh Pittsburgh, PA 15260						✓							
Point Park Coll Pittsburgh, PA 15222		✓											
Robert Morris Coll Coraopolis, PA 15108-1189			✓	✓	✓		✓			✓			
St. Vincent Coll Latrobe, PA 15650-2690			✓	✓	✓		✓	✓	✓	✓	✓		
Temple U Philadelphia, PA 19122-1803			✓	✓		✓			✓				
Thiel Coll Greenville, PA 16125	✓	✓	✓	✓	✓	✓			✓	✓	✓		
Valley Forge Christian Coll Phoenixville, PA 19460					✓								
Widener U Chester, PA 19013			✓	✓		✓							
Wilkes U Wilkes-Barre, PA 18766	✓	✓	✓	✓	✓				✓	✓	✓	✓	
York Coll of Pennsylvania York, PA 17403-3426						✓							

Puerto Rico

State/Institution	AG	AR	BU	CS	ED	EN	HP	HE	HU	NS	SB	TE	VA
Polytechnic U of Puerto Rico Hato Rey, PR 00919						✓							
Puerto Rico, U of, Bayamon Tech U Coll Bayamon, PR 00959-1919			✓	✓									✓
Puerto Rico, U of, Humacao U Coll Humacao, PR 00791					✓		✓			✓	✓		
Puerto Rico, U of, Mayaguez Mayaguez, PR 00681-5000		✓			✓				✓				

Rhode Island

State/Institution	AG	AR	BU	CS	ED	EN	HP	HE	HU	NS	SB	TE	VA
Johnson & Wales U Providence, RI 02903			✓										

State/Institution	AG	AR	BU	CS	ED	EN	HP	HE	HU	NS	SB	TE	VA
Rhode Island Coll Providence, RI 02908		✔	✔	✔	✔		✔		✔	✔	✔	✔	✔
Rhode Island, U of Kingston, RI 02881	✔	✔					✔						

South Carolina

State/Institution	AG	AR	BU	CS	ED	EN	HP	HE	HU	NS	SB	TE	VA
Benedict Coll Columbia, SC 29204						✔							
Charleston, Coll of Charleston, SC 29424			✔										
Clemson U Clemson, SC 29634-5124	✔		✔	✔	✔	✔			✔	✔			
Coker Coll Hartsville, SC 29550		✔	✔		✔		✔		✔	✔	✔		
Columbia Coll Columbia, SC 29203							✔						
Erskine Coll Due West, SC 29639						✔	✔						
Francis Marion U Florence, SC 29501-0547						✔						✔	
Lander U Greenwood, SC 29649			✔	✔									
Morris Coll Sumter, SC 29150-3599		✔	✔	✔			✔		✔	✔	✔		
Presbyterian Coll Clinton, SC 29325						✔							
South Carolina St U Orangeburg, SC 29117			✔			✔							
South Carolina, U of Columbia, SC 29208	✔	✔	✔			✔			✔	✔	✔		
South Carolina, U of, Aiken Aiken, SC 29801		✔	✔	✔	✔				✔	✔			
Southern Wesleyan U Central, SC 29630							✔						

State/Institution	AG	AR	BU	CS	ED	EN	HP	HE	HU	NS	SB	TE	VA
Voorhees Coll Denmark, SC 29042			✔	✔	✔				✔	✔	✔		
Winthrop U Rock Hill, SC 29733	✔	✔	✔	✔			✔	✔	✔	✔	✔	✔	

South Dakota

State/Institution	AG	AR	BU	CS	ED	EN	HP	HE	HU	NS	SB	TE	VA
Dakota St U Madison, SD 57042	✔	✔	✔				✔			✔			
Huron U Huron, SD 57350			✔										
Oglala Lakota Coll Kyle, SD 57752													✔
South Dakota Sch of Mines & Tech Rapid City, SD 57701-3995				✔		✔				✔			
South Dakota St U Brookings, SD 57007	✔		✔	✔	✔	✔		✔					

Tennessee

State/Institution	AG	AR	BU	CS	ED	EN	HP	HE	HU	NS	SB	TE	VA
Austin Peay St U Clarksville, TN 37044	✔		✔			✔							
Carson-Newman Coll Jefferson City, TN 37760			✔	✔									
Cumberland U Lebanon, TN 37087			✔										
David Lipscomb U Nashville, TN 37204-3951						✔	✔						
East Tennessee St U Johnson City, TN 37614-0002				✔								✔	
King Coll Bristol, TN 37620		✔	✔						✔		✔		
Lane Coll Jackson, TN 38301						✔							
Memphis Coll of Art Memphis, TN 38104		✔											

State/Institution	AG	AR	BU	CS	ED	EN	HP	HE	HU	NS	SB	TE	VA
Memphis, U of Memphis, TN 38152							✓						
Middle Tennessee St U Murfreesboro, TN 37132	✓	✓	✓	✓	✓		✓	✓	✓	✓	✓	✓	
Tennessee St U Nashville, TN 37209-1561	✓		✓	✓		✓				✓			
Tennessee Tech U Cookeville, TN 38505	✓	✓	✓	✓	✓	✓	✓	✓		✓	✓	✓	✓
Tennessee, U of, Chattanooga Chattanooga, TN 37403			✓			✓	✓			✓	✓		
Tennessee, U of, Knoxville Knoxville, TN 37996-0230	✓	✓	✓	✓		✓			✓				
Tennessee, U of, Martin Martin, TN 38238	✓		✓	✓	✓	✓	✓	✓	✓	✓	✓	✓	
Union U Jackson, TN 38305-3697			✓										

Texas

State/Institution	AG	AR	BU	CS	ED	EN	HP	HE	HU	NS	SB	TE	VA
Abilene Christian U Abilene, TX 79699-8465	✓					✓	✓						
Houston, U of Houston, TX 77004			✓	✓		✓			✓	✓	✓	✓	✓
Houston, U of, Clear Lake Houston, TX 77058			✓	✓					✓	✓			
Houston, U of, Downtown Houston, TX 77002			✓										
Howard Payne U Brownwood, TX 76801							✓						
Huston-Tillotson Coll Austin, TX 78702			✓	✓					✓	✓	✓		
Jarvis Christian Coll Hawkins, TX 75765			✓	✓	✓								
Lamar U Beaumont, TX 77710		✓					✓	✓					

State/Institution	AG	AR	BU	CS	ED	EN	HP	HE	HU	NS	SB	TE	VA
McMurry U Abilene, TX 79697							✔						
Northwood U, Texas Campus Cedar Hill, TX 75104-0058			✔										
Prairie View A&M U Prairie View, TX 77446	✔		✔	✔		✔						✔	
St. Edward's U Austin, TX 78704			✔	✔									
St. Thomas, U of Houston, TX 77006			✔										
Southern Methodist U Dallas, TX 75275						✔							
Southwestern Adventist Coll Keene, TX 76059			✔	✔						✔	✔	✔	
Texas A&M U, College Station College Station, TX 77843-1265	✔		✔	✔		✔	✔		✔	✔	✔	✔	
Texas A&M U, Corpus Christi Corpus Christi, TX 78412			✔	✔					✔	✔	✔	✔	
Texas A&M U, Kingsville Kingsville, TX 78363	✔							✔			✔		
Texas Southern U Houston, TX 77004													✔
Texas, U of, Arlington Arlington, TX 76019			✔			✔							
Texas, U of, Austin Austin, TX 78712-1157						✔			✔				
Texas Woman's U Denton, TX 76204			✔	✔									
Trinity U San Antonio, TX 78212-7200									✔				
Wayland Baptist U Plainview, TX 79072						✔							

State/Institution	AG	AR	BU	CS	ED	EN	HP	HE	HU	NS	SB	TE	VA
Utah													
Brigham Young U Provo, UT 84602	✔	✔	✔	✔	✔	✔	✔	✔	✔	✔	✔	✔	✔
Utah St U Logan, UT 84322-1600	✔	✔	✔	✔	✔	✔	✔	✔	✔	✔	✔	✔	✔
Utah, U of Salt Lake City, UT 84112			✔			✔			✔		✔		
Vermont													
Castleton St Coll Castleton, VT 05735		✔	✔	✔	✔	✔			✔	✔	✔		
Champlain Coll Burlington, VT 05402-0670			✔	✔		✔							
Goddard Coll Plainfield, VT 05667		✔			✔				✔		✔		
Lyndon St Coll Lyndonville, VT 05851-0919			✔		✔				✔	✔	✔		
Marlboro Coll Marlboro, VT 05344				✔									
Norwich U Northfield, VT 05663			✔			✔			✔			✔	
Southern Vermont Coll Bennington, VT 05201			✔				✔		✔		✔		
Vermont, U of Burlington, VT 05405-3596			✔			✔							
Virginia													
George Mason U Fairfax, VA 22030		✔	✔	✔	✔	✔			✔	✔	✔		✔
Hampton U Hampton, VA 23368	✔	✔	✔	✔	✔						✔		
Longwood Coll Farmville, VA 23909					✔	✔	✔				✔		

State/Institution	AG	AR	BU	CS	ED	EN	HP	HE	HU	NS	SB	TE	VA
Mary Washington Coll Fredericksburg, VA 22401-5358				✔									
Norfolk St U Norfolk, VA 23504		✔	✔	✔	✔	✔	✔	✔	✔	✔	✔	✔	✔
Old Dominion U Norfolk, VA 23529-0050		✔	✔	✔	✔	✔			✔	✔	✔	✔	
Randolph-Macon Coll Ashland, VA 23005-5505					✔	✔							
Randolph-Macon Woman's Coll Lynchburg, VA 24503						✔	✔						
St. Paul's Coll Lawrenceville, VA 23868			✔		✔					✔	✔		
Shenandoah U Winchester, VA 22601						✔	✔						
Virginia Commonwealth U Richmond, VA 23284-9005		✔	✔	✔	✔		✔		✔	✔	✔		
Virginia Polytechnic Inst & St U Blacksburg, VA 24061-0202	✔	✔	✔	✔		✔		✔	✔	✔	✔		
Virginia Union U Richmond, VA 23220			✔			✔			✔	✔	✔		

Washington

State/Institution	AG	AR	BU	CS	ED	EN	HP	HE	HU	NS	SB	TE	VA
Central Washington U Ellensburg, WA 98926		✔	✔	✔	✔			✔	✔	✔	✔	✔	
City U Bellevue, WA 98004			✔	✔	✔		✔		✔	✔	✔	✔	
Evergreen St Coll Olympia, WA 98505	✔	✔	✔		✔				✔	✔	✔		
Heritage Coll Toppenish, WA 98948			✔	✔			✔		✔	✔	✔		
Pacific Lutheran U Tacoma, WA 98447		✔	✔	✔	✔	✔	✔		✔	✔	✔		
Puget Sound, U of Tacoma, WA 98416		✔	✔	✔	✔		✔		✔	✔	✔		

State/Institution	AG	AR	BU	CS	ED	EN	HP	HE	HU	NS	SB	TE	VA
Seattle Pacific U Seattle, WA 98119	✔	✔	✔			✔		✔	✔	✔	✔		
Walla Walla Coll College Place, WA 99324			✔	✔	✔								
Washington, U of Seattle, WA 98195			✔			✔							
Whitworth Coll Spokane, WA 99251			✔	✔						✔			

West Virginia

State/Institution	AG	AR	BU	CS	ED	EN	HP	HE	HU	NS	SB	TE	VA
Charleston, U of Charleston, WV 25304	✔	✔				✔							
Davis & Elkins Coll Elkins, WV 26241		✔											
Marshall U Huntington, WV 25755		✔										✔	
Shepherd Coll Shepherdstown, WV 25443	✔	✔	✔					✔	✔	✔	✔		
West Virginia Inst of Tech Montgomery, WV 25136			✔	✔		✔						✔	
West Virginia St Coll Institute, WV 25112-1000	✔	✔	✔	✔		✔							
West Virginia U Morgantown, WV 26506-6009						✔							
West Virginia, Coll of Beckley, WV 25801			✔										

Wisconsin

State/Institution	AG	AR	BU	CS	ED	EN	HP	HE	HU	NS	SB	TE	VA
Cardinal Stritch Coll Milwaukee, WI 53217	✔	✔	✔	✔		✔					✔		
Carthage Coll Kenosha, WI 53140-1994						✔							
Concordia U Wisconsin Mequon, WI 53097	✔												

State/Institution	AG	AR	BU	CS	ED	EN	HP	HE	HU	NS	SB	TE	VA
Marian Coll of Fond du Lac Fond du Lac, WI 54935		✔	✔		✔		✔		✔	✔	✔		
Marquette U Milwaukee, WI 53233			✔	✔		✔				✔			
Milwaukee Inst of Art & Design Milwaukee, WI 53202		✔											
Mt Senario Coll Ladysmith, WI 54848			✔		✔						✔		
Northland Coll Ashland, WI 54806	✔		✔	✔	✔					✔	✔		
St. Norbert Coll DePere, WI 54115						✔							
Viterbo Coll LaCrosse, WI 54601-4797			✔		✔		✔						
Wisconsin, U of, Eau Claire Eau Claire, WI 54701			✔				✔		✔	✔	✔		
Wisconsin, U of, LaCrosse LaCrosse, WI 54601		✔	✔	✔			✔		✔				
Wisconsin, U of, Madison Madison, WI 53706	✔		✔		✔	✔		✔					
Wisconsin, U of, Milwaukee Milwaukee, WI 53201-0749						✔							
Wisconsin, U of, Platteville Platteville, WI 53818	✔		✔			✔						✔	
Wisconsin, U of, River Falls River Falls, WI 54022	✔												
Wisconsin, U of, Stout Menomonie, WI 54751		✔	✔	✔	✔	✔		✔	✔	✔	✔	✔	✔
Wisconsin, U of, Superior Superior, WI 54880		✔	✔										

Wyoming

State/Institution	AG	AR	BU	CS	ED	EN	HP	HE	HU	NS	SB	TE	VA
Wyoming, U of Laramie, WY 82071	✔	✔	✔	✔	✔	✔	✔	✔	✔	✔	✔	✔	

Getting the Most College for the Money: Cash Savers and Cash Makers

While the previous chapter told several ways that schools can provide more money for you to go to college, or even give you a discount on the price, this chapter is about ways to stretch your college dollars. It deals with innovative programs that the colleges are coming up with to help you meet their ever-increasing tuition. It also looks at ways you can save or even make money while getting your degree. But before we jump in, a word of warning: No program is set in stone. Schools change course. A program mentioned in this chapter, or elsewhere in this book, may no longer be in place when you check into it. At the same time, new programs are springing up all the time. So check out the full range of programs and payment options available at your school, or at the schools you're thinking of attending. The more you know, the better you'll do.

Innovative Tuition Plans

More and more colleges and universities are looking for ways to take the sting out of paying college tuition. For many of them, this means offering plans that make it possible to get around paying for college all in one formidable annual chunk. Many colleges now offer a range of payment plans. Washington University in St. Louis, a trailblazer in providing innovative payment programs, was early in offering a Tuition Stabilization Plan in 1979. That program freezes the cost of tuition for students who paid tuition up front; the school offered a loan program to make the huge payment possible. The vast majority of families involved in the program exercise the loan option, but the school keeps its default rate very low. Washington University has a broader loan program called the Cost Stabilization Program, which offers protection for tuition, room, and board. CSP offers parents a fixed-rate, low-interest, monthly pay-back plan that stretches out over ten years. Washington University requires no collateral on these loans.

Another school with a lot of payment plans to offer is the University of Pennsylvania. Its Penn Plan is a veritable smorgasbord of payment options that allow students to freeze their tuition by making hefty payments up front, or simply to pay tuition on a monthly basis instead of once a year. The school even offers a revolving line of credit (Visa card-style) for nontuition expenses.

There are as many programs as there are colleges, and programs at different schools that sound similar may have

significant differences between them. There's no substitute for getting the full description of all of your school's program from the school itself. However, if you would like a broad survey of programs available at different schools, you can order a chart-filled paper-back, *College Check Mate* from Octameron Associates (P.O. Box 2748, Alexandria, VA 22301).

Colleges are also getting smarter about giving students and their families more ways to pay for college. Many schools now allow tuition to be paid through regular electronic funds transfers from bank accounts or through credit cards. But look out for that interest rate on those credit cards! Some of the rates charged by banks on their cards would make a loan shark blush.

Paying on the Installment Plan

More schools are starting to allow families to pay tuition on the installment plan, or using their own endowments to make tuition loans that the families repay in installments. Schools ranging from the University of Michigan to Muskingum College in New Concord, Ohio, provide such plans, often with lower-than-commercial interest rates. The installments might run monthly, or as little as two per semester; they can be stretched out over several years. Check with your school for more details.

Banks and private companies are also working with colleges to create installment-plan tuition programs. Sometimes the colleges run the plans, and sometimes the private companies run them on their own.

Many private companies are willing to make a little money by acting as go-between for you and your school. Academic Management Services, Inc. of Pawtucket, R.I., makes the lump payment to the college for you; you then work out a schedule of repayment to the company, paying a $45 fee to the company that includes insurance on the life of the parent for the balance of the debt. Another is the Student Loan Marketing Association, SALLIE MAE, through its Family Education Financing program (1050 Thomas Jefferson Street, NW, Washington, DC 20007; (202) 333-8000). The NELLIE MAE, an organization focused in the Northeast, provides a range of loans (NELLIE MAE, 50 Braintree Hill Park, Suite 300, Braintree, MA 02184; (617) 849-1325). One such supplemental college loan which is available at many colleges, EXCEL, ranges from $2,000 to $20,000 annually with a cumulative maximum of $80,000 per student. The interest rates run between two and four percent higher than the prime rate, as published in the Wall Street Journal. NELLIE MAE also works with a group of 30 schools that make up the Consortium on Financing Higher Education to provide SHARE loans. The loan amounts are the same as EXCEL loans, as is the interest rate. Students who attend one of the consortium schools are eligible for SHARE loans; contact your financial aid office to see if your school is one of them. The Consortium schools read like a Who's Who of American Higher Education:

Amherst College
Barnard College
Brown University
Bryn Mawr College
Carleton College
Columbia University
Cornell University
Georgetown University
Harvard University
The Johns Hopkins University
Massachusetts Institute of Technology
Mount Holyoke College
Northwestern University
Oberlin College
Pomona College
Princeton University
Radcliffe College
Rice University
Smith College
Stanford University
Swarthmore College
Trinity College
The University of Chicago
University of Pennsylvania
The University of Rochester
Washington University
Wellesley College
Wesleyan University
Williams College
Yale University

You can get a list of other nationally available programs, along with local financial institutions that offer student loans, from your college financial aid office or state aid guarantee agency (see list on page 26).

Putting the Money Up Front

Schools like having money in the bank, and the sooner the better. They can earn interest on it, invest it, and otherwise have fun with it. That's why they are willing to make attractive offers in return for getting money quickly that you would eventually pay them anyway.

Tuition lock: Some schools eliminate the fear of tuition-hike shock by guaranteeing that incoming students will see no tuition increases for a set time. Most of these programs have a big catch: you have to pay all four years' worth of tuition up front. Harvard, George Washington, and Brandeis, among others, require full prepayment. Almost all of the colleges soften the blow by offering to lend the money or arrange financing through private lenders. Others will freeze tuition as an option so long as the family makes a deposit of several thousand dollars. Some schools, including Michigan State, go so far as to guarantee tuition won't rise any faster than inflation.

Prepayment discounts and bonuses: A number of schools offer discounts on tuition for students who pay their entire semester's worth (or year's worth) in a single up-front chunk. Kendall College in Illinois will give students a ten percent discount, as will West Coast University in Los Angeles. Other schools, like Cedarville College in Ohio and George Washington University in Washington, D.C., will give students a bonus for paying in advance. Again, check with your school to see if it offers such programs.

Getting a big head start: Tuition "futures": A few years ago, financial and education writers began singing the praises of a promising development for parents with young children: the pay now, learn later plan that was pioneered by Duquesne University. The program was part investment, part promise: if parents would prepay a certain amount many years before their child was to attend college, then the school would guarantee that the student's tuition would be paid in full by the time he or she arrived. The school would invest the cash. It also planned to make a little more money out of a tricky provision in Duquesne's plan. If the student couldn't get into the school or didn't want to attend, the parents would only get back the money they had originally invested—not the earned interest over those years. Despite the drawbacks, the innovative idea was widely hailed, and some states began looking into versions of the program that they could institute.

Now the future of the pay now, learn later plans seems less rosy. In 1987, less than three years after the plan was announced, Duquesne suspended its program until the world of investments looked more lucrative. But parent interest had been dropping off anyway, because the plan didn't make it easy to choose a school other than Duquesne—so tough luck if little Timmy has his heart set on Notre Dame. Critics of the Duquesne plan charge that the school jumped into the game with unrealistic pricing. About a dozen other private schools still have such plans in place, with varying degrees of success at keeping them going.

While the private sector seems to be reassessing its role in the education futures market, the states have been looking at ways to jump in. After all, tuition costs have become a hot issue politically as well as financially, and states have greater resources to help them weather future shocks. Many states have already enacted legislation to help give parents tuition guarantees or tax breaks. Several states now offer a local version of so-called "Baccalaureate Bonds." They act like zero-coupon bonds, which is to say your kids get no income—and pay no tax—until they mature. Illinois has created special tax-exempt savings bonds that pay extra interest if they are redeemed to pay educational expenses—a grant of up to $400 is added to the regular interest for each $5,000 of bonds. North Carolina has passed a similar program.

The federal government has stepped in, too. Series EE Savings Bonds are a stable, long-term college investment with some tax advantages. If you use those bonds to pay tuition or other educational fees for yourself or your family, the accrued interest on the redeemed bonds may be excluded from your reported income. There are a few requirements, of course. The law only applies to EE bonds issued after 1989, and the purchaser has to be older than 24. There are stringent income restrictions on these bonds: if your family income tops $60,000, the tax deduction fades away.

A handful of states have tuition guarantee plans so far. Most of the programs work pretty much like the Duquesne plan, except that students can use the tuition payments to attend any public school in the state. Michigan, Wyoming, Florida, Indiana, Maine, and Tennessee have such programs. Missouri passed its own savings plan, but with no guarantee that it would cover all of the costs of tuition when the bill came due, simply allowing parents to put away money without having to pay state income taxes on the interest. Illinois staked its hopes for the future on selling parents bonds that are exempt from federal taxes. Here's how it works: the families buy what are known as zero–coupon bonds. The state uses the money to do whatever states do; if the family holds on to the bond for five years and then cashes it in to pay college tuition, the state kicks in a supplemental interest payment over and above the interest that the state would normally pay. Illinois has sold a lot of bonds since starting the program in 1987, and many other states have adopted that approach.

One of the more interesting pay now, learn later options has been offered by a private bank, the College Savings Bank of Princeton, N.J. They call their idea the College Sure CD and it works this way: parents buy certificates of deposit, just like the CDs that people have been using as savings investments for years. But the rate on the College Sure CD is pegged to the average rate of inflation for tuition and other college costs. Unlike the Duquesne plan and its copies, the College Sure CD can be used at any college. However, the earnings rate is not as sexy as some of the higher-flying plans: to buy four years at Yale for one of today's second graders, parents would have to pay more than $90,000. The bank expects people to make regular payments into a CD account over time as a buffer against rising college costs, not to plunk down $90,000. And it promises stability: The instrument is a CD, fully insured by the Federal Deposit Insurance Board for up to $100,000. Right now the College Sure CD is sold through the bank and through PaineWebber.

Innovative Come-Ons

As we have already said, students are in rather short supply, especially where the smaller private colleges are concerned. Many of them have tried to find eye-catching ways to cut the cost of attendance. Some of the methods are almost hucksterish in nature, but if you already like the school, why not take advantage? Below we list a few that have been offered here and there; see if your school uses any of them:

Profiting by leadership: Some schools offer a tuition break for taking a leadership role in student organizations, from the school newspaper to the student government.

A legacy: Some schools reduce tuition for children of alumni/ae.

Lotteries: A few schools (or their student organizations) sponsor tuition lotteries: if your number comes up, your year is free. This is only for students who are already attending, of course.

Volume, volume, volume: Many schools now offer discounts for bringing other family members along. Fairleigh-Dickinson University in New Jersey gives a discount, while Lake Erie College in Ohio accepts twins for the price of one—a higher-ed twofer.

Bring a buddy: Several schools will give you a tuition discount for convincing a friend to attend.

Test the waters: Schools are letting prospective students try their first credits at a discount. Some, like John Brown University in Arkansas, even let high school juniors and seniors attend classes for free! They count as real courses, and are later transferable. Other come-ons are just as ingenious: Marian College of Fond du Lac, Wisconsin, offers its first part-time course for just $100.

Anniversary specials: A few years ago, Goucher College celebrated its centennial by offering one student a year's tuition at the same rate as students paid the year the school was founded.

Tuition matching: Some private schools now match tuition with public schools to stay competitive; Bard offers to charge students in the top ten percent of their high school graduating class anywhere in the U.S. the same tuition as they could get from a public school in their home state. (Remember, too, that many states now offer scholarship programs to equalize tuition rates between public and private schools.)

"Adopt-a-student" programs: In these programs, the school gets local companies to contribute. The companies participate to give something back to the community and to raise their public relations profile—but many of them get something more out of the deal. Sometimes these programs require the recipient to work at the company after graduation. This could be a back-door way for enterprising students to get the job they want and to make extra money while attending college. Check with your financial aid office or student employment office for details.

"Differential pricing": Schools are offering discounts for any number of odd reasons. Some give students a price break on less desirable housing—that could mean anything from teensy rooms to no air conditioning. Other schools let new students study for less than upper-classmen. Still other schools charge students less for some majors than for others. Options like these give you a little more control over how much your college education will cost. Your college financial aid office will be able to tell you if any of these benefits apply to you; you might also check with your campus housing and food service offices to see if any discounts are offered.

"Moral obligation scholarships": These are a gift from the school to you—granted with a "moral obligation" to pay the money back after graduation. Along with their feelgood charm, these programs pack a potent tax benefit: Since the payback is technically construed to be a gift to the school, the student gets a tax deduction. Bethel College in Indiana and Rice University in Texas are among a growing number of schools jumping on the moral obligation bandwagon.

Colleges are constantly thinking up new, headline-grabbing alternatives; keep an eye on the media for programs that pop up unexpectedly. A favorite we've run across lately is the Woz scholarship at the University of Colorado at Boulder, kicked off with a $100,000 grant from Apple Computer cofounder Steve Wozniack. It is intended to provide support for "hackers"—computer users who love to learn through exploring computer systems and programs—even those they're not supposed to get into. Wozniak calls these "mild social deviants" important because of the tremendous learning that comes from hacking forays. Deserving hackers get a tuition grant and a job in the computer science department, as well as extra computer time—on a computer system dedicated to their use, not the school's main computers.

A Warning: All Good Things Must Come to an End

It's a fact of life: many of the great college tuition plans end up running afoul of the IRS sooner or later. One previously popular method of saving for college, shifting assets to the children in order to take advantage of their lower taxation rate, has been all but eliminated by changes in the tax laws. And we have seen that the IRS is already taking a long look at the long-term tuition prepayment plans. We can expect the "moral obligation scholarships" to get the same kind of scrutiny. In fact, any program that promises to help people save money for college at low tax rates will attract the attention of the IRS. So it's important to check with the school to see if the IRS has ruled that the school's "too-good-to-be-true" program really is too good to be true.

Other Ways to Cut College Costs: Nontraditional Courses of Study

Cramming a Degree into a Shorter Time

A number of schools have found ways to cram the four-year college experience into three years. Middlebury College in Vermont, Albertus Magnus College in Connecticut, Valparaiso University in Indiana and Upper Iowa University all say you can do it in three years and save big. Some medical and law schools will allow you to enroll without having obtained an undergraduate degree. Most of these grad schools work together with their own campus' undergraduate schools to create a single compressed degree. Others simply require a certain list of courses; you can be accepted to the school upon completion of those courses, which fit into a three-year plan. Compressed degree plans aren't for the faint of heart: the pressure to pack it all in can be brutal. Also, the gains could be illusory if they are gotten at the price of studying through the summer and having to forego summer job income.

Credit and Degrees by Exam

The College Board has agreements with more than half of the nation's colleges to honor the program's AP exams and give credit or advanced placement. More than 150,000 students annually take AP exams, and two-thirds of them score high enough to place out. Needless to say, if you place out of a course, that is tuition saved. More than 10,000 students were eligible last year to place out of all freshman year courses. More than 20 tests are offered by AP, including English, calculus, American history, European history, biology, chemistry, physics, computer science, art, music, and many languages. Take the tests through your school for about $50 apiece, or contact the College Board, 45 Columbus Avenue, New York, NY 10023.

In addition, many schools offer some form of credit by examination: Opportunities range from selected courses to the entire course catalogue. Check the school's academic catalogue, or ask at individual departments.

Saving Money

Once a student gets to college, many ways to save money present themselves that may not have been apparent at home. Students are famous for living in near-poverty; unless you have joined a class-conscious clique, you find that near-poverty can be quite genteel. Buying used books not only saves money, it also can give you a head start on underlining your texts. Living in alternative housing like off-campus cooperative houses costs much less than dorms or apartments, and can build strong friendships as well—though your diet might suffer at the hands of housemates whose cooking leaves something to be desired. Buying food from organizations like food co-ops also saves a dollar here and there. Well-worn clothes and classy Goodwill castoffs can give a certain cachet and save money that would otherwise be spent on a costlier wardrobe. In other words, living poor pays.

A more upscale way to save money in college is to play the real estate game. Rather than giving money to a landlord, why not buy a campus-area condo or house? You can supplement your mortgage by renting out extra rooms, and can pay off a substantial amount of your college expenses if the property appreciates in value when you sell it. But the last point is a big "if." Despite the promises of real estate brokers, property values sometimes drop. There's no such thing as a no-risk deal. Still, if you have the money, owning your college home can be a very attractive option.

Some families try to save money by having the student live at home. This option saves dorm or apartment rental costs and looks very attractive on the surface. Yet there are a number of hidden costs to staying at home—not the least of which is losing out on a major part of the college social experience by not being at the center of things. Commuting costs can cut away at the money that living at home saves. Another reason why staying at home is more expensive than it looks: food. The student who stays at home won't be able to eat all meals at home; the odd hours that students keep will keep them away from home at mealtimes. So commuter students tend to spend a lot of money in campus-area eateries, while students in dorms buy a relatively inexpensive meal plan. Meal plans may be available for non-dormers and are worth looking into. Also, most parents won't stand for the poverty chic that can make student dollars stretch so far, and so will spend more money on clothing than the student would spend on his or her own.

Tapping into Family Resources

There are a few other sources of funds that you might not have considered for college financing—quiet assets that don't present themselves as obvious cash cows. But they are there. These include:

Home equity loans: These allow parents to draw on the increased value of their homes. The rates and repayment schedules can be more favorable then those offered on student loans from private sources and schools.

Company funds: Many employee pension funds and savings plans allow withdrawals for tuition. These withdrawals are often subject to rigid restrictions and stiff penalties, though some companies make the process easier—or even let parents borrow against the value of their savings plans. Check with your personnel office for details.

Barter and service deals: Some schools will make a deal with parents to exchange a wide range of gifts for tuition. Almost any type of property can be swapped under such a program. Even if the college can't use what you have to offer, it might resell it; this occurs often when corporations make odd gifts to schools, such as yachts, for tax purposes. Ask if the college has a barter program.

Making Money: The Job World Beyond Work-Study

Instead of relying on your college for a moderate-to-low-paying work-study job, why not strike out on your own? If you have an entrepreneurial flair, you might find that a little investment of time and effort can provide you with a comfortable living while you are in school—and after. Michael Dell began selling computers while he was in college—now his company sells millions of dollars worth of IBM-compatible computers each year under the Dell Computer logo. On a smaller scale, you might find plenty of opportunity among your fellow students. Students know students; once you have identified an item that you need, you can buy it in bulk and offer it to others who share your needs. This explains the proliferation of student-run services that offer discounts on everything from computer diskettes to lecture notes. One enterprising group of students even offered speedy delivery of birth control devices.

The clearinghouse for information on entrepreneurship in college is the Association of College Entrepreneurs, a group founded by college students in 1983 and which now numbers more than 4,500 members. It's based in Wichita, Kansas, but has local chapters nationwide. And your own campus business department might have people who can give you pointers: More than 600 schools across the nation have entrepreneurship courses.

For students interested in the entrepreneurial route, one book could serve as a wellspring of ideas: *How to Pay Your Way Through College (The Smart Way)* by John J. Lyons ($7.95, Banbury Books). This lively book presents more than 50 money-making opportunities for college students, ranging from resume writing to delivering birthday cakes and final exam "care packages." (The author's credentials are solid: as a college student he started a car-cleaning business aimed at luxury models. By the time he graduated he had opened franchises in Florida, Delaware, and California—and was making $50,000 a year.) Each plan is based on actual student experience, and Lyons even puts the reader on the way to forming a business plan by projecting the startup costs and materials needed.

Books like Lyons' can give you ideas on businesses you could start that won't require so much work that you'll flunk out—less of your time, at least, than nonpaying extracurricular activities such as working for the school newspaper or student government. Though these extracurriculars look good on your resume, working your way through college is an attractive resume item, too. And you might even be able to make your career interest pay. If your school doesn't have an established cooperative education program, you might be able to work something out on your own. Do you want to be a journalist? Write freelance articles. If your interest is politics, why not see if there are part-time positions in a nearby politician's office, or working with political consultants? You'll be lining your pocket and picking up real-life experience at the same time.

For another extreme version of college jobs, you might check out Heidi Mattson's 1995 memoir, *Ivy League Stripper*. Mattson said she turned to stripping when her financial aid fell through and her work-study professor made sexual advances. It's not the kind of part-time work that I'd ever recommend anyone engage in, but Mattson insists that without lucrative nights of topless dancing at the Foxy Lady, she could not have afforded her days pursuing a degree at Brown University.

A warning about entrepreneurship: Before you decide that starting your own business is the answer to all your financial needs, watch a few reruns of *The Honeymooners* or *Dobie Gillis*. Get-rich-quick schemes have long been the stock in trade of situation comedies because of their tendency to get the schemer into hot water—and into debt. It's time for a personal story to illustrate the point.

When I was in college, one roommate was always looking for the fast train to riches, like the time he went prospecting for gold in the American West. None of the schemes panned out, but he had fun—until he decided to make money on the historic rivalry between the University of Texas and Texas A&M. (Typical UT joke against an A&M student, known as an "Aggie": "How do you know when an Aggie has been using your word processor? There's Liquid Paper all over the screen.") My friend decided to sell a newspaper parody that made fun of UT on one side and made fun of A&M on the other, and distribute the publication at the big Thanksgiving football game between the two schools.

The idea sounded good, but it was a disaster. My buddy put in countless hours of writing and editing, and spent hundreds of dollars in printing costs. (These were the days before easy desktop publishing). But the paper bombed. The conservative alumni attending the game didn't know what to make of it; many who did buy it were offended by the jokes against their alma mater. Some of the jokes were funny, though, if you'd like to see a copy. I think my buddy still has a few thousand in a closet somewhere. But don't worry too much about him. He and a successful publishing executive met and fell in love, and these days he's living in a Manhattan penthouse. So things work out.

Putting Your Financial Aid PackageTogether

The Three Commandments of Applying for Financial Aid:

Before getting down to the nuts and bolts of applying for financial aid, it's worth keeping three "commandments" in mind. Without them, a hundred pages of instruction are useless. The three commandments are:

1: Be Prompt!

Read the deadlines below. Meet each deadline. Since many programs work from a fund of limited size, wasting time can waste money. Start applying for financial aid right after January 1—as soon after you receive your W-2 forms as possible. That's when you can begin filling out your IRS forms, too. That will make filling out the financial aid forms easier. Besides, if you have a refund coming you'll get it faster.

2: Be Accurate!

Fill in all of the blanks on every form, and fill them out accurately and legibly. Read the instructions fully. Any blank spaces or mistakes can cause the overworked aid agencies to send your form back to you to be filled in again. You'll not only have to do more work, but you'll delay the processing of your financial aid application—and that delay could keep you from receiving as much aid as you could have gotten.

3: Be Organized!

If there was ever a reason to get organized, this is it. You have to keep track of all of your applications to different colleges and the financial aid applications to those colleges. Make copies of every piece of correspondence you send out, keeping all of it in a fanfold organizer or file box, organized by school. Many financial aid guides go so far as to recommend sending all aid correspondence via certified mail so that you will have a record of having sent items and of their being received. The College Board, on the other hand, says registered mail is a bother and slows the application process. We say: If you are applying well in advance, spend the money for a little security.

Another reason for all this organization: By getting organized from the start, you will find it easier to fill out your forms again next year—and remember, you have to apply for aid every year.

The Timetable: Your Most Important Financial Aid Dates

Junior Year of High School

October: Take the PSAT exam. This important test will not only give you a taste of what's in store on the SAT; it will also qualify you for the National Merit Scholarship.

If you have not already begun to consider your college choices, you should be sending off for college brochures and financial aid information. Talk to friends from high school who have attended the colleges, and to alumni. It's a good time to begin touring the campuses that seem the most promising to you. While on campus, be sure to check out the financial aid office. Does it appear to be efficiently run? Does it look like the sort of place where you will get personalized service? If possible, schedule an interview with a financial aid adviser at the school to determine the school's resources and how much of your college costs your family will be expected to provide.

Senior Year of High School/Year Before Going to College

Fall: Begin narrowing down your college choices to the ones that interest you the most. Ask those schools for admissions applications and financial aid forms. Send in your applications for admission to your favorites well before the deadlines that each school lists. Be sure to take your time writing any essays the school requires; you want to stand out as a lucid thinker and a clear writer, not as someone who doesn't care enough to do a good job on an application.

January 1: You can't apply for financial aid before January 1 of the year you intend to go to college. But you should apply as soon as the ball drops in Times Square. People who file at the time of the deadline risk losing out on the college's own aid and those funds from campus-based federal financial aid programs. When you hear "Auld Lang Syne," think about your financial aid forms.

April 15: If you haven't done your financial aid forms yet because your IRS forms weren't done, you've probably just lost that excuse. Time's a-wastin'. A lot of students and their families have already turned in financial aid forms—and their tax forms besides. And they've probably already gotten their IRS refunds back, too.

May 1: Your aid application must be received by the processing agency listed on the form by the first of May. It's really very late by now—and the processing agency is still going to take four to six weeks to run your forms through, so it's later than you think. Still, better late than never. Before you buy the hot dogs for your Memorial Day picnic, make sure you've got the forms into the mail.

June 30: Your school's financial aid office must receive your application and your student aid report—the forms you get back from the processing agency—by this dead-line. If you are already in college, your deadline is the last day of enrollment for that year. Again, this is the absolute deadline. It's much better to get this in far ahead of time, and beginning January 1.

Freshman Year, Sophomore Year, Etc.

January 1: Apply for financial aid all over again. You need to do this every year.

Applying for Financial Aid: The Nuts and Bolts

Applying for financial aid begins with your applications at the federal level; other aid providers look to the information you provide to the federal government. Your school will tell you which forms to fill out, but the basics of applying for federal aid are the same for whatever form you use.

Are You Eligible for Financial Aid?

There are eligibility requirements for financial aid. You must be enrolled at least half-time to receive aid from the Direct or FFEL Program loan programs. Half-time enrollment is not required for the campus-based student aid programs such as Federal Supplemental Educational Opportunity Grants (FSEOG), Federal Work-Study (FWS), and Federal Perkins Loans. Individual schools have various qualifications for the campus-based programs. You must be what the government calls a "regular student," which means you are enrolled in an institution to get a degree or certificate, or are completing course work that enables you to qualify for admission.

Eligibility also depends on citizenship: You must be a citizen or an eligible noncitizen. If you are not a citizen, you must be a U.S. national or a U.S. permanent resident with an Alien Registration Receipt Card—or you must fall into one of the arcane categories listed in the glossary under "Citizen/Eligible Noncitizen." (For example, those whom the Immigration and Naturalization Service has designated "Cuban-Haitian entrant, status pending" are eligible for aid, while students on an F-1 or F-2 student visa are not.)

You can be knocked out of eligibility for any more federal student aid if you are in default. Uncle Sam will do his best to get his money back, too: You may find the government deducting payments from your paycheck, or your U.S. Internal Revenue Service refund might be redirected to the Treasury.

And to clinch your eligibility, you will have to sign several pieces of paper: You must sign a "statement of educational purpose" that promises you will use your federal student aid funds for school-related expenses only. You must also sign a "statement of registration status" that states you have registered for the draft, if you are required to do so. If you don't register, you can't get aid. (If you say you registered but you really didn't, there could be repercussions: The Education Department has begun to turn the list of liars over to the Justice Department.) After you have applied for aid and received your Student Aid Report (see page 116), you will have to add a "statement of updated information" to your aid request that certifies that the items listed in your Student Aid Report are still correct.

Dependent or Independent?

Few financial aid questions are as important as whether you will be considered a dependent or independent student. If you are considered a dependent student, your parents must report their income and assets along with yours (and with your spouse's, if you are married). If you are classified as an independent student, you report only your own income and assets (along with your spouse's, if you are married). Unless you are a rock star, you probably make less money than your parents, and you will be eligible for more aid if you can be certified as an independent student. You should answer these questions to see if you can make the independent classification:

Are you 24 years old or older? You will be automatically considered an independent student if you are 24 years old by December 31 of the year you receive the financial aid award.

Are you a vet? A veteran of the U.S. Armed Forces is also automatically considered an independent student. This doesn't apply to former National Guardsmen, Reservists, or to former members of the Armed Forces who received a dishonorable discharge.

Are both of your parents dead, or are you a ward of the court? Wards of the court are also independent, as are students whose parents are dead and who don't have an adoptive parent or legal guardian.

Do you have legal dependents other than a spouse? That includes your child, so long as the child gets at least half its support from you, or any other legal dependents who get more than half their support from you and who will continue to get that support through the award year.

Do your parents claim you as a tax exemption? If you are a SINGLE undergraduate student with no dependents and if your parents or guardian didn't claim you as a dependent on the previous two tax returns, you might qualify as an independent student. You must also prove that you had annual total resources, other than what the folks have kicked in, of more than $4,000 in those years. This includes wages, salaries, tips, student financial aid, personal loans for educational purposes, interest income, dividend income, and other income or benefits such as fellowships.

If you are MARRIED and can say that your parents or guardian won't claim you as a dependent on their next tax return, you will also be considered independent.

Living with your parents, by the way, does not automatically make you a dependent. But the school aid administrator can nonetheless take a hard look at the situation and can factor in the cost of room and board at home—among other support—to determine whether to increase the amount of parental contribution, the student contribution, or otherwise to fiddle with your financial aid package.

Your school's aid administrator can change your status from dependent to independent if he or she thinks circumstances warrant the switch. Though the financial aid officer has every reason to want to look to your parents to shoulder the burden of your financial aid, the switch to independent status occurs from time to time. See the passage below on dealing with financial aid officers.

Special Circumstances

If you don't qualify as an independent student by the basic rules outlined above but feel that special circumstances dictate that you should be considered as an independent student anyway, you will be happy to know that the school aid administrator has the power to reclassify you as he or she sees fit. The aid administrator has the power to adjust your family contribution, or some element of your cost of education, such as tuition at private schools. However, you shouldn't assume that just because that person has the power that you will get your status changed—far from it. So it would be especially foolish for you to fill out your aid application as an independent if you don't automatically qualify unless you have gotten specific instructions from your aid administrator. The procedure for making the change will depend on the aid applications used and the in-

dividual school's rules, so you definitely need to follow the lead of the aid administrator.

A radical change in your life will change the way the aid administrator sees you and your plea for aid. If one of your parents dies, you should list only the income of the surviving parent. If the parent dies after you have filed, you should contact the school's financial aid office, since the loss in family income certainly should be reflected in your aid package. If one of your parents becomes unemployed, that can also change your status. Losing benefits such as child support or Social Security can sway an administrator. Anything that makes you substantially poorer affects your chances to receive aid.

Other family issues that come up when filling out the forms include the following:

■ If you are a single student with dependent children and you provide more than half the support for the children, independent status is automatic. But if you and your dependent children live with your parents and they provide more than half the support, you probably won't be classified as independent.

■ If you are separated or divorced, give the aid administrator information that applies directly to you— report only your own share of the joint assets and liabilities.

■ If your parents are divorced, the aid administrator wants the information from the parent you have lived with for the most time over the year before you file. That parent should fill out the form as a single head of household, and only list his or her income and his or her portion of the joint assets and debts. If you didn't live with either parent, or you lived with each an equal amount of time, you should list the parent who gave you the most financial support in the year before you file. If you got no support from either parent or if you got equal support from each in that time, list the parent who gave the most in a previous, uneven year.

■ If you have a stepparent who has married the parent who supports you, you should provide that person's financial information along with that of your natural parent's.

Applying for Aid

The forms you need to fill out in order to apply for aid vary from state to state and from institution to institution, depending on the "need analysis service" used by the state or institution. Your school will let you know which forms you must complete and will provide them to you. The most common forms are:

■ The U.S. Department of Education's Free Application for Federal Student Aid (FAFSA), which is the main application for the Pell Grant. Some schools offer this grant application in electronic form, so you don't have to worry about your eraser rubbing through the paper;

■   The College Scholarship Service's Financial Aid Form (FAF);

■   The Pennsylvania Higher Education Assistance Agency's Application for Pennsylvania State Grant and Federal Student Aid (PHEAA);

■   The Student Aid Application for California (SAAC);

■   The Illinois State Scholarship Commission's Application for Federal and State Student Aid (AFSSA).

The forms, while not easy, are not impossible to fill out on your own.

The state forms tend to be shorter and easier to complete than the nationally distributed forms. You don't have to fill out the FAFSA if you are filling out one of the other forms; those forms let you apply for Pell Grants and other federal aid at the same time. Checking a box on the forms tells the state to send your financial information along to a federal processing center.

Your school's application instructions will give you the information you need about applying for other forms of aid—several states, for instance, require that you fill out still more forms to apply for their own aid programs. The school's own application, and the state applications, might have separate deadlines that you will have to pay heed to.

Once you have applied, the processing agency will take between four and six weeks to turn your application around. You may be asked to confirm information or to correct the forms and then return them to be processed again. (You didn't listen to the second commandment!) The reprocessing will add another two or three weeks to your wait.

After processing your data, you will begin to receive a lot of paper. Your application for federal aid through the FAFSA or the other forms will be used to generate a Student Aid Report, or SAR. The SAR puts your data into a financial aid Cuisinart and figures out whether you qualify for federal student aid. It generates a Student Aid Index number, which lets you know whether you qualify for a Pell Grant, and a Family Contribution number, which will be used to see whether you qualify for campus-based programs such as FSEOG, Federal Work-Study, Federal Perkins Loans, and the Stafford programs.

If you qualify for a Pell Grant, your SAR will arrive in three parts. The Information Summary, Part 1, will tell you how to check the SAR for errors. You use Part 2, the Information Review Form, to correct any errors in the SAR. Your school will use Part 3, Pell Grant Payment Document, to decide how much money you will receive. Immediately make copies of Part 1 and send one to the financial aid office of each school you are applying to. You'll submit all three parts of the SAR to the school you ultimately decide to attend.

Didn't get the Pell? Don't worry—very few applicants do. But now you have something very important: your family contribution number. Send that information to your financial aid administrator, who will use it to figure out whether you qualify for other federal student aid.

If you are very unlucky, the Department of Education or your school might decide that you need to submit to "verification." This is like an IRS audit. You may have to verify everything from income to household size to federal taxes paid. You may have a long one-on-one with your aid administrator, and have to produce documents or fill out a verification worksheet. If you don't comply, kiss your aid goodbye. Some schools require verification from every financial aid applicant.

How Need Analysis Works

How was it determined that you would or would not receive a Pell Grant?

By strict exercise of the Pell Grant Methodology. If you want to look it up, the Education Department publishes it each year in the Federal Register. But if you do look it up, you might be disappointed; it does not even purport to be an accurate look at your family's financial ability. It's just the numerical filter that the Education Department uses to ration the amount of Pell Grant money it has decided that it needs. As far as the Pell Grant Methodology goes, your school is only interested in whether your Student Aid Index qualifies you for a Pell, and pays little attention to what it purports to say about your financial status.

To figure out the family's financial strength, most schools now rely on what is known as the Uniform Methodology—or, in its latest form, the Congressional Methodology. Congress has mandated through the Higher Education Amendments of 1986 that schools will use the Congressional Methodology to determine the expected family contribution for campus-based and Stafford programs. Many schools are making the switch; get the lowdown from your school and familiarize yourself with the ins and outs of the evaluation process. So even though the next few paragraphs promise to be slow going, it's worth slogging through to understand how your school will judge your ability to pay.

For DEPENDENT STUDENTS, the expected family contribution (EFC) is broken down into four parts:

■   contribution from parental income
■   contribution from parental assets
■   contribution from student income
■   contribution from student assets

For INDEPENDENT STUDENTS, EFC boils down to:

■   contribution from student (and spouse, if any) income
■   contribution from student (and spouse, if any) assets

When families earn $15,000 or less, the need analysis excludes any consideration of assets. While the Pell Grant and Congressional methods both take into account required expenses such as taxes and unusual medical expenses, and while both let the family set aside a certain amount for retirement or emergencies, the two methodologies part ways when figuring out how that income and those assets can be sheltered, and how much. Also, both methodologies make allowances for the expected family contribution whenever another member of the family heads off to college.

Getting the Award Letter

Once the school has all the information it needs, it can put together an aid package that will probably include a combination of grants (precious few), loans (too many), and work-study employment. You will get your notification of what your aid package contains in an award letter. This document gives you an idea of your probable cost of attendance, how your need was determined, what your need turned out to be, and the composition of that aid package. If you are satisfied with the aid package, you sign the documents that come with the form and send them back to the school.

Even if you haven't decided which school to attend, you should move quickly to accept the aid package from each school that offers one. That's the only way to keep your options open. Schools set response deadlines: If you don't respond to your aid letter within that time, you could miss out on the funds that have been offered to you. Accepting the aid package does not obligate you to attend the school. This isn't to say you should keep a number of colleges on a string—choose your college as quickly as possible so that the schools you don't choose can distribute the money to other students.

But before you leap to accept that award letter, evaluate your offers with a cold eye. Don't be fooled by big numbers; pay special attention to how much of the offer is made up of grants and how much is made up of loans. Which schools are tossing in special awards for academic or athletic merit? If scholarships are offered, are they renewable or are they one-shot wonders that will leave you high and dry next year? Break out your calculator and compare the loan interest rates offered by different institutions, and check out whether the payback requirements for those loans are especially onerous. And as for work-study offers, keep in mind the study load before you and ask yourself whether you will be able to juggle work and school right off the bat. You may accept part of the award and reserve the right to appeal any objectionable parts.

Getting More: Appealing to the Financial Aid Officer

Say you want to attend a certain school, but the award letter was a major disappointment. Is there anything you can do to change the school's mind? As we have already seen, the aid officers have a degree of latitude within which to change their estimate of a student's need, especially in cases of hardship. If you are dissatisfied with your award, you might want to put together your case for more aid and present it to the school's financial aid officer. The sooner the better: As matriculation day approaches, the aid officer's discretionary power dries up with his or her funds.

Try for a face-to-face meeting, so long as (1) the travel expenses aren't prohibitive or (2) the school is not too big to provide that kind of personal service. If you get your foot in the door, politely present youself in the best possible light to the financial aid officer—make the school want you. Push your abilities and accomplishments and the reasons that you and the school make a good match.

You'll do best if you remember the old adage: It's nice to be nice. Financial aid officers suffer a lot of abuse. You do not want to add to the stress in your financial aid officer's life. Read your Dale Carnegie to polish those people skills, and take a look at a remarkably handy guide: "Financial Aid Officers:What They Do—To You and For You." Written by a financial aid officer, the $4.00 booklet outlines a winning strategy for helping a harried financial aid officer see your side of things. (Octameron Associates, P.O. Box 2748, Alexandria, VA 22301. They also require $2.00 for postage and handling chages.)

Glossary of Financial Aid Terms

Ability to Benefit: Applies to most students who are admitted to a postsecondary institution but who do not have a high school diploma or a GED high school diploma equivalency. To receive federal student aid, a student admitted on the basis of ability to benefit must fulfill one of the following conditions:

1.) Pass a standardized admissions test that measures the student's aptitude successfully to complete the course of study. If the student fails the test, he or she must complete step #2 to qualify for aid.

2.) Enroll in and successfully complete a remedial program that is required by the school and that does not exceed one academic year. If the student fails the admissions test mentioned in step #1, or if the student is admitted on the basis of counseling given by the school, he or she would be required to enroll in the remedial program.

3.) Receive a GED before graduating from the course of study or by the end of the first year of the course of study—whichever comes first.

Local financial aid administrators will have more information as to the specifics at your school.

Academic Year: The Federal government defines this as "A period of at least 30 weeks of instructional time during which a full-time student is expected to complete at least 24 semester or trimester hours, or at least 36 quarter hours, at an institution that measures program length in credit hours; or at least 900 clock hours at an institution that measures program length in clock hours."

Assets: Savings and checking accounts, home or business value, stocks, bonds, money market funds, mutual funds, real estate, trust funds, etc. Cars are not considered assets, nor are possessions such as stamp collections or musical instruments.

Campus-Based Programs: Federal Supplemental Educational Opportunity Grants (FSEOG's), Federal Work-Study (FWS), and Federal Perkins Loan Program. These federal programs are called campus-based because they're administered by the financial aid administrator at the school. Your financial aid package may contain aid from one or more of these programs.

Citizen/Eligible Noncitizen: You must be one of the following to receive federal student aid:

1.) U.S. citizen

2.) U.S. national

3.) U.S. permanent resident who has an I-151 or I-551 or I-551-C (Alien Registration Receipt Card)

If you're not in one of these categories, you must have a Departure Record (I-94) from the U.S. Immigration and Naturalization Service (INS) showing one of the following designations:

1.) "Refugee"

2.) "Asylum Granted"

3.) "Indefinite Parole" and/or "Humanitarian Parole"

4.) "Cuban-Haitian Entrant, Status Pending"

5.) "Conditional Entrant" (valid only if issued before April 1, 1980)

6.) Other eligible noncitizen with a Temporary Resident Card (I-688)

The Federal government says you can also be eligible based on the Family Unity Status category with an approved I-797 (Voluntary Departure and Immigrant Petition.)

Also, you're eligible for federal student aid if you have a suspension of deportation case pending before Congress.

You are NOT eligible for student financial aid if you only have a Notice of Approval to Apply for Permanent Residence (I-171 or I-464).

Only citizens and noncitizen nationals can receive Federal aid for study at a foreign institution, and only Direct or FFEL Program Loans can be used for foreign study.

Residents of Palau are eligible for Federal student aid programs. Some residents of the Federated States of Micronesia and the Marshall Islands may be eligible for Pell Grants, Federal Supplemental Educational Opportunity Grants (FSEOG's), or Federal Work-Study only. These residents should check with their financial aid administrators.

Consolidation Loan/Direct Consolidation Loan: You can get two kinds of consolidation loans: FFEL Consolidation Loans and Direct Consolidation Loans. Both allow you to bring together your different loans under one umbrella to simplify repayment. Loan payout can take from 10 to 30 years.

Cost of Education (or Cost of Attendance): The total amount it will cost a student to go to school. It is usually expressed as a yearly figure. The cost of education covers tuition and fees; on-campus room and board (or a housing and food allowance for off-campus students); and allowances for books, supplies, transportation, child care, costs related to a handicap, and miscellaneous expenses. Talk to the financial aid administrator at the school you're planning to attend if you have any unusual expenses that may affect your cost of education or your ability to pay that cost.

Default: Failure to repay a student loan according to the terms agreed to when you signed a promissory note. If you default on a student loan, your school, lender, state government, and the federal government all can take action to recover the money. Default may affect your future credit rating, and you won't be able to receive additional federal aid or a deferment of your loan repayments, if you decide to return to school. Also, you may be liable for expenses incurred in collecting the loan. Finally, the Internal Revenue Service may withhold your income tax refund so that your loan will be repaid.

Dislocated Worker: A person so classified by the appropriate state agency (such as the state employment service or job service). Generally, a dislocated worker is unemployed because 1.) He or she has been terminated or laid off; 2.) The plant or other facility where he or she worked has closed; 3.) He or she was self-employed, but is not now because of poor economic conditions in the community or because a natural disaster has occurred.

If one of these conditions applies to you, to your spouse, or to your parents, your (and/or their) financial circumstances will be specially considered in determining the ability to pay for your education.

To find out if you, your spouse, or one of your parents qualifies as a dislocated worker, contact your local state employment service or local Job Training Partnership Act (JTPA) service (listed under state agencies in the telephone book). Or contact your city or county employment and training program (listed under city or county agencies). If you have any trouble finding these offices, your financial aid administrator should have a list of Employment and Training offices you can contact.

Displaced Homemaker: Someone who—

1.) Has not worked in the labor force for a substantial number of years (for example, approximately five years or more), but during those years has worked in the home providing unpaid services for family members;

2.) Has depended on public assistance or on the income of another family member, but is no longer receiving that income, or who has been receiving public assistance because of dependent children in the home;

3.) Is unemployed or underemployed and is having trouble obtaining or upgrading employment. "Underemployed" means not working this week but being available for work and having made specific efforts to get a job sometime during the last four weeks. "Underemployed" means working part-time (even though full-time employment is desired), because work is slack or because only part-time work is available.

If all of these conditions apply to you, to your spouse, or to your parents, your (and/or their) financial circumstances will be specially considered in determining the ability to pay for your education.

Eligible Program: A course of study that leads to a degree or certificate at a school that takes part in one or more of the Federal student aid programs. To get federal aid, you must be enrolled in an eligible program. The same is true for a Direct Loan or an FFEL Program Loan, with a single exception: if your school has told you that you must take certain course work to qualify for admission into one of its

eligible programs, you can get a Direct Loan or an FFEL Program Loan (or parents can get a PLUS Loan) for up to 12 months while you're completing that course work, as long as you're attending at least half-time. You must also meet the usual student aid eligibility requirements.

Exit Interview: A counseling session you must attend before you leave your school, if you have any of the federal loans described in this book. At this session, your school will give you information on the average amount borrowers owe, the amount of your monthly repayment, and about deferment, refinancing, and loan consolidation options.

Expected Family Contribution (EFC): This figure is determined by a formula established by Congress. It indicates how much of your family's financial resources should be available to help pay for school. This amount is used to determine your eligibility for aid from the campus-based programs. This number is important because your financial aid administrator will subtract it from your cost of education to find out how much you can't pay. To determine your contribution, the information you fill in on an aid application is evaluated. Factors such as your (and your family's) taxable and nontaxable income, as well as assets such as savings or the net worth of a home, are considered in determining your family's financial strength. Certain allowances are subtracted from both income and assets to protect part of them for future needs. A portion of the remaining amount is considered available to help pay for postsecondary educational costs.

If you have any unusual expenses that may affect your family contribution, make sure that you notify your financial aid administrator.

Family Financial Statement (FFS): An American College Testing Program form to assess the student's need for monetary aid. If requested by the student, the need assessment will be sent to a college's financial aid office.

Financial Aid Form (FAF): Form provided by the College Board College Scholarship Service for assessing and informing specified colleges of a student's family's financial situation. It is generally available from high school guidance offices as well as from the colleges that prefer the results of this form.

Financial Aid Package: The total amount of financial aid a student receives. Federal and nonfederal aid such as loans, grants, or work-study are combined in a "package" to help meet the student's need. Using available resources to give each student the best possible package of aid is one of the major responsibilities of a school's financial aid administrator.

Financial Aid Transcript: A record of the Department of Education student aid you've received. If you've received federal student aid and you transfer, you must request that your old school(s) send your financial aid transcript to the school you'll be attending. If your new school doesn't receive a financial aid transcript from the old one(s), you won't receive aid from Department of Education programs.

Part 1 of the 1995–96 Student Aid Report contains a statement of registration status. You must sign either that one or a similar one prepared by your school. (Some schools require all students to sign a statement, indicating either that the student has registered or is not required to do so.)

NOTE: If you already have a statement on file with your school, you do not have to sign another one unless your registration status has changed.

Guaranty Agency: The organization that administers FFEL Programs in your state. The federal government sets loan limits and interest rates, but each state is free to set its own additional limitations, within federal guidelines. This agency is the best source of information on FFEL's in your state.

Half-time: You must be attending school at least half-time to be eligible to receive a Federal Pell Grant, a Federal Supplemental Educational Opportunity Grant (FSEOG), Federal Work-Study (FWS) and Federal Perkins Loan Programs. Half-time enrollment is not a requirement to receive aid from the campus-based programs.

At schools measuring progress by credit hours and academic terms (semesters, trimesters, or quarters), "half-time" means at least six semester hours or quarter hours per term. At schools measuring progress by credit hours but not using academic terms, "half-time" means at least 12 semester hours or 18 quarter hours per year. At schools measuring progress by clock hours, "half-time" means at least 12 hours per week. Note that schools may choose to set higher minimums than these.

Internship Deferment: A period during which loan payments can be deferred if a borrower is participating in a program of supervised practical training required to begin professional practice or service. For a new borrower, an internship also means a degree or certificate program offered by a postsecondary school, hospital, or health care facility with postgraduate training. If you're enrolled in an internship program, you may defer repayment of some loans for up to two years.

Parental Leave Deferment: A period of up to six months during which loan payments can be postponed if a borrower is pregnant, or if he or she is taking care of a newborn or newly adopted child. The borrower must be unemployed and not attending school. To get this deferment, you must apply within six months after you leave school or drop below half-time status.

Promissory Note: The legal document you sign when you get a student loan. It lists the conditions under which you're borrowing and the terms under which you agree to pay back the loan.

Regular Student: One who is enrolled in an institution to obtain a degree or certificate. (There are exceptions for some programs: See "Eligible Program.")

Satisfactory Progress: To be eligible to receive Federal student aid, you must maintain satisfactory academic progress. If you're enrolled in a program that is no longer than two years, the following definition of satisfactory progress applies to you: you must be maintaining a "C" average by the end of your second academic year of study or have an academic standing consistent with your institution's graduation requirements. You must continue to maintain satisfactory progress for the rest of your course of study.

If you're enrolled in a program that is shorter than two years, you must meet your school's written standard of satisfactory progress. Check with your school to find out what that standard is.

Selective Service Registration: If required by law, you must register or arrange to register with the Selective Service to receive federal student aid. A statement appears on the 1995–96 Student Aid Report (SAR) that lets you state that you have registered or to explain why you are not required to register. This requirement applies to males born on or after January 1, 1960 who are citizens or eligible noncitizens who are not currently on active duty in the armed forces. Also, citizens of the Federated States of Micronesia, the Marshall Islands or Palau are exempt.

Statement of Educational Purpose/Certification Statement on Refunds and Default: You must sign this statement in order to receive federal student aid. By signing it, you agree to use your student aid only for education-related expenses. Part 1 of the 1995–96 Student Aid Report (SAR) contains such a statement. You must sign either this one or a similar one prepared by your school.

Statement of Updated Information: You must sign a statement certifying that the following Student Aid Report (SAR) items are still correct at the time you submit your SAR to your school: your status as a dependent/independent student, the number of your family members, and the number of those members enrolled in postsecondary education at least half-time. If information for any items changes after you submit your application, you must update the information so that it is correct as of the date you sign your SAR. Otherwise, you will not be able to receive Federal student aid. The only exception to the requirement to update is when changes occur because your marital status changes. In that case, you need not update.

Student Aid Index (SAI): The number that appears on your Student Aid Report (SAR), telling you about your Pell Grant eligibility. The SAI is the result of a series of calculations based on the information you reported when you applied for federal student aid.

At-A-Glance Financial Aid Calendar

When

What To Do

Junior Year of High School

■ **October**

☞ Take PSAT

☞ Send for college brochures and financial aid information

☞ Begin campus tours; talk to financial aid advisers at colleges

Senior Year of High School

■ **September to December**

☞ Narrow down your college choices

☞ Ask schools for admission applications and financial aid forms

☞ Send in applications for admission

■ **January 1**

☞ Send in financial aid applications

■ **April 1**

☞ Most college acceptances and rejections have been sent out

■ **May 1**

☞ Your financial aid application must be received by the processing agency listed on the form

■ **June 30**

☞ Your school's financial aid office must have received your application and student aid report

Financial Aid Forms Update

At press time no Free Application for Federal Student Aid has been issued by the United States Department of Education for the 1996-97 school year. The form will be available in November of 1995. Information about the form, which is to be used for applying for federal aid and public funds like Pell Grants, Stafford Loans, or Perkins Loans, is available through a toll-free number: 1-800-4 FEDAID. Or you may write:

Federal Student Aid Information Center
P.O. Box 84
Washington, DC 20044

A number of changes have been announced by organizations supplying application forms for privately administered funds. The FFS, the Family Financial Statement, put out by the ACT, has been discontinued. The FAF, issued by the College Board, will also be discontinued as of Fall 1995. The FAF will be replaced by a new form, the CSS/PROFILE. Colleges and universities began to register with the College Board in the Spring of 1995 if they wanted their applicants to use the new form. Colleges will be responsible for notifying applicants if the new forms are required. Students may register for the service in September 1995, when registration forms will be available. It is a good idea for students applying for private or institutional funds to check with the schools they are interested in to see if additional forms are required or if other procedures must be followed.

Bibliography

Helpful Materials: General Guides

Online Resources

Colleges and universities have long been at the leading edge of computing and communications, so it's only natural that you can now find plenty of financial aid information online. You can get some of it even if your only access to the Internet is via electronic mail!

The easiest way to find information is through the World Wide Web (WWW), the part of the Internet that links far-flung computer systems effortlessly, and with lots of flashy multimedia enhancements. It's getting hard to find a college these days that doesn't have a "home page" on the WWW to advertise itself to prospective students; many of these pages have pointers to the school's financial aid information. Many financial aid offices also operate Gophers, which are systems on the Internet that make it easy to find information, but without the fancy bells and whistles of the Web. So if you have access to the Internet, surf over to your new school and check it out!

There are also plenty of online resources that provide general information on financial aid, available for free via the WWW. One of the best is the Financial Aid Information WWW Page, produced by Mark Kantrowitz, author of the *Prentice Hall Guide to Scholarships and Fellowships for Math and Science Students*, listed below. The WWW page is a gold mine: It includes access to scholarship and fellowship databases, information on grants and loans, an extensive bibliography, and links to school Web and Gopher systems. Like all good Web pages, this one contains links to most of the other important sources of financial aid information contained on other computer systems. So we won't go into a long list of Web page addresses here, since one leads to the other.

To find the Financial Aid Information Page, aim your Web browser toward this address, or URL: http://www.cs.cmu.edu/afs/cs/user/mkant/Public/FinAid/finaid.html.

Kantrowitz also produces a FAQ—short for "Frequently Asked Questions"—list that covers a lot of the basic information about financial aid. You can find it through the WWW page. If you don't have WWW access but do have simple electronic mail access, you can send an email message to: mail-server@rtfm.mit.edu, containing only the words "help" and "index" on separate lines. You will receive instructions for retrieving the financial aid FAQ (and others on thousands of topics, by the way—rtfm is a massive FAQ repository).

Signet Bank has even put the full text online of the current edition of the popular book, *Don't Miss Out: The Ambitious Student's Guide to Financial Aid* by Robert Leider and Anna Leider. (It's free, but contains many come-ons to buy other guides and services from their financial aid publishing house, Octameron Associates.) You can find it at the Signet Bank Student Loan Home Page: http://www.infi.net/collegemoney/index.html.

For a more activist page, wander over to Student Financial Aid Crisis in America!, which contains updates on legislation aimed at cutting financial aid programs and links to other political sites. You can find it at: http://www.access.digex.net/~rosati/studentaid.html.

A warning about Web sites: they change. The Internet is a very active place, and addresses can be ephermeral things. That's why it's important to familiarize yourself with the kinds of Internet search tools like Veronica (for gophering around) and WWW search engines like Lycos so that you can always find the kind of information you want without the hassles of following a rabbit trail in cyberspace.

Books and pamphlets

When a book is not generally available from bookstores or libraries, we have included the address to write for it directly. Since the cost of books rises as fast as the cost of tuition, it's worth writing or calling a publisher to confirm the price—and that the book is still in print. DON'T JUST SEND THEM MONEY IN AN ENVELOPE!! Then they get angry and write letters to ME.

Octameron Associates

P.O. Box 3437, Alexandria, VA 22303

This company publishes twelve booklets in all to help you plan out your college financial aid strategy and make yourself a more attractive college candidate. They are the brainchild of Robert and Anna Leider. If you want a shorter, quicker way into the financial aid process than you'll get from a large book, the Octameron booklets are as zippy as it gets. The best booklets aimed at the college financial aid process are:

Don't Miss Out: The Ambitious Student's Guide to Financial Aid/$7.00

The As and Bs of Academic Scholarships/$7.00

Financial Aid Officers: What They Do—To You and For You/$4.00

College Check Mate: Innovative Tuition Plans That Make You a Winner/$7.50

Other Publishers

How to Pay for Your Children's College Education/$12.95
Gerald Krefetz
College Board Publications
P.O. Box 886
New York, NY 10101

The College Cost Book/$16.00
College Board Publications
P.O. Box 886
New York NY 10101
(Costs of more than 3,000 schools, and more ways to stretch your education dollar.)

The College Board Guide to Going to College While Working: Strategies for Success/$9.95
Gene Hawes
College Board Publications
P.O. Box 886
New York, NY 10101

Need a Lift?/$2.00
American Legion Education Program
P.O. Box 1050
Indianapolis, IN 46206

The Student Loan Handbook: All About the Guaranteed Student Loan and Other Forms of Financial Aid
Betterway Publications
White Hall, VA 22987

Paying Less for College/$22.95
Susan Diets, Editor
Mark Yidyik, Data Editor
Peterson's Annual Guides
P.O. Box 2123
Princeton, NJ 08543-2123

The Right College/$22.00
Arco
1633 Broadway
New York, NY 10019

Princeton Review Student Access Guide: Paying for College/$14.00
Chany, Kalman
Random House

How to Put Your Kids Through College/$15.95
Consumer Reports Books Editors
Edelstein, Scott
Consumer Reports

College Costs Today/free
New York Life Insurance Company
51 Madison Avenue
New York NY 10010
(College costs at most American schools.)

The Public Ivys: A Guide to America's Best State Colleges & Universities/$19.95
Richard Moll
Penguin
120 Woodbine Street
Bergenfield, NJ 07621
(Essays on public schools whose quality rivals or exceeds that of the best private schools.)

The College Money Book: How to Get a High-Quality Education at the Lowest Possible Cost/(price not available)
David M. Brownstone, Gene R. Hawes
Macmillan

The Great American National Scholarships & Grants Guide/$12.95
Anthony Darby
DClaren Publishing
P.O. Box 250963
W. Bloomfield, MI 48325

Specific Areas of Interest

AFL–CIO Guide to Union Sponsored Scholarships; Awards and Student Financial Aid
Department of Publication, AFL–CIO
815 16th Street, NW
Washington, DC 20006
(202) 637-5000
(The best guide to union sponsored scholarships, with a good bibliography of financial aid sources.)

Army College Fund
U.S. Army Department of Defense
620 Central Avenue
Federal Center Building R
Alameda, CA 95401

Army ROTC Scholarships
Army ROTC/Department of Military Science
74 D Harmon Gym
UC Berkeley
Berkeley, CA 94720

Directory for the Arts/$6.00
Center for Arts Information
152 West 42nd Street
New York, NY 10036

Prentice Hall Guide to Scholarships & Fellowships for Math & Science Students: A Resource Guide for Students Pursuing Careers in Mathematics, Science, & Engineering/$29.95
Kantrowitz, Mark
Prentice-Hall
Englewood Cliffs, NJ

Directory of Athletic Scholarships/$29.95
Alan Green
Facts on File
460 Park Avenue South
New York, NY 10016

Federal Benefits for Veterans and Dependents/$3.75
Superintendent of Documents
P.O. Box 371954
Pittsburgh, PA 15250

Financial Aid for College Students/free
American Chemical Society/Education Department
1155 16th Street, NW
Washington, DC 20036

Grants, Fellowships and Prizes of Interest to Historians/$8.00 for members, $10.00 for non-members
American Historical Association
400 A Street, SE
Washington, DC 20003

National Directory of Internships
National Society for Experiential Education
3509 Haworth Drive, Suite 207
Raleigh, NC 27609

The Journalist's Road to Success
The Newspaper Fund
P.O. Box 300
Princeton, NJ 08543-0300

Publications Catalog (many titles)/free
National League of Nursing
30 Hudson Street
New York, NY 10014

Programs in Cooperative Education/free
The National Commission for Cooperative Education
300 Huntington Avenue
Boston, MA 02115

Student Financial Aid/free
American Speech, Language, and Hearing Association
Department of Public Information and Publications
Careers and Information Services Section
10801 Rockville Pike
Rockville, MD 20852

Financial Aid for the Disabled and their Families, 6th ed./$38.00
Reference Services Pr.

How to Find Money for College: The Disabled Student/$21.20
Schwartz, Saryl Z.
Path-College Affordable Prod.

Financial Aid for Minority Students

Garrett Park Press
P.O. Box 190, Garrett Park, MD 20766
(301) 946-2553
This company produces a number of guides to help minority students track down aid money. The titles cost $4.00. Titles include:

Financial Aid for Minorities in Business & Law

Financial Aid for Minorities in Education

Financial Aid for Minorities in Engineering and Sciences

Financial Aid for Minorities in Health Fields

Financial Aid for Minorities in Journalism/Mass Communications

Scholarship Listings

Free Money for College: A Guide to More than 1,000 Grants & Scholarships for Undergraduate Study, 3rd Ed./$24.95
Laura Blum
Facts on File

Financial Aids for Higher Education: A Catalog for Undergraduates
Oreon Keeslar
William C. Brown Publishers
2460 Kerper Boulevard
Dubuque, IA 52001

Keys to Financing a College Education/$4.95
Marguerite Dennis
Barron

The Scholarship Book: The Comprehensive Guide to Private-Sector Scholarships, Grants, and Loans for Undergraduates/$19.95
Daniel Cassidy, President, National Scholarship Research Service, and Michael J. Alves
Prentice-Hall, Inc.
P.O. Box 11074
Des Moines, IA 50336

Chronicle Student Aid Annual/$19.95
Chronicle Guidance Publications, Inc.
66 Aurora Street
Moravia, NY 13118

Scholarships, Fellowships, & Loans/$80.00
S. Norman Feingold/Marie Feingold
Bellman
P.O. Box 34937
Bethesda, MD 20817

Directory of Scholarships and Grants

How to Use the Scholarship Listings

In the following section, scholarships have been placed in categories by majors/fields of interest. A list of the group titles into which the categories are placed follows; the reader is also encouraged to review both the Category List (pages 129–130) that identifies which categories are included in each group, and the Index of Majors at the back of the book.

Agriculture/Animal Science
Allied Health
Business
Communications
Creative/Performing Arts
Education
Engineering/Technology
Language/Literature/Humanities
Medicine/Nursing
Science/Mathematics
Social Science/Political Science/Law
Other/Miscellaneous

Each scholarship may include the following information; if an item of data does not appear, the sponsoring organization has not supplied it.

Name of award
Address of sponsoring organization to be contacted
Telephone number of sponsoring organization
Average award and/or **Amount of award, Maximum award, Minimum award**: the average or set dollar amount, or range of dollar amounts within which the award falls
Number of awards given annually
Deadline: date by which applications for the award must be filed
College level: level in college or university student must have attained in order to be eligible for award
Majors/Fields: the majors or fields of interest for which the awards are given
Criteria: describes general information and requirements for the particular award, e.g. ethnic group, test scores, residency, renewability, etc.
Contact: name and/or title of person to contact for additional information, and address and/or telephone number if different from that of sponsoring organization

The following is a sample listing:

---

496   **Sharon Christa McAuliffe Memorial Teacher Education Award**

Maryland Higher Education Commission
State Scholarship Administration
16 Francis Street
Annapolis, MD 21401-1781
(410) 974-5370
Maximum award: $8,600
Minimum award: $2,000
Number of awards: 44
Deadline: December 1
College level: Junior, Senior, Graduate, Doctoral
Majors/Fields: Education
Criteria: Applicant must be a full-time undergraduate student, public school teacher, or part-time, degree-holding, nonteacher at a Maryland degree-granting institution with an approved teacher education program. Applicant must be a Maryland resident, have a minimum 3.0 GPA, and, if an undergraduate, must have at least 60 credit hours. Applicant must agree to teach one year in a critical shortage area in a Maryland public institution for each year of the award. Minimum 3.0 GPA is required to retain scholarship for one additional year. Awarded every year.
Contact: Michael Smith, Program Administrator.

Indexes

The **Index of Majors** (page 410) lists majors alphabetically within twelve major categories (see Category List on page 129). After each major is a list of the numbers of scholarships that list that major as a criterion for eligibility.

The **Index of Criteria** (page 415) lists other criteria required for scholarship eligibility. These may include academic record or National Merit status; parents' place of employment or involvement in an alumni/ae association, club, or union; handicap; gender; military affiliation; state, county, or city of residence; race or ethnic background; religion; or sport. The numbers of scholarships that require a particular criterion are listed after entry.

The **Index of Scholarships** (page 424) lists all awards alphabetically by the name of the award.

Category List

The following is a list of the major areas of study in which specific scholarships have been categorized. All scholarships with miscellaneous majors or which are categorized by criteria other than the major or field of interest have been placed in the **Other** category.

Agriculture/ Animal Science

Agribusiness
Agriculture
Agronomy/Land Management
Animal Science/Veterinary Medicine
Forestry
Horticulture/Plant Sciences
Wildlife Resources/Management

Allied Health

Allied Health
Dental/Medical Assistance
Dietetics/Food Science/Nutrition
Medical Technology
Pharmacy
Physical/Occupational Therapy
Respiratory Therapy

Business

Accounting
Business Administration/Management
Hospitality/Hospitality Administration
Human Resources Management
Insurance
Marketing/Sales/Retailing
Real Estate
Secretarial Studies
Transportation/Traffic Management

Communications

Communications
Communications Disorders
Journalism
Library Science
Photojournalism
Radio/TV Broadcasting
Speech/Forensics

Creative/Performing Arts

Architecture/Landscape Architecture
Art History
Creative/Performing Arts–General
Drama/Theatre
Fashion Design/Interior Decorating
Film/Photography
Fine Arts
Graphic Arts
Instrumental Music
Music–General
Voice

Education

Education–General
Elementary/Secondary Education
Special Education

Engineering/Technology

Aerospace/Aeronautical Engineering
Chemical Engineering
Civil/Environmental Engineering
Computer Science
Electrical/Electronic Engineering
Engineering–General
Industrial/Manufacturing Engineering
Mechanical Engineering
Mining/Metallurgical/Materials
   Engineering
Nuclear Engineering

Language/Literature/Humanities

Classical Studies
Cultural Studies
English/Literature/Writing
Foreign Languages
History
Humanities
Religion/Theology/Philosophy

Medicine/Nursing

Dentistry
Medicine
Nursing

Science/Mathematics

Atmospheric Sciences/Meteorology
Biology
Chemistry
Earth Science
Environmental Science
Life Sciences–General
Marine Science
Mathematics
Physical Sciences
Physics
Sciences–General

Social Science/Political Science/Law

Home Economics
Law
Military Science/ROTC
Political Science
Social Sciences–General
Sociology/Social Work
Urban Planning

Other/Miscellaneous

Academic/Leadership Ability
Athletic Ability
Automotive Studies
City/County of Residence
Club Affiliation
Corporate Affiliation
Culinary Arts/Baking
Ethnic/Race-Specific
Gender-Specific
Military Affiliation
Multiple Majors
National Merit
Other
Physically Handicapped
Religious Affiliation
State/Country of Residence
Textile Science
Union Affiliation
Vocational/Technical

Agriculture/Animal Science

Agribusiness

1 George Harris/San Antonio Livestock Exposition Scholarship

Southwest Texas State University
J. C. Kellam Building
San Marcos, TX 78666
(512) 245-2340
Average award: $2,000
Number of awards: 1
Deadline: March 15
College level: Freshman, Sophomore, Junior, Senior
Majors/Fields: Agricultural business
Criteria: Applicant must be a Texas resident majoring in agricultural business. Scholarship is renewable. Awarded every year. Award may be used only at sponsoring institution.
Contact: Scholarship Committee, Department of Agriculture, San Marcos, TX 78666, (512) 245-2315.

2 L.E. Mathers Memorial Scholarship

New Mexico State University
Box 30001
Department 5100
Las Cruces, NM 88003-0001
(505) 646-4105
Average award: Tuition
Deadline: March 1
College level: Junior
Majors/Fields: Agricultural economics, agricultural business
Criteria: Applicant must have at least half of the required credits for a major in the department of agricultural economics and agricultural business, have a minimum 2.8 GPA, demonstrate financial need, and be a U.S. citizen. Selection is based upon academic promise, character, and leadership. Preference is given to New Mexico residents. Awarded every year. Award may be used only at sponsoring institution.
Contact: College of Agriculture and Home Economics, (505) 646-1807.

3 NCFC Education Foundation Undergraduate Scholarship

National Council of Farmer Cooperatives
50 F Street, NW
Suite 900
Washington, DC 20001
(202) 626-8700
Average award: $1,000
Number of awards: 4
Deadline: June 15
College level: Sophomore, Junior, Senior
Criteria: Applicant must demonstrate a basic knowledge of cooperative business and express how cooperatives might be relevant in his or her life. Transcript, essay, and letter of recommendation are required. Awarded every year.
Contact: Undergraduate Scholarships, NCFC Education Foundation.

Agriculture

4 AACC Undergraduate Scholarships

American Association of Cereal Chemists (AACC)
3340 Pilot Knob Road
St. Paul, MN 55121-2097
Average award: $1,000
Maximum award: $1,500
Number of awards: 15
Deadline: April 3
College level: Sophomore, Junior, Senior
Majors/Fields: Cereal science
Criteria: Applicant must be a full-time student with a minimum 3.0 GPA, enrolled in a program emphasizing cereal science/technology, and recommended by department head or faculty advisor. Selection is based upon academic record, career interest, courses taken, jobs held (part- or full-time), active participation in student science club, and grades in science classes. Recipient must reapply on same basis as new applicants. Awarded every year.
Contact: Dr. Elwood F. Caldwell, Chairman, AACC Scholarship Jury, (612) 454-7250.

5 Agricultural Dean's Leadership Award

Utah State University
Logan, UT 84322-0160
(801) 750-1129
Average award: 75% of in-state tuition
Deadline: April 1
College level: Freshman, Sophomore, Junior, Senior
Majors/Fields: Agriculture
Criteria: Applicant must have served as or be currently serving as the Utah FFA president, have a minimum high school GPA of 3.0, and be enrolled full time in the Coll of Agriculture. Minimum 3.0 GPA is required to retain scholarship. Award may be used only at sponsoring institution.
Contact: Mark Tenhoeue, Director of High School and College Relations.

6 Arch E. McClanahan Agricultural Memorial Scholarship

University of Tennessee, Knoxville
Financial Aid Office
115 Student Services Building
Knoxville, TN 37994
(615) 974-3131
Average award: $3,000
Number of awards: 6
Deadline: December 1
College level: Freshman
Majors/Fields: Agriculture
Criteria: Applicant must be a Tennessee resident, have a minimum 3.5 GPA, minimum composite ACT score of 25 (combined SAT I score of 980), and demonstrate outstanding performance in school and community activities that support professional career development. Acceptable academic and leadership performance is required to retain scholarship. Awarded every year. Award may be used only at sponsoring institution.
Contact: Agricultural Sciences and Natural Resources, 310 Agricultural Engineering Building, Knoxville, TN 37996, (615) 974-7506.

7   Burroughs Foundation Annual Agricultural Scholarship

Clemson University
G-01 Sikes Hall
Clemson, SC 29634-5123
(803) 656-2280
Average award: $1,000
Number of awards: 2
Deadline: March 1
College level: Freshman
Majors/Fields: Agricultural sciences
Criteria: Applicant must be a resident of Horry County, S.C. Satisfactory GPA with at least 12 credits per semester is required to retain scholarship. Awarded every year. Award may be used only at sponsoring institution.
Contact: Marvin Carmichael, Director of Financial Aid.

8   Business Men's Assurance Company of America Scholarship

Future Farmers of America (FFA)
P.O. Box 15160
Alexandria, VA 22309-0160
(703) 360-3600
Average award: $1,000
Number of awards: 10
Deadline: February 15
College level: Freshman
Majors/Fields: Agriculture
Criteria: Applicant must be a FFA member pursuing a four-year degree in any area of agriculture, and be a resident of Alabama, Arizona, Arkansas, California, Colorado, Delaware, Florida, Georgia, Idaho, Illinois, Indiana, Iowa, Kansas, Kentucky, Louisiana, Maryland, Michigan, Minnesota, Mississippi, Missouri, Montana, Nebraska, Nevada, New Mexico, North Carolina, North Dakota, Ohio, Oklahoma, Oregon, Pennsylvania, South Carolina, South Dakota, Tennessee, Texas, Utah, Virginia, Washington, West Virginia, Wisconsin, or Wyoming. Selection is based upon academic standing, leadership ability, and financial need. Awarded every year.
Contact: National FFA Organizational Office.

9   California Farm Bureau Scholarship

California Farm Bureau Scholarship Foundation
1601 Exposition Boulevard – FB 13
Sacramento, CA 95815
(916) 924-4052
Average award: $1,000
Maximum award: $2,000
Number of awards: 33
Deadline: March 1
College level: Unspecified undergraduate
Majors/Fields: Agriculture
Criteria: Selection is based upon scholastic achievement, career goals, leadership skills, and determination. Recipient must reapply for renewal. Awarded every year.
Contact: Nina M. Danner, Scholarship Coordinator.

10   Cargill Scholarship for Rural America

Future Farmers of America (FFA)
P.O. Box 15160
Alexandria, VA 22309-0160
(703) 360-3600
Average award: $1,000
Number of awards: 250
Deadline: February 15
College level: Freshman
Criteria: Applicant must be from a family whose primary livelihood (at least half of income) is derived from farming, must demonstrate financial need, and be planning to enroll full-time in any accredited two- or four-year college, university, or vocational/technical school. Selection is based upon academic record, leadership, extracurricular activities, work experience, potential for success, recommendation, and statement of educational and career goals. Awarded every year.
Contact: National FFA Organizational Office.

11   Future Farmers of America Sweepstakes Award

New Mexico State University
Box 30001
Department 5100
Las Cruces, NM 88003-0001
(505) 646-4105
Average award: Tuition
Number of awards: 1
Deadline: March 1
College level: Freshman
Majors/Fields: Agriculture
Criteria: Applicant must have participated on one of the high school teams that won the sweepstakes award. Awarded every year. Award may be used only at sponsoring institution.
Contact: Greeley W. Myers, Director of Financial Aid.

12   George E. and Leila Giles Singleton Scholarship

Clemson University
G-01 Sikes Hall
Clemson, SC 29634-5123
(803) 656-2280
Average award: $1,200
Number of awards: 2
Deadline: March 1
College level: Freshman
Majors/Fields: Agricultural sciences
Criteria: Applicant must be a South Carolina resident and demonstrate financial need. Satisfactory GPA with at least 12 credits per semester is required to retain scholarship. Awarded every year. Award may be used only at sponsoring institution.
Contact: Marvin Carmichael, Director of Financial Aid.

13   Houston Livestock Show and Rodeo Scholarship

Southwest Texas State University
J. C. Kellam Building
San Marcos, TX 78666
(512) 245-2340
Maximum award: $1,500
Number of awards: 20
Deadline: March 15
College level: Sophomore, Junior, Senior
Majors/Fields: Agriculture
Criteria: Applicant must major in agriculture and demonstrate leadership, academic ability, and financial need. Scholarship is primarily for students with 30 or more semester hours. Awarded every year. Award may be used only at sponsoring institution.
Contact: Scholarship Committee, Department of Agriculture, San Marcos, TX 78666, (512) 245-2315.

14   J.W. Jones Endowed Agricultural Scholarship

Clemson University
G-01 Sikes Hall
Clemson, SC 29634-5123
(803) 656-2280
Average award: $3,500
Number of awards: 1
Deadline: March 1
College level: Freshman, Sophomore, Junior, Senior
Majors/Fields: Agricultural sciences
Criteria: Applicant must have a minimum 2.0 cumulative GPA in the Coll of Agricultural Sciences. Satisfactory GPA with at least 12 credits per semester is required to retain scholarship. Awarded every year. Award may be used only at sponsoring institution.
Contact: Marvin Carmichael, Director of Financial Aid.

15 Jack Wright Memorial Scholarship

University of Tennessee, Knoxville
Financial Aid Office
115 Student Services Building
Knoxville, TN 37994
(615) 974-3131
Maximum award: $1,200
Maximum number of awards: 6
Minimum number of awards: 5
Deadline: February 1
College level: Freshman
Majors/Fields: Agriculture
Criteria: Selection is based upon academic performance, leadership ability, and financial need. Award is for four years. Awarded every year. Award may be used only at sponsoring institution.
Contact: Agricultural Sciences and Natural Resources, 310 Agricultural Engineering Building, Knoxville, TN 37996, (615) 974-7506.

16 Jeremiah Milbank Sr. Memorial Scholarship

Clemson University
G-01 Sikes Hall
Clemson, SC 29634-5123
(803) 656-2280
Average award: $2,000
Number of awards: 1
Deadline: March 1
College level: Freshman, Sophomore, Junior, Senior
Majors/Fields: Agricultural sciences
Criteria: First priority is given to applicants from Jasper County; next priority is given to any South Carolina resident. Awarded every year. Award may be used only at sponsoring institution.
Contact: Marvin Carmichael, Director of Financial Aid.

17 Marlboro County Farm Bureau Scholarship in Agriculture

Clemson University
G-01 Sikes Hall
Clemson, SC 29634-5123
(803) 656-2280
Average award: $2,000
Number of awards: 1
Deadline: March 1
College level: Sophomore
Majors/Fields: Agriculture
Criteria: Applicant must be a resident of Marlboro County, S.C. Awarded every year. Award may be used only at sponsoring institution.
Contact: Marvin Carmichael, Director of Financial Aid.

18 Missouri Department of Agriculture Scholarship

Southwest Missouri State University
Student Financial Aid
901 South National Avenue
Springfield, MO 65804-0095
(417) 836-5000 or (800) 492-7900
Average award: $1,000
Number of awards: 2
Deadline: March 31
College level: Freshman
Majors/Fields: Agriculture
Criteria: Selection is based upon academic record, leadership, and citizenship. Minimum 2.5 cumulative GPA with at least 12 hours per semester is required to retain scholarship. Awarded every year. Award may be used only at sponsoring institution.
Contact: Scholarship Committee.

19 New Mexico Agricultural Chemical and Plant Food Association Scholarship

New Mexico State University
Box 30001
Department 5100
Las Cruces, NM 88003-0001
(505) 646-4105
Average award: Full tuition
Number of awards: 3
Deadline: March 1
College level: Freshman, Sophomore, Junior, Senior
Majors/Fields: Agriculture, agricultural economics, agricultural education, agronomy, entomology, extension education, home economics, horticulture, plant pathology, preforestry
Criteria: Selection is based upon financial need, scholarship potential, moral character, and leadership qualities. Recommendation of the scholarship committee is required to retain scholarship. Awarded every year. Award may be used only at sponsoring institution.
Contact: Greeley W. Myers, Director of Financial Aid.

20 Thomas Benton Young Sr. Memorial Annual Scholarship

Clemson University
G-01 Sikes Hall
Clemson, SC 29634-5123
(803) 656-2280
Average award: $1,000
Number of awards: 4
Deadline: March 1
College level: Freshman, Sophomore, Junior, Senior
Majors/Fields: Agricultural sciences
Criteria: First priority is given to applicants from the South Carolina counties of Clarendon, Darlington, Dillon, Florence, Georgetown, Horry, Lee, Marion, Marlboro, Sumter, or Williamsburg. Second priority is given to other South Carolina residents, and then to any other qualified applicants without regard to residency. Awarded every year. Award may be used only at sponsoring institution.
Contact: Marvin Carmichael, Director of Financial Aid.

21 UAL Scholarship

United Agribusiness League (UAL) Scholarship Program
54 Corporate Park
Irvine, CA 92714
(714) 975-1424
Average award: $2,500
Maximum award: $6,000
Minimum award: $1,000
Number of awards: 7
Deadline: April 15
College level: Sophomore, Junior, Senior, Graduate
Majors/Fields: Agriculture
Criteria: Applicant must be a UAL member. Recipient must reapply for renewal. Awarded every year.
Contact: Nancy Whitley, Director of Member Services.

22 W.L. Abernathy Jr. Scholarship

Clemson University
G-01 Sikes Hall
Clemson, SC 29634-5123
(803) 656-2280
Average award: $1,500
Number of awards: 4
Deadline: March 1
College level: Freshman, Sophomore, Junior, Senior
Majors/Fields: Agricultural sciences
Criteria: Applicant must be a South Carolina resident enrolled in the Coll of Agricultural Sciences. Awarded every year. Award may be used only at sponsoring institution.
Contact: Marvin Carmichael, Director of Financial Aid.

23 Wallace O. Hardee Scholarship

Clemson University
G-01 Sikes Hall
Clemson, SC 29634-5123
(803) 656-2280
Average award: $1,000
Number of awards: 12
Deadline: March 1
College level: Freshman, Sophomore, Junior, Senior
Majors/Fields: Agricultural sciences
Criteria: Applicant must be a South Carolina resident enrolled in the Coll of Agricultural Sciences. Satisfactory GPA with at least 12 credits per semester is required to retain scholarship. Awarded every year. Award may be used only at sponsoring institution.
Contact: Marvin Carmichael, Director of Financial Aid.

24 Walter B. McKinney Annual Scholarship

Clemson University
G-01 Sikes Hall
Clemson, SC 29634-5123
(803) 656-2280
Average award: $1,000
Number of awards: 5
Deadline: March 1
College level: Freshman, Sophomore, Junior, Senior
Majors/Fields: Agricultural sciences
Criteria: Applicant must be a South Carolina resident from a designated rural area as defined by the Farmer's Home Administration and must demonstrate financial need. Satisfactory GPA with at least 12 credits per semester is required to retain scholarship. Awarded every year. Award may be used only at sponsoring institution.
Contact: Marvin Carmichael, Director of Financial Aid.

25 William J. Oates Endowed Scholarship

Clemson University
G-01 Sikes Hall
Clemson, SC 29634-5123
(803) 656-2280
Average award: $1,200
Number of awards: 4
Deadline: March 1
College level: Freshman
Majors/Fields: Agricultural sciences, agricultural engineering
Criteria: Preference is given to applicants majoring in agricultural engineering. Satisfactory GPA with at least 12 credits per semester is required to retain scholarship. Awarded every year. Award may be used only at sponsoring institution.
Contact: Marvin Carmichael, Director of Financial Aid.

Agronomy/Land Management

26 Joe B. Douthit Memorial Soil and Water Conservation Scholarship

Clemson University
G-01 Sikes Hall
Clemson, SC 29634-5123
(803) 656-2280
Average award: $1,000
Number of awards: 4
Deadline: March 1
College level: Freshman, Sophomore, Junior, Senior
Majors/Fields: Agronomy, agricultural engineering
Criteria: Applicant must have a minimum 2.0 cumulative GPA and be interested in the conservation of soil and water. Satisfactory GPA with at least 12 credits per semester is required to retain scholarship. Awarded every year. Award may be used only at sponsoring institution.
Contact: Marvin Carmichael, Director of Financial Aid.

Animal Science/Veterinary Medicine

27 Adrian Berryhill Family Agriculture Scholarship

New Mexico State University
Box 30001
Department 5100
Las Cruces, NM 88003-0001
(505) 646-4105
Average award: $1,000
Number of awards: 2
Deadline: March 1
College level: Junior, Senior
Majors/Fields: Animal science, range science
Criteria: Applicant must be a New Mexico resident, preferably from a New Mexico ranching family. One award is given in animal science and one in range science. Awarded every year. Award may be used only at sponsoring institution.
Contact: College of Agriculture and Home Economics, (505) 646-1807.

28 AKC Veterinary Scholarship

American Kennel Clubs
51 Madison Avenue
New York, NY 10010
Average award: $2,500
Maximum award: $5,000
Minimum award: $1,000
Number of awards: 25
Deadline: May 1
College level: Veterinary students
Majors/Fields: Veterinary medicine
Criteria: Selection is based upon participation in the sport of purebred dogs, financial need, and scholastic achievement. Application must be made through the school's financial aid office. No school may submit more than four applications in any year. Reapplication is required to retain scholarship. Awarded every year.
Contact: Scholarships, (212) 696-8234.

29 Beville Hal Reagan Scholarship in Animal Science

University of Tennessee, Knoxville
Financial Aid Office
115 Student Services Building
Knoxville, TN 37994
(615) 974-3131
Average award: $2,000
Number of awards: 1
Deadline: February 1
College level: Freshman
Majors/Fields: Animal science
Criteria: Applicant must have actively participated in 4-H, FFA, or other youth agricultural programs and have a minimum composite ACT score of 24. Minimum 2.75 cumulative GPA and 3.25 GPA in animal science major is required to retain scholarship for third and fourth years. Applicant must participate in Animal Science Department's clubs and activities. Awarded every year. Award may be used only at sponsoring institution.
Contact: Agricultural Sciences and Natural Resources, 310 Agricultural Engineering Building, Knoxville, TN 37996, (615) 974-7506.

30   J. Frances Allen Scholarship

American Fisheries Society
5410 Grosvenor Lane
Suite 110
Bethesda, MD 20814-2199
Maximum award: $2,500
Number of awards: 1
Deadline: March 1
College level: Doctoral
Majors/Fields: Fisheries science
Criteria: Applicant must be a woman working towards her Ph.D. and must be a member of American Fisheries Society. Applicant must submit a vita, GRE scores, transcripts, and dissertation research proposal. Awarded every year.
Contact: Susan Monseur, Production Editor, *Fisheries*, (301) 897-8616.

31   National Zoological Park Minority Traineeships

Friends of the National Zoo
National Zoological Park
Washington, DC 20008
Maximum award: $2,400
Number of awards: 4
Deadline: February 21
Majors/Fields: Animal behavior, ecology, reproduction, nutrition, genetics, husbandry, exotic animal medicine, veterinary pathology, zoo graphics, public affairs, horticulture, facilities design, education, exhibit planning, exhibit evaluation
Criteria: Selection is based upon statement of interest, scholastic achievement, relevant experience, and letters of reference.
Contact: Traineeships.

32   National Zoological Park Research Traineeships

Friends of the National Zoo
National Zoological Park
Washington, DC 20008
Maximum award: $2,400
Number of awards: 10
Deadline: February 21
Majors/Fields: Animal behavior, ecology, reproduction, exotic animal medicine, veterinary pathology
Criteria: Selection is based upon statement of interest, scholarship achievement, relevant experience, and letters of reference.
Contact: Traineeships.

33   UDIA/Dairy Shrine Milk Marketing Scholarships

Dairy Shrine
100 MBC Drive
Shawano, WI 54166
(715) 526-2141
Maximum award: $1,000
Minimum award: $500
Number of awards: 3
Deadline: March 15
College level: Sophomore, Junior, Senior
Majors/Fields: Dairy science, milk marketing
Criteria: Awarded every year.
Contact: James Leuenberger, Secretary/Treasurer, (712) 526-2141.

Forestry

34   Charles E. Springs Annual Forestry Scholarship

Clemson University
G-01 Sikes Hall
Clemson, SC 29634-5123
(803) 656-2280
Average award: $1,000
Number of awards: 5
Deadline: March 1
College level: Freshman, Sophomore, Junior, Senior
Majors/Fields: Forestry
Criteria: Applicant must be a South Carolina resident from a designated rural area as defined by the Farmers' Home Administration and demonstrate financial need. Preference is given to entering freshmen. Satisfactory GPA with at least 12 credits per semester is required to retain scholarship. Awarded every year. Award may be used only at sponsoring institution.
Contact: Marvin Carmichael, Director of Financial Aid.

35   Edward S. Moore Foundation Scholarship

Clemson University
G-01 Sikes Hall
Clemson, SC 29634-5123
(803) 656-2280
Average award: $2,500
Number of awards: 1
College level: Freshman
Majors/Fields: Forestry
Criteria: Applicant must be a South Carolina resident and a member of a minority group. If all other factors are equal, financial need is considered. Minimum 2.5 GPA with at least 12 credits per semester is required to retain scholarship. Awarded every year. Award may be used only at sponsoring institution.
Contact: Marvin Carmichael, Director of Financial Aid.

36   Louisiana Forestry Foundation Scholarship

Louisiana Tech University
P.O. Box 7925
Ruston, LA 71272
(318) 257-2641
Maximum award: $1,200
Number of awards: 6
Deadline: March 1
College level: Freshman, Sophomore, Junior, Senior, Graduate, Doctoral
Majors/Fields: Forestry
Criteria: Minimum 2.5 GPA with at least eight hours per quarter is required to retain scholarship. Awarded every year. Award may be used only at sponsoring institution.
Contact: E. R. Winzer, Director of Student Financial Aid.

37   Ottis and Calista Causey Endowed Scholarship

Clemson University
G-01 Sikes Hall
Clemson, SC 29634-5123
(803) 656-2280
Average award: $2,000
Number of awards: 1
Deadline: March 1
College level: Freshman, Sophomore, Junior, Senior
Majors/Fields: Forestry
Criteria: Applicant must have a minimum 2.0 GPA. Satisfactory GPA with at least 12 credits per semester is required to retain scholarship. Awarded every year. Award may be used only at sponsoring institution.
Contact: Marvin Carmichael, Director of Financial Aid.

38 Sharp Academic Merit Scholarship

Mississippi State University
P.O. Box 6238
Mississippi State, MS 39762
(601) 325-7430
Average award: $3,000
Deadline: February 1
College level: Freshman
Majors/Fields: Forestry
Criteria: Applicant must have a minimum composite ACT score of 31. Selection is based upon ACT scores and high school academic record. Minimum 3.0 GPA in required forestry courses is required to retain scholarship. Awarded every year. Award may be used only at sponsoring institution.
Contact: Audrey S. Lambert, Director of Student Financial Aid.

39 TAPPI Technical Division Scholarships

Technical Association of the Pulp & Paper Industry (TAPPI)
Technology Park/Atlanta
P.O. Box 105113
Atlanta, GA 30348-5113
(404) 446-1400
Maximum award: $3,000
Minimum award: $500
Number of awards: 20
Deadline: January 31
College level: Freshman, Sophomore, Junior, Senior
Majors/Fields: Engineering, forest resources, nonwovens, packaging, paper, pulp, science
Criteria: Awarded every year.
Contact: Technical Services Department.

40 Virginia Forestry Association Scholarship

Virginia Forestry Association
1205 East Main Street
Richmond, VA 23219
(804) 644-8462
Average award: $1,000
Maximum award: $1,500
Number of awards: 8
Deadline: March 31
College level: Freshman, Sophomore, Junior, Senior
Majors/Fields: Forestry
Criteria: Applicant must major in forestry or any curriculum in the School of Forestry at Virginia Polytech Inst and State U. Selection is based upon, in order of importance: academic standing, motivation, apparent ability to contribute to the forestry profession, extracurricular activities, evidence of leadership, and financial need. Awarded every year. Award may be used only at sponsoring institution.
Contact: Charles F. Finley Jr., Executive Vice President.

Horticulture/Plant Sciences

41 A. Harvey and Mary E. Snell Scholarship

Clemson University
G-01 Sikes Hall
Clemson, SC 29634-5123
(803) 656-2280
Average award: $1,200
Number of awards: 2
Deadline: March 1
College level: Sophomore, Junior, Senior
Majors/Fields: Agricultural engineering, horticulture
Criteria: Applicant must have a minimum cumulative GPA of 3.0. Satisfactory GPA with at least 12 credits per semester is required to retain scholarhip. Awarded every year. Award may be used only at sponsoring institution.
Contact: Marvin Carmichael, Director of Financial Aid.

42 AHS Horticultural Career Intern Program

American Horticultural Society (AHS)
7931 East Boulevard Drive
Alexandria, VA 22308
(703) 768-5700
Maximum award: $5,760
Minimum award: $1,920
Number of awards: 3
Deadline: Three months prior to desired starting date
College level: Sophomore, Junior, Senior, Graduate, Nontraditional student changing career to horticulture
Majors/Fields: Horticulture
Criteria: Applicant must have a basic knowledge of horticulture, two years of horticulture education, writing ability, interest in working with the public, desire to learn about national horticulture and horticultural communications, and major in horticulture or related field. Awarded every year.
Contact: Intern Coordinator.

43 Anne Seaman PGMS Memorial Scholarship

Professional Grounds Management Society (PGMS)
120 Cockeysville Road
Suite 104
Hunt Valley, MD 21031
(410) 584-9754
Average award: $500
Maximum award: $1,000
Minimum award: $225
Number of awards: 3
Deadline: July 1
College level: Freshman, Sophomore, Junior, Senior
Majors/Fields: Grounds management
Criteria: Scholarship is renewable. Awarded every year.
Contact: Scholarships.

44 Carolinas Golf Association Scholarship

Clemson University
G-01 Sikes Hall
Clemson, SC 29634-5123
(803) 656-2280
Average award: $1,000
Number of awards: 5
Deadline: March 1
College level: Freshman, Sophomore, Junior, Senior
Majors/Fields: Turfgrass
Criteria: Applicant must have a minimum 2.0 GPA. Satisfactory GPA with at least 12 credits per semester is required to retain scholarship. Awarded every year. Award may be used only at sponsoring institution.
Contact: Marvin Carmichael, Director of Financial Aid.

45 Catherine H. Beattie Fellowship

Garden Club of America
598 Madison Avenue
New York, NY 10022
(212) 753-8287
Maximum award: $5,000
Number of awards: 1
Deadline: December 31
College level: Graduate, Doctoral
Majors/Fields: Horticulture, biology
Criteria: Award is for field research on rare plants. Preference is given to applicant whose project focuses on the endangered flora of the Carolinas and southeastern U.S. Awarded every year.
Contact: Ms. Peggy Olwell, Center for Plant Conservation, Missouri Botanical Garden, P.O. Box 299, Saint Louis, MO 63166-0299, (314) 577-9450.

46 Earl J. Small Growers Scholarship

Bedding Plants Foundation, Inc.
P.O. Box 27241
Lansing, MI 48909
(517) 694-8537
Average award: $2,000
Number of awards: 2
Deadline: April 1
College level: Sophomore, Junior, Senior
Majors/Fields: Horticulture
Criteria: Applicant must intend to pursue a career in greenhouse production and be a U.S. or Canadian citizen. Selection is based upon academic qualifications, financial need, and extracurricular activities. Awarded every year.
Contact: Sue Geopp, Executive Director.

47 GCA Award in Tropical Botany

Garden Club of America
598 Madison Avenue
New York, NY 10022
(212) 753-8287
Average award: $5,500
Number of awards: 2
Deadline: December 31
College level: Doctoral
Majors/Fields: Tropical botany
Criteria: Award is for field study in tropical botany by Ph.D. candidates. Awarded every year.
Contact: Ms. Lori Michaelson, World Wildlife Fund, 1250 24th Street, NW, Washington, DC 20037-1175, (202) 778-9714.

48 Gus Cunningham Wofford Memorial Scholarship

Clemson University
G-01 Sikes Hall
Clemson, SC 29634-5123
(803) 656-2280
Average award: $2,000
Number of awards: 1
Deadline: March 1
College level: Sophomore, Junior, Senior
Majors/Fields: Horticulture
Criteria: Preference is given to residents of Laurens County, S.C. Satisfactory GPA with at least 12 credits per semester is required to retain scholarship. Awarded every year. Award may be used only at sponsoring institution.
Contact: Marvin Carmichael, Director of Financial Aid.

49 Interchange Fellowship and Martin McLaren Scholarship

Garden Club of America
598 Madison Avenue
New York, NY 10022
(212) 753-8287
Number of awards: 2
Deadline: November 15
College level: Graduate, Doctoral
Majors/Fields: Horticulture, landscape architecture
Criteria: Fellowship provides a graduate academic year in the U.S. for a Briton and a work-study program for an American at universities and botanical gardens in the United Kingdom. Awarded every year.
Contact: Mrs. Monica Freeman.

50 James K. Rathmell, Jr. Memorial Scholarship

Bedding Plants Foundation, Inc.
P.O. Box 27241
Lansing, MI 48909
(517) 694-8537
Average award: $1,000
Maximum award: $2,000
Number of awards: 2
Deadline: April 1
College level: Junior, Senior, Graduate, Doctoral
Majors/Fields: Horticulture
Criteria: Award is for work and study of six months or longer abroad. Recipient must submit a written report upon return; 20 percent of funds are held until report is received. Awarded every year.
Contact: Sue Goepp, Executive Director.

51 Jerry Baker, America's Master Gardener, College Freshmen Scholarship

Bedding Plants Foundation, Inc.
P.O. Box 27241
Lansing, MI 48909
(517) 694-8537
Average award: $1,000
Number of awards: 2
Deadline: April 1
College level: Freshman
Majors/Fields: Gardening, horticulture, landscaping
Criteria: Selection is based upon academic qualifications, financial need, and extracurricular activities. Awarded every year.
Contact: Sue Goepp, Executive Director.

52 Katharine M. Grosscup Scholarship

Garden Club of America
598 Madison Avenue
New York, NY 10022
(212) 753-8287
Maximum award: $2,000
Deadline: February 15
College level: Junior, Senior, Graduate, Doctoral
Majors/Fields: Horticulture, agriculture
Criteria: Preference is given to applicants from Indiana, Michigan, Ohio, Pennsylvania, and West Virginia. Awarded every year.
Contact: Mrs. Nancy Stevenson, Grosscup Scholarship Committee, Garden Center of Greater Cleveland, 11030 East Boulevard, Cleveland, OH 44106, (216) 721-1600.

53 Mary Barratt Park Foundation Scholarship

Clemson University
G-01 Sikes Hall
Clemson, SC 29634-5123
(803) 656-2280
Average award: $1,000
Number of awards: 3
Deadline: March 1
College level: Freshman, Sophomore, Junior, Senior
Majors/Fields: Horticulture
Criteria: Applicant must have a minimum 2.0 cumulative GPA. Awarded every year. Award may be used only at sponsoring institution.
Contact: Marvin Carmichael, Director of Financial Aid.

54 National Council of State Garden Clubs Scholarship

New Mexico State University
Box 30001
Department 5100
Las Cruces, NM 88003-0001
(505) 646-4105
Average award: $4,000
Number of awards: 20
Deadline: November 1
College level: Freshman, Sophomore, Junior, Senior
Majors/Fields: Horticulture
Criteria: Applicant must have a minimum 3.0 GPA and be a resident of the state from which he or she is applying. Only one applicant may be submitted by each state annually. Awarded every year. Award may be used only at sponsoring institution.
Contact: College of Agricultural and Home Economics, (505) 646-1807.

55 National Council of State Garden Clubs Scholarship

National Council of State Garden Clubs
4401 Magnolia Avenue
St. Louis, MO 63110
(314) 776-7574
Average award: $4,000
Number of awards: 30
Deadline: December 1
College level: Freshman, Sophomore, Junior, Senior, Graduate, Doctoral
Majors/Fields: Horticulture, floriculture, land management, landscape design, urban planning
Criteria: Applicant must have the endorsement of the State Garden Club from the state in which he or she is a permanent resident. Satisfactory GPA and financial need are required to retain scholarship. Awarded every year.
Contact: Scholarship Chairman.

56 Scholarship in Turfgrass Management

Golf Course Superintendents Association of America
1421 Research Park Drive
Lawrence, KS 66049
(913) 841-2240
Average award: $1,500
Number of awards: 10
Deadline: October 1
College level: Sophomore, Junior, Senior
Majors/Fields: Botany, chemistry, forestry, golf course managment, horticulture, plant science, turfgrass science
Criteria: Applicant must have completed at least the first year of a collegiate turfgrass management program and be planning a career as a golf course superintendent. Selection is based upon academic excellence, extracurricular activities, and recommendations from college advisors and golf course superintendents or other employers. One award is available for an international applicant meeting the same criteria. Awarded every year.
Contact: Pat Jones, Director of Development.

57 Worcester County Horticultural Society

Worcester County Horticultural Society
Tower Hill Botanic Garden
Boylston, MA 01505-1008
(508) 869-6111
Maximum award: $2,000
Minimum award: $500
Number of awards: 5
Deadline: May 1
Majors/Fields: Horticulture
Criteria: Applicant must be a New England resident or be attending a New England college. Selection is based upon interest in horticulture, sincerity of purpose, academic performance, and financial need.
Contact: Awards.

Wildlife Resources/ Management

58 Andrew J. Boehm Fellowship

American Fishing Tackle Manufacturers Association
1250 Grove Avenue
Suite 300
Barrington, IL 60010
(708) 381-9490
Average award: $3,500
Maximum award: $5,000
Minimum award: $1,000
Number of awards: 4
Deadline: March 15
College level: Doctoral
Majors/Fields: Fisheries management
Criteria: Applicant must have a minimum 3.0 GPA and have made a commitment to a professional career in fisheries management or research. Selection is based upon research proposals designed for a M.S. or Ph.D. thesis. Research must involve some aspect of the life history, ecology, population dynamics, or behavior of some species of fish or fish-food organisms or their environmental requirements. Application must be submitted by the responsible supervising professor on behalf of the candidate. Proposals for research that has the potential of improving understanding or management of recreational fisheries will receive special consideration. Awarded every year.
Contact: Robert G. Kavanagh, President.

59 Rockefeller State Wildlife Scholarship

Louisiana Office of Student Financial Assistance
P.O. Box 91202
Baton Rouge, LA 70821-9202
(504) 922-1038
Average award: $1,000
Number of awards: 60
Deadline: April 1
College level: Freshman, Sophomore, Junior, Senior, Graduate, Doctoral
Majors/Fields: Forestry, wildlife, marine science
Criteria: Applicant must be a U.S. citizen or eligible noncitizen, be a resident of Louisiana, enroll full-time in a Louisiana public college or university, and have a minimum 2.5 GPA. FAFSA must be postmarked by March 15. Scholarship is renewable. Awarded every year.
Contact: Winona Kahao, Director of Scholarship/Grant Division, (504) 922-1150.

60 Wildlife Research Scholarship

Rob and Bessie Welder Wildlife Foundation Scholarship
P.O. Box 1400
Sinton, TX 78387-1400
(512) 364-2643
Average award: Scholarships for full-time students are $800 per month for M.S. candidates and $850 per month for Ph.D. candidates to cover living costs, tuition, fees, and books.
College level: Graduate, Doctoral
Majors/Fields: Animal behavior, biology, botany, conservation education, ecology, fisheries science, genetics, mammalogy, ornithology, parasitology, range science, veterinary pathology, wildlife science
Criteria: Applicant must have a minimum GRE score of 1100 and 3.0 GPA in the last two years of undergraduate or graduate work.
Contact: James G. Teer, Director.

Allied Health

Allied Health

61 AHA/AIA Fellowship in Health Facilities Design

American Hospital Association Division of Health Facilities
Management and Compliance
840 North Lake Shore Drive
Chicago, IL 60611
Average award: $7,000
Number of awards: 3
College level: Doctoral,
Majors/Fields: Architecture, health care
Criteria: Awarded every year.
Contact: Marietta B. Gaden, Director of Education, (312) 280-6409.

62 Barbara Thomas Enterprises Scholarship

Foundation of Record Education of American Health Information Management Association (AHIMA)
919 North Michigan Avenue
Suite 1400
Chicago, IL 60611-1683
(312) 787-2672
Minimum award: $5,000
Number of awards: 1
Deadline: July 1
College level: Sophomore, Junior, Senior, Graduate, Doctoral
Majors/Fields: Health information management, health information technology
Criteria: Applicant must be a single parent enrolled in a health information management or technology program. Awarded every year.
Contact: Scholarship Committee, (312) 787-2672, extension 302.

63 Constance L. Lloyd/ACMPE Scholarship

American College of Medical Practice Executives (ACMPE)
104 Inverness Terrace East
Englewood, CO 80112-5306
(303) 799-1111
Average award: $1,000
Deadline: June 1
College level: Freshman, Sophomore, Junior, Senior, Graduate, Doctoral
Majors/Fields: Heath care
Criteria: Applicant must be a woman enrolled at an accredited college or university in Georgia. Applicant must submit a letter stating career goals and objectives, a resume showing employment history with a brief narrative describing specific employment responsibilities in health care field, and three letters of recommendation. Reference letters should address performance, character, potential to succeed, and need for scholarship support. Awarded every year.
Contact: Laurie Draizen, Executive Assistant, (303) 799-1111, extension 206.

64 CRAHCA Data Analysis Scholarship

American College of Medical Practice Executives (ACMPE)
104 Inverness Terrace East
Englewood, CO 80112-5306
(303) 799-1111
Maximum award: $1,000
Deadline: None
Majors/Fields: Heath care administration, medical practice management
Criteria: Applicant must request specifics.
Contact: Laurie Draizen, Executive Assistant, (303) 799-1111, extension 206.

65 DeArce-Koch Scholarship

University of Toledo
Financial Aid Office
Toledo, OH 43606-3390
(419) 537-2056
Average award: $1,000
Number of awards: 40
Deadline: January 28
College level: Freshman
Majors/Fields: Health sciences, pharmacy
Criteria: Applicant must be majoring in any of the health sciences (including pharmacy) and be enrolled full time. Award is for four years. Awarded every year. Award may be used only at sponsoring institution.
Contact: Office of Financial Aid.

66 Fairfax County Medical Society Foundation Scholarship

Fairfax County Medical Society Foundation
8100 Oak Street
Dunn Loring, VA 22027
(703) 560-4855
Maximum award: $1,000
Number of awards: 10
Deadline: May 25
College level: Freshman, medical school applicants
Majors/Fields: Health, medicine
Criteria: Applicant must be a legal resident of Fairfax County, Va., and must intend to continue education in a medical or human health field. Selection is based upon financial need, scholastic achievement, and participation in school, community, and church activities. The Dr. Leon Block Scholarship is awarded to a deserving applicant who also has demonstrated talent in playing a musical instrument. Applicant must reapply each year. Awarded every year.
Contact: Diana C. Mills, Meetings Coordinator.

67 FFS Student Fellowships

Fight for Sight/The Research Division of Prevent Blindness America
500 East Remington Road
Schaumburg, IL 60173
(708) 843-2020
Maximum award: $1,500
Minimum award: $500
Number of awards: 15
Deadline: March 1
College level: Doctoral
Majors/Fields: Ophthalmology, visual sciences
Criteria: Applicant must be a U.S. or Canadian resident. Scholarship is renewable.
Contact: Program Coordinator.

68 FORE Graduate Scholarships

Foundation of Record Education (FORE) of American Health
Information Management Association (AHIMA)
919 North Michigan Avenue
Suite 1400
Chicago, IL 60611-1683
(312) 787-2672
Minimum award: $3,000
Number of awards: 1
Deadline: August 1
College level: Graduate, Doctoral
Majors/Fields: Health information management
Criteria: Applicant must be studying health information management
or a related field such as business, finance, information science,
education, law, or public health, hold a bachelor's degree, and be a
member of AHIMA. Awarded every year.
Contact: Graduate Scholarship Committee.

69 FORE Undergraduate Scholarship

Foundation of Record Education (FORE) of American Health
Information Management Association (AHIMA)
919 North Michigan Avenue
Suite 1400
Chicago, IL 60611-1683
(312) 787-2672
Average award: $1,500
Number of awards: 2
Deadline: July 1
College level: Sophomore, Junior, Senior
Majors/Fields: Health information management, health information
technology
Criteria: Applicant must have been accepted for admission into a CA-
HEA-approved program. Awarded every year.
Contact: Scholarship Committee, (312) 787-2672, extension 302.

70 Harry J. Harwick Scholarship

American College of Medical Practice Executives (ACMPE)
104 Inverness Terrace East
Englewood, CO 80112-5306
(303) 799-1111
Average award: $2,000
Number of awards: 1
Deadline: June 1
College level: Freshman, Sophomore, Junior, Senior, Graduate,
Doctoral
Majors/Fields: Health care administration, medical group practice
Criteria: Applicant must submit a letter stating career goals and ob-
jectives, a resume showing employment history with a brief narrative
describing specific employment responsibilities in health care field,
and three letters of recommendation. Reference letters should ad-
dress performance, character, potential to succeed, and need for
scholarship support. Awarded every year.
Contact: Laurie Draizen, Executive Assistant, (303) 799-1111, extension 206.

71 Health Careers Scholarship

International Order of the King's Daughters and Sons
6024 East Chicago Road
Jonesville, MI 49250
Maximum award: $1,000
Minimum award: $500
Number of awards: 50
Deadline: April 1
College level: Junior
Majors/Fields: Dentistry, medical technology, medicine, nursing, oc-
cupational therapy, pharmacy, physical therapy
Criteria: Applicant must be a U.S. or Canadian citizen enrolled in an
accredited school of study in the U.S. or Canada. Pre-med students
are not eligible. Enclose a stamped, self-addressed, business-sized
envelope with inquiry. Updated application, financial statement, and
transcript are required to retain scholarship. Awarded every year.
Contact: Alice Raber, Health Careers Director.

72 Health Professional Scholarship

Veterans Affairs Educational Assistance Program
Department of Veterans Affairs Central Office
810 Vermont Avenue, NW
Washington, DC 20420
(202) 535-7528
Maximum award: Tuition, fees, books, other related costs, and a tax-
free stipend of $621 per month
Deadline: Last Tuesday in May
College level: Junior, Senior, Graduate
Majors/Fields: Nursing, physical therapy, occupational therapy
Criteria: Applicant must be an undergraduate or graduate student in a
health care shortage area. Recipient is required to provide profes-
sional service for a designated period of time at a VA medical center.
Selection is based upon GPA, recommendations, career goals, and
work and/or volunteer recommendation and experiences. Scholar-
ship is renewable. Awarded every year.
Contact: Health Professional Scholarship Program.

73 Health Professions Scholarship

Indian Health Employee Scholarship
Federal Building
115 4th Avenue, SE
Aberdeen, SD 57401
(605) 226-7553
Number of awards: 720
Deadline: April 14
Majors/Fields: Health professions
Criteria: Applicant must prove Native American background. Schol-
arships have service obligations and payback requirements.
Awarded every year.
Contact: Alice L. LaFontaine, Scholarship Coordinator.

74 Health Service Corps Scholarship

New York State Higher Education Services Corporation
99 Washington Avenue
Albany, NY 12255
(518) 473-4563
Maximum award: $7,500
Number of awards: 250
Deadline: February
College level: Junior, Senior
Majors/Fields: Dental hygiene, midwife, nurse practitioner, occupational therapy, pharmacy, physical therapy, physician's assistant,
registered nursing, speech-language pathology
Criteria: Applicant must be enrolled full-time in an approved professional program, be within two years of becoming eligible for New York
state licensure in chosen field, and be a U.S. citizen or qualifying noncitizen. Selection is based upon academic achievement, previous
work experience, and demonstrated interest in working with institu-
tionalized populations. Recipient must work 18 months in a state-op-
erated facility or participating voluntary agency for each year of
scholarship support. Award is for two years. Awarded every year.
Contact: New York State Health Service Corps, Corning Tower,
Room 1602, Empire State Plaza, Albany, NY 12237, (518) 473-7019.

75 J.D. Archbold Memorial Hospital Scholarship

J. D. Archbold Memorial Hospital
Department of Education
P.O. Box 1018
Thomasville, GA 31799
(912) 228-2795
Average award: $2,000
Number of awards: 25
Deadline: None
College level: Junior, Senior
Majors/Fields: Health care
Criteria: Applicant must be in the last two years of an undergraduate
program in a health care field utilized by the hospital and must commit
to three years full-time employment at Archbold Medical Center after
graduation. Awarded every year.
Contact: Donna C. McMillan, Assistant to the Director of Education.

76 Midwest Section Scholarship

American College of Medical Practice Executives (ACMPE)
104 Inverness Terrace East
Englewood, CO 80112-5306
(303) 799-1111
Average award: $2,000
Maximum number of awards: 3
Minimum number of awards: 1
Deadline: June 1
College level: Freshman, Sophomore, Junior, Senior, Graduate, Doctoral
Majors/Fields: Health care administration, medical group management, medical practice management
Criteria: Applicant must reside in the Midwest section and submit a letter stating career goals and objectives, a resume showing employment history with a brief narrative describing specific employment responsibilities in health care field, and three letters of recommendation. Reference letters should address performance, character, potential to succeed, and need for schoalrship support. Awarded every year.
Contact: Laurie Draizen, Executive Assistant, (303) 799-1111, extension 206.

77 Professional Scholarship

Maryland Higher Education Commission
State Scholarship Administration
16 Francis Street
Annapolis, MD 21401-1781
(410) 974-5370
Maximum award: $1,000
Minimum award: $200
Number of awards: 386
Deadline: March 1
College level: Freshman, Sophomore, Junior, Senior, Graduate, Doctoral
Majors/Fields: Dentistry, law, medicine, nursing, pharmacy
Criteria: Applicant must attend an eligible Maryland institution and file FAFSA and SSA by March 1. Scholarship is renewable. Awarded every year.
Contact: Lula Caldwell, Program Administrator.

78 Rehabilitation Training Program

U.S. Department of Education Rehabilitation Services Administration
Division of Resource Development
Washington, DC 20202-2649
(202) 205-9400
Average award: $4,000
College level: Junior, Senior, Graduate, Doctoral
Majors/Fields: Rehabilitation
Criteria: Awards are granted to institutions of higher education, which in turn, award scholarships directly to students. Applicant should contact colleges directly to learn the availability and requirements for awards and contact RSA to obtain a list of colleges with RSA grants. All scholars must meet a work-or-repay requirement by working for a specified period after completing education in a state rehabilitation agency or related program. Scholarship is renewable.
Contact: Dr. Richard P. Melia, Director.

79 Reserve Member Stipend

Veterans Affairs Educational Assistance Program
Department of Veterans Affairs Central Office
810 Vermont Avenue, NW
Washington, DC 20420
(202) 535-7528
Maximum award: $400 per month while the reservist is enrolled in full-time course work.
Deadline: Last Tuesday in May
College level: Sophomore, Junior, Senior, Graduate
Majors/Fields: Nursing, physical therapy, occupational therapy
Criteria: Applicant must be a reservist, a member of the Selected Ready Reserves, eligible for the Reserve GI Bill, have scored above the 50th percentile on the Armed Forces Qualification Test, and be an undergraduate or entry-level graduate in a health care shortage area. Recipient is required to provide professional service for a designated period of time at a VA medical center. Selection is based upon GPA, recommendations, career goals, and work and/or volunteer recommendation and experiences. Scholarship is renewable. Awarded every year.
Contact: Reserve Member Stipend Program (143B).

80 St. Anthony Publishing, Inc. Julia LeBlond Memorial Scholarship

Foundation of Record Education of American Health Information Management Association (AHIMA)
919 North Michigan Avenue
Suite 1400
Chicago, IL 60611-1683
(312) 787-2672
Minimum award: $1,500
Number of awards: 2
Deadline: July 1 (undergraduate); August 1 (graduate)
College level: Sophomore, Junior, Senior, Graduate, Doctoral
Majors/Fields: Health information management, health information technology
Criteria: Applicant must have been accepted for admission into a CAHEA-approved program. Awarded every year.
Contact: Scholarship Committee, (312) 787-2672, extension 302.

81 State Health Service Corps Scholarship

New York State Health/Primary Care Service Corps
Room 1602, Corning Tower
Empire State Plaza
Albany, NY 12237
(518) 473-7019
Average award: $14,000
Number of awards: 130
Deadline: First week in February
College level: Junior, Senior
Majors/Fields: Registered professional nurse, physical therapist, occupational therapist, pharmacist, speech-language pathologist, physician assistant, dental hygienist, nurse practitioner, nurse midwife
Criteria: Applicant must submit evidence of enrollment in or acceptance for full-time study in a professional program at an institution approved by the New York State Board of Regents, be within 30 months of completing the program of study and becoming eligible to apply for a license, certificate, or registration in the profession of study, and meet the character and moral standards required for licensure. Recipient must maintain full-time attendance in approved program of study. Awarded every year.
Contact: Steve Swanson, Director.

82 Suburban Hospital Scholarship

Suburban Hospital Scholarship Program
Office of Personnel
8600 Old Georgetown Road
Bethesda, MD 20814
(301) 530-3850
Maximum award: $5,000
Number of awards: 8
Deadline: April 30
College level: Junior, Senior, Graduate
Majors/Fields: Medical technology, nursing, occupational therapy, physical therapy, physician assistant, radiology technology, respiratory therapy
Criteria: Applicant must reside in the metropolitan Washington, D.C. area, have a minimum 2.5 GPA, and be within four semesters of graduation in a medical technology, nursing, occupational therapy, physical therapy, physician assistant, radiology technology, or respiratory therapy program. Minimum 2.5 cumulative GPA is required to retain scholarship. Awarded every year.
Contact: Beth Murphy, Employment Manager.

83 Transcriptions, Ltd. Scholarship

Foundation of Record Education of American Health Information Management Association (AHIMA)
919 North Michigan Avenue
Suite 1400
Chicago, IL 60611-1683
(312) 787-2672
Maximum award: $3,000
Minimum award: $1,000
Number of awards: 2
Deadline: July 1
College level: Sophomore, Junior, Senior, Graduate, Doctoral
Majors/Fields: Health information management
Criteria: Applicant must be enrolled in a CAHEA-approved program. Awarded every year.
Contact: Scholarship Committee, (312) 787-2672, extension 302.

84 Western Section Scholarship

American College of Medical Practice Executives (ACMPE)
104 Inverness Terrace East
Englewood, CO 80112-5306
(303) 799-1111
Average award: $2,000
Maximum number of awards: 2
Minimum number of awards: 1
Deadline: June 1
College level: Sophomore, Junior, Senior, Graduate, Doctoral
Majors/Fields: Medical practice management
Criteria: Applicant must be a MGMA Western section member for two years. Applicant must submit a letter stating goals and objectives, a resume showing employment history with a brief narrative describing specific employment responsibilities in health care field, and three letters of recommendation. Reference letters should address performance, character, potential to succeed, and need for scholarship support. Awarded every year.
Contact: Laurie Draizen, Executive Assistant.

Dental/Medical Assistancy

85 ADHA Scholarship

American Dental Hygienists' Association (ADHA)
444 North Michigan Avenue
Suite 3400
Chicago, IL 60611
(312) 440-8900
Average award: $1,250
Maximum award: $1,500
Minimum award: $1,000
Number of awards: 34
Deadline: May 1
College level: Sophomore, Junior, Senior, Graduate, Doctoral
Majors/Fields: Dental hygiene
Criteria: Applicant must document financial need of at least $1,500, be enrolled in a full-time dental hygiene program in the U.S., have completed a minimum of one year of dental hygiene curriculum, have a minimum 3.0 GPA, and be an ADHA member. Awarded every year.
Contact: Cyndi Weingard, Associate Administrator, (312) 440-8944.

86 Annual Scholarship Program

Physician Assistant Foundation of the American Academy of Physician Assistants
950 N. Washington Street
Alexandria, VA 22314
(703) 836-2272, extension 3306
Maximum award: $5,000
Minimum award: $2,000
Number of awards: 33
Deadline: February 1
College level: Students enrolled in CAHEA-accredited PA Program
Majors/Fields: Physician assistant
Criteria: Applicant must be enrolled in a CAHEA-accredited physician assistant program, and be a member of the American Academy of Physician Assistants. Selection is based upon financial need, commitment/involvement to the profession, and academic record. Awarded every year.
Contact: Carolyn Blancos Losada, Administrator, (703) 836-2272.

87 Dental Assisting Scholarship

American Dental Association (ADA) Endowment and Assistance Fund, Inc.
211 East Chicago Avenue
17th Floor
Chicago, IL 60611-2678
(312) 440-2567
Average award: $1,000
Number of awards: 25
Deadline: September 1
College level: Freshman
Majors/Fields: Dental assisting
Criteria: Applicant must be a U.S. citizen entering a full-time, ADA-accredited program and have a minimum 2.8 GPA. Selection is based upon financial need, academic achievement, and personal and professional goals. Awarded every year.
Contact: Marsha Mountz, ADA Endowment Fund.

88   Dental Hygiene Scholarship

American Dental Association (ADA) Endowment and Assistance Fund, Inc.
211 East Chicago Avenue
17th Floor
Chicago, IL 60611-2678
(312) 440-2567
Average award: $1,000
Number of awards: 25
Deadline: August 15
College level: Freshman, Sophomore
Majors/Fields: Dental hygiene
Criteria: Applicant must be a U.S. citizen enrolled full-time as an entering or first-year student at an ADA-accredited dental hygiene school and have a minimum 2.8 GPA. Selection is based upon financial need, academic achievement, and personal and professional goals. Good academic standing is required to retain scholarship for one additional year. Awarded every year.
Contact: Marsha Mountz, ADA Endowment Fund.

89   Juliette A. Southard Dental Assistant Teacher Education Scholarship

American Dental Assistants Association (ADAA)
919 North Michigan Avenue
Chicago, IL 60611
(312) 664-3327
Maximum award: $2,000
Deadline: July 15
Majors/Fields: Dental assistant
Criteria: Applicant must be a U.S. citizen and an ADAA member currently certified or qualified for certification as a dental assistant. Renewable if satisfactory progress is maintained.
Contact: Scholarships.

Dietetics/Food Science/Nutrition

90   ADA Scholarship

American Dietetic Association Foundation
216 West Jackson
Chicago, IL 60606
(312) 899-0040
Average award: $1,000
Maximum award: $3,000
Minimum award: $350
Number of awards: 150
Deadline: February 15
College level: Senior, Graduate, Doctoral
Majors/Fields: Dietetics
Criteria: Selection is based upon financial need, academic standing, and professional potential. Awarded every year.
Contact: Linda Maraba, ADA Foundation Team.

91   IFT Freshman/Sophomore Scholarship

Institute of Food Technologists (IFT)
Scholarship Department
221 North LaSalle Street
Chicago, IL 60601
(312) 782-8424
Average award: $750
Maximum award: $1,000
Number of awards: 32
Deadline: February 15 (freshman); March 1 (sophomore)
College level: Freshman, Sophomore
Majors/Fields: Food science, food technology
Criteria: Applicant must be pursuing or transferring to an approved program in food science/technology. Freshman award applicant must be a scholastically outstanding high school graduate or senior entering college for the first time. Sophomore award applicant must have a minimum 2.5 GPA and recommendations from the department head and another faculty member. Reapplication is required to retain scholarship. Awarded every year.
Contact: Patti Pagliuco, Fellowship/Scholarship Program Administrator.

92   IFT Graduate Fellowship

Institute of Food Technologists (IFT)
Scholarship Department
221 North LaSalle Street
Chicago, IL 60601
(312) 782-8424
Average award: $4,000
Maximum award: $10,000
Minimum award: $1,000
Number of awards: 27
Deadline: February 1
College level: Graduate, Doctoral
Majors/Fields: Food packaging, food science, food technology, frozen foods, refrigeration
Criteria: Applicant must be a scholastically outstanding senior or graduate student with above average interest and aptitude in research who is enrolled in graduate studies at the effective date of the fellowship. Graduate research must be in food science or technology. The IFT Food Packaging Division fellowship is for research in food packaging; the IFT Refrigeration and Frozen Food Division Fellowship is for research in refrigeration and frozen foods. Reapplication is required to retain scholarship. Awarded every year.
Contact: Patti Pagliuco, Scholarship/Fellowship Program Administrator.

93   IFT Junior/Senior Scholarship

Institute of Food Technologists (IFT)
Scholarship Department
221 North LaSalle Street
Chicago, IL 60601
(312) 782-8424
Average award: $1,000
Maximum award: $2,000
Minimum award: $750
Number of awards: 54
Deadline: February 1
College level: Junior, Senior
Majors/Fields: Food engineering, food science, food technology, quality assurance
Criteria: Applicant must be a scholastically outstanding sophomore or junior enrolled in an approved food science/technology program, or a sophomore transfer into such a program. The IFT Food Engineering Division scholarship encourages the pursuit of activities in food engineering in an ABET-accredited engineering major or an IFT-approved program. Reapplication is required to retain scholarship. Awarded every year.
Contact: Patti Pagliuco, Scholarship Program Administrator.

94   Mildred B. Davis Fellowship

American Association of Family and Consumer Sciences
1555 King Street
Alexandria, VA 22314
(703) 706-4600
Average award: $3,000
Number of awards: 1
Deadline: January 16
College level: Graduate, Doctoral
Majors/Fields: Nutrition
Criteria: Applicant must be a U.S. citizen. Awarded every year.
Contact: Fellowships.

Medical Technology

95   ASCP/AMS Scholarship

American Society of Clinical Pathologists (ASCP)
2100 West Harrison Street
Chicago, IL 60612-3798
Maximum award: $1,000
Number of awards: 50
Deadline: October 28
College level: Students in final clinical year of study
Majors/Fields: Cytotechnology, histologic technician/histotechnologist, medical laboratory technician, medical technologist
Criteria: Applicant must be enrolled in an accredited program, demonstrate financial need and academic qualifications, and submit three recommendations. Awarded every year.
Contact: Jeanean Harris or ASCP Customer Services, Executive Assistant, (312) 738-1336.

96   Dental Lab Tech Scholarship

American Dental Association (ADA) Endowment and Assistance Fund, Inc.
211 East Chicago Avenue
17th Floor
Chicago, IL 60611-2678
(312) 440-2567
Average award: $1,000
Number of awards: 25
Deadline: August 15
College level: Freshman, Sophomore
Majors/Fields: Dental laboratory technology
Criteria: Applicant must be a U.S. citizen, an entering or first-year student at an ADA-accredited dental laboratory technology school, and have a minimum 2.8 GPA. Selection is based upon financial need, academic achievement, and personal and professional goals. Good academic standing is required to retain scholarship for one additional year. Awarded every year.
Contact: Marsha Mountz, ADA Endowment Fund.

Pharmacy

97   Advanced Predoctoral Fellowship in Pharmaceutics

Pharmaceutical Research and Manufacturers of America Foundation, Inc.
1100 15th Street, NW
Washington, DC 20005
(202) 835-3470
Average award: $12,500
Number of awards: 5
Deadline: October 1
College level: Doctoral
Majors/Fields: Pharmaceutics
Criteria: Applicant must hold a B.S. or Pharm.D. degree in pharmacy or a related area such as chemistry or biology from an accredited school in the U.S. Applicant should be enrolled in a Pharm.D./Ph.D. program and have completed the bulk of pre-dissertation requirements. Required clinical course work or clinical clerkships may not be taken during the tenure of the fellowship. Awarded every year.
Contact: Donna Moore, Director of Programs.

98   Advanced Predoctoral Fellowship in Pharmacology/Toxicology

Pharmaceutical Research and Manufacturers of America Foundation, Inc.
1100 15th Street, NW
Washington, DC 20005
(202) 835-3470
Average award: $12,500
Number of awards: 10
Deadline: September 15
College level: Doctoral
Majors/Fields: Pharmacology, toxicology
Criteria: Applicant must be a full-time, in-residence Ph.D. candidate in the field of pharmacology or toxicology who is enrolled in a school of medicine, pharmacy, dentistry, or veterinary medicine. Applicant should have completed the bulk of pre-thesis requirements. Those enrolled in an M.D./Ph.D. program should not be taking required clinical course work or clerkships during the tenure of the fellowship. Awarded every year.
Contact: Donna Moore, Director of Programs.

99   AFPE Fellowships

American Foundation for Pharmaceutical Education (AFPE)
618 Somerset Street
P.O. Box 7126
North Plainfield, NJ 07060
(908) 561-8077
Average award: $7,500
Number of awards: 85
Deadline: March 1
College level: Doctoral
Majors/Fields: Pharmacy
Criteria: Applicant must be a U.S. citizen or permanent resident and have completed at least one semester of graduate school. Some awards are for those interested in teaching at a pharmacy college. Scholarship is renewable.
Contact: Fellowship Program.

100   AFPE Gateway Scholarship

American Foundation for Pharmaceutical Education (AFPE)
618 Somerset Street
P.O. Box 7126
North Plainfield, NJ 07060
(908) 561-8077
Average award: $9,250
Number of awards: 1
Deadline: December 1
College level: Doctoral
Majors/Fields: Pharmacy
Criteria: Award is for undergraduate research and graduate study in a pharmacy program. Applicant must be a U.S. citizen or permanent resident.
Contact: Scholarships.

101   American Drug Stores Scholarship

University of Utah
Financial Aid and Scholarships Office
105 Student Services Building
Salt Lake City, UT 84112
(801) 581-6211
Average award: $1,250
Number of awards: 4
Deadline: February 1
College level: Junior, Senior
Majors/Fields: Pharmacy
Criteria: Applicant must be in the last two years of a B.S. pharmacy program, enroll for a minimum of 12 credit hours per quarter, and be interested in the community practice of pharmacy. Reapplication is required to retain scholarship. Awarded every year. Award may be used only at sponsoring institution.
Contact: Dr. Jan Bair, A050 University Hospital, Salt Lake City, UT 84112, (801) 581-2147.

102 Bergen Brunswig Drug Company Scholarship

University of Utah
Financial Aid and Scholarships Office
105 Student Services Building
Salt Lake City, UT 84112
(801) 581-6211
Average award: $2,500
Number of awards: 1
Deadline: February 1
College level: Junior, Senior
Majors/Fields: Pharmacy
Criteria: Applicant must be in the last two years of a B.S. pharmacy program and enroll for at least 12 credit hours per quarter. Selection is based upon scholastic ability and financial need. Reapplication is required to retain scholarship. Awarded every year. Award may be used only at sponsoring institution.
Contact: Dr. Jan Bair, A050 University Hospital, Salt Lake City, UT 84112, (801) 581-2147.

103 Ewart A. Swinyard Scholarship

University of Utah
Financial Aid and Scholarships Office
105 Student Services Building
Salt Lake City, UT 84112
(801) 581-6211
Maximum award: $1,500
Minimum award: $1,000
Number of awards: 7
Deadline: February 1
College level: Sophomore, Junior, Senior, Graduate, Doctoral
Majors/Fields: Pharmacy
Criteria: Applicant must enroll in the pharmacy program for at least 12 credit hours per quarter. Reapplication is required to retain scholarship. Awarded every year. Award may be used only at sponsoring institution.
Contact: Dr. Jan Bair, A050 University Hospital, Salt Lake City, UT 84112, (801) 581-2147.

104 Glaxo/AFPE Graduate Studies Scholarship

American Foundation for Pharmaceutical Education (AFPE)
618 Somerset Street
P.O. Box 7126
North Plainfield, NJ 07060
(908) 561-8077
Average award: $5,000
Maximum number of awards: 8
Minimum number of awards: 1
Deadline: May 1
College level: Doctoral
Criteria: Applicant must either be in the final year of a B.S. or Pharm.D. program at a pharmacy college or be a recent pharmacy program graduate planning to pursue a graduate or professional degree (not a Pharm.D.) in business administration, engineering, law, pharmaceutical sciences, or public health. Applicant must be a U.S. citizen or permanent resident and must submit the name of the graduate school (if known), transcript, a list of special honors, awards, and accomplishments, GRE scores, statement, and recommendations.
Contact: Scholarships.

105 Grace P. Swinyard Memorial Scholarship

University of Utah
Financial Aid and Scholarships Office
105 Student Services Building
Salt Lake City, UT 84112
(801) 581-6211
Maximum award: $1,500
Minimum award: $1,000
Number of awards: 7
Deadline: February 1
College level: Sophomore, Junior, Senior, Graduate, Doctoral
Majors/Fields: Pharmacy
Criteria: Applicant must enroll in the pharmacy program for at least 12 credit hours per quarter. Preference is given to female applicants. Reapplication is required to retain scholarship. Awarded every year. Award may be used only at sponsoring institution.
Contact: Dr. Jan Bair, A050 University Hospital, Salt Lake City, UT 84112, (801) 581-2147.

106 Kappa Epsilon/AFPE Nellie Wakeman Scholarship

American Foundation for Pharmaceutical Education (AFPE)
618 Somerset Street
P.O. Box 7126
North Plainfield, NJ 07060
(908) 561-8077
Average award: $4,000
Number of awards: 1
Deadline: May 1
College level: Graduate, Doctoral
Majors/Fields: Pharmacy
Criteria: Applicant must have completed one term of advanced studies in the pharmaceutical sciences, be a member in good standing of Kappa Epsilon, and be working toward a pharmacy M.S., a Ph.D., or a Pharm.D. (having previously earned a pharmacy B.S.). Applicant must submit an application form, transcript, and recommendations. Financial need is considered.
Contact: Scholarships, KE Executive Office, P.O. Box 870393, Stone Mountain, GA 33087-0010.

107 Pay Less Drugs Scholarship

University of Utah
Financial Aid and Scholarships Office
105 Student Services Building
Salt Lake City, UT 84112
(801) 581-6211
Average award: $3,000
Number of awards: 3
Deadline: February 1
College level: Junior, Senior
Majors/Fields: Pharmacy
Criteria: Applicant must be in the last two years of a B.S. pharmacy program, enroll for at least 12 credit hours per quarter, and be interested in the community practice of pharmacy. Reapplication is required to retain scholarship. Awarded every year. Award may be used only at sponsoring institution.
Contact: Dr. Jan Bair, A050 University Hospital, Salt Lake City, UT 84112, (801) 581-2147.

108 Presidential Scholarship

NARD Foundation
205 Daingerfield Road
Alexandria, VA 22314-6973
(703) 683-8200
Average award: $2,000
Number of awards: 14
Deadline: Spring
Majors/Fields: Pharmacy
Criteria: Selection is based upon academic achievement, leadership qualities, career objectives, and extracurricular accomplishments. Awarded every year.
Contact: Scholarships.

109 Sandoz/AFPE First-Year Graduate Scholarship

American Foundation for Pharmaceutical Education (AFPE)
618 Somerset Street
P.O. Box 7126
North Plainfield, NJ 07060
(908) 561-8077
Average award: $5,000
Number of awards: 2
Deadline: May 1
College level: Doctoral
Majors/Fields: Pharmacy
Criteria: Applicant must hold a B.S., Pharm.D., or equivalent degree, be planning to pursue a pharmaceutical Ph.D. at a pharmacy college, be a U.S. citizen or permanent resident, and demonstrate academic excellence and financial need. Applicant must submit the name of the graduate school (if known), transcript, list of special honors, awards, and accomplishments, GRE and SAT I scores, statement, and recommendations.
Contact: Scholarships.

110   Smith's Food and Drug Center Scholarship

University of Utah
Financial Aid and Scholarships Office
105 Student Services Building
Salt Lake City, UT 84112
(801) 581-6211
Average award: $2,500
Number of awards: 2
Deadline: February 1
College level: Junior, Senior
Majors/Fields: Pharmacy
Criteria: Applicant must be in the last two years of a B.S. Pharmacy program, enroll for at least 12 credit hours per quarter, and be interested in the community practice of pharmacy. Reapplication is required to retain scholarship. Awarded every year. Award may be used only at sponsoring institution.
Contact: Dr. Jan Bair, A050 University Hospital, Salt Lake City, UT 84112, (801) 581-2147.

111   SmithKline Beecham/AFPE First-Year Graduate Scholarship

American Foundation for Pharmaceutical Education (AFPE)
618 Somerset Street
P.O. Box 7126
North Plainfield, NJ 07060
(908) 561-8077
Average award: $5,000
Number of awards: 1
Deadline: May 1
College level: Doctoral
Majors/Fields: Pharmacy
Criteria: Applicant must hold a B.S., Pharm.D., or equivalent degree, be planning to pursue a pharmaceutical Ph.D. at a pharmacy college, be a U.S. citizen or permanent resident, and demonstrate academic excellence and financial need. Applicant must submit the name of the graduate school (if known), transcript, list of special honors, awards, and accomplishments, GRE and SAT I scores, statement, and recommendations.
Contact: Scholarships.

112   Undergraduate Research Fellowship in Pharmaceutics

Pharmaceutical Research and Manufacturers of America Foundation, Inc.
1100 15th Street, NW
Washington, DC 20005
(202) 835-3470
Average award: $5,000
Number of awards: 10
Deadline: October 1
College level: Pharmacy school students
Majors/Fields: Biology, chemistry, pharmacy
Criteria: Award is to stimulate undergraduate students to pursue advanced degrees in pharmaceutics. Awarded every year.
Contact: Donna Moore, Director of Programs, 1100 15th Street, Washington, DC 20005.

113   UpJohn/AFPE First Year Scholarship

American Foundation for Pharmaceutical Education (AFPE)
618 Somerset Street
P.O. Box 7126
North Plainfield, NJ 07060
(908) 561-8077
Average award: $5,000
Number of awards: 1
Deadline: May 1
College level: Doctoral
Majors/Fields: Pharmacy
Criteria: Applicant must hold a B.S., Pharm.D., or equivalent degree, be planning to pursue a pharmaceutical Ph.D. at a pharmacy college, be a U.S. citizen or permanent resident, and demonstrate academic excellence and financial need. Applicant must submit the name of the graduate school (if known), transcript, a list of special honors, awards, and accomplishments, GRE and SAT I scores, statement, and recommendations.
Contact: Scholarships.

Physical/Occupational Therapy

114   NSDAR Occupational Therapy Scholarships

National Society of the Daughters of the American Revolution
NSDAR Administration Building, Office of the Committees
1776 D Street, NW
Washington, DC 20006-5392
(202) 879-3292
Average award: $500
Number of awards: 10
Deadline: February 15, August 15
College level: Freshman, Sophomore, Junior, Senior, Graduate, Doctoral
Majors/Fields: Occupational therapy, physical therapy
Criteria: Applicant must be a U.S. citizen and submit a letter of sponsorship from a local DAR chapter. All inquiries must include a self-addressed, stamped envelope. Awarded every year.
Contact: Administrative Assistant.

115   Occupational Therapy Merit Fellowship

Washington University
One Brookings Drive
Campus Box 1089
St. Louis, MO 63130
(314) 935-6000 or (800) 638-0700
Average award: $16,750
Number of awards: 1
College level: Junior
Majors/Fields: Occupational therapy
Criteria: Applicant must be an outstanding student transferring into the occupational therapy program. Satisfactory academic performance is required to retain scholarship. Awarded every year. Award may be used only at sponsoring institution.
Contact: Program in Occupational Therapy, 4567 Scott Avenue, Campus Box 8066, Saint Louis, MO 63110, (314) 362-6911.

116   Physical and Occupational Therapists and Assistants Grant

Maryland Higher Education Commission
State Scholarship Administration
16 Francis Street
Annapolis, MD 21401-1781
(410) 974-5370
Maximum award: $2,000
Number of awards: 19
Deadline: July 1
College level: Freshman, Sophomore, Junior, Senior
Majors/Fields: Occupational therapy, occupational therapy assistant, physical therapy, physical therapy assistant
Criteria: Applicant must be a Maryland resident, attending an eligible Maryland institution on a full-time basis, and agree to serve as a therapist or assistant to handicapped children in Maryland public schools for one year for each year of the award. Scholarship is renewable. Awarded every year.
Contact: Margaret Riley, Program Administrator.

117   Physical Therapy Scholarship

Ordean Foundation
501 Ordean Building
Duluth, MN 55802
(218) 726-4785
Average award: $1,685
Maximum award: $2,000
Minimum award: $500
Number of awards: 10
Deadline: April 1
College level: Unspecified undergraduate
Majors/Fields: Physical therapy
Criteria: Applicant must be attending Coll of St. Scholastica, have a minimum 2.5 GPA, and be a resident of Duluth, Minn., or surrounding government entity in St. Louis County, Minn. Selection is based upon financial need. Renewal is based upon continuing financial need.
Contact: Jill Broman, Financial Aid Coordinator, College of Saint Scholastica, 1200 Kenwood Avenue, Duluth, MN 55811, (218) 723-4785.

Respiratory Therapy———

118 National AMBUCS Scholarship for Therapists
AMBUCS
P.O. Box 5127
High Point, NC 27262
(910) 888-6052
Maximum award: $1,500
Minimum award: $500
Deadline: April 15
College level: Junior, Senior, Graduate, Doctoral
Majors/Fields: Hearing audiology, music therapy, occupational therapy, physical therapy, speech language pathology, therapeutic recreation
Criteria: Applicant must be U.S. citizen with a minimum 3.0 GPA. Selection is based upon financial need, academic record, motivation, application form, and IRS Form 1040. Awarded every year.
Contact: Scholarships.

119 Robert M. Lawrence Scholarship
American Association for Respiratory Therapy
11030 Ables Lane
Dallas, TX 75229-4593
(214) 630-3540
Average award: $2,500
Number of awards: 1
Deadline: June 30
College level: Junior, Senior
Majors/Fields: Respiratory therapy
Criteria: Applicant must be enrolled full-time at an AMA-approved school of respiratory therapy and must submit an original essay on some facet of respiratory care. This essay is the major basis for selection. Awarded every year.
Contact: Scholarships.

120 William W. Burgin Scholarship
American Association for Respiratory Therapy
11030 Ables Lane
Dallas, TX 75229-4593
(214) 630-3540
Average award: $2,500
Number of awards: 1
Deadline: June 30
College level: Sophomore
Majors/Fields: Respiratory therapy
Criteria: Applicant must be enrolled full-time at an AMA-approved school of respiratory therapy and must submit an original essay on some facet of respiratory care. This essay is the major basis for selection. Awarded every year.
Contact: Scholarships.

Business

Accounting

121 AAA Fellowship

American Accounting Association (AAA)
5717 Bessie Drive
Sarasota, FL 34233
(813) 921-7747
Average award: $2,500
Deadline: February 1
College level: Graduate
Majors/Fields: Accounting
Criteria: Applicant must be accepted in a doctoral program at an AACBS-accredited institution at the Master's degree level. Applicant must be a resident of the U.S. or Canada, enrolled in a U.S. or Canadian school, and plan to teach in the U.S. or Canada. Applicant must submit the application form, recommendations, and graduate admissions test scores. Awarded every year.
Contact: Mary Cole, Office Manager.

122 Alumni Association of Coopers & Lybrand Scholarship

University of Calgary
2500 University Drive, NW
Calgary, Alberta, CN T2N 1N4
(403) 220-7872
Average award: $1,250
Number of awards: 2
Deadline: June 15
College level: Senior
Majors/Fields: Accounting, management
Criteria: Applicant must be interested in a career as a chartered accountant. Both awards are based upon academic merit; one also considers extracurricular activities which have demonstrated leadership ability. Awarded every year. Award may be used only at sponsoring institution.
Contact: J. Van Housen, Director of Student Awards & Financial Aid.

123 Artesia Data Systems, Inc. Scholarship

New Mexico State University
Box 30001
Department 5100
Las Cruces, NM 88003-0001
(505) 646-4105
Average award: Tuition
Number of awards: 2
Deadline: March 1
College level: Sophomore, Junior, Senior
Majors/Fields: Accounting, business computer systems
Criteria: Selection by the faculty is based upon academic performance and financial need. Awarded every year. Award may be used only at sponsoring institution.
Contact: Advising Center, College of Business Administration and Economics, (505) 646-4084.

124 Arthur H. Carter Scholarship

American Accounting Association (AAA)
5717 Bessie Drive
Sarasota, FL 34233
(813) 921-7747
Average award: $2,500
Maximum number of awards: 50
Minimum number of awards: 40
Deadline: April 1
College level: Junior, Senior, Graduate
Majors/Fields: Accounting
Criteria: Applicant must be a U.S. citizen, be enrolled for at least 12 semester hours in a school that is an Assembly Member of the AACSB, and take at least two accounting related courses. Awarded every year.
Contact: Mary Cole, Office Manager.

125 ASWA Scholarship

American Society of Women Accountants (ASWA)
1255 Lynnfield
Suite 257
Memphis, TN 38119-7235
(901) 680-0470
Average award: $2,000
Minimum award: $1,000
Number of awards: 3
Deadline: January 31
College level: Junior, Senior
Majors/Fields: Accounting
Criteria: Applicant must be a female accounting major with a minimum 3.0 GPA, have at least 60 semester hours, and demonstrate financial need. Awarded every year.
Contact: Scholarships.

126 Cynthia Ann Clark Thompson Memorial Scholarship

Louisiana Tech University
P.O. Box 7925
Ruston, LA 71272
(318) 257-2641
Average award: $1,000
Maximum award: $1,500
Minimum award: $500
Deadline: April 1
College level: Freshman, Sophomore, Junior, Senior, Graduate, Doctoral
Majors/Fields: Accounting
Criteria: Applicant must have worked full-time one summer, part-time while attending school, or full-time between high school and college. Applicant must not live with parents, must have greater financial need than others being considered, and must have qualities appropriate to accounting. Minimum 2.5 GPA is required to retain scholarship. Awarded every year. Award may be used only at sponsoring institution.
Contact: E. R. Winzer, Director of Student Financial Aid.

127 Ernst and Whinney Foundation Scholarship

Ernst and Whinney Foundation Scholarship
2000 National City Center
Cleveland, OH 44114
(216) 861-5000
Average award: $18,000
Maximum number of awards: 6
Minimum number of awards: 5
Deadline: June 1
Criteria: Applicant must plan to teach after studies are completed. Accounting applicants must have had three years of accounting work experience in the U.S. Awarded every year.
Contact: Scholarship.

128 IAIEF Scholarship

Independent Accountants International Educational Foundation (IAIEF), Inc.
9200 South Dadeland Boulevard
Suite 510
Miami, FL 33156
(305) 670-0580
Maximum award: $5,000
Minimum award: $250
Maximum number of awards: 15
Minimum number of awards: 14
Deadline: February 28
College level: Junior, Senior, Graduate, Doctoral
Majors/Fields: Accounting
Criteria: Awarded every year.
Contact: Pat Marsh, (305) 661-3580.

129 John T. Steed Accounting Scholarship

University of Oklahoma
University Affairs
900 Asp Avenue, Room 236
Norman, OK 73019-0401
(405) 325-1701
Average award: $2,500
Number of awards: 1
Deadline: February 8
College level: Freshman
Majors/Fields: Accounting
Criteria: Selection is based upon GPA, class rank, test scores, and commitment to accounting. Award is for four years. Awarded every year. Award may be used only at sponsoring institution.
Contact: School of Accounting, 200 Adams Hall, (405) 325-4221.

130 Kerr McGee Corporation Student Scholarship

University of Oklahoma
University Affairs
900 Asp Avenue, Room 236
Norman, OK 73019-0401
(405) 325-1701
Average award: $4,000
Number of awards: 1
Deadline: February 8
College level: Junior
Majors/Fields: Accounting
Criteria: Applicant must be an Oklahoma resident. Scholarship is renewable. Awarded every year. Award may be used only at sponsoring institution.
Contact: School of Accounting, 200 Adams Hall, (405) 325-4221.

131 Ledger & Quill Scholarship

DePaul University
25 East Jackson Boulevard
Suite 100
Chicago, IL 60604
(312) 362-8704
Average award: Full tuition
Number of awards: 2
Deadline: February 1
Majors/Fields: Accounting
Criteria: Applicant must rank in the top tenth of class, have a minimum composite ACT score of 27 or minimum combined SAT I score of 1100, and demonstrate strong leadership and extracurricular involvement. Minimum 3.4 GPA as a full-time student in the School of Accountancy is required to retain scholarship. Awarded every year. Award may be used only at sponsoring institution.
Contact: Jennifer Sparrow, Associate Director of Admissions.

132 Linda Weddle Memorial Scholarship

University of Oklahoma
University Affairs
900 Asp Avenue, Room 236
Norman, OK 73019-0401
(405) 325-1701
Average award: $1,000
Number of awards: 3
Deadline: February 8
College level: Freshman, Sophomore, Junior, Senior
Majors/Fields: Accounting
Criteria: Applicant must be a woman who is a U.S. citizen with demonstrated excellence in the classroom. Awarded every year. Award may be used only at sponsoring institution.
Contact: School of Accounting, 200 Adams Hall, Norman, OK 73019, (405) 325-4221.

133 Melvoin and Strobel Scholarships

DePaul University
25 East Jackson Boulevard
Suite 100
Chicago, IL 60604
(312) 362-8704
Average award: Half tuition
Number of awards: 2
Deadline: February 1
College level: Freshman
Majors/Fields: Accounting
Criteria: Applicant must have a minimum composite ACT score of 26 and rank in the top tenth of class. Scholarship is renewable. Awarded every year. Award may be used only at sponsoring institution.
Contact: Jennifer Sparrow, Associate Director of Admissions.

134 Michael J. McBride Scholarship

University of Northern Iowa
Financial Aid Office
Cedar Falls, IA 50613-0024
(319) 273-2700 or (800) 772-2736
Average award: $5,500
Number of awards: 1
Deadline: Spring
College level: Freshman, Sophomore, Junior, Senior
Majors/Fields: Accounting
Criteria: Selection is based upon financial need, strong academic credentials, and strong leadership and citizenship qualities. Satisfactory scholastic achievement is required to retain scholarship. Awarded whenever current recipient graduates. Award may be used only at sponsoring institution.
Contact: Evelyn Waack, Scholarship Coordinator, Financial Aid.

135 Minority Accounting Doctoral Support Program

KPMG Peat Marwick Foundation
Three Chestnut Ridge Road
Montvale, NJ 07645
Average award: $10,000
Number of awards: 15
Deadline: March 15
College level: Doctoral
Majors/Fields: Accounting
Criteria: Applicant must be an African-American, Hispanic-American, or Native American starting in a full-time accounting doctoral program. The institution must provide $5,000 annual stipend unrelated to teaching, waive tuition and fees, and provide teaching and research assistantships as appropriate for doctoral students. Renewable up to five years.
Contact: Bernard J. Milano, Secretary/Trustee, Minority Accounting Doctoral Support Program.

136 NSPA Scholarship Award

National Society of Public Accountants (NSPA) Scholarship Foundation
1010 North Fairfax Street
Alexandria, VA 22314-1574
(703) 549-6400
Average award: $1,000
Minimum award: $500
Number of awards: 26
Deadline: March 10
College level: Sophomore, Junior, Senior
Majors/Fields: Accounting
Criteria: Applicant must be majoring in accounting with a minimum "B" average in a full-time degree program at an accredited college or university. Awarded every year.
Contact: Susan E. Noell, Foundation Director.

137   Robert Kaufman Memorial Scholarship Fund

Independent Accountants International Educational Foundation (IAIEF), Inc.
9200 South Dadeland Boulevard
Suite 510
Miami, FL 33156
(305) 670-0580
Maximum award: $5,000
Minimum award: $250
Maximum number of awards: 20
Minimum number of awards: 12
Deadline: February 28
College level: Freshman, Sophomore, Junior, Senior, Graduate, Doctoral
Majors/Fields: Accounting
Criteria: Awarded every year.
Contact: Pat Marsh.

138   Scholarships for Minority Accounting Students

American Institute of Certified Public Accountants
1211 Avenue of the Americas
New York, NY 10036-8775
(212) 596-6200
Maximum award: $5,000
Deadline: July 1
College level: Sophomore, Junior, Senior, Graduate, Doctoral
Majors/Fields: Accounting
Criteria: Applicant must be a U.S. citizen, have a minimum 3.0 GPA, and be either African-American, Hispanic, Native American, or Pacific Islander. Selection is based upon merit and academic achievement. Financial need is considered. Recipient must reapply for renewal. Awarded every year.
Contact: Scholarships.

139   William Roy and Maxine R. Adams Scholarship for Academic Excellence

Louisiana Tech University
P.O. Box 7925
Ruston, LA 71272
(318) 257-2641
Average award: $1,250
Maximum award: $2,000
Minimum award: $500
Deadline: April 1
College level: Graduate
Majors/Fields: Accounting
Criteria: Applicant must be planning to pursue a master's degree, have a minimum 3.0 GPA, be at least in junior standing, and demonstrate good character. Award may be used only at sponsoring institution.
Contact: E. R. Winzer, Director of Student Financial Aid.

Business Administration/ Management

140   ABWA Severn River Chapter Scholarship

American Business Women's Association (ABWA) Severn River Chapter
P.O. Box 119
Severna Park, MD 21147
Average award: $1,000
Maximum number of awards: 2
Minimum number of awards: 1
Deadline: February 1
College level: Freshman, Sophomore, Junior, Senior
Majors/Fields: Business
Criteria: Applicant must be a woman who is a U.S. citizen and a resident of Anne Arundel County, Md. In addition, she must be seeking a business or professional career, have a minimum 3.0 GPA, and demonstrate financial need. Selection is based upon scholastic standing and number of applicants for any particular year. Awarded every year.
Contact: Education Chairman.

141   Administration and Business Alumni Scholarship

Louisiana Tech University
P.O. Box 7925
Ruston, LA 71272
(318) 257-2641
Average award: $1,000
Number of awards: 2
Deadline: December 1
College level: Freshman
Majors/Fields: Business
Criteria: Selection is based upon high academic qualifications, extracurricular activities, financial need, and potential for success in business. Awarded every year. Award may be used only at sponsoring institution.
Contact: E. R. Winzer, Director of Student Financial Aid.

142   Alexander Hamilton Life Insurance Scholarship

Utah State University
Logan, UT 84322-0160
(801) 750-1129
Average award: $1,000
Number of awards: 2
Deadline: March 1
College level: Sophomore, Junior, Senior
Majors/Fields: Business
Criteria: Awarded every year. Award may be used only at sponsoring institution.
Contact: Mark Tenhoeue, Director of High School/College Relations.

143   Alma-Hal Reagan MBA Fellowship

University of Tennessee, Knoxville
Financial Aid Office
115 Student Services Building
Knoxville, TN 37994
(615) 974-3131
Average award: $6,000
Deadline: February 1
College level: Graduate
Majors/Fields: Business administration
Criteria: Selection is based upon academic achievement. Scholarship is renewable. Awarded every year. Award may be used only at sponsoring institution.
Contact: Business Administration, 52 Glocker Business Administration Building, Knoxville, TN 37996, (615) 974-5096.

144   American Institute for Economic Research Fellowship–Summer Program

American Institute for Economic Research
Director of Education
Great Barrington, MA 01230
(413) 528-1216
Average award: $1,000
Number of awards: 12
Deadline: March 31
College level: Graduate, Doctoral
Majors/Fields: Economics
Criteria: Applicant must be a graduating senior applying to a doctoral program in economics or a student currently enrolled in such a program. Scholarship is renewable. Awarded every year.
Contact: Pamela P. Allard, Assistant to the Director.

145   Anthony Robert Scott Scholarship

Boise State University
1910 University Drive
Boise, ID 83725
(208) 385-1664
Minimum award: $1,000
Number of awards: 4
Deadline: March 1
College level: Sophomore, Junior, Senior
Majors/Fields: Business
Criteria: Applicant must be enrolled for 12 credits per semester and demonstrate financial need. Awarded every year. Award may be used only at sponsoring institution.
Contact: Chris Woodward, Financial Aid Counselor.

146 Arthur and Genevieve Roth Scholarship

Kosciuszko Foundation
15 East 65th Street
New York, NY 10021
(212) 734-2130
Average award: $1,000
Deadline: January 15
Majors/Fields: Banking, business administration, finance
Criteria: Awarded to U.S. citizens of Polish extraction. Preference is given to those who plan to attend the Arthur T. Roth Sch of Business Administration of Long Island U. Awarded every year.
Contact: Scholarships.

147 Bellingham Rotary Club Scholarship

Western Washington University
516 High Street
Bellingham, WA 98226-9006
(206) 650-3471
Maximum award: Tuition, books, and fees
Number of awards: 2
Deadline: March 31
College level: Junior, Senior
Majors/Fields: Business, economics
Criteria: Selection is based upon academic performance and extracurricular activities. Satisfactory progress is required to retain scholarship for an additional year. Awarded every year. Award may be used only at sponsoring institution.
Contact: College of Business and Economics, 419 Parks Hall, Bellingham, WA 98225, (206) 650-3896.

148 Ben Barnett Ph.D. Scholarship

University of Oklahoma
University Affairs
900 Asp Avenue, Room 236
Norman, OK 73019-0401
(405) 325-1701
Average award: $5,000
Number of awards: 2
Deadline: February 8
College level: Doctoral
Majors/Fields: Business administration
Criteria: Applicant must be a full-time student with high GMAT scores and GPA. Satisfactory progress is required to retain scholarship for two additional years. Awarded every year. Award may be used only at sponsoring institution.
Contact: Office of Graduate Programs, College of Business Administration, 307 West Brooks, Norman, OK 73019, (405) 325-4107.

149 Carthy Foundation Scholarship in Management

University of Calgary
2500 University Drive, NW
Calgary, Alberta, CN T2N 1N4
(403) 220-7872
Average award: $3,800
Number of awards: 1
Deadline: June 15
College level: Senior
Majors/Fields: Management
Criteria: Selection is based upon academic merit. Awarded every year. Award may be used only at sponsoring institution.
Contact: J. Van Housen, Director of Student Awards and Financial Aid.

150 Dean's Business Scholarship

DePaul University
25 East Jackson Boulevard
Suite 100
Chicago, IL 60604
(312) 362-8704
Average award: $3,500
Maximum award: $7,500
Minimum award: $1,500
Number of awards: 62
Deadline: February 1
College level: Freshman
Majors/Fields: Business, commerce
Criteria: Applicant must rank in the top tenth of secondary school class, have a minimum composite ACT score of 27 (combined SAT I score of 1100), and demonstrate leadership and a strong commitment to the study of business. Minimum 3.0 GPA as a full-time College of Commerce student is required to retain scholarship. Awarded every year. Award may be used only at sponsoring institution.
Contact: Jennifer Sparrow, Associate Director of Admissions.

151 Dean's Business Transfer Scholarship

DePaul University
25 East Jackson Boulevard
Suite 100
Chicago, IL 60604
(312) 362-8704
Average award: $3,000
Maximum award: $4,000
Minimum award: $1,500
Number of awards: 45
Deadline: July 1
College level: Transfer students
Majors/Fields: Commerce
Criteria: Applicant must be a transfer from an Illinois community college. Scholarship is renewable. Awarded every year. Award may be used only at sponsoring institution.
Contact: Jennifer Sparrow, Associate Director of Admissions.

152 Donald H. Cole Graduate Fellowship

Western Washington University
516 High Street
Bellingham, WA 98226-9006
(206) 650-3471
Maximum award: $3,000
Number of awards: 1
College level: Graduate
Majors/Fields: Business administration
Criteria: Applicant must be a student in the Masters of Business Administration program. Awarded every year. Award may be used only at sponsoring institution.
Contact: College of Business and Economics, 419 Parks Hall, Bellingham, WA 98225, (206) 650-3896.

153 Doug and Luella Glasgow Memorial Scholarship

Boise State University
1910 University Drive
Boise, ID 83725
(208) 385-1664
Minimum award: $1,000
Number of awards: 4
Deadline: March 1
College level: Freshman, Sophomore, Junior, Senior, Graduate
Majors/Fields: Management
Criteria: Applicant must be enrolled for 12 credits per semester. Awarded every year. Award may be used only at sponsoring institution.
Contact: Chris Woodward, Financial Aid Counselor.

154   Exceptional Student Fellowship

State Farm Companies Foundation
One State Farm Plaza
Bloomington, IL 61710
(309) 766-2161
Minimum award: $3,000
Number of awards: 50
Deadline: February 15
College level: Senior, Graduate
Majors/Fields: Business
Criteria: Applicant must be nominated by the dean of college or department head. Selection is based upon demonstrated leadership in extracurricular activities, scholarship, character, potential business administrative capacity, and recommendations. Applicant must be enrolled full-time, a U.S. citizen, and have a minimum 3.4 GPA. Awarded every year.
Contact: Lynne Tammeus, Senior Program Coordinator, One State Farm Plaza, SC-3, Bloomington, IL 61710, (309) 766-2039.

155   First Security Foundation Scholarship

Utah State University
Logan, UT 84322-0160
(801) 750-1129
Average award: $1,666
Number of awards: 2
Deadline: March 1
College level: Junior, Senior
Majors/Fields: Banking, finance
Criteria: Awarded every year. Award may be used only at sponsoring institution.
Contact: Mark Tenhoeue, Director of High School/College Relations.

156   Fleming Companies, Inc. Scholarship

University of Oklahoma
University Affairs
900 Asp Avenue, Room 236
Norman, OK 73019-0401
(405) 325-1701
Average award: $2,500
Number of awards: 2
Deadline: February 8
College level: Junior
Majors/Fields: Accounting, management information systems, marketing
Criteria: Applicant must have a minimum 3.0 GPA. Preference is given to women and minorities. Awarded every year. Award may be used only at sponsoring institution.
Contact: College of Business Administration, 108 Adams Hall, Norman, OK 73019-0450, (405) 325-6021.

157   Fukunaga Foundation Graduate Scholarship

Trustees of Fukunaga Foundation Scholarship
P.O. Box 2788
Honolulu, HI 96803
(808) 521-6511
Minimum award: $1,500
Deadline: April 15
College level: Graduate
Majors/Fields: Business administration
Criteria: Applicant must have a bachelor's degree with a minimum "B" average from an accredited business administration program, demonstrate financial need, and be a permanent resident of Hawaii. He or she must also demonstrate the ability, industriousness, dependability, and determination needed to succeed in business within the Pacific Basin area. Awarded every year.
Contact: Scholarship Selection Committee.

158   Fukunaga Foundation Scholarship

Trustees of Fukunaga Foundation Scholarship
P.O. Box 2788
Honolulu, HI 96803
(808) 521-6511
Minimum award: $1,500
Maximum number of awards: 15
Minimum number of awards: 10
Deadline: April 15
College level: Graduate, unspecified undergraduate
Majors/Fields: Business administration
Criteria: Applicant must rank in top quarter of class, have a minimum 3.0 GPA, demonstrate financial need, and be a permanent resident of Hawaii (at least one year). He or she must also demonstrate the ability, industriousness, dependability, and determination needed to succeed in business within the Pacific Basin area. Applicant must maintain a minimum 3.0 GPA and full-time status to retain award. Awarded every year.
Contact: Scholarship Selection Committee.

159   General Motors (GM) Scholarship

New Mexico State University
Box 30001
Department 5100
Las Cruces, NM 88003-0001
(505) 646-4105
Average award: Tuition, books, stipend, and summer internship
Deadline: March 1
College level: Sophomore, Junior, Senior
Majors/Fields: Business
Criteria: Applicant must be a U.S. citizen with a minimum 3.2 cumulative GPA. Selection by GM personnel is based upon academic record, extracurricular activities, and long-term interest in the auto industry. Awarded every year. Award may be used only at sponsoring institution.
Contact: Advising Center, College of Business Administration and Economics, (505) 646-4084.

160   Golden State Minority Foundation Scholarship

Golden State Minority Foundation
1055 Wilshire Boulevard
Los Angeles, CA 90017
(800) 666-4763
Average award: $2,000
Number of awards: 100
Deadline: November 1 (Northern California, Houston); April 1 (Southern California); March 1 (Michigan)
College level: Junior, Senior, Graduate, Doctoral
Majors/Fields: Business administration, economics
Criteria: Applicant must attend school in or be a resident of California, Michigan, or Houston, Tex., be black, Latino, or Native American, and be a U.S. citizen or permanent legal resident. Applicant must be enrolled full-time, employed no more than 25 hours per week, have a minimum 3.0 GPA, and be majoring in business administration, economics, or a related field at a four-year college or university. Scholarship is renewable. Awarded every year.
Contact: Ivan A. Houston, President.

161   Grants for Research

International Foundation of Employee Benefit Plans
P.O. Box 69
Brookfield, WI 53008-0069
(414) 786-6700
Average award: $5,000
Maximum award: $10,000
Deadline: None
College level: Doctoral, post doctoral work
Majors/Fields: Employee benefits
Criteria: Applicant must be a U.S. or Canadian citizen.
Contact: Ellen Mlada, Research Assistant, 18700 W. Bluemound Road, Brookfield, WI 53008-0069, (414) 786-6710, extension 440.

162 Greater San Antonio Builders Association/ National Association of Home Builders Scholarship

University of Texas at San Antonio
Office of Student Financial Aid
6900 North Loop 1604 West
San Antonio, TX 78249-0687
(210) 691-4011
Average award: $1,000
Number of awards: 2
Deadline: November 1; July 1
College level: Freshman, Sophomore, Junior, Senior
Majors/Fields: Building, management
Criteria: Applicant must be a Texas resident. Minimum 2.75 GPA is required to retain scholarship. Awarded every year. Award may be used only at sponsoring institution.
Contact: Office of the Dean, College of Business, HB 4.01.23, (210) 691-4313.

163 H. Gordon Martin Scholarship

Northern Kentucky University
Administrative Center 416
Nunn Drive
Highland Heights, KY 41099-7101
(606) 572-5144
Average award: In-state tuition
Deadline: February 1
College level: Freshman
Majors/Fields: Business
Criteria: Applicant must be a graduate of Ludlow, Ky., high school with a minimum composite ACT score of 18. Awarded every year. Award may be used only at sponsoring institution.
Contact: Robert E. Sprague, Director of Financial Aid.

164 Haggen/Western Association of Food Chains Scholarship

Western Washington University
516 High Street
Bellingham, WA 98226-9006
(206) 650-3471
Average award: $1,000
Number of awards: 5
Deadline: March 31
College level: Freshman, Sophomore, Junior, Senior
Majors/Fields: Business
Criteria: Applicant must be interested in a career in the food supply industry. Satisfactory academic performance is required to retain scholarship for an additional year. Awarded every year. Award may be used only at sponsoring institution.
Contact: College of Business and Economics, 419 Parks Hall, Bellingham, WA 98225, (206) 650-3896.

165 Hutchison Memorial Scholarship

Boise State University
1910 University Drive
Boise, ID 83725
(208) 385-1664
Minimum award: $1,000
Number of awards: 2
Deadline: March 1
College level: Freshman, Sophomore, Junior, Senior, Graduate
Majors/Fields: Business administration
Criteria: Awarded every year. Award may be used only at sponsoring institution.
Contact: Chris Woodward, Financial Aid Counselor.

166 J. Fred and Wilma D. Holly Fellowship Endowment in Economics

University of Tennessee, Knoxville
Financial Aid Office
115 Student Services Building
Knoxville, TN 37994
(615) 974-3131
Average award: Tuition, room and board
Deadline: February 1
College level: Graduate, Doctoral
Majors/Fields: Economics
Criteria: Selection is based upon full-time enrollment in the Coll of Business Administration, successful academic performance, and financial need. Scholarship is renewable. Awarded every year. Award may be used only at sponsoring institution.
Contact: Business Administration, 52 Glocker Business Administration Building, Knoxville, TN 37996, (615) 974-5096.

167 John M. Olin School of Business Dean's Scholarship

Washington University
One Brookings Drive
Campus Box 1089
St. Louis, MO 63130
(314) 935-6000 or (800) 638-0700
Maximum award: $8,375
College level: Freshman
Majors/Fields: Business
Criteria: Applicant must apply under the Early Decision or Early Action plans. Selection is based upon academic merit without regard to financial need. Satisfactory academic progress is required to retain scholarship. Awarded every year. Award may be used only at sponsoring institution.
Contact: Office of Undergraduate Admission.

168 John P. Eager Scholarship

Association for Information and Image Management
AIIM Headquarters
1100 Wayne Avenue, Suite 1100
Silver Spring, MD 20910
Average award: $5,000
Number of awards: 1
Deadline: December 30
College level: Freshman, Sophomore, Junior, Senior
Majors/Fields: Business management, business services, computer science, data processing, engineering, technical school, industrial design, library science, photography, photographic lab technician, photographic scientist, physical science, mathematics, micrographics, information management, trade, vocational
Criteria: Applicant must have a minimum 3.0 GPA and submit a minimum 2500-word essay. Awarded every year.
Contact: Maureen Heffernan, Manager of Chapter Relations, 1100 Wayne Avenue, Suite 1100, Silver Spring, MD 20910.

169 Langroise Scholarship

Boise State University
1910 University Drive
Boise, ID 83725
(208) 385-1664
Minimum award: $1,000
Number of awards: 10
Deadline: March 1
College level: Freshman, Sophomore, Junior, Senior, Graduate
Majors/Fields: Business
Criteria: Applicant must be enrolled for 12 credits per semester and demonstrate financial need. Awarded every year. Award may be used only at sponsoring institution.
Contact: Chris Woodward, Financial Aid Counselor.

170 Michael and Francesca Marinelli Scholarships

National Italian American Foundation (NIAF)
Educational Scholarship Program
1860 19th Street, NW
Washington, DC 20009-5599
(202) 638-2137
Maximum award: $2,000
Minimum award: $1,000
Maximum number of awards: 3
Minimum number of awards: 1
Deadline: May 31
College level: Students accepted at the American U in Rome or attending Nova U, Fla.
Majors/Fields: Science, business
Criteria: Applicant must be Italian-American and submit transcript and demonstration of financial need. An essay outlining applicant's objectives and rationale for choice of profession is required. Awarded every year. Award may be used only at sponsoring institution.
Contact: Dr. Maria Lombardo, Education Director.

171 National Doctoral Fellowship in Business and Management

University of Oklahoma
University Affairs
900 Asp Avenue, Room 236
Norman, OK 73019-0401
(405) 325-1701
Average award: $10,000 plus tuition
Minimum award: $10,000
Deadline: February 8
College level: Doctoral
Majors/Fields: Business administration
Criteria: Applicant must be a full-time Ph.D. student, have high GMAT scores and GPA, and be a U.S. or Canadian citizen. Awarded every year. Award may be used only at sponsoring institution.
Contact: Office of Graduate Programs, College of Business Administration, 307 West Brooks, Norman, OK 73019, (405) 325-4107.

172 Noble Foundation Scholarship

University of Oklahoma
University Affairs
900 Asp Avenue, Room 236
Norman, OK 73019-0401
(405) 325-1701
Maximum award: $5,000
Minimum award: $1,000
Deadline: February 8
College level: Graduate, Doctoral
Majors/Fields: Business administration, economics
Criteria: Applicant must be a U.S. resident, a full-time student, and score in the 85th percentile or above on the GMAT or GRE. Awarded every year. Award may be used only at sponsoring institution.
Contact: Office of Graduate Programs, College of Business Administration, 307 West Brooks, Norman, OK 73019, (405) 325-4107.

173 Ore-Ida Foods Business Scholarship

Boise State University
1910 University Drive
Boise, ID 83725
(208) 385-1664
Minimum award: $1,000
Number of awards: 3
Deadline: March 1
College level: Junior, Senior
Majors/Fields: Business
Criteria: Applicant must be enrolled for 12 credits per semester. Special consideration is given to children of Ore-Ida employees and minorities. Awarded every year. Award may be used only at sponsoring institution.
Contact: Chris Woodward, Financial Aid Counselor.

174 Phi Chi Theta Scholarship

Phi Chi Theta Foundation
8656 Totempole Drive
Cincinnati, OH 45249
Maximum award: $1,000
Number of awards: 3
Deadline: May 1
College level: Sophomore, Junior, Senior, Graduate, Doctoral
Majors/Fields: Business, economics
Criteria: Applicant must be a woman and demonstrate leadership, motivation, scholastic achievement, and financial need. Applicant should send a stamped, self-addressed envelope for the application. Transcript and recommendations are required. Reapplication is required in order to continue scholarship. Awarded every year.
Contact: Scholarship Chairman.

175 Quality Cup Scholarship

Rochester Institute of Technology
One Lomb Memorial Drive
Rochester, NY 14623
(716) 475-2186
Average award: $5,000
Number of awards: 10
Deadline: January 1
College level: Freshman
Majors/Fields: Business, engineering
Criteria: Applicant must be selected as an RIT/USA Today Quality Cup Medal Winner by a participating high school and participate in a scholarship competition on campus. Scholarship is renewable. Awarded every year. Award may be used only at sponsoring institution.
Contact: Verna Hazen, Director of Financial Aid.

176 Richard D. Irwin Doctoral Fellowship

Richard D. Irwin Foundation
1333 Burr Ridge Parkway
Burr Ridge, IL 60521
(708) 789-4000
Average award: $2,250
Maximum award: $2,500
Minimum award: $2,000
Number of awards: 20
Deadline: February 15
College level: Doctoral
Majors/Fields: Business, economics
Criteria: Applicant must be admitted into an accredited doctoral program at a school in the U.S. or Canada and have completed all work except writing the dissertation and passing final oral exams. Preference is given to applicants whose contribution to teaching is to be made in the U.S. or Canada. Awarded every year.
Contact: Gail Ryba, Agent for the Foundation.

177 Sam M. Walton Scholarship in Business

University of Missouri–Columbia
High School and Transfer Relations
219 Jesse Hall
Columbia, MO 65211
(800) 225-6075 (in-state), (314) 882-2456
Average award: $5,000
Deadline: March 1
College level: Freshman
Majors/Fields: Business, finance, management, marketing
Criteria: Applicant must intend to pursue a career in retailing and work part-time in retailing while attending the Coll of Business and Public Administration. Selection is based upon financial need, academic achievement, and an expressed interest in retailing. Satisfactory academic progress toward a business degree and fulfillment of requirements are required to retain scholarship. Awarded every year. Award may be used only at sponsoring institution.
Contact: Dr. Lissa Scheer, College of Business and Public Administration, 114 Middlebush Hall, (314) 882-3282.

178   Samuel D. Southern Scholarship

University of Calgary
2500 University Drive, NW
Calgary, Alberta, CN T2N 1N4
(403) 220-7872
Average award: $1,250
Number of awards: 2
Deadline: June 15
College level: Senior
Majors/Fields: Finance, management
Criteria: Selection is based upon academic merit. Applicant must have been a resident of the province of Alberta for at least five years. Awarded every year. Award may be used only at sponsoring institution.
Contact: J. Van Housen, Director of Student Awards & Financial Aid.

179   Shell Oil Scholarship

Utah State University
Logan, UT 84322-0160
(801) 750-1129
Average award: $2,000
Deadline: March 1
College level: Graduate, Doctoral
Majors/Fields: Business
Criteria: Awarded every year. Award may be used only at sponsoring institution.
Contact: Mark Tenhoeue, Director of High School/College Relations.

180   T.L. James Scholarship Internship

Louisiana Tech University
P.O. Box 7925
Ruston, LA 71272
(318) 257-2641
Average award: $1,250
Deadline: December 1
College level: Freshman
Majors/Fields: Business
Criteria: Applicant must have at least two of these qualifications: rank in top tenth of secondary school class, minimum composite ACT score of 25, or minimum 3.0 GPA. Consideration is given to financial need and leadership potential. Scholarship is renewable. Awarded every year. Award may be used only at sponsoring institution.
Contact: E. R. Winzer, Director of Student Financial Aid.

181   Texas Business Hall of Fame Scholarship

University of Texas at San Antonio
Office of Student Financial Aid
6900 North Loop 1604 West
San Antonio, TX 78249-0687
(210) 691-4011
Average award: $2,500
Number of awards: 1
Deadline: March 1
College level: Senior, Graduate
Majors/Fields: Business
Criteria: Applicant must be a U.S. citizen who is a graduating senior or a first-year M.B.A. student. Award is for four semesters. Awarded every year. Award may be used only at sponsoring institution.
Contact: Office of the Dean, College of Business, HB 4.01.23.

182   Thomas Dixon Scholarship

Boise State University
1910 University Drive
Boise, ID 83725
(208) 385-1664
Minimum award: $1,000
Number of awards: 4
Deadline: March 1
College level: Freshman, Sophomore, Junior, Senior, Graduate
Majors/Fields: Finance
Criteria: Applicant must be enrolled for 12 credits per semester and demonstrate financial need. Awarded every year. Award may be used only at sponsoring institution.
Contact: Chris Woodward, Financial Aid Counselor.

183   Walter D. Hershey Memorial Scholarship

Portland State University
P.O. Box 751
Portland, OR 97207-5252
(503) 725-5270
Maximum award: $1,200
Minimum award: $1,000
Number of awards: 4
Deadline: in February
College level: Junior
Majors/Fields: Business
Criteria: Awarded every year. Award may be used only at sponsoring institution.
Contact: Scholarships, School of Business Administration–Student Services, (503) 725-3712.

184   Western Association of Food Chains

Boise State University
1910 University Drive
Boise, ID 83725
(208) 385-1664
Minimum award: $1,000
Number of awards: 5
Deadline: March 1
College level: Freshman, Sophomore, Junior, Senior, Graduate
Majors/Fields: Business, food industry
Criteria: Applicant must be enrolled for 12 credits per semester and desire a career in the food industry. Awarded every year. Award may be used only at sponsoring institution.
Contact: Chris Woodward, Financial Aid Counselor.

185   William A. and Virginia Lomax Marbury Endowment for Business Scholarship

Louisiana Tech University
P.O. Box 7925
Ruston, LA 71272
(318) 257-2641
Average award: $1,200
Deadline: December 1
College level: Freshman
Majors/Fields: Business
Criteria: Selection is based upon academic performance and potential as well as financial need. Preference is given to applicants interested in insurance or banking. Continued financial need and satisfactory academic performance are required to retain scholarship. Awarded every year. Award may be used only at sponsoring institution.
Contact: E. R. Winzer, Director of Student Financial Aid.

Hospitality/Hospitality Administration

186   AHF Scholarship

American Hotel Foundation (AHF)
1201 New York Avenue, NW, Suite 600
Washington, DC 20005-3931
Maximum award: $1,000
Minimum award: $500
Number of awards: 150
College level: Sophomore, Junior, Senior
Majors/Fields: Hospitality, lodging program
Criteria: Applicant must be enrolled full time at an AHF approved two- or four-year college or university. Scholarship is renewable. Awarded every year.
Contact: Scholarships.

187   Capstone Hotel Scholarship

University of Alabama–Tuscaloosa
Box 870162
Tuscaloosa, AL 35487-0162
(205) 348-6756
Average award: $2,000
Number of awards: 2
Deadline: February 1
College level: Junior, Senior
Majors/Fields: Hospitality management, restaurant management
Criteria: One award is for a junior and one for a senior. Awarded every year. Award may be used only at sponsoring institution.
Contact: Dean, College of Human Environmental Sciences, Box 870158, Tuscaloosa, AL 35487-0158, (205) 348-6250.

188   HJ Heinz Graduate Degree Fellowship

Educational Foundation of the National Restaurant Association
250 South Wacker Drive
Suite 1400
Chicago, IL 60606-5834
(800) 765-2122
Maximum award: $2,000
Minimum award: $1,000
Number of awards: 7
Deadline: February 15
College level: Doctoral
Majors/Fields: Food service, hospitality
Criteria: Applicant must be a high school or college-level hospitality educator pursuing a postgraduate degree in a full-time program or on a substantial part-time basis.
Contact: Scholarship Program Coordinator.

189   IAHA Scholarship

International Association of Hospitality Accountants, Inc. (IAHA)
P.O. Box 203008
Austin, TX 78720-3008
(512) 346-5680
Average award: $1,000
Number of awards: 4
Deadline: March 31
College level: Sophomore, Junior, Senior
Majors/Fields: Accounting, hospitality management, management information systems
Criteria: Applicant must have a minimum 3.0 GPA. Selection is based upon resume, transcript, essay, references, and community involvement. Awarded every year.
Contact: Scholarship.

190   IFEC Foodservice Communicators Scholarship

International Foodservice Editorial Council
P.O. Box 491
Hyde Park, NY 12538
(914) 452-4345
Average award: $1,500
Maximum award: $2,000
Minimum award: $1,000
Number of awards: 4
Deadline: April 15
College level: Sophomore, Junior, Senior, Graduate, Doctoral
Majors/Fields: Communications arts, food service, hospitality
Criteria: Applicant must demonstrate financial need. Selection is based upon essay. Awarded every year.
Contact: Carol Metz, Executive Director.

191   Shelby Williams Fund for Excellence in Human Ecology

University of Tennessee, Knoxville
Financial Aid Office
115 Student Services Building
Knoxville, TN 37994
(615) 974-3131
Average award: $1,000
Deadline: February 1
College level: Freshman, Sophomore, Junior, Senior
Majors/Fields: Hotel administration, interior design, restaurant administration
Criteria: Preference is given to applicants who attended high school in the greater Morristown area. Length of awards varies. Awarded every year. Award may be used only at sponsoring institution.
Contact: College of Human Ecology, 112 Jesse Harris Building, Knoxville, TN 37996, (615) 974-6276.

192   Teacher Work Study Grants

Educational Foundation of the National Restaurant Association
250 South Wacker Drive
Suite 1400
Chicago, IL 60606-5834
(800) 765-2122
Average award: $2,000
Number of awards: 25
Deadline: February 15
College level: Educators and administrators
Majors/Fields: Food service, hospitality
Criteria: Applicant must be an educator or administrator who wishes to update his or her knowledge of the food service industry by obtaining eight weeks of hands-on experience in the industry.
Contact: Scholarship Program Coordinator.

193   Undergradute Scholarship Program

Educational Foundation of the National Restaurant Association
250 South Wacker Drive
Suite 1400
Chicago, IL 60606-5834
(800) 765-2122
Maximum award: $10,000
Minimum award: $500
Number of awards: 100
Deadline: March 1
College level: Sophomore, Junior, Senior
Majors/Fields: Food service, hospitality
Criteria: Applicant must have a minimum 3.0 GPA and 1,000 hours of work experience in the food service/hospitality industry. Awarded every year.
Contact: Scholarship Program Coordinator.

Human Resources Management

194   AP&ICS/E&R Fund Scholarship

American Production & Inventory Control Society, Inc.(AP&ICS)/ Education & Research (E&R) Foundation, Inc.
500 West Annandale Road
Falls Church, VA 22046-4274
(703) 237-8344, (800) 444-2742, extension 202 or 331
Maximum award: $1,750
Minimum award: $100
Number of awards: 162
Deadline: May 15
College level: Sophomore, Junior, Senior, Graduate, Doctoral
Majors/Fields: Resource management
Criteria: Applicant must be enrolled either part- or full-time at submission time. Reapplication is required for renewal. Awarded every year.
Contact: Michael H. Lythgoe or Wendy Whittaker, Director, E&R Foundation, (703) 237-8450.

Insurance

195 Actuarial Scholarships for Minority Students

Society of Actuaries/Casualty Actuarial Society
475 North Martingale Road
Suite 800
Schaumburg, IL 60173
(708) 706-3500
Average award: $1,200
Maximum award: $1,800
Minimum award: $600
Number of awards: 33
Deadline: May 1
College level: Freshman, Sophomore, Junior, Senior
Majors/Fields: Actuarial science
Criteria: Selection is based upon racial/ethnic background, financial need, and academic merit. Recipient must reapply for renewal. Awarded every year.
Contact: Susan Martz, Minority Recruiting Coordinator.

196 Calgary Life Underwriters Scholarship in Insurance and Risk Management

University of Calgary
2500 University Drive, NW
Calgary, Alberta, CN T2N 1N4
(403) 220-7872
Average award: $3,000
Number of awards: 1
Deadline: June 15
College level: Senior
Majors/Fields: Insurance, risk management
Criteria: Applicant must have a minimum 3.0 GPA. Selection is based upon academic merit, extracurricular activities, and interest in the life insurance industry. Awarded every year. Award may be used only at sponsoring institution.
Contact: J. Van Housen, Director of Student Awards & Financial Aid.

197 Doctoral Dissertation Award in Insurance/Business

State Farm Companies Foundation
One State Farm Plaza
Bloomington, IL 61710
(309) 766-2161
Minimum award: $10,000
Number of awards: 6
Deadline: March 31
College level: Doctoral
Majors/Fields: Business, insurance
Criteria: Award is available to doctoral candidates at the dissertation stage of insurance or business programs. Selection is based upon scholastic achievement, quality of doctoral dissertation proposal, and recommendations of director of doctoral program and other faculty members. Awarded every year.
Contact: Lynne Tammeus, Senior Program Coordinator.

198 Encon Scholarship

University of Calgary
2500 University Drive, NW
Calgary, Alberta, CN T2N 1N4
(403) 220-7872
Average award: $3,000
Number of awards: 1
Deadline: June 15
College level: Senior
Majors/Fields: Insurance, risk management
Criteria: Selection is based upon academic merit. Awarded every year. Award may be used only at sponsoring institution.
Contact: J. Van Housen, Director of Student Awards & Financial Aid.

Marketing/Sales/Retailing

199 Barber Dairies Scholarship

University of Alabama–Tuscaloosa
Box 870162
Tuscaloosa, AL 35487-0162
(205) 348-6756
Average award: $2,500
Number of awards: 3
Deadline: March 1
College level: Junior, Senior
Majors/Fields: Marketing
Criteria: Applicant must demonstrate financial need, enterprise, and campus leadership. Awarded every year. Award may be used only at sponsoring institution.
Contact: Department of Management and Marketing Scholarships, College of Commerce and Business Administration, Box 870225, Tuscaloosa, AL 35487-0225, (205) 348-6183.

200 Harry A. Applegate Memorial Scholarship

Distributive Education Clubs of America (DECA)
1908 Association Drive
Reston, VA 22091
(703) 860-5000
Average award: $1,000
Maximum award: $1,500
Maximum number of awards: 20
Minimum number of awards: 15
Deadline: Second Monday in March
College level: Freshman, Sophomore, Junior, Senior, Graduate
Majors/Fields: Marketing, marketing education, merchandising
Criteria: Applicant must be a DECA member. Selection is based upon academic record, SAT I or ACT scores, leadership, and financial need. Reapplication is required to retain scholarship. Awarded every year.
Contact: Tim Coffey, Director of Corporate Marketing.

201 NEDA Education Foundation Scholarship Fund

National Electronic Distributors Assocation (NEDA) Education Foundation
35 East Wacker Drive, Suite 3202
Chicago, IL 60601
Maximum award: $2,000
Minimum award: $1,000
Deadline: June 1
College level: Sophomore, Junior, Senior
Majors/Fields: Electronic distribution, industrial distribution, marketing, business administration
Criteria: Selection is based upon career goals, grades, college entrance exam scores, extracurricular activities, ability to communicate, and financial need. Recipient must submit completed application and referrals every year.
Contact: Scholarships.

202 Sonoco Annual Scholarship

Clemson University
G-01 Sikes Hall
Clemson, SC 29634-5123
(803) 656-2280
Average award: $1,250
Number of awards: 2
Deadline: March 1
College level: Freshman, Sophomore, Junior, Senior
Majors/Fields: Packaging science
Criteria: Applicant must have a minimum 2.0 cumulative GPA. Awarded every year. Award may be used only at sponsoring institution.
Contact: Marvin Carmichael, Director of Financial Aid.

Real Estate

203　Appraisal Institute Education Trust Scholarship

Appraisal Institute
875 North Michigan Avenue
Suite 2400
Chicago, IL 60611-1980
(312) 335-4100
Maximum award: $3,000
Minimum award: $2,000
Number of awards: 50
Deadline: March 15
College level: Sophomore, Junior, Senior, Graduate, Doctoral
Majors/Fields: Land economics, real estate, real estate appraisal
Criteria: Applicant must be a U.S. citizen and full-time undergraduate or graduate student. Applicant must submit recommendations, statement, transcripts, and proposed study program. Selection is based upon academic excellence. Financial need is not a factor. Awarded every year.
Contact: Charlotte Timms, Scholarship Coordinator, (312) 335-4136.

Secretarial Studies

204　NCRA Scholarship Fund

National Court Reporters Association
8224 Old Courthouse Road
Vienna, VA 22182-3808
(703) 556-6272
Maximum award: $1,500
Minimum award: $500
Number of awards: 3
Deadline: April 1
College level: Sophomore
Majors/Fields: Court reporting
Criteria: Selection is based upon essay and academic record. Awarded every year.
Contact: Penny Compher, Assistant Director for Education.

Transportation/Traffic Management

205　A.J. (Andy) Spielman Scholarship

American Society of Travel Agents (ASTA) Scholarship Foundation, Inc.
1101 King Street
Alexandria, VA 22314
(703) 739-2782
Average award: $2,000
Number of awards: 3
Deadline: June 23
College level: Proprietary travel school
Majors/Fields: Travel
Criteria: Applicant must be re-entering the work force in the field of travel and submit a 500-word essay. Reapplication is required for renewal. Awarded every year.
Contact: Scholarships.

206　A.L. Simmons Scholarship

American Society of Travel Agents (ASTA) Scholarship Foundation, Inc.
1101 King Street
Alexandria, VA 22314
(703) 739-2782
Average award: $2,000
Number of awards: 2
Deadline: June 23
College level: Doctoral
Majors/Fields: Tourism, travel
Criteria: Applicant must submit upper-level paper or thesis (15-50 pages) on a travel and tourism topic which has been or will be submitted to a professor. Reapplication is required for renewal. Awarded every year.
Contact: Scholarships.

207　Air Travel Card Grant

American Society of Travel Agents (ASTA) Scholarship Foundation, Inc.
1101 King Street
Alexandria, VA 22314
(703) 739-2782
Average award: $3,000
Number of awards: 1
Deadline: June 23
College level: Freshman, Sophomore, Junior, Senior
Majors/Fields: Business travel management, tourism, travel
Criteria: Applicant must submit a 500-word essay. Recipient must reapply for renewal. Awarded every year.
Contact: Scholarships.

208　Alaska Airlines Scholarship

American Society of Travel Agents (ASTA) Scholarship Foundation, Inc.
1101 King Street
Alexandria, VA 22314
(703) 739-2782
Average award: $1,000
Number of awards: 3
Deadline: June 23
College level: Sophomore, Junior, Senior
Majors/Fields: Travel, tourism
Criteria: Applicant must submit a 500-word essay. Preference is given to applicants from the U of Alaska and U of Washington. Reapplication is required for renewal. Awarded every year.
Contact: Scholarships.

209　American Express Travel Scholarship

American Society of Travel Agents (ASTA) Scholarship Foundation, Inc.
1101 King Street
Alexandria, VA 22314
(703) 739-2782
Average award: $2,500
Number of awards: 1
Deadline: June 23
College level: Freshman, Sophomore, Junior, Senior, proprietary travel school
Majors/Fields: Tourism, travel
Criteria: Applicant must submit a 500-word essay on the travel industry's future. Reapplication is required. Awarded every year.
Contact: Scholarships.

210　Arizona Chapter Gold

American Society of Travel Agents (ASTA) Scholarship Foundation, Inc.
1101 King Street
Alexandria, VA 22314
(703) 739-2782
Average award: $2,000
Number of awards: 1
Deadline: June 23
College level: Sophomore, Junior, Senior
Majors/Fields: Travel, tourism
Criteria: Applicant must be enrolled in an accredited four-year college in the state of Arizona and submit a 500-word essay. Reapplication is required for renewal. Awarded every year.
Contact: Scholarships.

211　Boeing Student Research Award

Travel & Tourism Research Association (TTRA)
Box 516
Pittsford, NY 14534
(716) 475-6061
Maximum award: $1,000
Minimum award: $250
Deadline: February 15
Majors/Fields: Travel research
Criteria: Selection is based upon quality of research, creativity of approach, relationship to travel/tourism, usefulness, applicability, and quality of presentation.
Contact: Dr. James F. Burke, Awards.

212 George Reinke Scholarship

American Society of Travel Agents (ASTA) Scholarship Foundation, Inc.
1101 King Street
Alexandria, VA 22314
(703) 739-2782
Average award: $1,000
Number of awards: 3
Deadline: June 23
College level: Proprietary travel school, junior college
Majors/Fields: Travel
Criteria: Applicant must demonstrate financial need and submit a 500-word essay. Reapplication is required for renewal.
Contact: Scholarships.

213 Holland-America Line Westours, Inc. Scholarship

American Society of Travel Agents (ASTA) Scholarship Foundation, Inc.
1101 King Street
Alexandria, VA 22314
(703) 739-2782
Average award: $1,200
Number of awards: 4
Deadline: June 23
College level: Freshman, Sophomore, Junior, Senior, Graduate, Doctoral, proprietary travel schools
Majors/Fields: Tourism, travel
Criteria: Applicant must submit a 500-word essay on the future of the cruise industry. Reapplication is required for renewal. Awarded every year.
Contact: Scholarships.

214 Joseph R. Stone Scholarships

American Society of Travel Agents (ASTA) Scholarship Foundation, Inc.
1101 King Street
Alexandria, VA 22314
(703) 739-2782
Average award: $2,400
Number of awards: 2
Deadline: June 23
College level: Freshman, Sophomore, Junior, Senior
Majors/Fields: Travel
Criteria: Applicant must be the child of a travel industry employee, have a minimum 3.0 GPA, and submit a 500-word essay. Reapplication is required for renewal. Awarded every year.
Contact: Scholarships.

215 NDTA Merit Scholarship

San Francisco Bay Area Chapter–National Defense Transportation Association
P.O. Box 24676
Oakland, CA 94623
(415) 872-4233
Average award: $2,000
Number of awards: 2
Deadline: March 31
College level: Freshman, Sophomore, Junior, Senior
Majors/Fields: Business, engineering, environmental studies, planning, transportation
Criteria: Applicant must be a U.S. citizen preparing for a career related to transportation. Selection is based upon scholastic ability, potential, professional interest, and character. Financial need is also considered. Awarded every year.
Contact: Scholarships.

216 Pollard Scholarship

American Society of Travel Agents (ASTA) Scholarship Foundation, Inc.
1101 King Street
Alexandria, VA 22314
(703) 739-2782
Average award: $1,500
Number of awards: 2
Deadline: June 23
Majors/Fields: Travel
Criteria: Applicant must be re-entering the job market, have been out of high school for at least five years, and submit a 500-word essay. Reapplication is required for renewal. Awarded every year.
Contact: Scholarships.

217 Princess Cruises and Princess Tours Scholarships

American Society of Travel Agents (ASTA) Scholarship Foundation, Inc.
1101 King Street
Alexandria, VA 22314
(703) 739-2782
Average award: $1,200
Number of awards: 2
Deadline: June 23
College level: Freshman, Sophomore, Junior, Senior, proprietary travel school
Majors/Fields: Travel, tourism
Criteria: Applicant must submit a 300-word essay on two features that cruise ships will need to offer passengers in the next ten years. Reapplication is required for renewal. Awarded every year.
Contact: Scholarships.

218 Southern California Chapter/Pleasant Hawaiian Holidays Scholarship

American Society of Travel Agents (ASTA) Scholarship Foundation, Inc.
1101 King Street
Alexandria, VA 22314
(703) 739-2782
Average award: $1,500
Number of awards: 2
Deadline: June 23
College level: Freshman, Sophomore, Junior, Senior
Majors/Fields: Travel, tourism
Criteria: Applicant must be a U.S. citizen, have a minimum 3.0 GPA, have at least one parent employed in the travel industry (car rental, airline, travel agency, hotel) in the southern California area, and submit a 1000-word essay. Reapplication is required for renewal. Awarded every year.
Contact: Scholarships.

219 TCI Memorial Scholarships

Transportation Clubs International (TCI) Scholarship
1275 Kamus Drive
Suite 101
Fox Island, WA 98333
(206) 549-2251
Minimum award: $1,000
Deadline: April 30
College level: Sophomore, Junior, Senior
Majors/Fields: Traffic management, transportation
Criteria: Applicant must be a TCI member or the dependent of a member. Selection is based upon scholastic ability, potential, professional interest, character, and financial need.
Contact: Transportation Clubs International Scholarships.

Communications

Communications

220   Alpha and Omega Fraternity Scholarship

Southwest Texas State University
J. C. Kellam Building
San Marcos, TX 78666
(512) 245-2340
Average award: $1,000
Deadline: March 15
College level: Junior, Senior
Criteria: Applicant must have a minimum 3.0 GPA and be active in journalism, theatre, speech, and/or communications. Award may be used only at sponsoring institution.
Contact: School of Fine Arts and Communications, San Marcos, TX 78666, (512) 245-2315.

221   Art Edgerton/Northwest Ohio Black Media Association Scholarship

University of Toledo
Financial Aid Office
Toledo, OH 43606-3390
(419) 537-2056
Average award: $2,000
Number of awards: 1
Deadline: January 28
College level: Freshman, Sophomore, Junior, Senior
Majors/Fields: Communication
Criteria: Applicant must be African-American. Selection is based on essay, interview, and demonstration of leadership. Awarded every year. Award may be used only at sponsoring institution.
Contact: Clyde Hughes, P.O. Box 9232, Toledo, OH 43697-9232, (419) 245-6000.

222   J. Kelly Sisk Communication Scholarship

University of Alabama-Tuscaloosa
Box 870162
Tuscaloosa, AL 35487-0162
(205) 348-6756
Average award: $1,000
Maximum number of awards: 7
Minimum number of awards: 6
Deadline: February 15
College level: Freshman, Sophomore, Junior, Senior
Majors/Fields: Communication
Criteria: Applicant must demonstrate academic excellence. Awarded every year. Award may be used only at sponsoring institution.
Contact: Scholarship Committee, College of Communication, Box 870172, Tuscaloosa, AL 35487-0172.

223   Jack B. Eckley Minority Scholarships in Telecommunications

University of San Francisco
2130 Fulton Street
San Francisco, CA 94117-1080
(415) 666-6771
Number of awards: 2
Deadline: June 30 (fall); November 30 (spring); April 30 (summer)
College level: Graduate students
Majors/Fields: Telecommunications
Criteria: Applicant must be a minority, a California resident, and a full-time student. Award may be used only at sponsoring institution.
Contact: Telecommunications Program, McLaren School of Business/University of San Francisco, 2130 Fulton Street, San Francisco, CA 94117-1080, (415) 666-2504.

224   Leonard M. Perryman Communications Scholarship for Ethnic Minority Students

Perryman Communications Scholarship for Ethnic Minority Students
United Methodist Communications
475 Riverside Drive, Suite 1901
New York, NY 10115
(212) 663-8900
Average award: $2,500
Number of awards: 1
Deadline: March 1
College level: Junior, Senior
Majors/Fields: Journalism, mass communications, religious communication
Criteria: Applicant must be an ethnic minority student intending to pursue a career in religious communication, including audio-visual media, and electronic and print journalism. Awarded every year.
Contact: Inday Day, Scholarship Coordinator.

225   STC Scholarship

Society for Technical Communication (STC)
901 North Stuart Street
Suite 904
Arlington, VA 22203-1854
(703) 522-4114
Average award: $2,000
Number of awards: 14
Deadline: February 15
College level: Sophomore, Junior, Senior, Graduate, Doctoral
Majors/Fields: Technical communication
Criteria: Applicant must be a full-time student in a technical communication program. Selection is based upon academic record and potential for contributing to the profession of technical communication. Awarded every year.
Contact: STC Office.

226   Whittle Communications Minority Scholarship

University of Tennessee, Knoxville
Financial Aid Office
115 Student Services Building
Knoxville, TN 37994
(615) 974-3131
Average award: Tuition, fees, room, board, books
Number of awards: 20
Deadline: February 1
College level: Freshman, Sophomore, Junior, Senior
Majors/Fields: Communications
Criteria: Applicant must be a minority Tennessee resident from an accredited Tennessee high school with a minimum 3.0 GPA and a minimum ACT English score of 24. Applicant will be able to intern at Whittle Communications while attending the university. Scholarship is renewable. Awarded every year. Award may be used only at sponsoring institution.
Contact: College of Communications, 302 Communications and Extension Building, Knoxville, TN 37996, (615) 974-3031.

Communications Disorders

227 Graduate Student Scholarship

American Speech-Language-Hearing Foundation
10801 Rockville Pike
Rockville, MD 20852
(301) 897-5700
Maximum award: $4,000
Minimum award: $2,000
Number of awards: 6
Deadline: June 15
College level: Graduate, Doctoral
Majors/Fields: Communication disorders, communication sciences
Criteria: Applicant must be a full-time graduate student. Selection is based upon academic promise and outstanding academic achievement. One scholarship gives priority to foreign or minority students studying in the continental U.S.; one scholarship gives priority to disabled students. Awarded every year.
Contact: Graduate Student Scholarship Competition.

228 Young Scholars Award for Minority Students

American Speech-Language-Hearing Foundation
10801 Rockville Pike
Rockville, MD 20852
(301) 897-5700
Average award: $2,000
Number of awards: 1
Deadline: June 15
College level: Graduate
Majors/Fields: Speech-language pathology, audiology
Criteria: Applicant must be a U.S. citizen, a minority, and be accepted for full-time study in a graduate program. Applicant must submit a formal paper. Awarded every year.
Contact: Graduate Student Scholarship Competition.

Journalism

229 *Modesto Bee* Internship

Modesto Bee Minority Intern Program
P.O. Box 3928
Modesto, CA 95352
(209) 578-2351
Average award: $3,500
Deadline: December 31
College level: Sophomore, Junior, Senior, Graduate
Majors/Fields: Journalism
Criteria: Applicant must submit a cover letter, a resume, three references, and five work samples to Sanders LaMont, Executive Editor, *The Modesto Bee,* P.O. Box 3928, Modesto, CA 95352. Awarded every year.
Contact: Internships.

230 AEJ Summer Internship Program, AEJ Minority Summer Internship Program

Association for Education in Journalism (AEJ)
NYU Institute of Afro-American Affairs
269 Mercer Street, Suite 601
New York, NY 10003
(212) 998-2130
Average award: $2,000
Number of awards: 15
Deadline: September 18
College level: Sophomore, Junior, Senior, Graduate
Majors/Fields: Journalism
Criteria: Applicant must be a full-time college student (with preference given to juniors), a member of a minority group (African-American, Asian, Hispanic, Native American, Pacific Islander), and demonstrate a commitment to journalism (staff position in campus media, previous internship).
Contact: Glenda Noel-Doyle, Program Coordinator, (212) 998-2134.

231 Albert Spiezny Journalism Scholarship

Kosciuszko Foundation
15 East 65th Street
New York, NY 10021
(212) 734-2130
Average award: $5,000
Number of awards: 2
Deadline: January 15
Majors/Fields: Journalism
Criteria: Awarded on a competitive basis to U.S. citizens of Polish extraction. Scholarships are connected with the possibility of apprentice editorship on the staff of *New Horizons* magazine, an English-language monthly devoted to Polish and Polish-American affairs. Award pays funds toward tuition expenses at the Graduate School of Journalism of Columbia U. Awarded every year.
Contact: Scholarships.

232 Art Peters Copy Editing Internship

Philadelphia Inquirer Minority Intern Program
P.O. Box 8263
Philadelphia, PA 19101
(215) 854-2419, (215) 854-2771
Average award: $493/week
Number of awards: 4
Deadline: December 15
College level: Sophomore, Junior, Senior
Majors/Fields: Print journalism
Criteria: Applicant must be black and have a strong interest in copy editing as a career. Work in college newspaper is preferred. Renewable if performance in first year of internship is satisfactory. Awarded every year.
Contact: Arlene Morgan, Senior Editor/Development, 400 North Broad Street, Philadelphia, PA 19101, (215) 854-2419.

233 Atlanta Press Club Journalism Grants

Atlanta Press Club
One CNN Center
Suite 358
Atlanta, GA 30303
(404) 577-7377
Minimum award: $500
Number of awards: 4
Deadline: April 1
College level: Freshman, Sophomore, Junior, Senior, Graduate, Doctoral
Majors/Fields: Journalism, communications
Criteria: Applicant must demonstrate interest in journalism and have financial need. Selection is also based upon academic performance. Awarded every year.
Contact: Liza Kaufman Hogan, Executive Director.

234 *Baltimore Sun* Scholarship for Minority Journalists

Baltimore Sun
501 North Calvert Street
Baltimore, MD 21278
(301) 332-6268
Average award: $5,000
Number of awards: 1
College level: Freshman
Majors/Fields: Journalism
Criteria: Applicant must be a member of a minority group and planning to attend the U of Maryland at College Park. Selection is based upon academic excellence, writing skills, participation in extracurricular activities, and the student's commitment to a career in journalism. Awarded every year.
Contact: Scholarships.

235　Bob Eddy Scholarship

Society of Professional Journalists
25 South Street
Fairfield, CT 06430
Maximum award: $2,000
Minimum award: $1,000
Number of awards: 3
Deadline: April 15
College level: Junior, Senior
Criteria: Applicant must be a Connecticut resident attending any college or a nonresident enrolled at a Connecticut college. Work samples (stories or tapes), essay about career goals, and college transcript are required. Awarded every year.
Contact: Cindy Simoneau, Chapter President, (203) 330-6391.

236　*Buffalo News* Scholarship

State University of New York at Buffalo
Buffalo, NY 14260
(716) 831-2000
Average award: $3,000
College level: Junior, Senior
Criteria: Applicant must submit an essay describing interest and goal in journalism, demonstrate journalistic ability, and file FAFSA. Preference is given to an underrepresented minority who is willing and able to accept a paid summer intership at the *Buffalo News.* Award may be used only at sponsoring institution.
Contact: Scholarships.

237　CABJ Scholarship

Chicago Association of Black Journalists
P.O. Box 11425
Chicago, IL 60611
(312) 836-5702
Average award: $1,000
Number of awards: 4
Deadline: June 30
College level: Junior, Senior, Graduate, Doctoral
Majors/Fields: Journalism
Criteria: Applicant must be an African-American with a minimum 2.5 GPA and be attending an accredited Illinois university. Selection is based upon potential for success as demonstrated through work samples, personal essay, and letters of recommendation. Awarded every year.
Contact: Maudlyne Ihejirika, Scholarship Chairwoman.

238　Chevron Journalism Economics Scholarship

University of Alabama–Tuscaloosa
Box 870162
Tuscaloosa, AL 35487-0162
(205) 348-6756
Average award: $1,500
Number of awards: 2
Deadline: February 15
College level: Sophomore, Junior
Majors/Fields: Journalism
Criteria: Applicant must be a journalism major minoring in economics. Awarded every year; may be used only at sponsoring institution.
Contact: Scholarship Committee, College of Communication, Box 870172, Tuscaloosa, AL 35487-0172, (205) 348-5520.

239　Donald W. Reynolds Foundations Scholarship

University of Oklahoma
University Affairs
900 Asp Avenue, Room 236
Norman, OK 73019-0401
(405) 325-1701
Average award: $2,500
Number of awards: 2
Deadline: February 1
College level: Junior
Majors/Fields: Print journalism
Criteria: Applicant must have a minimum 3.0 GPA, demonstrate financial need, and have a career goal to work on a community newspaper with a circulation of less than 50,000. Awarded every year. Award may be used only at sponsoring institution.
Contact: Director of School of Journalism and Mass Communication, 860 Van Vleet Oval, Norman, OK 73019, (405) 325-2721.

240　Dow Jones Newspaper Fund Editing Intern Program

Dow Jones Newspaper Fund
P.O. Box 300
Princeton, NJ 08543-0300
(609) 452-2820
Average award: $1,000
Number of awards: 65
Deadline: November 15
College level: Senior, Graduate
Criteria: Applicant must work the full summer at a copy desk of a daily newspaper (identified by DJNF) and will receive a $1,000 scholarship to apply toward his or her year in college. Recipient must attend a two-week training seminar before beginning the internship; seminar is paid for by the Newspaper Fund. Intern also receives regular wages from the newspaper for which he or she works. Applicant must be a U.S. citizen and request application between September 1 and November 1. Awarded every year.
Contact: Newspaper Editing Program.

241　Edward J. Nell Memorial Journalism Scholarships

Quill & Scroll Foundation
School of Journalism and Mass Communication
University of Iowa
Iowa City, IA 52242-1528
Minimum award: $500
Maximum number of awards: 10
Minimum number of awards: 8
Deadline: November 1 (yearbook contest); February 5 (writing/photo contest)
College level: Freshman
Majors/Fields: Journalism
Criteria: Applicant must be the winner of either the Yearbook Excellence Contest or the Writing/Photo Contest. Awarded every year.
Contact: Scholarships.

242　Ellen B. Scripps Fellowship

Scripps Howard Foundation
P.O. Box 5380
Cincinnati, OH 45201-5380
(513) 977-3035
Maximum award: $3,000
Deadline: February 25
College level: Graduate, Doctoral
Majors/Fields: Journalism
Criteria: Applicant must be a working journalist wanting to pursue further education in any field of graduate studies to become more proficient in chosen specialty in journalism. Applicant must demonstrate financial need, have good scholastic standing, demonstrate interest in the field of journalism, and be a U.S. citizen, resident alien, or hold a valid U.S. visa. Request application by December 20. Awarded every year.
Contact: Mary Lou Marusin, Executive Director.

243 F. Ward Just Scholarship

F. Ward Just Scholarship Foundation
5844 Heather Ridge Drive
Gurnee, IL 60031
(312) 680-7002
Average award: $4,000
Minimum award: $2,000
Number of awards: 2
Deadline: March 1
College level: Freshman
Majors/Fields: Journalism
Criteria: Applicant must demonstrate financial need, rank in top half of graduating class, be outstanding in character and promise, and show interest in a career in the newspaper business and broadcasting. Renewable if a minimum "C" average is maintained. Awarded every year.
Contact: Richard F. Kennedy, Vice President.

244 Fred Russell-Grantland Rice TRA Scholarship

Thoroughbred Racing Associations
420 Fair Hill Drive
Suite 1
Elkton, MD 21921
Average award: $10,000
Deadline: January 1
College level: Freshman
Criteria: Applicant must have a special interest in and demonstrate potential in the field of sports writing. Awarded every year.
Contact: Vanderbilt University, Coordinator of Special Scholarships, 2305 West End Avenue, Nashville, TN 37203, (615) 322-2561.

245 Freedom Forum Journalism Scholarship

Freedom Forum
1101 Wilson Boulevard
Arlington, VA 22209
(703) 284-2823
Maximum award: $4,000
Minimum award: $2,500
Number of awards: 50
Deadline: January 31
College level: Freshman, Sophomore, Junior, Senior, Graduate, Doctoral
Majors/Fields: Journalism, mass communications
Criteria: Applicant must plan to enter or be attending a four-year U.S. college on a full-time basis. Applicant must have career goals in print, broadcast journalism, or advertising. Three examples of journalistic work must be submitted. Awarded every year.
Contact: Karen R. Catone, Administrator of Awards and Initiatives.

246 GOEF Scholarship

Georgia Press Educational Foundation
3066 Mercer University Drive
Suite 200
Atlanta, GA 30341-4137
(404) 454-6776
Maximum award: $4,500
Minimum award: $1,500
Maximum number of awards: 7
Minimum number of awards: 2
Deadline: February 1
College level: Freshman, Sophomore, Junior, Senior
Majors/Fields: Print journalism
Criteria: Applicant must be a Georgia resident and attend a state school in Georgia. Awarded every year.
Contact: Scholarships.

247 Golf Writers Association of America Scholarship

California State University, Fullerton
P.O. Box 34080
Fullerton, CA 92634-9480
(714) 773-3128
Average award: $3,000
Number of awards: 1
Deadline: January
College level: Junior
Majors/Fields: Communications, print journalism
Criteria: Selection is based upon academic achievement and financial need. Awarded every year. Award may be used only at sponsoring institution.
Contact: Vickey Takeuchi, Scholarship Coordinator.

248 Inter American Press Association Scholarship

Inter American Press Association
Scholarship Fund
2911 Northwest 39th Street
Miami, FL 33142
(305) 634-2465
Average award: $10,000
Maximum award: Also includes health insurance for all recipients and round-trip airfare for Latin American and Caribbean scholars.
Number of awards: 5
Deadline: August 1
College level: Graduate, Doctoral
Majors/Fields: Journalism
Criteria: Applicant must be a journalism school graduate between 21 and 35 years of age with good command of the language he or she will use; U.S. and Canadian applicants must prove fluency in Spanish or Portuguese and Latin American applicants must take the TOEFL. Where experience is a prime consideration, three years of professional journalism is required. Award is for Latin American scholars to study for a year at a U.S. or Canadian journalism school and for U.S. and Canadian scholars to spend an academic year studying and reporting in Latin America or the Carribean. Study and work plan must be submitted for consideration. Awarded every year.
Contact: Scholarship Fund.

249 Jack Kassewitz/Garth Reeves Jr. Memorial Scholarships

Society of Professional Journalists South Florida Pro Chapter
c/o The Miami Herald
One Herald Plaza
Miami, FL 33132-1693
(305) 376-3564
Average award: $1,000
Minimum award: $500
Number of awards: 2
Deadline: March 1
College level: Freshman, Sophomore, Junior, Senior, Graduate
Majors/Fields: Journalism
Criteria: Applicant must be preparing for a career in journalism and be a resident of South Florida. Selection is based upon need, grades, participation in student publication, general character, and potential. Reapplication is required to continue scholarship. Awarded every year.
Contact: John D. Hopkins, Scholarship Chairman, SPJ.

250 John M. Will Memorial Scholarship

John M. Will Scholarship Foundation
P.O. Box 290
Mobile, AL 36601
(205) 432-6751
Maximum award: $3,000
Minimum award: $2,500
Number of awards: 2
Deadline: April 21
College level: Freshman, Sophomore, Junior, Senior, Graduate, Doctoral
Majors/Fields: Journalism
Criteria: Applicant must be a resident of Baldwin, Clarke, Conecuh, Escambia, Mobile, Monroe, or Washington counties in Alabama, Escambia or Santa Rosa counties in Florida, or George or Jackson counties in Mississippi. Applicant must submit the application form, cover letter, transcript, and recommendation. Recipient must reapply for renewal. Awarded every year.
Contact: Steele Holman II, Secretary of the Foundation.

251 Knight-Ridder Inc. Minority Scholarship

Detroit Free Press
321 W. Lafayette
Detroit, MI 48226
(313) 222-6873
Maximum award: $5,000
Minimum award: $1,000
Maximum number of awards: 4
Minimum number of awards: 3
Deadline: January 15
College level: Freshman
Majors/Fields: Journalism, communications
Criteria: Applicant must be a minority (Asian, black, Hispanic, or Native American) with a minimum 3.0 GPA.
Contact: Scholarships.

252 McMahon Memorial Scholarship

University of Oklahoma
University Affairs
900 Asp Avenue, Room 236
Norman, OK 73019-0401
(405) 325-1701
Average award: $5,000
Number of awards: 5
Deadline: February 15
College level: Freshman
Majors/Fields: Broadcast news, newswriting
Criteria: Selection is based upon test scores, GPA, and personal interview. Awarded every year. Award may be used only at sponsoring institution.
Contact: Director of School of Journalism and Mass Communication, 860 Van Vleet Oval, Norman, OK 73019, (405) 325-2721.

253 Minoru Yasui Memorial Scholarship for Broadcast Journalism

Asian American Journalists Association
1765 Sutter Street
Room 1000
San Francisco, CA 94115
(415) 346-2051
Average award: $1,000
Deadline: April 15
College level: Freshman, Sophomore, Junior, Senior, Graduate
Majors/Fields: Broadcast journalism
Criteria: Scholarship seeks to encourage Asian men to pursue on-air careers in broadcast journalism. Selection is based upon a commitment to the field of journalism, a sensitivity to Asian-American issues as demonstrated by community involvement, journalistic ability, scholastic ability, and financial need.
Contact: Lenore Espanola Ishida, Program Coordinator.

254 NAHJ Scholarship

National Association of Hispanic Journalists (NAHJ)
1193 National Press Building
Washington, DC 20045
(202) 662-7145
Average award: $1,000
Maximum number of awards: 25
Minimum number of awards: 20
Deadline: January 31
College level: Freshman, Sophomore, Junior, Senior, Graduate, Doctoral
Majors/Fields: Journalism, mass communication
Criteria: Applicant must submit a sample of best work, resume, recommendations, essay, transcript, and application. For application, send a self-addressed, stamped envelope with request. Awarded every year.
Contact: Rebecca K. Finley, Scholarships.

255 NAHJ/Newhouse Scholarship/Internship Program

National Association of Hispanic Journalists (NAHJ)
1193 National Press Building
Washington, DC 20045
(202) 662-7145
Average award: $5,000
Number of awards: 2
Deadline: January 31
College level: Junior, Senior
Majors/Fields: Journalism, mass communication
Criteria: Applicant must be enrolled full time. Award is given for two years. Recipient receives funding to attend the NAHJ convention as well as an internship during the summer between junior and senior year. Awarded every year.
Contact: Rebecca K. Finley, Scholarships.

256 National AAJA General Scholarship Fund

Asian American Journalists Association (AAJA)
1765 Sutter Street
Room 1000
San Francisco, CA 94115
(415) 346-2051
Maximum award: $2,000
Number of awards: 6
Deadline: April 15
College level: Freshman, Sophomore, Junior, Senior
Majors/Fields: Journalism
Criteria: Applicant must be enrolled full time. Selection is based upon a commitment to the field of journalism, a sensitivity to Asian-American issues as demonstrated by community involvement, journalistic ability, scholastic ability, and financial need.
Contact: Lenore Espanola Ishida, Program Coordinator.

257 Newhouse Scholarship

Asian American Journalists Association
1765 Sutter Street
Room 1000
San Francisco, CA 94115
(415) 346-2051
Average award: $2,000
Number of awards: 7
Deadline: April 15
College level: Freshman, Sophomore, Junior, Senior
Majors/Fields: Print journalism
Criteria: Historically underrepresented Asian-American groups including Southeast Asian, South Asian, Korean, Filipino, and Pacific Islander are encouraged to apply. Applicant must be enrolled full time. Selection is based upon commitment to the field of journalism, sensitivity to Asian-American issues as demonstrated by community involvement, journalistic ability, scholastic ability, and financial need.
Contact: Lenore Espanola Ishida, Program Coordinator.

258 NIAF Communications Scholarship

National Italian American Foundation (NIAF)
Educational Scholarship Program
1860 19th Street, NW
Washington, DC 20009-5599
(202) 638-2137
Minimum award: $5,000
Deadline: May 31
College level: Sophomore, Junior, Senior
Majors/Fields: Communications, journalism
Criteria: Applicant must submit transcript, demonstration of financial need, essay, and be Italian-American. Awarded every year.
Contact: Dr. Maria Lombardo, Education Director, 1860 19th Street, NW, Suite 800, Washington, DC 20009-5599.

259 Press Club of Dallas Foundation Scholarships

Press Club of Dallas Foundation
400 North Olive, LB 218
Dallas, TX 75201
(214) 740-9988
Average award: $1,000
Maximum award: $2,000
Minimum award: $500
Number of awards: 10
Deadline: May 1
College level: Junior, Senior, Graduate
Majors/Fields: Journalism, mass communications, public relations
Criteria: Applicant must attend school in Texas, provide samples of work, and demonstrate financial need. Recipient must reapply each year. Awarded every year.
Contact: Carol Wortham, Executive Director, 400 North Olive, LB 218, Dallas, TX 75201.

260 Quarton McElroy Broadcast Scholarship

Iowa Broadcasters Association
P.O. Box 71186
Des Moines, IA 50325
Average award: $2,000
Number of awards: 3
Deadline: April 10
College level: Freshman
Majors/Fields: Broadcast journalism, broadcasting
Criteria: Applicant must be a senior graduating from an Iowa high school who will attend an Iowa college or university. Awarded every year.

261 Scripps Howard Foundation Scholarship

Scripps Howard Foundation
P.O. Box 5380
Cincinnati, OH 45201-5380
(513) 977-3035
Maximum award: $3,000
Minimum award: $500
Deadline: February 25
College level: Freshman, Sophomore, Junior, Senior, Graduate, Doctoral
Majors/Fields: Broadcast journalism, print journalism
Criteria: Applicant must have good scholastic standing, show evidence of interest in the field of journalism, demonstrate financial need, and be a U.S. citizen, resident alien, or hold a valid U.S. visa. Evidence of journalism work on high school newspapers, magazines, radio or television stations, cable systems, or in private industry is required. Request application by December 20. Awarded every year.
Contact: Mary Lou Marusin, Executive Director.

262 South Carolina Press Association Foundation Newspaper Scholarship

South Carolina Press Association Foundation
P.O. Box 11429
Columbia, SC 29211
(803) 750-9561
Average award: $2,000
Maximum award: $2,500
Number of awards: 3
Deadline: June 1
College level: Junior, Senior
Criteria: Applicant must attend a South Carolina college and be interested in a career in newspapers. Selection is based upon grades, participation in journalistic activities in college, and recommendations of faculty members. Financial need may be considered. If applicant does not work in newspapers after graduation, scholarship becomes a loan and must be repaid. Satisfactory progress is required for renewal. Awarded every year.
Contact: Jennifer Roberts, Assistant Director.

263 Stoody-West Fellowship

United Methodist Communications
475 Riverside Drive, Suite 1901
New York, NY 10115
(212) 663-8900
Average award: $6,000
Deadline: February 15
College level: Graduate, Doctoral
Majors/Fields: Religious journalism
Criteria: Applicant must be a Christian. Selection is based upon Christian commitment and involvement in the church, academic achievement, recommendations, journalist experience and talent, goals, and potential professional usefulness as a religious journalist.
Contact: Fellowship Committee, Public Media Division, P.O. Box 320, Nashville, TN 37202.

264 Stoody-West Fellowship in Journalism

University of Oklahoma
University Affairs
900 Asp Avenue, Room 236
Norman, OK 73019-0401
(405) 325-1701
Average award: $6,000
Number of awards: 1
Deadline: January 16
College level: Graduate
Majors/Fields: Journalism, religious communications
Criteria: Applicant must be a Christian engaged in religious journalism or planning to enter the field. Applicant must study audio-visual, electronic, or print journalism. Awarded every year. Award may be used only at sponsoring institution.
Contact: Rev. Thad Holcombe, United Ministry Center, 1017 Elm, Norman, OK 73072, (405) 321-8682.

265 William B. Ruggles Scholarship

National Right to Work Committee
8001 Braddock Road
Suite 500
Springfield, VA 22160
(800) 325-7892, (703) 321-9820, extension 254
Minimum award: $2,000
Number of awards: 1
Deadline: March 31
College level: Sophomore, Junior, Senior, Graduate
Majors/Fields: Journalism
Criteria: Applicant must demonstrate high journalistic standards and an understanding of voluntarism and of the problems of compulsory unionism. Awarded every year.
Contact: Scholarships.

Library Science

266 Affirmative Action Scholarship

Special Libraries Association
1700 18th Street, NW
Washington, DC 20009
(202) 234-4700
Minimum award: $6,000
Number of awards: 1
Deadline: October 31
College level: Unspecified graduate
Majors/Fields: Library science
Criteria: Applicant must be a U.S. or Canadian citizen or submit evidence of becoming naturalized at the beginning of the award period, be a member of a minority group, and demonstrate financial need. Scholarship is renewable. Awarded every year.
Contact: Scholarships.

267 Bound-to-Stay-Bound Books Scholarship

American Library Association (ALA)
50 East Huron Street
Chicago, IL 60611
(800) 545-2433
Average award: $5,000
Number of awards: 2
Deadline: March 1
College level: Graduate, Doctoral
Majors/Fields: Library science
Criteria: Applicant must be a U.S. citizen, be enrolled in a library school accredited by the American Library Association, and must become a member of the ALA. Recipient is expected to accept a position after graduation in the field of library service to children for at least one year. Selection is based upon academic excellence, leadership qualities, and a desire to work with children. Awarded every year.
Contact: Susan Roman, Executive Director.

268 California State Library Multi-Ethnic Recruitment Scholarship

California State Library
Library Development Services Bureau
P.O. Box 942837
Sacramento, CA 94237-0001
(916) 653-5217
Average award: $2,500
Maximum award: $5,000
Number of awards: 38
Deadline: March 21
College level: Graduate
Majors/Fields: Library Science
Criteria: Applicant must be a minority student of African-American, Asian/Pacific Islander, Hispanic, or Native American descent in California who is pursuing a Master in Library Science degree at one of three accredited Schools of Library Science in California. Reapplication required to retain scholarship. Awarded every year.
Contact: Library Development Services Bureau.

269 Caroline M. Hewins Scholarship

Hartford Public Library
500 Main Street
Hartford, CT 06103
(203) 293-6076
Average award: $4,000
Number of awards: 1
Deadline: March 1
College level: Graduate
Majors/Fields: Library science
Criteria: Applicant must plan to specialize in library work with children and attend a library school accredited by the American Library Association. Preference is given to applicants who plan to pursue a career in public library service. Awarded every year.
Contact: Louise Blalock, Chief Librarian.

270 CLSI Scholarship in Library and Information Technology

Library and Information Technology Association
50 East Huron Street
Chicago, IL 60611
(312) 280-4270
Average award: $2,500
Number of awards: 1
Deadline: April 1
College level: Graduate
Majors/Fields: Library and information science
Criteria: Applicant must demonstrate academic excellence, leadership potential, evidence of commitment to career in library automation and information technology, and prior activities in library automation. Economic need is considered when all other criteria are equal. Awarded every year.
Contact: Tel Aviv V. Barbee, Administrative Secretary.

271 David H. Clift Scholarship

American Library Association (ALA)
50 East Huron Street
Chicago, IL 60611
(800) 545-2433
Average award: $3,000
Maximum number of awards: 2
Minimum number of awards: 1
Deadline: December
Majors/Fields: Library science
Criteria: Applicant must be a U.S. or Canadian citizen enrolled in a master's degree program in library education at an ALA-accredited institution. Selection is based upon academic excellence, leadership qualities, and a commitment to a career in librarianship. Awarded every year.
Contact: Scholarships.

272 Frederic G. Melcher Scholarship

American Library Association (ALA)
50 East Huron Street
Chicago, IL 60611
(800) 545-2433
Average award: $5,000
Number of awards: 2
Deadline: March 1
College level: Graduate
Majors/Fields: Library science
Criteria: Applicant must be a citizen of the U.S. or Canada, enrolled in an ALA-accredited master's degree program, and must become a member of the ALA. Applicant is expected to accept a position after graduation in the field of library service to children for at least two years. Selection is based upon academic excellence, leadership qualities, and desire to work with children in libraries. Awarded every year.
Contact: Susan Roman, Administrative Secretary.

273 Library Education & Human Resource Development Fellowship

U.S. Department of Education, Library Programs, Office of Educational Research/Improvement
ATTN: 84.036B
555 New Jersey Avenue, NW
Washington, DC 20208-5571
(202) 219-1315
Maximum award: $14,000
Number of awards: 200
College level: Graduate, Doctoral
Majors/Fields: Library science, information science
Criteria: Doctoral fellowships are awarded for three years. Awarded every year.
Contact: Jan Owens, Discretionary Library Program Division.

274 Library Scholarship for Law School Graduates

American Association of Law Libraries
Scholarships and Grants Committee
53 West Jackson Boulevard, Suite 940
Chicago, IL 60604
(312) 939-4764
Average award: $1,500
Number of awards: 8
Deadline: April 1
College level: Graduate, Doctoral
Majors/Fields: Library science
Criteria: Applicant must be a graduate of an accredited law school who is a degree candidate at an accredited library school. Awarded every year.
Contact: Ronda Bedrook, Scholarships and Grants Committee.

275 Library Scholarship for Non-Law School Graduates

American Association of Law Libraries
Scholarships and Grants Committee
53 West Jackson Boulevard, Suite 940
Chicago, IL 60604
(312) 939-4764
Average award: $1,000
Number of awards: 8
Deadline: April 1
College level: Graduate
Majors/Fields: Library science
Criteria: Applicant must be a college graduate with meaningful law library experience who is a degree candidate at an accredited library school. Awarded every year.
Contact: Ronda Bedrook, Scholarships and Grants Committee.

276 Louise Giles Minority Scholarship

American Library Association
50 East Huron Street
Chicago, IL 60611
(800) 545-2433
Average award: $3,000
Majors/Fields: Library science
Criteria: Applicant must be a U.S. or Canadian citizen who is a member of a principal minority group. Selection is based upon academic excellence, leadership qualities, and commitment to a career in librarianship. Awarded every year.
Contact: Scholarships.

277 Louisiana Library Association Scholarship

Louisiana Library Association
P.O. Box 3058
Baton Rouge, LA 70821
(504) 342-4928
Average award: $3,000
Number of awards: 2
Deadline: May 1
College level: Graduate
Majors/Fields: Library science
Criteria: Applicant must have been born in Louisiana, been a Louisiana resident for at least two years, or have a parent who has been a Louisiana resident for at least five years. Applicant must have a minimum undergraduate GPA of 3.2, minimum combined GRE score of 1050, submit recommendation from a librarian, attend a personal interview, and have unconditional admission to Louisiana State U School of Library and Information Science. Scholarship is renewable. Awarded every year.
Contact: Carol McMahan, Administrative Officer.

278 Medical Library Association Doctoral Fellowship

Medical Library Association (MLA)
Moore Library of Medicine
3300 Henry Avenue
Philadelphia, PA
(215) 842-6910
Minimum award: $1,000
Number of awards: 1
Deadline: February 1
College level: Doctoral
Majors/Fields: Library science
Criteria: Applicant must be a U.S. or Canadian citizen or permanent resident, enrolled in a Ph.D. program with emphasis on biomedical and health-related information science and be a graduate of an American Library Association-accredited, graduate library school. Fellowship may not be used to pay tuition fees, tuition-related expenses, equipment costs or expenses, clerical support, or living expenses. Awarded yearly when appropriate candidates apply.
Contact: Program Services .

279 Medical Library Association Minority Scholarship

Medical Library Association (MLA)
Moore Library of Medicine
3300 Henry Avenue
Philadelphia, PA
(215) 842-6910
Minimum award: $2,000
Number of awards: 1
Deadline: February 1
College level: Unspecified graduate
Majors/Fields: Library science
Criteria: Applicant must be an MLA member, be Asian, black, Hispanic, Native American, or Pacific Islander, be entering an American Library Association-accredited graduate library school, and have at least one half of his or her academic requirements to complete during the year following the granting of the scholarship. Citizenship or permanent resident status in the U.S. or Canada is required. Awarded each year that appropriate candidates apply.
Contact: Program Services .

280 Medical Library Association Scholarship

Medical Library Association
Moore Library of Medicine
3300 Henry Avenue
Philadelphia, PA
(215) 842-6910
Average award: $2,000
Number of awards: 1
Deadline: February 1
College level: Doctoral
Majors/Fields: Library science
Criteria: Applicant must be attending an American Library Association-accredited, graduate library school with at least half of the program completed and submit a statement of career objectives. Selection is based upon excellence in scholarship and potential for accomplishment in health sciences librarianship. Recipient will receive a student membership in the Medical Library Association. Citizenship or permanent resident status in the U.S. or Canada is required. Awarded each year that appropriate candidates apply.
Contact: Melinda Paquette, Clinical Librarian.

281 Minority Stipend

American Association of Law Libraries
Scholarships and Grants Committee
53 West Jackson Boulevard, Suite 940
Chicago, IL 60604
(312) 939-4764
Minimum award: $3,500
Number of awards: 2
Deadline: April 1
College level: Graduate, Doctoral
Majors/Fields: Library science, law
Criteria: Applicant must be a minority college graduate with law library experience who is a degree candidate at an accredited library or law school. Awarded every year.
Contact: Ronda Bedrook, Scholarships and Grants Committee.

282 OCLC Minority Scholarship in Library and Information Technology

Library and Information Technology Association
50 East Huron Street
Chicago, IL 60611
(312) 280-4270
Average award: $2,500
Number of awards: 1
Deadline: April 1
College level: Graduate
Majors/Fields: Library and information science
Criteria: Applicant must be a U.S. or Canadian citizen, have a strong commitment to the use of automation in libraries, desire to enter a career in the library automation field, and be a member of a qualified minority group (Native American, Alaskan Native, Asian or Pacific Islander, African-American, or Hispanic). Awarded every year.
Contact: Tel Aviv V. Barbee, Administrative Secretary.

283 Reference Service Press Fellowship

California Library Association
717 K Street, Suite 300
Sacramento, CA 95814
(916) 447-8541
Average award: $2,000
Number of awards: 1
Deadline: July 15
College level: Graduate
Majors/Fields: Library science
Criteria: Applicant must be accepted into an accredited master of library science program, be a California resident attending school in any state or a resident of any state attending school in California, be preparing for a career in reference or information science, and agree to take at least three classes specifically dealing with reference or information science. Awarded every year.
Contact: Fellowships.

284 REFORMA Scholarship

REFORMA
El Paso Community College
P.O. Box 20500
El Paso, TX 79998
(915) 594-2339, (915) 594-2132
Minimum award: $1,000
Number of awards: 3
Deadline: May 15
College level: Graduate, Doctoral
Majors/Fields: Library science
Criteria: Applicant must be a Spanish-speaking, U.S. citizen or permanent resident who displays character and leadership, has the potential for high academic standing, is committed to a career in librarianship, and demonstrates an understanding of and desire to serve the Spanish-speaking community. Awarded every year.
Contact: Luis Chaparro, Chair of Scholarship Committee.

285 Scholarship for Minority Students in Memory of Edna Yelland

California Library Association
717 K Street, Suite 300
Sacramento, CA 95814
(916) 447-8541
Average award: $2,000
Maximum number of awards: 2
Minimum number of awards: 1
Deadline: May 31
College level: Graduate
Majors/Fields: Library science
Criteria: Applicant must be a minority student pursuing a master of library science degree at an accredited California library school, be a California resident, be a U.S. citizen or permanent resident, attend an interview, and demonstrate financial need. Awarded every year.
Contact: Scholarships.

286 School Librarian's Workshop Scholarship

American Library Association
50 East Huron Street
Chicago, IL 60611
(800) 545-2433
Average award: $2,500
Number of awards: 1
Deadline: Febuary 1
College level: Graduate
Majors/Fields: Library science
Criteria: Applicant must have received a bachelor's degree with academic excellence, and be accepted to a full-time ALA-accredited library program or an NCATE-accredited unit. Applicant must have demonstrated interest in working with children or young adults in a public or private school and show leadership potential. Awarded every year.
Contact: Marie Settem, Coordinator for Membership and Affiliate Relations.

287 Special Libraries Association Scholarship

Special Libraries Association
1700 18th Street, NW
Washington, DC 20009
(202) 234-4700
Minimum award: $6,000
Number of awards: 3
Deadline: October 31
College level: Unspecified graduate
Majors/Fields: Library science
Criteria: Applicant must be U.S. or Canadian citizen, must demonstrate financial need, and must be a graduate or college senior with an interest in special librarianship. Work experience in a special library is helpful. Awarded every year.
Contact: Scholarships.

288 Tony Leisner Scholarship

American Library Association
50 East Huron Street
Chicago, IL 60611
(800) 545-2433
Average award: $3,000
Majors/Fields: Library science
Criteria: Applicant must be a U.S. or Canadian citizen who is currently working in a library and has at least one year of library experience. Selection is based upon academic excellence, leadership, and commitment to a career in librarianship. Awarded every year.
Contact: Scholarships.

289 World Book Incorporated Grant

Catholic Library Association
461 West Lancaster Avenue
Haverford, PA 19041
(215) 649-5250
Average award: $1,500
Number of awards: 2
Deadline: March 15
Majors/Fields: Library Science
Criteria: Grant is for continuing education in school or children's librarianship and will not be given to subsidize studies leading to a library science degree. Applicant must submit a report describing proposed program of study (attendance at special workshops, institutes, seminars, summer session at institutions of higher learning, or sabbaticals), including a statement of expense (tuition, room and board, and/or travel). Applicant must be a CLA member and have a M.L.S. Awarded every year.
Contact: Scholarship Committee.

Photojournalism

290   Joseph Ehrenreich Scholarship

National Press Photographers (NPP) Foundation
3200 Croasdaile Drive
Suite 306
Durham, NC 27705
(800) 289-6772
Average award: $1,000
Number of awards: 5
Deadline: March 1
College level: Sophomore, Junior, Senior
Majors/Fields: Photojournalism
Criteria: Applicant must have journalism potential, great financial need, photo aptitude, and academic ability. Portfolio is required. Applicant must be in a bachelor's degree program at a recognized four-year college or university with courses in photojournalism. Awarded every year.
Contact: Tony Spina, 3525 Squirrel Road, Bloomfield, MI 48304, (313) 646-7286.

291   W. Eugene Smith Memorial Fund Grant in Humanistic Photography

W. Eugene Smith Memorial Fund
c/o The International Center of Photography
1130 Fifth Avenue
New York, NY 10128
Maximum award: $20,000
Minimum award: $5,000
Number of awards: 3
Deadline: July 15
Criteria: Applicant must include a written proposal, which should be cogent, concise, journalistically realizable, visually translatable and humanistically driven.
Contact: Grants.

Radio/TV Broadcasting

292   ARRL Foundation Scholarships

American Radio Relay League (ARRL) Foundation
225 Main Street
Newington, CT 06111
(203) 666-1541
Minimum award: $1,000
Deadline: February 15
College level: Sophomore, Junior, Senior, Graduate, Doctoral
Majors/Fields: Communications, electrical engineering, electronics
Criteria: Applicant must have a general class radio license.
Contact: Mary Carcia.

293   Alabama Cable Television Association-Otto Miller Scholarship

University of Alabama-Tuscaloosa
Box 870162
Tuscaloosa, AL 35487-0162
(205) 348-6756
Average award: $2,000
Number of awards: 1
Deadline: February 15
College level: Junior
Majors/Fields: Telecommunication
Criteria: Preference is given to applicants interested in a career in cable television. Awarded every year. Award may be used only at sponsoring institution.
Contact: Scholarship Committee, College of Communication, Box 870172, Tuscaloosa, AL 35487-0172, (205) 348-5520.

294   Alexander M. Tanger Scholarship

Broadcast Education Association (BEA)
1771 N Street, NW
Washington, DC 20036-2891
(202) 429-5354
Average award: $2,500
Number of awards: 2
Deadline: January 15
College level: Junior, Senior, Graduate, Doctoral
Majors/Fields: Radio/TV broadcasting
Criteria: Applicant must be enrolled at a BEA-member institution. Selection is based upon substantial evidence of superior academic performance and potential to be an outstanding contributor to the field. Applicant should demonstrate interest in the general field of broadcasting and have a high order of integrity and sense of responsibility. Awarded every year.
Contact: Lara Sulimenko, Membership Services Assistant.

295   Broadcast Pioneers Scholarship

Broadcast Education Association (BEA)
1771 N Street, NW
Washington, DC 20036-2891
(202) 429-5354
Average award: $1,250
Number of awards: 2
Deadline: January 15
College level: Junior, Senior, Graduate, Doctoral
Majors/Fields: Broadcasting
Criteria: Applicant must be enrolled at a BEA-member instituiton. Selection is based upon substantial evidence of superior academic performance and potential to be an outstanding contributor to the field. Applicant should demonstrate interest in the general field of broadcasting and have a high order of integrity and sense of responsibility. Awarded every year.
Contact: Lara Sulimenko, Membership Services Assistant.

296   Carole Simpson Scholarship

Radio and Television News Directors Foundation, Inc.
1000 Connecticut Avenue, NW
Suite 615
Washington, DC 20036
(202) 659-6510
Average award: $2,000
Number of awards: 1
Deadline: March 15
College level: Sophomore, Junior, Senior, Graduate, Doctoral
Majors/Fields: Broadcast journalism
Criteria: Applicant must be a minority student enrolled in an electronic journalism sequence at an accredited or nationally recognized college or university. Awarded every year.
Contact: Gwen Lyda, Executive Assistant.

297   Charles N. Fisher Memorial Scholarship

ARRL Foundation
225 Main Street
Newington, CT 06111
(203) 666-1541
Minimum award: $1,000
Deadline: February 15
Majors/Fields: Communications, electronics
Criteria: Applicant must have a radio license. Preference is given to residents of the Southwestern Division (Arizona and Los Angeles, Orange County, San Diego, Santa Barbara, Calif.).
Contact: Mary Carcia.

298   Ed Bradley Scholarship

Radio and Television News Directors Foundation, Inc.
1000 Connecticut Avenue, NW
Suite 615
Washington, DC 20036
(202) 659-6510
Maximum award: $5,000
Number of awards: 1
Deadline: March 15
College level: Sophomore, Junior, Senior, Graduate, Doctoral
Majors/Fields: Broadcast journalism
Criteria: Applicant must be a minority student who desires a career in broadcast or cable news. Awarded every year.
Contact: Gwen Lyda, Executive Assistant.

299   Ewing C. Kelly Broadcast Scholarship

Kelly Television Company
4400 Steilacoom Boulevard, SW
P.O. Box 98828
Tacoma, WA 98499
(206) 582-8613
Average award: $1,000
Maximum award: $3,000
Minimum award: $500
Number of awards: 7
Deadline: April 15
College level: Junior, Senior, Graduate, Doctoral
Majors/Fields: Broadcasting
Criteria: Applicant must be career oriented, intend to pursue a career in broadcasting, and attend one of the following schools: Central Washington U, Eastern Washington U, Evergreen State Coll, Gonzaga U, Pacific Lutheran U, Seattle Pacific U, Seattle U, U of Puget Sound, U of Washington, Washington State U, Western Washington U, or Whitman Coll. Selection is based upon financial need, academic achievement, and demonstrated interest in a broadcasting career. Awarded every year.
Contact: Adel R. Hauck, Scholarship Coordinator.

300   Harold E. Ennes Scholarship

Society of Broadcast Engineers
8445 Keystone Crossing
Suite 140
Indianapolis, IN 46240
(317) 253-1640
Average award: $1,000
Maximum number of awards: 2
Minimum number of awards: 1
Deadline: July 1
College level: Freshman, Sophomore, Junior, Senior, Graduate
Majors/Fields: Broadcast engineering
Criteria: Applicant must have a career interest in the technical aspects of broadcasting and must be recommended by two members of the Society of Broadcast Engineers (SBE). Preference is given to SBE members. Awarded every year.
Contact: Linda Godby, Certification.

301   Harold E. Fellows Scholarship

Broadcast Education Association (BEA)
1771 N Street, NW
Washington, DC 20036-2891
(202) 429-5354
Average award: $1,250
Number of awards: 4
Deadline: January 15
College level: Junior, Senior, Graduate, Doctoral
Majors/Fields: Broadcasting
Criteria: Applicant must be enrolled at a BEA-member institution. Selection is based upon substantial evidence of superior academic performance and potential to be an outstanding contributor to the field. Applicant should demonstrate interest in the general field of broadcasting and provide evidence of a high order of integrity and sense of responsibility. Applicant must provide proof of employment or internship at a National Association of Broadcasters station. Awarded every year.
Contact: Lara Sulimenko, Membership Services Assistant.

302   James Lawrence Fly Scholarship

Broadcast Education Association (BEA)
1771 N Street, NW
Washington, DC 20036-2891
(202) 429-5354
Average award: $2,500
Number of awards: 1
Deadline: January 15
College level: Junior, Senior, Graduate, Doctoral
Majors/Fields: Media law
Criteria: Applicant must be enrolled at a BEA-member institution. Selection is based upon substantial evidence of superior academic performance and potential to be an outstanding contributor to the field. Applicant should communicate interest in the general field of broadcasting and have a high order of integrity and sense of responsibility. Awarded every year.
Contact: Lara Sulimenko, Membership Services Assistant.

303   National Broadcasting Company, Inc. National Fellowship

National Broadcasting Company, Inc.
30 Rockefeller Plaza
New York, NY 10112
(212) 664-4444
Average award: $15,000
Number of awards: 10
College level: Graduate, Doctoral
Criteria: Applicant must be attending one of the following participating institutions: Columbia U, Northwestern U, U of Georgia, U of Chicago, U of Southern California, and Case Western U. Scholarship is renewable. Awarded every year.
Contact: Financial Aid Office at participating university.

304   RTNDF Undergraduate Scholarship

Radio and Television News Directors Foundation (RTNDF)
1000 Connecticut Avenue, NW
Suite 615
Washington, DC 20036
(202) 659-6510
Average award: $1,000
Number of awards: 9
Deadline: March 15
College level: Sophomore, Junior, Senior
Majors/Fields: Broadcast journalism
Criteria: Applicant must be planning for a career in broadcast or cable news. Awarded every year.
Contact: Gwen Lyda, Executive Assistant.

305   Senator Barry Goldwater (K7UGA) Scholarship

ARRL Foundation
225 Main Street
Newington, CT 06111
(203) 666-1541
Minimum award: $5,000
Deadline: February 15
Criteria: Applicant must have at least a novice class radio license.
Contact: Mary Carcia.

306   Shane Media Scholarship

Broadcast Education Association (BEA)
1771 N Street, NW
Washington, DC 20036-2891
(202) 429-5354
Average award: $3,000
Number of awards: 1
Deadline: January 15
College level: Junior, Senior, Graduate, Doctoral
Majors/Fields: Radio broadcasting
Criteria: Applicant must be enrolled at a BEA-member institution. Selection is based upon substantial evidence of superior academic performance and potential to be an outstanding contributor to the field. Applicant should demonstrate interest in field of broadcasting and have high order of integrity and sense of responsibility. Awarded every year.
Contact: Lara Sulimenko, Membership Services Assistant.

307 Vincent T. Wasilewski Scholarship

Broadcast Education Association (BEA)
1771 N Street, NW
Washington, DC 20036-2891
(202) 429-5354
Average award: $2,500
Number of awards: 1
Deadline: January 15
College level: Junior, Senior, Graduate, Doctoral
Majors/Fields: Broadcasting
Criteria: Applicant must be enrolled at a BEA-member institution. Selection is based upon substantial evidence of superior academic performance and potential to be an outstanding contributor to electronic media. Applicant must communicate interest in the broadcasting industry, and show evidence of high integrity, personal responsibilty, and professional responsibility. Awarded every year.
Contact: Lara Sulimenko, Membership Services Assistant.

308 Walter Patterson Scholarship

Broadcast Education Association (BEA)
1771 N Street, NW
Washington, DC 20036-2891
(202) 429-5354
Average award: $1,250
Number of awards: 2
Deadline: January 15
College level: Junior, Senior, Graduate, Doctoral
Majors/Fields: Radio broadcasting
Criteria: Applicant must be enrolled at a BEA-member institution. Selection is based upon substantial evidence of superior academic performance and potential to be an outstanding contributor to the field. Applicant should demonstrate interest in the general field of broadcasting and have a high order of integrity and sense of responsibility. Awarded every year.
Contact: Lara Sulimenko, Membership Services Assistant.

309 WTOL-TV Broadcast and Communications Scholarship

University of Toledo
Financial Aid Office
Toledo, OH 43606-3390
(419) 537-2056
Average award: $3,000
Number of awards: 1
College level: Junior
Majors/Fields: Broadcast communications
Criteria: Applicant must be a black or Hispanic student. Minimum 3.0 GPA is preferred. Award is for two years. Awarded every year. Award may be used only at sponsoring institution.
Contact: J. C. Caldwell, 50 Men and Women of Toledo, Inc., P.O. Box 3557, Toledo, OH 43608, (419) 729-4654.

Speech/Forensics

310 Debate Scholarship

DePaul University
25 East Jackson Boulevard
Suite 100
Chicago, IL 60604
(312) 362-8704
Average award: $2,500
Maximum award: $4,000
Minimum award: $1,000
Number of awards: 10
Deadline: February 1
College level: Freshman
Criteria: Applicant must participate on the debate team. Scholarship is renewable. Awarded every year. Award may be used only at sponsoring institution.
Contact: Jennifer Sparrow, Associate Director of Admissions.

311 Forensics Regents Scholarship

Southwest Missouri State University
Student Financial Aid
901 South National Avenue
Springfield, MO 65804-0095
(417) 836-5000 or (800) 492-7900
Average award: $1,000
Number of awards: 12
Deadline: March 31
College level: Freshman, Sophomore, Junior, Senior
Criteria: Applicant must show promise for achievement in a prominent national debate program. Reapplication is required to retain scholarship. Awarded every year. Award may be used only at sponsoring institution.
Contact: Scholarship Committee, (417) 836-5262 or (800) 492-7900.

312 National Oratorical Contest Scholarship

American Legion
Education and Scholarships Program
P.O. Box 1055
Indianapolis, IN 46206
(317) 630-1200
Maximum award: $19,000
Minimum award: $1,000
Number of awards: 74
Deadline: December
College level: Freshman
Criteria: Applicant must be a U.S. citizen under 20 years of age, attending high school or junior high, and must compete in the American Legion oratorical contest at the national level. Scholarship must be used at a college or university in the U.S. for actual school costs, including tuition, room and board, fees, and books. Scholarship can be used over a period of eight years until the funds are exhausted. Awarded every year.
Contact: Steve Short, Assistant Director.

313 Oratorical Contest Scholarship

American Legion—Alabama
P.O. Box 1069
120 North Jackson Street
Montgomery, AL 36101-1069
(202) 262-6638
Average award: $1,170
Maximum award: $2,000
Minimum award: $500
Number of awards: 3
Deadline: State Finals in March
College level: Freshman
Criteria: Scholarship is awarded to the top three winners of the State Oratorical Contest. Awarded every year.
Contact: Department Adjutant.

314 Oratorical Contest Scholarship

American Legion—California
Department Adjutant
117 Veterans War Memorial Building
San Francisco, CA 94102
Maximum award: $1,000
Minimum award: $200
Number of awards: 6
College level: Freshman
Criteria: Scholarship is for the winners of the state oratorical contest; applicants are selected by schools and participate in district contests, followed by area and departmental finals. Applicant should see his or her local high school counselor for further information. Awarded every year.
Contact: Department Adjutant.

315 Oratorical Contest Scholarship

American Legion–Florida
Department Headquarters
P.O. Box 547936
Orlando, FL 32854-7936
(401) 295-2631
Average award: $1,333
Maximum award: $2,500
Minimum award: $1,000
Number of awards: 6
Deadline: October 1
College level: Freshman
Criteria: Applicant must be enrolled in any public, private, or parochial high school in grades 9 through 12 in the state of Florida. Award is for the first through sixth winners in the Oratorical Contest, a speaking contest based on the U.S. Constitution. Awarded every year.
Contact: Scholarships.

316 Oratorical Contest Scholarship

American Legion–Illinois
P.O. Box 2910
Bloomington, IL 61702
(309) 663-0361
Maximum award: $1,600
Minimum award: $1,000
Maximum number of awards: 10
Minimum number of awards: 5
Deadline: in January
College level: Freshman
Criteria: Applicant must be a student in ninth through twelfth grade at any accredited high school in Illinois and compete in the state oratorical contest. Awarded every year.
Contact: Department Headquarters.

317 Oratorical Contest Scholarship

American Legion–Indiana
Americanism Office
777 North Meridian Street
Indianapolis, IN 46204
(317) 635-8411 extension 264
Average award: $600
Maximum award: $2,200
Minimum award: $200
Number of awards: 8
Deadline: Early December
College level: Freshman
Criteria: Applicant must participate in local contests and must attend an Indiana high school. Speech must be on some aspect of the U.S. Constitution. Awarded every year.
Contact: Americanism Office.

318 Oratorical Contest Scholarship

American Legion–Iowa
Department Headquarters
720 Lyon Street
Des Moines, IA 50309
Maximum award: $2,000
Minimum award: $400
Number of awards: 3
Deadline: September
College level: Freshman
Criteria: Applicant must attend an accredited high school in Iowa, enter the contest at the local level, and must plan to attend a college or university in Iowa. Awarded every year.
Contact: Department Headquarters.

319 Oratorical Contest Scholarship

American Legion–Kansas
1314 Topeka Avenue
Topeka, KS 66612
(913) 232-9315
Maximum award: $1,000
Minimum award: $150
Number of awards: 4
College level: Freshman
Criteria: Awarded every year.
Contact: Scholarships.

320 Oratorical Contest Scholarship

American Legion–Maryland
War Memorial Building
101 North Gay Street
Baltimore, MD 21202
(410) 752-3104
Maximum award: $2,500
Minimum award: $100
Number of awards: 7
Deadline: October 1
College level: Freshman
Criteria: Applicant must be between the ages of 16 and 19. Awarded every year.
Contact: Robert N. Ford, Adjutant.

321 Oratorical Contest Scholarship

American Legion–Massachusetts
Room 546-2
State House
Boston, MA 02133
(617) 727-2966
Average award: $833
Maximum award: $1,000
Minimum award: $400
Number of awards: 4
Deadline: December 15
College level: Freshman
Criteria: Applicant must be a student under age 20 and enrolled in junior or senior high school at time of contest. Awarded every year.
Contact: W. J. Craven, Chairman, 46 Brickett Street, Springfield, MA 01119.

322 Oratorical Contest Scholarship

American Legion–Michigan
212 North Verlinden
Lansing, MI 48915
(517) 371-4720
Maximum award: $1,000
Minimum award: $500
Number of awards: 5
Deadline: February
College level: Freshman
Criteria: Applicant must be a finalist in the state oratorical contest. Awarded every year.
Contact: Department Adjutant.

323 Oratorical Contest Scholarship

American Legion–Minnesota
Education Committee
State Veterans Service Building
St. Paul, MN 55155
Maximum award: $1,200
Minimum award: $500
Number of awards: 8
Deadline: April 1
College level: Freshman
Criteria: Applicant must be a winner in the annual oratorical contest. Awarded every year.
Contact: Department Oratorical Chairman.

324 Oratorical Contest Scholarship

American Legion–Missouri
Department Adjutant
P.O. Box 179
Jefferson City, MO 65102
(314) 893-2353
Maximum award: $1,000
Minimum award: $400
Number of awards: 4
College level: Freshman
Criteria: Applicant must be a winner in the Missouri Annual Oratorical contest. Awarded every year.
Contact: Department Adjutant.

325 Oratorical Contest Scholarship

American Legion–Nebraska
Department Headquarters
P.O. Box 5205
Lincoln, NE 68505
(402) 464-6338
Maximum award: $1,000
Minimum award: $200
Number of awards: 4
College level: Freshman
Criteria: Applicant must be a winner of the Nebraska Department Oratorical Contest. Awarded every year.
Contact: Robert Craig, Department Adjutant.

326 Oratorical Contest Scholarship

American Legion–New Jersey
Department Adjutant
War Memorial Building
Trenton, NJ 08068
(609) 695-5418
Maximum award: $4,000
Minimum award: $500
Number of awards: 5
College level: Freshman
Criteria: Applicant must be a winner in the New Jersey Department Oratorical Contest. Awarded every year.
Contact: Department Adjutant.

327 Oratorical Contest Scholarship

American Legion–New York
Department Adjutant
112 State Street, Suite 400
Albany, NY 12207
(518) 463-2215
Maximum award: $6,000
Minimum award: $2,000
Number of awards: 5
College level: Freshman
Criteria: Applicant must be a winner in the New York Department Oratorical Contest. Awarded every year.
Contact: Richard M. Pedro, Department Adjutant.

328 Oratorical Contest Scholarship

American Legion–Tennessee
State Headquarters
215 Eighth Avenue, North
Nashville, TN 37203
(615) 254-0568
Average award: $2,500
Maximum award: $5,000
Minimum award: $1,500
Number of awards: 3
Deadline: January
College level: Freshman
Criteria: Applicant must attend high school in Tennessee and be a winner in the state oratorical contest. Contestant must speak 8 to 10 minutes on some phase of the U.S. Constitution, emphasizing the attendant duties and obligations of a citizen to our government. Awarded every year.
Contact: A. Mike Hammer, Department Adjutant.

329 Oratorical Contest Scholarship

American Legion–Texas
Department of Texas
P.O. Box 789
Austin, TX 78767
(512) 472-4138
Maximum award: $1,000
Minimum award: $250
Maximum number of awards: 4
Minimum number of awards: 4
Deadline: November
College level: Freshman
Criteria: Applicant must be a Texas resident, current high school student, be sponsored by an American Legion post, and be a winner in the state oratorical contest. Awarded every year.
Contact: Department Oratorical Chairman.

330 Oratorical Contest Scholarship

American Legion–Virginia
Department Adjutant
1805 Chantilly Street
Richmond, VA 23230
(804) 353-6606
Average award: $767
Maximum award: $1,100
Minimum award: $600
Number of awards: 3
Deadline: December 1
College level: Freshman
Criteria: Applicant must be a winner of the Virginia Department Oratorical contest and attend high school in Virginia. Awarded every year.
Contact: Department Adjutant.

331 Oratorical Contest Scholarship

American Legion–Wisconsin
Department Headquarters
812 East State Street
Milwaukee, WI 53202
Maximum award: $1,000
Minimum award: $300
Number of awards: 12
College level: Freshman
Criteria: Applicant must be a winner of the state or regional high school oratorical contests. Awarded every year.
Contact: Scholarships.

332 Voice of Democracy Audio-Essay Competition

Veterans of Foreign Wars
406 West 34th Street
Kansas City, MO 64111
(816) 968-1117
Maximum award: $20,000
Minimum award: $1,000
Number of awards: 39
Deadline: November 15
College level: Freshman
Criteria: Applicant must be a 10th-, 11th-, or 12th-year U.S. high school student or the dependent of a U.S. military or civilian service person in overseas schools. Awarded every year.
Contact: Gordon R. Thorson, National Director, Voice of Democracy, VFW Building.

Creative/Performing Arts

Architecture/Landscape Architecture

333   AIA Minority/Disadvantaged Scholarship

American Architectural Foundation
1735 New York Avenue, NW
Washington, DC 20006
Number of awards: 20
Deadline: January 15
Majors/Fields: Architecture
Criteria: Applicant must be a minority or disadvantaged U.S. resident nominated by an individual architect or firm, an AIA chapter, a community design center, a guidance counselor, a teacher, a dean or administrative head of an accredited school of architecture, or director of a community, civic, or religious organization. Scholarship is renewable.
Contact: Scholarships.

334   AIA New Jersey Scholarship

AIA New Jersey Scholarship Foundation, Inc.
900 Route Nine
Woodbridge, NJ 07095
(908) 636-5680
Average award: $500
Maximum award: $1,500
Minimum award: $250
Number of awards: 21
Deadline: April 16
College level: Sophomore, Junior, Senior, Graduate, Doctoral
Majors/Fields: Architecture
Criteria: Applicant must be pursing first professional or graduate degree in architecture at an accredited school. Awarded every year.
Contact: Katharine Shuler, Executive Director.

335   Dana Griffin Soper Memorial Scholarship

University of Colorado at Boulder
Campus Box 106
Boulder, CO 80309-0106
(303) 492-5091
Average award: $2,000
Number of awards: 1
Deadline: First Monday in March
College level: Graduate
Majors/Fields: Environmental design
Criteria: Applicant must be a full-time, environmental design major returning for third year of study. Selection is based upon performance, personality, character, service contribution to the college, and professional potential. Awarded every year. Award may be used only at sponsoring institution.
Contact: College of Environmental Design, Campus Box 314, Boulder, CO 80309-0314, (303) 492-7711.

336   Edward D. Stone, Jr. and Associates Minority Scholarship

Landscape Architecture Foundation
4401 Connecticut Avenue, NW #500
Washington, DC 20008
(202) 686-0068
Average award: $1,000
Number of awards: 2
Deadline: May 4
College level: Junior, Senior
Majors/Fields: Landscape architecture
Criteria: Applicant must be a minority student. Awarded every year.
Contact: Scholarships.

337   Fellowship in Health Facilities Design

American Institute of Architects (AIA)
1735 New York Avenue, NW
Washington, DC 20006
(202) 626-7300, (202) 626-7511
Average award: $8,500
Number of awards: 2
Deadline: January 15
College level: Senior, Graduate, Doctoral
Majors/Fields: Architecture, health facilities
Criteria: Applicant must be a U.S. or Canadian citizen interested in the field of health-care architecture. Fellowship is available for any of the following options: graduate study at an accredited school of architecture associated with a school of hospital administration or near hospital resources; independent graduate-level study, research, or design in the health facilities field; or travel within-residence research at hospitals in a predetermined area. Awarded every year.
Contact: Fellowship Coordinator, American Society for Health Care Engineering, Division of Health Facilities Management and Compliance, One North Franklin, Chicago, IL 60606, (312) 422-3807.

338   Fellowship in Landscape Architecture at the American Academy in Rome

Garden Club of America
598 Madison Avenue
New York, NY 10022
(212) 753-8287
Number of awards: 1
Deadline: November 15
College level: Certified landscape architect
Majors/Fields: Landscape architecture
Criteria: Applicant must be an American-certified landscape architect. Awarded every year.
Contact: Ms. Buff Kavelman, American Academy in Rome, 7 East 60th Street, New York, NY 10022, (212) 751-7200.

339   James W. Fitzgibbon Scholarship in Architecture

Washington University
One Brookings Drive
Campus Box 1089
St. Louis, MO 63130
(314) 935-6000 or (800) 638-0700
Average award: $17,750
Number of awards: 1
College level: Freshman
Majors/Fields: Architecture
Criteria: Selection is based upon academic merit without regard to financial need. Satisfactory academic performance is required to retain scholarship. Awarded every year. Award may be used only at sponsoring institution.
Contact: Office of Undergraduate Admission.

340   King and Johnson Scholarship

University of Tennessee, Knoxville
Financial Aid Office
115 Student Services Building
Knoxville, TN 37994
(615) 974-3131
Average award: $2,500
Number of awards: 1
Deadline: February 1
College level: Junior, Senior
Majors/Fields: Architecture
Criteria: Applicant must be a high school graduate and resident of Tennessee, show promise in architecture, and demonstrate financial need. Applicant also receives internship employment with King and Johnson Architects, Inc. Scholarship is renewable. Awarded every year. Award may be used only at sponsoring institution.
Contact: College of Architecture and Planning, 19 Art and Architecture Building, Knoxville, TN 37996, (615) 974-5265.

341 Lloyd Warren Fellowship

National Institute for Architectural Education
30 West 22nd Street
New York, NY 10010
(212) 924-7000
Average award: $2,000
Maximum award: $6,000
Minimum award: $500
Number of awards: 8
Deadline: May 12
College level: Senior, Graduate, Doctoral
Majors/Fields: Architecture
Criteria: Applicant must be earning his or her first professional degree in architecture and submit a design as outlined in the competition program. Awarded every year.
Contact: Fellowships.

342 Mark Kaminski Summer Internship

Smithsonian Institution Cooper-Hewitt Museum Internships
2 East 91st Street
MRC 553
New York, NY 10128
Average award: $2,500
Number of awards: 1
Deadline: March 31
College level: Sophomore, Junior, Senior, Graduate
Majors/Fields: Architecture, architectural history, design/criticism, museum education, museum studies
Criteria: Internship encourages promising young students to explore careers in the museum profession.
Contact: Kerry MacIntosh, Intern Coordinator, Cooper-Hewitt, National Museum of Design, 2 East 91st Street, New York, NY 10128.

343 Minority/Disadvantaged Scholarship

American Institute of Architects (AIA)
1735 New York Avenue, NW
Washington, DC 20006
(202) 626-7300, (202) 626-7511
Maximum award: $2,500
Minimum award: $1,000
Number of awards: 20
Deadline: January 14
College level: Freshman, Sophomore, transfer students
Majors/Fields: Architecture
Criteria: Applicant must be nominated by an architect, local AIA chapter, a community design center, guidance counselor or teacher, faculty member from an accredited architecture school, or director of a community or religious organization by December 3. Applicant must be a U.S. resident from a minority and/or disadvantaged background entering a degree program at a school of architecture approved by the National Architectural Accrediting Board. Good academic standing in an accredited school of architecture and financial need is required to retain scholarship. Awarded every year.
Contact: AIA/AAF Scholarship Program Director.

344 NSA/ASLA Student Competition in Landscape Architecture

National Stone Association
1415 Elliot Place, NW
Washington, DC 20007
(800) 342-1415
Maximum award: $2,000
Minimum award: $600
Number of awards: 3
Deadline: April 10
College level: Sophomore, Junior, Senior, Graduate
Majors/Fields: Landscape architecture
Criteria: Selection is based upon overall excellence in design, creativity, and sensitivity to community needs. Awarded every year.
Contact: Robert S. Brown, Jr., Director of Public Affairs.

345 Residential Fellowship in Byzantine, Pre-Columbian, and Landscape Architecture Studies

Dumbarton Oaks
1703 32nd Street, NW
Washington, DC 20007
(202) 342-3232
Maximum award: $34,700
Minimum award: $16,400
Number of awards: 40
Deadline: November 1
College level: Doctoral
Majors/Fields: Byzantine studies, landscape architecture, Pre-Columbian studies
Criteria: This is a research institute for scholars who are writing their dissertations or pursuing research at the postdoctoral level. In exceptional cases, applications are accepted from students before they pass their preliminary examinations. Junior, Regular, and Summer Fellowships are available. Reapplication for fellowship is possible after five years. Awarded every year.
Contact: Office of the Director.

346 Robert K. Fuller Scholarship for Graduate Study

University of Colorado at Boulder
Campus Box 106
Boulder, CO 80309-0106
(303) 492-5091
Average award: $2,000
Number of awards: 1
Deadline: First Monday in March
College level: Graduate, Doctoral
Majors/Fields: Architecture
Criteria: Applicant must have excellence in previous academic or professional work. Awarded every year. Award may be used only at sponsoring institution.
Contact: College of Environmental Design, Campus Box 314, Boulder, CO 80309-0314, (303) 492-7711.

347 RTKL Traveling Fellowship

American Institute of Architects (AIA)
1735 New York Avenue, NW
Washington, DC 20006
(202) 626-7300, (202) 626-7511
Average award: $2,500
Number of awards: 1
Deadline: February 14
College level: Senior
Majors/Fields: Architecture
Criteria: Applicant must be in the second-to-last year of a bachelor or master of architecture program and planning to travel outside the United States in an established school program or accepted in a professional degree program and planning foreign travel that will have a beneficial and direct relationship to educational goals. Selection is based upon statement of purpose, relevance of the travel plans to the educational goals, academic performance, and recommendations. Awarded every year.
Contact: Scholarships, (202) 626-7511.

348 Scholarship for Advanced Study and Research

American Institute of Architects (AIA)
1735 New York Avenue, NW
Washington, DC 20006
(202) 626-7300, (202) 626-7511
Maximum award: $2,500
Minimum award: $1,000
Number of awards: 15
Deadline: February 14
College level: Graduate, Doctoral
Majors/Fields: Architecture
Criteria: Applicant must be in the final year of a bachelor's or master's degree program, or an architect, intern, or teacher who wishes to pursue an advanced degree or conduct research at a U.S. university. Selection is based upon the merit of the proposed project. Awarded every year.
Contact: AIA/AAF Scholarship Program Director, (202) 626-7511.

349 Scholarship Program for Professional Degree Candidates

American Institute of Architects (AIA)
1735 New York Avenue, NW
Washington, DC 20006
(202) 626-7300, (202) 626-7511
Average award: $1,000
Maximum award: $2,500
Minimum award: $500
Number of awards: 230
Deadline: February 1
College level: Senior, Graduate
Majors/Fields: Architecture
Criteria: Applicant must attend a school accredited by the National Architectural Accrediting Board or recognized by the Royal Architectural Institute of Canada. Selection is based upon statement of goals, academic performance, recommendations, and financial need. Awarded every year.
Contact: Mary Felber, Scholarships.

Art History

350 AOS Fellowship for Study of Chinese Painting

American Oriental Society
The University of Michigan
Hatcher Graduate Library
Ann Arbor, MI 48109-1205
(313) 747-4760
Average award: $8,000
Number of awards: 1
Deadline: February 1
College level: Doctoral
Majors/Fields: Chinese art
Criteria: Applicant must have completed three years study of the Chinese language and all requirements for the Ph.D. except for research travel, the written dissertation, and its defense. Selection is based upon academic excellence and financial need. Awarded every year.
Contact: Jonathan Rodgers, Secretary.

351 Cloisters College Internship

Metropolitan Museum of Art
1000 Fifth Avenue
New York, NY 10028-0198
(212) 879-5500, extension 3710
Average award: $2,000
Number of awards: 8
Deadline: February 5
College level: Sophomore, Junior, Senior
Majors/Fields: Art history
Criteria: Recipient will conduct gallery workshops for groups of New York City day campers at the Cloisters, a medieval European branch museum. The nine-week internship runs from June to August and also includes intensive training in The Cloisters Collection and museum teaching techniques. Special consideration is given to first- and second-year students. Awarded every year.
Contact: College Internship Program, The Cloisters, Fort Tryon Park, New York, NY 10040, (212) 795-3640.

352 Henry Luce Foundation/ACLS Dissertation Fellowship in American Art History

American Council of Learned Societies
228 East 45th Street
New York, NY 10017-3398
(212) 697-1505
Maximum award: $15,000
Number of awards: 10
Deadline: November 15
College level: Doctoral
Majors/Fields: Art history
Criteria: Applicant must be a U.S. citizen or legal resident, have completed all requirements for the Ph.D. except the dissertation, have a dissertation topic focused on the history of visual arts of the U.S., and be a Ph.D. candidate in an Art History department. Applicant must not have received a grant of $5,000 or more previously from the Henry Luce Program. Awarded every year.
Contact: Office of Fellowships and Grants.

353 J. Clawson Mills Scholarship

Metropolitan Museum of Art
Attn: Internship Programs
1000 Fifth Avenue
New York, NY 10028-0198
(212) 879-5500, extension 3710
Average award: $10,500
Deadline: In November
College level: Doctoral
Criteria: Scholarship is for research in any branch of fine arts related to the Metropolitan Museum's collections and is usually reserved for mature scholars of demonstrated ability. Scholarship provides for study or research at the museum for one year with the possibility of renewal for a second year. Typed application must include name, present address and phone, full resume of education and employment, official transcripts, and a two-part statement not to exceed 1,000 words. Scholarship is renewable. Awarded every year.
Contact: Pia Quintano, Coordinator for Fellowships, (212) 570-3807.

354 Louise Wallace Hackney Fellowship for the Study of Chinese Art

American Oriental Society
The University of Michigan
Hatcher Graduate Library
Ann Arbor, MI 48109-1205
(313) 747-4760
Average award: $8,000
Number of awards: 1
Deadline: February 1
College level: Doctoral
Majors/Fields: Chinese art
Criteria: Applicant must be a U.S. citizen, have completed three years study of the Chinese language, and be a doctoral or postdoctoral student. Reapplication is required to retain scholarship. Awarded every year.
Contact: Jonathan Rodgers, Secretary.

355 Metropolitan Museum of Art Summer Internship

Metropolitan Museum of Art
Attn: Intership Programs
1000 Fifth Avenue
New York, NY 10028-0198
(212) 879-5500, extension 3710
Average award: $2,500
Number of awards: 14
Deadline: in January
College level: Senior, Graduate, Doctoral
Majors/Fields: Art history
Criteria: Applicant should have a strong background in art history. Undergraduate interns work on departmental projects, give gallery talks, and work at the Visitor Information Center. Graduate assistant is appointed to a specific department, participating in various projects and gaining practical, first-hand experience. Program runs ten weeks from June through August. Graduate applicant should have completed one year of graduate school. Scholarship is renewable. Awarded every year.
Contact: Linda Komaroff, Internship Coordinator, (212) 570-3710.

356 Norbert Schimmel Fellowship

Metropolitan Museum of Art
Attn: Intership Programs
1000 Fifth Avenue
New York, NY 10028-0198
(212) 879-5500, extension 3710
Average award: $10,500
Number of awards: 1
Deadline: in November
College level: Doctoral
Criteria: Award is for an annual fellowship to an outstanding graduate student who has been admitted to a doctoral program at a university in the U.S. and who has submitted a thesis outline about ancient Near Eastern art and archaeology or Greek and Roman art. Preference is given to the applicant who would profit most from access to the resources of the ancient Near Eastern art or Greek and Roman art departments. No application forms are required. Awarded every year.
Contact: Pia Quintano, Coordinator for Fellowships, (212) 570-3807.

357 Peter Krueger Summer Internship

Smithsonian Institution Cooper-Hewitt Museum Internships
2 East 91st Street
MRC 553
New York, NY 10128
Average award: $2,500
Number of awards: 6
Deadline: March 31
College level: Sophomore, Junior, Senior, Graduate
Majors/Fields: Art history, design, museum education, museum studies
Criteria: Internship encourages promising young students to explore careers in the museum profession.
Contact: Kerry MacIntosh, Intern Coordinator, Cooper-Hewitt, National Museum of Design, 2 East 91st Street, New York, NY 10128.

Creative/Performing Arts–General

358 Arts Recognition and Talent Search

National Foundation for Advancement in the Arts
800 Brickell Avenue
Suite 500
Miami, FL 33131
(305) 377-1140
Maximum award: $3,000
Minimum award: $100
Number of awards: 382
Deadline: June 1; October 1
College level: Freshman, 17- and 18-year old artists
Majors/Fields: Dance, music, theatre, visual arts, writing
Criteria: Applicant must be a U.S. citizen or permanent resident (except for the jazz category, which is international). Awarded every year.
Contact: Suzette L. Prude, Communications Officer.

359 Associates of the Faculty of Fine Arts 25th Anniversary Scholarship

University of Calgary
2500 University Drive, NW
Calgary, Alberta, CN T2N 1N4
(403) 220-7872
Average award: $1,000
Number of awards: 6
Deadline: June 15
College level: Freshman, Sophomore, Junior, Senior
Majors/Fields: Art, drama, music
Criteria: Selection is based upon academic merit. One award each is given for art, drama, and music. Awarded every year. Award may be used only at sponsoring institution.
Contact: J. Van Housen, Director of Student Awards and Financial Aid.

360 Creative and Performing Arts Scholarship

Indiana State University
217 North Sixth Street
Terre Haute, IN 47809
(812) 237-2121
Average award: $1,100
Number of awards: 25
Deadline: February 15
College level: Freshman
Criteria: Applicant must excel in art, creative writing, dance, music, or theatre. Audition or portfolio must be submitted. Satisfactory GPA and full-time status are required to retain scholarship. Awarded every year. Award may be used only at sponsoring institution.
Contact: Scholarships, Office of Admissions, (800) 742-0891.

361 Creative and Performing Arts Scholarship

Colorado State University
Financial Aid Office
108 Student Services Building
Fort Collins, CO 80523
(970) 491-6321
Average award: $1,000
Maximum award: $1,500
Minimum award: $500
Number of awards: 250
Deadline: February or March
College level: Freshman, Sophomore, Junior, Senior
Majors/Fields: Art (for art award)
Criteria: Applicant must have outstanding talent in art, creative writing, dance, forensics, music, or theatre. Audition may be required. Contact the awarding department for application information. Minimum 2.4 GPA, continued talent, and reapplication required for renewal. Awarded every year. Award may be used only at sponsoring institution.
Contact: Jeanne Snyder, Financial Aid Counselor.

362 Creative Arts Award

Kent State University
P.O. Box 5190
Kent, OH 44242-0001
(216) 672-2972
Maximum award: $1,800
Minimum award: $1,200
Deadline: October 31
College level: Freshman
Majors/Fields: Art, dance, fashion design, interior design, music, theatre
Criteria: Selection is based upon academic and artistic performance. Minimum 2.0 GPA is required to retain scholarship. Awarded every year. Award may be used only at sponsoring institution.
Contact: Theodore Hallenbeck, Director of Financial Aid, 103 Michael Schwartz Center.

363 Dance Tuition Waiver

Utah State University
Logan, UT 84322-0160
(801) 750-1129
Average award: Full tuition
Deadline: March 1
College level: Freshman, Sophomore, Junior, Senior
Majors/Fields: Dance
Criteria: Applicant must be a dance major or minor, demonstrate commitment to the dance program, and have high scholarship standards. Applicant must demonstrate talent in the area of performance, choreography, or teaching, and commitment to performing with the modern dance company DANCEWORKS. Minimum 3.7 GPA and reapplication are required to retain scholarship. Awarded every year. Award may be used only at sponsoring institution.
Contact: Mark Tenhoeue, Director of High School/College Relations.

364 Dean's Special Talent Scholarship

Ohio University
Office of Student Financial Aid and Scholarships
Athens, OH 45701
(614) 593-4141
Average award: $1,250
Maximum award: $1,500
Minimum award: $750
Number of awards: 80
Deadline: March 1
College level: Sophomore, Junior, Senior
Majors/Fields: Art, dance, music, theatre, visual communications
Criteria: Selection is based upon talent and academic qualifications. Awarded every year. Award may be used only at sponsoring institution.
Contact: Mrs. Yang-Hi Kim, Associate Director of Scholarships and Grants.

365   F. Lammont Belin Arts Scholarship

F. Lammont Belin Arts Scholarship
Waverly Community House, Inc.
P.O. Box 142
Waverly, PA 18471
(717) 586-8191
Average award: $9,000
Number of awards: 1
Deadline: December 15
College level: Graduate, Doctoral, artists not attending school
Majors/Fields: Architecture, dance, drama, fine arts, literature, music, painting, photography, sculpture
Criteria: Applicant must be a U.S. citizen, must reside or have resided in the Abingtons or Pocono Northeast region of Pennsylvania, and be an artist of outstanding aptitude and promise in the fine arts pursuing a career as a professional artist. Awarded every year.
Contact: Administrative Chair of Scholarship Committee.

366   Friends of Fine Arts Scholarship

Northern Kentucky University
Administrative Center 416
Nunn Drive
Highland Heights, KY 41099-7101
(606) 572-5144
Average award: In-state tuition
Deadline: February 1
College level: Freshman, Sophomore, Junior, Senior
Majors/Fields: Art, music, theatre
Criteria: Awarded every year. Award may be used only at sponsoring institution.
Contact: Robert E. Sprague, Director of Financial Aid.

367   In-School Players Scholarship

Southwest Missouri State University
Student Financial Aid
901 South National Avenue
Springfield, MO 65804-0095
(417) 836-5000 or (800) 492-7900
Average award: $1,000
Number of awards: 6
Deadline: March 31
College level: Freshman, Sophomore, Junior, Senior
Criteria: Applicant must have performance experience in acting and/or music. Reapplication and audition are required to retain scholarship. Awarded every year. Award may be used only at sponsoring institution.
Contact: Scholarship Committee, (417) 836-5262 or (800) 492-7900.

368   Junior and Community College Performing Arts Scholarship

Alabama Commission on Higher Education
3465 Norman Bridge Road
Montgomery, AL 36105-2310
(334) 281-1921
Maximum award: In-state tuition
College level: Freshman, Sophomore
Criteria: Applicant must attend a public junior or community college in Alabama on a full-time basis. Selection is based upon demonstrated talent determined through competitive auditions. Financial need is not considered. Awarded every year.
Contact: Dr. William H. Wall, Director of Grants and Scholarships.

369   National League of American Pen Women Grant

National League of American Pen Women, Inc. (NLAPW)
1300 Seventeenth Street, NW
Washington, DC 20036
Average award: $1,000
Number of awards: 3
Deadline: January 15
Majors/Fields: Art, Letters, Music
Criteria: Applicant must be a woman, at least 35 years of age, must submit background and creative use of the money. Send self-addressed, stamped envelope by August 1 of odd-numbered year to receive current information. Awarded in even-numbered years.
Contact: Shirley Holden Helberg, National Scholarship Chair, (717) 225-3023.

370   Performing and Creative Arts Scholarship

State University of New York at Buffalo
Buffalo, NY 14260
(716) 831-2000
Average award: $2,000
College level: Freshman, Sophomore, Junior, Senior
Majors/Fields: Arts
Criteria: Applicant must have a minimum combined SAT I score of 1150, maintain a minimum 90 unweighted average, and complete the audition process. Scholarship is renewable. Awarded every year. Award may be used only at sponsoring institution.
Contact: Josephine Capuana, Administrative Director, 214 Talbert Hall, Buffalo, NY 14260, (716) 645-3020.

371   Provost's Special Talent Scholarship

Ohio University
Office of Student Financial Aid and Scholarships
Athens, OH 45701
(614) 593-4141
Average award: $1,250
Maximum award: $1,500
Minimum award: $1,000
Number of awards: 50
Deadline: February 15
College level: Freshman
Majors/Fields: Art, music, theatre, visual communication, dance
Criteria: Applicant must be a student in the Coll of Fine Arts. Selection is based upon talent and academic qualifications. Awarded every year. Award may be used only at sponsoring institution.
Contact: Yang-Hi Kim, Associate Director of Scholarships & Grants.

372   Talent Scholarship

Wright State University
Coordinator of Scholarships
Dayton, OH 45435
(513) 873-5721
Average award: $1,000
Maximum award: $1,200
Minimum award: $500
Number of awards: 35
College level: Freshman
Majors/Fields: Music, theatre, dance
Criteria: Applicant must audition for music, dance, or theatre scholarship. Awarded every year. Award may be used only at sponsoring institution.
Contact: Judy Rose, Assistant Director of Financial Aid.

373 Visual and Performing Arts Scholarship

Washington State University
Office of Scholarship Services
Pullman, WA 99164-1728
(509) 335-1059
Maximum award: $1,500
Minimum award: $200
Number of awards: 50
Deadline: February 15
College level: Freshman, transfer students
Criteria: Applicant must have talent or skill in the visual or performing arts. Audition or portfolio may be required. Awarded every year. Award may be used only at sponsoring institution.
Contact: Johanna H. Davis, Assistant Director.

Drama/Theatre

374 Dean's Theatre Performance Scholarship

DePaul University
25 East Jackson Boulevard
Suite 100
Chicago, IL 60604
(312) 362-8704
Average award: $2,000
Number of awards: 8
College level: Freshman
Majors/Fields: Drama
Criteria: Applicant must posess strong academic credentials, demonstrate a strong interest in the theatre, and be admitted to the theatre studies program. Selection is based upon performance. Minimum 2.5 GPA as a full-time student in theatre studies is required to retain scholarship. Awarded every year. Award may be used only at sponsoring institution.
Contact: Jennifer Sparrow, Associate Director of Admissions.

375 Dean's Theatre Studies and Theatre Design and Technology Scholarships

DePaul University
25 East Jackson Boulevard
Suite 100
Chicago, IL 60604
(312) 362-8704
Average award: $3,300
Maximum award: $7,500
Minimum award: $2,000
Number of awards: 24
Deadline: February 1
College level: Freshman, transfer students
Majors/Fields: Costume construction, costume design, lighting design, production management, scene design, theatre studies, theatre technology
Criteria: Applicant must submit a portfolio of theatre-related projects, have strong academic credentials, and demonstrate a strong interest in theatre. Transfer applicant must have minimum 3.0 GPA. Minimum 2.5 GPA as a full-time theatre student in the conservatory program is required to retain scholarship. Awarded every year. Award may be used only at sponsoring institution.
Contact: Jennifer Sparrow, Associate Director of Admissions.

376 Theatre and Dance Activity Regents Scholarship

Southwest Missouri State University
Student Financial Aid
901 South National Avenue
Springfield, MO 65804-0095
(417) 836-5000 or (800) 492-7900
Average award: $1,000
Number of awards: 16
Deadline: March 31
College level: Freshman, Sophomore, Junior, Senior
Majors/Fields: Dance, theatre
Criteria: Applicant must have outstanding ability in acting, performance studies, technical theatre, dance, and related activities. New students must present a performance audition or technical interview. Reapplication, minimum 2.5 cumulative GPA, departmental recommendation, and participation in related activities are required to retain scholarship. Awarded every year. Award may be used only at sponsoring institution.
Contact: Scholarship Committee, (417) 836-5262 or (800) 492-7900.

Fashion Design/Interior Decorating

377 Dora Brahms Award

American Society of Interior Designers Educational Foundation, Inc.
608 Massachusetts Avenue, NE
Washington, DC 20002-6006
(202) 546-3480
Minimum award: $3,000
Number of awards: 1
Majors/Fields: Interior design
Criteria: Competition is open to educational institutions on behalf of their students in historic preservation and restoration studies. Awarded biennially.
Contact: Jennifer Wren, Student Programs Coordinator.

378 Erlaine Pitts Scholarship

Art Institute of Fort Lauderdale
1799 South 17th Street
Fort Lauderdale, FL 33316-3000
(800) 275-7603
Average award: $2,980
Number of awards: 1
College level: Freshman
Majors/Fields: Interior design
Criteria: Selection is based upon service to the school, academic progress, attendance, and professionalism. Awarded every year. Award may be used only at sponsoring institution.
Contact: Laura Waterman, Director of Student Financial Services, (305) 463-3000, extension 471.

379 Mabelle Wilhelmina Boldt Memorial Scholarship

American Society of Interior Designers Educational Foundation, Inc.
608 Massachusetts Avenue, NE
Washington, DC 20002-6006
(202) 546-3480
Average award: $3,500
Number of awards: 1
Deadline: April 11
College level: Graduate, Doctoral
Majors/Fields: Interior design
Criteria: Applicant must be a practicing designer for at least five years before going to/returning to graduate school. Applicant must submit transcript and recommendation. Selection is based upon academic and creative accomplishments. Preference is given to design research. Awarded every year.
Contact: Jennifer Wren, Student Affairs Coordinator.

380 S. Harris Memorial Scholarship

American Society of Interior Designers Educational Foundation, Inc.
608 Massachusetts Avenue, NE
Washington, DC 20002-6006
(202) 546-3480
Average award: $1,500
Number of awards: 2
Deadline: March 21
College level: Junior, Senior, Graduate
Majors/Fields: Interior design
Criteria: Applicant must submit transcript and recommendations. Selection is based upon financial need and academic and creative accomplishments. Awarded every year.
Contact: Jennifer Wren, Student Affairs Coordinator.

Film/Photography

381 University Film and Video Association Development Grants

University Film and Video Association
Drama and Communication Department, PAC 307
UNO Lakefront
New Orleans, LA 70148
(504) 286-6814
Maximum award: $4,000
Minimum award: $1,000
Deadline: January 15
College level: Sophomore, Junior, Senior, Graduate, Doctoral
Criteria: Applicant must be sponsored by a faculty member who is an active member of the University Film and Video Association.
Contact: J. Stephen Hank, Chairman.

Fine Arts

382 AICAD Scholarship Program

Alliance of Independent Colleges of Art and Design (AICAD)
1300 West Mount Royal Avenue
Baltimore, MD 21217
Deadline: January 1
College level: Freshman
Majors/Fields: Art
Criteria: Awarded by each member school of Alliance of Independent Colleges of Art and Design. Additional renewable funds may be available. Awarded every year.
Contact: Scholarships.

383 Alpha Delta Kappa Foundation Fine Arts Grants

Alpha Delta Kappa International Headquarters
1615 West 92nd Street
Kansas City, MO 64114
Maximum award: $5,000
Minimum award: $3,000
Deadline: June 1 of even-numbered years
Criteria: Awarded in even-numbered years.
Contact: Kareb Looney, Scholarship and Grants Coordinator.

384 Art Institute of Fort Lauderdale Scholarship

Art Institute of Fort Lauderdale
1799 South 17th Street
Fort Lauderdale, FL 33316-3000
(800) 275-7603
Average award: $2,980
Number of awards: 1
College level: Freshman
Criteria: Selection is based upon academic consideration, talent, and professionalism. Awarded every year. Award may be used only at sponsoring institution.
Contact: Laura Waterman, Director of Student Financial Services, (305) 463-3000, extension 417.

385 Art Student Grants

Liquitex Excellence in Art Student Grants
P.O. Box 431
1100 Church Lane
Easton, PA 18044-0431
(800) 272-9652
Maximum award: $1,000
Minimum award: $500
Number of awards: 200
Deadline: December 30
College level: Sophomore, Junior, Senior, Graduate, Doctoral
Majors/Fields: Visual arts
Criteria: Awarded every year.
Contact: Grants.

386 Bertha Langhorst Werner Scholarship

Art Academy of Cincinnati
1125 Saint Gregory Street
Cincinnati, OH 45202-1700
(513) 721-5205, (800) 323-5692
Average award: $1,500
Maximum award: $2,000
Minimum award: $500
Number of awards: 13
Deadline: May 1
College level: Sophomore, Junior, Senior
Criteria: Award may be used only at sponsoring institution.
Contact: Karen Geiger, Director of Financial Aid, (513) 562-8751.

387 Conway and Proetz Scholarships

Washington University
One Brookings Drive
Campus Box 1089
St. Louis, MO 63130
(314) 935-6000 or (800) 638-0700
Average award: $16,750
Number of awards: 2
College level: Freshman
Majors/Fields: Fine arts
Criteria: Selection is based upon academic merit without regard to financial need. Satisfactory academic performance is required to retain scholarship. Awarded every year. Award may be used only at sponsoring institution.
Contact: Office of Undergraduate Admissions.

388 Dean's Art Scholarship

DePaul University
25 East Jackson Boulevard
Suite 100
Chicago, IL 60604
(312) 362-8704
Maximum award: $7,000
Minimum award: $2,000
Deadline: February 1
College level: Freshman, Transfer
Majors/Fields: Art advertising, art history, design, studio art
Criteria: Applicant must demonstrate strong academic credentials and strong interest in the study of art. Transfer applicant must have minimum 3.0 GPA. Portfolio is required for design and studio majors; essay on an artist or period of art is required for art history majors. Minimum 2.5 GPA as a full-time art major is required to retain scholarship. Awarded every year. Award may be used only at sponsoring institution.
Contact: Admissions Office.

389 Elizabeth Greenshields Foundation Award

Elizabeth Greenshields Foundation
1814 Sherbrooke Street West
Montreal, Quebec, CN H3H 1E4
Average award: $10,000
Number of awards: 37
Deadline: None
College level: Sophomore, Junior, Senior, Graduate, Doctoral, practicing artists who have completed their formal art training
Majors/Fields: Drawing, painting, printmaking, sculpture
Criteria: Applicant must present work which is representational or figurative, be under 31 years of age, have already started or completed training in an established school of art, and demonstrate through past work and future plans a commitment to making art a lifetime career. Applicant must reapply and submit new work for renewal. Awarded every year.
Contact: Awards.

390 Ladies Auxiliary to the V.F.W. Art Scholarship

Ladies Auxiliary to the Veterans of Foreign Wars
406 West 34th Street
Kansas City, MO 64111
(816) 561-8655
Maximum award: $2,500
Minimum award: $300
Number of awards: 5
Deadline: May 1
College level: Freshman
Majors/Fields: Art
Criteria: Applicant must be a U.S. citizen, attend school in the same state as the sponsoring Auxiliary, and submit artwork for creative, patriotic art competition. Awarded every year.
Contact: Judy Millick, Public Relations Director.

391 Le Maxie Glover Scholarship

University of Toledo
Financial Aid Office
Toledo, OH 43606-3390
(419) 537-2056
Average award: $3,000
Number of awards: 1
Deadline: January 28
College level: Freshman
Majors/Fields: Art, art education, art history
Criteria: Applicant must be an African-American student enrolling in the art department at the Toledo Museum of Art. Award is for four years. Awarded every year. Award may be used only at sponsoring institution.
Contact: J.C. Caldwell, 50 Men and Women of Toledo, Inc., P.O. Box 3557, Toledo, OH 43608, (419) 729-4654.

392 NSS Scholarship

National Sculpture Society (NSS)
1177 Avenue of the Americas
New York, NY 10036
(212) 764-5645
Maximum award: $1,000
Minimum award: $1,000
Deadline: Early application recommended
College level: Freshman, Sophomore, Junior, Senior, Graduate, Doctoral
Majors/Fields: Figurative sculpture, realist sculpture
Criteria: Applicant must submit a brief biography and explanation of sculpture background, two recommendations, black and white 8" x 10" photos of at least three works, and demonstrate financial need. Reapplication is required for renewal. Awarded every year.
Contact: Gwen Pier, Executive Director.

393 Smithsonian Institution Internships and Fellowships

Smithsonian Institution Conservation Analytical Laboratory Interns
Museum Support Center
MRC 534
Washington, DC 20560
(301) 238-3700
Maximum award: $22,000
Minimum award: $13,000
Number of awards: 9
Deadline: February 15
College level: Graduate, Doctoral
Majors/Fields: Art conservation
Criteria: Awarded every year.
Contact: Carol Grissom, Coordinator of Training, (301) 238-3732.

394 Stacey Scholarship Fund

John F. and Anna Lee Stacey Testamentary Trust/National Academy of Western Art
1700 Northeast 63rd
Oklahoma City, OK 73111
Average award: $3,000
Minimum award: $1,000
Number of awards: 2
Deadline: February 1
College level: Freshman
Majors/Fields: Painting, drawing
Criteria: Applicant must be a U.S. citizen, an artist, between 18 and 35 years of age, who is skilled and devoted to the classical or conservative tradition of painting or drawing. Reapplication is required for renewal. Awarded every year.
Contact: Ed Muno.

395 Virginia Museum of Fine Arts Fellowship

Virginia Museum of Fine Arts
2800 Grove Avenue
Office of Education and Outreach
Richmond, VA 23221-2466
(804) 367-0824
Average award: $5,000
Maximum award: $8,000
Minimum award: $4,000
Number of awards: 9
Deadline: March 1
College level: Freshman, Sophomore, Junior, Senior, Graduate, Doctoral, professional artists
Majors/Fields: Art history, crafts, drawing, film, painting, photography, printmaking, sculpture, video, visual arts
Criteria: Applicant must be a legal resident of Virginia for one year prior to the deadline, and students must be enrolled full time at an accredited college, university, or school of the arts. Selection is based upon submission of a portfolio of ten works, or of three films, research papers, or published articles. Awarded every year.
Contact: Susan F. Ferrell, Fellowship Program Coordinator.

396 Visual Arts Scholarship

Northern Virginia Handcrafters' Guild
c/o Dorothy A. Hassfeld
Route 1, Box 51
Broad Run, VA 22014
Minimum award: $1,200
Number of awards: 2
Deadline: April 1
College level: Freshman
Criteria: Awarded to a student with interest and demonstrated talent in some crafts or art. Applicant must be a high school senior planning post-secondary level metalsmithing, fibrecrafts, glass, woodworking, pottery, drawing, or painting, and must live within a 60 mile radius of Merrifield, Va. No academic requirements are specified, but applicant must demonstrate reasonable chance of success in planned program of study. Financial need may be considered during the final selection process. Awarded every year.
Contact: Akiko Brilliant, (703) 978-0845.

Graphic Arts

397 Angelo Divencenzo Scholarship

Art Institute of Fort Lauderdale
1799 South 17th Street
Fort Lauderdale, FL 33316-3000
(800) 275-7603
Average award: $2,980
Number of awards: 1
College level: Freshman
Majors/Fields: Visual communications
Criteria: Selection is based upon academic excellence, attitude, and professionalism. Awarded every year. Award may be used only at sponsoring institution.
Contact: Laura Waterman, Director of Student Financial Services, (305) 463-3000, extension 471.

398 Art and Design Regents Scholarship

Southwest Missouri State University
Student Financial Aid
901 South National Avenue
Springfield, MO 65804-0095
(417) 836-5000 or (800) 492-7900
Average award: $1,000
Number of awards: 5
Deadline: February 26
College level: Freshman, Junior, Senior
Majors/Fields: Art/design
Criteria: Freshman applicant must have a minimum cumulative "B" grade average, three letters of recommendation, and submit a portfolio of art work. Upperclass applicant is judged on creative work and academic record; minimum 3.0 cumulative GPA is required. Satisfactory art work, academic progress, and financial need are required to retain scholarship. Awarded every year. Award may be used only at sponsoring institution.
Contact: Scholarship Committee, (417) 836-5262 or (800) 492-7900.

399 Colorado Institute of Art Scholarship

Colorado Institute of Art
200 East Ninth Avenue
Denver, CO 80203
(303) 837-0825
Average award: $11,480
Number of awards: 5
Deadline: January 31
College level: Freshman
Majors/Fields: Culinary arts, fashion design, industrial design, interior design, music/video business, photography, visual communication
Criteria: Applicant must submit slides of original artwork, actual photographs or written projects (depending on major). Selection is based upon merit, talent, and academic background. Minimum 2.5 GPA is required to retain scholarship. Awarded every year.
Contact: Barbara H. Browning, Director of Admissions.

400 CPIA Scholarship Trust Fund

Canadian Printing Industry Association
Fuller Building, Suite 906
75 Albert Street
Ottawa, Ontario, CN K1P 5E7
(613) 236-7208
Average award: $800
Number of awards: 50
Deadline: June 15
Majors/Fields: Graphic communications
Criteria: Applicant must attend school in Canada and be interested in a career in graphic communications. Renewable if minimum "B" average is maintained. Awarded every year.
Contact: Keith Jackson, President.

401 Edgar H. Snider Memorial Scholarship

Clemson University
G-01 Sikes Hall
Clemson, SC 29634-5123
(803) 656-2280
Average award: $1,000
Number of awards: 8
Deadline: March 1
College level: Freshman, Sophomore, Junior, Senior
Majors/Fields: Graphic communications
Criteria: Applicant must have a major or minor in graphic communications. Awarded every year. Award may be used only at sponsoring institution.
Contact: Marvin Carmichael, Director of Financial Aid.

402 Printing and Publishing Industry National Scholarship Program

National Scholarship Trust Fund
4615 Forbes Avenue
Pittsburgh, PA 15213-3796
(412) 621-6941
Maximum award: $1,000
Minimum award: $500
Maximum number of awards: 100
Minimum number of awards: 80
Deadline: January 15 (entering freshmen); March 15 (college students)
College level: Freshman, Sophomore, Junior, Senior
Majors/Fields: Graphic communications
Criteria: Selection is based upon a minimum 3.0 GPA, test scores, and recommendations. Minimum 3.0 GPA is required to retain scholarship. Awarded every year.
Contact: Ann Mayhew, Administrative Assistant.

403 Robert P. Scripps Graphic Arts Grant

Scripps Howard Foundation
P.O. Box 5380
Cincinnati, OH 45201-5380
(513) 977-3035
Maximum award: $3,000
Minimum award: $500
Deadline: February 25
College level: Freshman, Sophomore, Junior, Senior, Graduate, Doctoral
Majors/Fields: Graphic arts
Criteria: Applicant must be a U.S. citizen, resident alien, or hold a valid U.S. visa, have good scholastic standing, demonstrate interest in the field of journalism, demonstrate financial need, and major in graphic arts as applied to the newspaper industry, with the potential of becoming an administrator in newspaper production. Request application by December 20. Awarded every year.
Contact: Mary Lou Marusin, Executive Director.

404 TIME Education Program Student Art Competition for High School Students

TIME Education Program
Student Writing and Art Competition
P.O. Box 1000
Mount Kisco, NY 10549
(800) 882-0852
Average award: $2,500
Maximum award: $5,000
Minimum award: $1,250
Number of awards: 4
Deadline: March 1
College level: Freshman
Criteria: Applicant must be a high school student in the U.S. or Canada and submit a TIME cover design or political cartoon to be judged in the competition. Awarded every year.
Contact: Awards.

405 Traineeships in Exhibit Interpretation, Public Affairs, Education, Horticulture, Facilities Design, and Photography

Friends of the National Zoo
National Zoological Park
Washington, DC 20008
Maximum award: $2,400
Majors/Fields: Zoo graphics, photography, public affairs, education, horticulture, facilities design
Criteria: Selection is based upon statement of interest, scholastic achievement, relevant experience, and letters of reference.
Contact: Traineeships.

406 Young American Creative Patriotic Art Award

Young American Creative Patriotic Art Program
Ladies Auxiliary to the VFW
406 West 34th Street
Kansas City, MO 64111
(816) 561-8655
Maximum award: $3,000
Minimum award: $500
Number of awards: 5
Deadline: April 1
College level: Freshman, high school students in grades 9–12
Criteria: Applicant must be a high school student, U.S. citizen, and submit an unframed, patriotic art work on paper or canvas. Applicant must attend school in the same state as the sponsoring Auxiliary. Competition begins at the school level, then state, and national levels; awards are given on all levels. First- and second-place winners may not compete again; all others may compete again but must submit new entries. Awarded every year.
Contact: Judy Millick, Administrator of Programs.

Instrumental Music

407 Chopin Piano Scholarship

Kosciuszko Foundation
15 East 65th Street
New York, NY 10021
(212) 734-2130
Maximum award: $2,500
Minimum award: $1,000
Number of awards: 3
Deadline: March 31
Majors/Fields: Piano
Criteria: Award is designed to encourage highly talented American students of piano to study and play the works of Chopin. Competition is open to U.S. citizens and legal residents, regardless of ethnic background, who have demonstrated unusual musical ability but have not yet made extensive professional appearances. Contestant must be between the ages of 15 and 21 as of the opening date of the competition. Awarded every year.
Contact: Scholarships.

408 Honors String Awards

University of Colorado at Boulder
Campus Box 106
Boulder, CO 80309-0106
(303) 492-5091
Maximum award: $1,600
Minimum award: $1,400
Number of awards: 12
College level: Freshman, Sophomore, Junior, Senior
Majors/Fields: Instrumental music
Criteria: Applicant must be a performer in a string quartet. Awarded every year. Award may be used only at sponsoring institution.
Contact: Office of Financial Aid.

409 Isabel Rutter Endowment Scholarship

New Mexico State University
Box 30001
Department 5100
Las Cruces, NM 88003-0001
(505) 646-4105
Average award: Full tuition
Number of awards: 1
Deadline: March 1
College level: Sophomore, Junior, Senior
Majors/Fields: Violin
Criteria: Applicant must be a student of violin selected by the director of the Las Cruces Symphony. Awarded every year. Award may be used only at sponsoring institution.
Contact: College of Arts and Sciences, (505) 646-2001.

410 J.S. Bach International Competition

J.S. Bach International Competitions
1211 Potomac Street, NW
Washington, DC 20007
Maximum award: $4,000
Minimum award: $1,500
Number of awards: 3
Criteria: Competition is open to musicians of all countries, including foreigners who may be studying in the U.S. Applicant must be between the ages of 20 and 40. Enclose a self-addressed, stamped envelope with inquiry.
Contact: Competitions.

411 Joyce Margaret Locke Scholarship

University of Calgary
2500 University Drive, NW
Calgary, Alberta, CN T2N 1N4
(403) 220-7872
Average award: $1,000
Number of awards: 4
College level: Freshman, Sophomore, Junior, Senior
Majors/Fields: Music, string bass, viola, violin, violincello
Criteria: Selection is based upon performance before the spring jury or audition jury. Awarded every year. Award may be used only at sponsoring institution.
Contact: J. Van Housen, Director of Student Awards and Financial Aid.

412 Leonard Rose Cello Competition

Maryland Summer Institute for the Creative and Performing Arts
Summer & Special Programs
University of Maryland
College Park, MD 20742-5321
(301) 405-6540, (301) 405-6548
Maximum award: $20,000
Deadline: April 1
College level: Advanced cellists
Majors/Fields: Cello
Criteria: Major international music competition for the most advanced cellists only. Competition rounds examine solo repertoire and performance with symphony orchestra. Applicant must be between 18 and 30 years of age. Next competition will be held in 1997.
Contact: Donald Reinhold, Assistant Director, (301) 405-6548.

413   Marjorie Martin Caylor Scholarship

University of Oklahoma
University Affairs
900 Asp Avenue, Room 236
Norman, OK 73019-0401
(405) 325-1701
Average award: $1,000
Number of awards: 8
College level: Freshman, Sophomore, Junior, Senior
Majors/Fields: Keyboard
Criteria: Applicant must audition. Selection is based upon merit and talent on keyboard. Awarded every year. Award may be used only at sponsoring institution.
Contact: Director of School of Music, 560 Parrington Oval, Norman, OK 73019, (405) 325-2081.

414   Music Assistance Fund Scholarship

American Symphony Orchestra League
1156 Fifteenth Street, NW
Suite 800
Washington, DC 20005-1704
(202) 628-0099
Average award: $1,550
Maximum award: $2,500
Minimum award: $500
Number of awards: 55
Deadline: January 15
College level: Unspecified graduate, unspecified undergraduate
Majors/Fields: Music
Criteria: Applicant must be a U.S. citizen and an African-American who is currently attending or planning to attend a U.S. conservatory or school of music, and be a student of orchestral instruments majoring in music (peformance concentration desired). Piano, composition, conducting, or vocal majors are not eligible. Award allows recipient to attend a recognized summer program of music study and/or academic institution. Applicant should plan to pursue a career with a symphony orchestra. Selection is based upon need, recommendation, and talent. Audition is required. Renewal is based upon audition and need. Awarded every year.
Contact: Lorri Ward, Special Assistant to the President.

415   National Young Artists Competition in Organ Performance

American Guild of Organists
475 Riverside Drive, Suite 1260
New York, NY 10115
(212) 870-2310
Maximum award: $2,000
Minimum award: $750
Deadline: May 1
Majors/Fields: Organ
Criteria: Applicant must be an organist between 22 and 32 years of age, a member of the American Guild of Organists, and seriously interested in pursuing a recital career. Selection is based upon a comprehensive application procedure and three rounds of playing competition. Competition is held every other year.
Contact: Awards.

416   Pride Scholarship

University of Oklahoma
University Affairs
900 Asp Avenue, Room 236
Norman, OK 73019-0401
(405) 325-1701
Average award: $1,000
Maximum number of awards: 10
Minimum number of awards: 6
College level: Freshman, Sophomore, Junior, Senior
Majors/Fields: Music
Criteria: Applicant must be a member of the Pride of Oklahoma Marching Band. Awarded every year. Award may be used only at sponsoring institution.
Contact: Director of School of Music, 560 Parrington Oval, Norman, OK 73019, (405) 325-2081.

417   Regional Competitions for Young Organists

American Guild of Organists
475 Riverside Drive, Suite 1260
New York, NY 10115
(212) 870-2310
Maximum award: $1,000
Minimum award: $500
Majors/Fields: Organ
Criteria: Applicant may compete only in region of residence or school and must be 23 years of age or younger. Applicant need not be a member of the American Guild of Organists.
Contact: Awards.

418   Wallace F. Fiske Memorial Scholarship

University of Colorado at Boulder
Campus Box 106
Boulder, CO 80309-0106
(303) 492-5091
Average award: $1,800
Number of awards: 2
College level: Freshman, Sophomore, Junior, Senior
Majors/Fields: Instrumental music
Criteria: Awarded to the winners of a competition for excellence in performance in wind, brass, and percussion instruments. Awarded every year. Award may be used only at sponsoring institution.
Contact: Office of Financial Aid.

419   William Kapell Piano Competition

Maryland Summer Institute for the Creative & Performing Arts
Summer & Special Programs
University of Maryland
College Park, MD 20742-5321
(301) 405-6540, (301) 405-6548
Maximum award: $20,000
Deadline: April 1
College level: Advanced pianists
Majors/Fields: Piano
Criteria: Major international music competition for the most advanced pianists only. Competition rounds examine solo repertoire and performance with symphony orchestra. Applicant must be between 18 and 33 years of age. Competition will be held in 1996, 1998, 2000.
Contact: Donald Reinhold, Assistant Director, (301) 405-6548.

Music–General

420   ASCAP Foundation Grants to Young Composers

American Society of Composers, Authors, and Publishers
ASCAP Building, One Lincoln Plaza
New York, NY 10023
(212) 621-6327
Maximum award: $2,500
Minimum award: $250
Number of awards: 27
Deadline: March 15
College level: Freshman, Sophomore, Junior, Senior, Graduate, Doctoral
Criteria: Applicant must be a U.S. resident under 30 years of age. Awarded every year.
Contact: Frances Richard, Director.

421   Don Wright Prize

University of Calgary
2500 University Drive, NW
Calgary, Alberta, CN T2N 1N4
(403) 220-7872
Average award: $1,000
Number of awards: 2
College level: Freshman, Sophomore, Junior, Senior
Majors/Fields: Music
Criteria: Selection is based upon applicant's contribution to the musical life of the department in the previous academic year or on the recommendation of the audition jury. Awarded every year. Award may be used only at sponsoring institution.
Contact: J. Van Housen, Director of Student Awards & Financial Aid.

422   Eileen Phillips Cohen Music Scholarship

University of Wisconsin-Eau Claire
105 Garfield Avenue
Eau Claire, WI 54701
(715) 836-3373
Average award: $2,034
Number of awards: 3
Deadline: July 28
College level: Sophomore, Junior, Senior
Majors/Fields: Music
Criteria: Selection is based upon musical talent and good citizenship. Financial need is not necessarily a factor. Audition is required. Awarded every year. Award may be used only at sponsoring institution.
Contact: Melissa Vogler, Financial Aid Counselor.

423   Emily K. Rand Scholarship

Rand Memorial Trust Fund
c/o Joyce Chaplin
92 Raymond Road
Brunswick, ME 04011
(207) 725-1125
Average award: $800
Maximum award: $1,200
Minimum award: $500
Number of awards: 4
Deadline: May 6
College level: Freshman, Sophomore, Junior, Senior, Graduate, Doctoral
Majors/Fields: Music
Criteria: Applicant must be a resident of Cumberland, Oxford, or York counties, Maine, between 17 and 25 years of age at time of 10-minute audition. Audition should draw primarily from classical idiom. Applicant must have outstanding musical ability and good scholastic rating. Awarded every year.
Contact: Joyce Chaplin, Chairman.

424   F.L. Fenwick Scholarship in Music

University of Calgary
2500 University Drive, NW
Calgary, Alberta, CN T2N 1N4
(403) 220-7872
Average award: $2,500
Number of awards: 1
College level: Freshman, Sophomore, Junior, Senior
Majors/Fields: Music, pipe organ
Criteria: Awarded on the recommendation of the audition jury or the spring jury to a student studying the pipe organ. If no organist qualifies, students studying harpsichord will become eligible. Awarded every year. Award may be used only at sponsoring institution.
Contact: J. Van Housen, Director of Student Awards and Financial Aid.

425   GFWC of MA Music Scholarship

General Federation of Women's Clubs of Massachusetts
Box 679
Sudbury, MA 01776-0679
(508) 443-4569
Average award: $500
Number of awards: 5
Deadline: February 15
College level: Freshman
Majors/Fields: Instrument, music education, music therapy, piano
Criteria: Applicant must attend a Massachusetts high school and submit a letter of endorsement from the president of the sponsoring GFWC of MA club in the community of legal residence and a recommendation from either the music teacher or the high school principal. Audition is also required. Awarded every year.
Contact: Scholarships.

426   Glenn Miller Scholarship

Glenn Miller Birthplace Society
711 North Fourteenth Street
Clarinda, IA 51632
(712) 542-4439
Maximum award: $1,250
Minimum award: $500
Number of awards: 4
Deadline: March 15
College level: Freshman, Sophomore
Majors/Fields: Instrumental music, vocal music
Criteria: Applicant must intend to make music a central part of life. Awarded every year.
Contact: Scholarships.

427   Herbert and Golden Fitch Memorial Scholarship

Fort Collins Symphony Association
P.O. Box 1963
Fort Collins, CO 80522-1963
(303) 482-4823
Average award: $1,000
Majors/Fields: Music
Criteria: Applicant must be a music student at Colorado State U-Fort Collins who is available to play in the orchestra and is recommended by Maestro Will Schwartz. Scholarship is renewable. Awarded every year. Award may be used only at sponsoring institution.
Contact: Maestro Will Schwartz, Music Director, FCSU, P.O. Box 1963, Fort Collins, CO 80522.

428   Music Department Scholarship

University of Tennessee–Knoxville
Financial Aid Office
115 Student Services Building
Knoxville, TN 37994
(615) 974-3131
Average award: $1,500
Deadline: February 1
College level: Freshman, Sophomore, Junior, Senior
Majors/Fields: Music
Criteria: Length of awards varies. Awarded every year. Award may be used only at sponsoring institution.
Contact: Scholarship Coordinator, College of Liberal Arts, 220 Ayres Hall, Knoxville, TN 37996, (615) 974-4481.

429   Music Department Tuition Remission Scholarship

Portland State University
P.O. Box 751
Portland, OR 97207-0751
(503) 725-5270
Average award: $2,500
Deadline: in May
College level: Sophomore, Junior, Senior
Majors/Fields: Music
Criteria: Applicant must demonstrate outstanding musical skill. Renewable if minimum 3.0 GPA is maintained. Awarded every year. Award may be used only at sponsoring institution.
Contact: Scholarships, Music Department, (503) 725-3011.

430   Music Regents Scholarship

Southwest Missouri State University
Student Financial Aid
901 South National Avenue
Springfield, MO 65804-0095
(417) 836-5000 or (800) 492-7900
Average award: $1,000
Number of awards: 16
Deadline: March 31
College level: Sophomore, Junior, Senior
Majors/Fields: Music
Criteria: Selection is based upon audition. Minimum 2.5 cumulative GPA, with a 2.75 GPA in music courses, and continued promise of success in performance is required to retain scholarship. Awarded every year. Award may be used only at sponsoring institution.
Contact: Scholarship Committee, (417) 836-5262 or (800) 492-7900.

431   Nancy and Ted Anderson Music Scholarship

University of Colorado at Boulder
Campus Box 106
Boulder, CO 80309-0106
(303) 492-5091
Average award: $1,800
Number of awards: 20
College level: Freshman, Sophomore, Junior, Senior
Majors/Fields: Piano performance, voice performance
Criteria: Selection is by competition for excellence in piano performance and voice performance. Awarded every year. Award may be used only at sponsoring institution.
Contact: Office of Financial Aid.

432   National Orchestral Institute

Maryland Summer Institute for the Creative & Performing Arts
Summer & Special Programs
University of Maryland
College Park, MD 20742-5321
(301) 405-6540, (301) 405-6548
Maximum award: Tuition, room, and board for three-week program.
Deadline: February and March
Majors/Fields: Music
Criteria: Applicant must be between 18 and 30 years of age and be a talented musician on the threshold of professional career.
Contact: Donald Reinhold, Assistant Director.

433   Presser Foundation Scholarship

Western Washington University
516 High Street
Bellingham, WA 98226-9006
(206) 650-3471
Average award: $2,250
Number of awards: 1
College level: Senior
Majors/Fields: Music
Criteria: Applicant must be nominated by the Music Department faculty. Awarded every year. Award may be used only at sponsoring institution.
Contact: Music Department, 273 Performing Arts Center, Bellingham, WA 98225, (206) 650-3130.

434   Presser Scholarship

University of Colorado at Boulder
Campus Box 106
Boulder, CO 80309-0106
(303) 492-5091
Average award: $2,250
Number of awards: 1
College level: Senior
Majors/Fields: Music
Criteria: Applicant must excel in performance and scholastic achievement. Awarded every year. Award may be used only at sponsoring institution.
Contact: Office of Financial Aid.

435   Sorantin Young Artist Award

San Angelo Symphony Orchestra
P.O. Box 5922
San Angelo, TX 76902
(915) 658-5877
Maximum award: $2,000
Minimum award: $250
Number of awards: 6
Deadline: October 23
Majors/Fields: Piano, vocal, instrumental
Contact: Awards.

Voice

436   Altamura-Enrico Caruso Voice Competition, USA

Enrico Caruso Voice Competition, USA
Inter-Cities Performing Arts, Inc.
4000 Bergenline Avenue
Union City, NJ 07087
(201) 863-4211
Maximum award: $10,000
Deadline: May 31
Majors/Fields: Operatic studies
Criteria: Applicant must be a young professional majoring in operatic studies, currently performing in opera, and wishing to advance to the next level. Awarded every year.
Contact: Inter-Cities Performing Arts, Inc., 4000 Bergenline Avenue, Union City, NJ 07087.

437   Annual Operatic Vocal Competition for North American Artists

Baltimore Opera Company
1202 Maryland Avenue
Baltimore, MD 21201
(410) 625-1600
Maximum award: $10,000
Minimum award: $1,000
Number of awards: 8
Deadline: April 30
Majors/Fields: Opera, voice
Criteria: Applicant must be between 20 and 30 years of age. Prizes are awarded with the understanding that they will be used to further voice training, learn operatic roles, develop dramatic ability, or to perfect foreign languages. Scholarship is renewable. Scholarship is awarded every other year.
Contact: James Hard, Competition Coordinator.

438   Benton-Schmidt Scholarship

University of Oklahoma
University Affairs
900 Asp Avenue, Room 236
Norman, OK 73019-0401
(405) 325-1701
Maximum award: $3,000
Minimum award: $1,500
Number of awards: 7
College level: Graduate, Doctoral
Majors/Fields: Voice
Criteria: Applicant must audition. Selection is based upon merit and talent. Awarded every year. Award may be used only at sponsoring institution.
Contact: Director of School of Music, 560 Parrington Oval, Norman, OK 73019, (405) 325-2081.

439   Liederkranz Foundation Scholarship Award for Voice

Liederkranz Foundation
6 East 87th Street
New York, NY 10128
(212) 534-0880
Average award: $1,500
Maximum award: $3,500
Minimum award: $1,000
Number of awards: 20
Deadline: December 1
College level: Junior, Senior, Graduate, Doctoral
Majors/Fields: Vocal music
Criteria: Applicant must be 20–35 years old for general voice competition and 25–45 years old for Wagnerian voice competition. Applicant must audition; winners must perform at scholarship awards concert and a Liederkranz Foundation performance. $25 application fee is required. Awarded every year.
Contact: John Balme, Music Director.

440 **Marian Anderson Vocal Arts Competition**

Maryland Summer Institute for the Creative and Performing
Arts
Summer & Special Programs
University of Maryland
College Park, MD 20742-5321
(301) 405-6540, (301) 405-6548
Maximum award: $20,000
Deadline: April 1
College level: Advanced vocalists
Majors/Fields: Voice
Criteria: Major international music competition for the most advanced
vocalists only. Competition rounds examine solo repertoire and per-
formance with symphony orchestra. Applicant must be between 21
and 39 years of age. Competition is held in 1995 and 1999.
Contact: Donald Reinhold, Summer & Special Programs.

441 **Metropolitan Opera National Council Regional
Award**

Metropolitan Opera
National Council Auditions
Lincoln Center
New York, NY 10023
(212) 799-3100
Maximum award: $10,000
Minimum award: $400
Maximum number of awards: 5
Minimum number of awards: 1
Deadline: Varies
Majors/Fields: Music, voice
Criteria: Applicant must audition, have a voice with operatic poten-
tial, have musical training, should be able to sing in more than one
language, and be a U.S. citizen or resident for at least one year.
Scholarship is renewable. Awarded every year.
Contact: Awards.

442 **Robert Knauf Vocal Music Scholarship**

Northern Kentucky University
Administrative Center 416
Nunn Drive
Highland Heights, KY 41099-7101
(606) 572-5144
Average award: In-state tuition
Deadline: February 1
College level: Freshman, Sophomore, Junior, Senior
Majors/Fields: Vocal music
Criteria: Applicant must major in vocal music and submit two refer-
ence letters from former and/or present vocal instructors. Award is
renewable for 1–3 years. Awarded every year. Award may be used
only at sponsoring institution.
Contact: Robert E. Sprague, Director of Financial Aid.

443 **Sergio Franchi Music Scholarship in Voice
Performance**

National Italian American Foundation (NIAF)
Educational Scholarship Program
1860 19th Street, NW
Washington, DC 20009-5599
(202) 638-2137
Minimum award: $1,000
Deadline: May 31
College level: Sophomore, Junior, Senior, Graduate, Doctoral
Majors/Fields: Voice
Criteria: Applicant must be Italian-American, demonstrate financial
need, and submit transcript and tape of work.
Contact: Dr. Maria Lombardo, Education Director.

Education

Education–General

444   A. Martin and Ruth Zucker Memorial Scholarship

University of Toledo
Financial Aid Office
Toledo, OH 43606-3390
(419) 537-2056
Maximum award: $2,000
Maximum number of awards: 7
Minimum number of awards: 1
College level: Freshman, Sophomore, Junior, Senior
Majors/Fields: Education
Criteria: Awarded every year. Award may be used only at sponsoring institution.
Contact: Dean, College of Education and Allied Professions, Toledo, OH 43606, (419) 537-2025.

445   American Association of School Administrators Scholarship

American Association of School Administrators
1801 North Moore Street
Arlington, VA 22209
(703) 875-0714
Average award: $2,000
Number of awards: 5
Deadline: May 1
Majors/Fields: Education, administration
Criteria: Applicant should apply to the dean of education at his or her college in March. Awarded every year.
Contact: Molly Haden.

446   Child Care Provider Scholarship

Maryland Higher Education Commission
State Scholarship Administration
16 Francis Street
Annapolis, MD 21401-1781
(410) 974-5370
Maximum award: $2,000
Number of awards: 95
Deadline: June 30
College level: Freshman, Sophomore, Junior, Senior
Majors/Fields: Child development, early childhood education
Criteria: Applicant must be a Maryland resident with a minimum 2.0 GPA, file a completed Child Care Provider application, and be enrolled in a program leading to an associate or bachelor's degree or a Child Development Associate Credential. Applicant must agree to work one year in a Maryland childcare center as a day care provider or staff member for each year of the award. Reapplication is required to retain scholarship for three additional years. Awarded every year.
Contact: Michael Smith, Program Administrator.

447   Congressional Teacher Scholarship (NC)

Congressional Teacher Scholarship Program
Respective Schools of North Carolina
Average award: $5,000
Number of awards: 50
Majors/Fields: Education
Criteria: Applicant must be enrolled in good standing in an approved teacher education program, have ranked in top tenth of high school graduating class, and have interest in teaching in North Carolina. Applicants are nominated by deans of education at the 44 public and private schools in North Carolina with teacher education programs. Renewable if academic performance is maintained. Awarded every year.
Contact: Dean of Education.

448   David A. DeBolt Teacher Shortage Scholarship

Illinois Student Assistance Commission/Client Services
1755 Lake Cook Road
Deerfield, IL 60015-5209
(800) 899-ISAC, (708) 948-8500
Maximum award: $3,000
Deadline: May 1
College level: Sophomore, Junior, Senior, Graduate, Doctoral
Majors/Fields: Education
Criteria: Applicant must be a U.S. citizen or eligible noncitizen and a legal resident of Illinois. Applicant must be enrolled or accepted for enrollment on at least a half-time basis as an undergraduate in a qualified teacher education program at an approved Illinois institution in a teacher shortage discipline. Preference is given to minority applicants. Recipient must sign a contract promising to teach one year for each year of scholarship assistance or repay the money plus interest. Scholarship is renewable. Awarded every year.
Contact: Manager of Scholarships and Specialized Grants.

449   Dean William H. Washington and Miriam Betts Washington Scholarship

Clemson University
G-01 Sikes Hall
Clemson, SC 29634-5123
(803) 656-2280
Average award: $1,500
Number of awards: 2
Deadline: March 1
College level: Freshman, Sophomore, Junior, Senior
Majors/Fields: Education
Criteria: Applicant must demonstrate financial need and have a minimum 2.0 GPA. Awarded every year. Award may be used only at sponsoring institution.
Contact: Marvin Carmichael, Director of Financial Aid.

450   Dean's Education Scholarship

DePaul University
25 East Jackson Boulevard
Suite 100
Chicago, IL 60604
(312) 362-8704
Maximum award: $7,000
Minimum award: $2,000
Deadline: February 1
College level: Freshman, transfer students
Majors/Fields: Early childhood education, elementary education, secondary education
Criteria: Applicant must present strong academic credentials and a strong interest in teaching. Transfer applicant must have a minimum 3.0 GPA. Minimum 2.75 GPA freshman year and minimum 3.0 GPA thereafter as a full-time education major is required to retain scholarship. Awarded every year. Award may be used only at sponsoring institution.
Contact: Admissions Office.

451   Distinguished Scholar Teacher Education

Maryland Higher Education Commission
State Scholarship Administration
16 Francis Street
Annapolis, MD 21401-1781
(410) 974-5370
Average award: $3,000
Number of awards: 53
Deadline: July 1
College level: Freshman, Sophomore, Junior, Senior, Graduate
Majors/Fields: Education
Criteria: Applicant must be a distinguished scholar award recipient and must teach in a Maryland public school one year for each year of award. Minimum 3.0 GPA is required to retain scholarship. Awarded every year.
Contact: Margaret Riley, Program Administrator.

452   Future Teacher Conditional Scholarship

Washington Higher Education Coordinating Board
917 Lakeridge Way
P.O. Box 43430
Olympia, WA 98504-3430
(206) 753-3571
Maximum award: $3,000
Number of awards: 93
Majors/Fields: Education
Criteria: Applicant must demonstrate outstanding academic achievement. Preference is given to certain ethnic minorities. Scholarship is renewable for up to five years and requires a ten-year Washington public school teaching commitment or repayment of the scholarship plus interest. Scholarship is renewable. Awarded every year.
Contact: Elizabeth A. Gebhardt, Assistant Director of Student Financial Aid, (206) 753-4592.

453   Future Teachers Conditional Scholarship

Western Washington University
516 High Street
Bellingham, WA 98226-9006
(206) 650-3471
Average award: $3,000
Deadline: April 15
College level: Freshman, Sophomore, Junior, Senior
Majors/Fields: Education
Criteria: Applicant must be a Washington State resident, have a minimum cumulative high school GPA of 3.3 or college GPA of 3.0, and have declared intent to complete a program leading to initial teacher certification or additional teaching endorsements. Recipient must teach for ten years in a Washington public school or will be required to repay the scholarship. Selection is based upon academic excellence, commitment to teaching, leadership ability, community service involvement, and ability to act as a role model for children including targeted ethnic minorities. Satisfactory academic progress is required to retain scholarship for a maximum of five years. Awarded every year. Award may be used only at sponsoring institution.
Contact: Francine E. Titus, Scholarship Coordinator.

454   Indiana Minority Teacher Scholarship

State Student Assistance Commission of Indiana
150 West Market Street
Suite 500
Indianapolis, IN 46204-2811
(317) 232-2350
Maximum award: $4,000
Minimum award: $1,000
Maximum number of awards: 500
Minimum number of awards: 300
Deadline: Varies with college attended
College level: Freshman, Sophomore, Junior, Senior
Majors/Fields: Education
Criteria: Applicant must be a black or Hispanic Indiana resident with a minimum 2.0 GPA who agrees to teach in Indiana upon certification. Reapplication, minimum 2.0 GPA, and full-time enrollment are required to retain scholarship. Awarded every year.
Contact: Yvonne Heflin, Director of Special Programs.

455   J. Lloyd Rogers Family Scholarship

Southwest Texas State University
J. C. Kellam Building
San Marcos, TX 78666
(512) 245-2340
Average award: $1,000
Number of awards: 3
Deadline: March 1
College level: Junior, Senior
Majors/Fields: Education
Criteria: Applicant must be a man who has completed 60 hours of college-level work. Awarded every year. Award may be used only at sponsoring institution.
Contact: Elementary and Secondary Education Office.

456   Julia Victor and Leslie Carlisle McDonald Scholarship

Southwest Texas State University
J. C. Kellam Building
San Marcos, TX 78666
(512) 245-2340
Average award: $1,250
Number of awards: 2
Deadline: March 1
College level: Freshman, Sophomore, Junior, Senior
Majors/Fields: Education
Criteria: Applicant must have a minimum 3.0 GPA, be enrolled in the teacher education program for at least 12 hours, and be a member of at least one professional organization related to education. Awarded yearly subject to availability of funds. Award may be used only at sponsoring institution.
Contact: Elementary and Secondary Education Office, San Marcos, TX 78666-4602, (512) 245-2315.

457   LBJ Achievement Scholarship in Education

Southwest Texas State University
J. C. Kellam Building
San Marcos, TX 78666
(512) 245-2340
Average award: $1,000
Number of awards: 10
Deadline: November 15, March 15
College level: Junior, Senior
Majors/Fields: Education
Criteria: Applicant must be a black or Hispanic Texas resident enrolled full time with a minimum 3.0 GPA. Minimum 3.0 GPA is required to retain scholarship. Awarded every year. Award may be used only at sponsoring institution.
Contact: Coordinator of Scholarships, Office of Student Financial Aid, 601 University Drive, (512) 245-2315.

458   Mary Esther Lily Avis Scholarship

University of Calgary
2500 University Drive, NW
Calgary, Alberta, CN T2N 1N4
(403) 220-7872
Average award: $2,000
Number of awards: 8
Deadline: June 15
College level: Sophomore, Junior, Senior
Majors/Fields: Education
Criteria: Selection is based upon academic merit. Awarded every year. Award may be used only at sponsoring institution.
Contact: J. Van Housen, Director of Student Awards & Financial Aid.

459   Missouri Teacher Education Scholarship

Missouri Department of Elementary and Secondary Education
P.O. Box 480
Jefferson City, MO 65102
(314) 751-0300
Average award: $2,000
Number of awards: 250
Deadline: February 15
College level: Freshman, Sophomore, Junior, non-traditional students
Majors/Fields: Education
Criteria: Applicant must be a resident of Missouri, rank in the top 15% of high school class, or score in the top 15% on the SAT I, ACT, or SCAT exams. Applicant must agree to teach in the Missouri public schools (PreK-12) for five years after graduation. Awarded every year.
Contact: Karen Wunderlich, Supervisor.

460   New Mexico Space Grant Teacher Fellowship

New Mexico State University
Box 30001
Department 5100
Las Cruces, NM 88003-0001
(505) 646-4105
Maximum award: $10,000
Number of awards: 3
Deadline: March 1
College level: Freshman, Sophomore, Junior, Senior
Majors/Fields: Education, elementary education, math, science
Criteria: Applicant must be enrolled in a teacher certification program, have a minimum cumulative GPA of 3.25, be a U.S. citizen, and agree to work in the educational program at the Space Center in Alamogordo, N.Mex. Preference is given to women and minority students. Awarded every year. Award may be used only at sponsoring institution.
Contact: Greeley W. Myers, Director of Financial Aid.

461   Paul Douglas Conditional Scholarship

Western Washington University
516 High Street
Bellingham, WA 98226-9006
(206) 650-3471
Maximum award: $5,000
Deadline: Mid-January
College level: Freshman, Sophomore, Junior, Senior
Majors/Fields: Education
Criteria: Applicant must be a Washington State resident, rank in top tenth of high school class, and agree to teach for two years for each year the scholarship is received. Scholarship is renewable. Awarded every year. Award may be used only at sponsoring institution.
Contact: Francine E. Titus, Scholarship Coordinator.

462   Paul Douglas Teacher Scholarship

California Student Aid Commission
P.O. Box 510845
Sacramento, CA 94245-0845
(916) 445-0880
Maximum award: $5,000
Number of awards: 200
Deadline: July 1
College level: Sophomore, Junior, Senior
Majors/Fields: Education
Criteria: Applicant must be a U.S. citizen or eligible noncitizen, be a legal California resident, have graduated in the top tenth of class, or have GED equivalent, and have a minimum 3.0 GPA. Applicant must commit to teach two years in any subject area for each year of scholarship; one year per year of scholarship is required if applicant teaches in a subject shortage area. Renewable for up to four years. Awarded every year.
Contact: Brett Braidman, Editor of Publications.

463   Paul Douglas Teacher Scholarship

California State Polytechnic University, Pomona
3801 West Temple Avenue
Pomona, CA 91768-4019
(909) 869-3700
Average award: $5,000
Number of awards: 6
Majors/Fields: Education
Criteria: Award may be used only at sponsoring institution.
Contact: Crystal Steele, Financial Aid Counselor.

464   Paul Douglas Teacher Scholarship

District of Columbia Office of Postsecondary Education,
Research, and Assistance
2100 Martin Luther King Jr. Avenue, SE, Suite 401
Washington, DC 20020
(202) 727-3685
Average award: $5,000
Number of awards: 6
Deadline: Last Friday of June
College level: Freshman, Sophomore, Junior, Senior
Majors/Fields: Education
Criteria: Applicant must be a District of Columbia resident enrolled as full-time student with good academic standing, rank in the top tenth of graduating class, express an interest in teaching, demonstrate financial need, submit a recommendation, have an overall minimum GPA of 2.5, and have a minimum 3.0 GPA in math, science, and foreign languages. Reapplication is required to retain scholarship. Awarded every year.
Contact: Laurencia O. Henderson, Financial Assistance Specialist.

465   Paul Douglas Teacher Scholarship

Florida Department of Education
Office of Student Financial Assistance
1344 Florida Education Center
Tallahassee, FL 32399-0400
(904) 487-0049
Average award: $5,000
Deadline: April 15
College level: Freshman, Sophomore, Junior, Senior
Majors/Fields: Education
Criteria: Applicant must be a U.S. citizen or eligible noncitizen, rank in the top 10 percent of a Florida high school graduating class or have GED equivalent, and be enrolled full-time at an accredited institution in a program leading to teacher certification. Applicant must agree to teach two years for each year of the award. Satisfactory academic progress is required to retain scholarship. Awarded every year.
Contact: Office of Student Financial Assistance.

466   Paul Douglas Teacher Scholarship

Georgia Student Finance Commission
2082 East Exchange Place
Suite 200
Tucker, GA 30084
(404) 493-5405, (912) 751-6696, (800) 776-6878
Average award: $5,000
College level: Freshman, Sophomore, Junior, Senior
Majors/Fields: Education
Criteria: Applicant must be a Georgia resident, rank in the top tenth of class, and plan to teach. Preference is given to students in critical fields of education. Scholarship is renewable. Awarded every year.

467   Paul Douglas Teacher Scholarship

Idaho State Board of Education
Len B. Jordan Building, Room 307
P.O. Box 83720
Boise, ID 83720-0037
(208) 334-2270
Average award: $5,000
Number of awards: 2
Deadline: February 15
College level: Freshman, Sophomore, Junior, Senior
Majors/Fields: Education
Criteria: Applicant must be an Idaho resident pursuing a teaching degree full-time at an Idaho college or university, rank in the top tenth of graduating class, and commit to teach for two years for each year of scholarship award. Selection is based upon academic merit and interest in teaching. Scholarship is renewable. Awarded every year.
Contact: Caryl Smith, Scholarship Assistant.

468 Paul Douglas Teacher Scholarship

Illinois Student Assistance Commission/Client Services
1755 Lake Cook Road
Deerfield, IL 60015-5209
(800) 899-ISAC, (708) 948-8500
Average award: $4,536
Maximum award: $5,000
Minimum award: $2,459
Number of awards: 160
Deadline: August 1
College level: Freshman, Sophomore, Junior, Senior
Majors/Fields: Education
Criteria: Applicant must be a U.S. citizen or eligible noncitizen and a legal resident of Illinois. Applicant must rank in top tenth of high school class and be enrolled or accepted for enrollment, on a full-time basis, as an undergraduate in a qualified teacher education program at an approved Illinois institution. Recipient must sign a contract promising to teach two years for each year of scholarship assistance or repay the money plus interest. Scholarship is renewable. Awarded every year.
Contact: Manager of Scholarships and Specialized Grants.

469 Paul Douglas Teacher Scholarship

State Student Assistance Commission of Indiana
150 West Market Street
Suite 500
Indianapolis, IN 46204-2811
(317) 232-2350
Average award: $5,000
Number of awards: 72
Deadline: March 1
College level: Freshman, Sophomore, Junior, Senior
Majors/Fields: Education
Criteria: Applicant must be an Indiana resident. Reapplication, minimum 3.0 GPA, and full-time enrollment are required to retain scholarship. Awarded every year.
Contact: Yvonne Heflin, Director of Special Programs.

470 Paul Douglas Teacher Scholarship

Kansas Board of Regents
700 SW Harrison
Suite 1410
Topeka, KS 66603-3760
(913) 296-3517
Average award: $5,000
Number of awards: 30
Deadline: April 1
College level: Freshman, Sophomore, Junior, Senior, Graduate
Majors/Fields: Education
Criteria: Applicant must be a Kansas resident with high academic achievement who plans to enter the teaching profession. Applicant must agree to teach two years for each year of funding or repay the funds at the federally established rate. Good academic standing, completion of renewal contract, and continuation in teacher certification program are required to retain scholarship. Awarded every year.
Contact: Scholarships.

471 Paul Douglas Teacher Scholarship

Louisiana Office of Student Financial Assistance
P.O. Box 91202
Baton Rouge, LA 70821-9202
(504) 922-1038
Average award: $5,000
Number of awards: 56
Deadline: April 1
College level: Freshman, Sophomore, Junior, Senior, Graduate, Doctoral
Majors/Fields: Education
Criteria: Applicant must be a U.S. citizen or eligible noncitizen, rank in the top 10 percent of high school graduating class, be a resident of Louisiana, have a minimum composite ACT score of 23, and 3.0 GPA. FAFSA must be postmarked by March 15. Scholarship is renewable. Awarded every year.
Contact: Winona Kahao, Director of Scholarship/Grant Division, (504) 922-1107.

472 Paul Douglas Teacher Scholarship

Maryland Higher Education Commission
State Scholarship Administration
16 Francis Street
Annapolis, MD 21401-1781
(410) 974-5370
Maximum award: $5,000
Number of awards: 59
Deadline: March 31
College level: Freshman, Sophomore, Junior, Senior
Majors/Fields: Education
Criteria: Applicant must be a Maryland resident, a U.S. citizen or noncitizen eligible for assistance under Title IV, and must rank in the top tenth of high school class or the top tenth of GED scores. In addition, applicant must agree to teach in a Maryland public or private, nonprofit school or program for two years for each year of assistance. Scholarship is renewable. Awarded every year.
Contact: Michael Smith, Program Administrator.

473 Paul Douglas Teacher Scholarship

Michigan Higher Education Assistance Authority
Office of Scholarships and Grants
P.O. Box 30462
Lansing, MI 48909-7962
(517) 373-3394
Maximum award: $5,000
Number of awards: 45
Deadline: April 15
College level: Freshman, Sophomore, Junior, Senior
Majors/Fields: Education
Criteria: Applicant must rank in top ten percent of graduating class and attend college full time. Applicant must maintain satisfactory academic progress. Awarded every year.
Contact: Jean Maday, Director of Scholarship and Grant Programs.

474 Paul Douglas Teacher Scholarship

Mississippi Board of Trustees of State Institutions of Higher Learning
Student Financial Aid Office
3825 Ridgewood Road
Jackson, MS 39211-6453
(601) 982-6570
Maximum award: $5,000
College level: Freshman
Majors/Fields: Education
Criteria: Applicant must be a Mississippi resident, rank in the top tenth of class or have a minimum GED score of 62, be pursuing a Class "A" teaching certificate to be a preschool, elementary, or secondary education teacher, and be enrolled at an accredited public or private institution of higher education. Applicant must agree to teach two full-time semesters for each semester of award. Selection is based upon academic record and financial need. Renewable for up to four years. Awarded every year.
Contact: Mississippi Postsecondary Education Financial Assistance Board, (601) 982-6663.

475 Paul Douglas Teacher Scholarship

Missouri Coordinating Board of Higher Education
P.O. Box 6730
Jefferson City, MO 65102
(314) 751-3940
Average award: $5,000
Deadline: July 1
College level: Sophomore, Junior, Senior
Majors/Fields: Education
Criteria: Applicant must reapply and maintain satisfactory academic progress for renewal. Awarded every year.
Contact: Information Service Center, (800) 473-6757.

476 Paul Douglas Teacher Scholarship

Montana Commission on Higher Education
University of Montana
33 South Last Chance Gulch
Helena, MT 59620
(406) 444-6594
Average award: $5,000
Maximum number of awards: 10
Minimum number of awards: 5
College level: Unspecified undergraduate
Majors/Fields: Education
Criteria: Applicant must be a U.S. citizen, a resident of Montana, and must attend a program leading to the teaching profession in grades K-12. Rank in top tenth of secondary school class is required. Scholarship is renewable. Awarded every year.
Contact: Bill Lannan, Director, Montana Guaranteed Student Loan Program, (406) 444-6954.

477 Paul Douglas Teacher Scholarship

New Hampshire Postsecondary Education Commission
Student Financial Assistance Coordinator
2 Industrial Park Drive
Concord, NH 03301
(603) 271-2695
Average award: $5,000
Number of awards: 14
Deadline: May 1
College level: Freshman, Sophomore, Junior, Senior, Graduate
Majors/Fields: Education, elementary education, secondary education, preschool education
Criteria: Applicant must be a New Hampshire resident and rank in the top tenth of high school graduating class. Preference is given to applicants majoring in critical shortage areas as defined by the New Hampshire Department of Education. Scholarship is renewable. Awarded every year.
Contact: Judith Knapp, Student Financial Assistance Coordinator.

478 Paul Douglas Teacher Scholarship

New York State Education Department
Bureau of Postsecondary Grants Administration
Cultural Education Center
Albany, NY 12230
(518) 474-5705
Maximum award: $5,000
Deadline: March 1
College level: Freshman, Sophomore, Junior, Senior
Majors/Fields: Education
Criteria: Applicant must be a U.S. citizen or permanent resident, a New York State resident, rank in the top tenth of high school class, enroll in an education program leading to teacher certification, and agree to teach two years in any state for each annual payment received. Selection is based upon GPA, personal statement, recommendations, honors, achievements, grades in awarded field, honor or AP courses, and Regents courses. Scholarship is renewable. Awarded every year.
Contact: Office of Equity and Access.

479 Paul Douglas Teacher Scholarship

North Carolina State Department of Public Instruction
301 North Wilmington Street
Raleigh, NC 27601-2825
(919) 715-1120
Maximum award: $5,000
Maximum number of awards: 40
Minimum number of awards: 20
Deadline: in April
College level: Freshman, Sophomore, Junior, Senior
Majors/Fields: Education
Criteria: Applicant must be a U.S. citizen, a North Carolina resident, and rank in the top tenth of class. Selection is based upon academic standing, leadership, service, and interest in teaching. Preference is given to applicants who intend to teach disabled children, those with limited English proficiency, or preschool-age children, or teach in an inner-city, rural, or geographically isolated school. Scholarship is renewable. Awarded every year.
Contact: Scholarships, North Carolina State Education Assistance Authority, P.O. Box 2688, Chapel Hill, NC 27515.

480 Paul Douglas Teacher Scholarship

Ohio Student Aid Commission
309 South Fourth Street
Columbus, OH 43215-5445
(800) 837-6752 or (614) 466-8716
Average award: $5,000
Number of awards: 40
Deadline: Second Friday in March
College level: Freshman, Sophomore, Junior, Senior, Graduate, Doctoral
Majors/Fields: Education
Criteria: Applicant must be a U.S. citizen or eligible noncitizen, an Ohio resident attending an Ohio postsecondary school, must rank in the top tenth of class, be pursuing teacher certification, and attend school on a full-time basis. Applicant must not be in default on any student loan or owe a refund on any federal aid. Satisfactory academic progress is required to retain scholarship. Awarded every year.
Contact: Barbara Closser, Paul Douglas Teacher Scholarship Administrator, P.O. Box 16610, Columbus, OH 43216-6610, (800) 282-0820, extension 46629 or (614) 644-6629.

481 Paul Douglas Teacher Scholarship

University of Oklahoma
University Affairs
900 Asp Avenue, Room 236
Norman, OK 73019-0401
(405) 325-1701
Maximum award: $5,000
Deadline: June 4
College level: Freshman, Sophomore, Junior, Senior
Majors/Fields: Education
Criteria: Applicant must be an Oklahoma resident, rank in the top tenth of class, demonstrate financial need, and enroll in a teacher education program. Preference is given to applicants majoring in teaching education in a critical shortage area designated by the state. Award is for up to four years. Awarded every year. Award may be used only at sponsoring institution.
Contact: Student Services Center, College of Education, Room 137, ECH, Norman, OK 73019, (405) 325-2238.

482 Paul Douglas Teacher Scholarship

State Scholarship Commission (Oregon)
1500 Valley River Drive
Suite 100
Eugene, OR 97401-2146
(503) 687-7395
Minimum award: $1,000
Number of awards: 2
Deadline: March 1
College level: Freshman, Sophomore, Junior, Senior
Majors/Fields: Education
Criteria: Applicant must be an Oregon resident, rank in the top tenth of class, be enrolled full time at an Oregon school, and demonstrate financial need. Scholarship is renewable. Awarded every year.
Contact: Jim Beyer, Grant Program Director.

483 Paul Douglas Teacher Scholarship

Pennsylvania Higher Education Assistance Agency (PHEAA)
P.O. Box 8114
Harrisburg, PA 17105-8114
(717) 257-5220
Average award: $4,855
Maximum award: $5,000
Minimum award: $4,800
Number of awards: 120
Deadline: May 1
College level: Freshman, Sophomore, Junior, Senior
Majors/Fields: Education
Criteria: Applicant must rank in the top tenth of graduating class, be a Pennsylvania resident, and be enrolled in a teacher certification program. Academic progress required to retain scholarship. Awarded every year.
Contact: Sam Sobczak, Director of Teacher Education.

484 Paul Douglas Teacher Scholarship

Rhode Island Higher Education Assistance Authority
560 Jefferson Boulevard
Warwick, RI 02886
(401) 736-1100
Average award: $5,000
Number of awards: 11
Deadline: April 1
College level: Freshman, Sophomore, Junior, Senior
Majors/Fields: Education
Criteria: Applicant must be a Rhode Island resident and rank in top tenth of high school graduating class. Selection is based upon academic qualifications. Satisfactory academic progress and enrollment in full-time program that leads to teacher certification are required to retain scholarship. Awarded every year.
Contact: Mary Ann Welch, Director of Program Administration.

485 Paul Douglas Teacher Scholarship

Tennessee Student Assistance Corporation
Parkway Towers, Suite 1950
404 James Robertson Parkway
Nashville, TN 37243-0820
(615) 741-1346
Average award: $4,000
Maximum award: $5,000
Minimum award: $1,000
Number of awards: 10
Deadline: March 1
College level: Freshman, Sophomore, Junior, Senior, Graduate
Majors/Fields: Elementary education, secondary education
Criteria: Applicant must be a Tennessee resident, have graduated from a Tennessee high school in the top tenth of class, have a minimum 3.0 high school GPA, and sign an intent to teach statement. Recipient must teach two years for each year award is received. Minimum 3.0 GPA in a full-time teacher education program is required for renewal. Awarded every year.
Contact: Program Coordinator.

486 Paul Douglas Teacher Scholarship

Texas Higher Education Coordinating Board
Student Financial Assistance
P.O. Box 12788, Capitol Station
Austin, TX 78711-2788
(512) 483-6340
Average award: $4,698
Maximum award: $5,000
Number of awards: 250
Deadline: June 30
College level: Freshman, Sophomore, Junior, Senior
Majors/Fields: Education
Criteria: Applicant must rank in the top tenth of high school class, enroll full time in a program leading to teacher certification, and agree to teach two years for each year of the award or repay the award with interest. Satisfactory academic progress is required to retain scholarship. Awarded every year.
Contact: Connie Looper.

487 Paul Douglas Teacher Scholarship

University of Texas at San Antonio
Office of Student Financial Aid
6900 North Loop 1604 West
San Antonio, TX 78249-0687
(210) 691-4011
Average award: $5,000
Deadline: July 1
College level: Freshman, Sophomore, Junior, Senior
Majors/Fields: Education
Criteria: Applicant must be a Texas resident enrolled full time, a U.S. citizen, rank in the top tenth of class, have a minimum 3.0 GPA, demonstrate financial need, and make a commitment to teach after graduation. Minimum 3.0 GPA is required to retain scholarship for two additional years. Awarded every year. Award may be used only at sponsoring institution.
Contact: Scholarship Office, (210) 691-4855.

488 Paul Douglas Teacher Scholarship

University of Utah
Financial Aid and Scholarships Office
105 Student Services Building
Salt Lake City, UT 84112
(801) 581-6211
Maximum award: $5,000
Deadline: March 30
College level: Freshman
Majors/Fields: Education
Criteria: Applicant must be a Utah resident and rank in the top tenth of class. Preference is given to applicants planning to major in Utah-designated teacher shortage areas including math, science, and special education. Applicant must obtain teacher certification and teach full time for at least two years for each year of scholarship assistance received. Good academic standing and full-time enrollment are required to retain scholarship. Awarded every year. Award may be used only at sponsoring institution.
Contact: Dr. Mark Spencer, Utah System of Higher Education, 3 Triad Center, Suite 550, 355 West North Temple, Salt Lake City, UT 84180.

489 Paul Douglas Teacher Scholarship

State Council of Higher Education for Virginia
James Monroe Building, 10th Floor
101 North 14th Street
Richmond, VA 23219
(804) 786-1690
Maximum award: $5,000
College level: Freshman, Sophomore, Junior, Senior
Majors/Fields: Education
Criteria: Applicant must be a Virginia resident, attend a college or university in Virginia, and rank in the top tenth of class. Recipients must teach two years for each year the scholarship is received. Scholarship is renewable. Awarded every year.
Contact: Scholarships.

490 Paul Douglas Teacher Scholarship

Washington Higher Education Coordinating Board
917 Lakeridge Way
P.O. Box 43430
Olympia, WA 98504-3430
(206) 753-3571
Maximum award: $5,000
Number of awards: 70
Majors/Fields: Education
Criteria: Applicant must demonstrate academic merit, commitment to the teaching profession, and rank in top tenth of high school class. Recipient incurs the responsibility to teach for two years for each year of scholarship assistance or repay the amount received plus interest. Scholarship is renewable. Awarded every year.
Contact: Elizabeth A. Gebhardt, Assistant Director of Student Financial Aid, (206) 753-4592.

491 Paul Douglas Teacher Scholarship

State College and University Systems of West Virginia
Central Office
P.O. Box 4007
Charleston, WV 25364
(304) 347-1266
Maximum award: $5,000
Number of awards: 21
Deadline: April 1
College level: Freshman, Sophomore, Junior, Senior
Majors/Fields: Education
Criteria: Applicant must be a West Virginia resident, rank in top tenth of graduating class, and enroll full time at an institution of higher learning leading to teacher certification at the preschool, elementary, or secondary levels. Recipient must agree to teach in public or private schools for two years for each year of scholarship assistance. Repayment plus interest is required for failure to fulfill the teaching obligation. Minimum 3.0 GPA for freshmen and sophomores and 3.25 for juniors is required for renewal. Awarded every year.
Contact: Daniel Crockett, Scholarship Programs Coordinator.

492   Phi Delta Kappa Scholarship for Prospective Educators

Phi Delta Kappa
Eighth Street and Union Avenue
P.O. Box 789
Bloomington, IN 47402
(812) 339-1156
Average award: $1,000
Maximum award: $2,000
Number of awards: 46
Deadline: January 31
College level: Freshman
Majors/Fields: Education
Criteria: Applicant must rank in top third of graduating class. Selection is based upon scholarship, recommendations, written expression, interest in teaching as a career, and school and community activities. Awarded every year.
Contact: Howard D. Hill, Director of Chapter Programs.

493   Robert C. Byrd Honors Scholarship

North Carolina State Department of Public Instruction
301 North Wilmington Street
Raleigh, NC 27601-2825
(919) 715-1120
Maximum award: $1,500
Number of awards: 150
Deadline: in February
College level: Freshman
Majors/Fields: Education
Criteria: Applicant must be a North Carolina resident, have a minimum 3.0 GPA and combined SAT I score of 850, demonstrate outstanding academic achievement, and show promise of continued academic excellence. Priority is given to applicants who wish to teach in public schools, particularly in the areas of math and science. Renewable for up to four years if satisfactory academic progress with full-time enrollment is maintained. Awarded every year.
Contact: Scholarships.

494   Robert C. Byrd Honors Scholarship

Illinois Student Assistance Commission/
Client Support Services
1755 Lake Cook Road
Deerfield, IL 60015-5209
(800) 899-ISAC, (708) 948-8500
Average award: $1,500
Deadline: January 13
College level: Freshman, Sophomore, Junior, Senior
Majors/Fields: Education
Criteria: Applicant must be a U.S. citizen or eligible noncitizen, a legal resident of Illinois, rank in top two percent of class, have a minimum 3.8 GPA, and/or a minimum combined SAT I score of 1100 or composite ACT score of 27, and attend an Illinois institution. Recipient must sign a contract promising to teach two years for each year of scholarship assistance or repay the money plus interest. Renewable for up to four years. Awarded every year.
Contact: Manager of Scholarships and Specialized Grants.

495   Robert C. Byrd Honors Scholarship

State Student Assistance Commission of Indiana
150 West Market Street
Suite 500
Indianapolis, IN 46204-2811
(317) 232-2350
Average award: $1,500
Number of awards: 283
Deadline: April 15
College level: Freshman
Criteria: Scholarship is renewable if academic progress is satisfactory. Awarded every year.
Contact: Yvonne Heflin, Director of Special Programs.

496   Sharon Christa McAuliffe Memorial Teacher Education Award

Maryland Higher Education Commission
State Scholarship Administration
16 Francis Street
Annapolis, MD 21401-1781
(410) 974-5370
Maximum award: $8,600
Minimum award: $2,000
Number of awards: 44
Deadline: December 1
College level: Junior, Senior, Graduate, Doctoral
Majors/Fields: Education
Criteria: Applicant must be a full-time undergraduate student, public school teacher, or part-time degree-holding, nonteacher at a Maryland degree-granting institution with an approved teacher education program. Applicant must be a Maryland resident, have a minimum 3.0 GPA, and if an undergraduate must have at least 60 credit hours. Applicant must agree to teach one year in a critical shortage area in a Maryland public institution for each year of the award. Minimum 3.0 GPA is required to retain scholarship for one additional year. Awarded every year.
Contact: Michael Smith, Program Administrator.

497   Steffensen Cannon Scholarship

University of Utah
Financial Aid and Scholarships Office
105 Student Services Building
Salt Lake City, UT 84112
(801) 581-6211
Maximum award: $8,500
Minimum award: $6,500
Deadline: January 15
College level: Freshman, Sophomore, Junior, Senior, Graduate
Majors/Fields: Education
Criteria: Applicant must be enrolled in the Coll of Humanities, Graduate Sch of Education, or major in another discipline but intend to go into teacher education. Freshman applicant must rank in top quarter of class, undergraduate applicant must have a minimum 2.75 GPA, and graduate applicant must have a minimum 3.0 GPA. Priority is given to descendents of Ellen Christina Steffensen Cannon. Good academic standing is required to retain scholarship for an additional year. Awarded every year. Award may be used only at sponsoring institution.
Contact: Education Advising Center, 226 Milton Bennion Hall, Salt Lake City, UT 84112, (801) 581-7780.

498   Teacher Scholarship Program

American Association of Colleges for Teacher Education (AACTE)
One Dupont Circle
Suite 610
Washington, DC 20036-1186
(202) 293-2450
Minimum award: $2,500
Number of awards: 12
Deadline: March 20
College level: Freshman
Majors/Fields: Teacher education
Criteria: Applicant must live in or attend school in a National Basketball Association (NBA) city.
Contact: Mark Lewis, Program Associate.

499   Technology Scholarship Program for Alabama Teachers

Alabama Commission on Higher Education
3465 Norman Bridge Road
Montgomery, AL 36105-2310
(334) 281-1921
Average award: $848
Maximum award: $2,505
Minimum award: $279
College level: Doctoral, teachers taking graduate education courses for credit or non-credit
Majors/Fields: Technology courses
Criteria: Applicant must be a full-time, certified, Alabama public school teacher. Scholarship is renewable. Awarded every year.
Contact: Dr. William H. Wall, Director of Grants and Scholarship.

500 Tennessee Teacher Loan/Scholarship Program

Tennessee Student Assistance Corporation
Parkway Towers, Suite 1950
404 James Robertson Parkway
Nashville, TN 37243-0820
(615) 741-1346
Average award: $2,000
Maximum award: $2,026
Minimum award: $500
Number of awards: 170
Deadline: May 15
College level: Freshman, Sophomore, Junior, Senior, Graduate
Majors/Fields: Education
Criteria: Applicant must be a Tennessee resident, be pursuing teacher certification in high school math or science, or in elementary art or music, elementary education, or special education. Minimum 3.0 GPA is required for renewal. Awarded every year.
Contact: Program Coordinator.

501 Underwood-Smith Teacher Scholarship

State College and University Systems of West Virginia
Central Office
P.O. Box 4007
Charleston, WV 25364
(304) 347-1266
Average award: $4,464
Maximum award: $5,000
Minimum award: $1,373
Number of awards: 42
Deadline: April 1
College level: Freshman, Sophomore, Junior, Senior, Graduate, Doctoral
Majors/Fields: Education
Criteria: Applicant must be a West Virginia resident who will attend a West Virginia institution of higher education as a full-time student pursuing a course of study leading toward teacher certification at the preschool, elementary, or secondary level. Undergraduate applicant must rank in the top tenth of class, score in the top tenth statewide of those taking the ACT, or have a cumulative 3.25 GPA after successfully completing two years of course work at an approved institution. Graduate applicant must have graduated in the top tenth of college or class. Minimum 3.0 GPA is required for freshmen and sophomores and 3.25 for juniors for renewal. Awarded every year.
Contact: Daniel Crockett, Scholarship Programs Coordinator.

502 William Winter Teacher Scholar Program

Mississippi Board of Trustees of State Institutions of Higher Learning
Student Financial Aid
3825 Ridgewood Road
Jackson, MS 39211-6453
(601) 982-6570
Maximum award: $3,000
Minimum award: $1,000
College level: Freshman
Majors/Fields: Education
Criteria: Applicant must be a Mississippi resident. Renewable if 2.5 GPA is maintained. Awarded every year.
Contact: Mississippi Postsecondary Education Finanical Assistance Board, (601) 982-6663.

503 Woodring Scholarship

Western Washington University
516 High Street
Bellingham, WA 98226-9006
(206) 650-3471
Average award: $2,250
Number of awards: 10
Deadline: April 15
College level: Junior, Senior, Graduate, Doctoral
Majors/Fields: Education, elementary education, secondary education
Criteria: Applicant must have precollege test scores in the top ten percent, have at least 30 college credits, and be preparing for a career in public school teaching at the elementary or secondary school level. Awarded every year. Award may be used only at sponsoring institution.
Contact: Jill Clark, Scholarship Assistant.

Elementary/Secondary Education

504 Celia Koontz Findlay Scholarship in Elementary Education

University of Toledo
Financial Aid Office
Toledo, OH 43606-3390
(419) 537-2056
Maximum award: $1,400
Minimum award: $600
Number of awards: 2
College level: Sophomore, Junior, Senior
Majors/Fields: Elementary education
Criteria: Applicant must be a U.S. citizen and demonstrate academic achievement and financial need. Awarded every year. Award may be used only at sponsoring institution.
Contact: Dean, College of Education and Allied Professions, Toledo, OH 43606, (419) 537-2025.

505 Council on Public Higher Education Scholarship

Southwest Missouri State University
Student Financial Aid
901 South National Avenue
Springfield, MO 65804-0095
(417) 836-5000 or (800) 492-7900
Average award: $1,000
Number of awards: 10
Deadline: March 31
College level: Junior, Senior
Majors/Fields: Biology, chemistry, education, foreign language, mathematics, physics
Criteria: Applicant must have completed a minimum of 75 hours and be preparing for a career as a math, biology, chemistry, physics, or foreign language teacher at the elementary or secondary level. Financial need is not considered. Awarded every year. Award may be used only at sponsoring institution.
Contact: Scholarship Committee, (417) 836-5262 or (800) 492-7900.

506 Florence C. Painter Memorial Scholarship

Southwest Missouri State University
Student Financial Aid
901 South National Avenue
Springfield, MO 65804-0095
(417) 836-5000 or (800) 492-7900
Average award: $1,600
Number of awards: 2
Deadline: March 31
College level: Junior, Senior
Majors/Fields: Secondary education
Criteria: Applicant must have a minimum 3.0 cumulative GPA and demonstrate financial need. Preference is given to those planning to teach Spanish. Reapplication is required to retain scholarship. Awarded every year. Award may be used only at sponsoring institution.
Contact: Scholarship Committee, (417) 836-5262 or (800) 492-7900.

507 Gary Higgins Singleton Scholarship

Clemson University
G-01 Sikes Hall
Clemson, SC 29634-5123
(803) 656-2280
Average award: $1,200
Number of awards: 2
Deadline: March 1
College level: Freshman, Sophomore, Junior, Senior
Majors/Fields: Elementary education, secondary education
Criteria: Applicant must demonstrate financial need, plan to teach for at least two years after graduation, and be a resident of Anderson, Oconee, or Pickens counties. Preference is given to female applicants. Awarded every year. Award may be used only at sponsoring institution.
Contact: Marvin Carmichael, Director of Financial Aid.

508 Louisiana Education Majors Scholarship

Governor's Special Commission on Educational Services
P.O. Box 91202
Baton Rouge, LA 70821
(504) 922-1038
Average award: $2,000
Number of awards: 960
Deadline: March 1-Fall, December 31-Spring
College level: Unspecified undergraduate
Criteria: Applicant must have a minimum 3.0 GPA and a composite ACT score of 20, be a Louisiana resident, attend a Louisiana institution, and be a Louisiana high school graduate. Recipient must maintain a 3.0 GPA, agree to teach one year in Louisiana for each year of funding or repay the scholarship, and be a full-time student (12 semester or 8 quarter hours minimum). 3.0 GPA is required for renewal. Awarded every year.
Contact: Mona H. Durham, Scholarship/Grant Director.

509 Mary Emma Key McKinley Scholarship

University of Alabama–Tuscaloosa
Box 870162
Tuscaloosa, AL 35487-0162
(205) 348-6756
Average award: $1,000
Number of awards: 4
Deadline: March 15
College level: Freshman, Sophomore, Junior, Senior
Majors/Fields: Early childhood education
Criteria: Applicant must be enrolled full time and demonstrate an aptitude for and commitment to a career in early childhood education. Scholarship committee sets specific academic requirements. Awarded every year. Award may be used only at sponsoring institution.
Contact: Coordinator, Capstone College of Education Society, Box 870231, Tuscaloosa, AL 35487-0231, (205) 348-6881.

510 Math/Science/Foreign Language Scholarship

University of Utah
Financial Aid and Scholarships Office
105 Student Services Building
Salt Lake City, UT 84112
(801) 581-6211
Average award: $1,500
Maximum number of awards: 9
Minimum number of awards: 3
Deadline: March 1
College level: Sophomore, Junior, Senior, Graduate
Majors/Fields: Secondary education with major/minor in mathematics, biology, chemistry, computer science, geology, physics, French, German, Spanish
Criteria: Applicant must be pursuing teacher certification in Utah and have a minimum 3.0 cumulative GPA. Minimum 3.0 GPA and 12 credits per quarter are required to retain undergraduate scholarship. At least nine credit hours per quarter are required to retain graduate scholarship. Awarded every year. Award may be used only at sponsoring institution.
Contact: Education Advising Center, 226 Milton Bennion Hall, Salt Lake City, UT 84112, (801) 581-7780.

511 Mildred Ransdorf Donoghue Scholarship

California State University, Fullerton
P.O. Box 34080
Fullerton, CA 92634-9480
(714) 773-3128
Average award: $3,000
Deadline: September 30
College level: Graduate
Majors/Fields: Elementary education
Criteria: Applicant must be a woman, at least 30 years old, enrolled full-time in the multiple subject credential program or master's in education program with an elementary education concentration, and be a native-born North American citizen of British, French, German, Irish, Italian, Scandinavian, or Slavic descent. Awarded every year. Award may be used only at sponsoring institution.
Contact: Vickey Takeuchi, Scholarship Coordinator.

512 Stribik-Martin Scholarship

University of Colorado at Boulder
Campus Box 106
Boulder, CO 80309-0106
(303) 492-5091
Average award: $1,000
Number of awards: 2
Deadline: First Monday in March
College level: Sophomore, Junior, Senior
Majors/Fields: Applied mathematics, biology, chemistry, geology, mathematics, physics
Criteria: Applicant must be registered in the Coll of Arts and Sciences with a minimum cumulative GPA of 3.3 in 30 hours of course work. Applicant must intend to fulfill the requirements for secondary science or math teacher certification and the requirements for graduation from the Coll of Arts and Sciences. Awarded every year. Award may be used only at sponsoring institution.
Contact: Office of Financial Aid.

Special Education

513 Emily Nelson Moseley Memorial Scholarship

Southwest Missouri State University
Student Financial Aid
901 South National Avenue
Springfield, MO 65804-0095
(417) 836-5000 or (800) 492-7900
Average award: $2,400
Number of awards: 3
Deadline: March 31
College level: Junior, Senior
Majors/Fields: Special education
Criteria: Selection is based upon academic performance. Satisfactory academic progress is required to retain scholarship. Awarded every year. Award may be used only at sponsoring institution.
Contact: Scholarship Committee.

514 Graduate Study Scholarship for Handicapped Learner Certificate

Portland State University
P.O. Box 751
Portland, OR 97207-5252
(503) 725-5270
Maximum award: $8,000
Minimum award: $4,500
Number of awards: 10
Deadline: July 1
College level: Unspecified graduate
Criteria: Applicant must have a bachelor's degree and have previous experience with children and youth with disabilities. Admission to Special Education Program is required. Award may be used only at sponsoring institution.
Contact: Scholarships, Special Education Program, P.O. Box 751, Portland, OR 97207-0751, (503) 725-4632.

515 Special Education Services Scholarship

State Student Assistance Commission of Indiana
150 West Market Street
Suite 500
Indianapolis, IN 46204-2811
(317) 232-2350
Maximum award: $1,000
Number of awards: 75
Deadline: Determined by college or university
College level: Freshman, Sophomore, Junior, Senior
Majors/Fields: Occupational therapy, physical therapy, special education
Criteria: Applicant must be an Indiana resident with a minimum 2.0 GPA who agrees to teach in Indiana upon certification. Reapplication and satisfactory academic progress are required to retain scholarship. Awarded every year.
Contact: Yvonne D. Heflin, Director of Special Programs.

516 Teachers of Visually Impaired and Blind Students Scholarship

Portland State University
P.O. Box 751
Portland, OR 97207-5252
(503) 725-5270
Average award: $4,500
Number of awards: 10
Deadline: June 15
College level: Graduate
Majors/Fields: Special education
Criteria: Experience in education preferred. Awarded every year. Award may be used only at sponsoring institution.
Contact: Scholarships, Special Education Program, P.O. Box 751, Portland, OR 97207-0751, (503) 725-4632.

517 UCT Scholarship for Teachers of the Mentally Handicapped

Order of United Commercial Travelers of America (UCT)
632 North Park Street
P.O. Box 159019
Columbus, OH 43215-8619
(614) 228-3276
Average award: $500
Maximum award: $750
Minimum award: $100
Number of awards: 350
Deadline: None
College level: Senior, Graduate, Doctoral
Majors/Fields: Mental retardation
Criteria: Applicant must plan to be of service to the mentally handicapped in the U.S. or Canada. Preference is given to UCT members. Scholarship is renewable. Awarded every year.
Contact: Dianna Duhs, Scholarship Coordinator.

Engineering/Technology

Aerospace/Aeronautical Engineering

518   AAAA Scholarship Grant Program

AAAA Scholarship Foundation, Inc.
49 Richmondville Avenue
Westport, CT 06880-2000
Maximum award: $12,000
Minimum award: $1,000
Deadline: June 15
College level: Freshman
Criteria: Applicant planning on attending St. Louis U is eligible for a $3,000 scholarship. Applicant pursuing a four-year B.S. degree in an aeronautical-related science is eligible for a $4,000 scholarship. Selection is based upon academic merit and personal achievement. Awarded every year.
Contact: Scholarships.

519   AIAA Graduate Scholarship

American Institute of Aeronautics and Astronautics (AIAA)
Student Programs Department
370 L'Enfant Promenade, SW
Washington, DC 20024-2518
(202) 646-7400
Average award: $1,000
Number of awards: 4
Deadline: January 31
College level: Graduate
Majors/Fields: Aeronautical engineering, aerospace engineering, engineering, science
Criteria: Applicant must be a U.S. citizen or permanent resident, have a minimum 3.0 GPA, and major in some field of science or engineering encompassed by the technical activities of AIAA. Awarded every year.
Contact: Student Programs Department.

520   AIAA Undergraduate Scholarship

American Institute of Aeronautics and Astronautics (AIAA)
Student Programs Department
370 L'Enfant Promenade, SW
Washington, DC 20024-2518
(202) 646-7400
Average award: $1,000
Number of awards: 13
Deadline: January 31
College level: Sophomore, Junior, Senior
Majors/Fields: Aeronautical engineering, aerospace engineering, engineering, science
Criteria: Selection is based upon academic credentials, career goals, recommendations, and extracurricular activities. Applicant must be a U.S. citizen or permanent resident, have a minimum 3.0 GPA, and major in some field of science or engineering encompassed by the technical activities of the AIAA. Reapplication and minimum 3.0 GPA required to retain scholarship. Awarded every year.
Contact: Student Programs Department.

521   Air Traffic Control Association Scholarship

Air Traffic Control Association, Inc.
2300 Clarendon Boulevard
Suite 711
Arlington, VA 22201
(703) 522-5717
Average award: $2,000
Maximum award: $2,500
Minimum award: $1,500
Number of awards: 3
Deadline: August 1
College level: Freshman, Sophomore, Junior, Senior, Graduate, Doctoral, aviation career professional for part-time study
Majors/Fields: Aviation
Criteria: Applicant must be enrolled in an aviation-related course of study. Selection is based upon academic performance and financial need. Awarded every year.
Contact: Gabriel A. Hartl, President.

522   American Helicopter Society Scholarship

Vertical Flight Foundation
217 North Washington Street
Alexandria, VA 22314
(703) 684-6777
Average award: $2,000
Maximum number of awards: 10
Minimum number of awards: 1
Deadline: February 1
Majors/Fields: Aeronautical, aerospace
Criteria: Award is available to those interested in helicopter and vertical flight technology. Applicant must submit a current, official grade transcript, academic and character endorsements, and a black and white glossy photo of self with application. Piloting students are not eligible for the award. Awarded every year.
Contact: Scholarships.

523   Judith Resnik Memorial Scholarship

Society of Women Engineers (SWE)
120 Wall Street
11th Floor
New York, NY 10005-3902
(212) 509-9577
Average award: $2,000
Number of awards: 1
Deadline: February 1
College level: Senior
Majors/Fields: Aeronautical engineering, aerospace engineering
Criteria: Applicant must be a woman, have a 3.5 GPA, be a SWE member, studying in an engineering field with a space-related major, and be planning for a career in the space industry. Awarded every year.
Contact: Scholarship.

524   McAllister Memorial Scholarship

AOPA Air Safety Foundation
421 Aviation Way
Frederick, MD 21701
(301) 695-2170
Average award: $1,000
Maximum number of awards: 2
Minimum number of awards: 1
Deadline: March 31
College level: Junior, Senior
Majors/Fields: Aviation
Criteria: Applicant must have a minimum 3.25 GPA and submit a transcript and 250-word essay. Self-addressed, stamped envelope required to receive application. Awarded every year.
Contact: Robin Sharitz, Scholarship Coordinator.

525 National Air and Space Museum Internship Program

Smithsonian Institution National Air and Space Museum
Educational Services Department
MRC 305
Washington, DC 20560
Average award: $3,500
Deadline: February 15
College level: Sophomore, Junior, Senior, Graduate, Doctoral
Criteria: Applicant must have a strong academic performance. Awarded every year.
Contact: Coordinator of Student Services.

526 Space Industrialization Fellowship

Space Foundation Educational Grant Program
c/o Houston Advanced Research Center
4800 Research Forest Drive
The Woodlands, TX 77381
(713) 363-7944
Average award: $4,000
Number of awards: 1
Deadline: October 1
College level: Graduate, Doctoral
Majors/Fields: Disciplines related to the use of space resources through commercialization
Criteria: Applicant must be a superior graduate student with a bachelor's degree from an accredited school who intends to pursue a career dedicated to the furtherance of practical space research, engineering, business, or other application ventures. Awarded every year.
Contact: David J. Norton, Chairman.

527 Vertical Flight Foundation Scholarship

Vertical Flight Foundation
217 North Washington Street
Alexandria, VA 22314
(703) 684-6777
Average award: $2,000
Number of awards: 8
Deadline: February 1
College level: Freshman, Sophomore, Junior, Senior, Graduate, Doctoral
Majors/Fields: Aeronautical engineering, astronautical engineering, electrical engineering, engineering
Criteria: Applicant must be pursuing a career in some aspect of helicopter or vertical flight business, preferably majoring in aerospace engineering. In the event there are no qualified applicants in the opinion of the committee, no scholarships will be awarded. Awarded every year.
Contact: Janet Chaikin, Communications Manager.

Chemical Engineering

528 Conoco Fellowship

University of Oklahoma
University Affairs
900 Asp Avenue, Room 236
Norman, OK 73019-0401
(405) 325-1701
Average award: $8,800
Number of awards: 1
Deadline: March 1
College level: Graduate, Doctoral
Majors/Fields: Chemical engineering
Criteria: Applicant must be a U.S. citizen and not be on leave from a competing company. Selection is based upon merit. Awarded every year. Award may be used only at sponsoring institution.
Contact: Coordinator of Graduate Student Program, Chemical Engineering and Materials Science, 100 East Boyd Street, Energy Center, Norman, OK 73019, (405) 325-5811.

529 Department of Energy Summer Fellowship

Electrochemical Society
10 South Main Street
Pennington, NJ 08534-2896
Average award: $3,000
Number of awards: 5
Deadline: January 1
College level: Sophomore, Junior, Senior, Graduate, Doctoral
Majors/Fields: Electrochemical science/technology, solid state science/engineering
Criteria: Recipient must reapply for renewal. Awarded every year.
Contact: John Stanley, Meetings and Programs Assistant, (609) 737-1902.

530 Dr. Edward Groth, Jr. Memorial Scholarship

New Mexico State University
Box 30001
Department 5100
Las Cruces, NM 88003-0001
(505) 646-4105
Average award: Tuition
Deadline: March 1
College level: Junior, Senior
Majors/Fields: Chemical engineering
Criteria: Applicant must have a minimum 3.2 GPA, be involved in community organizations, and be an active member of the American Institute of Chemical Engineers. Awarded every year. Award may be used only at sponsoring institution.
Contact: College of Engineering, (505) 646-3547.

531 DuPont Fellowship

University of Oklahoma
University Affairs
900 Asp Avenue, Room 236
Norman, OK 73019-0401
(405) 325-1701
Average award: $4,000
Deadline: October 1
College level: Graduate, Doctoral
Majors/Fields: Chemical engineering
Criteria: Applicant must be a DuPont Designated Scholar. Selection is based upon merit. Awarded every year. Award may be used only at sponsoring institution.
Contact: Coordinator of Graduate Student Program, Chemical Engineering and Materials Science, 100 Boyd Street, Energy Center, Norman, OK 73019, (405) 325-5811.

532 Electrochemical Society Summer Fellowship

Electrochemical Society
10 South Main Street
Pennington, NJ 08534-2896
Average award: $3,000
Number of awards: 3
Deadline: January 1
College level: Sophomore, Junior, Senior, Graduate, Doctoral
Majors/Fields: Electrochemical science/technology, solid state science/engineering
Criteria: Recipient must reapply for renewal. Awarded every year.
Contact: John Stanley, Meetings and Programs Assistant, (609) 737-1902.

533 F.M. Becket Memorial Award

Electrochemical Society
10 South Main Street
Pennington, NJ 08534-2896
Average award: $3,500
Number of awards: 1
Deadline: January 1
College level: Doctoral
Majors/Fields: Electrochemical science/technology, solid science/technology
Criteria: Recipient must reapply for renewal. Awarded every other year.
Contact: John Stanley, Meetings and Programs Assistant, (609) 737-1902.

534   J. Waldo Smith Hydraulic Fellowship

American Society of Civil Engineers
345 East 47th Street
New York, NY 10017-2398
(212) 705-7667
Maximum award: $5,000
Minimum award: $4,000
Deadline: February 1
College level: Doctoral
Majors/Fields: Experimental hydraulics
Criteria: Applicant must be a graduate student, preferably an Associate Member of the Society. Scholarship is renewable. Awarded every third year.
Contact: Michael Peralta, Assistant Manager of Student Services.

535   NALCO Foundation Scholarship

National Society of Professional Engineers
Education Foundation
1420 King Street
Alexandria, VA 22314-2794
(703) 684-2800
Average award: $1,000
Number of awards: 2
College level: Freshman
Majors/Fields: Chemical engineering
Criteria: Applicant must be a U.S. citizen with a minimum 3.0 GPA and minimum SAT I scores of 600 math and 500 verbal (or ACT scores of 29 math and 25 English). One scholarship is for a Texas resident and the other is for an Illinois resident. Up to four years. Awarded every year.
Contact: Education Foundation.

536   Robert Davis Scholarship

New Mexico State University
Box 30001
Department 5100
Las Cruces, NM 88003-0001
(505) 646-4105
Average award: $1,000
Number of awards: 4
Deadline: March 1
College level: Freshman
Majors/Fields: Chemical engineering
Criteria: Selection is based upon academic standing, extracurricular activities, honors, career goals, and recommendations. Awarded every year. Award may be used only at sponsoring institution.
Contact: Greeley W. Myers, Director of Financial Aid.

537   Texas Eastman Kodak Scholarship

New Mexico State University
Box 30001
Department 5100
Las Cruces, NM 88003-0001
(505) 646-4105
Average award: Tuition
Deadline: March 1
College level: Sophomore
Majors/Fields: Chemical engineering
Criteria: Applicant must have a minimum 3.0 GPA and agree to work the summer between junior and senior years. Awarded every year. Award may be used only at sponsoring institution.
Contact: College of Engineering, (505) 646-3547.

Civil/Environmental Engineering

538   Abel Wolman Fellowship

American Water Works Association
6666 West Quincy Avenue
Denver, CO 80235
(303) 347-6210
Average award: $15,000
Number of awards: 1
Deadline: January 15
College level: Doctoral
Majors/Fields: Water supply, water treatment
Criteria: Applicant must be pursuing doctoral study and research related to the field of water supply and treatment. Applicant must have citizenship or permanent resident status in the U.S., Canada, or Mexico. Satisfactory progress required to retain scholarship. Awarded every year.
Contact: Scholarship Coordinator.

539   AGC Education and Research Foundation Graduate Award

Associated General Contractors (AGC) Education and Research Foundation
1957 E Street, NW
Washington, DC 20006
(202) 393-2040
Average award: $7,500
Number of awards: 6
Deadline: November 15
College level: Graduate, Doctoral
Majors/Fields: Civil engineering, construction engineering
Criteria: Applicant must pursue a graduate degree on a full-time basis and be a U.S. citizen or permanent resident. Selection is based upon grades, extracurricular activities, employment experience, financial need, and a demonstrated desire to pursue a construction career. Awarded every year.
Contact: Director of Programs.

540   AGC Education and Research Foundation Undergraduate Scholarship Program

Associated General Contractors (AGC) Education and Research Foundation
1957 E Street, NW
Washington, DC 20006
(202) 393-2040
Average award: $1,500
Number of awards: 86
Deadline: November 1
College level: Sophomore, Junior, Senior
Majors/Fields: Civil engineering, construction
Criteria: Applicant must plan to pursue a career in the construction industry, enroll in a four- or five-year program, and be a U.S. citizen or permanent resident alien. Selection is based upon grades, extracurricular activities, employment experience, financial need, and desire for a construction career. Renewable for up to four years if recipient maintains satisfactory GPA and employment in construction. Awarded every year.
Contact: Ernie Jones, Director of Programs.

541 American Society of Civil Engineers, Orange County Branch Scholarship

California State University, Fullerton
P.O. Box 34080
Fullerton, CA 92634-9480
(714) 773-3128
Maximum award: $2,000
Minimum award: $1,000
Number of awards: 2
Deadline: December 1
College level: Junior, Senior
Majors/Fields: Civil engineering
Criteria: Applicant must be a continuing upper-division student who has been an ASCE member for at least one year. Selection is based upon ASCE participation, academic achievement, and applicant's personal statement. Awarded every year. Award may be used only at sponsoring institution.
Contact: Vickey Takeuchi, Scholarship Coordinator.

542 Amoco Scholarship

University of Oklahoma
University Affairs
900 Asp Avenue, Room 236
Norman, OK 73019-0401
(405) 325-1701
Average award: $6,000
Number of awards: 1
Deadline: June 1
College level: Graduate
Majors/Fields: Civil engineering
Criteria: Selection is based upon merit. Awarded every year. Award may be used only at sponsoring institution.
Contact: Director of Civil Engineering and Environmental Science, College of Engineering, CEC, Room 334, Norman, OK 73019, (405) 325-5911.

543 Arthur S. Tuttle Memorial National Scholarship Fund

American Society of Civil Engineers (ASCE)
345 East 47th Street
New York, NY 10017-2398
(212) 705-7667
Maximum award: $5,000
Minimum award: $3,000
Deadline: March 1
College level: Doctoral
Majors/Fields: Civil Engineering
Criteria: Applicant must be a member of the National ASCE in good standing. Awarded every year.
Contact: Michael Peralta, Assistant Manager of Student Services.

544 ASCE Construction Engineering Scholarship and Student Prize

American Society of Civil Engineers (ASCE)
345 East 47th Street
New York, NY 10017-2398
(212) 705-7667
Average award: $1,000
Number of awards: 1
Deadline: April 1
College level: Sophomore, Junior, Senior
Majors/Fields: Engineering
Criteria: Applicant must be a member of an ASCE Student Chapter and also a National Student Member in good standing. The scholarship essay must deal with construction engineering. Scholarship is renewable. Awarded every year.
Contact: Michael Peralta, Assistant Manager of Student Services.

545 ASCE Research Fellowship

American Society of Civil Engineers (ASCE)
345 East 47th Street
New York, NY 10017-2398
(212) 705-7667
Maximum award: $15,000
Deadline: February 1
College level: Graduate, Doctoral
Majors/Fields: Civil engineering
Criteria: Applicant must be a National ASCE member in good standing, a U.S. citizen, and a graduate of an accredited program. Grants made annually when funding is provided in annual budget.
Contact: Michael Peralta, Assistant Manager of Student Services.

546 ASCE Research Initiation Scholarship

American Society of Civil Engineers (ASCE)
345 East 47th Street
New York, NY 10017-2398
(212) 705-7667
Average award: $20,000
Maximum number of awards: 2
Minimum number of awards: 1
Deadline: December 1
Majors/Fields: Civil Engineering
Criteria: Awarded on a competitive basis for a proposed research project. Applicant must be an ASCE member and have completed his or her doctoral degree within the last three years or have several years of industrial or postdoctoral experience and be within first two years as a full-time faculty member. Letter of reference required. Awarded every year.
Contact: Michael Peralta, Assistant Manager of Student Services.

547 ASDSO Scholarship

Association of State Dam Safety Officials (ASDSO)
450 Old East Vine Street
2nd Floor
Lexington, KY 40507-1544
(606) 257-5140
Average award: $2,500
Number of awards: 2
Deadline: January 15
College level: Junior, Senior
Majors/Fields: Civil engineering or other field of study relating to dam safety
Criteria: Scholarship is renewable. Awarded every year.
Contact: Lori Spragens, Executive Director.

548 Associated General Contractors Scholarship

Louisiana Tech University
P.O. Box 7925
Ruston, LA 71272
(318) 257-2641
Average award: $3,750
Maximum award: $6,000
Minimum award: $1,500
Number of awards: 1
College level: Freshman, Sophomore, Junior, Senior
Majors/Fields: Civil engineering, construction engineering technology
Criteria: Selection is through a national competition based upon GPA, class rank, and references. Scholarship is renewable. Awarded every year. Award may be used only at sponsoring institution.
Contact: E. R. Winzer, Director of Student Financial Aid.

549 California Council of Civil Engineers and Land Surveyors Scholarship

California State Polytechnic University, Pomona
3801 West Temple Avenue
Pomona, CA 91768-4019
(909) 869-3700
Average award: $1,000
Number of awards: 2
Criteria: Award may be used only at sponsoring institution.
Contact: Crystal Steele, Financial Aid Counselor, California State Polytechnic University, Pomona, 3801 West Temple Avenue, Pomona, CA 91768-3700.

550 Cohos Evamy Partners Design Competition

University of Calgary
2500 University Drive, NW
Calgary, Alberta, CN T2N 1N4
(403) 220-7872
Maximum award: $5,000
Deadline: June 15
College level: Junior, Senior
Majors/Fields: Civil engineering, structural engineering
Criteria: Applicant must be a Canadian citizen or permanent resident, have a minimum 3.0 GPA, and plan a career in structural engineering. Selection is based upon performance in the annual structural design competition. Awarded every year. Award may be used only at sponsoring institution.
Contact: J. Van Housen, Director of Financial Aid.

551 Dollar Rent-A-Car Scholarship

New Mexico State University
Box 30001
Department 5100
Las Cruces, NM 88003-0001
(505) 646-4105
Average award: $1,000
Number of awards: 5
Deadline: March 1
College level: Sophomore, Junior
Majors/Fields: Civil engineering
Criteria: Applicant must have a minimum 3.0 GPA and demonstrate financial need. Awarded every year. Award may be used only at sponsoring institution.
Contact: College of Engineering, (505) 646-3547.

552 Freeman Fellowship

American Society of Civil Engineers (ASCE)
345 East 47th Street
New York, NY 10017-2398
(212) 705-7667
Deadline: February 1
College level: Doctoral
Majors/Fields: Hydraulic construction
Criteria: Applicant must be a National ASCE member in good standing, under 45 years of age. Stipend will be awarded based on funds available from the endowment.
Contact: Michael Peralta, Assistant Manager of Student Services.

553 Helen Meeks McKerley Memorial Scholarship

Clemson University
G-01 Sikes Hall
Clemson, SC 29634-5123
(803) 656-2280
Average award: $1,000
Number of awards: 9
Deadline: March 1
College level: Sophomore, Junior, Senior
Majors/Fields: Civil engineering
Criteria: Applicant must have a minimum 2.0 cumulative GPA. Minimum 3.0 cumulative GPA with at least 12 credits per semester is required to retain scholarship. Awarded every year. Award may be used only at sponsoring institution.
Contact: Marvin Carmichael, Director of Financial Aid.

554 McDermott Incorporated Scholarship

Louisiana Tech University
P.O. Box 7925
Ruston, LA 71272
(318) 257-2641
Average award: $1,000
Number of awards: 2
Deadline: October 1
College level: Junior, Senior
Majors/Fields: Civil engineering
Criteria: Applicant must be in good academic standing. One award is for a junior and the other for a senior. Awarded every year. Award may be used only at sponsoring institution.
Contact: E. R. Winzer, Director of Student Financial Aid.

555 NAWIC Founders' Scholarship Foundation

National Association of Women in Construction (NAWIC)
327 Adams Street
Fort Worth, TX 76104
(817) 877-5551
Maximum award: $2,000
Minimum award: $500
Number of awards: 35
Deadline: February 1
College level: Sophomore, Junior, Senior
Majors/Fields: Construction
Criteria: Selection is based upon applicant's interest in construction, grades, extracurricular activities, employment experience, evaluations, and financial need. Scholarship is renewable. Awarded every year.
Contact: Scholarships.

556 NRF/Chicago Roofing Contractors Association

National Roofing Foundation (NRF)
10255 West Higgins Road
Suite 600
Rosemont, IL 60018-5607
(708) 299-9070
Average award: $2,000
Deadline: April 1
College level: Freshman, Sophomore, Junior, Senior
Criteria: Applicant must live in Cook, Lake, DuPage, Kane, Kendall, DeKalb, McHenry, or Will counties in Illinois. Scholarship is renewable.
Contact: Scholarship Coordinator, (708) 299-1183.

557 NRF/Roofing Industry Scholarship/Grant

National Roofing Foundation (NRF)
10255 West Higgins Road
Suite 600
Rosemont, IL 60018-5607
(708) 299-9070
Average award: $1,000
Number of awards: 2
Deadline: January 15
College level: Freshman, Sophomore, Junior, Senior
Criteria: Applicant must be an immediate family member of a regular contractor member of National Roofing Contractors Association. Scholarship is renewable.
Contact: Scholarship Coordinator.

558 O.H. Ammann Research Fellowship in Structural Engineering

American Society of Civil Engineers (ASCE)
345 East 47th Street
New York, NY 10017-2398
(212) 705-7667
Average award: $5,000
Number of awards: 1
Deadline: February 15
College level: Graduate, Doctoral
Majors/Fields: Structural engineering
Criteria: Applicant must be a National ASCE member in good standing. Award is to encourage the creation of new knowledge in the field of structural design and construction. Committee on Society Honors determines if scholarship may be retained. Awarded every year.
Contact: Michael Peralta, Assistant Manager of Student Services.

559 Peter D. Courtois Concrete Construction Scholarship

American Concrete Institute
22400 West Seven Mile Road
Detroit, MI 48219-1849
Average award: $1,000
Number of awards: 2
Deadline: January 10
College level: Senior
Majors/Fields: Construction, engineering
Criteria: Applicant must demonstrate interest and ability in the field of concrete construction and be a U.S. or Canadian citizen. Applicant must submit transcripts, recommendations, and essay. Awarded every year.
Contact: Dot Kirk, Secretary to Scholarship Council, P.O. Box 19150, Detroit, MI 48219-0150, (313) 532-2600.

560 R.A. McFarland Memorial Scholarship

Louisiana Tech University
P.O. Box 7925
Ruston, LA 71272
(318) 257-2641
Average award: $1,000
Number of awards: 2
Deadline: October 1
College level: Junior, Senior
Majors/Fields: Civil engineering
Criteria: Applicant must rank in the top quarter of class of civil engineering students, must have been at the university for at least two years, and have at least three quarters remaining before graduation. One award is for a junior and the other for a senior. Awarded every year. Award may be used only at sponsoring institution.
Contact: E. R. Winzer, Director of Student Financial Aid.

561 Samuel Fletcher Tapman ASCE Student Chapter Scholarship

American Society of Civil Engineers (ASCE)
345 East 47th Street
New York, NY 10017-2398
(212) 705-7667
Average award: $1,500
Number of awards: 3
Deadline: March 1
College level: Sophomore, Junior, Senior
Majors/Fields: Civil engineering
Criteria: Applicant must be an ASCE National Student Member; only one application per student chapter may be submitted. Selection is based upon the appraisal of the applicant's justification of the award, educational plans, academic performance, potential for development, leadership capacity, and financial need. Previous recipients are eligible to reapply. Awarded every year.
Contact: Michael Peralta, Assistant Manager of Student Services.

Computer Science

562 Adelle and Erwin Tomash Fellowship in the History of Information Processing

Charles Babbage Institute
University of Minnesota
103 Walter Library, 117 Pleasant Street, SE
Minneapolis, MN 55455
(612) 624-5050
Average award: $10,000
Number of awards: 1
Deadline: January 15
College level: Doctoral
Criteria: Applicant must submit biographical data, a research plan containing a statement and justification of research problem, discussion of procedure for research and writing, information on availability of research materials, evidence of faculty support for the project, three letters of reference, and certified transcripts of college credits. No special application form required. Priority consideration is given to students who have completed all requirements for the doctoral degree except research and writing of dissertation, but other graduate students may also apply. Awarded every year.
Contact: Robert Seidel, Director.

563 El Paso Natural Gas Company Scholarship

New Mexico State University
Box 30001
Department 5100
Las Cruces, NM 88003-0001
(505) 646-4105
Average award: $2,000
Number of awards: 1
Deadline: March 1
College level: Sophomore, Junior, Senior
Majors/Fields: Computer science
Criteria: Applicant must have a minimum 3.2 GPA. Selection is based upon scholastic ability and academic potential. Awarded every year. Award may be used only at sponsoring institution.
Contact: College of Arts and Sciences, (505) 646-2001.

564 Kerr McGee Scholarship

University of Oklahoma
University Affairs
900 Asp Avenue, Room 236
Norman, OK 73019-0401
(405) 325-1701
Average award: $4,000
Number of awards: 1
Deadline: February 8
College level: Junior
Majors/Fields: Management information systems
Criteria: Selection is based upon merit and financial need. Awarded every year. Award may be used only at sponsoring institution.
Contact: Coordinator of MIS Program, 206 Adams Hall, Norman, OK 73019, (405) 352-2651.

565 TRW Scholarship

California State University, Fullerton
P.O. Box 34080
Fullerton, CA 92634-9480
(714) 773-3128
Average award: $1,000
Maximum award: $1,500
Minimum award: $500
Number of awards: 3
Deadline: February 26
College level: Sophomore, Junior, Senior
Majors/Fields: Management science, management information systems
Criteria: Selection is based upon academic and career goals, and outstanding scholarship in management science and management information systems. Awarded every year. Award may be used only at sponsoring institution.
Contact: Vickey Takeuchi, Scholarship Coordinator.

Electrical/Electronic Engineering

566 AMOCO Foundation Doctorial Fellowship

University of Oklahoma
University Affairs
900 Asp Avenue, Room 236
Norman, OK 73019-0401
(405) 325-1701
Average award: $12,000 plus tuition and fees
Minimum award: $12,000
Number of awards: 1
Deadline: April 1
College level: Doctoral
Majors/Fields: Electrical engineering, computer science
Criteria: Applicant must be a U.S. citizen. Selection is based upon merit and financial need. Awarded every year. Award may be used only at sponsoring institution.
Contact: Associate Dean for Professional Programs and Research, College of Engineering, Room 107, CEC, (405) 325-2621.

567 Billy Mitchell Chapter Association of Old Crows Scholarship

University of Texas at San Antonio
Office of Student Financial Aid
6900 North Loop 1604 West
San Antonio, TX 78249-0687
(210) 691-4011
Average award: $1,000
Number of awards: 7
Deadline: None
College level: Junior, Senior
Majors/Fields: Electrical engineering
Criteria: Applicant must have a minimum 3.0 GPA. Reapplication and minimum 3.0 GPA are required to retain scholarship. Awarded every year. Award may be used only at sponsoring institution.
Contact: Office of the Director, Engineering Division, (210) 691-4490.

568 Clyde Farrar Fellowship

University of Oklahoma
University Affairs
900 Asp Avenue, Room 236
Norman, OK 73019-0401
(405) 325-1701
Average award: $5,000
Number of awards: 1
Deadline: April 1
College level: Graduate, Doctoral
Majors/Fields: Electrical engineering
Criteria: Selection is based upon merit. Awarded every year. Award may be used only at sponsoring institution.
Contact: Associate Dean for Professional Programs and Research, College of Engineering, Room 107, CEC, (405) 325-2621.

569 Julia Kiene Fellowship in Electrical Energy

Electrical Women's Round Table, Inc.
P.O. Box 292793
Nashville, TN 37229-2793
(615) 890-1272
Average award: $2,000
Number of awards: 1
Deadline: March 1
College level: Graduate, Doctoral
Majors/Fields: Communications, education, electrical engineering, journalism, marketing, radio/TV broadcasting
Criteria: Applicant must be a woman pursuing graduate work toward an advanced degree in any phase of electrical energy. Selection is based upon academic aptitude, vocational promise, character, financial need, and willingness to continue a career in a field related to electrical energy. These fields include communications, education, electrical engineering, electric utilities, extension work, housing and home furnishings, journalism, manufacturers of electrical household equipment, marketing, radio, research, and television. Recipient must reapply to retain scholarship. Awarded every year.
Contact: Ann Cox, Executive Director.

570 Robert W. Thunen Memorial Scholarship

Illuminating Engineering Society of North America
IES Golden Gate Section
460 Brannen Street, P.O. Box 77527
San Francisco, CA 94107-1527
Average award: $2,500
Minimum award: $1,000
Number of awards: 2
Deadline: March 27
College level: Junior, Senior, Graduate, Doctoral
Majors/Fields: Lighting, lighting application, lighting design
Criteria: Applicant must be a student at an accredited institution in northern California, Nevada, Oregon, or Washington and must submit a statement of purpose and three recommendations. Reapplication and continuation in previously approved program is required to retain scholarship. Awarded every year.
Contact: Linda M. Esselstein, Chairman of Thunen Fund, (415) 626-1950.

571 Schlumberger Collegiate Award Scholarship

Clemson University
G-01 Sikes Hall
Clemson, SC 29634-5123
(803) 656-2280
Average award: $3,000
Number of awards: 1
Deadline: March 1
College level: Junior, Senior
Majors/Fields: Electrical engineering
Criteria: Applicant must be an outstanding student. Awarded every year. Award may be used only at sponsoring institution.
Contact: Marvin Carmichael, Director of Financial Aid.

Engineering–General

572 Admiral Grace Murray Hopper Scholarship

Society of Women Engineers (SWE)
120 Wall Street
11th Floor
New York, NY 10005-3902
(212) 509-9577
Minimum award: $1,000
Number of awards: 2
Deadline: May 15
College level: Freshman
Majors/Fields: Computer science, engineering
Criteria: Applicant must be a woman and have a 3.5 GPA. Awarded every year.
Contact: Scholarships.

573 Air and Waste Management Association Scholarship Endowment Trust Fund

Air and Waste Management Association
One Gateway Center
Third Floor
Pittsburgh, PA 15222
(412) 232-3444
Average award: $3,000
Maximum award: $5,000
Minimum award: $1,000
Maximum number of awards: 6
Minimum number of awards: 4
Deadline: First week of December
College level: Doctoral
Majors/Fields: Air pollution control, waste management
Criteria: Applicant must be enrolled full time. Awarded every year.
Contact: International Headquarters.

574 Alex C. and Margaret Page Hood and Rotary Club of Las Cruces Scholarship

New Mexico State University
Box 30001
Department 5100
Las Cruces, NM 88003-0001
(505) 646-4105
Average award: Tuition
Number of awards: 2
Deadline: March 1
College level: Freshman, Sophomore, Junior, Senior
Majors/Fields: Engineering
Criteria: Applicant must demonstrate financial need, have a minimum 3.0 GPA, and have been a resident of New Mexico for at least one year. One applicant is selected by the Rotary Club and one by the Coll of Engineering. Reapplication is required to retain scholarship. Awarded every year. Award may be used only at sponsoring institution.
Contact: Greeley W. Myers, Director of Financial Aid.

575 Alex R. Cummings Bursary

University of Calgary
2500 University Drive, NW
Calgary, Alberta, CN T2N 1N4
(403) 220-7872
Average award: $2,500
Number of awards: 1
Deadline: July 15
College level: Freshman
Majors/Fields: Engineering
Criteria: Selection is based upon financial need and academic merit. Awarded every year. Award may be used only at sponsoring institution.
Contact: J. Van Housen, Director of Student Awards and Financial Aid.

576 Alexander S. Langsdorf Fellowship in Engineering and Applied Science

Washington University
One Brookings Drive
Campus Box 1089
St. Louis, MO 63130
(314) 935-6000 or (800) 638-0700
Average award: $19,250
Number of awards: 7
College level: Freshman
Majors/Fields: Applied science, engineering
Criteria: Applicant must apply under the Early Decision or Early Action plans. Selection is based upon academic merit without regard to financial need. Satisfactory academic performance is required to retain scholarship. Awarded every year. Award may be used only at sponsoring institution.
Contact: Office of Undergraduate Admissions, (800) 638-0700 or (314) 935-6000.

577 American Society of Naval Engineers Scholarship

American Society of Naval Engineers (ASNE)
1452 Duke Street
Alexandria, VA 22314-3458
(703) 836-6727
Average award: $2,000
Number of awards: 15
Deadline: February 15
College level: Senior, Graduate
Majors/Fields: Aeronautical engineering, electrical/electronic engineering, marine engineering, naval architecture, ocean engineering, physical sciences
Criteria: Applicant must be enrolled in a full-time, undergraduate or master's degree program or be a co-op student at an accredited college or university. Applicant must demonstrate or express a genuine interest in a career in naval engineering and be a U.S. citizen. Selection is based upon academic record, work history, professional promise, extracurricular activities, and recommendations. Financial need may be considered. Awarded every year.
Contact: Captain Dennis Pignotti, USN (Ret), Scholarships.

578 Anne Maureen Whitney Barrow Memorial Scholarship

Society of Women Engineers (SWE)
120 Wall Street
11th Floor
New York, NY 10005-3902
(212) 509-9577
Average award: $4,000
Number of awards: 1
Deadline: May 15
College level: Freshman
Majors/Fields: Engineering, engineering technology
Criteria: Applicant must be a woman and have a 3.5 GPA. Scholarship is renewable.
Contact: Scholarships.

579 ASHRAE Graduate Grant-in-Aid

American Society of Heating, Refrigerating, and Air Conditioning Engineers (ASHRAE)
1791 Tullie Circle, NE
Atlanta, GA 30329
(404) 636-8400
Minimum award: $7,500
Number of awards: 15
Deadline: December 15
College level: Graduate, Doctoral
Majors/Fields: Engineering
Criteria: Grant is intended to encourage the applicant to continue his or her preparation for service in the HVAC&R industry. Applicant must be a member of ASHRAE student chapter. The faculty advisor must submit an application form. Thesis for master's or doctoral degree must be in the field of heating, air conditioning, ventilation, refrigeration, or allied fields; relevance of the proposed research is a consideration for awarding the grant. Awarded every year.
Contact: William Seaton, Manager of Research.

580 ASHRAE Scholarship

American Society of Heating, Refrigerating, and Air Conditioning Engineers (ASHRAE)
1791 Tullie Circle, NE
Atlanta, GA 30329
(404) 636-8400
Average award: $3,000
Maximum award: $5,000
Minimum award: $2,000
Number of awards: 4
Deadline: December 15
College level: Freshman, Sophomore, Junior, Senior
Majors/Fields: Engineering in relation to the HVAC&R field
Criteria: Selection is based upon financial need, minimum 3.0 GPA, faculty recommendations, leadership ability, and potential service to the HVAC and/or refrigeration profession. Consideration is given to participation of the student and advisor in ASHRAE. Reapplication is required to retain scholarship. Awarded every year.
Contact: Rhonda Fowler, Staff Liaison, Scholarship Fund Trustees.

581 ASHRAE Undergraduate Grant-in-Aid

American Society of Heating, Refrigerating, and Air Conditioning Engineers (ASHRAE)
1791 Tullie Circle, NE
Atlanta, GA 30329
(404) 636-8400
Average award: $2,500
Number of awards: 12
Deadline: December 15
College level: Junior, Senior
Majors/Fields: Engineering
Criteria: Applicant must be involved in a research project in an area of HVAC, refrigeration, or a related field. Selection is based upon relevance of proposed research. Awarded every year.
Contact: William Seaton, Manager of Research.

582   ASSE Student Paper Awards

American Society of Safety Engineers (ASSE)
1800 E. Oakton Street
Des Plaines, IL 60018-2187
Maximum award: $1,000
Minimum award: $500
Number of awards: 3
Deadline: January 31
Majors/Fields: Safety engineering
Criteria: Applicant must be a full-time undergraduate student in a safety/health degree program. Selection is based upon the paper's relevance to important safety issues, persuasiveness, impact, quality of writing, technical accuracy, and feasibility.
Contact: Awards.

583   B. Charles Tiney Memorial ASCE Student Chapter Scholarship

American Society of Civil Engineers (ASCE)
345 East 47th Street
New York, NY 10017-2398
(212) 705-7667
Average award: $2,000
Number of awards: 1
Deadline: March 1
College level: Sophomore, Junior, Senior
Majors/Fields: Engineering
Criteria: Applicant must be an ASCE National Student Member in good standing and demonstrate financial need. Only one application per student chapter may be submitted. Awarded every year.
Contact: Michael Peralta, Assistant Manager of Student Services.

584   Cabot Corporation Graduate Fellowship

New Mexico State University
Box 30001
Department 5100
Las Cruces, NM 88003-0001
(505) 646-4105
Average award: $4,500
Number of awards: 2
Deadline: March 1
College level: Graduate, Doctoral
Majors/Fields: Chemical engineering, mechanical engineering
Criteria: Awarded every year. Award may be used only at sponsoring institution.
Contact: College of Engineering, (505) 646-3547.

585   Calvin M. Woodward Fellowship in Engineering and Applied Science

Washington University
One Brookings Drive
Campus Box 1089
St. Louis, MO 63130
(314) 935-6000 or (800) 638-0700
Average award: $8,375
Number of awards: 20
College level: Freshman
Majors/Fields: Applied science, engineering
Criteria: Applicant must apply under the Early Decision or Early Action plans. Selection is based upon academic merit without regard to financial need. Satisfactory academic performance is required to retain scholarship. Awarded every year. Award may be used only at sponsoring institution.
Contact: Office of Undergraduate Admissions.

586   Cecil C. Humphreys/Herff Engineering Scholarship

University of Memphis
Scates Hall 204
Memphis, TN 38152
(901) 678-3213
Maximum award: $4,200
Deadline: January 15
College level: Freshman
Majors/Fields: Engineering
Criteria: Applicant must have a minimum composite ACT score of 30 or combined SAT I score of 1200. Selection is based upon test scores, academic record, interview, excellence of performance in area of interest, and quantity and quality of extracurricular activities. Minimum 3.0 GPA for the first year, 3.25 GPA thereafter, and 10 service hours per year are required for renewal. Awarded every year. Award may be used only at sponsoring institution.
Contact: Dr. Sue Ann McClellan, Scholarship Coordinator.

587   Chevron Canada Resources Limited Scholarship in Engineering

University of Calgary
2500 University Drive, NW
Calgary, Alberta, CN T2N 1N4
(403) 220-7872
Average award: $1,500
Number of awards: 3
Deadline: June 15
College level: Senior
Majors/Fields: Chemical engineering, civil engineering, mechanical engineering
Criteria: Selection is based upon outstanding academic merit. Preference is given to Canadian citizens interested in oil production, drilling, design and construction, gas processing, or reservoir engineering. Awarded every year. Award may be used only at sponsoring institution.
Contact: J. Van Housen, Director of Student Awards and Financial Aid.

588   Chevron Scholarship

Society of Women Engineers (SWE)
120 Wall Street
11th Floor
New York, NY 10005-3902
(212) 509-9577
Average award: $2,000
Number of awards: 2
Deadline: February 1
College level: Sophomore, Junior
Majors/Fields: Chemical engineering, mechanical engineering, petroleum engineering
Criteria: Applicant must be a U.S. citizen, a woman, and be enrolled at a school, college or university with an accredited engineering program. Awarded every year.
Contact: Scholarships.

589   Christenson Engineering Corporation Scholarship

Western Washington University
516 High Street
Bellingham, WA 98226-9006
(206) 650-3471
Average award: $2,000
Number of awards: 1
Deadline: April 15
College level: Sophomore, Junior, Senior
Majors/Fields: Technology
Criteria: Applicant must be a full-time student with a declared major in a technical program of studies of the Technology Dept. GPA is considered. Awarded every year. Award may be used only at sponsoring institution.
Contact: Technology Department, 204 Ross Engineering Technology, Bellingham, WA 98225, (206) 650-3380.

590   Clemson-Sonoco Scholars Program

Clemson University
G-01 Sikes Hall
Clemson, SC 29634-5123
(803) 656-2280
Average award: $1,000
Number of awards: 3
Deadline: March 1
College level: Freshman, Sophomore, Junior, Senior
Majors/Fields: Chemical engineering, electrical engineering, industrial engineering, management, mechanical engineering
Criteria: Applicant must have a minimum 2.0 GPA. Scholarship is rotated among the departments of chemical engineering, electrical engineering, industrial engineering, management, and mechanical engineering. Awarded every year. Award may be used only at sponsoring institution.
Contact: Marvin Carmichael, Director of Financial Aid.

591   CR Resources Limited Entrance Scholarship

University of Calgary
2500 University Drive, NW
Calgary, Alberta, CN T2N 1N4
(403) 220-7872
Average award: $3,000
Number of awards: 1
Deadline: March 15
College level: Freshman
Majors/Fields: Engineering
Criteria: Applicant must be a Canadian citizen or permanent resident. Selection is based upon academic merit, contribution to school and community life, and academic promise. Awarded every year. Award may be used only at sponsoring institution.
Contact: J. Van Housen, Director of Student Awards and Financial Aid.

592   Digital Equipment Corporation, Inc. Scholarship

New Mexico State University
Box 30001
Department 5100
Las Cruces, NM 88003-0001
(505) 646-4105
Average award: $1,500
Number of awards: 2
Deadline: March 1
College level: Sophomore, Junior, Senior
Majors/Fields: Electrical engineering, mechanical engineering, industrial engineering
Criteria: Applicant must be American Indian or Hispanic. Awarded every year. Award may be used only at sponsoring institution.
Contact: College of Engineering, (505) 646-3547.

593   Dorothy Lemke Howarth Scholarship

Society of Women Engineers (SWE)
120 Wall Street
11th Floor
New York, NY 10005-3902
(212) 509-9577
Maximum award: $3,000
Minimum award: $1,000
Number of awards: 3
Deadline: February 1
College level: Sophomore
Majors/Fields: Engineering
Criteria: Applicant must be a U.S. citizen, a woman, and have a 3.5 GPA. Awarded every year.
Contact: Scholarships.

594   Dow Black Scholars Award

Mississippi State University
P.O. Box 6238
Mississippi State, MS 39762
(601) 325-7430
Average award: $2,500
Number of awards: 2
Deadline: February 1
College level: Freshman
Majors/Fields: Chemical engineering, mechanical engineering
Criteria: Applicant must be black and have a minimum composite ACT score of 21 or combined SAT I score of 860. Minimum 3.0 cumulative GPA is required to retain scholarship. Awarded every year. Award may be used only at sponsoring institution.
Contact: Audrey S. Lambert, Director of Student Financial Aid.

595   Dow Corning Scholarship

National Society of Professional Engineers
Education Foundation
1420 King Street
Alexandria, VA 22314-2794
(703) 684-2800
Average award: $3,000
Number of awards: 1
College level: Freshman
Majors/Fields: Engineering
Criteria: Applicant must be a resident of Illinois, Indiana, Ohio, or Wisconsin, rank in the top quarter of class, be of a minority background, have a minimum 3.0 GPA, and minimum SAT I scores of 500 verbal and 600 math (ACT scores of 22 English and 29 math). Award includes summer employment at the Dow Corning plant in Midland, Mich. Scholarship is renewable. Awarded every year.
Contact: Education Foundation.

596   Dual Degree Scholarship Program/ Undergraduate Scholarship Program

AT&T Bell Laboratories
University Relations
101 Crawfords Corner Road, Room 1E-213, P.O. Box 3030
Holmdel, NJ 07733-3030
(908) 949-4301
Maximum award: Full tuition, fees, room, board, book allowance, and summer employment (including travel expenses and housing)
Number of awards: 3
Deadline: June 10
College level: Freshman
Majors/Fields: Computer engineering, computer science, electrical engineering, mathematics, mechanical engineering, physics, systems engineering
Criteria: Applicant must be a U.S. citizen or permanent resident who is black, Hispanic, Native American, female Asian/Pacific Islander, or female Caucasian. Selection is based upon scholastic aptitude, academic performance, class rank, strength of high school curriculum, leadership, motivation, and ability. Applicant must attend Atlanta U, Clark U, Morehouse Coll, Morris Brown Coll, or Spelman Coll for three years or U of Alabama, Auburn U, Boston U, Georgia Inst of Tech, Rensselaer Polytech Inst, or Rochester Inst of Tech for two years. Scholarship is renewable. Awarded every year.
Contact: Scholarship Administrator.

597   El Paso Natural Gas Company (Engineering)

New Mexico State University
Box 30001
Department 5100
Las Cruces, NM 88003-0001
(505) 646-4105
Average award: $2,000
Number of awards: 2
Deadline: March 1
College level: Junior
Majors/Fields: Chemical engineering, mechanical engineering
Criteria: Applicant must have a minimum 3.0 cumulative GPA. Selection is based upon scholastic ability and academic potential with preference given to minority students. Awarded every year. Award may be used only at sponsoring institution.
Contact: College of Engineering, (505) 646-3547.

598   Employees at Duke Power Scholars Program

Clemson University
G-01 Sikes Hall
Clemson, SC 29634-5123
(803) 656-2280
Average award: $1,500
Number of awards: 5
Deadline: March 1
College level: Junior, Senior
Majors/Fields: Accounting, civil engineering, computer science, electrical engineering, mechanical engineering
Criteria: Preference, in the following order, is given to majors in electrical engineering, mechanical engineering, civil engineering, accounting, and computer science. Minimum 3.0 GPA with at least 12 credits per semester is required to retain scholarship. Awarded every year. Award may be used only at sponsoring institution.
Contact: Marvin Carmichael, Director of Financial Aid.

599   Engineering Scholarship Program/
Undergraduate Scholarship Programs

AT&T Bell Laboratories
University Relations
101 Crawfords Corner Road, Room 1E-213, P.O. Box 3030
Holmdel, NJ 07733-3030
(908) 949-4301
Average award: Full tuition, fees, room, board, book allowance, and summer employment (includes travel expenses and housing)
Number of awards: 15
Deadline: January 15
College level: Freshman
Majors/Fields: Computer engineering, computer science, electrical engineering, mechanical engineering, systems engineering
Criteria: Applicant must be a U.S. citizen or permanent resident who is black, Hispanic, Native American, female Asian/Pacific Islander, or female Caucasian. Selection is based upon scholastic aptitude, academic performance, class rank, strength of high school curriculum, leadership, motivation, and ability. Program is specifically intended for women and those ethnic groups that are underrepresented at AT&T; however, anyone may apply. Minimum "B" average and satisfactory performance during summer employment is required to retain scholarship. Awarded every year.
Contact: ESP Administrator.

600   Faculty of Engineering Associates Scholarship

University of Calgary
2500 University Drive, NW
Calgary, Alberta, CN T2N 1N4
(403) 220-7872
Average award: $3,000
Number of awards: 1
Deadline: March 15
College level: Freshman
Majors/Fields: Engineering
Criteria: Applicant must be a Canadian citizen or permanent resident. Selection is based upon academic merit, contribution to school and community life, and academic promise. Awarded every year. Award may be used only at sponsoring institution.
Contact: J. Van Housen, Director of Student Awards & Financial Aid.

601   Fluor Daniel Canada, Inc. Scholarship

University of Calgary
2500 University Drive, NW
Calgary, Alberta, CN T2N 1N4
(403) 220-7872
Average award: $2,000
Number of awards: 3
College level: Junior, Senior
Majors/Fields: Chemical engineering, civil engineering, electrical engineering, mechanical engineering
Criteria: Applicant must be a Canadian citizen or permanent resident and be enrolled full time. Selection is based upon academic merit. Awarded every year. Award may be used only at sponsoring institution.
Contact: J. Van Housen, Director of Student Awards & Financial Aid.

602   General Electric Foundation Scholarship

Society of Women Engineers (SWE)
120 Wall Street
11th Floor
New York, NY 10005-3902
(212) 509-9577
Average award: $1,000
Maximum award: $1,000 scholarship plus $500 to attend the National Convention/Student Conference.
Number of awards: 3
Deadline: May 15
College level: Freshman
Majors/Fields: Engineering
Criteria: Applicant must be a woman who is a U.S. citizen and has a 3.5 GPA. Continued academic achievement is required to retain scholarship for up to three additional years. Awarded every year.
Contact: Louise Bacon, Executive Assistant.

603   General Motors Foundation Scholarship

Society of Women Engineers (SWE)
120 Wall Street
11th Floor
New York, NY 10005-3902
(212) 509-9577
Average award: $1,000
Number of awards: 2
Deadline: February 1
College level: Junior
Majors/Fields: Automotive engineering, chemical engineering, electrical engineering, engineering technology, industrial engineering, manufacturing engineering, materials engineering, mechanical engineering
Criteria: Applicant must be a woman with a minimum 3.2 GPA, demonstrate leadership with a position of responsibility in a student organization, and have a career interest in the automotive industry and/or manufacturing environment. Scholarship is renewable. Awarded every year.
Contact: Scholarships.

604   General Motors Scholarship (Engineering)

New Mexico State University
Box 30001
Department 5100
Las Cruces, NM 88003-0001
(505) 646-4105
Average award: Tuition, book allowance, and stipend
Deadline: March 1
College level: Sophomore
Majors/Fields: Electrical engineering, industrial engineering, mechanical engineering
Criteria: Applicant must be a U.S. citizen with a minimum 3.2 cumulative GPA. Scholarship is renewable. Awarded every year. Award may be used only at sponsoring institution.
Contact: College of Engineering, (505) 646-3547.

605   George Swygert and Wilfred P. Tiencken
Endowed Scholarship

Clemson University
G-01 Sikes Hall
Clemson, SC 29634-5123
(803) 656-2280
Average award: $1,000
Number of awards: 2
Deadline: March 1
College level: Freshman, Sophomore, Junior, Senior
Majors/Fields: Engineering
Criteria: Applicant must have a minimum 2.0 cumulative GPA. Satisfactory GPA with at least 12 credits per semester is required to retain scholarship. Awarded every year. Award may be used only at sponsoring institution.
Contact: Marvin Carmichael, Director of Financial Aid.

606   Graduate Research Program for Women/ Cooperative Research Fellowship Program/ Ph.D. Fellowship Program

AT&T Bell Laboratories
University Relations
101 Crawfords Corner Road, Room 1E-213, P.O. Box 3030
Holmdel, NJ 07733-3030
(908) 949-4301
Average award: Full-tuition, fees, $13,200 annual stipend, book allowance, and summer employment (including travel expenses and housing)
Minimum award: $1,500
Number of awards: 44
Deadline: January 15 ; January 20 for Ph.D. program
College level: Graduate, Doctoral
Majors/Fields: Chemistry, chemical engineering, communications science, computer engineering, computer science, electrical engineering, information science, mathematics, mechanical engineering, physics, statistics
Criteria: Applicant must be a U.S. citizen or permanent resident who is black, Hispanic, Native American, female Asian/Pacific Islander or female Caucasian. Selection is based upon scholastic aptitude, academic performance, class rank, leadership, motivation, and ability. Ph.D. program is by invitation only. Scholarship is renewable. Awarded every year.
Contact: University Relations, (908) 949-2943.

607   Hearin-Hess Engineering Scholarship

Mississippi State University
P.O. Box 6238
Mississippi State, MS 39762
(601) 325-7430
Average award: $4,000
Number of awards: 7
Deadline: February 1
College level: Freshman
Majors/Fields: Engineering
Criteria: Applicant must have a minimum composite ACT score of 30 or combined SAT I score of 1240. Minimum 3.0 GPA in required engineering courses and enrollment in the Coll of Engineering are required to retain scholarship. Awarded every year. Award may be used only at sponsoring institution.
Contact: Audrey S. Lambert, Director of Student Financial Aid.

608   Hewlett-Packard Scholarship

Society of Women Engineers (SWE)
120 Wall Street
11th Floor
New York, NY 10005-3902
(212) 509-9577
Average award: $1,000
Number of awards: 7
Deadline: May 15
College level: Junior, Senior
Majors/Fields: Computer science, electrical engineering
Criteria: Applicant must be a woman, have a 3.5 GPA, and be an active supporter and contributor to SWE. Awarded every year.
Contact: Scholarships.

609   Hughes Bachelor of Science Scholarship

California State University, Fullerton
P.O. Box 34080
Fullerton, CA 92634-9480
(714) 773-3128
Average award: Salary, benefits and educational expenses
Deadline: March 15
College level: Junior, Senior
Majors/Fields: Aeronautical engineering, applied mathematics, computer science, electrical engineering, mechanical engineering, physics, systems engineering
Criteria: Applicant must have a minimum 3.0 GPA, be a U.S. citizen, and demonstrate academic achievement and professional promise. Scholarship program allows qualified applicants to complete their B.S. degree while beginning a technical career at Hughes Aircraft Company. Scholarship is renewable. Awarded every year. Award may be used only at sponsoring institution.
Contact: Vickey Takeuchi, Scholarship Coordinator.

610   Ivy Parker Memorial Scholarship

Society of Women Engineers (SWE)
120 Wall Street
11th Floor
New York, NY 10005-3902
(212) 509-9577
Average award: $2,000
Number of awards: 1
Deadline: February 1
College level: Junior, Senior
Majors/Fields: Engineering
Criteria: Applicant must be a woman, have a 3.5 GPA, and demonstrate financial need. Junior recipients may reapply for continued support for following year. Awarded every year.
Contact: Louise Bacon, Executive Assistant.

611   J.E. Sirrine Company Engineering Scholarship

Clemson University
G-01 Sikes Hall
Clemson, SC 29634-5123
(803) 656-2280
Average award: $1,000
Number of awards: 2
Deadline: March 1
College level: Freshman, Junior
Majors/Fields: Chemical engineering, civil engineering, electrical engineering, mechanical engineering
Criteria: Applicant must be an outstanding student. Awarded every year. Award may be used only at sponsoring institution.
Contact: Marvin Carmichael, Director of Financial Aid.

612   James A. "Shine" Milling Presidential Scholarship

Clemson University
G-01 Sikes Hall
Clemson, SC 29634-5123
(803) 656-2280
Average award: $5,500
Number of awards: 2
Deadline: March 1
College level: Freshman, Sophomore, Junior, Senior, Graduate
Majors/Fields: Engineering, industrial management
Criteria: Awarded every year. Award may be used only at sponsoring institution.
Contact: Marvin Carmichael, Director of Financial Aid.

613   John E. Anderson Safety Student of the Year Award

American Society of Safety Engineers (ASSE)
1800 E. Oakton Street
Des Plaines, IL 60018-2187
Minimum award: $1,500
Deadline: January 31
Majors/Fields: Safety engineering
Criteria: Applicant must be a full-time student and ASSE member. Selection is based upon the quality and scope of endorsements by the nominee's faculty advisor, appropriate chapter officer(s), and/or other faculty members, GPA, extracurricular safety activities, special safety-related projects or research, published articles, and demonstrated peer acceptance.
Contact: Awards.

614   Lillian Moller Gilbreth Scholarship

Society of Women Engineers (SWE)
120 Wall Street
11th Floor
New York, NY 10005-3902
(212) 509-9577
Average award: $5,000
Number of awards: 1
Deadline: February 1
College level: Junior, Senior
Majors/Fields: Engineering
Criteria: Applicant must be a woman with a 3.5 GPA who demonstrates outstanding potential and achievement. Awarded every year.
Contact: Louise Bacon, Executive Assistant.

615   Logistics Education Foundation Scholarship

Society of Logistics Engineers
8100 Professional Place, Suite 211
New Carrollton, MD 20785
(301) 459-8446
Average award: $1,000
Number of awards: 8
Deadline: April 15
College level: Freshman, Sophomore, Junior, Senior, Graduate, Doctoral
Majors/Fields: Logistics
Criteria: Awarded every year.
Contact: Richard A. Romer, Director of Professional Development.

616   Management of the Industrial Associates Minority Engineering Scholarship

Clemson University
G-01 Sikes Hall
Clemson, SC 29634-5123
(803) 656-2280
Average award: $1,000
Number of awards: 40
College level: Freshman
Majors/Fields: Engineering
Criteria: Applicant must be a minority student. Minimum 3.0 cumulative GPA with at least 12 credits per semester is required to retain scholarship. Awarded every year. Award may be used only at sponsoring institution.
Contact: Marvin Carmichael, Director of Financial Aid.

617   Men's Auxiliary of the Society of Women Engineers Memorial Scholarship

Society of Women Engineers (SWE)
120 Wall Street, 11th Floor
New York, NY 10005-3902
(212) 509-9577
Average award: $2,000
Number of awards: 2
Deadline: February 1
College level: Sophomore, Junior, Senior
Majors/Fields: Engineering
Criteria: Applicant must be a woman and have a 3.5 GPA. Selection is based upon scholarship and financial need. Awarded every year.
Contact: Scholarships.

618   Microsoft Corporation Scholarships

Society of Women Engineers (SWE)
120 Wall Street, 11th Floor
New York, NY 10005-3902
(212) 509-9577
Minimum award: $1,000
Number of awards: 10
Deadline: February 1
College level: Sophomore, Junior, Senior, Graduate
Majors/Fields: Computer engineering, computer science
Criteria: Applicant must be a woman with a career interest in the field of microcomputer software and have a 3.5 GPA. Awarded every year.
Contact: Scholarships.

619   MidCon Corporation Scholarship

New Mexico State University
Box 30001
Department 5100
Las Cruces, NM 88003-0001
(505) 646-4105
Average award: $2,000
Deadline: March 1
College level: Junior
Majors/Fields: Civil engineering, electrical engineering, mechanical engineering
Criteria: Applicant must have a minimum 2.5 GPA and accept a summer internship in the year the scholarship is granted. Awarded every year. Award may be used only at sponsoring institution.
Contact: College of Engineering, (505) 646-3547.

620   Minnesota Mining and Manufacturing Corporation Annual Scholarship

Clemson University
G-01 Sikes Hall
Clemson, SC 29634-5123
(803) 656-2280
Average award: $3,000
Number of awards: 2
Deadline: March 1
College level: Sophomore, Junior, Senior, Graduate, Doctoral
Majors/Fields: Engineering
Criteria: One award is an undergraduate scholarship and the other is a graduate fellowship. Awarded every year. Award may be used only at sponsoring institution.
Contact: Marvin Carmichael, Director of Financial Aid.

621   Minority Engineering and Sciences Scholarship

General Motors Corporation
3044 W. Grand Boulevard
Detroit, MI 48202
Maximum award: $5,000
Number of awards: 104
College level: Sophomore, Junior, Senior
Majors/Fields: Engineering, science
Criteria: Applicant must be a member of one of the following minority groups: Alaskan Native, American Indian, Asian-American, African-American/black, Mexican-American/Chicano, Hispanic, or Puerto Rican. Contact the engineering department to ask if the university participates in the scholarship program.
Contact: L.J. Wicker, Manager, Education Relations, (313) 556-3509.

622   Minority Engineering Program Scholarship

University of Utah
Financial Aid and Scholarships Office
105 Student Services Building
Salt Lake City, UT 84112
(801) 581-6211
Maximum award: $1,500
Minimum award: $500
Maximum number of awards: 6
Minimum number of awards: 4
Deadline: February 1
College level: Freshman, Sophomore, Junior, Senior
Majors/Fields: Engineering
Criteria: Applicant must be a U.S. citizen who is a member of an underrepresented ethnic or gender group. Reapplication is required to retain scholarship. Awarded every year. Award may be used only at sponsoring institution.
Contact: Kate Rhodes, MEP Director, 2220 Merrill Engineering Building, Salt Lake City, UT 84112, (801) 581-8954.

623   Norcen Energy Canadian Scholarship Series in Engineering

University of Calgary
2500 University Drive, NW
Calgary, Alberta, CN T2N 1N4
(403) 220-7872
Average award: $1,500
Number of awards: 6
Deadline: June 15
College level: Junior, Senior
Majors/Fields: Chemical engineering, mechanical engineering
Criteria: Applicant must be a Canadian citizen or permanent resident. Special consideration is given to applicants interested in a career in the oil and gas industry. Selection is based primarily upon academic merit. Financial need and extracurricular activities are considered. Awarded every year. Award may be used only at sponsoring institution.
Contact: J. Van Housen, Director of Student Awards & Financial Aid.

624   NRF General Scholarship

National Roofing Foundation (NRF)
10255 West Higgins Road
Suite 600
Rosemont, IL 60018-5607
(708) 299-9070
Average award: $2,000
Number of awards: 2
Deadline: January 15
College level: Freshman, Sophomore, Junior, Senior
Majors/Fields: Architecture, engineering
Criteria: Scholarship is renewable.
Contact: Scholarship Coordinator, 10255 W. Higgins, Suite 600, Rosemont, IL 60018-5607.

625   NSPE Auxiliary Scholarship

National Society of Professional Engineers (NSPE)
Education Foundation
1420 King Street
Alexandria, VA 22314-2794
(703) 684-2800
Average award: $1,000
Number of awards: 2
College level: Freshman
Majors/Fields: Engineering
Criteria: Applicant must be a woman, a U.S. citizen, have a minimum 3.0 GPA, rank in the top quarter of class, and have minimum SAT I scores of 500 verbal and 600 math (ACT scores of 22 English and 29 math). Selection is based upon scholarship and achievement. Renewable for four years. Awarded every year.
Contact: Education Foundation.

626   NSPE Student Chapter Member Award

National Society of Professional Engineers (NSPF)
Education Foundation
1420 King Street
Alexandria, VA 22314-2794
(703) 684-2800
Average award: $2,000
Number of awards: 6
College level: Sophomore, Junior, Senior
Majors/Fields: Engineering
Criteria: Applicant must be a U.S. citizen, have a minimum 3.0 GPA, submit two recommendations, and be a member in good standing of the NSPE Student Chapter. Awarded every year.
Contact: Education Foundation.

627   Olive Lynn Salembier Scholarship

Society of Women Engineers (SWE)
120 Wall Street
11th Floor
New York, NY 10005-3902
(212) 509-9577
Average award: $2,000
Number of awards: 1
Deadline: May 15
College level: Sophomore, Junior, Senior, Graduate, Doctoral
Majors/Fields: Engineering
Criteria: Applicant must be a woman who has been out of the engineering job market for a minimum of two years. Scholarship is to aid in obtaining the credentials necessary to re-enter the job market as an engineer. Awarded every year.
Contact: Louise Bacon, Executive Assistant.

628   PEG/PEPP Scholarships

National Society of Professional Engineers
Education Foundation
1420 King Street
Alexandria, VA 22314-2794
(703) 684-2800
Maximum award: $3,000
Minimum award: $2,000
Number of awards: 2
College level: Graduate
Majors/Fields: Management, engineering management
Criteria: Applicant must be a U.S. citizen, have a minimum 3.0 GPA, and submit two recommendations.
Contact: Education Foundation.

629   PEI Scholarship

National Society of Professional Engineers
Education Foundation
1420 King Street
Alexandria, VA 22314-2794
(703) 684-2800
Average award: $2,500
Number of awards: 1
College level: Junior, Senior
Majors/Fields: Engineering
Criteria: Applicant must be a U.S. citizen, have a minimum 3.0 GPA, and submit two recommendations. Awarded every year.
Contact: Education Foundation.

630   Peter Peterson/UT/EFO Scholarship

University of Toledo
Financial Aid Office
Toledo, OH 43606-3390
(419) 537-2056
Average award: $1,200
Number of awards: 4
Deadline: January 28
College level: Freshman
Majors/Fields: Engineering
Criteria: Applicant must be an outstanding graduate of an Ohio high school and demonstrate great potential in engineering. Scholarship is renewable. Awarded every year. Award may be used only at sponsoring institution.
Contact: Dean, College of Engineering, Toledo, OH 43606.

631   Petroleum Society of CIM (Calgary Section) Scholarship

University of Calgary
2500 University Drive, NW
Calgary, Alberta, CN T2N 1N4
(403) 220-7872
Average award: $1,500
Number of awards: 4
Deadline: June 15
College level: Junior, Senior
Majors/Fields: Engineering
Criteria: Selection is based upon academic merit and extracurricular activities. Awarded every year. Award may be used only at sponsoring institution.
Contact: J. Van Housen, Director of Student Awards and Financial Aid.

632 Phillips Petroleum Company Grant

National Society of Professional Engineers
Education Foundation
1420 King Street
Alexandria, VA 22314-2794
(703) 684-2800
Average award: $1,000
Number of awards: 2
College level: Freshman
Majors/Fields: Engineering
Criteria: Applicant must be a woman, a U.S. citizen, with a minimum 3.0 GPA, and minimum SAT I scores of 500 verbal and 600 math (or ACT scores of 22 English and 29 math). Awarded every year.
Contact: Education Foundation.

633 Piedmont Chapter of the South Carolina SPE Engineering Scholarship

Clemson University
G-01 Sikes Hall
Clemson, SC 29634-5123
(803) 656-2280
Average award: $1,000
Number of awards: 5
Deadline: March 1
College level: Sophomore, Junior, Senior
Majors/Fields: Engineering
Criteria: Applicant must be a South Carolina resident with a minimum 2.5 GPA. GPA requirement may be waived if financial need is a factor. Satisfactory GPA with at least 12 credits per semester is required to retain scholarship. Awarded every year. Award may be used only at sponsoring institution.
Contact: Marvin Carmichael, Director of Financial Aid.

634 ProNet Scholarship

National Society of Professional Engineers
Education Foundation
1420 King Street
Alexandria, VA 22314-2794
(703) 684-2800
Average award: $2,500
Number of awards: 1
College level: Junior, Senior
Majors/Fields: Engineering
Criteria: Applicant must be a U.S. citizen, with a minimum 3.0 GPA, and submit two recommendations. Awarded every year.
Contact: Education Foundation.

635 Quarry Engineering Scholarship

National Stone Association
1415 Elliot Place, NW
Washington, DC 20007
(800) 342-1415
Maximum award: $2,000
Number of awards: 5
Deadline: May 1
College level: Sophomore, Junior, Senior, Graduate
Majors/Fields: Civil engineering, geology, mining engineering
Criteria: Preference is given to applicants who have held summer employment in aggregates industry. Scholarship is renewable. Awarded every year.
Contact: Robert S. Brown, Jr., Director of Public Affairs.

636 Randall K. Nutt Engineering Scholarship

University of Tennessee, Knoxville
Financial Aid Office
115 Student Services Building
Knoxville, TN 37994
(615) 974-3131
Average award: Tuition and fees
Number of awards: 1
Deadline: February 1
College level: Freshman
Majors/Fields: Computer engineering, engineering
Criteria: Applicant must have a minimum 3.0 GPA and minimum composite ACT score of 23. Primary consideration is given to graduates of Farragut High School, Ooltewah High School, or Hohenwald High School, with other Tennessee residents secondary. Priority is given to applicants with financial need, without other aid, and those interested in electrical or computer engineering. Award is for four years. Awarded every year. Award may be used only at sponsoring institution.
Contact: College of Engineering, 118 Perkins Hall, Knoxville, TN 37996, (615) 974-2454.

637 Robert W. Cotton Memorial Scholarship Competition

Consulting Engineers Council of Metropolitan Washington
8811 Colesville Road, Suite G106
Silver Spring, MD 20910
(301) 588-6616
Maximum award: $5,000
Minimum award: $1,000
Number of awards: 10
Deadline: February 15
College level: Junior, Senior
Majors/Fields: Consulting engineering
Criteria: Applicant must be a U.S. citizen, rank in top half of class, and reside or study in the metropolitan Washington, D.C., area. Selection is based upon academic record, extracurricular activities, engineering-related job experience, and recommendations. Awarded every year.
Contact: Alpha Moore, Scholarship Coordinator.

638 Rockwell International Corporation Scholarship

Society of Women Engineers (SWE)
120 Wall Street
11th Floor
New York, NY 10005-3902
(212) 509-9577
Average award: $3,000
Number of awards: 2
Deadline: May 15
College level: Senior
Majors/Fields: Aerospace engineering, electronics engineering
Criteria: Applicant must be a woman, have a 3.5 GPA, and demonstrate financial need. Reapplication is required to retain scholarship for an additional year. Awarded every year.
Contact: Scholarships.

639 S.J. Cerny Engineering Scholarship

University of Oklahoma
University Affairs
900 Asp Avenue, Room 236
Norman, OK 73019-0401
(405) 325-1701
Average award: $3,000
Number of awards: 1
Deadline: March 15
College level: Freshman, Sophomore, Junior, Senior, Graduate, Doctoral
Majors/Fields: Engineering
Criteria: Applicant must be an Oklahoma resident, demonstrate financial need, have a minimum 3.0 GPA, and be a full-time engineering student. Preference is given to petroleum and geological engineering majors. Awarded every year. Award may be used only at sponsoring institution.
Contact: Associate Dean for Academic Programs, College of Engineering, Room 107, CEC, Norman, OK 73019, (405) 325-2621.

640 Safety Equipment Distributors Association Scholarship

American Society of Safety Engineers (ASSE)
1800 E. Oakton Street
Des Plaines, IL 60018-2187
Minimum award: $1,500
Number of awards: 2
Deadline: January 31
Majors/Fields: Safety engineering
Criteria: Applicant must be a full-time student, member of ASSE with at least one semester of studies left after announcement of results in May, and a minimum 2.75 GPA. Selection is based upon academic performance, career goals, extracurricular activities, and quality and scope of endorsement by nominee's faculty advisor, faculty member, and/or chapter officer.
Contact: Scholarships.

641 SHPE Foundation Educational Grant

Society of Hispanic Professional Engineers Foundation
5400 East Olympic Boulevard
Suite 210
Los Angeles, CA 90022
(213) 888-2080
Maximum award: $7,000
Minimum award: $300
Number of awards: 250
Deadline: April 15
College level: Freshman, Sophomore, Junior, Senior, Graduate, Doctoral
Majors/Fields: Engineering, science
Criteria: Reapplication is required to retain scholarship. Awarded every year.
Contact: Kathy Borunda, Manager of Corporate Development.

642 SNAME Scholarship

Society of Naval Architects and Marine Engineers (SNAME)
601 Pavonia Avenue
Jersey City, NJ 07306
(201) 798-4800
Maximum award: $10,000
Minimum award: $1,000
Number of awards: 5
Deadline: February 1
College level: Freshman, Sophomore, Junior, Senior, Doctoral
Majors/Fields: Marine engineering, naval architecture, ocean engineering
Criteria: Applicant must be a U.S. or Canadian citizen and an SNAME member in good standing. Undergraduate scholarships are available directly through Massachusetts Inst of Tech, U of Michigan, SUNY Maritime Coll, Florida Atlantic U, U of New Orleans, U of Newfoundland, Texas A&M U–College Station, Virginia Polytech Inst. UC–Berkeley offers an undergraduate grant-in-aid. Awarded every year.
Contact: Francis M. Cagliari, Executive Director.

643 Society for the Advancement of Material and Process Engineering, Orange County Chapter Scholarship

California State University, Fullerton
P.O. Box 34080
Fullerton, CA 92634-9480
(714) 773-3128
Maximum award: $2,000
Minimum award: $500
Deadline: April
Majors/Fields: Engineering, science
Criteria: Applicant must be a student member of SAMPE, or the child of a SAMPE member, enrolled full time. Selection is based upon academic achievement, recommendations, extracurricular activities, personal statement, and interest in materials and process engineering. Awarded every year. Award may be used only at sponsoring institution.
Contact: Vickey Takeuchi, Scholarship Coordinator.

644 Society of Women Engineers Orange County Chapter Scholarship

California State University, Fullerton
P.O. Box 34080
Fullerton, CA 92634-9480
(714) 773-3128
Maximum award: $2,000
Minimum award: $500
Number of awards: 2
Deadline: April
College level: Sophomore, Junior, Senior
Majors/Fields: Engineering
Criteria: Applicant must be a full-time, female engineering student. Selection is based upon academic achievement, leadership, professional activities, financial need, work experience, and recommendations. Awarded every year. Award may be used only at sponsoring institution.
Contact: Vickey Takeuchi, Scholarship Coordinator.

645 SPE Scholarship

Society of Plastics Engineers
14 Fairfield Drive
Brookfield Center, CT 06805
Average award: $3,500
Maximum award: $4,000
Minimum award: $3,000
Number of awards: 7
Deadline: December 15
College level: Sophomore, Junior, Senior
Majors/Fields: Plastics engineering
Criteria: Applicant must demonstrate financial need and academic qualifications. Recipient must maintain required GPA in major and reapply for renewal. Awarded every year.
Contact: Joan Godfrey, Education Assistant.

646 Stanley C. Pace Fellowship

Washington University
One Brookings Drive
Campus Box 1089
St. Louis, MO 63130
(314) 935-6000 or (800) 638-0700
Average award: $19,250
Number of awards: 1
College level: Freshman
Majors/Fields: Engineering, applied science
Criteria: Applicant must apply under the Early Decision or Early Action plans. Selection is based upon academic merit without regard to financial need. Satisfactory academic performance is required to retain scholarship. Awarded every year. Award may be used only at sponsoring institution.
Contact: Office of Undergraduate Admissions.

647 State Awards

National Society of Professional Engineers
Education Foundation
1420 King Street
Alexandria, VA 22314-2794
(703) 684-2800
Average award: $1,000
Number of awards: 54
College level: Freshman
Majors/Fields: Engineering
Criteria: Applicant must be a U.S. citizen, have a minimum 3.0 GPA, and minimum SAT I scores of 600 math and 500 verbal (or ACT scores of 29 math and 25 English). Awarded every year.
Contact: Education Foundation.

648   Stone and Webster Scholarship

Society of Women Engineers (SWE)
120 Wall Street
11th Floor
New York, NY 10005-3902
(212) 509-9577
Average award: $1,000
Number of awards: 5
Deadline: May 15
College level: Junior, Senior
*Majors/Fields:*Civil engineering, chemical engineering, electrical engineering, environmental engineering, mechanical engineering
Criteria: Applicant must be a U.S. citizen, a woman, and have a 3.5 GPA. One award is granted in each of the following engineering disciplines: chemical, civil, electrical, environmental, and mechanical. Awarded every year.
Contact: Scholarships.

649   Tau Beta Pi Association Scholarship

National Society of Professional Engineers
Education Foundation
1420 King Street
Alexandria, VA 22314-2794
(703) 684-2800
Average award: $1,000
Number of awards: 4
College level: Freshman
Majors/Fields: Engineering
Criteria: Applicant must be a U.S. citizen, have a minimum 3.0 GPA, and minimum SAT I scores of 500 verbal and 600 math (or ACT scores of 29 math and 22 English). Awarded every year.
Contact: Education Foundation.

650   Technical Minority Scholarship Program

Technical Minority Scholarship Program
Xerox Square-026
Rochester, NY 14644
Maximum award: $5,000
Minimum award: $4,000
Number of awards: 30
Deadline: September 1
College level: Sophomore, Junior, Senior, Doctoral
*Majors/Fields:*Computer science, engineering, mathematics, optics, physics, science
Criteria: Applicant must be a minority. Reapplication is required to retain scholarship. Awarded every year.
Contact: Scholarships.

651   Technology Regents Scholarship

Southwest Missouri State University
Student Financial Aid
901 South National Avenue
Springfield, MO 65804-0095
(417) 836-5000 or (800) 492-7900
Average award: $1,000
Number of awards: 5
Deadline: March 31
College level: Freshman
Majors/Fields: Technology
Criteria: Awarded every year. Award may be used only at sponsoring institution.
Contact: Scholarship Committee, (417) 836-5262 or (800) 492-7900.

652   Texaco Foundation Scholarship

Society of Women Engineers (SWE)
120 Wall Street
11th Floor
New York, NY 10005-3902
(212) 509-9577
Average award: $2,000
Number of awards: 2
Deadline: February 1
College level: Junior
*Majors/Fields:*Chemical engineering, civil engineering, electrical engineering, environmental engineering, petroleum engineering
Criteria: Applicant must be a U.S. citizen or authorized to work in the U.S., a woman, a SWE member, rank in the top fifth of class, and have a 3.5 GPA. Reapplication and rank in top fifth of class are required to retain scholarship. Awarded every year.
Contact: Scholarships.

653   Thomas M. Hunter Endowed Scholars Program

Clemson University
G-01 Sikes Hall
Clemson, SC 29634-5123
(803) 656-2280
Average award: $2,800
Number of awards: 1
College level: Freshman
Majors/Fields: Engineering
Criteria: Applicant must demonstrate high academic achievement, usually a minimum 3.75 GPA. Minimum 3.0 cumulative GPA with at least 12 credits per semester is required to retain scholarship. Awarded every year. Award may be used only at sponsoring institution.
Contact: Marvin Carmichael, Director of Financial Aid.

654   Thomas R. Camp Scholarship

American Water Works Association
6666 West Quincy Avenue
Denver, CO 80235
(303) 347-6210
Average award: $5,000
Number of awards: 1
Deadline: January 15
College level: Graduate, Doctoral
Majors/Fields: Water supply, water treatment
Criteria: Applicant must be doing applied research in the drinking water field at an institution of higher learning in the U.S., Canada, Guam, Puerto Rico, or Mexico. Selection is based upon academic record and leadership potential. Awarded every year.
Contact: Scholarship Coordinator.

655   Tony Neidermayer Memorial Bursary

University of Calgary
2500 University Drive, NW
Calgary, Alberta, CN T2N 1N4
(403) 220-7872
Average award: $1,500
Number of awards: 4
Deadline: June 15
College level: Sophomore, Junior, Senior
Majors/Fields: Engineering
Criteria: Selection is based upon academic merit and financial need. Awarded every year. Award may be used only at sponsoring institution.
Contact: J. Van Housen, Director of Student Awards & Financial Aid.

656 Transit Corps of Engineers Program

New York State Higher Education Services Corporation
99 Washington Avenue
Albany, NY 12255
(518) 473-4563
Number of awards: 50
Deadline: January 1, 1990
College level: Junior, Senior, Graduate
Criteria: Applicant must be an upper-division or graduate student enrolled in an engineering or technology program in a New York state college leading to licensure in engineering (30 awards) or be an employee of the New York City Transit Authority (NYCTA) (20 awards). Selection is based upon academic and professional achievement, interest in a career with the NYCTA, potential for employment by the NYCTA, willingness and ability to meet the service obligation, and affirmative action status relative to other applicants. Recipients are obligated for four years service with the New York City Transit Authority. Scholarship is renewable. Awarded every year.
Contact: New York City Transit Authority, Engineering Department, 370 Jay Street, Brooklyn, NY 11201, (718) 330-8699.

657 TRW Scholarship

Society of Women Engineers (SWE)
120 Wall Street
11th Floor
New York, NY 10005-3902
(212) 509-9577
Maximum award: $2,500
Deadline: May 15
College level: Freshman
Majors/Fields: Engineering
Criteria: Applicant must be a woman and have a 3.5 GPA. Recipients are chosen from the best national, regional, and new student sections. Awarded every year.
Contact: Scholarships.

658 United Negro College Fund Scholarship

General Motors Corporation
3044 W. Grand Boulevard
Detroit, MI 48202
Maximum award: $5,000
Number of awards: 8
College level: Sophomore, Junior, Senior
Majors/Fields: Engineering
Criteria: Applicant must be a member of one of the following minority groups: Alaskan Native, American Indian, Asian-American, African-American/black, Mexican-American/Chicano, Hispanic, or Puerto Rican. Contact the engineering department to ask if the university participates in the scholarship program.
Contact: L.J. Wicker, Manager, Education Relations, (313) 556-3509.

659 United Technologies Corporation Scholarship

Society of Women Engineers (SWE)
120 Wall Street
11th Floor
New York, NY 10005-3902
(212) 509-9577
Average award: $1,000
Number of awards: 2
Deadline: May 15
College level: Sophomore
Majors/Fields: Engineering
Criteria: Applicant must be a U.S. citizen, a woman, and have a 3.5 GPA. Continued academic achievement is required to retain scholarship for two additional years. Awarded every year.
Contact: Louise Bacon, Executive Assistant.

660 V.B. Higgins Engineering Fund Scholarship

Clemson University
G-01 Sikes Hall
Clemson, SC 29634-5123
(803) 656-2280
Average award: $1,000
Number of awards: 14
Deadline: March 1
College level: Sophomore, Junior, Senior
Majors/Fields: Engineering
Criteria: Applicant must have a minimum 2.0 cumulative GPA. Awarded every year. Award may be used only at sponsoring institution.
Contact: Marvin Carmichael, Director of Financial Aid.

661 WERC Fellowship

New Mexico State University
Box 30001
Department 5100
Las Cruces, NM 88003-0001
(505) 646-4105
Maximum award: $1,500
Minimum award: $500
Number of awards: 13
Deadline: March 15
College level: Sophomore, Junior, Senior
Majors/Fields: Engineering
Criteria: Applicant must be enrolled full-time in the Coll of Engineering, have a minimum cumulative GPA of 2.5, be a U.S. citizen or permanent resident, and agree to participate in and document results of a research project. Awarded every year. Award may be used only at sponsoring institution.
Contact: Dr. Ron Bhada, College of Engineering, (505) 646-3547.

662 Westinghouse Bertha Lamme Scholarship

Society of Women Engineers (SWE)
120 Wall Street
11th Floor
New York, NY 10005-3902
(212) 509-9577
Average award: $1,000
Number of awards: 3
Deadline: May 15
College level: Freshman
Majors/Fields: Engineering
Criteria: Applicant must be a U.S. citizen, a woman, and have a 3.5 GPA. Continued academic achievement is required to retain scholarship for three additional years. Awarded every year.
Contact: Louise Bacon, Executive Assistant.

663 Weyerhaeuser Black Scholars Award

Mississippi State University
P.O. Box 6238
Mississippi State, MS 39762
(601) 325-7430
Average award: $3,000
Number of awards: 1
Deadline: February 1
College level: Freshman
Majors/Fields: Chemical engineering, electrical engineering, mechanical engineering
Criteria: Applicant must be black and have a minimum composite ACT score of 21 or combined SAT I score of 860. Minimum 3.0 cumulative GPA is required to retain scholarship. Awarded every year. Award may be used only at sponsoring institution.
Contact: Audrey S. Lambert, Director of Student Financial Aid.

664 William Lemond Hamilton Bursary

University of Calgary
2500 University Drive, NW
Calgary, Alberta, CN T2N 1N4
(403) 220-7872
Average award: $2,000
Number of awards: 6
Deadline: June 15
College level: Freshman, Sophomore, Junior, Senior
Majors/Fields: Engineering, geology, geophysics, management
Criteria: Applicant must be a Canadian citizen planning a career in the resource industry. Selection is based upon financial need, extra-curricular activities, and academic merit. Awarded every year. Award may be used only at sponsoring institution.
Contact: J. Van Housen, Director of Student Awards & Financial Aid.

665 Women in Engineering Program

University of Colorado at Boulder
Campus Box 106
Boulder, CO 80309-0106
(303) 492-5091
Maximum award: $2,500
Minimum award: $250
College level: Freshman, transfer students
Majors/Fields: Engineering
Criteria: Applicant must be a woman. Selection is based upon academic merit. Financial need may be considered. Satisfactory GPA, full-time enrollment, and required curriculum are required to retain scholarship. Awarded every year. Award may be used only at sponsoring institution.
Contact: Office of the Dean, College of Engineering and Applied Science, Campus Box 422, Boulder, CO 80309-0422, (303) 492-5071.

Industrial/Manufacturing Engineering

666 Caterpillar Scholars Award

Society of Manufacturing Engineers (SME) Education Foundation
One SME Drive
P.O. Box 930
Dearborn, MI 48121
(313) 271-1500, extension 512
Minimum award: $2,000
Number of awards: 5
Deadline: March 1
College level: Sophomore, Junior, Senior
Majors/Fields: Manufacturing engineering technology, manufacturing technology
Criteria: Applicant must be enrolled full-time with a minimum 3.2 GPA. Awarded every year.
Contact: Dora Murray, Grants Coordinator.

667 Dwight D. Gardner Scholarship

Institute of Industrial Engineers (IIE)
Customer Service Center
25 Technology Park/Atlanta
Norcross, GA 30092
(404) 449-0460
Average award: $1,500
Number of awards: 5
Deadline: November 15
College level: Sophomore, Junior, Senior
Majors/Fields: Industrial engineering
Criteria: Applicant must be an active IIE member, be enrolled full-time, and have a minimum 3.4 GPA. Selection is based upon scholastic ability, character, leadership, potential service to the profession, and financial need. Awarded every year.
Contact: Member and Product Services.

668 Gianninoto Scholarship Fund

Industrial Designers Society of America
1142-E Walker Road
Great Falls, VA 22066
(703) 759-0100
Maximum award: $2,000
Minimum award: $1,000
Number of awards: 1
Deadline: April 30
College level: Doctoral
Majors/Fields: Industrial design
Criteria: Applicant must submit slide portfolio and letters of support. Awarded every year.
Contact: Celia Weinstein, Director of Internal Affairs.

669 Gilbreth Memorial Followship

Institute of Industrial Engineers (IIE)
Customer Service Center
25 Technology Park/Atlanta
Norcross, GA 30092
(404) 449-0460
Average award: $2,500
Number of awards: 5
Deadline: November 15
College level: Graduate, Doctoral
Majors/Fields: Industrial engineering
Criteria: Applicant must be an active IIE member, be enrolled full time, and have a minimum of 3.4 GPA. Selection is based upon scholastic ability, character, leadership, potential service to the profession, and financial need. Awarded every year.
Contact: Member and Product Services.

670 Myrtle and Earl Scholarship Fund

Society of Manufacturing Engineers (SME) Education Foundation
One SME Drive
P.O. Box 930
Dearborn, MI 48121
(313) 271-1500, extension 512
Minimum award: $500
Number of awards: 20
Deadline: March 1
College level: Sophomore, Junior, Senior
Majors/Fields: Manufacturing engineering, manufacturing engineering technology
Criteria: Applicant must have a minimum 3.2 GPA. Awarded every year.
Contact: Dora Murray, Grants Coorinator.

671 Pulp and Paper Merit Award

Pulp & Paper Foundation, Inc.
North Carolina State University
Box 8005
Raleigh, NC 27695-8005
(919) 515-5661
Maximum award: $3,700
Minimum award: $1,200
Maximum number of awards: 100
Minimum number of awards: 80
Deadline: January 15
College level: Freshman, Sophomore, Junior, Senior
Majors/Fields: Pulp/paper
Criteria: Applicant must be a U.S. citizen. Applicant must maintain a minimum 2.90 GPA. Awarded every year.
Contact: J. Ben Chilton, Executive Director.

672 **U.S. Department of Energy Predoctoral Fellowships in Integrated Manufacturing**

National Research Council
2101 Constitution Avenue
Washington, DC 20418
(202) 334-2872
Minimum award: $20,000
Number of awards: 12
Deadline: Early November
College level: Doctoral
Majors/Fields: Integrated manufacturing
Criteria: Fellowship is awarded for three years. Awarded every year.
Contact: Fellowship Office.

673 **United Parcel Services Scholarship for Female Students**

Institute of Industrial Engineers (IIE)
Customer Service Center
25 Technology Park/Atlanta
Norcross, GA 30092
(404) 449-0460
Average award: $2,500
Number of awards: 1
Deadline: November 15
College level: Sophomore, Junior, Senior
Majors/Fields: Industrial engineering
Criteria: Applicant must be a woman, an active IIE member, be enrolled full time, and have a minimum 3.4 GPA. Selection is based upon scholastic ability, character, leadership, potential service to the profession, and financial need. Awarded every year.
Contact: Member and Product Services.

674 **United Parcel Services Scholarship for Minority Students**

Institute of Industrial Engineers (IIE)
Customer Service Center
25 Technology Park/Atlanta
Norcross, GA 30092
(404) 449-0460
Average award: $2,500
Number of awards: 1
Deadline: November 15
College level: Sophomore, Junior, Senior
Majors/Fields: Industrial engineering
Criteria: Applicant must be a member of an minority group, an active IIE member, be enrolled full time, and have a minimum 3.4 GPA. Selection is based upon scholastic ability, character, leadership, potential service to the profession, and financial need. Awarded every year.
Contact: Member and Product Services.

675 **Wayne Kay Graduate Fellowship**

Society of Manufacturing Engineers (SME) Education Foundation
One SME Drive
P.O. Box 930
Dearborn, MI 48121
(313) 271-1500, extension 512
Average award: $5,000
Number of awards: 1
Deadline: March 1
College level: Graduate
Majors/Fields: Industrial engineering, manufacturing engineering
Criteria: Applicant must be a full-time student working for an advanced degree (M.S. or Ph.D.). Awarded every year.
Contact: Dora Murray, Grants Coordinator.

676 **Wayne Kay Scholarship**

Society of Manufacturing Engineers (SME) Education Foundation
One SME Drive
P.O. Box 930
Dearborn, MI 48121
(313) 271-1500, extension 512
Minimum award: $2,500
Number of awards: 8
Deadline: March 1
College level: Sophomore, Junior, Senior
Majors/Fields: Manufacturing engineering, manufacturing engineering technology
Criteria: Applicant must be enrolled full-time with a minimum 3.2 GPA. Awarded every year.
Contact: Dora Murray, Grants Coordinator.

Mechanical Engineering

677 **ASME Graduate Fellowship**

American Society of Mechanical Engineers (ASME)
Education Services Department
345 East 47th Street
New York, NY 10017-2392
(212) 705-7375
Average award: $5,000
Deadline: Fall
College level: Doctoral
Majors/Fields: Mechanical engineering
Criteria: Applicant must be pursuing a doctorate in mechanical engineering as a terminal degree, desire engineering education for a career, be a U.S. citizen or permanent resident, be a student member of ASME, and have an undergraduate degree from an ABET-accredited program. Women and minorities are encouraged to apply. Award is for a maximum of three years. Awarded every year.
Contact: Education Services Deparment, 345 East 47th Street, New York, NY 10017-2392.

678 **Babcock & Wilcox Annual Scholarship**

Clemson University
G-01 Sikes Hall
Clemson, SC 29634-5123
(803) 656-2280
Average award: $1,000
Number of awards: 2
Deadline: March 1
College level: Junior, Senior
Majors/Fields: Mechanical engineering
Criteria: Applicant must have a minimum 2.0 GPA. Satisfactory GPA with at least 12 credits per semester is required to retain scholarship. Awarded every year. Award may be used only at sponsoring institution.
Contact: Marvin Carmichael, Director of Financial Aid.

679 **Grothus-Pi Tau Sigma Award**

New Mexico State University
Box 30001
Department 5100
Las Cruces, NM 88003-0001
(505) 646-4105
Average award: Tuition
College level: Sophomore
Majors/Fields: Mechanical engineering
Criteria: Awarded for spring semester. Selection is made by department head and Pi Tau Sigma faculty advisors. Awarded every year. Award may be used only at sponsoring institution.
Contact: College of Engineering, (505) 646-3547.

680 International Gas Turbine Institute Scholarship

American Society of Mechanical Engineers (ASME)
Education Services Department
345 East 47th Street
New York, NY 10017-2392
(212) 705-7375
Average award: $1,000
Number of awards: 80
Majors/Fields: Mechanical engineering
Criteria: Applicant's school must apply and qualify; recipient is selected by ASME Student Section. Awarded every year.
Contact: Scholarships.

681 National Association of Plumbing-Heating-Cooling Contractors Educational Foundation Scholarship

National Association of Plumbing-Heating-Cooling
Contractors Scholarship Program
P.O. Box 6808
Falls Church, VA 22046
(703) 237-8100
Average award: $2,500
Number of awards: 3
Deadline: April 1
College level: Freshman, Sophomore
Majors/Fields: Business administration, construction management, mechanical engineering
Criteria: Applicant must be sponsored by a NAPHCC member who has been in good standing with the association for at least two consecutive years. Written request for continuance is required to retain scholarship. Awarded every year.
Contact: Jackie Hansmann, Scholarship Liaison.

682 Pellette & Associates Scholarship

New Mexico State University
Box 30001
Department 5100
Las Cruces, NM 88003-0001
(505) 646-4105
Average award: Tuition
Deadline: March 1
College level: Sophomore, Junior, Senior
Majors/Fields: Mechanical engineering
Criteria: Applicant must be enrolled full-time, have a minimum 2.5 GPA, be a New Mexico resident, and be a U.S. citizen. Awarded every year. Award may be used only at sponsoring institution.
Contact: College of Engineering, (505) 646-3547.

683 R.C. Baker Foundation Scholarship

Louisiana Tech University
P.O. Box 7925
Ruston, LA 71272
(318) 257-2641
Average award: $1,500
Number of awards: 2
Deadline: April 1
College level: Junior, Senior
Majors/Fields: Mechanical engineering
Criteria: Applicant must have a minimum 3.0 GPA, and demonstrate financial need, scholarship, leadership, and character. Awarded every year. Award may be used only at sponsoring institution.
Contact: E. R. Winzer, Director of Student Financial Aid.

684 Rice-Cullimore Scholarship

American Society of Mechanical Engineers (ASME)
Education Services Department
345 East 47th Street
New York, NY 10017-2392
(212) 705-7375
Average award: $2,000
Number of awards: 2
Deadline: February 15
College level: Graduate, Doctoral
Majors/Fields: Mechanical engineering
Criteria: Applicant must be a foreign student who qualifies in his or her home country and through the Institute of International Education. Awarded every year.
Contact: ASME Auxiliary.

685 Solid Waste Processing Division Scholarship

American Society of Mechanical Engineers (ASME)
Education Services Department
345 East 47th Street
New York, NY 10017-2392
(212) 705-7375
Maximum award: $2,000
Minimum award: $1,000
Number of awards: 5
Deadline: February 1
College level: Freshman, Sophomore, Junior, Senior, Graduate, Doctoral
Majors/Fields: Solid waste management
Criteria: Applicant must attend a North American college or university with an established program in solid waste management. Awarded every year.
Contact: Scholarships.

686 Sylvia W. Farny Scholarship

American Society of Mechanical Engineers (ASME)
Education Services Department
345 East 47th Street
New York, NY 10017-2392
(212) 705-7375
Average award: $1,500
Number of awards: 8
Deadline: February 15
College level: Senior
Majors/Fields: Mechanical engineering
Criteria: Selection is based upon academic achievement, financial need, and character. Awarded every year.
Contact: ASME Auxiliary.

687 Whetstone Scholarship

Louisiana Tech University
P.O. Box 7925
Ruston, LA 71272
(318) 257-2641
Average award: $1,000
Number of awards: 2
Deadline: April 1
College level: Freshman, Sophomore, Junior, Senior, Graduate, Doctoral
Majors/Fields: Mechanical engineering
Criteria: Applicant must have a minimum 3.0 GPA and be in good academic standing. Awarded every year. Award may be used only at sponsoring institution.
Contact: E. R. Winzer, Director of Student Financial Aid.

Mining/Metallurgical/ Materials Engineering

688 ASM Undergraduate Scholarship

ASM Foundation
Materials Park, OH 44073
(216) 338-5151, extension 506
Maximum award: $2,000
Minimum award: $500
Number of awards: 38
Deadline: June 15
College level: Sophomore
Majors/Fields: Materials science, metallurgy
Criteria: Applicant must be a U.S., Canadian, or Mexican citizen. Selection is based upon interest in metallurgy and materials science, motivation, achievement, scholarship, and potential. Some scholarships are renewable. Awarded every year.
Contact: Margaret Gilson, Scholarships.

689 Desk and Derrick Educational Trust Scholarship

Desk and Derrick Educational Trust
3840 South 103rd East Avenue
Suite 129
Tulsa, OK 74146-2445
(918) 622-1675
Average award: $1,000
Minimum award: $500
Number of awards: 12
Deadline: April 1
College level: Junior, Senior, Graduate
Majors/Fields: Chemical engineering, geology, petroleum engineering
Criteria: Applicant must be a woman and a U.S. or Canadian citizen. Financial need and minimum 3.0 GPA are required. Minimum 3.0 GPA is required to retain scholarship. Awarded every year.
Contact: Bettye Miller, Chairman, 8526 Deer Meadow, Houston, TX 77071, (713) 771-4003.

690 Geneva Steel Scholarship

University of Utah
Financial Aid and Scholarships Office
105 Student Services Building
Salt Lake City, UT 84112
(801) 581-6211
Maximum award: $2,200
Minimum award: $1,800
Number of awards: 2
Deadline: May 1
College level: Sophomore, Junior, Senior
Majors/Fields: Metallurgical engineering
Criteria: Awarded every year. Award may be used only at sponsoring institution.
Contact: Department of Metallurgical Engineering, 412 William C. Browning Building, Salt Lake City, UT 84112, (801) 581-5158.

691 H.E. "Eddie" Chiles Centennial Scholarship

University of Oklahoma
University Affairs
900 Asp Avenue, Room 236
Norman, OK 73019-0401
(405) 325-1701
Average award: $5,000
Number of awards: 1
Deadline: April 1
College level: Junior, Senior
Majors/Fields: Petroleum engineering
Criteria: Applicant must have a minimum 3.0 GPA and be enrolled on a full-time basis. Awarded every year. Award may be used only at sponsoring institution.
Contact: Scholarship Coordinator for Petroleum and Geological Engineering, T301 Energy Center, Norman, OK 73019-0628, (405) 325-2921.

692 Lou-Ark Society of Petroleum Engineers Scholarship

Louisiana Tech University
P.O. Box 7925
Ruston, LA 71272
(318) 257-2641
Average award: $1,650
Maximum award: $2,450
Number of awards: 1
Deadline: April 1
College level: Junior, Senior, Graduate
Majors/Fields: Petroleum engineering
Criteria: Applicant must demonstrate character, leadership, scholarship, and financial need. Awarded every year. Award may be used only at sponsoring institution.
Contact: E. R. Winzer, Director of Student Financial Aid.

693 Milton H. Ward Scholarship

University of Alabama-Tuscaloosa
Box 870162
Tuscaloosa, AL 35487-0162
(205) 348-6756
Average award: $2,400
Number of awards: 3
Deadline: March 1
College level: Sophomore, Junior, Senior
Majors/Fields: Mineral engineering
Criteria: Applicant must be a mineral engineering major with a mining specialization. Awarded every year. Award may be used only at sponsoring institution.
Contact: College of Engineering Dean's Office, 150 Mineral Industries Building, Box 870200, Tuscaloosa, AL 35487-0200, (205) 348-6408.

694 Petroleum and Geological Engineering Industrial Sponsored Scholarship

University of Oklahoma
University Affairs
900 Asp Avenue, Room 236
Norman, OK 73019-0401
(405) 325-1701
Maximum award: $7,000
Minimum award: $3,000
Maximum number of awards: 19
Minimum number of awards: 7
Deadline: April 1
College level: Graduate, Doctoral
Majors/Fields: Petroleum engineering, geological engineering
Criteria: Applicant must be a U.S. citizen or permanent resident. Selection is based upon merit. Scholarships are sponsored by Exxon, Phillips, Shell, Texaco, Union Pacific, International Petroleum Exposition, and O.H. & Ruth Verne Davis Reaugh. Awarded every year. Award may be used only at sponsoring institution.
Contact: Director of Petroleum and Geological Engineering, College of Engineering, Room F301, Energy Center, Norman, OK 73019, (405) 325-2921.

695 PGE Excellence in Engineering Distinguished Scholarship

University of Oklahoma
University Affairs
900 Asp Avenue, Room 236
Norman, OK 73019-0401
(405) 325-1701
Average award: $3,000
Maximum number of awards: 20
Minimum number of awards: 15
Deadline: April 1
College level: Freshman
Majors/Fields: Geological engineering, petroleum engineering
Criteria: Rank in top quarter of graduating class, minimum 3.0 GPA, and minimum ACT composite score of 25 are required. Selection is based upon extracurricular participation, leadership, recommendations, and essay. Awarded every year. Award may be used only at sponsoring institution.
Contact: Scholarship Coordinator for Petroleum and Geological Engineering, T301 Energy Center, Norman, OK 73019-0628, (405) 325-2921.

696   R.C. Baker Foundation Scholarship

University of Oklahoma
University Affairs
900 Asp Avenue, Room 236
Norman, OK 73019-0401
(405) 325-1701
Average award: $1,500
Number of awards: 6
Deadline: April 1
College level: Junior, Senior
Majors/Fields: Geological engineering, petroleum engineering
Criteria: Selection is based upon merit. Awarded every year. Award may be used only at sponsoring institution.
Contact: Scholarship Coordinator for Petroleum and Geological Enginering, T301 Energy Center, Norman, OK 73019-0628, (405) 325-2921.

697   RMCMI Scholarship

Rocky Mountain Coal Mining Institute (RMCMI)
3000 Youngfield Street, No. 324
Lakewood, CO 80215
(303) 238-9099
Minimum award: $750
Number of awards: 16
Deadline: February 1
College level: Junior
Majors/Fields: Civil engineering, electrical engineering, environmental engineering, geology, mechanical engineering, metallurgy, mineral processing, mining
Criteria: Applicant must be enrolled full time and be a resident of one of the RMCMI member states: Arizona, Colorado, Montana, New Mexico, North Dakota, Texas, Utah, or Wyoming. Applicant must maintain full-time status, have a satisfactory GPA, and be recommended by dean of college or university. Awarded every year.
Contact: Doris G. Finnie, Executive Director.

698   William C. Browning Scholarship

University of Utah
Financial Aid and Scholarships Office
105 Student Services Building
Salt Lake City, UT 84112
(801) 581-6211
Maximum award: $3,039
Number of awards: 20
Deadline: February 15
College level: Freshman, Sophomore, Junior, Senior
Majors/Fields: Mining engineering
Criteria: Applicant must be a U.S. citizen, have a minimum 3.0 GPA, and show a strong background in mathematics, physics, and chemistry. Selection is based upon GPA, ACT scores, and academic performance in math and science. Scholarship is renewable. Awarded every year. Award may be used only at sponsoring institution.
Contact: Dr. M. K. McCarter, 313 William C. Browning Building, Salt Lake City, UT 84112, (801) 581-8603.

Nuclear Engineering

699   ANS Scholarships

American Nuclear Society (ANS)
555 North Kensington Avenue
La Grange Park, IL 60525
(708) 352-6611
Maximum award: $3,500
Minimum award: $1,000
Number of awards: 45
Deadline: March 1
College level: Freshman, Sophomore, Junior, Senior, Graduate, Doctoral
Majors/Fields: Nuclear engineering, nuclear science
Criteria: Applicant must be a U.S. citizen or permanent resident enrolled in a U.S. institution. Applicant must be sponsored by an ANS local section, division, student branch, committee member, or organization member. Include self-addressed stamped envelope with request. Awarded every year.
Contact: Scholarship Coordinator.

Language/Literature/Humanities

Classical Studies

700 ACL/NJCL National Latin Examination Scholarship

ACL/NJCL National Latin Examination
PO Box 95
Mount Vernon, VA 22121
Average award: $1,000
Number of awards: 27
Deadline: May 15
College level: Freshman
Criteria: Applicant must take the ACL/NJCL National Latin Exam; applications for the $1,000 scholarship will automatically be mailed to the gold medal winners who qualify from the exam. Applicant must agree to take at least one year of Latin or classical Greek in college. Recipient must continue to take Latin or Greek to retain scholarship. Awarded every year.
Contact: Jane H. Hall, Chairman, (703) 360-4354.

701 Bliss Prize Fellowship in Byzantine Studies

Dumbarton Oaks
1703 32nd Street, NW
Washington, DC 20007
(202) 342-3232
Maximum award: $31,000
Deadline: November 1
College level: Graduate
Majors/Fields: Byzantine studies, Greek
Criteria: Applicant must have completed at least one year of Greek and be an applicant to a graduate school in any field or area of Byzantine studies. Fellowship is normally restricted to U.S. or Canadian college or university students. Satisfactory progress in Byzantine studies and continuing work in Greek are required to retain scholarship. Awarded every year.
Contact: Office of the Director.

702 Fellowship in Roman Studies

American Numismatic Society
Broadway at 155th Street
New York, NY 10032
(212) 234-3130
Maximum award: $5,000
Deadline: March 1
Criteria: Fellowship is for support of a substantive research project concerning the Roman world allowing for an extended residence in New York and work in the Society's cabinet and library, and consultation with relevant staff. Applicant must be a U.S. citizen, affiliated with a North American institution of higher learning, demonstrate academic competence, and submit a detailed proposal for project.
Contact: Fellowships.

703 Frances M. Schwartz Fellowship

American Numismatic Society
Broadway at 155th Street
New York, NY 10032
(212) 234-3130
Maximum award: $2,000
Deadline: March 1
College level: Graduate, Doctoral
Criteria: Applicant must hold a B.A. or equivalent. Fellowship is to educate qualified students in museum practice and to train them in numismatics, as well as to provide for curatorial assistance in the Greek, Roman, and Byzantine departments.
Contact: Fellowships.

704 NJCL Scholarship

American Classical League
National Junior Classical League (NJCL) Scholarships
Miami University
Oxford, OH 45056
(513) 529-7741
Maximum award: $1,000
Minimum award: $500
Number of awards: 6
Deadline: May 1
College level: Freshman
Majors/Fields: Classics
Criteria: Applicant must be a NJCL member who will enter college in upcoming academic year and plans to continue the study of the classics. Special consideration is given to applicants who plan to teach Greek, Latin, or classical humanities. Selection is based upon application, recommendations, grades, and service in the NJCL.
Contact: Scholarships, Miami University, Oxford, OH 45056.

Cultural Studies

705 ACLS/Chiang Ching-kuo Foundation Fellowships for Dissertation Research Abroad

American Council of Learned Societies (ACLS)
228 East 45th Street
New York, NY 10017-3398
(212) 697-1505
Maximum award: $15,000
Deadline: December 1
College level: Doctoral
Majors/Fields: Chinese studies
Criteria: Applicant must be a Ph.D. candidate whose dissertation is related to China, although it may be comparative in nature, and the research may be in any discipline of the humanities and social sciences or interdisciplinary. Fellowship is for research outside the U.S. in any country except the People's Republic of China. There are no citizenship restrictions, but foreign nationals must be enrolled as full-time Ph.D. candidates in U.S. institutions. Awarded every year.
Contact: Office of Fellowships and Grants.

706 Bolla Wines Scholarship

National Italian American Foundation (NIAF)
Educational Scholarship Program
1860 19th Street, NW
Washington, DC 20009-5599
(202) 638-2137
Minimum award: $1,000
Deadline: May 31
College level: Senior, Graduate, Doctoral
Majors/Fields: International studies, Italian-American history, Italian business
Criteria: Applicant must be an Italian-American of at least 21 years of age and must be able to demonstrate financial need. Transcript, a minimum 3.0 GPA. and an essay on "The Importance of Italy in Today's Business World" are required.
Contact: Dr. Maria Lombardo, Education Director, 1860 19th Street, NW, Washington, DC 20009.

707 Doctoral and Post-Doctoral Fellowships in the Humanities and Social Sciences

American Research Institute in Turkey
c/o University Museum
33rd and Spruce Streets
Philadelphia, PA 19104-6324
(215) 898-3474
Average award: $7,000
Maximum award: $30,000
Minimum award: $3,000
Number of awards: 7
Deadline: November 15
College level: Doctoral, post-doctoral study
Criteria: Applicant must be a U.S. citizen or permanent resident, affiliated with a U.S. or Canadian institution, with doctoral or postdoctoral research to be carried out in Turkey. Awarded every year.
Contact: Administrator, University Museum, American Research Institute in Turkey, 33rd and Spruce Streets, Philadelphia, PA 19104-6324.

708 E. Catherine Barclay Scholarship

University of Calgary
2500 University Drive, NW
Calgary, Alberta, CN T2N 1N4
(403) 220-7872
Average award: $3,000
Number of awards: 1
Deadline: February 15
College level: Sophomore, Junior, Senior
Criteria: Award is for a U of Calgary student to pursue studies by enrolling full time at the U de Bourgogne in Dijon, France. Selection is based upon academic merit, ability in oral French, and extracurricular activities demonstrating good citizenship. Awarded every year. Award may be used only at sponsoring institution.
Contact: J. Van Housen, Director of Student Awards & Financial Aid.

709 Endowment for Biblical Research and ASOR Summer Research Grants and Travel Scholarships

American Schools of Oriental Research (ASOR)
3301 N. Charles Street
Baltimore, MD 21218
(410) 516-3498
Maximum award: $1,500
Minimum award: $1,000
Number of awards: 9
Deadline: February 1
College level: Freshman, Sophomore, Junior, Senior, Graduate, Doctoral, post-doctoral
Majors/Fields: Archaeology, anthropology, linguistics, natural sciences
Criteria: Award is for travel or research to the Holy Land on archaeological or excavation projects, textual or linguistic study, anthropology or natural sciences studies, or interpretation or analysis of excavated material and manuscripts. Research in biblical periods is encouraged. Awarded every year.
Contact: Pamela Turner, Administrative Assistant.

710 Fellowships for the Bosphorus Summer Language Program in Advanced Turkish

American Research Institute in Turkey
c/o University Museum
33rd and Spruce Streets
Philadelphia, PA 19104-6324
(215) 898-3474
Average award: Travel, fees, and stipend
Maximum number of awards: 12
Minimum number of awards: 10
Deadline: February 15
College level: Junior, Senior, Graduate, Doctoral
Criteria: Applicant must be a U.S. citizen or permanent resident, currently enrolled in a degree program with a minimum "B" average and at least two years of Turkish language study or equivalent, and must pass proficiency exam. Awarded every year.
Contact: Professor Ahmet Karamustafa, Washington University, Campus Box 1230, One Brookings Drive, St. Louis, MO 63130-4899, (314) 935-4446.

711 Finlandia Foundation Trust Scholarship Exchange Program and Grants

Finlandia Foundation Trust
P.O. Box 2590
Grand Central Station
New York, NY 10163
Maximum award: $5,000
Minimum award: $1,000
Minimum number of awards: 40
Deadline: February 15
Majors/Fields: Finnish studies
Criteria: Applicant must be a U.S. or Finnish college student. Recipient must reapply to retain scholarship.
Contact: Grants.

712 German Marshall Fund of the United States Internship

German Marshall Fund of the United States
11 Dupont Circle, NW
Suite 750
Washington, DC 20036
(202) 745-3950
Average award: $10,150
Number of awards: 3
Deadline: January 31
College level: Graduate students and recent recipients of a B.A.
Criteria: Applicant must have a demonstrated interest in U.S.-European relations, strong research and writing skills, the ability to work independently, have academic work which concentrates on political science, public policy, economics, history, and/or European language(s), and must be a U.S. citizen or permanent resident. Two internships are in the Fund's Washington, D.C., office and one is in Berlin.
Contact: Internship Program.

713 Graduate Student East European Travel Grant

American Council of Learned Societies
228 East 45th Street
New York, NY 10017-3398
(212) 697-1505
Maximum award: $5,000
Deadline: February 1
College level: Doctoral
Criteria: Applicant must have completed at least one year of full-time graduate study in the Ph.D. program, be formulating a research program for a dissertation on Eastern Europe, and lack necessary field experience. Awarded every year.
Contact: Office of Fellowships and Grants.

714 Graduate/Postgraduate Study and Research in Poland

Kosciuszko Foundation
15 East 65th Street
New York, NY 10021
(212) 734-2130
Average award: Tuition, housing, and monthly stipend for living expenses
Deadline: January 15
College level: Graduate, Doctoral
Majors/Fields: Polish studies
Criteria: Applicant must be a U.S. graduate student who has a working knowledge of the Polish language. Selection is based upon academic performance, motivation for pursuing graduate studies in Poland, and quality of the research proposal. Awarded every year.
Contact: Domestic Grants Office.

715 Huntington Library, Art Collections, and Botanical Gardens Research Award

Huntington Library, Art Collections, and Botanical Gardens
1151 Oxford Road
San Marino, CA 91108-1299
(818) 405-2116
Maximum award: $9,000
Minimum award: $1,800
Number of awards: 100
Deadline: December 15
College level: Graduate, Doctoral, postdoctoral research
Majors/Fields: American studies, British studies
Criteria: Selection is based upon the value of the project, the ability of the applicant, and the degree to which special strengths of the library will be utilized. Recipients are expected to be in residence throughout their tenure. Awards are made only to persons who have demonstrated unusual abilities as scholars through publications of a high order of merit. Application should be in the form of a letter which includes an outline of the project, the period of proposed residence at the library, personal data, previous scholarly work, references, and financial need. Applicant must have three letters of support for the project prior to the deadline date. Reapplication is required to retain scholarship. Awarded every year.
Contact: Robert C. Ritchie, Director of Research.

716 IEC Summer in Australia, China, or Russia

International Education Center (IEC), Ltd.
Bowling Green Station
Box 843
New York, NY 10274
(800) 292-4452
Average award: $1,500
Number of awards: 150
College level: Freshman, Sophomore, Junior, Senior, Graduate, Doctoral, educators
Criteria: Fellowships are available towards programs offered by the International Education Center and only partially cover the program cost. IEC sponsors academic programs during the summer in culture, language, history, economics, politics, comparative education, research, and field study.
Contact: Jack Scheckner, Director.

717 Irish Way Scholarships

Irish American Cultural Institute
Irish Way
433 Raymond Boulevard
Newark, NJ 07105
Maximum award: $1,000
Minimum award: $250
Number of awards: 50
College level: Freshman, Sophomore
Majors/Fields: Irish studies
Criteria: Selection is based upon application information, recommendation from teacher(s)/counselor, and grades.
Contact: Scholarships.

718 Jennifer C. Groot Fellowship in the Archaeology of Jordan

American Schools of Oriental Research (ASOR)
3301 N. Charles Street
Baltimore, MD 21218
(410) 516-3498
Average award: $1,500
Maximum award: $2,000
Number of awards: 2
Deadline: February 1
College level: Junior, Senior, Graduate, Doctoral
Criteria: Applicant must be a U.S. or Canadian citizen with a desire to participate in an archaeological excavation in Jordan. Awarded every year.
Contact: Robin M. Brown, ASOR U.S. Representative, (410) 516-3495.

719 King Olav V Norwegian-American Heritage Fund

Sons of Norway Foundation
1455 West Lake Street
Minneapolis, MN 55408
(612) 827-3611
Average award: $580
Maximum award: $1,500
Minimum award: $250
Number of awards: 15
Deadline: March 1
College level: Freshman, Sophomore, Junior, Senior, Graduate, Doctoral
Majors/Fields: Norwegian studies
Criteria: Applicant must be an American, 18 years of age or older, who demonstrates a sincere interest in the Norwegian heritage or a Norwegian who demonstrates an interest in American heritage. Applicant must further the study of these heritages at a recognized educational institution. Selection is based upon GPA, participation in school and community activities, work experience, education and career goals, and personal and school references. Awarded every year.
Contact: Liv Dahl, Administrative Director, Heritage Programs.

720 Lorraine Allison Scholarship

Arctic Institute of North America
University of Calgary
2500 University Drive, NW
Calgary, Alberta, CN T2N 1N4
(403) 220-7515
Average award: $2,000
Number of awards: 1
Deadline: May 1
College level: Graduate, Doctoral
Criteria: Applicant must be enrolled at a Canadian university in a program of graduate study related to northern issues. Awarded to the applicant who best addresses academic excellence, a demonstrated commitment to northern Canadian research, and a desire for research results to benefit northerners, especially native northerners. Scholars from Yukon and the Northwest Territories are encouraged to apply. Satisfactory academic progress and reapplication required to retain scholarship. Awarded every year.
Contact: Michael P. Robinson, Executive Director.

721 Memorial Foundation for Jewish Culture Post-Rabbinical Scholarship

Memorial Foundation for Jewish Culture
15 East 26th Street
New York, NY 10010
(212) 679-4074
Minimum award: $2,000
Number of awards: 95
Deadline: November 30
College level: Unspecified graduate
Majors/Fields: Jewish studies
Criteria: Funds are for recently ordained rabbis to obtain advanced training for careers as head of Yeshivoth or other leadership positions. Awarded every year.
Contact: Scholarships.

722 National Welsh-American Foundation Exchange Scholarship

National Welsh-American Foundation
24 Essex Road
Scotch Plains, NJ 07076
Minimum award: $5,000
Number of awards: 1
Deadline: March 1
Majors/Fields: Welsh studies
Contact: Scholarships.

723 Queen Elizabeth Scholarship in Canadian Studies

University of Calgary
2500 University Drive, NW
Calgary, Alberta, CN T2N 1N4
(403) 220-7872
Average award: $1,000
Number of awards: 6
Deadline: June 15
College level: Freshman, Sophomore, Junior, Senior
Majors/Fields: Canadian studies
Criteria: Applicant must be a permanent resident of Canada who is focusing on the study of Canadian society, culture, or problems of particular relevance to Canadians. Selection is based upon number of Canadian courses taken and GPA in those courses. Preference is first given to majors in Canadian studies, then to minors in the field. Awarded every year. Award may be used only at sponsoring institution.
Contact: J. Van Housen, Director of Student Awards & Financial Aid.

724 Scholarship for Study in Japan

The Japan-America Society of Washington
1020 19th Street, NW
LL #40
Washington, DC 20036
(202) 833-2210
Maximum award: $6,000
Minimum award: $1,500
Deadline: March 1
Criteria: Applicant must have completed at least one year of college study in the U.S., begun studying the Japanese language and culture, and mobilized substantial financial support. Selection is based upon scholastic achievement, motivation, and financial need. Awarded every year.
Contact: Scholarships.

725 Soviet Jewry Community Service Scholarship

Memorial Foundation for Jewish Culture
15 East 26th Street
New York, NY 10010
(212) 679-4074
Deadline: November 30
College level: Freshman, Sophomore, Junior, Senior, Graduate, Doctoral
Majors/Fields: Jewish studies
Criteria: Applicant must be a Soviet Jew and commit to serve a community of Soviet Jews anywhere in the world for a minimum of three years. Awarded to students pursuing careers in the rabbinate, Jewish education, social and communal work, and as religious functionaries. Priority is given to applicants willing to serve in the former Soviet Union. Renewable in writing for a maximum of four years. Awarded every year.
Contact: Scholarships.

726 Study Abroad Scholarship

University of Utah
Financial Aid and Scholarships Office
105 Student Services Building
Salt Lake City, UT 84112
(801) 581-6211
Maximum award: $1,500
Minimum award: $750
Deadline: March 7 (summer and fall quarters); November 21 (winter and spring quarters)
College level: Sophomore, Junior, Senior
Criteria: Applicant must be a matriculated, full-time student with at least 36 credit hours and have a minimum 3.0 GPA. Award is for study abroad. Preference is given to applicants who will be sophomores or juniors during the time abroad and to applicants who have not previously received this scholarship. Awarded every year. Award may be used only at sponsoring institution.
Contact: International Center, 159 Olpin Union, Salt Lake City, UT 84112, (801) 581-5849.

727 Tuition Scholarship

Kosciuszko Foundation
15 East 65th Street
New York, NY 10021
(212) 734-2130
Deadline: January 15
College level: Graduate, Doctoral
Majors/Fields: Polish studies
Criteria: Applicant must be a full-time graduate student in the U.S. who is a U.S. citizen of Polish descent, a Pole who is a permanent resident of the U.S., or an American of non-Polish descent who is pursuing studies/research relating to Polish subjects. Selection is based upon academic excellence and evidence of identification with the Polish-American community. Reapplication is required to retain scholarship. Awarded every year.
Contact: Scholarships.

728 Year Abroad Program at Universities in Poland

Kosciuszko Foundation
15 East 65th Street
New York, NY 10021
(212) 734-2130
Average award: Tuition, housing, and monthly stipend for living expenses
Deadline: January 15
College level: Junior, Senior, Graduate, Doctoral
Majors/Fields: Polish studies
Criteria: Applicant must be an American student wishing to pursue an undergraduate course of Polish language, literature, history, and culture at a university in Poland. Students enrolled in an M.A. or Ph.D. program can apply if they are not at the dissertation level. Selection is based upon academic performance and motivation for pursuing studies in Poland. Awarded every year.
Contact: Scholarships.

English/Literature/Writing—

729 A.T.J. Cairns Memorial Undergraduate Scholarship

University of Calgary
2500 University Drive, NW
Calgary, Alberta, CN T2N 1N4
(403) 220-7872
Average award: $2,000
Number of awards: 4
Deadline: June 15
College level: Freshman, Sophomore, Junior, Senior
Majors/Fields: Creative writing, English literature
Criteria: Applicant must be registered full time with a major or minor in English. Two awards are for men and two for women. Selection is based upon academic merit in creative writing and English literature. Awarded every year. Award may be used only at sponsoring institution.
Contact: J. Van Housen, Director of Student Awards & Financial Aid.

730 Anthem Essay Contest

Ayn Rand Institute
Essay Contest Information
P.O. Box 6004 EF
Inglewood, CA 90312
(310) 306-9232
Maximum award: $1,000
Minimum award: $100
Number of awards: 31
Deadline: March 30
College level: High school freshman and sophomores
Criteria: Applicant must enter essay contest. Winning essay must demonstrate an outstanding grasp of the philosophic meaning of Ayn Rand's novelette *Anthem*. Awarded every year.
Contact: David Bombardier, Essay Contest Coordinator.

731 Conoco Scholarship Award

University of Oklahoma
University Affairs
900 Asp Avenue, Room 236
Norman, OK 73019-0401
(405) 325-1701
Average award: $4,000
Deadline: April 15
College level: Freshman, Sophomore, Junior, Senior
Majors/Fields: Geology, geophysics
Criteria: Selection is based upon merit and financial need. Awarded every year. Award may be used only at sponsoring institution.
Contact: Director of School of Geology and Geophysics, 100 East Boyd Street, Room G-114, EC, Norman, OK, (405) 325-3253.

732 Dog Writers' Educational Trust Scholarship

Dog Writers' Educational Trust
c/o Mary Ellen Tarman
P.O. Box E
Hummelstown, PA 17036-0199
(717) 566-7030
Average award: $2,500
Number of awards: 4
Deadline: December 31
College level: Freshman, Sophomore, Junior, Senior, Graduate, Doctoral
Criteria: Applicant must demonstrate involvement in dog-related activities. Selection is based upon dog-related activities (40%), academic performance (25%), financial need (20%), and future plans (15%). There is a $25 application fee. Awarded every year.
Contact: Mary Ellen Tarman, Executive Secretary.

733 Ewy English Scholarship

Boise State University
1910 University Drive
Boise, ID 83725
(208) 385-1664
Minimum award: $1,000
Number of awards: 2
Deadline: March 1
College level: Freshman, Sophomore, Junior, Senior, Graduate
Majors/Fields: English
Criteria: Selection is based upon financial need. Awarded every year. Award may be used only at sponsoring institution.
Contact: Chris Woodward, Financial Aid Counselor.

734 Fountainhead College Scholarship Essay Contest

Ayn Rand Institute
Essay Contest Information
P.O. Box 6004 EF
Inglewood, CA 90312
(310) 306-9232
Maximum award: $5,000
Minimum award: $500
Number of awards: 16
Deadline: April 15
College level: High school juniors and seniors
Criteria: Applicant must enter essay contest. Winning essay must demonstrate an outstanding grasp of the philosophical and psychological meaning of Ayn Rand's novel *The Fountainhead*. Awarded every year.
Contact: David Bombardier, Essay Contest Coordinator.

735 Guideposts Magazine's Youth Writing Contest

Guideposts
16 East 34th Street
New York, NY 10016
(212) 251-8100
Maximum award: $6,000
Minimum award: $1,000
Number of awards: 8
Deadline: November 30
College level: Freshman
Criteria: Applicant must be a high school junior or senior who submits an original first-person story of a memorable or moving actual experience. Selection is based upon the sincerity, writing ability, and story value of the manuscript. Preference is given to those with religious faith (no denominational requirement). Recipients must plan to attend college after high school, and awards are to be used within a five-year period as college scholarships only. Awarded every year.
Contact: Naomi Lawrence, Assistant to the Editorial Director.

736 Katherine Anne Porter Prize for Fiction

NIMROD, Arts and Humanities Council of Tulsa
2210 South Main Street
Tulsa, OK 74110-1190
(918) 584-3333
Maximum award: $1,000
Minimum award: $500
Number of awards: 4
Criteria: Awarded every year.
Contact: Awards.

737   Mary M. Sachoff Award

University of Colorado at Boulder
Campus Box 106
Boulder, CO 80309-0106
(303) 492-5091
Average award: $1,000
Number of awards: 2
College level: Graduate, Doctoral
Majors/Fields: English
Criteria: Applicant must be a graduate student in the English department. One award is for an original, creative, humorous work and one for an applicant who pursues the literary study of humor. Awarded every year. Award may be used only at sponsoring institution.
Contact: Department of English, Hellems 101, Campus Box 226, Boulder, CO 80309-0226, (303) 492-7381.

738   National Peace Essay Contest

United States Institute of Peace
1550 M Street, NW
Suite 700
Washington, DC 20005-1708
(202) 457-1700
Maximum award: $10,000
Minimum award: $250
Maximum number of awards: 163
Minimum number of awards: 141
Deadline: January 22
College level: Freshman
Criteria: Applicant must write a 1,500-word essay on a topic dealing with international conflict resolution. Topic changes yearly.
Contact: Heidi Schaeffer, Education Specialist.

739   Outdoor Writers Scholarship Award

Outdoor Writers Association of America (OWAA)
2017 Cato Avenue, Suite 101
State College, PA 16801-2768
(814) 234-1011
Minimum award: $2,000
Number of awards: 3
Deadline: March 1
College level: Junior, Senior, Graduate
Majors/Fields: Outdoor communications
Criteria: Selection is based upon clarity, organization, and originality. Awarded every year.
Contact: Executive Director.

740   Pablo Neruda Prize for Poetry

NIMROD, Arts and Humanities Council of Tulsa
2210 South Main Street
Tulsa, OK 74110-1190
(918) 584-3333
Maximum award: $1,000
Minimum award: $500
Number of awards: 4
Deadline: April 17
Criteria: Awarded every year.
Contact: Awards.

741   Robert H. Winner Memorial Award

Poetry Society of America
15 Gramercy Park
New York, NY 10003
(212) 254-9628
Average award: $2,500
Number of awards: 1
Deadline: December 22
Criteria: Award acknowledges original work being done in midlife by someone who has not yet had substantial recognition. Open to poets over 40 years of age who have not published or who have no more than one book. Applicant must submit a brief but cohesive manuscript of up to 10 poems or 20 pages. There is a $5 entry fee per contest for nonmembers. Send a self-addressed, stamped envelope (#10). Awarded every year.
Contact: Contests, Poetry Society of America.

742   Sarah Susannah Buchanan Philipps Memorial Scholarship for Study Abroad in England

University of Colorado at Boulder
Campus Box 106
Boulder, CO 80309-0106
(303) 492-5091
Average award: $2,500
Number of awards: 2
College level: Junior, Senior
Majors/Fields: English
Criteria: Applicant must have completed at least nine hours credit in English courses. Financial need is given significant consideration. Awarded every year. Award may be used only at sponsoring institution.
Contact: Tom Lyons, Professor of English, Hellems 116, Campus Box 226, Boulder, CO 80309-0226, (303) 492-7832.

743   TIME Education Program Student Writing Competition for College Students

TIME Education Program
Student Writing and Art Competition
P.O. Box 1000
Mount Kisco, NY 10549
(800) 882-0852
Maximum award: $5,000
Number of awards: 1
Deadline: March 1
College level: Sophomore, Junior, Senior
Criteria: Applicant must be a college student in the U.S. or Canada, be sponsored by a teacher, and submit an expository composition essay on the contest's theme. Grand prize winner receives a scholarship and a three-year subscription to TIME magazine. Awarded every year.
Contact: Awards.

744   TIME Education Program Student Writing Competition for High School Students

TIME Education Program
Student Writing and Art Competition
P.O. Box 1000
Mount Kisco, NY 10549
(800) 882-0852
Average award: $2,500
Maximum award: $5,000
Minimum award: $1,250
Number of awards: 4
Deadline: March 1
College level: Freshman
Criteria: Applicant must be a high school student in the U.S. or Canada and submit an original expository composition on one of the contest's themes. Awarded every year.
Contact: Awards.

745   Webster's NewWorld Writing Competition

Webster's NewWorld Dictionaries
1633 Broadway – Sixth Floor
New York, NY 10019
(212) 654-8989
Average award: $1,000
Number of awards: 2
Deadline: March 1
Criteria: Applicant must be a high school junior or senior in the U.S. or Canada and submit an original essay on the competition's subject.
Contact: Kathy Nebenhaus

746 **William B. Schallek Memorial Graduate Fellowship Award**

Richard III Society
P.O. Box 13787
New Orleans, LA 70185
Maximum award: $1,000
Minimum award: $500
Number of awards: 4
Deadline: February 28
College level: Doctoral
Majors/Fields: British studies
Criteria: Applicant must be a U.S. citizen or have applied for citizenship. Reapplication is required for renewal. Awarded every year.
Contact: Laura Blanchard, Fellowship Administrator, 303 Vine Street, Suite 106, Philadelphia, PA 19106-1143, (215) 574-1570.

747 **William Carlos Williams Award**

Poetry Society of America
15 Gramercy Park
New York, NY 10003
(212) 254-9628
Maximum award: $2,000
Minimum award: $500
Deadline: December 22
Criteria: Award is for a book of poetry published by a small press, nonprofit, or university press. Original works by a single author who is a U.S. permanent resident will be considered. Translations are ineligible. There is a $10 entry fee per book. Awarded every year.
Contact: Contests, Poetry Society of America, 15 Gramercy Park, New York, NY 10003.

748 **Writing Scholarship**

Scholastic Inc.
730 Broadway
New York, NY 10003
(212) 505-3404
Average award: $1,000
Number of awards: 4
Deadline: January 1
Majors/Fields: Writing
Criteria: Awards are offered to high school seniors who best show outstanding writing ability. Awarded every year.
Contact: Scholarships.

Foreign Languages

749 **American Association of Teachers of German Testing and Awards Program**

American Association of Teachers of German, Inc.
112 Haddontowne Court #104
Cherry Hill, NJ 08034
(609) 795-5553
Average award: All expenses paid, study trip to Germany.
Number of awards: 54
Deadline: February 26
Majors/Fields: German
Criteria: Applicant must score above the 90th percentile to be eligible for a Study Trip Award to Germany (one-month study trip, all expenses paid). Selection is based upon application, interview, and essay competition. Awarded every year.
Contact: Awards Program.

750 **Center for Contemporary German Literature Grant**

German Academic Exchange Service (DAAD)
950 Third Avenue
19th Floor
New York, NY 10022
(212) 758-3223
Average award: $3,000
Majors/Fields: German studies
Contact: Prof. Paul Michael Luetzeler, Director, Campus Box 1104, Washington University, St. Louis, MO 63130.

751 **East European Summer Language Training Grant**

American Council of Learned Societies
228 East 45th Street
New York, NY 10017-3398
(212) 697-1505
Maximum award: $2,500
Minimum award: $2,000
Deadline: February 1
College level: Graduate, Doctoral, Post-doctoral studies
Majors/Fields: Eastern European languages
Criteria: Applicant must desire to study any East European language (except the languages of the Commonwealth of Independent States) to use in his or her academic or other professional career. Awarded every year.
Contact: Office of Fellowships and Grants.

752 **Foreign Language and Area Studies Fellowship**

Portland State University
P.O. Box 751
Portland, OR 97207-5252
(503) 725-5270
Maximum award: $8,000 plus tuition and fees for the academic year
Minimum award: $1,500 plus tuition and fees for the summer session
Maximum number of awards: 4
Minimum number of awards: 2
Deadline: in Spring
College level: Graduate, Doctoral
Majors/Fields: Arabic languages/area studies, international studies
Criteria: Awarded every year. Award may be used only at sponsoring institution.
Contact: Scholarships, Middle East Studies Center, P.O. Box 751, Portland, OR 97207-0751, (503) 725-4074.

753 **Foreign Languages Regents Scholarship**

Southwest Missouri State University
Student Financial Aid
901 South National Avenue
Springfield, MO 65804-0095
(417) 836-5000 or (800) 492-7900
Average award: $1,000
Number of awards: 4
Deadline: March 31
College level: Sophomore, Junior, Senior
Majors/Fields: Foreign languages
Criteria: Applicant must have a minimum 3.0 cumulative GPA with at least 12 hours in a single foreign language and an "A" in each course. Applicant must agree to take two upper-division foreign language courses (one while on scholarship) and participate in departmental events. Awarded every year. Award may be used only at sponsoring institution.
Contact: Scholarship Committee, (417) 836-5262 or (800) 492-7900.

History

754 Alice E. Smith Fellowship

State Historical Society of Wisconsin
816 State Street
Madison, WI 53706-1488
(608) 264-6400
Average award: $2,000
Number of awards: 1
Deadline: July 15
College level: Doctoral, postgraduate work
Majors/Fields: U.S. history
Criteria: Applicant must be a female graduate student doing research in American history, with preference given to the history of Wisconsin or the Midwest. Applicant must submit four copies of a two-page letter stating qualifications and a summary of the research to be conducted. Awarded every year.
Contact: Michael E. Stevens, State Historian, (608) 264-6464.

755 Amy Louise Hunter Fellowship

State Historical Society of Wisconsin
816 State Street
Madison, WI 53706-1488
(608) 264-6400
Average award: $2,500
Number of awards: 1
Deadline: May 1
College level: Doctoral, postgraduate
Majors/Fields: History of women and public policy
Criteria: Applicant must submit a current resume and a letter of not more than two pages describing background and training in historical research plus a description of current research work. Preference is given to applicants doing research on Wisconsin topics or using the society's collections. Fellowship is awarded in even-number years.
Contact: Michael E. Stevens, State Historian, (608) 264-6464.

756 DAR American History Scholarship

National Society of the Daughters of the American Revolution
NSDAR Administration Building, Office of the Committees
1776 D Street, NW
Washington, DC 20006-5392
(202) 879-3292
Average award: $1,000
Maximum award: $2,000
Number of awards: 3
Deadline: February 1
College level: Freshman
Majors/Fields: American history
Criteria: Applicant must be a U.S. citizen and submit a letter of sponsorship from a local DAR chapter. Selection is based upon academic excellence, commitment to the field of American history, and financial need. All inquiries must include a self-addressed, stamped envelope. Annual transcript review and approval are required to retain scholarship. Awarded every year.
Contact: Administrative Assistant, NSDAR Office of the Committees/Scholarships.

757 Institute of Electrical and Electronics Engineers Fellowship in Electrical History

Center for the History of Electrical Engineering
Rutgers University
39 Union Street
New Brunswick, NJ 08903-5062
(908) 932-1066
Average award: $14,000
Deadline: February 1
College level: Graduate, Doctoral, post-doctoral students
Majors/Fields: History of electrical science and technology
Criteria: Applicant must have an undergraduate degree in engineering, the sciences, or the humanities and be doing full-time graduate work or postdoctoral research. Selection is based upon potential for pursuing research in and contributing to electrical history. Awarded every year.
Contact: Director, Center for the History of Electrical Engineering.

758 J.E. Caldwell Centennial Scholarship

National Society of the Daughters of the American Revolution
NSDAR Administration Building, Office of the Committees
1776 D Street, NW
Washington, DC 20006-5392
(202) 879-3292
Average award: $2,000
Number of awards: 1
Deadline: February 15
College level: Graduate
Majors/Fields: Historic preservation
Criteria: Applicant must be a U.S. citizen and be sponsored by a local DAR chapter. Selection is based upon academic excellence, commitment to historic preservation, and financial need. All inquiries must include a self-addressed, stamped envelope. Applicant may be male or female. Awarded every year.
Contact: Administrative Assistant, NSDAR Office of the Committees/Scholarships.

759 John C. Geilfuss Fellowship

State Historical Society of Wisconsin
816 State Street
Madison, WI 53706-1488
(608) 264-6400
Average award: $2,000
Number of awards: 1
Deadline: February 1
College level: Doctoral, postgraduate students
Majors/Fields: U.S. history, Wisconsin business history, Wisconsin economic history
Criteria: Applicant must be doing research at the graduate level or beyond in Wisconsin business or economic history or on U.S. business and economic history using the collections of the State Historical Society of Wisconsin. Applicant must submit four resumes and four copies of a two-page letter describing qualifications and research project. Awarded every year.
Contact: Michael E. Stevens, State Historian, (608) 264-6464.

760 McCarthy Memorial History Scholarship

Boise State University
1910 University Drive
Boise, ID 83725
(208) 385-1664
Minimum award: $1,000
Number of awards: 3
Deadline: March 1
College level: Sophomore, Junior, Senior
Majors/Fields: History
Criteria: Applicant must be an Idaho resident. Awarded every year. Award may be used only at sponsoring institution.
Contact: Chris Woodward, Financial Aid Counselor.

761 McGinty Undergraduate History Scholarship

Louisiana Tech University
P.O. Box 7925
Ruston, LA 71272
(318) 257-2641
Average award: $1,250
Maximum award: $2,000
Minimum award: $500
Deadline: February 15
College level: Freshman, Sophomore, Junior, Senior
Majors/Fields: History
Criteria: Freshman applicant must have a minimum composite ACT score of 26. Continuing applicant must have a minimum university 3.5 GPA. Minimum 3.0 GPA is required to retain scholarship. Awarded every year. Award may be used only at sponsoring institution.
Contact: E. R. Winzer, Director of Student Financial Aid.

762 Summerfield G. Roberts Award

Sons of the Republic of Texas
5942 Abrams Road
#222
Dallas, TX 75231
(214) 343-2145
Average award: $2,500
Number of awards: 1
Deadline: January 15
Criteria: Award is to encourage literary effort and research about historical events and personalities during the days of the Republic of Texas, 1836-1846, and to stimulate interest in this period. Manuscript must be written or published during the calendar year for which the award is given and it may be either fiction or nonfiction, poetry, essay, play, short story, novel, or biography. Competition is open to all writers everywhere. Awarded every year.
Contact: Awards, (214) 343-2146.

763 Texas History Essay Contest

Sons of the Republic of Texas
5942 Abrams Road
#222
Dallas, TX 75231
(214) 343-2145
Maximum award: $3,000
Minimum award: $1,000
Number of awards: 3
Deadline: February 6
College level: Freshman
Criteria: Applicant must submit a 1,500- to 2,000-word essay on Texas history and its relevance to the building of Texas. Selection is based upon depth of research into Texas history, originality of thought and expression, and organization. Awarded every year.
Contact: Maydee J. Scurlock, Executive Secretary, (214) 343-2146.

Humanities

764 American Numismatic Graduate Fellowship

American Numismatic Society
Broadway at 155th Street
New York, NY 10032
(212) 234-3130
Average award: $3,500
Number of awards: 1
Deadline: March 1
College level: Doctoral
Criteria: Fellowship is for support of doctoral dissertation work employing numismatic evidence.
Contact: Fellowships.

765 Andrew W. Mellon Fellowship in Humanistic Studies

University of Oklahoma
University Affairs
900 Asp Avenue, Room 236
Norman, OK 73019-0401
(405) 325-1701
Average award: $12,500 plus tuition and fees for first year of graduate study
Minimum award: $12,500
Number of awards: 80
Deadline: November 2
College level: Graduate
Criteria: Applicant must be a citizen or permanent resident of the U.S. or Canada, demonstrate outstanding academic promise, and desire a career of teaching and scholarship in a humanistic field of study. Scholarship is renewable. Awarded every year. Award may be used only at sponsoring institution.
Contact: Director of Honors Program, 347 Cate Center Drive, Norman, OK 73019, (405) 325-5291.

766 Bibliographical Society of America Fellowship

Bibliographical Society of America
P.O. Box 397
Grand Central Station
New York, NY 10163
(212) 647-9171
Maximum award: $2,000
Minimum award: $1,000
Number of awards: 9
Deadline: January 31
College level: Doctoral
Criteria: Award is for research into the history of the book trade and publishing. Eligible topics may concentrate on books and documents in any field, but should focus on the book or manuscript (the physical object) as historical evidence. Such topics may include establishing a text or studying the history of book production, publication, distribution, collecting, or reading. Awarded every year.
Contact: Marjory Zaik, Executive Secretary.

767 Bradley/Gamble Fellows Program in Population Studies

School for International Training
P.O. Box 676
Kipling Road
Brattleboro, VT 05302
(802) 257-7751
Average award: $5,000
Maximum award: $10,000
Minimum award: $2,500
Number of awards: 3
Deadline: April 1
College level: Bachelor's degree candidate, master's degree candidate
Criteria: Applicant must be a candidate for a Bachelor of International Studies or a Master of International Administration. Financial need may be considered. Applicant must maintain satisfactory academic progress and continue to demonstrate financial need. Awarded every year. Award may be used only at sponsoring institution.
Contact: Mary Henderson, Financial Aid Officer, (802) 258-3280.

768 Clara B. Small Scholarship

University of Wisconsin-Eau Claire
105 Garfield Avenue
Eau Claire, WI 54701
(715) 836-3373
Average award: $1,000
Number of awards: 2
Deadline: July 1
College level: Sophomore, Junior, Senior, Graduate, Doctoral
Majors/Fields: Arts, education, English, sciences
Criteria: Applicant must be a nontraditional student with a minimum 3.5 GPA who is enrolled at least half-time in the School of Arts and Sciences or Education. One award is for an English major. Awarded every year. Award may be used only at sponsoring institution.
Contact: Melissa Vogler, Financial Aid Counselor.

769 Community College International Studies Scholarship

School for International Training
P.O. Box 676
Kipling Road
Brattleboro, VT 05302
(802) 257-7751
Average award: $1,000
Maximum award: $1,500
Minimum award: $750
Number of awards: 2
Deadline: April 1
College level: Bachelor's degree candidate, tranfer student
Criteria: Applicant must be transferring from a community or junior college into the Bachelor of International Studies program. Financial need may be considered. Recipient must maintain satisfactory academic progress and continue to demonstrate financial need to retain scholarship. Awarded every year. Award may be used only at sponsoring institution.
Contact: Mary Henderson, Financial Aid Officer, (802) 258-3280.

770 George E. Mylonas Scholarship in the Humanities

Washington University
One Brookings Drive
Campus Box 1089
St. Louis, MO 63130
(314) 935-6000 or (800) 638-0700
Average award: $17,750
Number of awards: 3
College level: Freshman
Majors/Fields: Humanities
Criteria: Selection is based upon academic merit without regard to financial need. Satisfactory academic performance is required to retain scholarship. Awarded every year. Award may be used only at sponsoring institution.
Contact: Office of Undergraduate Admissions.

771 George T. Reynolds Fellowship

University of Colorado at Boulder
Campus Box 106
Boulder, CO 80309-0106
(303) 492-5091
Average award: $11,440 stipend and 7 hours tuition waiver
Minimum award: $11,440
Number of awards: 2
College level: Doctoral
Majors/Fields: Humanities, literature
Criteria: Applicant must be a Ph.D. candidate in the humanities. Preference is given to applicants in the field of literature and/or the oral interpretation of literature. Awarded every year. Award may be used only at sponsoring institution.
Contact: Office of Financial Aid.

772 Hagley Museum and Library Grants-in-Aid

Hagley Museum and Library
P.O. Box 3630
Wilmington, DE 19807
(302) 658-2400
Average award: $750
Maximum award: $2,000
Number of awards: 8
Deadline: March 31, June 30, October 31
College level: Doctoral
Criteria: Selection is based upon the best potential use of the Hagley Museum and Library's holdings. The short-term, grants-in-aid support visits to Hagley for scholarly research using the imprint, manuscript, pictorial, and artifact collections. Grants are designed to assist researchers with travel and living expenses while using the research collections. Stipends are for a minimum of two weeks and a maximum of two months at no more than $1,000 per month. Scholarship is renewable.
Contact: Carol Ressler Lockman, Center Coordinator.

773 Hagley/Winterthur Fellowships in Arts and Industries

Hagley Museum and Library
P.O. Box 3630
Wilmington, DE 19807
(302) 658-2400
Average award: $3,000
Maximum award: $6,000
Number of awards: 1
Deadline: November 15
College level: Doctoral
Criteria: Selection is based upon the best potential use of the collections of both Hagley and Winterthur. Fellowship is a cooperative program of short- to medium-term research fellowships for scholars interested in the historical and cultural relationships between economic life and the arts, including design, architecture, crafts, and the fine arts. Stipends are for a minimum of one month and a maximum of six months at no more than $1,000 per month. Awarded every year.
Contact: Carol Ressler Lockman, Center Coordinator.

774 Henry Belin du Pont Fellowship

Hagley Museum and Library
P.O. Box 3630
Wilmington, DE 19807
(302) 658-2400
Minimum award: $3,000
Number of awards: 5
Deadline: March 31; June 30; October 31
Criteria: Preference is given to applicants with highest travel costs to Hagley. Fellowships are to support scholars pursuing advanced research and study in the library, archival, and artifact collections of the Hagley Museum and Library. Fellows must devote full time to their studies and may not accept teaching assignments or undertake any other major activities during the tenure of their fellowships. Tenure must be continuous and last from two to six months. Stipends are for a minimum of two months and a maximum of six months at no more than $1,500 per month. Awarded every year.
Contact: Carol Ressler Lockman, Center Coordinator.

775 International Exchange, Study, or Work Abroad Scholarship

School for International Training
P.O. Box 676
Kipling Road
Brattleboro, VT 05302
(802) 257-7751
Average award: $1,000
Maximum award: $2,000
Number of awards: 3
Deadline: April 1
College level: Bachelor's degree candidate
Criteria: Applicant must have been a participant in an international exchange, study, or work abroad program. Financial need may be considered. Applicant must be enrolled in a degree program. Applicant must maintain satisfactory academic progress and continue to demonstrate financial need. Awarded every year. Award may be used only at sponsoring institution.
Contact: Mary Henderson, Financial Aid Officer, (802) 258-3280.

776 International Mathematics, Science, and Foreign Languages Summer Institute

International Educational Network (IEN)
3001 Veazey Terrace, NW
Washington, DC 20008
(202) 362-7855
Maximum award: $1,700
Number of awards: 10
College level: High school students 13 to 18 years of age.
Majors/Fields: Mathematics, science, foreign languages
Criteria: Applicant must be a high school student, 13 to 18 years of age.

777 Internship Programs

Solomon R. Guggenheim Museum
1071 Fifth Avenue
New York, NY 10128
(212) 727-6200
Deadline: February 1
Criteria: Internships are available in the archives, capital planning, conservation, curatorial, international curatorial, design, development, director's office, education, exhibition services, finance, information systems, learning through art, legal, library, membership/external affairs, personnel, photography, public affairs, publications, registrar, retail operations, security, special events, and visitor services departments.
Contact: Laurie Price, Staffing Coordinator, (212) 423-3516.

778 Kosciuszko Foundation New York Scholarship

Kosciuszko Foundation
15 East 65th Street
New York, NY 10021
(212) 734-2130
Average award: $1,000
Deadline: January 15
Criteria: Applicant must be a member or the dependent of a member of the Brooklyn Polish National Alliance. Awarded every year.
Contact: Scholarships.

779 Larry Temple Scholarship

University of Texas at Austin
Austin, TX 78713-7758
(512) 475-6200
Average award: $6,000
Number of awards: 7
Deadline: December 1 (preferred)
College level: Freshman, Sophomore, Junior, Senior
Criteria: Preference is given to applicant majoring in liberal arts, fine arts, or social work. Preference is also given to Texas residents. Awarded every year. Award may be used only at sponsoring institution.
Contact: Joe Wilcox, Financial Aid Officer.

780 Sidney Hillman Prize Award

Sidney Hillman Foundation Incorporated
15 Union Square
New York, NY 10003
(212) 242-0700
Average award: $1,000
Number of awards: 6
Deadline: January 16
Criteria: Award is given for outstanding contributions dealing with the themes of individual civil liberties, improved race relations, a strengthened labor movement, the advancement of social welfare and economic security, greater world understanding, and related problems. Contributions may be in the fields of daily or perodical journalism, non-fiction, radio, and television. Only work appearing in the year prior to the deadline is eligible for consideration. Unpublished manuscripts of any kind are not eligible.
Contact: Sidney Hillman Foundation.

781 SIT Fund

School for International Training (SIT)
P.O. Box 676
Kipling Road
Brattleboro, VT 05302
(802) 257-7751
Average award: $2,000
Maximum award: $4,000
Minimum award: $1,000
Number of awards: 40
Deadline: April 30 (fall semester); October 15 (spring semester)
College level: Undergraduate
Criteria: Applicant must be a participant in the semester-abroad program. Financial need is considered. Awarded every year. Award may be used only at sponsoring institution.
Contact: Mary Henderson, Financial Aid Officer, (802) 258-3280.

782 Student Diversity Scholarship

School for International Training
P.O. Box 676
Kipling Road
Brattleboro, VT 05302
(802) 257-7751
Average award: $1,000
Maximum award: $2,000
Minimum award: $500
Number of awards: 9
Deadline: April 1
College level: Degree candidate
Criteria: Applicant must have a world view or life experience which can enhance the diversity of the school's learning community. Financial need may be considered. Applicant must be enrolled in a degree program. Applicant must maintain satisfactory academic progress and continue to demonstrate financial need. Awarded every year. Award may be used only at sponsoring institution.
Contact: Mary Henderson, Financial Aid Officer, (802) 258-3280.

783 W.M. Keck Foundation Fellowship for Young Scholars

Huntington Library, Art Collections, and Botanical Gardens
1151 Oxford Road
San Marino, CA 91108-1299
(818) 405-2116
Maximum award: $6,900
Minimum award: $2,300
Number of awards: 14
Deadline: December 15
College level: Doctoral, postdoctoral research
Majors/Fields: American history, art, British history, literature
Criteria: Applicant must be a young scholar. Award is for study at the Huntington Library. Selection is based upon the value of the research project, ability of the applicant, and the degree to which the holdings of the Library will be utilized. Applicant must have three referees send a letter of support for the project prior to the deadline date. Awarded every year.
Contact: Robert C. Ritchie, W.M. Keck Foundation Director of Research, Fellowship Awards Committee, Huntington Library, San Marino, CA 91108.

Religion/Theology/ Philosophy

784 Benjamin E. Mays Scholarship for Ministry

Fund for Theological Education (FTE), Inc.
475 Riverside Drive
Suite 832
New York, NY 10115-0008
(212) 870-2058
Maximum award: Scholarship amount is based on financial need
Deadline: November 10
College level: Graduate
Majors/Fields: Divinity
Criteria: Applicant must be ordained or an official candidate for ordination, a black citizen of the U.S. or Canada, be a graduate of an accredited college or university, and be enrolled in a Master of Divinity program at a theological school fully accredited by the Association of Theological Schools in the United States and Canada. Applicant must be nominated by a church administrator, minister, member of a faculty or administration, or FTE alumni. High academic record and promise for ministerial effectiveness are required to retain scholarship. Awarded every year.
Contact: Joyce Johnson, Secretary.

785   Black North American Doctoral Scholarships for the Study of Religion

Fund for Theological Education, Inc.
475 Riverside Drive
Suite 832
New York, NY 10115-0008
(212) 870-2058
Maximum award: Scholarship amount is based on financial need
Deadline: February 10
College level: Doctoral
Majors/Fields: Religion
Criteria: Applicant must be a member of the Christian church, a black U.S. or Canadian citizen, and have completed one year of course-work in a Ph.D., Th.D., or Ed.D. degree program in fields of religious studies at an accredited university or seminary. Applicant must be nominated by a faculty member of a college, seminary, or university who holds a PH.D., Th.D., or Ed.D. degree. High academic perfor-mance and evidence of promise for teaching effectiveness are re-quired to retain scholarship. Awarded every year.
Contact: Joyce Johnson, Associate for Program.

786   Dissertation Year Scholarship for Doctoral Study for Black North Americans

Fund for Theological Education, Inc.
475 Riverside Drive
Suite 832
New York, NY 10115-0008
(212) 870-2058
Maximum award: Amount of scholarship is based on financial need
Deadline: February 10
College level: Doctoral
Majors/Fields: Religion, theology
Criteria: Applicant must be a member of the Christian church, a black U.S. or Canadian citizen, and have an approved dissertation propos-al. Applicant must be nominated by a faculty member of a college, seminary, or university who holds a Ph.D., Th.D., or Ed.D. degree; faculty member should be reasonably certain the applicant will com-plete dissertation during scholarship year. Awarded every year.
Contact: Joyce Johnson, Secretary.

787   International Doctoral Scholarship

Memorial Foundation for Jewish Culture
15 East 26th Street
New York, NY 10010
(212) 679-4074
Average award: $3,000
Maximum award: $5,000
Minimum award: $2,000
Number of awards: 75
Deadline: October 31
College level: Doctoral
Majors/Fields: Jewish studies
Criteria: Awarded to doctoral students specializing in Jewish fields. Priority is given to candidates at the dissertation level. Reapplication is required to retain scholarship. Awarded every year.
Contact: Dr. Jerry Hochbaum, Executive Vice President.

788   International Fellowship in Jewish Studies

Memorial Foundation for Jewish Culture
15 East 26th Street
New York, NY 10010
(212) 679-4074
Average award: $2,500
Maximum award: $4,000
Minimum award: $1,000
Deadline: October 31
College level: Any qualified scholar, researcher, or artist proposing a project in a field of Jewish specialization
Majors/Fields: Jewish studies
Criteria: Award is to assist well-qualified individuals in carrying out an independent scholarly, literary, or art project, in a field of Jewish spe-cialization, which makes a significant contribution to the understand-ing, preservation, enhancement, or transmission of Jewish culture. Recipient must request renewal in writing. Ordinarily, no more than two grants are made to one individual. Awarded every year.
Contact: Fellowships.

789   International Scholarship for Community Service

Memorial Foundation for Jewish Culture
15 East 26th Street
New York, NY 10010
(212) 679-4074
Average award: $2,000
Minimum award: $1,000
Number of awards: 50
Deadline: November 30
College level: Senior, Graduate, Doctoral
Majors/Fields: Jewish studies
Criteria: Award is to assist well-qualified individuals train for careers in the rabbinate, Jewish education, social work, and as religious functionaries in Diaspora Jewish communities in need of such per-sonnel. Applicant must undertake training in chosen field in a recog-nized yeshiva, teacher training seminary, school of social work, uni-versity or other educational institution, and commit to serve in a com-munity of need for two or three years. Students planning to serve in the U.S., Canada, or Israel are not eligible. Reapplication is required to retain scholarship. Awarded every year.
Contact: Dr. Jerry Hochbaum, Executive Vice President.

790   Word of Life Scholarship

Liberty University
P.O. Box 20000
Lynchburg, VA 24506-8001
(804) 582-2270
Average award: Tuition and general fees
Number of awards: 3
Deadline: June 1
College level: Freshman
Criteria: Applicant must be a graduate of the Word of Life Bible Inst in New York. Satisfactory academic progress is required to retain scholarship. Awarded every year. Award may be used only at spon-soring institution.
Contact: Penny Hutchison, Admissions Representative, (804) 582-2707.

Medicine/Nursing

Dentistry

791   AADR Student Research Fellowship

American Association for Dental Research (AADR)
1111 Fourteenth Street NW
Suite #1000
Washington, DC 20005
(202) 989-1050
Average award: $2,500
Number of awards: 27
Deadline: January 6
Majors/Fields: Dental hygiene
Criteria: Applicant must be enrolled in an accredited DDS/DMD or hygiene program at a health-associated dental institution within the U.S. and must be sponsored by a faculty member at that institution. Applicant must not have received the degree nor should it be awarded during the year of the fellowship. Recipient must submit a new research proposal for renewal of funding. Awarded every year.
Contact: Patricia J. Lewis, Executive Secretary, (202) 898-1050.

792   Board of Governors Dental Scholarship

North Carolina State Education Assistance Authority
Box 2688
Chapel Hill, NC 27515-2688
(919) 549-8614
Average award: $5,000
Number of awards: 8
College level: Doctoral
Majors/Fields: Dentistry
Criteria: Applicant must be a North Carolina resident, be accepted at the UNC School of Dentistry, demonstrate financial need, and intend to practice dentistry in North Carolina. Minorities are encouraged to apply. Satisfactory academic progress, financial need, and desire to practice dentistry in North Carolina are required to retain scholarship for a total of four years. Awarded every year.
Contact: UNC Dental School, Brauer Hall, Chapel Hill, NC 27514, (919) 966-4565.

793   Dental Student Scholarship

American Dental Association (ADA) Endowment and Assistance Fund, Inc.
211 East Chicago Avenue
17th Floor
Chicago, IL 60611-2678
(312) 440-2567
Average award: $2,500
Number of awards: 25
Deadline: June 15
College level: Entering, first-, and second-year dental students
Majors/Fields: Dentistry
Criteria: Applicant must be a U.S. citizen and have a minimum 3.0 GPA. Selection is based upon financial need, academic achievement, and personal and professional goals. Good academic standing is required to retain scholarship for one additional year. Awarded every year.
Contact: Marsha Mountz, ADA Endowment Fund.

794   Dr. Charles A. Vernale Student Loan Award

Connecticut State Dental Association
62-64 Rush Street
Hartford, CT 06106
(203) 278-5550
Average award: $2,000
Number of awards: 1
Deadline: June 30
College level: Dental students
Majors/Fields: Dentistry
Criteria: Applicant must be a Connecticut resident with a predoctoral degree in dental medicine. Awarded every year.
Contact: Noel Bishop, Executive Director.

795   Dr. Glayton Wilson Grier Scholarship

Dr. G. Wilson Grier Scholarship
c/o Peter K. Schaeffer, DDS
1071 South Governors Avenue
Dover, DE 19901
(302) 674-1080
Average award: $1,000
Number of awards: 3
Deadline: April 15
College level: Dental school
Majors/Fields: Dentistry
Criteria: Applicant must be a Delaware resident; first-year dental students are not eligible but postdoctoral students may apply. Selection is based upon grades. Financial need is considered. Reapplication required to retain scholarship. Awarded every year.
Contact: Peter K. Schaeffer, DDS, Chairperson.

796   Minority Dental Student Scholarship

American Dental Association (ADA) Endowment and Assistance Fund, Inc.
211 East Chicago Avenue
17th Floor
Chicago, IL 60611-2678
(312) 440-2567
Average award: $2,000
Maximum number of awards: 25
Minimum number of awards: 15
Deadline: July 1
College level: Entering, first-, and second-year dental students
Majors/Fields: Dentistry
Criteria: Applicant must be a U.S. citizen, have a minimum 2.5 GPA, and be one of the following minorities: African-American, Hispanic, or Native American. Selection is based upon financial need, academic achievement, and personal and professional goals. Good academic standing is required to renew scholarship for one additional year. Awarded every year.
Contact: Marsha Mountz, ADA Endowment Fund.

Medicine

797   AAOA Scholarship Award

Auxiliary to the American Osteopathic Association (AAOA)
142 East Ontario Street
Chicago, IL 60611
(312) 280-5800
Average award: $3,000
Deadline: April 15
College level: Sophomore
Majors/Fields: Osteopathic medicine
Criteria: Selection is based upon high scholastic standing (rank in top fifth of class), financial need, good moral character, good motivation, and aptitude for a career in osteopathic medicine. Recipient must not have a full tuition scholarship received from another source. Award is paid directly to the osteopathic college to be applied toward tuition, books, and equipment. Awarded every year.
Contact: Mrs. Judie Colwell, AAOA Scholarship Chairman, 4376 Shire Cove Road, Hilliard, OH 43026, (614) 876-2293.

798   Alvin and Mona Libin Scholarship in Medicine

University of Calgary
2500 University Drive, NW
Calgary, Alberta, CN T2N 1N4
(403) 220-7872
Average award: $10,000
Number of awards: 1
Deadline: August 1
College level: Doctoral
Majors/Fields: Medicine
Criteria: Applicant must be an Alberta resident entering the first year at the Faculty of Medicine M.D. program. Selection is based upon academic merit. Extracurricular activities and community involvement are considered. Awarded every year. Award may be used only at sponsoring institution.
Contact: J. Van Housen, Director of Student Awards & Financial Aid.

799   American Heart Association National Center Grant-in-Aid

American Heart Association National Center
7320 Greenville Avenue
Dallas, TX 75231-4599
(214) 373-6300
Average award: $30,000
Deadline: July 1
Criteria: Proposals are accepted from talented young investigators to support research projects broadly related to cardiovascular function and disease (including stroke) or to related fundamental problems. A doctoral degree is required at the time of award activation. At any given time an individual may hold only one grant-in-aid from the association's national program. Awarded every year.
Contact: Grants.

800   Board of Governors Medical Scholarship

North Carolina State Education Assistance Authority
Box 2688
Chapel Hill, NC 27515-2688
(919) 549-8614
Average award: $5,000
Maximum award: $5,000 plus tuition and fees
Number of awards: 20
College level: Doctoral
Majors/Fields: Medicine
Criteria: Applicant must be a North Carolina resident accepted for admission at a medical school in North Carolina, demonstrate financial need, and intend to practice medicine in North Carolina. Minorities are encouraged to apply. Satisfactory academic progress, financial need, and interest to practice medicine in North Carolina are required to retain scholarship for a total of four years. Awarded every year.
Contact: Medical School in North Carolina.

801   Clinical Scientist Award

American Heart Association National Center
7320 Greenville Avenue
Dallas, TX 75231-4599
(214) 373-6300
Average award: $35,000
Deadline: June 1
Majors/Fields: Cardiovascular medicine
Criteria: Three- to five-year awards are available for rigorous full-time clinical training of young M.D.'s. Applicant should have no more than two years of relevant postdoctoral research training at the time of the award. M.D./Ph.D. graduates with clinical training who are U.S. citizens or permanent residents are eligible. Applicant must have a sponsor in a clinical department and a preceptor for research training. Scholarship is renewable. Awarded every year.
Contact: Awards.

802   "Country Doctor" Scholarship Program

State Medical Education Board of Georgia
244 Washington Street, SW
Room 574J
Atlanta, GA 30334
(404) 656-2226
Average award: $10,000
Number of awards: 30
Deadline: May 15
College level: Doctoral
Majors/Fields: Medicine
Criteria: Applicant must be a Georgia resident and must attend an accredited U.S. medical school in preparation for licensure as an M.D. or D.O. in primary care. Applicant must agree to practice within the state of Georgia in a rural community of 15,000 people or less for at least four years after receiving degree. Financial need is required. Board approval and commitment to practice in designated areas are required to retain scholarship. Awarded every year.
Contact: Peggy H. Shull, Assistant Director.

803   Edward Livingston Trudeau Scholarship

American Lung Association
Medical Affairs Division
1740 Broadway
New York, NY 10019-4374
(212) 315-8793
Average award: $25,000
Deadline: October 2
College level: Unspecified graduate
Criteria: Awarded to holders of a M.D. or doctoral degree who have completed graduate training in lung disease and have appointments in schools of medicine or osteopathy. Awards are intended to give promising candidates an opportunity to stay in academic medicine and to prove themselves as teachers and investigators. Award requires supplement by the school. Applicant must be a U.S. or Canadian resident. Renewable for one additional year. Awarded every year.
Contact: Medical Affairs Director.

804   Elizabeth H. Miller Scholarship

University of Toledo
Financial Aid Office
Toledo, OH 43606-3390
(419) 537-2056
Maximum award: $1,000
Number of awards: 4
Deadline: April 1
College level: Freshman, Sophomore, Junior, Senior
Majors/Fields: Pre-medicine
Criteria: Selection is based upon academic achievement and financial need. Minimum 3.0 GPA is required to maintain scholarship. Awarded every year. Award may be used only at sponsoring institution.
Contact: Pre-Med Adviser, University Hall, Room 3000, Toledo, OH 43606, (419) 537-2102.

805   Established Investigators Award

American Heart Association National Center
7320 Greenville Avenue
Dallas, TX 75231-4599
(214) 373-6300
Average award: $35,000
Deadline: June 1
Criteria: This five-year award is to assist talented young physicians and scientists in developing careers in research, academic medicine, and biology. Applicants customarily have five to nine years of research experience following receipt of a doctoral degree. Applicant must be a U.S. citizen or permanent resident. Awarded every year.
Contact: Awards.

806   Family Practice Medical Scholarship

Maryland Higher Education Commission
State Scholarship Administration
16 Francis Street
Annapolis, MD 21401-1781
(410) 974-5370
Maximum award: $7,500
Number of awards: 2
Deadline: May 1
College level: Graduate, Doctoral
Majors/Fields: Family practice, medicine
Criteria: Applicant must have been admitted to the U of Maryland Sch of Medicine, demonstrate financial need, agree to enter family practice residency, enter a family medicine practice within six months of completion of residency, and practice family medicine for one year for each year of assistance in a Maryland area of acute need. Applicant must submit FAFSA by March 1. Reapplication is required to retain scholarship for three additional years. Awarded every year.
Contact: Linda Asplin, Program Administrator.

807   Fresno-Madera Medical Society Scholarship

Fresno-Madera Medical Society Scholarship Foundation
P.O. Box 31
Fresno, CA 93707
(209) 224-4224, extension 12
Average award: $1,000
Maximum award: $1,500
Number of awards: 12
Deadline: May 15
College level: Medical school students
Majors/Fields: Medicine
Criteria: Applicant must have been a resident of either Fresno or Madera counties for at least one year and be approved for matriculation in a medical school. Award will be sent to the school of matriculation to be administered towards tuition, lab fees, books, and any other valid educational expenses. Scholarship is renewable. Awarded every year.
Contact: Ellen Burton, Administrative Secretary.

808   Gina Finzi Memorial Student Summer Fellowship

Lupus Foundation of America
4 Research Place, Suite 180
Rockville, MD 20850-3226
(301) 670-9292
Average award: $2,000
Number of awards: 10
Deadline: February 1
College level: Senior, Graduate, Doctoral
Majors/Fields: Biology, chemistry, life science, psychosocial science, science
Criteria: Fellowship is given to foster interest in lupus erythematosus in the areas of basic, clinical, or psychological research under the supervision of an established investigator. Awarded every year.
Contact: Patricia S. Leisy, Director of Education Services.

809   Harvey E. Dowling, M.D. and Pearl Christie-Dowling, M.D. Bursary

University of Calgary
2500 University Drive, NW
Calgary, Alberta, CN T2N 1N4
(403) 220-7872
Average award: $2,000
Number of awards: 6
Deadline: August 1
College level: Doctoral
Majors/Fields: Medicine
Criteria: All awards are based upon financial need and are divided equally between male and female students who have been born and educated in Alberta. Three awards each are for second- and third-year students. Awarded every year. Award may be used only at sponsoring institution.
Contact: J. Van Housen, Director of Student Awards & Financial Aid.

810   Helen N. and Harold B. Shapira Scholarship

Shapira Scholarship Awards Fund
American Heart Association, Minnesota Affiliate
4701 West 77th Street
Minneapolis, MN 55435
(612) 835-3300
Average award: $1,000
Number of awards: 2
Deadline: April 1
College level: Unspecified graduate, unspecified undergraduate.
Majors/Fields: Medically related curriculum with application to the heart and blood vessel system
Criteria: Applicant must be attending a four-year college or university or a medical school in the state of Minnesota. Renewable if recipient maintains satisfactory scholastic progress. Awarded every year.
Contact: Joyce C. Lampion, Research Administrator.

811   Henry Viets Fellowship

Myasthenia Gravis Foundation of America, Inc.
222 South Riverside Plaza
Suite 1540
Chicago, IL 60606
(312) 258-0522, (800) 541-5454
Average award: $3,000
Number of awards: 4
Deadline: March 15
College level: Premedical and medical students
Criteria: Applicant must be planning to study in the area of myasthenia gravis. Awarded every year.
Contact: Fellowships, (800) 541-5454.

812   Honors Undergraduate Grant

National Institute of General Medical Sciences/
National Institute of Health
Minority Access to Research Careers (MARC) Program
Westwood Building, Room 950
Bethesda, MD 20892
(301) 496-7941
Maximum award: $6,504
Minimum award: $4,800
Deadline: January 10; May 10; September 10
College level: Freshman, Sophomore, Junior, Senior
Majors/Fields: Biomedical science
Criteria: Applicant must be a U.S. citizen or permanent resident, be committed to obtaining a doctoral degree in biomedical science, and be a minority student at a school with substantial minority enrollment. Renewable for a maximum of five years. Awarded every year.
Contact: Elward Bynum, MARC Program Director.

813   Howard H.M. Bowman Memorial Scholarship

University of Toledo
Financial Aid Office
Toledo, OH 43606-3390
(419) 537-2056
Maximum award: $1,000
Number of awards: 3
Deadline: April 1
College level: Freshman, Sophomore, Junior, Senior
Majors/Fields: Pre-medicine
Criteria: Selection is based upon academic achievement and financial need. Minimum 3.0 GPA is required to maintain scholarship. Awarded every year. Award may be used only at sponsoring institution.
Contact: Pre-Med Adviser, University Hall, Room 3000, Toledo, OH 43606, (419) 537-2102.

814 Irene and Daisy MacGregor Memorial Scholarship

National Society of the Daughters of the American Revolution
NSDAR Administration Building, Office of the Committees
1776 D Street, NW
Washington, DC 20006-5392
(202) 879-3292
Average award: $5,000
Number of awards: 2
Deadline: April 15
College level: Medical school
Majors/Fields: Medicine
Criteria: Applicant must be a U.S. citizen pursuing an M.D. to become a medical doctor and be sponsored by a local DAR chapter. Selection is based upon academic excellence, commitment to the field of medicine, and financial need. All inquiries must include a self-addressed, stamped envelope. Applicant may be male or female. Annual transcript review required to retain scholarship. Awarded every year.
Contact: Administrative Assistant, NSDAR Office of Committees/Scholarships.

815 Joseph Collins Foundation Scholarship

Joseph Collins Foundation
153 East 53rd Street
New York, NY 10022
Maximum award: $5,000
Minimum award: $2,000
Number of awards: 177
Deadline: March 1
College level: Doctoral
Majors/Fields: General practice, neurology, psychiatry
Criteria: Applicant must obtain application from the medical school authorities, complete it and return it to them for forwarding to the Foundation. Selection is based upon financial need, scholastic record and standing, demonstrated interest in arts and letters or other cultural pursuits outside the field of medicine, intention to specialize in neurology, psychiatry, or general practice, evidence of good moral character, and attendance at an accredited medical school located east of or contiguous to the Mississippi River. Renewal grants are made at the discretion of the Trustees. Awarded every year.
Contact: Augusta L. Packer, Secretary Treasurer.

816 Kermit Osserman Fellowship

Myasthenia Gravis Foundation of America, Inc.
222 South Riverside Plaza
Suite 1540
Chicago, IL 60606
(312) 258-0522, (800) 541-5454
Average award: $30,000
Number of awards: 3
Deadline: November 1
College level: Doctoral
Criteria: Applicant must be doing research in the area of myasthenia gravis. Awarded every year.
Contact: Fellowships.

817 Lawrence W. Mills Award

Auxiliary to the American Osteopathic Association (AAOA)
142 East Ontario Street
Chicago, IL 60611
(312) 280-5800
Average award: $5,000
Number of awards: 1
Deadline: April 15
College level: Sophomore
Majors/Fields: Osteopathic medicine
Criteria: Selection is based upon high scholastic standing (rank in top fifth of class), financial need, good moral character, good motivation, and aptitude for a career in osteopathic medicine. Recipient must not have a full tuition scholarship from another source. Award is given to the winner of the AAOA scholarship competition and is paid directly to the osteopathic college to be applied toward tuition, books, and equipment. Awarded every year.
Contact: Mrs. Judie Colwell, AAOA Scholarship Chairman, 4376 Shire Cove Road, Hilliard, OH 43026, (614) 876-2293.

818 Medical Student Research Fellowship

Pharmaceutical Research and Manufacturers of America Foundation, Inc.
1100 15th Street, NW
Washington, DC 20005
(202) 835-3470
Average award: $10,000
Number of awards: 5
Deadline: January 15
College level: Doctoral
Majors/Fields: Medicine
Criteria: Applicant must be enrolled in a U.S. medical or dental school, have finished at least one year of the school curriculum, and be sponsored by the pharmacology or clinical pharmacology program in which the investigative project is to be undertaken. Priority consideration will be given to those applicants who anticipate strong commitment to careers in the field of clinical pharmacology. Awarded every year.
Contact: Donna Moore, Director of Programs.

819 Predoctoral Fellowship

National Institute of General Medical Sciences/
National Institute of Health
Minority Access to Research Careers (MARC) Program
Westwood Building, Room 950
Bethesda, MD 20892
(301) 496-7941
Average award: $17,000
Maximum award: $28,000
Minimum award: $13,500
Number of awards: 9
Deadline: January 10; May 10; September 10
College level: Doctoral
Majors/Fields: Biomedicine
Criteria: Applicant must be a U.S. citizen or permanent resident, be accepted into an approved Ph.D. or combined M.D./Ph.D. program in the biomedical sciences, and be a minority student at a school with substantial minority enrollment. Renewal is based upon satisfactory academic standing. Awarded every year.
Contact: Elward Bynum, Director, MARC Program.

820 Ramsay and Elaine O'Neal Scholarship

Mississippi State University
P.O. Box 6238
Mississippi State, MS 39762
(601) 325-7430
Average award: $3,000
Number of awards: 1
Deadline: February 1
College level: Freshman
Criteria: Applicant must have a minimum composite ACT score of 28 or combined SAT I score of 1160, plan to enter medical or dental school, and participate in Scholarship Day. Minimum 3.5 cumulative GPA and 32 semester hours per year are required to retain scholarship. Awarded every year. Award may be used only at sponsoring institution.
Contact: Audrey S. Lambert, Director of Student Financial Aid.

821 Regents Health Care Scholarship for Medicine and Dentistry

New York State Education Department
Bureau of Postsecondary Grants Administration
Cultural Education Center
Albany, NY 12230
(518) 474-5705
Maximum award: $10,000
Minimum award: $1,000
Number of awards: 100
Deadline: March 15
College level: Graduate, Doctoral
Majors/Fields: Dentistry, medicine
Criteria: Applicant must attend or plan to attend an approved medical or dental program in New York state, have been a legal resident of New York state for at least one year prior to September 1, be a U.S. citizen or permanent resident, and be economically disadvantaged and/or a member of a minority group underrepresented in the medical or dental profession. Applicant must agree to a service commitment of one year for each year of award (minimum two years service) upon completion of all professional training. 80 percent of awards are for medicine and 20 percent for dentistry. Scholarship is renewable. Awarded every year.
Contact: Office of Equity and Access.

822 Richard L. Davis Scholarship

American College of Medical Practice Executives (ACMPE)
104 Inverness Terrace East
Englewood, CO 80112-5306
(303) 799-1111
Maximum award: $1,000
Maximum number of awards: 5
Minimum number of awards: 1
Deadline: June 1
College level: Sophomore, Junior, Senior, Graduate, Doctoral
Majors/Fields: Medical group management
Criteria: Applicant must submit a letter stating career goals and objectives, with an explanation of the individual's need for professional development such as gaps in formal education or changing health care environment, a resume showing employment history with a brief narrative describing specific employment responsibilities in health care field, and three letters of recommendation. Reference letters should address performance, character, potential to succeed, and need for scholarship support. Awarded every year.
Contact: Laurie Draizen, Executive Assistant, (303) 799-1111, extension 206.

823 Rock Sleyster Memorial Scholarship

American Medical Association
515 North State Street
Chicago, IL 60610
(312) 464-4691
Average award: $2,500
Number of awards: 20
Deadline: May 1
College level: Rising senior in medical school.
Majors/Fields: Psychiatry
Criteria: Applicant must be a U.S. citizen enrolled in an accredited U.S. or Canadian medical school and demonstrate financial need and an interest in psychiatry. Applicant must be nominated by the psychiatry department and dean's office and submit an application, recommendations, financial statement, and transcript. Awarded every year.
Contact: Harry S. Jonas, M.D., Assistant Vice President, Division of Undergraduate Medical Education, (312) 464-4657.

824 Scholars Program in Medicine

Washington University
One Brookings Drive
Campus Box 1089
St. Louis, MO 63130
(314) 935-6000 or (800) 638-0700
Average award: $8,375
Number of awards: 5
College level: Freshman
Majors/Fields: Pre-medical
Criteria: Applicant is provisionally accepted into the Sch of Medicine after four years in either the Coll of Arts and Sciences or Sch of Engineering and Applied Science. Applicant must apply under the Early Decision or Early Action plans. Selection is based upon academic merit without regard to financial need. Satisfactory academic performance is required to retain scholarship. Awarded every year. Award may be used only at sponsoring institution.
Contact: Office of Undergraduate Admissions.

825 Summer Fellowship

Parkinson's Disease Foundation
650 West 168th Street
New York, NY 10032
(212) 923-4700, (800) 457-6676
Average award: $2,000
Maximum award: $2,200
Minimum award: $1,800
Maximum number of awards: 9
Minimum number of awards: 6
Deadline: April 1
College level: Freshman, Sophomore, Junior, Senior, Graduate, Doctoral
Majors/Fields: Premedicine, science
Criteria: Applicant must find a sponsor. Fellowship program is for a ten-week work period in a lab setting. Awarded every year.
Contact: Patricia Ann Micek, Business Manager, 710 West 168th Street, 3rd Floor, Room 336, New York, NY 10032.

826 Torrison Medical Scholarship

Evangel Lutheran Church
8765 West Higgins Road
Chicago, IL 60631-4195
Maximum award: $5,000
Minimum award: $4,000
Maximum number of awards: 5
Minimum number of awards: 4
Deadline: April 15
College level: Doctoral
Majors/Fields: Medicine
Criteria: Applicant must be a member of the Evangelical Lutheran Church in America, accepted into a medical program, particularly in research in incurable diseases, and nominated by an ELCA college or university president or pastor. Awarded every year.
Contact: Eileen M. Heffner, Coordinator for Unit Services, Division for Higher Education and Schools, (312) 380-2843.

827 Venning Pre-Med Scholarship

Boise State University
1910 University Drive
Boise, ID 83725
(208) 385-1664
Minimum award: $1,000
Number of awards: 2
Deadline: March 1
College level: Sophomore, Junior, Senior
Majors/Fields: Pre-medicine
Criteria: Selection is based upon financial need. Awarded every year. Award may be used only at sponsoring institution.
Contact: Chris Woodward, Financial Aid Counselor.

828   Young Scientist Training Program

Life and Health Insurance Medical Research Fund
1001 Pennsylvania Avenue, NW
Suite 500
Washington, DC 20004-2599
(202) 624-2312
Average award: $16,000
Number of awards: 6
Deadline: March 1
College level: Doctoral, M.D./Ph.D. program
Majors/Fields: Medicine
Criteria: Applicant must be a U.S. citizen in the second year of medical school and be working toward a combined M.D./Ph.D. degree. Satisfactory progress report is required to retain scholarship. Awarded every year.
Contact: Jean Schlichting, Grants Coordinator.

Nursing

829   AACN Educational Advancement Scholarship for B.S.N. Students

American Association of Critical-Care Nurses (AACN)
Educational Advancement Scholarships
101 Columbia
Aliso Viejo, CA 92656-1491
(714) 362-2000 or (800) 899-2226, extension 376
Minimum award: $1,500
Number of awards: 37
Deadline: May 15
College level: Junior, Senior
Majors/Fields: Nursing
Criteria: Applicant must be a current American Association of Critical-Care Nurses member with an R.N. license who is currently working in a critical care unit or has worked in one for at least one of the last three years. Applicant must have a minimum 3.0 cumulative GPA and be currently enrolled in an N.L.N.-accredited baccalaureate degree program in nursing. A minimum of 20 percent of the awards will go to ethnic minority students. Recipient must reapply for one additional year. Awarded every year.
Contact: Mitzi Stiles, Education Secretary.

830   AACN Educational Advancement Scholarship for Graduate Students

American Association of Critical-Care Nurses (AACN)
Educational Advancement Scholarships
101 Columbia
Aliso Viejo, CA 92656-1491
(714) 362-2000 or (800) 899-2226, extension 376
Minimum award: $1,500
Number of awards: 18
Deadline: May 15
College level: Graduate, Doctoral
Majors/Fields: Nursing
Criteria: Applicant must be a current American Association of Critical-Care Nurses member with an R.N. license who is currently working in a critical care unit or has worked in one for at least one of the last three years. Applicant must have a minimum 3.0 cumulative GPA and have graduated from a baccalaureate degree program with proof of admission to a planned course of graduate study. A minimum of 20 percent of awards will be allocated to ethnic minorities. Recipient must reapply for one additional year.
Contact: Mitzi Stiles, Education Secretary.

831   Ailene C. Ewell Scholarship Award

Chi Eta Phi Sorority, Inc.
3029 Thirteenth Street, NW
Washington, DC 20009
Average award: $1,000
Maximum award: $2,000
Minimum award: $500
Maximum number of awards: 25
Minimum number of awards: 20
Deadline: February 28
College level: Senior
Majors/Fields: Nursing
Criteria: Applicant must be referred by a chapter of Chi Eta Phi Sorority. Selection is based upon financial need, scholastic ability, interest in nursing, and leadership potential. Satisfactory academic progress is required to retain scholarship. Awarded every year.
Contact: Scholarships.

832   ANA Minority Clinical and Research Training Fellowship

American Nurses Association (ANA)
600 Maryland Avenue, SW
Suite 100 West
Washington, DC 20024-2571
(202) 554-4444, extension 122
Maximum award: $9,000
Number of awards: 18
Deadline: January 15
College level: Doctoral
Majors/Fields: Behavioral science, psychiatric nursing
Criteria: Applicant must be a U.S. citizen or permanent resident, be a member of an ethnic or racial minority, and be a registered nurse in a full-time ANA-approved doctoral program. Scholarship is renewable. Awarded every year.
Contact: Dr. Carla S. Serlin, Director.

833   Caroline E. Holt Nursing Scholarship

National Society of the Daughters of the American Revolution
NSDAR Administration Building, Office of the Committees
1776 D Street, NW
Washington, DC 20006-5392
(202) 879-3292
Maximum award: $500
Number of awards: 10
Deadline: February 15; August 15
College level: Freshman, Sophomore, Junior, Senior
Majors/Fields: Nursing
Criteria: Applicant must be a U.S. citizen, studying nursing at the undergraduate level and be sponsored by a local DAR chapter. All inquiries must include a self-addressed, stamped envelope. Awarded every year.
Contact: Administrative Assistant, NSDAR Office of the Committees/Scholarships.

834 D.C. Nurses Training Corps Grant

District of Columbia Office of Postsecondary Education, Research, and Assistance
2100 Martin Luther King Jr. Avenue, SE
Suite 401
Washington, DC 20020
(202) 727-3685
Average award: $13,700
Maximum award: $22,000
Minimum award: $8,631
Number of awards: 16
Deadline: Last Friday in April
College level: Freshman, Sophomore, Junior, Senior
Majors/Fields: Nursing
Criteria: Applicant must be a District of Columbia resident, demonstrate financial need, have a minimum 2.5 GPA, be in good academic standing, and be accepted for or enrolled in a full-time nursing program at a District of Columbia institution. Reapplication, financial need, and good academic standing are required to retain scholarship. Awarded every year.
Contact: Laurencia O. Henderson, Financial Assistance Specialist.

835 Eight & Forty Nursing Scholarship

Eight & Forty Scholarship Program
P.O. Box 1055
Indianapolis, IN 46206
(317) 630-1212
Average award: $2,500
Number of awards: 22
Deadline: May 15
College level: R.N.
Majors/Fields: Nursing
Criteria: Applicant must be a U.S. citizen and a R.N. studying nursing with a lung and respiratory disease emphasis. Awarded every year.
Contact: William A. Pease, Program Manager, (317) 635-8411.

836 Eight and Forty Lung and Respiratory Nursing Scholarship

American Legion
The American Legion Education and Scholarships Program
P.O. Box 1055
Indianapolis, IN 46206
(317) 630-1200
Average award: $2,500
Number of awards: 20
Deadline: May 15
College level: Graduate, Doctoral
Majors/Fields: Nursing
Criteria: Applicant must be a registered nurse seeking advanced preparation for a full-time position in supervision, administration, or teaching with a direct relationship to lung and respiratory control. Awarded every year.
Contact: Education Program.

837 Elaine Potter Benfer Scholarship

New Mexico State University
Box 30001
Department 5100
Las Cruces, NM 88003-0001
(505) 646-4105
Maximum award: $2,400
Number of awards: 1
Deadline: March 1
College level: Sophomore, Junior, Senior
Majors/Fields: Nursing
Criteria: Applicant must be willing to volunteer with the Red Cross. Awarded every year. Award may be used only at sponsoring institution.
Contact: Greeley W. Myers, Director of Financial Aid.

838 Estelle Massey Osborne Scholarship

Nurses Educational Fund
555 West 57th Street
New York, NY 10019
(212) 582-8820, extension 806
Maximum award: $6,000
Minimum award: $2,500
Number of awards: 1
Deadline: March 1
College level: Graduate
Majors/Fields: Registered Nursing
Criteria: Applicant should be a black registered nurse who is a member of a national professional nursing association and enrolled in or applying to a full-time master's degree program in nursing approved by the National League for Nursing. Applicant must be U.S. citizen or have declared official intention of becoming one. Selection is based upon academic achievement and evidence of service to the profession. Send $5 check to cover postage and handling when requesting application. Applicant must submit GRE or MAT scores. Awarded every year.
Contact: Barbara Butler, Scholarship Coordinator.

839 Frances Topkins Scholarship

Foundation of the National Student Nurses' Association, Inc.
555 West 57th Street
Suite 1325
New York, NY 10019
(212) 581-2215
Maximum award: $2,500
Minimum award: $1,000
Deadline: February 1
College level: Sophomore, Junior, Senior, Graduate, Doctoral
Majors/Fields: Nursing
Criteria: Applicant must be enrolled at a state-approved school of nursing or pre-nursing in an associate degree, baccalaureate, diploma, generic doctorate, or generic master's program. Selection is based upon academic achievement, financial need, and involvement in student nursing organizations and community service related to health care. Applicant will automatically be considered for any specialty scholarships for which he or she is eligible. Awarded every year.
Contact: Scholarships.

840 George W. Nunn, Richard W. Stuhr, and Joseph Wallace Nursing Scholarship

University of Alabama–Tuscaloosa
Box 870162
Tuscaloosa, AL 35487-0162
(205) 348-6756
Average award: $2,000
Number of awards: 1
Deadline: March 15
College level: Freshman, Sophomore, Junior, Senior
Majors/Fields: Nursing
Criteria: Applicant must be enrolled full time in the Capstone Coll of Nursing. Awarded every year. Award may be used only at sponsoring institution.
Contact: Capstone College of Nursing, Box 8700358, Tuscaloosa, AL 35487-0358, (205) 348-6640.

841   Graduate Nursing Education Scholarship

Association of Brethren Caregivers
1451 Dundee Avenue
Elgin, IL 60120
Maximum award: $2,000
College level: Graduate, Doctoral
Majors/Fields: Nursing
Criteria: Applicant must be a member of the Chuch of the Brethren or employed by an agency of the Church of the Brethen. Renewable for up to $4,000.
Contact: Scholarships.

842   Hazel Corbin Assistance Fund

Maternity Center Association Foundation
48 East 92nd Street
New York, NY 10128-1397
(212) 369-7300
Average award: $1,000
Number of awards: 3
Deadline: Open
College level: Graduate
Majors/Fields: Midwifery, nursing
Criteria: Applicant must be a U.S. citizen. Selection is based upon financial need and willingness to practice in the U.S. for one year after graduation. Scholarships are awarded when funds are available.
Contact: Scholarship Coordinator.

843   Laura Moore Cunningham Nursing Scholarship

Boise State University
1910 University Drive
Boise, ID 83725
(208) 385-1664
Minimum award: $1,000
Number of awards: 2
Deadline: March 1
College level: Freshman, Sophomore, Junior, Senior, Graduate
Majors/Fields: Nursing
Criteria: Applicant must be an Idaho resident. Renewable if 3.0 GPA is maintained. Awarded every year. Award may be used only at sponsoring institution.
Contact: Chris Woodward, Financial Aid Counselor.

844   M. Elizabeth Carnegie Scholarship

Nurses Educational Fund
555 West 57th Street
New York, NY 10019
(212) 582-8820, extension 806
Maximum award: $10,000
Minimum award: $2,500
Number of awards: 1
Deadline: March 1
College level: Doctoral
Majors/Fields: Nursing
Criteria: Applicant must be a black registered nurse, member of a national professional nursing organization, and enrolled in a doctoral program in nursing or a nursing-related field, be a U.S. citizen or must have officially declared desire to become one. The award is nonrenewable and based upon academic achievement and evidence of service to the profession. Send $5 check to cover postage and handling when requesting application. Applicant must submit GRE or MAT scores. Awarded every year.
Contact: Barbara Butler, Scholarship Coordinator.

845   Mary L. Lewis Scholarship

Clemson University
G-01 Sikes Hall
Clemson, SC 29634-5123
(803) 656-2280
Average award: $1,000
Number of awards: 3
Deadline: March 1
College level: Freshman, Sophomore, Junior, Senior
Majors/Fields: Nursing
Criteria: Applicant must have a minimum 2.0 GPA. Minimum 3.0 GPA with at least 12 credits per semester is required to retain scholarship. Awarded every year. Award may be used only at sponsoring institution.
Contact: Marvin Carmichael, Director of Financial Aid.

846   McFarland Charitable Foundation Scholarship

Havana National Bank
112 South Orange Street
Havana, iL 62644
(309) 543-3361
Average award: $7,000
Maximum award: $12,000
Minimum award: $1,000
Number of awards: 5
Deadline: May 1
College level: Freshman, Sophomore, Junior, Senior
Majors/Fields: Registered nursing
Criteria: Applicant must contractually agree to practice registered nursing in the Havana, Ill., area for one year for each year of financing. Repayment is required for nonfulfillment of contractual obligation. Award is for several years. Awarded every year.
Contact: Linda M. Butler, Vice President and Senior Trust Officer.

847   Morrison Nursing Scholarship

Boise State University
1910 University Drive
Boise, ID 83725
(208) 385-1664
Minimum award: $1,000
Number of awards: 2
Deadline: March 1
College level: Freshman, Sophomore, Junior, Senior, Graduate
Majors/Fields: Nursing
Criteria: Awarded every year. Award may be used only at sponsoring institution.
Contact: Chris Woodward, Financial Aid Counselor.

848   Nagle Foundation Nursing Scholarship

Boise State University
1910 University Drive
Boise, ID 83725
(208) 385-1664
Minimum award: $1,000
Number of awards: 8
Deadline: March 1
College level: Freshman, Sophomore, Junior, Senior, Graduate
Majors/Fields: Nursing
Criteria: Awarded every year. Award may be used only at sponsoring institution.
Contact: Chris Woodward, Financial Aid Counselor.

849 National Health Service Corps Scholarship Program

Health Resources and Services Administration
Scholarship Programs Branch
4350 East West Highway, 10th Floor
Bethesda, MD 20814
(301) 594-4410
Average award: $9,552
Number of awards: 500
Deadline: Last Friday in March
Majors/Fields: Allopathic medicine, nurse midwifery, nurse practitioner, osteopathic medicine, physician assistant
Criteria: Applicant must be a U.S. citizen enrolled or accepted into an accredited school. Program carries requirement of one year of service for each year of support (two-year minimum) providing primary health services in high-priority Health Professional Shortage Area (HPSA) in the U.S. at sites approved by the Public Health Service.
Contact: National Health Service Corps Scholarship Program, 1010 Wayne Avenue, Suite 240, Silver Spring, MD 20910, (800) 638-0824.

850 Nurses MGF Research Fellowship

Myasthenia Gravis Foundation of America, Inc.
222 South Riverside Plaza
Suite 1540
Chicago, IL 60606
(312) 258-0522, (800) 541-5454
Maximum award: $2,000
Minimum award: $1,500
Deadline: February 1
College level: R.N.s
Criteria: Applicant must be planning research in the area of myasthenia gravis. Awarded every year.
Contact: Fellowships.

851 Nurses' Educational Fund Scholarship

Nurses Educational Fund
555 West 57th Street
New York, NY 10019
(212) 582-8820, extension 806
Maximum award: $10,000
Minimum award: $2,500
Number of awards: 16
Deadline: March 1
College level: Graduate, Doctoral
Majors/Fields: Nursing
Criteria: Applicant must be a registered nurse, member of a national professional nursing association, enrolled full-time in a master's or doctoral program accredited by National League for Nursing, and be a U.S. citizen or declare official intention of becoming one. Selection is based upon academic excellence; evidence of current and future service to the nursing profession is also important. Applicant must submit GRE or MAT scores. A $5.00 fee to cover postage and handling is required when requesting an application. Awarded every year.
Contact: Barbara Butler, Scholarship Coordinator.

852 Nursing Education Loan/Scholarship Program

Mississippi Board of Trustees of State Institutions of Higher Learning
Student Financial Aid
3825 Ridgewood Road
Jackson, MS 39211-6453
(601) 982-6570
Maximum award: $2,000
College level: Freshman
Majors/Fields: Nursing
Criteria: Applicant must be a Mississippi resident pursuing a B.S.Nurs. Renewable if 2.5 GPA is maintained. Awarded every year.
Contact: Mississippi Postsecondary Education Financial Assistance Board, (601) 982-6663.

853 Nursing Education Scholarship

Baptist Hospital
1000 West Moreno Street
Pensacola, FL 32501
(904) 434-4911
Average award: $1,500
Number of awards: 20
Deadline: November 30, April 30
College level: Unspecified undergraduate
Majors/Fields: Nursing
Criteria: Recipient must sign contractual agreement with Baptist Hospital agreeing to work one year as a nurse employed at the prevailing wage for each year the student is in the scholarship program. Should the graduate nurse decline to accept employment with Baptist Hospital upon graduation or be unable to pass the State Board Exam, the scholarship loan must be repaid with seven percent interest. Scholarship is renewable. Scholarship is awarded twice a year.
Contact: Pat Williams, Director of Nursing, Division II.

854 Nursing Fund Scholarship

State Student Assistance Commission of Indiana
150 West Market Street
Suite 500
Indianapolis, IN 46204-2811
(317) 232-2350
Average award: $500
Maximum award: $5,000
Maximum number of awards: 400
Minimum number of awards: 200
College level: Freshman, Sophomore, Junior, Senior
Majors/Fields: Nursing
Criteria: Applicant must be an Indiana resident and demonstrate financial need. Reapplication and satisfactory academic progress are required to retain scholarship. Awarded every year.
Contact: Yvonne D. Heflin, Director of Special Programs.

855 Nursing Grant Program for Persons of Color

Minnesota Higher Education Coordinating Board Division of Student Financial Aid
Suite 400, Capitol Square
550 Cedar Street
St. Paul, MN 55101
(800) 657-3866, (612) 296-3974
Average award: $2,500
Number of awards: 41
College level: Freshman, Sophomore, Junior, Senior
Majors/Fields: Nursing
Criteria: Applicant must be a U.S. citizen, meet state residency requirements, be Asian-/Pacific-American, African-American, American Indian, or Hispanic-American, be enrolled at least half-time, must not be in default on a student loan, demonstrate financial need, and be willing to serve in Minnesota for three years upon receipt of R.N. Applicant must reapply for renewal. Awarded every year.
Contact: Financial Aid Division Staff, (800) 657-3866.

856 Nursing Research Training Award

American Lung Association
Medical Affairs Division
1740 Broadway
New York, NY 10019-4374
(212) 315-8793
Maximum award: $11,000
Deadline: October 1
College level: Doctoral
Majors/Fields: Nursing
Criteria: Applicant must be a professional nurse who has a master's and is enrolled in a full-time doctoral program that has a focus relevant to lung disease. Priority given to those pursuing an academic career. Applicant must be a U.S. or Canadian resident. Renewable for one additional year. Awarded every year.
Contact: Scholarships.

857   Oconee Memorial Hospital Annual Scholarship

Clemson University
G-01 Sikes Hall
Clemson, SC 29634-5123
(803) 656-2280
Average award: $1,000
Number of awards: 3
Deadline: March 1
College level: Freshman, Sophomore, Junior, Senior
Majors/Fields: Nursing
Criteria: Applicant must have a minimum cumulative or predicted 3.0 GPA. Awarded every year. Award may be used only at sponsoring institution.
Contact: Marvin Carmichael, Director of Financial Aid.

858   Oncology Nursing Scholarships

Oncology Nursing Foundation
501 Holiday Drive
Pittsburgh, PA 15220-2749
(412) 921-7373
Maximum award: $3,000
Minimum award: $2,000
Number of awards: 40
Deadline: December 1
College level: Sophomore, Junior, Senior, Graduate Doctoral.
Majors/Fields: Oncology Nursing
Criteria: Applicant must be an R.N. or a nursing student with an interest in and a commitment to oncology nursing. Awarded every year.
Contact: Celia A. Hindes, Development Coordinator.

859   Primary Care Service Corps Scholarship

New York State Health/Primary Care Service Corps
Room 1602, Corning Tower
Empire State Plaza
Albany, NY 12237
(518) 473-7019
Maximum award: $15,000
Number of awards: 110
Deadline: Early April
College level: Junior, Senior
Majors/Fields: Midwife, nurse practitioner, physician assistant
Criteria: Applicant must submit evidence of enrollment in or acceptance for full- or part-time study in a professional program at an institution approved by the New York State Board of Regents, be within 24 months of completing the program for full-time and 48 months for part-time study, and becoming eligible to apply for a license, certificate, or registration in the profession of study, and meet the character and moral standards required for licensure. Recipient must maintain full- or part-time attendance in approved program of study. Awarded every year.
Contact: Phillip Passero, Assistant Director.

860   Registered Nurse Scholarship

Ordean Foundation
501 Ordean Building
Duluth, MN 55802
(218) 726-4785
Average award: $1,685
Maximum award: $2,000
Minimum award: $500
Number of awards: 37
Deadline: March 1
College level: Unspecified undergraduate
Majors/Fields: Nursing, radiation technology
Criteria: Applicant must demonstrate financial need, and be a resident of Duluth, Hermantown or Proctor, or of Canosia, Duluth, Midway, or Rice Lake in Saint Louis County, Minn. Renewable if there is continued financial need. Awarded every year.
Contact: Corrine Helman, Financial Aid Coordinator, Duluth Community College Center, 1309 Rice Lake Road, Duluth, MN 55811.

861   Scholarship for L.V.N.s Becoming Professional Nurses

Texas Higher Education Coordinating Board
Student Financial Assistance
P.O. Box 12788, Capitol Station
Austin, TX 78711-2788
(512) 483-6340
Average award: $1,724
Maximum award: $2,500
Minimum award: $1,500
Number of awards: 69
Deadline: July 15
College level: Freshman, Sophomore, Junior, Senior, Graduate, Doctoral
Majors/Fields: Nursing
Criteria: Applicant must be a Texas resident enrolled at least half time in a program leading to an associate's, bachelor's, or graduate degree in professional nursing at a Texas public or independent non-profit institution. Applicant may have been previously licensed to practice as a licensed vocational nurse. Recipient must reapply each year. No preference is given to renewals. Awarded every year.
Contact: Jane Caldwell, Director of Special Programs.

862   Scholarship for Rural B.S.N. or Graduate Nursing Students

Texas Higher Education Coordinating Board
Student Financial Assistance
P.O. Box 12788, Capitol Station
Austin, TX 78711-2788
(512) 483-6340
Average award: $2,500
Number of awards: 19
Deadline: July 15
College level: Freshman, Sophomore, Junior, Senior, Graduate, Doctoral
Majors/Fields: Nursing
Criteria: Applicant must be a Texas resident from a rural county enrolled at least half time in a program leading to a B.S.N. or graduate degree in professional nursing at any nonprofit public or independent institution in Texas. Recipient must reapply each year. No preference is given to renewals. Awarded every year.
Contact: Jane Caldwell, Director of Special Programs.

863   State Nursing Scholarship

Maryland Higher Education Commission
State Scholarship Administration
16 Francis Street
Annapolis, MD 21401-1781
(410) 974-5370
Maximum award: $2,400
Number of awards: 296
Deadline: March 1
College level: Freshman, Sophomore, Junior, Senior, Doctoral
Majors/Fields: Nursing
Criteria: Applicant must be a Maryland resident, have a minimum 3.0 GPA, and attend a Maryland college, university, or hospital program. Applicant must agree to serve as a full-time nurse in a shortage area of Maryland for one year for each year of award. FAFSA must be submitted by March 1. Minimum 3.0 GPA, satisfactory academic progress, and reapplication are required to retain scholarship. Awarded every year.
Contact: Lula Caldwell, Program Administrator.

864   Thomas S. Dobson Scholarship

University of Calgary
2500 University Drive, NW
Calgary, Alberta, CN T2N 1N4
(403) 220-7872
Average award: $2,500
Number of awards: 1
Deadline: July 15
College level: Freshman
Majors/Fields: Nursing
Criteria: Selection is based upon academic merit and extracurricular activities. Awarded every year. Award may be used only at sponsoring institution.
Contact: J. Van Housen, Director of Student Awards & Financial Aid.

Science/Mathematics

Atmospheric Sciences/Meteorology

865   AMS 75th Anniversary Campaign Scholarship

American Meteorological Society (AMS)
45 Beacon Street
Boston, MA 02108-3693
(617) 227-2426, extension 235
Average award: $2,500
Number of awards: 1
Deadline: June 17
College level: Senior
Majors/Fields: Atmospheric science, hydrologic science, meteorology, oceanic science
Criteria: Applicant must be a U.S. citizen or permanent resident enrolled in an accredited U.S. institution and show clear intent to make atmospheric science a career. Selection is based upon academic excellence and achievement. Awarded every year.
Contact: Stephanie Kehoe, Fellowship/Scholarship Coordinator.

866   AMS/Industry Graduate Fellowship

American Meteorological Society (AMS)
45 Beacon Street
Boston, MA 02108-3693
(617) 227-2426, extension 235
Average award: $15,000
Number of awards: 11
Deadline: January 15
College level: Graduate
Majors/Fields: Atmospheric science, hydrologic science, meteorology, oceanic science
Criteria: Applicant must be a U.S. citizen or permanent resident entering first year of graduate school at an accredited U.S. institution, and be pursuing a full-time course of study. Awarded every year.
Contact: Stephanie Kehoe, Fellowship/Scholarship Coordinator.

867   AMS/Industry Undergraduate Scholarship

American Meteorological Society (AMS)
45 Beacon Street
Boston, MA 02108-3693
(617) 227-2426, extension 235
Average award: $2,000
Deadline: February 15
College level: Junior, Senior
Majors/Fields: Atmospheric science, hydrologic science, meteorology, oceanic science
Criteria: Applicant must be a U.S. citizen or permanent resident, have a minimum 3.0 GPA, and show clear intent to pursue a career in the atmospheric or related oceanic or hydrologic sciences after graduation or graduate school. Satisfactory academic progress, full-time enrollment, and preparation for a career in the atmospheric or related sciences are required to retain scholarship. Awarded every year.
Contact: Stephanie Kehoe, Fellowship/Scholarship Coordinator.

868   Dr. Pedro Grau Undergraduate Scholarship

American Meteorological Society
45 Beacon Street
Boston, MA 02108-3693
(617) 227-2426, extension 235
Average award: $2,500
Number of awards: 1
Deadline: June 17
College level: Senior
Majors/Fields: Atmospheric science, hydrologic science, meteorology, oceanic science
Criteria: Applicant must be a U.S. citizen or permanent resident, enrolled in an accredited U.S. institution, and show clear intent to make atmospheric science a career. Selection is based upon academic excellence and achievements. Awarded every year.
Contact: Stephanie Kehoe, Fellowship/Scholarship Coordinator.

869   Howard T. Orville Scholarship in Meteorology

American Meteorological Society
45 Beacon Street
Boston, MA 02108-3693
(617) 227-2426, extension 235
Average award: $2,000
Number of awards: 1
Deadline: June 15
College level: Senior
Majors/Fields: Meteorology, atmospheric science, oceanic science, hydrologic science
Criteria: Applicant must have a minimum 3.0 GPA, be a U.S. citizen or permanent resident, be enrolled full-time in an accredited U.S. institution, and intend to make atmospheric science a career. Selection is based upon academic excellence and achievement. Awarded every year.
Contact: Stephanie Kehoe, Fellowship/Scholarship Coordinator.

870   Paul H. Kutschenreuter Scholarship

American Meteorological Society
45 Beacon Street
Boston, MA 02108-3693
(617) 227-2426, extension 235
Average award: $5,000
Number of awards: 1
Deadline: June 15
College level: Senior
Majors/Fields: Atmospheric science, hydrologic science, meteorology, oceanic science
Criteria: Applicant must be a U.S. citizen or permanent resident attending an accredited U.S. institution, have a minimum 3.0 GPA, and show clear intent to make the atmospheric or related sciences a career. Selection is based upon academic excellence, achievement, and financial need. Awarded every year.
Contact: Stephanie Kehoe, Fellowship/Scholarship Coordinator.

Biology

871   AFAR Scholarship

American Foundation for Aging Research (AFAR)
North Carolina State University
Box 7622
Raleigh, NC 27695
(919) 515-5679
Average award: $1,000
Minimum award: $500
Number of awards: 6
Deadline: None
College level: Junior, Senior, Doctoral
Majors/Fields: Biology, cell biology, immunology, molecular biology, neurobiology, virology
Criteria: Applicant must be enrolled in a U.S. degree-granting program. Selection is based upon research proposals. Award is for aging research, such as cancer research. $3 fee should accompany request for application. Recipient must make progress towards degree and research to maintain scholarship. Awarded every year.
Contact: Executive Secretary.

872   ASM/NCID Postdoctoral Research Program

American Society for Microbiology (ASM)
Office of Education and Training
1325 Massachusetts Avenue, NW
Washington, DC 20005
(202) 737-3600
Average award: $29,000
Maximum award: $33,000
Minimum award: $28,000
Number of awards: 9
Deadline: December 1
College level: Doctoral
Majors/Fields: Infectious diseases, public health microbiology
Criteria: Applicant must either hold a doctoral degree or have completed a primary residency within the last three years and be a U.S. citizen, permanent resident, or English speaking non-U.S. citizen. Research program lasts for two years. Awarded every year.
Contact: Dana Boyd, (202) 942-9299.

873   Biology Research Scholarship

University of Utah
Financial Aid and Scholarships Office
105 Student Services Building
Salt Lake City, UT 84112
(801) 581-6211
Maximum award: $1,500
Minimum award: $1,000
Number of awards: 20
Deadline: February 1
College level: Freshman, Sophomore, Junior, Senior
Majors/Fields: Biology
Criteria: Applicant must be interested in pursuing laboratory research leading to a career in biological research. Scholarship is renewable. Awarded every year; may be used only at sponsoring institution.
Contact: Biology Department, (801) 581-8921.

874   ESA Undergraduate Scholarship

Entomological Society of America (ESA)
9301 Annapolis Road
Lanham, MD 20706-3115
Maximum award: $1,500
Minimum award: $500
Number of awards: 2
Deadline: May 31
College level: Junior, Senior
Majors/Fields: Biology, entomology, zoology
Criteria: Applicant must be an undergraduate at a recognized university or college in the U.S., Mexico, or Canada. Applicant must have accumulated a minimum of 30 credit hours by the time the award is presented. Selection is based upon demonstrated enthusiasm, interest and achievement in biology, and academic achievements. Special consideration may be given to applicants demonstrating financial need. Awarded every year.
Contact: Scholarships, Education Committee, (301) 731-4535.

875   HHMI Traineeship Program

University of Texas at San Antonio
Office of Student Financial Aid
6900 North Loop 1604 West
San Antonio, TX 78249-0687
(210) 691-4011
Average award: $5,000
Number of awards: 6
Deadline: Open
College level: Freshman, Sophomore, Junior, Senior
Majors/Fields: Biology
Criteria: Applicant must be a U.S. citizen, have a minimum 3.0 GPA, and commit to a career in biomedical research. Minimum 3.0 GPA is required to retain scholarship. Awarded every year. Award may be used only at sponsoring institution.
Contact: Division of Life Sciences, MARC Office, Room 4.02.46 SB.

876   Howard Hughes Medical Institute Predoctoral Fellowships in Biological Sciences

National Research Council
2101 Constitution Avenue
Washington, DC 20418
(202) 334-2872
Minimum award: $14,500
Number of awards: 80
Deadline: Early November
College level: College seniors and graduate students who have completed less than one year of postbaccalaureate work toward a Ph.D. or Sc.D. following completion of undergraduate or medical degree.
Majors/Fields: Cell biology/regulation, genetics, immunology, neuroscience, structural biology
Criteria: Applicant must submit GRE scores and be a U.S. citizen. If not a citizen, applicant must attend U.S. educational institution and submit TOEFL scores if English is not primary language. Fellowship is for three years. Awarded every year.
Contact: Fellowship Office.

877   Jennifer Robinson Memorial Scholarship

Arctic Institute of North America
University of Calgary
2500 University Drive, NW
Calgary, Alberta, CN T2N 1N4
(403) 220-7515
Average award: $5,000
Number of awards: 1
Deadline: May 1
College level: Graduate, Doctoral
Majors/Fields: Biology
Criteria: Awarded to a graduate student in northern biology who best exemplifies the qualities of scholarship that the late Jennifer Robinson brought to her studies at the Institute's Kluane Lake Research Station. Scholarship committee looks for evidence of northern relevance and a commitment to field-oriented research. Submit brief statement of research objectives, three reference letters, curriculum vitae with transcripts, and list of current sources of research funding. Reapplication and satisfactory academic progress are required to retain scholarship. Awarded every year.
Contact: Michael P. Robinson, Executive Director.

878   John L. Gill Scholarship

New Mexico State University
Box 30001
Department 5100
Las Cruces, NM 88003-0001
(505) 646-4105
Average award: Tuition
Deadline: March 1
College level: Sophomore, Junior, Senior
Majors/Fields: Biology, health science, premedicine
Criteria: Applicant must be studying a medically-related field. Preference is given to premedical students who are graduates of a Las Cruces high school. Award is for up to three semesters. Awarded every year. Award may be used only at sponsoring institution.
Contact: College of Arts and Sciences, (505) 646-2001.

879 Minorities' Access to Research Careers Program Scholarship

New Mexico State University
Box 30001
Department 5100
Las Cruces, NM 88003-0001
(505) 646-4105
Average award: Tuition, travel to one scientific meeting, and $3,000 stipend
Minimum award: $3,000
Deadline: March 1
College level: Junior, Senior
Majors/Fields: Biology, biomedical science
Criteria: Applicant must be a minority, have a minimum 3.0 GPA, and demonstrate a strong commitment to a career in biomedical science. Awarded every year. Award may be used only at sponsoring institution.
Contact: College of Arts and Sciences, (505) 646-2001.

880 Predoctoral Minority Fellowship

American Society for Microbiology
Office of Education and Training
1325 Massachusetts Avenue, NW
Washington, DC 20005
(202) 737-3600
Maximum award: $10,000
Deadline: May 1
College level: Doctoral
Majors/Fields: Microbiological sciences
Criteria: Applicant must be a U.S. citizen or permanent resident and a minority predoctoral student. Fellowship begins on September 1 and lasts one year. Scholarship is renewable. Awarded every year.
Contact: Irene Hulede, (202) 942-9295.

881 Predoctoral Ortho-McNeil Fellowship

American Society for Microbiology
Office of Education and Training
1325 Massachusetts Avenue, NW
Washington, DC 20005
(202) 737-3600
Maximum award: $10,000
Deadline: May 1
College level: Doctoral
Majors/Fields: Antimicrobial agents
Criteria: Applicant must be a U.S. citizen or permanent resident and a minority predoctoral student. Fellowship begins on September 1 and lasts two years. Scholarship is renewable.
Contact: Irene Hulede, (202) 942-9295.

882 Summer Research Fellowship

American Society for Microbiology
Office of Education and Training
1325 Massachusetts Avenue, NW
Washington, DC 20005
(202) 737-3600
Average award: $2,000
Maximum award: Fellowship pays $2,000 stipend plus travel and housing.
Number of awards: 15
Deadline: February 1
College level: Junior, Senior, Graduate
Majors/Fields: Biological sciences
Criteria: Applicant must be a U.S. citizen or permanent resident and a third- or fourth-year undergraduate minority student planning to attend graduate school. Fellowship begins on June 1 and lasts eight to ten weeks. Scholarship is renewable.
Contact: Irene Hulede, (202) 942-9295.

883 Terminix Scholarship

Clemson University
G-01 Sikes Hall
Clemson, SC 29634-5123
(803) 656-2280
Average award: $1,600
Number of awards: 2
Deadline: March 1
College level: Freshman, Sophomore, Junior, Senior
Majors/Fields: Entomology
Criteria: Priority goes to entering freshmen, then outstanding juniors or seniors. Satisfactory GPA with at least 12 credits per semester is required to retain scholarship. Awarded every year. Award may be used only at sponsoring institution.
Contact: Marvin Carmichael, Director of Financial Aid.

884 Trustee Scholarship in Raptor Biology

Boise State University
1910 University Drive
Boise, ID 83725
(208) 385-1664
Minimum award: $1,000
Number of awards: 2
Deadline: March 1
College level: Doctoral
Criteria: Awarded every year. Award may be used only at sponsoring institution.
Contact: Chris Woodward, Financial Aid Counselor.

885 Undergraduate Research Fellowship

American Society for Microbiology
Office of Education and Training
1325 Massachusetts Avenue, NW
Washington, DC 20005
(202) 737-3600
Average award: $4,000
Minimum award: $2,500
Number of awards: 13
Deadline: February 1
College level: Sophomore, Junior
Majors/Fields: Microbiological sciences
Criteria: Applicant must be a U.S. citizen or permanent resident and a second- or third-year undergraduate student planning to attend graduate school. Fellowship begins June 1 and lasts three to six months. Reapplication is required for renewal. Awarded every year.
Contact: Dana Boyd, Education Coordinator, (202) 942-9299.

Chemistry

886 Annual Chemistry Scholarship

Clemson University
G-01 Sikes Hall
Clemson, SC 29634-5123
(803) 656-2280
Average award: $2,400
Number of awards: 1
College level: Freshman
Majors/Fields: Chemistry
Criteria: Selection is based upon admissions application. Minimum 3.0 GPA with at least 12 credits per semester is required to retain scholarship. Awarded every year. Award may be used only at sponsoring institution.
Contact: Marvin Carmichael, Director of Financial Aid.

887   Dow Scholarship in Chemistry

Southwest Texas State University
J. C. Kellam Building
San Marcos, TX 78666
(512) 245-2340
Average award: $2,000
Number of awards: 2
Deadline: March 15
College level: Freshman
Majors/Fields: Chemistry
Criteria: Applicant must have good ACT or SAT I scores, a strong high school record in science and mathematics, and have ability and show potential for advanced study in chemistry. Personal interview may be required. Minimum GPA and course load are required to retain scholarship. Awarded every year. Award may be used only at sponsoring institution.
Contact: Department of Chemistry, (512) 245-2315.

888   E.G. Coombe Family Bursary in Chemistry

University of Calgary
2500 University Drive, NW
Calgary, Alberta, CN T2N 1N4
(403) 220-7872
Average award: $1,500
Number of awards: 2
Deadline: June 15
College level: Sophomore, Junior, Senior
Majors/Fields: Chemistry
Criteria: Applicant must be a Canadian citizen or permanent resident. Selection is based primarily upon financial need. Academic merit and extracurricular activities are considered. Awarded every year. Award may be used only at sponsoring institution.
Contact: J. Van Housen, Director of Student Awards & Financial Aid.

889   Eugene T. Scafe Memorial Scholarship

Southwest Missouri State University
Student Financial Aid
901 South National Avenue
Springfield, MO 65804-0095
(417) 836-5000 or (800) 492-7900
Average award: $1,100
Number of awards: 3
Deadline: March 31
College level: Junior, Senior
Majors/Fields: Chemistry
Criteria: Applicant must have a minimum 3.0 cumulative GPA and at least 18 hours in chemistry with a minimum 3.0 GPA. Minimum 3.0 cumulative GPA is required to retain scholarship. Awarded every year. Award may be used only at sponsoring institution.
Contact: Scholarship Committee, (417) 836-5262 or (800) 492-7900.

890   Henry Kreider Memorial Scholarship

University of Toledo
Financial Aid Office
Toledo, OH 43606-3390
(419) 537-2056
Maximum award: $1,000
Number of awards: 3
College level: Junior, Senior
Majors/Fields: Chemistry
Criteria: Awarded every year. Award may be used only at sponsoring institution.
Contact: Chairman, Department of Chemistry.

891   Knapman Chemistry Scholarship

Western Washington University
516 High Street
Bellingham, WA 98226-9006
(206) 650-3471
Average award: $1,000
Number of awards: 2
Deadline: May 1
College level: Sophomore, Junior, Senior
Majors/Fields: Biochemistry, chemistry
Criteria: Applicant must have completed or be currently enrolled in Chemistry 353. Selection is based upon superior talent and achievement in chemistry or biochemistry. Awarded every year. Award may be used only at sponsoring institution.
Contact: Chemistry Department, 207 Haggard Hall, Bellingham, WA 98225, (206) 650-3070.

892   Project SEED College Scholarships

American Chemical Society
1155 16th Street, NW
Washington, DC 20036
Maximum award: $5,000
Minimum award: $4,000
Number of awards: 5
Deadline: February 1
College level: Freshman
Majors/Fields: Chemistry, chemical-related science
Criteria: Applicant must be an alumnus of American Chemical Society's Project SEED. Awarded every year.
Contact: Christine Brennan, Senior Staff Associate, (202) 872-4380.

Earth Science

893   AGI Minority Geoscience Graduate Scholarship

American Geological Institute (AGI)
4220 King Street
Alexandria, VA 22302-1507
(703) 379-2480
Maximum award: $4,000
Deadline: February 1
College level: Graduate, Doctoral
Majors/Fields: Earth science education, hydrology, geology, geophysics, hydrology, meteorology, physical oceanography, planetary geology
Criteria: Applicant must be a U.S. citizen who is black, Hispanic, or Native American (American Indian, Eskimo, Hawaiian, or Samoan). Selection is based upon academic excellence, financial need, and potential for professional success. Satisfactory GPA and three letters of recommendation are required to retain scholarship. Awarded every year.
Contact: Director, AGI Minority Geoscience Scholarships.

894   AGI Minority Geoscience Undergraduate Scholarship

American Geological Institute (AGI)
4220 King Street
Alexandria, VA 22302-1507
(703) 379-2480
Maximum award: $10,000
Number of awards: 30
Deadline: February 1
College level: Freshman, Sophomore, Junior, Senior
Majors/Fields: Earth science education, geochemistry, geology, geophysics, hydrology, meteorology, physical oceanography, planetary geology
Criteria: Applicant must be a U.S. citizen who is black, Hispanic, or Native American (American Indian, Eskimo, Hawaiian, or Samoan) with a minimum 2.8 GPA (minimum 3.0 GPA in science and mathematics). Selection is based upon academic excellence, financial need, and potential for professional success. Minimum 3.0 GPA and three letters of recommendation are required to retain scholarship. Awarded every year.
Contact: Director, AGI Minority Geoscience Scholarships.

895 AMAX Undergraduate Scholarship in Geology

University of Utah
Financial Aid and Scholarships Office
105 Student Services Building
Salt Lake City, UT 84112
(801) 581-6211
Average award: $1,000
Number of awards: 3
Deadline: February 1
College level: Freshman, Sophomore, Junior, Senior
Majors/Fields: Geology
Criteria: Applicant must be a field geology major. Awarded every year. Award may be used only at sponsoring institution.
Contact: Mrs. Donna M. Thomas, 717 William C. Browning Building, Salt Lake City, UT 84112-1183, (801) 581-7062.

896 American Association of Petroleum Geologists Grants-in-Aid

American Association of Petroleum Geologists
P.O. Box 979
Tulsa, OK 74101-0979
(918) 584-2555
Average award: $1,500
Maximum award: $2,000
Number of awards: 55
Deadline: November 1 (southern hemisphere), January 15 (northern hemisphere)
College level: Doctoral
Majors/Fields: Earth science aspects of the petroleum industry
Criteria: Applicant must reapply to continue grant. Awarded every year.
Contact: William A. Morgan, Chairman, Grants-in-Aid.

897 Amoco Foundation Fellowship

University of Utah
Financial Aid and Scholarships Office
105 Student Services Building
Salt Lake City, UT 84112
(801) 581-6211
Average award: $6,000
Number of awards: 1
Deadline: February 1
College level: Graduate, Doctoral
Majors/Fields: Geophysics
Criteria: Awarded every year. Award may be used only at sponsoring institution.
Contact: Mrs. Donna M. Thomas, 717 William C. Browning Building, Salt Lake City, UT 84112-1183, (801) 581-7062.

898 Conoco Scholarship

University of Oklahoma
University Affairs
900 Asp Avenue, Room 236
Norman, OK 73019-0401
(405) 325-1701
Average award: $1,000
Number of awards: 3
Deadline: February 8
College level: Freshman, Sophomore, Junior, Senior
Majors/Fields: Petroleum land management
Criteria: Selection is based upon merit, financial need, and involvement. Awarded every year. Award may be used only at sponsoring institution.
Contact: Director of Division of Petroleum Land Management, 103 Adams Hall, Norman, OK 73019, (405) 325-2551.

899 Geology and Geophysics Department Scholarship

University of Utah
Financial Aid and Scholarships Office
105 Student Services Building
Salt Lake City, UT 84112
(801) 581-6211
Average award: $1,000
Maximum number of awards: 6
Minimum number of awards: 2
Deadline: February 1
College level: Freshman, Sophomore, Junior, Senior, Graduate, Doctoral
Majors/Fields: Geophysics, geology, geoengineering
Criteria: Selection is based primarily upon GPA. Awarded every year. Award may be used only at sponsoring institution.
Contact: Mrs. Donna M. Thomas, 717 William C. Browning Building, Salt Lake City, UT 84112-1183, (801) 581-7062.

900 Geophysics Special Fund Scholarship

University of Utah
Financial Aid and Scholarships Office
105 Student Services Building
Salt Lake City, UT 84112
(801) 581-6211
Average award: $1,500
Number of awards: 5
Deadline: February 1
College level: Freshman, Sophomore, Junior, Senior, Graduate, Doctoral
Majors/Fields: Geophysics
Criteria: Applicant must be a matriculated geophysics major. Awarded every year. Award may be used only at sponsoring institution.
Contact: Dr. Allan A. Ekdale, 602 William C. Browning Building, Salt Lake City, UT 84112-1183, (801) 581-7162.

Environmental Science———

901 Donald A. Williams Scholarship

Soil and Water Conservation Society (SWCS)
7515 Northeast Ankeny Road
Ankeny, IA 50021-9764
(515) 289-2331
Average award: $1,500
Number of awards: 3
Deadline: April 1
College level: Sophomore, Junior
Majors/Fields: Agriculture, conservation, environmental studies, forestry
Criteria: Applicant must be an SWCS member for at least one year, with at least one year work experience, who wishes to improve technical or administrative competence in a conservation-related field through course work at an accredited college or through a program of special study. Attainment of a degree is not required. Financial need must be demonstrated. Awarded every year.
Contact: Scholarship, (800) 843-7645.

902 GCA Awards for Summer Enviromental Studies

Garden Club of America (GCA)
598 Madison Avenue
New York, NY 10022
(212) 753-8287
Average award: $1,500
Number of awards: 2
Deadline: February 15
College level: Sophomore, Junior, Senior
Majors/Fields: Ecology, environmental studies.
Criteria: Award is for a summer course in environmental studies. Preference is given to college students. Awarded every year.
Contact: Mrs. Monica Freeman.

903   Larson Aquatic Research Support Scholarship

American Water Works Association
6666 West Quincy Avenue
Denver, CO 80235
(303) 347-6210
Maximum award: $5,000
Minimum award: $3,000
Number of awards: 2
Deadline: November 15 (M.S.); January 15 (Ph.D.)
College level: Graduate, Doctoral
Majors/Fields: Analytical chemistry, aquatic chemistry, chemistry, civil engineering, environmental chemistry, water supply, water treatment
Criteria: Applicant must be studying at an institution of higher learning in the U.S., Canada, Guam, Puerto Rico, or Mexico. Selection is based upon academic record and leadership potential. Awarded every year.
Contact: Scholarship Coordinator.

904   Laurie Ircandia Memorial Scholarship

University of Calgary
2500 University Drive, NW
Calgary, Alberta, CN T2N 1N4
(403) 220-7872
Average award: $3,500
Number of awards: 1
Deadline: June 15
College level: Junior, Senior
Majors/Fields: Ecology, environmental protection, marine biology, zoology
Criteria: Applicant must intend to pursue graduate study. Selection is based upon academic merit and extracurricular activities in the fields of study. Awarded every year. Award may be used only at sponsoring institution.
Contact: J. Van Housen, Director of Student Awards & Financial Aid.

905   LIFE Scholarship Award

Land Improvement Foundation for Education (LIFE)
1300 Maybrook Drive
P.O. Box 9
Maywood, IL 60153-2434
(708) 344-0700
Minimum award: $1,000
Number of awards: 3
Deadline: March 15
College level: Sophomore, Junior, Senior
Majors/Fields: Conservation, environmental construction
Criteria: Applicant must have a minimum 2.5 GPA. Selection is based upon character worthiness and financial need. Scholarship is renewable.

906   Lindbergh Grant

Charles A. and Anne Morrow Lindbergh Foundation
708 South 3rd Street, Suite 110
Minneapolis, MN 55415-1141
(612) 338-1703
Maximum award: $10,580
Number of awards: 10
Deadline: June 13
Criteria: Selection is based upon the project that best addresses Lindbergh's vision of a balance between the advance of technology and preservation of the human/natural environment. Technical information provided in the application will also be considered. Award must go towards the cost of doing the proposal; it cannot be used for tuition, scholarships, or fellowships.
Contact: Grants Coordinator.

907   Robert A. Canham Scholarship

Water Environment Federation (WEF)
601 Wythe Street
Alexandria, VA 22314-1994
(703) 684-2400, extension 7366
Average award: $2,500
Number of awards: 1
Deadline: March 1
College level: Graduate, Doctoral
Majors/Fields: Water environment
Criteria: Applicant must be accepted into a graduate program in the water environment field and submit a detailed statement (750 to 1,000 words) of degree objectives as related to career goals. Recipient of the scholarship is expected to make a commitment to work in the environmental field for two years after completion of the degree.
Contact: Jennifer Northrop, Membership Development Specialist.

908   Scholarship in Conservation

Soil and Water Conservation Society (SWCS)
7515 Northeast Ankeny Road
Ankeny, IA 50021-9764
(515) 289-2331
Minimum award: $1,000
Number of awards: 12
Deadline: April 1
College level: Junior, Senior
Criteria: Award is for an undergraduate student enrolled in an agricultural or natural resource conservation-related curriculum, working towards a first B.S. degree. Minimum 2.5 GPA is required. Scholarship is renewable. Awarded every year.
Contact: Scholarships, (800) 843-7645.

909   Seiko Youth Challenge

Seiko Corporation of America
c/o DRB Communications
1234 Summer Street
Stamford, CT 06905
(800) 323-1550
Average award: $9,375
Maximum award: $25,000
Minimum award: $5,000
Number of awards: 5
Deadline: February 28
College level: Freshman
Criteria: Selection is based upon imagination and originality of approach, depth of research, methodology, practicality of implementation, and magnitude of local environmental impact. Applicant must identify, research, analyze, and propose a solution to a local environmental problem. Projects may be up to 10 pages in length with up to a 10-page appendix. Applicants must be in grades 9 through 12 working in teams of 2 to 4 people with the guidance of a faculty adviser. Awarded every year.
Contact: Robert Bigda, Program Administrator.

910   Student Paper Competition

Water Environment Federation (WEF)
601 Wythe Street
Alexandria, VA 22314-1994
(703) 684-2400, extension 7366
Maximum award: $1,000
Minimum award: $250
Number of awards: 12
Deadline: January 1
College level: Sophomore, Junior, Senior, Graduate, Doctoral
Majors/Fields: Water environment
Criteria: Selection is based upon relevancy of subject matter and originality of thoughts, concepts, and solutions presented. Papers may deal with any aspect of water pollution control, water quality problems, water-related concerns, or hazardous wastes. To enter, submit a 500- to 1,000-word abstract along with a completed application.
Contact: Jennifer Northrop, Membership Development Specialist.

Life Sciences–General

911   Porter Physiology Fellowships

American Physiological Society
9650 Rockville Pike
Bethesda, MD 20814
Average award: $7,000
Maximum award: $12,000
Minimum award: $2,500
Number of awards: 11
Deadline: June 15; January 15
College level: Doctoral
Majors/Fields: Physiological sciences
Criteria: Applicant must be a U.S. citizen or permanent resident and be a member of one of the following ethnic minority groups: African-American, Hispanic, Native Alaskan, Native American, or Pacific Islander. Renewable for one year if satisfactory progess is made. Awarded every year.
Contact: Dr. Eleanor L. Ison-Franklin, Co-Chairman, Porter Physiology Development Committee, Howard University, College of Medicine, Department of Physiology and Biophysics, 520 W Street, NW, Washington, DC 20059, (202) 806-6346.

Marine Science

912   International Women's Fishing Association Scholarship

International Women's Fishing Association Scholarship Trust
P.O. Drawer 3125
Palm Beach, FL 33480
(813) 689-2496
Average award: $1,000
Maximum award: $2,000
Minimum award: $500
Number of awards: 12
Deadline: March 1
College level: Doctoral
Majors/Fields: Marine science
Criteria: Applicant must be a graduate student in any marine science field studying anywhere in the world. Progress report is required to retain scholarship. Awarded every year.
Contact: Scholarship Trust Secretary.

913   Our World Underwater Scholarship

Our World Underwater Scholarship Society
P.O. Box 4428
Chicago, IL 60680
(312) 666-6846
Maximum award: $12,000
Number of awards: 1
Deadline: January 5
Criteria: Applicant must be a certified SCUBA diver between the ages of 21 and 24, have an associate or four-year degree with a good academic record, and pass a medical physical exam. Applicant should be interested in a career in marine science or a closely related field. Award is for a year of intensive travel. Awarded every year.
Contact: Scholarship Application Coordinator, (312) 666-6525.

914   Seaspace Scholarship

Seaspace, Inc.
P.O. Box 3753
Houston, TX 77253-3753
(713) 467-6675
Average award: $1,000
Number of awards: 19
Deadline: March 1
College level: Junior, Senior, Graduate, Doctoral
Majors/Fields: Marine science
Criteria: Applicant must have a minimum 3.5 undergraduate GPA or 3.0 graduate GPA. Financial need is considered. Awarded every year.
Contact: Judith Jones, Scholarship Coordinator.

Mathematics

915   Andree Memorial Scholarship

University of Oklahoma
University Affairs
900 Asp Avenue, Room 236
Norman, OK 73019-0401
(405) 325-1701
Maximum award: $2,000
Minimum award: $1,000
Maximum number of awards: 3
Deadline: March 20
College level: Graduate
Majors/Fields: Mathematics
Criteria: Applicant must be interested in computer-related mathematics. Selection is based upon academic record, financial need, and leadership as expressed through participation in the U of Oklahoma chapter of Pi Mu Epsilon. Awarded every year. Award may be used only at sponsoring institution.
Contact: Mathematics Department Graduate Advisor, 601 Elm, Norman, OK 73019, (405) 325-6711.

916   Eastman Scholarship in Mathematics

University of Nebraska, Lincoln
14th and R Streets
Lincoln, NE 68588
(402) 472-2030
Average award: $3,000
Maximum award: $4,000
Minimum award: $500
Number of awards: 12
Deadline: January 15
College level: Freshman, Sophomore, Junior, Senior
Majors/Fields: Mathematics
Criteria: Applicant must be a Nebraska high school graduate. Minimum 3.5 GPA, full-time enrollment, and satisfactory progress toward degree in math are required to retain scholarship. Awarded every year. Award may be used only at sponsoring institution.
Contact: Assistant Director of Scholarships.

Physical Sciences

917   AGA Educational Grant

American Gas Association (AGA)
1515 Wilson Boulevard
Arlington, VA 22209
(703) 841-8400
Average award: $1,000
Number of awards: 12
Deadline: April 1
College level: Junior, Senior
Criteria: Half of award is in the form of a loan. Applicant must submit a short essay (300 to 500 words) on the topic, "Why the Natural Gas Association should consider my field of study." Financial need must be demonstrated. Scholarship is renewable. Awarded every year.
Contact: Jane Nelson, Coordinator for Educational Programs.

918   Associated Western Universities–Department of Energy Graduate Fellowship

Associated Western Universities
4190 South Highland Drive, Suite 211
Salt Lake City, UT 84124
(801) 278-0799
Average award: $16,900
Number of awards: 50
Deadline: June 1 (priority)
College level: Doctoral
Majors/Fields: Science, engineering, mathematics
Criteria: Applicant must have completed all on-campus requirements except those related to thesis or dissertation research, preparation, and defense. Research project should be acceptable to the student's university advisor and the facility staff scientist. Applicant must be a U.S. citizen; in some cases, a permanent resident status may qualify. Tenurable only at DOE facilities. Renewable if academic and research performance is satisfactory. Awarded every year.
Contact: Dr. R. Norman Orava, Deputy Director.

919   EOSAT Award for Application of Digital Landsat TM Data

American Society for Photogrammetry and Remote Sensing
ASPRS Awards Program, Suite 210
5410 Grosvenor Lane
Bethesda, MD 20814-2160
(301) 493-0290
Maximum award: $4,000
Deadline: November 8
College level: Sophomore, Senior, Doctoral
Criteria: Applicant must be enrolled full-time at a college or university with image processing facilities. Awarded every year.
Contact: Christopher J. Dyer, Staff Student Liason.

920   Fannie and John Hertz Foundation Fellowship

Fannie and John Hertz Foundation
Box 5032
Livermore, CA 94551-5032
(510) 373-1642
Maximum award: $29,000
Minimum award: $25,000
Number of awards: 28
Deadline: October 20
College level: Doctoral
Majors/Fields: Applied physical sciences, engineering, mathematics
Criteria: Applicant must be a U.S. citizen, with a minimum "A-" grade average during the last two years of undergraduate work, and pursuing a graduate degree in the applied physical sciences (no biological sciences). Students in joint professional degree programs (e.g., M.D./Ph.D) are not eligible. Award is available only at the following institutions: California Inst of Tech, all U of California campuses, Carnegie-Mellon U, U of Chicago, Cornell U, Georgia Inst of Tech, Harvard U, U of Illinois, Johns Hopkins U, Massachusetts Inst of Tech, U of Minnesota, New York U, Polytech U (Brooklyn, NY), Princeton U, Rensselaer Polytech Inst, Rice U, U of Rochester, Stanford U, Texas A&M U, U of Texas-Austin, Vanderbilt U, U of Washington, U of Wisconsin, and Yale U. Renewable for up to five years. Adequate performance is required to retain fellowship. Awarded every year.
Contact: Dr. Wilson K. Talley, President.

921   Joseph F. Dracup Scholarship

American Congress on Surveying and Mapping
Awards Director
5410 Grosvenor Lane
Bethesda, MD 20814-2122
(301) 493-0200
Average award: $2,000
Number of awards: 1
Deadline: January 1
College level: Freshman, Sophomore, Junior, Senior
Majors/Fields: Geodetic surveying
Criteria: Applicant must be committed to a career in geodetic surveying. Awarded every year.
Contact: ACSM Awards Director.

922   Leica Inc. Surveying Scholarship

American Congress on Surveying and Mapping
Awards Director
5410 Grosvenor Lane
Bethesda, MD 20814-2122
(301) 493-0200
Average award: $1,000
Number of awards: 2
Deadline: January 1
College level: Freshman, Sophomore, Junior, Senior
Majors/Fields: Surveying
Criteria: Applicant must be enrolled in a four-year degree program. Scholarship recipient also earns a $2,000 credit for his or her school for purchase of Leica equipment and $500 credit to graduating senior for purchase of Leica equipment. Awarded every year.
Contact: ACSM Awards Director.

923   New Mexico Space Grant Graduate Fellowship

New Mexico State University
Box 30001
Department 5100
Las Cruces, NM 88003-0001
(505) 646-4105
Maximum award: $8,000
Number of awards: 3
Deadline: March 1
College level: Graduate, Doctoral
Majors/Fields: Astronomy, biology, chemistry, computer science, earth science, mathematics, physics
Criteria: Applicant must be a U.S. citizen enrolled in the Coll of Engineering or Coll of Arts and Sciences with a minimum cumulative GPA of 3.25. Preference is given to women and minority applicants. Awarded every year. Award may be used only at sponsoring institution.
Contact: Greeley W. Myers, Director of Financial Aid.

924   New Mexico Space Grant Undergraduate Scholarship

New Mexico State University
Box 30001
Department 5100
Las Cruces, NM 88003-0001
(505) 646-4105
Maximum award: $3,000
Number of awards: 5
Deadline: March 1
College level: Freshman, Sophomore, Junior, Senior
Majors/Fields: Astronomy, biology, chemistry, computer science, earth science, mathematics, physics
Criteria: Applicant must be a U.S. citizen, enroll in the Coll of Engineering or Coll of Arts and Sciences, and have a minimum cumulative GPA of 3.25. Preference is given to women and minority students. Awarded every year. Award may be used only at sponsoring institution.
Contact: Greeley W. Myers, Director of Financial Aid.

925   NPSC Graduate Fellowships for Minorities and Women

National Physical Science Consortium (NPSC)
New Mexico State University
Box 30001, Department 3NPS
Las Cruces, NM 88003-8001
(800) 952-4118, (505) 646-6038
Average award: Tuition and fees plus $10,000 for years one and two; $12,500 for years three and four; and $15,000 for years five and six. Fellowship is given for up to six years.
Maximum award: $15,000
Minimum award: $12,500
Number of awards: 27
Deadline: November 15
College level: Graduating seniors and students who have been out of graduate studies for at least a year and wish to return for a doctorate
Majors/Fields: Astronomy, chemistry, computer science, geology, materials science, mathematical sciences, physics
Criteria: Applicant must be a U.S. citizen, who is African-American, Hispanic, Native American, Eskimo, Aleut, Polynesian, and/or a woman. Applicant should have at a minimum 3.0 GPA and be eligible to pursue graduate study at a participating NPSC-member university. Applicant cannot be currently enrolled in graduate studies at a Ph.D.-granting institution which has field of study. Recipient must maintain acceptable academic standing and full-time status to retain fellowship. Awarded every year.
Contact: Ms. L. Nan Snow, Executive Director.

926   NSPS Scholarship

American Congress on Surveying and Mapping
Awards Director
5410 Grosvenor Lane
Bethesda, MD 20814-2122
(301) 493-0200
Average award: $1,000
Number of awards: 2
Deadline: January 1
College level: Freshman, Sophomore, Junior, Senior
Majors/Fields: Surveying
Criteria: Applicant must be enrolled in a four-year degree program.
Awarded every year.
Contact: ACSM Awards Director.

927   William A. Fischer Memorial Scholarship

American Society for Photogrammetry and Remote Sensing
ASPRS Awards Program, Suite 210
5410 Grosvenor Lane
Bethesda, MD 20814-2160
(301) 493-0290
Maximum award: $2,000
Number of awards: 1
Deadline: November 8
College level: Graduate, Doctoral
Majors/Fields: Remote sensing
Criteria: Applicant must use award to pursue graduate studies in new and innovative uses of remote sensing data/techniques that relate to the natural, cultural, or agricultural resources of the earth. Awarded when sufficient funds are available and qualified applicants apply.
Contact: Christopher J. Dyer, Staff Student Liaison, 5410 Grosvenor Lane, Suite 210, Bethesda, MD 20814-2160.

Physics

928   Congressional Science Fellowship

American Geophysical Union
2000 Florida Avenue, NW
Washington, DC 20009
Maximum award: $40,000
Number of awards: 1
Deadline: February 15
College level: Doctoral
Criteria: Applicant must be a member of the American Geophysical Union and a U.S. citizen or permanent resident. Financial need is not considered. Awarded every year.
Contact: Patricia Azriel, Administrative Secretary, (202) 462-6900.

929   Norcen Energy Canadian Scholarship Series in Geology and Geophysics

University of Calgary
2500 University Drive, NW
Calgary, Alberta, CN T2N 1N4
(403) 220-7872
Average award: $1,500
Number of awards: 2
Deadline: June 15
College level: Junior, Senior
Majors/Fields: Geology, geophysics
Criteria: Applicant must be a Canadian citizen or permanent resident. Special consideration is given to applicants expressing interest in the oil and gas industry. Selection is based upon academic merit, financial need, and extracurricular activities. Awarded every year. Award may be used only at sponsoring institution.
Contact: J. Van Housen, Director of Student Awards & Financial Aid.

930   Physics and Astronomy Undergraduate Work Grant

Southwest Missouri State University
Student Financial Aid
901 South National Avenue
Springfield, MO 65804-0095
(417) 836-5000 or (800) 492-7900
Average award: $1,000
Number of awards: 4
Deadline: March 31
College level: Sophomore, Junior, Senior
Majors/Fields: Astronomy, physics
Criteria: Applicant must demonstrate scholarship and an interest in science through projects and/or presentations. Reapplication is required to retain scholarship. Awarded every year. Award may be used only at sponsoring institution.
Contact: Scholarship Committee, (417) 836-5262 or (800) 492-7900.

931   SEG Foundation Scholarship

Society of Exploration Geophysicists (SEG) Foundation
P.O. Box 702740
Tulsa, OK 74170-2740
(918) 493-3516
Average award: $1,200
Maximum award: $3,000
Minimum award: $500
Number of awards: 80
Deadline: March 1
College level: Freshman, Sophomore, Junior, Senior, Graduate, Doctoral
Majors/Fields: Geophysics
Criteria: Applicant must intend to pursue a college course directed toward a career in exploration geophysics and have an interest in and aptitude for physics, mathematics, and geology. Financial need is considered, but the application is most important. Satisfactory scholastic standing, availability of funds, and a course of study leading to a career in exploration geophysics are required to retain scholarship. Awarded every year.
Contact: Marge Gerhart, Scholarship Coordinator, (918) 493-2074.

Sciences–General

932   AAAS Mass Media Science and Engineering Fellows Program

American Association for the Advancement of Science (AAAS)
1333 H Street, NW
Washington, DC 20005
(202) 326-6760
Maximum award: $4,000
Number of awards: 15
Deadline: January 15
College level: Advanced natural sciences, social sciences, and engineering students (graduate or outstanding junior or senior undergraduates)
Majors/Fields: Engineering, natural sciences, social sciences
Criteria: Applicant must be an advanced student (graduate or outstanding junior or senior undergraduate) in the natural sciences, social sciences, or engineering. Program places students as reporters, researchers, and production assistants for a ten-week period during the summer at radio stations, television stations, networks, newspapers, and magazines.
Contact: Amie E. Hubbard, Coordinator, (202) 326-6670.

933   AACC Graduate Fellowships

American Association of Cereal Chemists (AACC)
3340 Pilot Knob Road
St. Paul, MN 55121-2097
Average award: $2,000
Maximum award: $3,000
Minimum award: $1,000
Number of awards: 7
Deadline: April 3
College level: Graduate, Doctoral
Majors/Fields: Cereal science
Criteria: Applicant must be enrolled in a full-time graduate program or have been accepted to a full-time graduate program. Recipient must reapply on same basis as new applicants. Awarded every year.
Contact: Dr. Elwood F. Caldwell, Chairman, AACC Scholarship Jury, (612) 454-7250.

934   Achievement Reward for College Scientists (ARCS) Foundation Scholarship

University of Colorado at Boulder
Campus Box 106
Boulder, CO 80309-0106
(303) 492-5091
Average award: $2,000
Number of awards: 4
College level: Freshman, Sophomore, Junior, Graduate, Doctoral
Majors/Fields: Engineering, cellular biology, chemistry, developmental biology, molecular biology, physics
Criteria: Applicant must be a full-time student, exceptional in area of study, have a minimum 3.5 GPA, be a U.S. citizen, and have at least 18 months left towards degree. When a scholarship becomes available, each department recommends one candidate to the Office of Financial Aid. Award may be held for multiple years. Awarded every year. Award may be used only at sponsoring institution.
Contact: Office of Financial Aid.

935   American Association for Geodetic Surveying Fellowship

American Congress on Surveying and Mapping
Awards Director
5410 Grosvenor Lane
Bethesda, MD 20814-2122
(301) 493-0200
Average award: $2,000
Number of awards: 1
Deadline: January 1
College level: Graduate, Doctoral
Majors/Fields: Geodesy, geodetic surveying
Criteria: Applicant must be enrolled in a graduate study program. Awarded every year.
Contact: ACSM Awards Director, 5410 Grosvenor Lane, Bethesda, MD 20814-2122.

936   Arthur Holly Compton Fellowship in the Natural Sciences and Mathematics

Washington University
One Brookings Drive
Campus Box 1089
St. Louis, MO 63130
(314) 935-6000 or (800) 638-0700
Average award: $17,750
Number of awards: 6
College level: Freshman
Majors/Fields: Mathematics, natural science
Criteria: Selection is based upon academic merit without regard to financial need. Satisfactory academic performance is required to retain scholarship. Awarded every year. Award may be used only at sponsoring institution.
Contact: Office of Undergraduate Admissions.

937   Barry M. Goldwater Scholarship

Portland State University
P.O. Box 751
Portland, OR 97207-0751
(503) 725-5270
Maximum award: $7,000
Majors/Fields: Engineering, mathematics, natural science
Criteria: Applicant must have a minimum 3.0 GPA. Top quarter of class candidates are nominated by the university. Awarded every year. Award may be used only at sponsoring institution.
Contact: Scholarships, Mathematical Sciences Department, (503) 725-3432.

938   Behavioral Science Dissertation Grant

American Lung Association
Medical Affairs Division
1740 Broadway
New York, NY 10019-4374
(212) 315-8793
Maximum award: $21,000
Deadline: October 1
College level: Doctoral
Majors/Fields: Science
Criteria: Awarded to full-time doctoral students in the fields of science related to the social, behavioral, epidemiologic, psychological, and educational aspects of lung health. Applicant must have an academic career focus and be a U.S. or Canadian resident. Renewable for three years. Awarded every year.

939   Berntsen International Scholarship in Surveying Technology

American Congress on Surveying and Mapping
Awards Director
5410 Grosvenor Lane
Bethesda, MD 20814-2122
(301) 493-0200
Average award: $1,500
Number of awards: 1
Deadline: January 1
College level: Junior college/technical college
Majors/Fields: Surveying technology
Criteria: Applicant must be enrolled in a two-year program. Awarded every year.
Contact: ACSM Awards Director.

940   Boettcher Foundation Fellowship

University of Colorado at Boulder
Campus Box 106
Boulder, CO 80309-0106
(303) 492-5091
Average award: $6,000
Number of awards: 1
Deadline: First week in April
College level: Doctoral
Majors/Fields: Natural sciences, mathematics
Criteria: Selection is based upon academic merit. Awarded every year. Award may be used only at sponsoring institution.
Contact: Office of Financial Aid.

941 C. Louis and Thelma Ferrell Van Buren Scholarship

Southwest Missouri State University
Student Financial Aid
901 South National Avenue
Springfield, MO 65804-0095
(417) 836-5000 or (800) 492-7900
Average award: $1,300
Number of awards: 2
Deadline: March 31
College level: Junior, Senior
Majors/Fields: Mathematics, science
Criteria: Applicant must have a minimum 3.0 cumulative GPA. Participation in extracurricular activities is also considered. Reapplication is required to retain scholarship. Awarded every year. Award may be used only at sponsoring institution.
Contact: Scholarship Committee, (417) 836-5262 or (800) 492-7900.

942 Dean's Science Scholarship

DePaul University
25 East Jackson Boulevard
Suite 100
Chicago, IL 60604
(312) 362-8704
Maximum award: $7,000
Minimum award: $2,000
Deadline: February 1
College level: Freshman
Majors/Fields: Science
Criteria: Applicant must rank in the top tenth of class, have a minimum composite ACT score of 26 or combined SAT I score of 1050, and have a strong interest in the study of science. Minimum 2.75 GPA during first year, 3.0 GPA thereafter, is required to retain scholarship. Awarded every year. Award may be used only at sponsoring institution.
Contact: Admissions Office.

943 Dr. Robert H. Goddard Scholarship

National Space Club
655 Fifteenth Street, NW
Suite 300
Washington, DC 20005
Maximum award: $10,000
Number of awards: 1
Deadline: January 1
College level: Senior, Graduate, Doctoral
Majors/Fields: Aeronautics, engineering, science
Criteria: Applicant must be a U.S. citizen intending to pursue undergraduate or graduate studies in science or engineering. Selection is based upon college record, recommendations, accomplishments demonstrating creativity and leadership, scholastic plans for the aerospace sciences and technology, and proven past research in space-related science and engineering. Applicant is eligible to compete for a second year if circumstances and accomplishments are warranted. Awarded every year.
Contact: Stephen E. Dwornik, Chairman, Scholarship Committee.

944 Dupont Challenge/Science Essay Awards Program

General Learning Corporation
60 Revere Drive, Suite 200
Northbrook, IL 60062
(708) 205-3000
Maximum award: $1,500
Minimum award: $50
Number of awards: 54
Deadline: January 27
College level: Freshman
Majors/Fields: Science
Criteria: Applicant must be currently enrolled in a public or nonpublic school in the U.S., U.S. territories, or Canada in grades 7 through 12. A 700- to 1,000-word essay and official entry form are required. Awarded every year.
Contact: General Learning Corporation.

945 Duracell/National Science Teachers Association Scholarship Competition

National Science Teachers Association (NSTA)
1840 Wilson Blvd.
Arlington, VA 22201-3000
(703) 312-9258
Maximum award: $20,000
Minimum award: $100
Number of awards: 100
Deadline: Mid-January
College level: Freshman
Criteria: Applicant must be a student in grades 9-12, reside in the U.S. or its territories, and must create and build a working device powered by batteries that can perform a practical function. The top 100 finalists will send their actual devices in for judging. Awarded every year.
Contact: Eric Crossley, National Science Teachers Association.

946 Eloise Gerry Fellowship

Sigma Delta Epsilon/Graduate Women in Science
P.O. Box 19947
San Diego, CA 92159
Average award: $1,000
Maximum award: $5,000
Minimum award: $500
Number of awards: 4
Deadline: December 1
College level: Doctoral
Majors/Fields: Sciences
Criteria: Fellowship is for research or research support, not for tuition or scholarship support. Applicant may not apply for a Sigma Delta Epsilon Fellowship in the same year. Open to women only. Awarded every year.
Contact: Scholarships.

947 Ford Foundation Postdoctoral Fellowships for Minorities

National Research Council
2101 Constitution Avenue
Washington, DC 20418
(202) 334-2872
Minimum award: $25,000
Number of awards: 20
Deadline: Early January
College level: Postdoctoral work
Majors/Fields: Behavioral sciences, biology, engineering, humanities, mathematics, physical sciences, social sciences
Criteria: Applicant must have completed a Ph.D. or Sc.D. within seven years, be a U.S. citizen or national, and be an Alaskan Native, Native American, Black/African-American, Mexican-American, Pacific Islander, or Puerto Rican. Awarded every year.
Contact: Fellowship Office.

948 Ford Foundation Predoctoral and Dissertation Fellowships for Minorities

National Research Council
2101 Constitution Avenue
Washington, DC 20418
(202) 334-2872
Minimum award: $12,000
Number of awards: 75
Deadline: Early November
College level: College seniors and graduate students who have completed no more than 30 semester/45 quarter hours of graduate work in fields eligible for support
Majors/Fields: Behavioral sciences, biological sciences, engineering, humanities, mathematics, social sciences, physical sciences
Criteria: Applicant must be U.S. citizen or national who is an Alaskan Native, Native American, Black/African-American, Mexican American, Pacific Islander, or Puerto Rican. Fellowship is awarded for three years; continued support is based on recipient's progress. Awarded every year.
Contact: Fellowship Office.

949   Grants for Orchid Research

American Orchid Society
6000 South Olive Avenue
West Palm Beach, FL 33405
(407) 585-8666
Average award: $5,000
Maximum award: $10,000
Minimum award: $1,000
Number of awards: 2
Deadline: January 1; August 1
Majors/Fields: Orchid research
Criteria: Applicant must be associated with an accredited institution of higher education or an appropriate research institute and be qualified for research. Awarded every year.
Contact: Lee S. Cooke, Executive Director.

950   Horton Research Grant

American Geophysical Union
2000 Florida Avenue, NW
Washington, DC 20009
Average award: $10,000
Number of awards: 2
Deadline: March 1
College level: Ph.D. candidates
Majors/Fields: Hydrology, water resources
Criteria: Selection is based upon technical merits of the proposed dissertation topic and procedures, clarity of the presentation with respect to the study's objectives, and feasibility of meeting the objectives during the period of the award. Financial need is not considered. Awarded every year.
Contact: Patricia Azriel, Administrative Secretary, (202) 462-6900.

951   International Science and Engineering Fair

Science Service, Inc.
1719 N Street, NW
Washington, DC 20036
(202) 785-2255
Maximum award: $5,000
Minimum award: $1,000
College level: Freshman
Majors/Fields: Science, engineering
Criteria: Applicant must participate in an ISEF-affiliated fair. Awarded every year.
Contact: Director of Youth Programs.

952   Margaret Bush Wilson Scholarship

University of Missouri–Saint Louis
8001 Natural Bridge Road
Saint Louis, MO 63121
(314) 553-6396
Average award: $3,000
Number of awards: 15
Deadline: April 1
College level: Freshman
Majors/Fields: Biology, chemistry, computer science, mathematics, physics
Criteria: Applicant must have been heavily involved in the Bridge Program. Satisfactory academic progress and completion of 24 hours per year are required to retain scholarship. Awarded every year. Award may be used only at sponsoring institution.
Contact: James D. Reed, Financial Aid Advisor.

953   Minority Access for Research Careers Scholarship

University of Texas at San Antonio
Office of Student Financial Aid
6900 North Loop 1604 West
San Antonio, TX 78249-0687
(210) 691-4011
Average award: $7,004
Number of awards: 10
College level: Junior, Senior
Majors/Fields: Engineering, sciences
Criteria: Applicant must be a minority U.S. citizen or have a permanent visa, have a minimum 3.0 GPA, and make a commitment to graduate school and a career in biomedical research. Minimum 3.0 GPA is required to retain scholarship. Awarded every year. Award may be used only at sponsoring institution.
Contact: Division of Life Sciences, MARC Office, Room 4.02.46 SB.

954   Minority Biomedical Research Scholarship

University of Texas at San Antonio
Office of Student Financial Aid
6900 North Loop 1604 West
San Antonio, TX 78249-0687
(210) 691-4011
Maximum award: $7,500
Minimum award: $6,000
Number of awards: 28
College level: Freshman, Sophomore, Junior, Senior, Graduate, Doctoral
Majors/Fields: Engineering, science
Criteria: Applicant must be a U.S. citizen or have a permanent visa, have a minimum undergraduate GPA of 2.7 or minimum graduate GPA of 3.0, and make a commitment to a career in biomedical research. Minimum 2.7 GPA is required to retain scholarship. Awarded every year. Award may be used only at sponsoring institution.
Contact: Division of Life Sciences, MBRS Office, Room 4.02.46 SB.

955   National Institute of Health Minority High School Scholarship

University of Texas at San Antonio
Office of Student Financial Aid
6900 North Loop 1604 West
San Antonio, TX 78249-0687
(210) 691-4011
Average award: $4,000
Number of awards: 10
Deadline: April 1
College level: Freshman
Majors/Fields: Science
Criteria: Applicant must be a U.S. citizen. Scholarship is renewable. Awarded every year; may be used only at sponsoring institution.
Contact: Division of Life Sciences, MBRS Office, Room 4.02.46 SB.

956   National Science Foundation Graduate Research Fellowship

National Science Foundation Graduate Research Fellowship Program
Oak Ridge Associated Universities
P.O. Box 3010
Oak Ridge, TN 37831-3010
(615) 483-3344
Maximum award: $14,400
Number of awards: 1000
Deadline: November 4
College level: Graduate, Doctoral
Majors/Fields: Engineering, mathematics, science
Criteria: Applicant must be a U.S. citizen, national, or permanent resident alien. For the Minority Program, applicant must be a member of one of the following ethnic groups: American Indian, Black/African-American, Hispanic, Native Alaskan (Eskimo or Aleut), or Native Pacific Islander (Polynesian or Micronesian). Fellowships are awarded for study and research leading to master's or doctoral degrees in the mathematical, physical, biological, engineering, and behavioral and social sciences, including the history of science and the philosophy of science, and to research-based Ph.D. degrees in science education. Awarded every year.
Contact: Jeffrey Johnson, Operations Manager.

957   National Science Scholars Program

New York State Education Department
Bureau of Postsecondary Grants Administration
Cultural Education Center
Albany, NY 12230
(518) 474-5705
Maximum award: $5,000
College level: Freshman
Majors/Fields: Computer science, engineering, life science, mathematics, physical science
Criteria: Scholarships will be awarded to two students in each Congressional district of New York State, one of whom must be a woman. Applicant must be a high school senior or a student earning a GED diploma. Awarded every year.
Contact: Office of Equity and Access.

958   NSTF of the Graphic Arts Graduate Fellowship

Technical Association of the Graphic Arts
National Scholarship Trust Fund of the Graphic Arts
4615 Forbes Avenue
Pittsburgh, PA 15213-3796
(412) 621-6941
Maximum award: $4,000
Minimum award: $1,500
Deadline: January 10
College level: Graduate, Doctoral
Majors/Fields: Business technology, chemistry, engineering, industrial education, mathematics, physics
Criteria: Applicant must plan to seek employment at the managerial or educational level in the graphic communications industry, have demonstrated ability and special aptitude for advanced education in the sciences and education, and be admitted into a graduate program in an area of study that has potential application in the printing, publishing, and packaging industries. Selection is based upon academic record, recommendations, and test scores. Reapplication is required to retain scholarship. Awarded every year.
Contact: Peggy Dimperio, Business Manager.

959   Parkinson Scholarship in Technology

Boise State University
1910 University Drive
Boise, ID 83725
(208) 385-1664
Minimum award: $1,000
Number of awards: 3
Deadline: March 1
College level: Freshman, Sophomore, Junior, Senior, Graduate
Criteria: Awarded every year. Award may be used only at sponsoring institution.
Contact: Chris Woodward, Financial Aid Counselor.

960   Sigma Delta Epsilon Fellowship

Sigma Delta Epsilon/Graduate Women in Science
P.O. Box 19947
San Diego, CA 92159
Average award: $2,000
Maximum award: $4,000
Minimum award: $1,500
Deadline: December 1
College level: Doctoral
Majors/Fields: Sciences
Criteria: Fellowship is for research or research support, not for tuition or scholarship support. Applicant may not also apply for an Eloise Gerry Fellowship in the same year. Open to women only. For more information, send self-addressed, stamped ($0.55) business envelope. Awarded every year.

961   Sigma Xi Grants-in-Aid of Research

Sigma Xi, the Scientific Research Society
99 Alexander Drive
Research Triangle Park, NC 27709
Average award: $600
Maximum award: $2,500
Minimum award: $100
Number of awards: 879
Deadline: February 1, May 1, November 1
College level: Undergraduate and graduate students in degree programs
Majors/Fields: Scientic investigation
Criteria: Recipient must reapply for consideration.
Contact: Grants.

962   Southwestern Bell Scholarship

University of Missouri–Saint Louis
8001 Natural Bridge Road
Saint Louis, MO 63121
(314) 553-6396
Average award: $2,500
Number of awards: 2
Deadline: April 1
College level: Freshman
Criteria: Applicant must have a minimum cumulative 3.0 GPA and have participated in the Engelmann Math and Science Inst or the Bridge Program. Minimum 3.2 cumulative GPA is required to retain scholarship. Awarded every year. Award may be used only at sponsoring institution.
Contact: James D. Reed, Financial Aid Advisor.

963   SPIE Educational Grants and Scholarships in Optical Engineering

International Society for Optical Engineering (SPIE)
SPIE Scholarship Committee
P.O. Box 10
Bellingham, WA 98227-0010
(360) 676-3290
Maximum award: $5,000
Minimum award: $500
Number of awards: 20
Deadline: April 7
College level: Freshman, Sophomore, Junior, Senior, Graduate, Doctoral
Majors/Fields: Optical/opto-electronic applied science, optical/opto-electronic engineering
Criteria: Selection is based upon the long-range contribution which the granting of the award would make to optics and optical engineering. Financial need is not a factor. Awarded every year.
Contact: Susan M. Weihe, Scholarship Committee, P.O. Box 10, Bellingham, WA 98227-0010.

964   Tandy Technology Scholars Scholarship

Tandy Technology Scholars
P.O. Box 32897
TCU Station
Fort Worth, TX 76129
(817) 924-4087
Average award: $1,000
Number of awards: 100
Deadline: Mid-October
College level: Freshman
Criteria: Each enrolled school can nominate one applicant; schools with a senior class exceeding 300 may nominate two applicants. Applicant must excel in mathematics, science, or computer science. Nomination forms are mailed to enrolled high schools only, not individual students. Awarded every year.
Contact: Kaye Thornton, Program Coordinator.

965   Thomas Edison/Max McGraw Scholarship Program

National Science Supervisors Association
Edison/McGrow Scholarship
P.O. Box 380057
East Hartford, CT 06138-0057
(203) 633-5231, extension 490
Average award: $3,000
Maximum award: $5,000
Minimum award: $1,500
Number of awards: 10
Deadline: December 15
College level: Freshman, students in grades 9 through 12
Criteria: Reapplication with project is required for renewal. Awarded every year.
Contact: Dr. Kenneth R. Roy, NSSA Executive Director.

966   Utah Air Force Association Scholarship

Utah State University
Logan, UT 84322-0160
(801) 750-1129
Average award: In-state tuition
Deadline: March 1
College level: Junior, Senior
Majors/Fields: Engineering, science
Criteria: Applicant must have a minimum cumulative 3.0 GPA and 3.5 GPA in major. Application should include a description of how applicant has contributed or expects to contribute to the nation's aerospace efforts. Awarded every third year, with the next year being the 1997–98 academic year. Award may be used only at sponsoring institution.
Contact: Mark Tenhoeue, Director of High School/College Relations.

967   Westinghouse Science Talent Search

Science Service, Inc.
1719 N Street, NW
Washington, DC 20036
(202) 785-2255
Maximum award: $40,000
Minimum award: $1,000
Maximum number of awards: 40
Minimum number of awards: 40
Deadline: December 1
College level: Freshman
Majors/Fields: Science, mathematics, engineering
Criteria: Applicant must be in the last year of secondary school, and enter the competition by submitting a written report on an independent research project in science, mathematics, or engineering, along with standardized test scores, transcript, and official entry form. Satisfactory academic standing is required to retain scholarship. Awarded every year.
Contact: Director of Youth Programs.

968   William H. Greaves Undergraduate Scholarship

Northern Kentucky University
Administrative Center 416
Nunn Drive
Highland Heights, KY 41099-7101
(606) 572-5144
Average award: In-state tuition and books
Deadline: February 1
College level: Freshman, Sophomore, Junior, Senior
Majors/Fields: Computer science, electrical engineering technology, engineering, manufacturing technology, mathematics, science
Criteria: Freshman applicant must rank in top quarter of class and have a minimum ACT composite score of 25; upperclass applicant must have a minimum cumulative GPA of 3.0. Award is renewable for two to three years. Awarded every year. Award may be used only at sponsoring institution.
Contact: Robert E. Sprague, Director of Financial Aid.

Social Science/Political Science/Law

Home Economics

969   Alumni Research Grant

Phi Upsilon Omicron
208 Mount Hall, 1050 Carmack Road
The Ohio State University
Columbus, OH 43210
(614) 421-7860
Average award: $2,000
Number of awards: 1
Deadline: in March
College level: Post-graduate research
Majors/Fields: Home economics
Criteria: Applicant must be a Phi Upsilon Omicron member proposing postgraduate research work not necessarily leading to an advanced degree. Selection is based upon the use of money in applicant's research, value of research problem, and professional aims and goals. Awarded in odd numbered years.
Contact: National Office.

970   Candle Fellowship

Phi Upsilon Omicron
208 Mount Hall, 1050 Carmack Road
The Ohio State University
Columbus, OH 43210
(614) 421-7860
Average award: $1,000
Number of awards: 2
Deadline: March 1
College level: Graduate
Majors/Fields: Home economics
Criteria: Applicant must be a Phi Upsilon Omicron member. Selection is based upon scholastic record, honors, extracurricular activities, scholarly work, and statement of professional goals. Awarded every year.
Contact: National Office.

971   Diamond Anniversary Fellowships

Phi Upsilon Omicron
208 Mount Hall, 1050 Carmack Road
The Ohio State University
Columbus, OH 43210
(614) 421-7860
Average award: $1,000
Number of awards: 2
Deadline: March 1
College level: Graduate, Doctoral
Majors/Fields: Home economics
Criteria: Applicant must be a Phi Upsilon Omicron member. Selection is based upon scholastic record, honors, extracurricular activities, scholarly work, and statement of professional goals. Awarded every year.
Contact: National Office.

972   Gerber Companies Foundation Scholarship

Utah State University
Logan, UT 84322-0160
(801) 750-1129
Average award: Full tuition and fees
Number of awards: 2
Deadline: March 1
College level: Sophomore, Junior, Senior
Majors/Fields: Family life
Criteria: Applicant must be a female student in the Coll of Family Life who has one or more children of five years of age or younger. Preference is given to single parents. Awarded every year. Award may be used only at sponsoring institution.
Contact: Mark Tenhoeue, Director of High School/College Relations.

973   Hazel Putnam Roach Fellowship

American Association of Family and Consumer Sciences
1555 King Street
Alexandria, VA 22314
(703) 706-4600
Average award: $3,000
Number of awards: 1
Deadline: January 16
College level: Graduate
Majors/Fields: Home economics
Criteria: Applicant must be a U.S. citizen. Awarded every year.
Contact: Fellowships.

974   Jewell L. Taylor Fellowship

American Association of Family and Consumer Sciences
1555 King Street
Alexandria, VA 22314
(703) 706-4600
Average award: $5,000
Number of awards: 1
Deadline: January 16
College level: Graduate, Doctoral
Majors/Fields: Home economics
Criteria: Applicant must be a U.S. citizen. Awarded every year.
Contact: Foundation Associate.

975   Mary Irene Waters Scholarship

Montgomery County Association for Family and Community Education
18410 Muncaster Road
P.O. Box 5556
Derwood, MD 20855
(301) 590-9638
Maximum award: $2,000
Minimum award: $1,000
Maximum number of awards: 4
Minimum number of awards: 2
Deadline: March 31
College level: Sophomore, Junior, Senior, Graduate, Doctoral
Majors/Fields: Child care
Criteria: Applicant must be enrolled in a child care certificate program. Recipient must reapply and be interviewed for renewal. Awarded every year.
Contact: Marian D. Carey, Scholarship Chairman, 13011 Margot Drive, Rockville, MD 20853, (301) 942-6086.

Law

976   Alberta Law Foundation Scholarship

University of Calgary
2500 University Drive, NW
Calgary, Alberta, CN T2N 1N4
(403) 220-7872
Maximum award: $5,000
Minimum award: $3,500
Deadline: May 1
College level: Junior, Senior
Majors/Fields: Law
Criteria: Selection is based upon academic record, LSAT score, maturity, extracurricular activities, work experience, and community involvement. If possible, one award will be given to an Aboriginal Canadian. High academic standing is required to retain scholarship for two additional years. Awarded every year. Award may be used only at sponsoring institution.
Contact: J. Van Housen, Director of Student Awards & Financial Aid.

977　Ambrose H. Lindhorst Scholarship

Northern Kentucky University
Administrative Center 416
Nunn Drive
Highland Heights, KY 41099-7101
(606) 572-5144
Average award: $2,500
Deadline: February 1
College level: Graduate
Majors/Fields: Law
Criteria: Applicant must demonstrate a high level of academic promise. Awarded every year. Award may be used only at sponsoring institution.
Contact: Assistant Dean, Chase College of Law.

978　Anderson Publishing Company Minority Scholarship

Northern Kentucky University
Administrative Center 416
Nunn Drive
Highland Heights, KY 41099-7101
(606) 572-5144
Average award: $2,500
Deadline: February 1
College level: Graduate
Majors/Fields: Law
Criteria: Applicant must be a minority who is a resident of Cincinnati, Ohio. Scholarship is renewable. Awarded every year. Award may be used only at sponsoring institution.
Contact: Assistant Dean, Chase College of Law.

979　Bernard J. Seeman Scholarship

University of Colorado at Boulder
Campus Box 106
Boulder, CO 80309-0106
(303) 492-5091
Maximum award: $2,000
Minimum award: $1,000
Number of awards: 2
College level: Graduate
Majors/Fields: Law
Criteria: Applicant must be a top first-year law student with high potential and respect for the American system of justice. Awarded every year. Award may be used only at sponsoring institution.
Contact: Office of Financial Aid.

980　Busald, Funk, Zevely Scholarship

Northern Kentucky University
Administrative Center 416
Nunn Drive
Highland Heights, KY 41099-7101
(606) 572-5144
Average award: $2,500
Deadline: February 1
College level: Graduate
Majors/Fields: Law
Criteria: Applicant must demonstrate a high level of academic promise. Scholarship is renewable. Awarded every year. Award may be used only at sponsoring institution.
Contact: Assistant Dean, Chase College of Law.

981　Charles G. Coulson, Jr. Scholarship

Northern Kentucky University
Administrative Center 416
Nunn Drive
Highland Heights, KY 41099-7101
(606) 572-5144
Average award: $2,500
Deadline: February 1
College level: Graduate
Majors/Fields: Law
Criteria: Applicant must demonstrate financial need. Scholarship is renewable. Awarded every year. Award may be used only at sponsoring institution.
Contact: Assistant Dean, Chase College of Law.

982　Chase Activity Award

Northern Kentucky University
Administrative Center 416
Nunn Drive
Highland Heights, KY 41099-7101
(606) 572-5144
Average award: In-state tuition
Deadline: February 1
College level: Graduate
Majors/Fields: Law
Criteria: Applicant must be the president of the Student Bar Association, editor of the Law Review, or business manager of the Law Review. Awarded every year. Award may be used only at sponsoring institution.
Contact: Assistant Dean, Chase College of Law.

983　Chase Excellence Scholarship

Northern Kentucky University
Administrative Center 416
Nunn Drive
Highland Heights, KY 41099-7101
(606) 572-5144
Average award: In-state tuition
Deadline: February 1
College level: Graduate
Majors/Fields: Law
Criteria: Applicant must be a law student enrolled at least 8 credit hours. Awarded every year. Award may be used only at sponsoring institution.
Contact: Assistant Dean, Chase College of Law.

984　Chase Minority Educational Opportunity Tuition Award

Northern Kentucky University
Administrative Center 416
Nunn Drive
Highland Heights, KY 41099-7101
(606) 572-5144
Average award: In-state tuition
Deadline: February 1
College level: Graduate
Majors/Fields: Law
Criteria: Applicant must be a minority as defined by federal guidelines. Award is renewable for two to three years. Awarded every year. Award may be used only at sponsoring institution.
Contact: Assistant Dean, Chase College of Law.

985　CLEO Scholarship

Council on Legal Education Opportunity
1800 M Street, NW
Suite 160
Washington, DC 20006
(202) 785-4840
Average award: $5,000
Number of awards: 470
Deadline: February 1
College level: Doctoral
Majors/Fields: Law
Criteria: Applicant must be financially and educationally disadvantaged. Scholarship is renewable. Awarded every year.
Contact: Gretchen Wessel, Admissions Analyst.

986　Commonwealth Scholarship for Legal Studies

Northern Kentucky University
Administrative Center 416
Nunn Drive
Highland Heights, KY 41099-7101
(606) 572-5144
Average award: In-state tuition
Deadline: February 1
College level: Graduate
Majors/Fields: Law
Criteria: Applicant must be a Kentucky resident. Award is renewable for two to three years. Awarded every year. Award may be used only at sponsoring institution.
Contact: Assistant Dean, Chase College of Law.

987 Dietrich/Cross/Hanly Scholarship

Association of Former Agents of the United States Secret Service, Inc.
P.O. Box 11681
Alexandria, VA 22312
Average award: $1,000
Maximum award: $1,500
Minimum award: $500
Number of awards: 3
Deadline: April 30
College level: Junior, Senior, Graduate, Doctoral
Majors/Fields: Law enforcement
Criteria: Applicant must have completed at least one year of study in law enforcement and must be a U.S. citizen. Selection is based upon academic standing. Awarded every year.
Contact: P. Hamilton Brown, Executive Secretary.

988 E.W. Costello Entrance Scholarship

University of Calgary
2500 University Drive, NW
Calgary, Alberta, CN T2N 1N4
(403) 220-7872
Average award: $3,500
Number of awards: 1
Deadline: May 1
College level: Graduate
Majors/Fields: Law
Criteria: Selection is based upon academic record, LSAT score, maturity, extracurricular activities, work experience, and community involvement. High academic standing is required to retain scholarship for two additional years. Awarded every third year. Award may be used only at sponsoring institution.
Contact: J. Van Housen, Director of Student Awards & Financial Aid.

989 Ethel Tingley Scholarship

Northern Kentucky University
Administrative Center 416
Nunn Drive
Highland Heights, KY 41099-7101
(606) 572-5144
Average award: In-state tuition
Deadline: February 1
College level: Graduate
Majors/Fields: Law
Criteria: Applicant must be an entering female law student who demonstrates financial need. Award is for three years for full-time applicant and four years for a part-time applicant. Awarded every year. Award may be used only at sponsoring institution.
Contact: Assistant Dean, Chase College of Law.

990 Frederick T. Bonham Scholarship

University of Tennessee, Knoxville
Financial Aid Office
115 Student Services Building
Knoxville, TN 37994
(615) 974-3131
Average award: Total of $12,000 available for scholarships
Deadline: February 1
College level: Law students
Majors/Fields: Law
Criteria: Selection is based upon outstanding academic performance. Financial need and extracurricular activities are considered. Length of award is variable. Awarded every year. Award may be used only at sponsoring institution.
Contact: College of Law, 1505 West Cumberland Avenue, Knoxville, TN 37996, (615) 974-4131.

991 H. Gayle Weller Scholarship

University of Colorado at Boulder
Campus Box 106
Boulder, CO 80309-0106
(303) 492-5091
Average award: $2,500
Number of awards: 1
Deadline: As soon as possible after January 1
College level: Graduate
Majors/Fields: Law
Criteria: Applicant must be a second- or third-year law student who demonstrates high academic achievement and financial need. Awarded every year. Award may be used only at sponsoring institution.
Contact: Office of Financial Aid.

992 Holland & Hart Minority Scholarship

University of Colorado at Boulder
Campus Box 106
Boulder, CO 80309-0106
(303) 492-5091
Average award: $5,000
Number of awards: 2
Deadline: As soon as possible after January 1
College level: Graduate
Majors/Fields: Law
Criteria: Applicant must be a minority student whose achievements show promise of success in law school and the legal profession. Financial need is considered. Awarded every year. Award may be used only at sponsoring institution.
Contact: Office of Financial Aid.

993 Jean S. Breitenstein Law Clerks Scholarship

University of Colorado at Boulder
Campus Box 106
Boulder, CO 80309-0106
(303) 492-5091
Average award: $2,500
Number of awards: 1
Deadline: As soon as possible after January 1
College level: Graduate
Majors/Fields: Law
Criteria: Applicant must be a third-year law student, plan to practice law in Colorado, and demonstrate academic ability, achievement, and financial need. Awarded every year. Award may be used only at sponsoring institution.
Contact: Office of Financial Aid.

994 John W. Green Scholarship

University of Tennessee, Knoxville
Financial Aid Office
115 Student Services Building
Knoxville, TN 37994
(615) 974-3131
Maximum award: In-state tuition and fees
Deadline: February 1
College level: Law students
Majors/Fields: Law
Criteria: Selection is based upon merit of members of the three law classes who have unusual ability in the general development of character, ambition to excel, and interest in the general development and advancement of the ethical standards of the legal profession. Awarded every year. Award may be used only at sponsoring institution.
Contact: College of Law, 1505 West Cumberland Avenue, Knoxville, TN 37996, (615) 974-4131.

995   Kerr McGee Law Scholarship

University of Oklahoma
University Affairs
900 Asp Avenue, Room 236
Norman, OK 73019-0401
(405) 325-1701
Average award: $4,000
Number of awards: 1
Deadline: September 1
College level: Graduate
Majors/Fields: Law
Criteria: Applicant must have an interest in natural resources law and rank in the top fifth of class. Awarded on Law Day to be used for the second year of law school. Awarded every year. Award may be used only at sponsoring institution.
Contact: Admissions and Records, Law Center, Room 221, 300 Timberdell Road, Norman, OK 73019, (405) 325-4729.

996   Lasky Scholarship

University of Colorado at Boulder
Campus Box 106
Boulder, CO 80309-0106
(303) 492-5091
Average award: $1,000
Number of awards: 2
Deadline: As soon as possible after January 1
College level: Graduate
Majors/Fields: Law
Criteria: Applicant must be an outstanding second- or third-year law student who shows potential for making significant contributions to the legal profession as a lawyer or teacher and demonstrates financial need. Awarded every year. Award may be used only at sponsoring institution.
Contact: Office of Financial Aid.

997   Law School Scholarship for Library School Graduates

American Association of Law Libraries
Scholarships and Grants Committee
53 West Jackson Boulevard, Suite 940
Chicago, IL 60604
(312) 939-4764
Average award: $1,800
Number of awards: 6
Deadline: March 17
College level: Graduate
Majors/Fields: Law
Criteria: Applicant must be a library school graduate who is working toward a law degree at an accredited law school, has no more than 36 semester credit hours of study remaining before qualifying for the law degree, and who has meaningful law library experience. Awarded every year.
Contact: Ronda Bedrook, Scholarships and Grants Committee.

998   Leon and Dora Wolf Scholarship

University of Colorado at Boulder
Campus Box 106
Boulder, CO 80309-0106
(303) 492-5091
Average award: $2,500
Number of awards: 2
Deadline: As soon as possible after January 1
College level: Graduate
Majors/Fields: Law
Criteria: Applicant must be a third-year law student in the top 15 percent of the class. Preference is given to meritorious applicants who want to participate in the "Colorado Law Review" and require financial assistance to do so. Awarded every year. Award may be used only at sponsoring institution.
Contact: Office of Financial Aid.

999   May M. Walker Scholarship

University of Oklahoma
University Affairs
900 Asp Avenue, Room 236
Norman, OK 73019-0401
(405) 325-1701
Average award: $1,000
Number of awards: 5
Deadline: September 1
College level: Graduate
Majors/Fields: Law
Criteria: Applicant must be a full-time student, demonstrate financial need, and show evidence of ability to succeed. Awarded every year. Award may be used only at sponsoring institution.
Contact: Admissions and Records, Law Center, Room 221, 300 Timberdell Road, Norman, OK 73019, (405) 325-4729.

1000   Meredith L. Lawrence Scholarship

Northern Kentucky University
Administrative Center 416
Nunn Drive
Highland Heights, KY 41099-7101
(606) 572-5144
Average award: $2,500
Deadline: February 1
College level: Graduate
Majors/Fields: Law
Criteria: Applicant must be a first-time law student. Scholarship is renewable. Awarded every year. Award may be used only at sponsoring institution.
Contact: Assistant Dean, Chase College of Law.

1001   Merv Leitch, Q.C. Scholarship

University of Calgary
2500 University Drive, NW
Calgary, Alberta, CN T2N 1N4
(403) 220-7872
Average award: $3,500
Number of awards: 2
Deadline: May 1
College level: Senior, Graduate
Majors/Fields: Constitutional law, law, natural resources law
Criteria: Selection is based upon academic merit and extracurricular activities. One award is for a second-year student in constitutional law, and the other is for a third-year student in natural resources law. Awarded every year. Award may be used only at sponsoring institution.
Contact: J. Van Housen, Director of Student Awards & Financial Aid.

1002   National Association of Black Woman Attorneys Writing Scholarship

National Association of Black Woman Attorneys
724 9th Street, NW
Suite 206
Washington, DC 20001
(202) 637-3570
Maximum award: $5,000
Minimum award: $1,000
Number of awards: 4
Deadline: September 15
College level: Graduate
Majors/Fields: Law
Criteria: Applicant must be a black, female law student. Essay is required. The subject of the essay changes each year but always focuses on an issue of contemporary concern. Scholarship is renewable. Awarded every year.
Contact: Mabel D. Haden, Esq., President.

1003 Oklahoma Bar Foundation Scholarship

University of Oklahoma
University Affairs
900 Asp Avenue, Room 236
Norman, OK 73019-0401
(405) 325-1701
Average award: $2,500
Number of awards: 3
Deadline: September 1
College level: Graduate
Majors/Fields: Law
Criteria: Applicant must have an association with the state of Oklahoma, demonstrate financial need, and have an outstanding academic record. Awarded every year. Award may be used only at sponsoring institution.
Contact: Admissions and Records, Law Center, Room 221, 300 Timberdell Road, Norman, OK 73019, (405) 325-4729.

1004 Phillips Petroleum Scholarship

University of Colorado at Boulder
Campus Box 106
Boulder, CO 80309-0106
(303) 492-5091
Average award: $2,500
Number of awards: 1
Deadline: As soon as possible after January 1
College level: Graduate
Majors/Fields: Law
Criteria: Applicant must have a strong academic record and significant financial need. Awarded every year. Award may be used only at sponsoring institution.
Contact: Office of Financial Aid.

1005 Richard S. Nelson Scholarship

Northern Kentucky University
Administrative Center 416
Nunn Drive
Highland Heights, KY 41099-7101
(606) 572-5144
Average award: $2,500
Deadline: February 1
College level: Graduate
Majors/Fields: Law
Criteria: Applicant must be a resident of northern Kentucky. Scholarship is renewable. Awarded every year. Award may be used only at sponsoring institution.
Contact: Assistant Dean, Chase College of Law.

1006 Robert August Jung Scholarship

Northern Kentucky University
Administrative Center 416
Nunn Drive
Highland Heights, KY 41099-7101
(606) 572-5144
Average award: $2,500
Deadline: February 1
College level: Graduate
Majors/Fields: Law
Criteria: Applicant must be a first-time law student from Kentucky, Ohio or Indiana enrolled at least 12 credit hours per semester. Scholarship is renewable. Awarded every year. Award may be used only at sponsoring institution.
Contact: Assistant Dean, Chase College of Law.

1007 Robert J. Emery Student Support Fund

University of Oklahoma
University Affairs
900 Asp Avenue, Room 236
Norman, OK 73019-0401
(405) 325-1701
Average award: $5,000
Number of awards: 1
Deadline: September 1
College level: Graduate
Majors/Fields: Law
Criteria: Awarded to a second-year student on the basis of superior academic performance and financial need. Awarded every year. Award may be used only at sponsoring institution.
Contact: Admissions and Records, Law Center, Room 221, 300 Timberdell Road, Norman, OK 73019, (405) 325-4729.

1008 Ted Price Scholarship

Northern Kentucky University
Administrative Center 416
Nunn Drive
Highland Heights, KY 41099-7101
(606) 572-5144
Average award: $2,500
Deadline: February 1
College level: Graduate
Majors/Fields: Law
Criteria: Applicant must be a Kentucky resident. Scholarship is renewable. Awarded every year. Award may be used only at sponsoring institution.
Contact: Assistant Dean, Chase College of Law.

1009 Texas Sheriffs' Association Scholarship

Southwest Texas State University
J. C. Kellam Building
San Marcos, TX 78666
(512) 245-2340
Average award: $1,000
Number of awards: 2
Deadline: March 15
College level: Freshman, Sophomore, Junior, Senior
Majors/Fields: Criminal justice
Criteria: Applicant must have a minimum 2.5 GPA, have made a written commitment to a law enforcement career, and be eligible to serve as a peace officer. Personal interview is required. Awarded every year. Award may be used only at sponsoring institution.
Contact: Department of Criminal Justice, (512) 245-2315.

1010 W. Jeff Ward Scholarship

Northern Kentucky University
Administrative Center 416
Nunn Drive
Highland Heights, KY 41099-7101
(606) 572-5144
Average award: $2,000
Deadline: February 1
College level: Graduate
Majors/Fields: Law
Criteria: Applicant must demonstrate financial need; preference is given to residents of the Kentucky counties of Pike, Floyd, Johnson, Martin, Knott, or Perry. Awarded every year. Award may be used only at sponsoring institution.
Contact: Assistant Dean, Chase College of Law.

1011   William H. Greaves Scholarship

Northern Kentucky University
Administrative Center 416
Nunn Drive
Highland Heights, KY 41099-7101
(606) 572-5144
Average award: Full tuition
Deadline: February 1
College level: Graduate
Majors/Fields: Law
Criteria: Incoming student applicant will be selected by GPA and LSAT scores, along with other factors. Continuing student applicant must have a minimum 3.0 GPA. Award is renewable for two to three years. Awarded every year. Award may be used only at sponsoring institution.
Contact: Assistant Dean, Chase College of Law.

Military Science/ROTC

1012   Air Force ROTC Airman Scholarship and Commissioning Program (ASCP)

U.S. Air Force ROTC–HQ AFROTC/RROO
551 E. Maxwell Blvd.
Maxwell AFB, AL 36112-6106
(334) 953-2091
Maximum award: Type I scholarships pay full college tuition, incidental fees, plus a textbook allowance. All Air Force ROTC Cadets on scholarship receive a $100 monthly nontaxable allowance during the school year.
Minimum award: Type II scholarships pay the same benefits except tuition is capped at $8,000 per year.
College level: Active duty enlisted personnel
Majors/Fields: Engineering, pharmacy, physical therapy, pre-health, science
Criteria: Scholarship offers active duty enlisted personnel the opportunity to earn a commission while completing requirements for an undergraduate degree as an Air Force ROTC cadet. Applicant must be a U.S. citizen, under 25 years of age as of June 30 in year of graduation and commission, have letter of recommendation from immediate commander, have letter of acceptance and institutional evaluation of prior college credits from a school offering the AFROTC Four-Year Program, have a letter of academic eligibility from the AFROTC Commander at the college or university, have a minimum 2.5 GPA, be admitted to a school offering Air Force ROTC and the academic major of school, and be of good moral character. Scholarship is renewable. Awarded every year.
Contact: HQ AFROTC/RROO, 551 E. Maxwell Boulevard, Maxwell AFB, AL 36112-6106.

1013   Air Force ROTC Nursing Scholarships

U.S. Air Force ROTC–HQ AFROTC/RROO
551 E. Maxwell Blvd.
Maxwell AFB, AL 36112-6106
(334) 953-2091
Maximum award: Type I scholarships pay full college tuition, mandatory fees, plus a textbook allowance. All Air Force ROTC cadets on scholarships receive $100 monthly nontaxable allowance during the school year.
Minimum award: Type II scholarships pay the same benefits as Type I except tuition is capped at $8,000 per year. Targeted Scholarship pays full tuition and most required fees to a school designated on preference list on scholarship application (AF Form 113).
College level: Freshman
Majors/Fields: Nursing
Criteria: Air Force nursing scholarship program helps interested students pursue a nursing degree and earn an Air Force officer commission through Air Force ROTC. Applicant must gain acceptance to a school of nursing accredited by the National League of Nursing and submit a personal statement of interest and reasons for pursuing a nursing degree and an Air Force commission. Scholarship is renewable. Awarded every year.
Contact: HQ AFROTC, Scholarship Actions Sections.

1014   Air Force ROTC Scholarship

U.S. Air Force ROTC–HQ AFROTC/RROO
551 E. Maxwell Blvd.
Maxwell AFB, AL 36112-6106
(334) 953-2091
Average award: Type II scholarship pays the same benefits except tuition is capped at $8,000 per year.
Maximum award: Type I scholarship pays full college tuition, incidental and lab fees, plus a textbook allowance. All Air Force ROTC cadets on scholarship receive $100 monthly allowance during the school year.
Minimum award: Targeted scholarship pays full tuition and most required fees at a particular school based on the school preference listed by the applicant on the scholarship application (AF Form 113).
Deadline: December 1
College level: Freshman
Majors/Fields: Architecture, computer science, engineering, mathematics, meteorology, nursing, physics
Criteria: Applicant must be a U.S. citizen, have a minimum 2.5 GPA, rank in the top quarter of class, have a minimum composite ACT score of 24 or combined SAT I score of 1000, be a high school graduate, have never enrolled full-time at a college (except for joint high school/college programs), and be at least 17 years of age by October 31 of first college year and under 25 years of age by June 30 in the year of college graduation and Air Force commission. Awarded every year.
Contact: HQ AFROTC/RROO.

1015   Air Force ROTC Scholarship

University of Alabama–Tuscaloosa
Box 870162
Tuscaloosa, AL 35487-0162
(205) 348-6756
Average award: Tuition, lab fees, books and $100 per month
Deadline: December 1 (four year scholarship)
College level: Freshman, Sophomore, Junior
Criteria: Selection is based upon ACT or SAT I scores, GPA, personal interview, and leadership ability. Awards are for two, two-and-a-half, three, three-and-a-half, and four years. Awarded every year. Award may be used only at sponsoring institution.
Contact: AFROTC, Box 870258, Tuscaloosa, AL 35487-0258, (205) 348-5900.

1016   Air Force ROTC Scholarship

University of Colorado at Boulder
Campus Box 106
Boulder, CO 80309-0106
(303) 492-5091
Average award: Full in-state or out-of-state tuition, mandatory fees, books, $100 monthly allowance, and in some cases, health insurance; Type II awards have a maximum of $8,000 for tuition and fees
Deadline: December 1
College level: Sophomore, Junior
Criteria: Applicant must enroll in Air Force ROTC, attend college on a full-time basis, be physically qualified, and agree to serve four years of active duty as an Air Force officer upon graduation. Awards are for two, two and one-half, three, and three and one-half years. Awarded every year. Award may be used only at sponsoring institution.
Contact: Air Force ROTC, Campus Box 371, Boulder, CO 80309-0371, (303) 492-8351.

1017   Air Force ROTC Scholarship

University of Southern Mississippi
Office of Recruitment and Orientation
Box 5166
Hattiesburg, MS 39406-5166
(601) 266-5000
Average award: Full tuition, lab fees, books, incidental fees, and $100 per month allowance
College level: Freshman, Sophomore, Junior
Criteria: Selection is competitive. Award is available for two to four years. Awarded every year. Award may be used only at sponsoring institution.
Contact: Professor of Aerospace Studies, Box 5145, Hattiesburg, MS 39406-5145.

1018 Air Force ROTC Scholarship

New Mexico State University
Box 30001
Department 5100
Las Cruces, NM 88003-0001
(505) 646-4105
Average award: Tuition, books, fees, and $100 monthly stipend
Deadline: December 15
College level: Freshman, Sophomore, Junior
Criteria: Applicant must agree to enroll in the Air Force ROTC program and serve as an Air Force officer for four years active duty upon graduation. Awards are for two, two-and-a-half, three, three-and-a-half, and four years. Awarded every year. Award may be used only at sponsoring institution.
Contact: Department of Aerospace Studies, Las Cruces, NM 88003.

1019 Air Force ROTC Scholarship

University of Oklahoma
University Affairs
900 Asp Avenue, Room 236
Norman, OK 73019-0401
(405) 325-1701
Average award: Full tuition, fees, books, and $100 monthly allowance
Deadline: December 1 (entering freshman); January of sophomore year for others
College level: Freshman, Junior
Criteria: Applicant must be a U.S. citizen, meet medical and physical qualifications, and be under 25 years old at college graduation. High school applicant must have a minimum cumulative GPA of 2.5, rank in the top quarter of class, and have a minimum composite ACT score of 24. College applicant must have a minimum 2.5 GPA. Most scholarships are in engineering, nursing, and meteorology. Scholarship is renewable. Awarded every year. Award may be used only at sponsoring institution.
Contact: Professor of Aerospace Studies, 171 Felgar Street, Norman, OK 73019-0604, (405) 325-3211.

1020 Air Force ROTC Scholarship

Southwest Texas State University
J. C. Kellam Building
San Marcos, TX 78666
(512) 245-2340
Average award: Tuition, fees, book allowance, and $100 per month subsistence allowance
Deadline: March 15
College level: Freshman, Sophomore, Junior, Senior
Criteria: Selection is based upon scholarship, merit, and potential as a cadet corps member and future officer. Renewable for two to three-and-a-half years. Awarded every year. Award may be used only at sponsoring institution.
Contact: AFROTC Detachment 840, San Marcos, TX 78666, (512) 245-2182.

1021 Air Force ROTC Scholarship

University of Texas at San Antonio
Office of Student Financial Aid
6900 North Loop 1604 West
San Antonio, TX 78249-0687
(210) 691-4011
Average award: Tuition, books, fees, and $100 per month allowance
Deadline: December 1 (entering freshmen)
College level: Freshman, Sophomore, Junior
Criteria: Applicant must be a U.S. citizen, rank in the top quarter of class, and have a minimum composite ACT score of 24 or combined SAT I score of 1000. Award is for two to four years. Minimum 2.5 GPA is required to retain scholarship. Awarded every year. Award may be used only at sponsoring institution.
Contact: Air Force ROTC, 6900 North Loop 1604 West, San Antonio, TX 78249, (210) 691-4624.

1022 Air Force ROTC Science/Engineering Scholarship

University of Utah
Financial Aid and Scholarships Office
105 Student Services Building
Salt Lake City, UT 84112
(801) 581-6211
Average award: Full tuition, books, most lab fees, and $100 monthly stipend
Deadline: December 1
College level: Freshman, Sophomore, Junior
Majors/Fields: Architecture, civil engineering, computer science, electrical engineering, mathematics, mechanical engineering, meteorology, metallurgical engineering, nuclear engineering, physics
Criteria: Applicant must commit to being an Air Force officer after graduation and major in science or engineering. Award is for two to four years. Awarded every year. Award may be used only at sponsoring institution.
Contact: Capt. Cristen DeYoung, Air Force ROTC, 2009 Annex Building, Salt Lake City, UT 84112-1107, (801) 581-6236.

1023 Air Force ROTC/Villanova Scholars Award

Villanova University
Villanova, PA 19085
(215) 645-4010
Average award: $5,870
Number of awards: 2
Deadline: January 15
College level: Freshman
Criteria: Applicant must be receiving Level II AFROTC scholarship as designated by the Air Force. Academic eligibility must be maintained to retain scholarship. Awarded every year. Award may be used only at sponsoring institution.
Contact: George J. Walter, Director of Financial Aid.

1024 Air Force Scholarship

University of Arkansas, Fayetteville
Office of Scholarships and Financial Aid
114 Hunt Hall
Fayetteville, AR 72701
(501) 575-3806
Average award: Full tuition, books, fees, board, room, and $100 monthly
Deadline: December 1
College level: Freshman
Criteria: Selection is based upon test scores and GPA. Interview is required. Award is for two to four years. Awarded every year. Award may be used only at sponsoring institution.
Contact: Professor for Aerospace Studies, (501) 575-3651.

1025 Army National Guard/Army Reserve Force Duty Two-Year Scholarship

University of Oklahoma
University Affairs
900 Asp Avenue, Room 236
Norman, OK 73019-0401
(405) 325-1701
Average award: Tuition, lab fees, book allowance, classroom supplies, and $100 monthly allowance
Deadline: March 1
College level: Junior
Criteria: Applicant must be a National Guard or Army Reserve student and meet medical and administrative requirements. Selection is based upon academic performance and leadership potential. Award is for two years. Awarded every year. Award may be used only at sponsoring institution.
Contact: Professor of Military Science, 290 West Brooks, Armory Room 1, Norman, OK 73019-0220, (405) 325-2011.

1026 Army ROTC Four-Year Scholarship

University of Colorado at Boulder
Campus Box 106
Boulder, CO 80309-0106
(303) 492-5091
Average award: Tuition, fees, book allowance of $180 per semester, and $100 monthly allowance
Deadline: December 1
College level: Freshman
Criteria: Selection is based upon ACT or SAT I scores, high school academic standing, leadership abilities, extracurricular and athletic activities, and personal interview. Applicant must be a high school graduate, a U.S. citizen, meet physical fitness requirements, participate in Army ROTC, and agree to accept a commission as an Army regular or reserve officer. Award is for four years. Awarded every year. Award may be used only at sponsoring institution.
Contact: Army ROTC, P.O. Box 9000, Clifton, NJ 07015.

1027 Army ROTC Scholarship

University of Alabama–Tuscaloosa
Box 870162
Tuscaloosa, AL 35487-0162
(205) 348-6756
Average award: Tuition, books, lab fees, academic expenses and a $1,000 per year subsistence allowance
Deadline: in November (four-year scholarship); in March (two/three year scholarships)
College level: Freshman, Sophomore, Junior
Criteria: Selection is based upon ACT or SAT I scores, GPA, personal interview, extracurricular leadership, and athletic participation. Award is for two, three, or four years. Awarded every year. Award may be used only at sponsoring institution.
Contact: Army ROTC, Box 870260, Tuscaloosa, AL 35487-0260, (205) 348-5917.

1028 Army ROTC Scholarship

University of Southern Mississippi
Office of Recruitment and Orientation
Box 5166
Hattiesburg, MS 39406-5166
(601) 266-5000
Average award: Full tuition, fees, books, lab expenses, and $100 per month subsistence pay. Some four-year awards include room and board.
College level: Freshman, Sophomore, Junior
Criteria: Selection is competitive. Awards are for two, three, or four years. Awarded every year. Award may be used only at sponsoring institution.
Contact: Professor of Military Science, Box 5042, Hattiesburg, MS 39406-5042.

1029 Army ROTC Scholarship

Southwest Missouri State University
Student Financial Aid
901 South National Avenue
Springfield, MO 65804-0095
(417) 836-5000 or (800) 492-7900
Maximum award: Full fees, book allowance and $100 per month
Deadline: March 31
College level: Freshman, Sophomore, Junior, Senior
Criteria: Applicant must have a minimum 2.5 cumulative GPA and be a full-time student. Applicant must attend an interview, and pass a physical test, written exam, and free physical examination given by a local doctor. Recipient who accepts a two-, three-, or four-year scholarship will train to receive a commission as Second Lieutenant in the regular U.S. Army, Army Reserve, or Army National Guard. Scholarship is renewable. Awarded every year. Award may be used only at sponsoring institution.
Contact: Military Science Department, Southwest Missouri State University, Springfield, MO 65804, (417) 836-5262 or (800) 492-7900.

1030 Army ROTC Scholarship

New Mexico State University
Box 30001
Department 5100
Las Cruces, NM 88003-0001
(505) 646-4105
Average award: Tuition, books, supplies, fees, and $100 monthly stipend
Deadline: December 1 (entering freshman)
College level: Freshman, Sophomore, Junior, Senior
Criteria: Applicant must serve as a commissioned officer in the active army upon graduation. Awards are for one, two, three, or four years. Awarded every year; may be used only at sponsoring institution.
Contact: Department of Military Science, Las Cruces, NM 88003.

1031 Army ROTC Scholarship

Hofstra University
126 Memorial Hall
Hempstead, NY 11550
(516) 463-6677
Maximum award: $8,000
College level: Freshman, Sophomore, Junior, Senior
Criteria: Applicant must be a U.S. citizen, at least 17 years old, who is a high school graduate or has an equivalency certificate. Scholarship is renewable. Awarded every year. Award may be used only at sponsoring institution.
Contact: Army ROTC, 130 Hofstra University, Hempstead, NY 11550-1090, (516) 463-5648.

1032 Army ROTC Scholarship

University of Oklahoma
University Affairs
900 Asp Avenue, Room 236
Norman, OK 73019-0401
(405) 325-1701
Average award: Tuition, lab fees, book allowance, classroom supplies, and $100 monthly allowance
Deadline: March 1
College level: Freshman, Sophomore, Junior
Criteria: Applicant must meet medical and administrative requirements. Selection is based upon academic performance and leadership potential. Scholarship is available in engineering, nursing, and general studies. Award is for two, three, or four years. Awarded every year. Award may be used only at sponsoring institution.
Contact: Professor of Military Science, 290 West Brooks, Armory Room 1, Norman, OK 73019-0220, (405) 325-2011.

1033 Army ROTC Scholarship

Portland State University
P.O. Box 751
Portland, OR 97207-5252
(503) 725-5270
Average award: $4,500
Deadline: in January
College level: Sophomore, Junior, Senior
Criteria: Applicant must have a minimum 2.5 GPA, a minimum combined SAT I score of 850, and be physically and mentally sound. Half of awards are given on merit only; the other half include financial need. Scholarship is renewable. Award may be used only at sponsoring institution.
Contact: Scholarships, Department of Military Science, P.O. Box 751, Portland, OR 97207-0751, (503) 725-3212.

1034 Army ROTC Scholarship

Southwest Texas State University
J. C. Kellam Building
San Marcos, TX 78666
(512) 245-2340
Deadline: March 15
College level: Freshman, Sophomore, Junior, Senior
Criteria: Applicant must demonstrate potential as a future Army officer. Selection is based upon merit. Awarded for three or four years. Awarded every year. Award may be used only at sponsoring institution.
Contact: Professor of Military Science, Department of Military Science, San Marcos, TX 78666, (512) 245-3232.

1035   Army ROTC Scholarship

University of Texas at San Antonio
Office of Student Financial Aid
6900 North Loop 1604 West
San Antonio, TX 78249-0687
(210) 691-4011
Average award: Tuition, fees, books, $100 per month allowance
Deadline: December 1 (incoming freshmen)
College level: Freshman, Sophomore, Junior
Criteria: Applicant must be a U.S. citizen, have a minimum 2.5 GPA, and have a minimum combined SAT I score of 850 or composite ACT score of 17. Award is for two to four years. Minimum 2.0 GPA is required to retain scholarship. Awarded every year. Award may be used only at sponsoring institution.
Contact: Army ROTC, 6900 North Loop 1604 West, San Antonio, TX 78249-0687, (210) 691-4622.

1036   Army ROTC Scholarship

University of Utah
Financial Aid and Scholarships Office
105 Student Services Building
Salt Lake City, UT 84112
(801) 581-6211
Average award: Tuition, fees, allowance for books and supplies, and $100 monthly stipend
Maximum award: $22,500
Deadline: December 1 (incoming freshman), February 15 (continuing student)
College level: Freshman, Sophomore, Junior
Criteria: Applicant must be a U.S. citizen, demonstrate academic excellence, and meet established medical, physical, moral, and age criteria. Preference is given to technical and nursing majors. Applicant must agree to serve four years as a commissioned officer in the U.S. Army. Some two-year awards are available for Reserve Forces Duty only. Awards are for two, three, or four years. Awarded every year. Award may be used only at sponsoring institution.
Contact: Major Caryl Buford, Military Science Building, Salt Lake City, UT 84112, (801) 581-6716 or (801) 581-6717.

1037   Army ROTC Simultaneous Membership Program

New Mexico State University
Box 30001
Department 5100
Las Cruces, NM 88003-0001
(505) 646-4105
Average award: $3,000
Deadline: Before beginning of semester
College level: Freshman, Sophomore, Junior, Graduate, Doctoral
Criteria: Applicant must agree to accept a commission in the active Army, Army Reserve, or National Guard upon graduation and to participate in upper-division Army ROTC courses and National Guard or Reserve monthly drill meetings. Applicant must have a minimum 2.0 GPA, be between the ages of 17 and 28, enrolled full-time, and have at least two years of academic work remaining. Scholarship is renewable. Awarded every year. Award may be used only at sponsoring institution.
Contact: Greeley W. Myers, Director of Financial Aid.

1038   Army ROTC Supplemental Scholarship

Southwest Missouri State University
Student Financial Aid
901 South National Avenue
Springfield, MO 65804-0095
(417) 836-5000 or (800) 492-7900
Maximum award: On-campus room and board
Number of awards: 4
Deadline: March 31
College level: Freshman, Sophomore, Junior, Senior
Criteria: Applicant must be a recipient of a two-, three-, or four-year Army ROTC scholarship. Selection is based upon academic excellence, military potential, and financial need. Scholarship is renewable. Awarded every year. Award may be used only at sponsoring institution.
Contact: Military Science Department, Southwest Missouri State University, Springfield, MO 65804, (417) 836-5262 or (800) 492-7900.

1039   Army ROTC Two- and Three-Year Green to Gold Scholarship

University of Oklahoma
University Affairs
900 Asp Avenue, Room 236
Norman, OK 73019-0401
(405) 325-1701
Average award: Tuition, lab fees, book allowance, classroom supplies, and $100 monthly allowance
Deadline: March 15
College level: Sophomore, Junior
Criteria: Applicant must be enlisted on active duty with a minimum of two years on active duty as of date of discharge, and meet medical and administrative requirements. Selection is based upon academic performance and leadership potential. Award is for two or three years. Awarded every year. Award may be used only at sponsoring institution.
Contact: Professor of Military Science, 290 West Brooks, Armory Room 1, Norman, OK 73019, (405) 325-2011.

1040   Army ROTC Two- and Three-Year Scholarships

University of Colorado at Boulder
Campus Box 106
Boulder, CO 80309-0106
(303) 492-5091
Average award: $7,000 or 80% of tuition and fees, whichever is greater; book allowance of $180 per semester, and monthly allowance of $100
Deadline: February 1 (two-year); March 1 (three-year)
College level: Sophomore, Junior
Criteria: Applicant must be a U.S. citizen, meet age and physical fitness requirements, participate in Army ROTC, and accept a commission as an Army regular or reserve officer upon graduation. Selection is based upon college academic and military studies, personal interview, and motivation toward a career in the Army. Award is for two or three years. Awarded every year. Award may be used only at sponsoring institution.
Contact: Professor of Military Science, Campus Box 370, Boulder, CO 80309-0370, (303) 492-6495.

1041   Army ROTC Two-Year Camp Challenge Scholarship

University of Oklahoma
University Affairs
900 Asp Avenue, Room 236
Norman, OK 73019-0401
(405) 325-1701
Average award: Tuition, lab fees, book allowance, classroom supplies, and $100 monthly allowance
Deadline: April 30
College level: Junior
Criteria: Applicant must meet medical and administrative requirements, attend a six-week summer camp, and have a minimum of 55 undergraduate credit hours with no formal military training. Award is for two years. Awarded every year. Award may be used only at sponsoring institution.
Contact: Professor of Military Science, 290 West Brooks, Armory Room 1, Norman, OK 73019-0220, (405) 325-2011.

1042   Army ROTC/Villanova Scholars Award

Villanova University
Villanova, PA 19085
(215) 645-4010
Average award: $2,707
Maximum award: $2,774
Minimum award: $2,640
Number of awards: 2
Deadline: January 15
College level: Freshman
Criteria: Applicant must be selected by the Army for an 80-percent tuition scholarship. Minimum 3.25 GPA is required to retain scholarship. Awarded every year. Award may be used only at sponsoring institution.
Contact: George J. Walter, Director of Financial Aid.

1043   Naval-Marine ROTC College Scholarship

Naval Personnel Command
NMPC-602
Washington, DC 20370
Average award: Tuition, fees, books and $100 per month stipend
College level: Freshman, Sophomore, Junior, Senior
Criteria: Applicant must attend a civilian college with an NROTC unit on campus or one that is affiliated with an NROTC institution. Upon graduation, applicant becomes an officer in the Navy or Marine Corps. Awards are for two, three, or four years. Awarded every year.
Contact: Local Navy recruiter, (800) 327-NAVY.

1044   Naval ROTC Scholarship

University of Colorado at Boulder
Campus Box 106
Boulder, CO 80309-0106
(303) 492-5091
Average award: Full resident or nonresident tuition, fees, books, uniforms, and $100 monthly allowance
Deadline: March 1
College level: Sophomore, Junior, Senior
Criteria: Selection is based upon academic and professional merit. Applicant must enroll in Naval ROTC program, including summer activities, and agree to serve on active duty in the Navy or Marine Corps after graduation. Awards are for one, two, or three years. Awarded every year. Award may be used only at sponsoring institution.
Contact: Naval ROTC Office, Campus Box 374, Boulder, CO 80309-0374, (303) 492-8287.

1045   Naval ROTC Scholarship

University of Oklahoma
University Affairs
900 Asp Avenue, Room 236
Norman, OK 73019-0401
(405) 325-1701
Average award: Tuition, books, fees, and $1000 per year
Deadline: December 1
College level: Freshman, Sophomore, Junior, Senior
Criteria: Applicant must have a good academic record, be physically qualified, and have leadership potential. College students must have completed one year of calculus by the end of sophomore year. Award is for two, three or four years. Awarded every year. Award may be used only at sponsoring institution.
Contact: Professor of Naval Science, 290 West Brooks, Norman, OK 73019-0001, (405) 325-2021.

1046   Naval ROTC Scholarship

U.S. Naval Reserve Officers Training Corps (NROTC)
Navy Recruiting Command (Code 314)
801 N. Randolph Street
Arlington, VA 22203-1991
(703) 696-4581
Average award: $10,000
Maximum award: $20,000
Number of awards: 1000
Deadline: January 31
College level: Freshman
Criteria: Applicant must be a U.S. citizen, between 17 and 21 years of age, be physically qualified by Navy or Marine Corp standards, have no moral obligations or personal convictions that will prevent conscientious bearing of arms, and achieve qualifying scores on the SAT I or ACT. Applicant must maintain above-average grades to continue support. Awarded every year.
Contact: LCDR Doug Brazil, NROTC Program Manager, Naval Recruiting Command (Code 314), 801 North Randolph Street, Arlington, VA 22203-1991, (703) 393-4581.

1047   Navy Nurse Corps NROTC

Naval Personnel Command
NMPC-602
Washington, DC 20370
Average award: Tuition, lab fees, books and $100 per month subsistence allowance
College level: Freshman, Sophomore, Junior, Senior
Majors/Fields: Nursing
Criteria: Selection is based upon high school class standing, test scores, extracurricular activities, leadership qualities, and academic accomplishments. Applicant is commissioned as an ensign in the Navy Nurse Corps upon graduation. Awarded every year.
Contact: Local Navy recruiter, (800) 327-NAVY.

1048   U.S. Army Scholarship

University of Arkansas, Fayetteville
Office of Scholarships and Financial Aid
114 Hunt Hall
Fayetteville, AR 72701
(501) 575-3806
Average award: Full tuition, books, fees, room, board, and $100 monthly
Deadline: December 1
College level: Freshman
Criteria: Selection is based upon test scores and GPA. Interview is required. Award is for two to four years. Awarded every year. Award may be used only at sponsoring institution.
Contact: Professor of Military Science, (501) 575-4251.

Political Science

1049   Cortez A. M. Ewing Public Service Fellowship

University of Oklahoma
University Affairs
900 Asp Avenue, Room 236
Norman, OK 73019-0401
(405) 325-1701
Average award: $1,200
Maximum number of awards: 5
Minimum number of awards: 4
Deadline: Last day of classes, fall semester
College level: Sophomore, Junior, Senior
Majors/Fields: Political science
Criteria: Preference is given to students expecting to return to the U of Oklahoma campus in the fall following the summer congressional internship. Awarded every year. Award may be used only at sponsoring institution.
Contact: Political Science Department, 455 West Lindsey, Norman, OK 73019, (405) 325-2061.

1050   Harry S Truman Scholarship

Harry S Truman Scholarship Foundation
712 Jackson Place, NW
Washington, DC 20006
(202) 395-4831
Maximum award: $13,500
Minimum award: $3,000
Number of awards: 92
Deadline: December 1
College level: Senior
Majors/Fields: Public service
Criteria: Applicant must be a U.S. citizen or U.S. national, rank in top quarter of class, have outstanding leadership potential, and be planning to pursue graduate school study to prepare for a career in public service. Minimum "B" grade average is required to retain scholarship. Awarded every year.
Contact: Louis H. Blair, Executive Secretary.

1051 RAND/UCLA Center for Soviet Studies Fellowship

RAND/UCLA Center for Soviet Studies
1700 Main Street
Santa Monica, CA 90406
(213) 451-6961
Maximum award: $15,000
Minimum award: $11,000
Number of awards: 5
Deadline: February 1
College level: Doctoral
Criteria: Applicant must be accepted into the Ph.D. program at either the RAND graduate school or the political science, economics, or history departments at UCLA. Reading proficiency in Russian and knowledge of Soviet economics, history, politics, and foreign policy at the undergraduate level is required. Renewable for three years with satisfactory performance. Awarded every year.
Contact: Cara Gilbert, Administrative Director.

1052 United States Senate Youth Program

William Randolph Hearst Foundation
90 New Montgomery Street, Suite 1212
San Francisco, CA 94105
(415) 543-4057
Minimum award: $2,000
Number of awards: 104
Deadline: Late September or early October
College level: Freshman
Criteria: Applicant must be a high school junior or senior, permanent U.S. resident, hold elected student body position, and be selected to participate in the U.S. Senate Youth Program. Selection is based upon outstanding ability and demonstrated qualities of leadership. Awarded every year.
Contact: Rita A. Almon, Program Director, (800) 841-7048.

Psychology

1053 Ralph A. Tesseneer Scholarship

Northern Kentucky University
Administrative Center 416
Nunn Drive
Highland Heights, KY 41099-7101
(606) 572-5144
Average award: In-state tuition
Deadline: February 1
College level: Junior, Senior
Majors/Fields: Psychology
Criteria: Applicant must have a minimum 3.0 GPA. Awarded every year. Award may be used only at sponsoring institution.
Contact: Robert E. Sprague, Director of Financial Aid.

Social Sciences–General

1054 Anna C. and Oliver C. Colburn Fellowship

Archaeological Institute of America
656 Beacon Street
4th Floor
Boston, MA 02215-2010
(617) 353-9361
Average award: $11,000
Number of awards: 1
Deadline: February 1
College level: Doctoral, received Ph.D. within the last five years
Majors/Fields: Archaeology
Criteria: Fellowship is awarded contingent upon applicant's acceptance as an incoming associate member or student associate member of the American School of Classical Studies at Athens. Fellowship applicants must also apply to the American School. Applicant must be a U.S. or Canadian citizen or permanent resident and may not be a member of the American School during the year of application. Awarded in even-numbered years.
Contact: Fellowships.

1055 Arnold J. Lien Scholarship in Social Sciences

Washington University
One Brookings Drive
Campus Box 1089
St. Louis, MO 63130
(314) 935-6000 or (800) 638-0700
Average award: $17,750
Number of awards: 3
College level: Freshman
Majors/Fields: Social science
Criteria: Selection is based upon academic merit without regard to financial need. Satisfactory academic performance is required to retain scholarship. Awarded every year. Award may be used only at sponsoring institution.
Contact: Office of Undergraduate Admission.

1056 Dale and Coral Courtney Scholarship

Portland State University
P.O. Box 751
Portland, OR 97207-5252
(503) 725-5270
Average award: $2,000
Deadline: Mid-summer
College level: Unspecified graduate
Majors/Fields: Geography
Criteria: Applicant must submit an essay and faculty recommendations. Awarded every year. Award may be used only at sponsoring institution.
Contact: Scholarships.

1057 Enid Hall Griswold Memorial Scholarship

National Society of the Daughters of the American Revolution
NSDAR Administration Building, Office of the Committees
1776 D Street, NW
Washington, DC 20006-5392
(202) 879-3292
Average award: $1,000
Number of awards: 2
Deadline: February 15
College level: Junior, Senior
Majors/Fields: Economics, government, history, political science
Criteria: Applicant must be a U.S. citizen and submit a letter of sponsorship from a local DAR chapter. Selection is based upon academic excellence, commitment to field of study, and financial need. All inquiries must include a self-addressed, stamped envelope. Awarded every year.
Contact: Administrative Assistant, NSDAR Office of the Committees/Scholarships, 1776 D Street, NW, Washington, DC 20006-5392.

1058 Harriet and Leon Pomerance Fellowship

Archaeological Institute of America
656 Beacon Street
4th Floor
Boston, MA 02215-2010
(617) 353-9361
Average award: $3,000
Number of awards: 1
Deadline: Novermber 15
College level: Doctoral, received Ph.D. with the last five years
Majors/Fields: Archaeology
Criteria: Applicant must be a resident of the U.S. or Canada. Preference given to an applicant whose project requires travel to the Mediterranean for an individual project of scholarly nature related to Aegean Bronze Age archaeology. Awarded every year.
Contact: Fellowships.

1059   Helen M. Woodruff Fellowship of the Archaeological Institute of America

Archaeological Institute of America
656 Beacon Street
4th Floor
Boston, MA 02215-2010
(617) 353-9361
College level: Doctoral, post-doctoral study.
Majors/Fields: Archaeology, classical studies
Criteria: Combined with other funds from the American Academy in Rome, the fellowship will support a Rome Prize Fellowship. Applicant must be a U.S. citizen or permanent resident. Awarded every year.
Contact: American Academy in Rome, 41 East 65th Street, New York, NY 10021-6058, (212) 751-7200.

1060   Herbert H. Lehman Graduate Fellowship

New York State Higher Education Services Corporation
99 Washington Avenue
Albany, NY 12255
(518) 473-4563
Maximum award: $5,000
Minimum award: $4,000
Number of awards: 30
Deadline: May 1
College level: Graduate, Doctoral
Majors/Fields: Social sciences, public affairs, international affairs
Criteria: Applicant must be in a master's or doctoral degree program in social sciences, public affairs, or international affairs at a college in New York state. Program must be for the fellowship by the New York State Commissioner of Education. New York state residency is required if also applying for the Tuition Assistance Program. Selection is based upon academic merit. $4,000 for first year of study; $5,000 thereafter for up to three years. Awarded every year.
Contact: New York State Education Department, Higher and Professional Educational Testing, Cultural Education Center, Albany, NY 12230.

1061   Kenan T. Erim Award

Archaeological Institute of America
656 Beacon Street
4th Floor
Boston, MA 02215-2010
(617) 353-9361
Average award: $4,000
Number of awards: 1
Deadline: November 15
College level: Doctoral
Majors/Fields: Archaeology
Criteria: Applicant must be an American or international research and/or excavating scholar working on Aphrodisias material. Awarded every year.
Contact: Awards.

1062   Olivia James Traveling Fellowship

Archaeological Institute of America
656 Beacon Street
4th Floor
Boston, MA 02215-2010
(617) 353-9361
Average award: $15,000
Number of awards: 1
Deadline: November 15
College level: Doctoral, received Ph.D. within the last five years
Majors/Fields: Archaeology, architecture, classics, history, sculpture
Criteria: Applicant must be a U.S. citizen or permanent resident. Award is for travel and study in Greece, the Aegean Islands, Sicily, southern Italy, Asia Minor, or Mesopotamia. Preference given to projects of at least a half year's duration. Award is not intended to support field excavation projects. Awarded every year.
Contact: Fellowships.

Sociology/Social Work——

1063   Christie School Scholarship

Portland State University
P.O. Box 751
Portland, OR 97207-0751
(503) 725-5270
Average award: $3,000
Number of awards: 1
Deadline: June 1
Majors/Fields: Social work
Criteria: Appliant must serve a three-term, two-day-a-week internship at Christie Sch. Awarded every year. Award may be used only at sponsoring institution.
Contact: Scholarships, Graduate School of Social Work.

1064   Kerr Youth and Family Center Scholarship

Portland State University
P.O. Box 751
Portland, OR 97207-0751
(503) 725-5270
Average award: $7,000
Number of awards: 1
Deadline: June 1
Majors/Fields: Social Work
Criteria: Applicant must have a demonstrated interest in child and family mental health. Award involves a three-term, two-day-a-week field assignment at Kerr Center. Awarded every year. Award may be used only at sponsoring institution.
Contact: Scholarships, Graduate School of Social Work.

1065   Mt. Hood Community Mental Health Center Scholarship

Portland State University
P.O. Box 751
Portland, OR 97207-0751
(503) 725-5270
Maximum award: $10,000
Number of awards: 1
Deadline: June 1
Majors/Fields: Social work
Criteria: Applicant must fulfill a three-term, two-day-a-week field instruction at Mt. Hood Community Mental Health Center. Scholarship is renewable. Awarded every year. Award may be used only at sponsoring institution.
Contact: Scholarships, Graduate School of Social Work.

1066   Practicum Stipend in the Area of Developmental Disability Services

University of Oklahoma
University Affairs
900 Asp Avenue, Room 236
Norman, OK 73019-0401
(405) 325-1701
Average award: $4,000
Maximum award: $8,000
Number of awards: 11
Deadline: August 1 (undergraduate); November 1 (graduate)
College level: Junior, Senior, Graduate, Doctoral
Majors/Fields: Social work
Criteria: Applicant must be eligible to take SWK 4325 or 5820 Practica and be willing to seek professional positions with the division of Developmental Disabilities of the Oklahoma Department of Human Services. Awarded every year. Award may be used only at sponsoring institution.
Contact: School of Social Work, 217 RHYN, Norman, OK 73019, (405) 325-2821.

1067 Richard Klutznick Scholarship

B'nai B'rith Youth Organization
1640 Rhode Island Avenue, NW
Washington, DC 20036
(202) 857-6633
Average award: $2,500
Number of awards: 2
Deadline: April/May
College level: Graduate
Majors/Fields: Social work
Criteria: Applicant must be interested in working for Jewish agencies, have a positive attitude toward Jewish programs, demonstrate good scholarship, and attend an accredited school of social work majoring in group work. Applicant must accept employment with B'nai B'rith, if offered, and work for at least two years after graduation. Satisfactory GPA and reapplication are required to retain scholarship. Awarded every year.
Contact: Joseph Wittenstein, Assistant International Director.

1068 Social Work Scholarship

Portland State University
P.O. Box 751
Portland, OR 97207-0751
(503) 725-5270
Average award: $6,000
Number of awards: 1
Deadline: May 1
Majors/Fields: Social work
Criteria: Applicant must be a minority student who is interested in a career in child welfare services. Awarded every year. Award may be used only at sponsoring institution.
Contact: Scholarships, Graduate School of Social Work.

1069 Walter O. Cralle Memorial Scholarship

Southwest Missouri State University
Student Financial Aid
901 South National Avenue
Springfield, MO 65804-0095
(417) 836-5000 or (800) 492-7900
Average award: $1,000
Number of awards: 2
Deadline: March 31
College level: Junior, Senior
Majors/Fields: Anthropology, social work, sociology
Criteria: Applicant must have a minimum 3.5 cumulative GPA. Awarded every year. Award may be used only at sponsoring institution.
Contact: Scholarship Committee, (417) 836-5262 or (800) 492-7900.

Urban Planning

1070 American Planning Association Planning Fellowship

American Planning Association
1776 Massachusetts Avenue, NW
Washington, DC 20036
(202) 872-0611
Average award: $2,000
Maximum award: $3,500
Minimum award: $1,000
Maximum number of awards: 10
Minimum number of awards: 8
Deadline: May 15
College level: Graduate
Majors/Fields: Urban planning, regional planning
Criteria: Applicant must be a U.S. or Canadian citizen, demonstrate financial need, be enrolled in a graduate planning program that is accredited by the Planning Accreditation Board, and be African-American, Hispanic, or Native American. Awarded every year.
Contact: Mary Marcoux, Assistant for Divisions, Fellowships, and Council Administration.

1071 Charles Abrams Scholarship

American Planning Association
1776 Massachusetts Avenue, NW
Washington, DC 20036
(202) 872-0611
Average award: $2,000
Number of awards: 1
Deadline: April 30
College level: Graduate
Majors/Fields: Regional planning, urban planning
Criteria: Applicant must be a U.S. citizen, demonstrate financial need, and be accepted into the graduate planning program at one of the following schools: Columbia U, Harvard U, MIT, New Sch for Social Research (New York), or U of Pennsylvania. Awarded every year.
Contact: Mary Marcoux, Assistant for Divisions, Fellowships, and Council Administration.

1072 Maurie Clark Fellowship

Portland State University
P.O. Box 751
Portland, OR 97207-0751
(503) 725-5270
Average award: $5,600
Number of awards: 1
College level: Ph.D. candidate
Majors/Fields: Urban and Public Affairs
Criteria: Applicant must have an approved dissertation outline and intend to use the fellowship to support research activities. Awarded every year. Award may be used only at sponsoring institution.
Contact: Scholarships, School of Urban and Public Affairs.

1073 Patrick L. Monahan Memorial Scholarship

Western Washington University
516 High Street
Bellingham, WA 98226-9006
(206) 650-3471
Average award: $3,000
Deadline: April 15
College level: Freshman, Sophomore, Junior, Senior, Graduate, Doctoral
Majors/Fields: Geography, regional planning
Criteria: Applicant must demonstrate promise of significant professional contributions. Awarded every year. Award may be used only at sponsoring institution.
Contact: Geography Department, 217 Arntzen Hall, Bellingham, WA 98225, (206) 650-3284.

1074 Planning and Black Community Division Undergraduate Minority Scholarship Program

American Planning Association
1776 Massachusetts Avenue, NW
Washington, DC 20036
(202) 872-0611
Average award: $2,500
Number of awards: 1
Deadline: May 15
College level: Junior, Senior
Majors/Fields: Urban planning, regional planning
Criteria: Applicant must demonstrate financial need and be African-American, Hispanic, or Native American. Awarded every year.
Contact: Mary Marcoux, Assistant for Divisions, Fellowships, and Council Administration.

Other/Miscellaneous

Academic/Leadership Ability

1075   Academic Distinction Scholarship

Marquette University
1212 West Wisconsin Avenue
Milwaukee, WI 53233
(414) 288-7390
Average award: $4,000
Deadline: January 1 (priority)
College level: Freshman, transfer students
Criteria: Applicant must rank in the top tenth of high school class with comparable ACT or SAT I scores. Minimum 3.0 GPA and full-time enrollment are required to retain scholarship. Awarded every year. Award may be used only at sponsoring institution.
Contact: Anne Wingert, Assistant Director of Student Financial Aid.

1076   Academic Excellence Scholarship

University of Southern Mississippi
Office of Recruitment and Orientation
Box 5166
Hattiesburg, MS 39406-5166
(601) 266-5000
Average award: $1,500
Maximum award: $2,000
Minimum award: $1,000
Number of awards: 75
Deadline: April 1
College level: Freshman
Criteria: Applicant must have a minimum 3.0 GPA and have a minimum composite ACT score of 30 or be a National Merit or National Achievement semifinalist. Scholarship is renewable. Awarded every year. Award may be used only at sponsoring institution.
Contact: Dr. Homer Wesley, Director of Recruitment and Orientation.

1077   Academic Excellence Scholarship

University of Memphis
Scates Hall 204
Memphis, TN 38152
(901) 678-3213
Maximum award: $3,000
Minimum award: $2,800
Deadline: January 15
College level: Freshman
Criteria: Applicant must have a minimum 3.25 GPA, and a minimum composite ACT score of 30 or combined SAT I score of 1200. Minimum 3.0 GPA first year, 3.25 GPA each year thereafter, and service requirement of 20 hours per year are required to retain scholarship. Awarded every year; may be used only at sponsoring institution.
Contact: Dr. Sue Ann McClellan, Scholarship Coordinator.

1078   Academic Excellence Scholarship

University of Texas at Arlington
701 S. Nedderman Drive
P.O. Box 19199
Arlington, TX 76019
(817) 273-2197
Average award: $1,000
Number of awards: 4
Deadline: March 15
College level: Freshman
Criteria: Applicant must rank in the top quarter of graduating class and have a minimum combined SAT I score of 1300 or composite ACT score of 31. Minimum GPA of 3.5 and completion of 12 hours each fall and spring semester are required to retain scholarship. Awarded every year; may be used only at sponsoring institution.
Contact: Chris Woodyard, Scholarship Coordinator.

1079   Academic Grant

Colorado State University
Financial Aid Office
108 Student Services Building
Fort Collins, CO 80523
(970) 491-6321
Average award: $5,000
Number of awards: 37
Deadline: January 31
College level: Freshman
Criteria: Applicant is automatically considered based on application for admission. Minimum 2.0 cumulative GPA, nonresident status, and satisfactory progress are required to retain scholarship. Awarded every year; may be used only at sponsoring institution.
Contact: Jeanne Snyder, Financial Aid Counselor.

1080   Academic Honors Transfer Scholarship

Hofstra University
126 Memorial Hall
Hempstead, NY 11550
(516) 463-6677
Maximum award: $1,500
Minimum award: $1,000
Deadline: February 15
College level: Sophomore, Junior
Criteria: Applicant must be an incoming transfer student with a minimum of 24 hours from an accredited institution and a minimum 3.0 cumulative GPA. Applicant with 3.5 or greater GPA receives $1,500 and applicant with 3.0-3.499 GPA receives $1,000. Completion of 24 hours per year with a minimum of 18 hours of letter grades other than P is required to retain scholarship. Awarded every year. Award may be used only at sponsoring institution.
Contact: Joan Warren, Director of Financial Aid.

1081   Academic Opportunity Scholarship

Ferris State University
901 South State Street
Big Rapids, MI 49307
(616) 592-2110
Average award: $2,000
Number of awards: 10
Deadline: March 1
College level: Freshman
Criteria: Applicant must have a minimum 3.0 GPA. Minimum 2.75 GPA is required to retain scholarship. Awarded every year. Award may be used only at sponsoring institution.
Contact: Robert Bopp, Director of Scholarships and Financial Aid, 420 Oak Street, Big Rapids, MI 49307.

1082   Academic Scholarship

Indiana State University
217 North Sixth Street
Terre Haute, IN 47809
(812) 237-2121
Average award: $1,500
Number of awards: 200
Deadline: February 15
College level: Freshman
Criteria: Applicant must rank in the top tenth of graduating class. Satisfactory GPA and full-time status are required to retain scholarship. Awarded every year. Award may be used only at sponsoring institution.
Contact: Scholarships, Office of Admissions.

1083 Academic Scholarship for Frosh Students

University of Calgary
2500 University Drive, NW
Calgary, Alberta, CN T2N 1N4
(403) 220-7872
Average award: $1,000
Number of awards: 5
Deadline: July 15
College level: Freshman
Criteria: All five awards are based upon academic merit; one also considers extracurricular activities and achievements. Awarded every year. Award may be used only at sponsoring institution.
Contact: J. Van Housen, Director of Student Awards & Financial Aid.

1084 Achievement Class Award

University of Oklahoma
University Affairs
900 Asp Avenue, Room 236
Norman, OK 73019-0401
(405) 325-1701
Maximum award: $3,000
Minimum award: $1,200
Number of awards: 76
Deadline: February 15
College level: Freshman
Criteria: Selection is based upon merit and leadership. Ethnic minorities are encouraged to apply. Awarded every year. Award may be used only at sponsoring institution.
Contact: Prospective Student Services, Boyd House, 407 West Boyd Street, Norman, OK 73069, (405) 325-2151.

1085 Aduct Scholarship

University of Memphis
Scates Hall 204
Memphis, TN 38152
(901) 678-3213
Maximum award: $2,042
Minimum award: $1,200
Deadline: April 15
Criteria: Applicant must have academic potential evidenced by job achievement and community involvement. Minimum 2.5 GPA and 30 service hours per semester (15 hours for part-time recipients) are required to retain scholarship. Awarded every year. Award may be used only at sponsoring institution.
Contact: Dr. Sue Ann McClellan Scholarship Coordinator.

1086 Alumni Association of the University of Calgary Bursary

University of Calgary
2500 University Drive, NW
Calgary, Alberta, CN T2N 1N4
(403) 220-7872
Average award: $1,500
Number of awards: 10
Deadline: June 15
College level: Sophomore, Junior, Senior
Criteria: Selection is based upon financial need and academic merit. Awarded every year; may be used only at sponsoring institution.
Contact: J. Van Housen, Director of Student Awards & Financial Aid.

1087 Alumni Association Scholarship

Louisiana State University and Agricultural and Mechanical College
Baton Rouge, LA 70803-2750
(504) 388-3103
Maximum award: $7,995
Minimum award: $4,695
Number of awards: 100
Deadline: February 1
College level: Freshman
Criteria: Applicant must have excellent standardized test scores and high school academic record. Minimum 3.0 cumulative GPA and full-time enrollment are required to retain scholarship. Awarded every year. Award may be used only at sponsoring institution.
Contact: Kathleen Sciacchetano, Director of Financial Aid.

1088 Alumni Foundation Honor Scholarship

University of Toledo
Financial Aid Office
Toledo, OH 43606-3390
(419) 537-2056
Average award: $1,000
Number of awards: 10
Deadline: January 28
College level: Freshman
Criteria: Section is based upon academic achievement. Award is for four years. Awarded every year. Award may be used only at sponsoring institution.
Contact: Office of Financial Aid, Toledo, OH 43606-3390.

1089 Alumni Honor Scholarship

University of Toledo
Financial Aid Office
Toledo, OH 43606-3390
(419) 537-2056
Average award: $1,500
Number of awards: 5
College level: Sophomore, Junior, Senior
Criteria: Applicant must be invited to apply. Applicant must also be enrolled full time. Selection is based upon academic achievement, financial need, community service, and service to the university. Award is for up to three years. Awarded every year. Award may be used only at sponsoring institution.
Contact: Development Office, Toledo, OH 43606.

1090 Alumni Memorial Scholarship

Oakland University
101 North Foundation Hall
Rochester, MI 48309-4401
(810) 370-3360
Average award: $2,500
Number of awards: 1
Deadline: February 1
College level: Freshman
Criteria: Minimum 3.25 GPA is required to retain scholarship. Awarded every year. Award may be used only at sponsoring institution.
Contact: Stacy M. Penkala, Assistant Director of Admissions.

1091 Alumni Scholars Award

University of Colorado at Boulder
Campus Box 106
Boulder, CO 80309-0106
(303) 492-5091
Minimum award: $1,000
Maximum number of awards: 50
Minimum number of awards: 30
Deadline: March 1
College level: Freshman
Criteria: Applicant must rank in the top tenth of class. Selection is based upon academic merit, leadership, and community involvement. Financial need may be considered. Awarded every year. Award may be used only at sponsoring institution.
Contact: Office of Financial Aid.

1092 Alumni Scholarship

University of Houston
129 Ezekiel W. Cullen Building
Houston, TX 77204-2161
(713) 743-9051
Average award: $1,000
Number of awards: 57
Deadline: April 1
College level: Freshman
Criteria: Minimum 3.0 GPA and 14 hours per semester are required to retain scholarship. Awarded every year. Award may be used only at sponsoring institution.
Contact: Robert Sheridan, Director of Scholarships & Financial Aid.

1093   Alumni Scholarship

Indiana State University
217 North Sixth Street
Terre Haute, IN 47809
(812) 237-2121
Average award: Full tuition
Number of awards: 25
Deadline: February 15
College level: Freshman
Criteria: Applicant must rank in the top tenth of graduating class. Satisfactory GPA and full-time status are required to retain scholarship. Awarded every year. Award may be used only at sponsoring institution.
Contact: Scholarships, Office of Admissions, Terre Haute, IN 47809, (800) 742-0891.

1094   Alumni Scholarship

East Tennessee State University
P.O. Box 70722
Johnson City, TN 37614-0002
(615) 929-4300
Average award: $1,000
Number of awards: 19
Deadline: February 15
College level: Freshman, transfer students
Criteria: Freshman applicant must have a minimum composite ACT score of 29 or a combined SAT I score of 1150. Transfer applicant must be nominated by an area community or junior college president or his or her designee. Academic achievement required to retain scholarship. Awarded every year. Award may be used only at sponsoring institution.
Contact: Michael Jones, Financial Aid Counselor.

1095   Alumni Scholarship

University of South Carolina (Columbia)
Columbia, SC 29208
(803) 777-8134
Average award: $2,500
Number of awards: 30
Deadline: Early November
College level: Freshman
Criteria: Selection is based upon outstanding academic achievement. Minimum 3.0 GPA is required to retain scholarship. Awarded every year. Award may be used only at sponsoring institution.
Contact: Stewart Jones, Scholarship Coordinator.

1096   Alumni, Faculty and Staff Scholarships

Clemson University
G-01 Sikes Hall
Clemson, SC 29634-5123
(803) 656-2280
Average award: $1,000
Number of awards: 2
College level: Freshman
Criteria: Applicant must have outstanding academic potential. Minimum 3.0 GPA with at least 12 credits per semester is required to retain scholarship. Awarded every year. Award may be used only at sponsoring institution.
Contact: Marvin Carmichael, Director of Financial Aid.

1097   Alumni/Foundation Leadership Scholarship

Washington State University
Office of Scholarship Services
Pullman, WA 99164-1728
(509) 335-1059
Average award: $1,000
Number of awards: 30
Deadline: February 15
College level: Freshman
Criteria: Applicant must be a high school senior with a minimum 3.3 cumulative GPA who has been involved in leadership roles in school and/or community activities. Awarded every year. Award may be used only at sponsoring institution.
Contact: Johanna H. Davis, Assistant Director.

1098   American Council of Learned Societies Fellowship

American Council of Learned Societies
228 East 45th Street
New York, NY 10017-3398
(212) 697-1505
Maximum award: $20,000
Deadline: September 30
College level: Post-doctoral research
Criteria: Applicant must be a U.S. citizen or permanent legal resident, have held the Ph.D. for at least two years, and have not had a supported research leave for at least five years. Award is for postdoctoral research in all disciplines of the humanities and humanities-related social sciences. Awarded every year.
Contact: Office of Fellowships and Grants.

1099   American Wine Industry Research Scholarship

American Society for Enology & Viticulture
P.O. Box 1855
Davis, CA 95617
(916) 753-3142
College level: Senior
Majors/Fields: Agriculture
Criteria: Applicant must be a college junior majoring in a science basic to the wine industry with a minimum 3.0 GPA and plans to enter the American wine industry or related research. Scholarship is renewable.
Contact: Scholarships.

1100   Amigo Scholarship

University of New Mexico
Mesa Vista Hall
Room 1044
Albuquerque, NM 87131
(505) 277-6090
Average award: In-state tuition
Maximum number of awards: 350
Minimum number of awards: 70
Deadline: February 1
College level: Freshman, transfer students
Criteria: Applicant must be a nonresident of New Mexico and have a minimum 3.5 GPA with minimum composite ACT score of 23 or have a minimum 3.0 GPA with a minimum composite ACT score of 26. Minimum 3.0 GPA with 30 credit hours per year is required to retain scholarship. Awarded every year. Award may be used only at sponsoring institution.
Contact: Rita M. Padilla, Associate Director of Scholarships and Financial Aid.

1101   Angier B. Duke Scholarship

Duke University
P.O. Box 90397
Durham, NC 27706
(919) 684-6225
Average award: $18,400
Maximum award: $20,280
Number of awards: 15
Deadline: January 15
College level: Freshman
Criteria: Applicant must have high academic qualifications as determined by the A. B. Duke Selection Committee. A separate application is not required. Scholarship is renewable. Awarded every year. Award may be used only at sponsoring institution.
Contact: Christoph Guttentag, Director of Admissions, P.O. Box 90587, Durham, NC 27708-0587, (919) 684-3214.

1102   Anibal Excellence Scholarship

Oakland University
101 North Foundation Hall
Rochester, MI 48309-4401
(810) 370-3360
Average award: $2,500
Number of awards: 5
Deadline: February 1
College level: Freshman
Criteria: Minimum 3.25 GPA is required to retain scholarship. Awarded every year. Award may be used only at sponsoring institution.
Contact: Stacy M. Penkala, Assistant Director of Admissions.

1103   Art Academy of Cincinnati Entrance Scholarship

Art Academy of Cincinnati
1125 Saint Gregory Street
Cincinnati, OH 45202-1700
(513) 721-5205, (800) 323-5692
Average award: $3,500
Maximum award: $8,000
Minimum award: $1,000
Number of awards: 12
Deadline: March 15
College level: Freshman, Sophomore, Junior
Criteria: Selection is based upon talent, letters of recommendation, and artist's statement. Portfolio is required. Renewable if 3.0 GPA and full-time status are maintained. Awarded every year. Award may be used only at sponsoring institution.
Contact: Douglas Dobbins, Director of Admissions, (513) 562-8757.

1104   Association of Christian Schools International Scholarship

Liberty University
P.O. Box 20000
Lynchburg, VA 24506-8001
(804) 582-2270
Average award: $1,000
Number of awards: 4
Deadline: August 1; January 1
College level: Freshman
Criteria: Applicant must rank in the top 15% of an Association of Christian Schools International high school and have a minimum 3.0 GPA. Scholarship is renewable. Awarded every year. Award may be used only at sponsoring institution.
Contact: High School Administrator.

1105   Barry M. Goldwater Scholarship and Excellence in Education Program

Barry M. Goldwater Scholarship and Excellence in Education Foundation
6225 Brandon Avenue
Suite 315
Springfield, VA 22150-2519
(703) 756-6012
Maximum award: $7,000
Number of awards: 250
Deadline: December 15
College level: Junior, Senior
Majors/Fields: Engineering, mathematics, natural sciences
Criteria: Applicant must be a U.S. citizen, permanent resident, or resident alien who submits letter of intent to obtain U.S. citizenship, with a minimum "B" average, and rank in top quarter of class. Selection is based upon merit, outstanding potential, and intent to pursue career in mathematics, natural sciences, or engineering. Automatically renewed for sophomores. Awarded every year.
Contact: Goldwater Faculty Representative on campus, Scholarships.

1106   Bob Grainger Matriculation Bursary

University of Calgary
2500 University Drive, NW
Calgary, Alberta, CN T2N 1N4
(403) 220-7872
Average award: $2,000
Number of awards: 1
Deadline: July 15
College level: Freshman
Criteria: Selection is based upon academic merit, financial need, and extracurricular activities. Awarded every year. Award may be used only at sponsoring institution.
Contact: J. Van Housen, Director of Student Awards & Financial Aid.

1107   Bradley Distinguished Scholars Award

Marquette University
1212 West Wisconsin Avenue
Milwaukee, WI 53233
(414) 288-7390
Average award: Full tuition
Number of awards: 10
Deadline: February 1
College level: Freshman
Criteria: Applicant must rank in the top five percent of class, and have a minimum composite ACT score of 30 or combined SAT I score of 1300. Semifinalists are interviewed by a selection committee. Minimum 3.0 GPA and full-time enrollment are required to retain scholarship. Awarded every year. Award may be used only at sponsoring institution.
Contact: Anne Wingert, Assistant Director of Student Financial Aid.

1108   BSU Scholarship

Ball State University
Muncie, IN 47306
(317) 285-5600
Maximum award: $10,852
Minimum award: $6,472
Number of awards: 10
Deadline: April 1
College level: Freshman
Criteria: Applicant must rank in the top tenth of class and have a minimum combined SAT I score of 1200 or composite ACT score of 29. Scholarship is renewable. Awarded every year. Award may be used only at sponsoring institution.
Contact: Dr. Arno Wittig, Dean of Honors College, (317) 285-1024.

1109   Carl S. Ell Scholarship

Northeastern University
360 Huntington Avenue
Boston, MA 02115
(617) 373-2000
Maximum award: $21,834
Number of awards: 50
Deadline: March 1
College level: Freshman
Criteria: Applicant must have a minimum combined SAT I score of 1150 and rank in the top five percent of class. Minimum 3.25 GPA and participation in the Honor's program are required to retain scholarship. Awarded every year. Award may be used only at sponsoring institution.
Contact: Kevin Kelly, Dean of Admissions, 360 Huntington Ave, 150 Richard Hall, Boston, MA 02115, (617) 373-2200.

1110   Cecil C. Humphreys Merit Scholarship

University of Memphis
Scates Hall 204
Memphis, TN 38152
(901) 678-3213
Maximum award: $6,500
Deadline: January 15
College level: Freshman
Criteria: Applicant must be selected as a college-sponsored merit finalist and indicate the U of Memphis as first choice college with National Merit Scholarship Corporation. Scholarship is renewable. Awarded every year; may be used only at sponsoring institution.
Contact: Dr. Sue Ann McClellan, Scholarship Coordinator.

1111   Cecil C. Humphreys Presidential Scholarship

University of Memphis
Scates Hall 204
Memphis, TN 38152
(901) 678-3213
Maximum award: $4,200
Deadline: January 15
College level: Freshman
Criteria: Applicant must have a minimum composite ACT score of 30 or combined SAT score of 1200. Selection is competitive based upon test scores, high school transcript, interview, excellence of performance in an area of interest, and quantity and quality of extracurricular activities. Minimum 3.0 GPA for first year, 3.25 GPA thereafter, and service requirement of 10 hours per year are required to retain scholarship. Awarded every year. Award may be used only at sponsoring institution.
Contact: Dr. Sue Ann McClellan, Scholarship Coordinator.

1112   Centro Cultural Cubano Scholarship

University of Texas at San Antonio
Office of Student Financial Aid
6900 North Loop 1604 West
San Antonio, TX 78249-0687
(210) 691-4011
Average award: $1,000
Deadline: May 31
College level: Freshman, Sophomore, Junior, Senior
Criteria: Applicant must demonstrate financial need and have a minimum 2.75 GPA. Minimum 2.75 GPA is required to retain scholarship. Awarded every year. Award may be used only at sponsoring institution.
Contact: Scholarship Office, (210) 691-4855.

1113   Century III Leaders Program

National Association of Secondary School Principals
1904 Association Drive
Reston, VA 22091
Maximum award: $11,500
Minimum award: $100
Number of awards: 520
Deadline: October 17
College level: Freshman
Criteria: Applicant must be nominated by a high school principal or guidance counselor. Participation begins at local school level and progresses to statewide competition among all local school winners. Two winners from each state and the District of Columbia receive $1,500 scholarships and all-expense-paid trips to national Century III leaders meeting, and have the opportunity to win additional $10,000 scholarship. State alternates receive $500 scholarships. Selection is based upon leadership skills, school and community involvement, and innovative thinking about America's future. Awarded every year.
Contact: Awards.

1114   Chancellor Scholarship

University of Pittsburgh, Pittsburgh Campus
4200 Fifth Avenue
Pittsburgh, PA 15260
(412) 624-4141
Maximum award: $19,168
Minimum award: $9,982
Number of awards: 10
Deadline: January 15
College level: Freshman
Criteria: Selection is based upon high school performance, SAT I or ACT scores, essay, and interview. Minimum 3.0 GPA is required to retain scholarship. Awarded every year. Award may be used only at sponsoring institution.
Contact: Betsy A. Porter, Director of Admissions & Financial Aid, (412) 624-7164.

1115   Chancellor's Alumni Scholarship

Louisiana State University and Agricultural and Mechanical College
Baton Rouge, LA 70803-2750
(504) 388-3103
Maximum award: $9,595
Minimum award: $6,295
Number of awards: 10
Deadline: February 1
College level: Freshman
Criteria: Applicant must have an overall "A" average in high school English, math, social studies, and natural sciences. Interview and essay are required. Applicant must have a composite ACT score of 33, combined SAT I score of 1350, or a National Merit selection index score of at least 200. Minimum 3.0 cumulative GPA and full-time enrollment are required to retain scholarship. Awarded every year. Award may be used only at sponsoring institution.
Contact: Kathleen Sciacchetano, Director of Financial Aid.

1116   Chancellor's Leadership Class Scholarship

University of Nebraska, Lincoln
14th and R Streets
Lincoln, NE 68588
(402) 472-2030
Average award: $1,000
Number of awards: 75
Deadline: January 15
College level: Freshman
Criteria: Selection is based on outstanding leadership skills. Awarded every year. Award may be used only at sponsoring institution.
Contact: Debra Augustyn, Assistant Director of Scholarships and Financial Aid.

1117   Chancellor's Scholarship

University of Missouri–Saint Louis
8001 Natural Bridge Road
Saint Louis, MO 63121
(314) 553-6396
Average award: Full educational fees
Number of awards: 29
Deadline: April 1
College level: Freshman
Criteria: Applicant must rank in top quarter of class, score in a high percentile on a college entrance test, and enroll on a full-time basis. Awarded every year. Award may be used only at sponsoring institution.
Contact: James D. Reed, Financial Aid Advisor.

1118   Chancellor's Scholarship

Liberty University
P.O. Box 20000
Lynchburg, VA 24506-8001
(804) 582-2270
Average award: $1,000
Number of awards: 4
Deadline: August 1; January 1
College level: Freshman
Criteria: Applicant must be the valedictorian or salutatorian of a public or private high school. Satisfactory academic scholarship is required to retain scholarship. Awarded every year. Award may be used only at sponsoring institution.
Contact: Penny Hutchison, Admissions Representative, (804) 582-2707.

1119 Charles H. Hewitt Memorial Scholarship

Wright State University
Coordinator of Scholarships
Dayton, OH 45435
(513) 873-5721
Average award: $1,000
Number of awards: 40
Deadline: March 1
College level: Freshman
Criteria: Applicant must have two of the following: a minimum composite ACT score of 27 or combined SAT score of 1100, a minimum 3.4 GPA, or rank in the top tenth of class. Minimum 3.0 cumulative GPA is required to retain scholarship. Awarded every year. Award may be used only at sponsoring institution.
Contact: Judy Rose, Assistant Director of Financial Aid, (513) 873-2321.

1120 CIBA-GEIGY Scholarship

University of South Alabama
260 Administration Building
Mobile, AL 36688-0002
(334) 460-6231
Average award: $2,500
Deadline: Early application recommended
College level: Freshman
Majors/Fields: Engineering
Criteria: Applicant must be a resident of Washington County. Renewable for up to four years. Awarded every year. Award may be used only at sponsoring institution.
Contact: Catherine P. King, Director of Admissions.

1121 Civitan Shropshire Scholarship

Civitan International Foundation
P.O. Box 130744
Birmingham, AL 35213-0744
Average award: $1,000
Number of awards: 35
Deadline: February 1
College level: Freshman, Sophomore, Junior, Senior, Graduate, Doctoral, community college students
Criteria: Applicant must be a Civitan, the immediate relative of a Civitan, or a Junior Civitan for at least two years. Selection is based upon career goals. Awarded every year.
Contact: Rosemary Franklin, Administrative Manager, P.O. Box 130744, Birmingham, AL 35213-0744, (205) 591-8910, extension 111.

1122 Clarence A. McLendon and Julia C. McLendon Memorial Scholarship

Clemson University
G-01 Sikes Hall
Clemson, SC 29634-5123
(803) 656-2280
Average award: $2,000
Number of awards: 3
College level: Freshman
Criteria: Selection is based upon admissions application. Minimum 3.0 GPA with at least 12 credits per semester is required to retain to scholarship. Awarded every year. Award may be used only at sponsoring institution.
Contact: Marvin Carmichael, Director of Financial Aid.

1123 Class of '38 Golden Anniversary Scholarship

Clemson University
G-01 Sikes Hall
Clemson, SC 29634-5123
(803) 656-2280
Average award: $2,000
Number of awards: 5
Deadline: March 1
College level: Freshman, Sophomore, Junior, Senior
Criteria: Applicant must have a minimum 2.0 GPA. Satisfactory GPA with at least 12 credits per semester is required to retain scholarship. Awarded every year; may be used only at sponsoring institution.
Contact: Marvin Carmichael, Director of Financial Aid.

1124 Class of '39 Scholarship

Clemson University
G-01 Sikes Hall
Clemson, SC 29634-5123
(803) 656-2280
Average award: $2,310
Number of awards: 2
Deadline: March 1
College level: Freshman, Sophomore, Junior, Senior
Criteria: Applicant must have a minimum 2.0 GPA. Scholarships are rotated so that all of the university's colleges benefit in proportion to their total enrollment. Satisfactory GPA with at least 12 credits per semester is required to retain scholarship. Awarded every year. Award may be used only at sponsoring institution.
Contact: Marvin Carmichael, Director of Financial Aid.

1125 Class of '49 Alumni Scholars Endowment

Clemson University
G-01 Sikes Hall
Clemson, SC 29634-5123
(803) 656-2280
Average award: $3,000
Number of awards: 1
Deadline: March 1
College level: Freshman, Sophomore, Junior, Senior
Criteria: Applicant must have a minimum 2.0 GPA. Satisfactory GPA with at least 12 credits per semester is required to retain scholarship. Awarded every year; may be used only at sponsoring institution.
Contact: Marvin Carmichael, Director of Financial Aid.

1126 Class of 1936 Golden Anniversary Scholarship

Clemson University
G-01 Sikes Hall
Clemson, SC 29634-5123
(803) 656-2280
Average award: $2,000
Number of awards: 3
College level: Freshman
Criteria: Selection is based upon admissions application. Minimum 3.0 GPA is with at least 12 credits per semester is required to retain scholarship. Awarded every year. Award may be used only at sponsoring institution.
Contact: Marvin Carmichael, Director of Financial Aid.

1127 College of Arts and Sciences Scholarship

Washington University
One Brookings Drive
Campus Box 1089
St. Louis, MO 63130
(314) 935-6000 or (800) 638-0700
Average award: $8,375
Number of awards: 30
College level: Freshman
Majors/Fields: Natural sciences, mathematics, social sciences, humanities
Criteria: Selection is based upon academic merit without regard to financial need. Satisfactory academic performance is required to retain scholarship. Awarded every year. Award may be used only at sponsoring institution.
Contact: Office of Undergraduate Admissions.

1128 Colorado Scholars Award

Colorado State University
Financial Aid Office
108 Student Services Building
Fort Collins, CO 80523
(970) 491-6321
Average award: $1,000
Number of awards: 89
Deadline: February or March
College level: Freshman, Sophomore, Junior, Senior
Criteria: Applicant must have minimum 3.0 cumulative GPA. Reapplication and minimum 3.0 cumulative GPA are required to retain scholarship. Awarded every year. Award may be used only at sponsoring institution.
Contact: Peggy Meis, Financial Aid Counselor.

1129 Colorado Scholars President's Gold Award

Metropolitan State College of Denver
P.O. Box 173362
Denver, CO 80217-3362
(303) 556-3018
Average award: $1,000
Maximum award: $1,850
Minimum award: $950
Number of awards: 125
College level: Freshman
Criteria: Applicant must demonstrate outstanding high school achievement. Minimum 3.5 GPA is required to retain scholarship for four years. Awarded every year. Award may be used only at sponsoring institution.
Contact: Paul Cesare, Assistant Director of High School Relations.

1130 Community College Presidential Scholarship

University of Memphis
Scates Hall 204
Memphis, TN 38152
(901) 678-3213
Average award: $2,042
Deadline: April 1
College level: Junior
Criteria: Applicant must be recommended by the president of a Tennessee community college. Minimum 2.8 GPA is required to retain scholarship. Awarded every year. Award may be used only at sponsoring institution.
Contact: Dr. Sue Ann McClellan, Scholarship Coordinator.

1131 Community College Transfer Scholarship

Ferris State University
901 South State Street
Big Rapids, MI 49307
(616) 592-2110
Average award: $1,200
Number of awards: 29
Deadline: April 1
College level: Transfer with Associate degree
Criteria: Applicant must have an associate degree from a community college with a minimum 3.5 GPA. Minimum 3.25 GPA is required to retain scholarship. Awarded every year. Award may be used only at sponsoring institution.
Contact: Robert Bopp, Director of Scholarships and Financial Aid, 420 Oak Street, Big Rapids, MI 49307.

1132 Community College Transfer Scholarship

University of Memphis
Scates Hall 204
Memphis, TN 38152
(901) 678-3213
Average award: $2,442
Deadline: April 1
College level: Junior
Criteria: Applicant must have an associate degree with a minimum 3.5 GPA. Minimum 2.8 GPA and a service requirement of 30 hours per year are required to retain scholarship. Awarded every year. Award may be used only at sponsoring institution.
Contact: Dr. Sue Ann McClellan, Scholarship Coordinator.

1133 Competitive Scholarship for Transfers from Two-year Colleges

Marquette University
1212 West Wisconsin Avenue
Milwaukee, WI 53233
(414) 288-7390
Average award: $2,000
Number of awards: 30
Deadline: April 15 (fall); November 15 (spring)
College level: Transfer students from two-year colleges
Criteria: Selection is based upon academic qualifications, extracurricular activities, leadership, and a written essay. Minimum 3.0 GPA and full-time enrollment are required to retain scholarship. Awarded every year. Award may be used only at sponsoring institution.
Contact: Anne Wingert, Assistant Director of Student Financial Aid.

1134 Computer Based Honors Scholarship

University of Alabama–Tuscaloosa
Box 870162
Tuscaloosa, AL 35487-0162
(205) 348-6756
Average award: $2,000
Number of awards: 5
Deadline: December 20
College level: Freshman
Criteria: Applicant must have a minimum composite ACT score of 31 or combined SAT I score of 1300. Top 20 finalists visit the campus for interviews. Recipient will be able to work with the university computer facilities in course of study without majoring in computer science. Superior performance at the university and in the computer-based honors program is required to retain scholarship. Awarded every year. Award may be used only at sponsoring institution.
Contact: Molly Lawrence, Director of Financial Aid.

1135 Cullen Leadership Scholarship

University of Houston
129 Ezekiel W. Cullen Building
Houston, TX 77204-2161
(713) 743-9051
Average award: $2,000
Number of awards: 15
Deadline: April 1
College level: Freshman
Criteria: Applicant must provide essay detailing leadership activities and two letters of recommendation. Minimum 3.0 GPA and 14 hours per semester are required to retain scholarship. Awarded every year. Award may be used only at sponsoring institution.
Contact: Robert Sheridan, Director of Scholarships & Financial Aid.

1136 D. Paul Fansler Memorial Scholarship

Portland State University
P.O. Box 751
Portland, OR 97207-0751
(503) 725-5270
Average award: $1,000
Number of awards: 2
Deadline: May 1
College level: Junior, Senior
Criteria: Applicant must have a high promise of achievement in international affairs. Scholarship is renewable. Awarded every year. Award may be used only at sponsoring institution.
Contact: Scholarships, International Studies Program.

1137 David Scholarship

University of Nebraska, Lincoln
14th and R Streets
Lincoln, NE 68588
(402) 472-2030
Average award: $1,000
Number of awards: 135
Deadline: January 15
College level: Freshman
Criteria: Minimum 3.5 GPA with 24 credit hours per year is required to retain scholarship. Awarded every year. Award may be used only at sponsoring institution.
Contact: Debra Augustyn, Assistant Director of Scholarships.

1138 Dean's Scholarship

Indiana State University
217 North Sixth Street
Terre Haute, IN 47809
(812) 237-2121
Average award: $1,100
Number of awards: 110
Deadline: February 15
College level: Freshman
Criteria: Applicant must rank in the top quarter of graduating class. Satisfactory GPA and full-time status are required to retain scholarship. Awarded every year; may be used only at sponsoring institution.
Contact: Scholarships, Office of Admissions, (800) 742-0891.

1139 Dean's Scholarship

Ferris State University
901 South State Street
Big Rapids, MI 49307
(616) 592-2110
Average award: $2,500
Number of awards: 30
Deadline: January 10
College level: Freshman
Criteria: Applicant must have minimum 3.5 GPA and composite ACT score of 27. Minimum 3.25 GPA required to retain scholarship. Awarded every year. Award may be used only at sponsoring institution.
Contact: Robert Bopp, Director of Scholarships and Financial Aid, 420 Oak Street, Big Rapids, MI 49307.

1140 Dedman Distinguished Scholars Award

University of Texas at Austin
Austin, TX 78713-7758
(512) 475-6200
Average award: $3,000
Maximum award: $7,000
Minimum award: $1,000
Number of awards: 6
Deadline: December 1 (preferred)
College level: Freshman
Majors/Fields: Liberal arts
Criteria: Applicant must rank in the top five percent of class and be enrolled in the Coll of Liberal Arts. Satisfactory academic progress is required to retain scholarship. Awarded every year. Award may be used only at sponsoring institution.
Contact: Liberal Arts Interdisciplinary Programs, Office of the Dean.

1141 Departmental and General Scholarships

University of Texas at El Paso
Recruitment and Scholarship Office
500 West University Avenue
El Paso, TX 79968
(915) 747-5890
Maximum award: $2,000
Minimum award: $200
Number of awards: 150
Deadline: March 1
College level: Freshman, Sophomore, Junior, Senior, Graduate
Criteria: Applicant must have a minimum 3.0 college GPA or high school average of 90 and be enrolled full time. Some awards require financial need, specific majors, or ethnic minority status. Minimum 3.0 GPA and 30 credit hours per year are required to retain scholarship. Awarded every year. Award may be used only at sponsoring institution.
Contact: Barbara L. Nehring, Assistant Director for Scholarships.

1142 Departmental Scholarship

University of Central Oklahoma
100 North University
Edmond, OK 73034
(405) 341-2980, extension 3336
Average award: $1,000
Maximum award: $1,600
Number of awards: 10
Deadline: April 1
College level: Freshman, Sophomore, Junior, Senior, Graduate
Criteria: Applicant should contact department of major for specific details. Awarded every year. Award may be used only at sponsoring institution.
Contact: Margaret Howell, Scholarship Coordinator.

1143 DeVry Scholarship

DeVry Inc.
One Tower Lane
Oakbrook Terrace, IL 60181
Maximum award: Full tuition
Minimum award: Half tuition
Number of awards: 156
Deadline: March 20 for some scholarships.
College level: Freshman, Transfer
Criteria: Minimum 2.5 GPA is required for renewal. Awarded every year. Award may be used only at sponsoring institution.
Contact: Director of Admissions, DeVry Institute.

1144 Distinguished Academic Scholar Program

Hofstra University
126 Memorial Hall
Hempstead, NY 11550
(516) 463-6677
Maximum award: Full tuition
Deadline: February 15
College level: Freshman
Criteria: Applicant must have a minimum combined SAT I score of 1300 or composite ACT score of 29. Minimum 3.0 GPA at end of freshman year, 3.1 GPA at end of sophomore year, and 3.2 GPA at end of junior year are required to retain scholarship. Awarded every year. Award may be used only at sponsoring institution.
Contact: Joan Warren, Director of Financial and Academic Records.

1145 Distinguished Honors Scholarship

State University of New York–Buffalo
Buffalo, NY 14260
(716) 831-2000
Maximum award: $10,000
Number of awards: 20
College level: Freshman, Sophomore, Junior, Senior
Criteria: Applicant must rank in the top seven percent of class, have an unweighted average of 93, and have a minimum combined SAT I score of 1300. Scholarship is renewable. Awarded every year. Award may be used only at sponsoring institution.
Contact: Josephine Capuana, Administrative Director, 214 Talbert Hall, Box 601700, Buffalo, NY 14260-1700, (716) 645-3020.

1146 Distinguished Scholar Award

Colorado State University
Financial Aid Office
108 Student Services Building
Fort Collins, CO 80523
(970) 491-6321
Average award: $2,000
Number of awards: 81
Deadline: January 31
College level: Freshman
Criteria: Applicant is automatically considered based on application for admission. Minimum 3.5 cumulative GPA and participation in the Honors program required to retain scholarship. Awarded every year. Award may be used only at sponsoring institution.
Contact: Peggy Meis, Financial Aid Counselor.

1147 Distinguished Scholar Award

Central Missouri State University
Office of Admissions, Administration 104
Warrensburg, MO 64093
(816) 543-4541
Maximum award: $25,000
Number of awards: 25
Deadline: February 15
College level: Freshman
Criteria: Applicant must have a minimum composite ACT score of 28, and either rank in the top five percent of class or have a minimum cumulative GPA of 3.75 at the end of sixth or seventh high school semester. Renewable if minimum 2.0 GPA after first semester, minimum 3.5 GPA after second semester, or minimum 3.75 GPA after fourth semester is maintained and thereafter at least 12 hours per semester are taken. Awarded every year. Award may be used only at sponsoring institution.
Contact: Scholarships and Awards Officer, Admissions Office.

1148   Distinguished Scholar Award

University of Nebraska–Lincoln
14th and R Streets
Lincoln, NE 68588
(402) 472-2030
Average award: $1,000
Number of awards: 200
Deadline: January 15
College level: Freshman
Criteria: Applicant must be an outstanding student and/or National Merit Semifinalist. Selection is based upon standardized test scores. Recipient must maintain a 3.5 GPA and 24 credit hours per year to retain scholarship. Awarded every year. Award may be used only at sponsoring institution.
Contact: Debra Augustyn, Assistant Director of Scholarships and Financial Aid.

1149   DuSable Scholarship

Western Illinois University
One University Circle
Macomb, IL 61455
(309) 295-1414
Maximum award: $1,000
Number of awards: 4
Deadline: Early application recommended
College level: Freshman, transfer students
Criteria: Applicant must have a minimum composite ACT score of 22 and be a member of an under-represented group. Minimum 3.0 GPA is required to retain scholarship. Awarded every year. Award may be used only at sponsoring institution.
Contact: Janice Owens, Scholarship Coordinator, (309) 298-2446.

1150   E.I. and Minnie Pashby Scholarship

Colorado State University
Financial Aid Office
108 Student Services Building
Fort Collins, CO 80523
(970) 491-6321
Minimum award: $1,000
Number of awards: 3
Deadline: March 3
College level: Graduate, Doctoral
Criteria: Application must be a graduate student with need and ability. Reapplication required for renewal. Awarded every year. Award may be used only at sponsoring institution.
Contact: Jeanne Snyder, Financial Aid Counselor.

1151   Early Scholars Award

University of Memphis
Scates Hall 204
Memphis, TN 38152
(901) 678-3213
Maximum award: $2,442
Deadline: January 15
College level: Freshman
Criteria: Award is guaranteed to applicants with a minimum 3.5 high school GPA and a minimum composite ACT score of 27 or combined SAT I score of 1060. Minimum 3.0 GPA and a service requirement of 30 hours per year are required to retain scholarship. Awarded every year. Award may be used only at sponsoring institution.
Contact: Dr. Sue Ann McClellan, Scholarship Coordinator.

1152   Educational Communications Scholarship

Educational Communications Scholarship Foundation
721 North McKinley Road
Lake Forest, IL 60045-5002
Average award: $1,000
Number of awards: 150
Deadline: June 1
College level: Freshman
Criteria: Applicant must be a U.S. citizen and have taken the ACT or SAT I. Selection is based upon GPA, test scores, leadership qualifications, work experience, and essay evaluation. Some consideration given to financial need. Request for application must be made by March 15. Awarded every year.
Contact: Judy Casey, Assistant to the Chairman.

1153   Edwin F. Avery Memorial Scholarship

University of Alabama–Tuscaloosa
Box 870162
Tuscaloosa, AL 35487-0162
(205) 348-6756
Average award: $2,000
Number of awards: 2
Deadline: December 3
College level: Freshman
Criteria: Applicant must score in the top percentile on the ACT or SAT I. Minimum 3.0 GPA in residence is required to retain scholarship for up to four years. Awarded every year. Award may be used only at sponsoring institution.
Contact: Molly Lawrence, Director of Financial Aid.

1154   Edwin L. and Ruth Kennedy Distinguished Professor Scholarship

Ohio University
Office of Student Financial Aid and Scholarships
Athens, OH 45701
(614) 593-4141
Average award: Full tuition
Number of awards: 18
Deadline: No application is required
College level: Freshman, Sophomore, Junior, Senior
Criteria: Selection is based upon academic qualifications. Each Distinguished Professor personally selects recipient and determines specific major and academic program. Distinguished professor determines if scholarship is renewable. Awarded every year. Award may be used only at sponsoring institution.
Contact: Yang-Hi Kim, Associate Director of Scholarships & Grants.

1155   Elizabeth Coleman Honors Scholarship

University of Alabama–Tuscaloosa
Box 870162
Tuscaloosa, AL 35487-0162
(205) 348-6756
Average award: $2,000
Number of awards: 2
Deadline: February 15
College level: Freshman, Sophomore, Junior, Senior, Graduate
Criteria: Applicant must be an outstanding student. Minimum 3.0 GPA is required to retain scholarship. Awarded every year. Award may be used only at sponsoring institution.
Contact: Molly Lawrence, Director of Financial Aid.

1156   Elks National Foundation Most Valuable Student Award

Elks National Foundation
Average award: $1,000
Maximum award: $5,000
Number of awards: 500
Deadline: Mid-January
College level: Freshman
Criteria: Applicant must be a U.S. citizen, reside within the jurisdiction of the B.P.O. Elks of the U.S.A., have scholarship rating of 90%, and rank in upper five percent of his or her class. Selection is based upon scholarship, leadership, and financial need. Applications are available through local lodges in mid-November. Some scholarships are for four years. Awarded every year.
Contact: Contact local Elks for state association address.

1157 Elsa Jorgenson Award

Portland State University
P.O. Box 751
Portland, OR 97207-0751
(503) 725-5270
Average award: $6,000
Number of awards: 2
Deadline: April 15
College level: Doctoral, regularly admitted masters students
Majors/Fields: Engineering, English, foreign languages, mathematics, science
Criteria: Applicant must be a U.S. citizen or permanent resident. Selection is based upon statement of goals, academic merit, faculty recommendations, and financial need. One award is for English or foreign languages, the other is for science, engineering, or mathematics. Awarded every year. Award may be used only at sponsoring institution.
Contact: Scholarships, Office of Graduate Studies, (503) 725-3423.

1158 Emerging Leaders Scholarship

University of Memphis
Scates Hall 204
Memphis, TN 38152
(901) 678-3213
Maximum award: $2,442
Deadline: April 15
College level: Freshman, Sophomore, Junior, Senior
Criteria: Applicant must have a minimum 2.5 GPA, minimum composite ACT score of 20, demonstrate participation in school activities and leadership qualities. Recommendations and interview are required. Minimum 2.25 GPA for the first year, 2.5 GPA thereafter, full-time status, and enrollment in certain classes are required for renewal. Awarded every year. Award may be used only at sponsoring institution.
Contact: Dr. Sue Ann McClellan, Scholarship Coordinator.

1159 Endowed Scholarships

University of California, Los Angeles
A129 Murphy Hall
Box 951435
Los Angeles, CA 90095-1435
(310) 206-0404
Maximum award: $3,000
Minimum award: $100
Number of awards: 800
College level: Freshman, Sophomore, Junior, Senior
Criteria: Applicant with fewer than 20 units of university work must have a minimum 3.5 GPA; applicant with 20 or more units of work must have a minimum 3.3 GPA. Most scholarships are based on financial need and some have specific qualifications established by the donors. Awarded every year. Award may be used only at sponsoring institution.
Contact: Beverly LeMay, Assistant Director of Scholarships, (310) 206-0417.

1160 Esther L. Beyer Scholarship

University of Toledo
Financial Aid Office
Toledo, OH 43606-3390
(419) 537-2056
Average award: $1,000
Number of awards: 50
Deadline: January 28
College level: Freshman
Criteria: Applicant must have an excellent academic record and be enrolled full time. Awarded every year. Award may be used only at sponsoring institution.
Contact: Office of Financial Aid, Toledo, OH 43606-3390.

1161 Excellence Scholarship

University of Missouri–Columbia
High School and Transfer Relations
219 Jesse Hall
Columbia, MO 65211
(800) 225-6075 (in-state), (314) 882-2456
Average award: $1,000
Number of awards: 600
Deadline: August 15
College level: Freshman
Criteria: Applicant must rank in the top 15 percent of class, have a minimum composite ACT score of 27 or combined SAT I score of 1130, and enroll at the university the first semester after high school. Renewable for one additional year with a minimum 3.25 GPA. Awarded every year. Award may be used only at sponsoring institution.
Contact: High School and Transfer Relations.

1162 Foundation Scholarship

Oakland University
101 North Foundation Hall
Rochester, MI 48309-4401
(810) 370-3360
Average award: $5,000
Number of awards: 5
Deadline: February 1
College level: Freshman
Criteria: Minimum 3.25 GPA is required to retain scholarship. Awarded every year; may be used only at sponsoring institution.
Contact: Stacy M. Penkala, Assistant Director of Admissions.

1163 Founder's Scholarship

Ferris State University
901 South State Street
Big Rapids, MI 49307
(616) 592-2110
Average award: $6,000
Number of awards: 5
Deadline: January 10
College level: Freshman
Criteria: Applicant must have a minimum 3.7 GPA and minimum composite ACT score of 30. Minimum 3.25 GPA is required to retain scholarship. Awarded every year. Award may be used only at sponsoring institution.
Contact: Robert Bopp, Director of Scholarships and Financial Aid, 420 Oak Street, Big Rapids, MI 49307.

1164 Frank A. Burtner Scholarship

Clemson University
G-01 Sikes Hall
Clemson, SC 29634-5123
(803) 656-2280
Average award: $2,500
Number of awards: 1
Deadline: March 1
College level: Junior, Senior
Criteria: Applicant must have a minimum 2.0 GPA and demonstrate excellent leadership qualities. Awarded every year. Award may be used only at sponsoring institution.
Contact: Marvin Carmichael, Director of Financial Aid.

1165 Frank J. Jervey Alumni Scholarship

Clemson University
G-01 Sikes Hall
Clemson, SC 29634-5123
(803) 656-2280
Average award: $2,000
Number of awards: 2
College level: Freshman
Criteria: Selection is based upon admissions application. Minimum 3.0 cumulative GPA with at least 12 credits per semester is required to retain scholarship. Awarded every year. Award may be used only at sponsoring institution.
Contact: Marvin Carmichael, Director of Financial Aid.

1166   General Scholarship Program

University of Oregon
1242 University of Oregon
Eugene, OR 97403-1242
(503) 346-3044
Average award: $1,500
Maximum award: $2,100
Minimum award: $1,200
Number of awards: 200
Deadline: February 1
College level: Freshman, Sophomore, Junior, Senior, Graduate, Doctoral
Criteria: Selection is based upon academic standing, extracurricular activities, essay, and faculty recommendations. Awarded every year. Award may be used only at sponsoring institution.
Contact: Jim Gilmour, Associate Director of Financial Aid, (503) 346-1187.

1167   General Studies Scholarship for Academic Excellence

University of Calgary
2500 University Drive, NW
Calgary, Alberta, CN T2N 1N4
(403) 220-7872
Average award: $1,500
Number of awards: 2
Deadline: June 15
College level: Junior, Senior
Majors/Fields: General studies
Criteria: Selection is based upon academic merit. Awarded every year. Award may be used only at sponsoring institution.
Contact: J. Van Housen, Director of Student Awards & Financial Aid.

1168   Georgetown University Grant

Georgetown University
37th and O Streets, NW
Washington, DC 20057
(202) 687-4547
Average award: $10,000
Maximum award: $23,000
Minimum award: $500
Number of awards: 2134
Deadline: January 15 (entering freshmen); April 15 (others)
College level: Freshman, Sophomore, Junior, Senior, Graduate, Doctoral
Criteria: Applicant must demonstrate financial need. Renewable if financial need is still demonstrated. Awarded every year. Award may be used only at sponsoring institution.
Contact: Patricia McWade, Dean of Student Financial Services.

1169   Glenn Terrell Presidential Scholarship

Washington State University
Office of Scholarship Services
Pullman, WA 99164-1728
(509) 335-1059
Average award: $1,500
Maximum award: $3,000
Minimum award: $500
Number of awards: 350
Deadline: February 15
College level: Freshman, Sophomore, Junior, Senior
Criteria: Selection is based upon academic excellence as measured by GPA, standardized test scores, quality of required essay, and other indicators of scholarly achievement. Financial need is not considered. Scholarship is renewable. Awarded every year. Award may be used only at sponsoring institution.
Contact: Johanna H. Davis, Assistant Director.

1170   Graduate Scholarship

University of Texas at El Paso
Recruitment and Scholarship Office
500 West University Avenue
El Paso, TX 79968
(915) 747-5890
Maximum award: $9,600
Minimum award: $200
Number of awards: 150
Deadline: March 1
College level: Graduate, Doctoral
Criteria: Applicant must have a minimum 3.0 GPA and be enrolled full time. Some awards require financial need, specific major, or ethnic minority status. Awarded every year. Award may be used only at sponsoring institution.
Contact: Barbara L. Nehring, Assistant Director for Scholarships.

1171   Gulf Canada Centennial Scholarship

University of Calgary
2500 University Drive, NW
Calgary, Alberta, CN T2N 1N4
(403) 220-7872
Average award: $1,800
Number of awards: 2
Deadline: June 15
College level: Sophomore, Junior, Senior
Criteria: Selection is based upon academic merit. Awarded every year. Award may be used only at sponsoring institution.
Contact: J. Van Housen, Director of Student Awards & Financial Aid.

1172   Harlan M. Smith "Builders of a Better World" Scholarship

World Federalist Association
418 Seventh Street, SE
Washington, DC 20003
Average award: $1,000
Maximum number of awards: 5
Minimum number of awards: 3
Deadline: March 20
College level: Freshman, Sophomore, Junior, Senior, Graduate, Doctoral
Criteria: Applicant must be a young leader (under 28 years of age) intending to use the scholarship to futher his or her education, which could include international travel and study, internships, etc. Applicant must demonstrate high academic achievement, dedication to "building a better world" through a stronger and more effective United Nations, and currently live in the U.S. World Federalist Association members are strongly encouraged to apply. Selection is based upon application essay, recommendations, extracurricular activities, and leadership abilities. Awarded every year.
Contact: Scholarship Coordinator.

1173   Harry C. Tilotson Scholarship

University of Toledo
Financial Aid Office
Toledo, OH 43606-3390
(419) 537-2056
Maximum award: $1,500
Minimum award: $500
Number of awards: 50
Deadline: January 28
College level: Freshman
Criteria: Selection is based upon academic achievement. Award is for four years. Awarded every year. Award may be used only at sponsoring institution.

1174 Harry S Truman Scholarship

University of Oklahoma
University Affairs
900 Asp Avenue, Room 236
Norman, OK 73019-0401
(405) 325-1701
Maximum award: $27,000
Minimum award: $3,000
Number of awards: 3
Deadline: October 30
College level: Senior
Criteria: Applicant must rank in the top quarter of class. University selects three applicants to submit to the national office for this highly competitive national program. Awarded every year. Award may be used only at sponsoring institution.
Contact: Honors Program, Honors House, 347 Cate Center Drive, Norman, OK 73019, (405) 325-5291.

1175 Henry King Stanford Scholarship

University of Miami
P.O. Box 248187
Coral Gables, FL 33124-5240
(305) 284-5212
Average award: $8,670
Number of awards: 400
Deadline: January 15
College level: Freshman, transfer students
Criteria: Applicant must rank in the top five to eight percent of class, have a minimum 3.8 GPA, and have a minimum combined SAT I score of 1280 or composite ACT score of 30. Minimum 3.0 cumulative GPA and 24 credit hours per year are required to retain scholarship. Awarded every year; may be used only at sponsoring institution.
Contact: Martin J. Carney, Director, Financial Assistance Services.

1176 Hofstra Recognition Scholarship

Hofstra University
126 Memorial Hall
Hempstead, NY 11550
(516) 463-6677
Maximum award: $4,000
Minimum award: $1,500
Deadline: February 15
College level: Freshman
Criteria: Applicant must rank in the top tenth of class and have a minimum composite ACT score of 23 or combined SAT I score of 1000. Minimum 3.0 GPA by end of freshman year, 3.1 GPA by end of sophomore year, and 3.2 GPA by end of junior year are required to retain scholarship. Awarded every year. Award may be used only at sponsoring institution.
Contact: Joan Warren, Director of Financial and Academic Records.

1177 Honor Scholarship

Louisiana State University and Agricultural and Mechanical College
Baton Rouge, LA 70803-2750
(504) 388-3103
Average award: $3,945
Number of awards: 500
Deadline: February 1
College level: Freshman
Criteria: Applicant must have high standardized test scores and an excellemt academic record, especially in English and math. Minimum 3.0 cumulative GPA and full-time enrollment are required to retain scholarship. Awarded every year. Award may be used only at sponsoring institution.
Contact: Kathleen Sciacchetano, Director of Financial Aid.

1178 Honor Scholarship

University of Toledo
Financial Aid Office
Toledo, OH 43606-3390
(419) 537-2056
Average award: $1,000
Number of awards: 25
Deadline: February 28
College level: Freshman
Criteria: Applicant must have an excellent academic record. Award is for four years. Awarded every year. Award may be used only at sponsoring institution.
Contact: Office of Financial Aid, Toledo, OH 43606-3390.

1179 Honor Scholarship

Marquette University
1212 West Wisconsin Avenue
Milwaukee, WI 53233
(414) 288-7390
Average award: $3,000
Deadline: January 1 (priority)
College level: Freshman, transfer students
Criteria: Applicant must rank in top quarter of high school class with comparable ACT or SAT I scores. Minimum 2.0 GPA and full-time enrollment are required to retain scholarship. Awarded every year. Award may be used only at sponsoring institution.
Contact: Anne Wingert, Assistant Director of Student Financial Aid.

1180 Honors Scholarship

Wright State University
Coordinator of Scholarships
Dayton, OH 45435
(513) 873-5721
Average award: $1,500
Maximum award: $2,500
Minimum award: $500
Number of awards: 10
Deadline: February 1
College level: Freshman
Criteria: Award is competitive. Minimum 3.0 GPA in honors courses is required to retain scholarship. Awarded every year. Award may be used only at sponsoring institution.
Contact: Judy Rose, Assistant Director of Financial Aid, (513) 873-2321.

1181 Honors Scholarship

University of Akron
302 Buchtel Commons
Akron, OH 44325-6211
(216) 972-7032
Maximum award: $1,800
Minimum award: $900
Deadline: February 1
College level: Freshman
Criteria: Minimum 3.25 GPA is required to retain scholarship. Awarded every year. Award may be used only at sponsoring institution.
Contact: Doug McNutt, Director of Student Financial Aid.

1182 Ignatius Scholarship

Marquette University
1212 West Wisconsin Avenue
Milwaukee, WI 53233
(414) 288-7390
Average award: $5,000
Deadline: January 1 (priority)
College level: Freshman, transfer students
Criteria: Applicant must rank in the top five percent of high school class with comparable ACT or SAT I scores. Minimum 3.0 GPA and full-time enrollment are required to retain scholarship. Awarded every year. Award may be used only at sponsoring institution.
Contact: Anne Wingert, Assistant Director of Student Financial Aid.

1183   Illinois Department of Agriculture Scholarship

Western Illinois University
One University Circle
Macomb, IL 61455
(309) 295-1414
Maximum award: $1,000
Number of awards: 3
Deadline: Early application recommended
College level: Freshman
Majors/Fields: Agriculture
Criteria: Applicant must have a minimum composite ACT score of 25 and rank in the top fifth of class. Awarded every year. Award may be used only at sponsoring institution.
Contact: Janice Owens, Scholarship Coordinator, (309) 298-2001.

1184   Incentive Grant/Scholarship

Chowan College
P.O. Box 1848
Murfreesboro, NC 27855
(800) 488-4101
Average award: $2,875
Maximum award: $5,000
Minimum award: $1,500
Number of awards: 340
Deadline: August 1
College level: Freshman, Junior, Senior
Criteria: Selection is based on SAT I scores and GPA. Minimum 2.0 GPA is required to retain grant. Minimum 3.0 GPA is required to retain scholarship. Awarded every year. Award may be used only at sponsoring institution.
Contact: Austine Evans, Vice President for Enrollment Management.

1185   Indiana University of Pennsylvania Foundation Distinguished Scholars Award

Indiana University of Pennsylvania
308 Pratt Hall
Indiana, PA 15705
(412) 357-2218
Average award: $2,000
Minimum award: $1,500
Maximum number of awards: 35
Minimum number of awards: 11
Deadline: None
College level: Freshman
Criteria: Applicant must have a minimum combined SAT I score of 1100 or rank in the top tenth of class, and demonstrate leadership, extracurricular activities, and honors. Minimum 3.0 GPA is required to retain scholarship. Awarded every year. Award may be used only at sponsoring institution.
Contact: Patricia C. McCarthy, Assistant Director of Financial Aid.

1186   Isaac Bashevis Singer Scholarship

University of Miami
P.O. Box 248187
Coral Gables, FL 33124-5240
(305) 284-5212
Average award: $17,340
Number of awards: 10
Deadline: January 15
College level: Freshman
Criteria: Applicant must rank in the top one to two percent of class, have a minimum 3.9 GPA, and have a minimum combined SAT I score of 1400 or composite ACT score of 33. Minimum 3.0 cumulative GPA and 24 credit hours per year are required to retain scholarship. Awarded every year; may be used only at sponsoring institution.
Contact: Martin J. Carney, Director, Financial Assistance Services.

1187   J. Preston Levis Academic Scholarship

University of Toledo
Financial Aid Office
Toledo, OH 43606-3390
(419) 537-2056
Average award: $2,000
Number of awards: 5
Deadline: January 28
College level: Freshman
Criteria: Applicant must demonstrate outstanding citizenship, leadership, and academic achievement. Award is for four years. Awarded every year. Award may be used only at sponsoring institution.
Contact: Office of Financial Aid, Toledo, OH 43606-3390.

1188   Jack Warner Scholarship

University of Alabama–Tuscaloosa
Box 870162
Tuscaloosa, AL 35487-0162
(205) 348-6756
Average award: $1,000
Maximum number of awards: 4
Minimum number of awards: 2
College level: Freshman, Sophomore, Junior, Senior
Majors/Fields: Arts, business administration, commerce, engineering, sciences
Criteria: Selection is based upon academic excellence. Minimum 3.0 GPA is required to retain scholarship. Awarded every year. Award may be used only at sponsoring institution.
Contact: Molly Lawrence, Director of Financial Aid.

1189   Jay F. W. Pearson Scholarship

University of Miami
P.O. Box 248187
Coral Gables, FL 33124-5240
(305) 284-5212
Average award: $5,200
Number of awards: 310
Deadline: January 15
College level: Freshman, transfer students
Criteria: Selection is based upon academic achievement. Typically, applicant should rank in the top eight to twelve percent of class, have a minimum 3.6 GPA, and have a minimum combined SAT I score of 1200 or a composite ACT score of 28. Minimum 3.0 GPA and 24 credit hours per year are required to retain scholarship. Award may be used only at sponsoring institution.
Contact: Martin J. Carney, Director, Financial Assistance Services.

1190   Jaycee War Memorial Fund Scholarship

U.S. Junior Chamber of Commerce
4 West 21st Street
Tulsa, OK 74114-1116
Average award: $1,000
Number of awards: 20
Deadline: February 1
College level: Freshman, Sophomore, Junior, Senior, Graduate, Doctoral
Criteria: Applicant must be a U.S. citizen, possess academic potential and leadership traits, and show financial need. Enclose a self-addressed, business-sized, stamped envelope and a $5 application fee (check or money order made payable to JWMF) with request between July 1 and February 1. Awarded every year.
Contact: Jaycee War Memorial Fund Scholarship, Department 94922, Tulsa, OK 77194-0001.

1191 John F. Bannon Memorial Scholarship

Clemson University
G-01 Sikes Hall
Clemson, SC 29634-5123
(803) 656-2280
Average award: $1,500
Number of awards: 2
Deadline: March 1
College level: Freshman, Sophomore, Junior, Senior
Criteria: Applicant must have a minimum 2.0 GPA. Satisfactory GPA with at least 12 credits per semester is required to retain scholarship. Awarded every year. Award may be used only at sponsoring institution.
Contact: Marvin Carmichael, Director of Financial Aid.

1192 Julia Klug Scholarship

Colorado State University
Financial Aid Office
108 Student Services Building
Fort Collins, CO 80523
(970) 491-6321
Minimum award: $1,000
Number of awards: 4
Deadline: March 3
College level: Freshman, Sophomore, Junior, Senior, Graduate, Doctoral
Criteria: Applicant must demonstrate academic improvement, leadership, involvement in volunteer civic activities, and financial need. Reapplication is required for renewal. Awarded every year. Award may be used only at sponsoring institution.
Contact: Jeanne Snyder, Financial Aid Couselor.

1193 Junior College Honorary Scholarship

Washington University
One Brookings Drive
Campus Box 1089
St. Louis, MO 63130
(314) 935-6000 or (800) 638-0700
Average award: $16,750
Number of awards: 1
College level: Junior
Criteria: Applicant must be an outstanding student transferring from Saint Louis Community Coll. Satisfactory academic performance is required to retain scholarship. Awarded every year. Award may be used only at sponsoring institution.
Contact: Office of Undergraduate Admissions.

1194 Junior College Honors Scholarship

University of Alabama–Tuscaloosa
Box 870162
Tuscaloosa, AL 35487-0162
(205) 348-6756
Average award: Tuition
Number of awards: 5
Deadline: March 7
College level: Junior
Criteria: Applicant must be a transfer student from a junior college in Alabama with a minimum 3.5 GPA. Minimum 3.0 GPA is required to retain scholarship. Awarded every year. Award may be used only at sponsoring institution.
Contact: Molly Lawrence, Director of Financial Aid.

1195 Junior College Transfer Scholarship

University of South Alabama
260 Administration Building
Mobile, AL 36688-0002
(334) 460-6231
Average award: $1,000
Deadline: May 1
College level: Transfer students
Criteria: Applicant must have a satisfactory minimum cumulative GPA. Minimum 3.0 GPA is required to retain scholarship. Awarded every year. Award may be used only at sponsoring institution.
Contact: Catherine P. King, Director of Admissions.

1196 Kelso-Battle Scholarship

Ferris State University
901 South State Street
Big Rapids, MI 49307
(616) 592-2110
Average award: $4,000
Number of awards: 5
Deadline: March 1
College level: Freshman
Majors/Fields: Actuarial science, applied mathematics, biotechnology, computer information systems, industrial chemistry, industrial environment health management, pre-engineering, technology
Criteria: Applicant must have a minimum 3.5 GPA minimum, composite ACT score of 26, and demonstrate financial need. Minimum 3.25 GPA is required to retain scholarship. Awarded every year. Award may be used only at sponsoring institution.
Contact: Robert Bopp, Director of Scholarships and Financial Aid, 420 Oak Street, Big Rapids, MI 49307.

1197 Kerr-McGee Scholars Award

University of Oklahoma
University Affairs
900 Asp Avenue, Room 236
Norman, OK 73019-0401
(405) 325-1701
Average award: $4,000
Number of awards: 6
College level: Junior, Senior
Criteria: Applicant must be currently enrolled and have earned at least 30 hours at the university with a minimum 3.75 GPA. Applicant must not be currently receiving an academic award. Awarded every year. Award may be used only at sponsoring institution.
Contact: Kenneth Conklin, Office of Development, 730 College, Norman, OK 73019-0395.

1198 Leadership Program Teaching/Research Fellowship

University of Oklahoma
University Affairs
900 Asp Avenue, Room 236
Norman, OK 73019-0401
(405) 325-1701
Average award: $1,000
Number of awards: 18
Deadline: February 8
College level: Junior, Senior
Majors/Fields: Leadership program
Criteria: Applicant must be a member in good standing of the Leadership Program. Selection is based upon proposals for teaching and/or research submitted by the student and his or her faculty advisor. Awarded every year. Award may be used only at sponsoring institution.
Contact: Director of Leadership Program, Adams Hall 7B, Norman, OK 73019, (405) 325-2501.

1199 Lechner and McFadden Scholarships

Texas A&M University, College Station
College Station, TX 77843-4233
(409) 845-1957
Average award: $2,000
Number of awards: 200
Deadline: January 8
College level: Freshman
Criteria: Applicant must have a minimum combined SAT I score of 1300 or composite ACT score of 30 and rank in the top 10 percent of class or be a National Merit or National Achievement semifinalist. Academic achievement, rigor of curriculum, extracurricular activities, prizes and awards, leadership, and school recommendations will be considered. Minimum cumulative GPA of 3.0 is required to retain scholarship. Awarded every year. Award may be used only at sponsoring institution.
Contact: Dr. Dale T. Knobel, Executive Director of Honors Programs and Academic Scholarships.

1200 Lempert Scholarship

University of Toledo
Financial Aid Office
Toledo, OH 43606-3390
(419) 537-2056
Average award: $2,000
Number of awards: 17
Deadline: January 28
College level: Freshman
Criteria: Applicant must be enrolled full time. Selection is based upon outstanding academic achievement. Award is for four years. Awarded every year; may be used only at sponsoring institution.
Contact: Office of Financial Aid, Toledo, OH 43606-3390.

1201 Mary Coulter Clark Scholarship

Art Academy of Cincinnati
1125 Saint Gregory Street
Cincinnati, OH 45202-1700
(513) 721-5205, 800 323-5692
Average award: $1,000
Number of awards: 5
Deadline: May 1
College level: Sophomore, Junior, Senior, Graduate
Criteria: Selection is based upon GPA and financial need. Awarded every year. Award may be used only at sponsoring institution.
Contact: Karen Geiger, Director of Financial Aid, (513) 562-8751.

1202 McGill University Scholarship

McGill University
845 Sherbrooke Street West
Montreal, Quebec, CN H3A 2T5
(514) 398-4455
Maximum award: $7,000
Minimum award: $2,000
Deadline: January 15 (international students); March 15 (Canadians)
College level: Freshman, Sophomore, Junior, Senior, Graduate
Criteria: Application for all awards is submitted with the admissions application. Continuing students are automatically considered based upon high academic achievement. Applicant should rank in the top five percent of class. Scholarship is renewable. Awarded every year. Award may be used only at sponsoring institution.
Contact: Scholarships, Office of Admissions.

1203 Memorial Honors Scholarship

Hofstra University
126 Memorial Hall
Hempstead, NY 11550
(516) 463-6677
Maximum award: $7,500
Minimum award: $2,500
Deadline: February 15
College level: Freshman
Criteria: Applicant must rank in the top five percent of class and have a minimum combined SAT I score of 1350 or composite ACT score of 30. Minimum 3.0 GPA by end of freshman year, 3.1 GPA by end of sophomore year, and 3.2 GPA by end of junior year are required to retain scholarship. Awarded every year. Award may be used only at sponsoring institution.
Contact: Joan Warren, Director of Financial and Academic Records.

1204 Memorial Scholarship

University of Oklahoma
University Affairs
900 Asp Avenue, Room 236
Norman, OK 73019-0401
(405) 325-1701
Average award: $1,000
Maximum number of awards: 6
Minimum number of awards: 5
Deadline: March 1
College level: Freshman, Sophomore, Junior, Senior
Criteria: Selection is based upon academic merit and financial need. Awarded every year; may be used only at sponsoring institution.
Contact: Office of Financial Aid Services, 731 Elm, Norman, OK 73019-0230, (405) 325-4521.

1205 Monarch Merit Scholarship

Old Dominion University
Hampton Boulevard
Norfolk, VA 23529-0050
(804) 683-3683
Maximum award: $2,500
Number of awards: 45
Deadline: February 15
College level: Freshman
Criteria: Selection is based upon academic achievement and high school participation. Scholarship is renewable. Awarded every year. Award may be used only at sponsoring institution.
Contact: March A. Schutz, Assistant Director of Scholarships.

1206 National Alumni Association Honors Scholarship

University of Alabama–Tuscaloosa
Box 870162
Tuscaloosa, AL 35487-0162
(205) 348-6756
Maximum award: $4,172
Minimum award: In-state tuition
Number of awards: 30
Deadline: December 3
College level: Freshman
Criteria: Applicant must have a minimum composite ACT score of 30 or combined SAT I score of 1240 and have a minimum "B" average in high school. Top 20 applicants will be Alumni Honors Scholars with tuition and housing allowance; the next 10 recipients are Sesquicentennial Alumni Honors Scholars with tuition award only. Minimum 3.0 GPA is required to retain scholarship for four years. Awarded every year. Award may be used only at sponsoring institution.
Contact: Molly Lawrence, Director of Financial Aid.

1207 National Alumni Association Junior College Honors Scholarship

University of Alabama–Tuscaloosa
Box 870162
Tuscaloosa, AL 35487-0162
(205) 348-6756
Average award: $1,500
Number of awards: 10
Deadline: March 4
College level: Junior
Criteria: Applicant must be a junior college transfer student with a minimum 3.0 GPA and strong leadership activities. Minimum 3.0 GPA is required to retain scholarship. Awarded every year. Award may be used only at sponsoring institution.
Contact: Molly Lawrence, Director of Financial Aid.

1208 National Alumni Association Leadership Award

University of Alabama–Tuscaloosa
Box 870162
Tuscaloosa, AL 35487-0162
(205) 348-6756
Average award: In-state tuition
Number of awards: 50
Deadline: December 3
College level: Freshman
Criteria: Applicant must have a minimum composite ACT score of 22 or combined SAT I score of 920, have a minimum "B" average, demonstrate unique leadership ability in elected positions in school organizations, and have volunteered for or been elected to activities which benefit the community. Awarded every year. Award may be used only at sponsoring institution.
Contact: Molly Lawrence, Director of Financial Aid.

1209 National Alumni Association Past Presidents/ Crimson Scholarship

University of Alabama–Tuscaloosa
Box 870162
Tuscaloosa, AL 35487-0162
(205) 348-6756
Average award: $5,000
Number of awards: 1
Deadline: December 3
College level: Freshman
Criteria: Applicant must have a minimum composite ACT score of 30 or combined SAT I score of 1240 and an overall high school "B" average. Minimum 3.0 GPA is required to retain scholarship for four years. Awarded every year. Award may be used only at sponsoring institution.
Contact: Molly Lawrence, Director of Financial Aid.

1210 National Honor Society Scholarship

National Association of Secondary School Principals
1904 Association Drive
Reston, VA 22091
Average award: $1,000
Number of awards: 250
Deadline: February 3
College level: Freshman
Criteria: Each National Honor Society chapter may nominate two applicants based on leadership, scholarship, character, and service. Applicants must be high school seniors who have been nominated by their local chapter. Contact the National Honor Society advisor for further information. Awarded every year.
Contact: Awards.

1211 National Scholars Program

Eastern Michigan University
Office of Financial Aid
403 Pierce Hall
Ypsilanti, MI 48197
(313) 487-0455
Average award: $4,200
Number of awards: 100
Deadline: February 15
College level: Freshman
Criteria: Applicant must not be a resident of Michigan or Ohio and have a minimum 3.5 GPA and a combined SAT I score of 1050 or composite ACT score of 25. Minimum 3.5 GPA and 15 credit hours per semester are required to retain scholarship. Awarded every year. Award may be used only at sponsoring institution.
Contact: Cynthia Van Pelt, Assistant Director of Scholarships.

1212 Navy League Scholarship

Navy League of the United States
Scholarship Program
2300 Wilson Boulevard
Arlington, VA 22201-3308
Average award: $3,000
Number of awards: 3
Deadline: April 1
College level: Freshman
Criteria: Aapplicant must be a U.S. citizen and under 25 years of age. Selection is based upon academic performance, extracurricular activities, and financial need. Preference is given to children of active duty or deceased Coast Guard, Navy, Marine Corps, or Merchant Marine personnel, and applicants planning to major in engineering or science. Awarded every year.
Contact: Scholarships.

1213 Non-Resident Academic Scholarship

University of Memphis
Scates Hall 204
Memphis, TN 38152
(901) 678-3213
Average award: Registration fees, out-of-state tuition, and $300 book stipend
Deadline: January 15
College level: Freshman
Criteria: Applicant must have a minimum 3.25 GPA and a minimum composite ACT score of 30 (27 for minority applicant) or combined SAT I score of 1200 (1060 for minority applicant). Minimum 3.0 GPA and a service requirement of 30 hours per year are required to retain scholarship. Awarded every year. Award may be used only at sponsoring institution.
Contact: Dr. Sue Ann McClellan, Scholarship Coordinator.

1214 Oakland University Merit Scholarship

Oakland University
101 North Foundation Hall
Rochester, MI 48309-4401
(810) 370-3360
Average award: $1,766
Maximum award: $2,534
Minimum award: $998
Deadline: February 1
College level: Freshman
Criteria: Minimum 3.25 GPA is required to retain scholarship. Awarded every year; may be used only at sponsoring institution.
Contact: Stacy M. Penkala, Assistant Director of Admissions.

1215 Olliphant Scholarship

University of Southern Mississippi
Office of Recruitment and Orientation
Box 5166
Hattiesburg, MS 39406-5166
(601) 266-5000
Average award: $1,500
College level: Freshman
Criteria: Applicant must be an Honors College student who demonstrates outstanding leadership, commitment of service to society, and exemplary academic achievement. Award is for two years. Awarded every year; may be used only at sponsoring institution.
Contact: Office of Recruitment and Orientation.

1216 Oregon Laurels Graduate Tuition Remission Program

Portland State University
P.O. Box 751
Portland, OR 97207-0751
(503) 725-5270
Average award: $3,150
Maximum award: $2,808 part-time
Minimum award: $351
Number of awards: 103
Deadline: April 15
College level: Doctoral, regularly admitted masters students
Criteria: Applicant must be a U.S. citizen or permanent resident. Oregon residents are given preference. Selection is based upon academic merit, statement of goals, faculty recommendations, and gender and ethnicity as related to university's goals for achieving student diversity. Minimum 3.25 cumulative GPA and 27 credits for full-time students are required to retain scholarship. Awarded every year. Award may be used only at sponsoring institution.
Contact: Scholarships, Office of Graduate Studies, 303 Cramer Hall, Portland, OR 97207-0751, (503) 725-3423.

1217 Oregon Laurels Scholarship

Portland State University
P.O. Box 751
Portland, OR 97207-5252
(503) 725-5270
Average award: $1,800
Maximum award: $2,175
Minimum award: $1,200
Number of awards: 15
Deadline: March 1
College level: Freshman, Sophomore, Junior, Senior
Criteria: Applicant must have a minimum 3.25 GPA. Preference is given to Oregon residents. Minimum 3.0 GPA is required to retain scholarship. Awarded every year. Award may be used only at sponsoring institution.
Contact: Virginia McElroy, Scholarship Coordinator.

1218 Oregon Sports Lottery Graduate Scholarship

Portland State University
P.O. Box 751
Portland, OR 97207-5252
(503) 725-5270
Average award: $8,454
Maximum award: $10,782
Minimum award: $7,334
Number of awards: 8
Deadline: April 15
College level: Doctoral, regularly admitted master's students
Criteria: Applicant must be a U.S. citizen or permanent resident. All applicants are rated on academic merit, statement of goals, faculty recommendations, and departmental nominations. Half of awards are given on merit only; the other half include financial need. Reapplication, minimum 3.5 GPA, progress report, and at least 9 credits per term are required to retain scholarship. Awarded every year. Award may be used only at sponsoring institution.
Contact: Scholarships, Office of Graduate Studies, 303 Cramer Hall, Portland, OR 97207-0751, (503) 725-3423.

1219 Otey B. Paschall Scholarship

University of Oklahoma
University Affairs
900 Asp Avenue, Room 236
Norman, OK 73019-0401
(405) 325-1701
Average award: $1,000
Number of awards: 7
Deadline: March 1
College level: Freshman, Sophomore, Junior, Senior
Criteria: Selection is based upon scholarship, character, potential, and financial need. Awarded every year. Award may be used only at sponsoring institution.
Contact: Office of Financial Aid Services, 731 Elm, Norman, OK 73019-0230, (405) 325-4521.

1220 Peace Corps and Overseas Volunteer Scholarship

School for International Training
P.O. Box 676
Kipling Road
Brattleboro, VT 05302
(802) 257-7751
Average award: $1,000
Minimum award: $500
Number of awards: 8
Deadline: April 1
College level: Degree candidate
Criteria: Applicant must have completed a minimum of one year of volunteer service with the Peace Corps or a similar volunteer organization. Financial need may be considered. Applicant must be enrolled in a degree program. Applicant must maintain satisfactory academic progress and demonstrate financial need. Awarded every year. Award may be used only at sponsoring institution.
Contact: Mary Henderson, Financial Aid Officer, (802) 258-3280.

1221 Peer Mentor Scholarship

Portland State University
P.O. Box 751
Portland, OR 97207-0751
(503) 725-5270
Average award: $2,800
Number of awards: 30
College level: Sophomore, Junior
Criteria: Applicant must have a minimum 3.0 GPA and be enrolled full time. Personal interview is required. Recipient must assist faculty teaching Freshman Inquiry courses to retain scholarship. Awarded every year. Award may be used only at sponsoring institution.
Contact: Scholarships, Office of University Studies, (503) 725-5890.

1222 Phi Beta Kappa Scholarship

Hofstra University
126 Memorial Hall
Hempstead, NY 11550
(516) 463-6677
Maximum award: $7,500
Minimum award: $3,000
Deadline: February 15
College level: Freshman
Criteria: Applicant must graduate first in his or her high school class. Minimum 3.0 GPA by end of freshman year, 3.1 GPA by end of sophomore year, and 3.2 GPA by end of junior year are required to retain scholarship. Awarded every year. Award may be used only at sponsoring institution.
Contact: Joan Warren, Director of Financial and Academic Records.

1223 Phi Theta Kappa Scholarship

Marquette University
1212 West Wisconsin Avenue
Milwaukee, WI 53233
(414) 288-7390
Average award: $3,000
Number of awards: 15
Deadline: April 15 (fall); November 15 (spring)
College level: Transfer students from two-year colleges
Criteria: Selection is based upon academic qualifications, extracurricular activities, leadership, essay, and recommendation from applicant's Phi Theta Kappa advisor. Minimum 3.0 GPA and full-time enrollment are required to retain scholarship. Awarded every year. Award may be used only at sponsoring institution.
Contact: Anne Wingert, Assistant Director of Student Financial Aid.

1224 Portland Police Association Scholarship

Portland State University
P.O. Box 751
Portland, OR 97207-0751
(503) 725-5270
Average award: $1,000
Number of awards: 2
Deadline: Contact the Administration of Justice Department
College level: Senior
Criteria: Applicant must have a minimum 3.0 GPA and must not be related to any member of the Portland Police Association. Financial need must be demonstrated. Scholarships will be awarded to one male and one female student. Awarded every year. Award may be used only at sponsoring institution.
Contact: Scholarships, Department of Administration of Justice, (503) 725-4014.

1225 President's Endowed Scholarship

Texas A&M University, College Station
College Station, TX 77843-4233
(409) 845-1957
Average award: $3,000
Number of awards: 200
Deadline: January 8
College level: Freshman
Criteria: Applicant must have a minimum combined SAT I score of 1300 or composite ACT score of 30 and rank in the top tenth of class, or be a National Merit or National Achievement semifinalist. Academic achievement, rigor of curriculum, extracurricular activities, prizes and awards, leadership, and school recommendations are considered. Minimum 3.0 cumulative GPA is required to retain scholarship. Awarded every year. Award may be used only at sponsoring institution.
Contact: Dr. Dale T. Knobel, Executive Director of Honors Programs and Academic Scholarships.

1226 President's Honors Scholarship

State University of New York College at Buffalo
1300 Elmwood Avenue
Buffalo, NY 14222
(716) 878-5303
Average award: $1,000
Number of awards: 20
Deadline: January 15
College level: Freshman, Sophomore
Criteria: Selection is based upon high school average, SAT I scores, and class rank. Minimum high school average of 90 is required. Application includes listing of high school and community activities and an essay. Minimum 3.5 GPA and participation in honors courses as part of the All-College Honors Program are required to retain scholarship. Awarded every year. Award may be used only at sponsoring institution.
Contact: Kathryn A. Moran, Assistant Dean, Undergraduate Studies.

1227 President's Leadership Scholarship

University of Central Oklahoma
100 North University
Edmond, OK 73034
(405) 341-2980, extension 3336
Average award: $2,000
Maximum award: $3,000
Minimum award: $1,500
Number of awards: 20
Deadline: February 1
College level: Freshman
Criteria: Applicant must be active in three organizations, have a minimum 3.0 GPA, and be enrolled full time. Minimum 3.0 GPA, full-time enrollment, and participation in three campus organizations are required to retain scholarship. Awarded every year. Award may be used only at sponsoring institution.
Contact: Margaret Howell, Scholarship Coordinator.

1228 President's Leadership Scholarship

Marquette University
1212 West Wisconsin Avenue
Milwaukee, WI 53233
(414) 288-7390
Average award: $2,500
Deadline: January 1
College level: Freshman, transfer students
Criteria: Applicant must have demonstrated leadership ability and involvement in extracurricular activities. Academic achievement and SAT I or ACT scores are also considered. Minimum 2.0 GPA and full-time enrollment are required to retain scholarship. Awarded every year. Award may be used only at sponsoring institution.
Contact: Anne Wingert, Assistant Director of Student Financial Aid.

1229 President's Scholarship

Indiana State University
217 North Sixth Street
Terre Haute, IN 47809
(812) 237-2121
Average award: Full tuition, books, room and board
Number of awards: 15
Deadline: February 15
College level: Freshman
Criteria: Applicant must rank in the top tenth of graduating class. Satisfactory GPA and full-time status are required to retain scholarship. Awarded every year; may be used only at sponsoring institution.
Contact: Scholarships, Office of Admissions, Terre Haute, IN 47809, (800) 742-0891.

1230 President's Scholarship

Ferris State University
901 South State Street
Big Rapids, MI 49307
(616) 592-2110
Average award: $3,500
Number of awards: 10
Deadline: January 10
College level: Freshman
Criteria: Applicant must have a minimum 3.7 GPA, minimum composite ACT score of 30. Minimum 3.25 GPA is required to retain scholarship. Awarded every year. Award may be used only at sponsoring institution.
Contact: Robert Bopp, Director of Scholarships and Financial Aid, 420 Oak Street, Big Rapids, MI 49307.

1231 President's Scholarship

Central Missouri State University
Office of Admissions
Administration 104
Warrensburg, MO 64093
(816) 543-4541
Average award: $1,000
Number of awards: 400
Deadline: None
College level: Freshman
Criteria: Applicant must rank in the top quarter of class with a minimum composite ACT score of 22. Minimum 2.0 GPA with a least 12 hours per semester is required to retain scholarship. Awarded every year. Award may be used only at sponsoring institution.
Contact: Scholarships and Awards Officer, Office of Admissions.

1232 President's Scholarship

Ohio University
Office of Student Financial Aid and Scholarships
Athens, OH 45701
(614) 593-4141
Average award: $1,500
Number of awards: 10
Deadline: February 15
College level: Freshman
Criteria: Selection is based upon academic qualifications. Minimum 3.3 GPA and 16 credit hours per quarter are required to retain scholarship. Awarded every year. Award may be used only at sponsoring institution.
Contact: Yang-Hi Kim, Associate Director of Scholarships & Grants.

1233 Presidential Honors

State University of New York at Buffalo
Buffalo, NY 14260
(716) 831-2000
Average award: $2,000
Maximum award: $3,000
Minimum award: $1,000
College level: Freshman, Sophomore, Junior, Senior
Criteria: Applicant must have a minimum combined SAT I score of 1300, rank in the top seven percent of class, and have an unweighted average of 93. Scholarship is renewable. Awarded every year. Award may be used only at sponsoring institution.
Contact: Josephine Capuana, Administrative Director, 214 Talbert Hall, Box 601700, Buffalo, NY 14260-1700, (716) 645-3020.

1234 Presidential Scholars' Program

University of Toledo
Financial Aid Office
Toledo, OH 43606-3390
(419) 537-2056
Average award: Full tuition, fees, books, room and board
Number of awards: 4
Deadline: January 28
College level: Freshman
Criteria: Applicant must have a minimum 3.85 GPA or rank in top five percent of class, have a minimum composite ACT score of 30, and demonstrated leadership and citizenship. Essay and recommendations are required. Award is for four years. Awarded every year. Award may be used only at sponsoring institution.
Contact: Coordinator of Admissions Services for Scholars, (419) 537-2073.

1235 Presidential Scholarship

University of Alabama–Tuscaloosa
Box 870162
Tuscaloosa, AL 35487-0162
(205) 348-6756
Average award: Tuition
Number of awards: 100
Deadline: February 1
College level: Freshman
Criteria: Selection is based upon minimum composite ACT score of 30 or combined SAT I score of 1240, minimum 3.5 GPA, achievements, and leadership activities. Minimum 3.0 GPA is required to retain scholarship for four years. Awarded every year. Award may be used only at sponsoring institution.
Contact: Molly Lawrence, Director of Financial Aid.

1236 Presidential Scholarships

University of South Alabama
260 Administration Building
Mobile, AL 36688-0002
(334) 460-6231
Average award: $1,500, $3,000, or $5,000
Minimum number of awards: 50 in each category
Deadline: Late November
College level: Freshman
Criteria: Applicant must have a minimum composite ACT score of 27 (minimum scores of 30 or 33 required for larger awards) or comparable SAT I score and minimum 3.5 GPA as computed by the Office of Admissions. Minimum 3.0 GPA (3.3 or 3.5 for larger awards) is required to retain scholarship. Awarded every year. Award may be used only at sponsoring institution.
Contact: Catherine P. King, Director of Admissions.

1237 Presidential Scholarship

Georgia State University
P.O. Box 4040
Atlanta, GA 30302
(404) 651-2227
Average award: $2,800
Number of awards: 4
Deadline: April 1
College level: Freshman
Criteria: Selection is based upon academic qualifications. Minimum 3.5 cumulative GPA is required to retain scholarship. Awarded every year. Award may be used only at sponsoring institution.
Contact: Gwyn Francis, Director of Student Financial Aid.

1238 Presidential Scholarship

Southern Illinois University at Edwardsville
Box 1083
Edwardsville, IL 62026-1083
(618) 692-2000
Average award: $2,200
Number of awards: 20
Deadline: April 1
College level: Freshman, Sophomore, Junior, Senior
Criteria: Scholarship is renewable. Awarded every year. Award may be used only at sponsoring institution.
Contact: Director of Financial Aid.

1239 Presidential Scholarship

Western Illinois University
One University Circle
Macomb, IL 61455
(309) 295-1414
Maximum award: $1,000
Number of awards: 15
Deadline: December 14
College level: Freshman
Criteria: Applicant must have a minimum composite ACT score of 28 and rank in the top 15 percent of class. Minimum 3.5 GPA is required to retain scholarship. Awarded every year. Award may be used only at sponsoring institution.
Contact: Janice Owens, Scholarship Coordinator, (309) 298-2446.

1240 Presidential Scholarship

Ball State University
Muncie, IN 47306
(317) 285-5600
Maximum award: $3,622
Minimum award: $1,432
Number of awards: 404
Deadline: March 1
College level: Freshman
Criteria: Applicant must rank in the top fifth of high school class and have a minimum combined SAT I score of 1030 or ACT composite score of 24. Minimum 3.0 GPA is required to retain scholarship. Awarded every year; may be used only at sponsoring institution.
Contact: Ruth Vedvik, Director of Admissions, (317) 285-8300.

1241 Presidential Scholarship

University of Iowa
208 Calvin Hall
Iowa City, IA 52242
(319) 335-1450
Maximum award: $5,000
Number of awards: 20
Deadline: December 31
College level: Freshman
Criteria: Applicant must rank in top five percent of high school class and have a minimum composite ACT score of 30. Minimum 3.0 cumulative GPA and full-time enrollment are required to retain scholarship. Awarded every year. Award may be used only at sponsoring institution.
Contact: Judith Carpenter, Assistant Director, Student Financial Aid.

1242 Presidential Scholarship

University of Northern Iowa
Financial Aid Office
Cedar Falls, IA 50613-0024
(319) 273-2700 or (800) 772-2736
Average award: $5,400
Maximum award: $9,191
Number of awards: 15
Deadline: October 1
College level: Freshman
Criteria: Applicant must receive an invitation to apply; university must receive ACT score prior to August 1 of junior year. Applicant must have a minimum composite ACT score of 29 and rank in the top tenth of class. Special program of study is required to retain scholarship. Awarded every year. Award may be used only at sponsoring institution.
Contact: Carol Geiger, Administrative Assistant, Office of the Vice President for Education and Student Services, Cedar Falls, IA 50614-2700, (319) 273-2331.

1243 Presidential Scholarship

Eastern Michigan University
Office of Financial Aid
403 Pierce Hall
Ypsilanti, MI 48197
(313) 487-0455
Average award: $8,000
Number of awards: 10
Deadline: November 25
College level: Freshman
Criteria: Applicant must have a minimum high school GPA of 3.5 and a minimum composite ACT score of 25 or combined SAT I score of 1050. Applicant must attend the Presidential Scholarship competition held the first Saturday in December; this is a half-day comprehensive test, with the top 30 applicants being asked to return for an interview and write an essay. Minimum 3.5 GPA and 15 credit hours per semester are required to retain scholarship. Awarded every year. Award may be used only at sponsoring institution.
Contact: Cynthia Van Pelt, Assistant Director of Scholarships.

1244 Presidential Scholarship

Montana State University
Bozeman, MT 59717
(406) 994-2845
Maximum award: $7,335
Minimum award: $2,995
Number of awards: 20
Deadline: January 8
College level: Freshman
Criteria: Applicant must have intellectual or creative distinction. Selection is not based solely upon academic achievements. However most applicants have a minimum cumulative GPA of 3.8 and a minimum composite ACT score of 30, and combined SAT I score of 1300. Minimum 3.5 GPA is required to retain scholarship. Awarded every year. Award may be used only at sponsoring institution.
Contact: Victoria O'Donnell, Director of Honors Program, Montana State University, Quad D, Bozeman, MT 59717, (406) 994-4110.

1245 Presidential Scholarship

University of New Mexico
Mesa Vista Hall
Room 1044
Albuquerque, NM 87131
(505) 277-6090
Average award: $2,347
Number of awards: 200
Deadline: December 1
College level: Freshman
Criteria: Selection is based upon minimum 3.5 GPA, references, activities, class rank, minimum composite ACT score of 24 or SAT I equivalent, and leadership skills. Minimum 3.0 GPA with 30 hours per year is required to retain scholarship. Awarded every year. Award may be used only at sponsoring institution.
Contact: Rita M. Padilla, Associate Director for Scholarships & Financial Aid.

1246 Presidential Scholarship

Hofstra University
126 Memorial Hall
Hempstead, NY 11550
(516) 463-6677
Maximum award: $6,500
Minimum award: $2,000
Deadline: February 15
College level: Freshman
Criteria: Applicant must rank in the top fifth of his or her high school class and have a minimum combined SAT I score of 1200 or composite ACT score of 27. Minimum 3.0 GPA by end of freshman year, 3.1 GPA by end of sophomore year, and 3.2 GPA by end of junior year are required to retain scholarship. Awarded every year. Award may be used only at sponsoring institution.
Contact: Joan Warren, Director of Financial and Academic Records.

1247 Presidential Scholarship

Ohio State University–Columbus
Third Floor Lincoln Tower
1800 Cannon Drive
Columbus, OH 43210-1200
(614) 292-3980
Average award: $9,834
Deadline: January 15
College level: Freshman
Criteria: Applicant must rank in the top three percent of class, have a minimum composite ACT score of 29 or combined SAT I score of 1250. Competitive selection process begins in March of applicant's senior year. Minimum 3.2 GPA and satisfactory academic progress are required to retain scholarship. Awarded every year. Award may be used only at sponsoring institution.
Contact: Mary Haldane, Director of Financial Aid.

1248 Presidential Scholarship

Portland State University
P.O. Box 751
Portland, OR 97207-5252
(503) 725-5270
Average award: $1,800
Maximum award: $2,658
Number of awards: 10
Deadline: March 1
College level: Freshman
Criteria: Applicant must have minimum 3.5 GPA. Selection is based upon academic potential to succeed in college. Minimum 3.0 GPA is required to retain scholarship. Awarded every year. Award may be used only at sponsoring institution.
Contact: Virginia McElroy, Scholarship Coordinator.

1249 Presidential Scholarship

Texas Tech University
Lubbock, TX 79409
(806) 742-3144
Average award: $2,000
Deadline: March 1
College level: Freshman
Criteria: Applicant must rank in the top tenth of class and have a minimum combined SAT I score of 1350 or composite ACT score of 31. Minimum 3.5 GPA and 12 credit hours per semester are required to retain scholarship. Awarded every year. Award may be used only at sponsoring institution.
Contact: Ronny Barnes, Director of Financial Aid, Texas Tech University, Lubbock, TX 79409.

1250 Presidential Scholarship

University of Texas at El Paso
Recruitment and Scholarship Office
500 West University Avenue
El Paso, TX 79968
(915) 747-5890
Maximum award: $2,000
Minimum award: $750
Number of awards: 200
Deadline: March 1
College level: Freshman
Criteria: Applicant must have a minimum high school average of 90 and plan to enroll on a full-time basis. Selection is based upon GPA, class rank, and SAT I or ACT scores; top awards also consider leadership. Minimum GPA of 3.0 to 3.5, depending on size of award, and at least 30 credit hours per year are required to retain scholarship.
Contact: Barbara L. Nehring, Assistant Director for Scholarships.

1251 Principal's Leadership Award

National Association of Secondary School Principals
1904 Association Drive
Reston, VA 22091
Average award: $1,000
Number of awards: 150
Deadline: December 16
College level: Freshman
Criteria: Applicant must be a student leader. Awarded every year.

1252 Provost's Scholarship

Ohio University
Office of Student Financial Aid and Scholarships
Athens, OH 45701
(614) 593-4141
Average award: $1,250
Number of awards: 350
Deadline: February 15
College level: Freshman
Criteria: Selection is based upon academic qualifications. Awarded every year. Award may be used only at sponsoring institution.
Contact: Yang-Hi Kim, Associate Director of Scholarships & Grants.

1253 R. Boyd Gunning Scholarship

University of Oklahoma
900 Asp Avenue, Room 236
Norman, OK 73019-0401
(405) 325-1701
Average award: $2,000
Maximum number of awards: 20
Minimum number of awards: 10
Deadline: May 1
College level: Sophomore
Criteria: Applicant must be a full-time freshman with a minimum 3.7 GPA who entered the university directly from high school. Award is for three years. Awarded every year. Award may be used only at sponsoring institution.
Contact: Honors Program, 347 Cate Center Drive, Norman, OK 73019, (405) 325-5291.

1254 R.C. Easley National Scholarship

National Academy of American Scholars
Scholarship Committee
21343 Cold Spring Lane #600
Diamond Bar, CA 91765-3443
(909) 398-0554
Average award: $13,333
Maximum award: $25,000
Minimum award: $5,000
Number of awards: 13
Deadline: February 1
College level: Freshman
Criteria: Applicant must send a self-addressed stamped envelope with a $1.00 handling fee for application and information packet. Minimum 3.0 GPA or "B" average and full-time enrollment are required to retain scholarship. Awarded every year.
Contact: Scholarship Committee.

1255 R.F. Poole Alumni Scholarship

Clemson University
G-01 Sikes Hall
Clemson, SC 29634-5123
(803) 656-2280
Average award: $4,000
Number of awards: 7
College level: Freshman
Criteria: Selection is based upon admissions application. Minimum 3.0 cumulative GPA with at least 12 credits per semester is required to retain scholarship. Awarded every year. Award may be used only at sponsoring institution.
Contact: Marvin Carmichael, Director of Financial Aid.

1256 Recognition of Excellence Scholarship

Eastern Michigan University
Office of Financial Aid
403 Pierce Hall
Ypsilanti, MI 48197
(313) 487-0455
Average award: $1,500
Number of awards: 380
Deadline: January 15
College level: Freshman, Sophomore, Junior, Senior
Criteria: Applicant must have a minimum 3.3 GPA and composite ACT score of 21 or combined SAT I score of 900. Scholarship is renewable. Awarded every year. Award may be used only at sponsoring institution.
Contact: Cynthia Van Pelt, Assistant Director of Scholarships.

1257 Regents Scholarship

Eastern Michigan University
Office of Financial Aid
403 Pierce Hall
Ypsilanti, MI 48197
(313) 487-0455
Average award: $2,100
Number of awards: 350
Deadline: January 15
College level: Freshman, Sophomore, Junior, Senior
Criteria: Applicant must have a minimum 3.5 GPA and a composite ACT score of 25 or combined SAT I score of 1050. Minimum 3.5 GPA and 15 credit hours per semester are required to retain scholarship. Awarded every year. Award may be used only at sponsoring institution.
Contact: Cynthia Van Pelt, Assistant Director of Scholarships.

1258 Regents Scholarship

Central Missouri State University
Office of Admissions
Administration 104
Warrensburg, MO 64093
(816) 543-4541
Average award: $1,200
Number of awards: 500
Deadline: None
College level: Freshman
Criteria: Applicant must be the valedictorian or salutatorian, rank in the top tenth of class, have a minimum composite ACT score of 25, or have a minimum GED score of 310. Renewable if minimum 2.0 GPA at end of first semester, minimum 3.25 GPA at end of second semester, or minimum 3.5 GPA after fourth semester is maintained and thereafter at least 12 credits per semester are taken. Awarded every year. Award may be used only at sponsoring institution.
Contact: Scholarships and Awards Officer, Admissions Office.

1259 Regents Scholarship

University of New Mexico
Mesa Vista Hall
Room 1044
Albuquerque, NM 87131
(505) 277-6090
Average award: $6,200
Maximum number of awards: 60
Minimum number of awards: 15
Deadline: December 1
College level: Freshman
Criteria: Applicant must meet at least one of the following qualifications: minimum GPA of 3.9, minimum composite ACT score of 31 or the SAT I equivalent, class valedictorian, National Merit semifinalist, National Achievement scholar, National Hispanic scholar, extraordinary extracurricular activities, or excellent recommendations. Minimum 3.2 GPA after freshman year, and 3.5 GPA thereafter, with 30 credit hours per year is required to retain scholarship. Awarded every year. Award may be used only at sponsoring institution.
Contact: Rita M. Padilla, Associate Director for Scholarships & Financial Aid.

1260 Regents Scholarship

University of Memphis
Scates Hall 204
Memphis, TN 38152
(901) 678-3213
Maximum award: $2,042
Deadline: March 1
College level: Freshman
Criteria: Applicant must have a minimum 3.0 GPA and minimum composite ACT score of 26 or combined SAT I score of 1020. Minimum 2.8 GPA and a service requirement of 30 hours per semester are required to retain scholarship. Awarded every year. Award may be used only at sponsoring institution.
Contact: Dr. Sue Ann McClellan, Scholarship Coordinator.

1261 Resident Assistant

Liberty University
P.O. Box 20000
Lynchburg, VA 24506-8001
(804) 582-2270
Maximum award: $5,500
Deadline: Late January
College level: Junior, Senior
Criteria: Minimum 2.5 GPA, leadership ability, and spiritual maturity are required to retain scholarship. Awarded every year. Award may be used only at sponsoring institution.
Contact: Residence Housing Office.

1262 Robert C. Byrd Honors Scholarship

Alabama Commission on Higher Education
3465 Norman Bridge Road
Montgomery, AL 36105-2310
(334) 281-1921
Average award: $1,500
College level: Freshman
Criteria: Applicant must be an Alabama resident who demonstrates outstanding academic achievement. Awarded every year.
Contact: Rosemary Mobley, State Department of Education, (334) 242-8082.

1263 Robert C. Byrd Honors Scholarship

Florida Department of Education
Office of Student Financial Assistance
1344 Florida Education Center
Tallahassee, FL 32399-0400
(904) 487-0049
Average award: $1,500
Number of awards: 200
Deadline: April 15
College level: Freshman
Criteria: Applicant must be a U.S. citizen or eligible noncitizen, a Florida resident for at least six months, have a minimum cumulative GPA of 3.85, be ranked at least in the 75th percentile on the ACT or SAT I, and be enrolled at an eligible nonprofit postsecondary institution for a course of study at least one year in length. Awarded every year.
Contact: Office of Student Financial Assistance.

1264 Robert C. Byrd Honors Scholarship

University of Texas at San Antonio
Office of Student Financial Aid
6900 North Loop 1604 West
San Antonio, TX 78249-0687
(210) 691-4011
Average award: $1,500
Deadline: March 15
College level: Freshman
Criteria: Applicant must be a U.S. citizen or permanent resident, a Texas resident, rank in the top tenth of class, have a minimum composite ACT score of 24 or combined SAT I score of 1000, and demonstrate excellent academic achievement. Awarded every year. Award may be used only at sponsoring institution.
Contact: Scholarship Office, (210) 691-4855.

1265 Robert C. Byrd Honors Scholarship

Pennsylvania Higher Education Assistance Agency (PHEAA)
P.O. Box 8114
Harrisburg, PA 17105-8114
(717) 257-5220
Average award: $1,500
Number of awards: 546
Deadline: May 1
College level: Freshman
Criteria: Applicant must be a U.S. citizen and Pennsylvania resident, and meet the following academic requirements: (1) rank in top five percent of class, (2) minimum 3.5 GPA, (3) minimum combined SAT I score of 1100 or composite ACT score of 27. Eligible applicants are chosen by random selection in the 67 Pennsylvania counties. Normal progress must be maintained to continue scholarship. Awarded every year.
Contact: Sam Sobczak, Director of Teacher Education.

1266 Robert C. Edwards Scholarship

Clemson University
G-01 Sikes Hall
Clemson, SC 29634-5123
(803) 656-2280
Average award: $3,000
Number of awards: 2
College level: Freshman
Criteria: Applicant must be an outstanding student; preference is given to black applicants. Minimum 3.0 cumulative GPA with at least 12 credits per semester is required to retain scholarship. Awarded every year. Award may be used only at sponsoring institution.
Contact: Marvin Carmichael, Director of Financial Aid.

1267   Robert L. Nugent Scholarship

University of Arizona
Tucson, AZ 85721-0007
(602) 621-1858
Average award: $1,000
Maximum award: $1,500
Number of awards: 20
Deadline: March 1
College level: Freshman
Criteria: Selection is based upon academic ability, extracurricular activities, and community service. Minimum 3.0 cumulative GPA and full-time enrollment are required to retain scholarship. Awarded every year. Award may be used only at sponsoring institution.
Contact: Magdalen Vargas, Acting Associate Director of Scholarships.

1268   Schillig-Baird and Presidential Scholarship

University of Southern Mississippi
Office of Recruitment and Orientation
Box 5166
Hattiesburg, MS 39406-5166
(601) 266-5000
Average award: $5,496
Maximum award: $7,032
Minimum award: $5,112
Number of awards: 40
Deadline: February 1
College level: Freshman
Criteria: Applicant must be a National Merit finalist and have a minimum composite ACT score of 32 or combined SAT I score of 1330. Interview is required. Recipient must enroll in the Honors College. Scholarship is renewable. Awarded every year. Award may be used only at sponsoring institution.
Contact: Dr. Homer Wesley, Director of Recruitment and Orientation.

1269   Scholarship Foundation of America Honored Scholars Program

Scholarship Foundation of America
55 Hwy 35
Suite 5
Red Bank, NJ 07701
(908) 747-0028
Average award: $1,000
Maximum award: $5,000
Number of awards: 50
Deadline: None
College level: Freshman, Sophomore, Junior, Senior, Graduate, Doctoral
Criteria: Applicant must be a U.S. citizen, have taken the SAT I and received written results prior to application (minimum combined SAT I score of 1200), have a minimum 3.7 GPA, demonstrate outstanding academic achievement or excel in the visual/performing arts, and pursue full-time study at an accredited U.S. institution or participate in an approved foreign exchange program. Financial need is not considered. SAT I scores are not considered in visual/performing arts categories. Awarded every year.
Contact: Linda Paras, President.

1270   Sesquicentennial Faculty and Staff Scholarship

University of Alabama–Tuscaloosa
Box 870162
Tuscaloosa, AL 35487-0162
(205) 348-6756
Maximum award: $2,000
Minimum award: $1,000
Maximum number of awards: 2
Minimum number of awards: 1
Deadline: February 1
College level: Freshman
Criteria: Selection is based upon high school record, leadership, character, and other evidence of excellence. Awarded every year. Award may be used only at sponsoring institution.
Contact: Office of Admission Services, Box 870132, Tuscaloosa, AL 35487-0132.

1271   Sue and Sid Magnes Scholarship

University of South Alabama
260 Administration Building
Mobile, AL 36688-0002
(334) 460-6231
Average award: $2,000
Deadline: Early application recommended
College level: Freshman
Majors/Fields: Business
Criteria: Applicant must have a minimum composite ACT score of 21, a minimum 3.0 GPA, and be a resident of Mobile County, Ala. Renewable for up to three years if minimum 3.0 GPA is maintained. Awarded every year. Award may be used only at sponsoring institution.
Contact: Catherine P. King, Director of Admissions.

1272   Summer Honors Scholarship

Indiana State University
217 North Sixth Street
Terre Haute, IN 47809
(812) 237-2121
Average award: $1,100
Number of awards: 25
Deadline: February 15
College level: Freshman
Criteria: Applicant must be a graduate of the Summer Honor's Program of Indiana State U. Satisfactory GPA and full-time status are required to retain scholarship. Awarded every year. Award may be used only at sponsoring institution.
Contact: Scholarships, Office of Admissions, Terre Haute, IN 47809, (800) 742-0891.

1273   Texas Excellence Award

University of Texas at Austin
Austin, TX 78713-7758
(512) 475-6200
Average award: $3,000
Maximum award: $7,000
Minimum award: $1,000
Maximum number of awards: 36
Minimum number of awards: 10
Deadline: December 1 (preferred)
College level: Freshman, Sophomore, Junior, Senior
Criteria: Applicant must rank in top five percent of class. Satisfactory academic progress is required to retain scholarship. Awarded every year. Award may be used only at sponsoring institution.
Contact: Eleanor Moore, Director of Scholarships, Ex-Students Association, Austin, TX 78713, (512) 471-8083.

1274   Third Century Scholarship

Ohio University
Office of Student Financial Aid and Scholarships
Athens, OH 45701
(614) 593-4141
Average award: In-state tuition
Number of awards: 10
Deadline: February 15
College level: Freshman
Criteria: Selection is based upon academic qualifications. Minimum 3.3 GPA and 16 credit hours per quarter are required to retain scholarship. Awarded every year. Award may be used only at sponsoring institution.
Contact: Yang-Hi Kim, Associate Director of Scholarships & Grants.

1275   Tillotson Colorado Scholars Award

Colorado State University
Financial Aid Office
108 Student Services Building
Fort Collins, CO 80523
(970) 491-6321
Minimum award: $1,000
Number of awards: 4
Deadline: March 4
College level: Freshman
Criteria: Selection is based upon finanical need, test scores, GPA, extracurricular activities, and community service. Awarded every year. Award may be used only at sponsoring institution.
Contact: Jeanne Snyder, Financial Aid Counselor.

1276 Transfer Competitive Scholarship

Wright State University
Coordinator of Scholarships
Dayton, OH 45435
(513) 873-5721
Average award: $1,000
Number of awards: 20
Deadline: March 1
College level: Transfer students
Criteria: Applicant must have a minimum 3.5 cumulative GPA at present college and plan to enroll on a full-time basis at Wright State U. Minimum 3.0 GPA is required to retain scholarship.
Contact: Judy Rose, Assistant Director of Financial Aid.

1277 Trustees' Endowment Scholarship

University of South Carolina (Columbia)
Columbia, SC 29208
(803) 777-8134
Average award: $3,000
Number of awards: 10
Deadline: Early November
College level: Freshman
Criteria: Selection is based upon extraordinary academic achievement. Consideration is also given to needy and minority students who meet the academic requirement. Minimum 3.0 GPA is required to retain scholarship. Awarded every year. Award may be used only at sponsoring institution.
Contact: Stewart Jones, Scholarship Coordinator.

1278 Trustees' Scholarship

Brigham Young University
Scholarship Office, A-41 ASB
P.O. Box 21009
Provo, UT 84602-1009
(801) 378-4104
Average award: $2,450
Number of awards: 250
Deadline: January 15
College level: Freshman
Criteria: Applicant must have a minimum 3.85 GPA and combined SAT I score of 1300 or composite ACT score of 31. Selection is based upon high academic qualifications, leadership skills, and service. Minimum 3.5 GPA and fulfillment of attendance requirements are required to retain scholarship. Awarded every year. Award may be used only at sponsoring institution.
Contact: Duane L. Bartle, Scholarship Coordinator.

1279 Tuition Scholarship

University of Iowa
208 Calvin Hall
Iowa City, IA 52242
(319) 335-1450
Maximum award: $2,291
Number of awards: 1500
College level: Freshman, Sophomore, Junior, Senior
Criteria: Applicant must rank in the top tenth of class, have a minimum composite ACT score of 28, and demonstrate financial need. Minimum 3.0 cumulative GPA and financial need are required to retain scholarship. Awarded every year. Award may be used only at sponsoring institution.
Contact: Judith Carpenter, Assistant Director, Student Financial Aid.

1280 Two-Year College Academic Scholarship

Alabama Commission on Higher Education
3465 Norman Bridge Road
Montgomery, AL 36105-2310
(334) 281-1921
Average award: In-state tuition and books
College level: Freshman, Sophomore
Criteria: Applicant must be accepted for enrollment at a public, two-year, postsecondary educational institution in Alabama. Preference is given to Alabama residents. Selection is based upon academic merit. Financial need is not considered. Academic excellence is required to retain scholarship. Awarded every year.
Contact: Alabama Commission of Higher Education.

1281 U.S. Jaycee War Memorial Fund Scholarship

U.S. Jaycee War Memorial Fund
Department 94922
Tulsa, OK 74194-0001
Average award: $1,000
Number of awards: 20
Deadline: February 1
College level: Freshman, Sophomore, Junior, Senior, Graduate, Doctoral
Criteria: Applicant must be a U.S. citizen and demonstrate leadership, potential for academic success, and financial need. Request application by February 1 with $5.00 application fee and self-addressed, business-sized stamped envelope from JWMF, Dept. 94922, Tulsa, OK 74194-0001. Check or money order must be made payable to JWMF. Awarded every year.
Contact: Bob Guest, U.S. Junior Chamber of Commerce, Scholarship Program Administrator, P.O. Box 7, Tulsa, OK 74102-0007, (918) 584-2481.

1282 UC Davis Scholarship

University of California, Davis
Scholarship Office
Davis, CA 95616
(916) 757-3153
Average award: $1,500
Maximum award: $13,000
Minimum award: $1,000
Number of awards: 1500
Deadline: November 30
College level: Freshman, Sophomore, Junior, Senior
Criteria: Awarded every year. Award may be used only at sponsoring institution.
Contact: John Dixon, Coordinator of Undergraduate Scholarships.

1283 Undergraduate Scholarship

University of California, Berkeley
210 Sproul Hall
Berkeley, CA 94720
(510) 642-0645
Average award: $1,233
Maximum award: $3,000
Minimum award: $300
Number of awards: 1900
Deadline: March 2
College level: Freshman, Sophomore, Junior, Senior
Criteria: Selection is based solely upon financial need for entering freshmen; $300 honorary scholarships are available to academically qualifying upperclass students with no financial need. Satisfactory academic progress, GPA, and academic level are required to retain scholarship. Awarded every year. Award may be used only at sponsoring institution.
Contact: Linda Popofsky, Assistant Director of Financial Aid for Scholarships, (510) 642-6449.

1284 University Achievement Class Scholarship

University of Oklahoma
University Affairs
900 Asp Avenue, Room 236
Norman, OK 73019-0401
(405) 325-1701
Average award: $1,000
Number of awards: 85
Deadline: March 1
College level: Freshman
Criteria: Selection is based upon academic merit and leadership. Ethnic minorities are encouraged to apply. Awarded every year. Award may be used only at sponsoring institution.
Contact: High School and College Relations, (405) 325-2151.

1285 University Club of Portland Fellowship

Portland State University
P.O. Box 751
Portland, OR 97207-0751
(503) 725-5270
Average award: $5,000
Number of awards: 4
Deadline: April 15
College level: Graduate, Doctoral
Criteria: Applicant must be nominated by the Dean. Award may be used only at sponsoring institution.
Contact: Scholarships, Office of Academic Affairs.

1286 University of Calgary Senate Scholarship

University of Calgary
2500 University Drive, NW
Calgary, Alberta, CN T2N 1N4
(403) 220-7872
Average award: $2,500
Number of awards: 1
Deadline: June 15
College level: Sophomore, Junior, Senior
Criteria: Selection is based upon academic merit and involvement in campus and/or community activities. Awarded every year. Award may be used only at sponsoring institution.
Contact: J. Van Housen, Director of Student Awards & Financial Aid.

1287 University of Hawaii at Manoa Scholarship

University of Hawaii at Manoa
2600 Campus Road, Room #001
Honolulu, HI 96822
(808) 956-8975
Average award: $812
Maximum award: $2,500
Minimum award: $225
Number of awards: 166
College level: Freshman, Sophomore, Junior, Senior, Graduate, Doctoral
Criteria: Many different scholarships are offered. Award may be used only at sponsoring institution.
Contact: Financial Aid Services, (808) 956-7251.

1288 University Scholar Award

Central Missouri State University
Office of Admissions, Administration 104
Warrensburg, MO 64093
(816) 543-4541
Average award: $2,310
Maximum award: $2,772
Minimum award: $1,848
Number of awards: 47
College level: Freshman
Criteria: Applicant must have a minimum composite ACT score of 28 and either rank in the top five percent of class or have a minimum cumulative GPA of 3.75. Minimum 2.0 GPA after first semester, minimum 3.4 GPA at end of second semester, and minimum 3.6 GPA at end of fourth semester and thereafter, with at least 12 hours per semester are required to retain scholarship. Awarded every year.
Contact: Scholarships and Awards Officer, Admissions Office.

1289 University Scholarship

California State University, Northridge
18111 Nordhoff Street
Northridge, CA 91330-8307
(818) 885-3000
Average award: $1,000
Maximum award: $2,500
Minimum award: $250
Number of awards: 300
Deadline: March 1 (continuing students); April 1 (new students)
College level: Freshman, Sophomore, Junior, Senior, Graduate
Criteria: Applicant must have a minimum 3.0 GPA. Finanical need is considered. Reapplication is required to retain scholarship. Awarded every year. Award may be used only at sponsoring institution.
Contact: Lili Vidal, Scholarships/Work Study Office, (818) 885-4907.

1290 University Scholarship

University of California, Los Angeles
A129 Murphy Hall
Box 951435
Los Angeles, CA 90095-1435
(310) 206-0404
Maximum award: $1,200
Minimum award: $100
Number of awards: 70
College level: Freshman, Sophomore, Junior, Senior
Criteria: Applicant must demonstrate financial need. Freshman applicant must have a minimum 3.5 GPA and continuing student applicant must have a minimum 3.3 GPA. Awarded every year. Award may be used only at sponsoring institution.
Contact: Beverly LeMay, Assistant Director of Scholarships, (310) 206-0417.

1291 University Scholarship

University of Pittsburgh, Pittsburgh Campus
4200 Fifth Avenue
Pittsburgh, PA 15260
(412) 624-4141
Average award: $2,000
Maximum award: $6,000
Minimum award: $1,000
Number of awards: 200
Deadline: January 15
College level: Freshman
Criteria: Selection is based upon high school performance and test scores. Minimum 3.0 GPA is required to retain scholarship. Awarded every year. Award may be used only at sponsoring institution.
Contact: Betsy A. Porter, Director of Admissions and Financial Aid, (412) 624-7164.

1292 University Scholarship

University of South Carolina (Columbia)
Columbia, SC 29208
(803) 777-8134
Average award: $1,500
Number of awards: 200
Deadline: Early November
College level: Freshman
Criteria: Selection is based upon outstanding academic achievement. Minimum 3.0 GPA is required to retain scholarship. Awarded every year. Award may be used only at sponsoring institution.
Contact: Stewart Jones, Scholarship Coordinator.

1293 University Scholarship

Brigham Young University
Scholarship Office, A-41 ASB
P.O. Box 21009
Provo, UT 84602-1009
(801) 378-4104
Average award: $1,600
Maximum award: $2,450
Minimum award: $1,225
Number of awards: 1200
Deadline: February 15
College level: Freshman, transfer students
Criteria: Selection is based upon high academic qualifications. Awarded every year. Award may be used only at sponsoring institution.
Contact: Duane L. Bartle, Scholarship Coordinator.

1294   UNM Scholars Scholarship

University of New Mexico
Mesa Vista Hall
Room 1044
Albuquerque, NM 87131
(505) 277-6090
Average award: In-state tuition
Number of awards: 300
Deadline: February 1
College level: Freshman
Criteria: Applicant must rank in the top fifth of graduating class, have a minimum 3.0 GPA, and participate in activities. Minimum 3.0 GPA with 30 credit hours per year is required to retain scholarship. Awarded every year. Award may be used only at sponsoring institution.
Contact: Rita M. Padilla, Associate Director of Scholarships and Financial Aid.

1295   Upperclass Dean's Scholarship

Ohio University
Office of Student Financial Aid and Scholarships
Athens, OH 45701
(614) 593-4141
Average award: $1,000
Maximum award: $1,500
Minimum award: $750
Number of awards: 650
Deadline: March 1
College level: Sophomore, Junior, Senior
Criteria: Selection is based upon academic qualifications. Awarded every year. Award may be used only at sponsoring institution.
Contact: Yang-Hi Kim, Associate Director of Scholarships & Grants.

1296   Valedictorian and Salutatorian Scholarship

Wright State University
Coordinator of Scholarships
Dayton, OH 45435
(513) 873-5721
Average award: $2,000
Number of awards: 36
Deadline: March 1
College level: Freshman
Criteria: Applicant must rank first or second in a four-year high school. Minimum 3.0 cumulative GPA is required to retain scholarship. Awarded every year. Award may be used only at sponsoring institution.
Contact: Judy Rose, Assistant Director of Financial Aid, (513) 873-2321.

1297   Vulcan Scholarship

University of Alabama–Tuscaloosa
Box 870162
Tuscaloosa, AL 35487-0162
(205) 348-6756
Average award: $7,500
Number of awards: 1
Deadline: February 1
College level: Freshman
Criteria: Applicant must have a minimum composite ACT score of 32 or combined SAT I score of 1350, minimum GPA of 3.8, and demonstrate broad leadership experience. Essay is required. Top five finalists are interviewed on campus. Minimum 3.0 GPA is required to retain scholarship for four years. Awarded every year. Award may be used only at sponsoring institution.
Contact: Molly Lawrence, Director of Financial Aid.

1298   Wal-Mart Competitive Edge

Old Dominion University
Hampton Boulevard
Norfolk, VA 23529-0050
(804) 683-3683
Maximum award: $5,000
Number of awards: 1
Deadline: February 15
College level: Freshman
Majors/Fields: Technology-related area
Criteria: Applicant must have a minimum combined SAT I score of 1100 or composite ACT score of 27, a minimum 3.2 GPA, rank in top ten percent of class, demonstrate community service and leadership ability, and apply for finanical aid. Scholarship is renewable. Awarded every year. Award may be used only at sponsoring institution.
Contact: Mary A. Schutz, Assistant Director of Scholarships.

1299   Wallace Preston Greene Sr. Scholarship

Clemson University
G-01 Sikes Hall
Clemson, SC 29634-5123
(803) 656-2280
Average award: $2,100
Number of awards: 2
Deadline: March 1
College level: Freshman, Sophomore, Junior, Senior
Criteria: Applicant must demonstrate financial need. Preference is given to residents of Oconee County, S.C. Minimum 3.0 cumulative GPA with at least 12 credits per semester is required to retain scholarship. Awarded every year. Award may be used only at sponsoring institution.
Contact: Marvin Carmichael, Director of Financial Aid.

1300   Walter T. Cox Presidential Scholarship

Clemson University
G-01 Sikes Hall
Clemson, SC 29634-5123
(803) 656-2280
Average award: $4,500
Number of awards: 1
College level: Freshman
Criteria: Applicant must be the most promising entering freshman. Minimum 3.0 cumulative GPA with at least 12 credits per semester is required to retain scholarship. Awarded every year. Award may be used only at sponsoring institution.
Contact: Marvin Carmichael, Director of Financial Aid.

1301   Warren M. Anderson Scholarship

Indiana State University
217 North Sixth Street
Terre Haute, IN 47809
(812) 237-2121
Average award: $1,100
Number of awards: 50
Deadline: February 15
College level: Freshman
Criteria: Applicant must submit a list of high school and community service accomplishment and activities, and a recommendation from a high school counselor, civic leader, principal, or minister. Awarded to students of color. Satisfactory GPA and full-time status are required to retain scholarship. Awarded every year. Award may be used only at sponsoring institution.
Contact: Scholarships, Office of Admissions.

1302 William A. Kenyon Scholarship

Clemson University
G-01 Sikes Hall
Clemson, SC 29634-5123
(803) 656-2280
Average award: $2,500
Number of awards: 8
College level: Freshman
Criteria: Selection is based upon admissions application. Minimum 3.0 cumulative GPA with at least 12 credits per semester is required to retain scholarship. Awarded every year. Award may be used only at sponsoring institution.
Contact: Marvin Carmichael, Director of Financial Aid.

1303 William James Erwin Scholarship

Clemson University
G-01 Sikes Hall
Clemson, SC 29634-5123
(803) 656-2280
Average award: $1,500
Number of awards: 2
College level: Freshman
Criteria: Selection is based upon admissions application. Minimum 3.0 cumulative GPA with at least 12 credits per semester is required to retain scholarship. Awarded every year. Award may be used only at sponsoring institution.
Contact: Marvin Carmichael, Director of Financial Aid.

1304 WIU Foundation Honors Scholarship

Western Illinois University
One University Circle
Macomb, IL 61455
(309) 295-1414
Maximum award: $3,000
Number of awards: 4
Deadline: December 14
College level: Freshman
Criteria: Applicant must have a minimum composite ACT score of 30, rank in the top 15 percent of class, and reside on the Honors Floor. Minimum 3.5 GPA and participation in University Honors Program are required to retain scholarship. Awarded every year. Award may be used only at sponsoring institution.
Contact: Janice Owens, Scholarship Coordinator, (309) 298-2446.

1305 WIU Foundation Scholarship

Western Illinois University
One University Circle
Macomb, IL 61455
(309) 295-1414
Maximum award: $2,000
Number of awards: 10
Deadline: December 14
College level: Freshman
Criteria: Applicant must have a minimum composite ACT score of 28 and rank in the top 15 percent of class. Minimum 3.5 GPA is required to retain scholarship. Awarded every year. Award may be used only at sponsoring institution.
Contact: Janice Owens, Scholarship Coordinator, (309) 298-2446.

1306 Wives of the Class of '34 Endowed Scholarship

Clemson University
G-01 Sikes Hall
Clemson, SC 29634-5123
(803) 656-2280
Average award: $2,500
Number of awards: 1
College level: Freshman
Criteria: Selection is based upon admissions application. Minimum 3.0 cumulative GPA with at least 12 credits per semester is required to retain scholarship. Awarded every year. Award may be used only at sponsoring institution.
Contact: Marvin Carmichael, Director of Financial Aid.

1307 Yoshiyama Award

Hitachi Foundation
P.O. Box 19247
Washington, DC 20036-9247
Maximum award: $5,000
Maximum number of awards: 10
Minimum number of awards: 6
Deadline: April 1
College level: Freshman
Criteria: Award is to recognize exemplary service, community involvement, leadership, and civic responsibility. Awarded every year.
Contact: Yoshiyama Award.

Athletic Ability

1308 Al Thompson Junior Bowler Scholarship

Pro Bowlers Association
1720 Merriman Road
P.O. Box 5118
Akron, OH 44334-0118
(216) 836-5568
Maximum award: $1,500
Minimum award: $1,000
Number of awards: 2
Deadline: June 15
College level: Freshman
Criteria: Applicant must represent high school in bowling and other activities and have a minimum GPA of 2.5. Minimum 2.5 GPA is required to retain scholarship. Awarded every year.
Contact: Mark Gerberich, Deputy Commissioner.

1309 Amateur Athletic Union/Mars Milky Way High School All-American Award

Amateur Athletic Union
P.O. Box 68207
Indianapolis, IN 46268-0207
(317) 872-2900
Average award: $1,000
Maximum award: $20,000
Number of awards: 102
Deadline: January 9
College level: Freshman
Criteria: Selection is based upon academics, athletics, and community service. Awarded every year.
Contact: Tom Leix, Director of Special Projects, Department CGP.

1310 Athletic Scholarship

Georgetown University
37th and O Streets, NW
Washington, DC 20057
(202) 687-4547
Average award: $14,183
Maximum award: $26,856
Minimum award: $200
Number of awards: 140
Deadline: None
College level: Freshman, Sophomore, Junior, Senior
Criteria: Applicant must participate in baseball, lacrosse, track, or other sport. Renewable if participation in athletics is continued. Awarded every year. Award may be used only at sponsoring institution.
Contact: Patricia McWade, Dean of Student Financial Services.

1311 AWSEF Scholarship

American Water Ski Education Foundation (AWSEF)
799 Overlook Drive, SE
Winter Haven, FL 33884-1671
(813) 324-2472
Average award: $1,500
Number of awards: 6
Deadline: March 1
College level: Sophomore, Junior, Senior
Criteria: Applicant must be a U.S. citizen who is a current AWSEF donor member or American Water Ski Association member. Selection is based upon academic qualifications, leadership, extracurricular involvement, recommendations, financial need, and number of years of membership. Awarded every year.
Contact: Carole Lowe, Executive Director, P.O. Box 2957, Winter Haven, FL 33883-2957.

1312 Gloria Fecht Memorial Scholarship

Gloria Fecht Memorial Scholarship Fund
402 West Arrow Highway
Suite 10
San Dimas, CA 91773
(909) 592-1281
Average award: $2,000
Maximum award: $3,000
Minimum award: $1,000
Number of awards: 20
Deadline: March 1
College level: Freshman, Sophomore, Junior, Senior, Graduate
Criteria: Applicant must be a woman, have an active interest in golf, and be a Southern California resident or a resident of Northern California who attends school in Southern California. Minimum 3.0 GPA is required to retain scholarship. Awarded every year.
Contact: Mary Hicks, President.

1313 IPTAY Academic Scholarship Fund

Clemson University
G-01 Sikes Hall
Clemson, SC 29634-5123
(803) 656-2280
Average award: $2,000
Number of awards: 2
Deadline: March 1
College level: Freshman, Sophomore, Junior, Senior
Criteria: Applicant must not participate in intercollegiate athletics. Awarded every year. Award may be used only at sponsoring institution.
Contact: Marvin Carmichael, Director of Financial Aid.

1314 Junior and Community College Athletic Scholarship

Alabama Commission on Higher Education
3465 Norman Bridge Road
Montgomery, AL 36105-2310
(334) 281-1921
Maximum award: Tuition and books
College level: Freshman, Sophomore
Criteria: Applicant must attend a public junior or community college in Alabama on a full-time basis. Selection is based upon demonstrated athletic ability determined through try-outs. Financial need is not considered. Continued participation in designated sport is required to retain scholarship. Awarded every year.
Contact: Dr. William H. Wall, Alabama Commission of Higher Education.

1315 NATA Scholarship

National Athletic Trainers Association (NATA)
Grants and Scholarships Committee
2952 Stemmons
Dallas, TX 75247
(214) 637-6282
Minimum award: $1,500
Maximum number of awards: 80
Minimum number of awards: 40
Deadline: February 1
College level: Senior, Graduate, Doctoral
Majors/Fields: Athletic training
Criteria: Applicant must have a minimum 3.0 GPA, be a NATA member, pursue athletic training as a career, and be recommended by a certified athletic trainer. Awarded every year.
Contact: Briana Ebmeier, Foundation Manager.

1316 Olympic Tuition Grant

U.S. Olympic Committee
One Olympic Plaza
Colorado Springs, CO 80909
Average award: $1,200
Maximum award: $5,000
Number of awards: 450
Deadline: November 1; February 1; May 1; August 1
College level: High-performance athletes endorsed by their sport's national govering body, who are in a degree- or certificate-granting program
Criteria: Applicant must be a candidate for membership on the next U.S. Olympic or Pan American Games team and demonstrate financial need. Applicant must continue to perform at elite level and show need. Awarded every year.
Contact: Curt L. Hamakawa, Assistant Director, Athlete Support Department, (719) 578-4661.

1317 Peter A. McKernan Scholarship

Peter A. McKernan Scholarship Fund
P.O. Box 5601
Augusta, ME 04332-5601
(207) 582-2729
Average award: $2,000
Number of awards: 3
Deadline: May 1
College level: Freshman
Criteria: Applicant must have a minimum "C" average, have earned a varsity letter or its equivalent in a high school sport, submit an essay "What Friendship Means to Me," be nominated by high school, and demonstrate financial need. Each Maine high school may nominate two students, one who will be attending a four-year school and one for a vocational school. Awarded every year.
Contact: Judith Vigue, President.

1318 U.S. Ski Team Foundation Scholarship

United States Ski Education Foundation
P.O. Box 100
Park City, UT 84060
Average award: $1,000
Maximum award: $2,000
Deadline: May 1
College level: Freshman, Sophomore, Junior, Senior, Graduate, Doctoral
Criteria: Applicant must be a current or retired member of the U.S. Ski Team. Recipient must reapply for renewal. Awarded every year.
Contact: Laurie Beck, Academic and Career Counselor.

1319   Wendy's High School Heisman Award

National Association of Secondary School Principals
1904 Association Drive
Reston, VA 22091
Average award: $3,000
Maximum award: $5,000
Number of awards: 12
Deadline: September 30
College level: Freshman
Criteria: Applicant must demonstrate athletic ability, scholarship, and citizenship. Schools may nominate two seniors (1 male, 1 female). 12 national finalists will receive a trip to New York City for the Heisman Awards ceremony in December, and two of the finalists (1 male, 1 female) will be named the Wendy's High School Heisman Award winners. Awarded every year.

Automotive Studies

1320   Automotive Hall of Fame Scholarships

Automotive Hall of Fame
3225 Cook Road
P.O. Box 1727
Midland, MI 48641-1727
(517) 631-5760
Maximum award: $2,000
Minimum award: $250
Maximum number of awards: 24
Minimum number of awards: 16
Deadline: June 30
College level: Sophomore, Junior, Senior, Graduate, Doctoral
Criteria: Applicant must have a sincere interst in pursuing an automotive career upon graduation, regardless of major, and demonstrate satisfactory academic performance. Financial need is considered but not necessary. Awarded every year.
Contact: Margaret Gifford, Director of Educational Services.

1321   SEMA Scholarship Fund

Specialty Equipment Market Association (SEMA)
P.O. Box 4910
Diamond Bar, CA 91765-0910
(909) 396-0289
Maximum award: $2,500
Minimum award: $1,000
Number of awards: 13
Deadline: April 15
College level: Sophomore, Junior, Senior, Graduate, Doctoral
Criteria: Applicant must intend to enter the automotive aftermarket field. Scholarship is renewable.
Contact: Foundation Director.

1322   Universal Underwriters Scholarship

Automotive Hall of Fame
3225 Cook Road
P.O. Box 1727
Midland, MI 48641-1727
(517) 631-5760
Average award: $2,000
Number of awards: 4
Deadline: June 30
College level: Junior, Senior
Majors/Fields: Automotive studies
Criteria: Applicant must show a sincere interest in an automotive career and be enrolled as a full-time student at Northwood U. Awarded every year.
Contact: Margaret Gifford, Director of Educational Services.

1323   Walter W. Stillman Scholarship

Automotive Hall of Fame
3225 Cook Road
P.O. Box 1727
Midland, MI 48641-1727
(517) 631-5760
Maximum award: $2,000
Maximum number of awards: 3
Minimum number of awards: 1
Deadline: June 30
College level: Junior, Senior
Majors/Fields: Automotive studies
Criteria: Applicant must show a sincere interest in an automotive career, attend Northwood U, and maintain satisfactory academic progress. Financial need is considered. Preference is given to students from New Jersey. Awarded every year.
Contact: Margaret Gifford, Director of Educational Services.

City/County of Residence

1324   50 Men and Women of Toledo, Inc. Scholarship

University of Toledo
Financial Aid Office
Toledo, OH 43606-3390
(419) 537-2056
Maximum award: $3,000
Minimum award: $1,000
Number of awards: 1
Deadline: January 28
College level: Freshman
Criteria: Applicant must be an African-American graduate of a Toledo area high school. Award is for four years. Awarded every year. Award may be used only at sponsoring institution.
Contact: J.C. Caldwell, 50 Men and Women of Toledo, Inc., P.O. Box 3557, Toledo, OH 43608, (419) 729-4654.

1325   Alicia Patterson Grant

Newsday/Alicia Patterson Grant
235 Pinelawn Road
Long Island, NY 11747
Minimum award: $5,000
Criteria: Applicant must reside and attend school in Nassau or Suffolk counties, N.Y.
Contact: Angelica Jordan, Public Affairs Associate.

1326   Anna and Charles Stockwitz Children and Youth Fund

Jewish Family and Children's Services
1600 Scott Street
San Francisco, CA 94115
(415) 561-1226
Average award: $2,500
Maximum award: $5,000
Number of awards: 100
College level: Freshman, Sophomore, Junior, Senior, Graduate, Doctoral
Criteria: Applicant must be Jewish, under age 26, demonstrate financial need, and be a resident of Marin, Mountain View, Palo Alto, San Francisco, San Mateo, or Sonoma County, Calif. Scholarship is renewable. Awarded every year.
Contact: Ted Schreiber, Director of Loans and Grants Program.

1327   Anna Jones Scholarship

State Scholarship Commission (Oregon)
1500 Valley River Drive
Suite 100
Eugene, OR 97401-2146
(503) 687-7395
Minimum award: $1,000
Number of awards: 2
Deadline: March 1
College level: Freshman, Sophomore, Junior, Senior, Graduate
Criteria: Applicant must be a Lake County, Oreg., resident, a graduate of Paisley High School, be enrolled full time at an Oregon school, and demonstrate financial need. Awarded every year.
Contact: Jim Beyer, Grant Program Director.

1328   Aubrey Lee Brooks Scholarship

North Carolina State Education Assistance Authority
Box 2688
Chapel Hill, NC 27515-2688
(919) 549-8614
Average award: Half tuition
Maximum award: $3,500
Number of awards: 17
College level: Freshman
Criteria: Applicant must be a resident of one of the following North Carolina counties: Alamance, Bertie, Caswell, Durham, Forsyth, Granville, Guilford, Orange, Person, Rockingham, Stokes, Surry, Swain, or Warren; or reside in the cities of Greensboro or High Point. One award is for a senior at the North Carolina Sch of Science and Mathematics. Applicant must attend North Carolina State U, U of North Carolina at Chapel Hill, or U of North Carolina at Greensboro. Selection is based upon academic standing, character, leadership, financial need, and applicant's willingness to prepare for a career as a well-informed citizen. Good academic standing, financial need, and full-time enrollment at an eligible instutition are required to retain scholarship. Awarded every year.
Contact: High school guidance counselor.

1329   Big Thursday Golf Tournament Scholarship

Clemson University
G-01 Sikes Hall
Clemson, SC 29634-5123
(803) 656-2280
Average award: $1,000
Number of awards: 2
Deadline: March 1
College level: Freshman, Sophomore, Junior, Senior
Criteria: Applicant must be a resident of Richland County, a graduate from a Richland County high school, and have a minimum 3.0 GPA. Satisfactory GPA with at least 12 credits per semester is required to retain scholarship. Awarded every year. Award may be used only at sponsoring institution.
Contact: Marvin Carmichael, Director of Financial Aid.

1330   Bobby R. Hudson Endowed Scholarship

Clemson University
G-01 Sikes Hall
Clemson, SC 29634-5123
(803) 656-2280
Average award: $1,400
Number of awards: 2
Deadline: March 1
College level: Freshman, Sophomore, Junior, Senior
Criteria: Applicant must be a resident of Greenville County, S.C. Minimum 2.5 GPA with at least 12 credits per semester is required to retain scholarship. Awarded every year. Award may be used only at sponsoring institution.
Contact: Marvin Carmichael, Director of Financial Aid.

1331   Boston Youth Leadership Award

Northeastern University
360 Huntington Avenue
Boston, MA 02115
(617) 373-2000
Average award: $6,500
Number of awards: 5
Deadline: March 1
College level: Freshman
Criteria: Applicant must attend a Boston public, private, or parochial school, rank in the top quarter of class, and demonstrate outstanding community leadership and service. Minimum 3.0 GPA is required to retain scholarship. Awarded every year. Award may be used only at sponsoring institution.
Contact: Kevin Kelly, Dean of Admissions, (617) 373-2200.

1332   Broadcast Journalism

State Scholarship Commission (Oregon)
1500 Valley River Drive
Suite 100
Eugene, OR 97401-2146
(503) 687-7395
Minimum award: $1,000
Number of awards: 2
Deadline: March 1
College level: Freshman
Majors/Fields: Broadcast journalism
Criteria: Applicant must be an Oregon resident, be enrolled full time at an Oregon school, and demonstrate financial need. Awarded every year.
Contact: Jim Beyer, Grant Program Director.

1333   Community College Achievement Award

Southern California Edison Company
Educational Services, P.O. Box 800
Rosemead, CA 91770
(818) 302-9134 or (818) 302-0284
Maximum award: $4,000
Number of awards: 20
Deadline: March 1
College level: Junior, Senior
Criteria: Applicant must live in or attend a community college in the Southern California Edison service area, have a minimum 2.5 GPA, have sufficient transferrable units to enter a four-year college as a junior in the fall, and be a U.S. citizen or permanent resident. Dependents of Southern California Edison employees are not eligible. Selection is based upon career objectives and academic achievements. Recipients 18 years or older may also be eligible to participate in the Edison Summer Employment Program. Awarded every year.
Contact: Edison Scholarship Committee.

1334   Dane G. Hansen Foundation Leadership Scholarship

Dane G. Hansen Foundation
Logan, KS 67646
(913) 689-4832
Average award: $3,500
Number of awards: 6
Deadline: Fall of senior year in high school
College level: Freshman
Criteria: Applicant must be a graduating senior from a high school in the 26-county area of northwest Kansas and have a minimum 3.5 GPA. Renewable for up to three years if minimum "B" average is maintained. Awarded every year.
Contact: Raymond Lappin, Chairman of the Scholarship Committee.

1335 **Dorchester County Marketing Association Annual Scholarship**

Clemson University
G-01 Sikes Hall
Clemson, SC 29634-5123
(803) 656-2280
Average award: $1,500
Number of awards: 2
Deadline: March 1
College level: Freshman, Sophomore, Junior, Senior
Criteria: Applicant must be a resident of Dorchester County, S.C. First priority is given to students in the Coll of Agricultural Sciences, next to students in the Coll of Sciences, and then to any eligible applicant. Satisfactory GPA with at least 12 credits per semester is required to retain scholarship. Awarded every year. Award may be used only at sponsoring institution.
Contact: Marvin Carmichael, Director of Financial Aid.

1336 **Douglas County Community Scholarship**

State Scholarship Commission (Oregon)
1500 Valley River Drive
Suite 100
Eugene, OR 97401-2146
(503) 687-7395
Minimum award: $1,000
Number of awards: 2
Deadline: March 1
College level: Sophomore, Junior, Senior, Graduate
Criteria: Applicant must be an Oregon resident, a graduate of a Douglas County high school, be enrolled full time at a California, Idaho, Oregon, or Washington school, and demonstrate financial need. Awarded every year.
Contact: Jim Beyer, Grant Program Director.

1337 **DuPage Medical Society Foundation Scholarship**

DuPage Medical Society Foundation
498 Hillside Avenue #1
Glen Ellyn, IL 60137-4536
(708) 858-9603
Average award: $750
Maximum award: $1,000
Minimum award: $500
Number of awards: 5
Deadline: April 30
College level: Sophomore, Junior, Senior, Graduate, Doctoral, Medical school
Majors/Fields: Medicine, medical technical, nursing, dentistry, pharmacy
Criteria: Awards are for residents of DuPage County, Ill., who are majoring in health-related fields. Applicant must be in a professional education or technical training program at the time of application. Selection is based upon academic ability and financial need. Scholarship is renewable. Awarded every year.
Contact: Kirk G. McMurray, Executive Director, 498 Hillside Avenue, Glen Ellyn, IL 60137.

1338 **Edith McPherson Scholarship**

Colorado State University
Financial Aid Office
108 Student Services Building
Fort Collins, CO 80523
(970) 491-6321
Average award: $1,250
Maximum award: $1,500
Minimum award: $500
Number of awards: 14
Deadline: January 31
College level: Freshman
Criteria: Applicant is automatically considered based on application for admission. Applicant must be a San Luis Valley, Colo., resident, have strong academic potential, and demonstrate financial need. Satisfactory progress is required to retain scholarship. Awarded every year. Award may be used only at sponsoring institution.
Contact: Jeanne Snyder, Financial Aid Counselor.

1339 **Fay T. Barnes Scholarship**

Texas Commerce Bank of Austin
700 Lavaca
P.O. Box 550
Austin, TX 78789
(512) 479-2444
Average award: $2,500
Number of awards: 10
Deadline: January 1
College level: Freshman
Criteria: Applicant must be a resident of Travis or Williamson counties and plan to attend a college or university in Texas. Selection is based upon financial need and high school and community activities. Renewable if satisfactory GPA is maintained. Awarded twice per year.
Contact: Regina Knouse, Assistant Administrator, (512) 479-2644.

1340 **Frank Roswell Fuller Scholarship**

Frank Roswell Fuller Scholarship Fund
300 Summit Street
Hartford, CT 06106
(203) 297-2046
Average award: $2,500
Maximum award: $5,000
Minimum award: $1,500
Number of awards: 12
Deadline: May 15
College level: Freshman
Criteria: Applicant must be a graduate of a Hartford County, Conn., high school, demonstrate financial need, be a member of the Congregational Church, and attend a four-year college. Satisfactory academic progress and financial need are required to retain scholarship. Awarded every year.
Contact: Anne M. Zartarian, Manager.

1341 **Geographic Competitions Scholarship**

Marquette University
1212 West Wisconsin Avenue
Milwaukee, WI 53233
(414) 288-7390
Average award: $2,000
Deadline: February 15
College level: Freshman
Criteria: Applicant must rank in the top quarter of class and attend a high school in one of the following geographic areas: greater Chicago, Ill., greater Cleveland, Ohio, greater Detroit, Mich., greater Fox Valley, Wis., greater Milwaukee, Wis., greater Saint Louis, Mo., greater Twin Cities, Minn., greater Omaha, Nebr., the Caribbean, or Puerto Rico. Minimum 2.0 GPA and full-time enrollment are required to retain scholarship. Awarded every year. Award may be used only at sponsoring institution.
Contact: Anne Wingert, Assistant Director of Student Financial Aid.

1342 **George E. Andrews Scholarship**

Blackhawk State Bank
P.O. Box 719
Beloit, WI 53512-0719
(608) 364-8917
Average award: $3,000
Minimum award: $2,000
Number of awards: 1
Deadline: March 15
College level: Freshman
Criteria: In even-numbered years the award is made to a qualified senior at Beloit Memorial High School and in odd-numbered years to one at Beloit Catholic High School. Selection is based upon financial need, moral character, industriousness, and scholastic standing. Applicant must rank in top third of class. Scholarship is renewable. Awarded every year.
Contact: Dorothy L. Burton, Trust Officer.

1343 George J. Record School Foundation Scholarship

George J. Record School Foundation
P.O. Box 581
365 Main Street
Conneaut, OH 44030
(216) 599-8283
Average award: $2,500
Maximum award: $3,000
Minimum award: $500
Maximum number of awards: 82
Minimum number of awards: 64
Deadline: May 20 (freshmen); June 20 (others)
College level: Freshman, Sophomore, Junior, Senior
Criteria: Applicant must be a legal resident of Ashtabula County, Ohio, and plan to attend on a full-time basis a private, Protestant-based college approved by the Foundation. Financial need must be demonstrated. Six semesters or nine quarters of religion over the four years of college are required to retain scholarship. Awarded every year.
Contact: Charles N. Lafferty, Executive Director.

1344 George T. Welch Scholarship

George T. Welch Trust
Baker Boyer National Bank
P.O. Box 1796
Walla Walla, WA 99362
Maximum award: $2,500
Minimum award: $1,000
Number of awards: 60
College level: Freshman, Sophomore, Junior, Senior
Criteria: Applicant must be a resident of Walla Walla County, Wash., and demonstrate financial need. Scholarship is renewable. Awarded every year.
Contact: Holly T. Howard, Trust Officer.

1345 Greenville Clemson Club Annual Scholarship

Clemson University
G-01 Sikes Hall
Clemson, SC 29634-5123
(803) 656-2280
Average award: $1,000
Number of awards: 2
Deadline: March 1
College level: Freshman
Criteria: Applicant must be a resident of Greenville County, S.C. Minimum 2.5 cumulative GPA with at least 12 credits per semester is required to retain scholarship. Awarded every year. Award may be used only at sponsoring institution.
Contact: Marvin Carmichael, Director of Financial Aid.

1346 Harry and Devera Lerman Educational Trust Scholarship

University of Texas at San Antonio
Office of Student Financial Aid
6900 North Loop 1604 West
San Antonio, TX 78249-0687
(210) 691-4011
Average award: $2,000
Number of awards: 30
Deadline: April 30
College level: Freshman, Sophomore, Junior, Senior
Criteria: Applicant must rank in the top quarter of class, have a minimum 3.0 GPA, be a resident of Bexar County, Tex., be enrolled full time, demonstrate financial need, and not have other grants or scholarships. Minimum 3.0 GPA is required to retain scholarship. Awarded every year. Award may be used only at sponsoring institution.
Contact: Scholarship Office, (210) 691-4855.

1347 Hauss-Helms Foundation, Inc. Scholarship

Hauss-Helms Foundation, Inc.
P.O. Box 25
Wapakoneta, OH 45895
(419) 738-4911
Maximum award: $5,000
Minimum award: $400
Number of awards: 600
Deadline: April 15
College level: Freshman, Sophomore, Junior, Senior, Graduate, Doctoral
Criteria: Applicant must be a resident of Allen County or Auglaize County, Ohio, demonstrate financial need, and rank in the top half of graduating class or have a minimum 2.0 GPA. Awarded every year.
Contact: James E. Weger, President.

1348 Helen Bolton Scholarship

State Scholarship Commission (Oregon)
1500 Valley River Drive
Suite 100
Eugene, OR 97401-2146
(503) 687-7395
Minimum award: $1,000
Number of awards: 2
Deadline: March 1
College level: Freshman
Criteria: Applicant must be an Oregon resident, a graduate of North Medford, South Medford, or St. Mary's (Medford) high school, be enrolled full time at an Oregon school, and demonstrate financial need. Preference will be given to applicants entering the health care field. Awarded every year.
Contact: Jim Beyer, Grant Program Director.

1349 Hesslein Scholarship

University of Oklahoma
University Affairs
900 Asp Avenue, Room 236
Norman, OK 73019-0401
(405) 325-1701
Average award: $1,000
Maximum number of awards: 20
Minimum number of awards: 15
Deadline: March 1
College level: Freshman, Sophomore, Junior, Senior
Criteria: Applicant must be a resident of the Tulsa/Sand Springs, Okla., area and demonstrate financial need. Awarded every year. Award may be used only at sponsoring institution.
Contact: Office of Financial Aid Services, 731 Elm, Norman, OK 73019-0230, (405) 325-4521.

1350 Hispanic Community Scholarship

University of Toledo
Financial Aid Office
Toledo, OH 43606-3390
(419) 537-2056
Average award: $1,000
Number of awards: 2
Deadline: January 28
College level: Freshman
Criteria: Applicant must be a Hispanic graduate of a Toledo public school. Award is for four years. Awarded every year. Award may be used only at sponsoring institution.
Contact: Coordinator of Minority Admissions, Office of Admissions Services, Toledo, OH 43606, (419) 537-2073.

1351 Horace M. Kinsey and Maybelle McLaurin Kinsey Scholarship

Clemson University
G-01 Sikes Hall
Clemson, SC 29634-5123
(803) 656-2280
Average award: $1,200
Number of awards: 4
Deadline: March 1
College level: Freshman, Sophomore, Junior, Senior
Criteria: Applicant must be a worthy student; preference is given to residents of Colleton County, S.C. Awarded every year. Award may be used only at sponsoring institution.
Contact: Marvin Carmichael, Director of Financial Aid.

1352 Howard D. Folk Presidential Scholarship

Clemson University
G-01 Sikes Hall
Clemson, SC 29634-5123
(803) 656-2280
Average award: $1,000
Number of awards: 4
Deadline: March 1
College level: Freshman, Sophomore, Junior, Senior
Criteria: Applicant must be a graduate of Holly Hill Roberts High School or Holly Hill Academy. Satisfactory GPA with at least 12 credits per semester is required to retain scholarship. Awarded every year. Award may be used only at sponsoring institution.
Contact: Marvin Carmichael, Director of Financial Aid.

1353 Independent Colleges of Southern California Scholarship Program

Southern California Edison Company
Educational Services
P.O. Box 800
Rosemead, CA 91770
(818) 302-9134 or (818) 302-0284
Average award: $20,000
Number of awards: 2
College level: Freshman
Criteria: Applicant must reside in the Southern California Edison service area, be a member of an underrepresented ethnic group, be a U.S. citizen or permanent resident, demonstrate academic achievement and financial need, and plan to enter an ICSC school as a full-time undergraduate. Each member college selects two applicants based on academic performance, extracurricular activities, and demonstrated leadership. Preference is given to applicants who are the first generation to attend college. ICSC then selects finalists from these applicants. Dependents of Southern California Edison employees are not eligible. Awarded every year.
Contact: Edison Scholarship Committee.

1354 Jacob Rassen Memorial Scholarship Fund

Jewish Family and Children's Services
1600 Scott Street
San Francisco, CA 94115
(415) 561-1226
Average award: $1,000
Maximum award: $2,000
Minimum award: $500
Number of awards: 4
Deadline: None
College level: Freshman, Sophomore, Junior, Senior, Graduate
Criteria: Award is for a study trip to Israel for Jewish youth under age 22. Applicant must have demonstrated academic achievement, financial need, desire to enhance Jewish identity, and desire to increase knowledge of and connection to Israel. Applicant must be a resident of Marin County, San Francisco County, San Mateo County, Sonoma County, Palo Alto or Mountain View, Calif. Awarded every year.
Contact: Ted Schreiber, Director of Loans and Grants Program.

1355 Janesville Foundation Scholarship

Janesville Foundation
P.O. Box 8123
Janesville, WI 53547-8123
(608) 752-1032
Average award: $1,000
Number of awards: 8
Deadline: February 1
College level: Freshman
Criteria: Applicant must be graduating from either of Janesville, Wis., high schools; application must be made through the principal's office. Selection is based upon class rank, principal's recommendation, and college acceptance. Awarded every year.
Contact: Principals of Janesville, Wisconsin high schools.

1356 Jewish Foundation for Education of Women Scholarship

Jewish Foundation for Education of Women
330 West 58th Street
New York, NY 10019
(212) 265-2565
Average award: $1,000
Maximum award: $3,500
Minimum award: $500
Deadline: January 31 for coming year
College level: Unspecified undergraduate
Criteria: Scholarship is nonsectarian. Applicant must be a full-time student (minimum 12 credits) who lives within a 50-mile radius of New York City, including New Jersey and Long Island. Law or M.B.A. candidates are not eligible. Awarded every year.
Contact: Florence Wallach, Executive Director.

1357 Joe and Christine Callahan Scholarship

University of Alabama–Tuscaloosa
Box 870162
Tuscaloosa, AL 35487-0162
(205) 348-6756
Average award: $1,000
Number of awards: 2
Deadline: March 1
College level: Freshman
Criteria: Applicant must be enrolled full time. Preference is given to dependents of law enforcement officers. One award is for a graduate of a Clay County, Ala., high school and one for a graduate of a Calhoun County, Ala., high school. Awarded every year. Award may be used only at sponsoring institution.
Contact: Office of Student Financial Services.

1358 John H. Anderson Scholarship

University of Toledo
Financial Aid Office
Toledo, OH 43606-3390
(419) 537-2056
Average award: $2,000
Number of awards: 1
Deadline: January 28
College level: Freshman
Criteria: Applicant must be an African-American graduate of a Toledo area high school. Award is for four years. Awarded every year. Award may be used only at sponsoring institution.
Contact: J.C. Caldwell, 50 Men and Women of Toledo, Inc., P.O. Box 3557, Toledo, OH 43608, (419) 729-4654.

1359 John W. and Rose E. Watson Scholarship

John W. and Rose E. Watson Scholarship Foundation
5800 Weiss Street
Saginaw, MI 48603
(517) 797-6633
Average award: $1,200
Number of awards: 115
Deadline: April 1
College level: Freshman
Criteria: Applicant must be a graduate of a Saginaw, Mich., Catholic high school. Reapplication and satisfactory academic progress are required to retain scholarship. Awarded every year.
Contact: Jean Seman, Secretary.

1360   John W. Rowe Scholarship

Maine Community Foundation
210 Main Street
P.O. Box 148
Ellsworth, ME 04605
(207) 667-9735
Average award: $1,500
Maximum award: $5,000
Number of awards: 6
Deadline: May 1
College level: Freshman, Sophomore, Junior, Senior
Criteria: Applicant must be a the child of a Central Maine Power employee, enrolled in an accredited two- or four-year undergraduate institution, and be a graduate of a Maine secondary school. Selection is based upon personal aspirations, academic achievement, financial need, and school and community activities. Awarded every year.
Contact: Patti D'Angelo, Program Associate.

1361   Kingsley Alcid Brown Educational Fund

Maine Community Foundation
210 Main Street
P.O. Box 148
Ellsworth, ME 04605
(207) 667-9735
Maximum award: $2,000
Minimum award: $1,000
Number of awards: 1
Deadline: April 1
College level: Graduate, Doctoral
Criteria: Applicant must be a graduate of a Washington County, Me., high school pursuing a graduate-level degree. Awarded every year.
Contact: Patti D'Angelo, Program Associate.

1362   Lee C. Van Wagner Scholarship

Medical Society of the County of Chenango
P.O. Box 620
210 Clinton Road
New Hartford, NY 13413
(315) 735-2204
Average award: $2,000
Minimum award: $1,000
Maximum number of awards: 4
Minimum number of awards: 4
Deadline: June 1
College level: Doctoral
Majors/Fields: Medicine
Criteria: Applicant must be a legal resident of Chenango or Otsego counties, N.Y., be in an M.D. or D.O. degree program, and agree to practice in either Chanago or Otsego County for one year for each year of award, or repay the money within five years of graduation. Satisfactory grades are required to retain scholarship. Awarded every year.
Contact: Kathleen E. Dyman, Executive Director.

1363   Leonard H. Bulkeley Scholarship

Leonard H. Bulkeley Scholarship Fund
P.O. Box 1426
New London, CT 06320
(203) 447-1461
Maximum award: $1,000
Number of awards: 48
Deadline: April 1
College level: Freshman, Sophomore, Junior, Senior
Criteria: Applicant must be an undergraduate student between the ages of 16 and 25, who is a resident of New London, Conn. Selection is based upon academic standing, financial need, school and community activities, and a personal interview. Reapplication is required to retain scholarship. Awarded every year.
Contact: Gay Buths, Secretary.

1364   Madison Charitable Fund Scholarship

State Scholarship Commission (Oregon)
1500 Valley River Drive
Suite 100
Eugene, OR 97401-2146
(503) 687-7395
Minimum award: $1,000
Number of awards: 2
Deadline: March 1
College level: Freshman, Sophomore, Junior, Senior, Graduate
Criteria: Applicant must be an Oregon resident, a graduate of a Douglas County high school with a minimum 3.0 high school GPA, 2.5 college GPA, be enrolled full time at an Oregon school, and demonstrate financial need. Preference is given to Elkton High School graduates. Awarded every year.
Contact: Jim Beyer, Grant Program Director.

1365   Marcus and Theresa Levie Educational Fund

Jewish Vocational Service
One South Franklin
Chicago, IL 60606
(312) 357-4500
Average award: $5,000
Maximum number of awards: 40
Minimum number of awards: 35
Deadline: March 1
College level: Junior, Senior, Graduate, Doctoral
Majors/Fields: Helping professions
Criteria: Applicant must be a full-time Jewish student who is legally domiciled in Cook County, Ill. Applicant must be a superior student, demonstrate financial need, and show promise of significant contributions in a helping profession. Preprofessional students are not eligible. Reapplication is required to retain scholarship. Awarded every year.
Contact: Scholarship Secretary, One South Franklin Street, Chicago, IL 60606.

1366   Marie Mahoney Egan Scholarship

State Scholarship Commission (Oregon)
1500 Valley River Drive
Suite 100
Eugene, OR 97401-2146
(503) 687-7395
Minimum award: $1,000
Number of awards: 2
Deadline: March 1
College level: Freshman, Sophomore, Junior, Senior, Graduate
Criteria: Applicant must be a Lake County, Oreg., resident, a graduate of a Lake County high school, be enrolled full time at an Oregon school, and demonstrate financial need. Awarded every year.
Contact: Jim Beyer, Grant Program Director.

1367   Middlesex County (NJ) Medical Society Foundation Scholarship

Middlesex County (NJ) Medical Society Foundation
575 Cranbury Road, B-7
East Brunswick, NJ 08816
(908) 257-6800
Average award: $750
Maximum award: $1,000
Minimum award: $500
Maximum number of awards: 9
Minimum number of awards: 5
Deadline: February 1
College level: Medical school, nursing, and pharmacy students
Majors/Fields: Medicine, nursing, pharmacy
Criteria: Applicant must be a resident of Middlesex County, N.J., for at least five years and be studying medicine (both M.D. and D.O. programs), nursing, or pharmacy. Academic achievement and financial need are required to retain scholarship. Awarded every year.
Contact: Mary Alice Bruno, Executive Secretary.

1368   Mr. and Mrs. James M. Kirk Endowment

Clemson University
G-01 Sikes Hall
Clemson, SC 29634-5123
(803) 656-2280
Average award: $1,000
Number of awards: 3
Deadline: March 1
College level: Freshman
Criteria: Applicant must be a graduate of a Lancaster County high school. Awarded every year. Award may be used only at sponsoring institution.
Contact: Marvin Carmichael, Director of Financial Aid.

1369   Pacific Coca-Cola/Thriftway Stores Merit Award

Pacific Coca-Cola in Cooperation with Thriftway Stores
1150 124th Avenue, NE
P.O. Box C-93346
Bellevue, WA 98009-3346
(206) 455-2000
Average award: $1,500
Number of awards: 18
Deadline: Mid-April
College level: Freshman
Criteria: Applicant must be a high school senior in western Washington, Yakima, and Wenatchee areas with a minimum 3.5 GPA and plan to enroll full time in a participating college or university. Selection is based upon academic achievement, leadership potential, school and/or community involvement, employment, and family responsibility. Awarded every year.
Contact: Terry Conner, Key Account Representative.

1370   Parker Memorial Scholarship

Janesville Foundation
P.O. Box 8123
Janesville, WI 53547-8123
(608) 752-1032
Average award: $2,000
Number of awards: 4
Deadline: February 1
College level: Freshman
Criteria: Applicant must be graduating from either of Janesville, Wis., high schools; application must be made through the principal's office. Selection is based upon class rank, principal's recommendation, and college acceptance. Renewal is based upon scholastic achievement; payable only upon successful completion of first semester. Awarded every year.
Contact: Principals of Janesville, Wisconsin high schools.

1371   Pickens County Scholars Program

Clemson University
G-01 Sikes Hall
Clemson, SC 29634-5123
(803) 656-2280
Average award: $7,500
Number of awards: 2
College level: Freshman
Criteria: Applicant must be a graduate of a Pickens County high school. Preference is given to graduates of Liberty or Easley High School. Minimum 3.0 cumulative GPA with at least 12 credits per semester is required to retain scholarship. Awarded every year. Award may be used only at sponsoring institution.
Contact: Marvin Carmichael, Director of Financial Aid.

1372   Pinnacle Resources Ltd. Bursary

University of Calgary
2500 University Drive, NW
Calgary, Alberta, CN T2N 1N4
(403) 220-7872
Average award: $3,000
Number of awards: 1
Deadline: July 15
College level: Freshman
Criteria: Applicant must be a graduate of an Athabasca, Provost, or Westlock area high school. Selection is based upon academic merit, finanical need, and extracurricular activities. Awarded every year. Award may be used only at sponsoring institution.
Contact: J. Van Housen, Director of Student Awards & Financial Aid.

1373   Prince George's Chamber of Commerce Foundation Scholarship

Prince George's Chamber of Commerce Foundation, Inc.
4640 Forbes Boulevard
Suite 200
Lanham, MD 20706
(301) 731-5000
Average award: $2,000
Maximum award: $2,760
Minimum award: $1,000
Number of awards: 16
Deadline: May 15
College level: Freshman, Sophomore, Junior, Senior
Criteria: Applicant must be a Prince George's County, Md., resident. Minimum 2.5 GPA is required to retain scholarship. Awarded every year.
Contact: Robert Zinsmeister, Administrator.

1374   Regional Scholarship

Old Dominion University
Hampton Boulevard
Norfolk, VA 23529-0050
(804) 683-3683
Maximum award: $1,200
Number of awards: 25
Deadline: February 15
College level: Freshman
Criteria: Applicant must demonstrate financial need and be a resident of one of the following localities in Virginia: Accomack, Chesapeake, Hampton, Isle of Wight, Newport News, Portsmouth, Suffolk, Virginia Beach. Minimum 2.5 GPA, completion of 24 credit hours, and financial need are required to retain scholarship for one additional year. Awarded every year; may be used only at sponsoring institution.
Contact: Mary A. Schutz, Assistant Director of Scholarships.

1375   Reid-Baskin Scholarship

Clemson University
G-01 Sikes Hall
Clemson, SC 29634-5123
(803) 656-2280
Average award: $1,000
Number of awards: 6
Deadline: March 1
College level: Freshman, Sophomore, Junior, Senior
Majors/Fields: Engineering, liberal arts
Criteria: Preference is given to applicants majoring in liberal arts and engineering and to residents, in the following order, of Newberry and York Counties, S.C., and the Fredricksburg, Va., area. Awarded every year. Award may be used only at sponsoring institution.
Contact: Marvin Carmichael, Director of Financial Aid.

1376   Robert A. Hine Memorial Scholarship

Southern California Edison Company
Educational Services
P.O. Box 800
Rosemead, CA 91770
(818) 302-9134 or (818) 302-0284
Average award: $20,000
Number of awards: 1
Deadline: Take SAT I by first Saturday in December of senior year
College level: Freshman
Criteria: Applicant must reside in the Southern California Edison service area, be a member of an underrepresented ethnic group, be a U.S. citizen or permanent resident, demonstrate academic achievement, and plan to attend a four-year university as a full-time student. Preference is given to students with financial need. Dependents of Southern California Edison employees are not eligible. Top 100 applicants with the highest SAT I scores will be asked to complete an application for further evaluation. Awarded every year.
Contact: Educational Services.

1377   Robert Hardin Scholarship

East Tennessee State University
P.O. Box 70722
Johnson City, TN 37614-0002
(615) 929-4300
Average award: $1,000
Number of awards: 3
Deadline: February 15
College level: Freshman
Criteria: Applicant must be a graduating senior with the highest GPA from a high school in Carter, Elizabethton, Hampton, or Unicoi County, Tenn. Awarded every year. Award may be used only at sponsoring institution.
Contact: Michael Jones, Financial Aid Counselor.

1378   Roy T. Campbell Scholarship

East Tennessee State University
P.O. Box 70722
Johnson City, TN 37614-0002
(615) 929-4300
Average award: $1,000
Number of awards: 2
Deadline: February 15
College level: Freshman, Sophomore, Junior, Senior
Criteria: Applicant must be a resident of Cooke County, Tenn. Financial need is considered and a minimum 2.5 overall GPA is required. Awarded every year. Award may be used only at sponsoring institution.
Contact: Michael Jones, Financial Aid Counselor.

1379   Santa Barbara Scholarship

Santa Barbara Scholarship Foundation
P.O. Box 1403
Santa Barbara, CA 93102
(805) 965-7212
Average award: $1,300
Maximum award: $2,500
Minimum award: $1,000
Number of awards: 600
Deadline: February 1
College level: Freshman, Sophomore, Junior, Senior, Graduate, Doctoral
Criteria: Applicant must be a graduate of a Santa Barbara area high school and demonstrate financial need. Interview is required. Reapplication, demonstration of financial need, and a minimum 2.5 GPA are required to retain scholarship. Awarded every year.
Contact: Scholarships.

1380   Southern California Edison Company College Scholarship

Southern California Edison Company
Educational Services
P.O. Box 800
Rosemead, CA 91770
(818) 302-9134 or (818) 302-0284
Average award: $5,000
Number of awards: 4
Deadline: Take SAT I by first Saturday in December of senior year
College level: Freshman
Criteria: Applicant must live in or attend school in the Southern California Edison service territory and be a U.S. citizen or permanent resident. Dependents of Southern California Edison employees are not eligible. Applicant must be a high school senior or have met high school requirements to enter college full-time in the fall. Selection is by SAT I scores; the top 15 candidates in each of Edison's seven regions will be asked to submit applications. Recipients 18 years or older may also be eligible to participate in the Edison Summer Employment Program. Award is for four years. Awarded every year.
Contact: Edison Scholarship Committee.

1381   Stanley Olson Youth Scholarship Fund

Jewish Family and Children's Services
1600 Scott Street
San Francisco, CA 94115
(415) 561-1226
Average award: $1,500
Maximum award: $2,500
Number of awards: 3
Deadline: None
College level: Freshman, Sophomore, Junior, Senior, Graduate, Doctoral
Majors/Fields: Humanities
Criteria: Applicant must be a Jewish youth under age 26 with demonstrated academic achievement, have financial need, and be a resident of Marin County, San Francisco County, San Mateo County, Sonoma County, Palo Alto, or Mountain View, Calif. Scholarship is renewable. Awarded every year.
Contact: Ted Schreiber, Director of Loans and Grants Program.

1382   Street Family Scholarship

East Tennessee State University
P.O. Box 70722
Johnson City, TN 37614-0002
(615) 929-4300
Average award: $1,000
Number of awards: 9
Deadline: February 15
College level: Freshman, Sophomore, Junior, Senior
Criteria: Applicant must be a resident of one of the southwest Virginia counties of Buchanan, Dickenson, Lee, Russell, Scott, Washington, or Wise. Financial need and academic ability are also considered. Scholarship is renewable. Awarded every year. Award may be used only at sponsoring institution.
Contact: Michael Jones, Financial Aid Counselor.

1383   Thomas E. Sharpe Memorial Scholarship

Mount Vernon Urban Renewal Agency
9 South First Avenue
9th Floor
Mount Vernon, NY 10550
(914) 699-7230
Average award: $700
Maximum award: $1,000
Minimum award: $300
Number of awards: 156
Deadline: June 4
College level: Freshman, Sophomore, Junior, Senior
Criteria: Applicant must be a Mount Vernon, N.Y. resident, have a minimum 2.0 GPA, be enrolled on a full-time basis, and meet the income criteria. Reapplication is required to retain scholarship. Awarded every year.
Contact: Donna Fulco, Scholarship Program Manager.

1384　Tuscaloosa County Presidential Scholarship

University of Alabama-Tuscaloosa
Box 870162
Tuscaloosa, AL 35487-0162
(205) 348-6756
Maximum award: $1,500
Minimum award: $1,000
Maximum number of awards: 4
Minimum number of awards: 2
Deadline: February 1
College level: Freshman
Criteria: Applicant must be a graduate of a Tuscaloosa County, Ala., high school and demonstrate potential for academic success. Awarded every year. Award may be used only at sponsoring institution.
Contact: Office of Admission Services, Box 870132, Tuscaloosa, AL 35487-0132, (205) 348-5556.

1385　United Federation of Teachers College Scholarship

United Federation of Teachers
260 Park Avenue South
Sixth Floor
New York, NY 10010
(212) 598-9245
Average award: $1,000
Number of awards: 250
Deadline: Early December
College level: Freshman
Criteria: Award provides financial assistance to graduates of New York City public high schools who come from low-income families. Recipient must remain in good standing to retain scholarship. Awarded every year.
Contact: Neil M. Remland, Assistant Director.

1386　Virginia Kline Scholarship

University of Toledo
Financial Aid Office
Toledo, OH 43606-3390
(419) 537-2056
Average award: $1,000
Number of awards: 5
Deadline: January 28
College level: Freshman
Criteria: Applicant must be a graduate of Libbey or Waite high schools in Toledo, Ohio and enrolled full time. Selection is based upon academic achivement and financial need. Award is for four years. Awarded every year. Award may be used only at sponsoring institution.
Contact: Office of Financial Aid.

1387　Vivienne Camp College Scholarship

Jewish Family and Children's Services
1600 Scott Street
San Francisco, CA 94115
(415) 561-1226
Average award: $5,000
Number of awards: 4
College level: Freshman, Sophomore, Junior, Senior
Criteria: Awarded to two young Jewish men and two young Jewish women for undergraduate or vocational studies. Applicant must reside in Marin County, San Francisco County, San Mateo County, Sonoma County, Palo Alto, or Mountain View. Applicant should have demonstrated academic achievement, financial need, broad-based extracurricular activities, in-depth community involvement, and be accepted to a school in California. Scholarship is renewable. Awarded every year.
Contact: Ted Schreiber, Director of Loans and Grants Program.

1388　William B. Stokely Scholarship

East Tennessee State University
P.O. Box 70722
Johnson City, TN 37614-0002
(615) 929-4300
Average award: $1,000
Number of awards: 6
Deadline: February 15
College level: Freshman, Sophomore, Junior, Senior
Criteria: Applicant must be a resident of Cocke County, Tenn., demonstrate financial need, and have a strong academic record. Scholarship is renewable. Awarded every year. Award may be used only at sponsoring institution.
Contact: Michael Jones, Financial Aid Counselor.

1389　William F. Rohr Memorial Scholarship

University of Toledo
Financial Aid Office
Toledo, OH 43606-3390
(419) 537-2056
Average award: $1,000
Number of awards: 3
Deadline: February 28
College level: Freshman
Majors/Fields: Engineering
Criteria: Applicant must be a graduate of Woodward high school in Toledo, Ohio. Scholarship is renewable. Awarded every year. Award may be used only at sponsoring institution.

1390　Zee and Madge May Vincent Scholarship

University of Oklahoma
University Affairs
900 Asp Avenue, Room 236
Norman, OK 73019-0401
(405) 325-1701
Average award: $1,000
Maximum number of awards: 7
Minimum number of awards: 6
Deadline: March 1
College level: Freshman, Sophomore, Junior, Senior
Criteria: Selection is based upon merit and financial need. Preference is given to Logan County, Okla., residents. Awarded every year. Award may be used only at sponsoring institution.
Contact: Office of Financial Aid Services, 731 Elm, Norman, OK 73019-0230, (405) 325-4521.

Club Affiliation

1391　50 Men & Women of Toledo Scholarship

50 Men and Women of Toledo, Inc.
P.O. Box 3357
Toledo, OH 43608
(419) 729-4654
Average award: $1,500
Deadline: March 15
College level: Freshman
Criteria: Recipient must maintain a minimum 3.0 GPA. Awarded every year.
Contact: James C. Caldwell, President, P.O. Box 80056, Toledo, OH 43608-0056.

1392   Academic Year Ambassadorial Scholarship

Rotary Foundation of Rotary International
One Rotary Center
1560 Sherman Avenue
Evanston, IL 60201
(708) 866-3000
Maximum award: $21,500
College level: Junior, Senior, Graduate, Doctoral
Criteria: Applicant must apply for the scholarship through local Rotary club, have completed two years of university work or appropriate professional experience, and desire to study abroad for an academic year. Recipient must pass a language proficiency examination. Awarded every year.
Contact: Scholarships.

1393   Achievement Award

National 4-H Council
7100 Connecticut Avenue
Chevy Chase, MD 20815-4999
(301) 961-2800
Minimum award: $1,500
Number of awards: 9
Deadline: September 1
College level: Doctoral
Majors/Fields: 4-H knowledge, leadership
Criteria: Applicant must be a 4-H member. Awarded every year.
Contact: Local county extension 4-H office or state 4-H office.

1394   AGCO Corporation Scholarship

Future Farmers of America (FFA)
P.O. Box 15160
Alexandria, VA 22309-0160
(703) 360-3600
Maximum award: $2,000
Minimum award: $1,000
Number of awards: 3
Deadline: February 15
College level: Freshman
Majors/Fields: Agricultural engineering
Criteria: Applicant must be a FFA member. Awarded every year.
Contact: National FFA Organizational Office.

1395   Agricultural Career Awareness Scholarship to 1862 and 1890 Land-Grant

National 4-H Council
7100 Connecticut Avenue
Chevy Chase, MD 20815-4999
(301) 961-2800
Minimum award: $1,000
Number of awards: 10
Deadline: September 1
College level: Freshman, Sophomore
Majors/Fields: Agriculture studies
Criteria: Applicant must be a 4-H member. Scholarship is renewable. Awarded every year.
Contact: Local county extension 4-H office or state 4-H office.

1396   Agricultural Careers Scholarship

National 4-H Council
7100 Connecticut Avenue
Chevy Chase, MD 20815-4999
(301) 961-2800
Average award: $1,000
Number of awards: 6
Deadline: September 1
College level: Freshman, Sophomore, Junior, Senior
Majors/Fields: Advertising, agribusiness, conservation, farm management, farming, marketing
Criteria: Applicant must demonstrate participation and outstanding achievement in 4-H with a minimum membership of one year. Awarded every year.
Contact: Local county extension 4-H office or state 4-H office.

1397   Agricultural Careers Scholarship

National 4-H Council
7100 Connecticut Avenue
Chevy Chase, MD 20815-4999
(301) 961-2800
Minimum award: $1,000
Number of awards: 15
Deadline: September 1
College level: Doctoral
Majors/Fields: Agriculture studies
Criteria: Applicant must be a 4-H member. Awarded every year.
Contact: Local county extension 4-H office or state 4-H office.

1398   Agricultural Scholarship

National 4-H Council
7100 Connecticut Avenue
Chevy Chase, MD 20815-4999
(301) 961-2800
Average award: $1,000
Number of awards: 4
Deadline: September 1
College level: Doctoral
Majors/Fields: Agriculture
Criteria: Applicant must be a 4-H member. Awarded every year.
Contact: Local county extension 4-H office or state 4-H office.

1399   AKA Financial Assistance Scholarship

Alpha Kappa Alpha Sorority
5656 South Stony Island Avenue
Chicago, IL 60637-1902
Maximum award: $1,500
Deadline: February 15
College level: Sophomore, Junior, Senior
Criteria: Applicant must be currently enrolled in a course of study beyond the first year or in a Work in Process Program which may or may not be at a degree-granting institution.
Contact: Educational Advancement Foundation, 5656 South Stony Island, Chicago, IL 60637.

1400   AKA Merit Scholarship

Alpha Kappa Alpha Sorority
5656 South Stony Island Avenue
Chicago, IL 60637-1902
Average award: $1,000
Number of awards: 5
Deadline: February 15
College level: Sophomore, Junior, Senior
Criteria: Applicant must have completed a minimum of one year in an accredited, degree-granting program and must demonstrate exceptional academic achievement.
Contact: Educational Advancement Foundation, 5656 South Stony Island, Chicago, IL 60637.

1401   Alabama Power Foundation Scholarship

Future Farmers of America (FFA)
P.O. Box 15160
Alexandria, VA 22309-0160
(703) 360-3600
Average award: $1,500
Number of awards: 4
Deadline: February 15
College level: Freshman
Majors/Fields: Agribusiness, agriculture
Criteria: Applicant must be a FFA member, an Alabama resident, and demonstrate financial need. Awarded every year.
Contact: National FFA Organizational Office.

1402   Albert M. Lappin Scholarship

American Legion–Kansas
1314 Topeka Avenue
Topeka, KS 66612
(913) 232-9315
Average award: $1,000
Deadline: Febuary 15
College level: Freshman, Sophomore, Junior
Criteria: Applicant must be the child of an American Legion or Auxiliary member. Scholarship must be used at an approved Kansas college, university, or trade school. Awarded every year.
Contact: Scholarships.

1403   Albert W. Dent Scholarship

Foundation of the American College of Healthcare Executives
P.O. Box 95660
Chicago, IL 60694-5660
(312) 424-2800
Average award: $3,000
Deadline: March 31
College level: Graduate, Doctoral
Majors/Fields: Health care management
Criteria: Applicant must be a minority or handicapped student, a student associate of the American College of Healthcare Executives, a U.S. or Canadian citizen, and demonstrate financial need. Awarded every year.
Contact: Michelle Pluskota, Scholarships, (312) 424-2800, extension 1783.

1404   Alfa-Laval Agri Inc. Scholarship

Future Farmers of America (FFA)
P.O. Box 15160
Alexandria, VA 22309-0160
(703) 360-3600
Maximum award: $1,000
Minimum award: $500
Number of awards: 5
Deadline: February 15
College level: Freshman
Majors/Fields: Agricultural economics, agricultural engineering, agricultural marketing, agricultural technology, dairy science
Criteria: Applicant must be a FFA member interested in a career in dairy equipment dealer service and installation. Awarded every year.
Contact: National FFA Organizational Office.

1405   Allflex USA Inc. Scholarship

Future Farmers of America (FFA)
P.O. Box 15160
Alexandria, VA 22309-0160
(703) 360-3600
Average award: $1,000
Number of awards: 2
Deadline: February 15
College level: Freshman
Majors/Fields: Animal science
Criteria: Applicant must be a FFA member. Awarded every year.
Contact: National FFA Organizational Office.

1406   Allstate Scholarship

Boys and Girls Clubs of Chicago
625 West Jackson Boulevard, Suite 300
Chicago, IL 60661
(312) 627-2700
Average award: $800
Maximum award: $1,000
Number of awards: 20
Deadline: April 3
College level: Freshman
Criteria: Applicant must be a member of the Boys and Girls Clubs of Chicago. Application must be submitted by the club director. Selection is based upon financial need and grades. Renewable if satisfactory academic progress is maintained. Awarded every year.
Contact: Mary Ann Mahon-Huels, Asst. Vice President of Operations.

1407   America ConAgra Inc. Scholarship

Future Farmers of America (FFA)
P.O. Box 15160
Alexandria, VA 22309-0160
(703) 360-3600
Average award: $1,750
Number of awards: 6
Deadline: February 15
College level: Freshman
Majors/Fields: Agribusiness
Criteria: Applicant must be a FFA member, rank in the top 15 percent of class, demonstrate leadership through extracurricular activities, and demonstrate financial need. Applicant must plan to major in agribusiness in the Coll of Business Administration or Coll of Agriculture, Dept of Agricultural Economics at the U of Nebraska-Lincoln. Minimum 3.2 GPA and full-time enrollment as an agribusiness major is required to retain scholarship for four years. Awarded every year. Award may be used only at sponsoring institution.
Contact: National FFA Organizational Office.

1408   American Cyanamid Scholarship

Future Farmers of America (FFA)
P.O. Box 15160
Alexandria, VA 22309-0160
(703) 360-3600
Average award: $1,000
Number of awards: 5
Deadline: February 15
College level: Freshman
Majors/Fields: Agriculture, business
Criteria: Applicant must be a FFA member. Awarded every year.
Contact: National FFA Organizational Office.

1409   American Family Insurance Co. Scholarship

Future Farmers of America (FFA)
P.O. Box 15160
Alexandria, VA 22309-0160
(703) 360-3600
Average award: $1,000
Number of awards: 3
Deadline: February 15
College level: Freshman
Criteria: Applicant must be a FFA member pursuing a four-year degree at any accredited institution. One scholarship will be awarded to a resident from each of the following states: Wisconsin, Missouri, and Minnesota. Awarded every year.
Contact: National FFA Organizational Office.

1410   American Morgan Horse Institute Scholarship

Future Farmers of America (FFA)
P.O. Box 15160
Alexandria, VA 22309-0160
(703) 360-3600
Average award: $1,000
Minimum award: $500
Number of awards: 3
Deadline: February 15
College level: Freshman
Majors/Fields: Animal science
Criteria: Applicant must be a FFA member pursuing a degree in animal science with equine emphasis. Awarded every year.
Contact: National FFA Organizational Office.

1411   American National Cattlewomen Foundation Scholarship

Future Farmers of America (FFA)
P.O. Box 15160
Alexandria, VA 22309-0160
(703) 360-3600
Average award: $1,000
Number of awards: 2
Deadline: February 15
College level: Sophomore, Junior, Senior
Majors/Fields: Animal science, food science/nutrition
Criteria: Applicant must be a FFA member, a woman, and have a minimum 3.0 GPA. Awarded every year.
Contact: National FFA Organizational Office.

1412 American Seed Trade Association Inc. Scholarship

Future Farmers of America (FFA)
P.O. Box 15160
Alexandria, VA 22309-0160
(703) 360-3600
Maximum award: $1,000
Minimum award: $500
Number of awards: 4
Deadline: February 15
College level: Freshman
Majors/Fields: Agriculture, agronomy
Criteria: Applicant must be a FFA member. Awarded every year.
Contact: National FFA Organizational Office.

1413 Animal Science Scholarship

National 4-H Council
7100 Connecticut Avenue
Chevy Chase, MD 20815-4999
(301) 961-2800
Average award: $1,000
Number of awards: 4
Deadline: September 1
College level: Junior, Senior
Majors/Fields: Animal science
Criteria: Applicant must be a 4-H member for at least one year and demonstrate participation and outstanding achievement in 4-H. Awarded every year.
Contact: Local county extension 4-H office or state 4-H office.

1414 ARAM Scholarship Award

Association of Railroad Advertising & Marketing Scholarships (ARAM)
3706 Palmerstown Road
Shaker Heights, OH 44122
(216) 751-9673
Average award: $1,500
Maximum number of awards: 2
Minimum number of awards: 2
Deadline: Mid-April
College level: Freshman, Sophomore, Junior, Senior, Graduate
Criteria: Applicant must be the child or grandchild of an ARAM member. Awarded every year.
Contact: LaVira J. Boyarski, Scholarship Chairman, 1500 Kentucky Avenue, Paducah, KY 42003, (502) 444-4338.

1415 Arby's/Big Brothers/Big Sisters of America

Big Brothers/Big Sisters of America/Arby's/Hank Aaron Scholarships
230 North 13th Street
Philadelphia, PA 19107
Maximum award: $5,000
Number of awards: 2
Deadline: March 1
College level: Freshman, Sophomore, Junior, Senior, Graduate, Doctoral
Criteria: Applicant must have participated in a Big Brother/Big Sister program as a "Little." Scholarship is renewable. Awarded every year.
Contact: Violoa W. Bostic, Assistant National Executive Director for Marketing/Communicatio, (215) 567-7000.

1416 ASBOI Scholarship

Association of School Business Officials International
11401 North Shore Drive
Reston, VA 22090
Maximum award: $1,200
Number of awards: 3
Deadline: August 1
College level: Doctoral
Majors/Fields: Management
Criteria: Applicant must be an ASBOI member. Awarded every year.
Contact: Scholarships.

1417 Asgrow Seed Co. Scholarship

Future Farmers of America (FFA)
P.O. Box 15160
Alexandria, VA 22309-0160
(703) 360-3600
Average award: $1,000
Number of awards: 2
Deadline: February 15
College level: Freshman
Majors/Fields: Agribusiness, agricultural sales
Criteria: Applicant must be a FFA member who competed in the Agricultural Sales Contest above the local level. Awarded every year.
Contact: National FFA Organizational Office.

1418 Beacon/Woodstream Corp. Scholarship

Future Farmers of America (FFA)
P.O. Box 15160
Alexandria, VA 22309-0160
(703) 360-3600
Maximum award: $2,000
Minimum award: $500
Number of awards: 2
Deadline: February 15
College level: Freshman
Majors/Fields: Animal science
Criteria: Applicant must be a FFA member. Awarded every year.
Contact: National FFA Organizational Office.

1419 Beau Mitchell Memorial Scholarship

Colorado State University
Financial Aid Office
108 Student Services Building
Fort Collins, CO 80523
(970) 491-6321
Average award: $1,000
Minimum award: $700
Number of awards: 2
Deadline: March 3
College level: Freshman, Sophomore, Junior, Senior, Graduate, Doctoral
Criteria: Applicant should preferably be a nonresident with strong moral character, have an orientation toward the outdoors, and be a former member of the Boy Scouts of America. Reapplication is required to retain scholarship. Awarded every year. Award may be used only at sponsoring institution.
Contact: Jeanne Snyder, Financial Aid Counselor.

1420 Beef Award

National 4-H Council
7100 Connecticut Avenue
Chevy Chase, MD 20815-4999
(301) 961-2800
Minimum award: $1,000
Number of awards: 4
Deadline: September 1
College level: Doctoral
Majors/Fields: Beef industry studies, food industry studies
Criteria: Applicant must be a 4-H member. Awarded every year.
Contact: Local county extension 4-H office or state 4-H office.

1421 Beta Theta Pi Scholarships

Beta Theta Pi Foundation
P.O. Box 6277
Oxford, OH 45056
(513) 523-7591
Average award: $1,000
Maximum award: $1,500
Minimum award: $750
Number of awards: 46
Deadline: April 15
College level: Sophomore, Junior, Senior, Graduate, Doctoral
Criteria: Applicant must be a member of Beta Theta Pi. Selection is based upon academic achievement, undergraduate extracurricular activities, and financial need. Awarded every year.
Contact: Stephen B. Becker, Director of Advancement and Alumni Relations.

1422   Borden Foundation Inc. Scholarship

Future Farmers of America (FFA)
P.O. Box 15160
Alexandria, VA 22309-0160
(703) 360-3600
Average award: $1,000
Number of awards: 2
Deadline: February 15
College level: Freshman
Majors/Fields: Agricultural economics, dairy foods, food science, food technology
Criteria: Applicant must be a FFA member entering a degree program in food science and technology or agricultural engineering at Texas A&M U, or in food science and technology/dairy foods or agricultural engineering at Mississippi State U. Awarded every year.
Contact: National FFA Organizational Office.

1423   Bread Scholarship

National 4-H Council
7100 Connecticut Avenue
Chevy Chase, MD 20815-4999
(301) 961-2800
Average award: $1,500
Number of awards: 6
Deadline: September 1
College level: Doctoral
Majors/Fields: Grain products studies
Criteria: Applicant must be a 4-H member. Awarded every year.
Contact: Local county extension 4-H office or state 4-H office.

1424   BRIDGE Endowment Fund Scholarship

Future Farmers of America (FFA)
P.O. Box 15160
Alexandria, VA 22309-0160
(703) 360-3600
Average award: $5,000
Maximum award: $6,000
Maximum number of awards: 5
Minimum number of awards: 2
Deadline: February 15
College level: Freshman
Criteria: Applicant must be a physically disabled/handicapped FFA member. Preference is given to applicant majoring in agriculture. Awarded every year.
Contact: National FFA Organizational Office.

1425   BRIDGE Quaker Oats Foundation Scholarship

Future Farmers of America (FFA)
P.O. Box 15160
Alexandria, VA 22309-0160
(703) 360-3600
Average award: $1,000
Number of awards: 4
Deadline: February 15
College level: Freshman
Criteria: Applicant must be a physically disabled/handicapped FFA member. Awarded every year.
Contact: National FFA Organizational Office.

1426   Burlington Northern Foundation Scholarship

Future Farmers of America (FFA)
P.O. Box 15160
Alexandria, VA 22309-0160
(703) 360-3600
Average award: $1,000
Number of awards: 10
Deadline: February 15
College level: Freshman
Majors/Fields: Agribusiness, agriculture
Criteria: Applicant must be a FFA member who is a resident of Alabama, Arkansas, Colorado, Idaho, Illinois, Iowa, Kansas, Minnesota, Mississippi, Missouri, Montana, Nebraska, North Dakota, Oklahoma, Oregon, South Dakota, Tennessee, Texas, or Washington. Awarded every year.
Contact: National FFA Organizational Office.

1427   C-A-L Stores Company Inc. Scholarship

Future Farmers of America (FFA)
P.O. Box 15160
Alexandria, VA 22309-0160
(703) 360-3600
Average award: $1,000
Number of awards: 2
Deadline: February 15
College level: Freshman
Majors/Fields: Agribusiness
Criteria: Applicant must be a FFA member who is a resident of one of the following Idaho counties: Bannock, Bingham, Bear Lake, Blaine, Bonneville, Butte, Caribou, Cassia, Clark, Custer, Franklin, Fremont, Jefferson, Jerome, Lemhi, Lincoln, Madison, Minidoka, Oneida, Power, or Teton. Awarded every year.
Contact: National FFA Organizational Office.

1428   Carl M. Turner Rural Co-op Memorial Scholarship

New Mexico State University
Box 30001
Department 5100
Las Cruces, NM 88003-0001
(505) 646-4105
Average award: $1,000
Number of awards: 2
Deadline: March 1
College level: Freshman, Sophomore, Junior, Senior
Criteria: Applicant or his or her family must be a member of the New Mexico rural electric or telephone cooperative. Applicant must be a U.S. citizen with a minimum 2.5 GPA. Financial need is not considered. Awarded every year. Award may be used only at sponsoring institution.
Contact: Greeley W. Myers, Director of Financial Aid.

1429   Champion Laboratories Inc. Scholarship

Future Farmers of America (FFA)
P.O. Box 15160
Alexandria, VA 22309-0160
(703) 360-3600
Average award: $1,250
Number of awards: 4
Deadline: February 15
College level: Freshman
Majors/Fields: Agriculture
Criteria: Applicant must be a FFA member. Financial need is considered. Awarded every year.
Contact: National FFA Organizational Office.

1430   Champions Choice/AKZO Nobel Salt Scholarship

Future Farmers of America (FFA)
P.O. Box 15160
Alexandria, VA 22309-0160
(703) 360-3600
Average award: $1,000
Number of awards: 2
Deadline: February 15
College level: Freshman
Majors/Fields: Beef science, dairy science
Criteria: Applicant must be a FFA member who demonstrates financial need. Preference is given to applicants with outstanding leadership and agricultural-related work experience, and those who reside in the top ten dairy and beef states. Awarded every year.
Contact: National FFA Organizational Office.

1431 Charles P. Lake/Rain for Rent Scholarship

Future Farmers of America (FFA)
P.O. Box 15160
Alexandria, VA 22309-0160
(703) 360-3600
Average award: $1,000
Number of awards: 2
Deadline: February 15
College level: Sophomore, Junior, Senior
Majors/Fields: Agriculture
Criteria: Applicant must be a FFA member and a resident of Arizona, California, or Idaho. Preference is given to applicants who are specializing in irrigation and soil technology. Awarded every year.
Contact: National FFA Organizational Office.

1432 Chevy Trucks/Future Leaders Scholarship

Future Farmers of America (FFA)
P.O. Box 15160
Alexandria, VA 22309-0160
(703) 360-3600
Average award: $2,500
Number of awards: 10
Deadline: February 15
College level: Freshman, Sophomore, Junior, Senior
Criteria: Applicant must be a current, fully-paid FFA member, be recommended by the local FFA chapter advisor, participate in a Supervised Agricultural Experience (SAE), and demonstrate recruitment and leadership skills which have contributed to the local FFA chapter. Awarded every year.
Contact: National FFA Organizational Office.

1433 Chilean Nitrate Corp. Scholarship

Future Farmers of America (FFA)
P.O. Box 15160
Alexandria, VA 22309-0160
(703) 360-3600
Average award: $2,000
Number of awards: 1
Deadline: February 15
College level: Freshman
Majors/Fields: Agribusiness, agriculture
Criteria: Applicant must be a FFA member, a resident of North Carolina or Virginia, and have produced tobacco as part of SAE program. Preference may be given to agronomy majors. Awarded every year.
Contact: National FFA Organizational Office.

1434 Citizenship Scholarship

National 4-H Council
7100 Connecticut Avenue
Chevy Chase, MD 20815-4999
(301) 961-2800
Average award: $1,500
Number of awards: 9
Deadline: September 1
College level: Doctoral
Majors/Fields: Citizenship studies
Criteria: Applicant must be a 4-H member. Awarded every year.
Contact: Local county extension 4-H office or state 4-H office.

1435 Clothing and Textiles Schoalrship

National 4-H Council
7100 Connecticut Avenue
Chevy Chase, MD 20815-4999
(301) 961-2800
Average award: $1,500
Number of awards: 6
Deadline: September 1
College level: Doctoral
Majors/Fields: Fashion studies
Criteria: Applicant must be a 4-H member. Awarded every year.
Contact: Local county extension 4-H office or state 4-H office.

1436 Conservation of Natural Resources Award

National 4-H Council
7100 Connecticut Avenue
Chevy Chase, MD 20815-4999
(301) 961-2800
Minimum award: $1,500
Number of awards: 6
Deadline: September 1
College level: Doctoral
Majors/Fields: Natural resources conservation studies
Criteria: Applicant must be a 4-H member. Awarded every year.
Contact: Local county extension 4-H office or state 4-H office.

1437 Consumer Education Award

National 4-H Council
7100 Connecticut Avenue
Chevy Chase, MD 20815-4999
(301) 961-2800
Minimum award: $1,500
Number of awards: 6
Deadline: September 1
College level: Doctoral
Majors/Fields: Consumer studies
Criteria: Applicant must be a 4-H member. Awarded every year.
Contact: Local county extension 4-H office or state 4-H office.

1438 Cooperative Resources International Scholarship

Future Farmers of America (FFA)
P.O. Box 15160
Alexandria, VA 22309-0160
(703) 360-3600
Average award: $1,000
Number of awards: 2
Deadline: February 15
College level: Freshman
Majors/Fields: Dairy science
Criteria: Applicant must be a FFA member and a resident of Iowa, Minnesota, Nebraska, North Dakota, South Dakota, or Wisconsin. Awarded every year.
Contact: National FFA Organizational Office.

1439 Countrymark Cooperative Inc. Scholarship

Future Farmers of America (FFA)
P.O. Box 15160
Alexandria, VA 22309-0160
(703) 360-3600
Average award: $1,000
Number of awards: 3
Deadline: February 15
College level: Freshman
Majors/Fields: Agriculture
Criteria: Applicant must be a FFA member who is a resident of Indiana, Michigan, or Ohio. Preference is given to applicants who have outstanding leadership activities and work-related experience.
Contact: National FFA Organizational Office.

1440 Creswell, Munsell, Fultz & Zirbel Scholarship

Future Farmers of America (FFA)
P.O. Box 15160
Alexandria, VA 22309-0160
(703) 360-3600
Average award: $1,000
Number of awards: 7
Deadline: February 15
College level: Junior, Senior
Majors/Fields: Agricultural communications, agricultural journalism, agricultural marketing
Criteria: Applicant must be a current or former FFA member pursuing a degree toward a career in advertising, public relations, journalism, or communications. Applicant must be a student at Cay-Poly, Iowa State U, Kansas State U, North Carolina State U, Ohio State U, Purdue U, U of Illinois, U of Nebraska-Lincoln, U of Minnesota, U of Missouri, or U of Wisconsin-Madison. Selection is based upon GPA, high school and university activities, and community involvement. Awarded every year; may be used only at sponsoring institution.
Contact: National FFA Organizational Office.

1441 Cultural Ambassadorial Scholarship

Rotary Foundation of Rotary International
One Rotary Center
1560 Sherman Avenue
Evanston, IL 60201
(708) 866-3000
Average award: Round trip transporation, tuition, fees, living expenses
College level: Junior, Senior, Graduate, Doctoral
Criteria: Applicant must apply for scholarship through local Rotary club, have completed two years of university work or appropriate professional experience, and have at least one year of university training in preferred language. Scholarship is either for three or six months and is intended to provide an opportunity to refine language skills and engage in cultural immersion in another country. Awarded every year.
Contact: Scholarships, (708) 886-3000.

1442 D&B Supply Company Inc. Scholarship

Future Farmers of America (FFA)
P.O. Box 15160
Alexandria, VA 22309-0160
(703) 360-3600
Average award: $1,000
Number of awards: 2
Deadline: February 15
College level: Freshman
Majors/Fields: Agribusiness
Criteria: Applicant must be a FFA member. One award is given to a resident of Asotin County, Wash., or one of the following Idaho counties: Ada, Canyon, Cassia, Clearwater, Elmore, Gem, Gooding, Jerome, Lewis, Lincoln, Nez Perce, Owyhee, Payette, Twin Falls, Washington. The other award goes to a resident of one of the following Oregon counties: Baker, Malheur, Umatilla, Union.
Contact: National FFA Organizational Office.

1443 Dairy Award

National 4-H Council
7100 Connecticut Avenue
Chevy Chase, MD 20815-4999
(301) 961-2800
Minimum award: $1,000
Number of awards: 2
Deadline: September 1
College level: Doctoral
Majors/Fields: Dairy industry studies
Criteria: Applicant must be a 4-H member. Awarded every year.
Contact: Local county extension 4-H office or state 4-H office.

1444 Dairy Cattle Judging Scholarship

Future Farmers of America (FFA)
P.O. Box 15160
Alexandria, VA 22309-0160
(703) 360-3600
Average award: $1,000
Number of awards: 5
Deadline: February 15
College level: Freshman
Majors/Fields: Dairy science
Criteria: Applicant must be a FFA member who has competed in the Dairy Contest above the local level. Awarded every year.
Contact: National FFA Organizational Office.

1445 Dairy Foods Award

National 4-H Council
7100 Connecticut Avenue
Chevy Chase, MD 20815-4999
(301) 961-2800
Minimum award: $1,500
Number of awards: 6
Deadline: September 1
College level: Doctoral
Majors/Fields: Dairy foods, health studies
Criteria: Applicant must be a 4-H member. Awarded every year.
Contact: Local county extension 4-H office or state 4-H office.

1446 Dairy Foods Scholarship

Future Farmers of America (FFA)
P.O. Box 15160
Alexandria, VA 22309-0160
(703) 360-3600
Average award: $1,000
Number of awards: 2
Deadline: February 15
College level: Freshman
Majors/Fields: Agriculture, agribusiness
Criteria: Applicant must be a FFA member who has competed in the Dairy Foods Contest above the local level. Awarded every year.
Contact: National FFA Organizational Office.

1447 Dairy Goat Scholarship

National 4-H Council
7100 Connecticut Avenue
Chevy Chase, MD 20815-4999
(301) 961-2800
Average award: $1,000
Number of awards: 3
College level: Freshman, Sophomore, Junior, Senior
Majors/Fields: Agriculture, home economics
Criteria: Applicant must be a 4-H member for at least one year, demonstrate participation and outstanding achievement in 4-H, and have completed one year in a 4-H dairy goat project. Awarded every year.
Contact: Local county extension 4-H office or state 4-H office.

1448 Danish Sisterhood of America Scholarship

Danish Sisterhood of America
3429 Columbus Drive
Holiday, FL 34691
Minimum award: $1,000
Number of awards: 5
Deadline: February 28
College level: Freshman, Sophomore, Junior, Senior
Criteria: Applicant must be a Danish Sisterhood of America member or the child of a member. Selection is based upon academic achievement. Awarded every year.
Contact: Elizabeth K. Hunter, Scholarship Chairman and National Vice President.

1449 Darigold Scholarship

Future Farmers of America (FFA)
P.O. Box 15160
Alexandria, VA 22309-0160
(703) 360-3600
Average award: $1,000
Number of awards: 2
Deadline: February 15
College level: Freshman
Criteria: Applicant must be a FFA member with a dairy background who is a resident of California, Idaho, Oregon, or Washington. Preference is given to applicants majoring in dairy science or food technology. Awarded every year.
Contact: National FFA Organizational Office.

1450 DECA Scholarship

Distributive Education Clubs of America (DECA)
1908 Association Drive
Reston, VA 22091
(703) 860-5000
Average award: $1,000
Maximum award: $1,500
Minimum award: $500
Number of awards: 17
Deadline: Second Monday in March
College level: Freshman
Majors/Fields: Management, marketing, marketing education, merchandising
Criteria: Applicant must be an active member of DECA and rank in top third of class. Selection is based upon merit, club participation and accomplishments, leadership, responsibility, and character. Scholarship is renewable. Awarded every year.
Contact: Tim Coffey, Director of Corporate Marketing.

1451 DEKALB Genetic Corp. Scholarship

Future Farmers of America (FFA)
P.O. Box 15160
Alexandria, VA 22309-0160
(703) 360-3600
Average award: $1,000
Number of awards: 5
Deadline: February 15
College level: Freshman
Majors/Fields: Agribusiness, agricultural economics, agricultural sales, agronomy
Criteria: Applicant must be a FFA member. Awarded every year.
Contact: National FFA Organizational Office.

1452 Delta Gamma Foundation Fellowship

Delta Gamma Foundation
3250 Riverside Drive
P.O. Box 21397
Columbus, OH 43221-0397
(614) 481-8169
Average award: $2,500
Number of awards: 14
Deadline: April 1
Criteria: Applicant must be a member of Delta Gamma fraternity. Awarded every year.
Contact: Scholarships, Fellowships and Loans Chairman.

1453 Delta Gamma Foundation Scholarship

Delta Gamma Foundation
3250 Riverside Drive
P.O. Box 21397
Columbus, OH 43221-0397
(614) 481-8169
Average award: $1,000
Number of awards: 50
Deadline: March 1
Criteria: Applicant must be a member of Delta Gamma fraternity. Awarded every year.
Contact: Scholarships, Fellowships, and Loans Chairman.

1454 Descendants of the Signers of the Declaration of Independence Scholarship

Descendants of the Signers of the Declaration of Independence, Inc.
P.O. Box 224
Suncook, NH 03275-0224
Average award: $1,500
Maximum number of awards: 6
Minimum number of awards: 5
Deadline: March 15
College level: Freshman, Sophomore, Junior, Senior, Graduate, Doctoral
Criteria: Applicant must be a proven lineal descendant of a signer of the Declaration of Independence as attested by the Registrar-General, and be a full-time student at a four-year recognized U.S. college or university. Request must be made by January 15 in writing, with enclosed SASE, naming an ancestor signer to receive a reply. Recipient must reapply each year to retain scholarship. Awarded every year.
Contact: Mrs. Philip F. Kennedy, DSDI Scholarship Committee.

1455 Dog Care and Training Award

National 4-H Council
7100 Connecticut Avenue
Chevy Chase, MD 20815-4999
(301) 961-2800
Minimum award: $1,500
Number of awards: 6
Deadline: September 1
College level: Doctoral
Majors/Fields: Dog care studies, dog husbandry
Criteria: Applicant must be a 4-H member. Awarded every year.
Contact: Local county extension 4-H office or state 4-H office.

1456 Douglas Battery Manufacturing Scholarship

Future Farmers of America (FFA)
P.O. Box 15160
Alexandria, VA 22309-0160
(703) 360-3600
Average award: $1,000
Number of awards: 2
Deadline: February 15
College level: Freshman
Majors/Fields: Agriculture
Criteria: Applicant must be a FFA member and a resident of Forsyth County, N.C. Awarded every year.
Contact: National FFA Organizational Office.

1457 Douglas Products and Packaging Scholarship

Future Farmers of America (FFA)
P.O. Box 15160
Alexandria, VA 22309-0160
(703) 360-3600
Average award: $1,000
Number of awards: 2
Deadline: February 15
College level: Freshman
Majors/Fields: Agriculture
Criteria: Applicant must be a FFA member from Missouri. Awarded every year.
Contact: National FFA Organizational Office.

1458 Dragoco Scholarship

Future Farmers of America (FFA)
P.O. Box 15160
Alexandria, VA 22309-0160
(703) 360-3600
Average award: $1,000
Maximum award: $2,500
Minimum award: $500
Number of awards: 4
Deadline: February 15
College level: Freshman
Majors/Fields: Food science
Criteria: Applicant must be a FFA member. Awarded every year.
Contact: National FFA Organizational Office.

1459 Eagle Scout Scholarship

National Society of the Sons of the American Revolution
Eagle Scout Scholarship
1000 South Fourth Street
Louisville, KY 40203
(502) 589-1776
Maximum award: $5,000
Minimum award: $1,000
Number of awards: 2
Deadline: December 31
College level: Freshman
Criteria: Applicant must be in the current class of Eagle scouts (class year runs from July 1 to June 30 of each year). Awarded every year.
Contact: Lauren R. Bradley, National Chairman.

1460 Edwin T. Meredith Foundation

National 4-H Council
7100 Connecticut Avenue
Chevy Chase, MD 20815-4999
(301) 961-2800
Average award: $1,000
Number of awards: 3
Deadline: September 1
College level: Freshman, Sophomore, Junior, Senior
Criteria: Applicant must be a 4-H member for at least one year, demonstrate participation and outstanding achievement in 4-H, and be a resident of one of the following states: Illinois, Indiana, Iowa, Kansas, Michigan, Minnesota, Missouri, Nebraska, New York, North Dakota, Ohio, Oklahoma, Pennsylvania, South Dakota, Wisconsin. Awarded every year.
Contact: Local county extension 4-H office or state 4-H office.

1461   Electric Energy Award

National 4-H Council
7100 Connecticut Avenue
Chevy Chase, MD 20815-4999
(301) 961-2800
Minimum award: $1,000
Number of awards: 4
Deadline: September 1
College level: Doctoral
Majors/Fields: Electric energy studies
Criteria: Applicant must be a 4-H member. Awarded every year.
Contact: Local county extension 4-H office or state 4-H office.

1462   Energy Management Scholarship

National 4-H Council
7100 Connecticut Avenue
Chevy Chase, MD 20815-4999
(301) 961-2800
Average award: $1,500
Number of awards: 4
Deadline: September 1
College level: Doctoral
Majors/Fields: Energy management studies
Criteria: Applicant must be a 4-H member. Awarded every year.
Contact: Local county extension 4-H office or state 4-H office.

1463   Entomology Award

National 4-H Council
7100 Connecticut Avenue
Chevy Chase, MD 20815-4999
(301) 961-2800
Minimum award: $1,500
Number of awards: 6
Deadline: September 1
College level: Doctoral
Majors/Fields: Entomology studies
Criteria: Applicant must be a 4-H member. Awarded every year.
Contact: Local county extension 4-H office or state 4-H office.

1464   Farm Safety 4 Just Kids Scholarship

Future Farmers of America (FFA)
P.O. Box 15160
Alexandria, VA 22309-0160
(703) 360-3600
Average award: $2,000
Number of awards: 1
Deadline: February 15
College level: Freshman
Criteria: Applicant must be a FFA member, a member of the Farm Safety 4 Just Kids, and have served as the coordinator of the local FFA Chapter Safety Program. Awarded every year.
Contact: National FFA Organizational Office.

1465   Farmers Mutual Hail Insurance Company of Iowa Scholarship

Future Farmers of America (FFA)
P.O. Box 15160
Alexandria, VA 22309-0160
(703) 360-3600
Average award: $1,000
Number of awards: 14
Deadline: February 15
College level: Freshman
Majors/Fields: Agriculture
Criteria: Applicant must be a FFA member pursuing a four-year degree in any area of agriculture. Two awards are given in each of the following geographic areas: Iowa, Illinois, Wisconsin, Indiana/Ohio/Michigan, Minnesota/North Dakota, Nebraska, Missouri. Awarded every year.
Contact: National FFA Organizational Office.

1466   Fashion Revue Award

National 4-H Council
7100 Connecticut Avenue
Chevy Chase, MD 20815-4999
(301) 961-2800
Minimum award: $1,500
Number of awards: 4
Deadline: September 1
College level: Doctoral
Majors/Fields: Fashion design studies
Criteria: Applicant must be a 4-H member. Awarded every year.
Contact: Local county extension 4-H office or state 4-H office.

1467   Fastline Publications Scholarship

Future Farmers of America (FFA)
P.O. Box 15160
Alexandria, VA 22309-0160
(703) 360-3600
Maximum award: $1,000
Number of awards: 10
Deadline: February 15
College level: Freshman
Majors/Fields: Agricultural business management
Criteria: Applicant must be a FFA member who is a resident of Illinois, Indiana, Iowa, Kansas, Kentucky, Missouri, Nebraska, North Carolina, Ohio, South Carolina, Tennessee or Texas. Awarded every year.
Contact: National FFA Organizational Office.

1468   Fermenta Animal Health Co. Scholarship

Future Farmers of America (FFA)
P.O. Box 15160
Alexandria, VA 22309-0160
(703) 360-3600
Average award: $1,000
Number of awards: 5
Deadline: February 15
College level: Freshman
Majors/Fields: Agriculture
Criteria: Applicant must be a FFA member. Two awards are given nationwide, one award is for North Knox, Ind., FFA Chapter, one is for South Knox, Ind., FFA Chapter, and one is for Kansas City East Environmental Science/Agribusiness Magnet H.S. Awarded every year.
Contact: National FFA Organizational Office.

1469   FFA CARQUEST Corp. Scholarship

Future Farmers of America (FFA)
P.O. Box 15160
Alexandria, VA 22309-0160
(703) 360-3600
Average award: $1,000
Number of awards: 5
Deadline: February 15
College level: Freshman
Criteria: Applicant must be a FFA member from a chapter within a 25-mile radius of a CARQUEST store and be sponsored by its manager. Awarded every year.
Contact: National FFA Organizational Office.

1470   FFA Dodge Trucks Scholarship

Future Farmers of America (FFA)
P.O. Box 15160
Alexandria, VA 22309-0160
(703) 360-3600
Average award: $1,000
Number of awards: 4
Deadline: February 15
College level: Freshman
Majors/Fields: Agricultural mechanics, diesel mechanics
Criteria: Applicant must be a FFA member. Preference is given to applicants demonstrating financial need. Awarded every year.
Contact: National FFA Organizational Office.

1471   FFA FarmAid Scholarship

Future Farmers of America (FFA)
P.O. Box 15160
Alexandria, VA 22309-0160
(703) 360-3600
Average award: $1,000
Maximum award: $1,500
Minimum award: $500
Number of awards: 10
Deadline: February 15
College level: Freshman
Majors/Fields: Agriculture
Criteria: Applicant must be from a farm family, a FFA member, and demonstrate financial need. Minimum 2.0 GPA is required to retain scholarship for two additional years. Awarded every year.
Contact: National FFA Organizational Office.

1472   FFA/Johnson & Wales University Scholarship

Future Farmers of America (FFA)
P.O. Box 15160
Alexandria, VA 22309-0160
(703) 360-3600
Average award: Full tuition
Number of awards: 2
Deadline: February 15
College level: Freshman
Majors/Fields: Business, equine science, food service management, hospitality
Criteria: Applicant must be a FFA member attending Johnson & Wales U. Minimum 2.75 GPA with full-time enrollment is required to retain scholarship for up to four years. Awarded every year. Award may be used only at sponsoring institution.
Contact: National FFA Organizational Office.

1473   FFA Minority Scholarship

Future Farmers of America (FFA)
P.O. Box 15160
Alexandria, VA 22309-0160
(703) 360-3600
Maximum award: $10,000
Minimum award: $5,000
Number of awards: 4
Deadline: February 15
College level: Freshman
Majors/Fields: Agriculture
Criteria: Applicant must be a FFA member from any state, Puerto Rico, the U.S. Virgin Islands, or the District of Columbia. Applicant must be a member of an ethnic minority group. Minimum 2.0 GPA and full-time enrollment are required to retain $10,000 scholarship. Awarded every year.
Contact: National FFA Organizational Office.

1474   FFA National Pork Council Scholarship

Future Farmers of America (FFA)
P.O. Box 15160
Alexandria, VA 22309-0160
(703) 360-3600
Average award: $1,000
Number of awards: 4
Deadline: February 15
College level: Freshman
Majors/Fields: Agriculture
Criteria: Applicant must be a FFA member from a swine-producing family or involved in swine-production. Awarded every year.
Contact: National FFA Organizational Office.

1475   FFA Norfolk Southern Foundation Scholarship

Future Farmers of America (FFA)
P.O. Box 15160
Alexandria, VA 22309-0160
(703) 360-3600
Average award: $1,000
Minimum award: $500
Number of awards: 4
Deadline: February 15
College level: Freshman
Majors/Fields: Agriculture, agricultural education
Criteria: Applicant must be a FFA member. Awarded every year.
Contact: National FFA Organizational Office.

1476   FFA Souvenir Shirts Etc. Scholarship

Future Farmers of America (FFA)
P.O. Box 15160
Alexandria, VA 22309-0160
(703) 360-3600
Average award: $2,000
Number of awards: 2
Deadline: February 15
College level: Freshman
Majors/Fields: Agriculture
Criteria: Applicant must be a FFA member. Finanical need is considered. Awarded every year.
Contact: National FFA Organizational Office.

1477   FFA State Farm Companies Foundation Scholarship

Future Farmers of America (FFA)
P.O. Box 15160
Alexandria, VA 22309-0160
(703) 360-3600
Average award: $1,000
Number of awards: 4
Deadline: February 15
College level: Freshman
Majors/Fields: Agriculture, agribusiness
Criteria: Applicant must be a FFA member and an Illinois resident. Awarded every year.
Contact: National FFA Organizational Office.

1478   FFA Sun Company Scholarship

Future Farmers of America (FFA)
P.O. Box 15160
Alexandria, VA 22309-0160
(703) 360-3600
Average award: $1,000
Number of awards: 2
Deadline: February 15
College level: Freshman
Majors/Fields: Floriculture, horticulture
Criteria: Applicant must be a FFA member who has participated in the Floriculture Contest above the local level. Awarded every year.
Contact: National FFA Organizational Office.

1479   FFA United Feeds Scholarship

Future Farmers of America (FFA)
P.O. Box 15160
Alexandria, VA 22309-0160
(703) 360-3600
Average award: $1,000
Number of awards: 4
Deadline: February 15
College level: Freshman
Majors/Fields: Animal science
Criteria: Applicant must be a FFA member pursuing a four-year degree at Purdue U, Ohio State U, Michigan State U or U of Illinois and be a resident of Indiana, Ohio, Michigan or Illinois. Awarded every year. Award may be used only at sponsoring institution.
Contact: National FFA Organizational Office.

1480   FFA Wal-Mart Scholarship

Future Farmers of America (FFA)
P.O. Box 15160
Alexandria, VA 22309-0160
(703) 360-3600
Average award: $1,000
Number of awards: 50
Deadline: February 15
College level: Freshman
Majors/Fields: Agriculture
Criteria: Applicant must be a FFA member pursuing a four-year degree in any area of agriculture, and be a resident of Alabama, Arkansas, Arizona, California, Colorado, Connecticut, Delaware, Florida, Georgia, Hawaii, Idaho, Illinois, Indiana, Iowa, Kansas, Kentucky, Louisiana, Maine, Maryland, Michigan, Minnesota, Mississippi, Missouri, Montana, Nebraska, Nevada, New Hampshire, New Mexico, New York, North Carolina, North Dakota, Ohio, Oklahoma, Oregon, Pennsylvania, Puerto Rico, Rhode Island, South Carolina, South Dakota, Tennessee, Texas, Utah, Virginia, Washington state, West Virginia, Wisconsin, or Wyoming. Awarded every year.
Contact: National FFA Organizational Office.

1481   Fifth Marine Division Association Scholarship

Fifth Marine Division Association
Marine Corps Scholarship Foundation, Inc.
P.O. Box 3008
Princeton, NJ 08543-3008
(609) 921-3534
Average award: $2,000
Maximum award: $2,500
Minimum award: $500
Number of awards: 800
Deadline: February 1
College level: Freshman, Sophomore, Junior, Senior
Criteria: Applicant must be the child of Marine or Navy service member who served with the Fifth Marine Division and who has a current paid-up membership in the Fifth Marine Division Association. Inquiries must include sufficient data to establish parent's connection to the Fifth Marine Division Association and a self-addressed stamped envelope. Financial need is considered. Minimum 12 hours per semester with passing grades are required to retain scholarship. Awarded every year.
Contact: Scholarships.

1482   Firestone Agriculture Tire Division Scholarship

Future Farmers of America (FFA)
P.O. Box 15160
Alexandria, VA 22309-0160
(703) 360-3600
Maximum award: $2,000
Number of awards: 10
Deadline: February 15
College level: Freshman
Majors/Fields: Agriculture
Criteria: Applicant must be a FFA member. Awarded every year.
Contact: National FFA Organizational Office.

1483   FISCO Farm and Home Stores Scholarship

Future Farmers of America (FFA)
P.O. Box 15160
Alexandria, VA 22309-0160
(703) 360-3600
Average award: $1,000
Number of awards: 9
Deadline: February 15
College level: Freshman
Majors/Fields: Agriculture, agribusiness, animal science
Criteria: Applicant must be a FFA member from a California chapter within a 25-mile radius of a FISCO store, pursuing a four-year degree at a college or university within California. Selection is based upon FFA involvement, leadership, recommendation from FFA leader, academic record, and financial need. FISCO stores are located in Bakersfield, Chico, Lodi, Merced, Porterville, Tracy, Tulare, and Woodland, Calif. Awarded every year.
Contact: National FFA Organizational Office.

1484   Food and Nutrition Scholarship

National 4-H Council
7100 Connecticut Avenue
Chevy Chase, MD 20815-4999
(301) 961-2800
Average award: $1,500
Number of awards: 6
Deadline: September 1
College level: Doctoral
Majors/Fields: Food nutrition studies
Criteria: Applicant must be a 4-H member. Awarded every year.
Contact: Local county extension 4-H office of state 4-H office.

1485   Food Careers Scholarship (Kerr)

National 4-H Council
7100 Connecticut Avenue
Chevy Chase, MD 20815-4999
(301) 961-2800
Minimum award: $1,000
Number of awards: 6
Deadline: September 1
College level: Freshman
Criteria: Applicant must be a 4-H member. Awarded every year.
Contact: Local county extension 4-H office or state 4-H office.

1486   Food Careers Scholarship (Webster Industries)

National 4-H Council
7100 Connecticut Avenue
Chevy Chase, MD 20815-4999
(301) 961-2800
Maximum award: $1,000
Minimum award: $500
Number of awards: 6
Deadline: September 1
College level: Freshman
Criteria: Applicant must be a 4-H member and pursue studies in food technology, food and nutrition, food services, or a closely related field. Applicant must have participated in food preservation, canning, or freezing projects. Awarded every year.
Contact: Local county extension 4-H office or state 4-H office.

1487   Food Conservation, Preservation and Safety Scholarship

National 4-H Council
7100 Connecticut Avenue
Chevy Chase, MD 20815-4999
(301) 961-2800
Average award: $1,500
Number of awards: 4
Deadline: September 1
College level: Doctoral
Majors/Fields: Food conservation studies, food safety studies
Criteria: Applicant must be a 4-H member. Awarded every year.
Contact: Local county extension 4-H office or state 4-H office.

1488   Ford Motor Company Fund Scholarship

Future Farmers of America (FFA)
P.O. Box 15160
Alexandria, VA 22309-0160
(703) 360-3600
Average award: $1,200
Number of awards: 2
Deadline: February 15
College level: Freshman
Criteria: Applicant must be a FFA member pursuing a four-year degree. Awarded every year.
Contact: National FFA Organizational Office.

1489   Forestry Award

National 4-H Council
7100 Connecticut Avenue
Chevy Chase, MD 20815-4999
(301) 961-2800
Minimum award: $1,500
Number of awards: 6
Deadline: September 1
College level: Doctoral
Majors/Fields: Forest conservation studies, forest preservation studies
Criteria: Applicant must be a 4-H member. Awarded every year.
Contact: Local county extension 4-H office or state 4-H office.

1490   Foster G. McGaw Scholarship

Foundation of the American College of Healthcare Executives
P.O. Box 95660
Chicago, IL 60694-5660
(312) 424-2800
Average award: $3,000
Deadline: March 31
College level: Graduate, Doctoral
Majors/Fields: Health care management
Criteria: Applicant must be a student associate of the American College of Healthcare Executives, a U.S. or Canadian citizen, and demonstrate financial need. Awarded every year.
Contact: Michelle Pluskota, Scholarships, (312) 424-2800, extension 1783.

1491   Fraternal College Scholarship

Modern Woodmen of America
1701 1st Avenue
Rock Island, IL 61201
(309) 786-6481
Maximum award: $2,000
Minimum award: $500
Number of awards: 36
Deadline: January 1
College level: Freshman
Criteria: Applicant must be a beneficial member of Modern Woodmen of America for at least two years and be in the top half of graduating class. Selection is based upon character, leadership, academic activities, extracurricular activities, and scholastic records. Renewable for up to four years. Awarded every year.
Contact: Fraternal Scholarship Administrator.

1492   Fraternal Order of UDT/SEAL Scholarship

Fraternal Order of UDT/SEAL, Inc.
P.O. Box 5365
Virginia Beach, VA 23455
Average award: $1,000
Number of awards: 5
Deadline: March 15
College level: Freshman, Sophomore, Junior, Senior
Criteria: Applicant must be the dependent of an active member of the Fraternal Order of UDT/SEAL. Awarded every year.
Contact: Scholarships.

1493   Gardening and Horticulture Award

National 4-H Council
7100 Connecticut Avenue
Chevy Chase, MD 20815-4999
(301) 961-2800
Minimum award: $1,000
Number of awards: 5
Deadline: September 1
College level: Doctoral
Majors/Fields: Plant science studies
Criteria: Applicant must be a 4-H member. Awarded every year.
Contact: Local county extension 4-h office or state 4-H office.

1494   Georgia Boot Inc. Scholarship

Future Farmers of America (FFA)
P.O. Box 15160
Alexandria, VA 22309-0160
(703) 360-3600
Average award: $1,250
Number of awards: 2
Deadline: February 15
College level: Freshman
Majors/Fields: Agriculture
Criteria: Applicant must be a FFA member. Awarded every year.
Contact: National FFA Organizational Office.

1495   Georgia M. Hellberg Memorial Scholarship

Future Farmers of America (FFA)
P.O. Box 15160
Alexandria, VA 22309-0160
(703) 360-3600
Average award: $5,000
Number of awards: 8
Deadline: February 15
College level: Freshman
Majors/Fields: Soil/water conservation
Criteria: Applicant must be a FFA member pursuing a four-year degree in soil and water conservation or any major that leads to employment in that area. Awarded every year.
Contact: National FFA Organizational Office.

1496   Gertrude L. Warren Career Scholarship

National 4-H Council
7100 Connecticut Avenue
Chevy Chase, MD 20815-4999
(301) 961-2800
Average award: $1,000
Number of awards: 2
Deadline: September 1
College level: Freshman, Sophomore, Junior, Senior
Criteria: Applicant must be a 4-H member for at least one year, demonstrate participation and outstanding achievement in 4-H, and show evidence of 4-H influence on selection of future career.
Contact: Local county extension 4-H office or state 4-H office.

1497   Girls Incorporated Scholars Program

Girls Incorporated
30 East 33rd Street
New York, NY 10016-5394
(212) 689-3700
Maximum award: $10,000
Minimum award: $1,000
Number of awards: 17
Deadline: End of January
College level: Freshman
Criteria: Applicant must be a member of a Girls Incorporated affiliate and submit application for local judging. Awarded every year.
Contact: Louisa Anderson, Assoc. Director, Scholarships & Awards.

1498   Golden Harvest Seeds Inc. Scholarship

Future Farmers of America (FFA)
P.O. Box 15160
Alexandria, VA 22309-0160
(703) 360-3600
Average award: $1,000
Number of awards: 2
Deadline: February 15
College level: Freshman
Majors/Fields: Agronomy
Criteria: Applicant must be a FFA member and a U.S. citizen. One award is to an applicant from Illinois, Indiana, Michigan, Ohio or Wisconsin who is attending U of Illinois, Purdue U, Michigan State U, Ohio State U, or U of Wisconsin. Other award is to an applicant from Colorado, Iowa, Kansas, Minnesota, Missouri, Nebraska or South Dakota who is attending Colorado State U, Iowa State U, Kansas State U, U of Minnesota, U of Nebraska, or South Dakota State U. Awarded every year; may be used only at sponsoring institution.
Contact: National FFA Organizational Office.

1499   Graduate and Undergraduate Scholarships

Kappa Kappa Gamma Foundation
P.O. Box 38
Columbus, OH 43216
Maximum award: $1,500
Minimum award: $1,000
Number of awards: 38
Deadline: February 1
College level: Sophomore, Junior, Senior, Graduate, Doctoral
Criteria: Applicant must be a member of Kappa Kappa Gamma. Selection is based upon academic performance, contribution to chapter life, merit, and financial need. For more information and application materials, send a self-addressed stamped (55 cents) envelope to the above address and note membership. Awarded every year.
Contact: Scholarships.

1500   Graduate Student Award

Daughters of Penelope
Supreme Headquarters
1909 Q Street, NW, Suite 500
Washington, DC 20009
(202) 234-9741
Minimum award: $1,500
Deadline: June 20
College level: Graduate, Doctoral
Criteria: Applicant must be a woman, single, a member in good standing for at least two years of Daughters of Penelope or of Maids of Athena or the daughter of an Ahepan or Daughter of Penelope, a resident of the U.S., Canada, or Greece, and be enrolled for at least nine units per academic year. Selection is based upon scholastic records and extracurricular activities. Awarded every year.
Contact: Scholarship Committee, 1909 Q Street, NW, Suite 500, Washington, DC 20009.

1501   Guide Dog Raising/Training Scholarship

National 4-H Council
7100 Connecticut Avenue
Chevy Chase, MD 20815-4999
(301) 961-2800
Average award: $1,000
Number of awards: 3
Deadline: September 1
College level: Freshman, Sophomore, Junior, Senior
Criteria: Applicant must be a 4-H member for at least one year, demonstrate participation and outstanding achievement in 4-H, and have completed a project raising or training a guide dog puppy for a guide dog training facility that is currently supporting an accredited 4-H project. Applicant must live in Alaska, Arizona, California, Colorado, Idaho, Montana, Nevada, Oregon, Utah, or Washington. Awarded every year.
Contact: Local county extension 4-H office or state 4-H office.

1502   Gunild Keetman Assistance Fund

American Orff-Schulwerk Association
P.O. Box 391089
Cleveland, OH 44139-8089
(216) 543-5366
Maximum award: $999
Minimum award: $400
Number of awards: 10
Deadline: January 1
College level: Doctoral
Criteria: Applicant must be a AOSA member, a U.S. citizen or have resided in the U.S. for the past five years, and have financial need. Awarded every year.
Contact: Scholarships.

1503   Gustafson Inc. Scholarship

Future Farmers of America (FFA)
P.O. Box 15160
Alexandria, VA 22309-0160
(703) 360-3600
Average award: $2,500
Number of awards: 1
Deadline: February 15
College level: Freshman
Majors/Fields: Agronomy, seed technology
Criteria: Applicant must be a FFA member attending Colorado State U, Mississippi State U or Iowa State U. Preference is given to applicants with outstanding leadership and academic achievement. Awarded every year. Award may be used only at sponsoring institution.
Contact: National FFA Organizational Office.

1504   Harcourt General Insurance Co. Scholarship

Future Farmers of America (FFA)
P.O. Box 15160
Alexandria, VA 22309-0160
(703) 360-3600
Average award: $1,250
Number of awards: 4
Deadline: February 15
College level: Freshman
Majors/Fields: Agriculture
Criteria: Applicant must be a FFA member and a resident of California, Colorado, Illinois, Indiana, Iowa, Kentucky, Michigan, Minnesota, Missouri, Nebraska, North Dakota, Ohio, Oklahoma, Pennsylvania, South Dakota, Texas, or Wisconsin. Awarded every year.
Contact: National FFA Organizational Office.

1505   Health Award

National 4-H Council
7100 Connecticut Avenue
Chevy Chase, MD 20815-4999
(301) 961-2800
Minimum award: $1,500
Number of awards: 4
Deadline: September 1
College level: Doctoral
Majors/Fields: Health studies
Criteria: Applicant must be a 4-H member. Awarded every year.
Contact: Local county extension 4-H office or state 4-H office.

1506   Helena Chemical Company Scholarship

Future Farmers of America (FFA)
P.O. Box 15160
Alexandria, VA 22309-0160
(703) 360-3600
Average award: $1,000
Number of awards: 3
Deadline: February 15
College level: Freshman
Majors/Fields: Agribusiness, agricultural economics
Criteria: Applicant must be a graduating high school senior who is a FFA member and demonstrates financial need. One award is given for each of the following areas: (1) Arizona, California, Idaho, Montana, Nevada, Oregon, Utah, Washington; (2) Alabama, Arkansas, Florida, Georgia, Kentucky, Louisiana, Mississippi, New Mexico, North Carolina, Oklahoma, South Carolina, Tennessee, Texas; (3) Colorado, Connecticut, Delaware, Illinois, Indiana, Iowa, Kansas, Maine, Maryland, Massachusetts, Michigan, Minnesota, Missouri, Nebraska, New Hampshire, New Jersey, New York, North Dakota, Ohio, Pennsylvania, South Dakota, Vermont, Virginia, West Virginia, Wisconsin, Wyoming. Awarded every year.
Contact: National FFA Organizational Office.

1507 Hess & Clark Inc. Scholarship

Future Farmers of America (FFA)
P.O. Box 15160
Alexandria, VA 22309-0160
(703) 360-3600
Average award: $1,000
Number of awards: 3
Deadline: February 15
College level: Freshman
Majors/Fields: Dairy science
Criteria: Applicant must be a FFA member. Awarded every year.
Contact: National FFA Organizational Office.

1508 Horse Scholarship

National 4-H Council
7100 Connecticut Avenue
Chevy Chase, MD 20815-4999
(301) 961-2800
Average award: $1,000
Number of awards: 6
Deadline: September 1
College level: Doctoral
Majors/Fields: Horse studies
Criteria: Applicant must be a 4-H member. Awarded every year.
Contact: Local county extension 4-H office or state 4-H office.

1509 Hydro Agri North America Inc. Scholarship

Future Farmers of America (FFA)
P.O. Box 15160
Alexandria, VA 22309-0160
(703) 360-3600
Average award: $1,000
Number of awards: 4
Deadline: February 15
College level: Freshman
Majors/Fields: Agriculture
Criteria: Applicant must be a FFA member. Awarded every year.
Contact: National FFA Organizational Office.

1510 Illinois American Legion Scholarship Program

American Legion–Illinois
P.O. Box 2910
Bloomington, IL 61702
(309) 663-0361
Average award: $1,000
Number of awards: 20
Deadline: March 15
College level: Freshman
Criteria: Applicant must be the child of a member of an American Legion post in Illinois and have attended high school in Illinois. Selection is based upon scholarship and financial need. Awarded every year.
Contact: Scholarships.

1511 Inninois Cereal Mills Inc. Scholarship

Future Farmers of America (FFA)
P.O. Box 15160
Alexandria, VA 22309-0160
(703) 360-3600
Average award: $1,000
Number of awards: 2
Deadline: February 15
College level: Freshman
Criteria: Applicant must be a FFA member in an Illinois or Indiana chapter served by ICM Grain Company elevators. Awarded every year.
Contact: National FFA Organizational Office.

1512 J. Edgar Hoover Foundation Scholarship

Boy Scouts of America
J. Edgar Hoover Foundation Scholarships
1325 Walnut Hill Lane
Irving, TX 75038
(214) 580-2433
Maximum award: $1,000
Number of awards: 4
Deadline: March 15 to local council; March 31 to Boy Scouts of America office
College level: Freshman, students under 21 years of age
Majors/Fields: Criminal justice, law enforcement
Criteria: Applicant must be an active and registered member of an Explorer Law Enforcement post and a high school senior. Awarded every year.
Contact: Elaine Carlberg, Division Secretary–Exploring.

1513 J. Walter Thompson Scholarship

Future Farmers of America (FFA)
P.O. Box 15160
Alexandria, VA 22309-0160
(703) 360-3600
Average award: $1,000
Number of awards: 3
Deadline: February 15
College level: Freshman
Majors/Fields: Agronomy, food science
Criteria: Applicant must be a FFA member who has competed in the Cereal Grains Proficiency Program above the local level. Awarded every year.
Contact: National FFA Organizational Office.

1514 James W. and Margaret Grainger Clark Scholarship

Clemson University
G-01 Sikes Hall
Clemson, SC 29634-5123
(803) 656-2280
Average award: $2,400
Number of awards: 1
Deadline: March 1
College level: Freshman, Sophomore, Junior, Senior
Criteria: First priority is given to a graduate of Tamassee-Salem High School who resided at Tamassee DAR School in Tamassee, S.C., or a graduate of the Kate Duncan Smith DAR School in Grant, Ala. Next preference goes to the child of a member in good standing of the National Society of the Daughters of the American Revolution. Awarded every year. Award may be used only at sponsoring institution.
Contact: Marvin Carmichael, Director of Financial Aid.

1515 Jeanne E. Bray Memorial Scholarship

National Rifle Association (NRA)
11250 Waples Mill Road
Fairfax, VA 22030
Average award: $1,000
Number of awards: 6
Deadline: November 15
College level: Freshman, Sophomore, Junior, Senior
Criteria: Applicant must be the child of a full-time, commissioned peace officer and NRA member who is currently employed or who died in the line of duty. Selection is based upon academic achievement, honors and awards, school and community service, special accomplishments, work experience, and essay. Minimum 2.0 GPA is required to retain scholarship. Awarded every year.
Contact: Nicole Durand, Assistant to the Secretary, (703) 267-1634.

1516 John A. Anderson Scholarship

50 Men and Women of Toledo, Inc.
P.O. Box 3357
Toledo, OH 43608
(419) 729-4654
Average award: $1,000
Deadline: March 15
College level: Freshman
Criteria: Recipient must maintain a minimum 3.0 GPA.
Contact: James C. Caldwell.

1517 Jones-Laurence Award

Sigma Alpha Epsilon (SAE)
P.O. Box 1856
Evanston, IL 60204
(708) 475-1856
Maximum award: $3,500
Minimum award: $500
Number of awards: 3
Deadline: May 15
College level: Senior, Graduate
Criteria: Applicant must be a member of SAE who displays the most outstanding academic achievement and genuine concern for the academic welfare and success of his fraternity brothers. Awarded every year.
Contact: Michael J. Tschirret, Director of Education Programs.

1518 Junior Girls Scholarship

Ladies Auxiliary to the Veterans of Foreign Wars
406 West 34th Street
Kansas City, MO 64111
(816) 561-8655
Maximum award: $5,000
Minimum award: $3,000
Number of awards: 2
Deadline: April 15
College level: Freshman
Criteria: Applicant must have been an active member of the Ladies Auxiliary Junior Girls Unit for at least one year, have held an office in the unit, and be in grades 9–12. Selection is based upon participation in Junior Girls unit, community and school activities, and scholastic aptitude. Awarded every year.
Contact: Judy Millick, Public Relations Director.

1519 Kenneth and Ellen Nielsen Cooperative Scholarship

Future Farmers of America (FFA)
P.O. Box 15160
Alexandria, VA 22309-0160
(703) 360-3600
Average award: $1,000
Number of awards: 4
Deadline: February 15
College level: Freshman
Majors/Fields: Agriculture
Criteria: Applicant must be a FFA member who is a resident of and plans to attend school in Colorado, Illinois, Iowa, Kansas, Minnesota, Missouri, Nebraska, North Dakota, Oklahoma, South Dakota, Texas, Wisconsin, or Wyoming. Awarded every year.
Contact: National FFA Organizational Office.

1520 Kova Fertilizer Inc. Scholarship

Future Farmers of America (FFA)
P.O. Box 15160
Alexandria, VA 22309-0160
(703) 360-3600
Average award: $1,000
Number of awards: 2
Deadline: February 15
College level: Freshman
Criteria: Applicant must be a FFA member, an Indiana resident, and pursuing a four-year degree at Purdue U or a Purdue U affiliate. Preference is given to applicants from Decatur County or Jackson County. Awarded every year.
Contact: National FFA Organizational Office.

1521 Leadership Scholarship

National 4-H Council
7100 Connecticut Avenue
Chevy Chase, MD 20815-4999
(301) 961-2800
Average award: $1,500
Number of awards: 9
Deadline: September 1
College level: Doctoral
Majors/Fields: Leadership studies
Criteria: Applicant must be a 4-H member. Awarded every year.
Contact: Local county extension 4-H office or state 4-H office.

1522 LEICA Photogrammetric Fellowship Award

American Society for Photogrammetry and Remote Sensing
ASPRS Awards Program, Suite 210
5410 Grosvenor Lane
Bethesda, MD 20814-2160
(301) 493-0290
Average award: $1,000
Number of awards: 2
Deadline: November 8
College level: Graduate, Doctoral
Majors/Fields: Photogrammetry
Criteria: Applicant must be a ASPRS member and a U.S. citizen. Applicant must have completed at least one undergraduate course in surveying or photogrammetry. Selection is based upon applicant's educational and career plans for continued study in photogrammetry, scholastic ability, recommendations, and financial need. Awarded when sufficient funds are available and qualified applicants apply.
Contact: Christopher J. Dyer, Staff Student Liaison, 5410 Grosvenor Lane, Suite 210, Bethesda, MD 20814-2160, (301) 493-2160.

1523 Leo Burnett Co. Scholarship

Future Farmers of America (FFA)
P.O. Box 15160
Alexandria, VA 22309-0160
(703) 360-3600
Maximum award: $2,000
Minimum award: $1,000
Number of awards: 3
Deadline: February 15
College level: Freshman
Majors/Fields: Agriculture
Criteria: Applicant must be a FFA member and a member of a minority group: American Indian, Native Alaskan, Asian/Pacific Islander, Black, or Hispanic. Preference is given to applicants from the Midwest. Awarded every year.
Contact: National FFA Organizational Office.

1524 Lillian and Arthur Dunn Scholarship

National Society of the Daughters of the American Revolution
NSDAR Administration Building, Office of the Committees
1776 D Street, NW
Washington, DC 20006-5392
(202) 879-3292
Average award: $1,000
Maximum number of awards: 4
Minimum number of awards: 4
Deadline: February 15
College level: Freshman
Criteria: Applicant must be a graduating high school senior whose mother is a current DAR member. Applicant must be sponsored by his or her mother's DAR chapter and be a U.S. citizen. All inquiries must include a self-addressed, stamped envelope. Annual transcript review and approval are required to retain scholarship. Awarded every year.
Contact: Administrative Assistant, NSDAR Office of the Committees/Scholarships, 1776 D Street, Washington, DC 20006-5392.

1525 Marjorie Sells Carter Boy Scout Scholarship

Marjorie Sells Carter Boy Scout Scholarship Trust
P.O. Box 527
West Chatham, MA 02669
(508) 945-1225
Average award: $1,500
Number of awards: 30
Deadline: April 15
College level: Freshman, Sophomore
Criteria: Applicant must be a Boy Scout from one of the six New England states who has been active in scouting for at least two years. Award is highly competitive. Selection is based upon demonstrated leadership ability and financial need. Letter requesting second year aid and minimum "C" average are required to retain scholarship.
Contact: Mrs. B. J. Shaffer, Administrative Secretary.

1526 Meats Evaluation Scholarship

Future Farmers of America (FFA)
P.O. Box 15160
Alexandria, VA 22309-0160
(703) 360-3600
Average award: $1,000
Number of awards: 3
Deadline: February 15
College level: Freshman
Majors/Fields: Animal science, meat science
Criteria: Applicant must be a FFA member who has competed in the Meats Evaluation Contest above the local level. Awarded every year.
Contact: National FFA Organizational Office.

1527 Metropolitan Life Foundation Scholarship

Future Farmers of America (FFA)
P.O. Box 15160
Alexandria, VA 22309-0160
(703) 360-3600
Average award: $2,000
Number of awards: 5
Deadline: February 15
College level: Freshman
Majors/Fields: Agribusiness, agriculture
Criteria: Applicant must be a FFA member attending Iowa State U, Kansas State U, U of Missouri–Columbia, U of Nebraska–Lincoln, or Purdue U. Awarded every year.
Contact: National FFA Organizational Office.

1528 Mid-Ohio Chemical Co. Scholarship

Future Farmers of America (FFA)
P.O. Box 15160
Alexandria, VA 22309-0160
(703) 360-3600
Average award: $1,000
Number of awards: 3
Deadline: February 15
College level: Freshman
Majors/Fields: Agriculture
Criteria: Applicant must be a FFA member and a resident of Ohio, Indiana, or West Virginia. Awarded every year.
Contact: National FFA Organizational Office.

1529 Military Order of the Purple Heart Scholarship

Military Order of the Purple Heart, U.S.A.
5413-B Backlick Road
Springfield, VA 22151-3960
(703) 642-5360
Average award: $1,000
Number of awards: 4
Deadline: June 15
College level: Freshman, Sophomore, Junior, Senior, Graduate, Doctoral, vocational and professional school students
Criteria: Applicant must be a U.S. citizen and the child or grandchild of a recipient of the Purple Heart medal. Applicant must have graduated from an accredited school, demonstrate academic achievement, and be enrolled in a full-time program of studies. Financial need is considered. Minimum 2.5 GPA is required to retain scholarship.
Contact: Scholarship Program.

1530 Miller Meester Advertising Scholarship

Future Farmers of America (FFA)
P.O. Box 15160
Alexandria, VA 22309-0160
(703) 360-3600
Average award: $2,000
Number of awards: 1
Deadline: February 15
College level: Junior, Senior
Majors/Fields: Agricultural communications, agricultural journalism
Criteria: Applicant must be a FFA member. Awarded every year.
Contact: National FFA Organizational Office.

1531 Mills Fleet Farm Scholarship

Future Farmers of America (FFA)
P.O. Box 15160
Alexandria, VA 22309-0160
(703) 360-3600
Average award: $1,000
Number of awards: 4
Deadline: February 15
College level: Freshman
Majors/Fields: Agriculture
Criteria: Applicant must be a FFA member and a resident of Wisconsin or Minnesota. Selection is based upon academic achievement and leadership. Awarded every year.
Contact: National FFA Organizational Office.

1532 Morton Salt Scholarship

Future Farmers of America (FFA)
P.O. Box 15160
Alexandria, VA 22309-0160
(703) 360-3600
Average award: $1,000
Number of awards: 2
Deadline: February 15
College level: Freshman
Majors/Fields: Animal science, pre-veterinary medicine
Criteria: Applicant must be a FFA member. Preference is given to applicants displaying an interest in animal nutrition. Awarded every year.
Contact: National FFA Organizational Office.

1533 Multi-Year Ambassadorial Scholarship

Rotary Foundation of Rotary International
One Rotary Center
1560 Sherman Avenue
Evanston, IL 60201
(708) 866-3000
Maximum award: $10,000
College level: Junior, Senior, Graduate, Doctoral
Criteria: Applicant must have completed two years of university work or appropriate professional experience, and desire to pursue academic degree through study abroad. Award is for two or three years. Awarded every year.
Contact: Local Rotary club.

1534 NAPA Auto Parts Scholarship

Future Farmers of America (FFA)
P.O. Box 15160
Alexandria, VA 22309-0160
(703) 360-3600
Maximum award: $1,000
Number of awards: 10
Deadline: February 15
College level: Freshman
Majors/Fields: Agriculture
Criteria: Applicant must be a FFA member from a chapter within a 15-mile radius of a NAPA store. Applicant must visit with the local NAPA dealer and obtain the manager's signature as a sponsor. Awarded every year.
Contact: National FFA Organizational Office.

1535 National Agricultural Center & Hall of Fame/ Edith & Harry Darby Foundation

Future Farmers of America (FFA)
P.O. Box 15160
Alexandria, VA 22309-0160
(703) 360-3600
Average award: $2,000
Number of awards: 1
Deadline: February 15
College level: Freshman
Majors/Fields: Agriculture
Criteria: Applicant must be a FFA member and rank in top half of class. Awarded every year.
Contact: National FFA Organizational Office.

1536 National FFA Alumni Scholarship

Future Farmers of America (FFA)
P.O. Box 15160
Alexandria, VA 22309-0160
(703) 360-3600
Average award: $1,000
Number of awards: 5
Deadline: February 15
College level: Freshman, Junior, Senior
Majors/Fields: Agricultural education
Criteria: Applicant must be a current or former FFA member.
Contact: National FFA Organizational Office.

1537 National Fraternal Scholarship

Royal Neighbors of America
National Headquarters
230 Sixteenth Street
Rock Island, IL 61201-8645
(309) 788-4561
Minimum award: $2,000
Number of awards: 10
Deadline: December 1
College level: Freshman
Criteria: Applicant must be a high school senior who has been a beneficial member of the Royal Neighbors of America for at least two years, or who has received payment of the maturity value of his or her endowment certificate and since has continued to be a social member. Class rank must be in top quarter. Selection is based upon the relative merits of the applicant's qualities and leadership, both in school and in the royal neighbor camp, and scholastic records. Scholarship is for four years but subject to annual review. Awarded every year.
Contact: Betty Walsh, Manager of Fraternal Financial Department.

1538 Nationwide Insurance Enterprise Foundation Scholarship

Future Farmers of America (FFA)
P.O. Box 15160
Alexandria, VA 22309-0160
(703) 360-3600
Average award: $1,000
Number of awards: 3
Deadline: February 15
College level: Freshman
Majors/Fields: Agriculture
Criteria: Applicant must be a FFA member. Awarded every year.
Contact: National FFA Organizational Office.

1539 NCHA Scholarship

National Campers and Hikers Association (NCHA)
Scholarship Director
74 West Genesee Street
Skaneateles, NY 13152
(315) 685-5223
Average award: $1,000
Maximum award: $2,000
Minimum award: $500
Deadline: April 15
College level: Freshman, Sophomore, Junior, Senior
Criteria: Applicant must be a NCHA member, or the child of a member, for at least one year prior to application. Membership must be maintained during the award. High school applicant must rank in the top 40 percent of class; college applicant must have a minimum "B" average. Selection is based upon maturity, leadership, and activities and goals as related to the objectives of the NCHA. Special consideration is given to applicants majoring in fields related to conservation, ecology, or outdoor activities. Reapplication is required to retain scholarship. Awarded every year.
Contact: Barbara E. Harper, National Scholarship Director.

1540 Northrup King Company Scholarship

Future Farmers of America (FFA)
P.O. Box 15160
Alexandria, VA 22309-0160
(703) 360-3600
Average award: $1,000
Number of awards: 4
Deadline: February 15
College level: Freshman
Majors/Fields: Agriculture
Criteria: Applicant must be a FFA member who is a resident of Illinois, Iowa, Minnesota, Nebraska, or Wisconsin. Selection is based primarily upon academic achievement. Awarded every year.
Contact: National FFA Organizational Office.

1541 Off Highway Vehicle College Scholarship and Internship

National 4-H Council
7100 Connecticut Avenue
Chevy Chase, MD 20815-4999
(301) 961-2800
Maximum award: $5,000
Minimum award: $2,000
Number of awards: 7
College level: Senior, Graduate, Doctoral
Majors/Fields: Land manager
Criteria: Applicant must be a 4-H member. Awarded every year.
Contact: Local county extension 4-H office or state 4-H office.

1542 Owens-Illinois Scholarship

50 Men and Women of Toledo, Inc.
P.O. Box 3357
Toledo, OH 43608
(419) 729-4654
Average award: $1,500
Deadline: March 15
College level: Freshman
Criteria: Recipient must maintain a minimum 3.0 GPA. Awarded every year.
Contact: James C. Caldwell, President, P.O. Box 80056, Toledo, OH 43608.

1543 Parliamentary Procedure Scholarship

Future Farmers of America (FFA)
P.O. Box 15160
Alexandria, VA 22309-0160
(703) 360-3600
Average award: $1,000
Number of awards: 4
Deadline: February 15
College level: Freshman
Majors/Fields: Agribusiness, agriculture
Criteria: Applicant must be a FFA member who has competed in the Parliamentary Procedure Contest above the local level. Awarded every year.
Contact: National FFA Organizational Office.

1544 Pet Inc. Scholarship

Future Farmers of America (FFA)
P.O. Box 15160
Alexandria, VA 22309-0160
(703) 360-3600
Average award: $2,500
Number of awards: 2
Deadline: February 15
College level: Freshman
Majors/Fields: Agribusiness, food science/technology
Criteria: Applicant must be a FFA member. Awarded every year.
Contact: National FFA Organizational Office.

1545 Phi Kappa Phi Graduate Fellowships

The Honor Society of Phi Kappa Phi
Louisiana State University
P.O. Box 16000
Baton Rouge, LA 70893-6000
(504) 388-4917
Maximum award: $7,000
Minimum award: $1,000
Number of awards: 50
Deadline: February 1
College level: First-year graduate students
Criteria: Applicant must be an active member of Phi Kappa Phi. Awarded every year.
Contact: John W. Warren, Executive Director.

1546 Photography Award

National 4-H Council
7100 Connecticut Avenue
Chevy Chase, MD 20815-4999
(301) 961-2800
Minimum award: $1,500
Number of awards: 6
Deadline: September 1
College level: Doctoral
Majors/Fields: Photography studies
Criteria: Applicant must be a 4-H member. Awarded every year.
Contact: Local county extension 4-H office or state 4-H office.

1547 Poultry Scholarship

National 4-H Council
7100 Connecticut Avenue
Chevy Chase, MD 20815-4999
(301) 961-2800
Average award: $1,500
Number of awards: 2
Deadline: September 1
College level: Freshman, Sophomore, Junior, Senior
Majors/Fields: Animal science
Criteria: Applicant must be a 4-H member for at least one year, demonstrate participation and outstanding acheivement in 4-H, have participated in a poultry-related project, and be pursuing a career in poultry. Awarded every year.
Contact: Local county extension 4-H office or state 4-H office.

1548 Presidential Award

National 4-H Council
7100 Connecticut Avenue
Chevy Chase, MD 20815-4999
(301) 961-2800
Minimum award: $1,000
Number of awards: 12
Deadline: September 1
College level: Doctoral
Criteria: Applicant must be a 4-H member. Awarded every year.
Contact: Local county extension 4-H office or state 4-H office.

1549 Public Employees Public Service Scholarship

Public Employees RoundTable
P.O. Box 14270
Washington, DC 20044-4270
(202) 927-5000
Maximum award: $1,000
Minimum award: $500
Maximum number of awards: 12
Minimum number of awards: 8
Deadline: April or May
College level: Sophomore, Junior, Senior, Graduate, Doctoral
Criteria: Applicant must plan to enter public service and be enrolled in a four-year program with a minimum 3.5 GPA. Self-addressed, stamped envelope must be included in order to receive an application. Awarded every year.
Contact: Staff.

1550 Public Speaking Award

National 4-H Council
7100 Connecticut Avenue
Chevy Chase, MD 20815-4999
(301) 961-2800
Minimum award: $1,000
Number of awards: 6
Deadline: September 1
College level: Doctoral
Majors/Fields: Public Speaking Studies
Criteria: Applicant must be a 4-H member. Awarded every year.
Contact: Local county extension 4-H office or state 4-H office.

1551 Purina Mills Inc. Scholarship

Future Farmers of America (FFA)
P.O. Box 15160
Alexandria, VA 22309-0160
(703) 360-3600
Average award: $1,000
Number of awards: 5
Deadline: February 15
College level: Freshman
Majors/Fields: Agricultural business/economics, animal science
Criteria: Applicant must be a FFA member who has competed in the Livestock Contest at the district, state, or national level. Awarded every year.
Contact: National FFA Organizational Office.

1552 Quality Stores Inc. Scholarship

Future Farmers of America (FFA)
P.O. Box 15160
Alexandria, VA 22309-0160
(703) 360-3600
Average award: $1,000
Number of awards: 3
Deadline: February 15
College level: Freshman
Majors/Fields: Agribusiness
Criteria: Applicant must be a FFA member who is a resident of Indiana, Michigan or Ohio. Awarded every year.
Contact: National FFA Organizational Office.

1553   Resident Education Advisor Program

Sigma Alpha Epsilon (SAE)
P.O. Box 1856
Evanston, IL 60204
(708) 475-1856
Average award: $3,000
Minimum award: $2,000
Number of awards: 10
Deadline: April 15
College level: Graduate
Criteria: Applicant must be an SAE brother currently attending or planning to attend graduate school. He will serve 15–20 hours a week as a live-in educational advisor, take meals with the chapter, and will have room and board provided by the host chapter. Scholarship is renewable. Awarded every year.
Contact: Michael J. Tschirret, Director of Educational Programs, (708) 475-1856, extension 234.

1554   Rhone-Poulenc Animal Nutrition Scholarship

Future Farmers of America (FFA)
P.O. Box 15160
Alexandria, VA 22309-0160
(703) 360-3600
Average award: $1,000
Number of awards: 4
Deadline: February 15
College level: Freshman
Majors/Fields: Animal science, grain science, poultry science
Criteria: Applicant must be a FFA member. Two awards are for applicants who are pursuing a four-year degree in animal science/poultry science at a college or university in Alabama, Arkansas, California, Florida, Georgia, or North Carolina; applicant must also be a resident of one of these states. One award is for an applicant pursuing a four-year degree in grain science at Kansas State U. One award is for an applicant pursuing a four-year degree in animal science at Kansas State U, Iowa State U, U of Nebraska, Oklahoma State U, or Texas A&M. Awarded every year.
Contact: National FFA Organizational Office.

1555   Richard Heaney Scholarship

National Beverage Packaging Association
200 Daingerfield Road
Alexandria, VA 22314-2800
(703) 684-1080
Maximum award: $2,000
Minimum award: $1,000
Number of awards: 6
Deadline: July 1
College level: Junior, Senior, Graduate, Doctoral, second-year students at two-year technical colleges
Majors/Fields: Packaging
Criteria: Awarded every year.
Contact: Wesley Trochlil, Executive Director.

1556   Richard M. Proctor Memorial Bursary

University of Calgary
2500 University Drive, NW
Calgary, Alberta, CN T2N 1N4
(403) 220-7872
Average award: $1,200
Number of awards: 2
Deadline: July 15
College level: Freshman
Criteria: Applicant must have participated in the Big Brothers/Big Sisters program (formerly Uncles or Aunts-at-Large). If there are no eligible applicants, children of current Canadian Progress Club Calgary Downtown members are eligible. Selection is based upon academic merit and financial need. Awarded every year. Award may be used only at sponsoring institution.
Contact: J. Van Housen, Director of Student Awards & Financial Aid.

1557   Robert W. Woodruff Fellowship

Boys Clubs of America
771 First Avenue
New York, NY 11217
(212) 351-5962
Average award: $12,000
Maximum award: $15,000
Minimum award: $10,000
Number of awards: 1
Deadline: May 31
College level: Graduate
Criteria: Applicant must have a baccalaureate degree from an accredited college or university and be accepted for matriculation into an accredited graduate degree program. Applicant may choose area of academic specialization, but must be able to demonstrate the relevance of the chosen area to Boys Club work. Applicant must have a minimum of two years' full-time experience in a youth service agency, with preference be given to individuals with Boys Club experience, and must commit himself to minimum of two years of full-time employment with a Boys Club of America affiliated club after completion of the program. Renewal based on academic proficiency. Awarded every year.
Contact: Judith J. Carter, M.Ed., Director of Career Development.

1558   Safety Scholarship

National 4-H Council
7100 Connecticut Avenue
Chevy Chase, MD 20815-4999
(301) 961-2800
Average award: $1,000
Number of awards: 8
Deadline: September 1
College level: Doctoral
Majors/Fields: Industrial studies, family studies
Criteria: Applicant must be a 4-H member. Awarded every year.
Contact: Local county extension 4-H office or state 4-H office.

1559   Sandoz Agro Inc. Scholarship

Future Farmers of America (FFA)
P.O. Box 15160
Alexandria, VA 22309-0160
(703) 360-3600
Average award: $2,000
Number of awards: 3
Deadline: February 15
College level: Freshman
Majors/Fields: Agriculture
Criteria: Applicant must be a FFA member pursuing a four-year degree at U of Illinois, Cornell U, Purdue U, Iowa State U, U of Minnesota, Michigan State U, U of Wisconsin–Madison, Virginia Polytech Inst, U of California–Davis, or Florida A&M U. Awarded every year. Award may be used only at sponsoring institution.
Contact: National FFA Organizational Office.

1560   Sandoz Animal Health Scholarship

Future Farmers of America (FFA)
P.O. Box 15160
Alexandria, VA 22309-0160
(703) 360-3600
Average award: $2,000
Number of awards: 1
Deadline: February 15
College level: Freshman
Majors/Fields: Small-animal study
Criteria: Applicant must be a FFA member and attend one of the following schools: UC Davis–Sch of Veterinary Medicine, U of Florida–Coll of Veterinary Medicine, U of Georgia–Coll of Veterinary Medicine, Oklahoma State U–Coll of Veterinary Medicine, Texas A&M U–Coll of Veterinary Medicine, Tuskegee U–Sch of Veterinary Medicine. Awarded every year. Award may be used only at sponsoring institution.
Contact: National FFA Organizational Office.

1561 Santa Fe Pacific Foundation Scholarship

Future Farmers of America (FFA)
P.O. Box 15160
Alexandria, VA 22309-0160
(703) 360-3600
Average award: $1,000
Number of awards: 18
Deadline: February 15
College level: Freshman
Majors/Fields: Agriculture
Criteria: Applicant must be a FFA member majoring in any area of agriculture at a four-year college, and be a resident of Arizona, California, Colorado, Illinois, Kansas, Missouri, New Mexico, Oklahoma, or Texas. Recipient must agree to attend the National FFA Convention in Kansas City the year the scholarship is received; travel stipend will be provided. Awarded every year.
Contact: National FFA Organizational Office.

1562 Santa Fe Railway Scholarship

National 4-H Council
7100 Connecticut Avenue
Chevy Chase, MD 20815-4999
(301) 961-2800
Average award: $1,200
Number of awards: 27
Deadline: September 1
College level: Unspecified undergraduate
Criteria: Applicant must be a 4-H member, submit National 4-H Report Form and "My 4-H Story." Recipients must attend National 4-H Congress. Applicant must be a resident of Arizona, California, Colorado, Illinois, Kansas, Missouri, New Mexico, Oklahoma, or Texas. Awarded every year.
Contact: Local county extension 4-H office or state 4-H office.

1563 Scout of the Year Scholarship

American Legion
The American Legion Education and Scholarships Program
P.O. Box 1055
Indianapolis, IN 46206
(317) 630-1200
Maximum award: $8,000
Minimum award: $2,000
Number of awards: 4
Deadline: March 1
College level: Freshman
Criteria: Applicant must be a registered active member of a Boy Scout troop or Varsity Scout team sponsored by an American Legion post or auxiliary unit, or a registered active member of a duly chartered Boy Scout troop or Varsity Scout team and the son or grandson of an American Legion or auxiliary member. Award must be used within four years of graduation date at an accredited post-secondary school in the continental U.S. or a U.S. possession. Awarded every year.
Contact: Steve Short, National Americanism Commission.

1564 Scout of the Year

American Legion–Wisconsin
Department Headquarters
812 East State Street
Milwaukee, WI 53202
Maximum award: $8,000
Minimum award: $250
Deadline: March 1
College level: Freshman
Criteria: Applicant must be an Eagle Scout. Awarded every year.
Contact: Scholarships.

1565 Sheep Award

National 4-H Council
7100 Connecticut Avenue
Chevy Chase, MD 20815-4999
(301) 961-2800
Minimum award: $1,000
Number of awards: 4
Deadline: September 1
College level: Doctoral
Majors/Fields: Livestock studies
Criteria: Applicant must be a 4-H member. Awarded every year.
Contact: Local county extension 4-H office or state 4-H office.

1566 SIE Scholarships

Sigma Iota Epsilon (SIE) National Office
214 Wescott Blvd.
Florida State University
Tallahassee, FL 32306
(904) 644-6003
Average award: $775
Maximum award: $1,250
Minimum award: $500
Number of awards: 10
Deadline: May 10
College level: Junior, Senior, Graduate, Doctoral
Majors/Fields: Business administration, management
Criteria: Applicant must be an active SIE student member. Recipient must remain an active SIE student member. Awarded every year.
Contact: Mike Hankin, Administrator, 214 Westcott Blvd., Florida State University, Tallahassee, FL 32306.

1567 Sigma Chi Foundation Scholarship

Sigma Chi Foundation
P.O. Box 469
Evanston, IL 60204
(708) 869-3655
Average award: $1,000
Maximum award: $3,000
Minimum award: $500
Number of awards: 125
Deadline: May 15
College level: Junior, Senior, Graduate, Doctoral
Criteria: Applicant must be a full-time student and member of Sigma Chi fraternity. Selection is based upon GPA. There are general awards, as well as specific ones for medical science and graduate study in engineering. Satisfactory GPA is required to retain scholarship. Awarded every year.
Contact: Foundation Secretary.

1568 Slovenian Women's Union of America Scholarship

Slovenian Women's Union of America
Scholarship Program Director
7607 Blain Way
Indianapolis, IN 46254
(317) 298-9255
Average award: $1,000
Number of awards: 4
Deadline: March 20
College level: Freshman
Criteria: Applicant must have a three-year membership in the Slovenian Women's Union. Awarded every year.
Contact: Carita Girman, Scholarship Program Director.

1569   SmithKline Beecham Animal Health

Future Farmers of America (FFA)
P.O. Box 15160
Alexandria, VA 22309-0160
(703) 360-3600
Average award: $1,000
Number of awards: 4
Deadline: February 15
College level: Freshman
Majors/Fields: Pre-veterinary science
Criteria: Applicant must be a FFA member. Awarded every year.
Contact: National FFA Organizational Office.

1570   Sparks Co. Scholarship

Future Farmers of America (FFA)
P.O. Box 15160
Alexandria, VA 22309-0160
(703) 360-3600
Average award: $2,000
Number of awards: 1
Deadline: February 15
College level: Freshman
Majors/Fields: Animal science
Criteria: Applicant must be a FFA member attending Oklahoma State U. Awarded every year. Award may be used only at sponsoring institution.
Contact: National FFA Organizational Office.

1571   Spirit of Youth Scholarship

American Legion Auxiliary
777 North Meridian Street
Third Floor
Indianapolis, IN 46204
(317) 635-6291
Average award: $1,000
Number of awards: 5
Deadline: March 16
College level: Freshman
Criteria: Applicant must be a junior member of the ALA and have paid dues for the three preceding years. Applicant must maintain a minimum 3.0 GPA and continue membership in ALA to retain scholarship. Awarded every year.
Contact: National Secretary or National Treasurer, Scholarships.

1572   Stanley H. Stearman Scholarship Award

National Society of Public Accountants (NSPA) Scholarship Foundation
1010 North Fairfax Street
Alexandria, VA 22314-1574
(703) 549-6400
Average award: $2,000
Number of awards: 1
Deadline: March 10
College level: Sophomore, Junior, Senior, Graduate, Doctoral
Majors/Fields: Accounting
Criteria: Applicant must be the child, grandchild, niece, nephew, son-in-law, or daughter-in-law of an active National Society of Public Accountants member or deceased member. Applicant must be an accounting major with a minimum "B" average in a full-time degree program at an accredited college or university. Accounting major is required to retain scholarship for a total of three years. Awarded every year.
Contact: Susan E. Noell, Foundation Director.

1573   State Fraternal Scholarship

Royal Neighbors of America
National Headquarters
230 Sixteenth Street
Rock Island, IL 61201-8645
(309) 788-4561
Minimum award: $500
Maximum number of awards: 31
Minimum number of awards: 19
Deadline: December 1
College level: Freshman
Criteria: Applicant must be a high school senior who has been a beneficial member of Royal Neighbors of America for at least two years, or has received payment of the maturity value of his endowment certificate and continued to be a social member and rank in the top quarter of his class. Applicant must maintain membership in one of the state's Royal Neighbor camps but does not need to reside in the state. States offering this scholarship are California, Colorado, CMA Illinois, Florida, Northern Illinois, Southern Illinois, Indiana, Iowa, Kansas, Michigan, Minnesota, Missouri, Montana, Nebraska, North Dakota, Oklahoma, Oregon, South Dakota, Texas, Washington, Wisconsi and Wyoming. Awarded every year.
Contact: Betty Welsh, Manager of Fraternal Financial Department.

1574   Swine Scholarship

National 4-H Council
7100 Connecticut Avenue
Chevy Chase, MD 20815-4999
(301) 961-2800
Average award: $1,000
Number of awards: 7
Deadline: September 1
College level: Doctoral
Majors/Fields: Animal studies
Criteria: Applicant must be a 4-H member. Awarded every year.
Contact: Local county extension 4-H office or state 4-H office.

1575   Tau Beta Pi Fellowship

Tau Beta Pi Association
P.O. Box 8840
University Station
Knoxville, TN 37996-0002
(615) 546-4578
Maximum award: $7,500
Minimum award: $7,500
Number of awards: 22
Deadline: January 15
College level: Graduate
Majors/Fields: Engineering
Criteria: Applicant must be a Tau Beta Pi member. Awarded every year.
Contact: James D. Froula, P.E.

1576   Tau Beta Pi Laureate Award

Tau Beta Pi Association
P.O. Box 8840
University Station
Knoxville, TN 37996-0002
(615) 546-4578
Maximum award: $2,500
Minimum award: $2,500
Number of awards: 3
Deadline: March 15
College level: Graduate
Criteria: Applicant must be a Tau Beta Pi member who has excelled in nontechnical areas.
Contact: James D. Froula, P.E.

1577 Tau Beta Pi Scholarship

Tau Beta Pi Association
P.O. Box 8840
University Station
Knoxville, TN 37996-0002
(615) 546-4578
Average award: $5,000
Deadline: January 20
College level: Graduate
Majors/Fields: Business administration
Criteria: Applicant must be a Tau Beta Pi member who has been accepted at Rensselaer Polytech Inst, N.Y., in the M.B.A. program. Award may be used only at sponsoring institution.
Contact: James D. Froula, P.E.

1578 Theta Delta Chi Educational Foundation Scholarship

Theta Delta Chi Educational Foundation
135 Bay State Road
Boston, MA 02215
(617) 262-2815
Average award: $1,000
Number of awards: 15
Deadline: April 30
College level: Sophomore, Junior, Senior, Graduate, Doctoral
Criteria: Selection is based upon academic promise, service to Theta Delta Chi fraternity, and financial need. Awarded every year.
Contact: Scholarship Committee Chairperson.

1579 Thomas Wood Baldridge Scholarship

U.S. Jaycee War Memorial Fund
Department 94922
Tulsa, OK 74194-0001
Average award: $2,500
Number of awards: 1
Deadline: February 1
College level: Freshman, Sophomore, Junior, Senior, Graduate, Doctoral
Criteria: Applicant must be a Jaycee or the immediate family member of a Jaycee, a U.S. citizen, possess academic potential and leadership qualities, and demonstrated financial need. Request application by February 1 with $5.00 application fee and self-addressed, business-sized stamped envelope to War Memorial Fund, 4 West 21st Street, Tulsa, OK 74114-1116. Completed applications must be sent to applicants' respective state Junior Chamber organization by March 1. Awarded every year.
Contact: Bob Guest, U.S. Chamber of Commerce, Scholarship Program Administrator, P.O. Box 7, Tulsa, OK 74100-0007, (918) 584-2481.

1580 Toyota Motor Sales USA Inc. Scholarship

Future Farmers of America (FFA)
P.O. Box 15160
Alexandria, VA 22309-0160
(703) 360-3600
Average award: $5,000
Number of awards: 5
Deadline: February 15
College level: Freshman
Criteria: Applicant must be a FFA member. Preference is given to agricultural engineering or agricultural science/technology majors. Selection is based upon financial need, extracurricular/leadership activities, and scholastic achievement. Awarded every year.
Contact: National FFA Organizational Office.

1581 Tractor Supply Co. Scholarship

Future Farmers of America (FFA)
P.O. Box 15160
Alexandria, VA 22309-0160
(703) 360-3600
Average award: $2,500
Number of awards: 3
Deadline: February 15
College level: Freshman
Majors/Fields: Agriculture
Criteria: Applicant must be a FFA member planning to major in any area of agricultural sciences, and must demonstrate financial need. One scholarship will be awarded in each of three regions: (1) North Dakota, South Dakota, Minnesota, Nebraska, Iowa, Kansas, Missouri, Texas, Montana; (2) Illinois, Indiana, Kentucky, Tennessee, Arkansas, Mississippi, Wisconsin; (3) Michigan, Ohio, Pennsylvania, New York, Maryland. Minimum 2.0 GPA and full-time enrollment are required to retain scholarship for four years. Awarded every year.
Contact: National FFA Organizational Office.

1582 Transammonia Scholarship

Future Farmers of America (FFA)
P.O. Box 15160
Alexandria, VA 22309-0160
(703) 360-3600
Average award: $1,000
Number of awards: 5
Deadline: February 15
College level: Freshman
Majors/Fields: Agriculture
Criteria: Applicant must be a FFA member. Awarded every year.
Contact: National FFA Organizational Office.

1583 TROA Educational Assistance Program

The Retired Officers Association
201 North Washington Street
Alexandria, VA 22314-2529
(703) 838-8169
Average award: $2,000
Number of awards: 800
Deadline: March 1
College level: Freshman, Sophomore, Junior, Senior, Technical school
Criteria: Applicant must be under 24 years of age, never married, and the child of a TROA member. Officers who are eligible for TROA membership must be TROA members. Unmarried dependent sons and daughters of enlisted personnel are eligible. Minimum 3.0 GPA is required. Minimum 2.5 GPA is required for renewal. Awarded every year.
Contact: Janice E. Engler, Administrator.

1584 Unical 76 Scholarship

Future Farmers of America (FFA)
P.O. Box 15160
Alexandria, VA 22309-0160
(703) 360-3600
Average award: $1,000
Number of awards: 2
Deadline: February 15
College level: Freshman
Criteria: Applicant must be a FFA member and a resident of California or Washington. Awarded every year.
Contact: National FFA Organizational Office.

1585   United Dairymen of Idaho Scholarship

Future Farmers of America (FFA)
P.O. Box 15160
Alexandria, VA 22309-0160
(703) 360-3600
Average award: $1,600
Number of awards: 2
Deadline: February 15
College level: Freshman
Criteria: Applicant must be a FFA member. Preference is given to dairy-related majors. Awarded every year.
Contact: National FFA Organizational Office.

1586   Universal Dairy Equipment, Inc. Scholarship

Future Farmers of America (FFA)
P.O. Box 15160
Alexandria, VA 22309-0160
(703) 360-3600
Average award: $1,000
Number of awards: 2
Deadline: February 15
College level: Freshman
Majors/Fields: Agriculture
Criteria: Applicant must be a FFA member graduating from Kansas City East Environmental Sciences/Agribusiness Magnet High School and be pursuing a four-year degree in any agriculture-related major. Awarded every year.
Contact: National FFA Organizational Office.

1587   Valmont Irrigation Scholarship

Future Farmers of America (FFA)
P.O. Box 15160
Alexandria, VA 22309-0160
(703) 360-3600
Average award: $1,000
Number of awards: 5
Deadline: February 15
College level: Freshman
Majors/Fields: Agriculture
Criteria: Applicant must be a FFA member. Awarded every year.
Contact: National FFA Organizational Office.

1588   Veterinary Science Award

National 4-H Council
7100 Connecticut Avenue
Chevy Chase, MD 20815-4999
(301) 961-2800
Minimum award: $1,500
Number of awards: 6
Deadline: September 1
College level: Doctoral
Majors/Fields: Veterinary medicine studies
Criteria: Applicant must be a 4-H member. Awarded every year.
Contact: Local county extension 4-H office or state 4-H office.

1589   Viscosity Oil Company Scholarship

Future Farmers of America (FFA)
P.O. Box 15160
Alexandria, VA 22309-0160
(703) 360-3600
Average award: $3,500
Maximum award: $8,000
Minimum award: $2,000
Number of awards: 8
Deadline: February 15
College level: Freshman
Criteria: Applicant must be a FFA member. Financial need is considered. Awarded every year.
Contact: National FFA Organizational Office.

1590   Walco International Scholarship

Future Farmers of America (FFA)
P.O. Box 15160
Alexandria, VA 22309-0160
(703) 360-3600
Average award: $1,000
Number of awards: 3
Deadline: February 15
College level: Freshman
Majors/Fields: Animal science
Criteria: Applicant must be a FFA member. Awarded every year.
Contact: National FFA Oranizational Office.

1591   Washington Scholarship

SDX Foundation of Washington
U.S. News & World Report
2400 North Street, NW, Room 610
Washington, DC 20037
(202) 955-2330
Average award: $2,000
Maximum number of awards: 8
Minimum number of awards: 6
Deadline: March 1
College level: Sophomore, Junior
Criteria: Applicant must be a member of Sigma Delta Chi and be a full-time sophomore or junior at a college or university in metropolitan Washington, D.C. Demonstration of financial need is required. Scholarship is renewable. Awarded every year.
Contact: Scholarships, 2400 North Street, NW, Room 610, Washington, DC 20037.

1592   Western Farm Service Scholarship

Future Farmers of America (FFA)
P.O. Box 15160
Alexandria, VA 22309-0160
(703) 360-3600
Average award: $1,000
Number of awards: 5
Deadline: February 15
College level: Freshman
Majors/Fields: Crop production science
Criteria: Applicant must be a FFA member from the Central Valley of California, the coastal area of California, southern Idaho, the Willamette Valley of Oregon, or eastern Washington. Awarded every year.
Contact: National FFA Organizational Office.

1593   Western Seedmen's Association Scholarship

Future Farmers of America (FFA)
P.O. Box 15160
Alexandria, VA 22309-0160
(703) 360-3600
Average award: $1,000
Minimum award: $750
Number of awards: 2
Deadline: February 15
College level: Freshman
Majors/Fields: Agriculture education, agronomy
Criteria: Applicant must be a FFA member and a resident of Arizona, California, Colorado, Idaho, Iowa, Kansas, Minnesota, Missouri, Montana, Nebraska, Nevada, New Mexico, North Dakota, Oklahoma, Oregon, South Dakota, Texas, Utah, Washington, or Wyoming. Awarded every year.
Contact: National FFA Organizational Office.

1594   Wildlife and Fisheries Award

National 4-H Council
7100 Connecticut Avenue
Chevy Chase, MD 20815-4999
(301) 961-2800
Minimum award: $1,500
Number of awards: 15
Deadline: September 1
College level: Doctoral
Majors/Fields: Fisheries studies, wildlife studies
Criteria: Applicant must be a 4-H member. Awarded every year.
Contact: Local county extension 4-H office or state 4-H office.

1595 WIX Corporation Scholarship

Future Farmers of America (FFA)
P.O. Box 15160
Alexandria, VA 22309-0160
(703) 360-3600
Average award: $1,000
Number of awards: 4
Deadline: February 15
College level: Freshman
Majors/Fields: Agricultural engineering, agricultural mechanics
Criteria: Applicant must be a FFA member. Awarded every year.
Contact: National FFA Organizational Office.

1596 Women's Board Scholarship

Boys and Girls Clubs of Chicago
625 West Jackson Boulevard
Suite 300
Chicago, IL 60661
(312) 627-2700
Average award: $1,000
Maximum award: $2,000
Minimum award: $400
Number of awards: 21
Deadline: May 1
College level: Freshman
Criteria: Applicant must be a member of the Boys and Girls Clubs of Chicago with a minimum 2.5 GPA. Application must be submitted by the club director. Selection is based upon financial need and grades. Renewable if satisfactory academic performance is maintained and letter of request is sent. Awarded every year.
Contact: Mary Ann Mahon-Huels, Assistant Vice President of Operations.

1597 Wood Science Scholarship

National 4-H Council
7100 Connecticut Avenue
Chevy Chase, MD 20815-4999
(301) 961-2800
Average award: $1,000
Number of awards: 4
College level: Doctoral
Majors/Fields: Wood fiber products studies
Criteria: Applicant must be a 4-H member. Awarded every year.
Contact: Local county extension 4-H office or state 4-H office.

1598 Young American Bowling Alliance Coca-Cola Youth Bowling Championship

Young American Bowling Alliance
5301 South 76th Street
Greendale, WI 53129
(414) 421-4700
Maximum award: $3,000
Minimum award: $1,000
Number of awards: 18
Deadline: February 11
College level: Freshman, Sophomore, Junior, Senior
Criteria: Applicant must be a Young American Bowling Alliance Youth Division member under 21 years of age as of August 1 and compete in the tournament through local YABA league. Awarded every year.
Contact: Edward Gocha, Scholarship Administrator, (414) 423-3373.

1599 Youth Scholarship Fund of IBHA, Inc.

International Buckskin Horse Association (IBHA)
P.O. Box 268
Shelby, IN 46377
(219) 552-1013
Maximum award: $1,000
Minimum award: $500
Number of awards: 12
Deadline: March 1
College level: Freshman, Sophomore, Junior, Senior
Criteria: Applicant must hold membership in IBHA, participate in IBHA Youth events for at least two years, be 22 or younger with excellent test scores and strong recommendations, and participate in school and community activities. Minimum "C" average is required to maintain scholarship. Awarded every year.
Contact: Richard Kurzeja, Secretary, 3517 W. 231 Avenue, Lowell, IN 46356.

Corporate Affiliation

1600 AEJMC Correspondents Fund Scholarship in Journalism

Association for Education in Journalism and Mass Communication
1621 College Street
College of Journalism, U of South Carolina
Columbia, SC 29208-0251
(803) 777-2005
Average award: $2,000
Minimum award: $1,000
Number of awards: 12
Deadline: April 30
College level: Freshman, Sophomore, Junior, Senior, Graduate
Majors/Fields: Communications, journalism
Criteria: Applicant must be the child of a U.S. citizen who works or has worked for a bona fide news organization in a print or broadcast media as a foreign correspondent, including both American and non-American news organizations. Children of noncitizens who work as foreign correspondents for American news organizations are eligible as a secondary priority. Priority is given to journalism and mass communications majors or minors, or liberal arts studies emphasizing areas of background knowledge valuable to journalists. Reapplication is required to retain scholarship. Awarded every year.
Contact: Jennifer H. McGill, Executive Director.

1601 American Airlines/AMR Management Club Community/Leadership Scholarship

American Airlines/AMR Management Club
4200 Amon-Carter Boulevard
P.O. Box 2526 CP2
Fort Worth, TX 76155
Minimum award: $1,500
Number of awards: 2
Deadline: March 15
College level: Freshman
Criteria: Applicant must be the dependent of an AMR Corporation employee who works in the Dallas-Fort Worth metroplex area. Awarded every year.
Contact: Chris Thomas, Scholarship Committee Chairperson, (817) 963-6189.

1602   American National Can Company Scholarship

American National Can Company
8770 West Bryn-Mawr
Chicago, IL 60631-3542
(312) 399-3476
Average award: $1,000
Maximum award: $4,000
Minimum award: $500
Maximum number of awards: 27
Minimum number of awards: 1
Deadline: March 1
College level: Freshman
Criteria: Applicant must be the child of an employee or retiree of American National Can Company or its U.S. subsidiaries. Selection is based on PSAT/NMSQT scores, academic record, minimum 3.0 culmulative GPA, leadership and extracurricular activities. Program is administered by the National Merit Scholarship Corporation. Satisfactory academic progress is required to retain scholarship. Awarded every year.
Contact: J. Hatch, Director of Personnel.

1603   AMETEK/KETEMA College Scholarship

AMETEK Foundation Inc.
Station Square
Paoli, PA 19301
(215) 647-2121
Minimum award: $2,000
Maximum number of awards: 6
Minimum number of awards: 5
Deadline: December 1 of junior year
College level: Freshman
Criteria: Applicant must be the child of an AMETEK or KETEMA employee and take the PSAT/NMSQT in October of their junior year. Contact local AMETEK headquarters for additional information. Awarded every year.
Contact: Chelle Carlson.

1604   Auxiliary of Group Health Cooperative of Puget Sound Health Career Scholarship

Auxiliary of Group Health Cooperative of Puget Sound
1730 Minor #1520
Seattle, WA 98101
Average award: $1,000
Number of awards: 12
Deadline: Early February
College level: Freshman, Sophomore, Junior, Senior
Majors/Fields: Health
Criteria: Applicant must be an employee of the Group Health Cooperative of Puget Sound, a Washington state resident, attend an accredited school in Washington, and be pursuing a health career. Reapplication required to retain scholarship. Awarded every year.
Contact: E. H. Smith, Chair of Scholarships, c/o Sue Dinauer, G.H.C. Volunteer Services, 2400 Fourth Avenue, Seattle, WA 98121.

1605   Burlington Northern Railroad Scholarship

Burlington Northern Railroad
3000 Continental Plaza
777 Main Street
Fort Worth, TX 76102
(817) 878-3061
Maximum award: $2,500
Minimum award: $1,000
Number of awards: 25
Deadline: November 30
College level: Freshman
Criteria: Applicant must be the child of a full-time Burlington Northern employee having at least two consecutive years of service; children of deceased or retired employees are also eligible. Children can be natural, adopted, or step-children provided they are claimed under the IRS tax guidlines. Applicant must take the SAT I, rank in the top third of class, have a minimum 3.0 GPA, attend an accredited college or university, and agree to attend college for four consecutive years. Minimum 2.5 GPA and full-time enrollment required to retain scholarship. Awarded every year.
Contact: Lueretha Jones, Employee Services Coordinator.

1606   Butler Manufacturing Company Scholarship

Butler Manufacturing Company Foundation
BMA Tower, 31st and Southwest Trafficway
P.O. Box 419917
Kansas City, MO 64141-0917
(816) 968-3208
Average award: $2,000
Number of awards: 8
Deadline: February 19
College level: Freshman
Criteria: Applicant must be a U.S. citizen and the child of an employee of Butler Manufacturing Co. Financial need must be demonstrated. Minimum 2.0 GPA is required to retain scholarship. Awarded every year.
Contact: Barbara L. Fay, Foundation Administrator.

1607   Charles H. Hood Fund

Charles H. Hood Fund
500 Rutherford Avenue
Boston, MA 02129
(617) 242-0600, extension 2444
Average award: $4,000
Number of awards: 6
Deadline: January 15
College level: Freshman, Sophomore, Junior, Senior
Criteria: Applicant must be the child of a H.P. Hood, Inc. employee.
Contact: Awards.

1608   Coca-Cola Scholars Program

Coca-Cola Scholars Foundation, Inc.
P.O. Box 442
Atlanta, GA 30301-0442
(404) 733-5420
Maximum award: $5,000
Minimum award: $1,000
Number of awards: 150
Deadline: October 31
College level: Freshman
Criteria: Selection is based upon leadership, character, and merit. Applicant must attend a high school which is located in a participating bottler's territory. Scholarship is renewable. Awarded every year.
Contact: Scholarships, (800) 306-2653.

1609   Commission on Classified Staff Affairs Scholarship

Clemson University
G-01 Sikes Hall
Clemson, SC 29634-5123
(803) 656-2280
Average award: $1,000
Number of awards: 2
Deadline: March 1
College level: Freshman, Sophomore, Junior, Senior
Criteria: Applicant must be the child of a currently employed, permanent, classified Clemson U staff member and demonstrate financial need. Satisfactory GPA with at least 12 credits per semester is required to retain scholarship. Awarded every year. Award may be used only at sponsoring institution.
Contact: Marvin Carmichael, Director of Financial Aid.

1610   Cone Mills Corporation Four-Year or Vocational/Technical Scholarship

Cone Mills Corporation
1201 Maple Street
Greensboro, NC 27405
(910) 379-6697
Maximum award: $2,500
Minimum award: $500
Number of awards: 25
Deadline: November 30
College level: Freshman, vo-tech students
Criteria: Applicant must be enrolled on a full-time basis and the child of an active, retired, or deceased employee of Cone Mills Corp. with one or more years of experience. Children of corporate officers and divisional officers are not eligible. Renewal is based on adherence to college's academic standards. Awarded every year.
Contact: Cathy Coltrane, Corporate Personnel Manager and EEO Coordinator.

1611   Connie M. Maynard Education Fund Program

Golden Corral Corporation
P.O. Box 29502
Raleigh, NC 27626
(919) 881-4487
Average award: $1,800
Maximum award: $2,000
Minimum award: $500
Maximum number of awards: 50
Minimum number of awards: 30
Deadline: March 15
College level: Freshman, Sophomore, Junior, Senior, Graduate, Doctoral, vocational/technical degree programs
Criteria: Applicant must have at least 870 hours of work in a Golden Corral Corp. restaurant and a minimum 2.5 GPA. Selection is based upon academic achievement, community involvement, potential to achieve education and career goals, and recommendation. Financial need is not considered. Applicant must maintain a minimum 2.0 GPA and have at least 200 hours of work in a Golden Corral Restaurant. Awarded every year.
Contact: Joanne Martin, HR Coordinator.

1612   CSX Transportation Corporation Scholarship

CSX Transportation Corporation
P.O. Box 5151
Richmond, VA 23220-8151
(800) 533-GRAD
Average award: $2,500
Number of awards: 115
Deadline: May 1
College level: Freshman, Sophomore, Junior, Senior
Criteria: Applicant must be a dependent of a CSX employee. Recipients are selected by the Richmond Area Scholarship Program. Awarded every year.
Contact: Mila Spaulding, Administrator.

1613   Daniel Swarovski & Co. Scholarship

Gemological Institute of America (GIA)
Financial Aid Office
1660 Stewart Street
Santa Monica, CA 90404-4088
(310) 829-2991
Average award: $1,625
Number of awards: 6
Deadline: Quarterly
Majors/Fields: Gemology
Criteria: Applicant must have at least three years prior employment in the jewelry industry, demonstrate financial need, and submit three letters of recommendation. Awarded every year.
Contact: Financial Aid Office, (310) 829-2991, extension 355 or 266.

1614   Dravo Corporation Scholarship

Dravo Corporation
3600 One Oliver Plaza
Pittsburgh, PA 15222-2682
(412) 566-3000
Minimum award: $2,500
Maximum number of awards: 5
Minimum number of awards: 2
Deadline: April 9
College level: Freshman, Sophomore
Criteria: Applicant's parent must have been a full-time employee of the Dravo Corp. for at least one year. Award pays $2,500 a year for two years. Children of employees who are officers of the company are not eligible. Renewable for second year if recipient maintains satisfactory GPA. Awarded every year.
Contact: Corporate Employee Relations Department.

1615   Dun and Bradstreet Merit Scholarship

Dunn and Bradstreet Corporation
299 Park Avenue
New York, NY 10171
Maximum award: $2,000
Minimum award: $500
Number of awards: 4
Deadline: October 1
Criteria: Applicant must be the child of an active or retired employee of Dun and Bradstreet Corp. and its subsidiaries. He or she must take the PSAT/NMSQT exam during October of junior year of high school. Qualification selection is automatic through the procedures of the National Merit Scholarship Corporation on the basis of PSAT/NMSQT scores, need, and high school grades. Contact high school guidance counselor for information on the PSAT/NMSQT exam. Awarded every year.
Contact: Scholarships.

1616   Eastman Kodak Scholarship

University of Tennessee, Knoxville
Financial Aid Office
115 Student Services Building
Knoxville, TN 37994
(615) 974-3131
Average award: Tuition and fees
Number of awards: 5
Deadline: February 1
College level: Sophomore, Junior, Senior
Majors/Fields: Chemical engineering, electrical engineering, industrial engineering, mechanical engineering
Criteria: Applicant must be the child of an Eastman Kodak employee, U.S. citizen, rank in top quarter of class, and be a National Merit scholar. Selection is based upon academic excellence without regard to financial need. Scholarship is renewable. Awarded every year. Award may be used only at sponsoring institution.
Contact: College of Engineering, 118 Perkins Hall, Knoxville, TN 37996, (615) 974-2454.

1617   EEOC Endowed Scholarship

General Motors Corporation
3044 W. Grand Boulevard
Detroit, MI 48202
Maximum award: $2,500
Number of awards: 462
College level: Sophomore, Junior, Senior
Criteria: Applicant must be an employee or the child of an employee of General Motors Corp. and be a member of one of the following minority groups: Alaskan Native, American Indian, Asian-American, African-American/Black, Mexican-American/Chicano, Hispanic, Puerto Rican. Contact the university to ask if it participates in the scholarship program.
Contact: L.J. Wicker, Manager, Education Relations, (313) 556-3509.

1618   Faculty/Staff Tuition Benefits

Georgetown University
37th and O Streets, NW
Washington, DC 20057
(202) 687-4547
Average award: $14,780
Maximum award: $18,400
Minimum award: $1,830
Number of awards: 249
Deadline: Two months before registration
College level: Freshman, Sophomore, Junior, Senior, Graduate, Doctoral
Criteria: Applicant must be a dependent of or a full-time faculty or staff member. Scholarship is renewable. Awarded every year. Award may be used only at sponsoring institution.
Contact: Patricia McWade, Dean of Student Financial Services, G-19 Healy Hall.

1619   Francis Ouimet Scholarship

Francis Ouimet Scholarship Fund
190 Park Road
Weston, MA 02193-3401
Average award: $1,700
Maximum award: $5,000
Minimum award: $500
Number of awards: 240
Deadline: December 1
College level: Freshman, Sophomore, Junior, Senior
Criteria: Applicant must have worked at least three years at a Massachusetts golf course as a caddie, proshop worker, or green's crew worker. Minimum 2.0 GPA is required for renewal. Awarded every year.
Contact: Jennifer R. Gilvey, Scholarship Director.

1620   George A. Hormel and Company Scholarship

George A. Hormel and Company
P.O. Box 800
Austin, MN 55912
(507) 437-5611
Maximum award: $3,000
Minimum award: $750
Number of awards: 5
Deadline: January 11
College level: Freshman
Criteria: Applicant must be a high school student who is the child of an employee of George A. Hormel & Co. or its subsidiaries. Selection is by the National Merit Scholarship Corp. upon the basis of test scores, academic records, leadership, and extracurricular accomplishments. Applicant must take the PSAT and NMSQT exams during junior year of high school and attend a regionally accredited U.S. college. Scholarship is renewable. Awarded every year.
Contact: V. Allen Krejci, Scholarship Program Director.

1621   Gerber Companies Foundation Scholarship

Gerber Companies Foundation
445 State Street
Fremont, MI 49413-0001
Maximum award: $1,200
Minimum award: $1,200
Number of awards: 120
Deadline: March 31
College level: Freshman, Sophomore, Junior, Senior
Criteria: Applicant must be a dependent of an employee of Gerber Products Co. or its subsidiaries. Minimum 2.0 GPA is required to retain scholarship. Awarded every year.
Contact: Cynthia M. Ebert, Administrator, (616) 928-2759.

1622   Gibbs Scholarship

Gibbs Wire & Steel Company
Metals Drive
Southington, CT 06489
(203) 527-2027
Average award: $4,000
Number of awards: 4
Deadline: April 15
Criteria: Applicant must be the child of a Gibbs Wire & Steel employee. Scholarship is renewable. Awarded every year.
Contact: Robert B. Johnson, Vice President for Special Projects, (203) 621-0121.

1623   Gilbert Associates, Inc. Corporate Scholarship

Gilbert Associates Inc.
P.O. Box 1498
Reading, PA 19603
(215) 775-2600, extension 7094
Maximum award: $2,000
Number of awards: 6
Deadline: January 31
College level: Freshman
Criteria: Applicant must be a high school senior who is the dependent child of a regular, full-time employee of Gilbert Associates and its subsidiaries; employee must have completed one year of continuous service prior to May 31 of the scholarship year. Applicant must have participated in extracurricular activities, demonstrate motivation, self-discipline, and financial need. A personal interview is required. Awards are granted for one, two, three, or four years. Awarded every year.
Contact: Lillian A. Wilson, Scholarship Administrator.

1624   Halton Scholars

Halton Foundation
P.O. Box 3377
Portland, OR 97208
(503) 288-6411
Average award: $1,500
Maximum award: $3,100
Number of awards: 5
Deadline: January 31
College level: Freshman, Sophomore, Junior, Senior, Graduate, Doctoral
Criteria: Applicant must be less than 28 years of age and the child of a Halton Co. employee. Scholarship is renewable. Awarded every year.
Contact: Susan H. Findlay, Manager.

1625   Henry R. Towne Scholarship

Eaton Corporation
World Headquarters Eaton Center
Cleveland, OH 44114
(216) 523-5000
Maximum award: $3,000
Minimum award: $1,000
Number of awards: 12
Deadline: December 31
College level: Unspecified undergraduate
Criteria: Applicants must be the child of an Eaton Corp. employee and be a high school senior who has taken the PSAT/NMSQT. Selection is based upon test scores, academic record, class rank (top fifth), leadership, extracurricular activities, and other factors as determined by the National Merit Scholarship Corp. Scholarship is renewable. Awarded every year.
Contact: Thomas R. Freyberg, Human Resource Manager.

1626 James E. DeLong Foundation Scholarship

James E. DeLong Foundation, Inc.
1000 West Saint Paul Avenue
Waukesha, WI 53188
(414) 549-2773
Average award: $1,500
Number of awards: 2
Deadline: April 1
College level: Freshman
Criteria: Applicant must be the child of an employee of the Waukesha Engine Division, Waukesha, Wisc. Awarded every year.
Contact: Charles V. Zalewski, Secretary-Treasurer.

1627 John H. Mathis Scholarship

Lone Star Industries
300 First Stamford Place
Stamford, CT 06912-0014
(203) 969-8500
Minimum award: $2,000
Number of awards: 2
Deadline: March 31
College level: Freshman, Sophomore, Junior
Criteria: Applicant must rank in the top fifth of class and be a dependent son or daughter of a full-time Lone Star (or subsidiary) employee. Award is given to the two highest ranked applicants in the competition. Renewable for up to four years if good grades are maintained. Awarded every year.
Contact: Barbara Schroeder, Personnel Representative.

1628 Johnson Controls Foundation Scholarship

Johnson Controls Foundation
5757 North Green Bay Avenue
Box 591
Milwaukee, WI 53201
(414) 228-2296
Minimum award: $1,750
Number of awards: 16
Deadline: February 1
College level: Freshman, Sophomore, Junior, Senior
Criteria: Applicant must be the child of a Johnson Controls, Inc. employee. Satisfactory academic progress is required to retain scholarship. Awarded every year.
Contact: Human Resources Consultant, (414) 228-1200.

1629 Joseph and Virginia Altschuller Scholarship

University of Toledo
Financial Aid Office
Toledo, OH 43606-3390
(419) 537-2056
Average award: $2,500
Number of awards: 5
Deadline: March 1
College level: Freshman, Sophomore, Junior, Senior
Criteria: Applicant must be an employee or the dependent of an employee of Seaway Foodtown and enrolled full time. Award is for four years. Award may be used only at sponsoring institution.

1630 Kohler Co. College Scholarship

Kohler Co.
444 Highland Drive
Public Affairs Department
Kohler, WI 53044
(414) 457-4441
Average award: $1,667
Maximum award: $2,000
Minimum award: $500
Number of awards: 9
Deadline: February 15
College level: Freshman
Criteria: Applicant must be a U.S. citizen and an employee or the child of an employee of Kohler or its U.S. subsidiaries. Applicant should rank in the top tenth of class and have a near perfect GPA. Good academic standing, full-time enrollment, and continuing employment are required to retain scholarship. Awarded every year.
Contact: Peter J. Fetterer, Manager of Media and Civic Services.

1631 Luther A. Sizemore Foundation Scholarship

New Mexico State University
Box 30001
Department 5100
Las Cruces, NM 88003-0001
(505) 646-4105
Average award: Full tuition
Number of awards: 2
Deadline: March 1
College level: Freshman, Sophomore, Junior, Senior
Criteria: Preference is given to dependents of carpenters throughout New Mexico. Minimum 2.0 GPA and at least 12 credit hours per semester are required to retain scholarship. Awarded every year. Award may be used only at sponsoring institution.
Contact: Greeley W. Myers, Director of Financial Aid.

1632 M.A. Hanna Company Scholarships

M.A. Hanna Company
1301 East 9th Street, Suite 3600
Cleveland, OH 44114-1860
(216) 589-4000
Maximum award: $1,500
Number of awards: 50
Deadline: June 15
College level: Freshman, Sophomore, Junior, Senior
Criteria: Applicant must be the child, grandchild, or spouse of a full-time employee of M.A. Hanna Co. Scholarship is renewable. Awarded every year.
Contact: John S. Pyke, Jr., Vice President/Secretary.

1633 Maguire Educational Scholarships

Panhandle Eastern Corporation
P.O. Box 1642
Houston, TX 77252-1642
(713) 627-4608
Average award: $1,250
Number of awards: 10
Deadline: October 1
College level: Freshman, Sophomore, Junior, Senior
Criteria: Applicant must be the child of an employee or retiree of the Panhandle Eastern Corp. who has five years of service with the corporation. Children of officers and directors are not eligible. Scholastic standing acceptable to college must be maintained to continue scholarship. Awarded every year.
Contact: Dianne Wilson, Scholarship Coordinator.

1634 McDonnell Douglas Scholarship

McDonnell Douglas Scholarship Foundation
Mail Code 802-11
3855 Lakewood Boulevard
Long Beach, CA 90846
(310) 593-2612
Average award: $1,500
Maximum award: $4,000
Maximum number of awards: 56
Minimum number of awards: 30
Deadline: First Friday in March
College level: Freshman
Criteria: Applicant must be the dependent child, stepchild, or legally adopted child of an active, retired, disabled, or deceased employee of a McDonnell Douglas component company or subsidiary. Applicant must rank in the top third of class. Selection is based upon class standing, college entrance exams, leadership, lettering in varsity sports, extracurricular activities, community activity, and verifiable employment. Good academic standing is required to retain scholarship. Awarded every year.
Contact: Beverly A. Hoskinson, Administrator.

1635 Merit Gasoline Foundation Scholarship

Merit Gasoline Foundation Scholarship
551 West Lancaster Avenue
Haverford, PA 19041
Maximum award: $3,000
Minimum award: $1,000
Number of awards: 4
Deadline: May 15
College level: Freshman, Sophomore, Junior, Senior
Criteria: Applicant must be the child or stepchild of a full-time employee of the Merit Oil Corp. and/or its affiliates for at least two consecutive years. Also eligible are dependents of employees who are retired under the company's pension plan, totally disabled due to an accident or illness under the wage continuation program, or deceased, but fully qualified prior to death. Selection is based upon financial need, academic achievement, SAT I scores, and evaluation character, quality of leadership, work habits, and general interests. Satisfactory academic progress is required to retain scholarship. Awarded every year.
Contact: Executive Director.

1636 Olivia Jackson McGee Endowed Scholarship

Clemson University
G-01 Sikes Hall
Clemson, SC 29634-5123
(803) 656-2280
Average award: $2,000
Number of awards: 1
Deadline: March 1
College level: Freshman, Sophomore, Junior, Senior
Majors/Fields: Architecture, English
Criteria: Applicant must be the child or grandchild of a Clemson U tenured professor who is studying architecture or English; if no eligible applicant meets the criteria, the scholarship will be awarded to a student in architecture or English. Awarded every year. Award may be used only at sponsoring institution.
Contact: Marvin Carmichael, Director of Financial Aid.

1637 Outboard Marine Corporation Scholarship

Outboard Marine Corporation
100 Seahorse Drive
Waukegan, IL 60085-2195
(312) 689-6200
Average award: $1,000
Number of awards: 11
Deadline: March 30
College level: Freshman, Sophomore, Junior, Senior
Criteria: Applicant must be the child of a full-time employee of the Outboard Marine Corp. and meet minimum academic criteria. Scholarship is renewable. Awarded every year.
Contact: Denise Charts, Manager of Personnel and Corporate Employees.

1638 Pitney-Bowes Scholarship

Pitney-Bowes Inc.
One Elmcroft (52-11)
Stamford, CT 06926-0700
(203) 351-6203
Average award: $2,500
Number of awards: 30
Deadline: December 31
Criteria: Applicant must be a graduating high school senior, rank in top third of class, and be the dependent of a Pitney-Bowes employee. Selection is based upon high school class rank, SAT I scores, potential accomplishments, and financial need. Awarded every year.
Contact: Scholarships.

1639 President's Scholarship

Liberty University
P.O. Box 20000
Lynchburg, VA 24506-8001
(804) 582-2270
Average award: $1,000
Number of awards: 4
Deadline: August 1; January 1
College level: Freshman
Criteria: Applicant's parents must be employed full time in Christian ministry. Satisfactory academic progress is required to retain scholarship. Awarded every year. Award may be used only at sponsoring institution.
Contact: Penny Hutchison, Admissions Representative, (804) 582-2707.

1640 Prudential's Merit Scholarship

Prudential Insurance Company
P.O. Box 388
Fort Washington, PA 19034
Maximum award: $3,000
Minimum award: $500
Criteria: Applicant must be the child of an employee of the Prudential Insurance Company who scored in the upper percentile of the PSAT/NMSQT test given during the junior year of high school. Finalist's parent must be or have been a member of the home office or field staff (active or retired) on January 1st of the year in which the applicant will complete high school and be entering college. Awarded every year.
Contact: Scholarships.

1641 Rahr Foundation Scholarship

Rahr Malting Company
567 Grain Exchange Building
P.O. Box 15186
Minneapolis, MN 55414
(612) 332-5161
Average award: $2,000
Maximum number of awards: 2
Minimum number of awards: 4
Deadline: March 15
College level: Sophomore, Junior, Senior, Graduate
Criteria: Applicant must be the child of a current Rahr Malting Co. employee. Rahr branch offices have applications. Satisfactory GPA and full-time status are required to retain scholarship. Awarded every year.
Contact: Mary Gresham, Secretary and Director.

1642 Quaker Chemical Foundation Scholarship

Quaker Chemical Foundation
P.O. Box 809
Elm & Lee Streets
Conshohocken, PA 19428-0809
(215) 832-4313
Average award: $2,750
Maximum award: $4,000
Minimum award: $1,500
Number of awards: 8
Deadline: December
College level: Freshman, Sophomore, Junior, Senior
Criteria: Applicant must be the child of a Quaker Chemical employee in a baccalaureate or nonbaccalaureate degree program. Students at certain high schools designated by the Foundation as participating, may compete for a scholarship for baccalaureate degree programs, with the recommendation of their high school. Scholarship is renewable. Awarded every year.
Contact: Karen Miller, Secretary to the Foundation.

1643 Stanadyne Inc. Educational Grant

Stanadyne, Inc.
277 Woodland Avenue
Elyria, OH 44035
(216) 323-3341
Average award: $2,000
Number of awards: 12
Deadline: March 1
College level: Freshman
Criteria: Applicant must be the child of a full-time employee of Stanadyne, Inc. Awarded every year.

1644 State Farm Companies Foundation Scholarship

State Farm Companies Foundation
One State Farm Plaza
Bloomington, IL 61710
(309) 766-2161
Maximum award: $6,000
Minimum award: $2,000
Maximum number of awards: 75
Minimum number of awards: 75
Deadline: December 31
College level: Freshman
Criteria: Applicant must be the child of a full-time State Farm Insurance employee or agent. Applicant must meet National Merit Scholarship Corporation requirements. Awarded every year.
Contact: Lynne Tammeus, Senior Program Coordinator, (309) 766-2039.

1645 Stone Foundation Scholarship

Stone Foundation Scholarship
150 North Michigan Avenue
Chicago, IL 60601-7568
Average award: $2,000
Number of awards: 13
Deadline: April 1
College level: Freshman
Criteria: Applicant must be the child of a full-time Stone Container Corp. employee who has worked at the company for at least two years. Selection is based upon scholarship, character, community, and student activities. Financial need may be considered. Scholarship is renewable at the discretion of the scholarship committee. Recipient must maintain a minimum 2.0 GPA. Awarded every year.
Contact: Betsy Stetter, Personnel Supervisor, (312) 580-2291.

1646 Texaco Foundation Employee Scholarship

Texaco Foundation
2000 Westchester Avenue
White Plains, NY 10650
(914) 253-7584
Average award: $2,500
Number of awards: 100
Deadline: November 15
College level: Freshman
Criteria: Applicant must be the child of a Texaco employee or retiree who has been employed at least one year. Scholarship is renewable. Awarded every year.
Contact: Emma Damm, Coordinator for Corporate Contributions.

1647 Thomasville Furniture Industries Foundation Scholarship

Thomasville Furniture Industries Foundation
Wachovia Bank and Trust Company
P.O. Box 3099
Winston-Salem, NC 27102
Maximum award: $1,500
Minimum award: $150
Number of awards: 39
Criteria: Applicant must be the child of a regular employee of Thomasville Furniture Industries Inc. Awarded every year.
Contact: Scholarships, c/o Wachovia Bank and Trust Company.

1648 Walton Foundation Scholarship

Wal-Mart Foundation
702 South West 8th Street
Bentonville, AR 72716
(501) 273-6878
Average award: $1,500
Deadline: March 1
College level: Freshman
Criteria: Applicant must be the child of a Wal-Mart employee who has been a full-time associate for a full year prior to the deadline. Selection is based upon academic achievement, ACT or SAT I scores, extracurricular activities, leadership qualities, and financial need. Scholarship is renewable. Awarded every year.
Contact: Scott Jackson.

1649 Washington Post Thomas Ewing Memorial Education Grant

Washington Post
Thomas Ewing Memorial Carrier Scholarship
1150 15th Street, NW
Washington, DC 20079
(202) 334-5799
Average award: $1,000
Maximum award: $2,000
Number of awards: 35
Deadline: January 29
College level: Freshman, Sophomore, Junior, Senior, Graduate, Doctoral, technical or vocational school students
Criteria: Applicant must be a Washington Post carrier who has been on the route at least 18 months. Awarded every year.
Contact: Jay O'Hare or Mary McElroy, Sales Managers.

1650 Western Golf Association Evans Scholars Foundation Scholarship

Western Golf Association
Evans Scholars Foundation
Golf, IL 60029
(708) 724-4600
Average award: Full tuition and housing
Number of awards: 200
Deadline: November 1
College level: Freshman
Criteria: Applicant must have caddied for a minimum of two years at a Western Golf Association member club, rank in the top quarter of graduating class, have outstanding personal character, and demonstrate financial need. Scholarship is renewable. Awarded every year.
Contact: Scholarship Committee.

1651 Weyerhaeuser Company Foundation College Scholarship Program

Weyerhaeuser Company Foundation
CHIF31
Tacoma, WA 98477
(206) 924-2629
Maximum award: $4,000
Minimum award: $500
Number of awards: 30
Deadline: January 1 of high school junior year
College level: Freshman
Criteria: Applicant must be the child of a Weyerhaeuser employee who has had one year of continuous service by December 1 of the child's junior year in high school and be in service on March 1 of child's senior year of high school. Children of retired or deceased employees who had one year of continuous service prior to their death or retirement are also eligible. Interested applicants should take the PSAT/NMSQT exam in October of their junior year in high school. Selection is based upon PSAT/NMSQT scores, academic record, qualities of leadership, and extracurricular accomplishments. Satisfactory academic standing is required to retain scholarship for up to four years. Awarded every year.
Contact: Penny Paul, Program Manager.

1652 Weyerhaeuser Company Foundation Community Education Scholarship Program

Weyerhaeuser Company Foundation
CHIF31
Tacoma, WA 98477
(206) 924-2629
Maximum award: $1,500
Minimum award: $500
Number of awards: 17
Deadline: January 1 of high school senior year
College level: Freshman
Criteria: Applicant must be the child of a Weyerhaeuser employee who has had at least one year of continuous, full-time service by December 1 of the child's senior year in high school and is in service with the company on March 1 of the award year. Children of retired or deceased employees who had one year of continuous service with the company prior to their death or retirement are also eligible. Applicant must show career and academic potential as measured by a combination of factors such as past academic performance, school and community participation, advisor appraisal, work experience, and career objectives. Financial need is not a factor in selection and determines the amount of the award only. Applicant must plan to attend a community college. Two-year award is renewable and transferable to a four-year institution after one year. Awarded every year.
Contact: Penny Paul, Program Manager.

Culinary Arts/Baking

1653 Baking Industry Scholarships

American Institute of Baking
1213 Bakers Way
Manhattan, KS 66502
(913) 537-4750
Average award: $2,500
Maximum award: $3,300
Minimum award: $500
Number of awards: 40
Majors/Fields: Baking, maintenance engineering
Criteria: Applicant must be planning to seek new employment in the baking industry. Experience in the industry or approved substitute is required. Selection is based upon educational background, work experience, recommendations, and financial need. Applicant must be attending or accepted for admission to AIB's maintenance engineering or baking science and technology courses. Awarded every year. Award may be used only at sponsoring institution.
Contact: Ken Embers.

Ethnic/Race Specific

1654 A.T. Anderson Memorial Scholarship

American Indian Science & Engineering Society
Scholarship Coordinator
1630 30th Street, Suite 301
Boulder, CO 80301-1014
(303) 492-8658
Maximum award: $2,000
Minimum award: $1,000
Deadline: June 15
College level: Freshman, Sophomore, Junior, Senior, Graduate, Doctoral
Majors/Fields: Business, health, natural resources, science, engineering, math secondary education, science secondary education
Criteria: Applicant must be 25 percent American Indian or be recognized as a member of a tribe, have a minimum 2.0 GPA, be a full-time student, and be a member of the American Indian Science & Engineering Society. Awarded every year.
Contact: Roberta Manuelito, Scholarship Coordinator.

1655 AANO Scholarship

Albanian-American National Organization Fund, Inc.
395 Broadway
Unit #L3E
Cambridge, MA 02139
Maximum award: $1,000
Number of awards: 11
Deadline: April 30
College level: Freshman, Sophomore, Junior, Senior, Graduate, Doctoral
Criteria: Applicant must be of Albanian ethnicity and should be a U.S. or Canadian citizen. If applicant is not a U.S. or Canadian citizen, then he or she must have been enrolled in and attended two years of school (high school, college, or graduate school) in the U.S. or Canada. Awarded every year.
Contact: Sandra Kosta, Scholarship Chairperson.

1656 Academic Excellence Scholarship

University of Houston
129 Ezekiel W. Cullen Building
Houston, TX 77204-2161
(713) 743-9051
Average award: $1,500
Maximum award: $2,500
Minimum award: $1,000
Number of awards: 127
Deadline: April 1
College level: Freshman
Criteria: Applicant must be a black or Hispanic student. Minimum 2.0 GPA and 12 credit hours per semester are required to retain scholarship. Awarded every year. Award may be used only at sponsoring institution.
Contact: Robert Sheridan, Director of Scholarships & Financial Aid.

1657 Achievers Award

University of Oklahoma
University Affairs
900 Asp Avenue, Room 236
Norman, OK 73019-0401
(405) 325-1701
Maximum award: $3,000
Minimum award: $1,000
Number of awards: 139
Deadline: March 1
College level: Sophomore, Junior, Senior
Criteria: Applicant must be an ethnic minority. Selection is based upon academic achievement and leadership. Awarded every year. Award may be used only at sponsoring institution.
Contact: Student Support Services, Hester Hall, Room 200, Norman, OK 73019, (405) 325-3163.

1658   African-American/Black Students Scholarship

University of Southern Mississippi
Office of Recruitment and Orientation
Box 5166
Hattiesburg, MS 39406-5166
(601) 266-5000
Average award: $2,000
Deadline: April 1
College level: Freshman
Criteria: Applicant must be an African-American, have a minimum high school average of 90, and have a minimum composite ACT score of 25 (combined SAT I score of 1030). Awarded every year. Award may be used only at sponsoring institution.
Contact: Office of Recruitment and Orientation.

1659   AGBU Fellowship Program

Armenian General Benevolent Union
31 West 52nd Street
10th Floor
New York, NY 10019-6118
(212) 765-8260, extension 114
Average award: $8,000
Deadline: May 15
College level: Doctoral
Majors/Fields: Journalism, International Relations, Public Administration, Education Administration, Armenian Studies
Criteria: Applicant must be of Armenian heritage and be a full-time graduate student seeking a master's degree at a highly- or most-competitive U.S. institution. Awarded every year.
Contact: Maral Achian, Administrator of Scholarship Program

1660   Agnes Jones Jackson Scholarship

National Association for the Advancement of Colored People (NAACP)
4805 Mount Hope Drive
Baltimore, MD 21215-3297
(410) 358-8900
Average award: $1,500
Maximum award: $2,500
Deadline: April 30
College level: Freshman, Sophomore, Junior, Senior, Graduate, Doctoral
Criteria: Applicant must be a current, regular member of the NAACP for at least one year or a fully paid life member, and must not have reached age 25 by the April 30 deadline. Undergraduate applicant must have a minimum GPA of 2.5 and graduate applicant must have a minimum 3.0 GPA. Awarded every year.
Contact: Andrea E. Moss, Education Department.

1661   American Indian Endowed Scholarship

Washington Higher Education Coordinating Board
917 Lakeridge Way
P.O. Box 43430
Olympia, WA 98504-3430
(206) 753-3571
Average award: $1,000
Number of awards: 3
College level: Freshman, Sophomore, Junior, Senior
Criteria: Applicant must be a resident of Washington state, an American Indian, and show financial need. Awarded every year.
Contact: Elizabeth A. Gebhardt, Assistant Director of Student Financial Aid, (206) 753-4592.

1662   American Indian Scholarship Legislative Grant

North Carolina State Education Assistance Authority
Box 2688
Chapel Hill, NC 27515-2688
(919) 549-8614
Maximum award: $5,000
Minimum award: $700
College level: Freshman, Sophomore, Junior, Senior, Graduate, Doctoral
Criteria: Applicant must be a North Carolina resident, a member of an Indian tribe recognized by the state or federal government, demonstrate financial need, and be enrolled at one of the UNC constituent institutions. Good academic standing and continued financial need are required to retain scholarship. Awarded every year.
Contact: Financial aid office at eligible school.

1663   American Indian Tuition Waiver

University of Oklahoma
University Affairs
900 Asp Avenue, Room 236
Norman, OK 73019-0401
(405) 325-1701
Average award: $3,000
Deadline: July 15 (preferred)
College level: Freshman, Sophomore, Junior, Senior
Criteria: Applicant must be a nonresident American Indian who is affiliated with one of the 34 federally recognized Indian tribes located within the Oklahoma state boundaries. Award is for a maximum of five years. Awarded every year. Award may be used only at sponsoring institution.
Contact: Office of High School and College Relations, Boyd House, 407 West Boyd Street, Norman, OK 73019, (405) 325-2151.

1664   American-Scandinavian Foundation Fellowships and Grants

American-Scandinavian Foundation
725 Park Avenue
New York, NY 10021
(212) 879-9779
Maximum award: $15,000
Minimum award: $2,500
Number of awards: 30
Deadline: November 1
College level: Graduate, Doctoral, postdoctoral research
Criteria: Applicant must have completed undergraduate studies and have competence in the language of the country (Denmark, Finland, Iceland, Norway, or Sweden). U.S. citizenship or permanent residency is required. Recipient must reapply. Awarded every year.
Contact: Ellen McKey, Fellowship Program Administrator.

1665   Angela Scholarship

National Italian American Foundation (NIAF)
Educational Scholarship Program
1860 19th Street, NW
Washington, DC 20009-5599
(202) 638-2137
Minimum award: $2,500
Deadline: May 31
College level: Freshman
Criteria: Applicant must be Italian-American, demonstrate financial need, submit transcript, and be an entering freshman with an exemplary academic record showing social responsibilities during high school. Awarded every year.
Contact: Dr. Maria Lombardo, Education Director.

1666   APS Corporate-Sponsored Scholarship for Minority Undergraduate Students Who Major in Physics

American Physical Society
335 East 45th Street
New York, NY 10017-3483
(212) 682-7341
Average award: $2,000
Maximum award: $2000 awarded to applicant; $500 awarded to Physics department
Number of awards: 32
Deadline: February 26
College level: Freshman, Sophomore, Junior
Majors/Fields: Physics
Criteria: Applicant must be a U.S. citizen of black, Hispanic, or Native American descent. Applicant must major in physics with satisfactory GPA to retain scholarship for one additional year. Awarded every year.
Contact: Arlene Modeste, Program Coordinator.

1667   Armenian Students' Association Scholarship

Armenian Students Association of America, Inc.
395 Concord Avenue
Belmont, MA 02178
(617) 484-9548
Average award: $1,000
Maximum award: $1,500
Minimum award: $500
Maximum number of awards: 60
Minimum number of awards: 30
Deadline: March 15
College level: Sophomore, Junior, Senior, Graduate, Doctoral
Criteria: Applicant must be of Armenian ancestry, be a full-time student attending a four-year, accredited college or university in the U.S., and have completed at least the first year of college. Selection is based upon financial need, academic performance, ability for self help, and participation in extracurricular activities. Request scholarship application by January 15. Awarded every year.
Contact: Christine Williamson, Scholarship Administrator.

1668   Arnold CU Opportunity Scholarship

University of Colorado at Boulder
Campus Box 106
Boulder, CO 80309-0106
(303) 492-5091
Maximum award: $2,000
Minimum award: $1,000
Number of awards: 40
Deadline: March 1
College level: Freshman
Criteria: Applicant must be Asian-American, African-American, Hispanic, American Indian, or migrant. Minimum 2.3 GPA is required to retain scholarship for three additional years. Awarded every year. Award may be used only at sponsoring institution.
Contact: Office of Financial Aid.

1669   Benjamin Eaton Scholarship

National Foster Parent Association, Inc.
9 Dartmoor Drive
Crystal Lake, IL 60014-3297
(815) 455-2527
Maximum award: $1,000
Number of awards: 4
Deadline: March 1
College level: Freshman
Criteria: Applicant must be a foster, adoptive, or biological child in a licensed foster home and a member of the National Foster Parent Association. Awarded every year.
Contact: C.W. Black, Scholarships.

1670   Bert Price Scholarship

Grand Valley State University
Allendale, MI 49401
(616) 895-3234
Average award: $2,658
Number of awards: 90
Deadline: February 1
College level: Freshman, community college graduates
Criteria: Applicant must be a minority student with a disadvantaged background. Minimum 2.75 GPA is required to retain scholarship. Awarded every year. Award may be used only at sponsoring institution.
Contact: Ken Fridsma, Director of Financial Aid.

1671   Board of Governors Scholarship

Indiana University of Pennsylvania
308 Pratt Hall
Indiana, PA 15705
(412) 357-2218
Average award: $3,088
Maximum number of awards: 90
Minimum number of awards: 61
Deadline: None
College level: Freshman, Sophomore, Junior, Senior
Criteria: Applicant must be black or Hispanic, demonstrate leadership, rank in the top quarter of class, and have a minimum combined SAT I score of 1000. Minimum 2.5 GPA after freshman year, 2.75 GPA thereafter is required to retain scholarship. Awarded every year. Award may be used only at sponsoring institution.
Contact: Patricia C. McCarthy, Assistant Director of Financial Aid.

1672   Carmela Gagliardi Fellowships

National Italian American Foundation (NIAF)
Educational Scholarship Program
1860 19th Street, NW
Washington, DC 20009-5599
(202) 638-2137
Maximum award: $5,000
Number of awards: 4
Deadline: May 31
College level: Medical students
Majors/Fields: Medicine
Criteria: Applicant must be Italian-American, demonstrate financial need, rank in the top quarter of class, and submit transcript.
Contact: Dr. Maria Lombardo, Education Director.

1673   CERT Scholars Fund

Council of Energy Resource Tribes (CERT) Education Fund
1999 Broadway
Suite 2600
Denver, CO 80202-5726
(303) 297-2378
Average award: $1,000
Minimum award: $500
Number of awards: 50
Deadline: Mid-March, Mid-August
College level: Freshman, Sophomore, Junior, Senior, Graduate, Doctoral
Majors/Fields: Business, engineering, science
Criteria: Applicant must be a member of an American Indian tribe and must have successfully completed a high school summer transition program offered by CERT. Minimum 2.5 GPA is required to retain scholarship. Awarded every year.
Contact: Lesley Jackson, Education Director.

1674   Challenge Scholarship

University of Pittsburgh, Pittsburgh Campus
4200 Fifth Avenue
Pittsburgh, PA 15260
(412) 624-4141
Average award: $4,000
Minimum award: $1,000
Number of awards: 30
Deadline: January 15
College level: Freshman
Majors/Fields: Arts/sciences
Criteria: Applicant must be a minority student enrolled in the Coll of Arts and Sciences. Selection is based upon high school performance and test scores. Scholarship is renewable. Awarded every year. Award may be used only at sponsoring institution.
Contact: Betsy A. Porter, Director of Admissions & Financial Aid, (412) 624-7164.

1675   Chancellor's Minority Student Leadership Scholarship

East Carolina University
East Fifth Street
Greenville, NC 27858
(919) 757-6495
Average award: $1,000
Maximum number of awards: 15
Minimum number of awards: 10
College level: Freshman
Criteria: Applicant must be an African-American student committed to leadership development and community involvement. Awarded every year. Award may be used only at sponsoring institution.
Contact: Brian Haynes, Associate Vice Chancellor and Director of Minority Student Affairs.

1676   Charles B. Duffy Scholarship

State University of New York at Buffalo
Buffalo, NY 14260
(716) 831-2000
Average award: $2,554
College level: Doctoral
Criteria: Applicant must be of Polish descent. Scholarship is renewable. Awarded every year. Award may be used only at sponsoring institution.
Contact: Scholarships.

1677   Chicano Faculty/Staff Fund Scholarship

New Mexico State University
Box 30001
Department 5100
Las Cruces, NM 88003-0001
(505) 646-4105
Average award: $1,700
Deadline: April 1 (fall), October 1 (spring)
College level: Junior, Senior
Criteria: Applicant must be enrolled at least half time, demonstrate financial need, and have completed at least 24 credits with a minimum 2.0 GPA. Reapplication is required to retain scholarship. Awarded every year. Award may be used only at sponsoring institution.
Contact: Greeley W. Myers, Director of Financial Aid.

1678   Chinese Professional Club of Houston Scholarship

Chinese Professional Club of Houston
11302 Fallbrook Drive
Suite 304
Houston, TX 77065
(713) 955-0115
Average award: $1,000
Maximum award: $1,500
Minimum award: $600
Number of awards: 10
Deadline: November 15
College level: Freshman
Criteria: Applicant must be of Chinese descent and reside in the greater Houston metropolitan area. Awarded every year.
Contact: James Tang, M.D., Scholarship Committee Chairman.

1679   Clara B. Williams Scholarship

New Mexico State University
Box 30001
Department 5100
Las Cruces, NM 88003-0001
(505) 646-4105
Maximum award: $1,700
Deadline: March 1
College level: Freshman, Sophomore, Junior, Senior
Criteria: Applicant must be a black U.S. citizen with high academic merit. Awarded every year. Award may be used only at sponsoring institution.
Contact: Greeley W. Myers, Director of Financial Aid.

1680   Community College Minority Transfer Scholarship

University of Memphis
Scates Hall 204
Memphis, TN 38152
(901) 678-3213
Average award: $2,442
Deadline: April 1
College level: Junior
Criteria: Applicant must be African-American with an associate degree and a minimum 2.8 GPA. Minimum 2.8 GPA and a service requirement of 30 hours per year are required to retain scholarship. Awarded every year. Award may be used only at sponsoring institution.
Contact: Dr. Sue Ann McClellan, Scholarship Coordinator, 204 Scales Hall, Memphis, TN 38152.

1681   Congressional Hispanic Summer Internship Program

Congressional Hispanic Caucus Institute, Inc.
504 C Street, NE
Washington, DC 20002
(800) EXCEL DC
Minimum award: $1,000
Maximum number of awards: 30
Minimum number of awards: 30
Deadline: February 12
Criteria: Applicant must be a college-bound high school graduate or undergraduate with a minimum 3.0 GPA, excellent writing skills, who is active in his or her community, and is a Hispanic citizen or permanent resident of the U.S. or its territories. Fluency in English is required.
Contact: Internships.

1682   Daniel Memorial Fund Endowed Scholarship

Clemson University
G-01 Sikes Hall
Clemson, SC 29634-5123
(803) 656-2280
Average award: $1,500
Number of awards: 3
College level: Freshman
Criteria: Applicant must be a member of a minority group. Minimum 3.0 GPA with at least 12 credits per semester is required to retain scholarship. Awarded every year. Award may be used only at sponsoring institution.
Contact: Marvin Carmichael, Director of Financial Aid.

1683 Davis Scholarship

University of Nebraska, Lincoln
14th and R Streets
Lincoln, NE 68588
(402) 472-2030
Maximum award: Full cost of attendance
Minimum award: $1,500
Number of awards: 10
Deadline: January 15
College level: Freshman
Criteria: Applicant must be an underrepresented minority from Nebraska. Scholarship is renewable. Awarded every year. Award may be used only at sponsoring institution.
Contact: Debra Augustyn, Assistant Director of Scholarships.

1684 Displaced Homemaker Scholarships

Association on American Indian Affairs, Inc.
245 Fifth Avenue
New York, NY 10016
(212) 689-8720
Deadline: September 1
College level: Freshman, Sophomore, Junior, Senior
Criteria: Applicant must be an American Indian homemaker, male or female, who is unable to realize his or her educational goals. Applicant must submit application, essay, recommendations, personal monthly budget, most recent financial aid award letter, copy of certificate of degree of Indian Blood, or Tribal enrollment card, and transcript. Awarded every year.
Contact: Harriett Skye, Scholarship Coordinator.

1685 Distinction Scholarship

Ohio State University–Columbus
Third Floor Lincoln Tower
1800 Cannon Drive
Columbus, OH 43210-1200
(614) 292-3980
Average award: $9,834
Deadline: December 4
College level: Freshman
Criteria: Applicant must graduate from a chartered Ohio high school, rank in the top five-percent of class, have a minimum 3.75 GPA, and be African-American, Asian-American, Hispanic-American or Native American. If funding permits, out-of-state students will be considered. Scholarship is renewable. Awarded every year.
Contact: Office of Minority Affairs, (614) 292-0964.

1686 Diversity Scholarship

Oakland University
101 North Foundation Hall
Rochester, MI 48309-4401
(810) 370-3360
Average award: $2,500
Number of awards: 2
Deadline: February 1
College level: Freshman
Criteria: Minimum 2.5 GPA is required to retain scholarship. Awarded every year. Award may be used only at sponsoring institution.
Contact: Stacy M. Penkala, Assistant Director of Admissions.

1687 Diversity Scholarship

University of Wisconsin–Eau Claire
105 Garfield Avenue
Eau Claire, WI 54701
(715) 836-3373
Average award: $1,000
Number of awards: 5
Deadline: March 1
College level: Freshman, transfer students
Criteria: Applicant must be a minority student who ranks in the top quarter of graduating class. Transfer student must have a minimum 3.0 GPA. Awarded every year. Award may be used only at sponsoring institution.
Contact: Melissa Vogler, Financial Aid Counselor.

1688 EPA Tribal Lands Environmental Science Scholarship

American Indian Science & Engineering Society
Scholarship Coordinator
1630 30th Street, Suite 301
Boulder, CO 80301-1014
(303) 492-8658
Average award: $4,000
Deadline: June 15
College level: Junior, Senior, Graduate, Doctoral
Majors/Fields: Biochemistry, biology, chemistry, chemical engineering, entomology, environmental economics, environmental science, hydrology, toxicology
Criteria: Applicant must be Native American, have a minimum 2.0 GPA, and be enrolled on a full-time basis. Summer employment at an EPA facility and/or on an Indian reservation is also offered contingent upon the availability of resources. Awarded every year.
Contact: Roberta Manuelito, Scholarship Coordinator.

1689 Excellence Scholarship

Ohio State University–Columbus
Third Floor Lincoln Tower
1800 Cannon Drive
Columbus, OH 43210-1200
(614) 292-3980
Average award: $2,799
Deadline: December 4
College level: Freshman
Criteria: Applicant must rank in the top fifth of class, graduate from a chartered Ohio high school, have a minimum 3.0 GPA, and be an African-American, Asian-American, Hispanic-American or Native American. If funding permits out-of-state applicants will be considered. Scholarship is renewable. Awarded every year. Award may be used only at sponsoring institution.
Contact: Office of Minority Affairs, (614) 292-0964.

1690 Ferdinand Cinelli Etruscan Scholarship

National Italian American Foundation (NIAF)
Educational Scholarship Program
1860 19th Street, NW
Washington, DC 20009-5599
(202) 638-2137
Minimum award: $1,000
Deadline: May 31
College level: Sophomore, Junior, Senior, Graduate, Doctoral
Majors/Fields: Etruscan culture
Criteria: Applicant must be Italian-American, demonstrate financial need, submit transcript, demonstrate interest in Etruscan culture, and enroll in an Etruscan Foundation-approved program of research and study. Preference is given to those living or studying in Michigan. Awarded every year.
Contact: Dr. Maria Lombardo, Education Director

1691 FINE Fellowship

University of Oklahoma
University Affairs
900 Asp Avenue, Room 236
Norman, OK 73019-0401
(405) 325-1701
Maximum award: $10,000
Minimum award: $7,000
Deadline: in May (summer); in August (fall)
College level: Graduate, Doctoral
Majors/Fields: Education
Criteria: Applicant must be a Native American master's or doctoral student in education and demonstrate financial need. Awarded every year. Award may be used only at sponsoring institution.
Contact: College of Education, Room 105, ECH, Norman, OK 73019, (405) 325-1081.

1692 Frito-Lay Minority Business Scholarship

University of Tennessee, Knoxville
Financial Aid Office
115 Student Services Building
Knoxville, TN 37994
(615) 974-3131
Average award: $2,000
Deadline: February 1
College level: Sophomore
Majors/Fields: Business
Criteria: Applicant must be interested in a career in sales or sales management. Priority is given to applicants with an outstanding GPA and demonstrated leadership in extracurricular activities. Recipient participates in paid summer internship with Frito-Lay. Renewable for three years. Awarded every year. Award may be used only at sponsoring institution.
Contact: Business Administration, 52 Glocker Business Administration Building, Knoxville, TN 37996, (615) 974-5096.

1693 George C. Brooks Scholarship

University of Missouri–Columbia
High School and Transfer Relations
219 Jesse Hall
Columbia, MO 65211
(800) 225-6075 (in-state), (314) 882-2456
Average award: $7,000
Maximum award: $6,500 maximum for in-state residents; $9,500 maximum for out-of-state residents
Number of awards: 50
Deadline: March 1
College level: Freshman
Criteria: Applicant must be a minority, have a high composite ACT score, and have a sixth- or seventh-semester class rank in the top tenth of class. Minimum 2.5 GPA for 24 hours of graded course work is required to retain scholarship. Awarded every year. Award may be used only at sponsoring institution.
Contact: High School and Transfer Relations.

1694 Giargiari Fellowship

National Italian American Foundation (NIAF)
Educational Scholarship Program
1860 19th Street, NW
Washington, DC 20009-5599
(202) 638-2137
Minimum award: $5,000
Deadline: May 31
College level: Doctoral
Majors/Fields: Medicine
Criteria: Applicant must be Italian-American enrolled in an approved U.S. medical school, demonstrate financial need, and submit transcript. Awarded every year.
Contact: Dr. Maria Lombardo, Education Director.

1695 Graduate Minority Fellowship Grant

Western Washington University
516 High Street
Bellingham, WA 98226-9006
(206) 650-3471
Average award: $1,500
Number of awards: 3
Deadline: June 1
College level: Graduate, Doctoral
Criteria: Applicant must be a minority student with academic potential and financial need. Each fellow is required to work four hours per week for the Graduate School. Awarded every year. Award may be used only at sponsoring institution.
Contact: Francine E. Titus, Scholarship Coordinator.

1696 Greek Women's University Club Scholarship

Greek Women's University Club
9624 South Kolmar Avenue
Oak Lawn, IL 60453
(708) 366-8843
Average award: $750
Maximum award: $1,000
Minimum award: $500
Number of awards: 3
Deadline: July 17
College level: Junior, Senior, Graduate, Doctoral
Criteria: Applicant must be of Greek descent, a woman, full-time college student in sophomore, junior, or senior year, or graduate student, have a minimum 3.0 GPA, be a U.S. citizen and a permanent resident of the Chicago metropolitan area. Recipient must reapply to renew scholarship. Awarded every year.
Contact: Barbara Kariotis-Javaras, Scholarship Chairperson, 7223 Oak Street, River Forest, IL 60305, (708) 209-1355.

1697 Guido Zerilli-Marimo Fellowships

National Italian American Foundation (NIAF)
Educational Scholarship Program
1860 19th Street, NW
Washington, DC 20009-5599
(202) 638-2137
Minimum award: $5,000
Number of awards: 2
Deadline: May 31
College level: Unspecified undergraduate, unspecified graduate
Criteria: Applicant must be Italian-American, demonstrate financial need, submit transcript, be an undergraduate or graduate New York U student, and be accepted at an Italian university or at an American university with a school in Italy. Awarded every year.
Contact: Dr. Maria Lombardo, Education Director.

1698 Helen Faison Scholarship

University of Pittsburgh, Pittsburgh Campus
4200 Fifth Avenue
Pittsburgh, PA 15260
(412) 624-4141
Maximum award: $19,168
Minimum award: $9,982
Number of awards: 5
Deadline: January 15
College level: Freshman
Criteria: Applicant must be a minority student. Selection is based upon high school performance and test scores. Minimum 3.0 GPA is required to retain scholarship. Awarded every year. Award may be used only at sponsoring institution.
Contact: Betsy A. Porter, Director of Admissions and Financial Aid, (412) 624-7164.

1699 Herbert Lehman Scholarship

Herbert Lehman Education Fund
99 Hudson Street
Suite 1600
New York, NY 10013
(212) 219-1900, extension 511
Maximum award: $1,400
Minimum award: $1,400
Maximum number of awards: 60
Minimum number of awards: 50
Deadline: April 15
College level: Freshman
Criteria: Selection is based upon outstanding leadership potential and evidence of community service. Applicant must be an African-American, U.S. citizen who is entering a college or university that has an enrollment of African-American undergraduates that is less than eight percent of the total undergraduate enrollment. Preference is given to students planning to attend a southern school that was at one time segregated. Good academic standing and full-time enrollment are required to retain scholarship. Awarded every year.
Contact: G. Michael Bagley, Executive Director.

1700   Hispanic Scholarship Program

University of Central Florida
Office of Recruitment
Orlando, FL 32816
(407) 823-5439
Average award: $3,000
Maximum award: $4,000
Number of awards: 18
Deadline: March 15
College level: Freshman
Criteria: Applicant must be a finalist ($4,000 award) or semifinalist ($3,000 award) in the National Hispanic Scholarship Program. Minimum 3.0 GPA and full-time status required to retain scholarship. Awarded every year. Award may be used only at sponsoring institution.
Contact: Susan McKinnon, Assistant Director.

1701   Ibero-PYRD Scholarship

Rochester Institute of Technology
One Lomb Memorial Drive
Rochester, NY 14623
(716) 475-2186
Average award: $2,500
Number of awards: 15
Deadline: February 15
College level: Freshman
Criteria: Applicant must be a Hispanic student. Selection is based upon academic qualifications, leadership ability, and demonstrated financial need. Satisfactory academic progress is required to retain scholarship. Awarded every year. Award may be used only at sponsoring institution.
Contact: Verna Hazen, Director of Financial Aid.

1702   Indian Fellowship Program

U.S. Department of Education
Federal Student Aid Information Center
P.O. Box 84
Washington, DC 20044
(800) 433-3243
Average award: $12,590
Maximum award: $36,986
Minimum award: $1,728
Number of awards: 57
Deadline: January 25
College level: Freshman, Sophomore, Junior, Senior, Graduate, Doctoral
Majors/Fields: Business administration, clinical psychology, education, engineering, law, medicine, natural resources, psychology
Criteria: Applicant must be a U.S. citizen who is an American Indian, Eskimo, Aleut, or other Alaskan native. Fellowship is for undergraduate or advanced degree in business administration, engineering, natural resources, or related fields, or for postbaccalaureate degree in education, law, medicine, psychology, clinical psychology, or related fields. Awarded every year.
Contact: Dr. John Derby, Chief, Indian Fellowship Program, Office of Indian Education, Room 2177, FOB 6, 400 Maryland Avenue, SW, Washington, DC 20202-6335, (202) 401-1902.

1703   Indian Scholarship Program

North Dakota State Board for Indian Scholarships
State Capitol Building
Bismark, ND 58505
(701) 328-2166
Average award: $900
Maximum award: $2,000
Minimum award: $700
Maximum number of awards: 150
Minimum number of awards: 120
Deadline: July 15
College level: Freshman, Sophomore, Junior, Senior, Graduate, Doctoral
Criteria: Applicant must be a Native American North Dakota resident. Reapplication and submission of transcript and budget required to retain scholarship. Awarded every year.
Contact: Rhonda Schauer, Administrator.

1704   Interco Scholarship

University of Missouri–Saint Louis
8001 Natural Bridge Road
Saint Louis, MO 63121
(314) 553-6396
Average award: $2,500
Number of awards: 9
Deadline: April 1
College level: Freshman
Criteria: Applicant must be a minority student, be enrolled full time for at least 12 credit hours per semester, and demonstrate high academic achievement in high school. Scholarship is renewable. Awarded when funds are available. Award may be used only at sponsoring institution.
Contact: James D. Reed, Financial Aid Advisor.

1705   John and Anne Parente Scholarship

National Italian American Foundation (NIAF)
Educational Scholarship Program
1860 19th Street, NW
Washington, DC 20009-5599
(202) 638-2137
Minimum award: $2,000
Deadline: May 31
College level: Sophomore, Junior, Senior
Criteria: Applicant must be Italian-American, demonstrate financial need, and submit transcript. Preference is given to nonresidents of Pennsylvania. Awarded every year.
Contact: Dr. Maria Lombardo, Education Director.

1706   John B. Ervin Scholarship for Black Americans

Washington University
One Brookings Drive
Campus Box 1089
St. Louis, MO 63130
(314) 935-6000 or (800) 638-0700
Average award: $19,250
Number of awards: 10
College level: Freshman
Criteria: Applicant must be a black American. Selection is based upon academic merit without regard to financial need. Satisfactory academic performance is required to retain scholarship. Awarded every year. Award may be used only at sponsoring institution.
Contact: Office of Undergraduate Admissions, (800) 638-0700 or (314) 935-6000.

1707   John Newton Templeton Scholarship

Ohio University
Office of Student Financial Aid and Scholarships
Athens, OH 45701
(614) 593-4141
Average award: In-state tuition
Number of awards: 10
Deadline: February 15
College level: Freshman
Criteria: Applicant must be a minority student. Selection is based upon academic qualifications, talents, and leadership. Minimum 3.3 GPA and 16 credit hours per quarter are required to retain scholarship. Awarded every year. Award may be used only at sponsoring institution.
Contact: Yang-Hi Kim, Associate Director of Scholarships and Grants.

1708 Lancelot C. A. Thompson Minority Scholarship

University of Toledo
Financial Aid Office
Toledo, OH 43606-3390
(419) 537-2056
Average award: $3,000
Number of awards: 10
Deadline: January 28
College level: Freshman
Criteria: Applicant must be a minority student. Selection is based upon academic achievement, test scores, recommendations, essay, leadership, and citizenship. Award is for four years. Awarded every year. Award may be used only at sponsoring institution.
Contact: Coordinator of Minority Admissions, Office of Admissions Services, (419) 537-2073.

1709 Lavelle Scholarship

University of Pittsburgh, Pittsburgh Campus
4200 Fifth Avenue
Pittsburgh, PA 15260
(412) 624-4141
Maximum award: $17,202
Minimum award: $10,621
Number of awards: 1
Deadline: January 15
College level: Freshman
Criteria: Applicant must be a minority student enrolled in the Coll of Business Administration. Selection is based upon high school performance and test scores. Minimum 3.0 GPA is required to retain scholarship. Awarded every year. Award may be used only at sponsoring institution.
Contact: Betsy A. Porter, Director of Admissions and Financial Aid, (412) 624-7164.

1710 LBJ Achievement Scholarship

Southwest Texas State University
J. C. Kellam Building
San Marcos, TX 78666
(512) 245-2340
Average award: $1,000
Number of awards: 30
Deadline: March 15
College level: Freshman, first-time transfer students
Criteria: Applicant must be an African-American or Hispanic Texas resident enrolled on a full-time basis. Freshman applicant must have a minimum composite ACT score of 24 or combined SAT I score of 1000, or rank in the top quarter of class. Transfer applicant must have a minimum 3.5 GPA with at least 15 transferable hours or be listed in the Talent Roster of Outstanding Minority Community College Graduates for the year preceding the award. Awarded every year. Award may be used only at sponsoring institution.
Contact: Coordinator of Scholarships, Office of Financial Aid, 601 University Drive, San Marcos, TX 78666-4602, (512) 245-2315.

1711 Leonard M. Perryman Communications Scholarship for Ethnic Minority Students

United Methodist Communications
475 Riverside Drive, Suite 1901
New York, NY 10115
(212) 663-8900
Minimum award: $2,500
Number of awards: 1
Deadline: March 1
Majors/Fields: Religious communication
Criteria: Applicant must be an ethnic minority, undergraduate student who intends to pursue a career in religious communication. Awarded every year.
Contact: Scholarships, 475 Riverside Drive, Suite 1901, New York, NY 10115-1901.

1712 Lottie Conlan Scholarship

University of Oklahoma
University Affairs
900 Asp Avenue, Room 236
Norman, OK 73019-0401
(405) 325-1701
Average award: $1,000
Maximum number of awards: 7
Minimum number of awards: 6
Deadline: March 1
College level: Sophomore, Junior, Senior
Criteria: Applicant must have American Indian heritage and demonstrate financial need. Awarded every year. Award may be used only at sponsoring institution.
Contact: Office of Financial Aid Services, 731 Elm, Norman, OK 73019-0230, (405) 325-4521.

1713 Luso-American Education Foundation Scholarships

Luso-American Education Foundation
7080 Donlon Way
Suite 202
Dublin, CA 94568
(510) 828-3883
Average award: $500
Number of awards: 40
Deadline: March 1
College level: Freshman
Majors/Fields: Portuguese language/culture
Criteria: Applicant must be a California resident, under 21 years of age, have a minimum 3.0 GPA, demonstrate high moral character, good citizenship, and dedication to American ideals. Applicant must also satisfy one of the following: (1) be of Portuguese descent, (2) enroll in Portuguese classes in a four-year college or university, or (3) be a member of an organization whose scholarships are administered by the Luso-American Education Foundation. Selection is based upon potential for success in college, financial need, and leadership. Unusual talents will be recognized. Awarded every year.
Contact: Maria L. Sena, Administrative Director, PO Box 2967, Dublin, CA 94568.

1714 Margin of Quality Minority Scholarship

University of Oklahoma
University Affairs
900 Asp Avenue, Room 236
Norman, OK 73019-0401
(405) 325-1701
Average award: $1,000
Number of awards: 5
Deadline: February 8
College level: Freshman, Sophomore, Junior, Senior
Majors/Fields: Business
Criteria: Applicant must be a full-time student with a minimum 2.8 GPA, demonstrate financial need, and be black, Hispanic, Asian-American, or Native American. Awarded every year. Award may be used only at sponsoring institution.
Contact: Undergraduate Programs, 108 Adams Hall, Norman, OK 73019-0450, (405) 325-6021.

1715 Marian Oldham Scholarship

University of Missouri–Saint Louis
8001 Natural Bridge Road
Saint Louis, MO 63121
(314) 553-6396
Average award: $1,225
Number of awards: 2
Deadline: April 1
College level: Freshman
Criteria: Applicant must be a black, first-time freshman, rank in the top 15 percent of class, demonstrate leadership abilities, and show financial need. Scholarship is renewable. Awarded every year. Award may be used only at sponsoring institution.
Contact: James D. Reed, Financial Aid Advisor.

1716   Martin Luther King Scholarship

Southwest Texas State University
J. C. Kellam Building
San Marcos, TX 78666
(512) 245-2340
Average award: $2,000
Number of awards: 25
Deadline: July 1
College level: Freshman
Criteria: Applicant must be an African-American living in an on-campus residence hall, have a minimum combined SAT I score of 1000 or composite ACT score of 24, and rank in the top five percent of class or have a minimum 3.5 GPA. Awarded every year. Award may be used only at sponsoring institution.
Contact: Katrina Clanahan, Senior Admission Counselor.

1717   Martino Scholars Program

National Italian American Foundation (NIAF)
Educational Scholarship Program
1860 19th Street, NW
Washington, DC 20009-5599
(202) 638-2137
Minimum award: $1,000
Number of awards: 5
Deadline: May 31
College level: Graduate, Doctoral
Majors/Fields: Information sciences, multimedia technology, mathematics
Criteria: Applicant must be Italian-American, demonstrate financial need, submit transcript, and attend Chestnut Hill Coll, Penn., Georgetown U, D.C., Princeton U, N.J., MIT, or Harvard U, Mass. Awarded every year. Award may be used only at sponsoring institution.
Contact: Dr. Maria Lombardo, Education Director.

1718   Mellon Fellow Minority Scholarship

City University of New York, Queens College
65-30 Kissena Boulevard
Flushing, NY 11367
(718) 997-5000
Average award: $4,000
Maximum award: $6,000
Minimum award: $3,000
Number of awards: 5
College level: Junior, Senior
Criteria: Applicant must be commited to apply for full-time Ph.D. study after graduation from college. Excellent academic record must be maintained to retain scholarship. Awarded every year. Award may be used only at sponsoring institution.
Contact: Elaine P. Maimon, Dean, (718) 520-7762.

1719   MESBEC & NALE Scholarships

Native American Scholarship Fund, Inc.
8200 Mountain Road, NE
Suite 203
Albuquerque, NM 87110
(505) 262-2351
Maximum award: $5,000
Minimum award: $500
Deadline: September 15 (winter); March 15 (summer); April 15 (fall)
College level: Freshman, Sophomore, Junior, Senior, Graduate, Doctoral
Majors/Fields: Business, computers, education, engineering, mathematics, science
Criteria: Applicant must be a Native American with high GPA and test scores enrolled in a college or university seeking a baccalaureate degree, master's degree, or doctoral degree. Renewable if student maintains respectable GPA. Awarded every year.
Contact: Lynette C. Charlie, Director of Recruiting.

1720   Minority Academically Talented Scholarship

University of Central Florida
Office of Recruitment
Orlando, FL 32816
(407) 823-5439
Maximum award: $3,000
Minimum award: $1,000
Number of awards: 150
Deadline: March 15
College level: Freshman
Criteria: Applicant must be a minority student. Selection is based upon high school course work, weighted GPA, and SAT I or ACT scores. Minimum 2.5 GPA and full-time status are required to retain scholarship. Awarded every year. Award may be used only at sponsoring institution.
Contact: Susan McKinnon, Assistant Director.

1721   Minority Achievement Award

University of Utah
Financial Aid and Scholarships Office
105 Student Services Building
Salt Lake City, UT 84112
(801) 581-6211
Average award: $1,000
Number of awards: 25
Deadline: February 1
College level: Freshman, transfer students
Criteria: Applicant must be a minority student with outstanding academic achievement, extracurricular activities, and service records. Award is for a maximum of three quarters. Awarded every year. Award may be used only at sponsoring institution.
Contact: Financial Aid and Scholarships Office, 105 Student Services Building, Salt Lake City, UT 84112.

1722   Minority Achievement Program Scholarship

Western Washington University
516 High Street
Bellingham, WA 98226-9006
(206) 650-3471
Average award: $1,200
Number of awards: 40
College level: Freshman, transfer students
Criteria: Awarded to the most outstanding freshman and transfer Asian/Pacific Islander, African-American, Hispanic-American and Native American students. Separate application is not required. Awarded every year. Award may be used only at sponsoring institution.
Contact: Francine E. Titus, Scholarship Coordinator.

1723   Minority Advertising Intern Program

American Association of Advertising Agencies
666 Third Avenue
New York, NY 10017
(212) 986-4721
Average award: $3,000
Number of awards: 36
Deadline: January 15
Criteria: Applicant must be a minority U.S. citizen or permanent resident currently enrolled in an undergraduate or graduate program and have completed at least junior year. Minimum 2.5 GPA required. Selection is based upon application information, letters of recommendation, school transcripts, and supporting materials. Awarded every year.
Contact: Minority Advertising Intern Program.

1724 Minority Doctoral Study Grant

Oklahoma State Regents for Higher Education
500 Education Building
State Capitol Complex
Oklahoma City, OK 73105
(405) 524-9100
Average award: $6,000
Number of awards: 18
Deadline: May 1
College level: Doctoral
Criteria: Applicant must be a minority. Oklahoma residents receive preference. Reapplication is required to retain scholarship up to a maximum award of $24,000. Awarded every year.
Contact: Dawn Scott, Research Assistant, (405) 524-9153.

1725 Minority Educational Opportunity Tuition Award

Northern Kentucky University
Administrative Center 416
Nunn Drive
Highland Heights, KY 41099-7101
(606) 572-5144
Average award: Tuition
Deadline: February 1
College level: Freshman
Criteria: Applicant must be a minority U.S. citizen or permanent resident. Scholarship is renewable. Awarded every year. Award may be used only at sponsoring institution.
Contact: Robert E. Sprague, Director of Financial Aid.

1726 Minority Engineering Scholarship Program

University of Tennessee, Knoxville
Financial Aid Office
115 Student Services Building
Knoxville, TN 37994
(615) 974-3131
Average award: $2,200
Deadline: February 1
College level: Freshman
Majors/Fields: Engineering
Criteria: Applicant must be an African-American student with a minimum 3.0 GPA, minimum composite ACT score of 23 or combined SAT I score of 940, and at least 3.5 units of mathematics. Selection is based upon merit. Award is for five years with four co-op terms. Awarded every year. Award may be used only at sponsoring institution.
Contact: College of Engineering, 103 Estabrook Hall, Knoxville, TN 37996, (615) 974-2454.

1727 Minority Fellowship

American Sociological Association
1722 17th Street NW
Washington, DC 20036-2981
Average award: $10,008
Deadline: December 31
College level: Doctoral
Majors/Fields: Mental health
Criteria: Selection is based upon commitment to research in mental health/illness, scholarship, writing ability, research potential, financial need, and racial and ethnic minority identification. Fellowship is usually renewed for up to three years if productive and steady progess is made.
Contact: Frances M. Foster, Minority Affairs Program, (202) 833-3410, extension 322.

1728 Minority Incentive Award

Kent State University
P.O. Box 5190
Kent, OH 44242-0001
(216) 672-2972
Maximum award: $3,000
Minimum award: $1,500
Deadline: April 1
College level: Junior
Criteria: Applicant must be a minority transfer student admitted with junior status into a KSU major. Selection is based upon academic record. Satisfactory academic progress and full-time enrollment are required to retain scholarship for up to four semesters. Awarded every year. Award may be used only at sponsoring institution.
Contact: Theodore Hallenbeck, Director of Financial Aid, 103 Michael Schwartz Center.

1729 Minority Presence

North Carolina State Education Assistance Authority
Box 2688
Chapel Hill, NC 27515-2688
(919) 549-8614
Average award: $4,000
Maximum award: $4,500
College level: Graduate, Doctoral
Majors/Fields: Law, veterinary medicine
Criteria: Applicant must be a black North Carolina resident, demonstrate financial need, and be enrolled in a doctoral program at East Carolina U, North Carolina State U, U of North Carolina at Chapel Hill, or U of North Carolina at Greensboro, or in law school at U of North Carolina at Chapel Hill, or in the School of Veterinary Medicine at North Carolina State U. Awarded every year.
Contact: UNC General Administration, (919) 962-1000.

1730 Minority Scholar Award

Washington State University
Office of Scholarship Services
Pullman, WA 99164-1728
(509) 335-1059
Average award: $2,000
Maximum award: $3,000
Minimum award: $1,500
Number of awards: 100
Deadline: February 15
College level: Freshman, transfer students
Criteria: Applicant must be a U.S. citizen or permanent resident with a minimum 3.0 GPA, who is a Native American, Alaskan Native, Asian or Pacific Islander, African-American, or Hispanic-American. Financial need is not considered. Scholarship is renewable. Awarded every year. Award may be used only at sponsoring institution.
Contact: Johanna H. Davis, Assistant Director.

1731 Minority Scholars Award

State University of New York College at Buffalo
1300 Elmwood Avenue
Buffalo, NY 14222
(716) 878-5303
Average award: $1,000
Number of awards: 15
Deadline: Open
College level: Freshman, Sophomore, Junior, Senior
Criteria: Applicant must be an African-American, Latino, or Native American student. Incoming freshman applicant must have an unweighted high school average of 85. Continuing student must have a minimum 3.0 GPA. Minimum 3.0 GPA and attendance at scheduled meetings are required to retain scholarship. Awarded every year. Award may be used only at sponsoring institution.
Contact: Dr. Leon Smith, Director of Academic Standards.

1732   Minority Scholarship

University of Memphis
Scates Hall 204
Memphis, TN 38152
(901) 678-3213
Average award: $2,442
Deadline: March 1
College level: Freshman
Criteria: Applicant must be an African-American Tennessee resident. Selection is based upon test scores and high school record. Minimum composite ACT score of 20 or combined SAT I score of 780 and 3.0 GPA are recommended. Minimum 2.8 GPA and a service requirement of 30 hours per semester are required to retain scholarship. Awarded every year. Award may be used only at sponsoring institution.
Contact: Dr. Sue Ann McClellan, Scholarship Coordinator, 204 Scates Hall, Memphis, TN 38152.

1733   Minority Scholarship

East Tennessee State University
P.O. Box 70722
Johnson City, TN 37614-0002
(615) 929-4300
Average award: $1,000
Number of awards: 15
Deadline: February 15
College level: Freshman, Sophomore, Junior, Senior
Criteria: Applicant must be a new minority undergraduate student. Selection is based upon academic standing or academic potential. Scholarship is renewable. Awarded every year. Award may be used only at sponsoring institution.
Contact: Michael Jones, Financial Aid Counselor.

1734   Minority Student Scholarship

DePaul University
25 East Jackson Boulevard
Suite 100
Chicago, IL 60604
(312) 362-8704
Average award: $3,400
Maximum award: $7,500
Minimum award: $2,000
Number of awards: 35
Deadline: February 1
College level: Freshman
Criteria: Applicant must be African-American or Hispanic, with a minimum 3.0 GPA, rank in top quarter of class, and have a minimum composite ACT score of 24. Scholarship is renewable. Awarded every year. Award may be used only at sponsoring institution.
Contact: Jennifer Sparrow, Associate Director of Admissions.

1735   Minority Teachers of Illinois Scholarship

Illinois Student Assistance Commission/Client Support Services
1755 Lake Cook Road
Deerfield, IL 60015-5209
(800) 899-ISAC, 708 948-8500
Average award: $4,068
Maximum award: $5,000
Minimum award: $1,458
Number of awards: 38
Deadline: September 15
College level: Sophomore, Junior, Senior
Majors/Fields: Education
Criteria: Applicant must be a minority student of African-American, Hispanic, Asian-American or Native American origin. Applicant must be enrolled in a teacher education program or curriculum leading to initial teacher certification at a qualified Illinois institution of higher education. Recipient must sign a promissory note agreeing to fulfill teaching commitment or repay the scholarship with interest. Scholarship is renewable. Awarded every year.
Contact: Manager of Scholarships and Specialized Grants.

1736   Minority Transfer Scholarship

Rochester Institute of Technology
One Lomb Memorial Drive
Rochester, NY 14623
(716) 475-2186
Average award: $2,500
Number of awards: 15
Deadline: February 15
College level: Transfer students
Criteria: Applicant must be an African-American, Hispanic-American, or Native American student. Selection is based upon academic qualifications, leadership ability, and demonstrated financial need. Satisfactory academic progress is required to retain scholarship. Awarded every year. Award may be used only at sponsoring institution.
Contact: Verna Hazen, Director of Financial Aid.

1737   Minority Undergraduate Scholarship

University of Tennessee, Knoxville
Financial Aid Office
115 Student Services Building
Knoxville, TN 37994
(615) 974-3131
Maximum award: $2,000
Minimum award: $1,000
Deadline: February 15
College level: Freshman
Criteria: Applicant must be an African-American who is a National Achievement finalist, semifinalist, or commended student. Finalists and semifinalists receive $2,000; commended students and selected others with a minimum 3.0 GPA receive $1,000. Award is for four years. Awarded every year. Award may be used only at sponsoring institution.
Contact: Financial Aid Office.

1738   Morrison Center MSW Minority Scholarship

Portland State University
P.O. Box 751
Portland, OR 97207-0751
(503) 725-5270
Average award: $6,000
Number of awards: 1
Majors/Fields: Social work
Criteria: Applicant must be a minority student entering the second year of MSW program. Scholarship is renewable. Awarded every year. Award may be used only at sponsoring institution.
Contact: Scholarships, Graduate School of Social Work, (503) 725-4712.

1739   NAACP Willems Scholarship

National Association for the Advancement of Colored People (NAACP)
4805 Mount Hope Drive
Baltimore, MD 21215-3297
(410) 358-8900
Average award: $2,000
Maximum award: $3,000
Deadline: April 30
College level: Freshman, Sophomore, Junior, Senior, Graduate, Doctoral
Majors/Fields: Chemistry, computer science, engineering, mathematical science, physics
Criteria: Applicant must have a minimum 3.0 GPA and be a member of the NAACP. Undergraduate awards are for four years; graduate scholarships can be renewed. Awarded every year.
Contact: Andrea E. Moss, Education Department.

1740 National Hispanic Scholarship

University of Toledo
Financial Aid Office
Toledo, OH 43606-3390
(419) 537-2056
Average award: Full tuition, fees, room and board
Deadline: January 28
College level: Freshman
Criteria: Applicant must be a National Hispanic finalist. Award is for four years. Awarded every year. Award may be used only at sponsoring institution.
Contact: Coordinator of Admissions Services for Scholars, Office of Admissions Services, (419) 537-2073.

1741 National Hispanic Scholarship Fund Scholarship

National Hispanic Scholarship Fund
PO Box 728
Novato, CA 94948
(415) 892-9971
Average award: $1,000
Minimum award: $500
Number of awards: 3226
Deadline: June 15
College level: Sophomore, Junior, Senior, Graduate, Doctoral
Criteria: Applicant must be a U.S. citizen or permanent resident of Hispanic-American background, enrolled in a college or university in the U.S. or Puerto Rico on a full-time basis, and have completed a minimum of 15 units of college work. Selection is based upon academic achievement, personal strengths, leadership, and financial need. Applicant must reapply to continue scholarship. Awarded every year.
Contact: Selection Committee.

1742 NCR Annual Engineering Scholarship

Clemson University
G-01 Sikes Hall
Clemson, SC 29634-5123
(803) 656-2280
Average award: $2,500
Number of awards: 1
Deadline: March 1
College level: Freshman
Majors/Fields: Computer engineering, computer science, electrical engineering, engineering
Criteria: Applicant must be a black student with a minimum 3.0 GPA; preference is given to applicants intending to major in electrical engineering or computer engineering. Satisfactory GPA with at least 12 credits per semester is required to retain scholarship. Awarded every year. Award may be used only at sponsoring institution.
Contact: Marvin Carmichael, Director of Financial Aid.

1743 NIAF Law Fellowship

National Italian American Foundation (NIAF)
Educational Scholarship Program
1860 19th Street, NW
Washington, DC 20009-5599
(202) 638-2137
Minimum award: $1,000
Number of awards: 5
Deadline: May 31
College level: Doctoral
Majors/Fields: Law
Criteria: Applicant must be Italian-American, demonstrate financial need, and submit transcript and an essay of 750 words describing the contributions of Italian-Americans to the American judicial system. Awarded every year.
Contact: Dr. Maria Lombardo, Education Director.

1744 NIAF Scholarships

National Italian American Foundation (NIAF)
Educational Scholarship Program
1860 19th Street, NW
Washington, DC 20009-5599
(202) 638-2137
Minimum award: $1,000
Deadline: May 31
College level: Freshman, Sophomore, Junior, Senior, Graduate, Doctoral
Criteria: Applicant must be Italian-American, demonstrate financial need, and submit transcript. Inidividual scholarships available to women, to students in specific majors, and to applicants in various regions of the countries. Awarded every year.
Contact: Dr. Maria Lombardo, Education Director.

1745 Nicaraguan and Haitian Scholarship

Florida Department of Education
Office of Student Financial Assistance
1344 Florida Education Center
Tallahassee, FL 32399-0400
(904) 487-0049
Average award: $4,000
Maximum award: $5,000
Number of awards: 2
College level: Freshman, Sophomore, Junior, Senior
Criteria: Applicant must be a Nicaraguan or Haitian citizen (or have been born there) now living in Florida, with a minimum 3.0 GPA and demonstrated service to the community. Awarded every year.
Contact: Office of Student Financial Assistance.

1746 Oklahoma State Regents for Higher Education Doctoral Study Grant

University of Oklahoma
University Affairs
900 Asp Avenue, Room 236
Norman, OK 73019-0401
(405) 325-1701
Average award: $6,000 plus tuition and graduate assistantship
Minimum award: $6,000
Deadline: May 15
College level: Doctoral
Criteria: Applicant must be a minority. Preference is given to Oklahoma residents. Awarded every year. Award may be used only at sponsoring institution.
Contact: Graduate College, 1000 Asp Avenue, Room 313, Norman, OK 73019, (405) 325-3811.

1747 Opportunity at Iowa Scholarship

University of Iowa
208 Calvin Hall
Iowa City, IA 52242
(319) 335-1450
Maximum award: $5,000
Number of awards: 60
Deadline: March 1
College level: Freshman
Criteria: Applicant must be a minority student, rank in the top 30 percent of class, and have a minimum composite ACT score of 25. Minimum 3.0 cumulative GPA is required to retain scholarship. Awarded every year. Award may be used only at sponsoring institution.
Contact: Mark Warner, Director of Financial Aid.

1748   Oscar Ritchie Memorial Scholarship

Kent State University
P.O. Box 5190
Kent, OH 44242-0001
(216) 672-2972
Maximum award: Full tuition
Minimum award: $1,500
Deadline: April 1
College level: Freshman
Criteria: Applicant must be an academically talented minority student. Selection is based upon academic record, competitive exam given in spring of applicant's junior year in high school, and high school recommendations. Minimum 2.0 GPA is required to retain scholarship. Awarded every year. Award may be used only at sponsoring institution.
Contact: Theodore Hallenbeck, Director of Financial Aid, 103 Michael Schwartz Center.

1749   Outstanding Diverse Student Scholarship

Colorado State University
Financial Aid Office
108 Student Services Building
Fort Collins, CO 80523
(970) 491-6321
Average award: $1,300
Maximum award: $2,500
Minimum award: $500
Number of awards: 82
Deadline: January 31
College level: Freshman
Criteria: Applicant is automatically considered based on application for admission. Minimum 2.0 cumulative GPA and at least 12 credits is required to retain scholarship. Awarded every year. Award may be used only at sponsoring institution.
Contact: Peggy Meis, Financial Aid Counselor.

1750   Paragano Scholarship

National Italian American Foundation (NIAF)
Educational Scholarship Program
1860 19th Street, NW
Washington, DC 20009-5599
(202) 638-2137
Minimum award: $1,000
Number of awards: 2
Deadline: May 31
College level: Sophomore, Junior, Senior
Majors/Fields: Italian
Criteria: Applicant must be Italian-American, demonstrate financial need, submit transcript and be a New Jersey resident. Awarded every year.
Contact: Dr. Maria Lombardo, Education Director.

1751   Patricia Roberts Harris Fellowship

University of Oklahoma
University Affairs
900 Asp Avenue, Room 236
Norman, OK 73019-0401
(405) 325-1701
Average award: $10,000 plus tuition and books
Minimum award: $10,000
College level: Graduate, Doctoral
Criteria: Applicant must be a minority student. Selection is based upon merit and financial need. Awarded every year. Award may be used only at sponsoring institution.
Contact: Graduate College, 1000 Asp Avenue, Room 313, Norman, OK 73019, (405) 325-3811.

1752   Paul Laurence Dunbar Scholarship

Wright State University
Coordinator of Scholarships
Dayton, OH 45435
(513) 873-5721
Average award: $2,000
Number of awards: 15
Deadline: March 1
College level: Freshman
Criteria: Applicant must be an African-American, have a minimum composite ACT score of 20 or combined SAT I score of 870, have a minimum 3.0 cumulative GPA, rank in the top fifth of graduating class, and have completed college-preparatory course work. Minimum 3.0 cumulative GPA is required to retain scholarship. Awarded every year. Award may be used only at sponsoring institution.
Contact: Judy Rose, Assistant Director of Financial Aid, (513) 873-2321.

1753   Paul Phillips Scholarship

Grand Valley State University
Allendale, MI 49401
(616) 895-3234
Average award: $5,100
Maximum award: $6,638
Minimum award: $4,000
Number of awards: 3
Deadline: February 1
College level: Freshman
Criteria: Applicant must be a minority student. Minimum 3.0 GPA is required to retain scholarship. Awarded every year. Award may be used only at sponsoring institution.
Contact: Ken Fridsma, Director of Financial Aid.

1754   Pellegrini Scholarship Fund

Swiss Benevolent Society of New York
37 West Sixty-seventh Street
New York, NY 10023
Deadline: March 1
Criteria: Applicant must be of Swiss descent (one parent must be a Swiss national), with permanent residence in New York, New Jersey, Connecticut, Pennsylvania, or Delaware, demonstrate financial need, and have a good academic record.

1755   Piancone Family Agriculture Scholarship

National Italian American Foundation (NIAF)
Educational Scholarship Program
1860 19th Street, NW
Washington, DC 20009-5599
(202) 638-2137
Minimum award: $2,000
Deadline: May 31
College level: Sophomore, Junior, Senior, Graduate, Doctoral
Majors/Fields: Agriculture
Criteria: Applicant must be Italian-American, demonstrate financial need, submit transcript, and be a resident of Delaware, Maryland, Massachusetts, New Jersey, New York, Pennsylvania, Virginia, or Washington, DC.
Contact: Dr. Maria Lombardo, Education Director.

1756 Pilot Oil Corporation Minority Scholarship

University of Tennessee, Knoxville
Financial Aid Office
115 Student Services Building
Knoxville, TN 37994
(615) 974-3131
Average award: $1,500
Number of awards: 4
Deadline: February 1
College level: Freshman
Majors/Fields: Finance
Criteria: Applicant must be a full-time, minority undergraduate. Preference is given, in the following order, to residents of Knoxville area, Tenn., East Tennessee area, elsewhere in Tennessee, southeastern U.S., or other region. Award is for four years. Awarded every year. Award may be used only at sponsoring institution.
Contact: College of Business Administration, 52 Glocker Business Administration Building, Knoxville, TN 37996, (615) 974-5096.

1757 President's Achievement Award

Texas A&M University, College Station
College Station, TX 77843-4233
(409) 845-1957
Average award: $3,000
Minimum award: $2,500
Number of awards: 300
Deadline: January 8
College level: Freshman
Criteria: Applicant must be an academically successful African-American or Hispanic student. Academic achievement, rigor of curriculum, extracurricular activities, prizes and awards, leadership, and school recommendations are considered. Minimum cumulative GPA of 2.5 is required to retain scholarship. Awarded every year. Award may be used only at sponsoring institution.
Contact: Dr. Dale T. Knobel, Executive Director of Honors Programs and Academic Scholarships.

1758 President's Diversity Scholarship

University of Houston
129 Ezekiel W. Cullen Building
Houston, TX 77204-2161
(713) 743-9051
Average award: $2,000
Maximum award: $3,500
Minimum award: $500
Number of awards: 65
Deadline: April 1
College level: Transfer students
Criteria: Applicant must be a transfer student, have a minimum 3.0 GPA, have at least 30 credit hours, and be a member of a minority group (African-American, Hispanic, or Native American). Minimum 3.0 GPA and 15 credit hours each semester are required to retain scholarship. Awarded every year. Award may be used only at sponsoring institution.
Contact: Robert Sheridan, Director of Scholarships & Financial Aid.

1759 Presidential Scholarship for African-Americans

Villanova University
Villanova, PA 19085
(215) 645-4010
Average award: $18,200
Maximum award: $19,640
Minimum award: $15,740
Number of awards: 13
Deadline: December 15
College level: Freshman
Criteria: Applicant must be an African-American student, have an outstanding high school record and class rank, and a minimum combined SAT I score of 1200. Applicant must maintain high academic standards to retain scholarship. Award may be used only at sponsoring institution.
Contact: George J. Walter, Director of Financial Aid.

1760 Prestigious Scholarship

Ohio State University–Columbus
Third Floor Lincoln Tower
1800 Cannon Drive
Columbus, OH 43210-1200
(614) 292-3980
Average award: $3,299
Deadline: December 4
College level: Freshman
Criteria: Applicant must graduate from a chartered Ohio high school, rank in the top tenth of class, have a minimum 3.5 GPA, and be an African-American, Asian-American, Hispanic-American, or Native American. If funding permits out-of-state applicants will be considered. Scholarship is renewable. Awarded every year. Award may be used only at sponsoring institution.
Contact: Office of Minority Affairs, (614) 292-0964.

1761 Procter & Gamble Distributing Company Scholarship

Southwest Texas State University
J. C. Kellam Building
San Marcos, TX 78666
(512) 245-2340
Average award: $1,000
Number of awards: 2
Deadline: March 15
College level: Freshman, Sophomore, Junior, Senior
Criteria: Applicant must be a minority student with a minimum 2.75 GPA, be interested in a business career, and have demonstrated involvement and leadership in campus and/or civic activities. Awarded every year. Award may be used only at sponsoring institution.
Contact: Office of Minority Student Affairs, (512) 245-2315.

1762 Procter & Gamble Minority Scholarship

University of Tennessee, Knoxville
Financial Aid Office
115 Student Services Building
Knoxville, TN 37994
(615) 974-3131
Maximum award: $2,000
Minimum award: $1,000
Deadline: February 1
College level: Freshman, Sophomore, Junior, Senior
Criteria: Applicant must be a minority or handicapped student in the Coll of Business Administration. Length of awards varies. Awarded every year. Award may be used only at sponsoring institution.
Contact: College of Business Administration, 52 Glocker Business Administration Building, (615) 974-5096.

1763 Purnell-Fort Scholarship

University of Akron
302 Buchtel Commons
Akron, OH 44325-6211
(216) 972-7032
Maximum award: $4,000
Minimum award: $500
Deadline: February 1
College level: Freshman
Criteria: Applicant must be a minority student. Minimum 3.0 GPA is required to retain scholarship. Awarded every year. Award may be used only at sponsoring institution.
Contact: Doug McNutt, Director of Student Financial Aid.

1764   Ralph J. Bunche Scholarship

Northeastern University
360 Huntington Avenue
Boston, MA 02115
(617) 373-2000
Maximum award: $21,834
Number of awards: 12
Deadline: March 1
College level: Freshman
Criteria: Applicant must be African-American, rank in the top ten percent of class, and have a minimum combined SAT I score of 1050. Minimum 3.0 GPA is required to retain scholarship. Awarded every year. Award may be used only at sponsoring institution.
Contact: Kevin Kelly, Dean of Admissions.

1765   Reggie Lewis Memorial Scholarship

Northeastern University
360 Huntington Avenue
Boston, MA 02115
(617) 373-2000
Minimum award: $16,044
Number of awards: 7
Deadline: March 1
College level: Freshman
Criteria: Applicant must be a member of a minority group, rank in the top 20 percent of class, and have a minimum combined SAT I score of 1050. Minimum 3.0 GPA is required to retain scholarship. Awarded every year. Award may be used only at sponsoring institution.
Contact: Kevin Kelly, Dean of Admissions, (617) 373-2200.

1766   Reginaldo Howard Scholarship

Duke University
P.O. Box 90397
Durham, NC 27706
(919) 684-6225
Average award: $6,000
Number of awards: 7
Deadline: January 15
College level: Freshman
Criteria: Applicant must be African-American. Selection is based upon academic and extracurricular activities. A separate application is not required. Scholarship is renewable. Awarded every year. Award may be used only at sponsoring institution.
Contact: Christoph Guttentag, Director of Admissions, P.O. Box 90587, Durham, NC 27708-0587, (919) 684-3214.

1767   Richard and Jessie Barrington Educational Fund

Washoe Tribe of Nevada and California
Education Department
919 Highway 395 South
Gardnerville, NV 89410
(702) 265-4191
Average award: $1,000
Maximum award: $2,000
Minimum award: $800
Number of awards: 3
Deadline: August 15; December 15
College level: Freshman, Sophomore, Junior, Senior, Graduate
Criteria: Applicant must be a Washoe Tribe member with documented need. Awarded every year.
Contact: Sherry Smokey, Education Director.

1768   Robert J. Di Pietro Scholarship

National Italian American Foundation (NIAF)
Educational Scholarship Program
1860 19th Street, NW
Washington, DC 20009-5599
(202) 638-2137
Minimum award: $1,000
Number of awards: 2
Deadline: May 31
College level: Sophomore, Junior, Senior, Graduate, Doctoral
Criteria: Applicant must be Italian-American, 25 years of age or younger, demonstrate financial need, and submit transcript. Essay is required. Awarded every year.
Contact: Dr. Maria Lombardo, Education Director.

1769   Rosewood Family Scholarship

Florida Department of Education
Office of Student Financial Assistance
1344 Florida Education Center
Tallahassee, FL 32399-0400
(904) 487-0049
Average award: $4,000
Number of awards: 25
Deadline: April 1
College level: Freshman, Sophomore, Junior, Senior
Criteria: Applicant must be African-American, Hispanic, Asian, Pacific Islander, American Indian, or Alaskan Native. Strong preference is given to African-Americans who are direct descendants of the Rosewood families affected by the incidents of January 1923. Minimum 2.0 with at least 12 credit hour per term is required to retain scholarship. Awarded every year.
Contact: Office of Student Financial Assistance.

1770   Santa Fe Pacific Foundation Scholarship

American Indian Science & Engineering Society
Scholarship Coordinator
1630 30th Street, Suite 301
Boulder, CO 80301-1014
(303) 492-8658
Average award: $2,500
Deadline: March 31
College level: Freshman
Majors/Fields: Business, education, health administration, sciences
Criteria: Applicant must be a recent high school graduate, be at least 25 percent American Indian, have a minimum 2.0 GPA, be a full-time student, and reside in Arizona, Colorado, Kansas, New Mexico, Oklahoma, or in San Bernandino County, Calif. Scholarship is renewable. Awarded every year.
Contact: Roberta Manuelito, Scholarship Coordinator.

1771   Santa Fe Pacific Foundation Scholarship

Santa Fe Pacific Foundation
American Indian Science and Engineering Society
1630 30th Street, Suite 301
Boulder, CO 80301-1014
(303) 492-8658
Average award: $2,500
Number of awards: 5
Deadline: March 31
College level: Freshman
Majors/Fields: Business, education, health administration, sciences
Criteria: Applicant must show proof of at least 25 percent American Indian blood, plan to attend a four-year, accredited educational institution, and live in one of the states served by the Atchison, Topeka, and Santa Fe Railway (Arizona, Colorado, Kansas, New Mexico, Oklahoma, or San Bernardino County, Calif.). Two scholarships are designated for members of the Navajo tribe. Award is for four years or until baccalaureate degree is obtained. Awarded every year.
Contact: Roberta Manuelito, Director of College Programs.

1772   Seneca Nation of Indians

Seneca Nation of Indians
Seneca Nation of Higher Education
Box 231
Salamanca, NY 14779
(716) 945-1790
Minimum award: $5,000
Deadline: July 15 (Fall), December 31 (Spring), May 20 (Summer)
Criteria: Applicant must be an enrolled member of the Seneca Nation of Indians. Selection is based upon financial need. Scholarship is renewable.
Contact: Awards, Box 231, Salamanca, NY 14779.

1773   Sequoyah Graduate Fellowship

Association on American Indian Affairs, Inc.
245 Fifth Avenue
New York, NY 10016
(212) 689-8720
Average award: $1,500
Number of awards: 10
Deadline: September 13
College level: Graduate, Doctoral
Criteria: Applicant must be an enrolled member of an American Indian tribe or Alaskan Native corporation. Certification of degree of Indian blood and biography with career goals and interests must be submitted. Awarded every year.
Contact: Harriett Skye, Scholarship Coordinator.

1774   Sequoyah Heritage Award

University of Oklahoma
University Affairs
900 Asp Avenue, Room 236
Norman, OK 73019-0401
(405) 325-1701
Average award: $1,250
Number of awards: 4
Deadline: April
College level: Junior, Senior
Criteria: Applicant must be a Native American enrolled in an Arts and Sciences major with at least 30 hours of credit completed. Selection is based upon academic excellence, leadership, and potential for significant contributions to the American Indian community or the larger society. Awarded every year. Award may be used only at sponsoring institution.
Contact: Catherine Bishop, University Affairs, 900 Asp Avenue, Room 236, Norman, OK 73019-0401.

1775   Somas Hispanic American Scholarship

Portland State University
P.O. Box 751
Portland, OR 97207-0751
(503) 725-5270
Average award: $2,000
Number of awards: 2
College level: Graduate
Criteria: Applicant must be of Chicano or Latino descent. Awarded every year. Award may be used only at sponsoring institution.
Contact: Director, Educational Equity Programs and Services, (503) 725-4457.

1776   Sons of Italy Foundation National Leadership Grant

Sons of Italy Foundation
219 East Street NE
Washington, DC 20002
(202) 547-2900
Average award: $2,000
Maximum award: $5,000
Minimum award: $1,000
Number of awards: 12
Deadline: March 15
College level: Freshman, Sophomore, Junior, Senior, Graduate, Doctoral, Professional degree
Criteria: Applicant must be of Italian heritage and be a full-time student who has demonstrated exceptional leadership qualities and a distinguished level of scholastic achievement. Awarded every year.
Contact: Mark Dalessandro, Communications Manager and Project Coordinator.

1777   State Aid to Native Americans

New York State Higher Education Services Corporation
99 Washington Avenue
Albany, NY 12255
(518) 473-4563
Average award: $1,100
Minimum award: $456
Deadline: August 1; December 31; May 15
College level: Unspecified undergraduate
Criteria: Applicant must be on an official tribal roll of a New York State tribe or the child of an enrolled member, a resident of New York state, maintain good academic standing, and be enrolled in an approved postsecondary program in New York state. Awards are made to all eligible applicants. Scholarship is renewable. Awarded every year.
Contact: New York State Education Department, Native American Education Unit.

1778   State Scholarship Program

Southwest Texas State University
J. C. Kellam Building
San Marcos, TX 78666
(512) 245-2340
Average award: $1,000
Deadline: March 15
College level: Freshman, transfer students
Criteria: Applicant must be a minority Texas resident whose ethnic group makes up less than two-fifths of SWT's current enrollment. Applicant must rank in the top third of graduating class, or have a minimum combined SAT I score of 800 or composite ACT score of 18, or be a transfer student with a minimum 2.75 GPA. Financial need is required. Recipients of any form of athletic scholarship are not eligible. Awarded every year. Award may be used only at sponsoring institution.
Contact: Coordinator of Scholarships, Office of Student Financial Aid, 601 University Drive, San Marcos, TX 78666-4602, (512) 245-2315.

1779   Sutton Education Scholarship

National Association for the Advancement of Colored People (NAACP)
4805 Mount Hope Drive
Baltimore, MD 21215-3297
(410) 358-8900
Maximum award: $2,000
Minimum award: $1,000
Deadline: April 30
College level: Freshman, Sophomore, Junior, Senior, Graduate, Doctoral
Majors/Fields: Education
Criteria: Applicant must be a NAACP member. Undergraduate applicant must have a minimum GPA of 2.5 and graduate applicant must have a minimum 3.0 GPA. Renewable if satisfactory GPA is maintained. Awarded every year.
Contact: Andrea E. Moss, Education Department.

1780 Tennessee Higher Education Commission Scholarship

University of Tennessee, Knoxville
Financial Aid Office
115 Student Services Building
Knoxville, TN 37994
(615) 974-3131
Average award: $1,000
Maximum number of awards: 75
Minimum number of awards: 50
Deadline: February 1
College level: Freshman, Sophomore, Junior, Senior
Criteria: Applicant must be a minority with a minimum 3.0 GPA and minimum composite ACT score of 19 or combined SAT I score of 750. Scholarship is renewable. Awarded every year. Award may be used only at sponsoring institution.
Contact: Financial Aid Office.

1781 Tomas Rivera Admission Scholarship

Southwest Texas State University
J. C. Kellam Building
San Marcos, TX 78666
(512) 245-2340
Average award: $2,000
Number of awards: 25
College level: Freshman
Criteria: Applicant must be Hispanic and live in an on-campus residence hall, have a minimum combined SAT I score of 1000 or composite ACT score of 24, and rank in the top five percent of class or have a minimum 3.5 GPA. Awarded every year. Award may be used only at sponsoring institution.
Contact: Katrina Clanahan, Senior Admission Counselor, Admissions Office.

1782 Undergraduate Scholarships for Full-time Students of Swiss Descent

Swiss Benevolent Society of Chicago
6440 N. Bosworth Avenue
Chicago, IL 60626
Maximum award: $2,500
Minimum award: $750
Number of awards: 30
Deadline: March 6
College level: Freshman, Sophomore, Junior, Senior
Criteria: Applicant must be of Swiss descent, live in Illinois or southern Wisconsin, and have a minimum 3.5 GPA. High school seniors must have a minimum composite ACT score of 26 or combined SAT I score of 1050. Application must be requested between November 15 and February 1. Applicant must reapply for renewal. Awarded every year.
Contact: Scholarships.

1783 Underrepresented Minority Achievement Scholarship

Portland State University
P.O. Box 751
Portland, OR 97207-0751
(503) 725-5270
Average award: $3,060
Number of awards: 64
Deadline: March 1
College level: Freshman, Junior
Criteria: Applicant must be either African-American, Hispanic-American, or Native American. Renewable if minimum 2.5 GPA (2.7 GPA in major) is maintained. Awarded every year. Award may be used only at sponsoring institution.
Contact: Scholarships, Admissions Office, (503) 725-3511.

1784 UNCF Scholarship Program

United Negro College Fund (UNCF)
500 East 62nd Street
New York, NY 10021
(212) 326-1100
Average award: $2,500
Maximum award: $7,500
Minimum award: $500
Number of awards: 1200
Deadline: Rolling
College level: Graduate, unspecified undergraduate
Criteria: Applicant must attend one of 41 UNCF member institutions, have a minimum 2.5 GPA, demonstrate unmet financial need, and be nominated by the financial aid office of the UNCF institution student is attending. Renewal is based upon GPA, enrollment, and availability. Awarded every year.
Contact: UNCF Educational Services Department.

1785 U.S. Bank Minority Scholarship

Western Washington University
516 High Street
Bellingham, WA 98226-9006
(206) 650-3471
Average award: $2,000
Number of awards: 5
Deadline: March 31
College level: Freshman, Sophomore, Junior, Senior
Majors/Fields: Business, economics
Criteria: Applicant must be a declared major in a Coll of Business and Economics program, have a permanent residence in a community served by U.S. Bank, and demonstrate strong academic merit and potential. Applicant must be an African-American, Native American, Hispanic-American, or Asian/Pacific Islander. Awarded every year. Award may be used only at sponsoring institution.
Contact: Francine E. Titus, Scholarship Coordinator.

1786 US West "Beta" Scholarship

Portland State University
P.O. Box 751
Portland, OR 97207-0751
(503) 725-5270
Average award: $1,000
Number of awards: 3
College level: Sophomore, Junior, Senior
Criteria: Applicant must be of African-American heritage and demonstrate service, leadership, and financial need. Awarded every year. Award may be used only at sponsoring institution.
Contact: Scholarships, Educational Equity Programs and Services, (503) 725-4457.

1787 Urban League Scholarship

Rochester Institute of Technology
One Lomb Memorial Drive
Rochester, NY 14623
(716) 475-2186
Average award: $2,500
Number of awards: 15
Deadline: February 15
College level: Freshman
Criteria: Applicant must be an African-American, Hispanic-American or Native American. Selection is based upon academic qualifications, leadership potential, and demonstrated financial need. Satisfactory academic progress is required to retain scholarship. Awarded every year. Award may be used only at sponsoring institution.
Contact: Verna Hazen, Director of Financial Aid.

1788 Voices of Many Feathers Scholarship

Portland State University
P.O. Box 751
Portland, OR 97207-0751
(503) 725-5270
Average award: $2,000
Number of awards: 2
College level: Graduate, Doctoral
Criteria: Applicant must be of Native American descent and submit tribal enrollment numbers or other proof of descent. Selection is based upon academic record, community and/or university service, and leadership. Award may be used only at sponsoring institution.
Contact: Scholarships, Educational Equity Programs and Services, (503) 725-4457.

1789 Wasie Foundation Scholarship

Wasie Foundation
909 Foshay Tower
Minneapolis, MN 55402
(612) 332-3883
Average award: $1,500
Maximum award: $3,500
Minimum award: $500
Number of awards: 50
Deadline: April 15
College level: Freshman, Sophomore, Junior, Senior, Graduate, Doctoral
Criteria: Applicant must be a Christian, full-time student of Polish ancestry who intends to attend one of the following institutions in Minnesota: Coll of St. Benedict, Coll of St. Catherine, Coll of St. Scholastica, U of St. Thomas, Dunwoody Industrial Inst, Hamline U School of Law, St. John's U, St. Mary's Coll, U of Minnesota (Twin Cities), or William Mitchell Coll of Law. Selection is based upon academic ability, personal qualities, extracurricular activities, financial need, educational goals, and social conduct. Members of the Communist party are not eligible. Reapplication is required to retain scholarship. Awarded every year.
Contact: Ms. Lea M. Johnson, Scholarship Administrator.

1790 West Virginia Italian Heritage Festival Scholarship

National Italian American Foundation (NIAF)
Educational Scholarship Program
1860 19th Street, NW
Washington, DC 20009-5599
(202) 638-2137
Average award: $2,000
Number of awards: 3
Deadline: May 31
College level: Freshman, Sophomore, Junior, Senior
Criteria: Applicant must be Italian-American, a West Virginia resident, demonstrate financial need, and submit transcript. Awarded every year.
Contact: Dr. Maria Lombardo, Education Director.

1791 William Randolph Hearst Presidential Scholarship

Clemson University
G-01 Sikes Hall
Clemson, SC 29634-5123
(803) 656-2280
Average award: $5,000
Number of awards: 1
Deadline: March 1
College level: Freshman
Criteria: Applicant must be the most outstanding black entering freshman. Awarded every year. Award may be used only at sponsoring institution.
Contact: Marvin Carmichael, Director of Financial Aid.

1792 William Toto Scholarship

National Italian American Foundation (NIAF)
Educational Scholarship Program
1860 19th Street, NW
Washington, DC 20009-5599
(202) 638-2137
Minimum award: $1,000
Number of awards: 3
Deadline: May 31
College level: Junior
Majors/Fields: Business management, engineering
Criteria: Applicant must be Italian-American, demonstrate financial need, and submit transcript. Awarded every year.
Contact: Dr. Maria Lombardo, Education Director.

1793 Wisconsin HEAB Native American Student Grant

Wisconsin Higher Educational Aids Board (HEAB)
P.O. Box 7885
131 West Wilson Street
Madison, WI 53707-7885
(608) 266-0888
Maximum award: $2,200
College level: Freshman, Sophomore, Junior, Senior, Graduate, Doctoral
Criteria: Applicant must be a Wisconsin resident who is at least one quarter Native American and must attend a Wisconsin institution (public, private, and proprietary schools are all eligible). HEAB has an informal matching arrangement with grant funds awarded by the Federal Bureau of Indian Affairs and Wisconsin Tribal governments. Renewable for a maximum of ten semesters. Awarded every year.
Contact: Joyce Apfel, Grants Coordinator.

1794 Yakima Nation Tribal Scholarship

Yakima Indian Agency
Box 151
Toppenish, WA 98948
(509) 865-5121
Average award: $1,000
Deadline: July 1
College level: Unspecified undergraduate or graduate
Criteria: Applicant must be a member of the Yakima Indian Nation (enrolled tribal member). Recipient must attend an accredited two- or four-year college or university to receive degree in nonvocational area of study. Scholarship is renewable. Awarded every year.
Contact: Arlene Washines.

Gender Specific

1795 AARP Women's Initiative 10th Anniversary Scholarship

Business and Professional Women's Foundation
2012 Massachusetts Avenue, NW
Washington, DC 20036
(202) 293-1200
Maximum award: $3,000
Minimum award: $1,000
Number of awards: 15
Deadline: April 15
College level: Freshman, Sophomore, Junior, Senior
Criteria: Applicant must be a woman, at least 50 years of age, have financial need, and have a definite plan to use the desired training to enter or re-enter the work force or to move out of a low wage or obsolete job. Special consideration is given to women with critical financial need, sole supporters of household, women who have not earned a degree beyond high school, and/or AARP members. Enclose a self-addressed, double-stamped, business size envelope with request.
Contact: Scholarships.

1796 American Legion–Utah Auxiliary Scholarship

American Legion–Utah Auxiliary
Girls State Chairman
B-61 State Capitol Building
Salt Lake City, UT 84114
(801) 538-1014
Average award: Tuition
Number of awards: 4
College level: Freshman
Criteria: Applicant must attend Utah Girls State and demonstrate good citizenship. Scholarship must be used at Southern Utah State Coll. Awarded every year.
Contact: Girls State Chairman.

1797 America's Junior Miss

America's Junior Miss
P.O. Box 2786
Mobile, AL 36652-2786
(205) 438-3621
Average award: Tuition, room, board, and fees to each state winner
Maximum award: $30,000
Number of awards: 51
College level: Freshman
Criteria: Applicant must be a U.S. citizen, a high school senior, have never been married, and be a legal resident of the district or state she represents. Applicants are chosen locally, then advance to state competitions, and the 50 state winners compete for the national title. Selection is based upon panel evaluation (30 percent), scholastic achievement (20 percent), creative and performing arts (20 percent), fitness (15 percent), and poise (15 percent). Additionally, 215 colleges and universities throughout the U.S. give scholarship support to local, state, and national participants. Awarded every year.

1798 Avon Products Scholarship for Women in Business Studies

Business and Professional Women's Foundation
2012 Massachusetts Avenue, NW
Washington, DC 20036
(202) 293-1200
Average award: $1,000
Number of awards: 50
Deadline: April 15
College level: Sophomore, Junior, Senior, Graduate
Majors/Fields: Accounting, business, business administration, management, marketing, sales
Criteria: Applicant must be a woman, age 25 or older, a U.S. citizen, demonstrate financial need, and be officially accepted at an accredited U.S. institution. Applicant must use the training to upgrade skills for career advancement, train for a new career, or to enter or re-enter the job market. Applicant must graduate with a degree or certificate within 24 months of applying for the scholarship. Send a business-sized self-addressed, double-stamped envelope and enrollment verification. Awarded every year.
Contact: Scholarships.

1799 Betty Baum Hirschfield Scholarship

University of Oklahoma
University Affairs
900 Asp Avenue, Room 236
Norman, OK 73019-0401
(405) 325-1701
Average award: $3,500
Number of awards: 2
Deadline: March 1
College level: Returning student
Criteria: Applicant must be a single mother returning to school after an interruption at any stage of her education; equivalent of two semesters full-time work with a minimum "B" average must have been completed within the last five years. Selection is based upon likelihood of academic success and financial need. Awarded every year. Award may be used only at sponsoring institution.
Contact: Women's Studies Program, 530 PHSC, Norman, OK 73019, (405) 325-3481.

1800 BPW Career Advancement Scholarship

Business and Professional Women's Foundation
2012 Massachusetts Avenue, NW
Washington, DC 20036
(202) 293-1200
Average award: $1,000
Minimum award: $500
Number of awards: 200
Deadline: April 15
College level: Sophomore, Junior, Senior, Graduate
Majors/Fields: Computer science, engineering, paralegal studies, science, teacher education
Criteria: Applicant must be a woman, age 30 or older, a U.S. citizen, demonstrate critical financial need, and be officially accepted into a program of study at an accredited U.S. institution. Applicant must have a definite plan to use the training to upgrade skills for career advancement, train for a new career, or to enter or re-enter the job market. Applicant must graduate with a degree or certificate within 24 months of applying for the scholarship. Send a business-size (#10) self-addressed, double-stamped (first class) envelope and enrollment verification (copy of acceptance letter or most recent grade report). Awarded every year.
Contact: Scholarships.

1801 Chamberlain Memorial Scholarship

Montana State University
Bozeman, MT 59717
(406) 994-2845
Average award: $1,000
Maximum award: $1,500
Minimum award: $750
Maximum number of awards: 30
Minimum number of awards: 20
Deadline: March 1
College level: Sophomore, Junior, Senior
Criteria: Applicant must be a woman, a full-time student, a resident of Montana, and demonstrate financial need. Awarded every year. Award may be used only at sponsoring institution.
Contact: Rebecca S. Jones, Assistant Director for Scholarships & Grants, Financial Aid.

1802 Doris Mullen Memorial Scholarship

The Whirly-Girls, Inc.
Executive Towers 10-D
207 W. Clarendon Avenue
Phoenix, AZ 85013
(602) 263-0190
Average award: $4,500
Number of awards: 2
Deadline: November 15
College level: Helicopter flight trainees
Majors/Fields: Aviation
Criteria: Applicant must be a woman, demonstrate financial need, desire a career as a helicopter pilot, and hold a valid FAA pilot's license for an airplane, balloon, or glider. Scholarship is to be used only for helicopter flight training. Awarded every year.
Contact: Charlotte Kelley, President.

1803 Eleanor Roosevelt Teacher Fellowship

American Association of University Women Education Foundation
1111 16th Street N.W.
Washington, DC 20036-4873
(202) 728-7700
Maximum award: $5,000
Minimum award: $1,000
Deadline: December 1
College level: Teachers for specified education advancement
Criteria: Applicant must be a woman, elementary or secondary school teacher, U.S. citizen, dedicated to improving educational opportunities for women of all ages, and presently employed with at least five years full-time teaching experience and plans to continue teaching for the next five years.
Contact: Fellowships, 2401 Virginia Avenue, NW, Washington, DC 20037, (202) 728-7603.

1804 Frank McHale Memorial Scholarship

American Legion–Indiana
Americanism Office
777 North Meridian Street
Indianapolis, IN 46204
(317) 635-8411 extension 264
Average award: $2,300
Maximum award: $3,100
Minimum award: $2,100
Number of awards: 3
Deadline: May
College level: High school junior
Criteria: Applicant must be a boy finishing his junior year at an Indiana high school and must be a participant in Hoosier Boys State. Awarded every year.
Contact: Americanism Office.

1805 Holly A. Cornell Scholarship

American Water Works Association
6666 West Quincy Avenue
Denver, CO 80235
(303) 347-6210
Average award: $5,000
Number of awards: 1
Deadline: December 15
College level: Graduate
Majors/Fields: Water supply, water treatment
Criteria: Applicant must be a woman and/or minority student. Selection is based upon academic record and leadership potential. Awarded every year.
Contact: Scholarship Coordinator.

1806 Jeannette Rankin Foundation Award

Jeannette Rankin Foundation
P.O. Box 6653
Athens, GA 30604
Average award: $1,000
Maximum number of awards: 10
Minimum number of awards: 7
Deadline: March 1
College level: Sophomore, Junior, Senior, technical/vocational students
Criteria: Applicant must be a woman, 35 years or older, a U.S. citizen, and accepted or enrolled in a certified program of technical/vocational training or an undergraduate program. Financial need must be demonstrated. Request application between September 1 and January 15 and indicate age and level of study in letter of request; self-addressed stamped envelope is required. Awarded every year.
Contact: Awards.

1807 Karla Scherer Foundation Scholarship Program

Karla Scherer Foundation
100 Renaissance Center, Suite 1680
Detroit, MI 48243
Majors/Fields: Business
Criteria: Applicant must be a woman. When requesting an application, she should include the name(s) of school(s) she is applying (or attending), the courses she plans to take, and how she intends to use her education in her chosen career. If the request meets the preliminary criteria, then an application package will be mailed. Scholarship is renewable. Awarded every year.
Contact: Scholarships.

1808 Lt. William J. Scott Scholarship

University of Oklahoma
University Affairs
900 Asp Avenue, Room 236
Norman, OK 73019-0401
(405) 325-1701
Average award: $1,000
Maximum number of awards: 120
Minimum number of awards: 90
Deadline: March 1
College level: Freshman, Sophomore, Junior, Senior, Graduate, Doctoral
Criteria: Applicant must be an unmarried man and a U.S. citizen, born and residing in the U.S., who demonstrates financial need. Preference is given to Osage Indians. Awarded every year. Award may be used only at sponsoring institution.
Contact: Office of Financial Aid Services, 731 Elm, Norman, OK 73019-0230, (405) 325-4521.

1809 Mary Isabel Sibley Fellowship

Phi Beta Kappa Society
1811 Q Street, NW
Washington, DC 20009
(202) 265-3808
Average award: $10,000
Number of awards: 1
Deadline: January 15
College level: Doctoral, postdoctoral study
Majors/Fields: French language, French literature, Greek archaeology, Greek history, Greek language, Greek literature
Criteria: Applicant must be an unmarried woman between 25 and 35 years of age who has her doctorate or has fulfilled all requirements for it except the dissertation. Given in odd-numbered years for Greek language, literature, history, or archaeology; given in even-numbered years for French language or literature. Applicant must remain unmarried during the fellowship year. Awarded every year.
Contact: Linda D. Surles, Program Officer.

1810 Miss America Scholarship

Miss America Scholarship Foundation
P.O. Box 119
Atlantic City, NJ 08404
(609) 345-7571
Maximum award: $35,000
Minimum award: $2,500
Number of awards: 50
College level: Freshman, Sophomore, Junior, Senior, Graduate, Doctoral
Criteria: Applicant must enter a local competition, advance to the state competition, and then enter national competition. Applicant must be a woman, high school graduate, never been married, of good moral character, and a U.S. citizen. Awarded every year.
Contact: Karen Aarons, Executive Vice President.

1811 Miss Teenage America Annual Competition

Miss Teenage America Pageant
6420 Wilshire Blvd.
Los Angeles, CA 90048-5515
Maximum award: $15,000
Number of awards: 1
Deadline: July 15
College level: Freshman
Criteria: Selection is based upon applicant's scholastic achievement, individual accomplishment, community service, poise, appearance, and personality. Awarded every year.
Contact: Miss Teenage America Pageant.

1812   Nancy Ryles Scholarship

Portland State University
P.O. Box 751
Portland, OR 97207-0751
(503) 725-5270
Average award: $5,000
Number of awards: 1
Deadline: April 10
College level: Sophomore, Junior, Senior, Graduate
Criteria: Applicant must be a woman returning to school after break in education due to family responsibilities. Selection is based upon financial need and potential for academic success. Scholarship is renewable. Awarded every year. Award may be used only at sponsoring institution.
Contact: Virginia McElroy, Scholarship Coordinator.

1813   New York Life Foundation Scholarship for Women in the Health Professions

Business and Professional Women's Foundation
2012 Massachusetts Avenue, NW
Washington, DC 20036
(202) 293-1200
Maximum award: $1,000
Minimum award: $500
Number of awards: 100
Deadline: April 15
College level: Freshman, Sophomore, Junior, Senior
Majors/Fields: Health care
Criteria: Applicant must be a woman, age 25 years or older, a U.S. citizen, demonstrate critical financial need, and be officially accepted into a program of study at an accredited U.S. institution. Applicant must have a definite plan to use the training to upgrade skills for career advancement, train for a new career, or to enter or re-enter the job market. Applicant must graduate with a degree or certificate within 24 months from August 31 of the application year. Send a business-size (#10) self-addressed, double-stamped (first class) envelope and enrollment verification (copy of acceptance letter or most recent grade report). Awarded every year.
Contact: Scholarships.

1814   Olga V. Alexandria (Logan) Scholarship

University of Utah
Financial Aid and Scholarships Office
105 Student Services Building
Salt Lake City, UT 84112
(801) 581-6211
Maximum award: $2,000
Deadline: February 15
College level: Freshman, Sophomore, Junior, Senior
Majors/Fields: Ballet, business, law, medicine, theatre
Criteria: Applicant must be a woman and demonstrate financial need. Reapplication is required to retain scholarship. Awarded every year. Award may be used only at sponsoring institution.
Contact: Financial Aid and Scholarships Office.

1815   Project RENEW (Career Development) Grants

American Association of University Women Education Foundation
1111 16th Street N.W.
Washington, DC 20036-4873
(202) 728-7700
Maximum award: $5,000
Minimum award: $1,000
Deadline: January 1
College level: Doctoral, specified professional programs
Criteria: Applicant must be a woman, who, through higher education, is re-entering the job market or making a career change or advancement. Special consideration is given to AAUW members. Minority women are encouraged to apply. Applicant must be a U.S. citizen and pursuing course work at an institution accredited by the Federal Veteran's Administration. Awarded every year.
Contact: Grants, 2401 Virginia Avenue, NW, Washington, DC 20037, (202) 728-7603.

1816   Richard Cecil Hicks Educational Fund Scholarship

Clemson University
G-01 Sikes Hall
Clemson, SC 29634-5123
(803) 656-2280
Average award: $1,000
Number of awards: 4
Deadline: March 1
College level: Freshman, Sophomore, Junior, Senior
Majors/Fields: Architecture, engineering
Criteria: Applicant must be a man and a student in the Colleges of Architecture and Engineering and demonstrate financial need. Awarded every year. Award may be used only at sponsoring institution.
Contact: Marvin Carmichael, Director of Financial Aid.

1817   Sally Bragg Baker Scholarship

School for International Training
P.O. Box 676
Kipling Road
Brattleboro, VT 05302
(802) 257-7751
Average award: $2,666
Maximum award: $3,000
Minimum award: $2,000
Number of awards: 3
Deadline: April 30 (fall semester); October 15 (spring semester)
College level: Undergraduate
Criteria: Applicant must be a woman participating in the semester-abroad program and should demonstrate the qualities of international awareness and a desire to create a more peaceful world through international exchange. Financial need is considered. Awarded every year. Award may be used only at sponsoring institution.
Contact: Mary Henderson, Financial Aid Officer, (802) 258-3280.

1818   Spence Reese Foundation

Spence Reese Foundation
Boys & Girls Clubs of San Diego
3760 Fourth Avenue, Suite 1
San Diego, CA 92103
(619) 298-3520
Average award: $2,000
Number of awards: 4
Deadline: May 15
College level: Freshman
Majors/Fields: Engineering, law, medicine, political science
Criteria: Applicant must be a boy and a graduating high school senior, preferably residing within a 250-mile radius of San Diego. Selection is based upon academic standing, academic ability, financial ability, and potential for good citizenship. To request an application, send a self-addressed, stamped envelope and pertinent information. Awarded for four years.
Contact: John W. Treiber, President/CEO.

1819   Whirly-Girls Memorial Scholarship

The Whirly-Girls, Inc.
Executive Towers 10-D
207 W. Clarendon Avenue
Phoenix, AZ 85013
(602) 263-0190
Average award: $4,000
Number of awards: 1
Deadline: November 15
College level: Helicopter flight trainees
Majors/Fields: Aviation
Criteria: Applicant must be a woman, demonstrate financial need, desire a career as a helicopter pilot, and hold a valid FAA pilot's license for an airplane, balloon, or glider. Scholarship is to be used only for helicopter flight training. Awarded every year.
Contact: Charlotte Kelley, President.

1820 Women's Western Golf Scholarship

Women's Western Golf Foundation
Director of Scholarships
393 Ramsay Road
Deerfield, IL 60015
Average award: $2,000
Number of awards: 15
Deadline: March 15
College level: Freshman
Criteria: Applicant must be a woman and a U.S. citizen. Selection is based upon academic achievement, financial need, excellence of character, and involvement with the sport of golf. Skill or excellence in the sport of golf is not a criterion. Satisfactory GPA and financial need are required to retain scholarship. Awarded every year.
Contact: Mrs. Richard Willis, Director of Scholarships.

1821 Wyeth-Ayerst Scholarship for Women in Graduate Medical and Health Business Programs

Business and Professional Women's Foundation
2012 Massachusetts Avenue, NW
Washington, DC 20036
(202) 293-1200
Average award: $2,000
Deadline: April 15
College level: Graduate, Doctoral
Majors/Fields: Biomedical engineering, biomedical research, medical technology, pharmaceutical marketing, public health, public health policy
Criteria: Applicant must be a woman, age 25 or older, a U.S. citizen, demonstrate critical financial need, and be officially accepted into a program of study at an accredited U.S. institution. Applicant must have a definite plan to use the training to upgrade skills for career advancement, train for a new career, or to enter or re-enter the job market. Applicant must graduate with a degree or certificate with in 24 months of applying for the scholarship. Send a business-size (#10) self-addressed, double-stamped (first class) envelope and enrollment verification (copy of acceptance letter or most recent grade report). Awarded every year.
Contact: Scholarships.

Military Affiliation

1822 102nd Infantry Division Scholarship

102nd Infantry Division Association
1821 Shackleford Road
Nashville, TN 37215
(615) 292-2469
Maximum award: $1,200
Minimum award: $500
Number of awards: 14
Deadline: May 15
Criteria: Applicant's father or grandfather must have been an active member of 102rd Infantry Division between August 1942 and March 1946 and must be a dues-paying member of the association. If deceased, must have been a dues-paying member at time of death.
Contact: Scholarships.

1823 37th Infantry Division Award

37th Division Veterans Association
183 E. Mound Street
Suite 103
Columbus, OH 43215
(614) 228-3788
Average award: $1,000
Number of awards: 2
Deadline: April 1
College level: Freshman, Sophomore, Junior, Senior
Criteria: Applicant must be the son or daughter of a 37th Division veteran of World War I, World War II or the Korean conflict. (Name, address and unit father served in the 37th infantry division must be listed.) Award is based upon financial need. Scholarship is renewable. Awarded every year.
Contact: James W. Wallace, Secretary.

1824 Air Force Civilian Cooperative Work-Study Program

Air Force Civilian Cooperative Work-Study Programs
Air Force Material Command (DPCF)
Wright-Patterson Air Force Base
Dayton, OH 45433-5000
(513) 257-4136
College level: Sophomore, Junior, Senior, Graduate
Majors/Fields: Engineering, physical science, life science
Criteria: Applicant must be a college student preparing for a career in engineering, physical/life sciences, or other technical fields and enrolled in either an associate or bachelor's degree curriculum adapted to a cooperative work-study program that has a formal arrangement with the Air Force.
Contact: Cooperative Work-Study Program.

1825 Air Force Sergeants Association Scholarship

Air Force Sergeants Association (AFSA)
P.O. Box 50
Temple Hills, MD 20757-0050
(800) 638-0594
Average award: $2,000
Maximum award: $2,500
Number of awards: 12
Deadline: April 15
College level: Freshman, Sophomore, Junior, Senior
Criteria: Applicant must be an unmarried, dependent child, under age 23, of an AFSA member or AFSA Auxiliary member. Selection is based upon academic ability, character, leadership, writing ability, and potential for success. Financial need is not considered. Awarded every year.
Contact: Scholarship Administrator.

1826 Airmen Memorial Foundation CMSAF Richard D. Kisling Scholarship

Air Force Sergeants Association (AFSA)
P.O. Box 50
Temple Hills, MD 20757-0050
(800) 638-0594
Maximum award: $3,000
Minimum award: $1,000
Number of awards: 7
Deadline: April 15
College level: Freshman, Sophomore, Junior, Senior
Criteria: Applicant must be an unmarried, dependent child, under age 25, of an enlisted member serving in the U.S. Air Force, Air National Guard, or Air Force Reserve, or in retired status. Selection is based upon academic ability, character, leadership, writing ability, and potential for success. SAT I required. Send self-addressed, stamped (78 cents) envelope (#10 business) for application. Awarded every year.
Contact: Scholarship Administrator, Airmen Memorial Building, 5211 Auth Road, Suitland, MD 20746.

1827 Airmen Memorial Foundation Scholarship

Air Force Sergeants Association (AFSA)
P.O. Box 50
Temple Hills, MD 20757-0050
(800) 638-0594
Average award: $1,000
Number of awards: 20
Deadline: April 15
College level: Freshman, Sophomore, Junior, Senior
Criteria: Applicant must be an unmarried, dependent child, under age 25, of an enlisted member serving in the U.S. Air Force, Air National Guard, or Air Force Reserve, or in retired status. Send self-addressed, stamped envelope (#10 business) for application. Awarded every year.
Contact: Scholarship Administrator, Airmen Memorial Building, 5211 Auth Road, Suitland, MD 20746.

1828 Alabama G.I. Dependents' Scholarship Program

Alabama GI and Dependents Educational Benefit Act
Alabama State Department of Veterans Affairs
P.O. Box 1509
Montgomery, AL 36102-1509
(334) 242-5077
Maximum award: Tuition, books, and lab fees
Criteria: Applicant must be the dependent (child, stepchild, spouse, or unremarried widow[er]) of a disabled veteran . The veteran must have honorably served at least 90 days of continuous active federal military service, be rated 20 percent or more disabled due to service-connected disabilities or have held the qualifying rating at the time of death, or be a former prisoner of war, declared missing in action, or have died as the result of a service-connected disability or in the line of duty while on active duty. The veteran must have been a permanent civilian resident of the state of Alabama for at least one year immediately prior to (a) initial entry into active military service or (b) any subsequent period of military service in which a break in service occurred and civilian residency was established. Dependents of permanently disabled service-connected veterans rated at 100 percent may also qualify after the veteran has established at least five years of permanent residency in Alabama.
Contact: Alabama G.I. Dependents' Scholarship Program, Department of Veterans Affairs.

1829 Alabama GI Dependents' Educational Benefit Program

Alabama Commission on Higher Education
3465 Norman Bridge Road
Montgomery, AL 36105-2310
(334) 281-1921
Average award: Tuition, fees, and books
College level: Freshman, Sophomore, Junior, Senior
Criteria: Applicant must be the child or spouse of an eligible Alabama veteran and be attending a public postsecondary educational institution in Alabama. Scholarship is renewable. Awarded every year.
Contact: Alabama State Department of Veterans Affairs, P.O. Box 1509, Montgomery, AL 36102.

1830 Alabama National Guard Educational Assistance Program

Alabama Commission on Higher Education
3465 Norman Bridge Road
Montgomery, AL 36105-2310
(334) 281-1921
Average award: $560
Maximum award: $1,000
Minimum award: $50
College level: Freshman, Sophomore, Junior, Senior, Graduate
Criteria: Applicant must be a member of the Alabama National Guard attending an Alabama postsecondary institution. Scholarship is renewable. Awarded every year.
Contact: Jan B. Hilyer, Assistant Director for Grants and Scholarships, (334) 281-1921.

1831 American Legion–Alabama Auxiliary Scholarship

American Legion–Alabama
P.O. Box 1069
120 North Jackson Street
Montgomery, AL 36101-1069
(202) 262-6638
Average award: $850
Number of awards: 37
Deadline: May 1
College level: Freshman, Sophomore, Junior, Senior
Criteria: Applicant must be the child or grandchild of a veteran of World War I, World War II, Korean Conflict, Vietnam Conflict, Beirut/Granada Emergency, or Panama Emergency. Applicant must attend an Alabama state-supported college. Self-addressed, stamped envelope is required to receive application. Awarded every year.
Contact: Ray Andrews, Adjutant, American Legion Auxiliary Department Headquarters, 120 North Jackson Street, Montgomery, AL 36104, (205) 262-1176.

1832 American Legion–Alabama Scholarship

American Legion–Alabama
P.O. Box 1069
120 North Jackson Street
Montgomery, AL 36101-1069
(202) 262-6638
Average award: $850
Number of awards: 130
Deadline: May 1
College level: Freshman, Sophomore, Junior, Senior
Criteria: Applicant must be the child or grandchild of a veteran of World War I, World War II, Korean conflict, or Vietnam Conflict. Applicant must be a resident of Alabama and attend an Alabama college. Self-addressed, stamped envelope is required to receive application. Award is for four years. Awarded every year.
Contact: Department Adjutant.

1833 American Legion–Florida Auxiliary Scholarship

American Legion–Florida Auxiliary
American Legion Auxiliary
P.O. Box 547917
Orlando, Florida 32854-7917
Maximum award: $1,000
Minimum award: $500
Deadline: March 1
College level: Freshman, Sophomore, Junior, Senior, vocational/technical student
Criteria: Applicant must be sponsored by an Auxiliary Unit, be the child or grandchild of an honorably discharged veteran, be a Florida resident, and attend school in Florida. Application must be requested by January 1. Good scholastic record, financial need, and reapplication are required to retain scholarship. Awarded every year.
Contact: Secretary-Treasurer.

1834 American Legion–Maryland Auxiliary Scholarships

American Legion–Maryland Auxiliary
5205 East Drive
Suite R
Baltimore, MD 21227
(301) 242-9519
Maximum award: $2,000
Minimum award: $1,000
Number of awards: 2
Deadline: May 1
Majors/Fields: Arts, business, education, home economics, nursing, public administration, sciences
Criteria: Applicant must be a Maryland resident and the daughter of a veteran. One award is for an applicant planning to study arts, sciences, business, public administration, education, or home economics at a college or university in Maryland. One award is for an applicant age 16-22 training to be an R.N. who demonstrates financial need and has resided in Maryland for at least five years. Awarded every year.
Contact: Department Secretary.

1835 American Legion–Massachusetts Scholarship

American Legion–Massachusetts
Room 546-2
State House
Boston, MA 02133
(617) 727-2966
Maximum award: $1,000
Minimum award: $500
Number of awards: 15
Deadline: April 1
College level: Freshman
Criteria: Applicant must be the child of a Department of Massachusetts Legion member in good standing, or child of a deceased member who was in good standing at the time of death. One award is for nursing only. Awarded every year.
Contact: Department Scholarship Chairman, Room 542-2, State House, Boston, MA 02133.

1836 American Legion–Oregon Auxiliary Grant

American Legion–Oregon Auxiliary
P.O. Box 1730
Wilsonville, OR 97070-1730
(503) 682-3162
Average award: $1,000
Number of awards: 3
Deadline: April 1
College level: Freshman, Sophomore, Junior, Senior, Graduate, Doctoral
Criteria: Applicant must be the child or widow of a veteran, or the wife of a disabled veteran attending a college, university, business college, vocational school, or any accredited school in Oregon.
Contact: Chairman of Education.

1837 Amvets National Scholarship

Amvets National Headquarters
4647 Forbes Boulevard
Lanham, MD 20706-9961
(301) 459-9600
Average award: $1,000
Number of awards: 16
Deadline: April 15
College level: Freshman, Graduate, Doctoral
Criteria: Applicant must be a U.S. citizen and a veteran or the child of a veteran. Selection is based upon academic achievement and financial need. Scholarship is renewable.
Contact: Programs Department.

1838 Armed Forces Health Professions Scholarship

Naval Personnel Command
NMPC-602
Washington, DC 20370
Average award: Full tuition
College level: Doctoral
Majors/Fields: Medicine
Criteria: Applicant must be a qualified student attending an accredited medical school or school of osteopathy in the U.S. Graduates of the program become Navy medical officers. Award is for up to four years. Awarded every year.
Contact: Local Navy recruiter, (800) 327-NAVY.

1839 Casaday-Elmore Ministerial Scholarship

National Board Civil Air Patrol
HQ CAP-USAF/ETTC
105 S. Hansell St. Building 714
Maxwell Air Force Base, AL 36112-6332
(205) 293-5315
Maximum award: $1,500
Minimum award: $750
Deadline: October 1
College level: Freshman, Sophomore, Junior, Senior
Majors/Fields: Ministry
Criteria: Applicant must be a member of the Civil Air Patrol who has been accepted by an accredited college with plans to enter the ministry. CAP Form 95 must be submitted. Awarded every year.
Contact: Lt. Col. Bruce Gunn, Cadet Special Activity.

1840 Children of Prisoners of War or Persons Missing in Action Tuition Exemption

Texas Higher Education Coordinating Board
Student Financial Assistance
P.O. Box 12788, Capitol Station
Austin, TX 78711-2788
(512) 483-6340
Average award: $3,669
Number of awards: 3
College level: Freshman, Sophomore, Junior, Senior
Criteria: Applicant must be the dependent child of a Texas resident who is a POW or MIA; proof of parent's status from the Department of Defense is required. Applicant must attend a public college or university in Texas, and be under 21 years of age or under 25 years of age if majority of financial support is from parent. Scholarship is renewable. Awarded every year.
Contact: Mack Adams, Assistant Commissioner, Student Services.

1841 College Fee Waiver for California National Guard Dependents

State Department of Veterans Affairs
Division of Veterans Services
P.O. Box 942895
Sacramento, CA 94295-0001
(800) 952-5626
College level: Freshman, Sophomore, Junior, Senior, Graduate, Doctoral
Criteria: Applicant must be a dependent or unremarried surviving spouse of a member or the California National Guard who was killed or disabled resulting from an event that occured while in the active service of the state. Reapplication is required to retain scholarship. Awarded every year.
Contact: County Veterans Service Office.

1842 College Fee Waiver for Veteran's Dependents

State Department of Veterans Affairs
Division of Veterans Services
P.O. Box 942895
Sacramento, CA 94295-0001
(800) 952-5626
Maximum award: Waiver of fees
Deadline: None
College level: Freshman, Sophomore, Junior, Senior, Graduate
Criteria: Applicant must be the dependent of a veteran who has a service-connected disability or who died a service-related death. Veteran must have served during a period of war and been honorably discharged. Applicant must attain eligibility while under age 21 to continue until 27 years of age (30 if dependant is also a veteran); there is no age limit for surviving spouses. Applicant must attend a California state college, university, or community college. Reapplication is required to retain scholarship. Awarded every year.
Contact: Country Veterans Service Office.

1843 College Fee Waiver Program

State Department of Veterans Affairs
Division of Veterans Services
P.O. Box 942895
Sacramento, CA 94295-0001
(800) 952-5626
Maximum award: Waiver of fees
Deadline: None
College level: Freshman, Sophomore, Junior, Senior, Graduate, Doctoral
Criteria: Applicant must be the child of a veteran who has a service-connected disability or who died a service-related death. Applicant's annual income, including support from parents, can not exceed $7,000. Applicant must attend a California state college, university, or community college. Reapplication and meeting income requirements are required to retain scholarship. Awarded every year.
Contact: County Veterans Service Office.

1844 Colonel Hayden W. Wagner Memorial Fund

Daughters of the United States Army
Scholarship Chairman
7717 Rockledge Court
West Springfield, VA 22152
Average award: $1,000
Number of awards: 3
Deadline: March 31
College level: Freshman, Sophomore, Junior, Senior, Unspecified undergraduate
Criteria: Applicant must be the daughter, step-daughter, adopted daughter, or granddaughter of a career commissioned officer or warrant officer of the U.S. Army. Selection is based upon academic standing, test scores, school and community activities, and financial need. Letter of inquiry must include dates of the officer's active duty, with name, rank, and social security number, and a self-addressed, stamped envelope. Renewal is based upon continued achievement and financial need. Awarded every year.
Contact: Janet B. Otto, Scholarship Chairman.

1845 Col. Louisa Spruance Morse CAP Scholarship

National Board Civil Air Patrol
HQ CAP-USAF/ETTC
105 S. Hansell St. Building 714
Maxwell Air Force Base, AL 36112-6332
(205) 293-5315
Average award: $1,000
Number of awards: 5
Deadline: April 1
College level: Sophomore, Junior, Senior
Majors/Fields: Aviation
Criteria: Applicant must be a Civil Air Patrol member pursing an aviation education at Embry-Riddle Aeronautical U. CAP Form 95 must be submitted. Awarded every year.
Contact: Lt. Col. Bruce Gunn, Cadet Special Activities.

1846 Daughters of Cincinnati Scholarship

Daughters of Cincinnati
122 East 58th Street
New York, NY 10022
Average award: $1,000
Maximum award: $3,000
Minimum award: $500
Number of awards: 8
Deadline: March 15
College level: Freshman
Criteria: Applicant must be the daughter of a commissioned officer in the regular Army, Navy, Air Force, Coast Guard, or Marine Corps (active, retired, or deceased). Send parent's rank and branch of service with request for application. Selection is based upon a combination of financial need and merit. Satisfactory academic performance is required to retain scholarship. Awarded every year.
Contact: Scholarship Administrator.

1847 Department Scholarship

American Legion–Oregon Auxiliary
P.O. Box 1730
Wilsonville, OR 97070-1730
(503) 682-3162
Average award: $1,000
Deadline: March 15
College level: Freshman, Sophomore, Junior, Senior, Graduate, Doctoral
Criteria: Applicant must be the child or widow of a deceased veteran, or wife of a disabled veteran pursuing education at any accredited institution of higher education in Oregon. Awarded every year.
Contact: Chairman of Education.

1848 Dependents of Former Prisoners of War/ Missing in Action Scholarship

Minnesota Department of Veterans Affairs
Veterans Service Building
St. Paul, MN 55155-2079
(612)-296-2562
Maximum award: Full tuition
College level: Vocational/technical students
Criteria: Applicant must be the dependent of a POW or MIA who was a resident of Minnesota at the time of entry into the armed forces. Cite Minn. stat. 197.09, subd. 2. Applicant must enroll in a state-supported Vo-Tech institute. Awarded every year.
Contact: Minnesota Department of Veterans Affairs, (612) 296-2562.

1849 Dependents of Veterans Who Died of a Service-Connected Disability Scholarship

Minnesota Department of Veterans Affairs
Veterans Service Building
St. Paul, MN 55155-2079
(612)-296-2562
Average award: $350
Maximum award: Full tuition at a state university or institution.
College level: Freshman, Sophomore, Junior, Senior
Criteria: Applicant must be the child of a veteran who died of a service-connected disability. Cite Minn. stat. 197.75, subd. 1. Scholarship is renewable. Awarded every year.
Contact: Minnesota Department of Veterans Affairs, (612) 296-2562.

1850 Dolphin Scholarship

Dolphin Scholarship Foundation
405 Dillingham Boulevard
Norfolk Naval Station
Norfolk, VA 23511
(804) 451-3660
Minimum award: $1,750
Number of awards: 25
Deadline: April 15
College level: Freshman, Sophomore, Junior, Senior
Criteria: Applicant must be the dependent child (under age 24) of a member or former member of the submarine force who has (1) qualified in submarines and served in the Submarine Force for at least five years or (2) a Navy member who has served in submarine support activities for a minimum of six years, which need not be consecutive. No minimum period of service is required for personnel who died on active duty while in the Submarine Force. Selection is based upon scholastic proficiency, nonscholastic activities, character, all-around ability, and financial need. Renewable at discretion of the executive committee. Awarded every year.
Contact: Tomi Roeske, Secretary.

1851 Edward T. Conroy Memorial Grant

Maryland Higher Education Commission
State Scholarship Administration
16 Francis Street
Annapolis, MD 21401-1781
(410) 974-5370
Maximum award: $3,480
Number of awards: 63
Deadline: July 15
College level: Freshman, Sophomore, Junior, Senior, Graduate, Doctoral
Criteria: Applicant must attend a Maryland postsecondary institution. Award is available to children of deceased or 100-percent disabled U.S. Armed Forces personnel, to Maryland residents who were Vietnam-era POWs, and to state or local public safety personnel who are 100-percent disabled. Surviving spouses and children of safety personnel are also eligible. Renewable for up to 5 years full-time study or 8 years part-time study. Awarded every year.
Contact: Linda Asplin, Program Administrator.

1852 Eugenia Bradford Roberts Memorial Fund

Daughters of the United States Army
Scholarship Chairman
7717 Rockledge Court
West Springfield, VA 22152
Average award: $1,000
Number of awards: 3
Deadline: March 31
College level: Freshman, Sophomore, Junior, Senior, Unspecified undergraduate
Criteria: Applicant must be the daughter, step-daughter, adopted daughter, or granddaughter of a career commissioned officer or warrant officer of the U.S. Army. Selection is based upon academic standing, test scores, school and community activities, and financial need. Letter of inquiry must include dates of the officer's active duty, with name, rank, and social security number, and a self-addressed, stamped envelope. Renewal is based upon continued achievement and financial need. Awarded every year.
Contact: Janet B. Otto, Scholarship Chairman, 7717 Rockledge Court, West Springfield, VA 22152.

1853 Falcon Foundation Scholarships

Falcon Foundation
3116 Academy Drive #200
USAF Academy, CO 80840-4480
(719) 472-4096
Average award: $3,000
Number of awards: 100
Deadline: April 30
Criteria: Applicant must have potential for U.S. Air Force Academy education and desire for Air Force career but need further academic preparation before cadet appointment. Applicant must be unmarried and at least 17 years.
Contact: Scholarships.

1854   Fleet Reserve Association Scholarships

Fleet Reserve Association (FRA)
125 N. West Street
Alexandria, VA 22314-2754
Deadline: April 15
College level: Freshman, Sophomore, Junior, Senior
Criteria: Applicant must be the child, grandchild, or spouse of a member in good standing of the Fleet Reserve Association or the Ladies Auxiliary of the Fleet Reserve Association or of a member in good standing at time of death. Selection is based upon financial need, scholastic standing, character, and leadership qualities.
Contact: FRA Scholarship Administrator.

1855   Frank W. Garner Scholarship

Air Force Sergeants Association (AFSA)
P.O. Box 50
Temple Hills, MD 20757-0050
(800) 638-0594
Average award: $2,000
Number of awards: 12
Deadline: April 15
College level: Freshman, Sophomore, Junior, Senior
Criteria: Applicant must be an unmarried, dependent child, under age 23, of an Air Force Sergeants Association member or AFSA Auxiliary member. Selection is based upon academic ability, character, leadership, writing ability and potential for success. Financial need is not a consideration. Awarded every year.
Contact: Scholarship Administrator.

1856   Gen. Henry H. Arnold Education Grant

Air Force Aid Society
1745 Jefferson Davis Highway
Suite 202
Arlington, VA 22202
(703) 607-3072, extension 51
Average award: $1,000
Number of awards: 5000
Deadline: March 26
College level: Freshman, Sophomore, Junior, Senior
Criteria: Applicant must be the dependent child of an Air Force member in one of the following categories: on active duty, Title 10 Reservist on extended active duty, retired due to length of active duty service or disability, retired Guard/Reservist who is at least 60 years of age and receiving retirement pay, or deceased while on active duty or in retired status. Applicant must have a minimum 2.0 and be accepted or enrolled as a full-time student at an accredited college, university, or vocational/trade school. Awarded every year.
Contact: Education Assistance Department, (703) 607-3072, extension 24.

1857   Graduate Scholarships

National Board Civil Air Patrol
HQ CAP-USAF/ETTC
105 S. Hansell St. Building 714
Maxwell Air Force Base, AL 36112-6332
(205) 293-5315
Maximum award: $1,500
Minimum award: $750
Number of awards: 50
Deadline: October 1
College level: Graduate, Doctoral
Majors/Fields: Aerospace education, science
Criteria: Applicant must be a member of the Civil Air Patrol and submit CAP Form 95. Awarded every year.
Contact: Lt. Col. Bruce Gunn, Cadet Special Activity.

1858   Henry J. Reilly Memorial Graduate Scholarship

Reserve Officers Association (ROA) of the United States
One Constitution Avenue, N.E.
Washington, DC 20002-5624
(202) 479-2200
Average award: $500
Number of awards: 25
Deadline: April 15
College level: Graduate, Doctoral
Criteria: Applicant must be an active or associate ROA member, prove acceptance for graduate study at an accredited U.S. institution and enrollment in at least two graduate classes. If studying for a master's degree, applicant must have a minimum undergraduate GPA of 3.2. If continuing in a doctoral program, evidence of master's degree must be provided. A minimum 3.3 GPA in graduate work, curriculum vitae, and recommendations concerning the applicant's leadership and academic abilities are required. Scholarship is renewable. Awarded every year.
Contact: Reserve Officers Association of the United States.

1859   Henry J. Reilly Memorial Undergraduate Scholarship

Reserve Officers Association (ROA) of the United States
One Constitution Avenue, N.E.
Washington, DC 20002-5624
(202) 479-2200
Average award: $500
Number of awards: 75
Deadline: April 15
College level: Freshman, Sophomore, Junior, Senior
Criteria: Applicant must be the child or grandchild or an active or associate ROA or ROAL member or the child, age 21 or under, of a deceased member who was active and paid up at the time of death. Applicant must have registered for the draft, if eligible, have good moral character, and demonstrate leadership qualities. If a senior in high school, applicant must rank in top quarter of class, have minimum combined SAT I score of 1200, have at a minimum 3.3 GPA, and submit a 500-word essay (in student's own handwriting) on career goals. If already in undergraduate program, applicant must have a minimum 3.0 college GPA, 3.3 high school GPA, and combined SAT I score of 1200, and submit 500-word essay (in student's own handwriting) on career goals. Scholarship is renewable. Awarded every year.
Contact: Reserve Officers Association of the United States.

1860   Kathern F. Gruber Scholarship

Blinded Veterans Association (BVA)
477 H Street, NW
Washington, DC 20001-2694
(202) 371-8880
Maximum award: $2,000
Number of awards: 12
Deadline: April 15
College level: Freshman, Sophomore, Junior, Senior, Graduate, Doctoral
Criteria: Applicant must be the child or spouse of a legally blind veteran. Selection is based upon the application, transcript, three recommendations, and 300-word essay. Reapplication is required to retain scholarship. Awarded every year.
Contact: John Williams, Scholarships.

1861   Lawrence Luterman Memorial Scholarship

American Legion–New Jersey
Department Adjutant
War Memorial Building
Trenton, NJ 08068
(609) 695-5418
Average award: $1,000
Number of awards: 4
Deadline: February 15
College level: Freshman
Criteria: Applicant must be the natural or adopted descendant of a member of the American Legion, Department of New Jersey. Two scholarships are awarded for four years, two for one year. Awarded every year.
Contact: Department Adjutant, War Memorial Building, Trenton, NJ 08608.

1862   Maine Vietnam Veterans Scholarship

Maine Community Foundation
210 Main Street
P.O. Box 148
Ellsworth, ME 04605
(207) 667-9735
Average award: $700
Maximum award: $1,000
Number of awards: 3
Deadline: May 1
College level: Freshman, Sophomore, Junior, Senior
Criteria: First priority is given to Maine armed services veterans who served in the Vietnam Theater and their dependents; second priority is children of other Maine veterans. Selection is based upon financial need, community service, and academic achievement. Application must include a $3.00 processing fee. Awarded every year.
Contact: Patricia D'Angelo, Program Associate.

1863   Major General Lucas Beau Flight Scholarship

National Board Civil Air Patrol
HQ CAP-USAF/ETTC
105 S. Hansell St. Building 714
Maxwell Air Force Base, AL 36112-6332
(205) 293-5315
Maximum award: $1,500
Minimum award: $750
Deadline: April 1
Criteria: Award is to provide ground and air training toward a Federal Aviation Administration private pilot license. CAP Form 95 must be submitted. Awarded every year.
Contact: Lt. Col. Bruce Gunn, Cadet Special Activities.

1864   Margaret M. Prickett Scholarship

Daughters of the United States Army
Scholarship Chairman
7717 Rockledge Court
West Springfield, VA 22152
Average award: $1,000
Number of awards: 3
Deadline: March 31
College level: Freshman, Sophomore, Junior, Senior, Unspecified undergraduate
Criteria: Applicant must be the daughter, stepdaughter, adopted daughter, or granddaughter of a career commissioned officer or warrant officer of the U.S. Army. Selection is base upon academic standing, test scores, school and community activities, and financial need. Letter of inquiry must include dates of the officer's active duty, with name, rank, and social security number, and a self-addressed, stamped envelope. Renewal is based upon continued achievement and financial need. Awarded every year.
Contact: Janet B. Otto, Scholarship Chairman.

1865   Marianas Officers' Wives' Club Scholarship

Marianas Naval Officers' Wives' Club
Scholarship Chairwoman
PSC 489, Box 49 COMNAVMAR
FPO AP, 96536-0051
(671) 477-5405
Average award: $2,000
Number of awards: 11
Deadline: March 31
College level: Freshman, Sophomore, Junior, Senior, Graduate
Criteria: Applicant must be the dependent child or spouse of a regular or reserve Navy, Marine Corps, or Coast Guard member on active duty, retired with pay, deceased, or declared missing in action. Sponsor must have served on Guam for at least six consecutive months; current or past MNOWC members in good standing or their dependents are also eligible. Selection is based upon academic ability, community involvement, character, leadership ability, and financial need. Reapplication is required to retain scholarship. Awarded every year.
Contact: Scholarship Chairwoman.

1866   Marine Corps Scholarship

Marine Corps Scholarship Foundation
P.O. Box 3008
Princeton, NJ 08543
(609) 921-3534
Maximum award: $2,500
Minimum award: $500
Number of awards: 950
Deadline: February 1
College level: Unspecified undergraduate
Criteria: Applicant must be the child of a U.S. Marine on active duty, in the Reserve, or a former Marine or Reservist who has been honorably and/or medically discharged, is retired, or is deceased. Gross family income may not exceed $39,000 per year. Grants are for vocational, technical, or undergraduate college studies. A written request for an application should be made in September. Recipients must reapply each year for renewal. Awarded every year.
Contact: Scholarship Chairman.

1867   Mayward Jenson American Legion Memorial Scholarship

American Legion–Nebraska
Department Headquarters
P.O. Box 5205
Lincoln, NE 68505
(402) 464-6338
Average award: $500
Number of awards: 5
Deadline: March 1
College level: Freshman, Sophomore, Junior, Senior, Graduate, Doctoral
Criteria: Applicant must be the child or grandchild of a member of the American Legion or of a POW, MIA, KIA, or any deceased veteran, be a Nebraska resident, and attend a Nebraska institution of higher education. Awarded every year.
Contact: Department Headquarters.

1868   Medical and Teaching Scholarships

American Legion–New York Auxiliary
Department Secretary
112 State Street, Suite 409
Albany, NY 12207
Average award: $1,000
Number of awards: 10
Deadline: March 25
College level: Freshman
Majors/Fields: Medicine, education
Criteria: One scholarship is awarded in each of the ten Judicial Districts in New York. Applicant must be a high school senior or graduate under 20 years of age, a New York state resident, the child or grandchild of a veteran, and be pursuing a career in medical or teaching fields. Awarded every year.
Contact: American Legion Auxiliary Unit President.

1869   Merit and Memorial Scholarships

American Legion–Wisconsin Auxiliary
Department Executive Secretary
812 East State Street
Milwaukee, WI 53202-3493
(414) 271-0124
Average award: $1,000
Number of awards: 8
Deadline: March 15
College level: Freshman, Sophomore, Junior, Senior
Criteria: Applicant must be a Wisconsin resident, have a minimum 3.2 GPA, demonstrate financial need, attend an accredited school, and be the child, wife, or widow of a veteran. Granddaughters and great-granddaughters of veterans are eligible if they are American Legion Auxiliary members. Awarded every year.
Contact: Scholarships.

1870   Montgomery GI Bill

U.S. Army Reserve
P.O. Box 3219
Warminster, PA 18974-9844
(800) USA Army
Maximum award: $6,840
Deadline: Continually accepting applications
College level: Freshman, Sophomore, Junior, Senior
Criteria: Applicant must enlist in the Army Reserve for six years. Awarded every year.
Contact: U.S. Army Reserve.

1871   Montgomery GI Bill/Army College Fund

U.S. Army Reserve
P.O. Box 3219
Warminster, PA 18974-9844
(800) USA Army
Maximum award: $30,000
Deadline: Continually accepting applications
College level: Freshman, Sophomore, Junior, Senior, Graduate, Doctoral
Criteria: Applicant must enlist in the active Army for specified critical military skills. Individual must contribute $1,200, which is deducted from first year's pay. Awarded every year.
Contact: U.S. Army.

1872   National Fourth Infantry (IVY) Division Association Scholarship

National Fourth Infantry (IVY) Division Association
P.O. Box 276
Aquebogue, NY 11931
(516) 821-7284
Maximum award: $6,000
Number of awards: 6
College level: Freshman, Sophomore, Junior, Senior, Graduate, Doctoral, trade school students
Criteria: Applicant's parent must have died in action or in the line of duty in Vietnam while attached to the Fourth Infantry Division. Awarded every year.
Contact: William W. May, Secretary.

1873   National President's Scholarship

American Legion Auxiliary
777 North Meridian Street
Third Floor
Indianapolis, IN 46204
(317) 635-6291
Maximum award: $2,000
Minimum award: $1,500
Number of awards: 10
Deadline: March 16
College level: Freshman
Criteria: Applicant must be the child of a veteran who served in the U.S. Armed Forces in World War I, World War II, or the Korean, Vietnam, Panama, Grenada, or Persian Gulf conflicts and have financial need. Selection is based upon character, Americanism, leadership, scholarship, and need.
Contact: National Secretary or National Treasurer.

1874   National President's Scholarship

American Legion–California Auxiliary
Auxiliary Department Headquarters
401 Van Ness #113
San Francisco, CA 94102-4586
Average award: $1,500
Maximum award: $2,000
Minimum award: $500
College level: Freshman
Criteria: State winner competes in the Western Division. Applicant must be the child of a veteran of World War I, World War II, or the Korean, Vietnam, Grenada/Lebanon, Panama, or Desert Storm conflicts. Applicant must have been a resident of California for at least five years; if less, veteran must have been reported missing by government or hopitalized in the state. Awarded every year.
Contact: Auxiliary Department Headquarters.

1875   Naval Academy Women's Club Scholarship

Naval Academy Women's Club
Box 6417
Annapolis, MD 21401
(301) 267-7626
Average award: $1,000
Number of awards: 20
Deadline: March 31
College level: Freshman, Sophomore, Junior, Senior
Criteria: Applicant must meet one of the following requirements: be the child of a Navy or Marine Corps officer on active duty, retired, or deceased, who is or has been stationed as a commissioned officer at the U.S. Naval Academy Complex; the child of a faculty or senior staff member presently employed at the Naval Academy; the child of a Navy or Marine Corps enlisted person presently stationed at the Academy; or a current member of the Naval Academy Women's Club. Reapplication and satisfactory GPA are required to retain scholarship. Awarded every year.
Contact: Mary R. Seymour, Scholarship Chairman, NMPC-121D, Navy Department, Washington, MD 20370-5121.

1876   Navy Supply Corps Foundation Scholarship

Navy Supply Corps Foundation, Inc.
Navy Supply Corps School
1425 Prince Avenue
Athens, GA 30606-2205
(706) 354-4111
Average award: $2,000
Number of awards: 50
Deadline: February 15
College level: Freshman, Sophomore, Junior, Senior
Criteria: Applicant must be the child of a Navy Supply Corps Officer (including Warrant) or Supply Corps service member on active duty, in reserve status, retired-with-pay, or deceased. Selection is based upon scholastic ability. Minimum 3.0 GPA is required. Awarded every year.
Contact: Kaye Morris, Adminstrative Budget Officer.

1877   NCOA Scholarship

Non-Commissioned Officers Association (NCOA)
Scholarship Fund
P.O. Box 33610
San Antonio, TX 78265
Average award: $750
Number of awards: 35
Deadline: March 31
College level: Freshman, Sophomore, Junior, Senior
Criteria: Applicant must be the child, under age 25, or the spouse of a NCOA member and be attending an accredited college, university, or vocational training institute. A brief essay on Americanism is required. Reapplication and a minimum "B" average are required to retain scholarship. Awarded every year.
Contact: Scholarships.

1878   New Mexico Veterans Service Commission Scholarship Under Chapter 170

New Mexico Veterans Service Commission
P.O. Box 2324
Santa Fe, NM 87503
(505) 827-6300
Average award: Tuition waiver and $300
Maximum number of awards: 15
Minimum number of awards: 12
Deadline: None
College level: Freshman, Sophomore, Junior, Senior
Criteria: Applicant must be the child of a deceased veteran who was a New Mexico resident at the time of entry into the service and who served during a period of armed conflict and was killed in action or died as the result of such service. Scholarship is also available for some children of deceased state policemen or deceased National Guard members. Reapplication is required to retain scholarship. Awarded every year.
Contact: Alan T. Martinez, State Benefits.

1879 New York Council Navy League Scholarship

New York Council Navy League Scholarship Fund
375 Park Avenue
Suite 3408
New York, NY 10152
(212) 355-4960
Average award: $2,500
Number of awards: 4
Deadline: June 15
College level: Freshman, Sophomore, Junior, Senior
Criteria: Applicant must be the dependent of a regular/reserve Navy, Marine Corps, or Coast Guard service member who is serving on active duty, retired with pay, or died in the line of duty or after retirement. Applicant must also be a resident of Connecticut, New Jersey, or New York. "B-" average is required to retain scholarship. Awarded every year.
Contact: Donald Sternberg, Executive Administrator.

1880 Ohio War Orphans Scholarship

Ohio Student Aid Commission
309 South Fourth Street
P.O. Box 182452
Columbus, OH 43218-2452
(614) 466-1190
Maximum award: Full tuition at state schools
Number of awards: 400
Deadline: July 1
College level: Freshman, Sophomore, Junior, Senior
Criteria: Applicant must be the child of a veteran who served at least 90 days active duty during a period of war and must now be either disabled or deceased. Applicant must be an Ohio resident between the ages of 16 and 21 and attend a participating Ohio college or university. Satisfactory academic progress and full-time status are required to retain scholarship. Awarded every year.
Contact: Sue Minturn, Program Administrator.

1881 POW/MIA Scholarship

Boise State University
1910 University Drive
Boise, ID 83725
(208) 385-1664
Minimum award: $1,000
Number of awards: 3
Deadline: March 1
College level: Freshman, Sophomore, Junior, Senior, Graduate, Doctoral
Criteria: Applicant must be the child of a veteran who died in action or is a POW/MIA and who was an Idaho resident as of June 1, 1972. Copy of DD1300 is required. Awarded every year. Award may be used only at sponsoring institution.
Contact: Chris Woodward, Financial Aid Counselor.

1882 President's Scholarship

American Legion–Oregon Auxiliary
P.O. Box 1730
Wilsonville, OR 97070-1730
(503) 682-3162
Maximum award: $2,000
Minimum award: $1,500
Number of awards: 10
Deadline: April 3
College level: Freshman
Criteria: Applicant must be the child of a veteran who served in the Armed Forces during the eligibility dates for membership in the American Legion and be recommended by an American Legion unit. Awarded every year.
Contact: Chairman of Education.

1883 Richard D. Rousher Scholarship

Air Force Sergeants Association (AFSA)
P.O. Box 50
Temple Hills, MD 20757-0050
(800) 638-0594
Average award: $2,000
Deadline: April 15
College level: Freshman, Sophomore, Junior, Senior
Criteria: Applicant must be an unmarried, dependent child, under age 23, of an Air Force Sergeants Association member or AFSA Auxiliary member. Selection is based upon academic ability, character, leadership, writing ability, and potential for success. Financial need is not considered. Awarded every year.
Contact: Scholarship Adminstrator.

1884 SCAMP Grants & Scholarships

Scholarships for Children of American Military Personnel
136 South Fuller Avenue
Los Angeles, CA 90036
(213) 934-2288
Average award: $5,000
Minimum award: $3,500
Number of awards: 8
Deadline: July 31
College level: Freshman, Sophomore, Junior, Senior, Graduate, Doctoral
Criteria: Applicant must be the child of an American Armed Forces serviceperson who is a POW, MIA, or KIA in the Vietnam conflict or Desert Storm, who died challenging space, or implementing national policy objectives. Minimum 2.0 GPA and involvement in civic and community activities are required to renew scholarship. Awarded every year.
Contact: Leora M. Ostrow, Chairman of the Board.

1885 Scholarship for Children of Deceased, Disabled, or POW/MIA Veterans

Florida Department of Education
Office of Student Financial Assistance
1344 Florida Education Center
Tallahassee, FL 32399-0400
(904) 487-0049
Average award: Tuition and fees
Deadline: April 1
College level: Freshman, Sophomore, Junior, Senior
Criteria: Applicant must be a Florida resident, enrolled full time in a Florida public university, community college, or public vocational-technical center, have not yet received a bachelor's degree, and be between the ages of 16 and 22. Applicant must be the dependent child of a deceased or disabled Florida veteran or serviceman, or Florida serviceman classifed as a POW or MIA . The parent(s) of a dependent student must have been a Florida resident for five years if the veteran parent served in World War I, World War II, the Korean Conflict, or the Vietnam Era. If the veteran parent served in more recent operations, one year of residency is required. Minimum 2.0 cumulative GPA with 12 credit hours per term is required to retain scholarship. Awarded every year.
Contact: Office of Student Financial Assistance.

1886 Scholarship for Children of Disabled, Deceased and POW/MIA Veterans

North Carolina Division of Veterans Affairs
Albemarle Building, Suite #1065
325 North Salisbury Street
Raleigh, NC 27603
(919) 733-3851
Average award: $3,000
Minimum award: $1,200
Number of awards: 400
Deadline: May 31
College level: Freshman, Sophomore, Junior, Senior, Graduate, Doctoral
Criteria: Applicant must be the child of a desceased or disabled veteran or veteran listed as POW/MIA. The veteran must have been a legal resident of North Carolina at the time of entry into service, or the child must have been born in North Carolina and resided there continuously since birth. Award is for four years. Awarded every year.
Contact: Charles F. Smith, Assistant Secretary.

1887 Scholarship for Dependents of Deceased Servicemembers

Navy-Marine Corps Relief Society
Education Programs
801 North Randolph Street
Arlington, VA 22203-1978
(703) 696-4960
Maximum award: $2,000
Deadline: March 15
College level: Freshman, Sophomore, Junior, Senior
Criteria: Applicant must be the child of a Navy or Marine Corps servicemember who died while on active duty or in retired status. Satisfactory academic progress and financial need are required to retain scholarship. Awarded every year.
Contact: Education Programs.

1888 Scholarship Program for Dependent Children of Soldiers

Army Emergency Relief
Education Department
200 Stovall Street
Alexandria, VA 22332-0600
Average award: $800
Maximum award: $1,500
Minimum award: $500
Deadline: March 1
College level: Freshman, Sophomore, Junior, Senior
Criteria: Applicant must be the unmarried, dependent child of a soldier on active duty, retired, or deceased while on active duty or after retirement and must be under 22 years of age on June 1 preceding the school year for which the scholarship is requested. Selection is based upon financial need, academic achievements, and individual accomplishments. Applicant must maintain a minimum 2.0 GPA. Awarded every year.

1889 Seabee Memorial Scholarship Association Scholarship

Seabee Memorial Scholarship Association, Inc.
P.O. Box 6574
Silver Spring, MD 20916
(301) 871-3172
Average award: $1,300
Number of awards: 17
Deadline: April 15
College level: Freshman, Sophomore, Junior, Senior
Criteria: Applicant must be the child or grandchild of a regular, retired, reserve, or deceased officer or enlisted member of the Seabees. Selection is based upon financial need, citizenship, scholastic record, and good character. Fulfillment of scholarship contract is required to retain scholarship. Awarded every year.
Contact: LCDR Barbara Sisson, CEC, USNR, Assistant Vice President of Scholarships, (202) 586-4547.

1890 Second Marine Division Association Memorial Scholarship

Second Marine Division Association
PO Box 8180
Camp LeJeune, NC 28542
(919) 451-3167
Average award: $700
Maximum award: $1,400
Number of awards: 27
Deadline: April 1
College level: Freshman, Sophomore, Junior, Senior
Criteria: Applicant must be the unmarried child of a parent who served in the Second Marine Division or a unit attached to the Second Marine Division. Parents' taxable income should not exceed $30,000. Minimum 2.5 GPA is required to retain scholarship. Awarded every year.
Contact: Chuck Van Horne, Executive Secretary.

1891 South Carolina Free Tuition for Children of Certain Veterans

South Carolina Governor's Office, Division of Veterans Affairs
1205 Pendleton Street
Columbia, SC 29201
(803) 765-5104
Average award: Full Tuition
Deadline: None
College level: Freshman, Sophomore, Junior, Senior
Criteria: Applicant must be the child of a disabled or deceased American war veteran, POW, MIA, or Congressional Medal of Honor winner who was a South Carolina resident at the time of entry into the military or has been a resident of the state for at least one year. If deceased, veteran must have resided in South Carolina one year prior to death. Eligibility terminates upon the applicant's 26th birthday. Applicant must attend a South Carolina state-supported college, university, or post-high school technical educational institution. Scholarship is renewable. Awarded every year.
Contact: Jimmie L. Gresham, Field Office Supervisor.

1892 Southeast Asia POW/MIA Scholarship

Mississippi Board of Trustees of State Institutions of Higher Learning
Student Financial Aid
3825 Ridgewood Road
Jackson, MS 39211-6453
(601) 982-6570
Average award: Tuition, average cost of dorm room, and required fees
College level: Freshman, Sophomore, Junior, Senior
Criteria: Applicant must be the child of a Mississippi veteran presently or formerly listed as MIA in Southeast Asia who has been a prisoner of a foreign government as a result of the military action against the U.S. naval vessel Pueblo. Applicant is eligible until age 23 and must be enrolled in a Mississippi public college or university. POW/MIA must have been a Mississippi resident at the time of induction into the armed forces and at the time he was officially listed as POW or MIA; spouse must have been a Mississippi resident for at least ten years during her minority and at the time of the child's enrollment. Award is for a maximum of eight semesters. Awarded every year.
Contact: Student Financial Aid Office, (601) 982-6663.

1893 State President's Scholarship

American Legion–Wisconsin Auxiliary
Department Executive Secretary
812 East State Street
Milwaukee, WI 53202-3493
(414) 271-0124
Average award: $1,000
Number of awards: 3
Deadline: March 15
College level: Freshman
Criteria: Applicant must be a Wisconsin resident, have a minimum 3.2 GPA, demonstrate financial need, attend an accredited school, and be the child, wife, or widow of a veteran. Applicant or her mother must be a member of the American Legion Auxiliary. Awarded every year.
Contact: Scholarships.

1894 Technical/Vocational Scholarships

National Board Civil Air Patrol
HQ CAP-USAF/ETTC
105 S. Hansell St. Building 714
Maxwell Air Force Base, AL 36112-6332
(205) 293-5315
Maximum award: $1,500
Minimum award: $750
Number of awards: 50
Deadline: October 1
College level: Technical/vocational
Majors/Fields: Aerospace
Criteria: Applicant must be a member of the Civil Air Patrol and submit CAP Form 95. Awarded every year.
Contact: Lt. Col. Bruce Gunn, Cadet Special Activity.

1895　Undergraduate/Advanced Undergraduate College Scholarships

National Board Civil Air Patrol
HQ CAP-USAF/ETTC
105 S. Hansell St. Building 714
Maxwell Air Force Base, AL 36112-6332
(205) 293-5315
Maximum award: $1,500
Minimum award: $750
Number of awards: 50
Deadline: October 1
College level: Freshman, Sophomore, Junior, Senior
Majors/Fields: Education, engineering, humanities, science
Criteria: Applicant must be a member of the Civil Air Patrol and received the Billy Mitchell Award or the Senior Rating in Level II of the Senior Training Program. CAP Form 95 required. Awarded every year.
Contact: Lt. Col. Bruce Gunn, Cadet Special Activity.

1896　USO/Budweiser Scholarships

USO (United Service Organization)
601 Indiana Avenue, NW
Washington, DC 20004
Average award: $1,000
Number of awards: 15
Deadline: March 1
College level: Sophomore, Junior, Senior
Criteria: Applicant must be an immediate family member (son, daughter, or spouse only) of an active duty member of the U.S. Armed Forces and have graduated from high school within the past four years. Scholarships will not be awarded to students who received appointments to a service academy or ROTC scholarships. Selection is based upon scholastic record, test scores, and extracurricular activities. Awarded every year.
Contact: Donna de Levante, Assistant to Director, Programs and Affiliate Support, (202) 879-4735.

1897　U.S. Naval Academy Class of 1963 Foundation Scholarship

United States Naval Academy Class of 1963 Foundation
3309 Parkside Terrace
Fairfax, VA 22031
Average award: $2,500
Number of awards: 17
Deadline: None
College level: Freshman, Sophomore, Junior, Senior, Graduate, Doctoral, vocational school students
Criteria: Applicant must be the son or daughter of a deceased member of the U.S. Naval Academy class of 1963. Satisfactory academic progress is required to retain scholarship. Awarded every year.
Contact: J. Michael Lents, Chairman of Scholarship Committee.

1898　U.S. Submarine Veterans of World War II Scholarship

U.S. Submarine Veterans of World War II
405 Dillingham Boulevard
Norfolk Naval Station
Norfolk, VA 23511
(804) 451-3660
Minimum award: $1,750
Number of awards: 25
Deadline: April 15
College level: Freshman, Sophomore, Junior, Senior
Criteria: Applicant must be the dependent child, unmarried, and under age 24 of a paid-up, regular member of U.S. Submarine Veterans of World War II. Sponsor's membership card number must accompany application request. Good academic standing and reapplication are required for renewal. Awarded every year.
Contact: Tomi Roeske, Secretary.

1899　Veterans' Dependent Scholarship

Northern Kentucky University
Administrative Center 416
Nunn Drive
Highland Heights, KY 41099-7101
(606) 572-5144
Average award: Tuition
Deadline: February 1
College level: Freshman, Sophomore, Junior, Senior
Criteria: Applicant must be a dependent of a serviceman killed while in service or who died as a result of a service-connected disability. Scholarship is renewable. Awarded every year. Award may be used only at sponsoring institution.
Contact: Robert E. Sprague, Director of Financial Aid.

1900　Veterans' Dependent Scholarship (515)

Northern Kentucky University
Administrative Center 416
Nunn Drive
Highland Heights, KY 41099-7101
(606) 572-5144
Average award: Tuition
Deadline: February 1
College level: Freshman, Sophomore, Junior, Senior
Criteria: Applicant must be a dependent of a permanently disabled national guardsman, war veteran, prisoner of war, or serviceman missing in action. Award is to age 23, completion of degree or certification, or 36 months attendance, whichever comes first. Awarded every year. Award may be used only at sponsoring institution.
Contact: Robert E. Sprague, Director of Financial Aid.

1901　Vice Admiral E. P. Travers Scholarship

Navy-Marine Corps Relief Society
Education Programs
801 North Randolph Street
Arlington, VA 22203-1978
(703) 696-4960
Maximum award: $2,000
Number of awards: 500
Deadline: March 15
College level: Freshman, Sophomore, Junior, Senior
Criteria: Applicant must be the dependent child of an active duty Navy or Marine Corps servicemember and demonstrate financial need. Satisfactory academic progress and financial need are required to retain scholarship. Awarded every year.
Contact: Education Programs.

1902　War Orphans Education Program

West Virginia Department of Veterans Affairs
Charleston Human Resource Center
1321 Plaza East, Suite 101
Charleston, WV 25301-1400
(304) 558-3661
Average award: $250
Maximum award: Full tuition and fees, plus a monetary grant of up to $500.
Number of awards: 30
Deadline: Third Monday in July (fall); First Monday in December (spring)
College level: Freshman, Sophomore, Junior, Senior, Graduate, Doctoral
Criteria: Applicant must be the child of a veteran who died during wartime service or from an illness or injury resulting from wartime service. Applicant must be between age 16 and 23, a resident of West Virginia, attend school in West Virginia, and maintain a minimum 2.0 GPA. Awarded every year.
Contact: Susan E. Kerns, Secretary.

Multiple Majors

1903 H.A. Gorrell Memorial Bursary

University of Calgary
2500 University Drive, NW
Calgary, Alberta, CN T2N 1N4
(403) 220-7872
Average award: $2,000
Number of awards: 2
Deadline: June 15
College level: Senior
Majors/Fields: English, geology, geophysics
Criteria: Selection is based upon financial need, academic merit, and extracurricular activities. One award is made in English and one in geology/geophysics. Awarded every year. Award may be used only at sponsoring institution.
Contact: J. Van Housen, Director of Student Awards & Financial Aid.

1904 Henry I. and Thelma W. Sanders Endowed Scholarship

Clemson University
G-01 Sikes Hall
Clemson, SC 29634-5123
(803) 656-2280
Average award: $3,000
Number of awards: 2
Deadline: March 1
College level: Freshman, Sophomore, Junior, Senior
Majors/Fields: Chemistry, electrical engineering
Criteria: One award is for a chemistry major, the other for an electrical engineering major. Awarded every year. Award may be used only at sponsoring institution.
Contact: Marvin Carmichael, Director of Financial Aid.

1905 John and Anthony Pearson Memorial Bursary

University of Calgary
2500 University Drive, NW
Calgary, Alberta, CN T2N 1N4
(403) 220-7872
Average award: $2,000
Number of awards: 2
Deadline: June 15
College level: Junior, Senior
Majors/Fields: Engineering, management
Criteria: One award is for engineering and one for management. Selection is based primarily upon financial need. Academic merit is considered. Awarded every year. Award may be used only at sponsoring institution.
Contact: J. Van Housen, Director of Student Awards & Financial Aid.

1906 John F. Hardy Memorial Bursary

University of Calgary
2500 University Drive, NW
Calgary, Alberta, CN T2N 1N4
(403) 220-7872
Average award: $2,000
Number of awards: 4
Deadline: June 15
College level: Junior, Senior
Majors/Fields: Chemical engineering, geology, geophysics
Criteria: Selection is based primarily upon financial need. Academic achievement, leadership, and extracurricular activities are considered. Awarded every year. Award may be used only at sponsoring institution.
Contact: J. Van Housen, Director of Student Awards & Financial Aid.

1907 NSA Undergraduate Training Program

National Security Agency (NSA)
M322 (UTP)
Ft. Meade, MD 20755-6000
(800) 962-9398
Maximum award: Full-tuition
Deadline: November 10
College level: Freshman
Majors/Fields: Asian languages, computer science, computer engineering, electrical engineering, mathematics, Middle Eastern languages, Slavic languages
Criteria: Applicant must be a U.S. citizen, have a minimum combined SAT I score of 1000 (composite ACT score of 24), a minimum 3.0 GPA, leadership abilities, and extracurricular activities. Minorities are encouraged to apply. Scholarship is renewable. Awarded every year.
Contact: NSA Training Program.

1908 Sumitomo Machinery Corporation of America

Old Dominion University
Hampton Boulevard
Norfolk, VA 23529-0050
(804) 683-3683
Maximum award: $2,500
Number of awards: 2
Deadline: February 15
College level: Freshman, Sophomore, Junior, Senior
Majors/Fields: Arts/letters, engineering, technology
Criteria: Preference is given to applicant planning to major in engineering and international studies. Recipient will be eligible for work-study in Japan during junior year with appropriate employment and renumeration by Sumitomo Machinery Corp. Minimum 3.0 GPA and approval of award committee are required to retain scholarship. Awarded every year. Award may be used only at sponsoring institution.
Contact: Dr. A. Sidney Roberts, Chair of Dual Degree Committee, College of Engineering, Norfolk, VA 23529, (804) 683-3720.

National Merit

1909 Alumni National Merit Scholarship

University of Tennessee, Knoxville
Financial Aid Office
115 Student Services Building
Knoxville, TN 37994
(615) 974-3131
Maximum award: $2,000
Minimum award: $800
Deadline: February 1
College level: Freshman
Criteria: Applicant must be a National Merit finalist who selects U of Tennessee, Knoxville as first-choice school. Award is for four years. Awarded every year. Award may be used only at sponsoring institution.
Contact: Office of Alumni Affairs, 600 Andy Holt Tower, Knoxville, TN 37996-0210, (615) 974-3011.

1910 Beatrice National Merit Scholarship

Beatrice Foundation
Two North LaSalle Street
Chicago, IL 60602
(312) 558-4000
Maximum award: $2,500
Minimum award: $1,000
Number of awards: 10
Deadline: Take PSAT by fall of junior year
College level: Freshman
Criteria: Applicant must be the child of an employee of the Beatrice Company. Program is administered by the National Merit Scholarship Corporation. Applicants must take the PSAT/NMSQT in the fall of their junior year in high school. Scholarship is for four years. Awarded every year.
Contact: Lynda Robbins, Scholarship Administrator.

1911　Discovery Scholarship

Ohio State University–Columbus
Third Floor Lincoln Tower
1800 Cannon Drive
Columbus, OH 43210-1200
(614) 292-3980
Average award: $2,799
Deadline: February 15
College level: Freshman
Criteria: Applicant must be a National Merit or National Achievement scholar not receiving the Distinguished Scholarship. First priority is given to finalists designating Ohio State U as their first choice institution. Minimum 3.2 GPA and satisfactory academic progress are required to retain scholarship. Awarded every year. Award may be used only at sponsoring institution.
Contact: Mary Haldane, Director of Financial Aid.

1912　Distinguished Scholarship

Ohio State University–Columbus
Third Floor Lincoln Tower
1800 Cannon Drive
Columbus, OH 43210-1200
(614) 292-3980
Average award: $6,873
Deadline: February 15
College level: Freshman
Criteria: Applicant must be a National Merit or National Achievement scholar. First priority is given to finalists designating Ohio State U as their first choice institution. Minimum 3.2 GPA and satisfactory academic progress are required to retain scholarship. Awarded every year. Award may be used only at sponsoring institution.
Contact: Mary Haldane, Director of Financial Aid.

1913　Hallmark Scholarship

Western Kentucky University
Cravens Library 101
Bowling Green, KY 42101
(502) 745-2551
Average award: $3,104
Number of awards: 25
Deadline: February 15
College level: Freshman
Criteria: Applicant must be a National Merit, National Hispanic, or National Achievement semifinalist. Minimum 3.2 cumulative GPA is required to retain scholarship. Awarded every year. Award may be used only at sponsoring institution.
Contact: Dennis M. Smith, Assistant Director of Admissions.

1914　Merit Plus Scholarship

Texas A&M University, College Station
College Station, TX 77843-4233
(409) 845-1957
Average award: $2,000
Number of awards: 250
College level: Freshman
Criteria: Applicant must be a National Merit or National Achievement finalist or semifinalist, or a scholar or honorable mention scholar in the National Hispanic Scholar Recognition program. Awarded every year. Award may be used only at sponsoring institution.
Contact: Dr. Dale T. Knobel, Executive Director of Honors Programs and Academic Scholarships.

1915　National Achievement Scholarship

Texas A&M University, College Station
College Station, TX 77843-4233
(409) 845-1957
Average award: $1,000
Number of awards: 12
College level: Freshman
Criteria: Applicant must be a National Achievement finalist listing Texas A&M U as first-choice college. Satisfactory academic progress is required to retain scholarship. Awarded every year. Award may be used only at sponsoring institution.
Contact: Dr. Dale T. Knobel, Executive Director of Honors Programs and Academic Scholarships.

1916　National Achievement Scholarship

University of Toledo
Financial Aid Office
Toledo, OH 43606-3390
(419) 537-2056
Average award: Full tuition, fees, room and board
Deadline: January 28
College level: Freshman
Criteria: Applicant must be a minority National Achievement finalist. Award is for four years. Awarded every year. Award may be used only at sponsoring institution.
Contact: Coordinator of Admissions Services for Scholars, Office of Admissions Services, (419) 537-2073.

1917　National Achievement Scholarship Program

University of Central Florida
Office of Recruitment
Orlando, FL 32816
(407) 823-5439
Average award: $3,000
Maximum award: $5,000
Number of awards: 10
Deadline: March 15
College level: Freshman
Criteria: Applicant must be a National Achievement finalist ($5,000 award) or semifinalist ($3,000 award). Minimum 3.0 GPA and full-time status are required to retain scholarship. Awarded every year. Award may be used only at sponsoring institution.
Contact: Susan McKinnon, Assistant Director.

1918　National Achievement/University Scholarship

University of Texas at Austin
Austin, TX 78713-7758
(512) 475-6200
Average award: $1,250
Maximum award: $6,000
Maximum number of awards: 200
Deadline: May 31
College level: Freshman
Criteria: Applicant must be a finalist in the National Achievement competition and indicate U of Texas at Austin as first-choice institution. Satisfactory academic progress is required to retain scholarship. Awarded every year; may be used only at sponsoring institution.
Contact: Denise Briceno, National Merit Coordinator.

1919　National Merit/Achievement Scholarship

University of Missouri–Columbia
High School and Transfer Relations
219 Jesse Hall
Columbia, MO 65211
(800) 225-6075 (in-state), (314) 882-2456
Maximum award: $2,000
Minimum award: $1,000
Number of awards: 147
Deadline: December 1
College level: Freshman
Criteria: Applicant must be a National Merit or National Achievement finalist and designate U of Missouri–Columbia as the first choice. Applicant must enroll for at least 12 hours per semester. Scholarship is renewable. Awarded every year. Award may be used only at sponsoring institution.
Contact: High School and Transfer Relations.

1920　National Merit Finalist Scholarship

University of Toledo
Financial Aid Office
Toledo, OH 43606-3390
(419) 537-2056
Average award: Full tuition, fees, room and board
Deadline: January 28
College level: Freshman
Criteria: Applicant must be a National Merit finalist. Award is for four years. Awarded every year; may be used only at sponsoring institution.
Contact: Coordinator of Admissions Services for Scholars, Office of Admissions Services, (419) 537-2073.

1921 National Merit Scholarship

University of Arkansas, Fayetteville
Office of Scholarships and Financial Aid
114 Hunt Hall
Fayetteville, AR 72701
(501) 575-3806
Maximum award: $2,000
Minimum award: $750
College level: Freshman
Criteria: Applicant must be a National Merit finalist who indicates a preference to attend the U of Arkansas, Fayetteville. Good academic standing is required to retain scholarship. Awarded every year. Award may be used only at sponsoring institution.
Contact: Kelly Carter, Assistant Director.

1922 National Merit Scholarship

University of Central Florida
Office of Recruitment
Orlando, FL 32816
(407) 823-5439
Maximum award: $5,000
Minimum award: $3,000
Number of awards: 25
Deadline: March 15
College level: Freshman
Criteria: Applicant must be a National Merit finalist ($5,000 award) or semifinalist ($3,000 award). Minimum 3.0 GPA and full-time enrollment are required to retain scholarship. Awarded every year. Award may be used only at sponsoring institution.
Contact: Susan McKinnon, Assistant Director.

1923 National Merit Scholarship

Wichita State University
111 Jardine
Wichita, KS 67208-1595
(316) 689-3456
Average award: $3,000
Deadline: March 15
College level: Freshman
Criteria: Applicant must be a National Merit scholar. Minimum 3.2 GPA is required to retain scholarship. Awarded every year. Award may be used only at sponsoring institution.
Contact: Scholarships.

1924 National Merit Scholarship

Villanova University
Villanova, PA 19085
(215) 645-4010
Average award: $2,000
Number of awards: 14
Deadline: January 15
College level: Freshman
Criteria: Applicant must be a National Merit Scholarship Corporation finalist who designates Villanova U as his/her first choice. Recipient must maintain high academic standards to retain scholarship. Awarded every year; may be used only at sponsoring institution.
Contact: George J. Walter, Director of Financial Aid.

1925 National Merit Scholarship

Texas A&M University, College Station
College Station, TX 77843-4233
(409) 845-1957
Average award: $1,000
Number of awards: 191
College level: Freshman
Criteria: Applicant must be a National Merit finalist listing Texas A&M U as first-choice college. Satisfactory academic standing is required to retain scholarship. Awarded every year. Award may be used only at sponsoring institution.
Contact: Dr. Dale T. Knobel, Executive Director of Honors Programs and Academic Scholarships.

1926 National Merit Scholarship

Liberty University
P.O. Box 20000
Lynchburg, VA 24506-8001
(804) 582-2270
Maximum award: Full tuition, room and board, and general fees
Minimum award: 75% of tuition, room and board, and general fees
Number of awards: 4
Deadline: June 15; October 15
College level: Freshman
Criteria: Applicant is selected by the National Merit Foundation and must have a minimum 3.9 GPA. Awarded every year. Award may be used only at sponsoring institution.
Contact: Director of Honors Program.

1927 National Merit Supplemental Scholarship

University of Houston
129 Ezekiel W. Cullen Building
Houston, TX 77204-2161
(713) 743-9051
Average award: $5,800
Maximum award: $6,200
Minimum award: $3,700
Number of awards: 76
Deadline: April 1
College level: Freshman
Criteria: Applicant must have National Merit status. Minimum 3.2 GPA and 15 hours per semester are required to retain scholarship. Awarded every year; may be used only at sponsoring institution.
Contact: Robert Sheridan, Director of Scholarships & Financial Aid.

1928 National Scholarship

Wright State University
Coordinator of Scholarships
Dayton, OH 45435
(513) 873-5721
Average award: $6,672
Number of awards: 6
Deadline: March 1
College level: Freshman
Criteria: Applicant must be a National Merit finalist or National Achievement finalist. Minimum 3.0 cumulative GPA is required to retain scholarship. Awarded every year. Award may be used only at sponsoring institution.
Contact: Judy Rose, Assistant Director of Financial Aid.

1929 Northeastern University Merit Scholarships

Northeastern University
360 Huntington Avenue
Boston, MA 02115
(617) 373-2000
Minimum award: $16,044
Number of awards: 20
Deadline: March 1
College level: Freshman
Criteria: Applicant must be a National Merit finalist from New England and rank in the top 15 percent of class. Minimum 3.25 GPA is required to retain scholarship. Awarded every year. Award may be used only at sponsoring institution.
Contact: Kevin Kelly, Dean of Admissions, (617) 373-2200.

1930 Presidential Scholarship

Old Dominion University
Hampton Boulevard
Norfolk, VA 23529-0050
(804) 683-3683
Average award: $15,000
Deadline: February 15
College level: Freshman
Criteria: Applicant must be a National Merit or National Achievement finalist who designates Old Dominion U as first choice. Minimum 3.25 GPA is required to retain scholarship for three additional years. Awarded every year. Award may be used only at sponsoring institution.
Contact: Mary A. Schutz, Assistant Director of Scholarships.

1931 Stanley Works National Merit Scholarship

Stanley Works Scholarship Program
1000 Stanley Drive
New Britain, CT 06053
Maximum award: $4,000
Minimum award: $1,000
Number of awards: 4
Deadline: December 31
College level: Freshman
Criteria: Applicant must be a U.S. citizen and the child of a Stanley employee or retiree. Good academic and disciplinary standing required for renewal. Awarded every year.
Contact: Mona Zdun, Employee Relations Administrator, (203) 827-3872.

Physically Handicapped

1932 ACB Scholarship

American Council of the Blind (ACB)
1155 Fifteenth Street, NW
Suite 720
Washington, DC 20005
(202) 467-5081 or (800) 424-8666
Average award: $2,500
Maximum award: $4,000
Minimum award: $500
Number of awards: 20
Deadline: March 1
College level: Freshman, Sophomore, Junior, Senior, Graduate, Doctoral, vocational/technical school
Criteria: Applicant must be legally blind. Awarded every year.
Contact: Jessica Beach, Scholarship Coordinator.

1933 American Action Fund Scholarship

National Federation of the Blind
814 Fourth Avenue
Suite 200
Grinnell, IA 50112
(515) 236-3366
Average award: $10,000
Number of awards: 1
Deadline: March 31
College level: Freshman, Sophomore, Junior, Senior, Graduate, Doctoral
Criteria: Applicant must be legally blind and pursuing a full-time course of study. Selection is based upon academic excellence, service to the community, and financial need. Awarded every year.
Contact: Peggy Elliott, Chairman.

1934 Anne Pekar Memorial Scholarship

National Federation of the Blind
814 Fourth Avenue
Suite 200
Grinnell, IA 50112
(515) 236-3366
Average award: $4,000
Number of awards: 1
Deadline: March 31
College level: Freshman, Sophomore, Junior, Senior, Graduate, Doctoral
Criteria: Applicant must be a legally blind woman between the ages of 17 and 25 who is pursuing a full-time course of study. Selection is based upon academic excellence, service to the community, and financial need. Awarded every year.
Contact: Peggy Elliott, Chairperson.

1935 Blind and Deaf Students Tuition Exemption

Texas Higher Education Coordinating Board
Student Financial Assistance
P.O. Box 12788, Capitol Station
Austin, TX 78711-2788
(512) 483-6340
Average award: $666
Number of awards: 1,650
College level: Freshman, Sophomore, Junior, Senior, Graduate, Doctoral
Criteria: Applicant must provide certification of deafness or blindness from the appropriate state vocational rehabilitation agency where applicant is a client. Applicant must have a high school diploma or its equivalent, demonstrate high moral character, and meet entrance requirements for public colleges or universities in Texas. Scholarship is renewable. Awarded every year.
Contact: Mack Adams, Assistant Commissioner for Student Services, Capitol Station, P.O. Box 12788, Austin, TX 78711-2788.

1936 Chairscholars Foundation

Chairscholars c/o Hugo and Alicia Keim
Silverdollar Ranch #38
17000 Patterson Road
Odessa, FL 33556
Average award: $3,000
Number of awards: 3
Deadline: January 15
College level: Freshman, Sophomore
Criteria: Applicant must be in a wheelchair and have significant financial need. Selection is based upon GPA and community service. Renewable if a satifactory GPA is maintained. Awarded every year.
Contact: Hugo and Alicia Keim, President/Secretary, (813) 920-2737 (November 1–May 1), (914) 855-5499 (May 1–October 3.

1937 Children and Youth Scholarship

American Legion–Washington
P.O. Box 3917
Lacey, WA 98503
(360) 491-4373
Maximum award: $1,500
Minimum award: $1,000
Number of awards: 2
Deadline: April 1
College level: Freshman
Criteria: Applicant must be the child of an American Legion member or its auxiliary. Awarded every year.
Contact: Dallas Vaughan, Department Adjutant.

1938 Easter Seal of Iowa Disability Scholarships

Easter Seal Society of Iowa, Inc.
Disability Scholarship
P.O. Box 4002
Des Moines, IA 50333
(515) 289-1933
Maximum award: $1,000
Minimum award: $750
Number of awards: 2
Deadline: April 15
College level: Freshman
Criteria: Applicant must have a permanent disability, be a resident of Iowa, rank in the top 40 percent of class or have a cumulative GPA of 2.8, and demonstrate financial need. Awarded every year.
Contact: Scholarships.

1939 EIF Scholarship Fund

Electronic Industries Foundation
919 Nineteenth Street, NW, Suite 900
Washington, DC 20006
Minimum award: $2,000
Number of awards: 6
Majors/Fields: Technical fields, scientific fields
Criteria: Applicant must be a disabled U.S. citizen. Selection is based upon career goals, academic achievements, and financial need.
Contact: Scholarships.

1940   Ellen Setterfield Memorial Scholarship

National Federation of the Blind
814 Fourth Avenue
Suite 200
Grinnell, IA 50112
(515) 236-3366
Average award: $2,000
Number of awards: 1
Deadline: March 31
College level: Graduate, Doctoral
Majors/Fields: Social sciences
Criteria: Applicant must be legally blind and pursuing a full-time course of study. Selection is based upon academic excellence, service to the community, and financial need. Awarded every year.
Contact: Peggy Elliot, Chairman.

1941   Elsie Bell Grosvenor Scholarship Awards

Alexander Graham Bell Association for the Deaf
3417 Volta Place, NW
Washington, DC 20007-2778
(202) 337-5220
Maximum award: $1,000
Minimum award: $500
Number of awards: 2
Deadline: April 15
College level: Freshman, Sophomore, Junior, Senior, Graduate, Doctoral
Criteria: Applicant must be a deaf student residing in metropolitan Washington, D.C., who is planning on attending college outside the area or a deaf student who resides outside the metropolitan Washington D.C. area planning to attend college in the area. Renewable for one additional year. Awarded every year.
Contact: Scholarship Coordinator.

1942   Ezra Davis Memorial Scholarship

National Federation of the Blind
814 Fourth Avenue
Suite 200
Grinnell, IA 50112
(515) 236-3366
Average award: $10,000
Number of awards: 1
Deadline: March 31
College level: Freshman, Sophomore, Junior, Senior, Graduate, Doctoral
Criteria: Applicant must be legally blind and pursuing a full-time course of study. Selection is based upon academic excellence, service to the community, and financial need. Awarded every year.
Contact: Peggy Elliott, Chairperson.

1943   Frank Walton Horn Memorial Scholarship

National Federation of the Blind
814 Fourth Avenue
Suite 200
Grinnell, IA 50112
(515) 236-3366
Average award: $2,500
Number of awards: 1
Deadline: March 31
College level: Freshman, Sophomore, Junior, Senior, Graduate, Doctoral
Criteria: Applicant must be legally blind and pursing a full-time course of study. Preference is given to applicants studying architecture or engineering. Selection is based upon academic excellence, service to the community, and financial need. Awarded every year.
Contact: Peggy Elliott, Chairperson.

1944   Frederick A. Downes Scholarship

American Foundation for the Blind (AFB)
11 Penn Plaza
Suite 300
New York, NY 10001
(212) 502-7661
Average award: $2,500
Number of awards: 2
Deadline: April 3
College level: Freshman, Sophomore, Junior, Senior
Criteria: Applicant must be a U.S. citizen, legally blind, and 22 years of age or less. Selection is based upon transcript, three recommendations, and personal statement. Scholarship is renewable. Awarded every year.
Contact: Leslie Rosen, Director of Information Center/Scholarships, (212) 502-7661, (212) 620-2160.

1945   Grant Program for Physically Disabled Students in the Sciences

Foundation for Science and Disability
115 South Brainard Avenue
La Grange, IL 60525
Average award: $1,000
Number of awards: 3
Deadline: December 1
College level: Graduate, Doctoral
Majors/Fields: Computer science, engineering, mathematics, medicine, science
Criteria: Applicant must be physically disabled and submit a 250-word essay and recommendations. Recipient must reapply to renew scholarship. Awarded every year.
Contact: Rebecca F. Smith, Chairperson of the Science Student Grant Committee.

1946   Hermione Grant Calhoun Scholarship

National Federation of the Blind
814 Fourth Avenue
Suite 200
Grinnell, IA 50112
(515) 236-3366
Average award: $2,000
Number of awards: 1
Deadline: March 31
College level: Freshman, Sophomore, Junior, Senior, Graduate, Doctoral
Criteria: Applicant must be a legally blind woman pursuing a full-time course of study. Selection is based upon academic excellence, service to the community, and financial need. Awarded every year.
Contact: Peggy Elliott, Chairperson.

1947   Howard Brown Rickard Scholarship

National Federation of the Blind
814 Fourth Avenue
Suite 200
Grinnell, IA 50112
(515) 236-3366
Average award: $2,500
Number of awards: 1
Deadline: March 31
College level: Freshman, Sophomore, Junior, Senior, Graduate, Doctoral
Majors/Fields: Architecture, engineering, law, medicine, natural sciences
Criteria: Applicant must be legally blind and pursuing a full-time course of study. Selection is based upon academic excellence, service to the community, and financial need. Awarded every year.
Contact: Peggy Elliott, Chairperson.

1948　Kuchler-Killian Memorial Scholarship

National Federation of the Blind
814 Fourth Avenue
Suite 200
Grinnell, IA 50112
(515) 236-3366
Average award: $2,000
Number of awards: 1
Deadline: March 31
College level: Freshman, Sophomore, Junior, Senior, Graduate, Doctoral
Criteria: Applicant must be legally blind and pursuing a full-time course of study. Selection is based upon academic excellence, service to the community, and financial need. Awarded every year.
Contact: Peggy Elliott, Chairperson.

1949　Kurzweil Scholarship

National Federation of the Blind
814 Fourth Avenue
Suite 200
Grinnell, IA 50112
(515) 236-3366
Average award: $2,000
Number of awards: 1
Deadline: March 31
College level: Freshman, Sophomore, Junior, Senior, Graduate, Doctoral
Criteria: Applicant must be legally blind and pursuing a full-time course of study. Selection is based upon academic excellence, service to the community, and financial need. Awarded every year.
Contact: Peggy Elliott, Chairman.

1950　Lighthouse Career Incentive Awards Program

Lighthouse, Inc.
800 Second Avenue
New York, NY 10017
(212) 808-0077
Minimum award: $5,000
Number of awards: 5
Deadline: January 31
College level: Sophomore, Junior, Senior, Graduate, Doctoral
Criteria: Applicant must be a legally blind, U.S. citizen residing in the Northeast (New England, New Jersey, New York, Pennsylvania) and submit a 500-word essay. Financial need is not considered. Awarded every year.
Contact: Gilda Gold, Coordinator of Special Projects.

1951　Lucile A. Abt Scholarship

Alexander Graham Bell Association for the Deaf
3417 Volta Place, NW
Washington, DC 20007-2778
(202) 337-5220
Maximum award: $1,000
Number of awards: 5
Deadline: April 15
College level: Freshman, Sophomore, Junior, Senior, Graduate, Doctoral
Criteria: Applicant must be a deaf student who was born with a severe or profound hearing impairment or who suffered such a loss before acquiring language. He or she must use speech and residual hearing and/or speechreading (lipreading) as the preferred/customary form of communication and demonstrate a potential for leadership. Applicant must be accepted by or already enrolled in a regular, full-time college or university program for hearing students. Applicants who have serious handicaps in addition to their hearing impairments are encouraged to apply. Renewable for one additional year. Awarded every year.
Contact: Scholarship Coordinator.

1952　Maude Winkler Scholarship

Alexander Graham Bell Association for the Deaf
3417 Volta Place, NW
Washington, DC 20007-2778
(202) 337-5220
Maximum award: $1,000
Number of awards: 5
Deadline: April 15
College level: Freshman, Sophomore, Junior, Senior, Graduate, Doctoral
Criteria: Applicant must be an oral deaf student born with a severe or profound hearing impairment or who suffered such a loss before acquiring language. He or she must use speech and residual hearing and/or speechreading (lipreading) as the preferred/customary form of communication and demonstrate a potential for leadership. Applicant must be accepted by or already enrolled in a regular, full-time college or university program for hearing students. Applicants who have serious handicaps in addition to their hearing impairments are encouraged to apply. Renewable for one additional year. Awarded every year.
Contact: Scholarship Coordinator.

1953　Melva T. Owen Memorial Scholarship

National Federation of the Blind
814 Fourth Avenue
Suite 200
Grinnell, IA 50112
(515) 236-3366
Average award: $3,000
Number of awards: 1
Deadline: March 31
College level: Freshman, Sophomore, Junior, Senior, Graduate, Doctoral
Criteria: Applicant must be legally blind and pursuing a full-time course of study. Specific major is not required, except that it be directed towards attaining financial independence and shall exclude religion and those seeking only to further general or cultural education. Selection is based upon academic excellence, service to the community, and financial need. Awarded every year.
Contact: Peggy Elliott, Chairperson.

1954　Mozelle and Willard Gold Memorial Scholarship

National Federation of the Blind
814 Fourth Avenue
Suite 200
Grinnell, IA 50112
(515) 236-3366
Average award: $3,000
Number of awards: 1
Deadline: March 31
College level: Freshman, Sophomore, Junior, Senior, Graduate, Doctoral
Criteria: Applicant must be legally blind and pursuing a full-time course of study. Selection is based upon academic excellence, service to the community, and financial need. Awarded every year.
Contact: Peggy Elliott, Chairman.

1955　NFB Educator of Tomorrow Award

National Federation of the Blind
814 Fourth Avenue
Suite 200
Grinnell, IA 50112
(515) 236-3366
Average award: $2,500
Number of awards: 1
Deadline: March 31
College level: Freshman, Sophomore, Junior, Senior, Graduate, Doctoral
Majors/Fields: Education, elementary and secondary education
Criteria: Applicant must be legally blind and pursuing a full-time course of study toward a career in teaching. Selection is based upon academic excellence, service to the community, and financial need. Awarded every year.
Contact: Peggy Elliott, Chairperson.

1956 NFB Humanities Scholarship

National Federation of the Blind
814 Fourth Avenue
Suite 200
Grinnell, IA 50112
(515) 236-3366
Average award: $2,500
Number of awards: 1
Deadline: March 31
College level: Freshman, Sophomore, Junior, Senior, Graduate, Doctoral
Majors/Fields: Art, English, foreign languages, history, humanities, philosophy, religion
Criteria: Applicant must be legally blind and pursuing a full-time course of study. Selection is based upon academic excellence, service to the community, and financial need. Awarded every year.
Contact: Peggy Elliott, Chairperson.

1957 NFB Scholarship

National Federation of the Blind
814 Fourth Avenue
Suite 200
Grinnell, IA 50112
(515) 236-3366
Average award: $2,500
Maximum award: $4,000
Minimum award: $2,000
Number of awards: 14
Deadline: March 31
College level: Freshman, Sophomore, Junior, Senior, Graduate, Doctoral
Criteria: Applicant must be legally blind and pursuing a full-time course of study. Selection is based upon academic excellence, service to the community, and financial need. Awarded every year.
Contact: Peggy Elliott, Chairperson.

1958 Nordstorm Scholarship

President's Committee on Employment of People with Disabilities
1331 F Street, NW
Washington, DC 20004-1107
(202) 376-6200
Average award: $2,000
Number of awards: 5
Deadline: January 14
College level: Freshman, Sophomore, Junior, Senior
Majors/Fields: Business
Criteria: Applicant must be disabled as defined in the Americans with Disabilities Act (ADA).
Contact: Ellen Daly, Coordinator, Awards/Scholarship Progam.

1959 R.L. Gillette Scholarship

American Foundation for the Blind (AFB)
11 Penn Plaza
Suite 300
New York, NY 10001
(212) 502-7661
Average award: $1,000
Number of awards: 2
Deadline: April 3
College level: Freshman, Sophomore, Junior, Senior
Majors/Fields: Literature, music
Criteria: Applicant must be a woman who is legally blind and is a U.S. citizen. Selection is based upon transcript, three recommendations, and personal statement. Scholarship is renewable. Awarded every year.
Contact: Leslie Rosen, Director of Information Center/Scholarships.

1960 Robert and Rosemary Low Memorial Scholarship

Portland State University
P.O. Box 751
Portland, OR 97207-0751
(503) 725-5270
Average award: $3,633
Number of awards: 1
Deadline: April 15
College level: Doctoral, regularly admitted master's students
Criteria: Selection is based upon academic merit, statement of goals, faculty recommendations, and physical disability. Financial need is considered but not required. Reapplication with minimum of nine credits per term is required to retain scholarship. Awarded when funds are available. Award may be used only at sponsoring institution.
Contact: Scholarships, Office of Graduate Studies, 303 Cramer Hall, Portland, OR 97207-0751, (503) 725-3423.

1961 Robert M. Staley Scholarship

National Federation of the Blind of North Carolina
308 Carolina Avenue
Raleigh, NC 27606
Average award: $1,000
Number of awards: 2
College level: Freshman, Sophomore, Junior, Senior
Criteria: Applicant must be a legally blind student who is a North Carolina resident or is attending a postsecondary institution in North Carolina. Selection is based upon academic excellence, service to the community and financial need. Awarded every year.
Contact: Kathy G. Kannenbereg.

1962 Rudolph Dillman Memorial Scholarship

American Foundation for the Blind (AFB)
11 Penn Plaza
Suite 300
New York, NY 10001
(212) 502-7661
Average award: $2,500
Number of awards: 3
Deadline: April 3
College level: Sophomore, Junior, Senior, Graduate, Doctoral
Majors/Fields: Education, rehabilitation
Criteria: Applicant must be legally blind, provide proof of visual impairment in a statement from an optometrist, and be a U.S. citizen studying in the U.S. Selection is based upon transcript, three recommendations, and personal statement. Awarded every year.
Contact: Leslie Rosen, Director of Information Center/Scholarships.

1963 Sertoma Scholarship for Deaf or Hard of Hearing Students

Sertoma International
1912 East Meyer Boulevard
Kansas City, MO 64132
(816) 333-8300
Average award: $1,000
Number of awards: 10
Deadline: May 2
College level: Freshman, Sophomore, Junior, Senior
Criteria: Applicant must have a verifiable hearing loss, have a minimum 3.0 GPA, be a citizen or permanent resident of the U.S. or Canada, and be seeking a bachelor's degree from any U.S. or Canadian school. Recipient must reapply for renewal. Awarded every year.
Contact: Leslie A. Freese, Director of International Sponsorships.

1964 Stanley E. Jackson Scholarship

Foundation for Exceptional Children
1920 Association Drive
Reston, VA 22091
(703) 620-1054
Maximum award: $1,000
Minimum award: $500
Number of awards: 4
Deadline: February 1
College level: Freshman
Criteria: Applicant must be disabled and have demonstrated gifted and/or talented abilities in one or more of the following categories: general intellectual ability, specific academic aptitude, creativity, leadership, or visual or performing arts. One award is for a member of an ethnic minority group. Awarded every year.
Contact: Scholarship Department.

1965 Stanley E. Jackson Scholarship for Students with Disabilities

Foundation for Exceptional Children
1920 Association Drive
Reston, VA 22091
(703) 620-1054
Maximum award: $1,000
Number of awards: 2
Deadline: February 1
College level: Freshman
Criteria: Applicant must be disabled and intend to enroll in a full-time undergraduate program or vocational, technical, or fine arts training programs. One award is for a member of an ethnic minority group. Awarded every year.
Contact: Robert L. Silber, Executive Director.

1966 Wisconsin HEAB Visual and Hearing Impaired Program

Wisconsin Higher Educational Aids Board (HEAB)
P.O. Box 7885
131 West Wilson Street
Madison, WI 53707-7885
(608) 266-0888
Maximum award: $1,800
College level: Freshman, Sophomore, Junior, Senior
Criteria: Applicant must be a Wisconsin resident, legally deaf or blind, and demonstrate financial need. If the impairment prevents the student from studying in a Wisconsin institution, the grant can be used at an out-of-state institution that specializes in teaching the blind or deaf. Renewable for a maximum of ten semesters. Awarded every year.
Contact: Joyce Apfel, Grants Coordinator.

Religious Affiliation

1967 Bishop Charles P. Greco Graduate Fellowship

Knights of Columbus
P.O. Box 1670
Department of Scholarships
New Haven, CT 06507-0901
(203) 772-2130, extension 332
Average award: $1,000
Number of awards: 2
Deadline: May 1
College level: Graduate
Majors/Fields: Special education
Criteria: Applicant must be affiliated with the Knights of Columbus through membership or husband's or father's membership. Scholarship is for preparation of classroom teachers of mentally retarded children. Satisfactory academic performance is required to retain scholarship. Awarded every year.
Contact: Secretary of the Committee on Fellowships.

1968 Catholic Daughters of the Americas Graduate Scholarship

Catholic Daughters of the Americas
National Headquarters
10 West 71st Street
New York, NY 10023
Maximum award: $1,000
Minimum award: $500
Number of awards: 2
Deadline: June 1
College level: Graduate, Doctoral
Criteria: Applicant must be enrolled in a graduate program at a college or university, and submit official transcript of undergraduate work, letter of academic reference from one college or university, a list of reasons for applying for the scholarship, and her autobiography. Awarded every year.
Contact: Grace DiCairano, National Scholarship Chairman, 289 Pine Avenue, Manasquan, NJ 08736.

1969 David W. Self Scholarship

National Youth Ministry Organization (United Methodist) Scholarships
P.O. Box 840
Nashville, TN 37202-0840
(615) 340-7184
Maximum award: $1,000
Number of awards: 2
Deadline: June 1
College level: Freshman
Criteria: Applicant must be a United Methodist Youth intending to pursue a church-related career. Applicant must have a minimum 2.0 GPA. Selection is based upon finanical need and leadership. Awarded every year.
Contact: Angela Gay Kinkead, Executive Director.

1970 Italian Catholic Federation Scholarship Program

Italian Catholic Federation Central Council
1801 Vann Ness Avenue, Suite 300
San Francisco, CA 94109
Maximum award: $1,000
Minimum award: $350
Number of awards: 200
College level: Freshman
Criteria: Applicant must be Roman Catholic, wholly or partially of Italian ancestry, have a minimum 3.0 GPA, financial need, participation in church and community activities, and letters of recommendation.
Contact: Scholarships, 1801 Vann Ness Avenue, Suite 300, San Francisco, CA 94109.

1971 Jewish Community Centers Association Scholarship

Jewish Community Centers Association of North America
15 East 26th Street
New York, NY 10010-1579
(212) 532-4949
Average award: $5,000
Maximum award: $7,500
Minimum award: $2,500
Number of awards: 10
Deadline: February 1
College level: Graduate
Majors/Fields: Business administration, community service, Jewish education, physical education, social work
Criteria: Applicant must be Jewish, have a minimum 3.0 undergraduate GPA, demonstrate leadership potential, and agree to work in a JCCA-affiliated Jewish community center for three years after graduation. Applicant must major in a field applicable to work in a Jewish community center. Satisfactory academic record is required to retain scholarship. Awarded every year.
Contact: Stephen Bayer.

1972   Jewish W B Scholarship

Jewish W B
15 East 26th Street
New York, NY 10010
(212) 532-4949
Average award: $6,250
Maximum award: $7,500
Minimum award: $5,000
Number of awards: 8
Deadline: February 1
College level: Graduate
Criteria: Program is designed to aid master's degree candidates who are concentrating their studies in areas leading to professional careers in Jewish community centers and YMHAs/YWHAs. Applicant must have a Jewish background and commitment to Jewish community center work. Scholarship is renewable. Awarded every year.
Contact: Stephen Bayer, Scholarship Coordinator.

1973   Lutheran Brotherhood Member Scholarship

Lutheran Brotherhood
625 4th Avenue South
Box 857
Minneapolis, MN 55415
Average award: $1,000
Maximum award: $2,000
Minimum award: $500
Number of awards: 625
Deadline: January 29
College level: Freshman, Sophomore, Junior
Criteria: Applicant must be an eligible Lutheran Brotherhood member, the dependent of a Lutheran Brotherhood field force member, or the dependent of a home office employee. Recommended 3.25 GPA for incoming freshman, minimum 3.5 GPA for in-college applicant is required. Minimum 2.5 GPA is required to retain scholarship. Awarded every year.
Contact: Barbara White, Member Scholarship Coordinator, 625 Fourth Avenue South, Box 857, Minneapolis, MN 55415.

1974   National Presbyterian College Scholarship

Presbyterian Church (USA)
Office of Financial Aid
100 Witherspoon Street
Louisville, KY 40202-1396
(502) 569-5776
Maximum award: $1,400
Minimum award: $500
Deadline: December 1
College level: Freshman
Criteria: Applicant must be preparing full-time entrance to one of the participating colleges related to the Presbyterian Church (USA). Applicant must be a U.S. citizen or permanent resident, received by the session of the Presbyterian Church (USA), and take the SAT I or ACT no later than November 30th of senior year. Selection is based upon financial need. Scholarship is renewable. Awarded every year.
Contact: Mary Ann Folsom, Administrative Assistant.

1975   Native American Education Grant

Presbyterian Church (USA)
Office of Financial Aid
100 Witherspoon Street
Louisville, KY 40202-1396
(502) 569-5776
Maximum award: $1,500
Minimum award: $200
Deadline: June 1
College level: Sophomore
Criteria: Applicant must be an Alaskan Native or Native American, a member of the Presbyterian Church (USA), a U.S. citizen or permanent resident, have completed at least one semester of work at an accredited institution, and demonstrated financial need. Scholarship is renewable. Awarded every year.
Contact: Mary Ann Folsom, Administrative Assistant.

1976   Presidental Scholarship

Brigham Young University
Scholarship Office, A-41 ASB
P.O. Box 21009
Provo, UT 84602-1009
(801) 378-4104
Average award: $3,675
Maximum award: $4,675
Number of awards: 24
Deadline: January 15
College level: Freshman
Criteria: Applicant must be a member in good standing of The Church of Jesus Christ of Latter-day Saints, have a minimum high school GPA of 3.85, and a minimum composite ACT score of 31; leadership and service are also considered. Renewable if minimum 3.5 GPA is maintained and attendance requirements are met. Awarded every year. Award may be used only at sponsoring institution.
Contact: Duane L. Bartle, Scholarship Coordinator.

1977   Pro Deo and Pro Patria Scholarships

Knights of Columbus
P.O. Box 1670
Department of Scholarships
New Haven, CT 06507-0901
(203) 772-2130, extension 332
Average award: $1,500
Number of awards: 50
Deadline: March 1
College level: Freshman
Criteria: Applicant must be a member or the child of a member of the Knights of Columbus and must be attending a Catholic college. Selection is based upon academic excellence. Satisfactory academic performance required to retain scholarship. Awarded every year.
Contact: Fr. Donald Barry, S.J., Director of Scholarship Aid.

1978   Richard S. Smith Scholarship

National Youth Ministry Organization (United Methodist) Scholarships
P.O. Box 840
Nashville, TN 37202-0840
(615) 340-7184
Maximum award: $1,000
Deadline: June 1
College level: Freshman
Criteria: Applicant must be a United Methodist Youth intending to pursue a church-related career. Applicant must have a minimum 2.0 GPA. Selection is based upon financial need and leadership. Awarded every year.
Contact: Angela Gay Kinkead, Executive Director.

1979   Robert Schreck Memorial Award

Schreck Memorial Fund
c/o El Paso National Bank
P.O. Drawer 140
El Paso, TX 79980
Maximum award: $1,500
Minimum award: $475
Number of awards: 4
Criteria: Applicant must be entering the Episcopal ministry. Awarded every year.
Contact: El Paso National Bank, Awards, P.O. Drawer 140, El Paso, TX 79980.

1980   Shannon Scholarship

Trinity Episcopal Church
Second Street and Howard Avenue
Pottsville, PA 17901
(717) 622-8720
Average award: $2,500
Number of awards: 16
College level: Freshman
Criteria: Available to daughters of Episcopal priests residing in one of the five dioceses of Pennsylvania. Recipient may pursue field of choice at a two- or four-year institution. Awarded every year.
Contact: Scholarships.

1981   Sikh Education Aid Fund

Sikh Education Aid Fund
P.O. Box 140
Hopewell, VA 23860
(804) 541-9290
Average award: $1,400
Maximum award: $3,500
Minimum award: $600
Number of awards: 14
Deadline: June 20
College level: Freshman, Sophomore, Junior, Senior, Graduate, Doctoral
Criteria: Applicant must be of the Sikh faith or studying the Sikh faith with a minimum 3.0 GPA. Financial need is required. Recipient must maintain acceptable performance in academic programs to retain scholarship. Awarded every year.
Contact: Dr. G.S. Bhuller, Coordinator.

1982   Student Opportunity Scholarship

Presbyterian Church (USA)
Office of Financial Aid
100 Witherspoon Street
Louisville, KY 40202-1396
(502) 569-5776
Maximum award: $1,400
Minimum award: $100
Deadline: April 1
College level: Freshman
Criteria: Applicant must be African-American, Alaskan Native, Asian-American, Hispanic-American, or Native American, a member of the Presbyterian Church (USA), a U.S. citizen or permanent resident, and demonstrate financial need. Scholarship is renewable. Awarded every year.
Contact: Mary Ann Folsom, Administrative Assistant.

1983   Wolcott Foundation Fellowships

High Twelve International
11155-B2 South Towne Square
St. Louis, MO 63123
Average award: Fellowship pays for tuition and fees for 36 credit hours
Deadline: February 1
College level: Doctoral
Criteria: Fellowship is to prepare young men and women who have a background of Masonic ideals for careers in U.S. government service at the federal, state, and local levels as well as in selected private international business. Applicant must attend George Washington U in either the Sch of Business and Public Management or the Elliott Sch of International Affairs. Scholarship is renewable. Awarded every year. Award may be used only at sponsoring institution.
Contact: Roy E. Ludwig, International Secretary, 15456 Ivanhoe Drive, Visacia, CA 93892-9144.

1984   Women of the Evangelical Lutheran Church in America Scholarship

Women of the Evangelical Lutheran Church in America
8765 West Higgins Road
Chicago, IL 60631
(800) 638-3522
Maximum award: $2,000
Minimum award: $500
Number of awards: 6
Deadline: March 1
College level: Unspecified graduate, unspecified undergraduate
Criteria: All scholarships are for mature, Evangelical Lutheran Church in America women who for a number of years have been out of school, in the work force, or homemakers and are returning to school for vocational, academic training, or degrees. Cronk, Mehring, and Piero/Wade scholarships are for undergraduate, graduate, professional, or vocational courses of study. Kahler/Vickers/Raup scholarship is for medical school study. Kemp scholarship is for minority laywomen in graduate courses of study. Knudstrup scholarship is for occupation of service through graduate study. Awarded every year.
Contact: Scholarships.

1985   Zolp Scholarship

Loyola University, Chicago
380 Granada Centre
Chicago, IL 60626
(312) 508-3164
Average award: Full tuition
Deadline: None
College level: Freshman, Sophomore, Junior, Senior, Graduate, Doctoral
Criteria: Applicant must be Roman Catholic and have a last name spelled "Zolp." Scholarship is renewable. Award may be used only at sponsoring institution.
Contact: James G. Dwyer, Director of Financial Aid.

State/Country of Residence

1986   A.W. Bodine–Sunkist Memorial Scholarship

A.W. Bodine–Sunkist Memorial Scholarship
P.O. Box 7888
Van Nuys, CA 91409
(818) 379-7510
Average award: $3,000
Number of awards: 30
Deadline: April 30
College level: Freshman, Sophomore, Junior, Senior
Criteria: Applicant must have a background in Arizona or California agriculture, a minimum 3.0 GPA, and demonstrate financial need. Selection is based upon a combination of grades, ACT or SAT I scores, an essay, and references. Renewable if minimum 2.7 GPA is maintained, 12 units of study are taken, and financial need is demonstrated. Awarded every year.
Contact: Claire Peters, Scholarship Administrator.

1987   Academic Excellence Award Scholarship

Texas A&M University, College Station
College Station, TX 77843-4233
(409) 845-1957
Average award: $750
Maximum award: $1,500
Minimum award: $500
Number of awards: 600
Deadline: March 1
College level: Sophomore, Junior, Senior, Graduate, Doctoral
Criteria: Applicant must demonstrate financial need. Minimum 2.5 GPA and full-time enrollment are required to retain scholarship. Awarded every year. Award may be used only at sponsoring institution.
Contact: Molly Georgiades, Administrator for Scholarships and Student Employment, (409) 845-3982.

1988   Academic Scholars Program

Oklahoma State Regents for Higher Education
500 Education Building
State Capitol Complex
Oklahoma City, OK 73105
(405) 524-9100
Average award: $3,500
Maximum award: $5,000
Minimum award: $3,100
Number of awards: 1,125
Deadline: Mid-August
College level: Freshman
Criteria: Applicant must be an Oklahoma resident at or above the 99.5 percentile on ACT or SAT I, or be a resident or nonresident that is one of the following: National Merit scholar or finalist, National Achievement scholar or finalist, National Hispanic scholar or honorable mention awardee, or Presidential scholar. Minimum 3.25 GPA and full-time enrollment are required to retain scholarship. Awarded every year.
Contact: Dawn Scott, Research Assistant, (405) 524-9153.

1989 Advocacy Diversity Award

Colorado State University
Financial Aid Office
108 Student Services Building
Fort Collins, CO 80523
(970) 491-6321
Average award: $1,000
Number of awards: 56
Deadline: March 10
College level: Freshman, Sophomore, Junior, Senior
Criteria: Applicant must be a Colorado resident. Reapplication, minimum 2.0 cumulative GPA, Colorado residency, and satisfactory progress are required to retain scholarship. Awarded every year. Award may be used only at sponsoring institution.
Contact: Jeanne Snyder, Financial Aid Counselor.

1990 Alabama Scholarship for Dependents of Blind Parents

Alabama Commission on Higher Education
3465 Norman Bridge Road
Montgomery, AL 36105-2310
(334) 281-1921
Average award: Tuition and instructional fees
College level: Freshman, Sophomore, Junior, Senior
Criteria: Applicant must be an Alabama resident, attend an Alabama postsecondary instituition, and come from a family in which the head of the family is blind and whose family income is insufficient to provide educational benefits. Applicant must apply within two years of high school graduation. Scholarship is renewable. Awarded every year.
Contact: State of Alabama, Department of Education, Administrative and Financial Services Division, Gordon Persons Building, 50 North Ripley, Montgomery, AL 36130.

1991 Alan B. Holmes Memorial Scholarship

State Scholarship Commission (Oregon)
1500 Valley River Drive
Suite 100
Eugene, OR 97401-2146
(503) 687-7395
Minimum award: $1,000
Number of awards: 2
Deadline: March 1
College level: Freshman
Criteria: Applicant must be an Oregon resident, a graduate of Ashland, Butte Falls, Crater, Eagle Point, North Medford, South Medford, Phoenix, Prospect, or Rogue River high schools, be enrolled full time at an Oregon school, and demonstrate financial need. Applicant must submit an essay describing the contribution golf has made to his or her development. Awarded every year.
Contact: Jim Beyer, Grant Program Director.

1992 Alaska State Educational Incentive Grants

Alaska Commission on Postsecondary Education
Division of Student Financial Aid
3030 Vintage Blvd.
Juneau, AK 99801-7109
(907) 465-6741
Average award: $1,500
Minimum award: $100
Number of awards: 300
Deadline: May 31
College level: Freshman, Sophomore, Junior, Senior
Criteria: Awarded every year.
Contact: Program Coordinator.

1993 Alberta Heritage Louise McKinney Scholarship

University of Calgary
2500 University Drive, NW
Calgary, Alberta, CN T2N 1N4
(403) 220-7872
Maximum award: $4,000
Minimum award: $2,000
Deadline: June 15
College level: Sophomore, Junior, Senior
Criteria: Applicant must be an Alberta resident with outstanding academic ability. Awarded every year. Award may be used only at sponsoring institution.
Contact: J. Van Housen, Director of Student Awards & Financial Aid.

1994 Alice E. Wilson Award

Canadian Federation of University Women
P.O. Box 7250
Vanier Post Office
Vanier, Ontario, CN K1L 8E3
(613) 747-8154
Average award: $1,000
Number of awards: 3
Deadline: November 30
College level: Doctoral
Criteria: Award is to assist women doing refresher work, specialized study, or retraining in new techniques applicable to their field. Applicant must hold a bachelor's degree or the equivalent, be a woman, be a Canadian citizen, or have held landed immigrant status for at least one year. Special consideration is given to applicants returning to study after a few years. Awarded every year.
Contact: Awards.

1995 Alice Mellema

State Scholarship Commission (Oregon)
1500 Valley River Drive
Suite 100
Eugene, OR 97401-2146
(503) 687-7395
Minimum award: $1,000
Number of awards: 2
Deadline: March 1
College level: Freshman
Criteria: Applicant must be an Oregon resident, a graduate of Sheridan High School, be enrolled full time at an Oregon school, and demonstrate financial need. Awarded every year.
Contact: Jim Beyer, Grant Program Director.

1996 Alumni Past Presidents Scholarship

Clemson University
G-01 Sikes Hall
Clemson, SC 29634-5123
(803) 656-2280
Average award: $3,500
Number of awards: 1
College level: Freshman
Criteria: Preference is given to South Carolina resident. Minimum 3.0 GPA with at least 12 credits per semester is required to retain scholarship. Awarded every year. Award may be used only at sponsoring institution.
Contact: Marvin Carmichael, Director of Financial Aid.

1997 Alumni Scholarship

University of California, Los Angeles
A129 Murphy Hall
Box 951435
Los Angeles, CA 90095-1435
(310) 206-0404
Maximum award: $10,000
Minimum award: $1,000
Number of awards: 355
College level: Freshman, transfer students
Criteria: Freshman applicant must graduate from a California high school with a minimum 3.85 GPA and a minimum combined SAT I score of 1200. Transfer applicant must have at least 84 transferable quarter units from a California community college and have a minimum 3.5 GPA. Awarded every year. Award may be used only at sponsoring institution.
Contact: Beverly LeMay, Assistant Director of Scholarships, (310) 206-0417.

1998 Alumni Valedictorian Scholarship

University of Memphis
Scates Hall 204
Memphis, TN 38152
(901) 678-3213
Average award: $2,042
Deadline: March 1
College level: Freshman
Criteria: Applicant must be the top graduating student from any accredited or state-approved high school in Tennessee. Minimum 3.0 GPA is required to retain scholarship. Awarded every year. Award may be used only at sponsoring institution.
Contact: Dr. Sue Ann McClellan, Scholarship Coordinator.

1999 Amick Farms Scholarship

Clemson University
G-01 Sikes Hall
Clemson, SC 29634-5123
(803) 656-2280
Average award: $4,000
Number of awards: 1
Deadline: March 1
College level: Freshman, Sophomore, Junior, Senior
Criteria: Applicant must be a South Carolina resident; preference, in descending order, is given to residents of Saluda County, Lexington County, Edgefield County, or Newberry County. Preference is also given to minority students. Satisfactory GPA with at least 12 credits per semester is required to retain scholarship. Awarded every year. Award may be used only at sponsoring institution.
Contact: Marvin Carmichael, Director of Financial Aid.

2000 Archie and Hugh Bothner Bursaries

University of Calgary
2500 University Drive, NW
Calgary, Alberta, CN T2N 1N4
(403) 220-7872
Average award: $2,000
Number of awards: 3
Deadline: June 15
College level: Sophomore, Junior, Senior
Majors/Fields: Science
Criteria: Applicant must be a Canadian citizen or permanent resident. Selection is based upon academic merit and financial need. Awarded every year. Award may be used only at sponsoring institution.
Contact: J. Van Housen, Director of Student Awards & Financial Aid.

2001 Baird Foundation Scholarship

University of Arizona
Tucson, AZ 85721-0007
(602) 621-1858
Average award: $2,000
Number of awards: 80
Deadline: March 1
College level: Freshman
Criteria: Applicant must be an Arizona resident, a U.S. citizen or permanent resident, a National Merit finalist, and demonstrate academic excellence. Minimum 3.5 cumulative GPA and full-time enrollment are required to retain scholarship. Awarded every year. Award may be used only at sponsoring institution.
Contact: Magdalen Vargas, Acting Associate Director of Scholarships.

2002 Beverley Jackson Fellowship

Canadian Federation of University Women
P.O. Box 7250
Vanier Post Office
Vanier, Ontario, CN K1L 8E3
(613) 747-8154
Average award: $3,500
Number of awards: 1
Deadline: November 30
College level: Graduate, Doctoral
Criteria: Applicant must be over age 35, enrolled in graduate work at an Ontario university, and be a woman, a Canadian citizen, or have held landed immigrant status for at least one year. Awarded every year.
Contact: Fellowships.

2003 Bill Hudson Family Endowment Scholarship

Clemson University
G-01 Sikes Hall
Clemson, SC 29634-5123
(803) 656-2280
Average award: $4,000
Number of awards: 1
Deadline: March 1
College level: Freshman, Sophomore, Junior, Senior
Criteria: Applicant must be a South Carolina resident and demonstrate financial need. Satisfactory GPA with at least 12 credit hours per semester is required to retain scholarship. Awarded every year. Award may be used only at sponsoring institution.
Contact: Marvin Carmichael, Director of Financial Aid.

2004 Blount Scholarship

University of Alabama–Tuscaloosa
Box 870162
Tuscaloosa, AL 35487-0162
(205) 348-6756
Average award: $5,500
Number of awards: 1
Deadline: February 1
College level: Freshman
Majors/Fields: Arts, business administration, commerce, engineering, sciences
Criteria: Applicant must be an Alabama resident, have a minimum composite ACT score of 32 or combined SAT I score of 1350, minimum GPA of 3.8, and demonstrate broad leadership experience. Essay is required. Five finalists will be interviewed on campus. Minimum 3.0 GPA is required to retain scholarship for four years. Awarded every year. Award may be used only at sponsoring institution.
Contact: Molly Lawrence, Director of Financial Aid.

2005 Boettcher Foundation Scholarship

Boettcher Foundation
600 17th Street
Suite 2210 South
Denver, CO 80202-5422
(303) 534-1938
Maximum award: Award is dependent upon what school applicant choses to attend
Number of awards: 40
Deadline: February 1
College level: Freshman
Criteria: Applicant must have resided in Colorado during junior and senior year of high school. Renewable if 3.0 GPA is maintained. Awarded every year.
Contact: Scholarships.

2006 Burns Lions Club

State Scholarship Commission (Oregon)
1500 Valley River Drive
Suite 100
Eugene, OR 97401-2146
(503) 687-7395
Minimum award: $1,000
Number of awards: 2
Deadline: March 1
College level: Freshman
Criteria: Applicant must be an Oregon resident, a graduate of Burns or Crane High Schools, be enrolled full time at an Oregon school, and demonstrate financial need. Awarded every year.
Contact: Jim Beyer, Grant Program Director.

2007 C.G. Fuller Foundation Scholarship

C.G. Fuller Foundation
c/o NationsBank of South Carolina, N.A.
P.O. Box 448
Columbia, SC 29202
(803) 929-5879
Average award: $2,000
Number of awards: 15
Deadline: March 31
College level: Freshman
Criteria: Applicant must be a South Carolina resident attending a South Carolina college or university and demonstrate financial need. Renewable if minimum 3.0 GPA is maintained. Awarded every year.
Contact: Pamela S. Postal, Assistant Vice President, NationsBank of South Carolina, P.O. Box 448, Columbia, SC 29202.

2008 Carolina Scholars Award

University of South Carolina (Columbia)
Columbia, SC 29208
(803) 777-8134
Average award: $7,000
Number of awards: 20
Deadline: Early November
College level: Freshman
Criteria: Applicant must be a South Carolina resident and demonstrate extraordinary academic achievement, leadership, and character. Minimum 3.0 GPA is required to retain scholarship. Awarded every year. Award may be used only at sponsoring institution.
Contact: Stewart Jones, Scholarship Coordinator.

2009 Carolina Scholars Finalist Award

University of South Carolina (Columbia)
Columbia, SC 29208
(803) 777-8134
Average award: $3,000
Number of awards: 30
Deadline: Early November
College level: Freshman
Criteria: Applicant must be a South Carolina resident and demonstrate extraordinary academic achievement, leadership, and character. Minimum 3.0 GPA is required to retain scholarship. Awarded every year. Award may be used only at sponsoring institution.
Contact: Stewart Jones, Scholarship Coordinator.

2010 Carver Scholarship

University of Northern Iowa
Financial Aid Office
Cedar Falls, IA 50613-0024
(319) 273-2700 or (800) 772-2736
Average award: $3,600
Number of awards: 19
Deadline: March 16
College level: Junior
Criteria: Applicant must have a minimum 2.8 GPA, be a graduate of an Iowa high school, be a U.S. citizen, and have overcome some personal obstacle to have come this far in a college career (physical, financial, emotional, etc.). Applicant must have a minimum 2.8 GPA and socio-emotional situation must remain the same to retain scholarship. Awarded every year. Award may be used only at sponsoring institution.
Contact: Evelyn Waack, Scholarship Coordinator.

2011 Catherine Hainer McMartin Bursary

University of Calgary
2500 University Drive, NW
Calgary, Alberta, CN T2N 1N4
(403) 220-7872
Average award: $1,000
Number of awards: 8
Deadline: June 15
College level: Junior, Senior
Majors/Fields: Canadian studies, education, political science
Criteria: Applicant must be a Canadian citizen. Preference is given to applicants who aspire to leadership positions in education or public service. Awarded every year. Award may be used only at sponsoring institution.
Contact: J. Van Housen, Director of Student Awards & Financial Aid.

2012 CFUW Professional Fellowship

Canadian Federation of University Women
P.O. Box 7250
Vanier Post Office
Vanier, Ontario, CN K1L 8E3
(613) 747-8154
Average award: $3,000
Number of awards: 1
Deadline: November 30
College level: Graduate
Criteria: Applicant must have bachelor's degree or equivalent, intend to pursue graduate work below the Ph.D. level, and be accepted at the proposed place of study or research at the time of application. Applicant must be a female, Canadian citizen or have held landed immigrant status for one year. Fellowship may be used for study abroad. Awarded every year.
Contact: Fellowships.

2013 Chancellor's Club Scholarship

University of Calgary
2500 University Drive, NW
Calgary, Alberta, CN T2N 1N4
(403) 220-7872
Average award: $6,000
Number of awards: 10
Deadline: March 15
College level: Freshman
Criteria: Applicant must be a Canadian citizen or permanent resident. Selection is based upon academic merit, contribution to school and community life, and academic promise. Minimum 3.0 GPA and full course load are required to retain scholarship. Awarded every year. Award may be used only at sponsoring institution.
Contact: J. Van Housen, Director of Student Awards & Financial Aid.

2014   Children of Disabled Firemen and Peace Officers Tuition Exemption

Texas Higher Education Coordinating Board
Student Financial Assistance
P.O. Box 12788, Capitol Station
Austin, TX 78711-2788
(512) 483-6340
Average award: $865
Number of awards: 67
College level: Freshman, Sophomore, Junior, Senior
Criteria: Applicant must be the child of a deceased or disabled fireman, peace officer, custodial employee of the Department of Conservation, or game warden who died or was disabled in the line of duty while serving Texas. Applicant must apply prior to 21st birthday and attend a public college or university in Texas. Scholarship is renewable. Awarded every year.
Contact: Mack Adams, Assistant Commissioner, Student Services.

2015   Christa McAuliffe Memorial Scholarship

American Legion–New Hampshire
Department Adjutant
State House Annex
Concord, NH 03301
(603) 271-2211
Average award: $1,000
Deadline: May 1
College level: Freshman
Majors/Fields: Education
Criteria: Applicant must be a recent graduate of a New Hampshire high school who will be entering his or her first year of college to study education. Applicant must have been a resident of New Hampshire for at least three years. Awarded every year.
Contact: Herbert J. Geary, Department Adjutant.

2016   Christian A. Herter Memorial Scholarship

Massachusetts Higher Education Coordinator Council
1 Ashburton Place
McCormack Bldg., Rm 1401
Boston, MA 02108
(617) 727-7785
Average award: $9,721
Number of awards: 24
Deadline: March 31
College level: Freshman
Criteria: Applicant must be a permanent Massachusetts resident and have exhibited severe personal or family difficulties, medical problems, or have overcome a personal obstacle or hardship. Recipient must continue to demonstrate financial need and file a FAFSA to retain scholarship. Awarded every year.
Contact: Cynthia M. Gray, Scholarship Officer, Office of Student Financial Assistance, 330 Stuart Street, Boston, MA 02116, (617) 727-9420.

2017   Clemson Scholars Program

Clemson University
G-01 Sikes Hall
Clemson, SC 29634-5123
(803) 656-2280
Average award: $2,000
College level: Freshman
Criteria: Awarded to the top ranked student in each South Carolina public high school. If the top ranked student is not black, an additional scholarship is offered to the top ranked black student. Minimum 2.5 GPA with at least 12 credits per semester is required to retain scholarship. Awarded every year. Award may be used only at sponsoring institution.
Contact: Marvin Carmichael, Director of Financial Aid.

2018   Clifford T. Smith Scholarship

Clemson University
G-01 Sikes Hall
Clemson, SC 29634-5123
(803) 656-2280
Average award: $1,000
Number of awards: 10
Deadline: March 1
College level: Freshman, Sophomore, Junior, Senior
Majors/Fields: Agricultural sciences
Criteria: Applicant must be a South Carolina resident from a designated rural area as defined by the Farmers' Home Administration, and demonstrate financial need. Satisfactory GPA with at least 12 credits per semester is required to retain scholarship. Awarded every year. Award may be used only at sponsoring institution.
Contact: Marvin Carmichael, Director of Financial Aid.

2019   Community Action Grants

American Association of University Women Education
Foundation
1111 16th Street N.W.
Washington, DC 20036-4873
(202) 728-7700
Maximum award: $5,000
Minimum award: $1,000
Deadline: February 1
College level: Doctoral
Criteria: Applicant must be a U.S. citizen or permanent resident. Proposed activity must have direct community or public impact. Applicant may apply for one grant only.
Contact: Grants, 2401 Virginia Avenue, NW, Washington, DC 20037, (202) 728-7603.

2020   Copp Family Scholarship

University of Calgary
2500 University Drive, NW
Calgary, Alberta, CN T2N 1N4
(403) 220-7872
Average award: $3,000
Number of awards: 6
Deadline: March 15
College level: Freshman
Criteria: Selection is based upon academic merit, contribution to school and community life, and academic promise. Applicant must be a Canadian citizen or permanent resident. Awarded every year. Award may be used only at sponsoring institution.
Contact: J. Van Housen, Director of Student Awards & Financial Aid.

2021   Curators Scholarship

University of Missouri–Columbia
High School and Transfer Relations
219 Jesse Hall
Columbia, MO 65211
(800) 225-6075 (in-state), (314) 882-2456
Maximum award: $3,500
Number of awards: 400
Deadline: August 15
College level: Freshman
Criteria: Applicant must be a Missouri resident, rank in the top 5% of class, have a minimum composite ACT score of 28 or combined SAT I score of 1190, and enroll at the university the first semester after high school. Minimum 3.25 GPA is required to retain scholarship. Awarded every year. Award may be used only at sponsoring institution.
Contact: Office of the Curators Scholars Program, 306 Clark Hall, Columbia, MO 65211, (314) 882-6292.

2022 Dan Konnie Scholarship

State Scholarship Commission (Oregon)
1500 Valley River Drive
Suite 100
Eugene, OR 97401-2146
(503) 687-7395
Minimum award: $1,000
Number of awards: 2
Deadline: March 1
College level: Freshman
Criteria: Applicant must be an Oregon resident, a graduate of Elmira, Crow, or Triangle Lake high schools, be enrolled full time at an Oregon school, and demonstrate financial need. Awarded every year.
Contact: Jim Beyer, Grant Program Director.

2023 Delegate Scholarship

Maryland Higher Education Commission
State Scholarship Administration
16 Francis Street
Annapolis, MD 21401-1781
(410) 974-5370
Maximum award: In-state tuition and fees
Minimum award: $200
Number of awards: 2201
Deadline: Varies
College level: Freshman, Sophomore, Junior, Senior, Graduate, Doctoral
Criteria: Applicant must be a Maryland resident attending a college, university, or vocational school in Maryland on a full- or part-time basis; an out-of-state institution qualifies if the major is not offered in Maryland. Applicant must contact all three delegates in their state legislative district for application instructions. Reapplication is required to retain scholarship. Awarded every year.
Contact: Gail Fisher, Program Administrator.

2024 Department of New Hampshire Scholarship

American Legion–New Hampshire
Department Adjutant
State House Annex
Concord, NH 03301
(603) 271-2211
Average award: $1,000
Number of awards: 2
Deadline: May 1
College level: Freshman
Criteria: Applicant must be a graduate of a New Hampshire high school entering his or her first year of higher education and a New Hampshire resident for at least three years. Awarded every year.
Contact: Herbert J. Geary, Department Adjutant, State House Annex, Concord, NH 03301.

2025 Department President's Scholarship

American Legion–Ohio Auxiliary
1100 Brandywine Boulevard, Building D
P.O. Box 2279
Zanesville, OH 43702-2279
(614) 452-8245
Maximum award: $1,500
Minimum award: $1,000
Number of awards: 2
Deadline: March 15
College level: Freshman
Criteria: Applicant must be the child or grandchild of a living or deceased veteran who served in World War I, World War II, Korean, Vietnam, Lebanon, or Desert Storm conflicts. Applicant must be an Ohio resident and be sponsored by an American Legion Auxiliary unit. Awarded every year.
Contact: Doris Wainwright, Department Executive Secretary/Treasurer.

2026 Distinguished Scholar Award

Maryland Higher Education Commission
State Scholarship Administration
16 Francis Street
Annapolis, MD 21401-1781
(410) 974-5370
Maximum award: $3,000
Number of awards: 1429
Deadline: Varies
College level: Freshman
Criteria: Applicant must be a Maryland resident, attend a Maryland degree-granting institution, and be a National Merit finalist, National Achievement finalist, demonstrate superior academic achievement (3.7 GPA), or demonstrate superior talent in the arts. Applicant must be nominated by high school during second semester of junior year. Minimum 3.0 GPA is required to retain scholarship. Awarded every year.
Contact: Margaret Riley, Program Administrator.

2027 Dominion Merit Scholarship

Old Dominion University
Hampton Boulevard
Norfolk, VA 23529-0050
(804) 683-3683
Maximum award: $2,340
Number of awards: 5
Deadline: February 15
College level: Freshman
Criteria: Applicant must be a Virginia resident, rank in the top tenth of class, have a minimum combined SAT I score of 1200, and demonstrate potential for leadership. Minimum 3.25 GPA is required to retain scholarship for three additional years. Awarded every year. Award may be used only at sponsoring institution.
Contact: Mary A. Schutz, Assistant Director of Scholarships.

2028 Dorothy and Roy Malone Scholarship

Colorado State University
Financial Aid Office
108 Student Services Building
Fort Collins, CO 80523
(970) 491-6321
Maximum award: $1,250
Minimum award: $500
Number of awards: 5
Deadline: March 3
College level: Freshman, Sophomore, Junior, Senior
Criteria: Applicant must be a Pueblo County high school graduate, rank in the top third of class, demonstrate participation in extracurricular activities and financial need. Reapplication is required for renewal. Awarded every year; may be used only at sponsoring institution.
Contact: Jeanne Snyder, Financial Aid Counselor.

2029 Doyle and Donna Shepherd Scholarship

State Scholarship Commission (Oregon)
1500 Valley River Drive
Suite 100
Eugene, OR 97401-2146
(503) 687-7395
Minimum award: $1,000
Number of awards: 2
Deadline: March 1
College level: Freshman
Criteria: Applicant must be an Oregon resident, a graduate of Cottage Grove high school, be enrolled full time at an Oregon school, and demonstrate financial need. Awarded every year.
Contact: Jim Beyer, Grant Program Director.

2030   Dr. Marion Elder Grant Fellowship

Canadian Federation of University Women
P.O. Box 7250
Vanier Post Office
Vanier, Ontario, CN K1L 8E3
(613) 747-8154
Average award: $8,000
Number of awards: 1
Deadline: November 30
College level: Graduate, Doctoral
Criteria: Applicant must be a woman who is a Canadian citizen or who has held landed immigrant status for at least one year, and be enrolled full-time in Canada or abroad. All else being equal, preference will be given to holders of Acadia U degrees. Awarded every year.
Contact: Fellowships.

2031   Educational Assistance Grant

Maryland Higher Education Commission
State Scholarship Administration
16 Francis Street
Annapolis, MD 21401-1781
(410) 974-5370
Maximum award: $3,000
Minimum award: $200
Number of awards: 13376
Deadline: March 1
College level: Freshman, Sophomore, Junior, Senior
Criteria: Applicant must be a Maryland resident, a full-time student at a Maryland degree-granting institution, and demonstrate financial need. Selection is based upon finanical need and satisfactory academic progress. FAFSA must be submitted by March 1. Reapplication and financial need are required to retain scholarship. Awarded every year.
Contact: Karen Price, Program Manager.

2032   Educational Opportunity Grant

Washington Higher Education Coordinating Board
917 Lakeridge Way
P.O. Box 43430
Olympia, WA 98504-3430
(206) 753-3571
Average award: $2,500
Number of awards: 276
Criteria: Applicant must be an eligible placebound student, demonstrate financial need, and have an A.A. degree or its equivalent. Award is for upper-division study at an eligible institution. Awarded every year.
Contact: Elizabeth A. Gebhardt, Assistant Director of Student Financial Aid, (206) 753-4592.

2033   Edward Grisso Memorial Scholarship

University of Oklahoma
University Affairs
900 Asp Avenue, Room 236
Norman, OK 73019-0401
(405) 325-1701
Average award: $1,000
Maximum number of awards: 7
Minimum number of awards: 6
Deadline: March 1
College level: Junior
Criteria: Applicant must be a male Oklahoma resident who has made great academic improvement since freshman year and demonstrates financial need. Awarded every year. Award may be used only at sponsoring institution.
Contact: Financial Aid Services, 731 Elm, Norman, OK 73019-0230, (405) 325-4521.

2034   Edwin P. Rogers Sr. Scholarship

Clemson University
G-01 Sikes Hall
Clemson, SC 29634-5123
(803) 656-2280
Average award: $1,000
Number of awards: 10
Deadline: March 1
College level: Freshman, Sophomore, Junior, Senior
Majors/Fields: Agricultural sciences
Criteria: Applicant must be a South Carolina resident from a designated rural area as defined by the Farmers' Home Administration, and demonstrate financial need. Satisfactory GPA with at least 12 credits per semester is required to retained scholarship. Awarded every year. Award may be used only at sponsoring institution.
Contact: Marvin Carmichael, Director of Financial Aid.

2035   Elizabeth & James MacKenzie Andrews Bursary

University of Calgary
2500 University Drive, NW
Calgary, Alberta, CN T2N 1N4
(403) 220-7872
Maximum award: $3,500
Minimum award: $2,000
Number of awards: 4
Deadline: July 15
College level: Freshman
Majors/Fields: Education
Criteria: Applicant must have graduated from a high school in the province of Alberta. Selection is based upon financial need and academic merit. Minimum 2.6 GPA in the Faculty of Education is required to retain scholarship. Awarded every year. Award may be used only at sponsoring institution.
Contact: J. Van Housen, Director of Student Awards & Financial Aid.

2036   Farm Credit Scholarship

Clemson University
G-01 Sikes Hall
Clemson, SC 29634-5123
(803) 656-2280
Average award: $1,200
Number of awards: 4
Deadline: March 1
College level: Freshman, Sophomore, Junior, Senior
Majors/Fields: Agricultural economics, agricultural sciences
Criteria: Applicant must major in agricultural economics or any other agricultural sciences major with a business-related minor. Applicant must be a resident of Florida, George, North Carolina, or South Carolina. Satisfactory GPA with at least 12 credits per semester is required to retain scholarship. Awarded every year. Award may be used only at sponsoring institution.
Contact: Marvin Carmichael, Director of Financial Aid.

2037   First Generation Award

Colorado State University
Financial Aid Office
108 Student Services Building
Fort Collins, CO 80523
(970) 491-6321
Average award: $2,850
Number of awards: 68
Deadline: April 1
College level: Freshman, new transfer students
Criteria: Applicant must be a Colorado resident, a first-generation college student, and demonstrate financial need. Reapplication, minimum 2.0 cumulative GPA, and satisfactory progress are required to retain scholarship. Awarded every year. Award may be used only at sponsoring institution.
Contact: Peggy Meis, Financial Aid Counselor.

2038 Florida Undergraduate Scholars' Fund

Florida Department of Education
Office of Student Financial Assistance
1344 Florida Education Center
Tallahassee, FL 32399-0400
(904) 487-0049
Average award: $2,500
Maximum award: $4,000
Deadline: April 1
College level: Freshman, Sophomore, Junior, Senior
Criteria: Applicant must either (1) be a finalist in the National Merit or National Achievement Scholarship Program, (2) have a minimum 3.5 GPA and a minimum combined SAT I score of 1250 or composite ACT score of 29, (3) be designated by the State Board of Education as a Florida Academic Scholar, pursuant to the provisions of Section 232.2465, Florida Statutes, (4) have been awarded an International Baccalaureate Diploma from the International Baccalaureate Office, or (5) have participated in state-approved home education and have a minimum combined SAT I score of 1250 or composite ACT score of 30. Applicant must have a Florida high school diploma or its equivalent, be a Florida resident, and be enrolled at an eligible Florida institution. Minimum 3.2 GPA with 12 credit hours per term is required to retain scholarship. Awarded every year.
Contact: Office of Student Financial Assistance.

2039 Ford Family Foundation Scholarship

State Scholarship Commission (Oregon)
1500 Valley River Drive
Suite 100
Eugene, OR 97401-2146
(503) 687-7395
Minimum award: $1,000
Number of awards: 2
Deadline: March 1
College level: Freshman, Sophomore, Junior, Senior, Graduate
Criteria: Applicant must be an Oregon resident, have a minimum 3.0 GPA, be enrolled full time at a two- or four-year Oregon school, and demonstrate financial need. Awarded every year.
Contact: Jim Beyer, Grant Program Director.

2040 Freshman Achievement Scholarship

University of Central Oklahoma
100 North University
Edmond, OK 73034
(405) 341-2980, extension 3336
Average award: $750
Maximum award: Full tuition and fees up to 18 hours
Number of awards: 25
Deadline: April 1
College level: Freshman
Criteria: Applicant must be an Oklahoma resident enrolled for a minimum of 12 hours, have a minimum composite ACT score of 27, and have a minimum 3.0 GPA. Minimum 3.25 GPA with full-time status is required to retain scholarship. Awarded every year. Award may be used only at sponsoring institution.
Contact: Margaret Howell, Scholarship Coordinator.

2041 Gerald Roberts Mortimer and Victor Emanuel Mortimer Scholarships and Bursaries

University of Calgary
2500 University Drive, NW
Calgary, Alberta, CN T2N 1N4
(403) 220-7872
Average award: $1,400
Number of awards: 3
Deadline: July 15
College level: Freshman, Sophomore, Junior, Senior
Criteria: Applicant must have attended high school in the Judicial District of Canada, excluding the city of Calgary, for at least two consecutive years. Selection is based upon academic merit and financial need. Awarded every year; may be used only at sponsoring institution.

Contact: J. Van Housen, Director of Student Awards & Financial Aid.

2042 Good Neighbor Scholarship

Texas Higher Education Coordinating Board
Student Financial Assistance
P.O. Box 12788, Capitol Station
Austin, TX 78711-2788
(512) 483-6340
Average award: $3,326
Maximum award: Tuition at public colleges and universities in Texas
Number of awards: 300
Deadline: March 15
College level: Freshman, Sophomore, Junior, Senior, Graduate, Doctoral
Criteria: Applicant must be a native-born citizen and resident from another nation of the American hemisphere, certified by native country, and scholastically qualified for admission to a public college or university in Texas. Scholarship is renewable. Awarded every year.
Contact: Gustavo O. DeLeon, Director of Grant Programs.

2043 Gordon Edward Wright Scholarship

University of Calgary
2500 University Drive, NW
Calgary, Alberta, CN T2N 1N4
(403) 220-7872
Average award: $3,000
Number of awards: 1
Deadline: March 15
College level: Freshman
Criteria: Applicant must be a Canadian citizen or permanent resident. Selection is based upon academic merit, contribution to school and community, and academic promise. Awarded every year. Award may be used only at sponsoring institution.
Contact: J. Van Housen, Director of Student Awards & Financial Aid.

2044 Graduate Equity Fellowship

California State University, Fullerton
P.O. Box 34080
Fullerton, CA 92634-9480
(714) 773-3128
Average award: $3,000
Deadline: June 1
College level: Graduate, Doctoral
Criteria: Applicant must be a California resident, enrolled full-time, demonstrate financial need of at least $1,000, have a minimum 3.0 GPA, and be a member of an underrepresented group. Target groups include American Indian, African-American, Central American, Chicano, Filipino, Mexican-American, Pacific Islander, Puerto Rican, South American, disabled, and women for selected majors. Reapplication is required to retain scholarship for up to four semesters. Awarded every year. Award may be used only at sponsoring institution.
Contact: Vickey Takeuchi, Scholarship Coordinator.

2045 Graduate/Professional Fellowship

Ohio Student Aid Commission
309 South Fourth Street
P.O. Box 182452
Columbus, OH 43218-2452
(614) 466-1190
Maximum award: $3,500
Number of awards: 63
Deadline: March 1
College level: Graduate
Criteria: Applicant must graduate from an Ohio institution with a bachelor's degree and start graduate school in Ohio within the same year. Satisfactory academic progress and full-time enrollment are required to retain scholarship. Awarded every year.
Contact: Barbara Metheney, Program Administrator.

2046   Guaranteed Access Grant

Maryland Higher Education Commission
State Scholarship Administration
16 Francis Street
Annapolis, MD 21401-1781
(410) 974-5370
Maximum award: $6,000
Deadline: March 1
College level: Freshman
Criteria: Applicant must be a Maryland resident attending a Maryland institution, enrolled full-time, have a minimum 2.5 GPA, and have a total annual family income which qualifies for the federal Free Lunch Program. Applicant must file FAFSA and SSA by March 1. Minimum 2.5 GPA is required to maintain grant. Awarded every year.
Contact: Judy Colgan, Program Administrator.

2047   H. and N. Morgan Foundation Inc. Annual Scholarship

Clemson University
G-01 Sikes Hall
Clemson, SC 29634-5123
(803) 656-2280
Average award: $3,000
Number of awards: 2
College level: Freshman
Criteria: Applicant must be designated as a Palmetto Fellow by the South Carolina Commission on Higher Education. Minimum 3.0 cumulative GPA with at least 12 credits per semester is required to retain scholarship. Awarded every year. Award may be used only at sponsoring institution.
Contact: Marvin Carmichael, Director of Financial Aid.

2048   H.S. and Angeline Lewis Scholarship

American Legion–Wisconsin Auxiliary
Department Executive Secretary
812 East State Street
Milwaukee, WI 53202-3493
(414) 271-0124
Average award: $1,000
Number of awards: 6
Deadline: March 15
College level: Freshman, Sophomore, Junior, Senior, Graduate, Doctoral
Criteria: Applicant must be a Wisconsin resident, have a minimum 3.2 GPA, demonstrate financial need, attend an accredited school, and be the child, wife, or widow of a veteran. Granddaughters and great-granddaughters of veterans are eligible if they are American Legion Auxiliary members. Awarded every year.
Contact: Scholarships.

2049   Harland Cravat/Gray Johnson Scholarship

State Scholarship Commission (Oregon)
1500 Valley River Drive
Suite 100
Eugene, OR 97401-2146
(503) 687-7395
Minimum award: $1,000
Number of awards: 2
Deadline: March 1
College level: Freshman
Criteria: Applicant must be an Oregon resident, a graduate of Milwaukie High School, be enrolled full time at an Oregon school, and demonstrate financial need. Awarded every year.
Contact: Jim Beyer, Grant Program Director.

2050   Harry S. Truman Scholarship

University of Texas at San Antonio
Office of Student Financial Aid
6900 North Loop 1604 West
San Antonio, TX 78249-0687
(210) 691-4011
Average award: Tuition, books, fees, and $100 per month allowance
Deadline: October 14
College level: Junior, Senior
Criteria: Applicant must be a Texas resident, a U.S. citizen or U.S. national, have a minimum 3.0 GPA, aspire to a career in public service, and be nominated by his or her college. Minimum 3.0 GPA is required to retain scholarship. Awarded every year. Award may be used only at sponsoring institution.
Contact: Office of Student Financial Aid, 6900 North Loop 1604 West, San Antonio, TX 78249-0687, (512) 691-4011.

2051   Hebrew Immigrant Aid Society Scholarships

Hebrew Immigrant Aid Society
Scholarship Awards
333 Seventh Avenue
New York, NY 10001-5004
(212) 967-4100
Average award: $1,000
Maximum award: $2,500
Minimum award: $500
Number of awards: 36
Deadline: April 20
College level: Freshman, Sophomore, Junior, Senior, Graduate, Doctoral
Criteria: Applicant must have attended at least two semesters at an American high school or college. Applicant or his or her parent must be a Hebrew Immigrant Aid Society-assisted refugee who immigrated to the U.S. during or after 1985. Selection is based upon academic excellence, financial need, and community activity. Awarded every year.
Contact: Sally Hespe, Membership Associate, (212) 613-1358.

2052   Heisey Foundation Scholarship

Montana State University
Bozeman, MT 59717
(406) 994-2845
Average award: $1,000
Number of awards: 35
Deadline: March 1
College level: Sophomore, Junior, Senior
Criteria: Applicant must demonstrate financial need and have graduated from one of 31 designated high schools in Montana. Awarded every year. Award may be used only at sponsoring institution.
Contact: Rebecca S. Jones, Assistant Director for Scholarships & Grants, Financial Aid.

2053   Hemphill-Gilmore Scholarship

University of Texas at Arlington
701 S. Nedderman Drive
P.O. Box 19199
Arlington, TX 76019
(817) 273-2197
Average award: $1,000
Number of awards: 35
Deadline: March 31 (freshmen); June 1 (others)
College level: Freshman, Sophomore, Junior, Senior
Criteria: Financial need must be demonstrated. Awarded every year. Award may be used only at sponsoring institution.
Contact: Chris Woodyard, Scholarship Coordinator.

2054 Henry Sachs Foundation Scholarship

Henry Sachs Foundation
90 South Cascade Avenue
Suite 1410
Colorado Springs, CO 80903
(719) 633-2353
Average award: $3,000
Maximum award: $6,000
Minimum award: $1,500
Number of awards: 50
Deadline: March 1
College level: Freshman, Sophomore, Junior, Senior
Criteria: Applicant must be a black Colorado resident, have a minimum 3.4 GPA, and demonstrate financial need. Minimum 2.5 GPA and at least 12 credit hours per term are required to retain scholarship. Awarded every year.
Contact: Scholarships.

2055 Home Oil Company Limited Centennial Matriculation Bursary

University of Calgary
2500 University Drive, NW
Calgary, Alberta, CN T2N 1N4
(403) 220-7872
Average award: $1,000
Number of awards: 5
Deadline: July 15
College level: Freshman
Majors/Fields: Computer science, engineering, general studies, geology, geophysics, management
Criteria: Applicant must be a Canadian citizen or permanent resident. Selection is based upon financial need, academic merit, and extracurricular activities. Awarded every year. Award may be used only at sponsoring institution.
Contact: J. Van Housen, Director of Student Awards & Financial Aid.

2056 Home Oil Company Limited Centennial Undergraduate Bursary

University of Calgary
2500 University Drive, NW
Calgary, Alberta, CN T2N 1N4
(403) 220-7872
Average award: $1,000
Number of awards: 5
Deadline: June 15
College level: Sophomore, Junior, Senior
Majors/Fields: Management, engineering, general studies, computer science, geology, geophysics
Criteria: Applicant must be a Canadian citizen or permanent resident. Selection is based upon financial need, academic merit, and extracurricular activities. Awarded every year. Award may be used only at sponsoring institution.
Contact: J. Van Housen, Director of Student Awards & Financial Aid.

2057 Houston International Fund

School for International Training
P.O. Box 676
Kipling Road
Brattleboro, VT 05302
(802) 257-7751
Average award: $3,333
Maximum award: $5,000
Minimum award: $2,000
Number of awards: 3
Deadline: April 30 (fall semester); October 15 (spring semester)
College level: Undergraduate
Criteria: Applicant must be an undergraduate student from Houston, Tex., who is participating in the semester-abroad program. Financial need is considered. Minorities are strongly encouraged to apply. Awarded every year. Award may be used only at sponsoring institution.
Contact: Mary Henderson, Financial Aid Officer, (802) 258-3280.

2058 Howard Vollum American Indian Scholarship

State Scholarship Commission (Oregon)
1500 Valley River Drive
Suite 100
Eugene, OR 97401-2146
(503) 687-7395
Minimum award: $1,000
Number of awards: 2
Deadline: March 1
College level: Freshman, Sophomore, Junior, Senior, Graduate
Majors/Fields: Computer science, engineering, mathematics, science
Criteria: Applicant must be an American Indian, a resident of Clackamas, Multnomah, or Washington county, Oreg., or Clark County, Wash., be enrolled full time at an Oregon school, and demonstrate financial need. Awarded every year.
Contact: Jim Beyer, Grant Program Director.

2059 Incentive Scholarship

North Carolina State Education Assistance Authority
Box 2688
Chapel Hill, NC 27515-2688
(919) 549-8614
Maximum award: $3,000
College level: Freshman, Sophomore, Junior, Senior
Criteria: Applicant must be a resident of North Carolina, meet specified admission standards, and participate in required public service activities. Applicant must be a highly qualified student planning to enroll at Elizabeth City State U, Fayetteville State U, North Carolina Agricultural and Technical State U, North Carolina Central U, Pembroke State U, or Winston-Salem State U. Awarded every year.
Contact: Financial Aid office at eligible school.

2060 Independent School Scholars Program

Clemson University
G-01 Sikes Hall
Clemson, SC 29634-5123
(803) 656-2280
Average award: $2,000
College level: Freshman
Criteria: Applicant must be a student at an independent high school in South Carolina. Selection is based upon academic credentials and principal's nominations. Minimum 3.0 cumulative GPA with at least 12 credit hours per semester is required to retain scholarship. Awarded every year. Award may be used only at sponsoring institution.
Contact: Marvin Carmichael, Director of Financial Aid.

2061 International Student Essay Competition

International Group Services
10530 Rosehaven Street
Suite 350
Fairfax, VA 22030
(703) 591-9800
Maximum award: $2,000
Minimum award: $500
Number of awards: 4
Deadline: December 1
Criteria: Applicant must be an international student or scholar studying in the U.S. Awarded every year.
Contact: Mr. Chris Foster, Regional Marketing Manager.

2062 International Student Fee Remission Scholarship

Portland State University
P.O. Box 751
Portland, OR 97207-5252
(503) 725-5270
Maximum award: $9,000
Minimum award: $7,200
College level: Freshman, Sophomore, Junior, Senior, Graduate, Doctoral
Criteria: Applicant must hold legal, non-immigrant status and be an international student. Applicant must have a minimum 3.0 GPA, clearly defined degree goals, and meet all regular admissions requirements. Outstanding academic performance will be recognized. Renewable if minimum 3.0 GPA is maintained. Awarded every year. Award may be used only at sponsoring institution.
Contact: International Student Admissions Officer, (503) 725-3511.

2063 Jack F. Tolbert Memorial Grant

Maryland Higher Education Commission
State Scholarship Administration
16 Francis Street
Annapolis, MD 21401-1781
(410) 974-5370
Maximum award: $1,500
Minimum award: $200
Number of awards: 861
Deadline: March 1
College level: Private career school student
Majors/Fields: Vocational
Criteria: Applicant must be a Maryland resident, a full-time student at an approved private career school in Maryland, and demonstrate financial need. Apply to financial aid office at institution. FAFSA must be submitted by March 1. Awarded every year.
Contact: Gail Fisher, Program Administrator.

2064 Jack Shinin Memorial Scholarship

State Scholarship Commission (Oregon)
1500 Valley River Drive
Suite 100
Eugene, OR 97401-2146
(503) 687-7395
Minimum award: $1,000
Number of awards: 2
Deadline: March 1
College level: Freshman
Criteria: Applicant must be an Oregon resident, be African-American, Hispanic, or Native American, be enrolled full time at an Oregon school, and demonstrate financial need. Awarded every year.
Contact: Jim Beyer, Grant Program Director.

2065 Jack T. Wood Bursary

University of Calgary
2500 University Drive, NW
Calgary, Alberta, CN T2N 1N4
(403) 220-7872
Average award: $2,500
Number of awards: 1
Deadline: June 15
College level: Junior, Senior
Majors/Fields: Management
Criteria: Applicant must be a Canadian citizen, province of Alberta resident, and have made a contribution to a Faculty of Management student organization or other university activity. Selection is based upon outstanding academic merit, demonstrated leadership ability, and financial need. Awarded every year. Award may be used only at sponsoring institution.
Contact: J. Van Housen, Director of Student Awards & Financial Aid.

2066 James B. Pearson Fellowship

Kansas Board of Regents
700 SW Harrison
Suite 1410
Topeka, KS 66603-3760
(913) 296-3517
Maximum award: $10,000
Minimum award: $1,000
Deadline: April 1
College level: Graduate, Doctoral
Criteria: Applicant must be a Kansas resident attending a Kansas public university; preference is given to applicants whose studies are directly related to foreign affairs. Fellowship is to encourage graduate students to experience the global perspective gained from study abroad. Awarded every year.
Contact: Fellowships.

2067 James H. and Minnie M. Edmonds Educational Foundation Scholarship

University of Texas at Arlington
701 S. Nedderman Drive
P.O. Box 19199
Arlington, TX 76019
(817) 273-2197
Average award: $1,000
Number of awards: 20
Deadline: March 31 (freshmen); June 1 (continuing and transfer students)
College level: Freshman, Sophomore, Junior, Senior
Criteria: Applicant must be a Texas resident and a U.S. citizen. Financial need must be demonstrated. Awarded every year. Award may be used only at sponsoring institution.
Contact: Chris Woodyard, Scholarship Coordintor.

2068 James Lee Love Scholarship

North Carolina State Education Assistance Authority
Box 2688
Chapel Hill, NC 27515-2688
(919) 549-8614
Average award: $3,000
Number of awards: 16
College level: Freshman, Sophomore, Junior, Senior
Criteria: Applicant must be a North Carolina resident enrolled full-time at one of the 16 constituent institutions of the U of North Carolina, and demonstrate financial need approximately the same amount as the fixed stipend. Awarded every year.
Contact: Financial aid office at eligible school.

2069 James Roy Carter Jr. Endowed Presidential Scholarship

Clemson University
G-01 Sikes Hall
Clemson, SC 29634-5123
(803) 656-2280
Average award: $2,300
Number of awards: 2
Deadline: March 1
College level: Freshman, Sophomore, Junior, Senior
Criteria: Applicant must be a South Carolina resident. Preference is given to residents of Chester, York, or Lancaster County in the colleges of Agricultural Sciences, Engineering, and Forest and Recreation Resources. Awarded every year. Award may be used only at sponsoring institution.
Contact: Marvin Carmichael, Director of Financial Aid.

2070   John and Sarra Fabbro Scholarship

University of Calgary
2500 University Drive, NW
Calgary, Alberta, CN T2N 1N4
(403) 220-7872
Average award: $1,500
Number of awards: 2
Deadline: July 15
College level: Freshman
Criteria: Applicant must graduate from a separate school system in Alberta, have completed Italian 30, and have a minimum matriculation average of 75 percent. Awarded every year. Award may be used only at sponsoring institution.
Contact: J. Van Housen, Director of Student Awards & Financial Aid.

2071   Johnson/LaSelle Scholarship

State Scholarship Commission (Oregon)
1500 Valley River Drive
Suite 100
Eugene, OR 97401-2146
(503) 687-7395
Minimum award: $1,000
Number of awards: 2
Deadline: March 1
College level: Freshman
Criteria: Applicant must be an Oregon resident, a graduate of a Clackamas, Multnomah, or Washington county high school, be enrolled full time at a two- or four-year Oregon school, and demonstrate financial need. Awarded every year.
Contact: Jim Beyer, Grant Program Director.

2072   Jose Marti Scholarship Challenge Grant

Florida Department of Education
Office of Student Financial Assistance
1344 Florida Education Center
Tallahassee, FL 32399-0400
(904) 487-0049
Average award: $2,000
Deadline: April 1
College level: Freshman, Sophomore, Junior, Senior, Graduate, Doctoral
Criteria: Applicant must be a Florida resident, a U.S. citizen or eligible noncitizen, be enrolled full-time at an eligible Florida college or university, demonstrate financial need, have a minimum 3.0 GPA, and be an Hispanic-American or a person of Spanish culture with origins in the Caribbean, Central America, Mexico, South America, or Spain, regardless of race. Minimum 3.0 cumulative GPA with at least 12 credit hours per term is required to retain scholarship. Awarded every year.
Contact: Office of Student Financial Assistance.

2073   Joyce Margaret Wright Scholarship

University of Calgary
2500 University Drive, NW
Calgary, Alberta, CN T2N 1N4
(403) 220-7872
Average award: $3,000
Number of awards: 1
Deadline: March 15
College level: Freshman
Criteria: Applicant must be a Canadian citizen or permanent resident. Selection is based upon academic merit, contribution to school and community, and academic promise. Awarded every year. Award may be used only at sponsoring institution.
Contact: J. Van Housen, Director of Student Awards & Financial Aid.

2074   Junior and Community College Scholarship

University of Missouri–Columbia
High School and Transfer Relations
219 Jesse Hall
Columbia, MO 65211
(800) 225-6075 (in-state), (314) 882-2456
Average award: $1,114
Number of awards: 10
Deadline: February 1
College level: Junior
Criteria: Applicant must be a Missouri resident, transfer student, have an A.A. or A.S. degree, rank in the top tenth of public junior or community college class, and attend the university the semester immediately after graduation. Two awards are given for each public junior and community college. Awarded every year. Award may be used only at sponsoring institution.
Contact: Student Financial Aid Office, 11 Jesse Hall, Columbia, MO 65211, (800) 225-6075 (in-state), (314) 882-3795.

2075   Junior College Transfer Scholarship

University of Central Oklahoma
100 North University
Edmond, OK 73034
(405) 341-2980, extension 3336
Average award: Full tuition and fees
Maximum award: Full tuition and fees up to 18 hours
Number of awards: 28
Deadline: April 1
College level: Junior, Senior, Graduate
Criteria: Applicant must be an Oklahoma resident enrolled for a minimum of six hours, have 50 transferrable hours, and a minimum 3.6 GPA. Student activities are also considered. Minimum 3.6 GPA is required to retain scholarship. Awarded every year. Award may be used only at sponsoring institution.
Contact: Margaret Howell, Scholarship Coordinator.

2076   Kansas Minority Scholarship

Kansas Board of Regents
700 SW Harrison
Suite 1410
Topeka, KS 66603-3760
(913) 296-3517
Maximum award: $1,500
Number of awards: 200
Deadline: April 1
College level: Freshman, Sophomore, Junior, Senior
Criteria: Applicant must be an ethnic minority, Kansas resident, attend an eligible Kansas postsecondary institution full-time, and demonstrate financial need. Selection is based upon academic performance, ethnic category, and financial need. Minimum 2.0 GPA, demonstrated financial need, and reapplication are required to retain scholarship. Awarded every year.
Contact: Scholarships.

2077 Kansas Nursing Scholarship

Kansas Board of Regents
700 SW Harrison
Suite 1410
Topeka, KS 66603-3760
(913) 296-3517
Maximum award: $3,500
Minimum award: $2,500
Number of awards: 300
Deadline: April 1
College level: Freshman, Sophomore, Junior, Senior
Majors/Fields: Licensed practical nursing, registered nursing
Criteria: Applicant must be a Kansas resident, attend an eligible Kansas institution full-time, and secure sponsorship with a health care agency. After passing the licensing exam, applicant must be employed by sponsor for one year for each year of funding or repay the funds at 15 percent interest. Good academic standing and reapplication are required to retain scholarship. Awarded every year.
Contact: Scholarships.

2078 Kansas Osteopathy Scholarship

Kansas Board of Regents
700 SW Harrison
Suite 1410
Topeka, KS 66603-3760
(913) 296-3517
Maximum award: $15,000
Deadline: May 1
College level: Doctoral
Majors/Fields: Osteopathic medicine
Criteria: Applicant must be a Kansas resident enrolled in a nationally accredited osteopathy school; preference is given to first-year students. Applicant must repay one year of practice in a medically "underserved" area in Kansas for each year of assistance. Award is for up to four years. Awarded every year.
Contact: Scholarships.

2079 Kansas State Scholarship

Kansas Board of Regents
700 SW Harrison
Suite 1410
Topeka, KS 66603-3760
(913) 296-3517
Maximum award: $1,000
Minimum award: $50
Number of awards: 1,200
Deadline: April 1
College level: Freshman, Sophomore, Junior, Senior
Criteria: Applicant must be a Kansas resident, attend an eligible Kansas postsecondary institution full-time, have been designated during senior year of high school as a State Scholar, and demonstrate financial need. Minimum 3.0 GPA, demonstrated financial need, and reapplication are required to retain scholarship. Awarded every year.
Contact: Scholarships.

2080 Kansas Teacher Scholarship

Kansas Board of Regents
700 SW Harrison
Suite 1410
Topeka, KS 66603-3760
(913) 296-3517
Average award: $5,000
Number of awards: 100
Deadline: April 1
College level: Freshman, Sophomore, Junior, Senior
Majors/Fields: Education
Criteria: Applicant must be a Kansas resident with high academic credentials and attend a Kansas college or university full-time in a program leading to teacher certification in "hard to fill" discipline. Applicant must agree to teach in Kansas one year for each year of funding or repay the funds with 15 percent interest. Good academic standing, enrollment in selected teacher certification program, and completion of renewal contract are required to retain scholarship. Awarded every year.
Contact: Scholarships.

2081 Kansas Tuition Grant

Kansas Board of Regents
700 SW Harrison
Suite 1410
Topeka, KS 66603-3760
(913) 296-3517
Maximum award: $1,700
Minimum award: $200
Number of awards: 3500
Deadline: April 1
College level: Freshman, Sophomore, Junior, Senior
Criteria: Applicant must be a Kansas resident, atttend an eligible Kansas postsecondary institution full-time, and demonstrate financial need. Need-based grant assists students who choose Kansas independent or private institutions. Demonstrated financial need, and reapplication are required to retain grant. Awarded every year.
Contact: Grants.

2082 Katharine L. Morningstar Scholarship

Montana State University
Bozeman, MT 59717
(406) 994-2845
Average award: $1,200
Number of awards: 5
Deadline: March 1
College level: Sophomore, Junior, Senior
Criteria: Applicant must be a Montana resident and have a minimum 2.5 GPA. Awarded every year. Award may be used only at sponsoring institution.
Contact: Rebecca S. Jones, Assistant Director for Scholarships & Grants, Financial Aid.

2083 Kelly/Ebell Scholarship

State Scholarship Commission (Oregon)
1500 Valley River Drive
Suite 100
Eugene, OR 97401-2146
(503) 687-7395
Minimum award: $1,000
Number of awards: 2
Deadline: March 1
College level: Freshman
Majors/Fields: Agriculture science
Criteria: Applicant must be an Oregon resident, a graduate of Baker Senior High School, be enrolled full time at an Oregon school, and demonstrate financial need. Awarded every year.
Contact: Jim Beyer, Grant Program Director.

2084 Laurence R. Foster Scholarship

State Scholarship Commission (Oregon)
1500 Valley River Drive
Suite 100
Eugene, OR 97401-2146
(503) 687-7395
Minimum award: $1,000
Number of awards: 2
Deadline: March 1
College level: Freshman, Sophomore, Junior, Senior, Graduate
Majors/Fields: Public health
Criteria: Applicant must be an Oregon resident, be enrolled full time at an Oregon school, and demonstrate financial need. Awarded every year.
Contact: Jim Beyer, Grant Program Director.

2085 Law Enforcement Officers and Fireman Scholarship Program

Mississippi Board of Trustees of State Institutions of Higher Learning
Student Financial Aid
3825 Ridgewood Road
Jackson, MS 39211-6453
(601) 982-6570
Average award: Tuition, average cost of dorm room, and required fees
College level: Freshman, Sophomore, Junior, Senior
Criteria: Applicant must be the spouse or child of a full-time, Mississippi law enforcement officer or firefighter who was fatally injured or totally disabled from injuries that occured in the line of duty. Applicant must attend a Mississippi public college or university. Children are eligible until age 23. Awarded for a maximum of eight semesters. Awarded every year.
Contact: Student Financial Aid Office.

2086 Louisiana Honors Scholarship

Louisiana Office of Student Financial Assistance
P.O. Box 91202
Baton Rouge, LA 70821-9202
(504) 922-1038
Average award: Full tuition
Number of awards: 2,087
College level: Freshman
Criteria: Applicant must be a Louisiana resident, graduate in the top five percent of a Louisiana high school class, and enroll full-time in a Louisiana college or university. Scholarship is renewable. Awarded every year.
Contact: Winona Kahao, Director of Scholarship/Grant Division, (504) 922-1107.

2087 Louisiana Tuition Assistance Plan

Louisiana Office of Student Financial Assistance
P.O. Box 91202
Baton Rouge, LA 70821-9202
(504) 922-1038
Average award: Full-tuition.
Number of awards: 2,040
Deadline: April 1
College level: Freshman
Criteria: Applicant must have resided in Louisiana for at least two years, have a parent/guardian who is a resident of Louisiana, have graduated from high school within two years, have no criminal record other than misdemeanor traffic violations, enroll at a Louisiana two- or four-year public institution of higher education as a first-time, full-time undergraduate student, demonstrate financial need, have a minimum 2.5 GPA, and composite ACT score of 20. FAFSA must be postmarked by March 15. Minimum 2.5 GPA is required to renew scholarship. Awarded every year.
Contact: Winona Kahao, Director of Scholarship/Grant Division, (504) 922-1107.

2088 Maine Student Incentive Scholarship

Maine Education Assistance Division
Maine Student Incentive Scholarship Program
State House Station #119
Augusta, ME 04333
(800) 228-3734, (207) 287-2183
Maximum award: $1,000
Minimum award: $500
Number of awards: 9200
Deadline: May 1
College level: Freshman, Sophomore, Junior, Senior
Criteria: Applicant must be a Maine resident attending an eligible school in Alaska, Delaware, District of Columbia, Maine, Maryland, Massachusetts, New Hampshire, Pennsylvania, Rhode Island, Vermont, or Canada. Awarded every year.
Contact: Nancy Wasson, Consultant.

2089 Margaret McWilliams Pre-Doctoral Fellowship

Canadian Federation of University Women
P.O. Box 7250
Vanier Post Office
Vanier, Ontario, CN K1L 8E3
(613) 747-8154
Average award: $9,000
Number of awards: 1
Deadline: November 30
College level: Doctoral
Criteria: Applicant must hold master's degree or equivalent, with at least one year full-time study in the doctoral program, may be studying abroad, and must be a woman, a Canadian citizen, or have held landed immigrant status for one year. Awarded every year.
Contact: Fellowships.

2090 Margery M. Wilson Scholarship

Colorado State University
Financial Aid Office
108 Student Services Building
Fort Collins, CO 80523
(970) 491-6321
Average award: $1,000
Number of awards: 50
Deadline: March 3
College level: Freshman, Sophomore, Junior, Senior, Graduate, Doctoral
Criteria: Applicant must be a Colorado resident with financial need. Reapplication is required to retain scholarship. Awarded every year. Award may be used only at sponsoring institution.
Contact: Jeanne Snyder, Finanical Aid Counselor.

2091 Marguerite Ross Barnett Memorial Scholarship

Missouri Coordinating Board of Higher Education
P.O. Box 6730
Jefferson City, MO 65102
(314) 751-3940
Maximum award: $2,202
College level: Sophomore, Junior, Senior
Criteria: Applicant must attend school part time and work a minimum of 20 hours per week. Scholarship is renewable. Awarded every year.
Contact: Information Service Center, (800) 473-6757.

2092 Maria Jackson/General George White Scholarship

State Scholarship Commission (Oregon)
1500 Valley River Drive
Suite 100
Eugene, OR 97401-2146
(503) 687-7395
Minimum award: $1,000
Number of awards: 2
Deadline: March 1
College level: Freshman, Sophomore, Junior, Senior, Graduate
Criteria: Applicant must be an Oregon resident who has served or whose parents have served in the US Armed Forces, have a minimum 3.75 GPA, be enrolled full time at an Oregon school, and demonstrate financial need. Applicant must submit documentation such as DD93, DD214, or discharge papers. Awarded every year.
Contact: Jim Beyer, Grants Program Director.

2093   Marion J. Bagley Scholarship

American Legion–New Hampshire Auxiliary
Department Secretary
25 Capital Street, Room 29
Concord, NH 03301
Average award: $1,000
Deadline: May 1
College level: Freshman, Sophomore, Junior, Senior
Criteria: Applicant must be a high school graduate or equivalent and resident of New Hampshire. Awarded every year.
Contact: Department Secretary, 25 Capital Street, Room 29, Concord, NH 03301.

2094   Marshall Scholarship

British Government Marshall Scholarships
British Information Services
845 Third Avenue
New York, NY 10022
(212) 752-5747
Average award: $24,000
Number of awards: 40
Deadline: October 17
College level: Graduate, Doctoral
Criteria: Applicant must be a U.S. citizen under 26 years of age with a minimum 3.7 GPA for study leading to a degree at a British university.
Contact: Marshall Scholarships.

2095   Mary McLeod Bethune Scholarship Challenge Grant

Florida Department of Education
Office of Student Financial Assistance
1344 Florida Education Center
Tallahassee, FL 32399-0400
(904) 487-0049
Average award: $3,000
Deadline: April 30
College level: Freshman
Criteria: Applicant must be a Florida resident, demonstrate financial need, have a minimum 3.0 GPA, and be enrolled for at least 12 hours per term at Bethune-Cookman Coll, Edward Waters Coll, Florida A&M U, or Florida Memorial Coll. Minimum 3.0 GPA and continued full-time status is required to retain scholarship. Awarded every year.
Contact: Office of Student of Financial Assistance.

2096   Mary Morrow Scholarship

North Carolina Association of Educators
P.O. Box 27347
700 South Salisbury Street
Raleigh, NC 27611
(919) 832-3000
Average award: $1,000
Number of awards: 4
Deadline: January 22
College level: Senior
Majors/Fields: Education
Criteria: Applicant must be a North Carolina resident enrolled in a teacher education program in a North Carolina college or university and be willing to teach in the North Carolina public schools for at least two years following graduation. Awarded every year.
Contact: Linda Powell, Communications Department.

2097   Massachusetts State Scholarship Program

Massachusetts Higher Education Coordinator Council
1 Ashburton Place
McCormack Bldg., Rm 1401
Boston, MA 02108
(617) 727-7785
Average award: $1,100
Maximum award: $2,500
Minimum award: $250
Deadline: May 1
College level: Freshman, Sophomore, Junior, Senior
Criteria: Applicant must be a resident of Massachusetts, be enrolled as a full-time student, and demonstrate financial need. Applicant must demonstrate financial need and submit FAFSA. Awarded every year.
Contact: Clantha Carrigan McCurdy, Director of Student Financial Assisstance, Office of Student Financial Assistance, 330 Stuart Street, Boston, MA 02116, (617) 727-9420.

2098   Memorial Education Fellowship

General Federation of Women's Clubs of Massachusetts
Box 679
Sudbury, MA 01776-0679
(508) 443-4569
Average award: $2,000
Number of awards: 10
Deadline: March 1
College level: Graduate, Doctoral
Criteria: Specified fields of study change each year. Applicant must be a woman maintaining a legal residence in Massachusetts for at least five years and must be sponsored by the General Federation of Women's Clubs in Massachusetts club in their community of legal residence. Awarded every year.
Contact: Chairperson, Memorial Education Fund.

2099   Merit Recognition Scholarship

Illinois Student Assistance Commission/Client Services
1755 Lake Cook Road
Deerfield, IL 60015-5209
(800) 899-ISAC, 708 948-8500
Average award: $1,000
College level: Freshman
Criteria: Applicant must be a U.S. citizen or eligible noncitizen, a resident of Illinois, and rank in the top five percent of class at end of seventh semester. Applicant must attend an approved Illinois postsecondary institution as an undergraduate on at least a half-time basis, comply with Selective Service (draft) registration requirements, and claim the award within one year of high school graduation. Awarded every year.
Contact: Manager of Scholarships and Specialized Grants.

2100   Merit Scholarship

University of Central Oklahoma
100 North University
Edmond, OK 73034
(405) 341-2980, extension 3336
Average award: $1,000
Minimum award: $262
Number of awards: 350
Deadline: April 1
College level: Freshman, Sophomore, Junior, Senior, Graduate, Doctoral
Criteria: Applicant must be an Oklahoma resident enrolled for a minimum of six hours. Freshman applicant must have a minimum composite ACT score of 22; upperclass student must have a minimum 3.25 GPA. Reapplication is required for renewal. Awarded every year. Award may be used only at sponsoring institution.
Contact: Margaret Howell, Scholarship Coordinator.

2101 Michigan Competitive Scholarship Program

Michigan Higher Education Assistance Authority
Office of Scholarships and Grants
P.O. Box 30462
Lansing, MI 48909-7962
(517) 373-3394
Maximum award: $1,200
Minimum award: $100
Number of awards: 27,200
Deadline: February 21 (high school seniors); March 21 (college students)
College level: Freshman, Sophomore, Junior, Senior
Criteria: Applicant must receive a qualifying ACT score prior to attending college, attend a Michigan college (public or private), be a Michigan resident, complete FAFSA, and demonstrate need. Applicant cannot major in religious education. Minimum 2.0 GPA is required to maintain scholarship. Awarded every year.
Contact: Jean Maday, Director of Scholarship and Grant Programs.

2102 Michigan Tuition Grant Program

Michigan Higher Education Assistance Authority
Office of Scholarships and Grants
P.O. Box 30462
Lansing, MI 48909-7962
(517) 373-3394
Maximum award: $1,975
Minimum award: $100
Number of awards: 34,000
Deadline: September 1
College level: Freshman, Sophomore, Junior, Senior, Graduate, Doctoral
Criteria: Applicant must be a Michigan resident attending a private, independent, degree-granting, Michigan college, demonstrate financial need, and complete FAFSA. Applicant cannot major in religious education. Applicant must maintain satisfactory academic progress. Awarded every year.
Contact: Jean Maday, Director of Scholarship and Grant Programs.

2103 Minnesota State Grant

Minnesota Higher Education Coordinating Board Division of Student Financial Aid
Suite 400, Capitol Square
550 Cedar Street
St. Paul, MN 55101
(800) 657-3866, (612) 296-3974
Average award: $1,300
Maximum award: $5,889
Minimum award: $100
Number of awards: 60,000
Deadline: May 31
College level: Freshman, Sophomore, Junior, Senior
Criteria: Applicant must show need, be a U.S. citizen or permanent resident, meet state residency requirements, be in first four years of postsecondary education, not be in default on a student loan, and be current in child support obligation. Applicant must reapply and demonstrate need for renewal. Awarded every year.
Contact: Grants Staff.

2104 Minority Achievement Scholarship

University of Central Oklahoma
100 North University
Edmond, OK 73034
(405) 341-2980, extension 3336
Average award: $1,500
Maximum award: Full tuition and fees up to 18 hours
Number of awards: 15
Deadline: April 1
College level: Freshman
Criteria: Applicant must be a minority Oklahoma resident enrolled for a minimum of 12 hours, have a minimum composite ACT score of 24, and have a minimum GPA of 3.0. Minimum 3.0 GPA with full-time status is required to retain scholarship. Awarded every year. Award may be used only at sponsoring institution.
Contact: Margaret Howell, Scholarship Coordinator.

2105 Missouri Higher Education Assistance Scholarship

Missouri Coordinating Board of Higher Education
P.O. Box 6730
Jefferson City, MO 65102
(314) 751-3940 or (800) 473-6757
Average award: $2,000
College level: Freshman
Criteria: Applicant must score in the top three percent on the ACT or SAT I while in high school and attend an eligible Missouri college. Applicant must maintain satisfactory academic progress for renewal. Awarded every year.
Contact: Information Service Center.

2106 Missouri Student Grant Program

Missouri Coordinating Board of Higher Education
P.O. Box 6730
Jefferson City, MO 65102
(314) 751-3940 or (800) 473-6757
Maximum award: $1,500
Deadline: April 30
College level: Unspecified undergraduate
Criteria: Applicant must demonstrate financial need, be a U.S. citizen and legal Missouri resident, and be working toward his or her first undergraduate degree as a full-time student attending an approved non-profit Missouri institution. Students majoring in theology or divinity are not eligible. Renewable if financial need is continued. Awarded every year.
Contact: Missouri Student Grant Program.

2107 Moorman Company Fund Scholarships in Agriculture

Clemson University
G-01 Sikes Hall
Clemson, SC 29634-5123
(803) 656-2280
Average award: $1,000
Number of awards: 4
Deadline: March 1
College level: Freshman, Sophomore, Junior, Senior
Majors/Fields: Agricultural business, agricultural economics, agricultural education, agricultural mechanization, animal science, dairy science
Criteria: Applicant must be a South Carolina resident. Satisfactory GPA with at least 12 credits per semester is required to retain scholarship. Awarded every year. Award may be used only at sponsoring institution.
Contact: Marvin Carmichael, Director of Financial Aid.

2108 Nathan Family Scholarship

State Scholarship Commission (Oregon)
1500 Valley River Drive
Suite 100
Eugene, OR 97401-2146
(503) 687-7395
Minimum award: $1,000
Number of awards: 2
Deadline: March 1
College level: Freshman
Criteria: Applicant must be an Oregon resident, a graduate of Lincoln High School (Portland SD 1J), be enrolled full time at an Oregon school, and demonstrate financial need. Preference is given to African-American students. Awarded every year.
Contact: Jim Beyer, Grant Program Director.

2109   National Association of Water Companies– New Jersey Chapter Scholarship

National Association of Water Companies–
New Jersey Chapter
661 Shrewsbury Avenue
Shrewsbury, NJ 07702
(908) 842-6900
Maximum award: $2,500
Number of awards: 2
Deadline: April 1
College level: Freshman, Doctoral
Majors/Fields: Biology, business, chemistry, communication, computer science, engineering, environmental sciences, law, natural resource management
Criteria: Applicant must be a U.S. citizen, a New Jersey resident for at least five years, and pursuing a degree at a New Jersey college or university. Applicant must have a minimum 3.0 GPA and be pursuing a professional career in the water utility industry or any field related to it. Awarded every year.
Contact: Rae Marsico, NAWC-NJ Scholarship Committee Chairman, New Jersey-American Water Company.

2110   National Science Scholars Program

Florida Department of Education
Office of Student Financial Assistance
1344 Florida Education Center
Tallahassee, FL 32399-0400
(904) 487-0049
Maximum award: $5,000
College level: Freshman
Majors/Fields: Computer sciences, engineering, life sciences, mathematics, physical sciences
Criteria: Applicant must be a U.S. citizen or eligible noncitizen, a Florida resident, demonstrate academic achievement, be scheduled to graduate from a Florida public or private secondary school, and demonstrate potential and career motivation in the physical, life, or computer sciences, mathematics, or engineering. Scholarship is renewable. Awarded every year.
Contact: Office of Student Financial Assistance.

2111   Ned McWherter Scholars Program

Tennessee Student Assistance Corporation
Parkway Towers, Suite 1950
404 James Robertson Parkway
Nashville, TN 37243-0820
(615) 741-1346
Average award: $5,000
Number of awards: 55
Deadline: February 15
College level: Freshman
Criteria: Applicant must be a U.S. citizen, attend a participating college or university in Tennessee, be a Tennessee resident, have graduated from a Tennessee high school with a minimum 3.5 GPA, and rank in the top five percent nationally on the ACT or SAT I. High school grades, standardized test scores, leadership roles in high school, and difficulty of high school program are all considered; recipient is selected competitively. Minimum 3.2 GPA and full-time status are required to retain scholarship. Awarded every year.
Contact: Program Administrator.

2112   New Hampshire Charitable Foundation Statewide Student Aid Program

New Hampshire Charitable Foundation
Box 1335
Concord, NH 03302-1335
(603) 225-6641
Average award: $1,200
Maximum award: $2,500
Minimum award: $100
Number of awards: 667
Deadline: April 21
College level: Freshman, Sophomore, Junior, Senior, Graduate, Doctoral, non-traditional students
Criteria: Applicant must be a New Hampshire resident. Some funds have specific eligibility requirements such as field of study or residential area. Selection is made through a statewide competition and is based upon merit and financial need. Some awards are renewable. To retain aid, applicant must maintain a satisfactory GPA and still have financial need. Awarded every year.
Contact: Judith T. Burrows, Director of Student Aid Programs, 37 Pleasant Street, Concord, NH 03301-4005.

2113   New Mexico Scholars Program

New Mexico State University
Box 30001
Department 5100
Las Cruces, NM 88003-0001
(505) 646-4105
Average award: $1,700
Deadline: March 1
College level: Freshman
Criteria: Applicant must be a New Mexico resident, graduate from a New Mexico high school in the year of the award, plan to enroll full-time, and meet family income guidelines. Applicant must have a minimum composite ACT score of 25, combined SAT I score of 1050, or rank in the top five percent of class. Minimum 3.0 cumulative GPA is required to retain scholarship. Awarded every year. Award may be used only at sponsoring institution.
Contact: Greeley W. Myers, Director of Financial Aid.

2114   New Mexico Scholars Scholarship

University of New Mexico
Mesa Vista Hall, Room 1044
Albuquerque, NM 87131
(505) 277-6090
Average award: $2,440
Number of awards: 75
Deadline: February 1
College level: Freshman
Criteria: Applicant must be a New Mexico resident, have a minimum composite ACT score of 25, or combined SAT I score of 1020 and rank in top five percent of class, and have a family adjusted gross income of $30,000 ($40,000 if two members are in college). Minimum 3.0 GPA and 24 hours per year are required to retain scholarship. Awarded every year. Award may be used only at sponsoring institution.
Contact: Rita M. Padillo, Associate Director for Scholarships & Financial Aid.

2115 Non-AFDC Child Care Grant

Minnesota Higher Education Coordinating Board Division of
Student Financial Aid
Suite 400, Capitol Square
550 Cedar Street
St. Paul, MN 55101
(800) 657-3866, (612) 296-3974
Maximum award: $1,500
Minimum award: $100
Number of awards: 1,669
College level: Freshman, Sophomore, Junior, Senior
Criteria: Applicant must be pursuing a nonsectarian program, be a
U.S. citizen or permanent resident, meet state residency require-
ments, be enrolled at least half-time, be in the first four years of post-
secondary education, must not be in default on a student loan, must
not receive AFDC, must have a child 12 years or younger, and must
meet eligible income guidelines. Applicant must reapply for renewal.
Awarded every year.
Contact: Financial Aid Division Staff.

2116 Non-Resident Fee Waiver

Louisiana State University and Agricultural and Mechanical
College
Baton Rouge, LA 70803-2750
(504) 388-3103
Average award: $3,300
Number of awards: 150
Deadline: February 1
College level: Freshman, Sophomore, Junior, Senior
Criteria: Applicant must have a commendable academic record.
Minimum 3.0 cumulative GPA and full-time enrollment are required to
retain scholarship. Awarded every year. Award may be used only at
sponsoring institution.
Contact: Kathleen Sciacchetano, Director of Financial Aid.

2117 Non-Resident Scholar

University of Missouri–Columbia
High School and Transfer Relations
219 Jesse Hall
Columbia, MO 65211
(800) 225-6075 (in-state), (314) 882-2456
Maximum award: $4,000
Minimum award: $2,000
Number of awards: 150
Deadline: August 15
College level: Freshman
Criteria: Applicant must be in the top quarter of class and have a mini-
mum composite ACT score of 27 or combined SAT I score of 1130.
Minimum 2.5 GPA with at least 24 credit hours per academic year is
required to retain scholarship. Awarded every year. Award may be
used only at sponsoring institution.
Contact: Kathryn E. Bass, Assistant Director, 11 Jesse Hall, Colum-
bia, MO 65211.

2118 Non-Resident Tuition Exemption

Louisiana State University and Agricultural and Mechanical
College
Baton Rouge, LA 70803-2750
(504) 388-3103
Average award: $7,245
Number of awards: 159
Deadline: February 1
College level: Freshman, Sophomore, Junior, Senior
Criteria: Applicant must be a resident of a state other than Louisiana,
have high standardized test scores, and an excellent academic re-
cord, especially in English and math. Minimum 3.0 cumulative GPA
and full-time enrollment are required to retain scholarship, subject to
availability of funds. Awarded every year. Award may be used only at
sponsoring institution.
Contact: Kathleen Sciacchetano, Director of Financial Aid.

2119 North Carolina Association of Insurance Agents Scholarship

North Carolina Association of Insurance Agents
1506 Hillsborough Street
P.O. Box 10097
Raleigh, NC 27605
(919) 828-4371
Maximum award: $1,000
Number of awards: 60
Deadline: April 1
College level: Freshman, Sophomore, Junior, Senior
Criteria: Applicant must be a North Carolina resident pursuing a
bachelor's degree. Selection is based equally upon academic merit
and financial need. Applicant must be sponsored by an independent
insurance agent who belongs to the "Big I" association. Reapplication
is required to retain scholarship. Awarded every year.
Contact: Jeanne Hess Clin, Scholarship Coordinator.

2120 North Carolina Bar Association Scholarship

North Carolina Bar Association
P.O. Box 12806
Raleigh, NC 27605
(919) 828-0561
Maximum award: $2,000
Deadline: April 25
College level: Freshman, Sophomore, Junior, Senior, Graduate,
Doctoral
Criteria: Applicant must be child of a North Carolina law enforcement
officer who was killed or permanently disabled in the line of duty. Ap-
plication must be made before applicant turns 27 years old. Selection
is based upon financial need and merit. Renewable up to a maximum
of $8,000 over 4 years. Awarded every year.
Contact: Jackie Fountain, Administrative Assistant, (919) 677-0561.

2121 North Carolina Teaching Fellows Scholarship

North Carolina State Education Assistance Authority
Box 2688
Chapel Hill, NC 27515-2688
(919) 549-8614
Average award: $5,000
Number of awards: 400
College level: Freshman
Majors/Fields: Education
Criteria: Applicant must be a North Carolina resident planning to at-
tend Appalachian State U, East Carolina U, Elon College, Fayette-
ville State U, Meredith College, North Carolina A&T State U, North
Carolina Central U, North Carolina State U, UNC Asheville, UNC
Chapel Hill, UNC Charlotte, UNC Greensboro, UNC Wilmington,
Pembroke State U, or Western Carolina U. Selection is based upon
GPA, class rank, SAT I scores, writing samples, community service,
extracurricular activities, and references. Applicant must agree to
teach in a North Carolina public school one year for each year of
scholarship assistance they receive or repay the amount with ten
percent interest. Award is for four years. Awarded every year.
Contact: Public Schools Forum, North Carolina Teaching Fellows
Commission, Koger Center, Cumberland Bldg., 3739 National Drive,
Suite 210, Raleigh, NC 27612, (919) 781-6833.

2122 North Dakota State Board of Higher Education Scholarship

North Dakota University System
10th Floor, Capitol
600 East Boulevard
Bismark, ND 58505
(701) 224-2960
Average award: $1,800
Number of awards: 50
College level: Freshman
Criteria: Applicant must be a resident of North Dakota planning to attend college in North Dakota, rank in the top fifth of class, and score in
the top five percent of students taking the ACT. Minimum 3.6 GPA is
required for renewal. Awarded every year.

2123 North Dakota Undergraduate Scholarship

North Dakota University System
10th Floor, Capitol
600 East Boulevard
Bismark, ND 58505
(701) 224-2960
Average award: $1,100
Number of awards: 50
Deadline: April 1
Criteria: Applicant must score in at least the 95th percentile on the ACT. Awarded every year.

2124 Ohio Academic Scholarship

Ohio Student Aid Commission
309 South Fourth Street
P.O. Box 182452
Columbus, OH 43218-2452
(614) 466-1190
Average award: $1,000
Number of awards: 1,000
Deadline: February 23
College level: Freshman
Criteria: Applicant must be an Ohio resident, graduate from an Ohio chartered high school, and have full-time status in a participating Ohio college or university. Selection is based upon academic excellence in high school and ACT scores. Satisfactory academic progress and full-time enrollment are required to retain scholarship. Awarded every year.
Contact: Sue Minturn, Program Administrator.

2125 Ohio Academic Scholarship and Matching Program

University of Toledo
Financial Aid Office
Toledo, OH 43606-3390
(419) 537-2056
Average award: $2,500
Deadline: January 28
College level: Freshman
Criteria: Applicant must be an Ohio resident who has been awarded the Ohio Academic Scholarship from the Ohio Board of Regents. Selection is based upon academic achievement. Applicant must be enrolled full-time with a minimum 3.0 GPA for university funding and minimum 2.0 GPA for Ohio Academic Scholarship. Awarded every year. Award may be used only at sponsoring institution.
Contact: Office of Financial Aid.

2126 Opportunity Award Scholarship

Texas A&M University, College Station
College Station, TX 77843-4233
(409) 845-1957
Average award: $1,000
Maximum award: $2,000
Minimum award: $500
Number of awards: 600
Deadline: January 15
College level: Freshman
Criteria: Applicant must demonstrate financial need. A minimum 2.5 GPA and full-time enrollment are required to retain scholarship. Awarded every year. Award may be used only at sponsoring institution.
Contact: Molly Georgiades, Administrator for Scholarships and Student Employment, (409) 845-3982.

2127 Oregon Logging Conference Scholarship

Portland State University
P.O. Box 751
Portland, OR 97207-5252
(503) 725-5270
Average award: $1,000
Number of awards: 2
Deadline: October 10
College level: Graduate
Criteria: Applicant must be an Oregon resident with an interest in the Oregon timber industry and be enrolled full time. Awarded every year. Award may be used only at sponsoring institution.
Contact: Scholarships, College of Liberal Arts and Sciences, Dean's Office, P.O. Box 751, Portland, OR 97207-0751, (503) 725-3514.

2128 Oregon Need Grant

State Scholarship Commission (Oregon)
1500 Valley River Drive
Suite 100
Eugene, OR 97401-2146
(503) 687-7395
Average award: $1,594
Maximum award: $3,180
Minimum award: $756
Number of awards: 24200
College level: Sophomore, Junior, Senior, Graduate
Criteria: Applicant must be an Oregon resident, be enrolled full time at an Oregon school, and demonstrate financial need. Scholarship is renewable. Awarded every year.
Contact: Jim Beyer, Grant Program Director.

2129 Oregon Occupational Safety and Health Division Workers Memorial Scholarship

State Scholarship Commission (Oregon)
1500 Valley River Drive
Suite 100
Eugene, OR 97401-2146
(503) 687-7395
Minimum award: $1,000
Number of awards: 2
Deadline: March 1
College level: Freshman
Criteria: Applicant must be an Oregon resident, be enrolled full time at an Oregon school, demonstrate financial need, and be the dependent of an Oregon worker who incurred permanent total disability on the job or be receiving fatality benefits as the dependent of a fatally injured Oregon worker. Awarded every year.
Contact: Jim Beyer, Grant Program Director.

2130 Oregon Private 150 Scholarship

State Scholarship Commission (Oregon)
1500 Valley River Drive
Suite 100
Eugene, OR 97401-2146
(503) 687-7395
Minimum award: $1,000
Number of awards: 2
Deadline: March 1
College level: Junior, Senior
Majors/Fields: Business
Criteria: Applicant must be an Oregon resident, be enrolled full time at an Oregon school with a minimum 3.5 GPA, and demonstrate financial need. Awarded every year.
Contact: Jim Beyer, Grant Program Director.

2131 Palmetto Fellows Scholarship

Clemson University
G-01 Sikes Hall
Clemson, SC 29634-5123
(803) 656-2280
Maximum award: $2,500
Number of awards: 1
College level: Freshman
Criteria: Award is for the most outstanding entering freshman from South Carolina. Minimum 3.0 cumulative GPA with at least 12 credits per semester is required to retain scholarship. Awarded every year. Award may be used only at sponsoring institution.
Contact: Marvin Carmichael, Director of Financial Aid.

2132 Part-time Grant Program

Maryland Higher Education Commission
State Scholarship Administration
16 Francis Street
Annapolis, MD 21401-1781
(410) 974-5370
Maximum award: $1,000
Minimum award: $200
Number of awards: 2395
College level: Freshman, Sophomore, Junior, Senior, Graduate
Criteria: Applicant must attend a Maryland institution and take 6–11 credits. Scholarship is renewable. Awarded every year.
Contact: Financial Aid Office at Maryland college/universities.

2133 Patrick H. Johnson Memorial Scholarship

Marianas Naval Officers' Wives' Club
Scholarship Chairwoman
PSC 489, Box 49 COMNAVMAR
FPO AP, 96536-0051
(671) 477-5405
Average award: $3,000
Number of awards: 1
Deadline: March 31
College level: Freshman
Criteria: Applicant must be a graduating senior from an accredited high school on Guam; no military affiliation is required. Selection is based upon academic ability, character, leadership ability, community involvement, financial need, and the cost of the school.

2134 Paul L. Fowler Memorial Scholarship

Idaho State Board of Education
Len B. Jordan Building, Room 307
P.O. Box 83720
Boise, ID 83720-0037
(208) 334-2270
Average award: $2,830
Number of awards: 5
Deadline: January 31
College level: Freshman
Criteria: Applicant must be an Idaho resident who has demonstrated outstanding ability and willingness to work for a higher education. Selection is based upon class rank and ACT scores. Recipient must enroll full-time in an academic program. Awarded every year.
Contact: Caryl Smith, Scholarship Assistant.

2135 Phelps Dodge Corporation Scholarship

New Mexico State University
Box 30001, Department 5100
Las Cruces, NM 88003-0001
(505) 646-4105
Average award: $1,700
Number of awards: 2
Deadline: March 1
College level: Junior, Senior
Criteria: Applicant must be a New Mexico resident and a graduate of a New Mexico or Arizona high school. Preference is given to children of Phelps Dodge employees or employees of Phelps Dodge subsidiaries in New Mexico. Selection is based upon merit without regard to financial need. Awarded every year. Award may be used only at sponsoring institution.
Contact: Greeley W. Myers, Director of Financial Aid.

2136 Police Officers and Firefighters Survivor's Educational Assistance Program

Alabama Commission on Higher Education
3465 Norman Bridge Road
Montgomery, AL 36105-2310
(334) 281-1921
Average award: Tuition, fees, books, and supplies.
College level: Freshman, Sophomore, Junior, Senior
Criteria: Applicant must be the dependent or spouse of a police officer or firefighter killed in the line of duty in Alabama, and be enrolled at a public postsecondary educational institution in Alabama. Scholarship is renewable. Awarded every year.
Contact: Jan B. Hilyer, Assistant Director of Grants and Scholarships.

2137 Portland Teachers Credit Union

State Scholarship Commission (Oregon)
1500 Valley River Drive
Suite 100
Eugene, OR 97401-2146
(503) 687-7395
Minimum award: $1,000
Number of awards: 2
Deadline: March 1
College level: Sophomore, Junior, Senior, Graduate
Criteria: Applicant must be an Oregon resident, be enrolled full time at an Oregon school, be a member of the Portland Teachers' Credit Union, and demonstrate financial need. Awarded every year.
Contact: Jim Beyer, Grant Program Director.

2138 Potlatch Foundation for Higher Education Scholarship

Potlatch Foundation for Higher Education
P.O. Box 193591
San Francisco, CA 94119-3591
(510) 947-4725
Average award: $1,400
Number of awards: 70
Deadline: February 15
College level: Freshman, Sophomore, Junior, Senior
Criteria: Applicant must reside within 30 miles of a major Potlatch Corp. facility in Arkansas, California, Idaho, Minnesota, or Nevada or attend high school in such an area. Selection is based upon character, personality, leadership qualities, scholastic achievement and ability, and financial need. Application must be requested by December 15. Minimum 2.1 GPA is required to retain scholarship. Awarded every year.
Contact: Joyce O. Laboure, Corporate Programs Administrator.

2139 President's Associates Honors Scholarship

New Mexico State University
Box 30001
Department 5100
Las Cruces, NM 88003-0001
(505) 646-4105
Average award: $4,700
Number of awards: 5
Deadline: March 1
College level: Freshman
Criteria: Applicant must have a minimum 3.5 GPA with a minimum composite ACT score of 26 or combined SAT I score of 1090 or a minimum 3.0 GPA with a minimum composite ACT score of 28 or combined SAT I score of 1170. Applicant must be a graduate of a New Mexico high school. Selection is based upon academic achievement. Minimum 3.5 cumulative GPA is required to retain scholarship for four years. Awarded every year. Award may be used only at sponsoring institution.
Contact: Greeley W. Myers, Director of Financial Aid.

2140 President's Associates Scholarship

New Mexico State University
Box 30001
Department 5100
Las Cruces, NM 88003-0001
(505) 646-4105
Average award: $2,000
Number of awards: 10
Deadline: March 1
College level: Freshman
Criteria: Applicant must have a minimum 3.5 GPA with a minimum composite ACT score of 26 or combined SAT I score of 1090 or a minimum 3.0 GPA and a minimum composite ACT score of 28 or combined SAT I score of 1170. Applicant must be a graduate of a New Mexico high school. Selection is based upon academic achievement. Minimum 3.5 cumulative GPA is required to retain scholarship for four years. Awarded every year. Award may be used only at sponsoring institution.
Contact: Greeley W. Myers, Director of Financial Aid.

2141 President's Scholarship

Colorado State University
Financial Aid Office
108 Student Services Building
Fort Collins, CO 80523
(970) 491-6321
Average award: $1,000
Number of awards: 391
Deadline: Automatic consideration
College level: Sophomore, Junior, Senior, transfer students from two-year Colorado colleges
Criteria: Minimum 3.85 cumulative GPA is required to retain scholarship. Awarded every year. Award may be used only at sponsoring institution.
Contact: Jeanne Snyder, Financial Aid Counselor.

2142 Presidential Scholarship

University of Oregon
1242 University of Oregon
Eugene, OR 97403-1242
(503) 346-3044
Maximum award: $2,400
Number of awards: 50
Deadline: February 1
College level: Freshman
Criteria: Applicant must be an Oregon resident. Renewable if a minimum 3.25 GPA is maintained. Awarded every year. Award may be used only at sponsoring institution.
Contact: Jim Gilmour, Associate Director of Financial Aid, (503) 346-1187.

2143 Professional Land Surveyors of Oregon Scholarship

State Scholarship Commission (Oregon)
1500 Valley River Drive
Suite 100
Eugene, OR 97401-2146
(503) 687-7395
Minimum award: $1,000
Number of awards: 2
Deadline: March 1
College level: Junior
Majors/Fields: Land surveying
Criteria: Applicant must be an Oregon resident, be enrolled full time at an Oregon school, and demonstrate financial need. Awarded every year.
Contact: Jim Beyer, Grants Program Director.

2144 Professional Study Grant

Oklahoma State Regents for Higher Education
500 Education Building
State Capitol Complex
Oklahoma City, OK 73105
(405) 524-9100
Average award: $4,000
Number of awards: 30
Deadline: June 1
College level: Professional programs other than Ph.D.s
Majors/Fields: Health science, law, medicine, optometry, osteopathic medicine, veterinary medicine
Criteria: Applicant must be an Oklahoma resident enrolled in a professional program at an Oklahoma university. Renewable for one additional year. Awarded every year.
Contact: Dawn Scott, Research Assistant, (405) 524-9153.

2145 Public Safety Officers Survivor Grant

Minnesota Higher Education Coordinating Board Division of Student Financial Aid
Suite 400, Capitol Square
550 Cedar Street
St. Paul, MN 55101
(800) 657-3866, (612) 296-3974
Average award: $2,600
Maximum award: $4,849
Number of awards: 10
College level: Freshman, Sophomore, Junior, Senior
Criteria: Applicant must be the dependent child, under 23 years of age, or the surviving spouse of a public safety officer who was killed in the line of duty on or after January 1, 1973. Applicant must also be a U.S. citizen or permanent resident, meet state residency requirements, be enrolled at least half-time, be in the first four years of postsecondary education, and must not be in default on a student loan. Recipient must reapply each academic term for renewal. Awarded every year.
Contact: Diane Senkyr, Program Assistant, (612) 296-3974.

2146 Regents Professional Opportunity Scholarship

New York State Education Department
Bureau of Postsecondary Grants Administration
Cultural Education Center
Albany, NY 12230
(518) 474-5705
Maximum award: $5,000
Minimum award: $1,000
Number of awards: 220
Deadline: March 8
College level: Freshman, Sophomore, Junior, Senior, Graduate, Doctoral
Majors/Fields: Accounting, architecture, audiology, chiropractic, dental hygiene, engineering, landscape architecture, law, nursing, occupational therapy, occupational therapy assistant, ophthalmic dispensing, optometry, pharmacy, physical therapy, physical therapy assistant, physician assistant, psychology, social work, speech-language pathology, veterinary medicine
Criteria: Applicant must attend or plan to attend an approved licensure-qualifying program in New York state, be a legal resident of New York state for one year prior to September 1, be a U.S. citizen or permanent resident, and be economically disadvantaged or a member of a minority group underrepresented in one of the designated licensed professions. Applicant must agree to practice in New York state in chosen profession for 12 months for each annual payment received. Scholarship is renewable. Awarded when funding is available.
Contact: Office of Equity and Access.

2147 Regents Scholarship

University of Nebraska, Lincoln
14th and R Streets
Lincoln, NE 68588
(402) 472-2030
Average award: $1,968
Maximum award: $2,337
Minimum award: In-state tuition
Number of awards: 322
Deadline: January 15
College level: Freshman
Criteria: Applicant must be a graduate from a Nebraska high school. Minimum 3.5 GPA with 24 credits per year required to retain scholarship. Awarded every year; may be used only at sponsoring institution.
Contact: Debra Augustyn, Assistant Director of Scholarships.

2148 Regents Scholarships in Cornell University

New York State Education Department
Bureau of Postsecondary Grants Administration
Cultural Education Center
Albany, NY 12230
(518) 474-5705
Maximum award: $1,000
Minimum award: $100
Number of awards: 61
College level: Freshman, Sophomore, Junior, Senior
Criteria: Applicant must be a legal resident of New York state and meet admission requirements for Cornell U. Program allows students to attend the state's land-grant institution at reduced tuition. Scholarship is renewable. Awarded every year.
Contact: Office of Equity and Access.

2149 Regents' Scholarship

New Mexico State University
Box 30001, Department 5100
Las Cruces, NM 88003-0001
(505) 646-4105
Average award: Tuition
Deadline: March 1
College level: Freshman
Criteria: Applicant must have a minimum 3.0 GPA and either a minimum composite ACT score of 23 or combined SAT I score of 970 and rank in top tenth of class or have a minimum composite ACT score of 26 or combined SAT I score of 1090. Minimum 3.2 GPA at end of first semester and 3.5 GPA thereafter is required to retain scholarship. Awarded every year; may be used only at sponsoring institution.
Contact: Greeley W. Myers, Director of Financial Aid.

2150 Richard John Cowan Memorial Scholarship

State Scholarship Commission (Oregon)
1500 Valley River Drive, Suite 100
Eugene, OR 97401-2146
(503) 687-7395
Minimum award: $1,000
Number of awards: 2
Deadline: March 1
College level: Freshman
Criteria: Applicant must be an Oregon resident, be enrolled full time at an Oregon school, and demonstrate financial need. Applicant must have graduated from Burns or Crane High Schools within the last two years and not have previously attended college. Awarded every year.
Contact: Jim Beyer, Grant Program Director.

2151 Robert C. Byrd Honors Scholarship

Connecticut Department of Higher Education
Office of Student Financial Aid
61 Woodland Street
Hartford, CT 06105
(203) 566-2618
Average award: $1,500
College level: Freshman
Criteria: Applicant must be a Connecticut resident who ranks in the top three percent of class. Selection is based upon SAT I scores and class rank. Scholarship is renewable. Awarded every year.
Contact: Office of Student Financial Aid.

2152 Robert C. Byrd Honors Scholarship

Missouri Department of Elementary and Secondary Education
P.O. Box 480
Jefferson City, MO 65102
(314) 751-0300
Average award: $1,500
Number of awards: 130
Deadline: March 31
College level: Freshman
Criteria: Applicant must be a resident of Missouri, rank in the top 10 percent of graduating class, score in the top 10 percent on the ACT, and file with the school a statement certifying registration with the selective service. Recipient must remain in good standing with the college for scholarship to be renewed. Awarded every year.
Contact: Karen Wunderlich, Supervisor.

2153 Robert C. Byrd Honors Scholarship

New York State Education Department
Bureau of Postsecondary Grants Administration
Cultural Education Center
Albany, NY 12230
(518) 474-5705
Maximum award: $1,500
Number of awards: 400
College level: Freshman
Criteria: Applicant must be a legal resident of New York state and a senior in high school or a student earning a GED diploma by the end of February. Scholarship is renewable. Awarded every year.
Contact: Office of Equity and Access.

2154 Robert C. Byrd Honors Scholarship

North Carolina State Education Assistance Authority
Box 2688
Chapel Hill, NC 27515-2688
(919) 549-8614
Average award: $1,500
College level: Freshman
Criteria: Applicant must be a North Carolina resident who graduated from a North Carolina public or private secondary school. Selection is based upon outstanding academic achievement. Finanical need is not a factor. Renewable for up to four years of study. Awarded every year.
Contact: Department of Public Instruction, 301 N. Wilmington Street, Raleigh, NC 27601-2825, (919) 715-1120.

2155 Robert C. Byrd Honors Scholarship

Ohio Student Aid Commission
309 South Fourth Street
Columbus, OH 43215-5445
(800) 837-6752 or (614) 466-8716
Average award: $1,500
Number of awards: 260
College level: Freshman
Criteria: Applicant must be an Ohio resident, graduating high school senior, and an exceptional academic student who is admitted for enrollment at any institute of higher education. Eligibility is not need-based. Top 10 students in each of Ohio's 21 Congressional districts will be selected. Applicant must demonstrate outstanding academic achievement as indicated by class rank, test scores, and GPA. Satisfactory academic progress is required to retain scholarship. Awarded every year.
Contact: Cherie Look, Robert C. Byrd Program Administrator, P.O. Box 16610, Columbus, OH 43216-0610, (800) 282-0820, extension 29137 or (614) 752-9137.

2156   Robert C. Byrd Honors Scholarship

State Scholarship Commission (Oregon)
1500 Valley River Drive
Suite 100
Eugene, OR 97401-2146
(503) 687-7395
Minimum award: $1,000
Number of awards: 2
Deadline: March 1
College level: Freshman
Majors/Fields: Education
Criteria: Applicant must be an Oregon resident, have a minimum 3.85 GPA and minimum combined SAT I scores of 1150 or minimum GED score of 325, be enrolled full time at an Oregon school, and demonstrate financial need. Scholarship is renewable. Awarded every year.
Contact: Jim Beyer, Grant Program Director.

2157   Robert C. Byrd Honors Scholarship

Texas Higher Education Coordinating Board
Student Financial Assistance
P.O. Box 12788, Capitol Station
Austin, TX 78711-2788
(512) 483-6340
Average award: $1,500
Number of awards: 433
Deadline: March 15
College level: Freshman
Criteria: Selection is based upon GPA, class rank, and test scores. Financial need is not considered. Each Texas high school is allowed to nominate three candidates. Renewable when funds are available. Awarded every year.
Contact: Gustavo DeLeon, Director of Grant Programs.

2158   Robert C. Byrd Honors Scholarship

State College and University Systems of West Virginia
Central Office
P.O. Box 4007
Charleston, WV 25364
(304) 347-1266
Minimum award: $1,500
Number of awards: 90
Deadline: March 15
College level: Freshman, Sophomore
Criteria: Applicant must be a high school graduate enrolled at a nonprofit, degree-granting institution of higher education and must demonstrate outstanding academic achievement and show promise of continued achievement. Students apply for this award through high school counselors. Satisfactory academic progress is required to retain scholarship. Awarded every year.
Contact: Daniel Crockett, Scholarship Programs Coordinator.

2159   Sachs Foundation Scholarship

Sachs Foundation
90 South Cascade Avenue
Suite 1410
Colorado Springs, CO 80903
(719) 633-2353
Average award: $3,000
Maximum award: $6,000
Minimum award: $1,500
Number of awards: 50
Deadline: March 1
College level: Freshman, Sophomore, Junior, Senior, Graduate
Criteria: Applicant must be a U.S. citizen and a black resident of Colorado with a minimum GPA of 3.4. Minimum 2.5 GPA for 12 hours with no failures or incompletes is required to retain scholarship. Awarded every year.
Contact: Lisa Harris, Executive Assistant.

2160   Samuel W. O'Dell Scholarship

Clemson University
G-01 Sikes Hall
Clemson, SC 29634-5123
(803) 656-2280
Average award: $1,000
Number of awards: 5
Deadline: March 1
College level: Freshman, Sophomore, Junior, Senior
Majors/Fields: Agricultural sciences
Criteria: Applicant must be a South Carolina resident from a "designated rural area" as defined by the Farmer's Home Administration and demonstrate financial need. Satisfactory GPA with at least 12 credits per semester is required to retain scholarship. Awarded every year. Award may be used only at sponsoring institution.
Contact: Marvin Carmichael, Director of Financial Aid.

2161   Scholars Program

University of Missouri–Columbia
High School and Transfer Relations
219 Jesse Hall
Columbia, MO 65211
(800) 225-6075 (in-state), (314) 882-2456
Average award: $1,000
Number of awards: 90
Deadline: February 1
College level: Freshman
Criteria: Applicant must rank in top five percent of class, have a minimum composite ACT score of 27, be a Missouri resident, and enroll at the university the first semester after high school. One award is available for each Missouri high school. Minimum 3.25 GPA is required to retain scholarship for one additional year. Awarded every year. Award may be used only at sponsoring institution.
Contact: High School and Transfer Relations.

2162   Scholarship for Frosh Students Outside of Alberta

University of Calgary
2500 University Drive, NW
Calgary, Alberta, CN T2N 1N4
(403) 220-7872
Average award: $1,000
Number of awards: 3
Deadline: July 15
College level: Freshman
Criteria: Applicant must obtain matriculation outside Alberta. At least one award is available for applicants who complete high school outside Canada. All awards are based upon academic merit; one also considers extracurricular activities and achievements. Awarded every year. Award may be used only at sponsoring institution.
Contact: J. Van Housen, Director of Student Awards & Financial Aid.

2163   Scholarship for New Nebraskans

University of Nebraska, Lincoln
14th and R Streets
Lincoln, NE 68588
(402) 472-2030
Maximum award: Full tuition
Minimum award: $500
Deadline: Beginning of fall semester
College level: Freshman, transfer students
Criteria: Applicant must not be a resident of Nebraska. Satisfactory academic progress is required to retain scholarship. Awarded every year. Award may be used only at sponsoring institution.
Contact: Debra Augustyn, Assistant Director of Scholarships & Financial Aid.

2164 Scholarship for Rural Professional or Vocational Nursing Students

Texas Higher Education Coordinating Board
Student Financial Assistance
P.O. Box 12788, Capitol Station
Austin, TX 78711-2788
(512) 483-6340
Maximum award: $2,500
Minimum award: $1,500
Number of awards: 62
Deadline: July 15
College level: Freshman, Sophomore, Junior, Senior, Graduate, Doctoral
Majors/Fields: Nursing
Criteria: Applicant must be a Texas resident from a rural county, enrolled at least half time in a program leading to licensure as an L.V.N. or in an associate, bachelor, or graduate degree program in professional nursing. Applicant must attend a public or independent nonprofit institution in a nonmetropolitan county in Texas. Recipient must reapply each year. No preference is given to renewals. Awarded every year.
Contact: Jane Caldwell, Director of Special Programs.

2165 Scholastic Achievement Grant

Connecticut Department of Higher Education
Office of Student Financial Aid
61 Woodland Street
Hartford, CT 06105
(203) 566-2618
Maximum award: $2,000
Deadline: February 15
College level: Freshman
Criteria: Applicant must be a Connecticut resident, a U.S. citizen or national, rank in top fifth of high school class or have a minimum combined SAT I score of 1100, and attend a Connecticut college or a college in a state that has reciprocity agreements with Connecticut. Scholarship is renewable. Awarded every year.
Contact: Office of Student Financial Aid.

2166 Seminole and Miccosukee Indian Scholarship

Florida Department of Education
Office of Student Financial Assistance
1344 Florida Education Center
Tallahassee, FL 32399-0400
(904) 487-0049
Maximum award: Annual cost of education.
College level: Freshman, Sophomore, Junior, Senior, Graduate, Doctoral
Criteria: Applicant must be a Seminole or Miccosukee Indian, a Florida resident, have a high school diploma or equivalent, be enrolled at an eligible Florida college or university, and demonstrate financial need. Applicant can contact the tribal offices listed below: Miccosukee Tribe of Florida, c/o Higher Education Committee, P.O. Box 440021, Tamiami Station, Miami, FL 33144 or Seminole Tribe of Florida, c/o Higher Education Committee, 6073 Sterling Road, Hollywood, FL 33024. Minimum 2.0 GPA with at least 12 credit hours per term is required to retain scholarship. Awarded every year.
Contact: Office of Student Financial Assistance.

2167 Senator George J. Mitchell Scholarship Fund

Maine Community Foundation
210 Main Street
P.O. Box 148
Ellsworth, ME 04605
(207) 667-9735
Average award: $2,500
Number of awards: 20
Deadline: May 1
College level: Freshman, Sophomore, Junior, Senior
Criteria: Applicant must be a graduate of a Maine high school attending a Maine college or university. Awarded every year.
Contact: Patti D'Angelo, Program Associate.

2168 Senatorial Scholarship

Maryland Higher Education Commission
State Scholarship Administration
16 Francis Street
Annapolis, MD 21401-1781
(410) 974-5370
Maximum award: $2,000
Minimum award: $200
Number of awards: 8226
Deadline: March 1
College level: Freshman, Sophomore, Junior, Senior, Graduate, Doctoral
Criteria: Applicant must be a Maryland resident who is a full-time or part-time student at a college, university, or vocational school in Maryland; an out-of-state institution qualifies if the major is not offered in Maryland. Applicant should contact his or her state senator for additional information. Applicant must file FAFSA by March 1. Automatically renewed for three years. Awarded every year.
Contact: Karen Price, Program Manager.

2169 South Carolina Tuition Grants Program

South Carolina Higher Education Tuition Grants Commission
811 Keenan Building
P.O. Box 12159
Columbia, SC 29211
(803) 734-1200
Average award: $2,000
Maximum award: $3,260
Number of awards: 8460
Deadline: June 30
College level: Freshman, Sophomore, Junior, Senior
Criteria: Applicant must be a South Carolina resident attending a South Carolina independent college full-time. Recipient must complete 24 semester hours and meet institutional satisfactory progress requirements to retain scholarship. Awarded every year.
Contact: Edward M. Shannon, III, Executive Director.

2170 State Need Grant

Washington Higher Education Coordinating Board
917 Lakeridge Way
P.O. Box 43430
Olympia, WA 98504-3430
(206) 753-3571
Average award: $1,200
Number of awards: 38,000
Criteria: Applicant must be a Washington state resident with a low family income. Awarded every year.
Contact: Elizabeth A. Gebhardt, Assistant Director of Student Financial Aid, (206) 753-4592.

2171 State of Idaho Scholarship

Idaho State Board of Education
Len B. Jordan Building, Room 307
P.O. Box 83720
Boise, ID 83720-0037
(208) 334-2270
Average award: $2,700
Number of awards: 25
Deadline: January 31
College level: Freshman
Criteria: Applicant must take the ACT and be an Idaho resident planning to enroll full-time in an academic or vocational program at an Idaho college or university. Selection is based upon academic merit; 25 percent of initial awards are given to vocational students. Automatically renewed if recipient maintains a satisfactory GPA. Awarded every year.
Contact: Caryl Smith, Scholarship Assistant.

2172   State Scholarship for Ethnic Minorities in Professional/Vocational Nursing

Texas Higher Education Coordinating Board
Student Financial Assistance
P.O. Box 12788, Capitol Station
Austin, TX 78711-2788
(512) 483-6340
Average award: $1,973
Maximum award: $3,000
Minimum award: $1,500
Number of awards: 73
Deadline: July 15
College level: Freshman, Sophomore, Junior, Senior, Graduate, Doctoral
Majors/Fields: Nursing
Criteria: Applicant must be a member of an ethnic minority and a Texas resident enrolled at least half time in a program leading to licensure as an L.V.N. or in an associate, bachelor, or graduate degree program in professional nursing at an accredited Texas institution. Recipient must reapply each year. No preference is given to renewals. Awarded every year.
Contact: Jane Caldwell, Director of Special Programs.

2173   State Scholarship for Ethnic Recruitment

University of Texas at San Antonio
Office of Student Financial Aid
6900 North Loop 1604 West
San Antonio, TX 78249-0687
(210) 691-4011
Average award: $1,000
Deadline: September 15
College level: Freshman, transfer students
Criteria: Applicant must be a minority Texas resident, demonstrate financial need, rank in top third of class, have a minimum composite ACT score of 18 or combined SAT I score of 800, and not be receiving an athletic scholarship. Transfer applicant must have a minimum 2.75 GPA. Awarded every year. Award may be used only at sponsoring institution.
Contact: Scholarship Office, 6900 North Loop 1604 West.

2174   State Waiver of Tuition

Kentucky Center of Veterans Affairs
545 S. Third Street
Room 123
Louisville, KY 40202
(502) 595-4447
Average award: Waiver of tuition
Deadline: Apply at least three months before entering college
College level: State vocational/technical students
Criteria: Applicant must be the dependent of a veteran who served during a wartime period, must be rated 100 percent service connected or 100 percent permanently and totally disabled non-service connected, and resident of Kentucky. Awarded every year.
Contact: James E. Welch, Assistant Director.

2175   Student Life Scholarship

Oakland University
101 North Foundation Hall
Rochester, MI 48309-4401
(810) 370-3360
Average award: $1,000
Number of awards: 60
Deadline: February 1
College level: Freshman
Criteria: Applicant must live in residence halls on campus. Minimum 2.5 GPA is required to retain scholarship. Awarded every year. Award may be used only at sponsoring institution.
Contact: Stacy M. Penkala, Assistant Director of Admissions.

2176   Terry Foundation Scholarship

University of Texas at Austin
Austin, TX 78713-7758
(512) 475-6200
Average award: $5,000
Maximum award: $7,000
Minimum award: $1,000
Number of awards: 20
Deadline: December 1
College level: Freshman, Sophomore, Junior, Senior
Criteria: Applicant must be a Texas resident, demonstrate leadership, and have high SAT I or ACT scores. Financial need is considered. Satisfactory academic progress is required to retain scholarship. Awarded every year; may be used only at sponsoring institution.
Contact: Joe Wilcox, Financial Aid Officer.

2177   Texas Achievement Award

University of Texas at Austin
Austin, TX 78713-7758
(512) 475-6200
Average award: $2,000
Number of awards: 500
Deadline: December 1
College level: Freshman
Criteria: Applicant must be an African-American or Hispanic Texas resident, graduate of a Texas high school, and have a strong academic and leadership background. Satisfactory academic progress is required to retain scholarship. Awarded every year. Award may be used only at sponsoring institution.
Contact: Alicia Palacios, Special Programs Coordinator.

2178   Texas Achievement Honors Award

University of Texas at Austin
Austin, TX 78713-7758
(512) 475-6200
Average award: $5,000
Number of awards: 200
Deadline: December 1 (preferred)
College level: Freshman
Criteria: Applicant must be an African-American or Hispanic Texas resident, graduate from a Texas high school, and have strong academic and leadership background. Minimum cumulative GPA of 2.5 is required to retain scholarship. Awarded every year. Award may be used only at sponsoring institution.
Contact: Alicia Palacios, Special Programs Coordinator.

2179   Thelma and Harry Hair Scholarship

Clemson University
G-01 Sikes Hall
Clemson, SC 29634-5123
(803) 656-2280
Average award: $4,000
Number of awards: 1
Deadline: March 1
College level: Freshman, Sophomore, Junior, Senior
Criteria: First priority is given to applicants from Calhoun County and next to other South Carolina residents. Awarded every year. Award may be used only at sponsoring institution.
Contact: Marvin Carmichael, Director of Financial Aid.

2180   Thomas A. Folger Memorial Endowed Scholarship

Clemson University
G-01 Sikes Hall
Clemson, SC 29634-5123
(803) 656-2280
Average award: $2,000
Number of awards: 1
Deadline: March 1
College level: Freshman
Criteria: Applicant must be a South Carolina resident with priority given to Pickens County residents. Minimum 3.0 cumulative GPA with at least 12 credits per semester is required to retain scholarship. Awarded every year. Award may be used only at sponsoring institution.
Contact: Marvin Carmichael, Director of Financial Aid.

2181   Ty Cobb Scholarship

Ty Cobb Foundation
P.O. Box 725
Forest Park, GA 30051
Average award: $2,500
Maximum award: $3,000
Minimum award: $2,000
Number of awards: 100
Deadline: June 15
College level: Sophomore, Junior, Senior, medical and dental professional degrees
Criteria: Applicant must demonstrate financial need and be a resident of Georgia. Applicant must submit application, reason for requesting financial assistance, recommendation, and transcript. Minimum "B" average for 45 quarter or 30 semester hours is required to retain scholarship. Satisfactory academic progress is required for professional degree students to retain scholarship. Awarded every year.
Contact: Rosie C. Atkins, Secretary.

2182   Union Pacific Foundation Scholarship

Future Farmers of America (FFA)
P.O. Box 15160
Alexandria, VA 22309-0160
(703) 360-3600
Average award: $1,000
Number of awards: 16
Deadline: February 15
College level: Freshman
Majors/Fields: Agriculture
Criteria: Applicant must be a FFA member pursuing a four-year degree in any area of agriculture and a resident of Arkansas, California, Colorado, Idaho, Illinois, Iowa, Kansas, Louisiana, Missouri, Nebraska, Nevada, Oklahoma, Oregon, Texas, Utah, Washington or Wyoming. Awarded every year.
Contact: National FFA Organizational Office.

2183   Valedictorian Scholarship

University of South Carolina–Columbia
Columbia, SC 29208
(803) 777-8134
Average award: $3,000
Number of awards: 34
Deadline: None
College level: Freshman
Criteria: Applicant must be a valedictorian, South Carolina resident or a graduate of a South Carolina high school, and have a minimum combined SAT I score of 1000. Minimum 3.0 GPA is required to retain scholarship. Awarded every year. Award may be used only at sponsoring institution.
Contact: Stewart Jones, Scholarship Coordinator.

2184   Vermont Incentive Grant

Vermont Student Assistance Corporation
Champlain Mill
P.O. Box 2000
Winooski, VT 05404
(800) 642-3177 (in-state), (802) 655-9602
Average award: $1,071
Maximum award: $5,200
Minimum award: $400
Number of awards: 8869
Deadline: March 1 (priority)
College level: Unspecified undergraduate, unspecified graduate
Criteria: Applicant must be a Vermont resident and enrolled full-time at an approved postsecondary institution. Graduate applicants must be enrolled at the U of Vermont Medical Sch or at an approved school of veterinary medicine. Applicant should complete the ACT aid form or CSS financial aid form and have it sent to VSAC. Demonstration of financial need is required. Scholarship is renewable. Awarded every year.
Contact: Grant Department.

2185   Vocational Education Scholarship

Kansas Board of Regents
700 SW Harrison
Suite 1410
Topeka, KS 66603-3760
(913) 296-3517
Average award: $500
Number of awards: 120
Deadline: October 16, February 12
College level: Vocational programs
Criteria: Applicant must be a Kansas resident, attend an eligible Kansas postsecondary institution full-time, and be among the top 100 scorers taking the vocational exam. Renewable for up to two years. Awarded every year.
Contact: Scholarships.

2186   Vocational Gold Seal Endorsement Scholarship

Florida Department of Education
Office of Student Financial Assistance
1344 Florida Education Center
Tallahassee, FL 32399-0400
(904) 487-0049
Maximum award: $4,000
Deadline: April 1
College level: Freshman
Criteria: Applicant must receive a standard high school diploma with a Florida Gold Seal Endorsement from a Florida public high school, be a Florida resident for at least 12 months, and enroll in a degree or certificate program at an eligible Florida public or private, postsecondary vocational, technical, trade, or business school, or college or university for a minimum of 12 hours per term. Minimum 3.0 GPA with at least 12 credit hours per term is required to retain scholarship. Awarded every year.
Contact: Office of Student Financial Assistance.

2187   Walter C. and Marie C. Schmidt

State Scholarship Commission (Oregon)
1500 Valley River Drive
Suite 100
Eugene, OR 97401-2146
(503) 687-7395
Minimum award: $1,000
Number of awards: 2
Deadline: March 1
College level: Freshman, Sophomore, Junior, Senior, Graduate
Majors/Fields: Nursing
Criteria: Applicant must be an Oregon resident, be enrolled full time at an Oregon school, and demonstrate financial need. Applicant must submit, in writing, a statement of his or her desire to pursue a nursing career in geriatric health care. Awarded every year.
Contact: Jim Beyer, Grant Program Director.

2188   Washington Crossing Foundation

Washington Crossing Foundation
P.O. Box 17
Washington Crossing, PA 18977
(215) 493-6577
Maximum award: $5,000
Minimum award: $1,000
Number of awards: 16
Deadline: January 15
College level: Freshman
Majors/Fields: Government service
Criteria: Applicant must be a U.S. citizen with a career interest in government service. Scholarship is renewable. Awarded every year.
Contact: Eugene C. Fish, Esq., Vice Chairman.

2189   Washington Scholars

Washington Higher Education Coordinating Board
917 Lakeridge Way
P.O. Box 43430
Olympia, WA 98504-3430
(206) 753-3571
Average award: $2,532
Maximum award: Full tuition and fee waiver
College level: Freshman
Criteria: Award is intended to recognize and honor the accomplishments of three high school seniors from each legislative district. High school principals nominate the top one percent of the graduating senior class based upon academic accomplishment, leadership, and community service. Minimum 3.3 GPA is required for renewal. Awarded every year.
Contact: Elizabeth A. Gebhardt, Assistant Director of Student Financial Aid, (206) 753-4592.

2190   West Virginia Higher Education Grant

State College and University Systems of West Virginia
Central Office
P.O. Box 4007
Charleston, WV 25364
(304) 347-1266
Average award: $1,335
Maximum award: $1,944
Minimum award: $350
Maximum number of awards: 5,200
Minimum number of awards: 4,900
Deadline: March 1
College level: Freshman, Sophomore, Junior, Senior
Criteria: Applicant must demonstrate financial need, meet academic qualifications, be a U.S. citizen, have been a resident of the state of West Virginia for at least one year, and enroll as a full-time undergraduate student at an approved educational institution. Reapplication, financial need, and satisfactory academic performance are required for renewal. Awarded every year.
Contact: Robert E. Long, Grant Program Coordinator, (304) 347-1211.

2191   Weston Family Scholarship

State Scholarship Commission (Oregon)
1500 Valley River Drive
Suite 100
Eugene, OR 97401-2146
(503) 687-7395
Minimum award: $1,000
Number of awards: 2
Deadline: March 1
College level: Freshman
Criteria: Applicant must be an Oregon resident, a graduate of Astoria, Benson, Central Catholic, Cleveland, Franklin, Grant, Jefferson, La-Salle, Lincoln, Madison, Marshall, Roosevelt, St. Mary's Academy (Portland), or Wilson high school, be enrolled full time at an Oregon school, and demonstrate financial need. Awarded every year.
Contact: Jim Beyer, Grant Program Director.

2192   Wilfred Archibald Walter Bursary

University of Calgary
2500 University Drive, NW
Calgary, Alberta, CN T2N 1N4
(403) 220-7872
Average award: $2,000
Number of awards: 18
Deadline: June 15
College level: Sophomore, Junior, Senior
Criteria: Applicant must be a Canadian citizen or permanent resident. Selection is based upon academic merit and financial need. Awarded every year. Award may be used only at sponsoring institution.
Contact: J. Van Housen, Director of Student Awards & Financial Aid.

2193   William Keyte Memorial Bursary

University of Calgary
2500 University Drive, NW
Calgary, Alberta, CN T2N 1N4
(403) 220-7872
Average award: $2,000
Number of awards: 4
Deadline: July 15
College level: Freshman
Criteria: Applicant must be from the Special Areas District of Alberta. Selection is based primarily upon financial need if academic standing is satisfactory. Minimum 2.6 GPA is required to retain scholarship. Awarded every year; may be used only at sponsoring institution.
Contact: J. Van Housen, Director of Student Awards & Financial Aid.

2194   William P. Willis Scholarship

Oklahoma State Regents for Higher Education
500 Education Building, State Capitol Complex
Oklahoma City, OK 73105
(405) 524-9100
Average award: $1,650
Maximum award: $2,400
Minimum award: $1,560
Number of awards: 26
Deadline: Late May
College level: Freshman, Sophomore, Junior, Senior
Criteria: Applicant must be an Oklahoma resident and demonstrate financial need. Only one award is available per state institution. Applicant must obtain university president's nomination to retain scholarship. Awarded every year.
Contact: Dawn Scott, Research Assistant, (405) 524-9153.

Textile Science

2195   Amoco Foundation Scholarship

Clemson University
G-01 Sikes Hall
Clemson, SC 29634-5123
(803) 656-2280
Average award: $1,500
Number of awards: 2
Deadline: March 1
College level: Junior, Senior
Majors/Fields: Textiles
Criteria: Applicant must be a minority student with minimum 2.0 GPA. Awarded every year; may be used only at sponsoring institution.
Contact: Marvin Carmichael, Director of Financial Aid.

2196   Ben and Kitty Gossett Scholarship

Clemson University
G-01 Sikes Hall
Clemson, SC 29634-5123
(803) 656-2280
Average award: $2,000
Number of awards: 1
Deadline: March 1
College level: Freshman, Sophomore, Junior, Senior
Majors/Fields: Textiles
Criteria: Applicant must be a man and demonstrate financial need. Preference is given to applicants whose family is employed by the textile industry in South Carolina. Awarded every year. Award may be used only at sponsoring institution.
Contact: Marvin Carmichael, Director of Financial Aid.

2197 CIBA-Geigy Prestige Scholarship

Clemson University
G-01 Sikes Hall
Clemson, SC 29634-5123
(803) 656-2280
Average award: $5,000
Number of awards: 1
Deadline: March 1
College level: Freshman
Majors/Fields: Textile chemistry
Criteria: Applicant must have a minimum 2.0 GPA. Awarded every year. Award may be used only at sponsoring institution.
Contact: Marvin Carmichael, Director of Financial Aid.

2198 Comer Foundation Scholarship in Fashion and Design

University of Alabama-Tuscaloosa
Box 870162
Tuscaloosa, AL 35487-0162
(205) 348-6756
Average award: $2,500
Number of awards: 1
Deadline: February 1
College level: Freshman
Majors/Fields: Clothing design, textiles
Criteria: Scholarship is renewable. Award may be used only at sponsoring institution.
Contact: Dean, College of Human Environmental Sciences, Box 870158, Tuscaloosa, AL 35487-0158, (205) 348-6250.

2199 Daniel Keating Norris and Bessie Caldwell Norris Textile Scholarship

Clemson University
G-01 Sikes Hall
Clemson, SC 29634-5123
(803) 656-2280
Average award: $2,000
Number of awards: 3
Deadline: March 1
College level: Freshman, Sophomore, Junior, Senior
Majors/Fields: Textiles
Criteria: Applicant must be a South Carolina resident and demonstrate financial need. Awarded every year. Award may be used only at sponsoring institution.
Contact: Marvin Carmichael, Director of Financial Aid.

2200 Fieldcrest Foundation Scholarship

Clemson University
G-01 Sikes Hall
Clemson, SC 29634-5123
(803) 656-2280
Average award: $1,000
Number of awards: 2
Deadline: March 1
College level: Freshman, Sophomore, Junior, Senior
Majors/Fields: Textiles
Criteria: Preference is given to juniors. Minimum 2.5 GPA with at least 12 credits per semester is required to retain scholarship. Awarded every year. Award may be used only at sponsoring institution.
Contact: Marvin Carmichael, Director of Financial Aid.

2201 J.P. Stevens & Co. Inc. Foundation Scholarship

Clemson University
G-01 Sikes Hall
Clemson, SC 29634-5123
(803) 656-2280
Average award: $2,000
Number of awards: 3
College level: Freshman
Majors/Fields: Textiles
Criteria: Applicant must be a woman or minority student. Minimum 3.0 cumulative GPA with at least 12 credits per semester is required to retain scholarship. Awarded every year. Award may be used only at sponsoring institution.
Contact: Marvin Carmichael, Director of Financial Aid.

2202 Mary Josephine Cochran Fellowship

American Association of Family and Consumer Sciences
1555 King Street
Alexandria, VA 22314
(703) 706-4600
Average award: $3,000
Number of awards: 1
Deadline: January 16
College level: Graduate, Doctoral
Majors/Fields: Textiles/clothing
Criteria: Applicant must be a U.S. citizen. Awarded every year.
Contact: Fellowships.

2203 National Make It Yourself With Wool Contest

National Make It Yourself With Wool
2494 Morrison Avenue
Little Canada, MN 55117-1623
(612) 484-5871
Maximum award: $1,500
Minimum award: $500
Number of awards: 2
Deadline: In fall
Criteria: Applicant must be able to sew and model a garment constructed of at least 60-percent wool fabric. Awarded every year.
Contact: Sandy Schultz Ducharme.

2204 Sandoz Foundation Scholarship

Clemson University
G-01 Sikes Hall
Clemson, SC 29634-5123
(803) 656-2280
Average award: $2,000
Number of awards: 1
Deadline: March 1
College level: Freshman, Sophomore, Junior, Senior
Majors/Fields: Textiles, textile chemistry
Criteria: Minimum 2.5 cumulative GPA with at least 12 credits per semester is required to retain scholarship. Awarded every year. Award may be used only at sponsoring institution.
Contact: Marvin Carmichael, Director of Financial Aid.

2205 Tietex Corporation Scholarship

Clemson University
G-01 Sikes Hall
Clemson, SC 29634-5123
(803) 656-2280
Average award: $2,000
Number of awards: 3
Deadline: March 1
College level: Sophomore, Junior, Senior
Majors/Fields: Textiles
Criteria: Applicant must have a minimum 2.0 GPA. Awarded every year. Award may be used only at sponsoring institution.
Contact: Marvin Carmichael, Director of Financial Aid.

Union Affiliation

2206 Air Line Pilots Association Scholarship

Air Line Pilots Association
1625 Massachusetts Avenue, NW
Washington, DC 20036
(703) 689-2270
Average award: $3,000
Number of awards: 1
Deadline: April 1
College level: Freshman, Sophomore, Junior, Senior
Criteria: Applicant must be the child of medically retired or deceased pilot member of the Air Line Pilots Association. Academic capability and financial need are both considered. Renewable for up to four years if adequate academic standing is maintained. Awarded every year.
Contact: Jan Redden, Scholarship Program Monitor.

2207   Amalgamated Clothing and Textile Workers Scholarship

Amalgamated Clothing and Textile Workers Union
15 Union Square
New York, NY 10003
(212) 242-0700
Average award: $1,000
Number of awards: 3
Deadline: March 15
College level: Freshman
Criteria: Applicant must be the child of an Amalgamated Clothing and Textile Workers Union member who has been a member in good standing for at least two years. Renewable for one additional year. Awarded every year.
Contact: Scholarship Administrator.

2208   BC&TWIU Scholarship

Bakery, Confectionery, and Tobacco Workers International Union
10401 Connecticut Avenue
Kensington, MD 20895
(301) 933-8600
Average award: $1,000
Number of awards: 8
Deadline: December 31
College level: Freshman
Criteria: Applicant must be a member or the child of a member of the Bakery, Confectionery, and Tobacco Workers International Union. One scholarship is is designated for a Canadian applicant. The American Income Life Insurance Company awards a one-time $2,000 scholarship to the next in line of alternate winners after the eight regular winners have been selected. Renewable if satisfactory academic progress is maintained. Awarded every year.
Contact: Walter Pearson, Scholarship Administrator.

2209   Charlie Logan Scholarship for Dependents

Seafarers International Union
5201 Auth Way
Camp Springs, MD 20746
(301) 899-0675
Minimum award: $3,750
Number of awards: 4
Deadline: April 15
College level: Freshman
Criteria: Applicant must be age 25 or under, unmarried, and a dependent of a member of the Seafarers International Union. Parent must have credit for three years (1,095 days) of employment with an employer who is obligated to make contributions to the Seafarers' Welfare Plan on the employee's behalf. Recipient may attend any college or university in the U.S. Renewable for up to four years if minimum "B" average and a full course load are maintained. Awarded every year.
Contact: Lou Delma, Assistant Administrator, (301) 702-4405.

2210   Charlie Logan Scholarship for Seamen

Seafarers International Union
5201 Auth Way
Camp Springs, MD 20746
(301) 899-0675
Maximum award: $3,750
Minimum award: $3,000
Number of awards: 3
Deadline: April 15
College level: Freshman
Criteria: Available to active seamen who are high school graduates (or equivalent) and have credit for two years (730 days) of employment with an employer who is obligated to make contributions to the Seafarers Welfare Plan on the employee's behalf. Recipient may attend any institution (college or trade school) in the U.S. Renewal is based upon good scholastic standing. Awarded every year.
Contact: Lou Delma, Assistant Administrator, (301) 702-4405.

2211   College Vocational/Technical Scholarship

Loyal Christian Benefit Association
700 Peach Street
P.O. Box 13005
Erie, PA 16514-1305
(814) 453-4331
Average award: $1,000
Maximum number of awards: 10
Minimum number of awards: 5
Deadline: October
College level: Freshman
Criteria: Applicant must be a member in good standing of the Loyal Christian Benefit Association and be enrolled in a permanent LCBA insurance plan for one year prior to application with a minimum of $1,000 permanent insurance or have a term insurance certificate in force for three years. Minimum 3.0 GPA and financial need are required. Five college scholarships and five vocational/technical awards are offered. A LCBA certificate must remain in force during the entire scholarship period. Evidence of satisfactory progress must be submitted to Scholarship Committee for renewal. Awarded every year.
Contact: Eileen Jefferys, Branch Development Coordinator.

2212   CTA Scholarship

California Teachers Association
1705 Murchison Drive
P.O. Box 921
Burlingame, CA 94011-0921
(415) 697-1400
Average award: $2,000
Number of awards: 20
Deadline: February 15
College level: Freshman, Sophomore, Junior, Senior, Graduate, Doctoral
Criteria: Applicant must be an active member, the dependent child of an active member, or the dependent child of a deceased member of the CTA. Scholarship is renewable. Awarded every year.
Contact: Human Rights Department.

2213   David J. Fitzmaurice Scholarship

International Union of Electronic, Electrical, Salaried, Machine and Furniture Workers (IUE)
1126 16th Street, N.W.
Department of Social Action
Washington, DC 20036-4866
Average award: $2,000
Number of awards: 1
Deadline: April 15
College level: Freshman, Sophomore, Junior, Senior
Criteria: Applicant must be the child of an IUE member. Applicant must submit class rank, GPA, SAT I or ACT scores, copy of W-2 form, short statement of interest and goals, and three recommendations. Selection is based upon academic record, character, leadership ability, and a desire to improve and move ahead. Awarded every year.
Contact: Gloria T. Johnson, Director, Department of Social Action, 1126 16th Street, NW, Washington, DC 20036-4866.

2214   E.C. Hallbeck Memorial Scholarship Program

American Postal Workers Union
1300 L Street, NW
Washington, DC 20005
(202) 842-4268
Average award: $1,000
Number of awards: 5
Deadline: March 15
College level: Freshman
Criteria: Applicant must be the child of an active or deceased member of the American Postal Workers Union; the parent must have been a member in good standing for at least one year preceding application or death. Selection is based upon academic record, personal qualifications, SAT I or ACT scores, and total family income. Applicant may not accept more than $5,000 from other scholarships. Renewable for up to four years if academic progress is satisfactory. Awarded every year.
Contact: Scholarships.

2215 Evelyn Dubrow Post-Graduate Scholarship

International Ladies' Garment Workers' Union
1710 Broadway
Second Floor
New York, NY 10019
(212) 265-7000, extension 313
Average award: $5,000
Number of awards: 2
Deadline: April 1
College level: Graduate, Doctoral
Majors/Fields: Social science, human service, public service studies, labor movement studies
Criteria: Applicant must be the child of an ILGWU member in good standing for at least two years and be enrolled in a post graduate program of study related to public service and/or the labor movement. Scholarship is renewable for up to three years, subject to review. Awarded every year.
Contact: Michelle Payne, Scholarship Administrator, (212) 265-7000.

2216 Harry C. Bates Merit Scholarship

International Union of Bricklayers and Allied Craftsmen (BAC)
Education Department
815 15th Street, NW
Washington, DC 20005
(202) 783-3788
Maximum award: $2,000
Minimum award: $400
Number of awards: 3
Deadline: June 1 (Canada); mid-October (U.S.)
College level: Freshman
Criteria: Applicant must be the natural or legally adopted child of a current, retired, or deceased International Union of Bricklayers and Allied Craftsmen member. U.S. applicant must take PSAT/NMSQT during junior year of high school. If test results qualify applicant as a semifinalist, this information must be reported to the International Union by mid-October. Canadian applicant does not have to take a qualifying test. One U.S. award and two Canadian awards are given. Selection is based upon test scores (U.S. only), grades, leadership qualities, and extracurricular achievements. Canadian students can obtain an application from Mr. Brian Strickland, BAC Vice President, 161 Markwood Drive, Kitchener, ON N2M 2H3. Scholarship is renewable. Awarded every year.
Contact: Scholarships.

2217 IAM Scholarship

International Association of Machinists & Aerospace Workers
9000 Machinists Place
Room 117
Upper Marlboro, MD 20772-2687
(301) 967-4708
Maximum award: $2,000
Minimum award: $1,000
Number of awards: 10
Deadline: December 1
College level: Freshman, Sophomore, Junior, Senior
Criteria: Applicant must be either an IAM member with at least two years of continuous good-standing membership who is working full-time in a company under contract with the IAM, or be the son, daughter, stepchild, or legally adopted child of an IAM member. Child of IAM member must be a high school senior when applying. Scholarship is renewable. Awarded every year.
Contact: Charles E. Bradford, Director of Occupational Safety, Health, and Community Services.

2218 International Brotherhood of Teamsters Scholarship

International Brotherhood of Teamsters
25 Louisiana Avenue, NW
Washington, DC 20001
(202) 624-8735
Maximum award: $1,500
Minimum award: $1,000
Number of awards: 25
Deadline: December 15
College level: Freshman
Criteria: Applicant must be the child of a Teamsters member, rank in top 15 percent of class, have or expect to have excellent SAT I or ACT scores, and be able to demonstrate financial need. Application may be obtained from all Teamsters offices, from the scholarship fund, or by mailing the order form found in the summer and fall issues of the International Teamsters magazine. Applicant should complete the first part of the application and then forward it to the appropriate local union. Some awards are renewable. Awarded every year.
Contact: Scholarship Administrator.

2219 Iowa Federation of Labor AFL-CIO Graduate Assistantship

Iowa Federation of Labor AFL-CIO
2000 Walker Street, Suite A
Des Moines, IA 50317
(515) 262-9571
Average award: $3,800
Number of awards: 1
Deadline: March 30
College level: Graduate, Doctoral
Criteria: Applicant must be a member or the child of a member of a local union affiliated with the Iowa Federation of Labor AFL-CIO. Applicant must work ten hours per week at the U of Iowa Labor Center and be enrolled in a graduate program at the U of Iowa. Satisfactory academic performance is required to retain scholarship. Awarded every year.
Contact: Mark Smith, Secretary-Treasurer.

2220 James B. Carey Scholarship

International Union of Electronic, Electrical, Salaried, Machine and Furniture Workers (IUE)
1126 16th Street, N.W.
Department of Social Action
Washington, DC 20036-4866
Average award: $1,000
Number of awards: 9
Deadline: April 15
College level: Freshman, Sophomore, Junior, Senior
Criteria: Applicant must be the child of a IUE member. Applicant must submit class rank, GPA, SAT I or ACT scores, copy of W-2 form, short statement of interest and goals, and three recommendations. Selection is based upon academic record, character, leadership ability, and a desire to improve and move ahead. Awarded every year.
Contact: Gloria T. Johnson, Director, Department of Social Action.

2221 John H. Lyons, Sr. Scholarship

International Association of Bridge, Structural and Ornamental Ironworkers Union
1750 New York Avenue, NW
Suite 400
Washington, DC 20006
(202) 383-4830
Average award: $2,500
Number of awards: 2
Deadline: March 31
College level: Freshman
Criteria: Applicant must be the child, stepchild, or adopted child of an IABSOIU member who has five or more years of continuous membership or of a deceased member who was in good standing at the time of his or her death. Applicant must rank in the top half of class. Selection is based upon academic standing, SAT I or ACT scores, extracurricular activities, leadership, character reference, and citizenship. Satisfactory scholastic record and conduct, and IABSOIU affiliation are required to retain scholarship. Awarded every year.
Contact: Scholarship Committee.

2222   Joseph W. Childs Memorial Scholarship

United Rubber, Cork, Linoleum, and Plastic Workers of America (URW)
URW Fair Practices Department
570 White Pond Drive
Akron, OH 44320-1156
(216) 869-0320
Average award: $2,000
Number of awards: 4
Deadline: February 1
College level: Freshman
Criteria: Applicant's parent or guardian must be an URW member. Selection is based upon academic excellence, community involvement, and commitment to serve humanity. Awarded every year.
Contact: Lyle D. Skinner, Fair Practices Director.

2223   National College Award Program

International Ladies' Garment Workers' Union
1710 Broadway
Second Floor
New York, NY 10019
(212) 265-7000, extension 313
Average award: Each award is $2,500 over a four-year period.
Minimum award: $550
Number of awards: 20
Deadline: June 30
College level: Freshman
Criteria: Applicant must be the child of an ILGWU member in good standing for at least two years and be in an accredited high school preparing to enter an accredited four-year, undergraduate college or university. Satitisfactory GPA must be maintained for renewal. Awarded every year.
Contact: Michelle Payne, Scholarship Administrator.

2224   Nicholas C. Vrataric Scholarship

United Paperworkers International Union (UPIU)
Scholarship Awards Program
P.O. Box 1475
Nashville, TN 37202
(615) 834-8590
Average award: $1,000
Number of awards: 2
Deadline: March 15
College level: Any continuing education program
Criteria: Applicant must be an active UPIU member in good standing who is currently enrolled in a program to further his or her education. Selection is by random drawing. Awarded every year.
Contact: James H. Dunn, Secretary-Treasurer.

2225   School Food Service Foundation Scholarship

American School Food Service Association (ASFSA)
1600 Duke Street
7th Floor
Alexandria, VA 22314
(703) 739-3900
Average award: $500
Maximum award: $1,000
Minimum award: $100
Number of awards: 131
Deadline: April 15
College level: Freshman, Sophomore, Junior, Senior, Graduate, Doctoral
Majors/Fields: Dietetics, food science, food service management, nutrition
Criteria: Applicant must be a member or the child of an ASFSA member, plan to pursue a career in food service, and have a minimum 2.7 GPA. Reapplication, satisfactory academic progress, financial need, and potential required to retain scholarship. Awarded every year.
Contact: Nancy Motyka, School Food Service Foundation Assistant.

2226   Service Employees International Union Scholarship

Service Employees International Union (SEIU)
1313 L Street NW
Washington, DC 20005
(202) 898-3326
Average award: $750
Maximum award: $1,000
Number of awards: 9
Deadline: March 10
College level: Freshman, Sophomore, Junior, Senior, Graduate
Criteria: Applicant must be a high school senior or recent graduate who is a member or the child of a member of a SEIU local union. Applicant must have been a member for at least three years prior to September 1 of the year the award is presented. Officers and employees of the international union (non-local) and their families are not eligible. Selection is based upon high school grades, SAT I scores, achievements and honors, and personal character report. Renewal is based on satisfactory college transcript. Awarded every year.
Contact: SEIU Scholarship Committee, (202) 898-3200.

2227   Student CTA Scholarship

California Teachers Association
1705 Murchison Drive
P.O. Box 921
Burlingame, CA 94011-0921
(415) 697-1400
Average award: $2,000
Number of awards: 3
Deadline: February 15
College level: Freshman, Sophomore, Junior, Senior, Graduate, Doctoral
Majors/Fields: Education
Criteria: Applicant must be an active student CTA member enrolled in a teacher credential program. Awarded every year.
Contact: Human Rights Department.

2228   UFCW International Union Scholarship

United Food and Commercial Workers International Union
Education Office
1775 K Street, NW
Washington, DC 20006
(202) 223-3111
Average award: $1,000
Number of awards: 14
Deadline: December 31 (preliminary), March 15 (application)
College level: Freshman
Criteria: Applicant must be a UFCW union member in good standing for at least one year prior to December 31, or be the child of a member, and be less than 20 years old on March 15. Transcript and verification of enrollment must be sent to retain scholarship. Awarded every year.
Contact: Education Office.

2229   UPIU Scholarship

United Paperworkers International Union (UPIU)
Scholarship Awards Program
P.O. Box 1475
Nashville, TN 37202
(615) 834-8590
Average award: $1,000
Number of awards: 22
Deadline: March 15
College level: Freshman
Criteria: Applicant must be a senior in high school and the child of a living UPIU member in good standing. Selection is based upon scholastic aptitude, leadership, and good citizenship. UPIU is broken into eleven geographical regions, with two scholarships awarded in each region. Awarded every year.
Contact: James H. Dunn, Secretary-Treasurer.

2230 URW American Income Scholarship

United Rubber, Cork, Linoleum, and Plastic Workers (URW)
URW Fair Practices Department
570 White Pond Drive
Akron, OH 44320-1156
(216) 869-0320
Average award: $1,250
Number of awards: 4
Deadline: February 1
College level: Freshman
Criteria: Applicant's parent or guardian must be a URW member. Selection is based upon academic excellence, community involvement, and commitment to serve humanity. Awarded every year.
Contact: Lyle D. Skinner, Fair Practices Director.

2231 Utility Workers Union of America Scholarship

Utility Workers Union of America
815 16th Street, NW
Suite 605
Washington, DC 20006
(202) 347-8105
Average award: $1,500
Maximum award: $2,000
Minimum award: $500
Number of awards: 2
Deadline: January 1 of junior year
College level: Freshman
Criteria: Applicant's parent must be a member of the Utility Workers Union of America. Selection is made by the National Merit Scholarship Corp. Satisfactory academic progress is required to retain scholarship. Awarded every year.
Contact: Marshall M. Hicks, National President.

2232 William H. Bywater Scholarship

International Union of Electronic, Electrical, Salaried, Machine and Furniture Workers (IUE)
1126 16th Street, N.W.
Department of Social Action
Washington, DC 20036-4866
Average award: $3,000
Number of awards: 1
Deadline: April 15
College level: Freshman, Sophomore, Junior, Senior
Criteria: Applicant must be the child of a IUE local union elected official. Applicant must submit class rank, GPA, SAT I or ACT scores, copy of W-2 form, short statement of interest and goals, and three recommendations. Selection is based upon academic record, character, leadership ability, and a desire to improve and move ahead. Awarded every year.
Contact: Gloria T. Johnson, Department of Social Action.

Vocational/Technical

2233 AMT Scholarship

Association for Manufacturing Technology (AMT)
7901 Westpark Drive
McLean, VA 22102
(703) 893-2900
Maximum award: $2,000
Number of awards: 16
Deadline: March 15 (Company must commit to sponsorship by March 15.)
College level: Freshman, Sophomore
Majors/Fields: Manufacturing technology
Criteria: Applicant must be enrolled in an associate degree program and be interested in a career in the machine tool industry. Each participating AMT member company works with a regionally accredited college and high school in its geographic area to select a deserving applicant; company will provide work-training employment for the two summers of the scholarship. AMT does not grant scholarship directly; awards are made through the member company who serves as a sponsor. Award is for two years. Awarded every year.
Contact: Myrta Mason, Scholarship Administrator, (703) 827-5219.

2234 Lincoln Technical Institute Scholarship

Boys and Girls Clubs of Chicago
625 West Jackson Boulevard
Suite 300
Chicago, IL 60661
(312) 627-2700
Average award: $14,000
Deadline: October 1
College level: Freshman
Majors/Fields: Auto/diesel, automotive technician, diesel technician
Criteria: Applicant must be a current or former member of the Boys & Girls Clubs of Chicago. Applicant must submit application, a copy of high school diploma or GED certificate, and recommendation. Award may be used only at sponsoring institution.
Contact: Mary Ann Mahon-Huels, Asst. Vice President of Operations.

2235 Maryland Association of Private Career Schools Scholarship

Maryland Association of Private Career Schools
P.O. Box 209
Severna Park, MD 21146
(410) 974-4473
Average award: $1,000
Maximum award: $5,000
Minimum award: $500
Number of awards: 23
Deadline: March 31
College level: Freshman
Majors/Fields: Vocational/technical
Criteria: Applicant must be a Maryland high school graduate planning to attend a private career school. Selection is based upon academic qualifications. Awarded every year.
Contact: Midge Lee, Administrative Assistant.

Other

2236 Ben T. Huiet Endowment Fund Scholarship

Clemson University
G-01 Sikes Hall
Clemson, SC 29634-5123
(803) 656-2280
Average award: $1,000
Number of awards: 4
Deadline: March 1
College level: Freshman, Sophomore, Junior, Senior
Criteria: Applicant must have a minimum 2.0 GPA. Awarded every year. Award may be used only at sponsoring institution.
Contact: Marvin Carmichael, Director of Financial Aid.

2237 Charles H. Stone Scholarship

Clemson University
G-01 Sikes Hall
Clemson, SC 29634-5123
(803) 656-2280
Average award: $1,000
Number of awards: 4
Deadline: March 1
College level: Sophomore, Junior, Senior
Criteria: Applicant must demonstrate financial need and have a minimum 2.0 GPA. Awarded every year. Award may be used only at sponsoring institution.
Contact: Marvin Carmichael, Director of Financial Aid.

2238   College & Program Competition Scholarships

Marquette University
1212 West Wisconsin Avenue
Milwaukee, WI 53233
(414) 288-7390
Average award: $5,000
Deadline: End of January or beginning of February
College level: Freshman
Criteria: Competitions are held by program areas in arts and sciences, business administration, communication, journalism, performing arts, dental hygiene, engineering, medical laboratory technology, and nursing. Recipients must initially enroll in their winning program area. Minimum 3.0 GPA and full-time enrollment are required to retain scholarship. Awarded every year. Award may be used only at sponsoring institution.
Contact: Anne Wingert, Assistant Director of Student Financial Aid.

2239   Departmental Endowed Scholarships

Eastern Michigan University
Office of Financial Aid
403 Pierce Hall
Ypsilanti, MI 48197
(313) 487-0455
Average award: $1,000
Maximum award: $2,500
Minimum award: $150
Number of awards: 350
Deadline: January 15
College level: Freshman, Sophomore, Junior, Senior, Graduate
Criteria: Each scholarship has its own specifications. Awarded every year. Award may be used only at sponsoring institution.
Contact: Cynthia Van Pelt, Assistant Director, Scholarships.

2240   Dewitt T. and Mary Timmerman Hardin Endowment Fund Scholarship

Clemson University
G-01 Sikes Hall
Clemson, SC 29634-5123
(803) 656-2280
Average award: $1,000
Number of awards: 8
Deadline: March 1
College level: Freshman, Sophomore, Junior, Senior
Criteria: Applicant must be a worthy student. Awarded every year. Award may be used only at sponsoring institution.
Contact: Marvin Carmichael, Director of Financial Aid.

2241   Edgar A. Brown Foundation Scholarship

Edgar A. Brown Foundation
c/o NationsBank, N.A. (Carolinas)
SC3-230-03-03
Columbia, SC 29202-0448
(803) 929-5879
Average award: $1,500
Maximum award: $2,000
Minimum award: $1,000
Number of awards: 8
Deadline: March 1
College level: Freshman
Criteria: Applicant must attend Clemson U. Scholarship is renewable. Awarded every year. Award may be used only at sponsoring institution.
Contact: Marvin G. Carmichael, Director of Financial Aid, Clemson University, Box 345123, Clemson, SC 29631.

2242   Endowed Scholarships

Ohio University
Office of Student Financial Aid and Scholarships
Athens, OH 45701
(614) 593-4141
Average award: $750
Maximum award: $3,000
Minimum award: $250
Number of awards: 800
Deadline: February 15 (freshman); March 1 (upperclass applicant)
College level: Freshman, Sophomore, Junior, Senior
Criteria: Each scholarship has its own criteria, including parent's employment, organizational affiliation, financial need, religion, gender, academic qualifications, place of residence, or academic major. Reapplication is required to retain scholarship. Awarded every year. Award may be used only at sponsoring institution.
Contact: Yang-Hi Kim, Associate Director of Scholarships and Grants.

2243   James Corcoran and Mary Poats Littlejohn Memorial Scholarship

Clemson University
G-01 Sikes Hall
Clemson, SC 29634-5123
(803) 656-2280
Average award: $1,800
Number of awards: 3
Deadline: March 1
College level: Sophomore, Junior, Senior
Criteria: Applicant must demonstrate financial need and have a minimum 2.0 cumulative GPA. Satisfactory GPA with at least 12 credits per semester is required to retain scholarship. Awarded every year. Award may be used only at sponsoring institution.
Contact: Marvin Carmichael, Director of Financial Aid.

2244   Lillie Hawkins Floyd Trust Scholarship

Clemson University
G-01 Sikes Hall
Clemson, SC 29634-5123
(803) 656-2280
Average award: $2,000
Number of awards: 4
Deadline: March 1
College level: Freshman, Sophomore, Junior, Senior
Criteria: Applicant must be a single student and demonstrate financial need. Recipient must remain unmarried to retain scholarship. Awarded every year. Award may be used only at sponsoring institution.
Contact: Marvin Carmichael, Director of Financial Aid.

2245   Orville Redenbacher's Second Start Scholarship

Orville Redenbacher's Second Start Scholarships
P.O. Box 39101
Chicago, IL 60639
Average award: $1,000
Number of awards: 25
Deadline: May 1
College level: Adult students
Criteria: Applicant must be 30 years of age or older and returning to college or beginning for the first time.
Contact: Scholarships.

2246 Presidential Scholarship

Oakland University
101 North Foundation Hall
Rochester, MI 48309-4401
(810) 370-3360
Average award: $6,000
Number of awards: 2
Deadline: February 1
College level: Freshman
Criteria: Applicant must live in the residence halls on campus. Minimum 3.3 GPA is required to retain scholarship. Awarded every year. Award may be used only at sponsoring institution.
Contact: Stacy M. Penkala, Assistant Director of Admissions.

2247 Provost Scholarship

Southern Illinois University at Edwardsville
Box 1083
Edwardsville, IL 62026-1083
(618) 692-2000
Average award: $1,000
Maximum award: $2,200
Minimum award: $750
Number of awards: 94
Deadline: April 1
College level: Freshman, Sophomore, Junior, Senior
Criteria: Scholarship is renewable. Awarded every year. Award may be used only at sponsoring institution.
Contact: Director of Financial Aid.

2248 Raymond H. Kiefer Scholarship

University of Toledo
Financial Aid Office
Toledo, OH 43606-3390
(419) 537-2056
Average award: $2,500
Deadline: January 28
College level: Freshman
Criteria: Applicant must enroll on a full-time basis and demonstrate financial need. Awarded every year. Award may be used only at sponsoring institution.
Contact: Office of Financial Aid, Toledo, OH 43606-3390.

2249 Speck Farrar Scholarship

Clemson University
G-01 Sikes Hall
Clemson, SC 29634-5123
(803) 656-2280
Average award: $2,500
Number of awards: 10
Deadline: March 1
College level: Freshman, Sophomore, Junior, Senior
Criteria: Applicant must have a minimum 2.0 cumulative GPA and demonstrate financial need. Awarded every year. Award may be used only at sponsoring institution.
Contact: Marvin Carmichael, Director of Financial Aid.

2250 Tigerama Scholarship

Clemson University
G-01 Sikes Hall
Clemson, SC 29634-5123
(803) 656-2280
Average award: $1,000
Number of awards: 3
Deadline: March 1
College level: Freshman, Sophomore, Junior, Senior
Criteria: Scholarship fund was established by the Blue Key National Honor Fraternity. Awarded every year. Award may be used only at sponsoring institution.
Contact: Marvin Carmichael, Director of Financial Aid.

2251 Tuition Assistance Award

Liberty University
P.O. Box 20000
Lynchburg, VA 24506-8001
(804) 582-2270
Average award: $2,000
Minimum award: $1,000
Maximum number of awards: 4
Minimum number of awards: 2
Deadline: May 1; October 1
College level: Freshman
Criteria: Applicant must have substantial financial need. Satisfactory academic progress and financial need are required to retain scholarship. Awarded every year. Award may be used only at sponsoring institution.
Contact: Penny Hutchinson, Admissions Representative.

2252 William J. Neely Memorial Scholarship

Clemson University
G-01 Sikes Hall
Clemson, SC 29634-5123
(803) 656-2280
Average award: $1,000
Number of awards: 4
Deadline: March 1
College level: Freshman, Sophomore, Junior, Senior
Criteria: Applicant must have a minimum 2.0 cumulative GPA. Satisfactory GPA with at least 12 credits per semester is required to retain scholarship. Awarded every year. Award may be used only at sponsoring institution.
Contact: Marvin Carmichael, Director of Financial Aid.

Index of Majors

Agriculture/Animal Science

4-H Knowledge/Leadership, 1393, 1560

Agribusiness, 1, 2, 2107,1396, 1401, 1407, 1417, 1426, 1427, 1433, 1442, 1446, 1451, 1467, 1477, 1483, 1506, 1527, 1543, 1544, 1551, 1552

Agricultural Communications, 1440, 1530

Agricultural Economics, 2, 19, 1404, 1422, 1451, 1506, 1552, 2036, 2107

Agricultural Journalism, 1440, 1530

Agricultural Marketing, 1404, 1440

Agricultural Mechanics, 1470, 1595, 2107

Agricultural Sales, 1417, 1451

Agricultural Science, 7, 12, 14, 16, 20, 22, 23, 24, 25, 1580, 2018, 2034, 2036, 2083, 2160

Agricultural Technology, 1404, 1580

Agriculture/Agriculture Studies, 5, 6, 8, 9, 11, 13, 15, 17, 18, 19, 21, 52, 901, 908, 1099, 1183, 1395, 1397, 1398, 1401, 1408, 1412, 1424, 1426, 1429, 1431, 1433, 1439, 1446, 1447, 1456, 1457, 1465, 1468, 1471, 1473, 1474, 1475, 1476, 1477, 1480, 1482, 1483, 1494, 1503, 1504, 1509, 1519, 1523, 1527, 1528, 1531, 1534, 1535, 1538, 1540, 1543, 1559, 1561, 1581, 1582, 1586, 1587, 1755, 1987, 2126, 2182

Agronomy, 19, 26, 1412, 1451, 1498, 1503, 1513, 1593

Animal Science/Studies, 27, 29, 31, 32, 60, 1405, 1410, 1411, 1413, 1418, 1479, 1483, 1526, 1532, 1547, 1551, 1554, 1570, 1574, 1590, 2107

Beef /Meat Science, 1420, 1430, 1526

Cereal/Grain Science/Studies, 4, 933, 1423, 1554

Conservation, 901, 905, 908, 1396, 1436, 1495, 1539

Crop Production Science, 1592

Dairy Science/Industry, 33, 1404, 1422, 1430, 1438, 1443, 1444, 1445, 1449, 1507, 1585, 2107

Dog Husbandry, 1455

Equine Science/Horse Studies, 1472, 1508

Environmental Design, 335, 905

Environmental Economics, 1688

Environmental Sciences/Studies, 215, 901, 902, 904, 906, 1688, 2109

Fisheries, 30, 58, 60, 1594

Floriculture, 55, 1478

Forestry, 19, 34, 35, 36, 37, 38, 39, 40, 56, 59, 901, 1489

Gardening, 51

Grounds/Turfgrass Management, 43, 44, 56

Horticulture, 19, 31, 41, 42, 45, 46, 48, 49, 50, 51, 52, 53, 54, 55, 56, 57, 405, 1478

Land Management, 55, 203, 898, 1541

Landscape Architecture/Design, 49, 51, 55, 336, 338, 344, 345, 2146

Livestock Studies, 1565

Natural Resources, 1001, 1654, 1702, 2109, 1436

Plant Science, 19, 56, 949, 1493

Poultry Science, 1554

Range Science, 27, 60

Veterinary Medicine/Studies, 28, 31, 32, 60, 1532, 1569, 1588, 1729, 2144, 2146, 2184

Waste Management, 573, 685

Water Resources/Treatment, 538, 654, 903, 907, 910, 950, 1495, 1805

Wildlife Studies, 59, 60, 1594

Zoology, 874, 904

Allied Health

Dental Assistant, 87, 89

Dental Hygiene, 74, 81, 85, 88, 791, 2146, 2238

Dental Laboratory Technology, 96

Dietetics, 90, 2225

Food Conservation/Safety Studies, 92, 1487

Food Science/Nutrition, 31, 91, 92, 93, 94, 1411, 1422, 1458, 1484, 1486, 1513, 1544, 2225

Health Care/Administration, 61, 63, 64, 70, 76, 75, 337, 1348, 1403, 1490, 1770, 1771, 1813

Health Information Management, 62, 68, 69, 80, 83, 278

Health Science/Studies, 65, 66, 73, 878, 1012, 1445, 1505, 1604, 1654, 2144

Helping Professions, 1365

Medical Group Practice/Management, 64, 70, 76, 84, 822

Medical Laboratory Technology, 95, 2238

Medical Technology, 71, 82, 95, 1337, 1821

Mental Health, 1727

Music Therapy, 118, 425

Occupational Therapy, 71, 72, 74, 79, 81, 82, 114, 115, 116, 118, 515, 2146

Occupational Therapy Assistant, 116, 2146

Pharmacy/Pharmaceutics, 65, 71, 74, 77, 81, 97, 98, 99, 100, 101, 102, 103, 104, 105, 106, 107, 108, 109, 110, 111, 112, 113, 1012, 1337, 1367, 1821, 2146

Physical Therapy, 71, 72, 74, 79, 81, 82, 114, 116, 117, 118, 515, 1012, 2146

Physical Therapy Assistant, 116, 2146

Physician Assistant, 74, 81, 82, 86, 849, 859, 2146

Public Health, 872, 1821, 2084

Radiology Technology, 82, 860

Rehabilitation, 78, 1962

Respiratory Therapy, 82, 119, 120

Therapeutic Recreation, 118

Business

Accounting, 121, 122, 123, 124, 125, 126, 127, 128, 129, 130, 131, 132, 133, 134, 135, 136, 137, 138, 139, 156, 189, 598, 1572, 1798, 2146

Actuarial Science, 195, 1196

Administration, 445

Advertising, 1396

Banking, 146, 155

Business, 3, 140, 141, 142, 145, 147, 150, 154, 159, 163, 164, 167, 169, 170, 173, 174, 175, 176, 177, 179, 180, 181, 183, 184, 185, 197, 215, 1271, 1408, 1472, 1654, 1673, 1692, 1714, 1719, 1770, 1771, 1785, 1798, 1807, 1814, 1834, 1958, 1983, 2109, 2130

Business Administration, 143, 146, 148, 152, 157, 158, 160, 165, 168, 171, 172, 201, 681, 1188, 1566, 1577, 1702, 1709, 1792, 1798, 1971, 2004, 2238

Business Technology, 168, 958

Commerce, 150, 151, 168, 1188, 2004

Court Reporting, 204

Data Processing, 168

Economics, 144, 147, 160, 166, 172, 174, 176, 712, 1051, 1057, 1785

Exhibit Planning, 31

Finance, 146, 155, 177, 178, 182, 1756

Food Industry/Technology, 91, 92, 93, 164, 184, 1420,1422, 1449, 1486

Food Service/Management, 188, 190, 192, 193, 1472, 1486, 2225

Hospitality, 186, 187, 188, 189, 190, 191, 192, 193, 1472

Insurance, 196, 197, 198

Integrated Manufacturing, 672

Labor/Personnel, 161, 2215

Logistics, 615

Management, 122, 149, 153, 162, 177, 178, 375, 565, 590, 628, 664, 1416, 1450, 1566, 1798, 1905, 2055, 2056, 2065

Management Information Systems, 123, 156, 189, 564, 565

Marketing, 156, 177, 199, 200, 201, 569, 1396, 1450, 1798

Music/Video Business, 399

Packaging, 39, 202, 1555

Quality Assurance, 93

Real Estate, 203

Resource Management, 194

Restaurant Management, 191, 187

Sales, 1798

Telecommunications, 223, 293

Transportation, 215, 219

Travel/Tourism, 205, 206, 207, 208, 209, 210, 211, 212, 213, 214, 216, 217, 218

Communications

Broadcast Journalism, 253, 261, 296, 298, 304, 1332

Broadcasting, 260, 294, 295, 299, 301, 306, 307, 308, 309, 569

Communication Disorders, 74, 81, 118, 220, 227, 228, 2146

Communications, 190, 220, 221, 222, 225, 226, 227, 233, 247, 251, 258, 292, 297, 569, 606, 1717,. 1365, 1600, 2109, 2238

Journalism, 220, 224, 229, 230, 231, 233, 234, 235, 236, 237, 238, 240, 241, 242, 243, 245, 248, 249, 250, 251, 252, 254, 255, 256, 258, 259, 262, 264, 265, 569, 1600, 1659, 2238

Mass Communications, 224, 245, 252, 254, 255, 259

Outdoor Communications, 739

Photojournalism, 290, 291

Print Journalism, 232, 239, 246, 247, 257, 261

Public Relations, 259

Religious Communication, 224, 263, 264, 1711

Sports Writing, 244

Visual Communications, 364, 371, 397, 399

Creative/Performing Arts

Architecture, 61, 333, 334, 337, 339, 340, 341, 342, 343, 346, 347, 348, 349, 365, 624, 1014, 1022, 1062, 1636, 1816, 1943, 1947, 2146

Art, 350, 353, 354, 356, 359, 360, 361, 362, 364, 366, 369, 371, 382, 383, 384, 386, 390, 391, 396, 398, 406, 783, 1103, 1201, 1956

Art Advertising, 388

Art Conservation, 393

Art History, 351, 352, 355, 356, 357, 388, 391, 395

Arts, 370, 768, 1188, 1674, 1834, 2004, 2238

Creative Writing, 360, 729

Dance, 358, 360, 362, 363, 364, 365, 371, 372, 376, 1814

Drama/Theatre, 220, 358, 359, 360, 362, 364, 365, 366, 371, 372, 374, 375, 376, 1814

Drawing, 389, 394, 395, 396

Fashion Design/Studies/Costume Design, 362, 375, 399, 1435, 1466, 2198

Film/Video, 395

Fine Arts, 365, 387, 779

Graphic Arts/Communications, 400, 401, 402, 403

Instrumental Music, 407, 408, 409, 411, 412, 413, 415, 417, 418, 419, 424, 425, 426, 431, 435

Interior Design, 191, 362, 377, 378, 379, 380, 399

Lighting/Scene Design, 375, 570

Music, 358, 359, 360, 362, 364, 365, 366, 369, 371, 372, 411, 414, 416, 421, 422, 423, 424, 427, 428, 429, 430, 432, 433, 434, 441, 1959

Opera, 436, 437

Painting, 365, 389, 394, 395, 396

Performing Arts, 368, 373, 2238

Photography, 168, 365, 395, 399, 405, 1546

Pottery, 396

Printmaking, 389, 395

Sculpture, 365, 389, 392, 395, 1062

Studio Art, 388, 396

Visual Arts, 358, 373, 385, 395

Voice, 426, 431, 435, 437, 438, 439, 440, 441, 442, 443

Education

Aerospace Education, 1857

Agricultural Education, 19, 1475, 1536, 1593, 2107

Art Education, 391

Conservation Education, 60

Early Childhood Education, 446, 450, 509

Education, 31, 405, 444, 445, 447, 448, 449, 451, 452, 453, 454, 455, 456, 457, 458, 459, 460, 461, 462, 463, 464, 465, 466, 467, 468, 469, 470, 471, 472, 473, 474, 475, 476, 477, 478, 479, 480, 481, 482, 483, 484, 486, 487, 488, 489, 490, 491, 492, 493, 494, 495, 496, 497, 498, 499, 500, 501, 502, 503, 505, 569, 768, 1220, 1264, 1691, 1702, 1719, 1735, 1770, 1771, 1779, 1800, 1803, 1834, 1868, 1895, 1955, 1962, 2011, 2015, 2035, 2080, 2096, 2121, 2156, 2227

Educational Administration, 1659

Elementary Education, 450, 460, 477, 485, 503, 504, 507, 511, 1955
Earth Science Education, 893, 894
Extension Education, 19
Industrial Education, 958
Jewish Education, 1971
Marketing Education, 200, 1450
Math Secondary Education, 1654
Museum Education, 342, 357
Music Education, 425
Physical Education, 1971
Preschool Education, 477
Science Secondary Education, 1654
Secondary Education, 450, 477, 485, 503, 506, 507, 510, 1955
Spanish Education, 506
Special Education, 513, 515, 516, 1967

Engineering/Technology—

Aeronautical Engineering, 519, 520, 523, 527, 577, 609
Aeronautics, 518, 522, 943
Aerospace, 522, 1894
Aerospace Engineering, 519, 520, 523, 638
Agricultural Engineering, 25, 26, 41, 1394, 1404, 1580, 1595
Air Pollution Control, 573
Astronautical Engineering, 527
Automotive Engineering, 603
Aviation, 521, 524, 1802, 1819, 1845
Biomedical Engineering, 1821
Broadcast Engineering, 300
Chemical Engineering, 528, 530, 531, 535, 536, 537, 584, 587, 588, 590, 594, 595, 597, 601, 603, 606, 611, 623, 648, 652, 663, 689, 1616, 1688, 1906
Civil Engineering, 539, 540, 541, 542, 543, 545, 546, 547, 548, 550, 551, 553, 554, 560, 561, 587, 598, 601, 611, 619, 635, 648, 652, 697, 903, 1022
Computer Engineering, 596, 599, 606, 618, 636, 1742, 1907
Computer Science, 168, 510, 563, 566, 572, 596, 598, 599, 606, 608, 609, 618, 650, 923, 924, 925, 952, 957, 964, 968, 1014, 1022, 1196, 1719, 1739, 1742, 1800, 1907, 1945, 2055, 2056, 2058, 2109, 2110
Construction Engineering, 539
Construction/Technology, 162, 540, 548, 552, 555, 559, 681
Consulting Engineering, 637
Electrical Engineering, 292, 527, 566, 567, 568, 569, 571, 577, 590, 592, 596, 598, 599, 601, 603, 604, 606, 608, 609, 611, 619, 648, 652, 663, 697, 1022, 1616, 1742, 1904, 1907
Electrical Engineering Technology, 968, 1461
Electrochemical Science/Technology, 529, 532, 533
Electronic Distribution
Electronics, 201, 292, 297
Electronics Engineering, 577, 638
Energy Management Studies, 1462
Engineering, 39, 168, 175, 215, 519, 520, 527, 544, 559, 572, 574, 575, 576, 578, 579, 580, 581, 583, 585, 586, 591, 593, 600, 602, 605, 607, 610, 612, 614, 616, 617, 620, 621, 622, 624, 625, 626, 627, 629, 630, 631, 632, 633, 634, 636, 639, 641, 643, 644, 646, 647, 649, 650, 653, 655, 656, 657, 658, 659, 660, 661, 662, 664, 665, 918, 920, 932, 934, 937, 943, 947, 948, 951, 953, 954, 956, 957, 958, 966, 967, 968, 1012, 1014, 1019, 1032, 1105, 1120, 1157, 1188, 1196, 1212, 1365, 1375, 1389, 1567, 1575, 1654, 1673, 1702, 1719, 1726, 1739, 1742, 1792, 1800, 1816, 1818, 1824, 1895, 1905, 1908, 1943, 1945, 1947, 1987, 2004, 2055, 2056, 2058, 2109, 2110, 2126, 2146, 2238
Engineering Management, 628
Engineering Technology, 578, 603
Environmental Engineering, 648, 652, 697
Food Engineering, 93
Geoengineering, 899
Geological Engineering, 694, 695, 696
Industrial Engineering, 590, 592, 603, 604, 667, 669, 673, 674, 675, 1616
Industrial Design, 31, 168, 399, 405, 668
Industrial Studies, 201, 612, 1196, 1558
Information Sciences, 168, 270, 273, 282 562, 606, 1717
Maintenance Engineering, 1653
Manufacturing Engineering, 603, 670, 675, 676
Manufacturing Technology, 666, 670, 676, 968, 2233
Marine Engineering, 577, 642
Materials Engineering, 603
Materials Science, 688, 925
Mechanical Engineering, 584, 587, 588, 590, 592, 594, 596, 597, 598, 599, 601, 603, 604, 606, 609, 611, 619, 623, 648, 663, 677, 678, 679, 680, 681, 682, 683, 684, 686, 687, 697, 1022, 1616
Metallurgical Engineering, 690, 1022
Mineral Engineering, 693
Mineral Processing, 697
Mining, 693, 697
Mining Engineering, 635, 698
Nuclear Engineering, 699, 1022
Ocean Engineering, 577, 642
Optical/Opto-Electronic Engineering/Science, 963
Petroleum Engineering, 588, 652, 689, 691, 692, 694, 695, 696
Plastics Engineering, 645
Safety Engineering, 582, 613, 640
Solid State Science/Engineering, 529, 532, 533
Structural Engineering, 550, 558
Surveying, 922, 926, 939, 2143
Systems Engineering, 596, 599, 609
Technology, 168, 534, 589, 651, 656, 906, 1036, 1196, 1298, 1806, 1908, 1939, 2235
Vocational, 168, 1806, 2063, 2185, 2235

Language/Literature/ Humanities—

American Studies, 715
Arabic/Arabic Area Studies, 752
Armenian Studies, 1659
Arts/Letters, 369, 1908
Asian Languages, 1907
British Studies, 715, 746
Byzantine Studies, 345, 701, 703
Canadian Studies, 723, 2011
Chinese Studies, 705

Classics, 704, 1062, 1059
Design, 342, 357, 388, 398
Eastern European Languages/Studies, 713, 751
English, 729, 733, 737, 742, 768, 1157, 1636, 1903, 1956
Etruscan Culture, 1690
European Languages, 712
Finnish Studies, 711
Foreign Languages, 505, 753, 776, 1157, 1956
French, 510, 1809
General Studies, 1032, 1167, 2055, 2056
Geography, 1056, 1073
German, 510, 749, 750
Greek, 701, 1809
Greek Studies, 703, 1809
Humanities, 770, 771, 772, 773, 774, 777, 779, 947, 948, 1127, 1140, 1375, 1381, 1895, 1956
Irish Studies, 717
Italian, 1750
Jewish Studies, 721, 725, 787, 788, 789
Library Science, 168, 266, 267, 268, 269, 270, 271, 272, 273, 274, 275, 276, 277, 278, 279, 280, 281, 282, 283, 284, 285, 286, 287, 288, 289
Linguistics, 709
Literature, 365, 771, 783, 1959
Middle Eastern Languages, 1907
Museum Studies, 342, 357
Near Eastern Archaeology, 356
Poetry, 741, 747
Norwegian Studies, 719
Polish Studies, 714, 727, 728
Portuguese Language/Culture, 1713
Pre-Columbian Studies, 345
Roman Studies, 702, 703
Russian/Soviet Studies, 1051
Slavic Languages, 1907
Spanish, 510
Theology/Religion, 784, 785, 786, 1839, 1956
Turkish Studies, 707, 710
Welsh Studies, 722
Writing, 358, 736, 740, 748

Medicine/Nursing————

Chiropractic, 2146
Dentistry, 71, 77, 791, 792, 793, 794, 795, 796, 821, 1337, 2181
Medicine, 66, 71, 77, 798, 799, 800, 801, 802, 803, 805, 806, 807, 809, 810, 811, 814, 816, 818, 819, 821, 826, 828, 849, 850, 1337, 1362, 1367, 1567, 1672, 1694, 1702, 1814, 1818, 1838, 1868, 1945, 1947, 2144, 2181
Nurse/Midwife, 74, 81, 842, 849, 859
Nurse Practitioner, 74, 81, 849, 859
Nursing, 71, 72, 74, 77, 79, 81, 82, 829, 830, 831, 832, 833, 834, 835, 836, 837, 838, 839, 840, 841, 842, 843, 844, 845 846, 847, 848, 851, 852, 853, 854, 855, 856, 857, 858, 860, 861, 862, 863, 864, 1013, 1014, 1019, 1032, 1036, 1047, 1337, 1367, 1834, 1835, 2077, 2146, 2164, 2172, 2187, 2238
Ophthalmology, 67
Optometry, 2144, 2146
Osteopathic Medicine, 797, 817, 849, 2078, 2144
Psychiatry, 815, 823
Pre-Medicine, 804, 813, 824, 825, 827, 878

Science/Mathematics————

Applied Mathematics, 512, 609, 1196
Applied Science, 576, 585, 646
Astronomy, 923, 924, 925, 930
Atmospheric Science, 865, 866, 867, 868, 869, 870
Behavioral Science, 832, 947, 948
Biochemistry, 891, 1688
Biology/Life Sciences, 45, 60, 112, 505, 510, 512, 805, 808, 871, 873, 874, 875, 877, 878, 879, 882, 884, 923, 924, 947, 948, 952, 957, 1688,1824, 2109, 2110
Biomedical Science/Research, 278, 812, 871, 872, 876, 879, 881, 1821
Biotechnology, 1196
Botany, 56, 60
Cell Biology, 871, 876, 934
Chemistry, 56, 112, 505, 510, 512, 606, 808, 886, 887, 888, 889, 890, 891, 892, 903, 923, 924, 925, 934, 952, 958, 1196, 1688, 1739, 1904, 2109
Cytotechnology, 95
Developmental Biology, 934
Earth Science, 896, 923, 924
Ecology, 31, 32, 60, 902, 904, 1539
Entomology, 19, 874, 883, 1688, 1463
Gemology, 1613
Genetics, 31, 60, 876
Geochemistry, 894
Geodetic Surveying, 921, 935
Geology, 510, 512, 635, 664, 689, 697, 731, 893, 894, 895, 899, 925, 929, 1903, 1906, 2055, 2056
Geophysics, 664, 731, 893, 894, 897, 899, 900, 929, 931, 1903, 1906, 2055, 2056
Hydrology/Hydrologic Science, 865, 866, 867, 868, 869, 870, 893, 894, 950, 1688
Marine Biology, 904, 913
Marine Science, 59, 912, 914
Mathematics, 168, 195, 460, 505, 510, 512, 596, 606, 650, 776, 915, 916, 918, 920, 923, 924, 925, 936, 937, 940, 941, 947, 948, 952, 956, 957, 958, 964, 967, 968, 1014, 1022, 1105, 1127, 1157, 1365, 1717, 1719,1739, 1907, 1945, 2058, 2110
Metallurgy, 688, 697
Meteorology, 865, 866, 867, 868, 869, 870, 893, 894, 1014, 1019, 1022
Microbiological Sciences, 880, 885
Molecular Biology, 871, 934
Natural Science, 709, 932, 936, 937, 940, 1105, 1127, 1947
Neurobiology, 871
Neuroscience, 815, 876
Naval Architecture, 577, 642
Nuclear Science, 699
Oceanography/Oceanic Science, 865, 866, 867, 868, 869, 870, 893, 894, 913
Optics, 650
Physical Science, 168, 577, 911, 920, 947, 948, 957, 1824, 2110
Planetary Geology, 893, 894
Physics, 505, 510, 512, 596, 606, 609, 650, 923, 924, 925, 930, 934, 952, 958, 1014, 1022, 1666, 1739
Science, 39, 170, 460, 519, 520, 621, 641, 643, 650, 768, 776, 808, 825, 909, 918, 938, 941, 942, 943,

944, 946, 951, 953, 954, 955, 956, 960, 964, 961, 966, 967, 968, 1012, 1157, 1188, 1212, 1365, 1654, 1673, 1674, 1719, 1770, 1771, 1800, 1834, 1857, 1895, 1939, 1945, 1987, 2000, 2004, 2058, 2126, 2238

Statistics, 606

Structural Biology, 876

Textile Chemistry, 2197, 2204

Toxicology, 98, 1688

Tropical Botany, 47

Virology, 871

Social Science/Political Science/Law

American History, 756, 783

Anthropology, 709, 1069

Archaeology, 709, 718, 1054, 1058, 1059, 1061, 1062

British History, 783

Child Care/Development, 975, 446

Clinical Psychology, 1702

Criminal Justice/Law Enforcement, 987, 1009, 1512

Family Studies, 806, 972, 1558

Government, 1057, 1983, 2188

History, 706, 712, 755, 757, 760, 761, 1051, 1057, 1062, 1956

Home Economics, 19, 969, 970, 971, 973, 974, 1437, 1447, 1834

International Studies, 706, 752, 769, 775, 781, 782, 1060, 1136, 1220, 1659, 1817, 2057, 2066

Law, 77, 281, 302, 976, 977, 978, 979, 980, 981, 982, 983, 984, 985, 986, 988, 989, 990, 991, 992, 993, 994, 995, 996, 997, 998, 999, 1000, 1001, 1002, 1003, 1004, 1005, 1006, 1007, 1008, 1010, 1011,

1702, 1729, 1743, 1814, 1818, 1947, 2109, 2144, 2146

Midwestern History, 754

Paralegal Studies, 1800

Philosophy, 1956

Political Science, 712, 1049, 1051, 1057, 1818, 2011

Public Affairs/Administration, 31, 405, 712, 1050, 1060, 1072, 1659, 1834, 2215

Psychology, 1053, 1702, 2146

Regional/Urban Planning, 55, 215, 1070, 1071, 1073, 1074

Social Science 808, 932, 947, 948, 1055, 1060, 1127, 1940, 2215

Social Work, 779, 1063, 1064, 1065, 1066, 1067, 1068, 1069, 1738, 1971, 2146, 2215

Sociology, 1069

Texas History, 762, 763

U.S. History, 754, 759

Wisconsin History, 754

Other/Miscellaneous

Athletic Training, 1315

Automotive/Diesel Studies, 159, 1320, 1321, 1322, 1323, 1470, 2234

Citizenship Studies, 1434

Community Service, 1971

Culinary Arts/Baking, 399, 1653

Historic Preservation, 758

Leadership, 1198, 1521

Metalsmithing, 396

Textiles 39, 2195, 2196, 2198, 2199, 2200, 2201, 2202, 2204, 2205

Pulp/Paper/Wood Fiber Studies, 39, 671, 1597

Woodworking, 396

Index of Criteria

Academic Record

ACT composite score of 15 to 17, 1035

ACT composite score of 18 to 19, 163, 1778, 1780, 2173

ACT composite score of 20 to 21, 508, 594, 663, 1158, 1256, 1732, 1752, 2087

ACT composite score of 22 to 23, 471, 636, 1100, 1149, 1176, 1208, 1231, 1726, 2100, 2149

ACT composite score of 24 to 25, 6, 29, 180, 226, 695, 968, 1014, 1019, 1021, 1183, 1211, 1240, 1243, 1245, 1257, 1258, 1264, 1658, 1710, 1716, 1734, 1747, 1781, 1907, 2104, 2113, 2114

ACT composite score of 26 to 27, 131, 133, 150, 494, 761, 942, 1119, 1139, 1151, 1161, 1196, 1236, 1246, 1260, 1265, 1298, 1782, 2040, 2117, 2139, 2140, 2161

ACT composite score of 28 to 29, 820, 1094, 1108, 1144, 1147, 1189, 1239, 1242, 1247, 1279, 1288, 1305, 2021, 2038

ACT composite score of 30 to 31, 38, 586, 607, 1076, 1077, 1078, 1107, 1111, 1134, 1163, 1175, 1199, 1203, 1206, 1209, 1213, 1225, 1230, 1234, 1235, 1236, 1241, 1244, 1249, 1259, 1278, 1304, 1976

ACT composite score of 32 to 33, 1115, 1186, 1236, 1268, 1297, 2004

Class rank in top 1%, 1118, 1222, 1259, 1296, 1377, 1998, 2017, 2183, 2189

Class rank in top 2%, 494, 1186

Class rank in top 3%, 1247, 2151

Class rank in top 5%, 1107, 1109, 1140, 1147, 1156, 1182, 1202, 1203, 1234, 1241, 1265, 1273, 1288, 1685, 1716, 1781, 2021, 2086, 2099, 2113, 2114, 2161

Class rank in top 7%, 1145, 1233

Class rank in top 8%, 1175

Class rank in top 10%, 131, 133, 150, 180, 447, 461, 462, 464, 465, 466, 467, 468, 470, 471, 472, 473, 474, 476, 477, 478, 479, 480, 481, 482, 483, 484, 485, 486, 487, 488, 489, 490, 491, 501, 942, 1075, 1082, 1091, 1093, 1108, 1119, 1176, 1185, 1199, 1225, 1229, 1242, 1249, 1258, 1264, 1279, 1360, 1630, 1693, 1760, 1764, 2027, 2074, 2149, 2152

Class rank in top 12%, 1189

Class rank in top 15%, 459, 998, 1104, 1161, 1239, 1304, 1305, 1407, 1715, 1929, 2218

Class rank in top 20%, 652, 797, 817, 995, 1183, 1240, 1246, 1294, 1625, 1627, 1689, 1752, 1765, 2122, 2165

Class rank in top 25%, 3, 158, 497, 560, 595, 625, 632, 649, 695, 937, 968, 1014, 1019, 1021, 1050, 1078, 1105, 1117, 1138, 1174, 1179, 1231, 1331, 1341, 1346, 1537, 1573, 1616, 1650, 1671, 1672, 1687, 1710, 1734, 1859, 2117

Class rank in top 30%, 1747

Class rank in top 33%, 492, 1342, 1450, 1605, 1634, 1638, 1778, 2173

Class rank in top 40%, 1539, 1938

Class rank in top 50%, 243, 637, 1347, 1491, 1535, 2221

GPA 2.0, 12, 14, 16, 17, 20, 22, 23, 24, 25, 26, 34, 37, 44, 48, 53, 202, 401, 446, 449, 454, 507, 515, 553, 571, 590, 598, 605, 611, 620, 660, 678, 845, 883, 1037, 1123, 1124, 1125, 1164, 1191, 1254, 1286, 1317, 1330, 1335, 1345, 1347, 1351, 1352, 1375, 1383, 1609, 1636, 1654, 1677, 1688, 1770, 1816, 1856, 1902, 1904, 1969, 1978, 2003, 2018, 2034, 2036, 2107, 2160, 2179, 2180, 2195, 2196, 2197, 2199, 2200, 2204, 2205, 2236, 2237, 2240, 2243, 2244, 2249, 2250, 2252

GPA 2.5, 59, 82, 91, 117, 237, 464, 619, 633, 661, 682, 796, 834, 905, 908, 1009, 1012, 1013, 1014, 1019, 1029, 1033, 1035, 1158, 1308, 1333, 1378, 1428, 1596, 1611, 1660, 1723, 1779, 1784, 2046, 2082, 2087

GPA 2.6, 1086, 1106

GPA 2.7, 497, 954, 1112, 1761, 1778, 2173, 2225

GPA 2.8, 2, 87, 88, 96, 894, 1680, 1714, 1938, 2010

GPA 3.0, 3, 4, 41, 54, 58, 85, 118, 125, 136, 138, 139, 140, 156, 157, 158, 160, 168, 180, 189, 193, 196, 214, 218, 220, 226, 239, 251, 309, 375, 388, 398, 402, 450, 453, 456, 457, 462, 471, 485, 487, 493, 496, 506, 508, 510, 519, 520, 535, 537, 550, 551, 567, 574, 580, 595, 597, 609, 625, 626, 628, 629, 632, 634, 636, 639, 647, 649, 683, 687, 689, 691, 695, 698, 706, 710, 726, 753, 793, 829, 830, 857, 863, 867, 869, 870, 875, 879, 889, 925, 937, 941, 953, 962, 966, 968, 1011, 1053, 1076, 1080, 1081, 1099, 1100, 1104, 1105, 1128, 1141, 1170, 1195, 1206, 1207, 1208, 1209, 1221, 1224, 1226, 1227, 1250, 1260, 1271, 1289, 1294, 1312, 1315, 1329, 1346, 1363, 1364, 1391, 1411, 1516, 1539, 1542, 1572, 1583, 1602, 1605, 1658, 1681, 1687, 1689, 1696, 1713, 1726, 1730, 1731, 1732, 1734, 1737, 1739, 1742, 1745, 1752, 1758, 1780, 1799, 1876, 1907, 1963, 1970, 1971, 1981, 1986, 2039, 2040, 2044, 2050, 2062, 2070, 2072, 2095, 2104, 2109, 2139, 2140, 2149, 2211

GPA 3.2, 159, 277, 460, 501, 524, 530, 563, 603, 604, 666, 670, 676, 923, 924, 1077, 1213, 1214, 1217, 1298, 1869, 1893, 1973, 2013, 2020, 2048, 2100

GPA 3.3, 512, 1097, 1159, 1256, 1858, 1859

GPA 3.4, 154, 667, 669, 673, 674, 1119, 2054, 2159

GPA 3.5, 6, 523, 572, 578, 593, 602, 608, 610, 614, 617, 618, 627, 638, 648, 652, 657, 659, 662, 761, 768, 914, 934, 1069, 1131, 1132, 1139, 1151, 1194, 1196, 1211, 1235, 1236, 1243, 1245, 1248, 1257, 1265, 1276, 1290, 1334, 1369, 1549, 1710, 1716, 1760, 1781, 1782, 1997, 2038, 2111, 2130

GPA 3.6, 1189, 2075

GPA 3.7, 653, 920, 1147, 1163, 1197, 1230, 1253, 1269, 1288, 1685, 2026, 2092, 2094

GPA 3.8, 494, 1175, 1234, 1244, 1263, 1278, 1297, 1976, 2004, 2156

GPA 3.9, 1186, 1259, 1926

GPA 4.0, 1115
Grade average of 90.0, 370
Grade average of 93.0, 1145, 1233
SAT combined score of 700 to 800, 1732, 1778, 1780, 2173
SAT combined score of 801 to 900, 493, 594, 663, 1033, 1035, 1256, 1752
SAT combined score of 901 to 1000, 6, 1014, 1021, 1176, 1208, 1264, 1671, 1710, 1716, 1726, 1781, 1907, 2149, 2183
SAT combined score of 1001 to 1100, 131, 150, 494, 535, 595, 625, 632, 647, 649, 942, 1119, 1151, 1185, 1211, 1240, 1243, 1257, 1260, 1265, 1298, 1658, 1764, 1765, 1782, 2113, 2114, 2139, 2140, 2165
SAT combined score of 1101 to 1200, 370, 586, 820, 1077, 1094, 1108, 1109, 1111, 1161, 1189, 1213, 1246, 1269, 1759, 1859, 1997, 2021, 2027, 2117, 2156
SAT combined score of 1201 to 1300, 607, 1078, 1107, 1134, 1144, 1145, 1175, 1199, 1206, 1209, 1225, 1233, 1235, 1244, 1247, 1278, 2038
SAT combined score of 1301 to 1400, 1115, 1186, 1203, 1249, 1268, 1297, 2004

Business/Corporation Affiliation

American National Can Company, 1602
AMETEK, 1603
AMR Corporation, 1601
Beatrice Company, 1910
"Big I" Association, 2119
Boys Club of America, 1557
Burlington Northern Railroad, 1605
Butler Manufacturing Company, 1606
Carpentry, 1631
Central Maine Power, 1360
Christian Ministry, 1639
Clemson University, 1609, 1636
Cone Mills Corporation, 1610
CSX Transportation Corporation, 1612
Dravo Corporation, 1614
Dun and Bradstreet, 1615
Eastman Kodak, 1616
Eaton Corporation, 1625
Farming, 10, 1471
Foreign Correspondent, 1600
General Motors Corporation, 1617
George A. Hormel & Company, 1620
Georgetown University, 1618
Gerber Products, 1621
Gibbs Wire & Steel Company, 1622
Gilbert Associates Inc., 1623
Golden Corral Corporation, 1611
Golf Course, 1619
Group Health Cooperative of Puget Sound, 1604
H.P. Hood Inc., 1607
Halton Company, 1624
Johnson Controls Inc., 1628
KETEMA, 1603
Kohler, 1630
Lone Star Industries, 1627
M.A. Hanna Company, 1632
McDonnell Douglas, 1634
Merit Oil Corporation, 1635
National Association of Broadcasters, 301
Naval Academy, 1875
New York City Transit Authority, 656
Ore-Ida Foods, 173
Outboard Marine Corporation, 1637
Panhandle Eastern Corporation, 1633
Peace Officer, 1515
Phelps Dodge, 2135
Pitney-Bowes, 1638
Prudential Insurance Company, 1640
Quaker Chemical, 1642
Rahr Malting Company, 1641
Seaway Foodtown, 1629
Stanadyne Inc., 1643
Stanley, 1931
State Farm Insurance, 1644
Stone Container Corporation, 1645
Swine Production, 1474
Teaching, 499
Texaco, 1646
Thomasville Furniture Industries Inc., 1647
Travel Industry, 214, 218
Wal-Mart, 1648
Washington Post, 1649
Waukeska Engine Division, 1626
Weyerhaeuser Company, 1651, 1652

City/County of Residence

Abingtons (PA), 365, 1341
Accomack (VA), 1374
Ada County (ID), 1442
Alamance County (NC), 1328
Allen County (OH), 1347
Anderson County (SC), 507
Anne Arundel County (MD), 140
Ashtabula County (OH), 1343
Asotin County (WA), 1442
Athabasca area (Canada), 1372
Auglaize County (OH), 1347
Baker County (OR), 1442
Baldwin County (AL), 250
Bannock County (ID), 1427
Bear Lake County (ID), 1427
Beloit (WI), 1342
Bexar County (TX), 1346
Bingham County (ID), 1427
Blaine County (ID), 1427
Bonneville County (ID), 1427
Boston (MA), 1331
Buchanan County (VA), 1382
Butte County (ID), 1427
Calhoun County (AL), 1357
Calhoun County (SC), 2179
Canosia (MN), 860
Canyon County (ID), 1442
Caribou County (ID), 1427
Carter County (TN), 1377
Cassia County (ID), 1427, 1442
Caswell County (NC), 1328
Central Valley (CA), 1592

Cereal Alberta (Canada), 2193
Chanago County (NY), 1362
Chesapeake (VA), 1374
Chester (SC), 2069
Chicago (IL), 1341, 1696
Cincinnati (OH), 978
Clackamas County (OR), 2058, 2071
Clarendon County (SC), 20
Clark County (ID), 1427
Clark County (WA), 2058
Clarke County (AL), 250
Clay County (AL), 1357
Clearwater County (ID), 1442
Cleveland (OH), 1341
Coastal California, 1592
Cocke County (TN), 1378, 1388
Colleton County (SC), 1351
Conecuh County (AL), 250
Cook County (IL), 556, 1365
Cumberland County (ME), 423
Custer County (ID), 1427
Dallas-Fort Worth (TX), 1601
Darlington County (SC), 20
Decatur County (IN), 1520
DeKalb County (IL), 556
Detroit (MI), 1341
Dickenson County (VA), 1382
Dillon County (SC), 20
Dorchester County (SC), 1335
Douglas County (OR), 1336, 1364
Duluth (MN), 117, 860
DuPage County (IL), 556, 1337
Durham County (NC), 1328
East Tennessee, 1756
Eastern Washington, 1592
Edgefield County (SC), 1999
Elizabethton (TN), 1377
Elmore (ID), 1442
Escambia County (AL), 250
Escambia County (FL), 250
Fairfax County (VA), 66
Farragut (TN), 636
Florence County (SC), 20
Floyd County (KY), 1010
Forsyth County (NC), 1328, 1456
Fox Valley (WI), 1341
Franklin County (ID), 1427
Fredricksburg area (VA), 1375
Fremont County (ID), 1427
Fresno County (CA), 807
Gem County (ID), 1442
George County (MS), 250
Georgetown County (SC), 20
Gooding County (ID), 1442
Grant (AL), 1514
Granville County (NC), 1328
Greensboro (NC), 1328
Greenville County (SC), 1330, 1345
Guilford County (NC), 1328
Hampton (TN), 1377
Hampton (VA), 1374
Hanna Alberta (Canada), 2193

Hartford County (CT), 1340
Hermantown (MN), 860
High Point (NC), 1328
Hohenwald (TN), 636
Holly Hill (SC), 1352
Horry County (SC), 7, 20
Houston (TX), 160, 1678, 2057
Isle of Wight (VA), 1374
Jackson County (IN), 1520
Janesville (WI), 1355, 1370
Jasper County (SC), 16
Jefferson County (ID), 1427
Jerome County (ID), 1427, 1442
Johnson County (KY), 1010
Kane County (IL), 556
Kansas City (KS), 1586
Kendall County (IL), 556
Knott County (KY), 1010
Knoxville (TN), 1756
Lake County (IL), 556
Lake County (OR), 1327, 1366
Lancaster County (SC), 1368, 2069
Las Cruces (NM), 878
Laurens County (SC), 48
Lee County (SC), 20
Lee County (VA), 1382
Lemhi County (ID), 1427
Lewis County (ID), 1442
Lexington County (SC), 1999
Lincoln County (ID), 1427, 1442
Logan County (OK), 1390
Los Angeles County (CA), 297
Ludlow (KY), 163
Madera County (CA), 807
Madison County (ID), 1427
Malheur County (OR), 1442
Marin County (CA), 1326, 1354, 1381, 1387
Marion County (SC), 20
Marlboro County (SC), 17, 20
Martin County (KY), 1010
McHenry County (IL), 556
Merrifield (VA), 396
Middlesex County (NJ), 1367
Midway (MN), 860
Milwaukee (WI), 1341
Minidoka County (ID), 1427
Mobile County (AL), 250, 1271
Monroe County (AL), 250
Morristown (TN), 191
Mount Vernon (NY), 1383
Mountain View (CA), 1326, 1354, 1381, 1387
Multnomah County (OR), 2058, 2071
Nassau County (NY), 1325
New London (CT), 1363
New York (NY), 1356, 1385
Newberry County (SC), 1375, 1999
Newport News (VA), 1374
Nez Perce County (ID), 1442
North Knox (IN), 1468
Northeast Poconos (PA), 365
Northern Kentucky, 1005
Northwest Kansas, 1334
Oconee County (SC), 507, 1299

Omaha (NE), 1341
Oneida County (ID), 1427
Ooltewah (TN), 636
Orange County (CA), 297, 643
Orange County (NC), 1328
Otsego County (NY), 1362
Owyhee County (ID), 1442
Oxford County (ME), 423
Oyen Alberta (Canada), 2193
Palo Alto (CA), 1326, 1354, 1381, 1387
Payette County (ID), 1442
Perry County (KY), 1010
Person County (NC), 1328
Pickens County (SC), 507, 1371, 2180
Pike County (KY), 1010
Portsmouth (VA), 1374
Power County (ID), 1427
Prince George's County (MD), 1373
Proctor (MN), 860
Provost area (Canada), 1372
Pueblo County (CO), 2028
Rice Lake (MN), 860
Richland County (SC), 1329
Rockingham County (NC), 1328
Russell County (VA), 1382
Saginaw (MI), 1359
Saint Louis (MO), 1341
Saint Louis County (MN), 117
Saluda County (SC), 1999
San Bernardino County (CA), 1770, 1771
San Diego (CA), 1818
San Diego County (CA), 297
San Francisco County (CA), 1326, 1354, 1381, 1387
San Luis Valley (CO), 1338
San Mateo County (CA), 1326, 1354, 1381, 1387
Sand Springs (OK), 1349
Santa Barbara (CA), 297, 1379
Santa Rosa County (FL), 250
Scott County (VA), 1382
Sonoma County (CA), 1326, 1354, 1381, 1387
South Knox (IN), 1468
Southern California Edison service area, 1333, 1353, 1376, 1380
Southern Idaho, 1592
Stokes County (NC), 1328
Suffolk (VA), 1374
Suffolk County (NY), 1325
Surry County (NC), 1328
Tamassee (SC), 1514
Teton County (ID), 1427
Toledo (OH), 1350, 1386, 1389
Toledo area (OH), 1324, 1358
Travis County (TX), 1339
Tulsa (OK), 1349
Turtle Rock County (WI), 1342
Tuscaloosa County (AL), 1384
Twin Cities (MN), 1341
Twin Falls County (ID), 1442
Umatilla County (OR), 1442
Unicoi (TN), 1377
Union County (OR), 1442
Virginia Beach (VA), 1374

Walla Walla County (WA), 1344
Washington County (AL), 250, 1120
Washington County (ID), 1442
Washington County (ME), 1361
Washington County (OR), 2058, 2071
Washington County (VA), 1382
Washington metropolitan area (DC), 82
Waukesha (WI), 1626
Wenatchee area (WA), 1369
Western Washington, 1369
Westlock area (Canada), 1372
Will County (IL), 556
Willamette Valley (OR), 1592
Williamsburg County (SC), 20
Williamson County (TX), 1339
Wise County (VA), 1382
Yakima area (WA), 1369
York (SC), 2069
York County (ME), 423
York County (SC), 1375
Youngstown Alberta (Canada), 2193

Club Affiliation

4-H, 29, 1393, 1395, 1396, 1397, 1398, 1413, 1420, 1423, 1434, 1435, 1436, 1437, 1443, 1445, 1447, 1455, 1460, 1461, 1462, 1463, 1466, 1484, 1485, 1486, 1487, 1489, 1493, 1496, 1501, 1505, 1508, 1521, 1541, 1546, 1547, 1548, 1550, 1558, 1562, 1565, 1574, 1588, 1594, 1597
AAAA, 518
AHIMA, 62, 68, 80, 83
Air Force Sergeants Association, 1825, 1855, 1883
Air Force Sergeants Association Auxiliary, 1825
Alpha Kappa Alpha, 1399, 1400
American Academy of Physician Assistants, 86
American Association of Retired Persons, 1795
American Association of University Women, 1815
American Chemical Society, 892
American College of Healthcare Executives, 1403, 1490
American Dental Hygienists' Association, 85
American Fisheries Society, 30
American Geophysical Union, 928
American Guild of Organists, 415
American Home Economics Association, 974
American Indian Science & Engineering Society, 1654
American Institute of Chemical Engineers, 530
American Legion, 329, 1402, 1510, 1563, 1835, 1861, 1882, 1937
American Legion Auxiliary, 1402, 1563, 1571, 1869, 1893, 2025, 2048
American Library Association, 267, 272
American Nuclear Society, 699
American Orff-Schulwerk Association, 1502
American Radio Relay League, 292
American Society for Photogrammetry and Remote Sensing, 1522
American Society of Civil Engineers, 534, 541, 543, 544, 545, 546, 552, 558, 561, 583
American Society of Mechanical Engineers, 677, 680
American Society of Safety Engineers, 613, 640
American Water Ski Association, 1311

American Water Ski Educational Foundation, 1311
Association of Railroad Advertising and Marketing, 1414
Association of School Business Officials International, 1416
Aunts at Large, 1556
B.P. Elks of the U.S.A., 1156
Beta Theta Pi, 1421
Big Brothers, 1415, 1556
Big Sisters, 1415, 1556
Boy Scouts of America, 1419, 1459, 1512, 1525, 1563, 1564
Boys and Girls Clubs of Chicago, 1406, 1596, 2234
Brooklyn Polish National Alliance, 778
Canadian Progress Club Calgary, 1556
Catholic Library Association, 289
Chi Eta Phi Sorority, 831
Civitan International, 1121
Danish Sisterhood of America, 1448
Daughters of Penelope, 1500
Delta Gamma, 1452, 1453
Descendants of the Signers of the Declaration of Independence, 1454
Distributive Education Clubs of America, 200, 1450
Fifth Marine Division Association, 1481
Fraternal Order of UDT/SEAL, 1492
Future Farmers of America, 5, 8, 10, 29, 1394, 1401, 1404, 1405, 1407, 1408, 1409, 1410, 1411, 1412, 1417, 1418, 1422, 1424, 1425, 1426, 1427, 1429, 1430, 1431, 1432, 1433, 1438, 1439, 1440, 1442, 1444, 1446, 1449, 1451, 1456, 1457, 1458, 1464, 1465, 1467, 1468, 1469, 1470, 1471, 1472, 1473, 1474, 1475, 1476, 1477, 1478, 1479, 1480, 1482, 1483, 1488, 1494, 1495, 1498, 1503, 1504, 1506, 1507, 1509, 1511, 1513, 1519, 1520, 1523, 1526, 1527, 1528, 1530, 1531, 1532, 1534, 1535, 1536, 1538, 1540, 1543, 1544, 1551, 1552, 1554, 1559, 1560, 1561, 1569, 1570, 1580, 1581, 1582, 1584, 1585, 1586, 1587, 1589, 1590, 1592, 1593, 1595, 2182
General Federation of Women's Clubs of Massachusetts, 425, 2098
Girls Incorporated, 1497
High Twelve International, 1983
Institute of Industrial Engineers, 667, 669, 673, 674
International Buckskin Horse Association, 1599
Jaycee, 1579
Junior Girls Unit of the Ladies Auxiliary to the Veterans of Foreign Wars, 1518
Kappa Epsilon, 106
Kappa Kappa Gamma, 1499
Knights of Columbus, 1967, 1977
Loyal Christian Benefit Association, 2211
Lutheran Brotherhood, 1973
Maids of Athena, 1500
Military Order of the Purple Heart, 1529
Modern Woodmen of America, 1491
NAACP, 1660, 1739, 1779
National Association of Plumbing-Heating-Cooling Contractors, 681
National Athletic Trainers Association, 1315
National Campers and Hikers Association, 1539
National Foster Parent Association, 1669

National Honor Society, 1210
National Junior Classical League, 704
National Rifle Association, 1515
National Roofing Contractors Association, 557
National Society of Professional Engineers, 626
National Society of Public Accountants, 1572
National Society of the Daughters of the American Revolution, 114, 756, 758, 814, 833, 1057, 1514, 1524
Naval Academy Women's Club, 1875
New Mexico Rural Electric Cooperative, 1428
New Mexico Rural Telephone COOP, 1428
Order of Ahepa, 1500
Order of United Commercial Travelers of America, 517
Phi Theta Kappa, 1223
Phi Upsilon Omicron, 969, 970, 971
Pi Mu Epsilon, 915
Poetry Society of America, 741, 747
Pride of Oklahoma Marching Band, 416
Reserve Officers Association of the United States, 1858, 1859
Rotary, 574, 1392, 1441, 1533
Royal Neighbors of America, 1537
Sigma Alpha Epsilon, 1517, 1553
Sigma Chi, 1567
Sigma Delta Chi, 1591
Sigma Iota Epsilon, 1566
Society for the Advancement of Material and Process Engineering, 643
Society of Broadcast Engineers, 300
Society of Naval Architects and Marine Engineers, 642
Society of Women Engineers, 523, 608, 652
Soil and Water Conservation Society, 901
State Garden Club, 55
Tau Beta Pi, 1575, 1576, 1577
The Honor Society of Phi Kappa Phi, 1545
The Retired Officers Association, 1583
Theta Delta Chi, 1578
Transportation Clubs International, 219
Uncles at Large, 1556
University Film and Video Association, 381
Varisty Scout, 1563
World Federalist Association, 1172
Young American Bowling Alliance/Youth Division, 1598

Gender/Marital Status

Men, 253, 455, 1459, 1517, 1553, 1557, 1804, 1808, 1816, 1818, 1834, 2033, 2196
Single, 62, 972, 1500, 1583, 1797, 1799, 1808, 1809, 1810, 1825, 1826, 1827, 1853, 1855, 1883, 1888, 1890, 1898, 2209, 2244
Women, 30, 63, 105, 125, 132, 140, 156, 174, 369, 460, 507, 511, 523, 569, 572, 578, 588, 593, 596, 599, 602, 603, 606, 608, 610, 614, 617, 618, 622, 625, 627, 632, 638, 644, 648, 652, 657, 659, 662, 665, 673, 689, 754, 923, 924, 925, 946, 960, 972, 989, 1002, 1312, 1411, 1500, 1696, 1795, 1797, 1798, 1799, 1800, 1801, 1802, 1803, 1805, 1806, 1807, 1809, 1810, 1811, 1812, 1813, 1814, 1815, 1817, 1819, 1820, 1821, 1844, 1852, 1864, 1869,

1934, 1946, 1959, 1968, 1980, 1984, 1994, 2002, 2012, 2030, 2044, 2048, 2089, 2098, 2201

Handicapped Students —

Blind, 1932, 1933, 1934, 1935, 1940, 1942, 1943, 1944, 1946, 1947, 1948, 1949, 1950, 1953, 1954, 1955, 1956, 1957, 1959, 1961, 1962, 1966, 1990
Deaf, 1935, 1941, 1951, 1952, 1963, 1966
Disabled, 479, 1939, 1958, 1964, 1965, 2044
Handicapped, 1403, 1424, 1425, 1762
Hearing Impaired, 1941, 1951, 1952
Permanent Disability, 1938
Physically Disabled, 1424, 1425, 1936, 1945, 1960

Military Affiliation —

102rd Infantry Division, 1822
37th Infantry Division, 1823
Air Force, 1023, 1024, 1824, 1825, 1826, 1827, 1846, 1853, 1855, 1856, 1883
Air Force Reserve, 1825, 1826, 1827, 1855, 1883
Air Force ROTC, 1012, 1013, 1014, 1016, 1017, 1018, 1019, 1022
Air National Guard, 1825, 1826, 1827, 1855, 1883
Alabama National Guard, 1830
American Legion, 1867
Armed Forces, 1884, 1896, 2092
Army, 1030, 1036, 1042, 1048, 1844, 1846, 1852, 1864, 1888
Army Reserve, 1025, 1870
Army ROTC, 1026, 1028, 1029, 1032, 1033, 1034, 1038, 1039, 1040, 1041
Civil Air Patrol, 1839, 1845, 1857, 1863, 1894, 1895
Coast Guard, 1846, 1865, 1879
Deceased or Disabled Veteran, 1851
Deceased Veteran, 1828, 1842, 1843, 1867, 1880, 1881, 1885, 1886, 1891, 1899
Disabled Veteran, 1828, 1842, 1843, 1860, 1880, 1885, 1886, 1891, 1900
Fleet Reserve Association, 1854
Fourth Infantry Division, 1872
KIA, 1867, 1884
Ladies Auxiliary of the Fleet Reserve Association, 1854
Marine, 1481
Marine Corps, 1043, 1046, 1212, 1846, 1865, 1866, 1875, 1879, 1887, 1901
Medal of Honor winner, 1891
MIA, 1828, 1840, 1848, 1867, 1881, 1884, 1885, 1886, 1891, 1892
National Guard, 1025, 1841
Naval ROTC, 1044, 1045
Navy, 1043, 1046, 1047, 1212, 1481, 1838, 1846, 1850, 1865, 1875, 1879, 1887, 1897, 1901
Navy Supply Corps, 1876
Non Commissioned Officers Association, 1877
POW, 1828, 1840, 1848, 1867, 1881, 1884, 1885, 1886, 1891, 1892
Reserves, 79
ROTC, 1037
Seabees, 1889
Second Marine Division, 1890
U.S. Submarine Veterans of World War II, 1898

Veteran, 1829, 1831, 1832, 1833, 1834, 1835, 1836, 1837, 1847, 1849, 1862, 1868, 1869, 1873, 1874, 1878, 1882, 1893, 1902, 2025, 2048, 2174

National Merit Status —

Hispanic Honorable Mention Awardee, 1988
National Achievement Commended Student, 1737
National Achievement finalist, 1737, 1915, 1916, 1917, 1919, 1928, 1930, 1988, 2026, 2038
National Achievement scholar, 1259, 1911, 1912, 1988
National Achievement semifinalist, 1076, 1199, 1737, 1913, 1917
National Hispanic finalist, 1740
National Hispanic scholar, 1259, 1914, 1988
National Hispanic semifinalist, 1913
National Merit finalist, 1268, 1909, 1914, 1918, 1919, 1920, 1921, 1922, 1924, 1925, 1928, 1929, 1930, 1988, 2001, 2026, 2038
National Merit scholar, 1110, 1616, 1910, 1911, 1912, 1923, 1926, 1927, 1988
National Merit semifinalist, 1076, 1148, 1199, 1225, 1259, 1913, 1914, 1922
Presidential scholar, 1988

Race/Ethnicity —

Aboriginal Canadian, 976
Albanian, 1655
Aleut, 925, 956, 1702
American, 727
American Indian, 621, 658, 855, 893, 894, 956, 1523, 1617, 1661, 1684, 1702, 1727, 1769, 1773, 2044, 2058, 2076
Armenian, 1659, 1667
Asian, 251, 1727, 1769
Asian-American, 253, 256, 257, 621, 658, 1617, 1668, 1685, 1689, 1714, 1735, 1760, 1982
Asian/Pacific Islander, 138, 230, 257, 268, 279, 282, 596, 599, 606, 855, 911, 947, 948, 956, 1473, 1523, 1722, 1727, 1730, 1769, 1785, 2044, 2076
Black/African-American, 135, 138, 160, 221, 230, 232, 237, 251, 268, 279, 282, 309, 391, 414, 454, 457, 594, 596, 599, 606, 621, 658, 663, 784, 785, 786, 796, 838, 844, 855, 893, 894, 911, 925, 947, 948, 956, 1002, 1070, 1074, 1266, 1324, 1358, 1473, 1523, 1617, 1656, 1658, 1660, 1666, 1668, 1671, 1675, 1679, 1680, 1685, 1689, 1699, 1706, 1710, 1714, 1715, 1716, 1722, 1726, 1727, 1729, 1730, 1731, 1732, 1734, 1735, 1736, 1737, 1739, 1742, 1752, 1757, 1758, 1759, 1760, 1764, 1766, 1769, 1779, 1783, 1784, 1785, 1786, 1787, 1982, 2017, 2044, 2054, 2064, 2076, 2108, 2159, 2177, 2178
British, 511
Caribbean, 2072
Central American, 2044, 2072
Chicano, 1677, 1775, 2044
Chinese, 1678
Eskimo, 893, 894, 925, 956, 1702
Filipino, 257, 2044
French, 511
German, 511
Greek, 1696
Hawaiian, 893, 894

Hispanic, 135, 138, 160, 230, 251, 268, 279, 282, 309, 454, 457, 592, 596, 599, 606, 621, 658, 796, 855, 893, 894, 911, 925, 956, 1070, 1074, 1350, 1473, 1523, 1617, 1656, 1666, 1668, 1671, 1681, 1685, 1689, 1700, 1701, 1710, 1714, 1722, 1730, 1734, 1735, 1736, 1740, 1741, 1757, 1758, 1760, 1769, 1781, 1783, 1785, 1787, 1982, 2064, 2072, 2076, 2177, 2178

Irish, 511

Italian-American, 170, 258, 436, 443, 511, 706, 1665, 1672, 1690, 1694, 1697, 1705, 1717, 1743, 1744, 1755, 1768, 1776, 1790, 1792, 1970

Jewish, 1972, 2051

Korean, 257

Latino, 1727, 1731, 1775

Mexican-American/Chicano, 621, 658, 947, 948, 1617, 2044, 2072

Miccosukee Indian, 2166

Micronesian, 956

Minority, 35, 156, 173, 195, 223, 224, 226, 228, 234, 236, 266, 276, 281, 285, 296, 298, 336, 343, 448, 452, 460, 479, 595, 616, 622, 650, 674, 792, 800, 812, 819, 821, 829, 830, 832, 879, 880, 881, 882, 923, 924, 953, 978, 984, 992, 1068, 1084, 1149, 1301, 1353, 1376, 1403, 1657, 1670, 1674, 1682, 1683, 1687, 1693, 1695, 1698, 1704, 1707, 1708, 1709, 1711, 1720, 1721, 1723, 1724, 1725, 1728, 1733, 1738, 1746, 1747, 1748, 1751, 1753, 1756, 1758, 1761, 1762, 1763, 1765, 1778, 1780, 1805, 1907, 1916, 1964, 1965, 1999, 2057, 2104, 2146, 2172, 2173, 2195, 2201

Native Alaskan, 282, 621, 658, 911, 947, 948, 956, 1473, 1523, 1617, 1702, 1727, 1730, 1769, 1773, 1975, 1982, 2076

Native American, 73, 135, 138, 160, 230, 251, 268, 279, 282, 592, 596, 599, 606, 796, 893, 894, 911, 925, 947, 948, 1070, 1074, 1473, 1654, 1662, 1663, 1666, 1668, 1673, 1685, 1688, 1689, 1691, 1703, 1712, 1714, 1719, 1722, 1730, 1731, 1735, 1736, 1758, 1760, 1770, 1771, 1774, 1777, 1783, 1785, 1787, 1788, 1793, 1975, 1982, 2064

Osage Indian, 1808

Polish, 146, 231, 727, 1676, 1789

Polish-American, 727

Polynesian, 925, 956

Portuguese, 1713

Puerto Rican, 621, 658, 947, 948, 1617, 2044

Samoan, 893, 894

Scandinavian, 511

Seminole Indian, 2166

Seneca Indian, 1772

Slavic, 511

South American, 2044, 2072

Soviet Jew, 725

Spanish, 2072

Swiss, 1754, 1782

Washoe, 1767

Yakima Indian, 1794

Religious Affiliation

Christian, 263, 264, 1639, 1789

Christian Church, 784, 785, 786

Church of Jesus Christ of Latter-day Saints, 1976

Church of the Brethren, 841

Congregational, 1340

Episcopal, 1979, 1980

Evangelical Lutheran Church in America, 826, 1984

Jewish, 721, 725, 787, 788, 789, 1326, 1354, 1365, 1381, 1387, 1971

Mason, 1983

Presbyterian Church (USA), 1974, 1975, 1982

Roman Catholic, 1359, 1967, 1968, 1970, 1977, 1985

Sikh, 1981

United Methodist, 1969, 1978

Sports

Athletics, 1314

Basketball, 1310

Bowling, 1308, 1598

Golf, 247, 1312, 1650, 1820, 1991

Lacrosse, 1310

Pan American Games team, 1316

Track, 1310

United States Olympic Team, 1316

United States Ski Team, 1318

Water Skiing, 1311

State/Country of Residence

Alabama, 8, 313, 368, 499, 1262, 1280, 1314, 1401, 1426, 1480, 1506, 1554, 1829, 1830, 1831, 1832, 1990, 2004, 2136

Alaska, 84, 1501, 1992

Alberta, 178, 798, 809, 1993, 2035, 2041, 2065, 2070

Alberta Canada, 2193

American hemisphere countries, 2042

Arizona, 8, 84, 210, 297, 697, 1431, 1480, 1501, 1506, 1561, 1562, 1593, 1770, 1771, 1986, 2001

Arkansas, 8, 1426, 1480, 1506, 1554, 1581, 2138, 2182

California, 8, 84, 160, 223, 268, 283, 285, 462, 1312, 1431, 1449, 1480, 1483, 1501, 1504, 1506, 1554, 1561, 1562, 1573, 1584, 1593, 1713, 1841, 1842, 1843, 1874, 1986, 1997, 2044, 2138, 2182

Canada, 46, 67, 71, 121, 161, 171, 176, 178, 266, 271, 272, 276, 278, 279, 280, 282, 287, 288, 337, 400, 404, 517, 538, 550, 559, 587, 591, 600, 601, 623, 642, 654, 664, 688, 689, 701, 718, 719, 720, 723, 743, 744, 745, 765, 784, 785, 786, 803, 856, 874, 888, 903, 929, 938, 965, 1054, 1058, 1070, 1106, 1372, 1403, 1490, 1500, 1655, 1963, 1993, 1994, 2000, 2002, 2011, 2012, 2013, 2020, 2030, 2035, 2041, 2043, 2055, 2056, 2065, 2070, 2073, 2089, 2162, 2192, 2216

Caribbean, 1341

Colorado, 8, 84, 697, 1426, 1480, 1498, 1501, 1504, 1506, 1519, 1561, 1562, 1573, 1593, 1770, 1771, 1989, 2005, 2037, 2054, 2090, 2159, 2182

Connecticut, 235, 794, 1480, 1506, 1525, 1754, 1879, 2151, 2165

Delaware, 8, 795, 1480, 1506, 1754, 1755

District of Columbia, 464, 834

Finland, 711

Florida, 8, 315, 1263, 1480, 1506, 1554, 1573, 1745, 1833, 1885, 2036, 2038, 2072, 2095, 2110, 2166, 2186

Georgia, 8, 63, 246, 466, 802, 1480, 1506, 1554, 2036, 2181

Greece, 1500

Guam, 654, 903, 2133

Haiti, 1745

Hawaii, 84, 157, 158, 1480

Idaho, 8, 84, 467, 760, 843, 1426, 1431, 1449, 1480, 1501, 1506, 1593, 1881, 2134, 2138, 2171, 2182

Illinois, 8, 76, 151, 237, 316, 448, 468, 494, 535, 595, 1426, 1460, 1465, 1467, 1477, 1479, 1480, 1498, 1504, 1506, 1510, 1511, 1519, 1540, 1561, 1562, 1573, 1581, 1782, 2099, 2182

Indiana, 8, 52, 76, 317, 454, 469, 515, 595, 854, 1006, 1439, 1460, 1465, 1467, 1479, 1480, 1498, 1504, 1506, 1511, 1520, 1528, 1552, 1573, 1581, 1804

Iowa, 8, 76, 260, 318, 1426, 1438, 1460, 1465, 1480, 1498, 1504, 1506, 1519, 1540, 1573, 1581, 1593, 1938, 2010, 2182

Kansas, 8, 319, 470, 1426, 1460, 1467, 1480, 1498, 1506, 1519, 1561, 1562, 1573, 1581, 1593, 1770, 1771, 2066, 2076, 2077, 2078, 2079, 2080, 2081, 2182, 2185

Kentucky, 8, 986, 1006, 1008, 1467, 1480, 1504, 1506, 1581

Louisiana, 8, 59, 277, 471, 508, 1480, 1506, 2086, 2087, 2182

Maine, 1317, 1360, 1480, 1506, 1525, 1862, 2088, 2167

Maryland, 8, 116, 446, 472, 496, 863, 1480, 1506, 1581, 1755, 1834, 1851, 2023, 2026, 2031, 2046, 2063, 2132, 2168, 2235

Massachusetts, 425, 1506, 1525, 1755, 2016, 2097, 2098

Mexico, 538, 654, 688, 874, 903

Michigan, 8, 52, 76, 160, 473, 1439, 1460, 1465, 1479, 1480, 1498, 1504, 1506, 1552, 1573, 1581, 1690, 2101, 2102

Minnesota, 8, 76, 855, 1409, 1426, 1438, 1460, 1465, 1480, 1498, 1504, 1506, 1519, 1531, 1540, 1573, 1581, 1593, 1848, 1849, 2103, 2115, 2138, 2145

Mississippi, 8, 474, 502, 852, 1426, 1480, 1506, 1581, 1892, 2085

Missouri, 8, 459, 475, 1409, 1426, 1457, 1460, 1465, 1467, 1480, 1498, 1504, 1506, 1519, 1561, 1562, 1573, 1581, 1593, 2021, 2074, 2091, 2105, 2106, 2152, 2161, 2182

Montana, 8, 84, 476, 697, 1426, 1480, 1501, 1506, 1573, 1581, 1593, 1801, 2052, 2082

Nebraska, 8, 76, 916, 1426, 1438, 1460, 1465, 1467, 1480, 1498, 1504, 1506, 1519, 1540, 1573, 1581, 1593, 1683, 1867, 2147, 2182

Nevada, 8, 84, 570, 1480, 1501, 1506, 1593, 2138, 2182

New England, 57, 1929, 1950

New Hampshire, 477, 1480, 1506, 1525, 2015, 2024, 2093, 2112

New Jersey, 1323, 1506, 1750, 1754, 1755, 1861, 1879, 1950, 2109

New Mexico, 2, 8, 27, 84, 574, 682, 697, 1480, 1506, 1561, 1562, 1593, 1770, 1771, 1878, 2113, 2114, 2135, 2139, 2140, 2149

New York, 81, 478, 821, 957, 1460, 1480, 1506, 1581, 1754, 1755, 1777, 1868, 1879, 1950, 2146, 2148, 2153

Nicaragua, 1745

North America, 511

North Carolina, 8, 447, 479, 493, 792, 800, 1433, 1467, 1480, 1506, 1554, 1662, 1729, 1886, 1961, 2036, 2059, 2068, 2096, 2119, 2120, 2121, 2154

North Dakota, 8, 76, 697, 1426, 1438, 1460, 1465, 1480, 1504, 1506, 1519, 1573, 1581, 1593, 1703, 2122

Northern California, 570

Norway, 719

Ohio, 8, 52, 76, 480, 595, 630, 1006, 1439, 1460, 1465, 1467, 1479, 1480, 1498, 1504, 1506, 1528, 1552, 1581, 1685, 1689, 1760, 1880, 2025, 2045, 2124, 2125, 2155

Oklahoma, 8, 130, 481, 639, 1003, 1426, 1460, 1480, 1504, 1506, 1519, 1561, 1562, 1573, 1593, 1724, 1746, 1770, 1771, 1988, 2033, 2040, 2075, 2100, 2104, 2144, 2182, 2194

Oregon, 8, 84, 482, 570, 1216, 1217, 1332, 1348, 1426, 1449, 1480, 1501, 1506, 1573, 1593, 1991, 1995, 2006, 2022, 2029, 2039, 2049, 2064, 2071, 2083, 2084, 2092, 2108, 2127, 2128, 2129, 2130, 2137, 2142, 2143, 2150, 2156, 2182, 2187, 2191

Pennsylvania, 8, 52, 483, 1265, 1460, 1480, 1504, 1506, 1581, 1754, 1755, 1950, 1980

Poland, 727

Puerto Rico, 654, 903, 1341, 1480

Rhode Island, 484, 1480, 1525

South Carolina, 8, 12, 16, 20, 22, 23, 24, 34, 35, 262, 633, 1375, 1467, 1480, 1506, 1891, 1996, 1999, 2003, 2007, 2008, 2009, 2017, 2018, 2034, 2036, 2047, 2060, 2069, 2107, 2131, 2160, 2169, 2179, 2180, 2183, 2196, 2199

South Dakota, 8, 76, 1426, 1438, 1460, 1480, 1498, 1504, 1506, 1519, 1573, 1581, 1593

South Florida, 249

Southeastern United States, 1756

Southern Wisconsin, 1782

Tennessee, 6, 8, 226, 328, 340, 485, 500, 636, 1426, 1467, 1480, 1506, 1581, 1732, 1756, 1780, 1998, 2111

Texas, 1, 8, 162, 259, 329, 457, 487, 535, 697, 763, 779, 861, 862, 1264, 1426, 1467, 1480, 1504, 1506, 1519, 1561, 1562, 1573, 1581, 1593, 1710, 1778, 1840, 2014, 2050, 2067, 2157, 2164, 2172, 2173, 2176, 2177, 2178, 2182

United Kingdom, 49

Utah, 8, 84, 488, 697, 1480, 1501, 1506, 1593, 1796, 2182

Vermont, 1506, 1525, 2184

Virginia, 8, 330, 395, 489, 1374, 1433, 1480, 1506, 1755, 2027

Washington, 8, 84, 453, 461, 570, 1426, 1449, 1480, 1501, 1506, 1573, 1584, 1593, 1604, 1661, 2170, 2182, 2189

Washington D.C., 637, 1755, 1941

West Virginia, 8, 52, 491, 501, 1480, 1506, 1528, 1790, 1902, 2190

Wisconsin, 8, 76, 331, 595, 1342, 1409, 1438, 1460, 1465, 1480, 1498, 1504, 1506, 1519, 1531, 1540, 1573, 1581, 1793, 1869, 1893, 1966, 2048

Wyoming, 8, 84, 697, 1480, 1506, 1519, 1573, 1593, 2182

Union Affiliation

Air Line Pilots Association, 2206

Amalgamated Clothing and Textile Workers Union, 2207

American Association of Critical-Care Nurses, 829, 830

American Postal Workers Union, 2214

American School Food Service Association, 2225

American Society of Heating/Refrigeration/Air Conditioning Engineering, 579

Bakery/Confectionery/Tobacco Workers International Union, 2208

California Teachers Association, 2212, 2227

International Association of Bridge/Structural/Ornamental Ironworkers, 2221

International Association of Machinists and Aerospace Workers, 2217

International Brotherhood of Teamsters, 2218

International Ladies' Garment Workers' Union, 2215, 2223

International Union of Bricklayers and Allied Craftsmen, 2216

Intl. Union of Electronic/Electrical/Salaried/Machine/Furniture Workers, 2213, 2220, 2232

Iowa Federation of Labor AFL-CIO, 2219

Portland Teachers' Credit Union (OR), 2137

Seafarers International Union, 2209, 2210

Service Employees International Union, 2226

Slovenian Women's Union of America, 1568

United Food and Commercial Workers International Union, 2228

United Paperworkers International Union, 2224, 2229

United Rubber/Cork/Linoleum/Plastic Workers of America, 2222, 2230

Utility Workers Union of America, 2231

Index of Scholarships

A

A. Harvey and Mary E. Snell Scholarship, 41

A. Martin and Ruth Zucker Memorial Scholarship, 444

A.J. (Andy) Spielman Scholarship, 205

A.L. Simmons Scholarship, 206

A.T. Anderson Memorial Scholarship, 1654

A.T.J. Cairns Memorial Undergraduate Scholarship, 729

A.W. Bodine–Sunkist Memorial Scholarship, 1986

AAA Fellowship, 121

AAAA Scholarship Grant Program, 518

AAAS Mass Media Science and Engineering Fellows Program, 932

AACC Graduate Fellowships, 933

AACC Undergraduate Scholarships, 4

AACN Educational Advancement Scholarship for B.S.N. Students, 829

AACN Educational Advancement Scholarship for Graduate Students, 830

AADR Student Research Fellowship, 791

AANO Scholarship, 1655

AAOA Scholarship Award, 797

AARL Foundation Scholarships, 292

AARP Women's Initiative 10th Anniversary Scholarship, 1795

Abel Wolman Fellowship, 538

ABWA Severn River Chapter Scholarship, 140

Academic Distinction Scholarship, 1075

Academic Excellence Award Scholarship, 1987

Academic Excellence Scholarship, 1076, 1077, 1078, 1656

Academic Grant, 1079

Academic Honors Transfer Scholarship, 1080

Academic Opportunity Scholarship, 1081

Academic Scholars Program, 1988

Academic Scholarship, 1082

Academic Scholarship for Frosh Students, 1083

Academic Year Ambassadorial Scholarship, 1392

ACB Scholarship, 1932

Achievement Award, 1393

Achievement Class Award, 1084

Achievement Reward for College Scientists (ARCS) Foundation Scholarship, 934

Achievers Award, 1657

ACL/NJCL National Latin Examination Scholarship, 700

ACLS/Chiang Ching–kuo Foundation Fellowships for Dissertation Research Abroad, 705

Actuarial Scholarships for Minority Students, 195

ADA Scholarship, 90

Adelle and Erwin Tomash Fellowship in the History of Information Processing, 562

ADHA Scholarship, 85

Administration and Business Alumni Scholarship, 141

Admiral Grace Murray Hopper Scholarship, 572

Adrian Berryhill Family Agriculture Scholarship, 27

Aduct Scholarship, 1085

Advanced Predoctoral Fellowship in Pharmaceutics, 97

Advanced Predoctoral Fellowship in Pharmacology/Toxicology, 98

Advocacy Diversity Award, 1989

AEJ Summer Internship Program, AEJ Minority Summer Internship Program, 230

AEJMC Correspondents Fund Scholarship in Journalism, 1600

AFAR Scholarship, 871

Affirmative Action Scholarship, 266

AFPE Fellowships, 99

AFPE Gateway Scholarship, 100

African-American/Black Students Scholarship, 1658

AGA Educational Grant, 917

AGBU Fellowship Program, 1659

AGC Education and Research Foundation Graduate Award, 539

AGC Education and Research Foundation Undergraduate Scholarship Program, 540

AGCO Corporation Scholarship, 1394

AGI Minority Geoscience Graduate Scholarship, 893

AGI Minority Geoscience Undergraduate Scholarship, 894

Agnes Jones Jackson Scholarship, 1660

Agricultural Career Awareness Scholarship to 1862 and 1890 Land–Grant, 1395

Agricultural Careers Scholarship, 1396, 1397

Agricultural Dean's Leadership Award, 5

Agricultural Scholarship, 1398

AHA/AIA Fellowship in Health Facilities Design, 61

AHF Scholarship, 186

AHS Horticultural Career Intern Program, 42

AIA Minority/Disadvantaged Scholarship Program, 333

AIA New Jersey Scholarship, 334

AIAA Graduate Scholarship, 519

AIAA Undergraduate Scholarship, 520

AICAD Scholarship Program, 382

Ailene C. Ewell Scholarship Award, 831

Air and Waste Management Association Scholarship Endowment Trust Fund, 573

Air Force Civilian Cooperative Work–Study Program, 1824

Air Force ROTC Nursing Scholarships, 1013

Air Force ROTC Scholarship, 1014, 1015, 1016, 1017, 1018, 1019, 1020, 1021

Air Force ROTC Science/Engineering Scholarship, 1022

Air Force ROTC/Villanova Scholars Award, 1023

Air Force Scholarship, 1024

Air Force Sergeants Association Scholarship, 1825

Air Line Pilots Association Scholarship, 2206

Air Traffic Control Association Scholarship, 521

Air Travel Card Grant, 207

Airmen Memorial Foundation CMSAF Richard D. Kisling Scholarship, 1826

Airmen Memorial Foundation Scholarship, 1827

AKA Financial Assistance Scholarship, 1399

AKA Merit Scholarship, 1400

AKC Veterinary Scholarship, 28

Al Thompson Junior Bowler Scholarship, 1308

Alabama Cable Television Association/Otto Miller Scholarship, 293

Alabama G.I. Dependents' Scholarship Program, 1828

Alabama GI Dependents' Educational Benefit Program, 1829

Alabama National Guard Educational Assistance Program, 1830

Alabama Power Foundation Scholarship, 1401

Alabama Scholarship for Dependents of Blind Parents, 1990

Alan B. Holmes Memorial Scholarship, 1991

Alaska Airlines Scholarship, 208

Alaska State Educational Incentive Grants, 1992

Albert M. Lappin Scholarship, 1402

Albert Spiezny Journalism Scholarship, 231

Albert W. Dent Scholarship, 1403

Alberta Heritage Louise McKinney Scholarship, 1993

Alberta Law Foundation Scholarship, 976

Alex C. and Margaret Page Hood and Rotary Club of Las Cruces Scholarship, 574

Alex R. Cummings Bursary, 575

Alexander Hamilton Life Insurance Scholarship, 142

Alexander M. Tanger Scholarship, 294

Alexander S. Langsdorf Fellowship in Engineering and Applied Science, 576

Alfa-Laval Agri Inc. Scholarship, 1404

Alice E. Smith Fellowship, 754

Alice E. Wilson Award, 1994

Alice Mellema, 1995

Alicia Patterson Grant, 1325

Allflex USA Inc. Scholarship, 1405

Allstate Scholarship, 1406

Alma-Hal Reagan MBA Fellowship, 143

Alpha and Omega Fraternity Scholarship, 220

Alpha Delta Kappa Foundation Fine Arts Grants, 383

Altamura/Enrico Caruso Voice Competition, USA, 436

Alumni Association of the University of Calgary Bursary, 1086

Alumni Association of Coopers & Lybrand Scholarship, 122

Alumni Association Scholarship, 1087

Alumni, Faculty and Staff Scholarships, 1096

Alumni Foundation Honor Scholarship, 1088

Alumni/Foundation Leadership Scholarship, 1097

Alumni Honor Scholarship, 1089

Alumni Memorial Scholarship, 1090

Alumni National Merit Scholarship, 1909

Alumni Past Presidents Scholarship, 1996

Alumni Research Grant, 969

Alumni Scholars Award, 1091

Alumni Scholarship, 1092, 1093, 1094, 1095, 1997

Alumni Valedictorian Scholarship, 1998

Alvin and Mona Libin Scholarship in Medicine, 798

Amalgamated Clothing and Textile Workers Scholarship, 2207

Amateur Athletic Union/Mars Milky Way High School All-American Award, 1309

AMAX Undergraduate Scholarship in Geology, 895

Ambrose H. Lindhorst Scholarship, 977

America ConAgra Inc. Scholarship, 1407

America's Junior Miss, 1797

American Action Fund Scholarship, 1933

American Airlines/AMR Mananagement Club Community/Leadership Scholarship, 1601

American Association for Geodetic Surveying Fellowship, 935

American Association of Petroleum Geologists Grants-in-Aid, 896

American Association of School Administrators Scholarship, 445

American Association of Teachers of German Testing and Awards Program, 749

American Council of Learned Societies Fellowship, 1098

American Cyanamid Scholarship, 1408

American Drug Stores Scholarship, 101

American Express Travel Scholarship, 209

American Family Insurance Co. Scholarship, 1409

American Heart Association National Center Grant-in-Aid, 799

American Helicopter Society Scholarship, 522

American Indian Endowed Scholarship, 1661

American Indian Scholarship Legislative Grant, 1662

American Indian Tuition Waiver, 1663

American Institute for Economic Research Fellowship —Summer Program, 144

American Legion—Alabama Auxiliary Scholarship, 1831

American Legion—Alabama Oratorical Contest Scholarship, 313

American Legion—Alabama Scholarship, 1832

American Legion—Florida Auxiliary Scholarship, 1833

American Legion—Maryland Auxiliary Scholarships, 1834

American Legion—Massachusetts Scholarship, 1835

American Legion—Oregon Auxiliary Grant, 1836

American Legion—Utah Auxiliary Scholarship, 1796

American Morgan Horse Institute Inc. Scholarship, 1410

American National Can Company Scholarship, 1602

American National Cattlewomen Foundation Scholarship, 1411

American Numismatic Graduate Fellowship, 764

American Oriental Society Fellowship for Study of Chinese Painting, 350

American Planning Association Fellowship, 1070

American Seed Trade Association Inc. Scholarship, 1412

American Society of Civil Engineers, Orange County Branch Scholarship, 541

American Society of Naval Engineers Scholarship, 577

American Wine Industry Research Scholarship, 1099

American-Scandinavian Foundation Fellowships and Grants, 1664

AMETEK/KETEMA College Scholarship, 1603

Amick Farms Scholarship, 1999

Amigo Scholarship, 1100

Amoco Foundation Doctorial Fellowship, 566

Amoco Foundation Fellowship, 897

Amoco Foundation Scholarship, 2195

Amoco Scholarship, 542

AMS 75th Anniversary Campaign Scholarship, 865

AMS/Industry Graduate Fellowship, 866

AMS/Industry Undergraduate Scholarship, 867

AMT Scholarship, 2233

Amvets National Scholarship, 1837

Amy Louise Hunter Fellowship, 755

ANA Minority Clinical and Research Training Fellowship, 832

Anderson Publishing Company Minority Scholarship, 978

Andree Memorial Scholarship, 915

Andrew J. Boehm Fellowship, 58

Andrew W. Mellon Fellowship in Humanistic Studies, 765

Angela Scholarship, 1665

Angelo Divencenzo Scholarship, 397

Angier B. Duke Scholarship, 1101

Anibal Excellence Scholarship, 1102

Animal Science Scholarship, 1413

Anna and Charles Stockwitz Children and Youth Fund, 1326

Anna C. and Oliver C. Colburn Fellowship, 1054

Anna Jones Scholarship, 1327

Anne Maureen Whitney Barrow Memorial Scholarship, 578

Anne Pekar Memorial Scholarship, 1934

Anne Seaman PGMS Memorial Scholarship, 43

Annual Chemistry Scholarship, 886

Annual Operatic Vocal Competition for North American Artists, 437

Annual Scholarship Program, 86

ANS Scholarships, 699

Anthem Essay Contest, 730

Anthony Robert Scott Scholarship, 145

AP&ICS/E&R Fund Scholarship, 194

Appraisal Institute Education Trust Scholarship, 203

APS Corporate-Sponsored Scholarship for Minority Undergraduate Students Who Major in Physics, 1666

ARAM Scholarship Award, 1414

Arby's/Big Brothers/Big Sisters of America, 1415

Arch E. McClanahan Agricultural Memorial Scholarship, 6

Archie and Hugh Bothner Bursaries, 2000

Arizona Chapter Gold, 210

Armed Forces Health Professions Scholarship, 1838

Armenian Students' Association Scholarship, 1667

Army National Guard/Army Reserve Force Duty Two-Year Scholarship, 1025

Army ROTC Four-Year Scholarship, 1026

Army ROTC Scholarship, 1027, 1028, 1029, 1030, 1031, 1032, 1033, 1034, 1035, 1036

Army ROTC Simultaneous Membership Program, 1037

Army ROTC Supplemental Scholarship, 1038

Army ROTC Two- and Three-Year Green to Gold Scholarship, 1039

Army ROTC Two- and Three-Year Scholarships, 1040

Army ROTC Two-Year Camp Challenge Scholarship, 1041

Army ROTC/Villanova Scholars Award, 1042

Arnold CU Opportunity Scholarship, 1668

Arnold J. Lien Scholarship in the Social Sciences, 1055

Art Academy of Cincinnati Entrance Scholarship, 1103

Art and Design Regents Scholarship, 398

Art Edgerton/Northwest Ohio Black Media Association Scholarship, 221

Art Institute of Fort Lauderdale Scholarship, 384

Art Peters Copy Editing Internship, 232

Art Student Grants, 385

Artesia Data Systems, Inc. Scholarship, 123

Arthur and Genevieve Roth Scholarship, 146

Arthur H. Carter Scholarship, 124

Arthur Holly Compton Fellowship in the Natural Sciences and Mathematics, 936

Arthur S. Tuttle Memorial National Scholarship Fund, 543

Arts Recognition and Talent Search, 358

ASBOI Scholarship, 1416

ASCAP Foundation Grants to Young Composers, 420

ASCE Construction Engineering Scholarship and Student Prize, 544

ASCE Research Fellowship, 545

ASCE Research Initiation Scholarship, 546

ASCP/AMS Scholarship, 95

ASDSO Scholarship, 547

Asgrow Seed Co. Scholarship, 1417

ASHRAE Graduate Grant-in-Aid, 579

ASHRAE Scholarship, 580

ASHRAE Undergraduate Grant-in-Aid, 581

ASM Undergraduate Scholarship, 688

ASM/NCID Postdoctoral Research Associates Program, 872

ASME Graduate Fellowship, 677

ASSE Student Paper Awards, 582

Associated General Contractors Scholarship, 548

Associated Western Universities-Department of Energy Graduate Fellowship, 918

Associates of the Faculty of Fine Arts 25th Anniversary Scholarship, 359

Association of Christian Schools International Scholarship, 1104

ASWA Scholarship, 125

Athletic Scholarship, 1310

Atlanta Press Club Journalism Grants, 233

Aubrey Lee Brooks Scholarship, 1328

Automotive Hall of Fame Scholarships, 1320

Auxiliary of Group Health Cooperative of Puget Sound Health Career Scholarship, 1604

Avon Products Foundation Scholarship for Women in Business Studies, 1798

AWSEF Scholarship, 1311

B

B. Charles Tiney Memorial ASCE Student Chapter Scholarship, 583

Babcock & Wilcox Annual Scholarship, 678

Baird Foundation Scholarship, 2001

Baking Industry Scholarships, 1653

Baltimore Sun Scholarship for Minority Journalists, 234

Barbara Thomas Enterprises Scholarship, 62

Barber Dairies Scholarship, 199

Barry M. Goldwater Scholarship, 937

Barry M. Goldwater Scholarship and Excellence in Education Program, 1105

BC&TWIU Scholarship, 2208

Beacon/Woodstream Corp. Scholarship, 1418

Beatrice National Merit Scholarship, 1910

Beau Mitchell Memorial Scholarship, 1419

Beef Award, 1420

Behavioral Science Dissertation Grant, 938

Bellingham Rotary Club Scholarship, 147

Ben and Kitty Gossett Scholarship, 2196

Ben Barnett Ph.D. Scholarship, 148

Ben T. Huiet Endowment Fund Scholarship, 2236

Benjamin E. Mays Scholarship for Ministry, 784

Benjamin Eaton Scholarship, 1669

Benton-Schmidt Scholarship, 438

Bergen Brunswig Drug Company Scholarship, 102

Bernard J. Seeman Scholarship, 979

Berntsen International Scholarship in Surveying Technology, 939

Bert Price Scholarship, 1670

Bertha Langhorst Werner Scholarship, 386

Beta Theta Pi Scholarships, 1421

Betty Baum Hirschfield Scholarship, 1799

Beverley Jackson Fellowship, 2002

Beville Hal Reagan Scholarship in Animal Science, 29

Bibliographical Society of America Fellowship, 766

Big Thursday Golf Tournament Incorporated Annual Scholarship, 1329

Bill Hudson Family Endowment Scholarship, 2003

Billy Mitchell Chapter Association of Old Crows Scholarship, 567

Biology Research Scholarship, 873

Bishop Charles P. Greco Graduate Fellowship, 1967

Black North American Doctoral Scholarships for the Study of Religion, 785

Blind and Deaf Students Tuition Exemption, 1935

Bliss Prize Fellowship in Byzantine Studies, 701

Blount Scholarship, 2004

Board of Governors Dental Scholarship, 792

Board of Governors Medical Scholarship, 800

Board of Governors Scholarship, 1671

Bob Eddy Scholarship, 235

Bob Grainger Matriculation Bursary, 1106

Bobby R. Hudson Endowed Scholarship, 1330

Boeing Student Research Award, 211

Boettcher Foundation Fellowship, 940

Boettcher Foundation Scholarship, 2005

Bolla Wines Scholarship, 706

Borden Foundation Inc. Scholarship, 1422

Boston Youth Leadership Award, 1331

Bound-to-Stay-Bound Books Scholarship, 267

BPW Career Advancement Scholarship, 1800

Bradley Distinguished Scholars Award, 1107

Bradley/Gamble Fellows Program in Population Studies, 767

Bread Scholarship, 1423

BRIDGE Endowment Fund Scholarship, 1424

BRIDGE Quaker Oats Foundation Scholarship, 1425

Broadcast Journalism, 1332

Broadcast Pioneers Scholarship, 295

BSU Scholarship, 1108

Buffalo News Scholarship, 236

Burlington Northern Foundation Scholarship, 1426

Burlington Northern Railroad Scholarship, 1605

Burns Lions Club, 2006

Burroughs Foundation Annual Agricultural Scholarship, 7

Busald, Funk, Zevely Scholarship, 980

Business Men's Assurance Company of America Scholarship, 8

Butler Manufacturing Company Scholarship, 1606

C

C.G. Fuller Foundation Scholarship, 2007

C. Louis and Thelma Ferrell Van Buren Scholarship, 941

CABJ Scholarship, 237

Cabot Corporation Graduate Fellowship, 584

C-A-L Stores Company Inc. Scholarship, 1427

Calgary Life Underwriters Scholarship in Insurance and Risk Management, 196

California Council of Civil Engineers and Land Surveyors Scholarship, 549

California Farm Bureau Scholarship, 9

California State Library Multi-Ethnic Recruitment Scholarship, 268

Calvin M. Woodward Fellowship in Engineering and Applied Science, 585

Candle Fellowship, 970

Capstone Hotel Scholarship, 187

Cargill Scholarship for Rural America, 10

Carl M. Turner Rural COOP Memorial Scholarship, 1428

Carl S. Ell Scholarship, 1109

Carmela Gagliardi Fellowships, 1672

Carole Simpson Scholarship, 296

Carolina Scholars Award, 2008

Carolina Scholars Finalist Award, 2009

Carolinas Golf Association Scholarship, 44

Caroline E. Holt Nursing schoalrship, 833

Caroline M. Hewins Scholarship, 269

Carthy Foundation Scholarship in Management, 149

Carver Scholarship, 2010

Casaday-Elmore Ministerial Scholarship, 1839

Caterpillar Scholars Award, 666

Catherine H. Beattie Fellowship, 45

Catherine Hainer McMartin Bursary, 2011

Catholic Daughters of the Americas Graduate Scholarship, 1968

Cecil C. Humphreys/Herff Engineering Scholarship, 586

Cecil C. Humphreys Merit Scholarship, 1110

Cecil C. Humphreys Presidential Scholarship, 1111

Celia Koontz Findlay Scholarship in Elementary Education, 504

Center for Contemporary German Literature Grant, 750

Centro Cultural Cubano Scholarship, 1112

Century III Leaders Program, 1113

CERT Scholars Fund, 1673

CFUW Professional Fellowship, 2012

Chairscholars Foundation, 1936

Challenge Scholarship, 1674

Chamberlain Memorial Scholarship, 1801

Champion Laboratories Inc. Scholarship, 1429

Champions Choice/AKZO Nobel Salt Scholarship, 1430

Chancellor Scholarship, 1114

Chancellor's Alumni Scholarship, 1115

Chancellor's Club Scholarship, 2013

Chancellor's Leadership Class Scholarship, 1116

Chancellor's Minority Student Leadership Scholarship, 1675

Chancellor's Scholarship, 1117, 1118

Charles Abrams Scholarship, 1071

Charles B. Duffy Scholarship, 1676

Charles E. Springs Annual Forestry Scholarship, 34

Charles G. Coulson, Jr. Scholarship, 981

Charles H. Hewitt Memorial Scholarship, 1119

Charles H. Hood Fund, 1607

Charles H. Stone Scholarship, 2237

Charles N. Fisher Memorial Scholarship, 297

Charles P. Lake/Rain for Rent Scholarship, 1431

Charlie Logan Scholarship for Dependents, 2209

Charlie Logan Scholarship for Seamen, 2210

Chase Activity Award, 982

Chase Excellence Scholarship, 983

Chase Minority Educational Opportunity Tuition Award, 984

Chevron Canada Resources Limited Scholarship in Engineering, 587

Chevron Journalism Economics Scholarship, 238

Chevron Scholarship, 588

Chevy Trucks/Future Leaders Scholarship, 1432

Chicano Faculty/Staff Fund Scholarship, 1677

Child Care Provider Scholarship, 446

Children of Disabled Firemen and Peace Officers Tuition Exemption, 2014

Children of Prisoners of War or Persons Missing in Action Tuition Exemption, 1840

Children and Youth Scholarship, 1937

Chilean Nitrate Corp. Scholarship, 1433

Chinese Professional Club of Houston Scholarship, 1678

Chopin Piano Scholarship, 407

Christa McAuliffe Memorial Scholarship, 2015

Christenson Engineering Corporation Scholarship, 589

Christian A. Herter Memorial Scholarship, 2016

Christie School Scholarship, 1063

CIBA-Geigy Prestige Scholarship, 2197

CIBA-Geigy Scholarship, 1120

Citizenship Scholarship, 1434

Civitan Shropshire Scholarship, 1121

Clara B. Small Scholarship, 768

Clara B. Williams Scholarship, 1679

Clarence A. McLendon and Julia C. McLendon Memorial Scholarship, 1122

Class of '36 Golden Anniversary Scholarship, 1126

Class of '38 Golden Anniversary Scholarship, 1123

Class of '39 Scholarship, 1124

Class of '49 Alumni Scholars Endowment, 1125

Clemson Scholars Program, 2017

Clemson-Sonoco Scholars Program, 590

CLEO Scholarship, 985

Clifford T. Smith Scholarship, 2018

Clinical Scientist Award, 801

Cloisters College Internship, 351

Clothing and Textiles Scholarship, 1435

CLSI Scholarship in Library and Information Technology, 270

Clyde Farrar Fellowship, 568

Coca-Cola Scholars Program, 1608

Cohos Evamy Partners Design Competition, 550

College of Arts and Sciences Scholarship, 1127

College Fee Waiver for California National Guard Dependents, 1841

College Fee Waiver for Veteran's Dependents, 1842

College Fee Waiver Program, 1843

College and Program Competition Scholarships, 2238

College Vocational/Technical Scholarship, 2211

Colonel Hayden W. Wagner Memorial Fund, 1844

Colonel Louisa Spruance Morse CAP Scholarship, 1845

Colorado Institute of Art Scholarship, 399

Colorado Scholars Award, 1128

Colorado Scholars President's Gold Award, 1129

Comer Foundation Scholarship in Fashion and Design, 2198

Commission on Classified Staff Affairs Scholarship, 1609

Commonwealth Scholarship for Legal Studies, 986

Community Action Grants, 2019

Community College Achievement Award, 1333

Community College International Studies Scholarship, 769

Community College Minority Transfer Scholarship, 1680

Community College Presidential Scholarship, 1130

Community College Transfer Scholarship, 1131, 1132

Competitive Scholarship for Transfers from Two-year Colleges, 1133

Computer Based Honors Scholarship, 1134

Cone Mills Corporation Four-Year or Vocational/Technical Scholarship, 1610

Congressional Hispanic Summer Internship Program, 1681

Congressional Science Fellowship, 928

Congressional Teacher Scholarship, 447

Connie M. Maynard Education Fund Program, 1611

Conoco Fellowship, 528

Conoco Scholarship, 898

Conoco Scholarship Award, 731

Conservation of Natural Resources Award, 1436

Constance L. Lloyd/FACMPE Scholarship, 63

Consumer Education Award, 1437

Conway and Proetz Scholarships, 387

Cooperative Resources International Scholarship, 1438

Copp Family Scholarship, 2020

Cortez A. M. Ewing Public Service Fellowship, 1049

Council on Public Higher Education Scholarship, 505

Country Doctor Scholarship Program, 802

Countrymark Cooperative Inc. Scholarship, 1439

CPIA Scholarship Trust Fund, 400

CR Resources Limited Entrance Scholarship, 591

CRAHCA Data Analysis Scholarship, 64

Creative Arts Award, 362

Creative and Performing Arts Scholarship, 360, 361

Creswell, Munsell, Fultz & Zirbel Scholarship, 1440

CSX Transportation Corporation Scholarship, 1612

CTA Scholarship, 2212

Cullen Leadership Scholarship, 1135

Cultural Ambassadorial Scholarship, 1441
Curators Scholarship, 2021
Cynthia Ann Clark Thompson Memorial Scholarship, 126

D

D&B Supply Company Inc. Scholarship, 1442
D.C. Nurses Training Corps Grant, 834
D. Paul Fansler Memorial Scholarship, 1136
Dairy Award, 1443
Dairy Cattle Judging Scholarship, 1444
Dairy Foods Award, 1445
Dairy Foods Scholarship, 1446
Dairy Goat Scholarship, 1447
Dale and Coral Courtney Scholarship, 1056
Dan Konnie Scholarship, 2022
Dana Griffin Soper Memorial Scholarship, 335
Dance Tuition Waiver, 363
Dane G. Hansen Foundation Leadership Scholarship, 1334
Daniel Keating Norris and Bessie Caldwell Norris Textile Scholarship, 2199
Daniel Memorial Fund Endowed Scholarship, 1682
Daniel Swarovski & Co. Scholarship, 1613
Danish Sisterhood of America Scholarship, 1448
DAR American History Scholarship, 756
Darigold Scholarship, 1449
Daughters of Cincinnati Scholarship, 1846
David A. DeBolt Teacher Shortage Scholarship, 448
David H. Clift Scholarship, 271
David J. Fitzmaurice Scholarship, 2213
David Scholarship, 1137
David W. Self Scholarship, 1969
Davis Scholarship, 1683
Dean William H. Washington and Miriam Betts Washington Scholarship, 449
Dean's Art Scholarship, 388
Dean's Business Scholarship, 150
Dean's Business Transfer Scholarship, 151
Dean's Education Scholarship, 450
Dean's Scholarship, 1138, 1139
Dean's Science Scholarship, 942
Dean's Special Talent Scholarship, 364
Dean's Theatre Performance Scholarship, 374
Dean's Theatre Studies and Theatre Design and Technology Scholarships, 375
DeArce-Koch Scholarship, 65
Debate Scholarship, 310
DECA Scholarship, 1450
Dedman Distinguished Scholars Award, 1140
DEKALB Genetic Corp. Scholarship, 1451
Delegate Scholarship, 2023
Delta Gamma Foundation Fellowship, 1452
Delta Gamma Foundation Scholarship, 1453
Dental Assisting Scholarship, 87
Dental Hygiene Scholarship, 88
Dental Lab Tech Scholarship, 96
Dental Student Scholarship, 793
Department of Energy Summer Fellowship, 529
Department of New Hampshire Scholarship, 2024
Department President's Scholarship, 2025
Department Scholarship, 1847

Departmental Endowed Scholarships, 2239
Departmental and General Scholarships, 1141
Departmental Scholarship, 1142
Dependents of Former Prisoners of War/Missing in Action Scholarship, 1848
Dependents of Veterans Who Died of a Service Connected Disability Scholarship, 1849
Descendants of the Signers of the Declaration of Independence Scholarship, 1454
Desk and Derrick Educational Trust Scholarship, 689
DeVry Scholarship, 1143
Dewitt T. and Mary Timmerman Hardin Endowment Fund Scholarship, 2240
Diamond Anniversary Fellowships, 971
Dietrich/Cross/Hanly Scholarship, 987
Digital Equipment Corporation, Inc. Scholarship, 592
Discovery Scholarship, 1911
Displaced Homemaker Scholarships, 1684
Dissertation Year Scholarship for Doctoral Study for Black North Americans, 786
Distinction Scholarship, 1685
Distinguished Academic Scholar Program, 1144
Distinguished Honors Scholarship, 1145
Distinguished Scholar Award, 1146, 1147, 1148, 2026
Distinguished Scholar Teacher Education, 451
Distinguished Scholarship, 1912
Diversity Scholarship, 1686, 1687
Dr. Charles A. Vernale Student Loan Award, 794
Dr. Edward Groth, Jr. Memorial Scholarship, 530
Dr. Glayton Wilson Grier Scholarship, 795
Dr. Marion Elder Grant Fellowship, 2030
Dr. Pedro Grau Undergraduate Scholarship, 868
Dr. Robert H. Goddard Scholarship, 943
Doctoral and Post-Doctoral Fellowships in the Humanities and Social Sciences, 707
Doctoral Dissertation Award in Insurance/Business, 197
Dog Care and Training Award, 1455
Dog Writers' Educational Trust Scholarship, 732
Dollar Rent-A-Car Scholarship, 551
Dolphin Scholarship, 1850
Dominion Merit Scholarship, 2027
Don Wright Prize, 421
Donald A. Williams Scholarship, 901
Donald H. Cole Graduate Fellowship, 152
Donald W. Reynolds Foundations, Inc. Scholarship, 239
Dora Brahms Award, 377
Dorchester County Marketing Association Annual Scholarship, 1335
Doris Mullen Memorial Scholarship, 1802
Dorothy Lemke Howarth Scholarship, 593
Dorothy and Roy Malone Scholarship, 2028
Doug and Luella Glasgow Memorial Scholarship, 153
Douglas Battery Manufacturing Scholarship, 1456
Douglas County Community Scholarship, 1336
Douglas Products and Packaging Scholarship, 1457
Dow Black Scholars Award, 594
Dow Corning Scholarship, 595
Dow Jones Newspaper Fund Editing Intern Program, 240
Dow Scholarship in Chemistry, 887
Doyle and Donna Shepherd Scholarship, 2029
Dragoco Scholarship, 1458

Dravo Corporation Scholarship, 1614

Dual Degree Scholarship Program/Undergraduate Scholarship Program, 596

Dun and Bradstreet Merit Scholarship, 1615

DuPage Medical Society Foundation Scholarship, 1337

DuPont Challenge/Science Essay Awards Program, 944

DuPont Fellowship, 531

Duracell/National Science Teachers Association Scholarship Competition, 945

DuSable Scholarship, 1149

Dwight D. Gardner Scholarship, 667

E

E.C. Hallbeck Memorial Scholarship Program, 2214

E. Catherine Barclay Scholarship, 708

E.G. Coombe Family Bursary in Chemistry, 888

E.I. and Minnie Pashby Scholarship, 1150

E.W. Costello Entrance Scholarship, 988

Eagle Scout Scholarship, 1459

Earl J. Small Growers Scholarship, 46

Early Scholars Award, 1151

East European Summer Language Training Grant, 751

Easter Seal of Iowa Disability Scholarships, 1938

Eastman Kodak Scholarship, 1616

Eastman Scholarship in Mathematics, 916

Ed Bradley Scholarship, 298

Edgar A. Brown Foundation Scholarship, 2241

Edgar H. Snider Memorial Scholarship, 401

Edith McPherson Scholarship, 1338

Educational Assistance Grant, 2031

Educational Communications Scholarship, 1152

Educational Opportunity Grant, 2032

Edward D. Stone, Jr. and Associates Minority Scholarship, 336

Edward Grisso Memorial Scholarship, 2033

Edward J. Nell Memorial Journalism Scholarships, 241

Edward Livingston Trudeau Scholarship, 803

Edward S. Moore Foundation Scholarship, 35

Edward T. Conroy Memorial Grant, 1851

Edwin F. Averyt Memorial Scholarship, 1153

Edwin L. and Ruth Kennedy Distinguished Professor Scholarship, 1154

Edwin P. Rogers Sr. Scholarship, 2034

Edwin T. Meredith Foundation, 1460

EEOC Endowed Scholarship, 1617

EIF Scholarship Fund, 1939

Eight & Forty Lung and Respiratory Nursing Scholarship, 836

Eight & Forty Nursing Scholarship, 835

Eileen Phillips Cohen Music Scholarship, 422

El Paso Natural Gas Company (Engineering), 597

El Paso Natural Gas Company Scholarship, 563

Elaine Potter Benfer Scholarship, 837

Eleanor Roosevelt Teacher Fellowship, 1803

Electric Energy Award, 1461

Electrochemical Society Summer Fellowship, 532

Elizabeth Coleman Honors Scholarship, 1155

Elizabeth Greenshields Foundation Award, 389

Elizabeth H. Miller Scholarship, 804

Elizabeth and James MacKenzie Andrews Bursary, 2035

Elks National Foundation Most Valuable Student Award, 1156

Ellen B. Scripps Fellowship, 242

Ellen Setterfield Memorial Scholarship, 1940

Eloise Gerry Fellowship, 946

Elsa Jorgenson Award, 1157

Elsie Bell Grosvenor Scholarship Awards, 1941

Emerging Leaders Scholarship, 1158

Emily K. Rand Scholarship, 423

Emily Nelson Moseley Memorial Scholarship, 513

Employees at Duke Power Scholars Program, 598

Encon Scholarship, 198

Endowed Scholarships, 1159, 2242

Endowment for Biblical Research (Boston) and ASOR Summer Research Grants and Travel Scholarships, 709

Energy Management Scholarship, 1462

Engineering Scholarship Program/Undergraduate Scholarship Programs, 599

Enid Hall Griswold Memorial Scholarship, 1057

Entomology Award, 1463

EOSAT Award for Application of Digital Landsat TM Data, 919

EPA Tribal Lands Environmental Science Scholarship, 1688

Erlaine Pitts Scholarship, 378

Ernst and Whinney Foundation Scholarship, 127

ESA Undergraduate Scholarship, 874

Established Investigators Award, 805

Estelle Massey Osborne Scholarship, 838

Esther L. Beyer Scholarship, 1160

Ethel Tingley Scholarship, 989

Eugene T. Scafe Memorial Scholarship, 889

Eugenia Bradford Roberts Memorial Fund, 1852

Evelyn Dubrow Post-Graduate Scholarship, 2215

Ewart A. Swinyard Scholarship, 103

Ewing C. Kelly Broadcast Scholarship, 299

Ewy English Scholarship, 733

Excellence Scholarship, 1161, 1689

Exceptional Student Fellowship, 154

Ezra Davis Memorial Scholarship, 1942

F

F.L. Fenwick Scholarship in Music, 424

F. Lammont Belin Arts Scholarship, 365

F.M. Becket Memorial Award, 533

F. Ward Just Scholarship, 243

Faculty of Engineering Associates Scholarship, 600

Faculty/Staff Tuition Benefits, 1618

Fairfax County Medical Society Foundation Scholarship, 66

Falcon Foundation Scholarships, 1853

Family Practice Medical Scholarship, 806

Fannie and John Hertz Foundation Fellowship, 920

Farm Credit Scholarship, 2036

Farm Safety 4 Just Kids Scholarship, 1464

Farmers Mutual Hail Insurance Company of Iowa Scholarship, 1465

Fashion Revue Award, 1466

Fastline Publications Scholarship, 1467

Fay T. Barnes Scholarship, 1339

Fellowship in Health Facilities Design, 337
Fellowship in Landscape Architecture at the American Academy in Rome, 338
Fellowship in Roman Studies, 702
Fellowships for the Bosphorus Summer Language Program in Advanced Turkish, 710
Ferdinand Cinelli Etruscan Scholarship, 1690
Fermenta Animal Health Co. Scholarship, 1468
FFA CARQUEST Scholarship, 1469
FFA Dodge Trucks Scholarship, 1470
FFA FarmAid Scholarship, 1471
FFA Johnson and Wales University Scholarship, 1472
FFA Minority Scholarship, 1473
FFA National Pork Council Scholarship, 1474
FFA Norfolk Southern Foundation Scholarship, 1475
FFA Souvenir Shirts Etc. Scholarship, 1476
FFA State Farm Companies Foundation Scholarship, 1477
FFA Sun Company Scholarship, 1478
FFA United Feeds Scholarship, 1479
FFA Wal-Mart Scholarship, 1480
FFS Student Fellowships, 67
Fieldcrest Foundation Scholarship, 2200
Fifth Marine Division Association Scholarship, 1481
50 Men & Women of Toledo Scholarship, 1391
50 Men and Women of Toledo, Inc. Scholarship, 1324
FINE Fellowship, 1691
Finlandia Foundation Trust Scholarship Exchange Program and Grants, 711
Firestone Agriculture Tire Division Scholarship, 1482
First Generation Award, 2037
First Security Foundation Scholarship, 155
FISCO Farm and Home Stores Scholarship, 1483
Fleet Reserve Association Scholarships, 1854
Fleming Companies, Inc. Scholarship, 156
Florence C. Painter Memorial Scholarship, 506
Florida Undergraduate Scholars' Fund, 2038
Fluor Daniel Canada, Inc. Scholarship, 601
Food Careers Scholarship (Kerr), 1485
Food Careers Scholarship (Webster Industries), 1486
Food Conservation, Preservation and Safety Scholarship, 1487
Food and Nutrition Scholarship, 1484
Ford Family Foundation Scholarship, 2039
Ford Foundation Postdoctoral Fellowships for Minorities, 947
Ford Foundation Predoctoral and Dissertation Fellowships for Minorities, 948
Ford Motor Company Fund Scholarship, 1488
FORE Graduate Scholarships, 68
FORE Undergraduate Scholarship, 69
Foreign Language and Area Studies Fellowship, 752
Foreign Languages Regents Scholarship, 753
Forensics Regents Scholarship, 311
Forestry Award, 1489
Foster G. McGaw Scholarship, 1490
Foundation Scholarship, 1162
Founder's Scholarship, 1163
Fountainhead Essay Contest, 734
Frances M. Schwartz Fellowship, 703
Frances Topkins Scholarship, 839
Francis Ouimet Scholarship, 1619
Frank A. Burtner Scholarship, 1164

Frank J. Jervey Alumni Scholarship, 1165
Frank McHale Memorial Scholarship, 1804
Frank Roswell Fuller Scholarship, 1340
Frank W. Garner Scholarship, 1855
Frank Walton Horn Memorial Scholarship, 1943
Fraternal College Scholarship, 1491
Fraternal Order of UDT/SEAL Scholarship, 1492
Fred Russell-Grantland Rice TRA Scholarship, 244
Frederic G. Melcher Scholarship, 272
Frederick A. Downes Scholarship, 1944
Frederick T. Bonham Scholarship, 990
Freedom Forum Journalism Scholarship, 245
Freeman Fellowship, 552
Freshman Achievement Scholarship, 2040
Fresno-Madera Medical Society Scholarship, 807
Friends of Fine Arts Scholarship, 366
Frito-Lay Minority Business Scholarship, 1692
Fukunaga Foundation Graduate Scholarship, 157
Fukunaga Foundation Scholarship, 158
Future Farmers of America Sweepstakes Award, 11
Future Teacher Conditional Scholarship, 452
Future Teachers Conditional Scholarship, 453

G

Gardening and Horticulture Award, 1493
Gary Higgins Singleton Scholarship, 507
GCA Award in Tropical Botany, 47
GCA Awards for Summer Environmental Studies, 902
Gen. Henry H. Arnold Education Grant, 1856
General Electric Foundation Scholarship, 602
General Motors (GM) Foundation Scholarship, 603
General Motors (GM) Scholarship, 159
General Motors (GM) Scholarship (Engineering), 604
General Scholarship Program, 1166
General Studies Scholarship for Academic Excellence, 1167
Geneva Steel Scholarship, 690
Geographic Competitions Scholarship, 1341
Geology and Geophysics Department Scholarship, 899
Geophysics Special Fund Scholarship, 900
George A. Hormel and Company Scholarship, 1620
George C. Brooks Scholarship, 1693
George E. Andrews Scholarship, 1342
George E. and Leila Giles Singleton Scholarship, 12
George E. Mylonas Scholarship in the Humanities, 770
George Harris/San Antonio Livestock Exposition Scholarship, 1
George J. Record School Foundation Scholarship, 1343
George Reinke Scholarship, 212
George Swygert and Wilfred P. Tiencken Endowed Scholarship, 605
George T. Reynolds Fellowship, 771
George T. Welch Scholarship, 1344
George W. Nunn, Richard W. Stuhr, and Joseph Wallace Nursing Scholarship, 840
Georgetown University Grant, 1168
Georgia Boot Inc. Scholarship, 1494
Georgia M. Hellberg Memorial Scholarship, 1495
Gerald Roberts Mortimer and Victor Emanuel Mortimer Scholarships and Bursaries, 2041
Gerber Companies Foundation Scholarship, 972, 1621

German Marshall Fund of the United States Internship, 712

Gertrude L. Warren Career Scholarship, 1496

GFWC of MA Music Scholarship, 425

Gianninoto Scholarship Fund, 668

Giargiari Fellowship, 1694

Gibbs Scholarship, 1622

Gilbert Associates, Inc. Corporate Scholarship, 1623

Gilbreth Memorial Fellowship, 669

Gina Finzi Memorial Student Summer Fellowship, 808

Girls Incorporated Scholars Program, 1497

Glaxo/AFPE Graduate Studies Scholarship, 104

Glenn Miller Scholarship, 426

Glenn Terrell Presidential Scholarship, 1169

Gloria Fecht Memorial Scholarship, 1312

GOEF Scholarship, 246

Golden Harvest Seeds Inc. Scholarship, 1498

Golden State Minority Foundation Scholarship, 160

Golf Writers Association of America Scholarship, 247

Good Neighbor Scholarship, 2042

Gordon Edward Wright Scholarship, 2043

Grace P. Swinyard Memorial Scholarship, 105

Graduate Equity Fellowship, 2044

Graduate Minority Fellowship Grant, 1695

Graduate Nursing Education Scholarship, 841

Graduate/Postgraduate Study and Research in Poland, 714

Graduate/Professional Fellowship, 2045

Graduate Research Program for Women/Cooperative Research Fellowship Program/Ph.D. Fellowship Program, 606

Graduate Scholarship, 1170

Graduate Scholarships, 1857

Graduate Student Award, 1500

Graduate Student East European Travel Grant, 713

Graduate Student Scholarship, 227

Graduate Study Scholarship for Handicapped Learner Certificate, 514

Graduate and Undergraduate Scholarships, 1499

Grant Program for Physically Disabled Students in the Sciences, 1945

Grants for Orchid Research, 949

Grants for Research, 161

Greater San Antonio Builders Association/National Association of Home Builders Scholarship, 162

Greek Women's University Club Scholarship, 1696

Greenville Clemson Club Annual Scholarship, 1345

Grothus-Pi Tau Sigma Award, 679

Guaranteed Access Grant, 2046

Guide Dog Raising/Training Scholarship, 1501

Guideposts Magazine's Youth Writing Contest, 735

Guido Zerilli-Marimo Fellowships, 1697

Gulf Canada Centennial Scholarship, 1171

Gunild Keetman Assistance Fund, 1502

Gus Cunningham Wofford Memorial Scholarship, 48

Gustafson Inc. Scholarship, 1503

H

H.A. Gorrell Memorial Bursary, 1903

H.E. Eddie Chiles Centennial Scholarship, 691

H. Gayle Weller Scholarship, 991

H. Gordon Martin Scholarship, 163

H. and N. Morgan Foundation Inc. Annual Scholarship, 2047

H.S. and Angeline Lewis Scholarship, 2048

Haggen/Western Association of Food Chains Scholarship, 164

Hagley Museum and Library Grants-in-Aid, 772

Hagley/Winterthur Fellowships in Arts and Industries, 773

Hallmark Scholarship, 1913

Halton Scholars, 1624

Harcourt General Insurance Scholarship, 1504

Harlan M. Smith Builders of a Better World Scholarship, 1172

Harland Cravat/Gray Johnson Scholarship, 2049

Harold E. Ennes Scholarship, 300

Harold E. Fellows Scholarship, 301

Harriet and Leon Pomerance Fellowship, 1058

Harry A. Applegate Memorial Scholarship, 200

Harry C. Bates Merit Scholarship, 2216

Harry C. Tilotson Scholarship, 1173

Harry and Devera Lerman Educational Trust Scholarship, 1346

Harry J. Harwick Scholarship, 70

Harry S. Truman Scholarship, 1050, 1174, 2050

Harvey E. Dowling, M.D. and Pearl Christie-Dowling, M.D. Bursary, 809

Hauss-Helms Foundation, Inc. Scholarship, 1347

Hazel Corbin Assistance Fund, 842

Hazel Putnam Roach Fellowship, 973

Health Award, 1505

Health Careers Scholarship, 71

Health Professional Scholarship, 72

Health Professions Scholarship, 73

Health Service Corps Scholarship, 74

Hearin-Hess Engineering Scholarship, 607

Hebrew Immigrant Aid Society Scholarships, 2051

Heisey Foundation Scholarship, 2052

Helen Bolton Scholarship, 1348

Helen Faison Scholarship, 1698

Helen M. Woodruff Fellowship of the Archaeological Institute of America, 1059

Helen Meeks McKerley Memorial Scholarship, 553

Helen N. and Harold B. Shapira Scholarship, 810

Helena Chemical Company Scholarship, 1506

Hemphill-Gilmore Scholarship, 2053

Henry Belin du Pont Fellowship, 774

Henry I. and Thelma W. Sanders Endowed Scholarship, 1904

Henry J. Reilly Memorial Graduate Scholarship, 1858

Henry J. Reilly Memorial Undergraduate Scholarship, 1859

Henry King Stanford Scholarship, 1175

Henry Kreider Memorial Scholarship, 890

Henry Luce Foundation/ACLS Dissertation Fellowship in American Art History, 352

Henry R. Towne Scholarship, 1625

Henry Sachs Foundation Scholarship, 2054

Henry Viets Fellowship, 811

Herbert and Golden Fitch Memorial Scholarship, 427

Herbert H. Lehman Graduate Fellowship, 1060

Herbert Lehman Scholarship, 1699

Hermione Grant Calhoun Scholarship, 1946

Hess & Clark Inc. Scholarship, 1507

Hesslein Scholarship, 1349

Hewlett-Packard Scholarship, 608
HHMI Traineeship Program, 875
Hispanic Community Scholarship, 1350
Hispanic Scholarship Program, 1700
HJ Heinz Graduate Degree Fellowship, 188
Hofstra Recognition Scholarship, 1176
Holland-America Line Westours, Inc. Scholarship, 213
Holland & Hart Minority Scholarship, 992
Holly A. Cornell Scholarship, 1805
Home Oil Company Limited Centennial Matriculation Bursary, 2055
Home Oil Company Limited Centennial Undergraduate Bursary, 2056
Honor Scholarship, 1177, 1178, 1179
Honors Scholarship, 1180, 1181
Honors String Awards, 408
Honors Undergraduate Grant, 812
Horace M. Kinsey and Maybelle McLaurin Kinsey Scholarship, 1351
Horse Scholarship, 1508
Horton Research Grant, 950
Houston International Fund, 2057
Houston Livestock Show and Rodeo Scholarship, 13
Howard Brown Rickard Scholarship, 1947
Howard D. Folk Presidential Scholarship, 1352
Howard H.M. Bowman Memorial Scholarship, 813
Howard Hughes Medical Institute Predoctoral Fellowships in Biological Sciences, 876
Howard T. Orville Scholarship in Meteorology, 869
Howard Vollum American Indian Scholarship, 2058
Hughes Bachelor of Science Scholarship, 609
Huntington Library, Art Collections, and Botanical Gardens Research Award, 715
Hutchison Memorial Scholarship, 165
Hydro Agri North America Inc. Scholarship, 1509

I

IAHA Scholarship, 189
IAIEF Scholarship, 128
IAM Scholarship, 2217
Ibero-PYRD Scholarship, 1701
IEC Summer in Australia, China, or Russia, 716
IFEC Foodservice Communicators Scholarship, 190
IFT Freshman/Sophomore Scholarship, 91
IFT Graduate Fellowship, 92
IFT Junior/Senior Scholarship, 93
Ignatius Scholarship, 1182
Illinois American Legion Scholarship Program, 1510
Illinois Department of Agriculture Scholarship, 1183
In-School Players Scholarship, 367
Incentive Grant/Scholarship, 1184
Incentive Scholarship, 2059
Independent Colleges of Southern California Scholarship Program, 1353
Independent School Scholars Program, 2060
Indian Fellowship Program, 1702
Indian Scholarship Program, 1703
Indiana Minority Teacher Scholarship, 454
Indiana University of Pennsylvania Foundation Distinguished Scholars Award, 1185
Inninois Cereal Mills Inc. Scholarship, 1511

Institute of Electrical and Electronics Engineers Fellowship in Electrical History, 757
Inter American Press Association Scholarship, 248
Interchange Fellowship and Martin McLaren Scholarship, 49
Interco Scholarship, 1704
International Brotherhood of Teamsters Scholarship, 2218
International Doctoral Scholarship, 787
International Exchange, Study, or Work Abroad Scholarship, 775
International Fellowship in Jewish Studies, 788
International Gas Turbine Institute Scholarship, 680
International Mathematics, Science, and Foreign Languages Summer Institute, 776
International Scholarship for Community Service, 789
International Science and Engineering Fair (ISEF), 951
International Student Essay Competition, 2061
International Student Fee Remission Scholarship, 2062
International Women's Fishing Association Scholarship, 912
Internship Programs, 777
Iowa Federation of Labor AFL-CIO Graduate Assistantship, 2219
IPTAY Academic Scholarship Fund, 1313
Irene and Daisy MacGregor Memorial Scholarship, 814
Irish Way Scholarships, 717
Isaac Bashevis Singer Scholarship, 1186
Isabel Rutter Endowment Scholarship, 409
Italian Catholic Federation Scholarship Program, 1970
Ivy Parker Memorial Scholarship, 610

J

J. Clawson Mills Scholarship, 353
J.D. Archbold Memorial Hospital Scholarship, 75
J.E. Caldwell Centennial Scholarship, 758
J.E. Sirrine Company Engineering Scholarship, 611
J. Edgar Hoover Foundation Scholarship, 1512
J. Frances Allen Scholarship, 30
J. Fred and Wilma D. Holly Fellowship Endowment in Economics, 166
J. Kelly Sisk Communication Scholarship, 222
J. Lloyd Rogers Family Scholarship, 455
J.P. Stevens & Co. Inc. Foundation Scholarship, 2201
J. Preston Levis Academic Scholarship, 1187
J.S. Bach International Competition, 410
J.W. Jones Endowed Agricultural Scholarship, 14
J. Waldo Smith Hydraulic Fellowship, 534
J. Walter Thompson Scholarship, 1513
Jack B. Eckley Minority Scholarships in Telecommunications, 223
Jack F. Tolbert Memorial Grant, 2063
Jack Kassewitz/Garth Reeves Jr. Memorial Scholarships, 249
Jack Shinin Memorial Scholarship, 2064
Jack T. Wood Bursary, 2065
Jack Warner Scholarship, 1188
Jack Wright Memorial Scholarship, 15
Jacob Rassen Memorial Scholarship Fund, 1354
James A. Shine Milling Presidential Scholarship, 612
James B. Carey Scholarship, 2220

James B. Pearson Fellowship, 2066

James Corcoran and Mary Poats Littlejohn Memorial Scholarship, 2243

James E. DeLong Foundation Scholarship, 1626

James H. and Minnie M. Edmonds Educational Foundation Scholarship, 2067

James K. Rathmell, Jr. Memorial Scholarship, 50

James Lawrence Fly Scholarship, 302

James Lee Love Scholarship, 2068

James Roy Carter Jr. Endowed Presidential Scholarship, 2069

James W. Fitzgibbon Scholarship in Architecture, 339

James W. and Margaret Grainger Clark Scholarship, 1514

Janesville Foundation Scholarship, 1355

Jay F. W. Pearson Scholarship, 1189

Jaycee War Memorial Fund Scholarship, 1190

Jean S. Breitenstein Law Clerks Scholarship, 993

Jeanne E. Bray Memorial Scholarship, 1515

Jeannette Rankin Foundation Award, 1806

Jennifer C. Groot Fellowship in the Archaeology of Jordan, 718

Jennifer Robinson Memorial Scholarship, 877

Jeremiah Milbank Sr. Memorial Scholarship, 16

Jerry Baker, America's Master Gardener, College Freshmen Scholarship, 51

Jewell L. Taylor Fellowship, 974

Jewish Community Centers Association Scholarship, 1971

Jewish Foundation for Education of Women Scholarship, 1356

Jewish W B Scholarship, 1972

Joe B. Douthit Memorial Soil and Water Conservation Scholarship, 26

Joe and Christine Callahan Scholarship, 1357

John A. Anderson Scholarship, 1516

John and Anne Parente Scholarship, 1705

John and Anthony Pearson Memorial Bursary, 1905

John B. Ervin Scholarship for Black Americans, 1706

John C. Geilfuss Fellowship, 759

John E. Anderson Safety Student of the Year Award, 613

John F. Bannon Memorial Scholarship, 1191

John F. Hardy Memorial Bursary, 1906

John H. Anderson Scholarship, 1358

John H. Lyons, Sr. Scholarship, 2221

John H. Mathis Scholarship, 1627

John L. Gill Scholarship, 878

John M. Olin School of Business Dean's Scholarship, 167

John M. Will Memorial Scholarship, 250

John Newton Templeton Scholarship, 1707

John P. Eager Scholarship, 168

John and Sarra Fabbro Scholarship, 2070

John T. Steed Accounting Scholarship, 129

John W. and Rose E. Watson Scholarship, 1359

John W. Green Scholarship, 994

John W. Rowe Scholarship, 1360

Johnson Controls, Inc. Foundation Scholarship, 1628

Johnson/LaSelle Scholarship, 2071

Jones-Laurence Award, 1517

Jose Marti Scholarship Challenge Grant, 2072

Joseph Collins Foundation Scholarship, 815

Joseph Ehrenreich Scholarship, 290

Joseph F. Dracup Scholarship, 921

Joseph R. Stone Scholarships, 214

Joseph and Virginia Altschuller Scholarship, 1629

Joseph W. Childs Memorial Scholarship, 2222

Joyce Margaret Locke Scholarship, 411

Joyce Margaret Wright Scholarship, 2073

Judith Resnik Memorial Scholarship, 523

Julia Kiene Fellowship in Electrical Energy, 569

Julia Klug Scholarship, 1192

Julia Victor and Leslie Carlisle McDonald Scholarship, 456

Juliette A. Southard Dental Assistant Teacher Education Scholarship, 89

Junior College Honorary Scholarship, 1193

Junior College Honors Scholarship, 1194

Junior College Transfer Scholarship, 1195, 2075

Junior and Community College Athletic Scholarship, 1314

Junior and Community College Performing Arts Scholarship, 368

Junior and Community College Scholarship, 2074

Junior Girls Scholarship, 1518

K

Kansas Minority Scholarship, 2076

Kansas Nursing Scholarship, 2077

Kansas Osteopathy Scholarship, 2078

Kansas State Scholarship, 2079

Kansas Teacher Scholarship, 2080

Kansas Tuition Grant, 2081

Kappa Epsilon/AFPE Nellie Wakeman Scholarship, 106

Karla Scherer Foundation Scholarship Program, 1807

Katharine L. Morningstar Scholarship, 2082

Katharine M. Grosscup Scholarship, 52

Katherine Anne Porter Prize for Fiction, 736

Kathern F. Gruber Scholarship, 1860

Kelly/Ebell Scholarship, 2083

Kelso-Battle Scholarship, 1196

Kenan T. Erim Award, 1061

Kenneth and Ellen Nielsen Cooperative Scholarship, 1519

Kermit Osserman Fellowship, 816

Kerr McGee Corporation Student Scholarship, 130

Kerr McGee Law Scholarship, 995

Kerr McGee Scholars Award, 1197

Kerr McGee Scholarship, 564

Kerr Youth and Family Center Scholarship, 1064

King and Johnson Scholarship, 340

King Olav V Norwegian-American Heritage Fund, 719

Kingsley Alcid Brown Educational Fund, 1361

Knapman Chemistry Scholarship, 891

Knight-Ridder Inc. Minority Scholarship, 251

Kohler Co. College Scholarship, 1630

Kosciuszko Foundation New York Scholarship, 778

Kova Fertilizer Inc. Scholarship, 1520

Kuchler-Killian Memorial Scholarship, 1948

Kurzweil Scholarship, 1949

L

L.E. Mathers Memorial Scholarship, 2
Ladies Auxiliary to the V.F.W. Art Scholarship, 390
Lancelot C. A. Thompson Minority Scholarship, 1708
Langroise Scholarship, 169
Larry Temple Scholarship, 779
Larson Aquatic Research Support Scholarship, 903
Lasky Scholarship, 996
Laura Moore Cunningham Nursing Scholarship, 843
Laurence R. Foster Scholarship, 2084
Laurie Ircandia Memorial Scholarship, 904
Lavelle Scholarship, 1709
Law Enforcement Officers and Fireman Scholarship
    Program, 2085
Law School Scholarship for Library School Graduates,
    997
Lawrence Luterman Memorial Scholarship, 1861
Lawrence W. Mills Award, 817
LBJ Achievement Scholarship, 1710
LBJ Achievement Scholarship in Education, 457
Le Maxie Glover Scholarship, 391
Leadership Program Teaching/Research Fellowship,
    1198
Leadership Scholarship, 1521
Lechner and McFadden Scholarships, 1199
Ledger & Quill Scholarship, 131
Lee C. Van Wagner Scholarship, 1362
Leica Inc. Photogrammetric Fellowship Award, 1522
Leica Inc. Surveying Scholarship, 922
Lempert Scholarship, 1200
Leo Burnett Co. Scholarship, 1523
Leon and Dora Wolf Scholarship, 998
Leonard H. Bulkeley Scholarship, 1363
Leonard M. Perryman Communications Scholarship
    for Ethnic Minority Students, 224, 1711
Leonard Rose Cello Competition, 412
Library Education & Human Resource Development
    Fellowship, 273
Library Scholarship for Law School Graduates, 274
Library Scholarship for Non-Law School Graduates,
    275
Liederkranz Foundation Scholarship Award for Voice,
    439
Lt. William J. Scott Scholarship, 1808
LIFE Scholarship Award, 905
Lighthouse Career Incentive Awards Program, 1950
Lillian and Arthur Dunn Scholarship, 1524
Lillian Moller Gilbreth Scholarship, 614
Lillie Hawkins Floyd Trust Scholarship, 2244
Lincoln Technical Institute Scholarship, 2234
Linda Weddle Memorial Scholarship, 132
Lindbergh Grant, 906
Lloyd Warren Fellowship, 341
Logistics Education Foundation Scholarship, 615
Lorraine Allison Scholarship, 720
Lottie Conlan Scholarship, 1712
Lou-Ark Society of Petroleum Engineers Scholarship,
    692
Louise Giles Minority Scholarship, 276
Louise Wallace Hackney Fellowship for the Study of
    Chinese Art, 354
Louisiana Education Majors Scholarship, 508

Louisiana Forestry Foundation Scholarship, 36
Louisiana Honors Scholarship, 2086
Louisiana Library Association Scholarship, 277
Louisiana Tuition Assistance Plan, 2087
Lucile A. Abt Scholarship, 1951
Luso-American Education Foundation Scholarships,
    1713
Luther A. Sizemore Foundation Scholarship, 1631
Lutheran Brotherhood Member Scholarship, 1973

M

M. Elizabeth Carnegie Scholarship, 844
M.A. Hanna Company Scholarships, 1632
Mabelle Wilhelmina Boldt Memorial Scholarship, 379
Madison Charitable Fund Scholarship, 1364
Maguire Educational Scholarships, 1633
Maine Student Incentive Scholarship, 2088
Maine Vietnam Veterans Scholarship, 1862
Major General Lucas Beau Flight Scholarship, 1863
Management of the Industrial Associates Minority
    Engineering Scholarship, 616
Marcus and Theresa Levie Educational Fund, 1365
Margaret Bush Wilson Scholarship, 952
Margaret M. Prickett Scholarship, 1864
Margaret McWilliams Pre-Doctoral Fellowship, 2089
Margery M. Wilson Scholarship, 2090
Margin of Quality Minority Scholarship, 1714
Marguerite Ross Barnett Memorial Scholarship, 2091
Maria Jackson/General George White Scholarship,
    2092
Marian Anderson Vocal Arts Competition, 440
Marian Oldham Scholarship, 1715
Marianas Officers' Wives' Club Scholarship, 1865
Marie Mahoney Egan Scholarship, 1366
Marine Corps Scholarship, 1866
Marion J. Bagley Scholarship, 2093
Marjorie Martin Caylor Scholarship, 413
Marjorie Sells Carter Boy Scout Scholarship, 1525
Mark Kaminski Summer Internship, 342
Marlboro County Farm Bureau Scholarship in Agri-
    culture, 17
Marshall Scholarship, 2094
Martin Luther King Scholarship, 1716
Martino Scholars Program, 1717
Mary Barratt Park Foundation Scholarship, 53
Mary Coulter Clark Scholarship, 1201
Mary Emma Key McKinley Scholarship, 509
Mary Esther Lily Avis Scholarship, 458
Mary Irene Waters Scholarship, 975
Mary Isabel Sibley Fellowship, 1809
Mary Josephine Cochran Fellowship, 2202
Mary L. Lewis Scholarship, 845
Mary M. Sachoff Award, 737
Mary McLeod Bethune Scholarship Challenge Grant,
    2095
Mary Morrow Scholarship, 2096
Maryland Association of Private Career Schools
    Scholarship, 2235
Massachusetts State Scholarship Program, 2097
Math/Science/Foreign Language Scholarship, 510
Maude Winkler Scholarship, 1952
Maurie Clark Fellowship, 1072
May M. Walker Scholarship, 999

Mayward Jenson American Legion Memorial Scholarship, 1867

McAllister Memorial Scholarship, 524

McCarthy Memorial History Scholarship, 760

McDermott Incorporated Scholarship, 554

McDonnell Douglas Scholarship, 1634

McFarland Charitable Foundation Scholarship, 846

McGill University Scholarship, 1202

McGinty Undergraduate History Scholarship, 761

McMahon Memorial Scholarship, 252

Meats Evaluation Scholarship, 1526

Medical Library Association Doctoral Fellowship, 278

Medical Library Association Minority Scholarship, 279

Medical Library Association Scholarship, 280

Medical Student Research Fellowship, 818

Medical and Teaching Scholarships, 1868

Mellon Fellow Minority Scholarship, 1718

Melva T. Owen Memorial Scholarship, 1953

Melvoin and Strobel Scholarships, 133

Memorial Education Fellowship, 2098

Memorial Foundation for Jewish Culture Post-Rabbinical Scholarship, 721

Memorial Honors Scholarship, 1203

Memorial Scholarship, 1204

Men's Auxiliary of the Society of Women Engineers Memorial Scholarship, 617

Meredith L. Lawrence Scholarship, 1000

Merit Gasoline Foundation Scholarship, 1635

Merit and Memorial Scholarships, 1869

Merit Plus Scholarship, 1914

Merit Recognition Scholarship, 2099

Merit Scholarship, 2100

Merv Leitch, Q.C. Scholarship, 1001

MESBEC & NALE Scholarships, 1719

Metropolitan Life Foundation Scholarship, 1527

Metropolitan Museum of Art Summer Internship, 355

Metropolitan Opera National Council Regional Award, 441

Michael and Francesca Marinelli Scholarships, 170

Michael J. McBride Scholarship, 134

Michigan Competitive Scholarship Program, 2101

Michigan Tuition Grant Program, 2102

Microsoft Corporation Scholarships, 618

Mid-Ohio Chemical Co. Scholarship, 1528

MidCon Corporation Scholarship, 619

Middlesex County (NJ) Medical Society Foundation Scholarship, 1367

Midwest Section Scholarship, 76

Mildred B. Davis Fellowship, 94

Mildred Ransdorf Donoghue Scholarship, 511

Military Order of the Purple Heart Scholarship, 1529

Miller Meester Advertising Scholarship, 1530

Mills Fleet Farm Scholarship, 1531

Milton H. Ward Scholarship, 693

Minnesota Mining and Manufacturing Corporation Annual Scholarship, 620

Minnesota State Grant, 2103

Minorities' Access to Research Careers Program Scholarship, 879

Minority Academically Talented Scholarship, 1720

Minority Access for Research Careers Scholarship, 953

Minority Accounting Doctoral Support Program, 135

Minority Achievement Award, 1721

Minority Achievement Program Scholarship, 1722

Minority Achievement Scholarship, 2104

Minority Advertising Intern Program, 1723

Minority Biomedical Research Support Scholarship, 954

Minority Dental Student Scholarship, 796

Minority Doctoral Study Grant, 1724

Minority Educational Opportunity Tuition Award, 1725

Minority Engineering and Sciences Scholarship, 621

Minority Engineering Program Scholarship, 622

Minority Engineering Scholarship Program, 1726

Minority Fellowship, 1727

Minority Incentive Award, 1728

Minority Presence, 1729

Minority Scholar Award, 1730

Minority Scholars Award, 1731

Minority Scholarship, 1732, 1733

Minority Stipend, 281

Minority Student Scholarship, 1734

Minority Teachers of Illinois Scholarship, 1735

Minority Transfer Scholarship, 1736

Minority Undergraduate Scholarship, 1737

Minority/Disadvantaged Scholarship, 343

Minoru Yasui Memorial Scholarship for Broadcast Journalism, 253

Miss America Scholarship, 1810

Miss Teenage America Annual Competition, 1811

Missouri Department of Agriculture Scholarship, 18

Missouri Higher Education Assistance Scholarship, 2105

Missouri Student Grant Program, 2106

Missouri Teacher Education Scholarship, 459

Mr. and Mrs. James M. Kirk Endowment, 1368

Modesto Bee Internship, 229

Monarch Merit Scholarship, 1205

Montgomery GI Bill, 1870

Montgomery GI Bill/Army College Fund, 1871

Moorman Company Fund Scholarships in Agriculture, 2107

Morrison Center MSW Minority Scholarship, 1738

Morrison Nursing Scholarship, 847

Morton Salt Scholarship, 1532

Mt. Hood Community Mental Health Center Scholarship, 1065

Mozelle and Willard Gold Memorial Scholarship, 1954

Multi-Year Ambassadorial Scholarship, 1533

Music Assistance Fund Scholarship, 414

Music Department Scholarship, 428

Music Department Tuition Remission Scholarship, 429

Music Regents Scholarship, 430

Myrtle and Earl Scholarship Fund, 670

N

NAACP Willems Scholarship, 1739

Nagle Foundation Nursing Scholarship, 848

NAHJ Scholarship, 254

NAHJ/Newhouse Scholarship/Internship Program, 255

NALCO Foundation Scholarship, 535

Nancy Ryles Scholarship, 1812

Nancy and Ted Anderson Music Scholarship, 431

NAPA Auto Parts Scholarship, 1534

NATA Scholarship, 1315

Nathan Family Scholarship, 2108

National AAJA General Scholarship Fund, 256

National Achievement Scholarship, 1915, 1916, 1917

National Achievement/University Scholarship, 1918

National Agricultural Center & Hall of Fame/Edith & Harry Darby Foundation, 1535

National Air and Space Museum Internship Program, 525

National Alumni Association Honors Scholarship, 1206

National Alumni Association Junior College Honors Scholarship, 1207

National Alumni Association Leadership Award, 1208

National Alumni Association Past Presidents/Crimson Scholarship, 1209

National AMBUCS Scholarship for Therapists, 118

National Association of Black Woman Attorneys Writing Scholarship, 1002

National Association of Plumbing-Heating-Cooling Contractors Educational Foundation Scholarship, 681

National Association of Water Companies-New Jersey Chapter Scholarship, 2109

National Broadcasting Company, Inc. National Fellowship, 303

National College Award Program, 2223

National Council of State Garden Clubs Scholarship, 54, 55

National Doctoral Fellowship in Business and Management, 171

National FFA Alumni Scholarship, 1536

National Fourth Infantry (IVY) Division Association Scholarship, 1872

National Fraternal Scholarship, 1537

National Health Service Corps Scholarship Program, 849

National Hispanic Scholarship, 1740, 1741

National Honor Society Scholarship, 1210

National Institute of Health Minority High School Scholarship, 955

National League of American Pen Women Grant, 369

National Make It Yourself With Wool Contest, 2203

National Merit/Achievement Scholarship, 1919

National Merit Finalist Scholarship, 1920

National Merit Scholarship, 1921, 1922, 1923, 1924, 1925, 1926

National Merit Supplemental Scholarship, 1927

National Oratorical Contest Scholarship, 312

National Orchestral Institute, 432

National Peace Essay Contest, 738

National Presbyterian College Scholarship, 1974

National President's Scholarship, 1873, 1874

National Scholars Program, 1211

National Scholarship, 1928

National Science Foundation Graduate Research Fellowship, 956

National Science Scholars Program, 957, 2110

National Welsh-American Foundation Exchange Scholarship, 722

National Young Artists Competition in Organ Performance, 415

National Zoological Park Minority Traineeships, 31

National Zoological Park Research Traineeships, 32

Nationwide Insurance Enterprise Foundation Scholarship, 1538

Native American Education Grant, 1975

Naval Academy Women's Club Scholarship, 1875

Naval ROTC Scholarship, 1044, 1045, 1046

Navy League Scholarship, 1212

Navy-Marine ROTC College Scholarship, 1043

Navy Nurse Corps NROTC, 1047

Navy Supply Corps Foundation Scholarship, 1876

NAWIC Founders' Scholarship Foundation, 555

NCFC Education Foundation Undergraduate Scholarship, 3

NCHA Scholarship, 1539

NCOA Scholarship, 1877

NCR Annual Engineering Scholarship, 1742

NCRA Scholarship Fund, 204

NDTA Merit Scholarship, 215

Ned McWherter Scholars Program, 2111

NEDA Education Foundation Scholarship Fund, 201

New Hampshire Charitable Foundation Statewide Student Aid Program, 2112

New Mexico Agricultural Chemical and Plant Food Association Scholarship, 19

New Mexico Scholars Program, 2113

New Mexico Scholars Scholarship, 2114

New Mexico Space Grant Graduate Fellowship, 923

New Mexico Space Grant Teacher Fellowship, 460

New Mexico Space Grant Undergraduate Scholarship, 924

New Mexico Veterans Service Commission Scholarship Under Chapter 170, 1878

New York Council Navy League Scholarship, 1879

New York Life Foundation Scholarship for Women in the Health Professions, 1813

Newhouse Scholarship, 257

NFB Educator of Tomorrow Award, 1955

NFB Humanities Scholarship, 1956

NFB Scholarship, 1957

NIAF Communications Scholarship, 258

NIAF Law Fellowship, 1743

NIAF Scholarships, 1744

Nicaraguan and Haitian Scholarship, 1745

Nicholas C. Vrataric Scholarship, 2224

NJCL Scholarship, 704

Noble Foundation Scholarship, 172

Non-AFDC Child Care Grant, 2115

Non-Resident Academic Scholarship, 1213

Non-Resident Fee Waiver, 2116

Non-Resident Scholar, 2117

Non-Resident Tuition Exemption, 2118

Norbert Schimmel Fellowship, 356

Norcen Energy Canadian Scholarship Series in Engineering, 623

Norcen Energy Canadian Scholarship Series in Geology and Geophysics, 929

Nordstorm Scholarship, 1958

North Carolina Association of Insurance Agents Scholarship, 2119

North Carolina Bar Association Scholarship, 2120

North Carolina Teaching Fellows Scholarship, 2121

North Dakota State Board of Higher Education Scholarship, 2122
North Dakota Undergraduate Scholarship, 2123
Northeastern University Merit Scholarships, 1929
Northrup King Company Scholarship, 1540
NPSC Graduate Fellowships for Minorities and Women, 925
NRF/Chicago Roofing Contractors Association, 556
NRF General Scholarship, 624
NRF/Roofing Industry Scholarship/Grant, 557
NSA Undergraduate Training Program, 1907
NSA/ASLA Student Competition in Landscape Architecture, 344
NSDAR Occupational Therapy Scholarships, 114
NSPA Scholarship Award, 136
NSPE Auxiliary Scholarship, 625
NSPE Student Chapter Member Award, 626
NSPS Scholarship, 926
NSS Scholarship, 392
NSTF of the Graphic Arts Graduate Fellowship, 958
Nurses MGF Research Fellowship, 850
Nurses' Educational Fund Scholarship, 851
Nursing Education Loan/Scholarship Program, 852
Nursing Education Scholarship, 853
Nursing Fund Scholarship, 854
Nursing Grant Program for Persons of Color, 855
Nursing Research Training Award, 856

O

102nd Infantry Division Scholarship, 1822
O.H. Ammann Research Fellowship in Structural Engineering, 558
Oakland University Merit Scholarship, 1214
Occupational Therapy Merit Fellowship, 115
OCLC Minority Scholarship in Library and Information Technology, 282
Oconee Memorial Hospital Annual Scholarship, 857
Off Highway Vehicle College Scholarship and Internship, 1541
Ohio Academic Scholarship, 2124
Ohio Academic Scholarship and Matching Program, 2125
Ohio War Orphans Scholarship, 1880
Oklahoma Bar Foundation Scholarship, 1003
Oklahoma State Regents for Higher Education Doctoral Study Grant, 1746
Olga V. Alexandria (Logan) Scholarship, 1814
Olive Lynn Salembier Scholarship, 627
Olivia Jackson McGee Endowed Scholarship, 1636
Olivia James Traveling Fellowship, 1062
Olliphant Scholarship, 1215
Olympic Tuition Grant, 1316
Oncology Nursing Scholarships, 858
Opportunity Award Scholarship, 2126
Opportunity at Iowa Scholarship, 1747
Oratorical Contest Scholarship, 314, 315, 316, 317, 318, 319, 320, 321, 322, 323, 324, 325, 326, 327, 328, 329, 330, 331
Ore-Ida Foods Business Scholarship, 173
Oregon Laurels Graduate Tuition Remission Program, 1216
Oregon Laurels Scholarship, 1217
Oregon Logging Conference Scholarship, 2127

Oregon Need Grant, 2128
Oregon Occupational Safety and Health Division Workers Memorial Scholarship, 2129
Oregon Private 150 Scholarship, 2130
Oregon Sports Lottery Graduate Scholarship, 1218
Orville Redenbacher's Second Start Scholarship, 2245
Oscar Ritchie Memorial Scholarship, 1748
Otey B. Paschall Scholarship, 1219
Ottis and Calista Causey Endowed Scholarship, 37
Our World Underwater Scholarship, 913
Outboard Marine Corporation Scholarship, 1637
Outdoor Writers Scholarship Award, 739
Outstanding Diverse Student Scholarship, 1749
Owens-Illinois Scholarship, 1542

P

Pablo Neruda Prize for Poetry, 740
Pacific Coca-Cola/Thriftway Stores Merit Award, 1369
Palmetto Fellows Scholarship, 2131
Paragano Scholarship, 1750
Parker Memorial Scholarship, 1370
Parkinson Scholarship in Technology, 959
Parliamentary Procedure Scholarship, 1543
Part-Time Grant Program, 2132
Patricia Roberts Harris Fellowship, 1751
Patrick H. Johnson Memorial Scholarship, 2133
Patrick L. Monahan Memorial Scholarship, 1073
Paul Douglas Conditional Scholarship, 461
Paul Douglas Teacher Scholarship, 462, 463, 464, 465, 466, 467, 468, 469, 470, 471, 472, 473, 474, 475, 476, 477, 478, 479, 480, 481, 482, 483, 484, 485, 486, 487, 488, 489, 490, 491
Paul H. Kutschenreuter Scholarship, 870
Paul L. Fowler Memorial Scholarship, 2134
Paul Laurence Dunbar Scholarship, 1752
Paul Phillips Scholarship, 1753
Pay Less Drugs Scholarship, 107
Peace Corps and Overseas Volunteer Scholarship, 1220
Peer Mentor Scholarship, 1221
PEG/PEPP Scholarships, 628
PEI Scholarship, 629
Pellegrini Scholarship Fund, 1754
Pellette & Associates Scholarship, 682
Performing and Creative Arts Scholarship, 370
Pet Inc. Scholarship, 1544
Peter A. McKernan Scholarship, 1317
Peter D. Courtois Concrete Construction Scholarship, 559
Peter Krueger Summer Internship, 357
Peter Peterson/UT/EFO Scholarship, 630
Petroleum and Geological Engineering Industrial Sponsored Scholarship, 694
Petroleum Society of CIM (Calgary Section) Scholarship, 631
PGE Excellence in Engineering Distinguished Scholarship, 695
Phelps Dodge Corporation Scholarship, 2135
Phi Beta Kappa Scholarship, 1222
Phi Chi Theta Scholarship, 174
Phi Delta Kappa Scholarship for Prospective Educators, 492
Phi Kappa Phi Graduate Fellowships, 1545

Phi Theta Kappa Scholarship, 1223
Phillips Petroleum Company Grant, 632
Phillips Petroleum Scholarship, 1004
Photography Award, 1546
Physical and Occupational Therapists and Assistants Grant, 116
Physical Therapy Scholarship, 117
Physics and Astronomy Undergraduate Work Grant, 930
Piancone Family Agriculture Scholarship, 1755
Pickens County Scholars Program, 1371
Piedmont Chapter of the South Carolina SPE Engineering Scholarship, 633
Pilot Oil Corporation Minority Scholarship, 1756
Pinnacle Resources Ltd. Bursary, 1372
Pitney-Bowes Scholarship, 1638
Planning and Black Community Division Undergraduate Minority Scholarship Program, 1074
Police Officers and Firefighters Survivor's Educational Assistance Program, 2136
Pollard Scholarship, 216
Porter Physiology Fellowships, 911
Portland Police Association Scholarship, 1224
Portland Teachers Credit Union, 2137
Potlatch Foundation for Higher Education Scholarship, 2138
Poultry Scholarship, 1547
POW/MIA Scholarship, 1881
Practicum Stipend in the Area of Developmental Disability Services, 1066
Predoctoral Fellowship, 819
Predoctoral Minority Fellowship, 880
Predoctoral Ortho-McNeil Fellowship, 881
President's Achievement Award, 1757
President's Associates Honors Scholarship, 2139
President's Associates Scholarship, 2140
President's Diversity Scholarship, 1758
President's Endowed Scholarship, 1225
President's Honors Scholarship, 1226
President's Leadership Scholarship, 1227, 1228
President's Scholarship, 1229, 1230, 1231, 1232, 1639, 1882, 2141
Presidential Award, 1548
Presidential Honors, 1233
Presidential Scholars' Program, 1234
Presidential Scholarship, 108, 1235, 1237, 1238, 1239, 1240, 1241, 1242, 1243, 1244, 1245, 1246, 1247, 1248, 1249, 1250, 1930, 1976, 2142, 2246
Presidential Scholarship for African-Americans, 1759
Presidential Scholarships, 1236
Press Club of Dallas Foundation Scholarships, 259
Presser Foundation Scholarship, 433
Presser Scholarship, 434
Prestigious Scholarship, 1760
Pride Scholarship, 416
Primary Care Service Corps Scholarship, 859
Prince George's Chamber of Commerce Foundation Scholarship, 1373
Princess Cruises and Princess Tours Scholarships, 217
Principal's Leadership Award, 1251
Printing and Publishing Industry National Scholarship Program, 402
Pro Deo and Pro Patria Scholarships, 1977

Procter & Gamble Distributing Company Scholarship, 1761
Procter & Gamble Minority Scholarship, 1762
Professional Land Surveyors of Oregon Scholarship, 2143
Professional Scholarship, 77
Professional Study Grant, 2144
Project RENEW (Career Development) Grants, 1815
Project SEED College Scholarships, 892
ProNet Scholarship, 634
Provost Scholarship, 2247
Provost's Scholarship, 1252
Provost's Special Talent Scholarship, 371
Prudential's Merit Scholarship, 1640
Public Employees Public Service Scholarship, 1549
Public Safety Officers Survivor Grant, 2145
Public Speaking Award, 1550
Pulp and Paper Merit Award, 671
Purina Mills Inc. Scholarship, 1551
Purnell-Fort Scholarship, 1763

Q

Quaker Chemical Foundation Scholarship, 1642
Quality Cup Scholarship, 175
Quality Stores Inc. Scholarship, 1552
Quarry Engineering Scholarship, 635
Quarton McElroy Broadcast Scholarship, 260
Queen Elizabeth Scholarship in Canadian Studies, 723

R

R.A. McFarland Memorial Scholarship, 560
R. Boyd Gunning Scholarship, 1253
R.C. Baker Foundation Scholarship, 683, 696
R.C. Easley National Scholarship, 1254
R.F. Poole Alumni Scholarship, 1255
R.L. Gillette Scholarship, 1959
Radio and Television News Directors Foundation Undergraduate Scholarship, 304
Rahr Foundation Scholarship, 1641
Ralph A. Tesseneer Scholarship, 1053
Ralph J. Bunche Scholarship, 1764
Ramsay and Elaine O'Neal Scholarship, 820
RAND/UCLA Center for Soviet Studies Fellowship, 1051
Randall K. Nutt Engineering Scholarship, 636
Raymond H. Kiefer Scholarship, 2248
Recognition of Excellence Scholarship, 1256
Reference Service Press Fellowship, 283
REFORMA Scholarship, 284
Regents Health Care Scholarship for Medicine and Dentistry, 821
Regents Professional Opportunity Scholarship, 2146
Regents Scholarship, 1257, 1258, 1259, 1260, 2147, 2149
Regents Scholarships in Cornell University, 2148
Reggie Lewis Memorial Scholarship, 1765
Reginaldo Howard Scholarship, 1766
Regional Competitions for Young Organists, 417
Regional Scholarship, 1374
Registered Nurse Scholarship, 860
Rehabilitation Training Program, 78
Reid-Baskin Scholarship, 1375
Reserve Member Stipend, 79

Resident Assistant, 1261

Resident Education Advisor Program, 1553

Residential Fellowship in Byzantine, Pre-Columbian, and Landscape Architecture Studies, 345

Rhone-Poulenc Animal Nutrition Scholarship, 1554

Rice-Cullimore Scholarship, 684

Richard Cecil Hicks Educational Fund Scholarship, 1816

Richard D. Irwin Doctoral Fellowship, 176

Richard D. Rousher Scholarship, 1883

Richard Heaney Scholarship, 1555

Richard and Jessie Barrington Educational Fund, 1767

Richard John Cowan Memorial Scholarship, 2150

Richard Klutznick Scholarship, 1067

Richard L. Davis Scholarship, 822

Richard M. Proctor Memorial Bursary, 1556

Richard S. Nelson Scholarship, 1005

Richard S. Smith Scholarship, 1978

RMCMI Scholarship, 697

Robert A. Canham Scholarship, 907

Robert A. Hine Memorial Scholarship, 1376

Robert August Jung Scholarship, 1006

Robert C. Byrd Honors Scholarship, 493, 494, 495, 1262, 1263, 1264, 1265, 2151, 2152, 2153, 2154, 2155, 2156, 2157, 2158

Robert C. Edwards Scholarship, 1266

Robert Davis Scholarship, 536

Robert H. Winner Memorial Award, 741

Robert Hardin Scholarship, 1377

Robert J. Di Pietro Scholarship, 1768

Robert J. Emery Student Support Fund, 1007

Robert K. Fuller Scholarship for Graduate Study, 346

Robert Kaufman Memorial Scholarship Fund, 137

Robert Knauf Vocal Music Scholarship, 442

Robert L. Nugent Scholarship, 1267

Robert M. Lawrence Scholarship, 119

Robert M. Staley Scholarship, 1961

Robert P. Scripps Graphic Arts Grant, 403

Robert and Rosemary Low Memorial Scholarship, 1960

Robert Schreck Memorial Award, 1979

Robert W. Cotton Memorial Scholarship Competition, 637

Robert W. Thunen Memorial Scholarship, 570

Robert W. Woodruff Fellowship, 1557

Rock Sleyster Memorial Scholarship, 823

Rockefeller State Wildlife Scholarship, 59

Rockwell International Corporation Scholarship, 638

Rosewood Family Scholarship, 1769

Roy T. Campbell Scholarship, 1378

RTKL Traveling Fellowship, 347

Rudolph Dillman Memorial Scholarship, 1962

S

S. Harris Memorial Scholarship, 380

S.J. Cerny Engineering Scholarship, 639

Sachs Foundation Scholarship, 2159

Safety Equipment Distributors Association Scholarship, 640

Safety Scholarship, 1558

St. Anthony Publishing, Inc. Julia LeBlond Memorial Scholarship, 80

Sally Bragg Baker Scholarship, 1817

Sam M. Walton Scholarship in Business, 177

Samuel D. Southern Scholarship, 178

Samuel Fletcher Tapman ASCE Student Chapter Scholarship, 561

Samuel W. O'Dell Scholarship, 2160

Sandoz/AFPE First Year Graduate Scholarship, 109

Sandoz Agro Inc. Scholarship, 1559

Sandoz Animal Health Scholarship, 1560

Sandoz Foundation Scholarship, 2204

Santa Barbara Scholarship, 1379

Santa Fe Pacific Foundation Scholarship, 1561, 1770, 1771

Santa Fe Railway Scholarship, 1562

Sarah Susannah Buchanan Philipps Memorial Scholarship for Study Abroad in England, 742

SCAMP Grants & Scholarships, 1884

Schillig-Baird and Presidential Scholarship, 1268

Schlumberger Collegiate Award Scholarship, 571

Scholars Program, 2161

Scholars Program in Medicine, 824

Scholarship for Advanced Study and Research, 348

Scholarship for Children of Deceased, Disabled, or POW/MIA Veterans, 1885

Scholarship for Children of Disabled, Deceased, and POW/MIA Veterans, 1886

Scholarship in Conservation, 908

Scholarship for Dependents of Deceased Servicemembers, 1887

Scholarship Foundation of America Honored Scholars Program, 1269

Scholarship for Frosh Students Outside of Alberta, 2162

Scholarship for L.V.N.s Becoming Professional Nurses, 861

Scholarship for Minority Students in Memory of Edna Yelland, 285

Scholarship for New Nebraskans, 2163

Scholarship Program for Dependent Children of Soldiers, 1888

Scholarship Program for Professional Degree Candidates, 349

Scholarship for Rural B.S.N. or Graduate Nursing Students, 862

Scholarship for Rural Professional or Vocational Nursing Students, 2164

Scholarship for Study in Japan, 724

Scholarship in Turfgrass Management, 56

Scholarships for Minority Accounting Students, 138

Scholastic Achievement Grant, 2165

School Food Service Foundation Scholarship, 2225

School Librarian's Workshop Scholarship, 286

Scout of the Year Scholarship, 1563, 1564

Scripps Howard Foundation Scholarship, 261

Seabee Memorial Scholarship Association Scholarship, 1889

Seaspace Scholarship, 914

Second Marine Division Association Memorial Scholarship, 1890

SEG Foundation Scholarship, 931

Seiko Youth Challenge, 909

SEMA Scholarship Fund, 1321

Seminole and Miccosukee Indian Scholarship, 2166
Senator Barry Goldwater (K7UGA) Scholarship, 305
Senator George J. Mitchell Scholarship Fund, 2167
Senatorial Scholarship, 2168
Seneca Nation of Indians, 1772
Sequoyah Graduate Fellowship, 1773
Sequoyah Heritage Award, 1774
Sergio Franchi Music Scholarship in Voice Performance, 443
Sertoma Scholarship for Deaf or Hard of Hearing Students, 1963
Service Employees International Union Scholarship, 2226
Sesquicentennial Faculty and Staff Scholarship, 1270
Shane Media Scholarship, 306
Shannon Scholarship, 1980
Sharon Christa McAuliffe Memorial Teacher Education Award, 496
Sharp Academic Merit Scholarship, 38
Sheep Award, 1565
Shelby Williams Fund for Excellence in Human Ecology, 191
Shell Oil Scholarship, 179
SHPE Foundation Educational Grant, 641
Sidney Hillman Prize Award, 780
SIE Scholarships, 1566
Sigma Chi Foundation Scholarship, 1567
Sigma Delta Epsilon Fellowship, 960
Sigma Xi Grants-in-Aid of Research, 961
Sikh Education Aid Fund, 1981
SIT Fund, 781
Slovenian Women's Union of America Scholarship, 1568
Smith's Food and Drug Center Scholarship, 110
SmithKline Beecham Animal Health, 1569
SmithKline Beecham-AFPE First Year Graduate Scholarship, 111
Smithsonian Institution Internships and Fellowships, 393
SNAME Scholarship, 642
Social Work Scholarship, 1068
Society for Technical Communication Scholarship, 225
Society for the Advancement of Material and Process Engineering, Orange County Chapter Scholarship, 643
Society of Women Engineers Orange County Chapter Scholarship, 644
Solid Waste Processing Division Scholarship, 685
Somas Hispanic American Scholarship, 1775
Sonoco Annual Scholarship, 202
Sons of Italy Foundation National Leadership Grant, 1776
Sorantin Young Artist Award, 435
South Carolina Free Tuition for Children of Certain Veterans, 1891
South Carolina Press Association Foundation Newspaper Scholarship, 262
South Carolina Tuition Grants Program, 2169
Southeast Asia POW/MIA Scholarship, 1892
Southern California Chapter/Pleasant Hawaiian Holidays Scholarship, 218
Southern California Edison Company College Scholarship, 1380

Southwestern Bell Scholarship, 962
Soviet Jewry Community Service Scholarship, 725
Space Industrialization Fellowship, 526
Sparks Co. Scholarship, 1570
SPE Scholarship, 645
Special Education Services Scholarship, 515
Special Libraries Association Scholarship, 287
Speck Farrar Scholarship, 2249
Spence Reese Foundation, 1818
SPIE Educational Grants and Scholarships in Optical Engineering, 963
Spirit of Youth Scholarship, 1571
Stacey Scholarship Fund, 394
Stanadyne Inc. Educational Grant, 1643
Stanley C. Pace Fellowship, 646
Stanley E. Jackson Scholarship, 1964
Stanley E. Jackson Scholarship for Students with Disabilities, 1965
Stanley H. Stearman Scholarship Award, 1572
Stanley Olson Youth Scholarship Fund, 1381
Stanley Works National Merit Scholarship, 1931
State Aid to Native Americans, 1777
State Awards, 647
State Farm Companies Foundation Scholarship, 1644
State Fraternal Scholarship, 1573
State Health Service Corps Scholarship, 81
State of Idaho Scholarship, 2171
State Need Grant, 2170
State Nursing Scholarship, 863
State President's Scholarship, 1893
State Scholarship for Ethnic Minorities in Professional/ Vocational Nursing, 2172
State Scholarship for Ethnic Recruitment, 2173
State Scholarship Program, 1778
State Waiver of Tuition, 2174
Steffensen Cannon Scholarship, 497
Stone and Webster Scholarship, 648
Stone Foundation Scholarship, 1645
Stoody-West Fellowship, 263
Stoody-West Fellowship in Journalism, 264
Street Family Scholarship, 1382
Stribik-Martin Scholarship, 512
Student CTA Scholarship, 2227
Student Diversity Scholarship, 782
Student Life Scholarship, 2175
Student Opportunity Scholarship, 1982
Student Paper Competition, 910
Study Abroad Scholarship, 726
Suburban Hospital Scholarship, 82
Sue and Sid Magnes Scholarship, 1271
Sumitomo Machinery Corporation of America, 1908
Summer Fellowship, 825
Summer Honors Scholarship, 1272
Summer Research Fellowship, 882
Summerfield G. Roberts Award, 762
Sutton Education Scholarship, 1779
Swine Scholarship, 1574
Sylvia W. Farny Scholarship, 686

T

T.L. James Scholarship Internship, 180
Talent Scholarship, 372
Tandy Technology Scholars Scholarship, 964

TAPPI Technical Division Scholarships, 39
Tau Beta Pi Association Scholarship, 649
Tau Beta Pi Fellowship, 1575
Tau Beta Pi Laureate Award, 1576
Tau Beta Pi Scholarship, 1577
TCI Memorial Scholarship, 219
Teacher Scholarship Program, 498
Teacher Work Study Grants, 192
Teachers of Visually Impaired and Blind Students Scholarship, 516
Technical Minority Scholarship Program, 650
Technical/Vocational Scholarships, 1894
Technology Regents Scholarship, 651
Technology Scholarship Program for Alabama Teachers, 499
Ted Price Scholarship, 1008
Tennessee Higher Education Commission Scholarship, 1780
Tennessee Teacher Loan/Scholarship Program, 500
Terminix Scholarship, 883
Terry Foundation Scholarship, 2176
Texaco Foundation Employee Scholarship, 1646
Texaco Foundation Scholarship, 652
Texas Achievement Award, 2177
Texas Achievement Honors Award, 2178
Texas Business Hall of Fame Foundation Scholarship, 181
Texas Eastman Kodak Scholarship, 537
Texas Excellence Award, 1273
Texas History Essay Contest, 763
Texas Sheriffs' Association Scholarship, 1009
Theatre and Dance Activity Regents Scholarship, 376
Thelma and Harry Hair Scholarship, 2179
Theta Delta Chi Educational Foundation Scholarship, 1578
Third Century Scholarship, 1274
37th Infantry Division Award, 1823
Thomas A. Folger Memorial Endowed Scholarship, 2180
Thomas Benton Young Sr. Memorial Annual Scholarship, 20
Thomas Dixon Scholarship, 182
Thomas E. Sharpe Memorial Scholarship, 1383
Thomas Edison/Max McGraw Scholarship Program, 965
Thomas M. Hunter Endowed Scholars Program, 653
Thomas R. Camp Scholarship, 654
Thomas S. Dobson Scholarship, 864
Thomas Wood Baldridge Scholarship, 1579
Thomasville Furniture Industries Foundation Scholarship, 1647
Tietex Corporation Scholarship, 2205
Tigerama Scholarship, 2250
Tillotson Colorado Scholars Award, 1275
TIME Education Program Student Art Competition for High School Students, 404
TIME Education Program Student Writing Competition for College Students, 743
TIME Education Program Student Writing Competition for High School Students, 744
Tomas Rivera Admission Scholarship, 1781
Tony Leisner Scholarship, 288
Tony Neidermayer Memorial Bursary, 655

Torrison Medical Scholarship, 826
Toyota Motor Sales USA Inc. Scholarship, 1580
Tractor Supply Co. Scholarship, 1581
Traineeships in Exhibit Interpretation, Public Affairs, Education, Horticulture, Facilities Design, and Photography, 405
Transammonia Scholarship, 1582
Transcriptions, Ltd. Scholarship, 83
Transfer Competitive Scholarship, 1276
Transit Corps of Engineers Program, 656
TROA Educational Assistance Program, 1583
Trustee Scholarship in Raptor Biology, 884
Trustees Endowment Scholarship, 1277
Trustees Scholarship, 1278
TRW Scholarship, 565, 657
Tuition Assistance Award, 2251
Tuition Scholarship, 727, 1279
Tuscaloosa County Presidential Scholarship, 1384
Two-Year College Academic Scholarship, 1280
Ty Cobb Scholarship, 2181

U

UAL Scholarship, 21
UC Davis Scholarship, 1282
UCT Scholarship for Teachers of the Mentally Handicapped, 517
UDIA/Dairy Shrine Milk Marketing Scholarships, 33
UFCW International Union Scholarship, 2228
UNCF Scholarship, 658
UNCF Scholarship Program, 1784
Undergraduate Research Fellowship, 885
Undergraduate Research Fellowship in Pharmaceutics, 112
Undergraduate Scholarship, 1283
Undergraduate Scholarships for Full-time Students of Swiss Descent, 1782
Undergraduate/Advanced Undergraduate College Scholarships, 1895
Undergradute Scholarship Program, 193
Underrepresented Minority Achievement Scholarship, 1783
Underwood-Smith Teacher Scholarship, 501
Unical 76 Scholarship, 1584
Union Pacific Foundation Scholarship, 2182
United Dairymen of Idaho Scholarship, 1585
United Federation of Teachers College Scholarship, 1385
United Parcel Services Scholarship for Female Students, 673
United Parcel Services Scholarship for Minority Students, 674
U.S. Army Scholarship, 1048
U.S. Bank Minority Scholarship, 1785
U.S. Department of Energy Predoctoral Fellowships in Integrated Manufacturing, 672
U.S. Jaycee War Memorial Fund Scholarship, 1281
U.S. Naval Academy Class of 1963 Foundation Scholarship, 1897
U.S. Senate Youth Program, 1052
U.S. Ski Team Foundation Scholarship, 1318
U.S. Submarine Veterans of World War II Scholarship, 1898
United Technologies Corporation Scholarship, 659
Universal Dairy Equipment, Inc. Scholarship, 1586

Universal Underwriters Scholarship, 1322
University Achievement Class Scholarship, 1284
University of Calgary Senate Scholarship, 1286
University Club of Portland Fellowship, 1285
University Film and Video Association Development Grants, 381
University of Hawaii at Manoa Scholarship, 1287
University Scholar Award, 1288
University Scholarship, 1289, 1290, 1291, 1292, 1293
UNM Scholars Scholarship, 1294
UPIU Scholarship, 2229
UpJohn/AFPE First Year Scholarship, 113
Upperclass Dean's Scholarship, 1295
Urban League Scholarship, 1787
URW American Income Scholarship, 2230
US West Beta Scholarship, 1786
USO/Budweiser Scholarships, 1896
Utah Air Force Association Scholarship, 966
Utility Workers Union of America Scholarship, 2231

V

V.B. Higgins Engineering Fund Scholarship, 660
Valedictorian and Salutatorian Scholarship, 1296
Valedictorian Scholarship, 2183
Valmont Irrigation Scholarship, 1587
Venning Pre-Med Scholarship, 827
Vermont Incentive Grant, 2184
Vertical Flight Foundation Scholarship, 527
Veterans' Dependent Scholarship, 1899, 1900
Veterinary Science Award, 1588
Vice Admiral E. P. Travers Scholarship, 1901
Vincent T. Wasilewski Scholarship, 307
Virginia Forestry Association Scholarship, 40
Virginia Kline Scholarship, 1386
Virginia Museum of Fine Arts Fellowship, 395
Viscosity Oil Company Scholarship, 1589
Visual Arts Scholarship, 396
Visual and Performing Arts Scholarship, 373
Vivienne Camp College Scholarship, 1387
Vocational Education Scholarship, 2185
Vocational Gold Seal Endorsement Scholarship, 2186
Voice of Democracy Audio-Essay Competition, 332
Voices of Many Feathers Scholarship, 1788
Vulcan Scholarship, 1297

W

W. Eugene Smith Memorial Fund Grant in Humanistic Photography, 291
W. Jeff Ward Scholarship, 1010
W.L. Abernathy Jr. Scholarship, 22
W.M. Keck Foundation Fellowship for Young Scholars, 783
Wal-Mart Competitive Edge, 1298
Walco International Scholarship, 1590
Wallace F. Fiske Memorial Scholarship, 418
Wallace O. Hardee Scholarship, 23
Wallace Preston Greene Sr. Scholarship, 1299
Walter B. McKinney Annual Scholarship, 24
Walter C. and Marie C. Schmidt, 2187
Walter D. Hershey Memorial Scholarship, 183
Walter O. Cralle Memorial Scholarship, 1069

Walter Patterson Scholarship, 308
Walter T. Cox Presidential Scholarship, 1300
Walter W. Stillman Scholarship, 1323
Walton Foundation Scholarship, 1648
War Orphans Education Program, 1902
Warren M. Anderson Scholarship, 1301
Washington Crossing Foundation, 2188
Washington Post Thomas Ewing Memorial Education Grant, 1649
Washington Scholars, 2189
Washington Scholarship, 1591
Wasie Foundation Scholarship, 1789
Wayne Kay Graduate Fellowship, 675
Wayne Kay Scholarship, 676
Webster's New World Writing Competition, 745
Wendy's High School Heisman Award, 1319
WERC Fellowship, 661
West Virginia Higher Education Grant, 2190
West Virginia Italian Heritage Festtival Scholarship, 1790
Western Association of Food Chains, 184
Western Farm Service Scholarship, 1592
Western Golf Association Evans Scholars Foundation Scholarship, 1650
Western Section Scholarship, 84
Western Seedmen's Association Scholarship, 1593
Westinghouse Bertha Lamme Scholarship, 662
Westinghouse Science Talent Search, 967
Weston Family Scholarship, 2191
Weyerhaeuser Black Scholars Award, 663
Weyerhaeuser Company Foundation College Scholarship Program, 1651
Weyerhaeuser Company Foundation Community Education Scholarship Program, 1652
Whetstone Scholarship, 687
Whirly-Girls Memorial Scholarship, 1819
Whittle Communications Minority Scholarship, 226
Wildlife and Fisheries Award, 1594
Wildlife Research Scholarship, 60
Wilfred Archibald Walter Bursary, 2192
William A. Fischer Memorial Scholarship, 927
William A. Kenyon Scholarship, 1302
William A. and Virginia Lomax Marbury Endowment for Business Scholarship, 185
William B. Ruggles Scholarship, 265
William B. Schallek Memorial Graduate Fellowship Award, 746
William B. Stokely Scholarship, 1388
William C. Browning Scholarship, 698
William Carlos Williams Award, 747
William F. Rohr Memorial Scholarship, 1389
William H. Bywater Scholarship, 2232
William H. Greaves Scholarship, 1011
William H. Greaves Undergraduate Scholarship, 968
William J. Neely Memorial Scholarship, 2252
William J. Oates Endowed Scholarship, 25
William James Erwin Scholarship, 1303
William Kapell Piano Competition, 419
William Keyte Memorial Bursary, 2193
William Lemond Hamilton Bursary, 664
William P. Willis Scholarship, 2194
William Randolph Hearst Presidential Scholarship, 1791

William Roy and Maxine R. Adams Scholarship for Academic Excellence, 139

William Toto Scholarship, 1792

William W. Burgin Scholarship, 120

William Winter Teacher Scholar Program, 502

Wisconsin HEAB Native American Student Grant, 1793

Wisconsin HEAB Visual and Hearing Impaired Program, 1966

WIU Foundation Honors Scholarship, 1304

WIU Foundation Scholarship, 1305

Wives of the Class of '34 Endowed Scholarship, 1306

WIX Corporation Scholarship, 1595

Wolcott Foundation Fellowships, 1983

Women in Engineering Program, 665

Women of the Evangelical Lutheran Church in America Scholarship, 1984

Women's Board Scholarship, 1596

Women's Western Golf Foundation Scholarship, 1820

Wood Science Scholarship, 1597

Woodring Scholarship, 503

Worcester County Horticultural Society, 57

Word of Life Scholarship, 790

World Book Incorporated Grant, 289

Writing Scholarship, 748

WTOL-TV Broadcast and Communications Scholarship, 309

Wyeth-Ayerst Scholarship for Women in Graduate Medical and Health Business Programs, 1821

Y

Yakima Nation Tribal Scholarship, 1794

Year Abroad Program at Universities in Poland, 728

Yoshiyama Award, 1307

Young American Bowling Alliance Coca-Cola Youth Bowling Championship, 1598

Young American Creative Patriotic Art Award, 406

Young Scholars Award for Minority Students, 228

Young Scientist Training Program, 828

Youth Scholarship Fund of IBHA, Inc., 1599

Z

Zee and Madge May Vincent Scholarship, 1390

Zolp Scholarship, 1985